HANDBOOK
OF
READING
RESEARCH

VOLUME III

HANDBOOK
OF
READING
RESEARCH

Volume III

Edited by

Michael L. Kamil
Stanford University

Peter B. Mosenthal
Syracuse University

P. David Pearson
Michigan State University

Rebecca Barr
National-Louis University

LAWRENCE ERLBAUM ASSOCIATES, PUBLISHERS
2000   Mahwah, New Jersey   London

Lawrence Erlbaum Associates, Inc., Publishers
10 Industrial Avenue
Mahwah, New Jersey 07430-2262

Cover design by Kathryn Houghtaling Lacey

Library of Congress Cataloging-in-Publication Data

Handbook of reading research / [edited by] Michael L. Kamil ... [et al.].
        p. cm.
    Includes bibliographical references and index.
    ISBN 0-8058-2398-0 (cloth) 0-8058-2399-9 (paper)
    1. Reading. 2. Reading—Research—Methodology. I. Kamil, Michael, L.
LB1050.H278 2000
428.4'072—dc20   96-10470
                                                                      CIP

Books published by Lawrence Erlbaum Associates are printed
on acid-free paper, and their bindings are chosen for strength
and durability

Printed in the United States of America
10 9 8 7 6

CONTENTS

PART III: LITERACY PROCESSES

PART IV: LITERACY PRACTICES

PART V: LITERACY POLICIES

PREFACE

Where the telescope ends, the microscope begins. Which of the two has the grander view?
—Victor Hugo, Les Misérables (1862)

In 1893, Frederick Jackson Turner completed his momentous work, *The Significance of the Frontier in American History*. In this work, he re-directed historians' attention away from the genealogy-ridden chronicles of the Atlantic seaboard and refocused their attention on men and women taming the new western frontier. Coupled with Horace Greeley's dictum of "Go West, young man," Turner sparked our imagination in what he called the "the hither edge of free land."

This "hither edge" represented what Daniel Boorstin (1987) called a "verge," i.e., a "place of encounter between something and something else" (p. xv). Boorstin noted that America's history has been much more than just the verge between Turner's east and west; rather it has been a broad succession of verges:

> America (has always been) a land of verges—all sorts of verges, between kinds of landscape or seascape, between stages of civilization, between ways of thought and ways of life. During our first centuries we experienced more different kinds of verges, and more extensive and more vivid verges, than any other great modern nation. The long Atlantic coast, where early colonial settlements flourished was, of course, a verge between the advanced European civilization and the stone-age culture of the American Indians, between people and wilderness....

> As cities became sprinkled around the continent, each was a new verge between the ways of the city and those of the countryside. As immigrants poured in from Ireland, Germany, and Italy, from Africa and Asia, each group created new verges between their imported ways and the imported ways of their neighbors and the new-grown ways of the New World. Each immigrant himself lived the verge encounter between another nation's ways of thinking, feeling, speaking, and living and the American ways. (xv–xvi)

It was Alexis de Tocqueville (1872) who noted that America's appreciation for verges was not shared by its European counterparts. At the time of his observations, the national pride of the English, French, Germans, and Italians was rooted in the grandeur of their homogeneous traditions rather than in the heterogeneous contradictions posed by proliferating verges. For these countries, national vitality was based on preserving the best of the rich past rather than pursuing the novelty of the unknown.

In contrast, America, with hardly any historical past (at least compared to that of Europe's), has always been different. Its vitality has largely been in its verges—in its new mixtures and confusions. Yet, as Alfred North Whitehead (1935) so shrewdly observed, it is one's ability to tolerate such confusion that enables progress to occur. "The progress of man [kind] depends largely on his ability to accept superficial paradoxes to see that what at first looks like a contradiction need not always remain one." (p. 354)

In designing the third volume of *Handbook of Reading Research*, the editors were mindful of the need to preserve the continuity of the past. It is the obligation of any handbook editor to maintain the traditions of the discipline he or she represents. And so in this *Handbook*, as in Volumes I and II, the editors have included the classic topics of reading—from vocabulary and comprehension to reading instruction in the classroom. In addition, the editors instructed each contributor to provide a brief history that chronicles the legacies within each of the volume's many topics.

On the whole, however, this volume of the *Handbook of Reading Research* is not about tradition. Rather, it is a book that explores the verges of reading research from the time chapters were written for Volume II in 1989 and the research conducted after this date. During this decade, the fortified borderlands and imperial reigns of reading research of old have given way to border crossings and new participants in the reading research of new. In this time, "we" (i.e., the common collective of reading researchers) have replaced the orthodoxy of research with the need to secure a voice for validating our own individual experiences and opinions. We, in essence, have established a new self-awareness of who we are as individuals, how we think, and what we value.

Moreover, we have become more receptive to novelty and change. In this regard, we have come to embrace the idea of "what is possible" than fixate on the idea of "what is." We have come to realize that not only can things be different but we, as researchers and reading educators, can make that difference happen. In Northrop Frye's words (1954), we have come to realize that we "can enlarge upon the imagination" to raise new options that never before existed. In so doing, we must not only envision change, but we must act to realize it.

And perhaps most important, we have become more community-conscious. As part of creating new possibilities and exploring the unfamiliar, we have set about transforming not only ourselves but the very research community that sustains us. It is a community that, in becoming more inclusive, offers greater reassurance that difference and similarity both have their merits.

For the past decade, these three prevailing characteristics of the reading research community have created a bounty of new verges. In conceptualizing this volume of the *Handbook*, the editors contemplated long and hard on how to best address these minglings of the margins. In some instances, the editors adopted the strategy of asking contributors of this handbook to address these verges using the lens of a telescope, tracing the trends of reading research across entire countries and continents. In other instances, the editors invited contributors to address these verges using the lens of a microscope, focusing on the complexities and patterns inherent within a single topic of reading research. In the process, it is the editors' hope to have spanned the verge between the breadth and depth of new developments in the field.

The editors also realized that they needed to do more than simply pass the responsibility to the *Handbook's* contributors of discerning verges. New verges suggested the need to rethink what topics should be included in the *Handbook of Reading Research* that ushers in a new millennium. In undertaking this responsibility, the editors began by extensively reviewing the reading research literature from 1989 to 1995 from a wide array of research and practitioner-based journals and books. Based on this review, the editors identified two broad themes that appeared to represent the myriad verges that have emerged since Volumes I and II were published. Based on particulars of these themes, new topics for Volume III were identified. These themes are briefly discussed below.

THEME 1: BROADENING THE DEFINITION
OF READING

In Volumes I and II of the *Handbook*, reading was largely defined in terms of the so-cial-science discipline of psychology. The new view advanced in the 1980s was that reading was no longer a single product that varied according to properties inherent in written text. Instead, reading was now viewed by many as a process involving cogni-tive construction. As this view advanced, the number of reading studies in psychology journals increased exponentially. However, with the publication of Volume II of the *Handbook* in 1991, a new verge emerged. Reading researchers began to draw from a va-riety of social-science disciplines—most noticeably, sociology and anthropology. In the process, reading took on social, cultural, and multicultural dimensions.

Moreover, reading researchers began to interpret reading in terms of critical literary theory, as well as in terms of the politics of the times (thus uniting reading and political science). Concomitantly, with new devices for observing brain activities, interest was rekindled in understanding the neurological bases of reading. In these shifts, the verge of reading has become one that stretches between the highly reductionist belief that reading is a matter of brain chemistry to the largely constructivist belief that reading is a constitutive process. To address this verge, the editors saw the need to present read-ing from the perspective of multiple social-science disciplines, as well as from the per-spectives of neurology and critical literary theory.

In Volume II of the *Handbook*, chapters were included on reading-writing relations and response to literature. The inclusion of these chapters attempted to address the ob-servation that, in responding to text, readers often do more than speak or write in sim-ple one-word or short-phrase responses. Rather, readers may construct elaborate, open-ended responses that may involve readers reading multiple passages at different points in time. Within the past decade, many researchers have come to view reading as but one part of the classroom communication continuum that involves complex mean-ing exchanges between students and teachers operating from different social and po-litical stances.

In this shift, the verge of reading has become one that stretches between viewing reading as the primary modality for learning to viewing reading as but one aspect of how teachers and students communicate in classrooms. To address this verge, the edi-tors saw the need to expand reading-writing relations to include reading as part of a much broader dimension of communication including all four modalities of speaking, writing, listening, and reading.

In Volume I, the editors included a chapter on quantitative experimental design in reading research as well as one on ethnographic approaches to doing reading research. In Volume II, no specific chapters reflecting innovations in reading research methodol-ogy were included. In assessing the advancements in educational research methodol-ogy writ large since Volume II, the editors found extensive development straddling the verge between quantitative and qualitative research.

On the quantitative side, new advances have been made in such areas as hierarchi-cal regression, path analysis, and item response theory. On the qualitative side, many new advances have been made in the areas of discourse analysis, single subject design, case study, and narrative analysis. In the editors' review of reading research over the past 9 years, they saw the field incorporating many of the new advances in qualitative methodology. In contrast, they saw the field incorporating few such advances in its use of quantitative methodology. For Volume III the editors chose to include the qualita-tive aspect of the methodological verge because of the greater impact that qualitative methodologies have had. The lack of similar impact of quantitative methodologies, in turn, led to the decision to forego such a review for Volume III.

A final area where the expansion of the definition of reading has brought with it the proliferation of verges has been in the areas of media and technology. In Volume I, reading was largely defined as "reading the printed page." In Volume II, reading was extended to include the "reading of diagrams," consideration of "page typology," and "the use of computers in reading instruction." In the past decade, the verge between reading a single instance of print to reading as the exploration of all forms of representation in multi-media and hypermedia formats has become as prominent as the one between Turner's eastern homefront and the prairie frontier. To address this verge, the editors included several chapters on media and technology in this volume. In addition, many of the contributors took it upon themselves to consider the implications of this verge in light of developing their respective topics.

THEME 2: BROADENING THE READING RESEARCH AGENDA

Agendas are plans of actions. They include goals to be achieved (i.e., ideal outcomes) or problems to be solved (i.e., removing blocks to ideal outcomes). They are set for the purpose of benefiting some, often at the neglect of others. In any arena, certain individuals or groups are granted the authority to set agendas; others are not. In order to achieve goals (or solve problems) in a way that is beneficial for intended individuals or groups, agenda setters prescribe actions to be taken. In implementing these agendas, prescribed actions become the blueprint for actions actually taken, and assessment, or evaluation, is conducted to determine the extent to which actions taken match the actions prescribed. Moreover, an assessment may be conducted to determine whether the outcomes actually achieved from implementing an agenda correspond with the ideal outcomes originally proposed in setting the agenda.

Over the past decade, the editors have found a variety of verges arising due to changes in the nature of *who* sets the reading research agenda and *how* this agenda is set. Until the end of the 1980s, it was largely university professors who conducted reading research, sat on editorial boards, and oversaw grant RFPs. In sum, university professors were the "acknowledged authorities" who set and implemented reading research agendas. In this scenario, the teachers' primary role was, with the help of researchers, to translate research findings into practice. In the process, the goal of the researcher became the unspoken goal of the teacher: If the goal of the reading researcher was to increase automaticity of word recognition this, too, became the goal of the reading teacher.

Over the past 9 years, this unwritten rule has been challenged as teachers have begun to engage in their own research associated with the goals and problems of their particular instructional agendas. Moreover, teachers' representation on editorial boards and RFP review boards at state and national levels has increased significantly. Such changes have created an important verge between "practitioner research" and "academic research."

An added dimension to this verge of who sets reading agendas has arisen as policy makers have also begun to significantly influence the reading research agenda. In part, they have accomplished this by funding selective research that most closely supports their view of what constitutes the best reading-instruction agenda. And in part, they have accomplished this by organizing research review panels that tend to promote their view of what reading research "should be." Taken together, academicians, teachers, and policy makers constitute competing elements of this verge as they each lay their claim as the legitimate diviners of what the reading research agenda should be and how this agenda should relate to the reading instruction agenda. To address this verge, the editors saw the need to include a new chapter on action research, as well as build into several chapters the issue of how policy merges as a verge with academic research and classroom practice.

Between Volume I and Volume II of the *Handbook*, researchers began to realize that just as research informs practice, practice informs research. This partnering was supposedly accomplished by first, deciding what the goal of reading should be; second, deciding whose goal this was and who would most benefit by its attainment; and third, how this goal might best be realized through the careful prescription of strategic actions. The assumption here was that researchers would set the research agenda, then implement it, and finally assess its effectiveness as it played out in various instructional settings.

In recent years, an alternative approach to setting reading agendas has been identified, creating yet another verge. In this approach, policy makers at the state level begin by arguing the need for performance standards. They create assessment instruments that are then administered to students. They then receive the results of these assessments and set a political cut point that distinguishes those who "have met the standards" versus those who "have failed the standards." Given the high consequences for failing to meet the standards, teachers and school districts revise their instructional agendas by aligning them with the state assessment. In this manner, teachers end up teaching to the assessments that policy makers create, thus prompting local school districts to bring their instructional curricula more in line with the agenda of state policy makers, regardless of whether or not research supports those changes.

This strategy on the part of state policy makers has created yet another verge in the reading agenda. Instead of agenda setting proceeding at local levels with assessment following the determination of local instructional goals, agenda setting in reading now also must proceed at state levels with instructional goals following assessment criteria. To address this verge, the editors have included several chapters on assessment with due consideration of the assessment-instruction relation.

Indeed, in reviewing the reading research over the past two decades, the editors of the three handbook volumes would argue that verges have multiplied exponentially in the past 10 years. While such verges often lead to contradictions and confusion, they provide the critical basis for continually rethinking the answers to "What is possible?" and "What should be?" in reading research, practice, and policy. As long as these questions continue to be fiercely debated, reading will likely remain the prominent educational issue among researchers, practitioners, and policy makers alike. Should the verges disappear and agreement on all issues prevail, reading would quickly lose its prominence, no doubt giving way to disciplines whose frontiers represent more fertile verges for exploration.

Volume III represents a different type of verge. The editors and the individual authors of the chapters have decided to forego royalties and honoraria for their work. In conjunction with The National Reading Conference, a fund has been established to promote reading research. The fund will operate on the royalty and fee income from this and subsequent volumes of the *Handbook*.

In contemplating Volume IV of the *Handbook*, we, as editors, considered what was not included in Volume III. We negotiated for more chapters than we received. In particular, we did not get all of the chapters that dealt with reading research around the globe. We did not represent the large and growing concerns with adult and workplace literacy.

The editors anticipate that verges of the next 10 years are likely to be different and will continue to expand in increasing orders of magnitude. Yet, Volume IV (like Volumes I and II) will hopefully continue to address the timeless verges between what we know and what we don't know, between what we do and what we should do. In sum, our task as reading researchers remains one of continuing to create new frontiers of thought, keeping the borders of verges open for all who are willing and imaginative enough to undertake the exploration. And in the process of creating confusion, we will have ever present the opportunity to discern what James Glick (1992) called the "broader underlying pattern of our shared chaos."

ACKNOWLEDGMENTS

Finally, we want to acknowledge the efforts of many of our colleagues, students, spouses, and others who have worked to make Volume III a reality. We extend special recognition to the editorial work of Naomi Silverman who kept us (roughly) on time and on task; the assistance of Lori A. Hawver was also invaluable in reminding us when we were lagging behind; and Robin Marks Weisberg provided important support in production. We also want to acknowledge Lawrence Erlbaum for creating a new home for the *Handbook of Reading Research*. Most particularly, we, as editors, want to extend our great appreciation for all of the authors around the world who made this work a reality. We look forward to Volume IV.

REFERENCES

Barr, R. , Kamil, M. L., & Mosenthal, P. B. (Eds.). (1984). *Handbook of reading research* (Vol. I). New York: Longman.
Boorstin, D. J. (1989). *Hidden history: exploring our secret past*. New York: Vintage Books.
de Tocqueville, A. (1945). *Democracy in America*. New York: Knopf. (Original work published 1872)
Frye, N. (1964). *Educated imagination*. Bloomington: Indiana University Press.
Glick, J. (1988). *Chaos: Making a new science*. New York: Penguin.
Hugo, V. (1982). *Les miserables*. New York: Penguin. (Original work published 1873)
Pearson, P. D., Barr, R., Kamil, M. L., & Mosenthal, P. B. (Eds.). (1984). *Handbook of reading research* (Vol. I). New York: Longman.
Turner, F. J. (1976). *The frontier in American history*. New York:
Whitehead, A. N. (1968). *Essays in science and philosophy*. New York: Greenwood Publishing.

PART I

Literacy Research Around the World

CHAPTER 1

Reading Research in Australia and Aotearoa/New Zealand

Ian A. G. Wilkinson*
The Ohio State University

Peter Freebody
Griffith University

John Elkins
The University of Queensland

This overview of research focuses on reading, but occasionally moves into the broader field of literacy. It has been decided to present the picture from Australia first, though the international influence of New Zealand research has probably been as great, particularly through the work of Clay in reading development (Clay, 1991) and through the widespread adoption of Reading Recovery (Clay, 1993). Some Australian research, particularly in the area of genre, has been treated lightly because its influence has been greater in writing research and applied linguistics than in reading. Halliday and Hasan's (1976, 1985) development of systemic functional linguistics spawned many Australian studies of the development of genre (e.g., Painter & Martin, 1986) and of cohesion (Anderson, 1982, 1983; Smith & Elkins, 1985, 1992). Kidston and Elkins (1992) reviewed research and practice up to the past decade. They found a strong so-called "psycholinguistic" tradition, closely related to Goodman's miscue analysis and whole-language theory. Cambourne (1984, 1988, Cambourne & Brown, 1987) was the most active researcher of this type. Research on adult literacy has not been reviewed because of space limitations.

AUSTRALIA

Context

Australia's population is mostly people of European ancestry, though over one third are recent migrants or their children, including many from Asia. Indigenous people, Aboriginals and Torres Strait Islanders, represent less than 2%. The Australian Commonwealth comprises states and territories with constitutional responsibility for edu-

---

*At the time this chapter was written, Wilkinson was on faculty at The University of Auckland.

cation. What has characterized policy related to literacy education over the last 10 years, however, has been an increasingly interventionist Commonwealth Government. This process began to be shown explicitly in 1989 with the development and publication of the Commonwealth's policy paper on literacy education (Dawkins, 1990). This policy entailed, among other things, a redirection of school-directed funds to language and literacy education, culminating in the gradual collapsing of Commonwealth support for other services (e.g., a "disadvantaged schools" program and programs relating to English as a second language, ESL) into programs more explicitly targeted at literacy education. That 10-year period has as well seen a shift of the Commonwealth's interest initially toward adult literacy and ESL programs and more recently back toward the school years, with particular enthusiasm for early literacy.

These changes brought to the surface a long tradition in Australia of considering literacy education to be intrinsically bound up with questions of equity and access to public goods and services, including productive employment pathways and an active voice in political processes. In contrast, the Commonwealth's interest has been made constitutionally legitimate partly through a linking of literacy education and the economic well-being and cultural cohesion of Australia, a focus on functionality rather than participation. This partial reformulation of literacy in economistic terms, as a component of human capital, has therefore been in contest with both the personalist and social justice conceptions of the nature and value of literacy education that had long shaped the field (Green, Hodgens, & Luke, 1994). In that regard, states and territories and the Commonwealth share responsibilities for migrant services and indigenous education. The composition of Australian society has long been multicultural and multilingual, but it has been in the last 30 years or so that the consequences of such a cultural and linguistic environment for literacy education have become part of the foreground of research efforts.

Trends and Issues

In many respects, the issues that have occupied the field of reading research in Australia parallel those found in other English-speaking countries: Questions about the relative significance of skills- and meaning-based instruction, developmental sequences in reading acquisition, and the role of reading capability across the school curriculum have been prominent. However, these have been given distinctive inflections in this context due to two features of the history of literacy education in Australia: The first concerns access to literacy in a culturally and linguistically diverse environment and the optimal role of educational providers for both children and adults; the second relates to the tendency in Australian schools and preservice teacher education programs to work with a variety of pedagogical methods and literacy instruction materials, partly because they have been, to date, relatively free from commercial instructional programs and, until recently, from government-imposed testing regimes. Government priorities for literacy research can be discerned in a recent "map" of research on children's literacy (Gunn, 1996), which indicates those areas that have received significant funding over the last 10 years or so. The following is a sample of those areas:

- Literacy for students with bilingual or non-English-speaking background.
- The relationship of oral language development to literacy with special focus on classroom interaction as a literacy-learning site.
- The impact of various literacy programs.
- The nature of the interface between home and school culture and its consequences for literacy learning.

We briefly illustrate each of these prominent areas with a necessarily selective sample of studies. We collect these examples under the headings of skills approaches and cultural/critical approaches, terms derived from a Commonwealth-funded study of teacher education programs in literacy by Christie et al. (1991).

Skills Approaches.   The role of alphabetic and phonological knowledge in early reading development has been, in Australia (Bowey 1996; Bowey & Underwood, 1996; Bowey, Vaughan, & Hansen, 1998) as elsewhere, a matter of contention in theoretical as well as professional circles. Major Australian contributors to this debate have included Byrne and Fielding-Barnsley, who based their theorization of early reading on Chomsky's approach to linguistic knowledge. In a series of publications (Byrne & Fielding-Barnsley, 1989, 1991, 1995; and see Byrne, 1992, 1998), they have explored the development of phonemic awareness in young children and documented its teachability. In the 1991 study, they evaluated the effects of a program (called Sound Foundations) aimed at enhancing phonemic awareness, and 3 years later explored its longer term outcomes. Preschoolers (aged about 4 years) who were trained for 12 weeks showed greater gains than a control group who used similar materials without a focus on phonemic awareness. The authors also found transfer to unfamiliar sounds favoring the trained group, and transfer as well to superior performance on a forced-choice word recognition test, indicating that the trained group could use their knowledge to decode unfamiliar printed words, a transfer outcome also noted in Jorm and Share (1983).

In the follow-up study, Byrne and Fielding-Barnsley (1995) found that, compared to control group, the trained children were superior in reading comprehension 3 years after the training. Byrne and Fielding-Barnsley took this to offer support for Juel's (1988) "simple view" of reading—that reading comprehension comprises a simple additive relation of decoding to listening comprehension.

Under this heading as well can be grouped much of the research that has been occasioned by the endorsement by several state education authorities of the implementation of Reading Recovery programs. The research effort directed at this intervention has confirmed findings reported elsewhere: The program has strong immediate effects that diminish proportionately with the duration of the follow-up period. Comparably to some New Zealand research (e.g., Glynn, Bethune, Crooks, Ballard & Smith, 1992), Centre, Wheldhall, Freeman, Outhred, and McNaught (1995) found the Reading Recovery group was superior to control students on all tests measuring reading achievement; at 15 weeks follow-up the advantage over the control group was sustained with the exception of those tests assessing metalinguistic skills; and at 30 weeks follow-up, almost all of the original advantages had been lost. More recent research by Crevola and Hill (1998) has taken the need for Reading Recovery as a given, and sought to improve the first wave of literacy education by drawing on the effective schools literature. Another current research project involves the adaptation of Slavin's Success for All for Australian schools. Termed SWELL, this whole-class early literacy intervention has produced encouraging results (Center & Freeman, 1997).

Research on assessment has had several threads. National and state testing has seen the adoption of Rasch scaling rather than traditional psychometric theory (Masters & Forster, 1997), and a wider grasp of literacy by including writing, speaking, and listening with reading. Classroom assessment, particularly portfolios, has been studied by van Kraayenoord (1994, 1997) and her colleagues (Dilena & van Kraayenoord, 1996; Maxwell, van Kraayenoord, Field, & Herschell, 1995). Some recent work on criterion-related assessment has seen attention paid to benchmarks. Testing receives greater attention at times when "standards" receive political attention, as occurred in the mid 1990s. Research responses appear to have little impact on the claims that standards of reading or spelling are inadequate, and substantial politicizing of the literacy standards debate has occurred (McGaw, 1998).

In the Australian context, psychologists and remedial educators with an interest in literacy education have actively pursued research aimed principally at establishing the need for systematic attention in classrooms to phonological and phonemic awareness. The strong argument that instruction is necessary for the full development of appropriate levels of awareness, and that these domains of awareness are in turn necessary for early reading acquisition, is still debated and motivates much research, as does the even stronger argument that these domains of awareness are both necessary and sufficient for early reading acquisition.

Cultural Approaches.   As an example of a distinctively Australian study under the first of the headings just given, Clayton, Barnett, Kemelfield and Mulhauser (1996) studied the use of oral and written English and various Australian Aboriginal languages in the desert regions of South Australia, Western Australia, and the Northern Territory. Among their findings was that language and literacy development in English for young Aboriginal people is a major priority for the communities. Achieving appropriate levels of proficiency through schooling, however, was made difficult by a complex interaction of factors relating, on one hand, to socioeconomic circumstances and the language ecology of communities and, on the other, to the remoteness and difficulties in resourcing characteristic of desert schools. These researchers also noted that Aboriginal communities expressed the desire that the English language and literacy development of their children not be at the expense of local indigenous languages. In Australia, indigenous languages have been vanishing for 200 years, and the Aboriginal community members who participated in this study made it clear that they wanted "both ways" learning, with English and Aboriginal languages to be "equal and level, not one rising above the other."

The dilemma facing bilingual and multilingual parents with respect to the cultural and linguistic context of their children in school was reflected as well in a study by Breen et al. (1995). They provided documentation of reading and writing practices in six urban and rural communities, with case studies of 23 families, across Western Australia. One notable finding from this study was that the remarkable diversity found among the family literacy practices contrasted sharply with the uniformity of the classroom practices aimed at reading and writing that the children encountered in school. The nature and amount of reading activities in the homes, although not consistent across the 23 case study families, showed a mixture of reading for pleasure, for parent and child home study, for parental occupation, for sports and hobbies, and for religion. The schools were found to use a common set of tasks within whole-language-based classroom strategies, texts that were almost uniformly monocultural and sometimes ethnocentric, and programs that often assumed specifically Australian cultural knowledge, thereby educationally but also culturally marginalizing some of the children in the case studies. As in the study by Clayton and others, the parents in this study saw English oracy and literacy as means of attaining a good education and possibly better employment for their children, but were keen to avoid losing their distinctive cultural background, an outcome that would accompany their children's loss of the home languages.

In line with a renewal of interest in the early schooling and a belief in its critical role in later reading development, Hill, Comber, Louden, Rivalland, and Reid (1998) documented the literacy development of 20 preschool children in five different locations, and followed them into the first year of school. They found substantial variation in the reading capabilities of children entering school. Among many relevant findings, they showed that many children have knowledge about books (and how to read with a "book reading tone"), letters, and how to attend to print before entering school, but that the first year of schooling is associated with significant gains in word concepts, punctuation, sentence writing, and a critical awareness that reading is necessarily associated with decoding. They draw out one important implication of this, in the light of moves to assess literacy capabilities among very young children:

> This points to a possible danger with testing programs being used too early or interpreted as evidence of "risk," when in fact the children may simply have not had the opportunities to learn what is being tested. Early testing programs conducted before school may inaccurately label children or indicate inexperience with school literate practices rather than anything more. (Hill et al., 1998, p. 13)

These studies of literacy as a set of cultural practices have served to provide a descriptive basis for debates about reading curriculum, policy and classroom practice. They also signal a widespread move in Australian reading research toward the study of reading education in naturalistic settings, using combinations of quantitative and qualitative research methods. As noted earlier, compared to other countries, Australian literacy educators tend to use a variety of methods, mixing and matching hybrids of genre-based, meaning-based, and skills-based approaches (van Kraayenoord & Paris, 1994). In that light, Australian literacy research in general is characterized by a move into the classroom and to the study of the details of interactions in and around reading materials. This work is exemplified by the work of Baker (1991, 1997), who has shown, through close attention to transcripts of reading lessons, how such lessons constitute simultaneously the relations between teachers and students, the contents of various cultural domains, and procedures that are taken to count as successful reading for and in school. Baker's work serves as a caution against conducting research in reading that is based on "theories, abstractions or idealisations" (1991, p. 184) of pedagogy rather than on the details of lessons themselves. There has also been a substantial amount of research on critical literacy (Luke, 1994) and on gender issues in literacy (Alloway & Gilbert, 1997; Gilbert, 1988, 1998; Gilbert & Taylor, 1991), but space constrains our dealing with this here.

Conclusions

From this brief sample of studies, a number of substantive and methodological observations can be made. First, as a field of study, "reading" has been subsumed in the Australian research context under more general studies of *literacy*. It is significant, for example, that the Australian Reading Association recently changed its name to the Australian Literacy Educators Association, and its journal from the *Australian Journal of Reading* to *Australian Journal of Language and Literacy*. This is more than cosmetic. It reflects a change in how the reading enterprise is defined and conceptually arranged, from being next to other curriculum areas in the primary school program (e.g., social studies) to being next to other foundational psychological and sociocultural capabilities (e.g., numeracy).

This change has been brought about partly by the significant incursions into the study of reading by linguists, ethnographers, and cultural theorists (including cross-culturalists). There are positive and negative corollaries to this: On the positive side, the notion of reading is now located in terms of its direct and inextricable relationship to writing, a connection established by much research and by teachers' professional understandings. This realignment now enables impact from adjacent disciplines on the matter of reading (e.g., critical theory). Finally, the change provides a constant reminder that the linguistic and sociocultural aspects of understanding shape the nature of what is read and how various kinds of reading practices are shaped by social processes in homes and schools.

On the negative side, easier access to the "output data" (especially linguistic output) of writing compared to reading has tended to direct many empirically oriented educators away from the systematic study of reading; the realignment has also heightened the disciplinary divides within the literacy field in Australia (put somewhat too simply, reading is for psychologists, writing for linguists and ethnographers). This increased disciplinary divide itself leads to increased difficulty in staging focused debates across disciplinary divisions, and a reversion among some to unsophisticated notions of reading outcomes because of their readier measurability (e.g., spelling).

AOTEAROA/NEW ZEALAND

Context

Unlike Australia, New Zealand has a unified national education system, although with a high degree of management at the local school level. In 1989, the government implemented reforms involving radical decentralization of educational administration while retaining the accountability of schools to agencies of central government. The reforms, termed *Tomorrow's Schools* (Lange, 1988), were designed to enhance the responsiveness of schools to their local communities, to improve parental choice in education, and to increase the overall quality of schooling. Ten years on, only some of these goals have been realized. Heavy emphases on local control and marketization of education have come at the cost of increased inequity of educational opportunities for students from schools in "rich" and "poor" areas (see Gordon, 1994; Wylie, 1997).

These reforms have come at a time when there have been dramatic shifts in the cultural and linguistic environment for literacy education. New Zealand has a strong bicultural heritage, and Maori, the indigenous people of New Zealand, make up 14.5% of the population. Pakeha (a Maori term used to describe New Zealanders of European descent) comprise 71.7% (Statistics New Zealand, 1997). Both Maori and English are official languages, and there is an emphasis on Maori culture in education and social policy. In the last 30 years, high levels of migration to New Zealand of people from the Pacific Islands and Asia have made for a more multicultural and multilingual society. Pacific Islanders and Asians, as well as Maori, because of their younger age structures, now make up large proportions of the school-age population. In 1998, 20% of school students were Maori, 7% were Pacific Islanders, and almost 6% were Asian (Ministry of Education, 1998). At least 7% of students came from non-English-speaking backgrounds.

There have also been dramatic changes in the socioeconomic structure of New Zealand. In 1984, the government introduced a program of economic and social restructuring in the pursuit of free-market reforms described as "more radical than those of any other industrialized country" ("The mother of all reformers," 1993, p. 20). State expenditures were cut, unemployment rose, and income inequalities increased (Kelsey, 1995). This restructuring has had a negative impact on the well-being of many New Zealand families and, it may be conjectured, on the home literacy backgrounds of children entering school.

Trends and Issues

As a result of these changes, the single biggest challenge confronting literacy education in New Zealand today is the issue of equity in the face of increasing ethnic, language, and socioeconomic diversity (Wilkinson, 1998). Although New Zealand continues to maintain high levels of literacy, there is a growing body of evidence of large inequities in outcomes. Results of the 1990–1991 survey of reading literacy conducted by the International Association for the Evaluation of Educational Achievement (IEA) showed that variation in achievement among 14-year-old students in New Zealand was the largest of any other country participating in the survey (Elley & Schleicher, 1994). New Zealand had more good readers than any other country, but it also had a large number of poor readers. Variation in achievement among 9-year-olds was also very large. The majority of poor readers were Maori, Pacific Islanders, and other children whose home language was not English, and boys at an early age (Wagemaker, 1993). More recent data collected by the National Education Monitoring Project (Flockton & Crooks, 1997) suggest that gaps in students' reading achievement between different ethnic, income, and gender groups continue to be cause for concern (see also Fergusson & Horwood, 1997; Nicholson, 1995; Nicholson & Gallienne, 1995). There is also evidence of large gaps in literacy levels between these groups in the adult population (Ministry of Education, 1997).

Educational responses to the challenge posed by increasing diversity have primarily centered on emergent and early literacy and have taken several forms. One response has been to regard the problems as solely societal and to hold on to current practices but with redoubled efforts to address the needs of low-performing subgroups. Nevertheless, there is growing concern that "more of the same" will not be enough (Ministry of Education, 1999). Another response has been to suggest that the societal changes require more concerted approaches to improving equity in literacy education. Yet another response has been to suggest that the problems signal weaknesses in current methods of teaching literacy and that wholesale changes in methodology are required. Research indicative of these three approaches is considered in turn.

Strengthening Current Practices.   Clay (1997) and Elley (1997) have argued that New Zealand teachers need to hold on to practices currently used in the junior school (the first 2 to 3 years) but show greater sensitivity to the needs of students from disadvantaged subgroups (e.g., those for whom English is not the home language, young boys). Current practices offer at least two tiers of support for children with reading difficulties.

The first tier comprises the regular classroom reading program in which the major components are language experience activities, reading aloud to children, shared-book experiences, and book-based activities involving high-interest natural language texts. Elley (1989) documented the benefits of reading aloud to children in terms of gains in vocabulary knowledge, especially for lower ability students (although for more conservative evidence, see Nicholson & Whyte, 1992; Penno, 1997). Elley (1991; Elley & Foster, 1996) also documented the benefits of book-based programs in combination with language experience and shared-reading activities for improving the word recognition and comprehension of students for whom English is a second language.

The second tier of support is Reading Recovery (Clay, 1993), an early-intervention program designed to accelerate progress of children who are experiencing difficulties learning to read after 1 year of school. Reading Recovery is now available in 72% of state-funded primary schools and serves approximately 18% of 6-year olds (Kerslake, 1998). Evaluations by Clay (1987, 1990) suggest that the program is highly successful at least in the short term (see also Clay & Tuck, 1991). Smith (1994) has documented its success with children for whom English is a second language.

Recently, a third tier of support for the 1% to 2% of children who do not become successful readers following regular classroom instruction and Reading Recovery has been developed and evaluated by Phillips and Smith (1997). This is a very specialized program in which children (average age 6 years 11 months) who are identified as the lowest achieving "hardest-to-teach" children are given one-on-one tutoring by specially trained teachers who receive ongoing support and monitoring. The tutoring procedures are based on those of Reading Recovery but are more finely tuned to the needs of individual children and are more consistently delivered. Results of Phillips and Smith's (1997) evaluation showed that almost 80% of the 23 children who completed the program achieved reading levels commensurate with average levels of their peers, and the majority of children achieved this in an average of 20.4 lessons. In other results that the developers themselves described as "unexpected," gains were particularly marked for Maori children and children from non-English-speaking backgrounds.

Improving Equity.   Another response to the challenge posed by diversity, represented especially in the work of McNaughton (1995) and colleagues, has been to suggest that societal changes require more concerted approaches to improving equity in literacy education. These approaches include improving the equity of resources for literacy learning, improving equity of access to effective literacy instruction, and improving equity of processes occurring within instructional activities.

Equity of resources for literacy learning refers to both psychological and physical resources. Wylie, Thompson, and Hendricks (1996) documented major disparities in the home literacy backgrounds of children from different ethnic and income groups prior to entry to school. In one finding, they noted that only 58% of Maori and 29% of Pacific Islands children were read to at least once a day, compared with 78% of Pakeha children. The Alan Duff Charitable Foundation has implemented a *Books in Homes* program to foster children's ownership of books and to promote a literate culture among families from disadvantaged communities. The program donates books to students in low-income areas and operates in 150 schools nationwide. Students take the books home and share them with their families. The program has been successful in improving the reading attitudes and habits of children and has led to modest gains in reading achievement (Elley, 1998).

Other attempts have been made to improve the equity of access to effective instruction. Working from a sociocultural perspective, McNaughton (1995) has argued that effective forms of instruction are those that allow children to engage with activities using familiar forms of expertise and that provide bridges between home and school. McNaughton and colleagues (Phillips & McNaughton, 1990; Tagoilelagi, 1992; Wolfgramm, 1991) have identified styles of storybook reading used by Maori, Pacific Islands, and Pakeha families and have noted that different styles enable some children to engage with classroom instruction more than others (see also McNaughton, Ka'ai, & Wolfgramm, 1993). McNaughton and colleagues have worked with families to augment their repertoires of reading styles to create closer connections between home and school literacy activities (e.g., Wolfgramm, McNaughton, & Afeaki, 1997). Conversely, these researchers have also tried to augment classroom practices to make them more compatible with the home-based activity structures of certain minority cultures (e.g., Hohepa, Smith, Smith, & McNaughton, 1992; Hohepa, McNaughton, & Jenkins, 1996).

Still other attempts have been made to address the equity of processes occurring within instructional activities. Early studies by Clay (1985) and Kerin (1987) noted the problems experienced by Pakeha teachers in conducting extended conversations with New Entrant (Kindergarten) Maori children during reading and writing sessions. Cazden (1992) related these problems to features of classroom organization, discourse, and topic knowledge. Goodridge and McNaughton (1997) have illustrated similar difficulties encountered by teachers in their interactions with Maori and Pacific Islands children. Glasswell, Parr, and McNaughton (1996) have also revealed patterns of interactions between teachers and low-ability children in writing conferences that prevent children from fully participating in the activities because of a lack of shared understanding of the goals and nature of the activity. These studies suggest that teachers need awareness of different strategies for working with children with diverse backgrounds and experiences.

Changing Methods.   A third response to the challenge posed by diversity has been to suggest that the problems signal weaknesses in current methods of teaching literacy and that changes in methodology are required. Nicholson (1999), and Tunmer and Chapman (1996) have argued that the problems experienced by low-progress readers are due to lack of explicit attention to phonemic awareness and phonics in beginning reading instruction in New Zealand (see also, Thompson, 1995; Thompson & Johnston, 1993). At issue seems to be the relative contribution of sentence context and graphophonemic cues in the identification of unfamiliar words. Current practices advocate that beginning readers use sentence context as the primary source of information for identifying unfamiliar words and use graphophonemic cues simply to confirm hypotheses based on context. Critics, on the other hand, argue that the strategies should be reversed—beginning readers should look for familiar spelling patterns first and use context only to confirm hypotheses based on word-level information (Tunmer & Chapman, 1998). This recommendation is gaining currency (Ministry of Education, 1999).

Nicholson has conducted two small-scale interventions on the benefits of adding explicit instruction in phonemic awareness and phonics to New Entrant reading programs. One study with children from mostly middle-class backgrounds evaluated the effects of adding phonemic awareness training alone (Castle, Riach, & Nicholson, 1994). Another study with children from low-income backgrounds examined the effects of adding phonemic awareness training combined with alphabet knowledge and knowledge of simple letter–sound correspondences (Nicholson, 1997). Children in both studies made gains in phonemic awareness, although these gains showed only modest transfer to measures of reading.

Tunmer, Chapman, Prochnow, and Ryan (1997) have conducted one of the most comprehensive intervention studies of beginning reading instruction in New Zealand. Working collaboratively with classroom teachers, they adapted, developed, and tested supplementary materials and procedures designed to help students, especially low-achieving students, acquire the phonological processing skills and word identification strategies necessary for literacy development. New Entrant children from seven schools participated in the year-long intervention. Results showed superior gains in reading achievement by the end of the year (the locus of the effects and the long-term benefits have yet to be examined).

The work of these critics has also threatened Reading Recovery's dominance as the second tier of defense against reading failure. Nicholson (1989) has criticized the methodology used in early evaluations of the program, and Tunmer and colleagues (Chapman & Tunmer, 1991; Iverson & Tunmer, 1993; Tunmer, 1990, 1992) have argued that there should be greater emphasis on phonological awareness, phonological recoding, and syntactic awareness in the program. The Glynn et al. (1992) evaluation has also cast doubt on the long-term benefits of Reading Recovery, as mentioned previously, and revealed that many children completing the program are placed in their regular classroom at reading levels well below those they had attained at discontinuation. Tunmer, Chapman, Prochnow, and Ryan (1997) reported similar findings.

Conclusions

If New Zealand is to meet the challenge of equity in literacy education, the dilemma is how to maintain its child-centered pedagogy in the face of economic rationalist pressures and the demands placed on the educational system by increasing diversity. New Zealand's literacy practices have a history of association with a developmental constructivist bias in teaching and learning. There is a general commitment to the centrality of the child in teaching and to a view of learning as proceeding from the child along developmentally appropriate pathways under guidance or support of the teacher; direct instruction of specific knowledge and skills according to prespecified routines finds little favor.

Given this developmental constructivist bias, attempts to strengthen current practices and to improve equity of resources, access to effective instruction, and processes have a natural home in the New Zealand literacy landscape. Nevertheless, the dominance of Reading Recovery as the second tier of defense against reading failure may be weakened in the future, not only because of the research criticizing the program's pedagogy and its effects but also because of the enormity of the demands being placed on the educational system by low-performing subgroups. The shift toward school-based management and the fundamental inability of Reading Recovery (as it is presently constituted) to deal with low performance at a schoolwide level may mean that Reading Recovery becomes one of a number of options that individual schools choose for dealing with reading problems.

Moreover, among those who argue for strengthening current practices and improving equity, there is broad agreement that programs for literacy instruction of 8- to 12-year-olds need closer attention (Clay, 1997; Education Review Office, 1997). Some have argued for a second catch-up effort, following on from Reading Recovery, at about 10 or 11 years (Clay, 1997; Henson, 1991). One example of such an effort is local adaptations of reciprocal teaching (Palincsar & Brown, 1984). Moore and colleagues (Gilroy & Moore, 1988; Kelly, Moore, & Tuck, 1994; Le Fevre, 1996) have reported robust comprehension gains from reciprocal teaching for students in the middle and upper primary school, particularly those with diverse language and ethnic backgrounds.

If wholesale changes in methodology of reading instruction are to take hold, New Zealand educators will need to resolve the tension between explicit instruction and a developmental constructivist bias. Suggestions for specific guidance and tutoring do not sit easily with a constructivist framework, unless they can be construed within a sociocultural framework that ascribes an active role to social and cultural processes as well as to the child (McNaughton, 1996) (as has been achieved with Reading Recovery and reciprocal teaching). For the issues of phonemic awareness and phonics, this means that classroom teachers may need to find ways of providing more explicit assistance to children in the phonetic structure of language, and in letter–sound correspondences, but without distracting them from engagement with the functions of language and literacy (Johnston, 1997).

SYNTHESIS

It seems to us remarkable how little connection exists between the literacy researchers and topics of the two neighbors. Even where common concerns for equity and the literacy of indigenous students exist, there seems to be little cooperative effort. Each country has high levels of general literacy, but major areas where improvement is needed. Each is struggling with a historical commitment to student-centered literacy education, in the face of economic rationalist pressures toward improving functional literacy as an instrument of national economic responses to globalization. Each has made significant contributions to reading research, although New Zealand work may be better known overseas at present. Australian research in critical literacy, and applications of systemic functional linguistics, seem likely to be more widely acknowledged in coming years.

REFERENCES

Alloway, N. & Gilbert, P. (1997). Boys and literacy: Lessons from Australia. *Gender and Education, 9*(1), 49–58.

Anderson, J. (1982). Cue Systems, cohesion and comprehending. *Australian Journal of Remedial Education, 14,* 56–59.

Anderson, J. (1983). Cohesion and the reading teacher. *Australian Journal of Reading, 6,* 3–4.

Baker, C. D. (1991). Literacy practices and social relations in classroom reading events. In C. D. Baker & A. Luke (Eds.), *Towards a critical sociology of reading pedagogy* (pp. 161–190). Amsterdam: John Benjamins.

Baker, C. D. (1997). Literacy practices and classroom order. In S. Muspratt, A. Luke, & P. Freebody (Eds.), *Constructing critical literacies: Teaching and learning textual practice* (pp. 243–262). Cresskill, NJ: Hampton Press.

Bowey, J. A. (1996). Phonological sensitivity as a proximal contributor to phonological recoding skills in children's reading. *Australian Journal of Psychology, 48,* 113–118.

Bowey, J. A., & Underwood, N. (1996). Further evidence that orthographic rime usage in nonword reading increases with word level reading proficiency. *Journal of Experimental Child Psychology, 63,* 526–562.

Bowey, J. A., Vaughan, L., & Hansen, J. (1998). Beginning readers' use of orthographic analogies in word reading. *Journal of Experimental Child Psychology, 68,* 108–133.

Breen, M., Louden, W., Barratt-Pugh, C., Rivalland, J., Rohl, M., Rhydwen, M., Lloyd S., & Carr T. (1995). *Literacy in its place: Literacy practices in urban and rural communities.* Report to the Commonwealth Department of Employment, Education, Training and Youth Affairs, Canberra, as part of the Children's Literacy National Projects Program. Perth, WA: Edith Cowan University.

Byrne, B. (1992). Studies in the acquisition procedure for reading: Rationale, hypotheses and data. In P. B. Gough, L. C. Ehri, & R. Treiman (Eds.), *Reading acquisition* (pp. 1–34). Hillsdale, NJ: Lawrence Erlbaum Associates.

Byrne, B. (1998). *The foundation of literacy.* Hove, UK: Psychology Press.

Byrne, B., & Fielding-Barnsley, R. (1989). Phonemic awareness and letter knowledge in the child's acquisition of the alphabetic principle. *Journal of Educational Psychology, 81,* 313–321.

Byrne, B., & Fielding-Barnsley, R. (1991). Evaluation of a program to teach phonemic to young children. *Journal of Educational Psychology, 83,* 451–455.

Byrne, B., & Fielding-Barnsley, R. (1995). Evaluation of a program to teach phonemic awareness to young children: A 2- and 3-year follow-up and a new preschool trial. *Journal of Educational Psychology, 87,* 488–503.

Cambourne, B. (1984). Language, learning and literacy. In A. Butler & J. Turbill (Eds.), *Towards a reading-writing classroom* (pp. 5–10). Sydney, NSW: Primary English Teachers' Association.

Cambourne, B. (1988). *The whole story: Natural learning and the acquisition of literacy in the classroom.* Auckland, NZ: Ashton Scholastic.

Cambourne, B., & Brown, H. (1987). *Read and Retell: A strategy for the whole language classroom.* North Ryde, NSW: Methuen, Australia.

Castle, J. M., Riach, J., & Nicholson, T. (1994). Getting off to a better start in reading and spelling: The effects of phonemic awareness instruction within a whole language program. *Journal of Educational Psychology, 86,* 350–359.

Cazden, C. B. (1992). Differential treatment in New Zealand classrooms. *Whole language plus: Essays on literacy in the United States and New Zealand* (pp. 211–233). New York: Teachers College Press.

Center, Y., & Freeman L. (1997). A trial evaluation of SWELL (Schoolwide Early Language and Literacy): A whole class early literacy program for at-risk and disadvantaged children. *International Journal of Disability, Development and Education, 44,* 21–40.

Center, Y., Wheldhall, K., Freeman, L., Outhred, L., & McNaught, M. (1995). An evaluation of Reading Recovery. *Reading Research Quarterly, 30,* 240–263.

Chapman, J. W., & Tunmer, W. E. (1991). Recovering "reading recovery." *Australia and New Zealand Journal of Developmental Disabilities, 17,* 59–71.

Christie, F., Devlin, B., Freebody, P., Luke, A., Martin, J. R., Threadgold, T., & Walton, C. (1991). *Teaching English literacy.* Report of a Project of National Significance to the Commonwealth Department of Employment, Education, and Training on the preservice preparation of teachers for teaching English literacy. Canberra, ACT: Department of Employment, Education & Training.

Clay, M. M. (1985). Engaging with the school system: A study of the interactions in new entrant classrooms. *New Zealand Journal of Educational Studies, 20,* 20–38.

Clay, M. M. (1987). Implementing Reading Recovery: Systematic adaptations to an educational innovation. *New Zealand Journal of Educational Studies, 22,* 35–58.

Clay, M. M. (1990). The Reading Recovery programme, 1984–1988: Coverage, outcomes and Education Board district figures. *New Zealand Journal of Educational Studies, 25,* 61–70.

Clay, M. M. (1991). *Becoming literate: The construction of inner control.* Auckland, NZ: Heinemann.

Clay, M. M. (1993). *Reading recovery: A guidebook for teachers in training.* Portsmouth, NH: Heinemann.

Clay, M. M. (1997). *Future directions and challenges.* A talk to the Auckland Council of the New Zealand Reading Association. Auckland, NZ: Auckland Reading Association.

Clay, M. M., & Tuck, B. (1991). *A study of Reading Recovery subgroups: Including outcomes for children who did not satisfy discontinuing criteria.* Report to Ministry of Education, University of Auckland, Auckland, NZ.

Clayton, J., Barnett, J., Kemelfield, G., & Mulhauser, P. (1996). *Desert schools: An investigation of English language and literacy among young aboriginal people in seven communities.* Report to the Commonwealth Department of Employment, Education, Training and Youth Affairs, Canberra, as part of the Children's Literacy Projects Program. Canberra, ACT: Department of Employment, Education, Training and Youth Affairs.

Crevola, C. A., & Hill, P. W. (1998). Evaluation of a whole-school approach to prevention and intervention in early literacy. *Journal of Education for Students Placed at Risk, 3,* 133–157.

Dawkins, J. (1990). *Australian literacy and language policy.* Canberra, ACT: Australian Government Publishing Service.

Dilena, M., & van Kraayenoord, C. E. (1996). *Whole school approaches to literacy assessment and reporting: Executive summary.* Canberra, ACT: Department of Employment, Education, Training and Youth Affairs.

Education Review Office. (1997). Literacy in New Zealand schools: Reading. *Education Evaluation Report,* No. 5.

Elley, W. B. (1989). Vocabulary acquisition from listening to stories. *Reading Research Quarterly, 24,* 176–186.

Elley, W. B. (1991). Acquiring literacy in a second language: The effect of book-based programs. *Language Learning, 41,* 375–411.

Elley, W. B. (1997). A perspective on New Zealand reading programmes. In J. Biddulph (Ed.), *Language/literacy education: Diversity and challenge* (Report on the New Zealand Council for Teacher Education language/literacy teacher education conference) (pp. 33–43). Hamilton, NZ: School of Education, University of Waikato.

Elley, W. B. (1998). *Evaluation of "Books in Homes" programme: Final report.* Wellington: Ministry of Education.

Elley, W. B., & Foster, D. (1996). *Sri Lanka Books in Schools project.* London: International Book Development.

Elley, W. B., & Schleicher, A. (1994). International differences in achievement levels. In W. B. Elley (Ed.), *The IEA study of reading literacy: Achievement and instruction in thirty-two school systems* (pp. 35–63). Oxford: Pergamon.

Fergusson, D. M., & Horwood, J. (1997). Gender differences in educational achievement in a New Zealand birth cohort. *New Zealand Journal of Educational Studies, 32,* 83–96.

Flockton, L., & Crooks, T. (1997). *Reading and speaking assessment results, 1996.* Dunedin, NZ: Educational Assessment Research Unit, University of Otago.

Gilbert, P. (1988). Stoning the romance: Girls as resistant readers and writers. *Curriculum Perspectives, 8*(2), 13–19.

Gilbert, P. (1998). Gender and schooling in new times: The challenge of boys and literacy. *Australian Educational Researcher, 25*(1), 15–36.

Gilbert, P., & Taylor, S. (1991). *Fashioning the feminine: Girls, popular culture and schooling.* Sydney, NSW: Allen & Unwin.

Gilroy, A., & Moore, D. (1988). Reciprocal teaching of comprehension-fostering and comprehension-monitoring activities with ten primary school girls. *Educational Psychology, 8,* 41–49.

Glasswell, K., Parr, J., & McNaughton, S. (1996, December). *Developmental pathways in the construction of writing expertise.* Paper presented at the annual conference of the New Zealand Association for Research in Education, Nelson, NZ.

Glynn, T., Bethune, N., Crooks, T., Ballard K., & Smith, J. (1992). Reading Recovery in context: Implementation and outcome. *Educational Psychology, 12,* 249–261.

Goodridge, M. J., & McNaughton, S. (1997). *Early literacy experience in families.* Unpublished manuscript, University of Auckland, Auckland, NZ.

Gordon, L. (1994). "Rich" and "poor" schools in Aotearoa. *New Zealand Journal of Educational Studies, 29,* 113–125.

Green, B., Hodgens, J., & Luke, A. (1994). *Debating literacy in Australia: A documentary history, 1945–1994.* deet, Canberra, ACT: Australian Literacy Federation.

Gunn, S. (1996). *Children's literacy research map.* Report to the Commonwealth Department of Employment, Education, Training and Youth Affairs, Canberra, as part of the Children's Literacy National Projects Program. Canberra, ACT: Department of Employment, Education, Training and Youth Affairs.

Halliday, M., & Hasan, R. (1976). *Cohesion in English.* London: Longman.

Halliday, M., & Hasan, R. (1985). *Language, context and text: Aspects of language in a social-semiotic perspective.* Waurn Ponds, Vic.: Deakin University Press.

Henson, N. (1991). *Reading in the middle and upper primary school: A report of an investigation undertaken on behalf of the Ministry of Education.* Wellington, NZ: Ministry of Education.

Hill, S., Comber, B., Louden, W., Rivalland, J., & Reid, J. (1998). *100 Children go to school: Connections and disconnections in literacy development in the first year prior to school and the first year of school.* Report to the Commonwealth Department of Employment, Education, Training and Youth Affairs, Canberra, as part of the

Children's Literacy National Projects Program. Canberra, ACT: Department of Employment, Education, Training and Youth Affairs.

Hohepa, M., McNaughton, S., & Jenkins, K. (1996). Maori pedagogies and the roles of the individual. *New Zealand Journal of Educational Studies, 31,* 29–40.

Hohepa, M., Smith, G. H., Smith, L. T., & McNaughton, S. (1992). Te Kohanga Reo hei tikanga ako i te Reo Maori: Te Kohanga Reo as a context for language learning. *Educational Psychology, 12*(3,4), 323–346.

Iverson, S., & Tunmer, W. (1993). Phonological processing skills and the Reading Recovery programme. *Journal of Educational Psychology, 85,* 112–126.

Johnston, P. (1997). Language/literacy education—An international perspective. In J. Biddulph (Ed.), *Language/literacy education: Diversity and challenge* (Report on the New Zealand Council for Teacher Education language/literacy teacher education conference) (pp. 3–18). Hamilton, NZ: School of Education, University of Waikato.

Jorm, A., & Share, D. (1983). Phonological recoding and reading acquisition. *Applied Psycholinguistics, 4,* 103–147.

Juel, C. (1988). Learning to read and write: A longitudinal study of 54 children from first through fourth grades. *Journal of Educational Psychology, 80,* 437–447.

Kelly, M., Moore, D. W., & Tuck, B. F. (1994). Reciprocal teaching in a regular primary school classroom. *Journal of Educational Research, 88,* 53–61.

Kelsey, J. (1995). *The New Zealand experiment: A world model for structural adjustment?* Auckland, NZ: Auckland University Press with Bridget Williams Books.

Kerin, A. (1987). *One to one interaction in junior classes.* Unpublished master's thesis, University of Auckland, Auckland, NZ.

Kerslake, J. (1998). Reading Recovery data for 1996. *Research Bulletin* (no 8). Wellington, NZ: Ministry of Education, Research Division.

Kidston, P., & Elkins, J. (1992). Australia. In J. Hladczuk & W. Eller (Eds.), *International handbook of reading education* (pp. 1–24). Westport, CT: Greenwood Press.

Lankshear, C. (1994). *Critical literacy.* Belconnen, ACT: Australian Curriculum Studies Association.

Lange, D. (1988). *Tomorrow's schools.* Wellington, NZ: Government Printer.

Le Fevre, D. (1996). *Tape-assisted reciprocal teaching for readers with poor decoding skills.* Unpublished master's thesis, University of Auckland, Auckland, NZ.

Luke, A. (1994). *The social construction of literacy in the primary school.* South Melbourne, Vic.: Macmillan Education Australia.

Masters, G., & Forster, M. (1997). *Mapping literacy achievement: Results of the 1996 National English Literacy Survey.* Canberra, ACT: Department of Employment, Education, Training and Youth Affairs.

Maxwell, G. S., van Kraayenoord, C. E., Field, C., & Herschell, P. (1995). *Developing an assessment framework: A planning guide for schools.* Brisbane, LD: Southern Vales School Support Centre, Department of Education, Queensland.

McGaw, B. (1998). Politicising the standards debate. *ACER Newsletter Supplement, 92,* 1–4.

McNaughton, S. (1995). *Patterns of emergent literacy: Processes of development and transition.* Auckland, NZ: Oxford University Press.

McNaughton, S. (1996). Commentary: Co-constructing curricula: A comment on two curricula (*Te Whariki* and the English Curriculum) and their developmental bases. *New Zealand Journal of Educational Studies, 31,* 189–196.

McNaughton, S., Ka'ai, T., & Wolfgramm, E. (1993, March). *The perils of scaffolding: Models of tutoring and sociocultural diversity in how families read storybooks to preschoolers.* Paper presented at the biennial conference of the Society for Research in Child Development, New Orleans, LA.

Ministry of Education. (1997). *Adult literacy in New Zealand: Results from the international adult literacy survey.* Wellington, NZ: Author.

Ministry of Education. (1998). *Education Statistics News Sheet* (Vol. 8, No. 11).

Ministry of Education. (1999). *Report of the Literacy Taskforce.* Wellington, NZ: Author.

The mother of all reformers. (1993, October 16). *Economist,* p. 20.

Muspratt, S., Luke, A., & Freebody, P. (Eds.). (1997). *Constructing critical literacies: Teaching and learning textual practices.* Cresskill, NJ: Hampton Press.

Nicholson, T. (1989). A comment on Reading Recovery. *New Zealand Journal of Educational Studies, 24,* 95–97.

Nicholson, T. (1995). Research note: More news on rich and poor schools, and the news is still not good. *New Zealand Journal of Educational Studies, 30,* 227–228.

Nicholson, T. (1997). Closing the gap on reading failure: Social background, phonemic awareness and learning to read. In B. A. Blachman (Ed.), *Foundations of reading acquisition and dyslexia: Implications for early intervention* (pp. 381–408). Mahwah, NJ: Lawrence Erlbaum Associates.

Nicholson, T. (1999). Literacy in the family and society. In G. B. Thompson & T. Nicholson (Eds.), *Learning to read: Beyond phonics and whole language* (pp. 1–22) New York: Teachers College Press.

Nicholson, T., & Gallienne, G. (1995). Struggletown meets Middletown: A survey of reading achievement levels among 13-year-old pupils in two contrasting socioeconomic areas. *New Zealand Journal of Educational Studies, 30,* 15–24.

Nicholson, T., & Whyte, B. (1992). Matthew effects in learning new words while listening to stories. In C. K. Kinzer & D. J. Leu (Eds.), *Literacy research, theory, and practice: Views from many perspectives* (pp. 499–503). Chicago: National Reading Conference.

Painter, C., & Martin, J. R. (Eds.). (1986). *Writing to mean: Teaching genres across the curriculum.* Applied Linguistics Association of Australia, Occasional Papers No. 9, Sydney, NSW: University of Sydney.

Palincsar, A. S., & Brown, A. L. (1984). Reciprocal teaching of comprehension-fostering and comprehension-monitoring activities. *Cognition and Instruction, 1,* 117–175.

Penno, J. (1997). *Vocabulary acquisition from teacher explanation and repeated exposure to stories: Does it overcome the Mathew effect?* Unpublished master's thesis, University of Auckland, Auckland, NZ.

Phillips, G., & McNaughton, S. (1990). The practice of storybook reading to preschool children in mainstream New Zealand families. *Reading Research Quarterly, 25,* 196–212.

Phillips, G., & Smith, P. (1997). *A third chance to learn: The development and evaluation of specialised interventions for young children experiencing the greatest difficulty in learning to read.* Wellington, NZ: New Zealand Council for Educational Research.

Smith, J., & Elkins, J. (1985). The use of cohesion by underachieving readers. *Reading Psychology, 6,* 13–25.

Smith, J., & Elkins, J. (1992). Coherence and the sharing of meaning: Supporting underachieving readers. *International Journal of Disability, Development and Education, 39,* 239–249.

Smith, P. E. (1994). Reading Recovery and children with English as a second language. *New Zealand Journal of Educational Studies, 29,* 141–159.

Statistics New Zealand. (1997). *1996 Census of population and dwellings: Ethnic groups.* Wellington, NZ: Author.

Tagoilelagi, F. (1992). *The role of the Samoan culture* (fa'a Samoa) *in its children's literacy skills.* Unpublished master's thesis, University of Auckland, Auckland, NZ.

Thompson, G. B. (1993). Appendix: Reading instruction for the initial years in New Zealand schools. In G. B. Thompson, W. E. Tunmer, & T. Nicholson (Eds.), *Reading acquisition processes* (pp. 148–154). Clevedon, UK: Multilingual Matters.

Thompson, G. B., & Johnston, R. S. (1993). The effects of type of instruction on processes of reading acquisition. In G. B. Thompson, W. E. Tunmer, & T. Nicholson (Eds.). *Reading acquisition processes* (pp. 74–90). Clevedon, UK: Multilingual Matters.

Tunmer, W. E. (1990). The role of language prediction skills in beginning reading. *New Zealand Journal of Educational Studies, 25,* 95–114.

Tunmer, W. E. (1992). Phonological processing and Reading Recovery: A reply to Clay. *New Zealand Journal of Educational Studies, 27,* 203–217.

Tunmer, W., & Chapman, J. (1996). Whole language or whole nonsense. *New Zealand Journal of Educational Studies, 31,* 77–84.

Tunmer, W., & Chapman, J. (1998). Language prediction skill, phonological recoding ability, and beginning reading. In C. Hulme & R. M. Joshi (Eds.), *Reading and spelling: Development and disorders* (pp. 33–67). Mahwah, NJ: Lawrence Erlbaum Associates.

Tunmer, W., Chapman, J., Prochnow, J., & Ryan, H. (1997, July). *Language-related and cognitive-motivational factors in beginning literacy achievement: An overview.* Paper presented at the conference Reading on Track: Research Results for Teaching Reading, Massey University, Palmerston North, NZ.

van Kraayenoord, C. E. (1994). Toward self-assessment of literacy learning. *Australian Journal of Language and Literacy, 17,* 45–55.

van Kraayenoord, C. E. (1997). The value of classroom-based performance assessment of literacy learning. *SET Special 1997: Language and Literacy,* No. 13, 1–4. Camberwell, Vic.: Australian Council for Educational Research.

van Kraayenoord, C. E., & Paris, S. G. (1994). Literacy instruction in Australian primary schools. *Reading Teacher, 48,* 218–228.

Wagemaker, H. (Ed.). (1993). *Achievement in reading literacy: New Zealand's performance in a national and international context* (pp. 186–188). Wellington, NZ: Ministry of Education.

Wilkinson, I. A. G. (1998). Dealing with diversity: Achievement gaps in reading literacy among New Zealand students. *Reading Research Quarterly, 33,* 144–167.

Wolfgramm, E. (1991). *Becoming literate: The activity of book reading to Tongan preschoolers in Auckland.* Unpublished master's thesis, University of Auckland, Auckland, NZ.

Wolfgramm, E., McNaughton, S., & Afeaki, V. (1997). Story reading programme in a Tongan language group. *Set special: Language and literacy, 7.*

Wylie, C. (1997). *Self-managing schools seven years on: What have we learnt?* Wellington, NZ: New Zealand Council for Educational Research.

Wylie, C., Thompson, J., & Hendricks, A. (1996). *Competent children at 5: Families and early education.* Wellington, NZ: New Zealand Council for Educational Research.

CHAPTER 2

Reading Research in the United Kingdom

Colin Harrison
University of Nottingham

There are dangers as well as difficulties in attempting an overview of research. I share the opinion of those who would argue that any authors, no matter how carefully they attempt to review a field with impartiality and rigor, are unable to shake off the effects of their own personal history and ideology. This does not mean that it is futile to make the attempt, but rather that in these postmodern times it can be helpful to acknowledge that a review of research is bound to be idiosyncratic (Harrison & Gough, 1996).

The 1930s would be one possible point at which to begin an historical overview of reading research in the United Kingdom, because it was in 1932 that Sir Frederick Bartlett published his landmark study of the psychology of memory, *Remembering*, which for 60 years was one of the most cited in the field, because of its pioneering analysis of cross-cultural intrusions on story recall (Bartlett, 1932). Equally, the 1960s would be another point to begin, because it was during this decade that UKRA was established, and the journal *Reading* was founded. This journal went on to publish for over 20 years an annual review of reading research in Great Britain, which has left us with a valuable record of research findings that would in many cases no longer be accessible (see Goodacre, 1969, for an early example, and Raban, 1990, for one that demonstrates the explosion of research activity that occurred during the intervening years). One further archival source for information on reading research would be the *Journal of Research in Reading*, which was established by UKRA under the inspirational leadership of Tony Pugh in 1978. The *Journal of Research in Reading* remains the only journal in Europe wholly devoted to reading research.

In order to facilitate comparisons with research and practice in other countries, however, the remainder of this chapter focuses on contemporary issues and themes in reading research in the United Kingdom, using the three coordinating concepts of processes, practices and policies. Broadly speaking, research into reading processes has been carried out by psychologists, and research into practice has been carried out by scholars in university schools of education, whereas policy-driven research has been directed and funded by government agencies. It is worth mentioning in this context that although UKRA covers England, Northern Ireland, Scotland, and Wales, Scotland and Northern Ireland have their own government departments for education, and thus have more independence in policy and practice than is the case in England and Wales. From 1988, the point at which a national curriculum was introduced, these latter two countries endured a decade of unprecedented government-initiated change, which has impinged on both research and practice, and to which I give attention later in the chapter. I am acutely aware that on a conservative estimate some 1,600 books and perhaps 4,000 journal articles on reading have been published in the United Kingdom during the period 1960–1998, and that this chapter refers directly to no more than 40 of these. In order to keep within the word limit for the chapter, I made the difficult decision not to attempt to summarize research into neurological processes or into reading in a second language, even though I believe that much important and exciting work has been done in these areas in the United Kingdom.

RESEARCH INTO READING PROCESSES

If one were to pose the question, "What phrase had the greatest impact on teachers' understanding of the reading process in the United Kingdom over the 1990s?" the consensus answer would probably be "phonological awareness." In the 1970s, the insights of Kenneth Goodman (1967) and Frank Smith (1973), both frequent visitors to England, came to dominate the discourse of reading, at least in schools and in the education departments of universities and colleges, and the phrase *psycholinguistic guessing game* became a key element in teachers' accounts of the reading process. During the 1980s, this dominance prevailed, but was augmented by Marie (now Dame Marie) Clay's emphasis on "concepts of print" and the principles of Reading Recovery (Clay, 1985). But during the 1990s, the phrases *phonological awareness* and *phonemic awareness* came to assume a centrality that might seem surprising, at least to those unfamiliar with the cyclical nature of reading research and pedagogy. In the United Kingdom, these phrases are particularly associated with the work of Peter Bryant, notably in his collaborations with Lynette Bradley (Bradley & Bryant, 1983; Bryant & Bradley, 1985) and Usha Goswami (Goswami & Bryant, 1990). I discuss the impact of these studies on pedagogy later in this chapter; for the moment, my focus is the reading process.

In the early 1980s, Bradley and Bryant (1983; Bryant & Bradley, 1985) reported on a 4-year longitudinal study of the reading of 368 children, which had begun when the children were either 4 or 5 years old. The study gave particular attention to prereading abilities, especially those that preceded children's knowledge of letters and letter names (children who showed any sign of being able to read were excluded from the study), and sought to establish which variables were the best predictors of subsequent success in reading. Bradley and Bryant used regression procedures to eliminate from the analysis achievement attributable to intelligence, memory, and vocabulary, and produced one central finding: that children's sensitivity to rhyme was the best single predictor of subsequent success in reading. The test that Bradley and Bryant used was an alliteration oddity test, in which the child was asked to say which word in a list of three or four was the odd one out: the words might be *pin, win, sit,* and *fin,* for example, with *sit* being the odd one out. The argument Bryant developed was that the child's sensitivity to rhyme and alliteration was a causal factor in progress in learning to read and spell in the following 3 years. The finding was a specific one: Sensitivity to rhyme predicted subsequent reading ability, but it did not predict skill in arithmetic. A second more detailed longitudinal study (Bryant, Bradley, Maclean, & Crossland, 1989), starting at age 3 years and following 64 children over 3 years, also showed a strong predictive relationship between sensitivity to rhyme and progress in reading. The effects of intelligence, vocabulary knowledge, and social background were controlled, and once again a very specific effect was found: Rhyme awareness predicted success in reading but not mathematical skills. It is important to stress that Bryant and his co-workers regarded sensitivity to rhyme as an ability that developed independently from other forms of phonological awareness, and they argued that other experimenters who conflated scores on phonological variables such as rhyme awareness, phoneme detection, and letter–sound knowledge had produced highly questionable conclusions in some cases.

Bryant's argument was supported by the research of Ellis and Large (1987), who reported that many 4-year-old children with a high IQ but poor rhyme-detection skills went on to become poor readers, whereas those with high IQ and good rhyme-detection skills were much more likely to become good readers. Stuart and Masterson (1992) also carried out longitudinal studies of young children, beginning at age 4 years with a battery of six tests of rhyme detection and phoneme awareness. Unlike Bryant, Stuart and Masterson found that their six phonological measures intercorrelated so highly that it was reasonable to combine them into a single factor. What they found was that this phonological score was a better predictor of reading ability at age 10 than was IQ at age 6. Phonological awareness at age 4 was also a better predictor of subsequent spelling ability than was IQ. Like Bryant, Stuart and Masterson found that phonological awareness was a specific rather than a general ability; it was not a strong predictor of subsequent vocabulary knowledge, for example. Correlation is not causation, however, and they point out that, although having a lower than average phonological score at age 4 is extremely likely to be followed by below-average attainment in reading, there is no guarantee that having an above-average phonological score will lead inevitably to success in reading (Stuart & Masterson, 1995, p. 182).

Bryant was aware that correlational data do not provide evidence of a causal relationship, and he set out to establish such a relationship through intervention studies, the most widely cited of which was the one that appeared in *Nature* (Bradley & Bryant, 1983); this is generally held to be the one that led to the foregrounding of the issue of phonological awareness for teachers in the United Kingdom. It is important, therefore, to stress that this training study, which is widely understood to have shown that teaching 6-year-olds about rhyme brings about significant improvement in reading ability, actually produced findings that were rather less clear-cut than this. First, there were not one but two experimental groups, the second of which received specific training in recognizing letter–sound relationships, using plastic letters. This is of course a very different intervention from one that sets out simply to improve children's ability to recognize and manipulate sounds. There were also two control groups, one of which was given additional time on vocabulary development through categorizing word families. In the event, the groups performed as one might have predicted on Bryant's model: The dual-treatment experimental group (phonological training plus letter–sound training) did best, the single-treatment experimental group (phonological training only) came second, the vocabulary development group came third, and the no-treatment control came fourth. This rank order was consistent across the three tests of word reading, passage reading, and spelling. However, although the means supported Bryant's hypothesis, the within-group variance was high, and this meant that the crucial group difference—that between the phonological training only versus the vocabulary training—fell short of statistical significance. In fact, the difference in group mean scores between the two experimental groups was greater on all three tests than the difference between the phonological training only group and the vocabulary development control group. The case that developing young children's rhyme awareness leads to improved reading had received support, but the results from Bradley and Bryant's dual-treatment experimental group strongly suggested that the most powerful teaching method is one that combines training in phonological categorization with training in letter–sound relationships.

One seminal strand of United Kingdom research into the reading process that explores more deeply the issue of how children make use of their knowledge of phonology has been the work of Usha Goswami (1986, 1990) into how analogies are used to decode new words. Goswami focused on the onset-rime distinction (between the first consonants in a word and the remainder of the word, e.g., str-ing), and examined children's potential for decoding previously unfamiliar words at age 5, 6, and 7. She used an elegant experimental procedure, establishing first that a word was unfamiliar, then teaching it and noting how the child was subsequently able to generalize using onset-rime analogies. Children in all three age groups demonstrated an ability to use analogies to help recognize unfamiliar words, but their ability to do so developed over time, and Goswami's experiments provided an detailed account of the developmental sequence, as children learned to form analogies first using the rime (recognizing *weak*, having been taught *beak*), then the onset (recognizing *trap*, having been taught *trim*), and finally just part of the rime (recognizing *harp* having been taught *hark*).

Goswami and Bryant's (1990) views on the importance of the onset-rime distinction have not gone unchallenged. Muter, Hulme, Snowling, and Taylor (1997) argued that not all measures of phonological awareness are equally good predictors of later reading, and that rhyme awareness, which comes early, is a weaker predictor than phoneme segmentation, which develops later. Muter and her colleagues carried out a longitudinal study of children from age 4, giving a battery of phonological tests that enabled a factor analysis to be carried out. This produced two factors: a *rhyming factor* (rhyme detection, rhyme production) and a *segmentation factor* (phoneme segmentation, deletion and blending). They then carried out multiple-regression path analyses, which came up with a result that appears to inflict severe damage on the Goswami and Bryant model: Their path diagrams showed significant weightings at the beginning of the study for IQ and segmentation ability in predicting achievement a year later in segmentation, reading, and spelling. In their analysis, rhyming ability failed to make a significant independent contribution to either reading or spelling. Muter et al. also reported that letter knowledge made a further significant contribution to both reading and spelling in year 2, and identified one final key element—a separate interaction effect based on the product of letter-knowledge × segmentation, which exerted a small additional effect on reading, and a massive additional effect on spelling. The authors' interpretation of these findings was to emphasize that it is necessary to teach children in such a way that explicit links are formed between their underlying phonological awareness and their experiences in learning to read. The Hatcher, Hulme, and Ellis (1994) intervention study reported later in this chapter provides a detailed test of these claims.

Research into reading comprehension has been much less prominent in the United Kingdom, but important work on reading comprehension processes was carried out by Briggs, Austin, and Underwood (1984), who extended the widely cited study of West and Stanovich (1978) on readers' use of context in reading by offering a closer examination of differences between younger and older, and good and poor readers. They found a more complex pattern of interactions related to children's use of context than what would have been predicted by Stanovich's Interactive-Compensatory model of the reading process. Stanovich proposed a two-process model of reading, in which readers either used automatic (unattended) word recognition, which freed up processing capacity for comprehension, or a slower, attentional pathway, which was more reliant on context for word recognition. Good readers, it was hypothesized, would be less reliant on context, and less influenced by it than poor readers. This was not what Briggs et al. found, however. Skilled readers at age 11 appear to go through a phase in which they are influenced by context, but in a somewhat disabling way (though it should be noted that in the Briggs et al. study the reading ability of the good readers was at the level of the "less skilled" readers in West and Stanovich study). Perhaps the best interpretation is that it is only as readers approach adulthood that they are able to consciously repress context effects in order to activate the more rapid automatic word recognition pathway to word recognition.

RESEARCH INTO READING PEDAGOGY AT HOME AND SCHOOL

Early years education in the United Kingdom saw something of a revolution over the two decades that followed the publication of a seminal study of the importance of stories in the linguistic development of potential readers (Wells, 1978), and as schools have come to see parents as allies and partners in the teaching of reading (Bloom, 1990).

Two research projects that monitored the results of encouraging parents to read with their children came to have national significance; these were the Haringey project (Tizard et al., 1982) and the Belfield project (Hannon & Jackson, 1987). The actual experimental results of both projects were relatively modest in scale and effect size, but both received dramatic levels of publicity in the press, and Hannon reported that the Belfield team felt impelled to go into the production of booklets to help meet parents' needs for information. Hannon (1995) conducted a useful review of research and practice in parents' involvement in the teaching of literacy, and he reviewed all the major initiatives, offering a helpful gloss on the methodological options related to evaluation and program development in this field. He argued that the multiplicity of contextual variables available tends to make traditional testing approaches and methodologies invalid, and argued instead for *evaluation by participants*, and a qualitative analysis of the following issues: take-up, participation rate, implementation, involvement processes, teachers' views, and parents' views.

A related strand of research activity has been that of Keith Topping (see Topping & Lindsay, 1992, for a review), a former school educational psychologist who conducted a series of studies on the effectiveness of *paired reading* (peer tutoring of reading, usually based on student–student interaction). Much of Topping's work focused on peer relationships within schools, but Hannon (1995, p. 25) pointed out that many of those advocating parent involvement have made use of Topping's approach, and often use the terms *paired reading*, *shared reading*, *home reading*, and *parent listening* interchangeably.

Topping's approach is essentially one of having a more experienced reader provide immediate encouragement and support for the less experienced, as the two readers read together, with the tutor gradually withdrawing support as the tutee gains in confidence. Paired reading has been used with readers of all ages from age 6 to adult. The approach has been widely evaluated, in over 150 small projects involving over 2,300 participants, and the results have been very positive. Brooks, Flanagan, Henkhuzens, and Hutchinson (1998), however, in their review of the effectiveness of early intervention schemes in the United Kingdom, commented that Topping's claim of overall effect size (0.87 for reading accuracy, over 34 projects) may be an overestimate, because Topping calculated his effect sizes using a nonstandard metric.

Research into the development of reading abilities beyond the early years is relatively new field in the United Kingdom, and it is worth reviewing it in some detail, because the studies initiated in the 1970s are still having an impact on practice. Research into extending reading development first received funding at national level in 1973, when the Schools Council (the government-funded national curriculum development agency, which was closed down by Margaret Thatcher when she became Secretary of State for Education) launched two research projects, Extending Beginning Reading (Southgate, Arnold, & Johnson, 1981) and The Effective Use of Reading (Lunzer & Gardner, 1979). These projects looked respectively at reading in a representative sample of schools in the age ranges 7–9, and 10–15, across the countries of England and Wales. Southgate's project reported some significant findings, the import of which is still being felt. She stated that teachers gave far too much time to listening to children read, that teachers did not use that time well, and that while teachers were devoting time to hearing children read, children spent up to a third of their time off-task. As an alternative to listening to children read, more sustained and less frequent interactions were recommended, in which comprehension development, reading progress, and reading interests could all be explored (Southgate et al., 1981, p. 320). One startling research finding was that students in the school in which the teachers spent the least amount of time listening to individual children read made the most progress in reading (Southgate et al., 1981, p. 319).

Southgate's findings found support in the research of Hazel Francis (1987), who in another widely cited study concluded that teachers needed to have a much clearer understanding of the intentions and pedagogical goals in hearing children read. She suggested that in their desire to avoid making the experience an unpleasant one for children, teachers tended to hold back from correcting, and thus from explicit teaching, and that it was this that made the practice seem limited to an outside observer.

The Lunzer and Gardner (1979) project carried out the most extensive investigation ever undertaken in the United Kingdom into the place of reading at the end of elementary schooling and in the first 4 years of secondary school, and producing findings that are still regarded as important and valid. The study investigated:

- The nature of reading comprehension subskills (a unitary model was proposed, with comprehension defined as *the ability and willingness to reflect on what is read*).
- The readability of school texts (a cross-validation study found that pooled teacher estimates of readability were highly reliable, and that in general, the harder a text, the more likely a student would be to have to read it at home, without the availability of teacher or peer support).
- How reading occurred in the classroom (reading took up about 10–15% of a student's day; outside of English, or Language Arts, however, this percentage dropped to 8–11%).
- Reading for homework (there was more sustained reading at home than in school; even when the texts were difficult, children tended to rate the reading they were assigned for homework as easy).
- The use of commercial reading development programs (in a study of 1,018 children, at ages 11, 12 and 15, a 3-month intensive course using commercial reading materials produced highly significant gains in experimental groups, which were sustained in a late posttest 6 months later; gains were particularly large in the case of groups of weaker readers).
- The use of small-group discussion activities to develop comprehension subsequently called DARTs—Directed Activities Related to Texts (these were found to be useful in a range of subject areas, promoting close reading, and increasing confidence).

Lunzer and Gardner also reported on how teachers sought to develop reading at junior high school level (broadly speaking, they didn't), how children read in class (generally in bursts that summed to less than 15 sec in 1 min, even in text-intensive subjects as history and geography), and the tasks that teachers offered students for "research" (these were often too often inauthentic).

The two Schools Council studies appeared at a time when reading development was about to become a focal issue for teachers. One important reason for this was the democratization of schooling that accompanied government moves during the 1970s to decrease selective and increase comprehensive schooling, which drew the attention of a much greater number of teachers to the needs of weaker readers. Another was the contribution of the Open University's courses for teachers. During the 15 years that followed the publication of the government's report on the teaching of English (DES, 1975) thousands of teachers participated in the Open University's distance-learning courses on reading, many at master's level, and all carrying out classroom-based research into reading activities and reading development.

During the 1980s, Lunzer and Gardner received funding to extend and further evaluate the DARTs activities (Davies & Green, 1984; Lunzer & Gardner, 1984). What was significant in these studies was that teachers within each content area devised small-group reading development activities, which were formatively evaluated before inclusion in the report. Although the evaluation did not explore whether the DARTs activities were associated with gains in reading achievement, the authors did report increased attention to text, increases in reflective reading, improved comprehension, and readers who used DARTs activities needing to ask fewer questions of the teacher.

RESEARCH INTO EARLY INTERVENTION

There was a great deal of research activity related to the evaluation of early intervention in the United Kingdom during the 1990s, much of which may be attributed directly or indirectly to the government initiatives referred to later in this chapter. The United Kingdom government gave substantial support for a pilot implementation and evaluation of Reading Recovery (Clay, 1993) in 21 local authorities, and also supported an evaluation of a range of family literacy projects (Brooks, Gorman, Harman, Hutchison, & Wilkin, 1996). Other projects arose out of the work by psychologists into reading processes. Of particular importance were intervention studies designed to assess the effectiveness of various types of phonological training. The Sylva and Hurry (1995) evaluation of Reading Recovery included an alternative treatment group that received phonological training, and in Cumbria, a county in the north of England, Hatcher et al. (1994) evaluated a program that compared the effectiveness of phonological training with and without a complementary program of individualized activities broadly similar to those offered in a Reading Recovery session.

Brooks et al. (1998) undertook a meta-analysis of these studies, and of approximately 50 more (many of which were too descriptive to be capable of inclusion in the meta-analysis). In a lucid and authoritative monograph, the authors reviewed and compared the 20 studies, which they felt provided useful answers to the question of which interventions have been effective. Where a particular intervention had been the subject of numerous evaluations, some of which had been reported in insufficient detail to enable effects to be judged on any statistical basis, the authors adopted the useful expedient of reporting the most meticulously designed and reported. In the remainder of this section, I draw heavily on the Brooks et al. (1998) analysis.

In some respects it is difficult to generalize from the evaluations of Reading Recovery in the United Kingdom. All of the 21 local authorities in which Reading Recovery was implemented produced an evaluation report, but many were descriptive and did not report outcome measures other than in relation to Marie Clay's diagnostic survey instrument, or through data on how many students were "successfully discontinued" from the program. These measures are not easy to relate to standardized tests. The most comprehensive evaluation (Sylva & Hurry, 1995), however, did use standardized tests, and reported on the implementation of Reading Recovery in six London boroughs and in Surrey, a county bordering south London. All the children in this study were age 7 at the start of the project, and had already failed to make a good start in reading. A total of 89 children across the seven authorities were given Reading Recovery. An alternative treatment based on developing phonological awareness was given to a total of 91 children in a second set of schools, and the design also included a no-treatment control group in a third set of schools in the same authorities.

The evaluation showed Reading Recovery to be expensive, but effective: The experimental group made mean gains of 16 months in word reading over the 8.5 months of the intervention (with an effect size of 0.75), and these gains were sustained. By contrast, the no-treatment controls made only an 8-month gain. A very important finding of the study was that the alternative treatment groups, which had been given a sustained program to develop phonological awareness, made only modest progress: Their mean reading gain was 10 months over the 8.5 months of the intervention (with an effect size close to zero). The clear implication from the Sylva and Hurry study is that, although phonological awareness may be a good predictor of future success in reading, interventions for poor readers that focus on phonological awareness alone will have very limited success.

A very similar conclusion was drawn by Hatcher et al. (1994) in their study in Cumbria. This study had three experimental groups and one no-treatment control group, with 31 children 7 years old (±1) in each group. The treatments were a "phonology alone" program, a "reading and phonology" program, and a "reading alone" program. Controls to minimize differences attributable to teacher's style and other unintended interactions were exemplary, and the results were dramatic: The "reading and phonology" group showed significant gains in word reading, reading accuracy, and reading comprehension, with effect sizes in the range 0.45 to 1.60. Just as importantly, neither of the other treatment groups showed any significant gains over the normal schooling group. Hatcher et al. (1994) argue that there is a powerful interaction effect when phonology and reading are taught together, and that this was what made the mixed program effective. The mixed program was modeled on Marie Clay's (1985) procedures, but included additional phonological activities.

Brooks et al. drew the following conclusions from their meta-analysis:

- Normal schooling ("no treatment") does not enable slow readers to catch up.
- Work on phonological skills should be embedded within a broad approach.
- Children's comprehension skills can be improved if directly targeted.
- Working on children's self-esteem and reading in parallel has definite potential.
- Approaches using information technology (such as integrated learning systems) only work if they are precisely targeted.
- Large-scale schemes, such as the Basic Skills Agency Family Literacy project (Brooks et al., 1996) and Reading Recovery, although expensive, can give good value for money.
- Where reading partners are available and can be given appropriate training, partnership approaches can be very effective.
- Most of the schemes, which incorporate follow-up studies, continued to show gains (Brooks et al., 1998, p. 14).

READING RESEARCH AND POLICY ISSUES

The period 1988–1998 was a cataclysmic one in the United Kingdom in terms of the impact of government policies on schools (Harrison, 1995), particularly in England and Wales, and to a lesser extent in Scotland and Northern Ireland. During the period 1988–1991 the National Curriculum was established in England and Wales, and teachers were given a statutory duty to administer and test it, focusing on achievement at the end of three "key stages," corresponding to years 2, 6, 9, and 11 in the English school system (grades 1, 5, 8, and 10 in the United States).

The rationale for these changes was a concern to raise educational standards, but some of the government's strategies were difficult to reconcile with these goals. For example, in 1990 the Thatcher government abolished the Assessment of Performance Unit, the language monitoring group of which had been based in the National Foundation for Educational Research since its establishment in 1980. This group had been responsible for developing nationally validated tests of reading, writing, speaking, and listening in English and Welsh schools, and was by far the best placed to report on any changes in national standards of literacy (Gorman, White, Brooks, Maclure, & Kispal, 1987).

The government's thinking was that if all parents were able to receive information on the performance of their own children, using tests administered in school, with performance related to National Curriculum standards, then there would be no need for national surveys (K. Clarke, personal communication, February 11, 1991). But unfortunately, the task of devising completely new sets of classroom-based assessment materials to perform simultaneously the job of diagnostic and summative assessment, in English, mathematics, and science, at a number of age levels, proved too great, and the result was administrative chaos, teacher disaffection, a record number of teachers taking premature retirement, and a national boycott of the government's tests (Harrison, 1995; Harrison, Bailey, & Dewar, 1998). Some innovative approaches to classroom-based assessment were piloted and then rejected before the evaluations of them had even been submitted (Vincent & Harrison, 1998), whereas independent evaluations of the government's new tests (released 2 years after the reports had been submitted) showed that they fell short of acceptable standards of rigor in terms of validity and reliability (Ruddock et al., 1995).

During the middle and later 1990s, an uneasy truce developed, and the government's testing program was reduced, which permitted test development to occur at a less frantic pace and a dialogue to be opened between those responsible for enacting government policy and academics with testing expertise (Horner, 1998; Brooks, 1998; Vincent & Harrison, 1998). The Labour government, which came to power in 1997, was no less interventionist than the Conservative government that preceded it, and in 1998 government's Literacy Task Force announced that every elementary school in England and Wales would be required to deliver a Literacy Hour each day, following a strict set of pedagogical goals that were sent out to schools, and that were to be accompanied by in-service teacher development activities, some of which have been supported by additional government funds.

Scotland and Northern Ireland have fared somewhat better than England and Wales, in terms of direct government intervention in literacy teaching and assessment. In Scotland, for example, a suggested national program for literacy development for the age group 5–14 years was put forward, and although most schools decided that it would be unwise not to "volunteer" to adopt the new curriculum, it has been launched in a much more collegial climate than its English counterpart (in England, the national curriculum was drawn up by officers of the Schools Curriculum and Assessment Agency, reporting directly to ministers; in Scotland, the curriculum and the suggested assessment arrangements to accompany it were written by schools inspectors, who collaborated closely with academics, teachers and local authority personnel to ensure that the curriculum would be likely to receive wide support).

Innovative assessment arrangements have also been developed in Scotland in a more collaborative atmosphere than has been the case in England. The approach in Scotland has been to help teachers to become more skilled at formative evaluation of literacy development, and to this end a *Diagnostic Procedures* handbook was developed by a group of teachers working closely with members of the schools inspectorate and academics (Haywood & Spencer, 1998).

It is important to end this section with a mention of two reports that produced significant data on trends in reading standards in the United Kingdom. Government initiatives to raise standards are generally predicated on the assumption that reading standards are in decline, and certainly the press in the United Kingdom gave sustained support to this belief during the early 1990s. The available data did not support such a view, however. Two reports that appeared during the 1990s gave strong evidence that this was not the case in the United Kingdom. Brooks (1997) reviewed all the national survey data on reading in the United Kingdom over 50 years, and concluded that literacy standards have changed very little over that period. He noted that standards of reading in England appeared to dip slightly at the end of the 1980s (when teachers were grappling ineffectually with the demands of the new curriculum, and an unprecedented number of teachers in primary schools took premature retirement), but recovered in the early 1990s. International comparisons suggest that the British educational system produces high standards of literacy, with middle and upper ability children performing at a level comparable to the most successful countries in the world; more worrying is the longer "tail" of underperformance in the United Kingdom, which some commentators have ascribed to the elitist nature of the United Kingdom educational system.

The other important study was a replication of the Whitehead, Capey, and Madden (1977) study of the voluntary reading habits of 8,000 children aged 10, 12, and 14 (Hall & Coles, 1997). reported very similar findings to those of Whitehead, and emphasized that there was no evidence of a widespread decline in voluntary reading. Boys and girls at age 10 and girls at age 12 were reading more than boys at 12 and girls at 14 were reading about the same amount as their counterparts 25 years previously; only boys at age 14 had a mean significantly below that of Whitehead's population, and this was only a reduction of 0.3 books read in the previous month. What was worrying was that boys still read far less than girls, at all age levels, a finding that perhaps goes some way toward explaining the highly significant gender differences in reading achievement noted in the large-scale APU studies of the 1980s (Gorman et al., 1987).

FINAL WORD: NEW LITERACY STUDIES

As I suggested in the introduction to this chapter, research into reading processes in the United Kingdom has been carried out mostly by psychologists, research into practice has been led for the most part by scholars in university schools of education, whereas policy-driven research has been directed and funded by government agencies. Nearly all the research reported in this chapter falls within the paradigms of traditional psychometric research, classroom-based research, or policy research.

This situation is changing: Street (1995) has argued compellingly that traditional or "commonsense" definitions of literacy are only a privileged subset of the available models. He argues that such commonsense models, whether they be those used by researchers to conceptualize literacy as a technical activity or those used by politicians to characterize literacy as a kind of economic activity, are limiting and hegemonic. He contrasts these commonsense models, which he describes as *autonomous*, because of their tendency to render invisible alternative models, with *ideological* models that admit of diversity in definition, and that open up the field of literacy research to a fresh perspective: the study of literacy practices. On such an analysis, literacy research can become a branch of cultural studies, with the task of the researcher being to lay bare for analysis both the power relations that make up the landscape of literacy practices within a culture, and the discourses that map them.

A related if not directly similar approach has been adopted by researchers at the University of Lancaster (Fairclough, 1995; Hamilton, Barton, & Ivanic, 1994). Around the terms *critical discourse analysis* and *new literacy studies*, these colleagues and a number of co-workers have created a series of perspectives on literacy and literacy practices that are not only potentially powerful; they are ones which have found a ready audience with teachers and teacher educators, because they offer tools for critical analysis in the literacy field that many have found liberating. Studies of the social aspects of literacy seem set to become an area of growth in the future.

ACKNOWLEDGMENTS

I am grateful to Greg Brooks, Hazel Francis, Peter Hannon, Maggie Snowling and Morag Stuart, who assisted in the preparation of this chapter by sending me copies of papers, and to Roger Beard and Maggie Snowling, who also suggested key issues and themes. I also wish to thank Lisa Coulson, who conducted a valuable literature search.

REFERENCES

Bartlett, F. C. (1932). *Remembering: A study in experimental and social psychology.* Cambridge: Cambridge University Press.

Bloom, W. (1990). *Parents as partners in reading.* London: Hodder and Stoughton.

Briggs, P., Austin, S., & Underwood, G. (1984). The effects of sentence context in good and poor readers: A test of Stanovich's interactive-compensatory model. *Reading Research Quarterly, 20*, 54–61.

Brooks, G. (1997, September). *Trends in standards of literacy in the United Kingdom, 1948–1996.* Paper presented at the British Educational Research Association's annual conference, University of York.

Brooks, G. (1998). New emphasis on old principles: The need for clarity of purpose and of assessment method in national testing and for national monitoring. In C. Harrison & T. Salinger (Eds.), *Assessing reading I: Theory and practice* (pp. –). New York: Routledge.

Brooks, G., Gorman, T. P., Harman, J., Hutchison, D., & Wilkin, A. (1996). *Family literacy works: The NFER evaluation of the Basic Skills Agency's Family Literacy Programmes.* London: Basic Skills Agency.

Brooks, G, Flanagan, N., Henkhuzens, Z., & Hutchison, D. (1998). *What works for slow readers? The effectiveness of early intervention schemes.* Slough, UK: National Foundation for Educational Research.

Bradley, L., & Bryant, P. E. (1983). Categorising sounds and learning to read: A causal connexion. *Nature, 301*, 419–421.

Bryant, P. E., & Bradley, L. (1985). *Children's reading problems: Psychology and education.* Oxford: Basil Blackwell.

Bryant, P. E., Bradley, L., Maclean, M., & Crossland, J. (1989). Nursery rhymes, phonological skills and reading. *Journal of Child Language, 16*, 407–428.

Clay, M. (1985). *The early detection of reading difficulties: A diagnostic survey with recovery procedures,* 3rd ed. Aukland, NZ: Heinemann.

Clay, M. M. (1993). *Reading Recovery: A guidebook for teachers in training.* Aukland, NZ: Heinemann.

Davies, F., & Greene, T. (1984). *Reading for learning in the sciences.* Edinburgh: Oliver and Boyd.

Department for Educational Science. (1975). *A language for life* (The Bullock Report). London: HMSO.

Ellis, N. C., & Large, B. (1987). The development of reading: As you seek so shall you find. *British Journal of Developmental Psychology, 78*, 128.

Fairclough, N. (1995). *Critical discourse analysis: The critical study of language.* London: Longman.

Francis, H. (1987). Hearing beginning readers read: problems of relating practice to theory in interpretation and evaluation. *British Educational Research Journal, 13*(3), 215–226.

Goodacre, E. (1969). Reading research—Where is it reported? *Reading, 3*(1), 11–15.

Goodman, K. (1967). Reading: A psycholinguistic guessing game. *Journal of the Reading Specialist, 6*, 266–271.

Gorman, T. P., White, J., Brooks, G., Maclure, M., & Kispal, A. (1987). *Language performance in schools: Review of language monitoring, 1979–83.* London: DES.

Goswami, U. (1986). Children's use of analogy in learning to read. *Journal of Experimental Child Psychology, 42*, 73–83.

Goswami, U. (1990). Phonological priming and orthographic analogies in reading. *Journal of Experimental Child Psychology, 49*, 323–340.

Goswami, U., & Bryant, P. (1990). *Phonological skills and learning to read.* East Sussex: Lawrence Erlbaum Associates.

Hall, C., & Coles, M. (1997). Gendered readings: Helping boys develop as critical readers. *Gender and Education, 9*, 1, 61–68.

Hamilton, M., Barton, D., & Ivanic, R. (Eds.). (1994). *Worlds of literacy.* Clevedon, UK: Multilingual Matters.

Hannon, P. (1995). *Literacy, home and school*. London: Falmer.

Hannon, P., & Jackson, A. (1987). *The Belfield Reading Project: Final report*. London: National Children's Bureau.

Harrison, C. (1995). Youth and white paper: The politics of literacy assessment in the United Kingdom. *English Journal, 84*(2), 115–119.

Harrison, C., Bailey, M., & Dewar, A. (1998). Responsive reading assessment: Is postmodern assessment of reading possible? In C. Harrison & T. Salinger (Eds.), *Assessing reading I: Theory and practice* (pp. –). New York: Routledge.

Harrison, C., & Gough, P. (1996). Compellingness in reading research. *Reading Research Quarterly, 31*(3), 334–341.

Hatcher, P. J., Hulme, C., & Ellis, A. W. (1994). Ameliorating early reading failure by integrating the teaching of reading and phonological skills: the phonological linkage hypothesis. *Child Development, 65*, 1, 41–57.

Haywood, L., & Spencer, E. (1998). Taking a closer look: A Scottish perspective on reading assessment. In C. Harrison & T. Salinger (Eds.), *Assessing reading I: Theory and practice* (pp. –). New York: Routledge.

Horner, S. (1998). Assessing reading in the English National Curriculum. In C. Harrison & T. Salinger (Eds.), *Assessing reading I: Theory and practice* (pp. –). New York: Routledge.

Lunzer, E. A., & Gardner, W. (1979). *The effective use of reading*. London: Heinemann.

Lunzer, E .A., & Gardner, W. (1984). *Learning from the written word*. Edinburgh: Oliver and Boyd.

Muter, V., Hulme, C., Snowling, M., & Taylor, S. (1997). Segmentation, not ryhming, predicts early progress in learning to read. *Journal of Experimental Child Psychology 65*, 370–396.

Raban, B. (1990). Reading research in Great Britain 1988. *Reading, 24*(3), 107–127.

Ruddock, G., Brooks, G., Harris, D., Salt, S., Putman, K., & Schagen, I. (1995). *Evaluation of national curriculum assessment in English and technology at Key Stage 3: 1993*. Slough, Berkshire: National Foundation for Educational Research.

Smith, F. (1973). *Psycholinguistics and reading*. New York: Holt, Reinhart and Winston.

Southgate, V., Arnold, H., & Johnson, S. (1981). *Extending beginning reading*. London: Heinemann, for the Schools Council.

Street, B. (1995). *Social literacies: Critical approaches to literacy in development, ethnography and education*. London: Longman.

Stuart, M., & Masterson, J. (1992). Patterns of reading and spelling in 10-year-old children related to prereading phonological abilities. *Journal of Experimental Child Psychology, 54*, 168–187.

Sylva, K., & Hurry, J. (1995). *The effectiveness of Reading Recovery and phonological training for children with reading problems: Full report*. London: SCAA.

Tizard, J., Schofield, W. N., & Hewison, J. (1982). Collaboration between teachers and parents in assisting children's reading. *British Journal of Educational Psychology, 52*, 1–15.

Topping, K., & Lindsay, G. (1992). Paired reading: A review of the literature. *Research Papers in Education, 7*, 199–246.

Vincent, D., & Harrison, C. (1998). Curriculum-based assessment of reading in England and Wales: A national pilot study. In C. Harrison & T. Salinger (Eds.), *Assessing reading I: Theory and practice* (pp. –). New York: Routledge.

Wells, G. (1978). Language use and educational success: An empirical response to Joan Tough's "The Development of Meaning." *Research in Education, 18*, 9–34.

West, R. F., & Stanovich, K. E. (1978). Automatic and contextual facilitation inj readers of three ages. *Child Development, 49*, 717–727.

Whitehead, F., Capey, A., & Madden, J. (1977). *Children and their books*. London: Macmillan.

CHAPTER 3

Education in Transition: Trends in Central and Eastern Europe

Kurtis S. Meredith
Jeannie L. Steele
University of Northern Iowa

The close of the 20th century witnessed an explosion of new democracies. These fledgling democracies emerged in a part of the world thought destined to totalitarian rule well into the 21st century. But the general euphoria in the West over the rise in democratic expression has subsided recently with the realization that these democracies are tenuous at best, with many of the newly founded democratic republics slipping toward autocratic or totalitarian governments and, in some instances, near chaos. Thought has now centered on considering by what means democracies can be established, and what role schooling plays in supporting civil society. Coincidentally, many Western societies have begun to examine these same issues (Oldenquist, 1996; Smith, 1995; Soder, 1996) as concern develops regarding Western adherence to democratic principles and practices.

It has long been understood, especially by totalitarian regimes, that control of schools, and the minds of young people, is essential to controlling the population. During 45 years of Soviet domination, Central and Eastern European (CEE) schools were subjected to systematic manipulation (Organization for Economic Cooperation and Development, 1996; Harangi & Toth, 1996) and a Soviet-style education system was imposed. Soviet control over schools reached to the heart of education, affecting daily classroom practices and relations between teachers and students. Through intimidation, teachers became conduits and students passive receptors of information and ideology (Karsten & Majoor, 1994; Stech, 1994; Rust, Knost, & Wichman, 1994).

Meredith and Steele (1995), based on their work in CEE, stated in their presentation to the European Conference of the International Reading Association in Budapest, "These formally subordinated nations are now struggling to establish democratic institutions. Amid the turmoil of transition it is becoming increasingly apparent that the hope for democracy rests with the schools and in the minds and hearts of young people." Schools in the region are engaged in a titanic struggle for identity and heart amidst the collapse of former regimes and their imposed curricular manifestos (Döbert & Manning, 1994). Schools are caught in the crossfire of (a) recovering from the sudden collapse of socialism and (b) leading the way into the future without a road map (Stech, 1994). Thus, the evolving CEE societies are contending simultaneously with assembling civil societies and with restructuring schools so they will sustain and nurture a new social order. Any consideration of trends in education during this transitory period must be linked to considerations of this aqueous cultural, social, economic, and political milieu. Moreover, although similarities exist among nations of the region, so do substantial differences, which prevent broad characterizations.

In this chapter we first describe the history and continuing tensions of education in Central and Eastern Europe. Our portrayal of the region describes the Soviet legacy, the beginnings of school reform, and Central and Eastern European schools today. Second, we elaborate in some detail on the links between literacy, democracy, and school reform. Reform has dominated CEE educational communities since 1989. Reforms have encountered some resistance or have been inadequately conceptualized and/or implemented, leaving behind few successes. The authors, living in CEE and working with schools and universities for over 5 years, are actively engaged in two successful education reform efforts. These school reform initiatives are briefly described as examples of reform efforts effecting change. Third, we explore university reform and the present status of academic research. Research has suffered a particularly egregious fate during the second half of the 20th century. We will explicate the plight of academic research, describe current research practices, and consider future research needs. Finally, some conclusions are drawn about public schooling, university teacher preparation programs, and research trends.

HISTORY OF EDUCATION IN CENTRAL AND EASTERN EUROPE

The Soviet Legacy

Ample evidence exists that the historical, sociological, linguistic, political, economic, and moral characteristics of any society are inseparable from its collective cultural context. This reality is no more apparent than in Central and Eastern Europe, where history, politics, culture, and economics lie at the vortex of all issues, including education and educational research in general, and literacy and learning in particular (Mitter, 1996). It is impossible to understand present or future research trends without first becoming aware of the historically significant realities that impinge on current educational practices and constructs (Karsten & Majoor, 1994).

It may be helpful to begin by defining the geographic boundaries of CEE. Although there is debate as to just who may lay claim to a European context, the most inclusive definition of Europe, beyond the boundaries of "Western" Europe, was proposed by Mitter (1996) and incorporates the former Soviet satellite nations cut off from "Western Europe" after World War II plus the newly independent states (NIS) of the former Soviet Union that lie between the Central European corridor and Russia. To these is then added Russia. This vast array of cultures and peoples has often been seen as a largely homogeneous group. Under Soviet domination, this view was superficially true (Rust et al., 1994). However, as nationalist tendencies of the post-1989 collapse of Soviet domination have revealed, the region is a mosaic of peoples as various in culture, habit, and language as anywhere on earth. Perhaps the two most distinctive features these nations now share are (a) a recent past during which the imposition of Soviet rule and Marxist ideology nearly crushed their respective economic, cultural, and social infrastructures (Revel, 1993), and (b) an attempt since 1989 to transition to a different, mostly democratic social order, revitalizing or recreating their cultural, social, economic, and political foundations (Rust et al., 1994).

During the period of Soviet domination, a universal Soviet system of education was imposed. The hallmark of this system was centralized control (Döbert & Manning, 1994; OECD, 1996; Szebenyi, 1992). The school system model typically included extensive kindergartens (preschool programs for children ages 2–6), 8- year basic schools, and vocationally focused secondary programs based on internal employment needs. Consequently, some students were directed toward gymnasia for eventual university training, whereas others attended technical schools for subsequent work in industries or attendance at technical universities. Service schools such as restaurant and hotel schools and, in some countries such as Romania, elementary teacher training high schools, and other vocational schools were established according to centrally determined employment needs. Curriculum was centrally controlled, commingling general content with Marxist ideology. Educational research was removed from universities and housed in research academies. Research was formulated by state authorities and was generally intended to show support for the imposed political system. University faculty were not allowed to pursue independent research agendas.

Karsten and Majoor (1994) described the impact of the Soviet model more starkly, suggesting that under Communism, substantial damage was done to educational systems in four fundamental ways: damage to *knowledge* through neglect, oppression, controlled access and pervasive censorship; damage to *thinking* through limitations in experimentation with new ideas; damage to the *teaching profession* through loss of prestige, lack of respect for roles and by requiring schools to transfer ideology; and damage to *values* by imposing a pseudo-value structure. Stech (1994), decrying the Czech experience with the Soviet model, wrote, "The past school system model brought us not only pain, but became anchored deeply in our consciousness and can be linked to some [prescribed] values accepted by people in everyday life" (p. 71).

Beginnings of School Reform

The primary task for students throughout the system was to memorize vast amounts of information and prepare for exhaustive examinations administered with alarming frequency. The curriculum was extremely dense, and students were under enormous pressure to perform. Initial reforms were inspired by the belief that schools needed to become more humane. Cracks, however, began to appear in this uniform educational model in the early 1980s as Hungary moved toward decentralization (Harangi & Toth, 1996; Németh & Pukánsky, 1994; Szebenyi, 1992). Although accomplishing more on paper than in practice, it was a benchmark in education reform.

Even with the rigid delivery of an almost exclusively information-driven curriculum, the education system was a source of great pride in most nations. Numerous achievements were credited to the system. In many countries of the region, schooling was not universally available until after World War II. The Soviet model was egalitarian, and compulsory education was established. Literacy rates throughout the region continue to be among the highest in the world. Schools were well-disciplined, calm, and secure places where students came with respect for learning. Academic performance, as measured by standardized test, often placed CEE students near the top in global comparisons.

Despite these apparent successes, education was targeted for reform shortly after 1989 by nearly every nation in the region. The initial reform movement focused on six basic goals:

1. Rewriting the curriculum, removing Marxist ideology and rewriting historical accounts, broadening the literature base, and increasing textbook choices.

2. Restructuring schools to better serve newly established democratic institutions, initially targeting changes in civic education curriculum.
3. Humanizing schools so students would have more opportunity for active learning.
4. Preparing schools for Western evaluations, bringing schools up to "Western European" standards for eventual membership in the European Union.
5. Decentralizing school management, giving local authorities greater decisionmaking authority.
6. Reestablishing a university-based research agenda.

Agreement to remove Marxist ideology from textbooks was reached with relatively ease. Rust et al. (1994) stated, "The educational adjustments taking place throughout the region are significant and there is striking uniformity of educational changes taking place, all related in one way or another to a rejection of the communist ideology that has dominated education for the past four decades" (p. 283). Restructuring schools so they would better support civil societies and humanizing schools by introducing alternative instructional practices proved more difficult. Most CEE nations have adopted independent reform agendas, often supported by Western organizations such as the World Bank, Open Society Institutes, the European Union, United States Agency for International Development (USAID), and the United States Information Agency (USIA). New civic education curricula have been developed with varying degrees of implementation success. As the push for entry into the European Union intensifies, the need, especially for universities, to have in place systems and standards consistent with Western European standards has prompted the call for more rapid change. However, adoption of a comprehensive pedagogical research agenda has been slower to materialize due to shortages of funding, separation of schools from universities, and a shortage of skilled researchers.

School decentralization has experienced only limited success. Many countries have struggled with issues of local control, with resistance coming from many quarters. Many opponents of decentralization believe in the necessity of a national curriculum to maintain standards. Those opposed to decentralization suggest there is little expertise in rural communities to run schools. Schools also continue to be seen as political mechanisms. Allowing local control means letting go of a potentially productive political asset.

What is clear is that schools and universities are presently engaged in fundamental change and that school reform is inexorably linked to economic, political, and social reform. The massive reforms underway are, however, meeting resistance within the schools. Under the previous regime (Kaufman, 1997), school reform usually meant greater bureaucracy without real change. Yet most educators recognize that real reform is essential. As one Hungarian teacher told Kaufman, "Traditional reform is not the answer. The only reform that stands a chance is one that will aid in overcoming crisis. Any new education policy must help reform the economy. Students may need both more education and a different education" (Kaufman, 1997, p. 91). In fact, reform is not simply important, it is paramount. The rejection of the Soviet model has left a void. After 45 years of a single model, few instructional alternatives are readily available. What is needed (Meredith, Steele, & Shannon, 1994) is long-term systemic school restructuring intended to provide a coherent education system open to all stakeholders and responsive to the compelling academic, social, and economic imperatives of the region.

Central and Eastern European Schools Today

Bennett (1996), describing present day Russian schools, could have been describing the entire former sphere of Soviet influence. She wrote, "Today the old monolith, in which every Soviet pupil turned the same page of the same textbook on the same day in every school across eleven time zones, has been pulled apart" (Bennett, 1996, p. A22). Svecova (1994) noted that there is a universal understanding that the remains of the Soviet education system cannot adequately support students in the new, market-driven, civil societies now emerging.

At a 1997 conference on school reform held at Lake Balaton, Hungary (Temple, Meredith, Steele, & Walter, 1997), educators from 11 CEE and Central Asian nations presented their views on the status of education in their respective countries. The overwhelming majority identified the same factors influencing the quality of education. Those factors included overcrowded classrooms (up to 50 students per class), poor quality textbooks, rigid instructional practices, teacher-dominated classrooms, emphasis on rote memorization of factual information, absence of practical application of knowledge, absence of critical thinking, overburdened curriculum, limited resources, poor school/parent relations, shortened school day, low teacher salaries, centralized control, and unresponsive university pedagogical programs.

Tremendous variation exists in the conditions of schools and universities throughout the region. The Balkans have suffered the most since 1989 (Open Society Institute, 1997). The conflicts in the former Yugoslav Federation have left schools in Bosnia in need of rebuilding literally from the ground up. Civil unrest in 1992 and 1994 and again in 1997 in Albania left over 1,000 schools destroyed. Those that remained were heavily vandalized and their meager supplies looted (Meredith, 1997; Meredith & Steele, 1998). Other nations of CEE have fared better. Although routinely underfunded, schools and universities in Slovakia, the Czech Republic, Russia, Poland, and Hungary have maintained standards and pushed ahead with school reform (Open Society Institute, 1997). The Baltic states have also pursued innovative education initiatives, perhaps more successfully than others in the region (Temple et al., 1997).

What is evident is that throughout the region tremendous energy is being expended on education reforms. Although continuing to labor under remnants of Soviet structure, drastic changes are being implemented. Despite the devastation of schools in Albania, educators are engaged in an array of initiatives (Meredith, 1996; Meredith & Steele, 1998; Musai, 1997). Four model kindergarten programs have been implemented. A major school construction program financed by the Soros Foundation (Musai, 1997; Open Society Institute, 1997) and a textbook revision program to replace outdated texts across all grades are underway. In Bucharest, Romania, elementary schools often operate three shifts a day, each shift operating for 3 hours. Yet Romania has embarked upon an ambitious restructuring effort in cooperation with the World Bank, including teacher and administrator in-service, curriculum development, textbook production, and university/school cooperation. Slovakia has moved forward with teacher and administrator recertification legislation (Steele, Meredith, & Miklušiáková, 1996), linking continuing education with salary increases. The Slovak Ministry of Education has also recognized nontraditional, innovative, in-service programs for teachers and administrators as qualified recertification programs.

LITERACY, DEMOCRACY, AND SCHOOL REFORM

For school reform to be effective, it must be conceptualized within the prevailing context of post 1989 Central and Eastern Europe where schools and society are reformulating out of a legacy of Communist totalitarianism, a social reengineering never before attempted in history. It is a context of uncertainty. The Hungarian film director Ibolya Fekete (1997) best described the context in which her East European peers survive when she declared, "You [East Europeans] have lost everything you used to be, and now you have to find a new place. It is a basic human struggle" (p. 56). Jozef Miklušiák, a former member of the Slovak parliament, succinctly stated this idea in relation to school reform in 1993. He said, "Our children are having difficulty finding their sense of life. We need help guiding our schools so children can find their place in life in a democracy and to see for themselves a future within a democratic society" (J.Miklušiák, personal communication, May 1993).

The discussion about schooling has inevitably led to discussions about creating and sustaining democratic impulses. Perhaps one of the more significant educational legacies of the collapse of the Soviet empire will be the sudden imperative to juxtapose education and democracy within, as Fekete has said, this "basic life struggle," thereby demanding that the discussion become immediately manifest in instructional practice. The links between literacy and life-long learning on one hand and literacy and democracy through empowerment and constructive meaning making on the other have placed the language and literature of literacy at the center of the discourse on democracy and schooling. This linkage has become more transparent through the writings of theorists such as Giroux (1993), Rényi (1993), and Soder (1996). Within CEE, a growing number of scholars are examining this relationship in the context of ongoing school reform (Mieszalski, 1994; Parizek, 1992; Sandi, 1992).

The connections between literacy and democracy, although now more transparent, are not necessarily intuitive (Meredith, Steele, & Athanassoula, 1996; Steele, 1996). Certainly the connections between literacy and democratic participation at what Dewey (1938) suggested as an institutional or superficial level is intuitively obvious. That is, such literacies as political literacy will contribute to voter choice. Less intuitive is the linkage recent literacy pedagogy theories and practices have established at a more fundamental and personal level. It has been suggested (Meredith, 1996) that literacy pedagogy can foster democratic communities within schools, thereby nurturing civil societies. This thinking arises from the belief that democracy embodies a set of behaviors and values that guide daily life so that citizens within a democratic society behave in ways that sustain democratic experience. Schools are thought to be well situated to establish a democratic climate and provide genuine experiences with democratic interchange.

Many would argue that one of the central tasks of literacy is meaning making (Rosenblatt, 1978)—that is, to engage students in constructing meanings so as to succor innovation. Classrooms are paradigmatic settings for democratic culture because they have the capacity to engender unlimited diversity of ideas, reflections, opinions, and meanings. Meaning making becomes the defining act for democracy because it is the basis for valuing and the platform for self-reflection, opinion formation, and decision making.

In many instances education reform has not meaningfully entered the classroom. Teachers and students continue the process of passive information transfer. Critical thinking, opinion formation, initiative, collaborative problem solving, development of respect and tolerance, consensus building, constructive conflict resolution, and participatory decision making all await systematic and consistent introduction. The very foundational behaviors of democratic life remain apart from daily instruction.

Two reform efforts about which the authors are aware attempt to address reform through a model based on literacy pedagogy and principles of systemic engagement. The Orava Project (http://www.uni.edu/coe/orava) in the Republic of Slovakia is a model program that is succeeding at the most fundamental level of education restructuring precisely because it does systematically address and model teacher behaviors and instructional practices that are fundamental to the needed changes and because it is collaborative, avoiding the imposition of ideas in favor of a sharing model consistent with Nel Noddings's (1992) notions of caring. The project is a complex, systematic endeavor intended to effect permanent changes that are reflected in the interaction of people in their daily lives. Primary efforts include the establishment of core teacher leaders (CTLs) as teacher trainers for dissemination of democratic instructional practices, and introduction of these instructional practices into university teacher preparation programs.

The Reading and Writing for Critical Thinking Project (http://www.uni.edu/coe/rwct) introduces a comprehensive teacher in-service program focusing on critical thinking into an ongoing school reform context that was designed specifically for the participating countries by local educators from those nations. Both reform efforts bring together educators from around the world to share instructional practices that engender democratic behavior and maximize student learning.

The rapidly changing cultural climate of the region necessitates school change. There is historically a tradition of school transformation (Anweiler, 1992), which, although dormant during the communist era, is reawakening. The immediate needs of these transforming societies have put enormous pressures on schools to respond quickly. Those who consider restructuring schooling as fundamental to sustaining democracy have an even greater sense of urgency. Democracy's hold in the region is tenuous. Many consider today's elementary students as the pivotal population who will either embody democratic interchange and secure its place in the social order or fail to embody essential behaviors, allowing democracy to slip from the political landscape.

UNIVERSITY REFORM AND ACADEMIC RESEARCH

Reform at the university level has been complicated by numerous factors. One factor is the extent to which various university faculties were exposed to Western thought. Prior to 1989, exposure to outside ideas and influences differed widely according to both discipline and access of a particular country to Western thought. Scholars in mathematics and the natural sciences, which were not considered political, were permitted much greater access to Western knowledge. Many learned English or German and read scholarly work in those languages. Social scientists and educators, in contrast, were regarded with far greater suspicion and were more restricted. While others studied abroad, these professionals remained behind the iron curtain where ideas were easier to control. Consequently, before 1989, many scholars in education were unaware of trends and theories emerging in the west.

Before 1989, university faculty were not permitted to conduct independent research. Instead, research institutes were created. Research in these institutes was hampered by three factors:

1. The state typically determined the research questions.
2. Source material was limited or nonexistent, reducing literature searches to a few relevant texts.
3. A research tradition based on a foundation of sound empirical research models was absent.

Since 1989, there has been renewed interest in academic research. However, opportunity and financial support lag behind interest, leaving many potential researchers frustrated. Computers for data collection and data analysis have only recently become uniformly available. The lack of availability of translated software has compounded the problem. For nations with larger populations, and thus more viable markets, software is now available in the local language.

In many nations of CEE, research institutes continue to exist. They are typically detached from the education community and offer little insight into effective instructional practices, continuing to be more content to focus on theory development and so called "scientific pedagogy." Azarov, cited in Furjaeva (1994), called for dramatic change in pedagogical research, suggesting, "The teacher needs living pedagogical knowledge" (p. 143). And Furjaeva (1994) suggested the calls for "new research approaches" were an inevitable consequence of the failures of the reform movements of the 1980s.

Despite the continuing presence of research institutes, there has been a steady increase in university-based academic research. Significant CEE-initiated research is beginning to appear in local and international publications. Further, cooperative research between CEE and Western university faculties is increasing, creating a valuable comparative research literature (Comparative Education Society in Europe, [CESE] Conference, 1996).

The 1996 CESE and the 1997 EARLI (European Association for Research on Learning and Instruction) conferences provided a representative sampling of the research topics and methods emerging in the region. These two conferences provided a forum for 53 CEE research projects addressing a wide array of research topics, including cognitive processes in learning, effective civics education curricula, cognitive skills in reading, evaluation of school reform effectiveness, reading comprehension, achievement outcomes, academic assessment practices, school violence, motivation, reasoning and thinking, learning styles and strategies, school transformation, schools and globalization, and teacher education practices.

Research methods varied considerably. Much of the comparative research conducted with Western researchers was empirically based using formal research design techniques. Other independent research was more observational or the result of surveys, interviews, and literature reviews. Much of the school reform research reported is anecdotal, reporting teacher and student reactions to reform efforts. Few systematic intermediate or long-term school reform outcomes studies are being reported. The gulf between schools and universities also continues to limit the amount of school-based research being conducted (Furjaeva, 1994; Meredith & Steele, 1995).

In conversations with education ministry leaders from Estonia to Albania the lament is the same. During the past half century only a few researchers were able to engage in informative education research. Existing research traditions were lost. Now research needs are enormous, with effectiveness research on school reform efforts one of the greatest needs. The strengths and weaknesses of existing education programs are only acknowledged anecdotally. Ministries are making systemic decisions and developing guiding school policy without adequate data for decision making. The number of researchers remains small, whereas research needs exist in every area of education and schooling.

CONCLUSION

Educators in Central and Eastern Europe are engaged in a critical reexamination of their role in society. Teachers, previously marginalized by manipulative political agendas, are now adjusting to a new reality (Rust et al., 1994). For those educators who understand their central role in social construction, the pressure for change is enormous. There is, among these nations, a long history of commitment to education. Students come to school eager to learn, prepared to embrace new ideas, in a hurry to develop ways of knowing that will bring them comfort within their amorphous cultural milieu.

The trend in education in CEE is to both move away from education of the recent past and toward an as yet undefined schooling that prepares young people for their future. It will remain undefined if only because one significant lesson learned from the previous system is that a fixed system cannot survive, and, indeed, should not survive, because it ultimately fails to serve either political or social ends.

Schools and universities are engaged in a transformation process that began with the opening of the Hungarian border to Austria, through the fall of the Berlin Wall and the 1997 uprising in Albania. The nations of the region are forever linked by this common bond. Yet it would be a fateful mistake to consider this a region of homogeneous peoples moving toward shared goals along the same path with similar sentiments and intentions. Establishing a living democracy has been an all-consuming effort since the revolutions that shook this region. But democracy is not a set of describable entities, laws, or conditions. What is emerging is not a democracy but democracies (Rengger, 1994). By their very nature, democracies necessarily reflect the differences of the people who shape them. The education community is attempting to respond to this massive social restructuring. Reform efforts have challenged, frightened, disappointed, and invigorated the educational culture. Obstacles to reform are numerous and severe, yet reforms move forward, compelled by the sheer thrust of necessity and the reality that each day in each classroom a teacher stands before a group of expectant students and must engage those students in some manner.

Universities are at a crossroads. Fifty years of limited access to pedagogical information and theoretical evolution as well as severe brain drain have left them in a state of intellectual shock. Western university faculty immersed in a literacy-rich and research-intensive community of scholars, without direct observation of the devastation Soviet policy wrecked on research traditions, have difficulty fully appreciating the enormity of the resulting void in existing education research and expertise. It is understandable. Václav Havel (1992), president of the Czech Republic wrote, "Often we ourselves are unable to appreciate fully the existential dimension of this bitter experience and all its consequences" (p. 126). Thus, among the paramount needs of the education community are the development of university research traditions, improved research skills, and the capacity of writers and researchers to translate theory and research into practice. Research is urgently needed to determine school change effectiveness. There need to be systematic studies of the impact of school reform on student achievement, teacher effectiveness, and student and teacher attitudes toward teaching and learning. In some countries there exists only limited documentation of the number of school reform efforts currently underway (Meredith & Steele, 1998). Documentation of newly implemented forms of teacher education and instructional practices is needed. For now, there also exist four generations of people representing vastly differing educational experiences. The oldest generation has memory of the time before Communism and what education was like then. Time is running out on this collective memory, and little written documentation has survived World War II and the intervening Communist years. The children and grandchildren of this oldest generation were schooled under the Communist method. Now the youngest generation has experienced 10 years of a transforming school culture. Among these generations there is a wealth of insight and an abundance of extraordinarily informative tales to be told about academic life. Someone needs to listen to these stories before it is too late.

Basic research about schools and schooling is desperately needed. There is a shortage of research about school and student performance teacher training programs, school culture, developmental and child health needs, special education practices, curriculum development, school management practices, in-service training, and other issues that guide political decision makers and policy developers. Finally, teachers have been excluded from the emerging resurgence in education research. Their engagement is critical to countermand the isolation of university researchers and to build bridges between research and practice. Action research by classroom teachers is needed to inform teachers about their own practices and to offer other teachers the kind of practical, relevant pedagogical information that so-called "scientific pedagogy" research fails to provide. Without more practical research, university research will continue to be marginalized as functionally irrelevant.

One of the most eloquent guides to the psyche of the Central and Eastern European mind is the Czech playwright and president Václav Havel. His insights have illuminated the path of transition and made coherent some of the seemingly imponderable events circumscribing this great transition. In his book *Summer Meditations*, Havel (1992) looked into the "soul" of the transformation process and saw both despair and hope. He wrote:

> The most basic sphere of concern is schooling. Everything else depends on that.... Most important is a new concept of education. At all levels, schools must cultivate a spirit of free and independent thinking in students. Schools will have to be humanized, both in the sense that their basic component must be the human personalities of the teachers, creating around themselves a "force field" of inspiration and example.... The role of the school is not to create "idiot-specialists" to fill the special needs of different sectors of the national economy, but to develop the individual capabilities of the students in a purposeful way, and to send out into life thoughtful people capable of thinking about the wider social, historical, and philosophical implications of their specialties. (p. 117)

It is in this context that teachers teach and children go to school. It is a time of enormous change and uncertainty. Clearly much of the burden for tapping that potential for goodwill, for deciding where to begin, for determining how to find meaningful outlets, for nurturing citizens toward "freely accepting responsibility for the whole of society" falls to the schools as caretakers and guides of the next generation of citizens.

REFERENCES

Anweiler, O. (1992). Some historical aspects of educational change in the former Soviet Union and Eastern Europe. In D. Phillips & M. Kaser (Eds.), *Education and economic change in Eastern Europe and the former Soviet Union* (pp. 29–39). Wallingford, UK: Triangle Books.

Bennett, V. (1996, October 24). Old-world educators preparing a generation of new Russians. *Star Tribune*, p. A22.

Comparative Education Society in Europe (CESE) Conference. (1997, August). *Abstract*. 17th CESE Conference, Athens, Greece.

Dewey, J. (1938). *Experience in education*. New York: Macmillan.

Döbert, H., & Manning, S. (1994). The transformation of the East German school and its relation to international developments in education. In V. D. Rust, P. Knost, & J. Wichmann (Eds.), *Education and the values crisis in Central and Eastern Europe* (pp. 3–25). Frankfurt am Main, Germany: Peter Lang.

Fekete, I. (1997, September 8). The perils of freedom. *Newsweek, CXXX*, p. 56.

Furjaeva, T. (1994). Children and youth in the policy, science and practice of a society in transition: Russia. In V. D. Rust, P. Knost, & J. Wichmann (Eds.), *Education and the values crisis in Central and Eastern Europe* (pp. 131–157). Frankfurt am Main, Germany: Peter Lang.

Giroux, H. A. (1993). *Living dangerously*. New York: Peter Lang.

Harangi, L., & Toth, J. S., (1996). Hungary. In S. Haddad (Ed.), *International review of education* (Vol. 42, Nos. 1–3, pp. 59–74). Hamburg, Germany: UNESCO Institute for Education.

Havel, V. (1992). *Summer meditations*. New York: Vintage Books.

Karsten, S., & Majoor, D. (Eds.). (1994). *Education in East and Central Europe: Changes after the fall of Communism*. Munster, Germany: Waxmann.

Kaufman, C. (1997, February). Transformation education in Hungary. *Social education*, 89–92.

Meredith, K. S. (1996, December). *Personalizing democracy through critical literacy*. Paper presented at the 46th Annual Meeting of the National Reading Conference, Charleston, SC.

Meredith, K. S. (1997). *Education in Albania: The status of education and education reform*. Report prepared for United States Agency for International Development, Orava Foundation for Democratic Education, Bratislava, Slovakia.

Meredith, K. S., & Steele, J. L. (1995, July). *Pedagogical practice and the ethic of democracy*. Paper presented at the 9th Annual European Conference of the International Reading Association, Budapest, Hungary.

Meredith, K. S., & Steele, J. L. (1998). *Multilevel reform of the Albanian education system: Obstacles and opportunities*. Report prepared for United Stated Agency for International Development, Orava Association for Democratic Education, Bratislava, Slovakia.

Meredith, K. S., Steele, J. L., & Athanassoula, A. (1996, October). *Instruction of democratic behavior in a world-system of a civil society*. 17th Comparative Education Society in Europe Conference Abstract, p. 6.

Meredith, K. S., Steele, J. L., & Shannon, P. (1994, December). *Critical literacy as a foundation for critical democracy*. Paper presented at the National Reading Conference, San Diego, CA.

Mieszalski, S. (1994). Polish education: Face to face with challenges and threats. In V. D. Rust, P. Knost, & J. Wichmann (Eds.), *Education and the values crisis in Central and Eastern Europe* (pp. 57–69). Frankfurt am Main, Germany: Peter Lang.

Mitter, W. (1996). Democracy and education in Central and Eastern Europe. In A. Oldenquist (Ed.), *Can democracy be taught?* (pp. 129–154). Bloomington, IN: Phi Delta Kappa Educational Foundation.

Musai, B. (1997). *A brief description of the Albanian education system and teacher training.* Elbasan, Albania. Albania Education Development Program, Tirana, Albania.

Németh, A., & Pukánsky, B. (1994). Tendencies and reforms in the Hungarian school system in historical perspective. In V. D. Rust, P. Knost, & J. Wichmann (Eds.), *Education and the values crisis in Central and Eastern Europe* (pp. 37–55). Frankfurt am Main, Germany: Peter Lang.

Noddings, N. (1992). *The challenge to care in schools.* New York: Teachers College Press.

Oldenquist, A. (Ed.). (1996). *Can democracy be taught?* Bloomington, IN: Phi Delta Kappa Educational Foundation.

Open Society Institute. (1997). *Regional programs.* Budapest, Hungary, New York: Author.

Organization for Economic Cooperation and Development. (1996). *Reviews of national policies for education—Czech Republic.* Paris: Commission of the European Communities, OECD.

Parizek, V. (1992). Education and economic change in Czechoslovakia. In D. Phillips & M. Kaser (Eds.), *Education and economic change in Eastern Europe and the former Soviet Union* (pp. 71–82). Wallingford, UK: Triangle Books.

Rengger, N. J. (1994). Towards a culture of democracy? Democratic theory and democratization in Eastern and Central Europe. In G. Pridham, E. Herring, & G. Sanford (Eds.), *Building democracy?* (pp. 60–86). New York: St. Martin's Press.

Rényi, J. (1993). *Going public: Schooling for a diverse democracy.* New York: New Press.

Revel, J.-F. (1993). *Democracy against itself.* New York: Free Press, Macmillan.

Rosenblatt, L. M. (1978). *The reader, the text, the poem.* Carbondale and Edwardsville, IL: Southern Illinois University Press.

Rust, V. D., Knost, P., & Wichmann, J. (Eds.). (1994). *Education and the values crisis in Central and Eastern Europe.* Frankfurt am Main, Germany: Peter Lang.

Sandi, A. M. (1992). Processes of educational change in Romania. In D. Phillips & M. Kaser (Eds.), *Education and economic change in Eastern Europe and the former Soviet Union* (pp. 83–93). Wallingford, UK: Triangle Books.

Smith, H. (1995, winter). It's education for, not about, democracy. *Educational Horizons, 73*(2), 62–69.

Soder, R. (Ed.). (1996). *Democracy, education, and the schools.* San Francisco, CA: Jossey-Bass.

Stech, S. (1994). Values changes in the Czech school system: Looking beyond the ideological bias. In V. D. Rust, P. Knost, & J. Wichmann (Eds.). *Education and the values crisis in Central and Eastern Europe* (pp. 71–85). Frankfurt am Main, Germany: Peter Lang.

Steele, J. L. (1996, December). *Empowering professionals as teacher leaders.* Paper presented at the 46th Annual Meeting of the National Reading Conference, Charleston, SC.

Steele, J. L., Meredith, K. S., & Miklušiáková, E. (1996, July). *Projekt Orava: Empowering educators as leaders.* Paper presented at the 16th World Congress of International Reading Association, Prague, Czech Republic.

Svecova, J. (1994). Czechoslovakia. In S. Karsten & D. Majoor (Eds.), *Education in East Central Europe: Educational changes after the fall of Communism* (pp. 77–119). Munster, Germany: Waxmann.

Szebenyi, P. (1992). State centralization and school autonomy: Processes of educational change in Hungary. In D. Phillips & M. Kaser (Eds.), *Education and economic change in Eastern Europe and the former Soviet Union* (pp. 57–70). Wallingford, UK: Triangle Books.

Temple, C., Meredith, K. S., Steele, J. L., & Walter, S. (1997). *Report on the Reading and Writing for Critical Thinking Institute.* Washingotn, DC: Consortium for Democratic Education, International Reading Association International Division.

CHAPTER 4

Literacy Research
in Latin America

Ileana Seda Santana
Universidad Nacional Autónoma de México

In the story *Dos Palabras* [*Two Words*] by Isabel Allende, Belisa Crepusculario accidentally discovered the power of words during her escape journey from misery. Her discovery took place when she curiously inquired about the small "fly's legs" on a brittle
newspaper page. The man told her that those were words and what it said. Belisa concluded that words "roam free" and anyone with some imagination may own them.
Thus, she decided to make a living by selling words to anyone who would buy them
(Allende, 1990).

Universal literacy is a major aspiration of educational systems in every nation. During the 1960s, developing nations launched multiple programs aimed at eradicating illiteracy. Their general premise was that industrialized countries have high levels of
literacy, and therefore reading and writing were necessary conditions for national development. It has become evident over time that being able to read and write may be a
necessary but not a sufficient condition for socioeconomic advancement and development. More important seem to be group histories (Rodríguez, 1995) and the functions
and functionality of literacy as viewed and experienced by the illiterate themselves
(White, 1979). Thus literacy movements in Latin America have had to address the tensions between histories and literacy, of learning versus owning the word, and of the
need to affect one's reality, like Allende's character (Freire, 1969, 1970).

In this chapter, a brief historical context sets the scene for the substance of the discussion, followed by a theoretical consideration of language, literacy, and culture. In the
third section I describe literacy programs in Latin America in terms of mainstream education and alternative education programs that relate to language, literacy and education issues. In the fourth section I discuss the research scenario. Finally, an agenda for
research and development attempts to identify gaps and propose areas in which to
move forward.

HISTORY AND CULTURE

A common denominator among Latin American countries is European colonization.
Countries located in the "connected" lands of North, Central, and South America also

share long pre-Columbian histories of advanced civilizations, some of which are esti-mated to date from 3000 B.C. Today, long history and old civilizations still exert their weight in the region's culture along with colonization and modern world influences.

The present political and economic status of Latin America is considered by some analysts to be in a necessary transition that will have major effects on the region's edu-cational systems (Marini, 1994). One major change is decentralization of totally cen-tralized systems. Mainly driven by economic demands, the decline of military governments, administrative manageability, and weakening of monolithic sindicalists organizations are also pressing factors (Namo de Mello, 1996; Rodríguez, 1995; Rodríguez & Bernal, 1990; Schiefelbein, 1993; Schiefelbein & Tedesco, 1995).

Tensions between neoliberal ideology, Marxist traditions, and long cultural histo-ries, particularly in the "connected lands" of Latin America, create new demands for change in the socioeconomic and political structures. Marini (1994), analyzing the situ-ation from a Marxist perspective, maintained that Latin America entered into a cycle two decades ago that will still entail sudden changes and unexpected situations. These include increased competition among countries, accelerated industrial development, and the emergence of newly industrialized countries—presently the case of Mexico and Brazil—which will expand to the majority of countries in the region. As a result, there will be greater gaps between social classes and greater demands for higher levels of training, thus altering the structure of the labor force and of employment conditions.

The path however, is a necessary one for developing countries' integration into the new world economy. Influenced by neoliberal ideology, demands for reduction of state controls and of a larger private sector are and will continue to be present. How-ever, Latin American nations' need to be competitive also requires creative means to strengthen their inner forces and to establish more favorable economic terms for them-selves (Marini, 1994).

In this scenario, education is a major enabling factor for nations developing their own technologies, economic models, and cultural advances. They need to move forward through balanced developments in various fronts while imperiously maintaining their own identities. Latin America, as a greater society, is richly diverse and pluralistic both among and within countries. Although Spanish and Portuguese are the major official languages, the presence of linguistically diverse indigenous populations places com-plex demands on educational systems. Geographically, it expands over a vast region in the American continent: from North America (Mexico) through Central to South Amer-ica and the Caribbean. In the literature, though, the geographical boundaries are not clear. Organizations and publications concerned with the region focus mainly on coun-tries of Spanish and Portuguese colonization histories. Sometimes they include coun-tries of British and French histories like Jamaica and Haiti.

To follow suit, in this chapter the discussion focuses on countries of Spanish and Portuguese colonization histories, which include the leading and larger nations in the region: Mexico, Brazil, and Argentina. Particularities about each country are necessar-ily used as examples in order to address commonalities. At the risk of simplification, the intent is to do as much justice to all as possible.

LANGUAGE, LITERACY, AND CULTURE

In the Spanish language, the word *literacy* in its current use has no direct equivalent. The closest term is *letrado* which corresponds to *learned person*, whereas *iletrado* [*illiter-ate*] corresponds to *analfabeta*, literally *someone who cannot read or write* or figuratively, *ignorant*. The opposite, *alfabetizado*, usually refers to someone who has "acquired" the written code. *Alfabetizado* and *alfabetización* (the process of becoming *alfabetizado*) are the common terms used in Latin American literature. In recent times the meaning seems to be expanding toward the *letrado* connotation.

Any discussion about literacy and education in Latin America needs to address language issues. The diversity of indigenous groups and languages within the region requires special educational efforts for most nations. To illustrate, in Mexico the indigenous population has been estimated to be 5 million representing 56 vernacular languages (Secretaría de Educación Pública [SEP], 1986; Nahmad, 1975). In the Vaupues territory of the Colombian Amazon, an area of approximately 65 square kilometers, the indigenous population was estimated in 1985 to be five times larger than the white population for a total of 19,000. The norm is for the indigenous to be bilingual and most likely multilingual. Many languages may be spoken by less than a thousand people, some by less than a hundred, and print is most likely nonexistent (Alfonso, Oltheten, Ooijens, & Thybergin, 1988).

Policies concerning national languages and language of instruction have traditionally been sensitive issues (Heath, 1972). Literacy programs in countries of Spanish colonialism were originally termed as programs of *castellanización*, that is, of learning Castillian. Today, educational systems make efforts to provide education to the indigenous populations and to graphically encode some of the vernacular languages. However, most programs continue to be transitional into the prestige languages (Larson & Davis, 1981; SEP, 1986; F. P. Secundino, personal communication, 1997; Troike & Modiano, 1975).

By the same token, mainstream education has been met with overt resistance by some indigenous groups, whereas others, indigenous and the poor in general, find themselves excluded from educational systems. In a meeting sponsored by the Centro Regional para el Fomento del Libro en America Latina y el Caribe (CERLAC, Regional Center to Promote [the use of] Books in Latin America and the Caribbean) in 1995, a group of specialists advised Latin American governments to establish policies of literacy. To that effect, Rodríguez (1995) wrote that although understandable from an access to modernity perspective, the recommendation does not take into account neoliberal thought and a natural resistance to legislate literacy. More significantly, he continued, are the "limits and conditionings" of cultures. He argued for a communicative attitude (rather than a legislative one), which takes into account the subjective, objective, and social worlds of groups and cultures.

Indigenous education is immersed in the complexities of many cultures and many languages. At the same time, teachers who have the educational, cultural, and linguistic backgrounds are very scarce. Often the solution is to opt for a sort of induction education of youths who finish secondary level education and who are members of the target groups. But the solution has its problems, among them that the many variations of vernaculars are often mutually incomprehensible. Felipe Patricio Secundino, a member of the Hñahñu and supervisor of indigenous education for the state of Querétaro in Mexico, in a personal communication (1997) pointed out that these young teachers are often assigned to remote rural areas, which they abandon as soon as they find more accessible settings. Thus, lack of continuity and development due to teacher mobility is one of the major obstacles in creating a substantial contingency of teachers to service indigenous groups (Secundino, personal communication, 1997). Also, the norm is for children to abandon school around Grade 4, which in turn affects community development and inhibits the continuous supply of teachers.

In a different cultural and political context, language has historically been a source of tension for Puerto Rico's educational system. After the Spanish American War when Puerto Rico became a territory of the United States as Estado Libre Asociado [literally, Free Associated State], the language of instruction, Spanish versus English, became a thorny issue. Today, tensions still exist, and as recently as 1992 and 1993 policies and laws about the official language were in question, finally opting for two official languages, although Spanish continues to be the language of instruction and English is taught as a necessary curricular subject (Scarano, 1993; Seda-Santana, 1987).

In essence, the particular linguistic code in which to address literacy and illiteracy is a varied and complex landscape requiring both encompassing and specific solutions for each nation and its people. Infused by cultural, political, and economic demands, solutions will need to be encompassing if they are to be effective while maintaining national unity and economic advancement.

LITERACY PROGRAMS IN LATIN AMERICA

Latin America's education seems to be in constant crisis (Puiggrós, 1995; Rivera-Pizarro, 1991; UNESCO, 1974; UNICEF, 1979). Such crisis may be explained by present political and economic dilemmas (Marini, 1994) as well as historical, social, and demographic complexities.

Public education efforts in Latin America aim toward universal education. Thus, education systems have expanded as central governments have accepted responsibility for many and varied educational functions and the search for the necessary and appropriate resources (UNESCO, 1974; UNICEF, 1979). Besides formal education, nations have undertaken open education, distance education, and nonformal education programs (Puiggrós, 1995). Some programs are geared for school-age children, youth, and unschooled and poorly schooled/illiterate adults, in urban, rural, urban marginal settings (in the peripheries of cities), remote rural areas, and urban shantytowns (Rivera-Pizarro, 1991; Rockwell, 1996; SEP, 1986; UNESCO, 1974; UNICEF, 1979). This monumental task is compounded by the ethnic and linguistic diversity of recipients.

Mainstream Education

The official discourse of government documents and of education professionals about school literacy is clearly influenced by current theories from developed nations. At the same time, there seems to be a revival of some ideological traditions of education in the region, mainly a critical perspective. Definitions of literacy, however, seem to fluctuate from Heath's (1991) *literate behaviors to* Cicero's *learned person to* the Middle Ages conception of *minimal ability in reading* as discussed by Venezky (1991).

In school learning the common term for reading and writing is *lecto-escritura* [read-write], which may signify as a unit (Seda-Santana, 1993). Although *lecto-escritura* suggests a wholistic view, in reality reading and writing are viewed and taught as separate processes (Braslavsky, 1995). For example, once a learner has command of the letter–sound correspondence and can decode words, the person is considered *alfabetizado*.

Official Spanish language curricula and government frameworks for elementary teaching of *lecto-escritura* suggest a *being literate* view with emphasis on *literacy skills* and *literate behaviors* (Heath, 1991) (see, e.g., Braslavsky, 1995, for Argentina; Gómez-Palacio, 1982, and SEP, 1992, for Mexico; Dirección de Educación Primaria/UNESCO, 1994, for Nicaragua; de Romero & de García, 1994, for Paraguay). Thus, in spite of the wholistic perspective espoused by the official discourse, in instructional practice atomistic and behaviorist tendencies prevail.

Alternative Education

Alternative education as used here refers to any program outside of traditional schools, albeit under the auspices of government institutions. It includes popular, indigenous, bilingual, adult, and community education. A prime objective of alternative education is community organization and development, as well as completion of basic education.

Conceptions about education often fluctuate ideologically between education for national development (characterized by technification, reason, efficiency, and development of human resources) and as a path to dependency versus liberation (Castro, 1994; Rodríguez, 1995; Torres-Novoa, 1977). The latter is evident in formal education programs, be it for national development or personal empowerment.

An important theoretical influence in educational systems in Latin America is Freirian thought. The Freirian ideal of education as liberation (Freire, 1969, 1970) aspires for participants to develop a critical conscience and to develop a commitment to decision making, and for effective actions to affect one's reality. Education for liberation typifies an important segment of the pedagogical movements in Latin America (Castro, 1994).

The word in relation to *the world* is central in Freire (Freire & Macedo, 1989), and basic education has not escaped its influence. Liberation is mediated by means of *the word* in written and oral forms (Freire & Macedo, 1989), and *dialogue* is viewed as the means to establish authentic pedagogical relationships essential to the goal of critical conscience. In essence, *lecto-escritura* is important but it is not a means to an end; rather, it may be a need stemming from the development of critical conscience.

It is in alternative education, a long-time staple in Latin America, that Freirian thought is most evident, such as Peru's Nucleos Educativos Comunales (NEC, Community Educational Nuclei), Honduras's schools by radio, the Acción Popular Cultural Hondureña (APCH, Honduran Popular Cultural Movement), and Mexico's Cursos Comunitarios (Community Education). These programs have moved into rural communities and have become important means for community development and organization. At the same time, the programs allow participants to obtain certification of their basic education studies (Castro, 1994; Rockwell, 1996, White, 1979).

Alternative education represents a major effort to reach universal education and *alfabetización*. Alternative education programs of different countries tend to be identified with *alfabetización* as the major goal. Examples of such programs are:

1. Panama's schools of production, a work-study approach for basic education.
2. Guatemala's bilingual education for indigenous populations, characterized by beginning reading in the vernacular language and then in Spanish.
3. Colombia's Popular and Bank Schools as alternatives to mainstream education.
4. Colombia's Radio Sutatenza, which began in 1947 with nationwide broadcast of Acción Popular Cultural (ACPO, Popular Cultural Action Program), and includes distribution of weekly printed material.
5. El Salvador's televised education of basic school years.
6. Venezuela's basic literacy and education program.
7. Haiti's Radio Docteur.

With few exceptions, alternative education and programs for *alfabetización* in general are government sanctioned and funded. The programs, as might be expected, have had various degrees of success and duration. Initially stemming from local efforts, once programs expand and become official they begin to suffer some of the same problems of formal education, mainly bureaucratization and inflexibility (Rockwell, 1996; UNICEF, 1979). On the positive side, officialization enables certification of studies.

A major source of difficulty for alternative education programs is the need for teachers with appropriate training and sensitivity to work in the target communities. Often called *promotores*, promoters, they need pedagogical education as well as a wholistic education that sensitizes them about their target contexts and prepares them for their community leadership roles. The challenge is how to prepare *promotores* for a specific type of praxis to enable them to act both as active participants and leaders within the group (Cetrulo, 1988).

Promotores have traditionally been outsiders who gradually insert themselves into the communities. The major difficulty is the short duration of their involvement, which impedes acquisition of the necessary cultural wisdom to work their way up to be accepted by the communities and become effective leaders within them.

Recently, efforts have been made to gain continuity by involving and preparing members of the target groups as *promotores*. Although in principle a good solution, sometimes other problems arise, such as lack of training and experience for the demands of their roles.

Adult Education: *Alfabetización* and *Post-Alfabetización*

In Latin America, adult education programs for *alfabetización* may subsume other movements like popular education and indigenous-bilingual education while maintaining their own space, particularly in *alfabetización*. Adult education, however requires a broad definition of "adult" in the context of alternative education and of marginalized groups. An adult may be anyone of any age who actively participates in group or family production or in a subsistence economy and is not attending school. This is often the case in remote rural areas (Infante, 1983; Isáis-Reyes, 1957; Schmelkes, 1990). Thus, in adult education, the socioeconomic characteristics of individuals and their geographical location determine eligibility.

Traditionally, programs for adult *alfabetización* tended to view literacy as a good in and of itself and as the ability to "break the code." That is, once individuals learned the alphabetic code, they became members of the literate society, which would translate into national progress (Isáis-Reyes, 1957). Soon it was understood that access to the alphabetic code by no means guarantees national or personal progress (Infante, 1983; Marini, 1994; Rodríguez, 1995; Schiefelbein, 1993; Schmelkes, 1990). The necessary learnings are more related to *literate behaviors* and *being literate* (Heath, 1991) and to being able to act upon one's reality (Freire, 1969, 1970).

Freire and Macedo (1989) argued that those who have previously developed a critical conscience and a need to modify their own reality (liberation) may acquire a need to break the code. Thus, programs for *alfabetización* will have the most impact when individuals understand the need for and the functionality of literacy.

However, a major difficulty for programs of *alfabetización* is the loss of acquired abilities due to the lack of practice and of printed material in the communities (Ferreiro, 1997; Infante, 1983). Recent works in *post-alfabetización* programs have attempted to reach some understanding about the results of adult education programs and their impact in the lives of participants (Schmelkes, 1990).

Post-alfabetización, in a strict sense, refers to programs of postacquisition of *lecto-escritura* to reinforce functional skills and avoid their loss (Medina-Ureña, 1982). In a broader sense, *post-alfabetización* refers to programs that help individuals advance forward in their lives and not just to maintain skills—that is, to "advance toward higher personal goals and to ease participants' introduction into new social and occupational roles" (Nagel & Rodríguez, 1982, p. 51). They have emerged from varied needs and demands: government, private, joint government and private initiatives, and community efforts.

Evaluation of impact of *post-alfabetización* programs is based on problem solution and productivity, in community organization and community outcomes. *Alfabetización* here is clearly a means to an end, and some of the observed outcomes in communities are modifications in agrarian structures, alternative economies, organization of land laborers, a supply of skilled labor to the formal economic sectors, creation of alternative means of production, particularly among women, and work skills for the younger productive segments of the population.

Educación Popular

The *educación popular* [popular education], in essence, refers to education for social movements (Bengoa, 1988; Ortíz-Cáceres, 1990). It "is characterized by its political-pedagogical nature with the intent of turning education into a vehicle of support to popular organization, and to increase for its people their participatory capabilities in decision-making processes which affect their daily lives" (Sirvent, 1993, p. 19, my translation). In this view, education should promote critical thought and should have its effects in the social organizations of its recipients (Ortíz-Cáceres, 1990; Sirvent, 1993; Torres-Novoa, 1977).

Popular education programs in Latin America represent important movements of social organizations. Literacy is a major goal of the programs; however, promoters and organizations have begun to recognize that literacy is only one of many components to address in situations of marginalization. Other components related to helplessness and access within a major society also need to be addressed.

THE RESEARCH SCENARIO

Educational research in developing countries necessarily differs ideologically from research in industrialized nations. In 1979, Mexico's Centro de Estudios Educativos (CEE, Center of Educational Studies) and the U.S. Comparative and International Education Society (CIES) sponsored a meeting of researchers from the American continent. The goal was to reach some understanding of the nature and ideology of research in the different regions of the continent.

Conclusions pointed to the fact that research is a social practice and its characteristics and definition depend on its context. Patricio Carriola, from the Centro de Investigaciones y Desarrollo Educativo (CIDE, Center for Research and Educational Development) of Santiago de Chile, warned against trying to adopt research models from the industrialized nations that are not suitable to the contexts of other nations. The dangers are that research is transformed by problems and questions that are alien to the contexts to which it should respond (CEE, 1979).

It was concluded that a major difference between the research practices of the northernmost (industrialized) nations and the southernmost (developing) nations is that in industrialized nations research as praxis may or may not have a clear relation to practice. When it does, implementation is conducted by others not necessarily involved in the praxis of research. In Latin America the relationship between educational research and policy is surrounded by an aura of immediacy. Researchers are frequently immersed in the practical applications of research and in policy decisions. Thus, Carriola called for establishing a *common ground of understanding* between researchers of the American continent.

In turn, Joseph P. Farrell from the CIES called for efforts across nations to try to better contextualize research to its settings, that is, *to relate its function to the context* rather than to an a priori concept of science. The immediate nature of research in Latin America has been an impetus to develop specific paradigms in its praxis (CEE, 1979), although they presently share a broad common ground.

Twenty years after the CEE and CIES meeting and in the era of free trade agreements, the value of immediacy still pervades the research. Research intended to effect change, including qualitative, participant, and critical research, allows a good fit with the context (Montero-Sieburth, 1991; Sirvent, 1993). Qualitative research paradigms in general and their historical leftist tradition find fertile ground in the Marxist and Freirian influenced thought of educational movements in Latin America (Montero-Sieburth, 1991). Recently these research paradigms have also been expanded to include research in classrooms and schools (see Beltrán-Rueda & Campos, 1992; Campos-Saborio, 1990; Montero-Sieburth, 1992) and to gender studies (Montero-Sieburth, 1992).

In light of immediacy, the content of Latin American research has focused mainly on (a) program development and implementation, and (b) evaluation of educational programs. Furthermore, the immediacy of problem solution within formal schooling, a traditionally closed setting, has opened itself to analyses of these sorts.

In contrast, education and psychology research methods courses in higher education follow predominantly a logical-positivist ideology of experimental research and statistical methods. This may be due to the prevailing notions among academics of neutrality and objectivity, as well as an a priori notion of science mainly modeled after "alien universes" as pointed out by Farrell (CEE, 1979).

Presently there are clear indications of openness and change in higher education. Yet at the same time the sociopolitical ideological roots of qualitative methods, its association to leftist and feminist research, and the need to adopt a particular position toward the construction of knowledge seem "unscientific" to more traditional scholars.

Literacy research in Latin America has been and is responding to its context. Present theoretical influences from developed nations are creating new demands and needs for literacy research in the region, but old demands and needs still have to be addressed. Among the latter are the generalized alternative education demands that the region's diverse populations require. The following examples of recent research should help illustrate.

A study by Rockwell (1991) in Mexico suggested that it is less likely that children become literate in school due to instruction from which they mainly acquire *skills* than through a variety of experiences that she referred to as *extrainstructional* activities. She presented evidence suggesting that children appropriate for themselves the reading and writing processes in spite of instruction. Convergent evidence for the Rockwell work is the fact that, as a topic of discussion, instruction of *lecto-escritura* virtually disappears from the literature about formal education after Grade 3, although by no means from educational concerns and evaluation studies (Colbert & Arboleda, 1990; Velez, 1992).

In Chile, Ortíz-Cáceres (1990) compared and characterized three different popular education programs for adults. She found that the "pedagogical discourse" in these programs is slanted toward collective conscience, group organization, and participation in the greater society. She concluded that the positive effects of these programs were mainly on three fronts:

1. Participants acquired a more realistic perspective (social representation) about social mobility.
2. They were exposed to alternatives to the societal "free rider" notion.
3. They generated internal group norms favorable to collective action, which were monitored within the group.

Schmelkes (1990) compared 76 *post-alfabetización* programs of 13 countries in the region. In her conclusions she established a direct link between education and work. The mission of one group of programs was preparation for work, and work skills were added to the curriculum. The mission of the other programs was production of goods, and educational activities were a necessary ingredient to achieve program goals.

For the first group of programs Schmelkes found that it was difficult to link educational efforts with work objectives in their implementation. In the second group of programs there was a close link between the contents of instruction and the need to be productive. In these, instruction became instrumental and functional to the goals of participants, thus extending implementation beyond the normal activities of the programs (Schmelkes, 1990).

These examples, represent the tenor of most of the existing research literature: that is, of analyses of programs in existence, of program implementations in quantitative terms (Rivera-Pizarro, 1991), or to discuss sociopolitical and philosophical issues (Rodríguez & Bernal, 1990; Rodríguez, 1995).

Basic research related to school literacy is less common, although there are important contributions from Ferreiro (1989, 1997), Ferreiro and Teberosky (1979), Braslavsky (1983, 1995), and Rojas-Drummond and colleagues (Rojas-Drummond, Hernández, Velez, & Villagrán, 1998), to name a few. Other research consists of general analyses of school programs and program implementations such as those by Barocio-Quijano (1990), Braslavsky (1995), and Rockwell (1991).

AGENDA FOR RESEARCH AND DEVELOPMENT

In the midst of multiple demands, research has not been a major priority for Latin American countries. Although many efforts and advances have been made in the educational field, the ground is fertile both for research and for development. At the forefront of educational endeavors is the demand for universal literacy where alternative education programs have offered the most interesting settings and activities for researchers in general. Moreover, an analysis of the literature of both formal and alternative education reveals several areas in need of exploration, of which I address only some—those especially pertinent to literacy education.

Of prime importance is research on teachers and teacher education, particularly in formal education settings. National efforts to advance education lean heavily toward program development and program evaluation, but little is done to effectively bridge the gap between national programs and teacher education (i.e., Braslavsky, 1983; Campos-Saborio, 1990; Dirección de Educación Primaria de Nicaragua/UNESCO, 1994; Ferreiro, 1997; Rivera-Pizarro, 1991). Theoretical influences such as those related to reflection and action in one's reality (Freire, 1969, 1970, 1996; Schön, 1983) are emerging in the literature of formal education; however, detailed analyses of processes of change and educational practice are virtually nonexistent. They only appear tangentially, mostly in relation to program implementation (i.e., Barocio-Quijano, 1990; Campos-Saborio, 1990; Dirección de Educación Primaria de Nicaragua/UNESCO, 1994).

In keeping with the immediacy of research in Latin America and paradigms of participant and critical research, research on teachers and teacher research would be a natural candidate. Although such intrusions are surrounded by strong resistance both by researchers and on the school side (Seda-Santana, 1994), the possibilities are wide open, and some efforts are also beginning to emerge (Macotela-Flores, Seda-Santana, & Flores-Macías, 1997; Rojas-Drummond et al., 1998). Researchers will need to clearly establish within their design the direct practical benefits of each specific research initiative to the context in which it is to be conducted.

In relation to the complex ethnic, linguistic, and geographical landscape of the region, research addressing possible alternative routes to literacy is also virtually nonexistent. Printed material in general is scarce in remote areas, but at the same time popular literature such as comic books, tabloid magazines, and newspapers is common in cities and towns, and it is all written in the dominant language. Because bilingualism is common among the cities' marginalized populations, studies of whether and how literacies exist or are part of their lives would provide useful information to understand alternative processes of *alfabetización* and to inform alternative education programs. Specifically, programs of *post-alfabetización* may benefit from information on alternative routes to *alfabetización* and the uses of literacy among specific populations.

Popular literature in and of itself is a source of multiple researchable questions in relation to its social role and alternative routes to literacy. Existing work has addressed the sociopolitical aspects and domination ideology of comic books (Dorfman & Mattelart, 1980; Emmanuelli, 1991; Ortíz, 1991; Zalpa-Ramírez, 1997), but not in relation to literacy learning and development. Popular literature is most likely the only literature, if any, available to marginalized groups.

Recent movements in educational systems, such as decentralization, need to be researched for specific outcomes and impact on national economic systems and educational effectiveness. Of particular interest may be a movement's impact on alternative education programs and on national curricula. By the same token, some experiments involving government-subsidized private education for the lower socioeconomic groups in Chile reveal that educational efforts that model the ways of the higher socioeconomic groups are not necessarily practical solutions to level off differences in acquired abilities in reading, writing, and arithmetic (Schiefelbein & Tedesco, 1995). Thus, practical experiments that apply some of Latin America's own theoretical perspectives to educational contexts and to today's demands are necessary.

To summarize, literacy research in Latin American ought to maintain and respond to the immediacy of its context and address problems to be solved. At the same time, it needs to move forward in researching questions and situations that take advantage of existing knowledge bases and contribute to addressing questions of a finer and more detailed grain than exists thus far. Issues of ownership and functionality in particular, as suggested in Allende's character, are important for alternative education movements to move more directly into Freire's ideal (1996) of a pedagogy of hope.

REFERENCES

Alfonso, L. A., Oltheten, T., Ooijens, J., & Thybergin, A. (1988). *Educación, participación e identidad cultural: Una experiencia educativa con las comunidades indígenas del nordeste amazónico* [*Education, participation and cultural identity: An educational experience with the indigenous communities of the Amazonic northeast*]. La Haye, The Netherlands: Centro para el Estudio de la Educación en Paises en Desarrollo (CESO).

Allende, I. (1990). *Cuentos de Eva Luna* [*Eva Luna's Stories*] (pp. 11–20). México: Diana Literaria.

Barocio-Quijano, R. (1990). El currículo con orientación cognoscitiva: Una alternativa para la educación de los niños preescolares [Cognitively oriented curriculum: An alternative for preschool education]. *Revista Latinoamericana de Estudios Educativos, XX*(2), 79–93.

Beltrán-Rueda, M., & Campos, M. A. (1992). *Investigación etnográfica en educación* [*Ethnographic research in education*]. México, D.F.: Universidad Nacional Autónoma de México.

Bengoa, J. (1988). La Educación para los movimientos sociales [Education for social movements]. In A. van Dam, J. Ooijens, & G. Peter (Eds.), *Educación popular en América Latina: La teoría en la práctica* [*Popular education in Latin America: Theory into practice*] (pp. 7–42). La Haye, The Netherlands: Centro para el Estudio de la Educación en Paises en Vías de Desarrollo (CESO).

Braslavsky, B. P. (1983). *La lectura en la escuela* [*Reading in school*]. Buenos Aires: Kapelusz.

Braslavsky, B. P. (1995). La lectura inicial: Ensayo de un paradigma didáctico [Beginning reading: Rehearsal of an instructional paradigm]. *Revista Latinoamericana de Innovaciones Educativas, VII*(19), 45–95.

Campos-Saborío, N. (1990). *Learning-teaching styles in classrooms of schools located in marginal urban areas.* San José, Costa Rica: Universidad de Costa Rica, Instituto pare el mejoramiento de la Educación Costarricense.

Castro, I. (1994). Propuesta pedagógica y organización escolar en América Latina [Proposal for school organization and pedagogy in Latin America]. *Revista Latinoamericana de Estudios Educativos, XXIV*(1–2), 129–144.

Cetrulo, R. (1988). La formación de promotores: Aspectos teóricos y metodológicos [Education of promotores: Theoretical and methodological perspectives]. In A. van Dam, J. Ooijens, & G. Peter (Eds.), *Educación popular en América Latina: La teoría en la práctica* [*Popular education in Latin America: Theory into practice*] (pp. 43–70). La Haye: The Netherlands: CESO.

Colbert, V., & Arboleda, J. (1990). *Universalization of primary education in Colombia.* Paris: UNESCO/UNICEF.

Centro de Estudios Educativos. (1979). *Perspectivas de la Educación en América Latina* [*Perspectives of Education in Latin America*]. México, D.F.: Author.

de Romero, A. T., & de García, M. C. (1994). La reforma educativa en el aula [Educational reform in the classroom]. *Revista Latinoamericana de Innovaciones Educativas, VI*(18), 119–167.

Direccion de Educacion Primaria de Nicaragua/UNESCO. (1994). Sistematización del proyecto PAM-PALE: Propuesta pare el aprendizaje de las matemáticas y de la lengua escrita [Systematization of project PAM-PALE: Proposal for learning mathematics and written language]. *Revista Latinoamericana de Innovaciones Educativas, VI*(18), 69–84.

Dorfman, A., & Mattelart, A. (1980). *Para leer al Pato Donald. Comunicación de masa y colonialismo [To read Donald Duck. Mass communication and colonialism]*. México, D.F.: Siglo XXI.

Emmanuelli, J. (1991). El comic de la mujer [The woman's comic book]. *Cupey, VIII*(1–2), 109–128.

Ferreiro, E. (Ed.). (1989). *Los hijos del analfabetismo: Propuesta para la Alfabetización escolar en América Latina [Children of illiteracy: Proposal for school "alfabetización" in Latin America]*. México, D.F.: Siglo XXI.

Ferreiro, E. (1997). *Alfabetizacion: Teoria y práctica [Literacy: Theory and practice]*. México, D.F.: Siglo XXI.

Ferreiro, E., & Teberosky, A. (1979). *Literacy before schooling*. Portsmouth, NH: Heinemann.

Freire, P. (1969). *La educación como práctica de la libertad [Education and liberation]*. México, D.F.: Siglo XXI.

Freire, P. (1970). *Pedagogía del oprimido [Pedagogy of the oppressed]*. México, D.F.: Siglo XXI.

Freire, P. (1996). *Pedagogía de la esperanza [Pedagogy of hope]*. México, D.F.: Siglo XXI.

Freire, P., & Macedo, D. (1989). *Alfabetización: Lectura de la palabra y lectura de la realidad [Alfabetización: Reading the word and reading reality]*. Barcelona, Spain: Paidós.

Gómez-Palacio, M. (1982). *Propuesta de aprendizaje para la lengua escrita [A learning proposal for written language]*. México, D.F.: Secretaría de Educación Publica (SEP).

Heath, S. B. (1972). *Telling tongues: Language policy in Mexico, colony to nation*. New York: Teachers College Press.

Heath, S. B. (1991). The sense of being literate: Historical and cross-cultural features. In R. Barr, M. L. Kamil, P. B. Mosenthal, & P. D. Pearson (Eds.), *Handbook of reading research II* (pp. 3–25). New York: Longman.

Infante, M. I. (1983). *Educación, comunicación y lenguaje: Fundamentos para la alfabetización de adultos de América Latina [Education, communication and language: Bases for adult literacy in Latin America]*. México, D.F.: Centro de Estudios Educativos.

Isáis-Reyes, J. M. (1957). *Algunas ideas sobre alfabetización [Some ideas about literacy]*. Pátzcuaro, Michoacán, México: Centro Regional de Educación Fundamental para la América Latina (CREFAL).

Larson, M. L., & Davis, P. M. (Eds.). (1981). *Bilingual education: An experience in the Peruvian Amazonia*. Washington, D.C.: Center for Applied Linguistics.

Macotela-Flores, G. S., Seda-Santana, I., & Flores-Macías, R. C. (1997). *Desarrollo y evaluación de un programa de colaboración entre maestros de aula y maestros de apoyo y su relación con el logro académico de niños de primaria [Development and evaluation of a collaborative program between regular and resource teachers and its relation to children's academic achievement]*. Unpublished manuscript, Facultad de Psicología, Universidad Nacional Autónoma de México (CONACyT Reference No. 26369-H).

Marini, R. M. (1994). Latin America at the crossroads. *Latin American Perspectives, 21*(1), 99–114.

Medina-Ureña, G. (1982). *La postalfabetización en América Latina [Postalfabetizacion in Latin America]*. Pátzcuaro, Michoacán, México: CREFAL.

Montero-Sieburth, M. (1991, October). *Corrientes, enfoques, e influencias de la investigación cualitativa para Latinoamerica [Trends, perspectives and influences of qualitative research in Latin America]*. Paper presented at the First Latin American Conference on Qualitative Research, San José, Costa Rica.

Montero-Sieburth, M. (1992). Models and practice of curriculum change in developing countries. *Comparative Education Review, 36*(2), 175–193.

Nagel, J. A., & Rodríguez, E. (1982). *Alfabetización: Politicas y estrategias en América Latina y el Caribe [Alfabetizacion: Policies and strategies in Latin America and the Caribbean]*. Santiago de Chile: UNESCO-OREALC.

Nahmad, S. (1975). La política educativa en regiones interculturales de México [Educational policy in the intercultural regions of México]. In R. C. Troike & N. Modiano (Eds.), *Proceedings of the First Inter-American Conference of Bilingual Education* (pp. 15–24). Arlington, VA: Center for Applied Linguistics.

Namo de Mello, G. (1996). Autonomía de la escuela: Posibilidades, límites y condiciones [School autonomy: Possibilities, limits and conditions]. *Revista Latinoamericana de Estudios Educativos, VII*(22), 11–46.

Ortíz, J. C. (1991). Canales y la contralectura de las felices parejas: Mujer, matrimonio y marginalidad [Channels and the counterreading of the happy couples: Women, marriage and maginalization]. *Cupey, VIII*(1–2), 101–108.

Ortíz-Cáceres, M. (1990). Educación popular y acción colectiva. Estudio de los efectos educativos [Popular education and collective action. A study of its educational effects]. *Revista Latinoamericana de Estudios Educativos, XX*(2), 95–109.

Puiggrós, A. (1995). America Latina: Crisis y prospectiva de la educación [Latin America: Educational crisis and prospectus]. Cuadernos, Argentina: Instituto de Estudios y Acción Social.

Rivera-Pizarro, J. (Ed.). (1991). *Investigación sobre educación en algunos paises de América Latina [Educational research in some Latin American countries]*. Canada: International Development Research Center.

Rockwell, E. (1991). Los usos escolares de la lengua escrita [School uses of written language]. In E. Ferreiro & Gómez-Palacio (Eds.), *Nuevas perspectivas sobre los procesos de lecto-escritura [New perspectives about read-write processes]*, (pp. 296–320). México, D.F.: Siglo XXI.

Rockwell, E. (1996). Cursos comunitarios: Una primaria alternativa para el medio rural [Community courses: An alternative primary education program for rural areas]. *Revista Latinoamericana de Innovaciones Educativas, VIII*(22), 111–135.

Rojas-Drummond, S., Hernández, G., Velez, M., & Villagrán, G. (1998). Cooperative learning and the appropriation of procedural knowledge by primary school children. *Learning and Instruction, 30*(1), 37–61.

Rodríguez, P. G. (1995). Política nacional de lectura: Meditación en torno a sus límites y condicionamientos [National reading policy? Reflection about its limits and conditioning factors]. *Revista Latinoamericana de Estudios Educativos, XXV*(3), 25–53.

Rodríguez, P. G., & Bernal, E. (1990). Razón y alfabetización [Reason and literacy]. *Revista Latinoamericana de Estudios Educativos, XX*(3), 97–109.

Scarano, F. A. (1993). *Puerto Rico: Cinco siglos de historia* [*Puerto Rico: Five centuries of history*]. San Juan: McGraw-Hill.

Schiefelbein, E. (1993). Desafíos, mitos, avances y posibilidades de la educación básica [Challenges, myths, advances and possibilities of basic education]. *Memoria del seminario de análisis sobre política educativa nacional* [*Proceedings from the seminar for the analysis of national educational policy*] (Vol. 1, pp. 9–26). México, D.F.: Fundación SNTE.

Schiefelbein, E., & Tedesco, J. C. (1995). Las nuevas lineas de la transformación educativa [The new lines of educational transformation]. *Revista Latinoamericana de Innovaciones Educativas, VII*(21), 11–32.

Schmelkes, S. (1990). *Post-alfabetización y trabajo en America Latina* [*Post-alfabetización and work in Latin America*]. México, D.F.: Oficina Regional de Educación para América Latina y el Caribe (OREALC) de la UNESCO & Centro Regional de Educación Fundamental para la América Latina (CREFAL).

Schön, D. A. (1983). *The reflective practitioner.* New York: Basic Books.

Secretaría de Educación Pública. (1986). *Bases generales de la educación indígena* [*General bases for indigenous education*]. México, D.F.: Author.

Secretaría de Educación Pública. (1992). *Acuerdo Nacional para la modernización de la educación básica* [*National agreement for modernization of basic education* (primary and secondary education)]. México, D.F.: Author.

Seda-Santana, I. (1987). *The history of English instruction in Puerto Rico.* Unpublished manuscript, University of Illinois, Urbana-Champaign.

Seda-Santana, I. (1993, December). ¿Qué es la lecto-escritura? [What is read-write? (as one)]. *En línea: Órgano informativo de la maestría en educación, I*(4). Monterrey, N.L., México: Instituto Tecnológico de Estudios Superiores de Monterrey.

Seda-Santana, I. (1994). La investigación participativa: Un testimonio. [Participant research: A testimony]. *Contextos I*(5), 6–9.

Sirvent, M. T. (1993). La investigación participativa aplicada a la renovación curricular [Participant research applied to curricular change]. *Revista Latinoamericana de innovaciones educativas, XI*, 11–74.

Torres-Novoa, C. A. (1977). *La praxis educativa de Paolo Freire* [*Paolo Freire's educational praxis*]. México, D.F.: Ediciones Guernika.

Troike, R. C., & Modiano, N. (Eds.). (1975). *Proceedings of the First Inter-American Conference on Bilingual Education.* Arlington, VA: Center for Applied Linguistics.

UNESCO. (1974). *Evolución reciente de la educación en America Latina I: Progresos escollos y soluciones* [*Recent evolution of education in Latin America I: Progress, difficulties and solutions*]. México, D.F.: Author and SEP Setentas.

UNICEF. (1979). *Situación de la infancia en América Latina y el Caribe* [*Children's situation in Latin America and the Caribbean*]. Santiago, Chile: Author.

Velez, E. (1992). *Factors affecting achievement in primary education.* Mexico, D. F.: World Bank.

Venezky, R. L. (1991). The development of literacy in the industrialized nations of the west. In R. Barr, M. L. Kamil, P. B. Mosenthal, & P. D. Pearson (Eds.), *Handbook of reading research II* (pp. 46–67). New York: Longman.

White, R. A. (1979). Alfabetismo: ¿Causa o efecto del desarrollo social? [Literacy: Cause or effect of social advancement?]. In CEE (Ed.), *Perspectivas de la Educación en America Latina* [*Educational perspectives in Latin America*] (pp. 111–128). México, D.F.: CEE.

Zalpa-Ramírez, G. (1997). Comicidad y sociedad: El mundo imaginario de la historieta [Humor and society: The imaginary world of the comic book]. *Caleidoscopio, I*(1), 9–36.

CHAPTER 5

Trends in Reading Research in the United States: Changing Intellectual Currents Over Three Decades

Janet S. Gaffney
Richard C. Anderson
University of Illinois at Urbana-Champaign

Life can only be understood backwards. It must be lived forwards.

—Soren Kierkegaard

Our charge was to construct an interpretive analysis of trends in reading research in the United States. We wanted to distinguish historically and currently contending issues in school-based literacy and understand the interplay between reading and writing research and theoretical perspectives, teaching practices, and school policies. What are the intellectual currents that flow through and shape our perspectives and how have they changed, changed us, and changed our actions over time? And, of course, we wanted to frame answers to these questions differently from our predecessors in order to offer a fresh view of the past and to project a future that honors the past but is not bounded by it.

We became archeologists using the last three decades of researcher and practitioner journals from two major professional organizations as our artifacts. Guzzetti, Anders, and Neuman (1999) reviewed the topics, methods, and special features of the *Journal of Reading Behavior/Journal of Literacy Research*, expanding on the analyses of publications of the National Reading conference by Baldwin and his associates (Baldwin et al., 1992). We selected the International Reading Association (IRA) and the Council for Exceptional Children (CEC) due to their prominence in education, parallel missions, and membership configurations in their respective fields of reading and special education.

Information about both organizations was located in the *Encyclopedia of Associations* (Jaszczak, 1997). The organizations have corresponding purposes, and each sponsors major journals focused on research and practice. Each organization sponsors a major annual conference, distributes print and nonprint media, operates as a clearinghouse for information, and serves an advocacy role for children and youth, parents, and professionals.

IRA was founded in 1956, the product of a merger of the International Council for the Improvement of Reading and Instruction and the National Association for Remedial Teachers. This professional organization is comprised of 94,000 members including teachers, reading specialists, consultants, administrators, supervisors, researchers, psychologists, librarians, and parents interested in promoting literacy. The goal of the organization is to improve the quality of reading instruction and to promote literacy worldwide. IRA disseminates information on adult literacy, early childhood and literacy development, international education, literature for children and adolescents, and teacher education and professional development (Jaszczak, 1997, p. 894).

From the four journals published by IRA, we selected *Reading Research Quarterly* as the research journal and *The Reading Teacher* as the journal focused on practice. *Reading Research Quarterly* is a peer-reviewed journal that publishes original research reports and articles on theory in teaching reading and learning to read and "is intended to provide a forum for the exchange of information and opinion on theory, research, and practice in reading" (*Reading Research Quarterly*, front inside cover). The first issue of volume 1 was published in the fall of 1965.

The Reading Teacher is a peer-reviewed journal that is published eight times per year and contains articles on current theory, research, and practice in literacy education of preschool and elementary school children (Jaszczak, 1997; *Reading Teacher*, 1998, p. v). *The Reading Teacher* was published by the International Council for the Improvement of Reading Instruction beginning in 1947, with continuing publication by IRA at the inception of the organization in 1956.

Founded in 1922, CEC is a professional organization of 54,000 members including administrators, teachers, parents, and others who work on behalf of children with disabilities and those who are gifted. The goal of the organization is to improve the educational outcomes of children, youth, and young adults with disabilities and those with gifts and talents. CEC is an advocate for appropriate government policies, provides information to the media, operates as a clearinghouse for information on disabilities and gifted education, and supports professional development (Jaszczak, 1997, p. 902).

CEC publishes two journals: *Exceptional Children* (bimonthly) and *TEACHING Exceptional Children* (quarterly).[1] *Exceptional Children* is the primary forum for "original research on the education and development of persons with disabilities of all ages from infants to young adults and articles on professional issues of concern to special educators" (*Exceptional Children*, 1995, inside cover). All kinds of research are solicited in the journal's statement of purpose, and submissions undergo blind peer-review. "The journal welcomes manuscripts reflecting qualitative or quantitative methodologies using group or single-subject research designs. Articles appropriate for publication include data-based research, data-based position papers, research integration papers, and systematic analyses of policy or practice. The journal also includes reports of official actions of the governing bodies of CEC" (*Exceptional Children*, 1995). *Exceptional Children* was first published in 1934 under the title *The Journal of Exceptional Children* and in 1951 switched to the abbreviated title in use today.

---

[1] Other specialized journals are published under the auspices of Divisions of CEC.

TEACHING Exceptional Children is specifically designed for teachers of children with disabilities and children who are gifted. Articles that deal with practical methods and materials for classroom use are featured and are subjected to a field-review process. The statement of purpose is explicit that *TEACHING Exceptional Children* is not research oriented but welcomes data-based descriptions of techniques, equipment, and procedures for teacher application with students with exceptionalities (*TEACHING Exceptional Children*, 1995). *TEACHING Exceptional Children* was first published in 1968.

Essentially, our approach was to look at changes over three decades in patterns of language use in these professional journals. The pivotal assumption for our approach is this: *The words people use reveal the assumptions they make.* In a fascinating book about computers and cognition, Winograd and Flores (1987) proposed a view of language that is importantly constructive. In their view, not unlike that of Foucault (1973), we design ourselves in language. Thus, they advocate "a shift from language as description to language as action" (p. 76). In language, we create a mutual orientation to the world. Over time, the consensual language forms the background of our conversations. Like white noise, present but unattended, the background constituted in language becomes invisible to us. According to Winograd and Flores, when problems arise they rub against the invisible background and our assumption-embedded language reveals itself. The rubs, therefore, are the interesting places to look.

To find the rubs, our method was to look at what people say and what they do not say, what they once said but no longer say, what they now say that they did not say before. Both what was said and what was left unsaid informed our search, peeled back layers to reveal the always present but usually invisible background, and uncovered the changing voices in the field over the last three decades.

PROCEDURES FOR ANALYSIS

Our analysis of the four journals began with issues published in 1965. This was the first year of publication of *Reading Research Quarterly* and the year that Chall completed her influential report, *Learning to Read: The Great Debate*, which was published in 1967. As educational researchers with professional and personal histories in the field of reading, we shared our hypotheses about themes and issues that we expected to be prominent at different points in time. We discussed the social, cultural, economic, political, and directly educational influences that were present during each decade since 1965. We generated a bibliography of classic books, chapters, and articles about reading and the teaching of reading that we read to augment our shared knowledge.

But we went beyond the conventional approach of scattered, selective reading and tried a perhaps innovative empirical approach to chart the landscape of the last three decades of reading research. We used a multifaceted approach that sought both depth and breadth of analysis: (a) Using the qualitative software NUD*IST, we did intensive studies of all of the research articles published during each of 4 years a decade apart. (b) Using the search engine OVID, we did extensive studies of the ERIC database for two of the journals in our purview. We were able to switch easily from macro to micro levels of analysis, providing a series of checks and balances—a process of triangulation—for developing and proving hypotheses about trends.

We chose for intensive analysis every article in the two research journals, *Reading Research Quarterly* and *Exceptional Children*, published in 1965, 1975, 1985, and 1995. Only two issues of Volume 1 of the *Reading Research Quarterly* were published in 1965, fall and winter, so to fill out the sample we supplemented the 1965 issues with subsequent issues published in 1966. The moldy smell of the earliest issues reinforced the

TABLE 5.1

Total Number of Articles in *Reading Research Quarterly*
and *Exceptional Children* by Year

Year	Reading Research Quarterly	Exceptional Children
1965	11[a]	44
1975	10	27
1985	15	45
1995	32	31
Total	68	147

[a]Two issues of *Reading Research Quarterly* were drawn from 1966.

sense that we were on an archeological dig. The total number of articles included in the sample for each journal and year is reported in Table 5.1. Neither of the practitioner journals publishes abstracts, so we chose to reserve them for the subsequent broader but shallower analysis.

The titles and author-written abstracts of the 215 *Reading Research Quarterly* and *Exceptional Children* articles from 1965, 1975, 1985, and 1995 were imported into NUD*IST (Qualitative Solutions and Research, 1997). We agreed on initial categories for coding the articles, but each of us created new categories as we proceeded. As we read the articles that we were coding, we were able to add our own notes about the content and emerging ideas through the memo and appending tools of the NUD*IST program.

Once the documents were collected, stored in electronic form, coded, and supplemented with our notes and evolving thoughts, we were ready to explore the rich data. With relative ease, we could create reports based on the coding categories that we created and also easily search the titles and text of documents for actual words and phrases. An advantage of NUD*IST is that one can readily view terms in context in order to distinguish, for instance, between *teaching strategies* and *learning strategies*. Both of us undertook exploratory sweeps of the documents guided by a priori hypotheses, searching for specific words or word strings. Results of searches were saved so that they could be analyzed by journal and year, allowing the identification of patterns. We pursued our hunches and conducted independent analyses. We often shared our results, generated ideas for new directions, and brainstormed alternative word strings with similar meanings to ensure that we were finding all occurrences of keywords. For example, a search for documents having to do with teaching included

[teach | teacher | teachers | teaching | instruct | instructor | instructors | instruction]

and in a search for documents addressing children with reading difficulties the following descriptors were used:

[below average | poor | slow | disability | disabilities | disabled | handicapped | retarded | blind | deaf | impaired | special | exceptional | low intelligence | low IQ | dyslexic | dyslexia]

To be comprehensive, we sometimes needed to search using terminology that is not acceptable in the late twentieth century, such as *retarded* and *handicapped*. As a result, however, we were able to track changes over time in usage of such terms in technical writing.

The broad analysis involved the entire set of 697 *Reading Research Quarterly* articles and 3,018 *Reading Teacher* articles published from January 1966[2] through April 1998 that are included in the ERIC databases. The databases were examined online using the OVID search tools. For each article, the source material available to be searched online consisted of the title, descriptive codes and identifiers assigned by ERIC indexers, and a succinct ERIC-written abstract.

CHANGING CONCEPTIONS OF RESEARCH

To plunge immediately into our results, consider the vignette that follows. The italicized terms are ones that were more frequent in 1965 than in 1995, or vice versa, based on counts from the intensive analysis of articles in the *Reading Research Quarterly* in 1965, 1975, 1985, and 1995. For instance, the word *experiment* [includes *experiments, experimental*; in this and subsequent examples, closely related terms are incorporated] appeared in 55% of the articles published in 1965 but only 22% of the articles published in 1995, whereas *study* appeared in 18% of the 1965 articles and 59% of the 1995 articles.

> In 1965, an investigator reported a *conclusion* about a *theory* or *hypothesis* by performing *statistical* analyses of *data* from *tests* administered during an *experiment*. By 1995, an investigator announced a *finding* based on a *study* motivated by a *model* or maybe a *framework*, *view*, or *premise*.

Anyone who has been a professional in the field over these years is well aware that the conception of educational research has broadened, so our finding is not surprising, but it is gratifying that the trend is so clearly documented by our methods. The unsurprising finding in this case will increase our confidence in making negative inferences when trends do not appear in other cases.

We must caution that our analysis does not fully warrant the conclusion that the field's conception of research has changed. It might be that the same proportion of scholars are performing experiments on aspects of reading now as in earlier decades, only now more experimentalists are publishing in journals such as the *Journal of Educational Psychology* or, more recently, *Scientific Studies of Reading*, instead of *Reading Research Quarterly*. The only way to tell for sure would be to canvass all of the journals that publish reading research, broadly defined. Another, possibly transient, influence is who the editors of a journal are in a certain era. In 1995, the editors of the *Reading Research Quarterly* were Judith Green, Robert Tierney, and Michael Kamil, who had an announced policy of broadening the journal (Tierney, Kamil, & Green, 1992). Against the idea that 1995 was perhaps atypical because of editorial policy is the fact that generally the key terms in the vignette just given changed progressively over the three decades, including during the tenure of Philip Gough and his fellow editors, known not to be enemies of experimental research.

We turn now to the question whether it is possible to document, on the basis of the language used in journal articles, changes in theoretical paradigm over the past three decades. Our sense is that the major theoretical changes in the reading field are captured like this:

Behaviorist → Cognitive → Sociocultural

The transition from behaviorism to cognitive science was assuredly a paradigm shift, if any change in world view in the history of the human sciences deserves this label.

---

[2]Although *The Reading Teacher* and *Reading Research Quarterly* were published earlier, documentation of publications in ERIC begins with 1966.

Some would call the transition from a cognitive to a sociocultural view a paradigm shift, but we believe it is more appropriate to call it a paradigm elaboration.

During the 1960s, behaviorism is ascendent at the intersection of education and psychology. B. F. Skinner is god, although Jerome Brunner keeps an altar candle burning for a cognitive perspective in the *Process of Education*. Cognitive trends are well underway in academic disciplines that relate to education. Linguistics is flourishing and the hybrid field of psycholinguistics is emerging. Information-processing psychology develops rapidly and dominates experimental psychology by the end of the decade. Educational psychologists such as Robert Glaser, Lauren Resnick, and Richard Anderson, who began the decade as behaviorists, end it as cognitive psychologists. Research on text processing is pioneered by Ernst Rothkopf, who uses the concept of mathemagenic behavior to rationalize research on adjunct questions.

Interestingly, analysis of the language of journal articles suggests that the reading field is not now and never has been manifestly behaviorist. The evidence for this claim is the extremely low rate of the terms *reinforcement, programmed instruction* [or *programed instruction*], *operant, behavior analysis, behavioral analysis* in the *Reading Research Quarterly* or *The Reading Teacher*. Some might argue that behaviorism is or was latent, but it seems few in the reading field were ever self-conscious Skinnerians.

In the 1970s, cognitive science—the amalgam of psychology, linguistics, and computer science—is born; one of the founders, Herbert Simon, wins a Nobel Prize. Allan Paivio makes mental imagery respectable. John Bransford shows that all language processing is meaningful. Bonnie Meyer establishes the psychological reality of text structure. Nancy Stein and Jean Mandler introduce story grammars. The concept of schema is reinvented. Text processing research flourishes under the leadership of such figures as Walter Kintsch. John Flavell and Ann Brown make metacognition an exciting new theme. Postmodernism and deconstructionism take hold in humanities departments. Del Hymes, Courtney Cazden, and John Gumperz push the new discipline of sociolinguistics into education; they extend linguistic competence to "communicative competence." The 1970s are the Golden Era for school effectiveness and teacher effectiveness research.

In the 1980s, and on into the 1990s, educational scholarship takes a social and political turn. By late 1980s, the avant garde are social constructivists. James Wertsch and Barbara Rogoff promulgate the ideas of Vygotsky and Baktin. Michael Apple makes neo-Marxist critiques of technical rationality in the schools. Situated cognition, blending cognitive and sociocultural concepts, moves to the forefront. Psychologists study increasingly complex phenomena such as computer programming and scientific understanding. Connectionism emerges as a significant rival to rationalist cognitive psychology. Cooperative learning is a thriving educational research topic. Increasing numbers now do qualitative research instead of experimental or quantitative research. Teacher-as-researcher is a rallying cry in educational scholarship.

We were able to find traces of the cognitive revolution and the sociocultural turn in the language of journal abstracts and titles. Interestingly, again, theoretically juicy terms such as *schema, metacognitive,* and *constructive* are rare. The evidence for paradigm change is less direct. It can be traced in the changing frequency of words and phrases such as *comprehension, background knowledge, reading strategy, context, social,* and *culture.* These words and their implications are reviewed fully in the next section.

Reading researchers take a curiously atheoretical—we might say positivist—stance toward their work. They stick to "facts" that are presented as though they can be verified by the senses alone, eschewing subjective or theoretical terms. Evidence for this comes from the high frequency of use of the verbs *show, reveal,* and *indicate,* as in "Study 1 revealed that …" and "The data show that …" We believe that the unproblematical use of these verbs implies that the authors assume (or judge they must pretend to assume) that conclusions are simply there to be seen, without an active human agent who understands, interprets, or explains in terms of a theoretical framework. The percentage of *Reading Research Quarterly* articles using *show, reveal,* or *indicate* in this manner ranged between 45 and 50% from 1965 through 1985 and then declined sharply in 1995 to 13%, which may mean that positivism is falling out of favor. However, agentless uses of related forms such as *suggest* and *imply,* as in "The data suggest" and "The results imply," remained high in 1995.

Authors almost never identify themselves in *Reading Research Quarterly* articles as the agents in sentences containing verbs of knowing, believing, or valuing. We found no instance of *We, author, investigator, researcher, experimenter* (there are no instances of the personal pronoun *I* in the corpus) paired with *know, believe, think, contend, maintain, suspect, feel, argue, interpret, explain, judge.* We did find two instances in which authors identified themselves as the agents of an act of concluding, as in "The investigators conclude that" Writers go to amazing lengths to avoid making themselves the agents of knowledge claims, as in the awkward circumlocution, "It is suggested that."

The positivist stance helps us to explain the relative absence in *Reading Research Quarterly* corpus of *schema* or the prefix *meta-,* as in *metacognition* and *metalinguistic awareness.* These terms are embarrassingly theory laden. If our analysis is correct, when writing, if not when thinking, authors retreat to terms they feel are less theoretical, more everyday, more sense based, like *prior knowledge* and *strategy.*

Word identification is the one subspecialty in reading that we could find in 1995 in which investigators consistently and self-consciously evaluated competing explanations for data. This indicates a studied awareness that conclusions do not just "show" themselves in data. Ironically, most people in reading would say that word identification is the most positivist area of reading research, which leads one to wonder what people mean by "positivism," anyway.

Why positivism might persist in reading research is perfectly understandable. Those of us who came of age during the era of radical behaviorism were taught that a theory is a needless ornament that distracts from the elegant simplicity of human beings. Since that era, the field has rushed headlong to the view that human beings, individually and severally, are exceedingly complex, so complex that truths are seen as always contingent, transient, and context bound. A strong theory of how a process works is not thought to be possible, or even desirable. So, we have come full circle, around again to the view that theory is a dangerous thing. You have your position and I have mine, but we can at least agree on the plain facts.

Remember, though, that journal abstracts were our primary source documents. Quite possibly, whole articles do not have the positivist skew of abstracts. Analyzing a corpus of whole articles is a bigger job for another day, however.

CHANGING CONCEPTIONS OF READING

This section summarizes analyses that reveal aspects of change in conceptions of the nature of the reading process and ideas about the teaching of reading. We attempt to explain changes in the field of reading in terms of preceding and concurrent social, political, and intellectual developments. Trends in reading are associated with, and presumptively caused by, multiple forces: (a) large scale social, economic, and political developments, (b) developments in cognate fields, (c) general developments within education, and (d) developments specific to reading education. Taking heed of the work of organizational theorists, Venezky (1987) cautioned those who are studying curriculum history to bear in mind the complex factors that impinge upon schools. He contended that if schools are vulnerable to external pressures, then reading instruction is doubly vulnerable. "No other component of the curriculum has been subjected throughout its history to such intense controversy over both its basic methods and its content" (Venezky, 1987, p. 159).

The remainder of this section foregrounds the results of 12 searches of the corpus of articles accessible through ERIC and published in *Reading Research Quarterly* and *The Reading Teacher* from 1996 through April 1998. These 12 represent a small subset of the searches that we conducted. These searches were given priority because they revealed something interesting that could, in most cases, be corroborated in part in the more intensive analysis from selected years. With one exception, the searches are summarized in bar graphs that present the percentage of articles containing words or word strings in each 5-year period since 1965. We imagine the bar graphs to be aerial photographs of the temporal landscape of the reading field. The graphic depictions of the data reveal the movements in the field as they swell and crest and wane.

Considered first is the question of which units of language have preoccupied researchers and practitioners. Figure 5.1 charts the percentage of articles that mention word (e.g., *word, verb*) and subword units (e.g., *letter, syllable, prefix*). Figure 5.2 shows the percentage of articles mentioning a whole text unit (e.g., *story, book, poem*). There are no figures for the classes of units that would include *phrase* and *sentence* or *paragraph* and *passage* because such units are rare in the corpus.

Looking at Fig. 5.1, it is apparent that there was a steady decline in mentions of letters, syllables, and other word and subword units in *The Reading Teacher*. That references to these units of language were relatively high in 1966–1970 is perhaps attributable to Chall's *Learning to Read: The Great Debate* and the fact that the received wisdom of the day was represented in basic skills management plans such as the Wisconsin Design. We ascribe the decline since 1966–1970 to the lure of competing ideas. Kenneth Goodman first introduced the idea of reading as a psycholinguistic guessing game in the late 1960s. Frank Smith's influential books began appearing in 1971.

Still looking at Fig. 5.1, references to word and subword units in *Reading Research Quarterly* jumped in 1976–1980 and have remained high ever since. We believe that the best explanation for the jump in 1976–1980 is a burst of new ideas (phonemic awareness, dual route lexical access, and decoding by analogy), new experimental methods (priming, lexical decision), and new empirical findings (regularity × frequency interaction) at approximately that time.

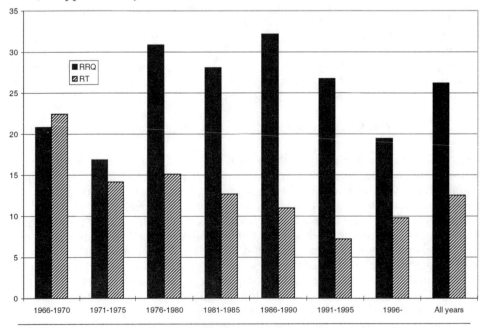

FIG. 5.1. Percentage of articles referring to word and subword units of language.

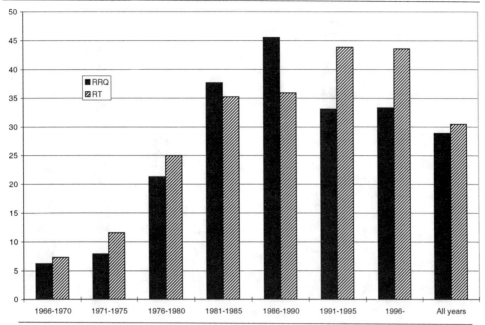

FIG. 5.2. Percentage of articles referring to whole texts.

Figure 5.2 shows references to whole text units. Such references increased dramatically in both journals between 1966–1970 and 1986–1990. Since then, references in *The Reading Teacher* have gone even higher, whereas those in *Reading Research Quarterly* have declined somewhat. The sharp upward trend from 1966–1970 we impute to a confluence of forces from within the field and cognate disciplines, again a wave of new ideas, methods, and findings. As we mentioned in the preceding section, the 1970s was the period during which reading was construed as a constructive process, when ideas of schema, script, text structure, and story grammar took hold. In 1976, the first federally funded center focused on reading, the Center for the Study of Reading, was established, with a charter to examine comprehension, not decoding. The whole language movement was gaining momentum during this period.

Figure 5.3 charts references to *phonics* (including *decoding, word identification*, etc.). The trends very closely match those that appear in Fig. 5.1 with respect to word and subword units. This is only to be expected, of course, but it does provide converging evidence for an underlying theme, since the word strings searched were not the same.

Figure 5.4 shows the occurrences of comprehension (narrowly defined to include just *comprehension, comprehend, comprehends,* and *comprehending*) whereas Fig. 5.5 shows occurrences of *strategy* (*reading strategy, learning strategy*, etc.). Looking at Fig. 5.4, the data for *Reading Research Quarterly* can be interpreted as showing that research on comprehension peaked during the 1980s, when more than half the articles contained the term, and then dropped sharply during the 1990s. *The Reading Teacher* shows a similar but weaker pattern. Durkin's (1978–1979) exposé showing little direct comprehension instruction in schools may have been a specific catalyst for the peak in the 1980s.

As would be expected, the trends in Fig. 5.4 for comprehension and Fig. 5.5 for strategy roughly corroborate the trend portrayed in Fig. 5.2 for whole text units. A difference is that mentions of whole text units in *The Reading Teacher* continued to climb during the 1990s, whereas mentions of comprehension and strategies in this journal were falling. Our explanation is that *Reading Research Quarterly* was riding currents in text processing research and discourse psycholinguistics. *The Reading Teacher* was in-

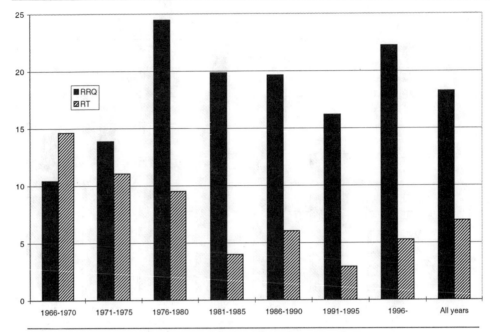

FIG. 5.3. Percentage of articles referring to phonics.

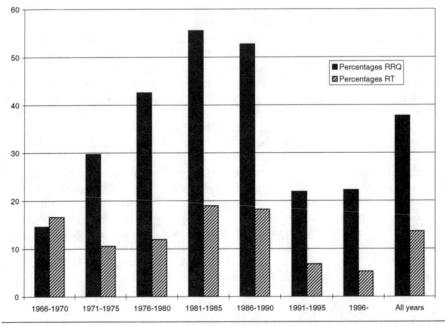

FIG. 5.4. Percentage of articles containing *comprehension*.

fluenced to some extent by the same currents, but was also responsive to the whole-language and literature-based instruction movements, which continued to be vigorous into the 1990s.

Figure 5.6 shows the occurrences of *schema* (including *schemas* and *schemata* and re-lated terms such as *existing knowledge* and *topic knowledge*). The occurrences are plotted on a finer scale than that in other figures for a couple of reasons, one of which is simply that there are not enough of them to show percentages. The figure shows that follow-ing its first appearance in 1978, *schema* got a fair amount of play until the late 1980s, when its use tailed off to one or two occurrences every several years, approximating the pattern for more general, and much more frequent, terms such as *comprehension*.

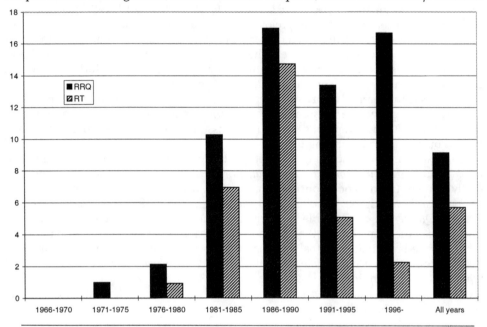

FIG. 5.5. Percentage of articles referring to reading strategies.

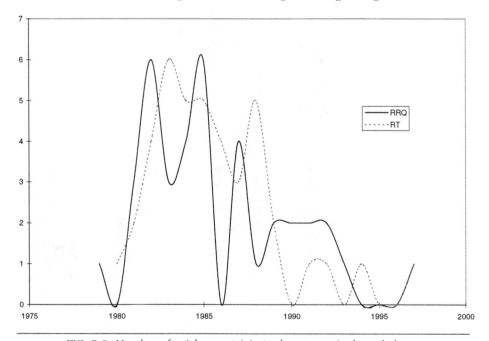

FIG. 5.6. Number of articles containing *schema* or *prior knowledge*.

The idea of schema reflects the surge of interest in comprehension, and indeed, probably to some extent, was actually one cause of rising interest. The low frequency of schema-related terms, nonetheless, suggests to us that most in the field did not commit themselves to the specific theoretical content associated with *schema* and, instead, took the general idea in various directions.

The occurrences of *whole language* (just this phrase) are displayed in Fig. 5.7. It is apparent that whole language was at the peak of its influence in the decade beginning in 1986. The rate of mentions in *Reading Research Quarterly* during 1991–1995 is inflated; a series of related commentaries and rejoinders account for over half of the occurrences. The overall rate of *whole language* may seem low, but we would not make any strong inference from this about the influence of the whole-language movement. We found similarly low rates for other named methods or approaches— including DISTAR, reciprocal teaching, process writing, Reading Recovery, and Success for All. One reason for this is that named approaches tend not to be explicitly mentioned in ERIC abstracts, although whole language became prominent enough to be assigned a descriptive ERIC code that our search encompassed. Whole language appears to have waned in the period beginning in 1996.

Changing directions now, Fig. 5.8 pictures trends in use of the terms *social* and *cultural* (including *culture, context, contextual*, words beginning with *socio-*, etc.). The generally upward trend in both journals is consistent with the idea of a change toward a sociocultural paradigm. We believe that the surge in 1976–1980 references in *Reading Research Quarterly* is attributable to the rising influence of sociolinguistics and anthropology of education during that period. A contributing influence may have been schema-based research, which always had a sociocultural dimension. In fact, the first *Reading Research Quarterly* article to use the word *schemata* used it in the phrase *cultural schemata* (Steffenson, Joag-Dev, & Anderson, 1978). The peak in use of sociocultural words in *Reading Research Quarterly* in 1991–1995 is possibly an effect of the deliberate policy of the editors to broaden the journal.

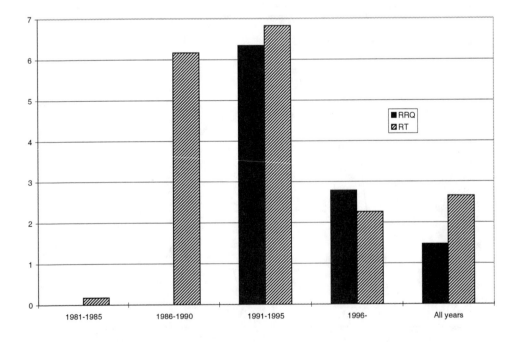

FIG. 5.7. Percentage of articles referring to whole language.

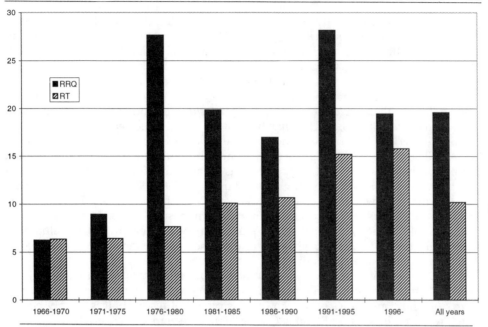

FIG. 5.8. Percentage of articles containing *social* or *cultural*.

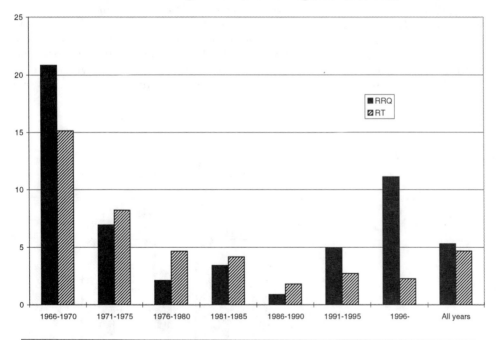

FIG. 5.9. Percentage of articles containing words about race, class, or dialect.

Figure 5.9 presents trends in the use of words referring to race, class, and dialect. The high rate of these words in the 1960s undoubtedly reflects the Civil Rights movement, the strong tide toward school integration, and the launching of Great Society programs such as Head Start and Follow Through. All of this inevitably captured the attention of the reading field. Guzzetti et al. (1999) confirmed that attention to socioeconomic status and ethnicity peaked during the first decade (1969–1978) of publication of the *Journal of Reading Behavior/Journal of Literacy Research*. What is not as easy to understand is the steadily declining references to race, class, or dialect since the 1960s (with an upturn recently). Considering Figs. 5.8 and 5.9 together, one possibility is that terms for race, class, and dialect got swept under the sociocultural rubric.

Finally, we present data on three topics that are discussed more frequently in *The Reading Teacher* than in *Reading Research Quarterly*. Mentions of writing (includes *write, writer, writes, wrote*, and *writing*, but not *written*) are plotted in Fig. 5.10. In *The Reading Teacher*, the trend in references to writing turned up in 1981–1985, surged in 1986–1990, and has declined since then, although remaining at a level higher than any period before the 1980s. This pattern is weakly mirrored in *Reading Research Quarterly*, except for the continuing upward trend in 1996–1998. It is tempting to surmise that the trend was stronger in *The Reading Teacher* than in *Reading Research Quarterly* because leaders in the process writing movement such as Don Graves and Lucy Calkins spoke directly to teachers, bypassing a long research and development phase. Questions of whether, when, or under what circumstances research "leads" practice are taken up again in the next section.

Figure 5.11 shows references to *cooperative learning* or *learning centers*. Except in 1996–1998, there are more references in *The Reading Teacher* than in *Reading Research Quarterly*. These are topics on which there is plenty of research. It is simply not research reported in *Reading Research Quarterly* until recently.

Figure 5.12 graphs occurrences of words about motivation or interest. Again, except in 1996–1998, there are more references in *The Reading Teacher* than in *Reading Research Quarterly*. Perhaps it is obvious that a journal for teachers would not ignore motivation. At the same time, it is apparent that motivation, emotion, and affect do not comprise a major theme in reading research. This finding would not surprise motivational researchers, such as Mark Lepper or Carole Ames, who have often complained of the hegemony of cool cognition. The rise in occurrences of motivational

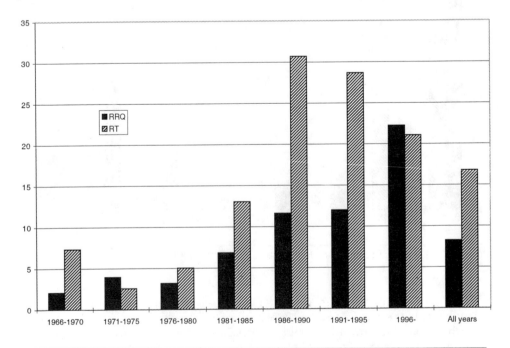

FIG. 5.10. Percentage of articles referring to writing.

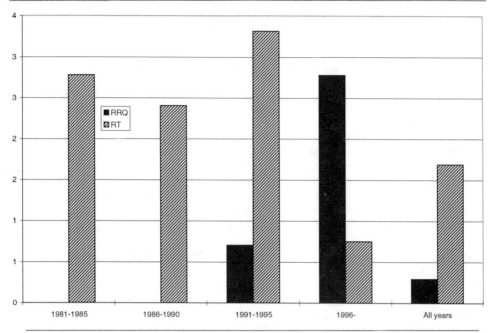

FIG. 5.11. Percentage of articles mentioning *cooperative learning*.

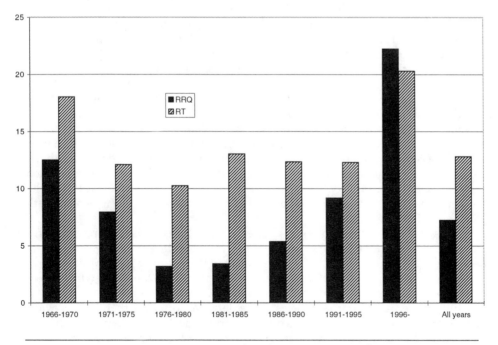

FIG. 5.12. Percentage of articles containing words
about motivation or interest.

terms in 1996–1998 may reflect, in part, the influence of the National Reading Research Center at the University of Georgia and the University of Maryland which
made engagement one of its principal themes.

ON THE CONNECTION BETWEEN RESEARCH
AND PRACTICE

In the her most recent update of *Learning to Read*, Chall (1996) wrote that

> The use of research and theory for improving practice has not been consistent. While research continues to produce findings in the same direction, practice seems to move back and forth. More often than not, it moves in a direction that is not supported by the research and theory. It would seem that the time has come to give more serious attention to why practice has been so little influenced by existing research. (p. xx)

Chall expressed the lament of many educational researchers, teacher educators, and staff developers. A plethora of reasons have been offered as to why teachers do not implement research-based practices, such as: (a) lack of effort or commitment because the innovation "won't be here long," or the fad phenomenon (Slavin, 1989); (b) lack of knowledge of research, or issues of dissemination (Gallagher, 1998) and access (Kennedy, 1997); (c) not enough time or inadequate material, personnel, and financial resources; (d) poor implementation, what Gallagher (1998) characterizes as "teacher error"; (e) lack of teacher knowledge or skill (National Commission on Teaching & America's Future, 1996); and (f) insufficient systemic support and weak leadership (Fullan, 1993).

Recently, two authors proposed reasons for the presumed research–practice gap that are distinct from those commonly listed. Robinson (1998) viewed confusion over the nature of methods as the primary reason for the research–practice gap. In her problem-solving-based theory, methods are activities that solve problems that confront teachers in their practice. She contends that often methods recommended on the basis of research do not solve the problems in ways that are responsive to the particular constraints on teachers' work. Rather, the solutions are dominated by the abstract viewpoint espoused by researchers.

A related explanation is put forward by Gallagher (1998), who maintained that law-like generalizations that emerge from research, in this case in special education, inaccurately represent and exaggerate scientific claims. Gallagher's logic led her to dismiss the often repeated reasons for lack of research-based practice. In her view, teachers need to be responsive to concrete features of the context and of individual students' learning rather than suppose that it is possible to implement errorless practices based on scientific authority. Thus, "we would begin to make teacher craft knowledge the centerpiece of our efforts to improve both practice and teacher education" (Gallagher, 1998, p. 500).

Interestingly, all of these hypotheses are based on the premise that research should affect practice and does not do so often enough or to a sufficient degree. The next question we wanted to ask of our data revolved around these same issues. What is the direction and extent of influence between research and practice? We explore whether, when, and under what conditions research could be said to *lead* practice.

Using the corpus of journal articles as the data, we could say that there is evidence that research *leads* practice if there is a buildup of references to a topic in research journals followed by a buildup of references to this topic in practitioner journals. There are two caveats. First, there is a weak and a strong sense of *lead*. The weak sense is to precede in time. The strong sense is to cause. Frustrating though it is to us, we are never going to be able to prove causation using our methods. The second caveat is that our data is several steps removed from actual classroom practice. An article in a journal such as *The Reading Teacher* contains ideas that the authors and editors think that teachers should know, that teachers will find useful, and that teachers will want to know, which is closer to classroom practice than most research articles, but still not realized practice itself.

Scanning the charts introduced in the previous section, there are several instances in which we can say research has led practice, in the weak sense. Clearest is the pattern of references marking a sociocultural perspective (Fig. 5.8). Without stretching too much, comprehension (Fig. 5.4), whole texts (Fig. 5.2), and reading strategies (Fig. 5.5) also appear to be topics where research has led practice.

When research *leads* in the weak sense, it could *lead* in the strong sense—that is, certain research development could be the cause or a contributing cause of a practical innovation. So when the weak criterion is met, checking further entailments of a causal relationship could be worthwhile. One additional entailment is that the supposed effect follows the supposed cause by an interval within the response time of the physical or social system. For instance, one would not want to say that flipping a switch caused a light to go off, if the light goes off an hour after the switch was flipped. We have no good idea about the response time of the social system that includes articles in *Reading Research Quarterly* and *The Reading Teacher*, but it takes more or less a year to write an article and get it published if everything goes smoothly.

The one analysis that we have presented on a time scale of a year is occurrences of *schema* and related terms, which appears in Fig. 5.6. Close scrutiny of this figure reveals that the first appearance of schema in *Reading Research Quarterly* preceded the first appearance in *The Reading Teacher* by a year; then six appearances in *Reading Research Quarterly* preceded six appearances in *The Reading Teacher* by a year. Thus, the timing of events is not inconsistent with a causal relationship. Please be clear that we are not angling toward the conclusion that a particular journal article provides the ideas and inspiration that causes another particular journal article to be written. What we would like to be able to conclude instead is that number of references to a theme in a journal is an indicator of the strength and direction of flow of a social and intellectual process that encompasses various communication channels with various response-time characteristics, including speeches, discussion, letters, preprint circulation, and, in recent years, e-mail notes and Web postings, as well as published articles. The timing of events is not inconsistent with this general process either, although how long it should take for presumed effects to show themselves becomes murky.

In the case of *schema*, there is another way to reason about whether research led practice. Best available information about the uses of *schema* supports a lack-of-other-explanation inference. We have never heard reports of unprompted discussions among teachers about how schemata provide the ideational scaffolding for the ready assimilation of new information.

Clear cases in which research has not led practice are the topic of word and subword units (Fig. 5.1) and the correlated topic of phonics (Fig. 5.3). References to these topics surged in *Reading Research Quarterly*, but there was not a corresponding subsequent surge in *The Reading Teacher*. As we have already remarked, writing may be another topic in which research, at least research reported in *Reading Research Quarterly*, did not lead practice. A similar story is plausible for whole language, which by all reports was a grass-roots movement.

At the beginning of this section, we quoted Chall's (1996) statement that "More often than not, it [practice] moves in a direction which is not supported by theory and research" (p. xx). Our analysis supports this statement in the notable instance of phonics. Insofar as frequency of mention is a valid indicator, attention to phonics in *The Reading Teacher* has steadily declined over the past three decades, whereas attention first climbed and then remained high in *Reading Research Quarterly*. However, according to our analysis, Chall's statement is not generally true. More often than not, practice moves in synchrony with research. Nor does our analysis support Chall's belief that practice "moves back and forth" to a greater extent than research. Most topic changes in *The Reading Teacher* are slow and sustained over long periods of time. In contrast, topic changes in *Reading Research Quarterly* are more frequently abrupt. Pronounced changes in direction are to be expected in a research journal; papers that contain no news will not be published.

THE CASE OF SPECIAL EDUCATION

Historically, general and special education have operated on parallel paths, insulated from one another. At its core, special education serves an advocacy function for gaining access first and then appropriate education services for children and youth with physical, sensory, intellectual, and behavioral disabilities that range in degree from mild to severe. Parent organizations such as the Association for Retarded Children (now the Association for Retarded Citizens) and Association for Children with Learning Disabilities (now the Learning Disabilities Association of America), were central to generating the public and political support necessary for the conduct of litigation and the passage of major legislation, such as the Education for All Handicapped Children Act (Public Law 94-142, 1975) and Individuals with Disabilities Education Act (Public Law 101-476, 1990). These political roots continue to be central to the nature of special education. Trends in the field can be readily tracked through changes in legislative mandates that are accompanied by alterations in language used to refer to persons with disabilities and to the services they receive. New legislation incorporates the evolving language in the field, and the new terms are authorized by their inclusion in the law and subsequent rules and regulations.

As reflected in the changes of the names of the laws and organizations, special educators have shifted the language that is used to refer to those who they are intended to benefit. An analysis of the titles and abstracts of every article in *Exceptional Children* in 1965, 1975, 1985, and 1995 shows the history of the transition in terminology. In 1965 and 1975, *handicapped* was the dominant descriptor. The transition in special-education terminology occurred in 1985 when the terms *handicapped* and *disabled* were used equally. By 1995, the field had completely shifted to "person-first" language and the only expressions found were of the form *student with a disability*.

Since the inception of the field, advocates of special education have been concerned with issues of exclusion and inclusion in general education (Gaffney, 1998). Initially, focus was on obtaining access for school-age students in general education settings and in providing appropriate services. The call was for the *mainstreaming* of students with special needs who had been receiving their education in separate classes and schools. Public Law 94-142 provided the impetus and legal weight for mainstreaming; when it was passed in 1975, the articles on legislative issues were most prominent in *Exceptional Children* in 1965.

Functionally, mainstreaming had the effect of shifting students with disabilities one step in the direction of the least restrictive environment. In other words, a student in a special school would likely be moved to a self-contained special class and a student receiving services in a special class might be placed in a resource room, receiving some but not all services with general-education peers. The term *mainstreaming* seeps into the special-education language in 1975 and is the dominant term in *Exceptional Children* in 1985. In 1995, however, another term, *inclusion*—which had never appeared previously—eclipses all other terms. *Inclusion* raises the ante for the integration of students with disabilities by advancing the notion that *every* student ought to be educated within the general education environment. The inclusion paradigm encompasses all students with disabilities, regardless of the nature or the severity of their condition. Distinguished from mainstreaming, its conceptual predecessor, inclusion puts the burden of proof on those who propose placement in settings other than general education and with goals other than those used in the general curriculum.

Based on the coding of the 147 articles in *Exceptional Children* published in 1965, 1975, 1985, and 1995, 71 (48%) are research based and 32 (22%) are essays that do not report research. These essays fall into categories such as practical advice, policy analyses, reviews or syntheses of research, and commentaries and rejoinders. The percentage of articles published in *Exceptional Children* that are research based by year is: 1965 (32%), 1975 (19%), 1985 (53%), and 1995 (90%). The type of research has changed over the three decades. Over half (57%) of the research articles published in 1995 were based on surveys and interviews, which far exceeds any other year.

Exceptional Children has undergone a dramatic shift toward qualitative and naturalistic research. These types account for 32% of the research in 1995. Not a single instance of qualitative or naturalistic research had appeared in any of the previous years. Quantitative methodology reached a high in 1985, under the editorship of James Ysseldyke, when it was employed in 42% of the research studies, with a steep decline to 10% in 1995. In any given year, only two or three studies employing empirical methods included a control group. Surprising to us, based on our a priori assumptions about research methodology in special education, was the fact that only two case studies were reported, one each in 1965 and 1975, and the fact that single-subject methodology was not employed in any study reported in Exceptional Children in any of the 4 years that were examined.

The fields of special education and reading intersect in the area of reading difficulties. Over 75–80% of school-age students with mild disabilities (i.e., learning disabilities, mild mental retardation, emotional disturbance, and behavioral disorders) experience significant problems in basic language and reading skill (Ellis & Cramer, 1994). Based on a review of national studies, a report by the National Center for Learning Disabilities (1996) indicates that as many as one in six elementary students encounters reading difficulties. The majority of students with mild disabilities are identified in third and fourth grades, once the discrepancy between an individual student's performance and national standards is significant and sensitive to testing. In fact, based on longitudinal data, approximately 74% of third graders with learning disabilities had reading difficulties that persisted through the ninth grade (Francis, Shaywitz, Steubing, Shaywitz, & Fletcher, 1994).

Despite the prevalence of reading difficulties among students with mild disabilities, the sample of 147 articles across the 4 years of *Exceptional Children* yielded only 13 (9%) articles that included terms related to reading or writing in the title or abstract. One article published in 1965 and one published in 1975 addressed both reading and writing. Reading was the central focus of only 4 of the 13 articles mentioning reading. This number seems shockingly small, considering the prevalence of reading difficulties among students with disabilities and the importance of reading as a life skill.

In a search for terms that would tap into theory, none were found in the total corpus of abstracts and titles in *Exceptional Children*. It seems that special education researchers are empiricists and pragmatists, not much given to theorizing and not very interested in the theories of others.

CONCLUDING REMARKS

What did we learn from our excavation of three decades worth of reading research? What did we unearth? What is worth preserving and what should be buried with honor? Most scholarship confirms established knowledge. This is regrettable because the excitement for the scholar comes from the unexpected archeological "finds" and figuring out how they came to be located at the site at a particular time in history. It was only reasonable to suppose that most of our findings would confirm the conventional wisdom about reading research, but we did have some surprises.

Using computer-aided document analysis, we got clear evidence of a major shift in conceptions of research over the last three decades. A parallel increase in number of qualitative articles published in the third decade (1989–1998) of *Journal of Reading Be-*

havior/Journal of Literacy Research has been noted by Guzzetti et al. (1999). Researchers are increasingly likely to use qualitative and naturalistic methods and increasingly less likely to use experimental and quantitative methods. This finding does not disturb the conventional wisdom.

Going beyond the conventional wisdom, perhaps, is our discovery of a certain skittishness about theory. Reading researchers avoid using theory-laden terms, in journal abstracts at least. Reading education and, certainly, special education seem to be fields where people want the simple facts, never mind the interpretation. This stance may reflect the supposed viewpoint of schoolteachers, who have been seen as impatient with theory since Lortie's (1975) famous study.

Our inquiry suggests that most ideas come and go within a rather short period of time. Some intellectual currents that seemed extraordinarily strong to those of us who swam in them leave only faint traces that can be detected with our methods. *Schema* (and its inflections) rarely appears in the corpus of *Reading Research Quarterly* and *The Reading Teacher* articles. Even when related terms such as *previous knowledge* and *prior knowledge* are included in a search, there are at most a half dozen articles a year for a period of no more than 8 years that refer to the concept of schema. The same is true of *whole language;* the expression was frequently used for a period of only about 10 years. Even terms for processes that seem to be integral to the very nature of reading, such as *comprehension*, ebb and flow on a short cycle. Most cycles are shorter and more pronounced in *Reading Research Quarterly* than in *The Reading Teacher.*

Our analysis of 30 odd years of articles in *Reading Research Quarterly* and *The Reading Teacher* suggests that, on most topics, the waves in practitioner journals are synchronized with waves in research journals. More often than not, *research leads practice*, meaning that a buildup of references to a topic in research journals precedes a buildup of references to this topic in practitioner journals. Notable exceptions to this rule were the topics of phonics, writing, and whole language. On these topics, authors of *The Reading Teacher* articles were not writing in a rhythm echoing the one in *Reading Research Quarterly.*

Some trends proved true in both special education, as represented in *Exceptional Children*, and general reading education. One similar trend is the broadening conception of research. Another similarity is the atheoretical stance toward research. Our most dismaying finding about special education research is that it so seldom focuses on reading.

Overall, we end up being pleased with the method of online search for words in representative documents as a means for revealing the trends in a field. We are less pleased with our insight into the tangled skein of social and intellectual causation that might account for the trends. Our accounts boil down to: It was in the nature of things, the time was ripe, it was happening everywhere.

Behind the broadened conception of ways of doing research documented in our analysis are changing assumptions about the nature of knowledge. We are struck by the contrasting kinds of knowledge that are endorsed as "truth." The shifts from behaviorism to cognitivism to socioculturalism reflect an increasingly complex picture of literacy, which surely must be closer to the "truth," in some sense of the word. Acknowledgment of this complexity is associated with a postmodern conception of science and whether science, variously conceived, is the best way to extend knowledge about literacy.

The most radical formulation of the postmodern view is that *all knowledge is local.* Gallagher's position (1998) regarding the knowledge base of special education represents the outermost perspective. She contended that law-like generalizations about teaching practices are problematic and that the terms *science* and *scientific* are invoked merely to lend status to claims. In her words:

We may find that the methods of science have served more to obscure than enlighten our current educational practices. Conversely, we may also find that research based on the suggested alternative perspective offers us a more viable means to understand the complexity involved with educational contexts, individual learning processes, teaching practices, educational policies, and innovations. (Gallagher, 1998, p. 500)

If all knowledge were truly local, then, other things being equal, first-hand knowledge would inevitably lead to better decisions than those based on statistical generalization from other cases. However, Paul Meehl (1954/1996) and his colleagues (Grove & Meehl, 1996) demonstrated that, to the contrary, decisions based on statistical generalizations are consistently superior to clinical decisions based on first-hand knowledge. Meehl's findings pose a challenge for the claim that all knowledge is local. Either the claim is false or it has to be understood impressionistically on a phenomenological or existential plane of discourse.

To evaluate whether "classroom actions are so situated that generalization across contexts is next to impossible" (p. 363), Chinn and his colleagues (Chinn, Waggoner, Anderson, Schommer, & Wilkinson, 1993) completed a detailed analysis of 3,008 oral reading error episodes in 72 small-group reading lessons in six second- and third-grade classrooms. Chinn et al. concluded that the data did

> not support radical contextualism, the champions of which sometimes talk as though no generalizations across situations are tenable. Although there were certainly differences among between classrooms in this study, the behavior of teachers and students during oral reading error episodes proved to be highly predictable, and certain features of the behavior proved to be stereotyped …. Generalizations across people and situations … were replicated rather well in the six classrooms in this study and … are generally consistent with the findings of previous studies. (p. 390)

A problem with radical contextualism is that if the ecology of every class of children is unique, then teachers will be unable to benefit from principles gleaned from research conducted in other classrooms or even from narratives about the practices of other teachers. To invoke complexity may mean to excuse inaction. One of us invited classroom teachers enrolled in a graduate course to discuss an exemplary research study that they had been assigned to read. The study reported striking benefits from a writing intervention for children with learning disabilities. Nonetheless, the teachers seemed determined to dismiss the study. Their grounds for dismissing it were that the students who participated in the study were different from their students. When asked "different in what respects?" they could not describe any consequential difference, just "different," as though that were all that needed to be said. Admitting that the study was generalizable would have entailed changing their teaching practice or acknowledging that theirs was not best practice. Insisting that the students in the study were different from their own left them a way out.

Our concluding thought is that generalizations that transcend time and circumstance are both possible and desirable. To conclude otherwise is, in the words of N. L Gage (1996), the "counsel of despair."

REFERENCES

Baldwin, S., Readence, J., Shumm, J. S., Konopak, J., Konopak, B., & Klinger, J. (1992). Forty years if NRC publications: 1952–1991. *Journal of Reading Behavior, 24,* 505–532.

Chall, J. S. (1967). *Learning to read: The great debate.* New York: McGraw-Hill.

Chall, J. S. (1996). *Learning to read: The great debate* (3rd ed.). Orlando, FL: Harcourt Brace.

Chinn, C., Waggoner, M., Anderson, R. C., Schommer, M., & Wilkinson, I. A. G. (1993). Situated actions during reading lessons: A microanalysis of oral reading error episodes. *American Educational Research Journal, 30*(2), 361–392.

Durkin, D. (1978–1979). What classroom observations reveal about reading comprehension instruction. *Reading Research Quarterly, 14*, 481–533.

Ellis, W., & Cramer, S. C. (1994). *Learning disabilities: A national responsibility.* Report of the Summit on Learning Disabilities in Washington, DC September 20–21. New York: National Center for Learning Disabilities.

Exceptional Children (1995). Reston, VA: Council for Exceptional Children.

Foucault, M. (1973). *The order of things: The archaeology of the human sciences.* New York: Random House.

Francis, D. J., Shaywitz, S. E., Steubing, K. K., Shaywitz, B. A., & Fletcher, J. M. (1994). Measurement of change: Assessing behavior over time and within a developmental context. In G. R. Lyon, D. B. Gray, J. F. Kavanagh, & N. A. Krasnegor (Eds.), *Frames of reference for the assessment of learning disabilities: New views on measurement issues* (pp. 29–58). Baltimore, MD: Paul H. Brookes.

Fullan, M. (1993). *Change forces: Probing the depths of educational reform.* Bristol, PA: Falmer Press.

Gaffney, J. S. (1998). The prevention of reading failure: Teach reading and writing. In J. Osborn & F. Lehr (Eds.), *Literacy for all: Issues in teaching and learning* (pp. 100–110). New York: Guilford Press.

Gage, N. L. (1996). Confronting counsels of despair for the behavioral sciences. *Educational Researcher, 25*(3), 5–15.

Gallagher, D. J. (1998). The scientific knowledge base of special education: Do we know what we think we know? *Exceptional Children, 64*, 493–502.

Grove, W. M., & Meehl, P. E. (1996). Comparative efficiency of informal (subjective, impressionistic) and formal (mechanical, algorithmic) prediction procedures: The clinical-statistical controversy. *Psychology, Public Policy, & Law, 2*, 293–323.

Guzzetti, B., Anders, P. L., & Neuman, S. B. (1999). Thirty years of JRB/JLR: A retrospective of reading/literacy research. *Journal of Literacy Research, 31*, 67–92.

Jaszczak, S. (1997). *Encyclopedia of associations* (32nd ed.). Detroit, MI: Gale Research, Inc.

Kennedy, M. (1997). The connection between research and practice. *Educational Researcher, 26*, 4–12.

Lortie, D. C. (1975). *Schoolteacher: A sociological study.* Chicago: University of Chicago Press.

Meehl, P. E. (1996). *Clinical versus statistical prediction: A theoretical analysis and a review of the evidence.* Northvale, NJ: Jason Aronson. (Original work published in 1954)

National Center for Learning Disabilities. (1996, Summer). Learning to read/reading to learn *NCLD News*, p. 6.

National Commission on Teaching & America's Future. (1996). *What matters most: Teaching for America's future.* New York: Teachers College.

Qualitative Solutions and Research. (1997). *QSR NUD*IST 4* (2nd ed.). Thousand Oaks, CA: SCOLARI/Sage.

The Reading Teacher (1998). Newark, DE: International Reading Association.

Robinson, V. M. K. (1998). Methodology and the research–practice gap. *Educational Researcher, 27*, 17–26.

Slavin, R. E. (1989). PET and the pendulum: Faddism in education and how to stop it. *Phi Delta Kappan, 70*, 752–758.

Steffensen, M. S., Joag-dev, C., & Anderson, R. C. (1979). A cross-cultural perspective on reading comprehension. *Reading Research Quarterly, 15*, 10–29.

TEACHING Exceptional Children (1995). Reston, VA: Council for Exceptional Children.

Tierney, R. J., Kamil, M. L., & Green, J. L. (1992). Editorial. *Reading Research Quarterly, 27*, 8–10.

Venezky, R. L. (1987). Steps toward a modern history of American reading instruction. *Review of Research in Education, 13*, 129–167.

Winograd, T., & Flores, F. (1987). *Understanding computers and cognition: A new foundation for design.* Reading, MA: Addison-Wesley.

PART II

Methods of Literacy Research

CHAPTER 6

Making Sense of Classroom Worlds: Methodology in Teacher Research

James F. Baumann
University of Georgia

Ann M. Duffy-Hester
University of North Carolina at Greensboro

> *We had such a hard time finding methods that we thought were practical and feasible. To this day, I have not been able to master the use of a teaching journal. The idea of being videotaped gives me hives .... None of the traditional methods of collecting data were inviting to me .... I thought of what strategies I could fit into my existing classroom structure and what wouldn't drive me insane.*
>
> —teacher researcher Debby Wood (cited in Baumann, Shockley-Bisplinghoff, & Allen, 1997, p. 138)

The 1990s have been marked by the resurgence and coming of age of teacher research (McFarland & Stansell, 1993). The recent renaissance of teacher research has resulted in the publication of numerous compendia (e.g., Bissex & Bullock, 1987; Donoahue, Van Tassell, & Patterson, 1996), full-length books (e.g., Allen, Michalove, & Shockley, 1993), and essays on classroom research (e.g., Cochran-Smith & Lytle, 1993; Goswami & Stillman, 1987). In spite of the proliferation of published teacher research studies, relatively little attention has been given to methodology processes and how they evolve and mature (Calkins, 1985). Perhaps it comes as no surprise that teacher researchers like Debby Wood and her colleagues sometimes struggle to find research methods appropriate to the unique demands of their classroom studies.

Many teacher researchers have successfully wrestled with vexing methodological issues, however, by selecting, adapting, or creating procedures that accommodate their specific research needs (Baumann et al., 1997). But what are the methodological solutions? What is the nature of methodologies teacher researchers have employed in classroom-based inquiries into literacy? We address these questions in this chapter by presenting a qualitative analysis of published literacy teacher-research studies. We begin with a discussion of theoretical issues, followed by a description of our research methods. Next, we present and discuss the categories and themes of teacher-research methodology our analysis uncovered. Finally, we address limitations and conclusions, and we consider whether teacher inquiry is a new research genre.

THEORETICAL ISSUES

Defining Teacher Research

Defini... but most include several common ... rtle & Cochran-Smith, 1994a, 1994b ... vironment, teacher researchers have ... process. This provides them a uniqu... (Cochran-Smith & Lytle, 1993, p. 43... blurred in teacher research (Coch... 986). It is this mixture of reflection a... r's personal theory and theory within ... stone of teacher research is that it is p... flecting on one's teaching and practi... ng action to improve or alter it (Burt... 1994).

Te... hulman, 1997), which means it is inte... iously initiate and implement their ... analysis. Teacher research embrace ... ch traditions (e.g., qualitative, quan... mation collection and interpretation ... .g., personal narrative, formative e... l but nonetheless still regular, ordered modes of inquiry (Lytle & Cochran-Smith, 1994b). Drawing from these principles and extending Lytle and Cochran-Smith's (1994b, p. 1154) definition of teacher research, we conceive of teacher research as "reflection and action through systematic, intentional in... ...life." (B... et al., 1997, p. 125).

Methods Ve[rsus Methodology]

In our explor... method and methodology. Accordi... ogy involves how a researcher com... a researcher's beliefs about the nat... s by which a researcher gains knowle... for teacher researchers involves thei... hildren, and classroom life. Methods, ... rcher employs in an inquiry: the pl... reducing or synthesizing data, and ... f information. Methods are determir... ay in Baumann, Dillon, Shockley, Al...

The impl... ion of methodology in teacher rese... ous types of research de-

Handwritten annotations:

Defining Teacher Research
- insider perspective
  ↳ participant role in inquiry
- theory & practice interrelated blurred
- reflection & practice intertwine (own theory and field theory)
- pragmatic & action oriented
- disciplined inquiry
- pieces and parts of other methods in a ordered way
- "reflection and action through systematic intentional inquiry about classroom life."
- qualitative & quantitative
- interpretation procedures

- Methodology: means by which a researcher gains knowledge about the world
  *for teachers: beliefs about world of teaching, learning, children, and classroom life
- Methods: procedures and tools a researcher employs in an inquiry → who, what, plan, when, why
- Methods are determined by methodological decisions
- examine general characteristics of teacher research, process of inquiry, and nature of classroom inquire, methods used in their studies widely

Methods vs. Methodology

CHAPTER 6

Making Sense of Classroom Worlds: Methodology in Teacher Research

James F. Baumann
University of Georgia

Ann M. Duffy-Hester
University of North Carolina at Greensboro

> *We had such a hard time finding methods that we thought were practical and feasible. To this day, I have not been able to master the use of a teaching journal. The idea of being videotaped gives me hives …. None of the traditional methods of collecting data were inviting to me …. I thought of what strategies I could fit into my existing classroom structure and what wouldn't drive me insane.*
>
> —teacher researcher Debby Wood (cited in Baumann, Shockley-Bisplinghoff, & Allen, 1997, p. 138)

The 1990s have been marked by the resurgence and coming of age of teacher research (McFarland & Stansell, 1993). The recent renaissance of teacher research has resulted in the publication of numerous compendia (e.g., Bissex & Bullock, 1987; Donoahue, Van Tassell, & Patterson, 1996), full-length books (e.g., Allen, Michalove, & Shockley, 1993), and essays on classroom research (e.g., Cochran-Smith & Lytle, 1993; Goswami & Stillman, 1987). In spite of the proliferation of published teacher research studies, relatively little attention has been given to methodology processes and how they evolve and mature (Calkins, 1985). Perhaps it comes as no surprise that teacher researchers like Debby Wood and her colleagues sometimes struggle to find research methods appropriate to the unique demands of their classroom studies.

Many teacher researchers have successfully wrestled with vexing methodological issues, however, by selecting, adapting, or creating procedures that accommodate their specific research needs (Baumann et al., 1997). But what are the methodological solutions? What is the nature of methodologies teacher researchers have employed in classroom-based inquiries into literacy? We address these questions in this chapter by presenting a qualitative analysis of published literacy teacher-research studies. We begin with a discussion of theoretical issues, followed by a description of our research methods. Next, we present and discuss the categories and themes of teacher-research methodology our analysis uncovered. Finally, we address limitations and conclusions, and we consider whether teacher inquiry is a new research genre.

THEORETICAL ISSUES

Defining Teacher Research

Definitions of teacher research vary (Threat et al., 1994), but most include several common characteristics (Cochran-Smith & Lytle, 1993; Lytle & Cochran-Smith, 1994a, 1994b). Being present daily in the research and work environment, teacher researchers have an insider, or *emic*, perspective on the research process. This provides them a unique, situation-specific, participant role in an inquiry (Cochran-Smith & Lytle, 1993, p. 43). Theory and practice are interrelated and blurred in teacher research (Cochran-Smith & Lytle, 1993; Kincheloe, 1991; Lather, 1986). It is this mixture of reflection and practice, or *praxis*, in which a teacher-researcher's personal theory and theory within a field converge and affect one another. A cornerstone of teacher research is that it is *pragmatic* and *action oriented*; that is, it involves reflecting on one's teaching and practice, inquiring about it, exploring it, and then taking action to improve or alter it (Burton, 1991; Patterson & Shannon, 1993; Wells et al., 1994).

Teacher research must involve disciplined inquiry (Shulman, 1997), which means it is *intentional* and *systematic*. Teacher researchers consciously initiate and implement their inquiries and have a plan for data gathering and analysis. Teacher research embraces both inquiries steeped in conventional research traditions (e.g., qualitative, quantitative) that have well-articulated, accepted information collection and interpretation procedures and evolving research paradigms (e.g., personal narrative, formative experiment, memoir) that involve less traditional but nonetheless still regular, ordered modes of inquiry (Lytle & Cochran-Smith, 1994b). Drawing from these principles and extending Lytle and Cochran-Smith's (1994b, p. 1154) definition of teacher research, we conceive of teacher research as "reflection and action through systematic, intentional inquiry about classroom life" (Baumann et al., 1997, p. 125).

Methods Versus Methodology

In our exploration of teacher research, we distinguish between method and methodology. According to Denzin and Lincoln (1994, p. 99), epistemology involves how a researcher comes to know about the world; ontology involves a researcher's beliefs about the nature of reality; and methodology involves the means by which a researcher gains knowledge about the world. Consequently, *methodology* for teacher researchers involves their beliefs about the world of teaching, learning, children, and classroom life. *Methods*, in contrast, are the procedures and tools a researcher employs in an inquiry: the plans for gathering information, the mechanisms for reducing or synthesizing data, and the techniques for analyzing and making sense of information. Methods are determined by methodological decisions (see Dillon essay in Baumann, Dillon, Shockley, Alvermann, & Reinking, 1996).

The implication of this distinction is that our examination of methodology in teacher research involves more than simply reporting the various types of research designs, data collection procedures, and analysis techniques (i.e., methods) teacher researchers have employed. Rather, it requires that we put on a wide-angle lens to examine the general characteristics of teacher research, the process of teacher inquiry, and the nature of classroom inquiry dissemination, along with the actual methods classroom teachers use in their studies.

Literature on Methodology in Teacher Research

Teacher research has a long, rich, and varied tradition, and we refer readers to other sources to glean a full historical perspective (e.g., Cochran-Smith & Lytle, 1990; Lytle & Cochran-Smith, 1994a; McFarland & Stansell, 1993; Olson, 1990). Here we briefly trace selected works germane to methodology in teacher research.

Early in the 20th century, one finds references to the importance of teacher contributions to the knowledge base on teaching (Dewey, 1929) as well as discussions of methods appropriate for research involving teachers (Buckingham, 1926). Concurrent with the mid-century action research movement (e.g., Corey, 1953; Elliott, 1991; Stenhouse, 1973, 1975) were discussions about appropriate methodology for teacher research (Corman, 1957; Hodgkinson, 1957). More recently, authors have described various methods, tools, and procedures for engaging in teacher research (e.g., Brause & Mayher, 1991; Calhoun, 1994; Hopkins, 1993; Hubbard & Power, 1993a, 1999; Kincheloe, 1991; Mohr & Maclean, 1987; Myers, 1985; Nixon, 1981; Sagor, 1992).

Given the long-standing interest in the conduct and publication of teacher research and the more recent works describing methods and tools, it is interesting that there have been relatively few analyses of methodological perspectives employed in teacher research. Reviewers of the history or tradition of teacher research (e.g., Cochran-Smith & Lytle, 1993; Hollingsworth & Sockett, 1994; McFarland & Stansell, 1993; Olson, 1990) have commented on the methods employed and some methodological themes, but systematic analyses have been rare. Baumann et al. (1997) examined in detail the methodological perspectives employed in three specific teacher-research environments, but their cases do not provide any sense of the breadth of methodologies teacher researchers employ. The purpose of this chapter is to begin to fill this void. The following question guided our research: What is the nature of methodologies teacher researchers have employed in published classroom-based inquiries in literacy?

METHOD

Theoretical and Researcher Perspectives

This research is a qualitative study of teacher-research methodology in literacy education. Through an application of the constant comparative method to written documents (Glaser & Strauss, 1967), we analyzed 34 purposively selected teacher-research studies. Through this analysis, we generated categories and themes of teacher-research methodology that captured the essence of our sample.

We have both had experience with teacher research. Jim engaged in teacher research when taking a sabbatical from his university position to teach second-grade (Baumann & Ivey, 1997). He also worked within a teacher-research community (Baumann, Allen, & Shockley, 1994) and reflected on teacher-research methods (Baumann, 1996). Ann, a former elementary school classroom teacher and reading specialist, conducted teacher research as the instructor of a university- and field-based elementary reading education course (Duffy, 1997) and as the teacher of a summer reading program for second-grade, struggling readers (Duffy-Hester, 1999).

We believe that good teachers of literacy are theoretical as they utilize extant literacy research that informs their practice and produce new theories of teaching and learning through their teacher-research endeavors. We see teacher researchers as linking research and practice, the embodiment of reflective practitioners (Schon, 1983). We know from our own teacher research that engaging in classroom inquiry can transform an educator's views on teaching and learning.

Sampling

We selected literacy-based, teacher-research studies that were consistent with our definition of teacher research (i.e., reflection, action, and systematic intentional inquiry). We accomplished this selection through the process of *theoretical sampling*, which is "the process of data collection for generating theory whereby the analyst jointly collects, codes, and analyzes his data and decides what data to collect next and where to find them, in order to develop his theory as it emerges" (Glaser & Strauss, 1967, p. 45).

To obtain a broadly based sample of teacher-research studies, our theoretical sampling was guided by three selection criteria: (a) publication source, including journal articles, chapters in edited books, and full-length books; (b) age and grade level, including early childhood (preschool to Grade 2), elementary school (Grades 3–5), middle and junior high school (Grades 6–8), high school (Grades 9–12), and college-age students; and (c) research topic foci, including comprehension, discussion, integrated language arts, literature response, oral language, reading, spelling, writing, and whole language. We identified studies that reflected the range of diversity specified by each criterion.

As our analysis proceeded, we revisited and reevaluated our definition of teacher research, deleted studies from our list that did not seem to meet our evolving definition, and added new studies to broaden our sample. Midway through our sampling and analysis process, we created a matrix to determine whether we had adhered to our three sampling criteria of publication outlet, age/grade level, and research topic focus. We added and deleted studies as necessary so that the sample reflected our criteria and hence the broader universe of published teacher-research studies. We also shared the study sample and our criteria with a person experienced and highly published in literacy teacher research. We asked this educator to assess the sample in relation to our criteria. Based on her evaluation and suggestions, we deleted and added several studies. Table 6.1 presents the 34 teacher-research studies in our final sample.

Analysis

Our data analysis proceeded through five phases. In Phase I, *initial coding and category creation*, we independently read a subset of studies in the sample, writing researcher memos (LeCompte & Preissle, 1993) such as observer comments, methodological memos, and analytic memos. We then independently analyzed our notes to glean the emerging categories and met to discuss and create a list of common categories. In Phase II, *category refinement and theme creation*, we read additional studies, modified the existing categories, and identified emerging clusters of categories as themes. We concluded the analysis in Phase III, *data saturation*, that is, when neither of us modified or added to the 16 categories and 4 themes we had identified at this point.

In Phase IV, *establishing credibility*, we independently reread the studies and listed page numbers for which we found evidence of each category, resulting in an interrater agreement score of 88.6% across all 16 categories and 34 studies. Disagreements about a particular category were discussed and resolved in conference. In Phase V, *audit*, we provided a doctoral student trained in qualitative research methodology and knowledgeable in literacy teacher research copies of the studies, sampling and analysis procedures, data reduction and analysis documents, and a list of guiding questions (modeled after Halpern, 1983; cited in Lincoln & Guba, 1985) that evaluated the completeness, comprehensibility, utility, and linkages in our research. After reviewing six

TABLE 6.1
Teacher-Research Studies Analyzed

1. Allen, Janet. (1995). *It's never too late: Leading adolescents to lifelong literacy.* B, H, I

2. Allen, Jennifer. (1997). Exploring literature through student-led discussions. *Teacher Research: The Journal of Classroom Inquiry.* A, EL, D/LR

3. Allen, JoBeth; Michalove, Barbara; & Shockley, Betty. (1993). *Engaging children: Community and chaos in the lives of young literacy learners.* B, EC/EL, I

4. Allen, Sara. (1992). Student-sustained discussion: When students talk and the teacher listens. *Students teaching, teachers learning.* C, H, D/LR

5. Atwell, Nancie. (1987). Everyone sits at a big desk: Discovering topics for writing. *English Journal.* A, M, W

6. Avery, Carol S. (1987). Traci: A learning-disabled child in a writing-process classroom. *Seeing for ourselves: Case-study research by teachers of writing.* C, EC, W

7. Bryan, Leslie Hall. (1996). Cooperative writing groups in community college. *Journal of Adolescent & Adult Literacy.* A, C, W

8. Caulfield, Judy. (1996). Students telling stories: Inquiry into the process of learning stories. *Research in the classroom: Talk, texts, and inquiry.* C, EL/M, O

9. Christensen, Linda; & Walker, Barbara J. (1992). Researching one's own teaching in a reading education course. *Literacy research and practice: Foundations for the year 2000.* C, C, R

10. Cline, Dawn M. (1993). A year with reading workshop. *Teachers are researchers: Reflection and action.* C, M, R

11. Clyde, Jean Anne; Condon, Mark W. F.; Daniel, Kathleen; & Sommer, Mary Kenna. (1993). Learning through whole language: Exploring book selection and use with preschoolers. *Teachers are researchers: Reflection and action.* C, EC, WL

12. Commeyras, Michelle; Reinking, David; Heubach, Kathleen M.; & Pagnucco, Joan. (1993). Looking within: A study of an undergraduate reading methods course. *Examining central issues in literacy research, theory, and practice.* C, C, R

13. Cone, Joan Kernan. (1994). Appearing acts: Creating readers in a high school English class. *Harvard Educational Review.* A, H, R

14. Donoahue, Zoe. (1996). Collaboration, community, and communication: Modes of discourse for teacher research. *Research in the classroom: Talk, texts, and inquiry.* C, EL, S

15. Feldgus, Eileen Glickman. (1993). Walking to the words. *Inside/outside: Teacher research and knowledge.* C, EC, W

16. Grattan, Kristin Walden. (1997). They can do it too! Book club with first and second graders. *The book club connection: Literacy learning and classroom talk.* C, EC, D/LR

17. Grimm, Nancy. (1990). Tutoring dyslexic college students: What these students teach us about literacy development. *The writing teacher as researcher: Essays in the theory and practice of class-based research.* C, C, W

18. Harvey, Stephanie; McAuliffe, Sheila; Benson, Laura; Cameron, Wendy; Kempton, Sue; Lusche, Pat; Miller, Debbie; Schroeder, Joan; & Weaver, Julie. (1996). Teacher-researchers study the process of synthesizing in six primary classrooms. *Language Arts.* A, EC, C

19. Johnston, Patricia. (1993). Lessons from the road: What I learned through teacher research. *Inside/outside: Teacher research and knowledge.* C, M, D

(Continues)

TABLE 6.1 (Continued)

20.   Maher, Ann. (1994). An inquiry into reader response. *Changing schools from within: Creating communities of inquiry.* C, EL, LR

21.   Mosenthal, James. (1995). A practice-oriented approach to methods coursework in literacy teaching. *Perspectives on literacy research and practice.* C, C, I

22.   Murphy, Paula. (1994). Antonio: My student, my teacher: My inquiry begins. *Teacher Research: The Journal of Classroom Inquiry.* A, M, I

23.   Newton, Marianne; Nash, Doris; & Ruffin, Loleta. (1996). A whole language trilogy: The covered bridge connection. *Teachers doing research: Practical possibilities.* C, EC, WL

24.   Paley, Vivian Gussin. (1997). *The girl with the brown crayon.* B, EC, LR

25.   Phinney, Margaret Yatsevitch; & Ketterling, Tracy. (1997). Dialogue journals, literature, and urban Indian sixth graders. *Teacher Research: The Journal of Classroom Inquiry.* A, M, LR/W

26.   Pils, Linda J. (1993). "I love you, Miss Piss." *Reading Teacher.* A, EC, W

27.   Ray, Lucinda C. (1987). Reflections on classroom research. *Reclaiming the classroom: Teacher research as an agency for change.* C, H, W

28.   Richards, Jane. (1987). Rx for editor in chief. *Seeing for ourselves: Case-study research by teachers of writing.* C, H, W

29.   Saunders, Laura. (1995). Unleashing the voices we rarely hear: Derrick's story. *Teacher Research: The Journal of Classroom Inquiry.* A, M, LR

30.   Sega, Denise. (1997). Reading and writing about our lives: Creating a collaborative curriculum in a class of high school misfits. *Teacher Research: The Journal of Classroom Inquiry.* A, H, I

31.   Swift, Kathleen. (1993). Try Reading Workshop in your classroom. *Reading Teacher.* A, M, R

32.   Thomas, Sally; & Oldfather, Penny. (1995). Enhancing student and teacher engagement in literacy learning: A shared inquiry approach. *Reading Teacher.* A, EL/M, I

33.   Von Dras, Joan. (1990). Transitions toward an integrated curriculum. *Talking about books: Creating literate communities.* C, EL, I

34.   Wood, Katie. (1993). A case study of a writer. *Teachers are researchers: Reflection and action.* C, M, W

Note. Each teacher-research study analyzed is presented in an abbreviated reference format that includes author(s), publication date, title, and publication outlet. The reference list at the end of the chapter includes complete citations for each entry in this table. We have included authors' first names in this table to fully acknowledge the identity of all teacher researchers whose work is cited. Following each entry is a three-part code. The first part identifies the type of teacher-research publication (A = journal article; B = full book; C = chapter in an edited book). The second part identifies the age or grade of research participants (EC = early childhood, including preschool, kindergarten, and Grades 1–2 children; EL = elementary children in Grades 3–5; M = middle school or junior high students in Grades 6–8; H = high school students in Grades 9–12; C = college-age students). The third part identifies the content foci for the studies (C = comprehension, D = discussion, I = integrated language arts, LR = literature response, O = oral language, R = reading, S = spelling, W = writing, WL = whole language). We acknowledge the limits and subjectivity of our classification system, particularly with respect to the content focus designations.

representative studies, the auditor concluded that the analysis procedures and inquiry path were clear, although she indicated that we had misclassified one study in the category "Teacher researchers supplement qualitative research methods with quantitative methods." To address this concern, we reviewed all 34 studies, finding evidence for this category in 3 additional studies.

RESULTS AND DISCUSSION

Our analysis of met̶ ~~gories~~, which cluste̶ search, (b) the proce̶ and reporting class̶

tables

charts

numbering

labeling

bullet points

boldface

̶iction of 16 cate- ̶es of teacher re- , and (d) writing categories.

To facilitate refere̶ ing system. For exan̶ vide a brief reference For example, **Instru̶** students," within Th within this chapter, ̶ numbers in Table 6.1

̶/category label- ̶e 2. We also pro- type in Table 6.2. learn from their in citing studies ̶ the identifying

Table 6.3 presents of a bullet indicates ̶ The final two colum̶ study, followed by th̶ gories, a 75% occurre̶ egory (e.g., Category

̶ly. The presence ̶articular study. ̶t emerged for a ̶6 possible cate- data but by cat- % occurrence).

Table 6.3 reveals s̶ sentation across stuc̶ ond, there was variation by study, ranging from a 56% occurrence (Study 28) to 100%

̶ad high repre- ccurrence. Sec-

TABLE 6.2
Themes and Categories Emerging From Analysis
of Published Teacher-Research Studies

Theme 1: General attributes of teacher research

A. **Questions from within**: Teacher research is prompted by the problems teachers face and the questions they pose within their own classrooms. (100%)

B. **Question evolution**: Research questions are modified as teachers conceptualize and implement a classroom study. (59%)

C. **Theoretically driven**: Existing theory—presented through written texts or collegial dialogue—inspires, guides, supports, or informs teachers in their own inquiries (i.e., theory → teacher research). (97%)

D. **Theoretically productive**: Engaging in teacher research leads to the creation or development of theories of teaching, learning, and schooling (i.e., teacher research→ theory). (94%)

E. **Reflective**: Teacher researchers are reflective practitioners. (100%)

Theme 2: Process of teacher inquiry

A. **Collaborative**: Teacher researchers conduct research with peers, students, families, or college faculty as coresearchers or collaborators. (91%)

B. **Instructive**: Teacher researchers learn from their students. (100%)

C. **Clarifying**: Classroom inquiry enables teachers to make sense of their classroom worlds. (94%)

D. **Unsettling**: Because classroom inquiry involves change and risk-taking, teacher researchers may feel uneasiness with innovations or changes they examine in their classrooms. (62%)

E. **Compatible or discordant**: Engaging in research and teaching are mutually reinforcing processes for some teacher researchers, whereas others experience tension between them. (26%)

(Continues)

TABLE 6.2 (Continued)

Theme 3: Teacher-research methods

A. **Pragmatic**: Teacher researchers employ methods on the basis of their practicality and efficiency for addressing research questions. (100%)

B. **Versatile**: Teacher researchers select, adapt, or create qualitative research methods for collecting and analyzing data. (100%)

C. **Complementary**: Teacher researchers supplement qualitative research methods with quantitative methods. (26%)

Theme 4: Writing and reporting classroom inquiry

A. **Narrative**: Teacher researchers employ a narrative style when reporting classroom inquiries. (94%)

B. **Illustrative**: Teacher researchers document findings by including excerpts of transcripts
and interviews or reproducing student work and artifacts in research reports. (91%)

C. **Figurative**: Teacher researchers use research vignettes or metaphors to convey key points
and ideas. (94%)

Note. Parenthetic percentages indicate the frequency with which a category was present across the 34
studies examined.

(Study 1). Third, there was variation by category, with frequencies ranging from 26%
to 100%.

This variation is also captured, in part, in Table 6.4 (see p. 87), which presents three
sets of categories clustered according to their frequency of occurrence. *Defining categories* were the most frequent features (91%–100% occurrence). *Discriminating categories*
were those features that distinguished some studies from others (59%–62% occurrence). *Negative-case categories* were features of teacher research that, although low in
frequency (26% occurrence), were retained because they helped define teacher research methodology through exceptions, much in the way negative-case qualitative
analysis procedures (Kidder, 1981) are used to clarify and refine categories and properties. We now turn to a theme-by-theme presentation of categories with supporting data
for each.

Theme 1: General Attributes of Teacher Research

[Handwritten notes at bottom of page:]

Theme 1: General Attributes of Teacher Research

4 "Teacher research is prompted by the problems teachers face and the questions they pose w/in their own classes."

2 "Research questions are modified as teachers conceptualize and implement a classroom study."

3 "Existing theory—presented through written texts or collegical dialogue—inspires, guides, supports, or informs teachers in their own inquiries (i.e., theory → teacher research)."

4 "Engaging in teacher research leads to the creation or development of theories of teaching, learning, and schooling (i.e., teacher research → theory)."

5 "Teacher researchers are reflective practitioners."

4 Questions from w/in
2 Question Evolution
3 Theoretically Driven
4 Theoretically Productive
5 Reflective

TABLE 6.3

Themes and Categories by Study

Study ID/Author	General Attributes					Process of TR					TR Methods			Writing TR			n	%
	1A	1B	1C	1D	1E	2A	2B	2C	2D	2E	3A	3B	3C	4A	4B	4C		
1. Allen, Janet	•	•	•	•	•	•	•	•	•	•	•	•	•	•	•	•	16	100
2. Allen, Jennifer	•	•	•		•	•	•	•	•	•	•	•	•	•	•	•	15	94
3. Allen, JoBeth, et al.	•	•	•		•	•	•	•	•		•	•		•	•	•	12	75
4. Allen, Sara	•	•	•	•	•	•	•	•	•	•	•	•		•	•	•	15	94
5. Atwell, Nancie	•	•			•	•	•	•	•		•	•		•	•	•	12	75
6. Avery, Carol. S	•	•			•	•	•	•	•		•	•		•	•	•	12	75
7. Bryan, Leslie Hall	•	•	•		•	•	•	•	•		•	•		•	•		12	75
8. Caulfield, Judy	•	•	•	•	•	•	•	•	•		•	•	•	•	•	•	15	94
9. Christensen & Walker	•	•	•	•	•	•	•	•	•		•	•		•	•	•	14	88
10. Cline, Dawn M.	•	•	•		•	•	•	•	•		•	•	•	•	•	•	14	88
11. Clyde, Jean Anne, et al.	•	•	•		•	•	•	•	•	•	•	•		•	•	•	14	88
12. Commeyras, Michelle, et al.	•	•	•		•	•	•	•	•		•	•		•	•		12	75
13. Cone, Joan Kernan	•	•	•	•	•	•	•	•	•		•	•	•	•	•	•	15	94
14. Donoahue, Zoe	•	•	•		•	•	•	•	•		•	•			•	•	12	75
15. Feldgus, Eileen Glickman	•	•	•		•	•	•	•	•		•	•		•	•	•	13	81
16. Grattan, Kristin Walden	•	•	•		•	•	•	•	•		•	•		•	•	•	13	81
17. Grimm, Nancy	•	•	•		•	•	•	•	•		•	•		•	•	•	13	81
18. Harvey, Stephanie, et al.	•	•	•		•	•	•	•	•		•	•		•	•	•	13	81

(Continues)

TABLE 6.3 (Continued)

Study ID/Author	General Attributes					Process of TR					TR Methods			Writing TR				
	1A	1B	1C	1D	1E	2A	2B	2C	2D	2E	3A	3B	3C	4A	4B	4C	n	%
19. Johnston, Patricia	●	●	●	●	●	●	●	●	●	●	●	●		●	●	●	15	94
20. Maher, Ann	●	●	●	●	●	●	●	●			●	●		●	●	●	13	81
21. Mosenthal, James	●	●	●	●	●	●	●	●	●		●	●		●	●	●	12	75
22. Murphy, Paula	●	●	●	●	●	●	●	●			●	●		●	●	●	13	81
23. Newton, Marianne, et al.	●	●	●		●	●	●		●	●	●	●	●	●		●	13	81
24. Paley, Vivian Gussin	●	●	●	●	●	●	●	●			●	●		●	●	●	13	81
25. Phinney & Ketterling	●	●	●	●	●	●	●	●	●	●	●	●		●	●	●	15	94
26. Pils, Linda J.	●	●	●	●	●	●	●	●	●	●	●	●		●	●	●	13	81
27. Ray, Lucinda C.	●	●	●	●	●	●	●	●	●		●	●	●	●	●	●	14	88
28. Richards, Jane	●		●		●	●	●	●			●	●		●		●	9	56
29. Saunders, Laura	●	●	●	●	●	●	●	●	●	●	●	●		●	●	●	15	94
30. Sega, Denise	●	●	●	●	●	●	●	●			●	●		●	●	●	11	69
31. Swift, Kathleen	●	●	●	●	●	●	●	●	●	●	●	●		●	●	●	14	88
32. Thomas & Oldfather	●	●		●	●	●	●	●	●	●	●	●	●		●	●	14	88
33. Von Dras, Joan	●	●	●	●	●	●	●	●	●		●	●		●	●	●	12	75
34. Wood, Katie	●	●	●	●	●	●	●	●	●		●	●		●	●	●	14	88
n	34	20	33	32	34	31	34	32	21	9	34	34	9	32	31	32	452	
%	100	59	97	94	100	91	100	94	62	26	100	100	26	94	91	94		83

TABLE 6.4

**Teacher Research Categories Clustered
by Overall Frequency Across Studies**

Cluster 1: Defining categories (category present in 91%–100% of all studies)	1A	**Questions from within:** Teacher research is prompted by the problems teachers face and the questions they pose within their own classrooms.
	1C	**Theoretically driven:** Existing theory—presented through written texts or collegial dialogue—inspires, guides, supports, or informs teachers in their own inquiries (i.e., theory → teacher research).
	1D	**Theoretically productive:** Engaging in teacher research leads to the creation or development of theories of teaching, learning, and schooling (i.e., teacher research → theory).
	1E	**Reflective:** Teacher researchers are reflective practitioners.
	2A	**Collaborative:** Teacher researchers conduct research with peers, students, families, or college faculty as coresearchers or collaborators.
	2B	**Instructive:** Teacher researchers learn from their students.
	2C	**Clarifying:** Classroom inquiry enables teachers to make sense of their classroom worlds.
	3A	**Pragmatic:** Teacher researchers employ methods on the basis of their practicality and efficiency for addressing research questions.
	3B	**Versatile:** Teacher researchers select, adapt, or create qualitative research methods for collecting and analyzing data.
	4A	**Narrative:** Teacher researchers employ a narrative style when reporting classroom inquiries.
	4B	**Illustrative:** Teacher researchers document findings by including excerpts of transcripts and interviews or reproducing student work and artifacts in research reports.
	4C	**Figurative:** Teacher researchers use research vignettes or metaphors to convey key points and ideas.
Cluster 2: Discriminating categories (category present in 59%–62% of all studies)	1B	**Question evolution:** Research questions are modified as teachers conceptualize and implement a classroom study.
	2D	**Unsettling:** Because classroom inquiry involves change and risk-taking, teacher researchers may feel uneasiness with innovations or changes they examine in their classrooms.
Cluster 3: Negative-case categories (category present in 26% of all studies)	2E	**Compatible or discordant:** Engaging in research and teaching are mutually reinforcing processes for some teacher researchers, whereas others experience tension between them.
	3C	**Complementary:** Teacher researchers supplement qualitative research methods with quantitative methods.

Category B: Question Evolution. *Research questions are modified as teachers conceptualize and implement a classroom study.* Kathleen Swift's (31) inquiry about the impact Reading Workshop had on the attitudes of her sixth graders led her to new questions: "What was happening to students' reading skills as a result of Reading Workshop? I wondered how well Reading Workshop strengthened and built comprehension. What effect did it have on the learning disabled students and below-grade-level readers?" (p. 367). University teacher researchers Linda Christiansen and Barbara J. Walker (9) likewise reported that "taking a closer look at one's teaching has led both to restructuring courses and providing questions for further research" (p. 63). Lucinda C. Ray's (27) four initial research questions grew along with her inquiry: "I learned some answers to these questions…. I learned to ask some new questions which I hadn't anticipated" (p. 222).

Although research question evolution is common (Baumann, Allen, & Shockley, 1994), Hubbard and Power (1993b) argued that "many teachers have to do some wandering to get to their wonderings" (p. 21). Our findings support this process.

Category C: Theoretically Driven.   *Existing theory—presented through written texts or collegial dialogue—inspires, guides, supports, or informs teachers in their own inquiries (i.e., theory → teacher research).* Some teacher researchers demonstrate their familiarity and use of existing theory through literature reviews. Marianne Newton, Doris Nash, and Loleta Ruffin (23) found that by reading the professional literature, they were able to make "natural *connections* between the research others had done and what we were trying to do with the children in our classrooms" (p. 83–84). Theoretical grounding also came in the form of personal contacts. Sara Allen (4) reported how her department chair challenged her to engage in classroom inquiry, and Nancie Atwell (5) related how a research consultant brought "authority as a teacher and researcher [and] a wealth of knowledge" (p. 179) to their research team.

Teacher research is not atheoretical. Teacher researchers confer with colleagues, take courses and attend workshops on research, and read professional materials (Cochran-Smith & Lytle, 1993). We found this linkage of extant theory to classroom inquiry an almost universal characteristic of teacher research.

Category D: Theoretically Productive.   *Engaging in teacher research leads to the creation or development of theories of teaching, learning, and schooling (i.e., teacher research → theory).* Carol S. Avery's (6) case study of a learning-disabled, first-grade child led to modification of her teaching philosophy and practices, and Joan Kernan Cone's (13) research led her to "know high school reading instruction in a way that would dramatically change the way I teach" (p. 87). Others reported that teacher research affirmed their theories, such as Eileen Glickman Feldgus (15), who found that her study of kindergartners strengthened several of her "personal beliefs" and "convictions" about emergent readers and writers (p. 177).

Teacher research involves a recursive relationship between theory and practice. Ann Keffer described how this notion of praxis played out for her daily: "Classroom research is not something one gets through with. Instead, it is a different approach to teaching in which theory informs practice and *practice informs theory* continually and immediately right in the classroom" (cited in Baumann et al., 1997, p. 139).

Category E: Reflective.   *Teacher researchers are reflective practitioners.* Reflection was evident in all studies examined. Laura Saunders (29) described introspection in relation to her case study of an eighth-grade student: "As I reflect upon my decision making where Derek was concerned …" (p. 56). Kristin Walden Grattan (16) wrote about her research with primary-grade children: "As I reflect on my journey of exploring and modifying Book Club to meet my classroom needs, I realize that it was a rather bumpy road" (p. 279). Leslie Hall Bryan (7), in the midst of her research with developmental studies college students, mused: "At this point I reflected on the process as a whole and the direction I wanted to go for the last weeks of the term" (p. 191). Lucinda C. Ray (27) stated that "reflection … describes the impact of the study on me as a researcher and learner" (p. 222).

All who have analyzed the teacher-research process (Goswami & Stillman, 1987) or the development of teacher-research communities (Lytle & Cochran-Smith, 1992) acknowledge the centrality of reflective practice (Schon, 1983). Our data further reinforce this conclusion.

Theme 2: Process of Teacher Inquiry

Category A: Collaborative.   *Teacher researchers conduct research with peers, students, families,* (Donoahue (14) described an inquiry group, a university-based ' (p. 91), and school/university rese… metimes parents became involved i raci's mother to help collect case stuc middle school (19), and high school (… example, Sally Thomas and Penny C about motivation for literacy across th

Gosw …searchers "collaborate with their stu ing on community resources in new a evalence and power of teach-ers colla research process.

Cate *rom their students.* Carol S. Avery (… ng from her students: "They are sucl received help from her high school… pelling and punctuation, and Ann M… ponse began to seriously unfold when she began "listening to the children" (p. 85).

Denise … across the front of her high school classroom that read, "W 11). She reported that once she reali veryone's learning, including her … old me, I listened, and we learned" researchers learn from and along w

Cate eachers to make sense of their classroom ens for viewing the instructional e utorial program for dyslexic college stioned developmental models of li Murphy's (22) exploration of Antoni tivity and knowledge about what it nority adolescent reader. The analys lucted on preservice literacy teache own teaching: "Undertaking this st ur department" (p. 304).

Brit nes involves inquiry, resulting in "so ew discoveries that teacher researchers learn to understand their classroom and how to improve them as learning environments.

Category D: Unsettling.   *Because classroom inquiry involves change and risk-taking, teacher researchers may feel uneasiness with innovations or changes they examine in their*

[Handwritten annotations:]

"Theme 2: Process of Teacher Inquiry"

"Teacher researchers conduct research with peers, students, families, or college faculty as co-researchers or collaborators."

"Teacher researchers learn from their students,"

"Classroom inquiry enables teachers to make sense of their classroom worlds."

"Because classroom inquiry involves change and risk-taking, teacher researchers may feel uneasiness with innovations or changes they examine in their classrooms."

"Engaging in research and teaching are mutually reinforcing processes for some teacher researchers, whereas others experience tensions between them."

classrooms. Marianne Newton and colleagues (23) referred to their application of whole-language practices in their classrooms as "an unsettling exploration into our own philosophies of education," but they soon "discovered that our hesitancies and uncertainties were a natural part of our learning" (p. 83). Sara Allen (4) anticipated uneasiness in her research on engaging her senior students with English literature, explaining that "I knew I might be in for some chaos." But Allen proceeded anyway, clarifying that "I was willing to risk that [the chaos]. I was desperate" (p. 82).

The exploration of dialogue journals between Margaret Yatsevitch Phinney's university students and Tracy Ketterling's sixth-grade students (25) yielded successes and "some things that *didn't* work" (p. 24), leading them to "recognize that teaching and learning are imperfect activities" (p. 40). Thus, unsettling as classroom inquiry may be, teacher researchers accept the uncertainty and learn from it.

Category E: Compatible or Discordant. *Engaging in research and teaching are mutually reinforcing processes for some teacher researchers, whereas others experience tension between them.* Jennifer Allen (2) noted how she "shifted back and forth between the roles of researcher and teacher" (p. 124), but she also related how she eventually "balanced the roles of researcher and teacher" (p. 138). Some teacher researchers described how inquiry became an inseparable part of what it meant to teach students (e.g., see Shockley essay in Baumann et al., 1996); others reported a bit of discord. Patricia Johnston (19) commented, "I found that the doing and the being of teacher research are at once second nature to me and somehow touching on foreign soil" (p. 178), and Linda Pils (26) talked about how research involved "both an inward and outward struggle" (p. 648).

O'Dell (1987) argued that teacher research "arises from a sense of dissonance or conflict or uncertainty" (p. 129). Laura Saunders (29) commented that "the tension between conducting classroom inquiry and the daily demands of a classroom teacher transformed my ability to teach and learn" (p. 57). Thus, the tension can be beneficial by clarifying methodological, ethical, and pragmatic issues for teacher researchers (Baumann, 1996).

Theme 3: Teacher-Research Methods

Category A: Pragmatic *Teacher researchers employ methods on the basis of their prac-*
*ticality and efficien~~~ f~~~ d researcher James
Mosenthal (21) st cesses of one of his
students by exam m to reconstruct a
"history of the exp d Tracy Ketterling
(25) selected meth ts that affected the
project positively that she included
excerpts from inte because her [Jo's]
responses are so tl (pp. 106–107).

Shulman (1997) ding the one best
method but of care investigator and
the field and then into it" (p. 4). Our
data suggest that te al and efficient in
answering their re

Category B: Ver ualitative research
methods for collectin y variations constituted the methc s we examined.
JoBeth Allen, Barba borative investi-

[Handwritten notes overlaid:]

Theme 3: Teacher-Research Methods.

• Pragmatic - Teacher researchers employ methods on the basis of their practicality and efficiency for addressing research questions.

• Versatile - Teacher researchers select, adapt, or create qualitative research methods for collecting and analyzing data.

• Complementary - Teacher researchers supplement qualitative research methods with quantitative methods.

gation of the effects of a whole-language curriculum on students who struggled with literacy development, identified methods used by other literacy researchers (Almy & Genishi, 1979; Hansen, 1989) and adapted them to suit their unique needs. Sara Allen (4) reported that she "developed and refined" (p. 83) qualitative data collection procedures. Well into her study, Judy Caulfield (8) revamped her analysis of students' storytellings, moving away from counting false starts to looking at students' storytelling attempts as forms of rehearsal and elaboration.

Nocerino (1993) argued that "it is flexibility that encourages the exploration, development, and refinement of meaningful research" (p. 91). We found that teacher researchers employed flexible, selective, and adaptive qualitative research methods in their studies.

Category C: Complementary. *Teacher researchers supplement qualitative research methods with quantitative methods.* Some teacher researchers used quantitative data to support qualitative data. Judy Caulfield (8) counted the number of false starts students made in storytelling. Michelle Commeyras and colleagues (12) used inferential statistics to analyze questionnaires. Dawn M. Cline (10) analyzed students' grades, grade-point averages, and SAT scores. Other researchers analyzed student test scores (23, 31), used percentages and pie charts to present interview data (1), or computed frequencies when analyzing conference data (27).

Qualitative researchers Miles and Huberman (1994) commented that "we have to face the fact that numbers and words are *both* needed if we are to understand the world" (p. 40). Clearly, some of the teacher researchers in our sample reached the same conclusion.

Theme 4: Writing and Reporting Classroom Inquiry

Category A: Narrative. *Teacher researchers employ a narrative style when reporting classroom inquiries.* Paula Murphy (22) told the story of one of her students in a compensatory reading ed[...] ntonio's world" (p. 79). Vivian Paley [...] d in her class who falls in love with [...] eeny's story that is told in these pag[...] fe, Laura Benson, Wendy Cameron, [...] hroeder, and Julie Weaver (18) used [...] s while describing their collaborative [...]

A narrative styl[...] lassrooms (Carter, 1993; Connelly & [...] erted that "within the details of the st[...] a theory of organization and meani[...] allow teacher researchers to conve[...] t and meaning of these events.

Category B: Ill[...] s by including excerpts of transcripts [...] facts in research reports. Joan Von Dr[...] dren were able to connect with and [...] dfather (32) illustrated students' en[...] one child's drawing showing "My 1[...] avorite books" and various dialogue journal exchanges between Sally and her students. Linda Pils (26) integrated excerpts of the writing of Gary, one of her first-grade students, along with her own journal to document Gary's growth.

Booth, Colomb, and Williams (1995) recommend that researchers "offer readers evidence that *they* will consider reliable in support of a claim that *they* will judge specific

[Handwritten annotation:]
Theme 4: Writing and Reporting Classroom Inquiry
- Narrative – Teacher researchers employ a narrative style when reporting classroom inquiries
- Illustrative – Teacher researchers document findings by including excerpts of transcripts and interviews or reproducing student work and artifacts in research reports
- Figurative – Teacher researchers use research vignettes or metaphors to convey key points and ideas.

and contestable" (p. 126). Through the inclusion of many and varied illustrative data clips, teacher researchers enable their audiences to judge and interpret their research.

Category C: Figurative.   *Teacher researchers use research vignettes or metaphors to convey key points and ideas.* Paula Murphy (22) used a vignette to describe how she met Antonio, the student whose learning she chronicled, and Laura Saunders (29) used an excerpt from Derrick's autobiography to introduce her inquiry involving dialogue journals. Jean Anne Clyde, Mark W. F. Condon, Kathleen Daniel, and Mary Kenna Sommer (11) used an opening vignette that described how deaf, preschool children and their teachers used oral and written texts during dramatic play. Patricia Johnston (19) described teacher research metaphorically as "embarking on a journey toward making sense of classroom practice," relating how "this adventure through uncharted territory revealed much about student response" (p. 178). Marianne Newton, Doris Nash, and Loleta Ruffin (23) used the metaphor of a covered bridge to describe their exploration of whole language, explaining their initial uneasiness ("old bridges can feel shaky," p. 83) and how they supported one another in their research ("it was not an easy decision to cross this bridge together," p. 85).

Dey (1993) asserted that "using metaphors can enrich an account by conveying connotations which elaborate on and illuminate our basic meaning" (p. 245). Teachers often use such rhetorical devices to express and interpret what they learn from their inquiries.

LIMITATIONS

Our study is limited in several ways. First, our inquiry is limited to the sample of teacher-research studies we analyzed. Although we selected a diverse set of research reports that we believe reflect the full range of published teacher inquiry, we cannot claim transferability to the complete body of teacher research. Second, the results are limited by the information the authors provided in their reports. We identified categories only when an author provided explicit or highly implied evidence of their presence. We acknowledge that researchers may not have chosen to provide certain content because it was not relevant to their research presentation, thus resulting in possible underrepresentation of some categories. Third, our inquiry is limited by the qualitative research paradigm we employed, including the personal perspectives we brought to it (Alvermann, O'Brien, & Dillon, 1996). Thus, we leave it to readers to assess the dependability and credibility of our results and conclusions, or to offer alternate explanations for them.

CONCLUSIONS

We present the overall findings from our study through the medium of *substantive theory,* which describes "everyday-world situations" that have "a specificity and hence usefulness to practice" (Merriam, 1998, p. 17). This notion of everyday practice is philosophically and practically suited for an overall framework of methodology in teacher research.

Our findings confirm that methodology in teacher research reflects both commonality and diversity. The defining categories (see Table 6.4) reflect several common methodological traits of teacher research. The internal locus of questions (1A) and the theoretical nature of classroom research—both driving an inquiry (1C) and subsequent classroom instruction (1D)—characterize the methodology teacher researchers employ. Our data support most definitions of teacher research, which typically involve the reflective nature of classroom inquiry (1E), how the research process helps teachers make sense of their classroom worlds (2C), and how teachers learn from and with their students while engaging in research (2B). We found research collaborations (2A) a common occurrence. There are also commonalities in the methods teacher researchers employ. Teachers select pragmatic, useful methods for collecting and analyzing data (3A), and they are creative in selecting, adapting, or inventing qualitative methods that suit their resea[…] ch reports typically possessed sev[…] g a storytelling form (4A); the inclu[…] ipts, journal entries, students' wor[…] use of figurative devices such as me[…]

But teacher resea[…] iverse in process, method, and reporti[…] ative-case categories. Although ques[…] the sine qua non of teacher research, […] questions underwent change throug[…] ut not all, teacher researchers indicate[…] ith classroom exploration (2D). In a […] bility between the responsibility they […] e in classroom research: Some indic[…] tionship between teaching and resear[…] ion between them at times (2E). Ever[…] er research, some teachers also used […] gs (3C).

Unlike other, lo[…] any of which involve fairly forma[…] s an almost paradoxical combination of theme and individuality. The themes involve the attributes, processes, methods, and dissemination structures we extracted from the corpus of studies examined. But because of the reflective, action-oriented nature of inquiry into classroom life that defines teacher research, it simultaneously exudes a character that defies definition. Therefore, rather than there being a single portrait of teacher research, we suggest that teacher research is represented by a family album that includes many members who possess ancestry resemblance but are also readily distinguishable from one another.

A NEW GENRE?

Teacher research has been characterized "as its own genre" (Coch[…] ith & Lytle, 1993, p. 10), as a "new […] s "a unique genre of research" (Patt[…] Lytle (1993) argued that teacher rese[…] p. 10) when compared to research co[…] support the "new genre" and "distin[…] ch.

One distinctive featu[…] teacher research. We found teacher[…] revising existant methodological para[…] d practical, versatile research perspe[…] in conventional research on teachi[…] e, purpose, and publication outlet. Al[…] ars in professional periodicals that […] teacher research are usually differen[…] d serials or books, outlets that reach[…] chers and school personnel.

Finally, classroom inqu[…] nsibilities faced by a teacher research[…] quantita-

Handwritten annotations:

— Methodology in teacher research reflects both commonality and diversity — not homologous form of inquiry — diverse in process, method, and reporting

— own genre — own research paradigm — unique genre of research → evolutionary nature of methodology → choosing, discarding, revisiting, revising → audience, purpose, and publication outlet different → qualitative not quantitative

tive methods to conduct classroom experiments both historically (Olson, 1990) and contemporarily (Santa & Santa, 1995), our analysis indicates that teacher researchers tend to employ qualitative methods. But does that plant teacher research squarely within the qualitative methodology tradition? We think not. Teacher researchers, like qualitative researchers, are immersed in the research environment, but there are important distinctions. Qualitative researchers are first and foremost *researchers*, with participation being a planned means to achieve insight into the social setting under study. In contrast, teacher researchers are first and foremost *teachers*, who are responsible for the learning and well-being of the students assigned to them. Teacher research is not an ethnographic field study in which the researcher lives in the community; a teacher researcher not only lives in the community but works in and has responsibility for it. Erickson (1986) characterized a teacher researcher's role as "not that of the participant observer who comes from the outside world to visit, but that of an unusually observant participant who deliberates inside the scene of action" (p. 157). The insider role of teacher researcher brings with it a unique combination: the power associated with first-person insight, the limitation of participant perspective, and perhaps a bit of tension involved with trying to simultaneously teach and study one's teaching environment. It is this unique combination of qualities, we believe, that gives teacher research its individuality and status as a new research genre.

In his introduction to the second edition of *Complementary Methods for Research in Education* (Jaeger, 1997), Shulman (1997) described the promise of "the creation of forms of 'teacher research,'" predicting that the teacher research movement "will grow sufficiently in strength to provide another new paradigm for educational research" (pp. 19–20). We agree that teachers are in the best position to explore their own practice and to make sense of the classroom worlds "because they are full-time inhabitants of those settings rather than episodic visitors" (p. 21). We disagree with Shulman, however, about the tense. Rather than anticipating that teacher research "will grow" to provide a new paradigm, we believe that teacher research has already achieved a new educational research genre status. As such, we look forward not only to the use of *teacher research* without quotation marks in the future, but also to the inclusion of a chapter on teacher research methodology in the third edition of *Complementary Methods*.

ACKNOWLEDGMENTS

We thank JoBeth Allen and Ruth Shagoury Hubbard for their review of our sample of teacher-research studies and their useful suggestions for how to make it more representative of the diversity within published teacher research. We thank Cheri Triplett for her detailed, thoughtful, and critical evaluation of our analysis procedures and emerging themes and categories.

REFERENCES

Allen, J. (1995). *It's never too late: Leading adolescents to lifelong literacy.* Portsmouth, NH: Heinemann.
Allen, J. (1997). Exploring literature through student-led discussions. *Teacher Research: The Journal of Classroom Inquiry, 4*(2), 124–139.
Allen, J., Michalove, B., & Shockley, B. (1993). *Engaging children: Community and chaos in the lives of young literacy learners.* Portsmouth, NH: Heinemann.
Allen, S. (1992). Student-sustained discussion: When students talk and the teacher listens. In N. A. Branscombe, D. Goswami, & J. Schwartz (Eds.), *Students teaching, teachers learning* (pp. 81–92). Portsmouth, NH: Boynton/Cook.
Almy, M., & Genishi, C. (1979). *Ways of studying children.* New York: Teachers College Press.
Alvermann, D. E., O'Brien, D. G., & Dillon, D. R. (1996). On writing qualitative research. *Reading Research Quarterly, 31,* 114–120.

Atwell, N. (1987). Everyone sits at a big desk: Discovering topics for writing. In D. Goswami & P. R. Stillman (Eds.), *Reclaiming the classroom: Teacher research as an agency for change* (pp. 178–187). Upper Montclair, NJ: Boynton/Cook.

Atwell, N. (1993). Forward. In Patterson, L., Santa, C. M., Short, K. G., & Smith, K. (Eds.), *Teachers are researchers: Reflection and action* (pp. vii–xii). Newark, DE: International Reading Association.

Avery, C. S. (1987). Traci: A learning-disabled child in a writing-process classroom. In G. L. Bissex & R. H. Bullock (Eds.), *Seeing for ourselves: Case-study research by teachers of writing* (pp. 59–75). Portsmouth, NH: Heinemann.

Baumann, J. F. (1996). Conflict or compatibility in classroom inquiry? One teacher's struggle to balance teaching and research. *Educational Researcher, 25*(7), 29–36.

Baumann, J. F., Allen, J., & Shockley, B. (1994). Questions teachers ask: A report from the National Reading Research Center School Research Consortium. In D. J. Leu & C. K. Kinzer (Eds.), *Multidimensional aspects of literacy research, theory, and practice*, 43rd Yearbook of the National Reading Conference (pp. 474–484). Chicago: National Reading Conference.

Baumann, J. F., Dillon, D. R., Shockley, B. B., Alvermann, D. A., & Reinking, D. (1996). Perspectives for literacy research. In L. Baker, P. P. Afflerbach, & D. Reinking (Eds.), *Developing engaged readers in school and home communities* (pp. 217–245). Mahwah, NJ: Lawrence Erlbaum Associates.

Baumann, J. F., & Ivey, G. (1997). Delicate balances: Striving for curricular and instructional equilibrium in a second-grade, literature/strategy-based classroom. *Reading Research Quarterly, 32*(3), 244–275.

Baumann, J. F., Shockley-Bisplinghoff, B., & Allen, J. (1997). Methodology in teacher research: Three cases. In J. Flood, S. B. Heath, & D. Lapp (Eds.), *Handbook of research on teaching literacy through the communicative and visual arts* (pp. 121–143). New York: Macmillan.

Bissex, G. L. (1987). What is a teacher-researcher? In G. L. Bissex & R. H. Bullock (Eds.), *Seeing for ourselves: Case-study research by teachers of writing* (pp. 3–5). Portsmouth, NH: Heinemann.

Bissex, G. L., & Bullock, R. H. (Eds.). (1987). *Seeing for ourselves: Case-study research by teachers of writing.* Portsmouth, NH: Heinemann.

Booth, W. C., Colomb, G. G., & Williams, J. M. (1995). *The craft of research.* Chicago: University of Chicago Press.

Brause, R. S., & Mayher, J. S. (Eds.). (1991). *Search and re-search: What the inquiring teacher needs to know.* London: Falmer.

Britton, J. (1987). A quiet form of research. In D. Goswami & P. R. Stillman (Eds.), *Reclaiming the classroom: Teacher research as an agency for change* (pp. 13–19). Upper Montclair, NJ: Boynton/Cook.

Bryan, L. H. (1996). Cooperative writing groups in community college. *Journal of Adolescent & Adult Literacy, 40*, 188–193.

Buckingham, B. R. (1926). *Research for teachers.* New York: Silver, Burdett.

Burton, F. R. (1991). Teacher-researcher projects: An elementary school teacher's perspective. In J. Flood, J. M. Jensen, D. Lapp, & J. R. Squire (Eds.), *Handbook of research on teaching the English language arts* (pp. 226–230). New York: Macmillan.

Calhoun, E. F. (1994). *How to use action research in the self-renewing school.* Alexandria, VA: Association for Supervision and Curriculum Development.

Calkins, L. M. (1985). Forming research communities among naturalistic researchers. In B. W. McClelland & T. R. Donovan (Eds.), *Perspectives on research and scholarship in composition* (pp. 125–144). New York: Modern Language Association.

Carter, K. (1993). The place of story in the study of teaching and teacher education. *Educational Researcher, 22*(1), 5–12.

Caulfield, J. (1996). Students telling stories: Inquiry into the process of learning stories. In Z. Donoahue, M. A. Van Tassell, & L. Patterson (Eds.), *Research in the classroom: Talk, texts, and inquiry* (pp. 51–64). Newark, DE: International Reading Association.

Christensen, L., & Walker, B. J. (1992). Researching one's own teaching in a reading education course. In N. D. Padak, T. V. Raskinski, & J. Logan (Eds.), *Literacy research and practice: Foundations for the year 2000*, 14th Yearbook of the College Reading Association (pp. 57–64). Kent, OH: College Reading Association.

Cline, D. M. (1993). A year with reading workshop. In L. Patterson, C. M. Santa, K. G. Short, & K. Smith (Eds.), *Teachers are researchers: Reflection and action* (pp. 115–121). Newark, DE: International Reading Association.

Clyde, J. A., Condon, M. W. F., Daniel, K., & Sommer, M. K. (1993). Learning through whole language: Exploring book selection and use with preschoolers. In L. Patterson, C. M. Santa, K. G. Short, & K. Smith (Eds.), *Teachers are researchers: Reflection and action* (pp. 42–50). Newark, DE: International Reading Association.

Cochran-Smith, M., & Lytle, S. L. (1990). Research on teaching and teacher research: The issues that divide us. *Educational Researcher, 19*(2), 2–11.

Cochran-Smith, M., & Lytle, S. L. (Eds.). (1993). *Inside/outside: Teacher research and knowledge.* New York: Teachers College Press.

Commeyras, M., Reinking, D., Heubach, K. M., & Pagnucco, J. (1993). Looking within: A study of an undergraduate reading methods course. In D. J. Leu & C. K. Kinzer (Eds.), *Examining central issues in literacy research, theory, and practice*, 42nd Yearbook of the National Reading Conference (pp. 297–304). Chicago: National Reading Conference.

Cone, J. K. (1994). Appearing acts: Creating readers in a high school English class. *Harvard Educational Review, 64*(4), 450–473.

Connelly, F. M., & Clandinin, D. J. (1990). Stories of experience and narrative inquiry. *Educational Researcher, 19*(5), 2–14.

Corey, S. M. (1953). *Action research to improve school practices.* New York: Teachers College Bureau of Publications, Columbia University.

Corman, B. R. (1957). Action research: A teaching or a research method? *Review of Educational Research, 27,* 545–547.

Denzin, N. K., & Lincoln, Y. S. (1994). Part II: Major paradigms and perspectives. In N. K. Denzin & Y. S. Lincoln (Eds.), *Handbook of qualitative research* (pp. 99–104). Thousand Oaks, CA: Sage.

Dewey, J. (1929). *The sources of a science of education.* New York: Liveright.

Dey, I. (1993). *Qualitative data analysis: A user-friendly guide for social scientists.* New York: Routledge.

Donoahue, Z. (1996). Collaboration, community, and communication: Modes of discourse for teacher research. In Z. Donoahue, M. A. Van Tassell, & L. Patterson (Eds.), *Research in the classroom: Talk, texts, and inquiry* (pp. 91–107). Newark, DE: International Reading Association.

Donoahue, Z., Van Tassell, M. A., & Patterson, L. (Eds.). (1996). *Research in the classroom: Talk, texts, and inquiry.* Newark, DE: International Reading Association.

Duffy, A. (1997, December). *Outstanding elementary school preservice teachers' perceptions of, learnings about, and work with struggling readers.* Paper presented at the 47th Annual Meeting of the National Reading Conference, Scottsdale, AZ.

Duffy-Hester, A. M. (1999). *Effects of a balanced literacy program on the reading growth of elementary school struggling readers.* Unpublished doctoral dissertation, University of Georgia.

Elliott, J. (1991). *Action research for educational change.* Milton Keynes, England: Open University Press.

Erickson, F. (1986). Qualitative methods in research on teaching. In M. C. Wittrock (Ed.), *Handbook of research on teaching* (3rd ed., pp. 119–161). New York: Macmillan.

Feldgus, E. G. (1993). Walking to the words. In M. Cochran-Smith & S. Lytle (Eds.), *Inside/outside: Teacher research and knowledge* (pp. 170–177). New York: Teachers College Press.

Glaser, B. G., & Strauss, A. L. (1967). *The discovery of grounded theory: Strategies for qualitative research.* Hawthorne, NY: Aldine de Gruyter.

Goswami, D., & Stillman, P. (Eds.). (1987). *Reclaiming the classroom: Teacher research as an agency for change.* Upper Montclair, NJ: Boynton/Cook.

Grattan, K. W. (1997). They can do it too! Book club with first and second graders. In S. I. McMahon & T. E. Raphael (Eds.), *The book club connection: Literacy learning and classroom talk* (pp. 267–283). New York: Teachers College Press.

Grimm, N. (1990). Tutoring dyslexic college students: What these students teach us about literacy development. In D. A. Daiker & M. Morenberg (Eds.), *The writing teacher as researcher: Essays in the theory and practice of class-based research* (pp. 336–342). Portsmouth, NH: Boynton/Cook.

Halpern, E. S. (1983). *Auditing naturalistic inquiries: The development and application of a model.* Unpublished doctoral dissertation, Indiana University.

Hansen, J. (1989). Anna evaluates herself. In J. Allen & J. Mason (Eds.), *Risk makers, risk takers, risk breakers* (pp. 19–29). Portsmouth, NH: Heinemann.

Harvey, S., McAuliffe, S., Benson, L., Cameron, W., Kempton, S., Lusche, P., Miller, D., Schroeder, J., & Weaver, J. (1996). Teacher-researchers study the process of synthesizing in six primary classrooms. *Language Arts, 73,* 564–574.

Hodgkinson, H. L. (1957). Action research: A critique. *Journal of Educational Sociology, 31*(4), 137–153.

Hollingsworth, S., & Sockett, H. (Eds.). (1994). *Teacher research and educational reform,* 93rd Yearbook of the National Society for the Study of Education, Part 1. Chicago: University of Chicago Press.

Hopkins, D. (1993). *A teacher's guide to classroom research* (2nd ed.). Buckingham, England: Open University Press.

Hubbard, R. S., & Power, B. M. (1993a). *The art of classroom inquiry: A handbook for teacher-researchers.* Portsmouth, NH: Heinemann.

Hubbard, R. S., & Power, B. M. (1993b). Finding and framing a research question. In L. Patterson, C. M. Santa, K. G. Short, & K. Smith (Eds.), *Teachers are researchers: Reflection and action* (pp. 19–25). Newark, DE: International Reading Association.

Hubbard, R. S., & Power, B. M. (1999). *Living the questions: A guide for teacher-researchers.* York, ME: Stenhouse.

Jaeger, R. M. (Ed.). (1997). *Complementary methods for research in education* (2nd ed.). Washington, DC: American Educational Research Association.

Johnston, P. (1993). Lessons from the road: What I learned through teacher research. In M. Cochran-Smith & S. Lytle (Eds.), *Inside/outside: Teacher research and knowledge* (pp. 178–184). New York: Teachers College Press.

Kidder, L. H. (1981). Qualitative research and quasi-experimental frameworks. In M. B. Brewer & R. E. Collins (Eds.), *Scientific inquiry and the social sciences* (pp. 226–256). San Francisco: Jossey-Bass.

Kincheloe, J. L. (1991). *Teachers as researchers: Qualitative inquiry as a path to empowerment.* London: Falmer.

Krall, F. R. (1988). From the inside out—personal history as educational research. *Educational Theory, 38,* 467–479.

Lather, P. (1986). Research as praxis. *Harvard Educational Review, 56,* 257–277.

LeCompte, M. D., & Preissle, J. (1993). *Ethnography and qualitative design in educational research* (2nd ed.). New York: Academic Press.

Lincoln, Y. S., & Guba, E. G. (1985). *Naturalistic inquiry.* Newbury Park, CA: Sage.

Lytle, S., & Cochran-Smith, S. L. (1992). Teacher research as a way of knowing. *Harvard Educational Review, 62*(4).

Lytle, S. L., & Cochran-Smith, M. (1994a). Inquiry, knowledge, and practice. In S. Hollingsworth & H. Sockett (Eds.), *Teacher research and educational reform*, 93rd Yearbook of the National Society for the Study of Education, Part 1 (pp. 22–51). Chicago: University of Chicago Press.

Lytle, S. L., & Cochran-Smith, M. (1994b). Teacher research in English. In A. C. Purves (Ed.), *Encyclopedia of English studies and language arts* (pp. 1153–1155). New York: Scholastic.

Maher, A. (1994). An inquiry into reader response. In G. Wells, L. Bernard, M. A. Gianotti, C. Keating, C. Konjevic, M. Kowal, A. Maher, C. Mayer, T. Moscoe, E. Orzechowska, A. Smieja, & L. Swartz (Eds.), *Changing schools from within: Creating communities of inquiry* (pp. 81–97). Portsmouth, NH: Heinemann.

McFarland, K. P., & Stansell, J. C. (1993). Historical perspectives. In L. Patterson, C. M. Santa, K. G. Short, & K. Smith (Eds.), *Teachers are researchers: Reflection and action* (pp. 12–18). Newark, DE: International Reading Association.

Merriam, S. B. (1998). *Qualitative research and case study applications in education.* San Francisco: Jossey-Bass.

Miles, M. B., & Huberman, A. M. (1994). *An expanded sourcebook: Qualitative data analysis* (2nd ed.). Thousand Oaks, CA: Sage.

Mohr, M., & Maclean, M. (1987). *Working together: A guide for teacher-researchers.* Urbana, IL: National Council of Teachers of English.

Mosenthal, J. (1995). A practice-oriented approach to methods coursework in literacy teaching. In K. A. Hinchman, D. J. Leu, & C. K. Kinzer (Eds.), *Perspectives on literacy research and practice*, 44th Yearbook of the National Reading Conference (pp. 358–367). Chicago: National Reading Conference.

Murphy, P. (1994). Antonio: My student, my teacher: My inquiry begins. *Teacher Research: The Journal of Classroom Inquiry, 1*(2), 75–88.

Myers, M. (1985). *The teacher-researcher: How to study writing in the classroom.* Urbana, IL: National Council of Teachers of English.

Newton, M., Nash, D., & Ruffin, L. (1996). A whole language trilogy: The covered bridge connection. In G. Burnaford, J. Fischer, & D. Hobson (Eds.), *Teachers doing research: Practical possibilities* (pp. 82–90). Mahwah, NJ: Lawrence Erlbaum Associates.

Nixon, J. (1981). *A teacher's guide to action research.* London: Grant McIntyre.

Nocerino, M. A. (1993). A look at the process. In L. Patterson, C. M. Santa, K. G. Short, & K. Smith (Eds.), *Teachers are researchers: Reflection and action* (pp. 86–91). Newark, DE: International Reading Association.

O'Dell, L. (1987). Planning classroom research. In D. Goswami & P. R. Stillman (Eds.), *Reclaiming the classroom: Teacher research as an agency for change* (pp. 128–160). Upper Montclair, NJ: Boynton/Cook.

Olson, M. W. (1990). The teacher as researcher: A historical perspective. In M. W. Olson (Ed.), *Opening the door to classroom research* (pp. 1–20). Newark, DE: International Reading Association.

Paley, V. G. (1997). *The girl with the brown crayon.* Cambridge, MA: Harvard University Press.

Patterson, L., & Shannon, P. (1993). Reflection, inquiry, action. In L. Patterson, C. M. Santa, K. G. Short, & K. Smith (Eds.), *Teachers are researchers: Reflection and action* (pp. 7–11). Newark, DE: International Reading Association.

Phinney, M. Y., & Ketterling, T. (1997). Dialogue journals, literature, and urban Indian sixth graders. *Teacher Research: The Journal of Classroom Inquiry, 4*(2), 22–41.

Pils, L. J. (1993). "I love you, Miss Piss." *Reading Teacher, 46,* 648–653.

Ray, L. C. (1987). Reflections on classroom research. In D. Goswami & P. R. Stillman (Eds.), *Reclaiming the classroom: Teacher research as an agency for change* (pp. 219–242). Upper Montclair, NJ: Boynton/Cook.

Richards, J. (1987). Rx for editor in chief. In G. L. Bissex & R. H. Bullock (Eds.), *Seeing for ourselves: Case-study research by teachers of writing* (pp. 139–142). Portsmouth, NH: Heinemann.

Sagor, R. (1992). *How to conduct collaborative action research.* Alexandria, VA: Association for Supervision and Curriculum Development.

Santa, C. M., & Santa, J. L. (1995). Teacher as researcher. *JRB: A Journal of Literacy, 27,* 439–451.

Saunders, L. (1995). Unleashing the voices we rarely hear: Derrick's story. *Teacher Research: The Journal of Classroom Inquiry, 3*(1), 55–68.

Schon, D. A. (1983). *The reflective practitioner: How professionals think in action.* New York: Basic Books.

Sega, D. (1997). Reading and writing about our lives: Creating a collaborative curriculum in a class of high school misfits. *Teacher Research: The Journal of Classroom Inquiry, 4*(2), 101–111.

Shulman, L. S. (1997). Disciplines of inquiry in education: A new overview. In R. M. Jaeger (Ed.), *Complementary methods for research in education* (2nd ed., pp. 3–29). Washington, DC: American Educational Research Association.

Stenhouse, L. (1973). The humanistic curriculum project. In H. Butcher & H. Pont (Eds.), *Educational research in Britain 3* (pp. 149–167). London: University of London Press.

Stenhouse, L. (1975). *An introduction to curriculum research and development.* London: Heinemann.

Swift, K. (1993). Try Reading Workshop in your classroom. *Reading Teacher, 46,* 366–371.

Thomas, S., & Oldfather, P. (1995). Enhancing student and teacher engagement in literacy learning: A shared inquiry approach. *Reading Teacher, 49,* 192–202.

Threatt, S., Buchanan, J., Morgan, B., Strieb, L. Y., Sugarman, J., Swenson, J., Teel, K., & Tomlinson, J. (1994). Teachers' voices in the conversation about teacher research. In S. Hollingsworth & H. Sockett (Eds.), *Teacher research and educational reform*, 93rd Yearbook of the National Society for the Study of Education, Part 1 (pp. 222–244). Chicago: University of Chicago Press.

Von Dras, J. (1990). Transitions toward an integrated curriculum. In K. G. Short & K. M. Pierce (Eds.), *Talking about books: Creating literate communities* (pp. 121–133). Portsmouth, NH: Heinemann.

Wells, G., Bernard, L., Gianotti, M. A., Keating, C., Konjevic, C., Kowal, M., Maher, A., Mayer, C., Moscoe, T., Orzechowska, E., Smieja, A., & Swartz, L. (Eds.). (1994). *Changing schools from within: Creating communities of inquiry.* Toronto: Oise Press.

Wood, K. (1993). A case study of a writer. In L. Patterson, C. M. Santa, K. G. Short, & K. Smith (Eds.), *Teachers are researchers: Reflection and action* (pp. 106–114). Newark, DE: International Reading Association.

CHAPTER 7

Designing Programmatic Interventions

Therese D. Pigott
Loyola University, Chicago

Rebecca Barr
National-Louis University, Chicago

The purpose of this chapter is to think carefully about how literacy scholars can conduct useful evaluation studies of literacy interventions. Literacy interventions represent an important class of studies where theory, practice, and policy intersect. The history of evaluation research highlights many issues salient to the study of programmatic interventions. The tensions between the use of evaluation findings to inform local practice versus higher level policy, the difficulties in comparing different approaches to alleviate a problem, and the conflict between the purposes of basic research and evaluation research have been in existence since the first attempts at intervention studies.

Recognizing the struggles inherent in evaluation research emphasizes both the importance and the difficulty in designing and implementing research on programmatic interventions. As shown in this chapter, studies of literacy interventions differ in the extent to which they pursue implications for practice, theory development and policy; most often, interest in practice and policy prevails over that in theory. We argue that evaluations of programmatic interventions can, in fact, contribute to the three areas of theory, practice, and policy through careful design and a grounding in both literacy theory and classroom practice, a view not held by all concerned with evaluation (see Wolf, 1990).

This chapter provides a historical overview of evaluation research and its transformation during the past decade to include interpretive and formative modes of research. Throughout, studies by literacy researchers are discussed that have as their goal the assessment of programmatic interventions. The development of three approaches is considered: (a) experimental or quasi-experimental studies to compare the effectiveness of developed programs, (b) qualitative documentation to understand how a program works, and (c) formative modes of evaluation to enhance the design and development of programs. In the final section of the chapter, we draw conclusions and discuss ways in which literacy researchers can design studies of programmatic interventions with theoretical, practical, and policy implications.

TRADITIONAL PROGRAM EVALUATIONS

Much of the early writing on evaluation began with Smith and Tyler's (1942) Eight Year Study of curriculum changes in secondary schools. Smith and Tyler located the importance of this work in practice, seeking to gather information that would help teachers understand their influence on student behavior. Smith and Tyler did not mention policymakers as major stakeholders in the process of developing and improving programs, and were not concerned with the theoretical implications that might derive from assessing the relative merits of several options to alleviate a given problem.

With the expansion of programs to aid the poor during the Great Depression and the simultaneous development of new statistical techniques, interest in evaluation increased. The advent of federally funded evaluation studies in the 1960s brought a change in both the design and audience of evaluations. Where Smith and Tyler (1942) were concerned with providing empirical data for teachers to improve student achievement, the focus of large-scale evaluations centered on providing quantitative data for policymakers to make decisions about program effectiveness. Experimental design, influenced by Campbell and Stanley (1963), was the guiding principle for evaluation research. The methods Campbell and Stanley advocated were based on the random assignment of participants to a "treatment" and a "control" group in order to make causal inferences about the effects of an intervention. When random assignment was not feasible (a common occurrence), Campbell and Stanley suggested a number of quasi-experiments where a nonrandomly assigned "treatment" group is compared to a nonrandomly assigned control group such as the teacher's class from a previous year or a comparable class from a nearby school. A second type of quasi-experiment—an interrupted time-series design—compares an individual or a class during intervention with performance on multiple measures before and after the intervention. Discontinuities in the pattern of responses before and after an intervention are evidence for the treatment's effect. In this manner, a class or individual serves as its own control.

The results of experimental or quasi-experimental evaluation research provided policymakers with evidence about whether a program causes particular outcomes. The goal of many evaluation studies such as First Grade Reading and Head Start was to make value judgments about the relative merit of several different approaches to alleviate a social problem. Cronbach (1963) wrote about the usefulness of evaluations for making decisions about programs, especially about the large national projects from the 1960s, stressing the need to look at a wide range of possible consequences of programs, both intended and unintended by the program designers.

Program evaluations in the reading research literature since the 1900s have also been driven by the question: Which method is best? Based on the research approaches of psychologists and others following analytic science traditions, literacy researchers have tended to use quasi-experimental designs to establish the causal impact of programs on student outcomes (Pressley & Harris, 1994). In the reading research literature, traditional evaluation studies fall into two main groups: (a) smaller scale local studies comparing one or several experimental programs motivated by considerations of practice and sometimes theory, and (b) large-scale assessments of programs serving policy and accountability functions.

Small-Scale Intervention Studies

Studies conducted in the first half of the century, often by doctoral students, tended to be small-scale comparisons of an innovative method with a traditional approach in several matched classrooms. Chall (1967/1983/1995), for example, summarized that portion of the early literature that pertains to beginning reading methods. Although programmatic comparisons have long been the mainstay of literacy research, they were reinvigorated by research on reading processes in the 1970s and early 1980s. Once knowledge and strategies characterizing proficient reading were identified, attempts were made to see whether less proficient students could be taught this knowledge and learn to use these strategies. Although research of this sort focuses on many aspects of literacy, two areas in particular have received concentrated attention: (a) phonemic awareness and beginning reading methods (see the chapters by Blachman and Hiebert & Taylor in this volume) and (b) metacognitive and comprehension strategy research (see the chapter by Pressley in this volume). The goal of these studies was to determine the optimal methods to foster the literacy development of individuals with a focus on classroom practice.

This research differs from large-scale interventions (to be discussed next) in scope and sometimes in duration. Typically a series of instructional activities is developed to elaborate, but not replace, ongoing instruction. The duration of these activities may vary from a few days to a semester or a year. More recent studies have shifted in focus to longer term and more comprehensive content-specific strategy programs in such areas as literacy, social studies, history, science, and math (e.g., Bereiter & Bird, 1985; Gaskins, Anderson, Pressley, Cunicelli, & Sallow, 1993; Guthrie et al., 1996; Morrow, Pressley, Smith, & Smith, 1997; Paris & Oka, 1986; Pressley et al., 1992; Siegel & Fonzi, 1995). We are making a distinction between the use of experimental methods in evaluation of interventions and experimental research in general. Intervention studies have as their express purpose the evaluation of a program for improving instruction. The broader field of experimental research in education and the social sciences includes intervention studies, but also may include experiments focused on questions not related to a classroom or instructional intervention.

Many validity concerns characterize these smaller scale studies. Lysynchuk, Pressley, d'Ailly, Smith, and Cake (1989) examined 38 studies of comprehension strategy instruction in elementary schools that had been published in selective educational research journals. They found a variety of internal validity flaws including "(a) not assigning subjects randomly to treatment and control conditions, (b) not exposing experimental and control subjects to the same training materials, (c) not providing information about the amount of time spent on dependent variable tasks, (d) not including checks on the success of the manipulation and process measures, (e) not using the appropriate units of analysis, and (f) not assessing either long-term effects or the generalization of the strategies to other tasks and materials" (p. 458). Unfortunately, as they noted, some studies with major flaws limiting the conclusions that can be drawn have already influenced theory and practice (see Ridgeway, Dunston, & Qian, 1993, for similar findings for research conducted in secondary schools).

Until recently, it has been common practice not to observe the experimental and control instruction; thus it has not been possible to know whether the theoretically based ideal program has been realized and the extent to which its manifestation varies across classes for different pupils and situational conditions. As Lysynchuk and colleagues (1989) found, another common design error of small-scale studies has been to treat the individual student as the unit of analysis, rather than the class (or school or district). Yet, when the class is used as the unit of analysis, with only two or three classes involved in each condition, there is insufficient power to detect a reliable difference between treatment and control conditions.

Some smaller scale case studies by literacy researchers use variations on traditional experimental designs, such as the interrupted time-series and control series designs (Campbell, 1963; 1969). Yaden (1995) described what he referred to as "reversal designs" involving a time series including a period in which baseline data are taken, a period of intervention during which the same response data are taken, followed by a period in which the intervention is withdrawn. Smolkin, Yaden, Brown, and Hofius (1992), for example, used time series measures during parent–child read-alouds to assess the effect of such features of texts as genre, visual design choices, and discourse. Rose and Beattie (1986) used a base period followed by an intervention to assess the effects of teacher-directed versus taped previewing on oral reading. Single-subject experimental research involving an individual child, a group, or a class is becoming more common as a useful means to assess the effects of literacy programs (Neuman & McCormick, 1995).

Large-Scale Evaluation Studies in the Reading Literature

The 1960s also saw an emphasis on large-scale summative evaluations of literacy programs. Prompted by the Russian launching of Sputnik (Pearson, 1997) and perhaps by concerns pertaining to the relatively low literacy achievement of minority groups (Willis & Harris, 1997), federal funding for the First Grade Reading Studies was provided to address, once and for all, the best way to teach beginning reading (Bond & Dykstra, 1967; Dykstra, 1968). The large number of classrooms representing each method promised enough statistical power to detect differences between methods even when the classroom served as the unit of analysis. A common set of tests of pupil prereading ability permitted assessment of the comparability of samples across project sites and methods before and after the intervention.

Despite the attention to experimental design issues, comparisons between basal and nonbasal approaches to reading produced mixed results. The experimental group outperformed the comparison group on only some of the outcome measures, and these results varied across sites (Bond & Dykstra, 1967). The failure to discern differences in effectiveness among methods may have been due to the large variation found in learning outcomes within methods. This variation suggests that treatment implementation may have been inconsistent and/or that situational factors may have had a strong influence on the way methods developed locally. Because instruction was not observed, these possibilities could not be confirmed. In addition, the theoretical implications of the evaluation were limited because the measures used, although common across sites, were not tied conceptually to the unique characteristics of the programs.

Similarly, in the 1970s, evaluations of the Follow Through interventions in primary grades designed to provide support for at-risk children (Stallings, 1975; Stebbins, St. Pierre, Proper, Anderson, & Cerva, 1977) addressed the problem of how to compare curricula that differed widely in philosophies and goals. The comparisons involved multiple measures and multiple outcomes, not all of which were shared by each program. Observational evidence describing what the treatment was and who the children were revealed that the instruction children experienced was not uniform across all sites. Variability occurred both in the implementation of the study design and in the programs themselves, lessening the confidence of researchers in the potential of large-scale evaluation to influence and create policy.

Large-scale evaluations such as the First Grade Reading Studies and Follow Through also suffered from a number of threats to internal validity due to the selection of students from the low end of a test-score distribution. These threats include statistical regression to the mean, subject selection bias, and mortality issues. Recent reviews of the evaluations of Reading Recovery (Hiebert, 1994; Shanahan & Barr, 1995) identified such concerns as limiting confidence in conclusions that can be drawn about program effectiveness. Large-scale evaluations of federally funded programs for at-risk students, such as the Chapter and Title programs, suffer from similar threats to internal validity.

QUALITATIVE DOCUMENTATION OF PROGRAMS

The equivocal results of evaluations based on a quasi-experimental model led many to call for considering descriptions of programs and the perceptions of participants as part of evaluations. Weiss (1972) argued that decisions about a given program rarely focus on a summative judgment, such as a choice between a program and no program. Often, what is of interest to policymakers, teachers, and other stakeholders centers on what aspects of particular programs are related to the program's intended and unintended consequences (what Weiss calls a "process model"). Cook and Reichardt (1979) edited a monograph advocating the joining of qualitative and quantitative forms of evaluation. Even earlier, from a sociological perspective, Hyman, Wright, and Hopkins (1962) argued for the importance of including evidence that described the nature of programs, participant perspectives, and unanticipated outcomes. Understanding what aspects of a program are optimal and what are less than desirable requires intimate knowledge of the students, teachers, and classroom processes from both the evaluator and participants' perspectives.

Since the mid 1980s, the frustration with the lack of use of evaluation studies by policymakers has paralleled that in the broader field of educational research (see, e.g., Peterson, 1998), leading to discussions about the nature of social reality, and ultimately to discussions about the most appropriate methodology for examining a program or intervention. Stake (1975) was one of the first evaluators to question the exclusive use of strategies focusing on the identification of input-output relationships in evaluation research. Influenced by Stake's perspective, researchers such as Guba and Lincoln (1989) rejected the premises underlying experimental and quasi-experimental studies altogether, arguing that there is no single social reality to be discovered by empirical research, but instead that individuals in a situation construct their own meanings and interpretations of a given context. Thus, researchers using interpretive data collection methods see the goal of research to understand and document a given situation or context. Although evaluators such as Patton (1990), Eisner (1991), and Pitman and Maxwell (1992) agree with Guba and Lincoln's emphasis on gathering participants' perceptions and observations as the primary method for data collection, each takes a slightly different approach to evaluating programs that reflects various concerns about the field of evaluation and social science research.

In literacy research, qualitative evaluation methods have been used in two ways: (a) to provide a description of the nature of the experimental instruction in the context of traditional evaluation studies, and (b) to represent interpretively the perceptions and experiences of participants concerning the program. For both, a guiding question may be "How does the program work?" but the assumptions underlying the two approaches differ.

Experimental Program Documentation

Literacy researchers, recognizing the limitations of skeletal descriptions of instruction, have begun to observe program implementation and solicit the perceptions of program participants (see, e.g., Alvermann, O'Brien, & Dillon, 1990; Beck, McKeown, Sandora, Kucan, & Worthy, 1996; Gaskins et al., 1993; Goldenberg, 1992; Guzzetti & Williams, 1996; Pressley et al., 1992; Saunders, O'Brien, Lennon, & McLean, 1998). Although the basic evaluation goal continues to focus on determining whether a program accounts for learning outcomes, the inclusion of more comprehensive descriptions of programs empowers researchers to understand why certain results have occurred. Robinson (1998), in her discussion of research methods for bridging the research-practice gap, argued that the understanding of practice requires the acknowledgment that classroom practices are context dependent.

In their comparison of skills-based or whole language classroom programs, for example, Dahl and Freppon (1995) examined how inner-city children in the United States made sense of their beginning reading and writing instruction. Data were gathered through field notes, audio recordings of reading and writing episodes, student papers, and the pre/post written language measures. In addition, Dahl and Freppon identified important instructional differences based on their ethnographic observation.

Teaching approaches were characterized in terms of learning opportunities in the areas of phonics, writing, and response to literature. These descriptions suggested that both sets of teachers taught in these areas, but did so in different ways. In the area of phonics, for example, skills-based teachers addressed letter–sound relations in skill lessons, by showing students how to sound out words, and having students sound out words as they read aloud. Whole-language teachers also demonstrated sounding out procedures, but during whole group instruction with big books, and provided practice on letter–sound relations during reading and writing. In addition to validating adherence to a theoretically based method, such observations enable researchers to understand how students learn, and to assess how other conditions may affect the outcomes.

Interpretive Approaches to Evaluation Research

As discussed earlier, some qualitative researchers argue that the preoccupation of evaluation researchers with linear and causal relations misrepresents the complexity of the interaction that occurs between instruction programs and student development. As an alternative, interpretive researchers such as Guba and Lincoln (1989) and Eisner (1991) argued for seeing evaluation as a value-laden activity that is inherently social and political. Studies of response to literature, with origins in the theoretical and empirical work of scholars from the reader response tradition within literacy theory, tend to reflect evaluation models that are interpretive in form (see, e.g., Brock, 1997; Hickman, 1983; Marshall, 1987; McMahon, 1997).

To illustrate, Eeds and Wells (1989) in their study of "grand conversations" sought to describe patterns of classroom discussion and how teachers and students responded to text and to each other. They compared what actually occurred in groups with an idealized model that they referred to as "grand conversation." By this, they meant the construction and disclosure of "deeper meaning, enriching understanding for all participants" (p. 5). Focus in this form of evaluation research is on the relation between "intents or goals," as implicit in the notion of "grand conversations," and what was experienced by participants in groups as described through journal responses and observation. The intentions become the standard against which judgments are made about the success and appropriateness of the group activities. This approach entails a description of programs as seen through the eyes of participants, and allows for differences to emerge in goals (those of program developers vs. those of teachers or students), as well as in constructions of program interaction (those of observers and those of participants).

FORMATIVE APPROACHES TO PROGRAM EVALUATION

A final shift in thinking about evaluation research has occurred recently. Instead of conceptualizing evaluation as an experimental or an interpretive portrayal of an established program, researchers have argued that it is more useful to use evaluation in a formative way to enhance program effectiveness as it is being developed. This approach comes to education via the design sciences developed by technological researchers. In considering the many technologies introduced into classrooms, Collins (1991) noted that remarkably little systematic knowledge has accumulated to guide the design of future innovations. He described the importance of developing "a methodology for carrying out design experiments, to study the different ways of using technology in classrooms and schools" (p. 17). Similarly, Newman (1990, 1991) argued for the usefulness of what he referred to as formative experiments. These new approaches are more akin to the design sciences of aeronautics and artificial intelligence than the analytic sciences of physics and psychology. That is, they seek to focus on what teaching and learning is going on as students interact in the context of a new program, rather than the more traditional question of whether certain programs are better or worse for certain types of learners or for certain types of content.

In a design experiment or a formative experiment, a researcher might, for example, identify two comparably effective teachers with differences in style of teaching (activity centers vs. whole-class instruction) who wish to teach a selected unit developed by the researchers. Assuming the teachers teach multiple classes, each would be asked to use the specially developed unit with half their classes and their own curriculum with the other half. Evaluation of the experiment might include pre- and posttests of student understanding, structured interviews with students, class observations, teacher daily notes, and follow-up after a year or two to determine student retention of learning and teacher practice. Such an approach holds the promise for addressing issues of practice and theory, as well as policy.

Although not yet a common evaluation approach in the field of literacy, several researchers have conducted evaluation research of this sort. Brown (1992) stated, "As a design scientist in my field, I attempt to engineer innovative educational environments and simultaneously conduct experimental studies of those innovations" (p. 141). Based on Newman's (1990) description of formative experiments, Reinking and colleagues (Reinking & Pickle; 1993; Reinking & Watkins, 1997) implemented a time-series evaluation through which they assessed ways in which multimedia book reviews could be enhanced to increase the independent reading of fourth graders. Instead of the conventional book review, Reinking and his collaborators developed a multimedia book review designed, because of its novelty, to enhance student involvement in reading. They collected baseline data on students' reading prior to the intervention, as well as measures of students attitudes toward reading, field observations, focus-group interviews, parent questionnaires, and teacher logs. Given this evidence, they discovered that the intervention had unanticipated effects on students' writing. One was that poor readers in one class avoided creating the multimedia book reviews, which they attributed to the public nature of the database. The solution they tried was to encourage all students to consider entering reviews of easy books for lower grade children to read. Although the implications of formative experiments and design experiments for practice are clear and immediate, their consequence for theory and policy will be easier to assess once more studies using this approach have been conducted and reported.

IMPLICATIONS FOR THEORY, PRACTICE, POLICY, AND RESEARCH

Debates about the use of experimental designs, interpretive data analysis, and formative approaches to evaluation continue. How can we design evaluation studies to be useful to multiple audiences at the local and policy levels, and how can evaluation studies provide information that can be useful to practice, policy, and theory? At the local, practice level, usefulness implies that the evaluation provides information about the program, its implementation, and its effectiveness for a specific classroom or a particular school with particular children. At the policy level, usefulness encompasses information about the program that can influence decision making, such as information about the benefits and costs of a program and its potential for alleviating a social problem. At the level of theoretical development, however, expectations have been more limited about whether evaluation studies could contribute to knowledge about teaching and learning. Because of the emphasis on usefulness to local and policy stakeholders, many evaluations have been atheoretical, unconcerned with how the information gathered in the evaluation of a particular program may help educational researchers think about issues of classroom learning and teaching.

The expense and importance of conducting evaluation research require attention to the design of evaluations that can contribute to theory, practice, and policy. Although it may be difficult to serve all three purposes, inattention to many of these issues has left the field in a crisis of credibility. Evaluation studies provide an important opportunity to work at the intersection of practice, theory, and policy because the research is inherently concerned with how an intervention "works" in a given context. These ideas are not new; August and Hakuta (1997), in a review of studies on educating language-minority children, called for similar measures to strengthen the research literature on this issue and to develop the potential for research to have a larger influence on public policy. As shown in the previous examples, a number of issues must be addressed in an evaluation in order to contribute to theory, practice, and policy.

First, the intervention and evaluation should both be grounded in theory. The intervention should have some demonstrated connection to literacy theory, which will in turn influence decisions about the design of the evaluation itself. For example, the data to be collected, whether involving tests and scales or observations and interviews, should be selected while keeping the nature of the intervention(s) in mind. One lesson from the early large-scale assessment studies is the danger of using measures that are not sensitive to the particular goals of the program.

Second, the question of "what works" is an important one for studying programmatic interventions, but needs to be modified. As Venezky (personal communication, 1997) wrote, the question should be "for whom does it work, and why?" The translation from theory to practice is not linear—information about the implementation of the intervention, how it works in a given setting, and whether teachers and students experience differential effects of the program (including unintended and potentially harmful effects) allows a deeper understanding not only of practice but also of how theory might be improved as a result of practice. The large-scale evaluation studies provide an example of the importance of understanding implementation issues. Knowing *if* the program works is not enough. How the program works, under what conditions, and for what particular students and teachers provides the information needed to contribute to theory, practice and policy.

Third, the study must be well designed, with attention to alternative explanations for results, and possible confounding factors. Campbell and Stanley (1963) and Cook and Campbell (1979) detailed these threats in experimental and quasi-experimental studies. Descriptive studies are not immune to these issues. Multiple sources of information allow a fuller description of the programmatic innovation, and decrease the risk of the evaluation missing other perspectives on the program. Although the goal of these studies may not be to generalize to a wide group, attention to competing views of the program increases the likelihood of assessing important outcomes and addressing implementation issues.

The development of evaluation research methods that can provide theoretically based knowledge to inform both practice and policy will continue. Recently, writing about evaluation and the relationship between research, policy, and practice focused on the importance of collaborations of participants at differing levels of the educational system. Patton (1997) summarized his theory of utilization-focused evaluation by emphasizing that evaluations should be driven by the intended use of the results for the intended users. As Hargreaves (1996) wrote, "Policy is therefore best secured ... through communities of people within and across schools who create policies, talk about them, process them, inquire into them, and reformulate them, bearing in mind the circumstances and the children they know best" (p. 115). For evaluation research to contribute to educational research, policy, and practice, we need both carefully designed studies and collaborative participation from all those who care about research, policy, and practice.

REFERENCES

Alvermann, D. E., O'Brien, D. G., & Dillon, D. R. (1990). What teachers do when they say they're having discussions of content area reading assignments: A qualitative analysis. *Reading Research Quarterly, 25,* 296–322.

August, D., & Hakuta, K. (1997). Program evaluation. In D. August & K. Hakuta (Eds.), *Educating language minority children* (pp. 55–71). National Research Council Institute of Medicine. Washington, DC: National Academy Press.

Beck, I. L., McKeown, M. G., Sandora, C., Kucan, L., & Worthy, J. (1996). Questioning the author: A yearlong classroom implementation to engage students with text. *Elementary School Journal, 96,* 385–414.

Bereiter, C., & Bird, M. (1985). Use of thinking aloud in identification and teaching of reading comprehension strategies. *Cognition and Instruction, 2,* 131–156.

Bond, G. L., & Dykstra, R. (1967). The Cooperative Research Program in first-grade reading instruction. *Reading Research Quarterly, 2,* 5–142.

Brock, C. (1997). Exploring the use of Book Club with second-language learners in mainstream classrooms. In S. I. McMahon, & T. E. Raphael (Eds.), *The Book Club connection: Literacy learning and classroom talk* (pp. 141–158). New York: Teachers College Press.

Brown, A. L. (1992). Design experiments: Theoretical and methodological challenges in creating complex interventions in classroom settings. *Journal of the Learning Sciences, 2,* 141–178.

Campbell, D. T. (1963). From description to experimentation: Interpreting trends as quasi-experiments. In C. W. Harris (Ed.), *Problems in measuring change* (pp. 212–242). Madison: University of Wisconsin Press.

Campbell, D. T. (1969). Reforms as experiments. *American Psychologist, 24,* 409–429.

Campbell, D. T., & Stanley, J. C. (1963). *Experimental and quasi-experimental designs for research.* Chicago: Rand McNally.

Chall, J. S. (1995). *Learning to read: The areas debate.* New York: McGraw-Hill. (Original work published 1968 and 1983)

Collins, A. (1991). Toward a design science of education. In E. Scanlon & T. O'Shea (Eds.), *New directions in educational technology* (pp. 15–22). New York: Springer-Verlag.

Cook, T. D., & Campbell, D. T. (1979). *Quasi-experimentation: Design and analysis issues for field settings.* Chicago: Rand McNally.

Cook, T. D., & Reichardt, C. S. (Eds.). (1979). *Qualitative and quantitative methods in evaluation research.* Beverly Hills, CA: Sage.

Cronbach, L. J. (1963). Course improvement through evaluation. *Teachers College Record, 64,* 672–684.

Dahl, K. L., & Freppon, P. A. (1995). A comparison of inner-city children's interpretations of reading and writing instruction in the early grades in skills-based and whole language classrooms. *Reading Research Quarterly, 30,* 50–74.

Dykstra, R. (1968). Summary of the second grade phase of the Cooperative Research Program in primary reading instruction. *Reading Research Quarterly, 4,* 49–70.

Eeds, M., & Wells, D. (1989). Grand conversations: An explanation of meaning construction in literature study groups. *Research in the Teaching of English, 23,* 4–29.

Eisner, E. W. (1991). *The enlightened eye: Qualitative inquiry and the enhancement of educational practice.* New York: Macmillan.

Gaskins, I. W., Anderson, R. C., Pressley, M., Cunicelli, E. A., & Sallow, E. (1993). Six teachers' dialogue during cognitive process instruction. *Elementary School Journal, 93,* 277–304.

Goldenberg, C. (1992). Instructional conversations: Promoting comprehension through discussion. *Reading Teacher, 46,* 316–326.

Guba, E. G., & Lincoln, Y. S. (1989). *Fourth generation evaluation.* Newbury Park, CA: Sage.

Guthrie, J. T., Van Meter, P., McCann, A. D., Wigfield, A., Bennett, L., Poundstone, C .C., Rice, M. E., Faibisch, F. M., Hunt, B., & Mitchell, A. M. (1996). Growth of literacy engagement: Changes in motivations and strategies during concept-oriented reading instruction. *Reading Research Quarterly, 31,* 306–332.

Guzzetti, B. J., & Williams, W. O. (1996). Gender, text, and discussion: Examining intellectual safety in the science classroom. *Journal of Research in Science Teaching, 22,* 5–20.

Hargreaves, A. (1996). Transforming knowledge: Blurring the boundaries between research, policy, and practice. *Educational Evaluation and Policy Analysis, 18,* 105–122.

Hickman, J. (1983). Everything considered: Response to literature in an elementary school setting. *Journal of Research and Development in Education, 16,* 8–13.

Hiebert, E. H. (1994). Reading Recovery in the United States: What difference does it make to an age cohort? *Educational Researcher, 23*(9), 15–25.

Hyman, H. H., Wright, C. R., & Hopkins, T. K. (1962). *Applications of methods of evaluation: Four studies of the encampment for citizenship.* Berkeley: University of California Press.

Lysynchuk, L. M., Pressley, M., d'Ailly, H., Smith, M., & Cake, H. (1989). A methodological analysis of experimental studies of comprehension strategy instruction. *Reading Research Quarterly, 24,* 458–470.

Marshall, J. D. (1987). The effects of writing on students' understanding of literary texts. *Research in the Teaching of English, 21,* 30–63.

McMahon, S. I. (1997). Reading in the Book Club program. In S. I. McMahon & T. E. Raphael (Eds.), *The Book Club connection* (pp. 47–68). New York: Teachers College Press.

Morrow, L. M., Pressley, M., Smith, J. K., & Smith, M. (1997). The effect of a literature-based program integrated into literacy and science instruction with children from diverse backgrounds. *Reading Research Quarterly, 32*, 55–76.

Neuman, S. B., & McCormick, S. (Eds.). (1995). Single-subject experimental research: *Applications for literacy.* Newark, DE: International Reading Association.

Newman, D. (1990). Opportunities for research on the organizational impact of school computers. *Educational Researcher, 19*, 8–13.

Newman, D. (1991). Formative experiments on the convolution of technology and the educational environment. In E. Scanlon & T. O'Shea (Eds.), *New directions in educational technology* (pp. 15–22). New York: Springer-Verlag.

Paris, S. G., & Oka, E. R. (1986). Children's reading strategies, metacognition, and motivation. *Developmental Review, 6*, 25–56.

Patton, M. Q. (1990). *Qualitative evaluation and research methods* (2nd ed.). London: Sage.

Patton, M. Q. (1997). *Utilization-focused evaluation* (3rd ed.). Thousand Oaks, CA: Sage.

Pearson, P. D. (1997). The First-Grade Studies: A personal reflection. *Reading Research Quarterly, 32*, 428–432.

Peterson, P. L. (1998). Why do educational research? Rethinking our roles and identified, our texts and contexts. *Educational Researcher, 27*(3), 4–10.

Pitman, M. A., & Maxwell, J. A. (1992). Qualitative approaches to evaluation: Models and methods. In M. D. LeCompte, W. L. Millroy, & J. Preissle (Eds.), *The handbook of qualitative research in education* (pp. 729–770). New York: Academic Press.

Pressley, M., El-Dinary, P. B., Gaskins, I., Schuder, T., Bergman, J., Almasi, L., & Brown, R. (1992). Beyond direct explanation: Transactional instruction of reading comprehension strategies. *Elementary School Journal, 92*, 511–554.

Pressley, M., & Harris, K. R. (1994). Increasing the quality of educational intervention research. *Educational Psychology Review, 6*, 191–208.

Reinking, D., & Pickle, J. M. (1993). Using a formative experiment to study how computers affect reading and writing in classrooms. In D. J. Leu & C. K. Kinzer (Eds.), *Examining central issues in literacy research, theory, and practice* (pp. 263–270). Chicago, IL: National Reading Conference.

Reinking, D., & Watkins, J. (1997). *Balancing change and understanding in literacy research through formative experiments.* Paper presented at the meeting of the National Reading Conference, Scottsdale, AZ.

Ridgeway, V. G., Dunston, P. J., & Qian, G. (1993). A methodological analysis of teaching and learning strategy research at the secondary school level. *Reading Research Quarterly, 28*, 335–349.

Robinson, V. M. J. (1998). Methodology and the research-practice gap. *Educational Researcher, 27*, 17–26.

Rose, T. L., & Beattie, J. R. (1986). Relative effects of teacher-directed and taped previewing on oral reading. *Learning Disabilities Quarterly, 9*, 193–199.

Saunders, W., O'Brien, G., Lennon, D., & McLean, J. (1998). Making the transition to English literacy successful: Effective strategies for studying literature with transition students. In R. Gersten & R. Jimenez (Eds.), *Effective strategies for teaching language minority students* (pp. 99–132). Belmont, CA: Wadsworth.

Siegel, M., & Fonzi, J. M. (1995). The practice of reading in an inquiry-oriented mathematics class. *Reading Research Quarterly, 30*, 632–673.

Shanahan, T., & Barr, R. (1995). Reading Recovery: An independent evaluation of the effects of an early instructional intervention for at risk learners. *Reading Research Quarterly, 30*, 958–996.

Smith, E. R., & Tyler, R. W. (1942). *Appraising and recording student progress.* New York: Harper & Row.

Smolkin, L. B., Yaden, D. B., Brown, L., & Hofius, B. (1992). The effects of genre, visual design choices, and discourse structure on preschoolers' responses to picture books during parent-child read-alouds. In C. K. Kinzer & D. J. Leu (Eds.), *Literacy research, theory and practice: Views from many perspectives* (pp. 291–301). Chicago: National Reading Conference.

Stake, R. E. (Ed.). (1975). *Evaluating the arts in education: A responsive approach.* Columbus, OH: Merrill.

Stallings, J. (1975). Implementation and child effects of teaching practices in Follow Through classrooms. *Monographs of the Society for Research in Child Development, 40.*

Stebbins, L. B., St. Pierre, R. G., Proper, E. G., Anderson, R. B., & Cerva, T. R. (1977). *Education as experimentation: A planned variation model. Vol. IV-A. An evaluation of Follow Through.* Cambridge, MA: Abt Associates.

Weiss, C. H. (1972). *Evaluation research: Methods for assessing program effectiveness.* Englewood Cliffs, NJ: Prentice Hall.

Willis, A. I., & Harris, V. J. (1997). Expanding the boundaries: A reaction to the First-Grade Studies. *Reading Research Quarterly, 32*, 439–445.

Wolf, R. M. (1990). *Evaluation in education: Foundations of competency assessment and program review* (3rd ed.). New York: Praeger.

Yaden, D. B. (1995). Reversal designs. In S. B. Neuman & S. McCormick (Eds.), *Single subject experimental research: Applications for literacy* (pp. 32–46). Newark, DE: International Reading Association.

CHAPTER 8

Undertaking Historical Research in Literacy

E. Jennifer Monaghan
Brooklyn College of the City University of New York

Douglas K. Hartman
University of Pittsburgh

VALUES OF STUDYING THE HISTORY OF LITERACY

The value of history has its own history. Called *historiodicy*, this justification of the study of the past has been an essential practice of historians for almost 3,000 years (Marrou, 1966). Their work has been shouted down, burned up, declared evil, proclaimed prophetic, forgotten, and ignored. It is this marginalization of historical work, especially as it relates to the literacy community, that moves us to sketch briefly several reasons why studying the history of literacy is of value (Moore, Monaghan, & Hartman, 1997).

The most time-honored rationale for knowing and doing history is that we can learn from the past. The challenge, however, is in knowing which lessons to draw on and how best to make use of them. Making straightforward, one-on-one applications of the past to the present can distort the unique dimensions of each event and lead to erroneous conclusions. Even judiciously constructed lessons are no guarantee of what to do or decide in the present. Thomas Jefferson, for example, wrote that the lessons of history were better for preventing a repeat of past follies than for divining wise future directions (cited in Gagnon, 1989, p. 113). So the pedagogical value of historical research on literacy is that it provides us with possible rather than probable understandings, and the ability to take precautions rather than control possible futures.

There are other reasons for undertaking historical work. One is that history provides yet another layer of context for understanding events by locating them in specific times and places. Understanding a particular reading method, for instance, requires more than simply knowing about it: It must be located in the milieu of its times. Moreover, historical research helps us to identify who we are as a community. History is a vital sign of any community's maturity, vitality, and growing self-awareness, and it provides the basis for a collective sense of direction and purpose. By creating a set of connections between past and present, we see ourselves as part of a drama larger than our own particular interests, areas of study, or organizational affiliations. As members of the reading community, in particular—a community that has neglected its own past—we need to gain a clearer picture of who we are by examining where we have been.

Historical research also promotes interdisciplinarity. To answer the questions that matter in our past brings us in contact with a wider circle of colleagues and their work, from librarians to antiquarians. In addition, studying history is intellectually enriching and challenging. The most thought-provoking history asks the "why" questions. Why did progressive education fail? Why did the *McGuffey Readers* become the most popular school readers of the 19th century? Why were women in colonial America taught to read, but less often to write? And why is the book shaped as it is? Answering questions like these forces us to theorize, search for and weigh evidence, make inferences, and draw conclusions. All social scientists do this, of course, but the work of history is especially adept at asking and answering questions that are not amenable to experimental, observational, or case study approaches. Finally, historical research is fun. What other discipline allows one to snoop into the concerns of others and label the product serious scholarly work?

Perhaps the biggest disadvantage associated with literacy history is that its messages for the present are equivocal. Indeed, this may have been why it has taken a profession wedded to presentism so long to embrace it.

A SHORT HISTORY OF HISTORIOGRAPHY

Not only do the values of history have a history, but the methods of doing history have one as well. Called *historiography*, this self-conscious practice of thinking about the development of historical scholarship traces the ways in which history has been undertaken back to the oldest known artifacts of human activity. The historical practices of early human beings were very different from those of today. By their oral telling of myths, legends, and fables, humans attempted to explain the unpredictable happenings of the world as products of supernatural causes. And their written records recounted long lists of deeds done in warfare, sometimes chronologically, but mostly in registers of isolated pieces of information that offered no interpretation or analysis (Butterfield, 1981).

Historical work took on some measure of analytic detachment with the Jews of ancient Israel. Their reports in the books of the Old Testament displayed a capacity for assembling information from many sources with an eye toward accurate appraisals, but their accounts were still primarily the product of religious experience rather than any kind of analytic inquiry (Momigliano, 1990).

The first move toward an analytic approach that looked into the facts and determined their accuracy was undertaken by the Greeks. Herodotus and Thucydides, for example, departed from the practice of explaining human events as the outcome of divine will and interpreted the human affairs of governance and warfare as the product of human wills. They did so by checking information against participant and eyewitness reports, consulting archived documents, and thinking carefully about the motivations and causations for actions and events. And when they wrote, they wrote to instruct others, anticipating parallel future circumstances that could be avoided or taken. The underlying assumption in all their work was that history repeated itself through endless cycles (Grant, 1970).

The Romans, influenced by the Greeks, further developed practices for writing biography and memoir. But the emerging Christian view of history that was taking hold within the Roman empire melded the religious and analytic historical practices of the past. Early on, Christians compiled the Gospels in such a way that their beliefs, grounded in what they held were actual occurrences, could be defended against challenges and used to display the continuities of the New Testament with the Old. Later they developed universalist histories that located all human activity under the hand of God from Creation, in Genesis, to Armageddon, in Revelation. These were followed by ecclesiastical histories that detailed the rise of Christianity throughout the Mediterranean world after the Roman Emperor Constantine converted in the fourth century (Gay & Cavanaugh, 1972).

But St. Augustine's *The City of God* provided the most influential statement of the Christian interpretation of history. He rejected outright the Greek idea of cyclical history movements and reframed history as a progression along a line with a clear beginning, middle, and end—from Creation, through this world, to the eternal world, as God worked out his will through history (Barker, 1982).

Augustine's method of using analytic tools within this religious framework was followed closely by medieval historians for 10 centuries. They faithfully informed readers of their information sources, but relied unquestioningly on information from earlier accounts, rarely using original sources to check and cross-check the accuracy of historical statements or the truthfulness of earlier assertions. To question the accuracy and motives of earlier historical accounts would be to question God's providence itself (Dahmus, 1982).

Historical methods in the modern age developed gradually from the 14th through the 19th centuries. The fundamental change entailed a shift away from supernatural explanations of history toward secular approaches (Breisach, 1983/1994). By the early 20th century, academic history had become completely secularized, and the history of the United States was viewed as a steady march toward perfection (American "triumphalism").

But, ironically, at a time when verification of sources was easier than it had ever been, the validity of historical knowledge itself came under public attack. Public confidence in history as the purveyor of "truth" yielded to skepticism, as younger historians presented conflicting versions of reality: Was Christopher Columbus the heroic seafarer of the older history or the purveyor of genocide of the new? Historians became aware of how their own predilections, and even language itself, influenced their scholarship.

Since the late 1950s, historians have moved through a succession of reconceptualizations of their craft. First came the new social history of the 1960s and 1970s, which made quantitative research the norm and the lives of the marginalized its target. Then followed, in the 1970s and 1980s, investigations of the intersections among history, language, and thought. These are associated with the work of Michel Foucault (1972), who insisted on the importance of discoursing about discourse, and with that of Jacques Derrida (1967/1976, 1978), who challenged the authority of text by positing that each reader reads (deconstructs) text differently. Both writers, in making language itself an object of study, cast doubt on language's ability to represent reality. Finally, the "postmodernism" of the 1990s elevated culture to a level of importance once held by the supernatural.

In response to these transformations of the field, Joyce Appleby urged, as do we, that historians of the new histories should continue to be "cultural translators," interpreting our past for consumers of history while new questions lead to new answers "through the mediating filter of culture" (Appleby, 1998, pp. 11, 12; cf. Appleby, Hunt, & Jacob, 1994).

AN ANALYSIS OF PAST METHODOLOGIES IN RESEARCHING THE HISTORY OF LITERACY

The historiography of literacy has been influenced by these shifting currents. Disciplines other than the reading professional community have approached the history of literacy in a variety of ways. The first, and oldest, of these have been histories of schooling, which discussed literacy within the larger framework of formal education and as a feature of American triumphalism (e.g., Cubberley, 1919/1934). The work, however, of Bernard Bailyn (1960) and Lawrence Cremin (1970, 1980, 1988) moved educational historians away from considering formal schooling as the chief agency of education toward including other educating agencies, such as churches, the community, and the family. (An ironic consequence has been a reduced interest on the part of educational historians in the role of schooling in literacy acquisition.)

A few decades later another group, generally known as "literacy historians," began to pursue a second, and different, approach, by applying the quantitative methodologies of the social historians to the topic of literacy. In order to discuss the relationship between literacy and society, they estimated the number of literates by comparing the proportion of those who could sign their names to a document with those who could only make a mark. The signature was hailed as a proxy for literacy: a uniform and quantifiable measure that was constant over time. This was more plausible during those centuries in which reading was taught at an earlier age than writing, so that reading acquisition could be inferred from signing ability. (For examples of discussions based mainly on signature counts, see Cressy, 1980, for 16th- and 17th-century England, and Lockridge, 1974, for colonial New England.)

The signature/mark approach, however, had its problems. Quite apart from the fact that, up to the 19th century, it seriously underestimated the number of those who could read even though they could not write (E. J. Monaghan, 1989), it only identified the minimally literate without showing how or why literates used their literacy. Nonetheless, the discovery of steadily increasing signature literacy up to the present time stimulated debates about the role played by literacy in different cultures. (For an overview, see Venezky, 1991.) Some historians have integrated signature counts into a variety of other sources in order to comment on popular culture (e.g., Vincent, 1989).

A third major approach has been to quantify not who was literate but what was read. The French historians of the "Annales school" provided the socioeconomic framework for the founders of the "histoire de livre" or history of the book, seeking, in Robert Darnton's words, to "discover the literary experience of ordinary readers" (1989, p. 28). Their number includes scholars such as Lucien Febvre and Henri-Jean Martin (1958/1976) and Roger Chartier (1994) in France, and Robert Darnton (1989) and David Hall (1996) in the United States. Book historians have examined what people read (numbers and kinds of books), paying particular interest to "low-culture" reading interests. This "history of the book" approach has now broadened its scope and fostered the investigation of all the links among books and their readers, from the creative act of the author, through the physical process of editing, publishing, and selling, to the book's reception by its reader. It has also sparked a series of publications on the history of the book in different countries (e.g., Amory & Hall, 2000).

The fourth and most recent trend, however, which represents a further evolution of the history of the book scholarship, has been an emphasis on a history of audiences (Rose, 1992). Studies of books alone rely for their generalizations on presumed or inferred effects upon readers, but historians now search for readers/writers who have reported on the meanings of their literacy. This approach is therefore dependent on qualitative data found in primary sources such as diaries, autobiographies, and letters. For instance, Barbara Sicherman (1989) used family letters and published memoirs to evaluate the role played by reading in the lives of the daughters of an upper-middle-class family at Fort Wayne, Indiana, in the late 19th century. This last approach, which ideally combines qualitative with quantitative data, may prove to be the prevalent one for some time to come for historians of the book.

LITERACY HISTORY AND THE READING RESEARCH COMMUNITY

There is now a large body of work on the history of reading and literacy, but most of it has been undertaken by scholars who are outside the reading research community. (For examples, see works cited in Moore, Monaghan, & Hartman, 1997.) In contrast to the historical approaches used by scholars from the social sciences and literature arenas, those in the reading professional community have used fewer and more limited approaches. The few reading researchers who have approached the history of literacy have traditionally done so through an examination of the textbooks used to teach reading (e.g.. Hoffman & Roser, 1987; Reeder, 1900; Robinson, Faraone, Hittleman, & Unruh, 1990; Smith, 1965).

The best known study of this kind remains that of Nila Banton Smith. Her study began as a published dissertation and received successive updates (1934, 1965, 1986). Although of value even today, Smith's work is inevitably a creature of its time. Her discussions of the contents of American reading instructional textbooks are innocent of any consideration of how literacy instruction has been mediated by gender, class, or race—themes that preoccupy contemporary historians.

Courses in the history of literacy created by reading professionals within schools of education have been influenced by the history of the book scholarship (e.g., Cranney & Miller, 1987), but this scholarship has yet to make a major impact on researchers in the reading professional community, in spite of Richard Venezky's call for a new history of reading instruction (1987b). In fact, little interest has been shown by most of the reading community in doing historical research, whatever the approach.

There are, however, a few important exceptions. Bernardo Gallegos's work (1992) on the links between literacy and society in early New Mexico used both qualitative and quantitative data—such as a letter by a friar describing how he taught the Indians and signature evidence from military enlistment papers. Allan Luke integrated content analysis into his history of the Canadian "Dick and Jane" experience (1988). Other studies have also demonstrated a broader scope of approach, especially in terms of sources and topics. They include biographical studies of well-known reading experts such as William S. Gray (Mavrogenes, 1985; H. M. Robinson, 1985) or Laura Zirbes (Moore, 1986); studies of the history of a particular reading methodology (Balmuth, 1982) or content area (Moore, Readence, & Rickelman, 1983); oral histories of teachers and students (Clegg, 1997), and studies of what literacy has meant to certain communities of readers (Weber, 1993). Moreover, Venezky's (1987a) review of the history of American readers sets them in a broad historical context.

UNDERTAKING HISTORICAL RESEARCH IN LITERACY

Notwithstanding these contributions, the history of literacy remains wide open to research by the reading community. Before we review these different approaches to the topic in more detail, it may be useful to clarify some terminology regarding sources.

Primary, Secondary, and Original Sources

It is important to distinguish between *primary* and *secondary* sources. Primary sources are documents or artifacts generated by the persons actually involved in, or contemporary to, the events under investigation. In this sense, a curriculum guide to reading instruction and a diary discussion of what the diarist's children are reading are both primary sources. Secondary sources are the products of those who try to make sense of primary sources—historians. But a source may be primary or secondary, depending on what the researcher is looking for. Smith's *American Reading Instruction* (1965), for instance, is obviously a secondary source: She wrote her history basing her generalizations mainly on the study of a large number of textbooks that she had personally examined. Her book could also, however, be used as a primary source: It would be an indispensable source if Smith herself and her views on reading instruction were the object of investigation.

The distinction also needs to be made between *primary* and *original* sources. It is by no means always necessary, and all too often it is not possible, to deal only with original sources. Printed copies of original sources, provided they have been undertaken with scrupulous care (such as the published letters of the Founding Fathers), are usually an acceptable substitute for their handwritten originals. Again, it depends on the researcher's purpose. If the researcher wishes to study the spelling of the founding fathers, a reproduction will do, but if the penmanship of the Founding Fathers is the object of study, no printed substitute will suffice. In either case, primary sources are the bedrock of historical research.

Historiographers generally use both primary and secondary sources. Although it is certainly possible to produce useful and important historical work based only on secondary sources (Balmuth, 1982, for instance, used mainly secondary sources), much of the excitement of historical work lies in entering the world of the past through primary sources, including those used by other historians before. Historical advances are made not only by using sources seldom used by others but by looking at familiar material in new ways—ways made possible because the world view of the researcher has changed from that of earlier historians. In the last four decades, for instance, we have come to appreciate the importance of gender, race, and class as constructs that have influenced literacy instruction.

Four Approaches to the Past

The four approaches to the past detailed next all use primary sources as their chief database. We have identified them as qualitative and quantitative approaches, content analysis, and oral history.

The first approach may be termed *qualitative*. This is what most laypersons think of as "history": the search for a story inferred from a range of written or printed evidence. The resultant written/published history is organized chronologically and presented as a factual tale: a tale of a person who created reading textbooks, such as a biography of William Holmes McGuffey (Sullivan, 1994) or of Lindley Murray and his family (C. Monaghan, 1998). The sources of qualitative history are various, ranging from manuscripts such as account books, school records, marginalia, letters, diaries, and memoirs to imprints such as textbooks, children's books, journals, and other books of the time period under consideration. In qualitative history, the researcher inevitably draws inferences from what is all too often an incomplete body of data and makes generalizations on the basis of relatively few pieces of evidence.

The second approach is *quantitative*. Here, rather than relying on "history by quotation," as the former approach has been pejoratively called, researchers deliberately look for evidence that lends itself to being counted and that is therefore presumed to have superior validity and generalizability. In literacy studies, as we noted earlier, a prime example of the quantitative approach has been the tabulation of signatures and marks to estimate the extent of literacy. Other researchers have sought to estimate the popularity of a particular textbook by tabulating the numbers printed, based on the author's copyright records (e.g., E. J. Monaghan, 1983). These studies seek to answer the question, among others, of "How many?" The assumption is that broader questions (e.g., the relationship between literacy and industrialization, or between textbooks and their influence on children) can then be addressed more authoritatively.

Armed with numbers, historians can perform statistical analyses to establish correlations, as did Soltow and Stevens (1981), between schooling and literacy.

A third approach is *content analysis*. Here the text itself is the object of scrutiny. This approach takes as its data published works (in the case of literacy history, these might be readers, penmanship manuals, or examples of children's literature) and subjects them to a careful analysis that usually includes both quantitative and qualitative aspects. Smith (1965), for example, paid attention to such quantitative features as the size of a given textbook, the proportion of illustration to text, and the number of pages devoted to different content categories. In contrast, Lindberg (1976) used a qualitative approach to draw implications from the changing contents of the *McGuffey Eclectic Readers* in successive editions and comment on topics such as their attitude to slavery or their shift in theological viewpoint. Content analysis has been particularly useful in investigating constructs such as race (e.g., Larrick, 1965; MacCann, 1998) or gender (Women on Words and Images, 1972).

All three of these approaches—qualitative, quantitative, and content—use written or printed text as their database. (For examples of all three approaches, see Kaestle, Damon-Moore, Stedman, Tinsley, & Trollinger, 1991.) In contrast, the fourth approach, *oral history*, turns instead to living memory. Oral historians ask questions of those who are willing to talk about the past. For instance, oral historians interested in literacy look for those who can remember their early schooling or teaching (e.g., Clegg, 1997). These four approaches are not, of course, mutually exclusive. (Most content analyses, for instance, involve tabulation.) Indeed, historians avail themselves of as many of these as their question, topic, and time period permit. Arlene Barry (1992) and Thecla Spiker (1997) both used all four approaches in their dissertations.

The integrative use of approaches is made possible because the nature of historical research cuts across all genres of approaches, all of which begin with the identification of a topic and the framing of a question.

Identifying the Topic/Framing the Question.   As in experimental research, the investigator has a question or problem that he or she wishes to answer or solve. (The classic beginner's mistake is to ask too large a question.) The complexity of the question and the breadth of the investigation are guided by the anticipated historiographical outcome—the written report.

Questions will be proportionate in scope to the anticipated length of the answer. One study asked what prominent variations of the phonics/whole-word debate in the late 1960s appeared in contemporary readers, but restricted its time frame to 5 years (Iversen, 1997). The result was a master's thesis. Another, probing deeper, asked what had led to the creation, development, and discontinuance of an entire textbook series, the *Cathedral Basic Readers*, over a half century (Spiker, 1997). Yet another asked how the inhabitants of a small, rural, midwestern community used printed information over a 30-year period (Pawley, 1996). Both these became doctoral dissertations. Other studies probed the professional life of a progressive reading educator, Laura Zirbes (Moore, 1986); the literacy of a small group of Wampanoag Indians (E. J. Monaghan, 1990); the family literacy of a particular 18th-century Boston family (E. J. Monaghan, 1991); and the meaning reading held for American farm wives at the turn of the 20th century (Weber, 1993). These, focusing intently on a limited topic, were all published in scholarly journals.

Identifying Undergirding Theories.   Just as social science researchers do, historians proceed from a theoretical position, whether this is articulated or not. Smith (1965), for instance, was heavily influenced by the measurement movement of her time: She provided considerable detail on the size of the textbooks she studied, the number of their pages, how many pages were devoted to which topic, and so forth. Today, literacy historians are much more likely to be explicit about their theoretical positions, and invoke, say, modernization theory, or their stances on gender, race, and class, as the theories undergirding their approach.

A related issue is researcher stance. All of us are located within the particular perspectives of our own time and setting, and it might appear that if we are explicit about where we come from, this will militate against the possibility of observer bias. However, what we are looking for dictates what we will find. Some studies clearly have a particular perspective that may slant the conclusions drawn and even restrict the data considered worthy of study. Some authors pursue particular goals—heroic ones such as using history "to provide a sense of legitimacy for those who seek a different kind of literacy" (Shannon, 1990, p. x), or, at the other end of the political spectrum, political ones such as promoting a conservative agenda (e.g., Blumenthal, 1973). Any predetermined agenda runs the risk of slanting the evidence to its own needs. What emerges may be "the truth," but it is less likely to be close to "the whole truth," even if there were such a thing, because it may not do justice to opposing points of view.

Identifying and Locating Potential Sources.   Although, for simplicity of exposition, we have discussed the issue of the researcher's question/problem first, there are in fact strictly practical decisions that affect the choice of topic from the outset—namely, where are the sources to be found? If most of the relevant sources are half a continent away, the practical difficulties of expense and time will preclude a particular topic, however appealing it is to the researcher. Most historical research takes place in the manuscript and rare book rooms of public, private, and university libraries or at state and town historical societies, so the researcher has to have the time and money to get there. Considerations like these may guide the researcher to one approach rather than another: A content analysis of a textbook owned by the author, housed in a local library, or amenable to photocopying, for instance, may be more feasible than attempting a biography of an author whose letters and records are housed on the other side of the country. (See http://www.historyliteracy.org/research/archives/index.html for archives relating to the history of literacy.)

As researchers debate the merits of potential topics, they need to make an initial mental survey of all the possible relevant primary sources. In terms of manuscripts, are there any letters, diaries, or journals written by the target person or related to the target topic? What about school records at the local, town, or state level? What exists in printed form? Have any of the manuscripts been published? Are there schoolbooks, children's books, contemporary educational journals, contemporary books? Where are they, and how can access be obtained? Are there still people alive who would remember the event or the person or the book or the approach being investigated?

Fortunately, problems of access to the written/printed word are diminishing as time passes. Access to materials housed in distant libraries is being increasingly provided by interlibrary loans, photocopies, and microfilms. A collection of 844 primers and other introductory reading materials is available in microfiche form (*American Primers*, 1990; Venezky, 1990), and textbooks are being put on microfilm at Harvard University. And now there is the Internet, where the World Wide Web has already given access to works not restricted by copyright protection. The obverse of this coin is that immediate access to the original manuscripts is also diminishing—and with it some of the pleasure of the research. There is no emotional substitute for reading the original letter, with its faded ink on a yellowed page, removed from the hand that penned it only by the passage of time.

The ease of finding sources once again depends on the topic. The names of persons are by far the easiest to research: They are always indexed by libraries, particularly if a person is well known. A search for material on, say, William Holmes McGuffey will produce a wealth of entries. Subjects such as "adult reading" are far harder to research, for they may not be listed under the rubric one expects—or they may not be catalogued at all. This is where a reference librarian is indispensable in guiding the novice to the relevant Library of Congress subject headings or to key words to be used in the search. Nowadays, posting a request for help on an Internet listserv (such as the History of Reading Special Interest Group of the International Reading Association's HoRSIG or the Society for the History of Authorship, Reading and Publishing's SHARP-L) can recruit informed others in your search for relevant sources. In addition, a comprehensive bibliography of historical sources in American reading education for the 1900–1970 period is under preparation (R. D. Robinson, in press).

Once the topic has been pinned down, what is equivalent to the literature review of experimental research should begin. Dissertations are a key resource here, along with articles and books. Secondary sources will normally provide clues that will lead back to more primary sources.

Much is made, in some of the few "how-to" pages on historical research that are occasionally included in textbooks on undertaking educational research, of establishing the authenticity of the sources, refusing to accept any but triangulated sources, and so on. In fact, although the question of authenticity is certainly important, and forgeries do turn up from time to time, in general the authentication of sources has already been undertaken by experts at the libraries where the documents are housed. And in most cases, triangulation is neither possible nor desirable.

Collecting and Recording the Data.   Now, armed with a wish list of what you want to explore, precise information on where it is, and your professional identification for easy library admission, comes the time for data collection. Although the old method was to record the relevant material in pencil (because all manuscript/rare book rooms prohibit the use of pens), usually by copying selected passages for later analysis, the advances in computerization of libraries—and the computer skills of scholars—over the past few years are making this obsolete. Many libraries are equipped with electric outlets for laptop computers. (It is prudent to call ahead and bring old-fashioned equipment in case all the outlets are in use.) Data collected electronically has the great advantage of only needing to be entered once. Note-taking, filing, and organizing are all made easier by the aid of the word processor. Scanning an original text into your own computer with a hand scanner may be the next technological leap.

Material taken down by hand, of course, will have to be entered into a computer at a later date. If you prefer the hand route, or if the absence of electrical outlets mandates it, think carefully about the surface on which you plan to record data. Many historians used to use large 5 by 7 inch note cards, which helped organize data by topic. One major drawback of these was that, at the same time, the chronology and sequence of the data were lost. An approach that preserves both of these is to record everything in a notebook or on numbered sheets of paper, and then index it all topically (most efficiently done on a word processor) at your workplace. It is also helpful to record the date and place of a given piece of research at the top of each page of notes.

Here are some more practical hints. First, it can be helpful, and especially so if your topic is obscure, to alert the librarian ahead of time to your research interests, so that the librarian can be thinking about sources for you, as well as confirm whether you can use your laptop. Second, always bring with you to the library all the equipment that you need on the spot. Libraries of historical societies, in particular, may be sited in neighborhoods that have few computer supply or stationery stores nearby. Manuscript rooms will provide you with the occasional pencil (and a pencil sharpener is always on site), but not paper.

Third, treat every entry as if this is the last time you will ever set eyes on it. Although it is relatively easy to backtrack one's bibliographical omissions for books, it is much harder to figure out what collection a manuscript came from. In fact, even with the manuscript in front of you, you may not be able to tell. Record all the identifying material on something that will not be surrendered to the librarian *before* you hand in your request slip. Fourth, pay lavishly for photocopying and—the latest technology, which allows for the reproduction of pages from books too fragile to be subjected to the rigors of xeroxing—computer scanning. Better yet, see if you can borrow the text itself through interlibrary loan, or purchase a contemporary reproduction. Nothing is more helpful than having the text in your possession at your own workspace.

The collection of oral histories deserves a chapter to itself. Here we can only note that there are particular challenges, as well as joys, for the researcher who relies on the memories of the living as his or her sources. Memories are fallible, and cross-verification often difficult to obtain. The resultant data, however, may be of such intrinsic interest or charm that researchers often publish their reminiscences with little interpretation (e.g., Terkel, 1970), so providing, in essence, primary sources for further study.

Oral history takes much more time than one would think. The next technological breakthrough, already underway, will be the translation of speech directly into print; until this is perfected, however, painstaking transcription by hand from the audiotape is the only method available. For detailed information, including legal caveats, we suggest joining the Oral History Association (see the Research Resources of the web page of the History of Reading Special Interest Group of the International Reading Association, 1999, for professional associations relevant to historians of literacy). There are also tips and bibliographies on oral history that have been prepared by reading researchers (e.g., King & Stahl, 1991; Stahl, Hynd, & Henk, 1986; Stahl, King, Dillon, & Walker, 1994).

Interpreting the Data.   Once the work of data collection is completed—or, more accurately, you have called a halt to it—the work of analysis begins. Sources should not be taken at face value.

Two kinds of analysis are necessary. The first is an analysis of internal aspects of the data. This is the point at which one detects bias within the sources themselves. Given the self-serving nature of our species, autobiographies and diaries need particular scrutiny. Oral histories, too, pose unusual problems of verification, because the data provided are removed at a distance of time of perhaps as much as a half century from the period under investigation, and are filtered through the fallible and limited human memory.

The second kind of analysis is external to the sources themselves: It is the work of interpretation and organization. Historical research can be considered a kind of anthropology of the past. The historian looks for patterns and themes, and compares, combines, and selects material that will support generalizations and answer the questions or problems that motivated the study. No matter what questions the study began with, others will inevitably arise from the data itself. If the initial focus of the study changes with any newfound information, it is well worth the effort to pursue the new direction.

Communicating Interpretations/Writing the Results.   What historians discover as they pore over their data commits them to one kind of organization over another. Organization can be a function of the source's chronology, as is the case in a biography; or it may be both chronological and conceptual, with the topics that emerged later in time also appearing later in the book; or it could be largely topical. Given that so much history is a study of causes and effects, and that cause always animates effect, the chronological element will undergird the telling of the history.

Once the organization is in place and writing begun, the social science researcher must confront issues of documentation. The purpose of documentation is to allow readers of the history to scrutinize, if they choose, the actual sources, in order to satisfy themselves that a particular source has been invoked in a way that accurately reflects its content. Reading researchers are comfortable and familiar with the American Psychological Association (APA) style (used, in fact, throughout this volume), which simply cites author and date within the body of the text and provides the complete reference at the end. As an adequate reference system in the writing of history, however, APA has several severe disadvantages. APA does have a mechanism for direct quotation, but if the historian has paraphrased instead of quoting, the standard APA procedure is simply to refer to the entire book. In these cases the reader has to search through the whole book to find the few relevant pages. There is also no short way, in APA, to cite manuscripts. And over and above these technical objections, there are aesthetic and cognitive ones: Within-text citations encumber the text greatly. Some paragraphs in a historical text or even individual sentences are based not on one source but on many; citing them in APA style produces a visual clutter that distracts greatly from the meaning and stylistic integrity of the writing.

This explains why historians document their assertions by using numbered notes, which appear as superscripts in the body of the text and are fully referenced in footnotes or endnotes. *The Chicago Manual of Style* (1993), now in its 14th edition, or some variation of it is by far the most popular style sheet for historical work. Footnotes are out of favor these days; instead, endnotes appear at the end of the work.

Nonetheless, the APA habit is so strong that the great majority of theses and dissertations sponsored by schools of education have used the APA style. We recommend that dissertation chairs advocate historical referencing for historical writing and support their students in doing battle with the establishment on its behalf.

Publication.   The final objective of historical research is, as in behavioral research, publication. Although historical research is still a fledgling enterprise among reading researchers, several studies that began as theses or dissertations within the reading community have reached the pages of literacy journals or appeared in book form. For example, Barry's article (1994) on high school remedial reading programs and Gallegos' book (1992) on literacy and society in early New Mexico both stem from doctoral dissertations. Books on the history of reading are often published by university presses (Association of American University Presses, 1999). There is unquestionably a market out there for historical work.

FINAL WORD

The time for historical research in reading to take its rightful place with other methodologies is, in our opinion, long overdue. There is a need to site reading history within the larger contexts of its times. But it is not easy to become a good historian overnight. Those who wish to pursue this genre of research should consider sitting in on a course on historical methods given at their own institution and joining appropriate historical societies. We particularly recommend the History of Reading Special Interest Group of the International Reading Association, which supports a web page, www.historyliteracy.org, that offers many research resources.

REFERENCES

Amory, H., & Hall, D. D. (Eds.). (2000). *A history of the book in America. Vol. 1: The colonial book in the Atlantic world.* Cambridge: Cambridge University Press & American Antiquarian Society.

American Primers. (1990). (Microform.) Frederick, MD: University Publications of America.

Appleby, J. (1998). The power of history. *American Historical Review, 103,* 1–14.

Appleby, J., Hunt, L., & Jacob, M. (1994). *Telling the truth about history.* New York: Norton.

Association of American University Presses. (1999). *Association of American University Presses: Directory, 1999–2000.* New York: Author.

Bailyn, B. (1960). *Education in the forming of American society: Needs and opportunities*. Chapel Hill, NC: Institute of Early American History and Culture.

Balmuth, M. (1982). *The roots of phonics: A historical introduction*. New York: McGraw-Hill.

Barker, J. (1982). *The superhistorians: Makers of our past*. New York: Charles Scribner.

Barry, A. (1992). *The evolution of high school remedial reading programs in the United States*. Unpublished doctoral dissertation, University of Wisconsin, Madison.

Barry, A. L. (1994). The staffing of high school remedial reading programs in the United States since 1920. *Journal of Reading, 38*, 14–22.

Blumenthal, S. L. (1973). *The new illiterates—And how you can keep your children from becoming one*. New Rochelle, NY: Arlington House.

Breisach, E. (1994). *Historiography: Ancient, medieval, and modern*, (2nd ed.). Chicago: University of Chicago. (Original work published 1983)

Butterfield, H. (1981). *The origins of history*. New York: Basic Books.

Chartier, R. (1994). *The order of books: Readers, authors and libraries in Europe between the fourteenth and eighteenth centuries* (L. G. Cochrane, Trans.). Stanford, CA: Stanford University Press.

Chicago Manual of Style (14th ed.). (1993). Chicago: University of Chicago Press.

Clegg, L. B. (1997). *The empty schoolhouse: Memories of one-room Texas schools*. College Station: Texas A & M University Press.

Cranney, A. G., & Miller, J. [A]. (1987). History of reading: Status and sources of a growing field. *Journal of Reading, 30*, 388–398.

Cremin, L. A. (1970). *American education: The colonial experience, 1607–1783*. New York: Harper & Row.

Cremin, L. A. (1980). *American education: The national experience, 1783–1876*. New York: Harper & Row.

Cremin, L. A. (1988). *American education: The metropolitan experience, 1876–1980*. New York: Harper & Row.

Cressy, D. (1980). *Literacy and the social order: Reading and writing in Tudor and Stewart England*. New York: Cambridge University Press.

Cubberley, E. P. (1934). *Public education in the United States: A study and interpretation of American educational history* (Rev. ed.). Boston: Houghton Mifflin. (Original work published 1919)

Dahmus, J. H. (1982). *Seven medieval historians: An interpretation and a bibliography*. Chicago: Nelson Hall.

Darnton, R. (1989). What is the history of books? In C. N. Davidson (Ed.), *Reading in America: Literature and social history* (pp. 27–52). Baltimore, MD: Johns Hopkins University Press.

Derrida, J. (1976). *Of grammatology* (G. C. Spivak, Trans.). Baltimore, MD: Johns Hopkins University Press. (Original work published 1967)

Derrida, J. (1978). *Writing and difference* (A. Bass, Trans.). Chicago: University of Chicago Press.

Febvre, L. P. V., & Martin, H. -J. (1976). *The coming of the book: The impact of printing 1450–1800*. London: N.L.B. (Original work published 1958)

Foucault, M. (1972). *The archaeology of knowledge* (A. M. S. Smith, Trans.). New York: Pantheon.

Gagnon, R. (1989). *Historical literacy: The case for history in American education*. New York: Collier Macmillan.

Gallegos, B. P. (1992). *Literacy, education, and society in New Mexico, 1693–1821*. Albuquerque: University of New Mexico Press.

Gay, P., & Cavanaugh, G. J. (1972). *Historians at work: From Herodotus to Froissart* (Vol. 1). New York: Harper & Row.

Grant, M. (1970). *The ancient historians*. New York: Charles Scribner.

Hall, D. D. (1996). *Cultures of print: Essays in the history of the book*. Amherst: University of Massachusetts Press.

History of Reading Special Interest Group of the International Reading Association. (1999). *History of Literacy* [Online]. Available: http://www.historyliteracy.org.

Hoffman, J. V., & Roser, N. (Eds.). (1987). The basal reader in American reading instruction [Special issue]. *Elementary School Journal, 87*(3).

Iversen, S. J. (1997). *Initial reading instruction in United States' schools: An exploratory examination of the history of the debate between whole-word and phonic methods, 1965 through 1969*. Unpublished Master's thesis, Ohio State University.

Kaestle, C. F., Damon-Moore, H., Stedman, L. C., Tinsley, K., & Trollinger, W. V., Jr. (1991). *Literacy in the United States: Readers and reading since 1880*. New Haven, CT: Yale University Press.

King, J. R., & Stahl, N. A. (1991). Oral history as a critical pedagogy: Some cautionary issues. In B. L. Hayes & K. Camperell (Eds.), *Yearbook of the American Reading Forum, 11*, 219–226.

Larrick, N. (1965, September 11). The all-white world of children's books. *Saturday Review*, pp. 63–65, 84–85.

Lindberg, S. W. (1976). *The annotated McGuffey: Selections from the McGuffey Eclectic Readers, 1836–1920*. New York: Van Nostrand Reinhold.

Lockridge, K. A. (1974). *Literacy in colonial New England: An enquiry into the social context of literacy in the early modern West*. New York: Norton.

Luke, A. (1988). *Literacy, textbooks and ideology: Postwar literacy and the mythology of Dick and Jane*. New York: Falmer.

MacCann, D. (1998). *White supremacy in children's literature: Characterizations of African Americans, 1830–1900*. New York: Garland.

Marrou, H. I. (1966). *The meaning of history* (R. J. Olsen, Trans.). Baltimore, MD: Helicon.

Mavrogenes, N. A. (1985). William S. Gray: The person. In J. A. Stevenson (Ed.), *William S. Gray: Teacher, scholar, leader* (pp. 1–23). Newark, DE: International Reading Association.

Momigliano, A. (1990). *The classical foundations of modern historiography.* Berkeley, CA: University of California Press.

Monaghan, C. (1998). *The Murrays of Murray Hill.* Brooklyn, NY: Urban History Press.

Monaghan, E. J. (1983). *A common heritage: Noah Webster's blue-back speller.* Hamden, CT: Archon Books.

Monaghan, E. J. (1989). Literacy instruction and gender in colonial New England. In C. N. Davidson (Ed.), *Reading in America: Literature and social history* (pp. 53–80). Baltimore, MD: Johns Hopkins University Press.

Monaghan, E. J. (1990). "She loved to read in good Books": Literacy and the Indians of Martha's Vineyard, 1643–1725. *History of Education Quarterly, 30,* 493–521.

Monaghan, E. J. (1991). Family literacy in early 18th-century Boston: Cotton Mather and his children. *Reading Research Quarterly, 26,* 342–370.

Moore, D. W. (1986). Laura Zirbes and progressive reading instruction. *Elementary School Journal, 86,* 663–672.

Moore, D. W., Monaghan, E. J., & Hartman, D. K. (1997). Values of literacy history. *Reading Research Quarterly, 32,* 90–102.

Moore, D. W., Readence, J. E., & Rickelman, R. J. (1983). An historical exploration of content area reading instruction. *Reading Research Quarterly, 18,* 419–438.

Pawley, C. (1996). *Reading on the middle border: The culture of print in Osage, Iowa, 1870–1900.* Unpublished doctoral dissertation, University of Wisconsin.

Reeder, R. R. (1900). *The historical development of school readers and of method in teaching reading.* New York: Macmillan.

Robinson, H. M. (1985). William S. Gray: The scholar. In J. A. Stevenson (Ed.), *William S. Gray: Teacher, scholar, leader* (pp. 24–36). Newark, DE: International Reading Association.

Robinson, H. A., Faraone, V., Hittleman, D. R., & Unruh, E. (1990). *Reading comprehension instruction, 1783–1987: A review of trends and research.* Newark, DE: International Reading Association.

Robinson, R. D. (in press). *Historical sources in U.S. reading education: 1900–1970.* Newark, DE: Internatinal Reading Association.

Rose, J. (1992). Rereading the English common reader: A preface to a history of audiences. *Journal of the History of Ideas, 51,* 47–70.

Shannon, P. (1990). *The struggle to continue: Progressive reading instruction in the United States.* Portsmouth, NH: Heinemann.

Sicherman, B. (1989). Sense and sensibility: A case study of women's reading in late-Victorian America. In C. N. Davidson (Ed.), *Reading in America: Literature and social history* (pp. 201–225). Baltimore, MD: Johns Hopkins University Press.

Smith, N. B. (1934). *American reading instruction: Its development and its significance in gaining a perspective on current practices in reading.* New York: Silver, Burdett.

Smith, N. B. (1965). *American reading instruction.* Newark, DE: International Reading Association.

Smith, N. B. (1986). *American reading instruction* (Prologue by L. Courtney, FSC, and epilogue by H. A. Robinson). Newark, DE: International Reading Association.

Soltow, L., & Stevens, E. (1981). *The rise of literacy and the common school in the United States: A socioeconomic analysis to 1870.* Chicago: University of Chicago Press.

Spiker, T. M. W. (1997). *Dick and Jane go to church: A history of the Cathedral Basic Readers.* Unpublished doctoral dissertation, University of Pittsburgh.

Stahl, N. A., Hynd, C. R., & Henk, W. A. (1986). Avenues for chronicling and researching the history of college reading and study skills instruction. *Journal of Reading, 29,* 334–341.

Stahl, N. A., King, J. R., Dillon, D., & Walker, J. R. (1994). The roots of reading: Preserving the heritage of a profession through oral history projects. In E. G. Sturtevant & W. M. Linek (Eds.), *Pathways for literacy: Learners teach and teachers learn. The sixteenth yearbook of the College Reading Association* (pp. 15–24). Commerce, TX: College Reading Association.

Sullivan, D. P. (1994). *William Holmes McGuffey: Schoolmaster to the nation.* Rutherford, NJ: Fairleigh Dickinson University Press.

Terkel, S. (1970). *Hard times: An oral history of the Great Depression.* New York: Pantheon.

Venezky, R. L. (1987a). A history of the American reading textbook. *Elementary School Journal, 87,* 247–265.

Venezky, R. L. (1987b). Steps toward a modern history of reading instruction. In E. Z. Rothkopf (Ed.), *Review of research in education* (Vol. 13, pp. 129–167). Washington, DC: American Educational Association.

Venezky, R. L. (1990). *American primers: Guide to the microfiche collection; Introductory essay.* Frederick, MD: University Publications of America.

Venezky, R. L. (1991). The development of literacy in the industrialized nations of the West. In R. Barr, M. L. Kamil, P. B. Mosenthal, & P. D. Pearson (Eds.). *Handbook of reading research* (Vol. II, pp. 46–67). New York: Longman.

Vincent, D. (1989). *Literacy and popular culture: England, 1750–1914.* New York: Cambridge University Press.

Weber, R. (1993). Even in the midst of work: Reading among turn-of-the-century farmers' wives. *Reading Research Quarterly, 28,* 293–302.

Women on Words and Images. (1972). *Dick and Jane as victims: Sex stereotyping in children's readers.* Princeton, NJ: Author.

CHAPTER 9

Narrative Approaches

Donna E. Alvermann
University of Georgia

> *The telling of stories can be a profound form of scholarship moving serious study close to the frontiers of art.*
>
> — Joseph Featherstone (1989, p. 377)

Presently researchers in the social sciences are engaged in the telling of stories[1] that span a range of narrative approaches (e.g., autobiography, autoethnographies, biography, personal narratives, life histories, oral histories, memoirs, and literary journalism). A growing number of these researchers (e.g., Lawrence-Lightfoot & Davis, 1997; Richardson, 1993, 1997) are writing their storied narratives in ways that combine empirical and aesthetic descriptions of the human condition, thus pushing at "the frontiers of art" to which Featherstone earlier alluded. Still others (e.g., Denzin, 1997; hooks, 1991) are critiquing the notion that one should ever rightfully assume the authority to tell other people's stories. This chapter is about these researchers and their work, as well as the work of other researchers who use narrative approaches to study literacy. It is also about issues that currently encompass narrative inquiry as a way of knowing and writing, and the implications of such issues for research and practice in the field of literacy education.

Thematically speaking, the issues discussed in this chapter cluster around what is commonly referred to as the *postmodern* or *poststructural critique* of narrative inquiry. This critique is concerned primarily with three major issues—those dealing with subjectivity, truth claims, and representation. Although the term *postmodern* is troublesome in some circles, Marcus's (1994) assessment of the situation is that theorists in the social sciences have absorbed much of postmodernism's preoccupation with these

---

[1]Following Polkinghorne (1995), I use the term *story* in the sense of a storied narrative that combines a succession of events that are alleged to have occurred. Polkinghorne's definition of a storied narrative is "the linguistic form that preserves the complexity of human action with its interrelationship of temporal sequence, human motivation, chance happenings, and changing interpersonal and environmental contexts" (p. 7).

three issues without necessarily laying claim to its label.[2] For example, present interest in subjectivity and the turn toward self-critical reflexivity mark a departure from earlier times when it was simply assumed that researchers would strive to maintain a distance between the knower (narrator) and the known (narrated). Similarly, researchers are having to rethink what it means to be concerned about truth claims when aspects of the global are now encompassed by the local—when "the scientist and the artist are both claiming that *in the particular resides the general*" (Lawrence-Lightfoot, 1997, p. 14). Finally, the current interest in re-presenting others' representations marks a departure from a time when researchers could count on the fact that discovering new truths was valued over gaining critical insights into existing interpretations.

Before examining these issues in greater depth and the implications they hold for literacy research and practice, I first situate narrative inquiry historically. After that, I provide several examples of how literacy researchers are using this form of inquiry to understand their own lives and the lives of others whom they study both in and out of school.

NARRATIVE INQUIRY: FROM PAST TO PRESENT

What counts as narrative inquiry varies widely across researchers and those who critique their work. Although there are traces of various forms of narrative mixing with philosophy as early as the 18th century (Lawrence-Lightfoot & Davis, 1997), narrative inquiry as a method of analysis is thought to have taken hold during the 20th century with the Russian formalists' study of fairy tales and Levi-Strauss's analysis of myths (Manning & Cullum-Swan, 1994). More recent work, often referred to as the "new narrative research" (Casey, 1995, p. 211), focuses specifically on lives and lived experience. In this chapter, I use the term *narrative inquiry* to refer to a variety of research practices ranging from those that tell a story of how individuals understand their actions through oral and written accounts of historical episodes (Riessman, 1993) to those that explore certain methodological aspects of storytelling (Richardson, 1997).

Narrative inquiry's recent emphasis on how people understand themselves and their experiences began in the mid 1970s, according to Bruner (1986), when "the social sciences had moved away from their traditional positivist stance towards a more interpretive posture" (p. 8). The move toward a teller's point of view has not been limited to storytelling in the strict linguistic sense of the term. For example, some narratives have neither protagonists nor culminating events, but instead depict snapshots of past events that are linked thematically. Others depict the interconnectedness and meaning of seemingly random activities that social groups perform as part of daily living (Polkinghorne, 1988; Riessman, 1993).

There has been a tendency of late among education researchers to elevate narrative inquiry, especially that dealing with teachers' thinking and collaborative research, to new heights—to what some would say is a privileged way of knowing. This practice continues to draw criticism from both teacher educators (e.g., Carter, 1993; de la Luna & Kamberelis, 1997) and research methodologists (e.g., Constas, 1998; Emihovich, 1995). Presently the more general critique of narrative inquiry, however, has focused on issues made increasingly visible by the postmodern turn and its preoccupation with the loss of innocence in academic writing. For example, researchers working from a postmodernist narrative perspective are becoming more critically reflexive in locating their own subjectivities in the stories they write. Richardson (1997) captured the gist of this critique in her questioning of the academy's adherence to outdated canons of writing practices:

---

[2] Although internal critiques of research traditions typically associated with the natural sciences had already begun in literature, history, sociology, anthropology, philosophy, and law before the advent of postmodernity in the early 1980s, Marcus (1994) argued that it took postmodernism's intersection with those developing critiques to both radicalize and consolidate them.

We are restrained and limited by the kinds of cultural stories available to us. Academics are given the "story line" that the "I" should be suppressed in their writing, that they should accept homogenization and adopt the all-knowing, all-powerful voice of the academy. But contemporary philosophical thought raises problems that exceed and undermine the academic story line. We are always present in our texts, no matter how we try to suppress ourselves. (p. 2)

Similar critiques related to the twin crises of legitimation (truth claims) and representation abound (Britzman, 1995; Denzin, 1994, 1997; Lather & Smithies, 1997; Lenzo, 1995; Tierney & Lincoln, 1997). In one form or another, these same issues occupy the very center of researchers' thinking in a variety of disciplines that use narrative inquiry as a way of understanding life and lived experiences (Cortazzi, 1993). However, in keeping with this handbook's focus, the examples of narrative approaches that I include in the next chapter section are limited to those involving literacy research. In an effort to avoid overlapping with other chapters in the handbook that focus on teacher research, case studies, and ethnographic approaches, I have omitted literacy teachers' memoirs (e.g., Hankins, 1998), first- and second-hand accounts of teachers' classroom literacy experiences (Cochran-Smith & Lytle, 1993; Lalik, Dellinger, & Druggish, 1996), and ethnographic accounts of literacy teaching and learning (Allen, Michalove, & Shockley, 1993; Dyson, 1997; Fishman, 1988; Heath, 1983). The examples that are included illustrate how literacy researchers are presently using narrative inquiry to understand their own lives and the lived experiences of others.

UNDERSTANDING LIVES AND LIVED EXPERIENCE THROUGH STORYTELLING

We must lay in waiting for ourselves.
Throughout our lives.
Abandoning the pretense that we know.

— William F. Pinar (1976a, p. viii)

This quotation from Pinar's introduction to a book he coauthored with Madeleine Grumet (Pinar & Grumet, 1976) on curriculum reform aptly illustrates a central need in the stories we tell about ourselves—namely, the need to be vigilant in recovering the forgotten or suppressed memories that are the autobiographical antecedents of our professional lives. Kathryn Au, whose research focuses on how students of diverse backgrounds become literate while maintaining a connection to their cultural identities, recalled the following childhood memory in a chapter she wrote for Neumann and Peterson's (1997) edited volume on the life histories of notable women researchers in education. In Au's (1997) words:

Until I was a teenager, I spent all of my summer vacations at the house in Paia [the location of a Hawaiian sugar plantation on which Au's maternal grandfather, Hew Sing Cha, worked as a cook and baker]. After dinner, Grandmother Hew and the adult relatives often 'talked story,' reminiscing and gossiping in a mixture of Hakka and English. My grandmother was a skillful storyteller with an excellent memory, and others in the circle often turned to her with questions. As a child I did not participate in these discussions, but I developed an appreciation for uses of language and literacy that did not necessarily involve English or a printed text. (p. 74)

In a later section that dealt with her development as a researcher, Au (1997) told of an incident that led her to hypothesize a connection between Hawaiian children's lively interactive styles in reading circle and the talk-story style of communicating that she had observed while seated among her adult relatives in her Grandmother Hew's house. Au wrote:

> My attitudes toward schooling and literacy were shaped by the experiences of family members.... As a Chinese American with an interest in my own cultural heritage, I have explored avenues of bringing students to high levels of literacy through forms of class-room instruction respectful of their cultures.
>
> One conclusion to be drawn from my research on talk-story-like reading lessons is that effective instruction may take more than one form. Definitions of effective teaching need to be broad enough to take into account a range of practices beyond those typically seen in mainstream settings. Another conclusion growing from my research is that students of diverse backgrounds can become excellent readers and writers when they receive well-conceived, culturally responsive instruction. (pp. 87–88)

Biography is another form of narrative inquiry. In a dissertation titled *Jane's Story: A Description of One Deaf Person's Experiences with Literacy*, Robert Perry (1995) told the story of his wife's virtual isolation from the spoken language around her since she was 6 months of age. Suffering from a severe skin ailment, Jane had been administered three shots of streptomycin within a week's time in the early 1950s. (Streptomycin was one of several antibiotics later shown to damage the neural structure of infants' ears.) Relying primarily on lipreading until she became an adult and learned American Sign Language, Jane and her mother collaborated with Perry to tell a story that spans two continents, two spoken languages, and a lifetime of experiences related to learning to read. Included are a number of comprehension and vocabulary strategies that Jane developed without formal instruction, a history of her development as a concert pianist, an original poem by Jane titled "The Artist's Life," and a thoughtful discussion of how her deafness has limited the knowledge she needs to make inferences while reading. Much of what Jane has shared in her role as coresearcher on this biography project is interpreted within a theoretical framework that honors the social nature of language and literacy.

Two other approaches to narrative inquiry can be found in Lorri Neilsen's writings on literacy and educational change. The first is a book of narrative essays by Neilsen (1994) titled *A Stone in My Shoe: Teaching Literacy in Times of Change*. In one of the essays, "Bring on the Children," Neilsen began her story this way:

> I had a sassy red planbook, a teaching certificate, and a nameplate on my door. I had a storehouse of language arts guides, a fat file of mimeographed story starters, boxes of paint and clay, and a black light poster of the Beatles. At twenty-one, I was prepared to transform children's minds through language and art. Bring on the children. (p. 1)

After tracing several changes in her thinking about what makes a good literacy teacher, Neilsen concluded by saying:

> But what I now know about teaching reading and writing, I know not only in my mind, but in my bones. This knowing transcends words on the page and goes deep into that twilight zone that makes all researchers wary: personal knowledge. Because this wisdom of practice is difficult to see, label, measure, count, or stamp, we call it intuition, sixth sense, or—strangely, considering its status—common sense. It is the essence of good teaching, the root source of improvisation, and traditionally the most undervalued knowledge in the educational enterprise. (p. 5)

Elsewhere, Neilsen (1998) experimented with performative texts as a narrative approach to understanding how two adolescents (one of them her 15-year-old son) experience literacy in and out of school. As Neilsen described this approach, performance and role playing were central to what she hoped the reader would take from her study:

Some of this study is reported as stage setting, some as conventional discursive analysis, and some as dialogue and monologue. The play, as it were, is in the reading of the juxtaposed texts. Readers become both participants and audience as these texts weave through one another. As narrator and participant, I become, as does the reader, part of the intertextual dynamics. The players, the texts, the readings, and the contexts are presented in an attempt to create an interplay that is not linear—a text about text that does not adhere to Western rhetorical and narrative conventions. (p. 5)

The use of narrative inquiry to understand one's own life and the lives of others is but part of the story. Literacy researchers are also exploring a variety of narrative devices that have potential for opening up new ways of making visible to their reading audiences how the choices they make in collecting, analyzing, and representing their data reflect the theoretical frameworks within which they work. Three examples of such devices are presented next, the first of which is an *aside*.

According to *The American Heritage Dictionary*, an *aside* is a theatrical term used to denote "a piece of dialogue intended for the audience and supposedly not heard by the other actors on stage" or "a parenthetical departure; a digression" (Soukhanov, 1996, p. 108). A few researchers in literacy related areas have begun to use the aside as a narrative device—as a textual method of discovery. For instance, St. Pierre (1997), working from Deleuze and Guattari's (1980/1987) theoretical image of the nomad deterritorializing space, used the aside in search of her warrant for credibility in studying how older, white Southern women care for their intellectual and literary selves. Upon returning to the site where she originally had collected her data, St. Pierre wrote:

> *Aside*: I have been to Milton since I last wrote. I returned to collect more data, to get a "feel" for the place, so that I could refresh and deploy my ethnographic authority in this aside, my warrant for credibility that Clifford (1988) describes as an "accumulated savvy and a sense of the style of a people or a place" (p. 35). I wanted to look around again and listen to the women talk so that I could write with what Geertz (cited in Olson, 1991) describes as that "sense of circumstantiality and of power in reserve … [so that] an anecdote or an example doesn't sound strained but sounds like you've got fifty others and this is the best one you chose" (p. 191). I know, however, that I am always an "unreliable narrator" (Visweswaran, 1994, p. 62) and can never produce a traditional authoritative account. Nevertheless, I might manage to construct some semblance of Essex County women for you in this space.
>
> During my days there, I was much concerned about this telling and rehearsed first one story and then another and composed bits of text in my head as I tried once again to put myself in the dubious scientific position of participant-observer. I am just about ready to give up on that signifier, since I am always sucked right into the middle of things, barely able to maintain the status of fieldworker, once more just Bettie Adams, come home to celebrate her mother's birthday. (p. 372)

In this aside, which continues for several more paragraphs, St. Pierre laid out in narrative form why she is suspicious of ethnographic methods and how they intrude on her interactions with the women of Essex County. Offered in a narrative aside, her critique of ethnography as a viable methodology for her own work is meant to speak to her audience of readers only if they wish to attend to it. Those not wishing to attend need only skip over the aside to get to the rest of her article.

The aside has also been used to provide a temporary release from the constraints of academic writing. For example, Young (1998) used asides at the beginning of each of her chapters in her dissertation on the critical literacies of young adolescent boys who were part of a home schooling project that she initiated. In introducing the aside in Chapter 1 of her dissertation, Young advised her readers that what she wrote would add context to her study—in fact, would tell another story—but only if they chose to read it. The asides were used to share her personal thoughts as a writer, a researcher, and the mother of two of the boys in the project.

A second narrative device that has been used by literacy researchers involves what Fitzgerald and Noblit (1999) described as a "think scene"—that is, "think how I [the researcher] can *show* this, not tell it" (p. 60). Showing (rather than merely talking about) their data was Fitzgerald and Noblit's way of conveying to their reading audience what their field notes and videotapes revealed about the two English-language learners, Roberto and Carlos, who were at the center of their study on emergent reading. As Fitzgerald and Noblit worked to analyze their data within what is referred to as the "I-witnessing" or "confessional" narrative genre (Geertz, 1988; Van Maanen, 1988), they orally constructed stories about the "think scenes" that they had identified as being representative of their year-long study.

In similar fashion, Schaafsma (1993) shared stories orally with members of his research team—stories that he had originally jotted in his journal while teaching in an inner-city Detroit summer writing program. Later, in writing about this kind of oral-sharing activity, which he "re-presented" narratively in his book, *Eating on the Street: Teaching Literacy in a Multicultural Society,* Schaafsma made visible to his readers how his perspective on literacy as social action influenced the way he collected and analyzed the data.

A third narrative device, a layered participant profile for representing the multiple views of a multiple author team, was developed by my colleagues and me (Alvermann, Commeyras, Young, Randall, & Hinson, 1997) in our study of gendered discursive practices in text-oriented classroom discussions. Although I wrote the first layer of each of five profiles, the other four members of the research team wove their own views into that initial layer. Profiling the participants' personal histories in this way was a conscious effort to interrupt the modernist emphasis on individualism, wherein *I* is separable and identifiable from *we* (Harre & Gillet, 1994). Identities were blurred as we wrote about ourselves, one over the other, until we had confounded our individual voices—a practice in keeping with the two theoretical constructs that framed our study: Messer-Davidow's (1985) perspectivity and Alcoff's (1988) positionality. In the following truncated version of one of the five participants' profiles (that of David Hinson), David's contributions are italicized to distinguish his views from those of the other four authors.

> He [David] told us there are two kinds of teachers. One is the "guide on the side," whereas the other is the "sage on the stage." He sees himself as the latter.... David's vision of himself as a sage on the stage seems ... [congruent with] his life as a disc jockey. For 9 years, he was accustomed to playing the winners and shelving the losers. He wouldn't have kept his job any other way. Is it David the disc jockey or David the teacher we are observing? Both descriptions ... imply that David is an actor and performs daily for his students. *How unusual is this? I like the give-and-take with an audience. For me, it's more enjoyable to view teaching as "show business."* And he's good! I think that is one reason why I never voiced any of my criticism about his tendency to control students' discussions. *Why should I criticize something that was working for David and his class? What exactly was there to criticize?* I feel I have not been honest with David. I remember being shocked when I heard David say he finds himself having to fight the tendency to call on the attractive, verbose students over the unattractive, passive students during class discussions. Later, I thought it was good David was aware of his biases and wanted to alter them. (pp. 81–82)

In sum, as this brief overview suggests, literacy researchers are engaged in a variety of narrative approaches. Although grounding their studies in a narrative framework necessarily put these researchers in touch with issues related to subjectivity, truth claims, and representation, by and large the published reports of their work (mostly chapters or journal length articles) did not permit an extended discussion of how they dealt with these issues. The dual purpose, therefore, of the remaining two sections of this chapter is to provide a detailed look at the three issues in terms of how they may influence a study's findings, and the implications they hold for future research and practice.

A DETAILED LOOK AT THREE CURRENT ISSUES

Knowledge grounded in stories is suspect in some people's minds. As one critic (Cizek, 1995) observed, "if all knowledge is a personalized construction ... then can any interpretivist claims be rejected?" (p. 27). This question of whether or not narrative research is falsifiable is also reflected in Fenstermacher's (1994) question, "How, in the use of stories and narratives, are such problems as self-deception, false claims, and distorted perceptions confronted and resolved?" (p. 218). In an attempt to address some of the concerns raised by Cizek and Fenstermacher, I turn to a body of literature that deals with subjectivity and the twin problems of legitimation and representation.

Subjectivity and the Reflexive Self

The concern that a distinction be made between what seems apparent to us and what is in fact "reality" has been part of humankind's search for truth and certainty since ancient times. In forging notions of the need to maintain a distance between the knower and what can be known or between one's personal orientations and the scientific project, scholars writing from the empiricist tradition have demonstrated little patience with narrative approaches. Generally, they have tended to regard interactions between researchers and their research participants (or between researchers and narrators in the case of storytelling approaches) as potential sources of distortion and bias (Jansen & Peshkin, 1992). For instance, literary critic Linda Kauffman (1993) warned that because in autobiographical work "there is something fatally alluring about personal testimony" (p. 132), it behooves us to be wary of a rear-view mirror enchantment with ourselves. This allusion to autobiographers' purportedly narcissistic tendencies has been challenged by scholars sympathetic to the idea that "autobiographical reflection is not a symptom of but a solution to contemporary psychosocial problems" (Casey, 1995, p. 217). Sympathetic to this view, Pinar (1988) argued, "Understanding of self is not narcissism; it is a precondition and concomitant condition to the understanding of others" (p. 150).

Other criticisms involving charges of solipsism and risk of alienation have also been leveled against narrative inquiry. To counter the charge that such inquiry assumes the self is the only thing that can be known and verified, researchers have relied upon a technique they call *methodological reflexivity*. Perhaps one of the better known illustrations of this technique is Wolf's (1992) *A Thrice Told Tale* in which the author records the same set of events using three different forms of writing: a narrative (short story), a social science article, and her anthropological field notes. The assumption is that this type of reflexive writing forces one to turn a critical eye to one's own prejudices and distortions (or at least as the self perceives them). In Wolf's case, "The Hot Spell" was written as a piece of fiction in which the narrator revealed her biases and her state of mind (boredom, discomfort, insecurity) during a dramatic unfolding of events that took place while she was doing fieldwork in Taiwan in 1960. Wolf's field notes, which cover the events written about in the short story, and the article she published some 30 years later in *American Ethnologist* (Wolf, 1990) can be read against and within the short story as a way of locating the author's subjective involvement and the attention she paid it.

A second criticism—the potential for self-revelations to invite alienation—stems from the fact that narrative tellings often diminish the teller, or, equally damaging, they turn the teller into a crafty narrator. In Grumet's (1987) words, "Our stories are the masks through which we can be seen, and with every telling we stop the flood and swirl of thought so someone can get a glimpse of us, and maybe catch us if they can" (p. 322). Acknowledging the politics of personal knowledge and the potentially alienating aspects of the self-story, Grumet made it a practice to use Pinar's (1976b) method of *currere* in her work with teachers who examine their own practices through autobiographical writing. This method requires that, instead of a single text, the teachers write three separate accounts of their lives—a triple retelling organized into past experience, present situation, and future images. Grumet used this approach to autobiographical writing as a way of partially addressing the dangers involved in asking others to reveal themselves in a single telling, for as she pointed out, if multiple accounts undermine the authority of the teller, they at least protect him or her "from being captured by the reflection provided in a single narrative" (p. 324).

Finally, an ethical concern posed by those who work within narrative as a form of inquiry is the degree to which we should expect our work to enable those who tell us their stories to take actions that will change their own conditions or the conditions of others living in similar circumstances. In *Troubling the Angels: Women Living with HIV/AIDS* (Lather & Smithies, 1997), the researchers held themselves accountable as the authors of the text for getting the women's stories out to the general public in what was called the "K-Mart" version of the later published work. The women, whose stories Lather and Smithies told, served as the authors' editorial board. In this capacity, the women had final say as to how they would be portrayed and to whom they would speak (e.g., their choice of the general public, not the academic world, as their initial audience). In making the personal lives of these women who were living with HIV/AIDS part of their scholarship, Lather and Smithies found ways of textually representing the relationship between themselves and the women's selves. For example, they used split pages on which the women's voices were positioned above their own, and they boxed in the women's poems as a way of setting them apart, out of reach of their own authorial control.

In summary, the relationship between the knower and the known is made less obscure and perhaps "safer" when researchers practice reflexivity and take steps to ensure that ethical consideration is given to their participants' needs. However, in the long run, as Haraway (1991) cogently pointed out, our subjectivities are "always constructed and stitched together imperfectly" (p. 193)—a point that one might argue also suggests that narrative approaches are no more susceptible to problems of self-deception than are other forms of research. Or, as Nespor and Barber (1995) succinctly put it, "No one is detached or 'neutral'" (p. 53).

Crisis of Legitimation (Truth Claims)

The belief that "truth and validity claims reflect historically determined values and interests of different groups … [and that] reality is mediated by conceptual schemes (Kant), ideologies (Marx), language games (Wittgenstein), and paradigms (Kuhn)" (Jansen & Peshkin, 1992, p. 688) is part of a tradition that views knowledge as being at least partially dependent on the knower. It is a tradition influenced in post-World War II Europe by existentialist thinking according to Casey (1995), who, in her analysis of the education field's current enthusiasm for narrative research, finds a connection between certain narrative approaches and existentialism's emphasis on the need for individuals to make sense of a senseless world.

But how is one to address the issues surrounding validity in current-day discussions of the so-called legitimation crisis? I suggest that French literary theorist Helene

Cixous's (Cixous & Calle-Gruber, 1997) interpretation of Archimedes' thoughts on Truth is a good starting place:

> Archimedes is someone who never believed in the truth of something;
> that something was the truth, no.
> To believe in the Truth as tension, as movement, yes.
> — Helene Cixous (Cixous & Calle-Gruber, 1997, p. 5)

Viewing the Truth as tension, as movement, seems a good way to characterize contemporary writers' handling of narrative inquiry and truth claims. Although some narrative analysts (see Cortazzi, 1993) assume that the language used by their participants captures the reality of lived experiences, others view language as actually constituting that reality (Denzin, 1997; Gilbert, 1993). Still others (The Personal Narratives Group, cited in Riessman, 1993) believe that people fabricate their stories, not so much with an intent to deceive as with a desire to make their fictions become realities. In describing this phenomenon, Riessman (1993) noted that interpretive narratives require interpretation:

> When talking about their lives, people lie sometimes, forget a lot, exaggerate, become confused, and get things wrong. Yet they *are* revealing truths. These truths don't reveal the past "as it actually was," aspiring to a standard of objectivity. They give us instead the truths of our experiences.... Unlike the Truth of the scientific ideal, the truths of personal narratives are neither open to proof nor self-evident. We come to understand them only through interpretation, paying careful attention to the contexts that shape their creation and to the world views that inform them. Sometimes the truths we see in personal narratives jar us from our complacent security as interpreters "outside" the story and make us aware that our own place in the world plays a part in our interpretation and shapes the meanings we derive from them. (The Personal Narratives Group, cited in Riessman, 1993, p. 22)

The criteria that might be applied in determining a narrative's authority, legitimacy, or trustworthiness (Denzin, 1997; Riessman, 1993) vary with the type of narrative under consideration (e.g., oral, first-person, written, biographical, and so on). Generally, those who work with narrative forms of inquiry agree that valid[3] research is well grounded and supportable—it has what Polkinghorne (1988) referred to as *verisimilitude*, or the appearance of truth.

Transgressive validity (Richardson, 1997), as its name implies, violates what many working within the narrative paradigm would consider "acceptable" social science. In transforming her notes of an oral history of an unwed mother into the poem "Louisa May," Richardson (1997), in her words, transgressed "the normative constraints for social science writing" (p. 167). She crossed the invisible line separating social science from literary craft (Manning, 1987). Although she initially found her work trivialized and vulnerable to dismissal among colleagues in her field (sociology), today Richardson's scholarship is considered an important move in engaging narrative researchers in serious discussions of authorship, authority, validity, and aesthetics (Lenzo, 1995).

One such discussion focuses on Lawrence-Lightfoot's (1997) recounting of a paradox that argues for a very different way of thinking about validity and generalization. She contextualized this paradox within her own method of inquiry, portraiture, which

---

[3]Here, Polkinghorne (1988) used the ordinary, or nontechnical, meaning of *valid*, as in well-grounded and supportable. He distinguished its ordinary meaning from two of its more technical ones—the first being a valid conclusion drawn in the context of formal logic, and the second being a valid relationship between an instrument and the concept it purports to measure.

blends aesthetics and empiricism while drawing on features of the narrative, case study, and ethnography. In her words:

> Not only is the portraitist interested in developing a narrative that is both convincing and authentic, she is also interested in recording the subtle details of human experience. She wants to capture the specifics, the nuance, the detailed description of a thing, a gesture, a voice, an attitude as a way of illustrating more universal patterns. A persistent irony—recognized and celebrated by novelists, poets, playwrights—is that as one moves closer to the unique characteristics of a person or a place, one discovers the universal.... Eudora Welty (1983) offers a wonderful insight gained from her experience as a storyteller. She says forcefully: "What discoveries I have made in the process of writing stories, all begin with the particular, never the general." Clifford Geertz (1973) puts it another way when he refers to the paradoxical experience of theory development, the emergence of concepts from the gathering of specific detail. Geertz (1973) says, "Small facts are the grist for the social theory mill" (p. 23). The scientist and the artist are both claiming that *in the particular resides the general*. (Lawrence-Lightfoot, 1997, p. 14)

In summary, in the same way that traditional concerns for validity and generalizability can get in the way of how narrative researchers like to tell their stories, so also can the evolving notions of what ought to constitute truth claims beget angst among the traditionalists (Smith, 1997). In the end, however, it may be the work of individuals such as those whose research has just been described that will prevent the balkanization of education research. For if agreement can be reached on how to accept and work from one another's stories, it will be due in no small measure to their ability, and ours, to see Truth as tension, and as movement.

Crisis of Representation

Making problematic the assumed link between experience and text has created what is known in anthropology circles as the crisis of representation (Clifford & Marcus, 1986; Denzin, 1994). An argument that supports the existence of such a crisis is this: Because we can never suppress ourselves in the texts we write (or read), we in fact create the persons we write about. An example of the dilemma that the crisis of representation poses for researchers can be found in Denzin's (1989) work on the crisis of representation in biographical studies:

> When a writer writes a biography, he or she writes him[self] or herself into the life of the subject written about. When the reader reads a biographical text, that text is read through the life of the reader. Hence, writers and readers conspire to create the lives they write and read about. Along the way, the produced text is cluttered by the traces of the life of the "real" person being written about. (p. 26)

Questioning the assumed link between a narrative that tells about a real person's life and the text which represents that life (or, as Denzin noted, "traces of [that] life") opens the door to exploring two related phenomena. The first has to do with performance and the inadequacy of written texts for depicting lived experience (Denzin, 1997; Eisner, 1997) and the second with the blurring of genres (Geertz, 1980, 1983).

The inadequacy of written texts for depicting lived experience has led some researchers to explore ways of presenting their data through various performance modes. For example, Neilsen (1998) represented a series of in-depth interviews on teenagers' literate experiences as a play; Paget (1995) offered a dramatic reading of her research on conversations between a doctor and a patient; and Richardson (1993) performed an oral rendition of her data poem, "Louisa May," before a group of her peers at a national meeting of sociologists. By performing their texts, Neilsen, Paget, and Richardson established a different kind of communicative relation with their audiences.

Even so, by its very nature, performance relies on language to mediate experience—a point Denzin (1997) makes in drawing from Derrida (1976) to explain why neither the written word nor the performance (that is, no text) is ever final or complete:

> There is no clear window into the inner life of a person, for any window is always filtered through the glaze of language, signs, and the process of signification. And language, in both its written and spoken forms, is always inherently unstable, in flux, and made up of the traces of other signs and symbolic statements. Hence, there can never be a clear, unambiguous statement of anything, including an intention or a meaning. (Denzin, 1997, p. 14)

The publication of Geertz's two books, *The Interpretation of Cultures* (1973) and *Local Knowledge* (1983), helped to usher in the crisis of representation by introducing the notion of blurred genres. Although the first of these two volumes set the stage for reconceptualizing interpretive research generally, it is the latter, with its chapter on blurred genres, and Pratt's (1986) work on the relation of narrative to ethnographic writing that are at the heart of the representational crisis in narrative inquiry. This crisis, which dismisses the assumption that narrative approaches directly capture lived experience, argues instead that the texts written by researchers using these approaches create such experience (Denzin, 1997). Just as importantly, the work of Geertz (1983) and Pratt (1986) is recognized for having elevated storytelling from mere anecdotal writing to its current status as a vehicle in which empirical and aesthetic descriptions of the human condition find articulation. For example, Pratt (1986) has advocated blurring the genre boundaries between the personal narrative and ethnographic writing:

> I think it is fairly clear that personal narrative persists alongside objectifying description in ethnographic writing because it mediates a contradiction within the discipline between personal and scientific authority, a contradiction that has become especially acute since the advent of fieldwork as a methodological norm.... Fieldwork produces a kind of authority that is anchored to a large extent in subjective, sensuous experience. One experiences the indigenous environment and lifeways for oneself, sees with one's own eyes, even plays some roles, albeit contrived ones, in the daily life of the community. (p. 32)

In a move to extend Pratt's (1986) endorsement of blurring narrative and ethnographic boundaries as a means of circumventing problems associated with texts that separate the researcher from the researched and the literary from the scientific,[4] Richardson (1997) and Eisner (1997) argued for a style of academic writing that blurs narrative knowing, sociological telling, poetry, and film making. Although both Richardson and Eisner personally research and write in ways that displace (and, at times, erase) boundaries between art and science, both are also fully cognizant of the need to avoid turning this new approach to narrative inquiry into a petrified discourse—one that is no longer open to resistance and rewriting.

In sum, exploring alternative ways of representing ourselves and the people we write about in our research comes at a defining moment in the history of narrative inquiry—when the question of what counts (or should count) as legitimate research has been settled to some degree by what Eisner (1997) described as the long-overdue insight that "research [does] not belong to science alone" (p. 5). Although this insight is not recognized as such in all corners of the research world, Eisner's thinking, which is grounded in Geertz's (1983) work on blurred genres, lends credence to the continuing

---

[4]In 16th-century European travel accounts, first-person narrations of the traveler's journey predominated over the empirical descriptions of the flora and fauna of the regions he or she described. Ironically, "the descriptive portions were sometimes seen as dumping grounds for the 'surplus data' that could not be fitted into the narrative" (Pratt, 1986, p. 33).

search for better ways of representing lived experience, given the inadequacy of all texts, written and performed, for depicting such experience presently.

IMPLICATIONS

Of interest here are the implications of the issues raised by the postmodern or poststructural turn in narrative inquiry. Specifically, how has this turn affected the way researchers and practitioners think about subjectivity, truth claims, and representation? For instance, what methodological considerations do researchers need to take into account when using narrative approaches? Who might be an audience for academic writing that purposefully blurs borders separating the scholarly from the everyday world of practice, and why might this audience be a valuable one to seek?

Research

Regardless of the type of narrative inquiry undertaken, the postmodern critique calls attention to the researcher's presence and why it must be taken into account from the start (Brodkey, 1987). Such an accounting involves making decisions about whose stories to tell, which parts of a story to omit when it comes time to publish the research, how much of the narrator's voice to include, when to interrupt that voice with the researcher's commentary, and so on. The implications such reflexive practices hold for literacy researchers are numerous. Perhaps understanding the complex system of power relations embedded in the narrative interview is as good a starting point as any. As Emihovich (1995) noted, the interview process is complicated by the privileged position of the researcher in relation to the researched (e.g., the researcher can leave the scene after recording the narrator's story, whereas the narrator often does not have this choice). A more subtle form of privilege is to be found in the decisions that lead to the researcher taking on the voice of the narrator/storyteller. Such decisions often alter the way in which the voice of the storied participant can be heard (Polkinghorne, 1997).

Another aspect of the power relationship present in the narrative interview that has implications for literacy researchers is documented by Scheurich (1995) in his postmodernist critique of the traditional interview process. Arguing from the perspective that "the researcher has multiple intentions and desires, some of which are consciously known and some of which are not" (p. 240), as does the person being interviewed, Scheurich believed we should highlight, not hide, the so-called baggage that is brought to the interview process. Admitting that it is simply impossible to name all that baggage, Scheurich opted for what he termed "a reasonably comprehensive statement of disciplinary training, epistemological orientation, social positionality, institutional imperatives, and funding sources and requirement" (pp. 249–250). Providing readers with such a statement is, to Scheurich's way of thinking, a way of enabling them to make their own evaluations of the research enterprise.

Experimenting with alternative ways of writing, such as those encountered in the newer forms of narrative research in education (see Casey, 1995, for a comprehensive listing of these forms and examples of each), is never without controversy. But it is especially the case when such experimentation crosses boundaries traditionally thought to separate academic scholarship from the more mundane world in which we all live. This kind of boundary crossing has appeal for literacy researchers working in areas where representing in writing what their participants tell them is not viewed as simply a matter of mirroring lived experience, as if that were possible in the first place. As Denzin (1997), following Derrida (1976), pointed out, "Language and speech do not mirror experience; they create experience and in the process of creation constantly transform and defer that which is being described" (p. 5).

For theorists writing about narrative inquiry, however, the issue lies not so much with representation per se as with the truth claims that can be made about one's story (Bruner, 1987; Gilmore, 1994; Tonkin, 1992; Trinh, 1991). Rejecting the notion that narrative texts need only "move us" to establish their truth claims, Riessman (1993, p. 64) and Polkinghorne (1995) argued for judging a text's authority in terms of its coherence (explanatory power), correspondence (achieved through member checks), persuasiveness, and pragmatic use (the insights and understandings it provides the field). That there is no agreement on what constitutes the legitimacy of narrative texts is part of the larger debate surrounding the notion of truth as both tension and movement. Nowhere is this debate more evident than in our own field. In literacy research, the criteria used in establishing truth claims for narratives are numerous, ranging from those that refuse to endorse any single interpretation of the data to those that seek convergence, if not consensus (Alvermann & Hruby, 2000).

Opening up our research agendas in literacy education to include alternative forms of data representation typically associated with narrative inquiry can increase the variety of questions we ask about reading and writing as processes and about literacy instruction in general. As Eisner (1997) pointed out, agendas open to alternative forms of data representation hold promise for developing a field's awareness in ways that may lead to new ways of thinking:

> Put another way, our capacity to wonder is stimulated by the possibilities that new forms of representation suggest. As we learn to think within the medium we choose to use, we also become more able to raise questions that the media themselves suggest; tools, among other things, are also heuristics. (p. 8)

But with this opening up of agendas to include new forms of data representation comes a need to avoid substituting creativity and cleverness for substance. In Eisner's (1997) words, "We need to be our own toughest critics" (p. 9). This advice seems sound if the goal is to experiment with less technical forms of scientific writing but not at the expense of methodological rigor.

Practice

To whom do we tell our stories as literacy researchers engaged in narrative inquiry? More often than not, these stories are shared professionally with a relatively small group of like-minded peers. As Lawrence-Lightfoot (1997) reminded us in her introduction to *The Art and Science of Portraiture*, rarely does the work produced in the academy reach beyond its walls:

> Academicians tend to speak to one another in a language that is often opaque and esoteric. Rarely do the analyses and texts we produce invite dialogue with people in the "real world." Instead, academic documents—even those that focus on issues of broad public concern—are read by a small audience of people in the same disciplinary field, who often share similar conceptual frameworks and rhetoric. (pp. 9–10)

However, this situation appears to be changing. A growing number of scholars working within the realm of narrative inquiry are beginning to argue forcefully for reaching out to audiences other than one's academic peer group. For example, Tierney (1997) pressed for an openness in narrative writing, one that enables others to exercise greater awareness of the debates that rage in the academic community. He also pushed for dissertation committees to consider experimental fiction as a viable form of doctoral research. Although less radical in his approach to reaching out to audiences beyond the academic community, Polkinghorne (1997) posited that "by changing their voice to storyteller, researchers will also change the way in which the voices of their 'subjects' or participants can be heard" (p. 3). This change has implications, in turn, for what those outside the academic community "hear" and value or reject in our research. Polkinghorne also advocated writing separate reports for different audiences, thus improving the chances that one's story is read beyond the academic community.

Implications of the socially constructed nature of narrative inquiry for literacy teaching and learning are also numerous. For example, the potential for storytelling to renew and regulate our ways of ordering and naming literacy practices at all levels of instruction is profound, as Gilbert (1989, 1993) repeatedly showed. This renewal process continually provides the framework through which we act as we go about our work in search of different story lines for language research. In Gilbert's (1993) words:

> In our personal lives, we tell stories as a way of structuring and giving significance to lived experience, and as a way of positioning ourselves in particular ways with our friends, our colleagues, our families. And this is not only so for our personal lives. It applies equally to our professional lives and to the stories that sustain us there. We tell stories of our research experiences, stories of the texts we read, stories of our classrooms, and stories of the children we teach. And our stories keep changing as our ways of reading stories (and therefore of making new stories) change. (p. 211)

Narrative research that is grounded in the everyday world of literacy and teaching provides entry into that world. Stories of how local knowledge of literacy conditions can help shape policy decisions are few and far between; however, where they do exist (e.g., Quint, 1996; Rist, 1994), they signal still further the collapsing of boundaries once thought to separate the research community from the world of practice—the knower from the known. In the wake of this collapse, at least two key questions have surfaced that have implications for the field of practice. First is the question of whether or not a level of discourse can be found that encourages communication between researchers and practitioners in literacy education. A second question asks what impact narrative research is having on classroom literacy practices. To some degree, the difficulty in answering these questions lies with literacy researchers' partial, as opposed to full, specification of the educational phenomena that they observe. More generally, however, the difficulty seems to stem from the literacy community's disinclination (or inability) to set a collective research agenda (Mosenthal, 1985, 1993). For whatever reason, the situation is made even more complex by postmodernist critiques that challenge the authority of the author–storyteller–researcher.

Writing in a different context, but on a theme related to decentering the author–storyteller–researcher's authority, Grumet (1987) made the following observation about truth claims in relation to first-person narratives:

> Viewed against the background of bureaucratic, depersonalized institutions, storytelling seems pretty authentic, or at least expressive. It seems natural to assume that the first person is closer to us than the third, an intimacy that Sartre [1972] repudiates emphatically in *The Transcendence of the Ego*, arguing that we do not know ourselves any better than we know others, and reminding us not to confuse familiarity with knowledge. (p. 321)

This observation calls to mind one of Eisner's (1997) several cautions concerning the use of alternative forms of data representation. In essence, Eisner is concerned that narrative researchers—in their effort to paint classroom life and all its complexities in a way that is understandable to the general public—all too often settle for a kind of ambiguity in their reporting that is reminiscent of the Rorschach syndrome. That is, "Everyone confers his or her own idiosyncratic meaning on the data. No consensus is possible. The data mean whatever anyone wants them to mean; or worse, no [one] knows what they mean" (Eisner, 1997, p. 9).

On a more positive ending note, it is important to bear in mind educational philosopher Maxine Greene's (1994) thinking on the postmodernist critique of narrative inquiry and how we might choose to respond to the problem that Eisner (1997) has identified. Writing from the perspective of someone who has observed many changes come and go in the name of educational research, Greene quoted Kathy Carter (1993) on the place of story in teaching and teacher education to make the point that what matters is not the label of one's truth claims but rather the problems such claims pose for representing one's data:

> We may need, [Carter wrote], to continue to challenge the tradition of truth claims that largely ignored context, character, contradiction, and complexity. We may have to run against the winds of the sometimes warped ways of gaining acceptance by the scientific community, a community that has systematically excluded particular problematics, voices, values, and experiences from its intellectual pursuits. (Carter, cited in Greene, 1994, p. 455)

The appealing nature of Carter's argument notwithstanding, to Greene's way of thinking (and, I might add, my own), the "problems of relativism and representation will have to be confronted" (Greene, 1994, p. 455) if the metanarratives of yesteryear are not to replace the stories of today. This chapter is offered as an invitation to the conversation surrounding these problems, or at least as I have interpreted them.

REFERENCES

Alcoff, L. (1988). Cultural feminism versus post-structuralism: The identity crisis in feminist theory. *Signs, 13*, 405–436.

Allen, J., Michalove, B., & Shockley, B. (1993). *Engaging children*. Portsmouth, NH: Heinemann.

Alvermann, D. E., & Hruby, G. G. (2000). Mentoring and reporting research: A concern for aesthetics. *Reading Research Quarterly, 35*(1).

Alvermann, D. E., Commeyras, M., Young, J. P., Randall, S., & Hinson, D. (1997). Interrupting gendered discursive practices in classroom talk about texts: Easy to think about, difficult to do. *Journal of Literacy Research, 29*, 73–104.

Au, K. H. (1997). Schooling, literacy, and cultural diversity in research and personal experience. In A. Neumann & P. L. Peterson (Eds.), *Women, research, and autobiography in education* (pp. 71–90). New York: Teachers College Press.

Britzman, D. (1995). "The question of belief": Writing poststructural ethnography. *Qualitative Studies in Education, 8*, 233–242.

Brodkey, L. (1987). Writing ethnographic narratives. *Written Communication, 4*, 25–50.

Bruner, J. (1986). *Actual minds, possible worlds*. Cambridge, MA: Harvard University Press.

Bruner, J. (1987). Life as narrative. *Social Research, 54*(1), 11–32.

Carter, K. (1993). The place of story in the study of teaching and teacher education. *Educational Researcher, 22*(1), 5–18.

Casey, K. (1995). The new narrative research in education. In L. Darling-Hammond (Ed.), *Review of research in education* (Vol. 21, pp. 211–253). Washington, DC: American Educational Research Association.

Cixous, H., & Calle-Gruber, M. (1997). *Helene Cixous rootprints: Memory and life writing*. London: Routledge.

Cizek, G. J. (1995). Crunchy granola and the hegemony of the narrative. *Educational Researcher, 24*(2), 26–28.

Clifford, J. (1988). *The predicament of culture: Twentieth-century ethnography, literature, and art*. Cambridge, MA: Harvard University Press.

Clifford, J., & Marcus, G. E. (Eds.). (1986). *Writing culture*. Berkeley: University of California Press.

Cochran-Smith, M., & Lytle, S. L. (Eds.). (1993). *Inside/outside: Teacher research and knowledge*. New York: Teachers College Press.

Constas, M. A. (1998). The changing nature of educational research and a critique of postmodernism. *Educational Researcher, 27*(2), 26–33.

Cortazzi, M. (1993). *Narrative analysis*. London: Falmer.

de la Luna, L., & Kamberelis, G. (1997). Refracted discourses/disrupted practices: Possibilities and challenges of collaborative action research in classrooms. In C. K. Kinzer, K. A. Hinchman, & D. J. Leu (Eds.), *Inquiries in literacy theory and practice: 46th Yearbook of the National Reading Conference* (pp. 213–228). Chicago: National Reading Conference.

Deleuze, G., & Guattari, F. (1987). *A thousand plateaus: Capitalism and schizophrenia* (B. Massumi, Trans.). Minneapolis, MN: University of Minnesota Press. (Original work published 1980)

Denzin, N. (1989). *Interpretive biography.* Newbury Park, CA: Sage.

Denzin, N. (1994). Evaluating qualitative research in the poststructural moment: The lessons James Joyce teaches us. *International Journal of Qualitative Studies in Education, 7,* 295–308.

Denzin, N. (1997). *Interpretive ethnography.* Thousand Oaks, CA: Sage.

Derrida, J. (1976). *Of grammatology.* (G. C. Spivak, Trans.). Baltimore, MD: Johns Hopkins University Press.

Dyson, A. H. (1997). *Writing superheroes: Contemporary childhood, popular culture, and classroom literacy.* New York: Teachers College Press.

Eisner, E. W. (1997). The promise and perils of alternative forms of data representation. *Educational Researcher, 26*(6), 4–10.

Emihovich, C. (1995). Distancing passion: Narratives in social science. *International Journal of Qualitative Studies in Education, 8,* 37–48.

Featherstone, J. (1989). To make the wounded whole. *Harvard Educational Review, 59,* 367–378.

Fenstermacher, G. D. (1994). Argument: A response to "Pedagogy, virtue, and narrative identity in teaching." *Curriculum Inquiry, 24,* 215–220.

Fishman, A. (1988). *Amish literacy: What and how it means.* Portsmouth, NH: Heinemann.

Fitzgerald, J., & Noblit, G. (1999). About hopes, aspirations, and uncertainty: First-grade English-language learners' emergent reading. *Journal of Literacy Research, 31*(2), 133–182.

Geertz, C. (1973). *The interpretation of cultures.* New York: Basic Books.

Geertz, C. (1980). Blurred genres. *American Scholar, 49,* 165–179.

Geertz, C. (1983). *Local knowledge: Further essays in interpretive anthropology.* New York: Basic Books.

Geertz, C. (1988). *Works and lives.* Stanford, CA: Stanford University Press.

Gilbert, P. (1989). *Writing, schooling and deconstruction: From voice to text in the classroom.* London: Routledge.

Gilbert, P. (1993). Narrative as gendered social practice: In search of different story lines for language research. *Linguistics and Education, 5,* 211–218.

Gilmore, L. (1994). *Autobiographics.* Ithaca, NY: Cornell University Press.

Greene, M. (1994). Epistemology and educational research: The influence of recent approaches to knowledge. In L. Darling-Hammond (Ed.), *Review of research in education* (Vol. 20, pp. 423–464). Washington, DC: American Educational Research Association.

Grumet, M. (1987). The politics of personal knowledge. *Curriculum Inquiry, 17,* 319–329.

Hankins, K. H. (1998). Cacophony to symphony: Memoirs in teacher research. *Harvard Educational Review, 68,* 80–95.

Haraway, D. J. (1991). *Simians, cyborgs, and women.* New York: Routledge.

Harre, R., & Gillet, G. (1994). *The discursive mind.* Thousand Oaks, CA: Sage.

Heath, S. B. (1983). *Ways with words: Language, life, and work in communities and classrooms.* New York: Cambridge University Press.

hooks, b. (1991). Narratives of struggle. In P. Mariani (Ed.), *Critical fictions: The politics of imaginative writing* (pp. 53–61). Seattle, WA: Bay.

Jansen, G., & Peshkin, A. (1992). Subjectivity in qualitative research. In M. D. LeCompte, W. L. Millroy, & J. Preissle (Eds.), *The handbook of qualitative research in education* (pp. 681–725). New York: Academic Press.

Kauffman, L. S. (1993). The long goodbye: Against personal testimony, or an infant grifter grows up. In G. Greene & C. Kahn (Eds.), *Changing subjects: The making of feminist literary criticism* (pp. 129–146). London: Routledge.

Lalik, R., Dellinger, L., & Druggish, R. (1996). Appalachian literacies at school. In D. J. Leu, C. K. Kinzer, & K. A. Hinchman (Eds.), *Literacies for the 21st century: Research and practice: 45th Yearbook of the National Reading Conference* (pp. 345–358). Chicago: National Reading Conference.

Lather, P., & Smithies, C. (1997). *Troubling the angels: Women living with HIV/AIDS.* Boulder, CO: Westview Press.

Lawrence-Lightfoot, S. (1997). A view of the whole: Origins and purposes. In S. Lawrence-Lightfoot & J. H. Davis (Eds.), *The art and science of portraiture* (pp. 1–16). San Francisco, CA: Jossey-Bass.

Lawrence-Lightfoot, S., & Davis, J. H. (1997). *The art and science of portraiture.* San Francisco: Jossey-Bass.

Lenzo, K. (1995). Validity and self-reflexivity meet poststructuralism: Scientific ethos and the transgressive self. *Educational Researcher, 24*(4), 17–23, 45.

Manning, P. K. (1987). *Semiotics and fieldwork.* Newbury Park, CA: Sage.

Manning, P. K., & Cullum-Swan, B. (1994). Narrative, content, and semiotic analysis. In N. K. Denzin & Y. S. Lincoln (Eds.), *Handbook of qualitative research* (pp. 463–477). Thousand Oaks, CA: Sage.

Marcus, G. E. (1994). What comes (just) after "post"? In N. K. Denzin & Y. S. Lincoln (Eds.), *Handbook of qualitative research* (pp. 563–574). Thousand Oaks, CA: Sage.

Messer-Davidow, E. (1985). Knowers, knowing, knowledge: Feminist theory and education. *Journal of Thought, 20,* 8–24.

Mosenthal, P. B. (1985). Defining progress in educational research. *Educational Researcher, 14*(9), 3–9.

Mosenthal, P. B. (1993). Understanding agenda setting in reading research. In A. P. Sweet & J. I. Anderson (Eds.), *Reading research into the year 2000* (pp. 115–128). Hillsdale, NJ: Lawrence Erlbaum Associates.

Neilsen, L. (1994). *A stone in my shoe: Teaching literacy in times of change.* Winnipeg, Canada: Peguis.

Neilsen, L. (1998). Playing for real: Performative texts and adolescent identities. In D. E. Alvermann, K. A. Hinchman, D. W. Moore, S. F. Phelps, & D. R. Waff (Eds.), *Reconceptualizing the literacies in adolescents' lives* (pp. 3–26). Mahwah, NJ: Lawrence Erlbaum Associates.

Nespor, J., & Barber, L. (1995). Audience and the politics of narrative. *International Journal of Qualitative Studies in Education, 8,* 49–62.

Neumann, A., & Peterson, P. L. (1997). *Learning from our lives: Women, research, and autobiography in education.* New York: Teachers College Press.

Olson, G. A. (1991). The social scientist as author: Clifford Geertz on ethnography and social construction [Interview with Clifford Geertz]. In G. A. Olson & I. Gale (Eds.), *(Inter)views: Cross-disciplinary perspectives on rhetoric and literacy* (pp. 187–210). Carbondale, IL: Southern Illinois University Press.

Paget, M. A. (1995). Performing the text. In J. Van Maanen (Ed.), *Representation in ethnography* (pp. 222–244). Thousand Oaks, CA: Sage.

Perry, R. C. (1995). *Jane's story: A description of one deaf person's experiences with literacy.* Unpublished dissertation, University of Georgia, Athens.

Pinar, W. F. (1976a). Introduction. In W. F. Pinar & M. R. Grumet, *Toward a poor curriculum* (pp. iii–viii). Dubuque, IA: Kendall/Hunt.

Pinar, W. F. (1976b). The method. In W. F. Pinar & M. R. Grumet, *Toward a poor curriculum* (pp. 51–65). Dubuque, IA: Kendall/Hunt.

Pinar, W. F. (1988). "Whole, bright, deep with understanding": Issues in qualitative research and autobiographical method. In W. Pinar (Ed.), *Contemporary curriculum discourses* (pp. 134–153). Scottsdale, AZ: Gorsuch Scarisbrick.

Pinar, W. F., & Grumet, M. R. (1976). *Toward a poor curriculum.* Dubuque, IA: Kendall/Hunt.

Polkinghorne, D. E. (1988). *Narrative knowing and the human sciences.* Albany: State University of New York Press.

Polkinghorne, D. E. (1995). Narrative configuration in qualitative analysis. *International Journal of Qualitative Studies in Education, 8,* 5–23.

Polkinghorne, D. E. (1997). Reporting qualitative research as practice. In W. G. Tierney & Y. S. Lincoln (Eds.), *Representation and the text: Re-framing the narrative voice* (pp. 3–21). Albany: State University of New York Press.

Pratt, M. L. (1986). Fieldwork in common places. In J. Clifford & G. E. Marcus (Eds.), *Writing culture: The poetics and politics of ethnography* (pp. 27–50). Berkeley: University of California Press.

Quint, S. (1996). "Cause you talkin' about a whole person": A new path for schooling and literacy in troubled times and spaces. *Journal of Literacy Research, 28,* 310–319.

Richardson, L. (1993). Poetics, dramatics, and transgressive validity: The case of the skipped line. *Sociological Quarterly, 35,* 695–710.

Richardson, L. (1997). *Fields of play: Constructing an academic life.* New Brunswick, NJ: Rutgers University Press.

Riessman, C. K. (1993). *Narrative analysis.* Newbury Park, CA: Sage.

Rist, R. (1994). Influencing the policy process with qualitative research. In N. K. Denzin & Y. S. Lincoln (Eds.), *Handbook of qualitative research* (pp. 545–557). Thousand Oaks, CA: Sage.

Sartre, J. P. (1972). *The transcendence of the ego* (F. Williams & R. Kirkpatrick, Trans.). New York: Octagon Books.

Schaafsma, D. (1993). *Eating on the street: Teaching literacy in a multicultural society.* Pittsburgh, PA: University of Pittsburgh Press.

Scheurich, J. J. (1995). A postmodernist critique of research interviewing. *International Journal of Qualitative Studies in Education, 8,* 239–252.

Smith, J. K. (1997). The stories educational researchers tell about themselves. *Educational Researcher, 26*(5), 4–11.

Soukhanov, A. H. (1996). *The American heritage dictionary of the English language* (3rd ed.) Boston: Houghton Mifflin.

St. Pierre, E. A. (1997). Nomadic inquiry in the smooth spaces of the field: A preface. *International Journal of Qualitative Studies in Education, 10,* 365–383.

Tierney, W. G. (1997). Lost in translation: Time and voice in qualitative research. In W. G. Tierney & Y. S. Lincoln (Eds.), *Representation and the text: Re-framing the narrative voice* (pp. 23–36). Albany: State University of New York Press.

Tierney, W. G., & Lincoln, Y. S. (Eds.). (1997). *Representation and the text: Re-framing the narrative voice.* Albany: State University of New York Press.

Tonkin, E. (1992). *Narrating our pasts: The social construction of oral history.* Cambridge, UK: Cambridge University Press.

Trinh, T. M-ha. (1991). *When the moon waxes red: Representation, gender and cultural politics.* New York: Routledge.

Van Maanen, J. (Ed.). (1988). *Tales of the field.* Chicago: University of Chicago Press.

Visweswaran, K. (1994). *Fictions of feminist ethnography.* Minneapolis: University of Minnesota Press.

Welty, E. (1983). *One writer's beginnings.* Cambridge, MA: Harvard University Press.

Wolf, M. (1990). The woman who didn't become a shaman. *American Ethnologist, 17,* 419–430.

Wolf, M. (1992). *A thrice-told tale.* Stanford, CA: Stanford University Press.

Young, J. P. (1998). *Critical literacy, homeschooling, and masculinities: Young adolescent boys talk about gender.* Unpublished doctoral dissertation, University of Georgia, Athens.

CHAPTER 10

Critical Approaches

Marjorie Siegel
Teachers College, Columbia University

Susana Laura Fernandez
University of Buenos Aires

Why is it that there is so much intellectual activity around issues of power and politics in the social sciences and the humanities, yet so little of it has influenced theory, research, and practice in the field of literacy education? This is indeed a curious situation, especially when we consider that by 1984—the publication year of the first *Handbook of Reading Research* (Pearson, Barr, Kamil, & Mosenthal, 1984)—critical perspectives on teaching, curriculum, and schooling had begun to take hold in schools of education. The publication of books like *Knowledge and Control* (Young, 1971) and *Schooling in Capitalist Society* (Bowles & Gintis, 1976) challenged the long-standing fiction that schooling is a neutral activity, and proposed, instead, that teaching and curriculum are political practices inasmuch as they produce knowledge for purposes of social regulation. As such, critical approaches represent a critique of widely held functionalist views about the role of schooling in society, which suggest that schooling is "an efficient and rational way of sorting and selecting talented people so that the most able and motivated attain the highest status positions" (Hurn, 1993, p. 45). For example, the image of schooling as an opportunity for social mobility based on merit is replaced, in critical thought, by one that shows how schools reproduce the unequal distribution of wealth and power that is the hallmark of capitalist societies, and in so doing contribute to the maintenance of the status quo (Shannon, 1996).

Even a brief consideration of why "critical approaches" are just beginning to find a place in the discourse on literacy will allow us to highlight some of the themes that distinguish critical approaches from those theories and methods that have dominated reading research thus far. We begin, therefore, with a brief look at what was included and excluded from the first two volumes of the *Handbook of Reading Research* (hereafter *HRR1* and *HRR2*), and then turn to the problem of defining critical approaches, working historically from the critical theory of the Frankfurt School, to Paulo Freire's work on literacy as the development of critical consciousness, to contemporary critical scholarship, especially the ideas of Michel Foucault. We conclude with some observations on current trends in critical studies of literacy education. In taking on the challenge of mapping the discourse on critical approaches to reading and literacy education, we are mindful of the fact that chapters such as these are "acts of cultural production" (Noblit & Pink, 1995, cited in Apple, 1997, p. xi) that construct the field they purport to "describe." Hence, our reading of this rapidly expanding field of studies is by no means definitive but, rather, suggestive of the multiple meanings critical approaches have today.

CRITICAL APPROACHES AND THE DISCOURSE ON READING

However problematic the exclusion of critical approaches from the discourse on reading and literacy may seem to us now, the reasons for this exclusion become clear when we consider the history of reading research. From its earliest beginnings as a field of study, reading research has followed the currents of academic psychology (cf. Luke & Freebody, 1997a; Venezky, 1984), resulting in a particular view of both the object of study and the method for studying it. This dominance is evident in *HRR1* (Pearson et al., 1984), which can be read as a tribute to psychological theories and methods and a celebration of the knowledge about reading they produced. With few exceptions, the chapters constructed reading as an autonomous (Street, 1984), psychological process unrelated to any of the social, political, cultural, and economic patterns that shape schooling, and thus treated science, schooling, and language unproblematically as neutral, rational activities unaffected by power and ideology. The few chapters that interrupted this narrative (e.g., ethnographic approaches [Guthrie & Hall, 1984], sociolinguistic directions [Bloome & Green, 1984], and social and motivational influences [Wigfield & Asher, 1984]) were quite important, as they introduced ways of conceptualizing reading and reading research drawn from anthropology and sociology. In these chapters, reading was characterized as a social and cultural activity, research methods emphasized meanings and contexts, and schools were found to play a role in producing the low levels of reading achievement among African-American and Hispanic students, although explanations for this finding tended toward theories of cultural discontinuity rather than structural inequalities (Au, 1993).

The interpretative turn that refigured the social sciences in the 1970s was fully evident when *HRR2* (Barr, Kamil, Mosenthal, & Pearson) appeared in 1991, and this shift was marked by an expanded vocabulary: *literacy*, not just *reading*, had become an object of study. For some, this meant that in addition to a psychological dimension, "literacy has acquired … a sociopolitical dimension, associated with its role within society and the ways in which it is deployed for political, cultural, and economic ends" (Venezky, 1991, p. 46). Yet, the meaning of *sociopolitical* remained largely unexamined, as evidenced by the field's uncritical acceptance of the "literacy myth," that is, the belief that literacy leads to economic and political progress (Graff, 1987). Absent from the historical treatment of literacy in *HRR2* was research that showed how literacy was used to "solidify the social hierarchy, empower elites and ensure that people lower on the hierarchy accept the values, norms, and beliefs of the elites, even when it is not in their interest to do so" (Gee, 1990, p. 40). Even when an overtly economic topic was examined, as in the chapter on the production of commercial materials (Chall & Squire, 1991), the ideological process whereby cultural material is selected and shaped for consumption in schools was taken for granted. From this brief discussion, it seems clear that although the study of reading was no longer decontextualized, the meaning of context had not yet been expanded to include the political and economic contexts. In light of this, it should probably not be surprising to find that Paulo Freire's work on critical literacy received only one mention in *HRR2*, despite the worldwide acclaim that *Pedagogy of the Oppressed* had received since its publication in 1970.

Patrick Shannon's chapter, "Politics, Policy, and Reading Research" (1991), was the one exception to this, and his opening comments on educational policy analysis can provide an introduction to the meaning of *critical* in critical approaches. He argued that educational policy analysis:

> can no longer be discussed as the natural evolution of scientific progress, neutral or benign. Rather, with political discussions included, specific policies can be identified as particular historical constructions negotiated among people with unequal power and authority to make decisions, often pursuing differing visions of how we should live together in and out of schools. (p. 47)

What makes this characterization of policy analysis "critical" is its rejection of naturalism (the assumption that policies represent unmediated reality), rationality (the assumption that policies are the result of science and logic), neutrality (the assumption that policies are not reflective of any particular interests), and individualism (the assumption that policies affect individuals without regard for their membership in particular social groups) (Popkewitz, 1990). Critical policy research, instead, assumes that educational problems must be conceptualized as part of the social, political, cultural, and economic patterns by which schooling is formed, patterns that reflect the unequal power and access of some groups in society. As Shannon noted, "critical" policy research employs a range of methods, but what sets this work apart from that of liberal and conservative policy research are the assumptions researchers make, the questions they pursue, and the value commitments they bring to their work. He wrote:

> In their attempts to identify how this imbalance of power exerts itself in specific situations, critical policy researchers use history to access the past policy negotiations and social relations that set the parameters for the current negotiations; they employ survey and statistical analyses to gather information about how the larger social structure affects all reading policies; and they utilize naturalistic methods to understand how both the powerful and the powerless cope with policy negotiations and the consequent situations.... This sense of injustice and the advocacy position in favor of teachers and students leads critical policy researchers to select questions that illuminate the power relations of reading policy and programs ... and that can expose the contradictions in reading education policy as opportunities for change. (p. 164)

Embedded in this description of critical policy research are themes that are characteristic of critical approaches to the study of literacy education: the emphasis on historical analyses of the social construction of educational problems, policies, and practices; the awareness of schooling as a site for the production and reproduction of social, economic, and political inequities; and the desire to use research to achieve social change. With these themes in mind, we turn now to the problem of understanding critical approaches.

UNDERSTANDING CRITICAL APPROACHES

There are a number of difficulties in attempting to understand "critical approaches." First, there is no single "critical approach." The word *critical* has begun to appear as a descriptor for approaches to research that are already common in education, as in "critical" ethnography (Anderson, 1989; Carspecken, 1996; Quantz, 1992; Simon & Dippo, 1986), "critical" discourse analysis (Bloome & Talwalkar, 1997; Fairclough, 1989, 1992; Gee, 1990; Luke, 1995), and "critical" action research (Carr & Kemmis, 1986; Noffke, 1997). Is there something that these approaches could be said to share? Would that shared element be "critical theory," "critical literacy," or "critical pedagogy," or perhaps a commitment to aligning purpose and method (Gitlin, Siegel, & Boru, 1989)?

These questions point to a second difficulty in understanding critical approaches, and that is that the word *critical* has no single meaning. Although it is tempting to seek a single meaning, doing so may result in forcing a uniformity of meaning where none exits or smoothing over what is in fact contested (Kincheloe & McLaren, 1994; Lankshear & McLaren, 1993). In light of these difficulties, we have chosen to present a brief overview of the historical formation of the meaning of the word *critical* because we believe understanding "critical approaches" depends on understanding the multiple meanings this word has in educational discourse. In this regard, we think it important to keep in mind Martin Jay's (1973) observation on the work of the Frankfurt School: "At the very heart of Critical Theory was an aversion to closed philosophical systems. To present it as such would therefore distort its essentially open-ended, probing, and unfinished quality" (p. 41).

The Critical Theory of the Frankfurt School

Any discussion of the meaning of *critical* must begin with a reference to the critical theory of the Frankfurt School, a group of scholars—including Max Horkheimer, Theodor Adorno, and Herbert Marcuse, among others—who formed the Institute of Social Research at the University of Frankfurt in 1923. Although the rise of Nazism forced the Institute into exile in 1935, first at Columbia University and later in California, their writings were not translated into English until the 1960s. Hence, the impact of their ideas only began to be felt when they captured the attention of students and intellectuals in the 1960s and 1970s, and later through the writings of Jurgen Habermas (Held, 1980).

Critical theory had two major thrusts: (a) a critique of positivism, which, by reducing reasoning to instrumental rationality and separating fact from values, had not only linked science to new forms of domination, but had privileged forms of reasoning that gave little emphasis to human consciousness and action; and (b) a concern for the relationship of theory and society, seeking a theory that would connect institutions, the activities of daily life, and the forces that shape the larger society—that is, connections among the economy, the culture industry, and the psychology of individuals.

Horkheimer set the stage for the idea of critical theory in his 1932 essay "Notes on Science and the Crisis" (1972), and introduced the term itself in 1937 in "Traditional and Critical Theory" (1972). The crisis that concerned Horkheimer was the failure of science to contribute to the betterment of society as a whole, and the source of this crisis was positivism (i.e., the description, classification, and generalization of facts). Horkheimer criticized positivists for reducing reasoning to formal logic, for making a fetish of facts, and for pretending to have "disentangled facts from values" (Jay, 1973, p. 62). The result, he argued, was "the abdication of reflection ... and the reification of the existing order" (Jay, 1973, p. 62). In short, science had become scientistic, something set apart from the workings of society; questions about value (i.e., deciding which problems should be addressed, deciding which course of action to take) were set aside in favor of questions about technique. Horkheimer argued that human reasoning could not simply involve passive sense-perception of reality because the world is "a product of the activity of society as a whole" (p. 200)—something made rather than given. In the following passage, Horkheimer rejected the idea of naturalism and highlighted the historical formation of both the objects perceived and the individual:

> The facts which our senses present to us are socially performed in two ways: through the historical character of the object perceived and through the historical character of the perceiving organ. Both are not simply natural; they are shaped by human activity, and yet the individual perceives himself [sic] as receptive and passive in the act of perception. (p. 200)

A central criticism of positivism, therefore, was that treating things as natural placed "questions about the genesis, development, and normative nature of the conceptual systems that select, organize, and define the facts" (Giroux, 1981, p. 14) outside the purview of science. Because the facts could not be questioned, the evaluative dimension of theory was eliminated and science became a tool of prevailing interests.

What was needed, instead, was a theory that served an unmasking function and could be used to "penetrate the world of things to show the underlying relations between persons ... and demystify the surface forms of equality" (Aronowitz, 1972, p. xiii). This involved both immanent critique and dialectical thought (Giroux, 1981). Immanent critique is the analysis of "reality" by comparing "the pretensions of bourgeois ideology with the reality of its social conditions" (Jay, 1973, p. 63) or the appearance of a social fact (e.g., money, consumption, production) and what lay behind it. Dialectical thought was a style of analysis that attempted to trace out the historical formation of facts and their mediation by social forces. The goal of this analysis was not only to unmask the connections between knowledge, power, and domination, but to construct a more just society through praxis, defined as a kind of "self-creating action" (Jay, 1973, p. 4) that was both informed by theory and controlled by people. To summarize, reason and praxis were the two poles of critical theory (Jay, 1973). One could not separate knowledge from either values or action; moreover, the researcher was never a disinterested investigator inasmuch as the investigator's reasoning was mediated by the very social categories that were the focus of study. It was this striving for critical awareness of the historical formation of human thinking and social relations that would serve as the starting point for emancipation from exploitative and oppressive social conditions.

The influence of critical theory was not felt in American intellectual circles until the 1960s, when sociologists of education (among others) grew disenchanted with the optimism of the functionalist view of schooling, and skeptical of the benefits of science and technology. Arguing that "we live in a divided and conflict-ridded society [and] groups who compete for control of schooling use the rhetoric of societal needs to conceal the fact that it is their interests and their demands they are trying to advance" (Hurn, 1993, p. 57–58), scholars began to enunciate a conflict view of schooling that questioned the rhetoric of equal opportunity and pointed out the role schools played in reproducing inequalities. Correspondence (Bowles & Gintis, 1976) and reproduction (Bourdieu & Passeron, 1977) theories offered Marxist analyses of schooling that purported to show that schools met "the needs of capital by mirroring the class-differentiated, alienated social relations of the workplace" (Wexler, 1987, p. 40). Members of the Frankfurt School rejected orthodox Marxism as overly deterministic and lacking a consideration of human consciousness, and their empirical work focused on the psychology of domination and the creation of mass deception by the emerging culture industry. Sociologists of education drew on this work to criticize the economic reductionism of correspondence and reproduction theories (e.g., Bowles & Gintis, 1976); culture, not just the economy, thus became a focal point in the cultural reproduction theory neo-Marxist scholars developed. These theories suggested that schools reproduced class relations by selecting and transmitting the culture of dominant groups as if it were universal and legitimate knowledge. Willis (1977) later argued that cultural reproduction theory ignored human agency and the internal contradictions and forms of resistance that served as sources for social change, and schools eventually came to be seen as sites for production as well as reproduction, a perspective that allowed for struggle and possibility (Wexler, 1987).

Paulo Freire and the Idea of Critical Literacy

Among literacy educators, the person most associated with critical approaches is Paulo Freire, the Brazilian philosopher and teacher whose death in 1997 was mourned by radical educators around the world. Freire's work emerged from social and political conditions that existed in Brazil in the 1960s, which he described as stratified by race and class, with a very large and very poor working class population with little or no education. He argued, further, that Brazil's history of colonialism "bred the habits of domination and dependence which still prevail among us in the form of paternalistic approaches to problems" (1973, p. 22) and "did not constitute the cultural climate necessary for the rise of democratic regimes" (1973, p. 29). In this context, Freire began to develop a pedagogy of liberation, working with adults to break what he called "the culture of silence" (1973, p. 24) and enable them to overcome the oppression they experienced. Working from Marxist theory, he rejected the idea that the "oppressed" are "marginals" living "outside" of society, and argued, instead, that "they have always been 'inside'—inside the structure which made them 'beings for others'" (Freire, 1970, p. 55). "Illiteracy" is thus regarded not as an individual failing but as a historically constructed product of a society structured to produce inequality. Freire's first literacy campaign, carried out in northeast Brazil where 15 of the 25 million people in the region were illiterate, was so successful (300 workers became literate in 45 days) that the government decided to apply his method throughout Brazil. From these experiences, Freire developed a theory of education that was radical both in its politics and its methods, and successful enough as to become a threat to those in power. When a right-wing government came to power in 1964, Freire was jailed and then exiled.

The starting point of his theory was the observation that humans, unlike animals, are culture makers who use language to mediate their world. Freire argued that the human capacity to name the world enables humans to reflect on their worlds and become aware of their social and political location in those worlds, and this awareness, in turn, creates the urge to act on the world and remake culture. This kind of awareness, which he called *conscientizacao* or critical consciousness, cannot be developed through education practiced as banking because such practices regard knowledge as "a gift bestowed" (Freire, 1970, p. 53) and students as objects into which knowledge is deposited. In contrast, problem-posing education starts with people's knowledge and, through a dialogue among equals, attempts to expose—"demythologize"—the historical conditions that create their reality so that they may act to transform those conditions. It is in this way that education becomes the practice of freedom.

The method Freire developed to engage people in dialogues that would lead to critical consciousness was grounded in language. He wrote:

> Consistent with the liberating purpose of dialogical education, the object of investigation is not persons … but rather the thought-language with which men and women refer to reality, the levels at which they perceive that reality, and their view of the world, in which their generative themes are found. (1970, p. 78)

By examining a series of generative themes represented pictorially (what Freire called codifications of the participants' world), participants in the culture circles can begin to name their world and by decoding it begin to transform that reality. This is followed by work with syllables carefully selected for their ability to generate a range of words that can be used to examine the codifications. As even this brief description indicates, this approach to teaching literacy does not treat reading as a technical matter of reading words, but a political matter of reading the world and rewriting that world (Freire, 1987). Critical literacy can thus be defined as the practice of demystifying the conditions that oppress and working toward the transformation of those conditions. From this has come the idea of critical pedagogy as "classroom practice consistent with liberatory politics" (Gore, 1993, p. 42), a definition that attends "both to social vision and to instruction" (p. 42).

Contemporary Perspectives on the Meaning of "Critical"[1]

In recent years, these interpretations of *critical* have themselves been criticized, due in part to what these perspectives have ignored as well as to new social theories that have been taken up in the academy. Feminists, for example, have argued that Freire's theory emphasizes forms of oppression that result from an inequitable class structure over those that result from gender and racial inequalities. By speaking about oppression in abstract and universal terms, Freire ignores the ways in which gender and race, as well as class, serve as oppressive forces (Weiler, 1991). Feminists, among others, have also argued that critical pedagogy, which was meant to serve as a "pedagogy of hope" against the despair of reproduction theories of education, became as dominating and limiting as more traditional educational practices (e.g., Ellsworth, 1989; Gore, 1993; Knoblach & Brannon, 1993; Luke & Gore, 1992). Critical scholars have also argued that critical theory needs to be rethought or modified, given the shift from industrialism to postindustrialism, and the limitations of structuralism and modernism (Gee, 1990; Lankshear & McLaren, 1993; Wexler, 1987). Indeed, critical approaches have been profoundly reshaped by postmodernism, which critiques grand narratives about the direction of history (e.g., the Marxist narrative of class conflict and revolution), poststructuralism, which critiques the Enlightenment idea of progress, reason, and power (Popkewitz & Brennan, 1998), and postcolonialism, which rereads western knowledge as forged in the context of relationships between the west and the non-west. Because Michel Foucault's work has been so influential in reformulating critical scholarship, we comment briefly on his contributions to contemporary critical approaches.

Although Foucault knew the work of the Frankfurt School, and regarded its examination of rationality important, he did not accept its belief that enlightenment—the development of consciousness—would free people. As Popkewitz and Brennan (1998) explained, the philosophy of consciousness, the cornerstone of critical theory and critical literacy as well as of functionalist views of schooling, was rooted in two ideas from 19th-century thought: (a) the idea that rational knowledge was the engine of progress, and (b) the idea that the avenue of social progress was through individual human consciousness and action. Foucault upset these foundations of knowing and rationality when he suggested that our very concepts (such as individual agency, reason, abnormality, the child, etc.) were already *effects* of power; thus he questioned whether critical theory hid more than it revealed. As a result of this inquiry, he shifted his emphasis from human consciousness and agency to the changing ways in which knowledge and humanness were historically constituted. This approach to studying knowledge as a social practice is called *decentering the subject* and provides a way to understand how the subject is produced by systems of ideas that relate power and knowledge. Foucault called these systems of ideas *discourses* and turned his attention from the study of "autonomous" subjects to the study of how discourses, as historical practices, construct objects. Discourses operate both across disciplinary boundaries (e.g., across medicine, law, education, and social work) and within material practices across social locations (e.g., juvenile courts, hospitals, schools, and social service agencies).

Another aspect of critical theory and critical literacy that Foucault reconceptualized was power. In these theories, power is regarded as something people do or do not have, but Foucault (1977) argued that power is diffused through all social relationships in concrete and detailed specificity (pp. 115–116). Thus, he rejected the notion that power is primarily repressive and juridical, and proposed, instead, that power "tra-

---

[1]The contemporary landscape of critical work is more complex than what we can present here; our hope is that this brief overview can give a sense of the issues being developed in the discourse.

verses and produces things, it induces pleasure, forms knowledge, produces discourse. It needs to be considered as a productive network which runs through the whole social body" (p. 119). Knowledge or truth, on the other hand,

> isn't outside power or lacking in power.... Truth is a thing of this world: it is produced only by virtue of multiple forms of constraint. And it induces regular effects of power. Each society has its regime of truth, its "general politics" of truth: that is, the types of discourse which it accepts and makes function as true; the mechanisms and instances which enable one to distinguish true and false statements, the means by which each is sanctioned; the techniques and procedures accorded value in the acquisition of truth; the status of those who are charged with saying what counts as true. (p. 131)

Knowledge and power are thus inextricably intertwined in that what counts as knowledge is related to and may indeed arise from the ways in which power is diffused throughout society and within social relationships. From a Foucauldian perspective, then, "*critical* refers to a broad band of disciplined questioning of the ways in which power works through the discursive practices and performances of schooling" (emphasis in the original, Popkewitz & Brennan, 1998, p. 4).

CRITICAL APPROACHES TO STUDYING LITERACY EDUCATION

Locating the literature that could be characterized as *critical* within the field of literacy education is not as straightforward as it may seem, largely because, until quite recently, there were few such studies, and those that were published tended to appear as books, book chapters, and articles in general educational journals (e.g., *Harvard Educational Review*) and practitioner-oriented journals (e.g., *Rethinking Schools*) rather than in the mainstream research journals in the field (e.g., *Reading Research Quarterly, Journal of Literacy Research*). Despite these problems, several lines of work can be identified. One line of work, inspired by neo-Marxist critical theory, examines the political economy of reading instruction (a study of the historical relations between means of production and state structures) in order to show the ideological dimensions of what are thought to be neutral technologies (i.e., commercially published materials and instructional practices) of reading instruction (Luke, 1989, 1991; Shannon, 1989). Shannon (1989) extended his work on basal reading materials by examining the ways these materials serve to deskill teachers, whereas Luke (1988, 1989), showed how particular literacy practices come to be selected and authorized in the official discourse on literacy education.

A second line of work attempts to move beyond cultural discontinuity explanations for the low levels of reading achievement among African-American and Hispanic students by considering issues of power and politics as well as cultural differences. Drawing on Freire's theory, this work explores the ways that students' positioning in the larger society intersects with school literacy practices to silence them and construct them as school failures rather than literate persons, or, in other cases, to enable them to give voice to their knowledge and begin to read their world and rewrite it (e.g., Mitchell & Weiler, 1991; Walsh, 1991a). Other literacy scholars have woven together Freirean ideas with those of Russian language and social philosopher Mikhail Bakhtin to show how power works through language and how acknowledging students' voices can inform pedagogy and expand students' possibilities (e.g., Gutierrez, Rymes, & Larson, 1995; Walsh, 1991b). A few progressive literacy educators (e.g., Edelsky, 1991) have used critical theory and Freirean theory to articulate their underlying political commitment to challenging social and economic inequalities, something others are less sanguine about because they believe whole language and process writing instruction have taken hold, in part, because they serve corporate interests in an information society (Willinsky, 1990).[2]

One of the most fertile strands of critical work on literacy education is inspired by poststructuralist theories, as indicated by the interest in critical discourse analysis (e.g., Bloome & Talwalkar, 1997; Fairclough, 1989, 1992; Gee, 1990; Luke, 1995) and in feminist poststructuralist studies of literacy education (e.g., Davies, 1989, 1993; Gilbert, 1991, 1993, 1997). In some cases, this work combines critical theory, sociocultural theories of literacy (e.g., Street, 1984), and poststructuralist theory to critique progressive literacy pedagogies such as process writing and whole language (Luke & Freebody, 1997a, 1997b). This line of scholarship points up the contradictions in these practices and shows that what are thought to be "natural," "authentic," and "empowering" pedagogies may unintentionally reinforce the status quo by valorizing particular kinds of literacy practices or allowing oppressive practices to enter the classroom in an attempt to value students' "voices" or encourage teachers to serve as "facilitators" (e.g., Gilbert, 1991, 1997).

Despite the differences in the meaning of *critical* within critical scholarship on literacy education, we can (tentatively) note some themes that this work seems to share. One is that literacy is conceptualized as a social and political practice rather than a set of neutral, psychological skills. Another is that critical approaches look beyond the taken-for-granted explanations of practices and policies to understand their historical formation, especially the ways in which discourses—systems of ideas traditionally thought to be "outside" of schooling—work to construct the instructional practices and social relations that constitute literacy education in schools. And, finally, critical approaches seek to challenge and transform the status quo by engaging people in a "collective process of re-naming, re-writing, re-positioning oneself in relation to coercive structures" (Davies, 1993, p. 199).

CONCLUDING THOUGHTS

We began this chapter by asking why critical approaches had been excluded from the discourse on literacy education, and this question continues to trouble us, especially at a time when bilingual education and affirmative action are under attack. Why have we agreed not to frame literacy education as political? One explanation is that we, as a field, have made a fetish of the search for the "correct" methods of teaching reading. Yet, as Bartolome (1994) noted, this "methods fetish" only serves to deflect our attention from questions about the inequalities and injustices that persist in schools and society. Critical approaches to the study of literacy education examine the ways in which literacy instruction participates in the production of these persistent inequalities but also how literacy instruction may become a site for contesting the status quo. Although this line of scholarship is just beginning to receive attention within the field of literacy education, the need for work that addresses these issues is more urgent than ever as new literacies, along with new modes of exploitation, multiply in our increasingly globalized and digitalized world.

---

[2]This debate reflects the ambiguous legacy of the Progressivism (the social movement critical of the urban, capitalist, industrial society that was emerging at the turn of the 20th century); although progressives were committed to social progress and believed in equality, efficiency, and science, there is disagreement as to whether this movement was liberal or conservative because, it is argued, it helped consolidate the emerging corporate capitalism (Wexler, 1976).

ACKNOWLEDGMENTS

We acknowledge the contributions of Desiree Baird, Nadine Bryce, Peggy McNamara, Anastasia Maroulis, Hannah Schneewind, and Susan Stires—whose efforts to locate the literature on critical approaches to literacy research did much to shape this chapter. Special thanks go to Nancy Lesko and Michelle Knight for their careful readings and constructive comments on an earlier draft of this chapter, and to David Pearson for his support and patience.

REFERENCES

Anderson, G. (1989). Critical ethnography in education: Origins, current status, and new directions. *Review of Educational Research, 59*, 249–270.

Apple, M. (1997). Introduction. In M. Apple (Ed.), *Review of research in education* (Vol. 22, pp. xi–xxi). Washington, DC: American Educational Research Association.

Aronowitz, S. (1972). Introduction. In M. Horkheimer, *Critical theory: Selected essays* (pp. xi–xxi). New York: Herder & Herder.

Au, K. (1993). *Literacy instruction in multicultural settings.* Fort Worth, TX: Harcourt Brace.

Barr, R., Kamil, M., Mosenthal, P., & Pearson, P. D. (Eds.). (1991). *Handbook of reading research* (Vol. 2). New York: Longman.

Bartolome, L. (1994). Beyond the methods fetish: Toward a humanizing pedagogy. *Harvard Educational Review, 64*(2), 173–194.

Bloome, D., & Green, J. (1984). Directions in the sociolinguistic study of reading. In P. D. Pearson (Ed.), *Handbook of reading research* (Vol. 1, pp. 395–422). New York: Longman.

Bloome, D., & Talwalkar, S. (1997). Critical discourse analysis and the study of reading and writing. *Reading Research Quarterly, 32*(1), 104–112.

Bourdieu, P., & Passeron, J. (1977). *Reproduction in education, society, and culture.* London: Sage.

Bowles, S., & Gintis, H. (1976). *Schooling in capitalist America.* New York: Basic Books.

Carr, S., & Kemmis, W. (1986). *Becoming critical: Education, knowledge, and action research.* London: Falmer Press.

Carspecken, P. (1996). *Critical ethnography in educational research.* New York: Routledge.

Chall, J., & Squire, J. (1991). The publishing industry and textbooks. In R. Barr, M. Kamil, P. Mosenthal, & P. D. Pearson (Eds.), *Handbook of reading research* (Vol. 2, pp. 120–146). New York: Longman.

Davies, B. (1989). *Frogs and snails and feminist tales: Preschool children and gender.* Sydney: Allen & Unwin.

Davies, B. (1993). *Shards of glass: Children reading and writing beyond gendered identities.* Cresskill, NJ: Hampton Press.

Edelsky, C. (1991). *With literacy and justice for all.* London: Falmer Press.

Ellsworth, E. (1989). Why doesn't this feel empowering?: Working through the repressive myths of critical pedagogy. *Harvard Educational Review, 59*(3), 297–324.

Fairclough, N. (1989). *Language and power.* London: Longman.

Fairclough, N. (1992). *Discourse and social change.* Cambridge: Polity Press.

Foucault, M. (1977). *Power/knowledge: Selected interviews and other writings (1972–1977)* (C. Gordon, L. Marshall, J. Mepham, & K. Soper, Trans.). New York: Pantheon Books.

Freire, P. (1970). *Pedagogy of the oppressed.* New York: Continuum.

Freire, P. (1973). *Education for critical consciousness.* New York: Continuum.

Freire, P. (1987). *Literacy: Reading the word and the world.* South Hadley, MA: Bergin & Garvey.

Gee, J. P. (1990). *Social linguistics and literacies: Ideologies in discourses.* London: Falmer Press.

Gilbert, P. (1991, June). *The story so far: Gender, literacy and social regulation.* Paper presented at the Rejuvenation Conference of the Center for the Expansion of Language and Thinking, Amherst, MA.

Gilbert, P. (1993). Dolly fictions: Teen romance down under. In L. Christian-Smith (Ed.), *Texts of desire: Essays on fiction, femininity and schooling* (pp. 69–86). London: Falmer Press.

Gilbert, P. (1997). Discourses on gender and literacy: Changing the stories. In S. Muspratt, A. Luke, & P. Freebody (Eds.), *Constructing critical literacies: Teaching and learning textual practice* (pp. 59–75). Cresskill, NJ: Hampton Press.

Giroux, H. (1981). *Critical theory and educational practice.* Victoria, Australia: Deakin University Press.

Gitlin, A., Siegel, M., & Boru, K. (1989). The politics of method: From leftist ethnography to educative research. *International Journal of Qualitative Studies in Education, 2*(3), 237–253.

Gore, J. (1993). *The struggle for pedagogies: Critical and feminist pedagogies as regimes of truth.* New York: Routledge.

Graff, H. (1987). *The legacies of literacy: Continuities and contradictions in western culture and society.* Bloomington, IN: Indiana University Press.

Guthrie, L., & W. Hall. (1984). Ethnographic approaches to reading research. In P. D. Pearson (Ed.), *Handbook of reading research* (Vol. 1, pp. 91–110). New York: Longman.

Gutierrez, K., Rymes, B., & Larson, J. (1995). Script, counterscript, and underlife in the classroom: James Brown *versus* Brown v. Board of Education. *Harvard Educational Review, 65*(3), 445–471.

Held, D. (1980). *Introduction to critical theory: Horkheimer to Habermas.* Berkeley: University of California Press.

Horkheimer, M. (1972). *Critical theory: Selected essays.* New York: Herder & Herder.

Hurn, C. (1993). *The limits and possibilities of schooling* (3rd ed.). Boston: Allyn & Bacon.

Jay, M. (1973). *The dialectical imagination: A history of the Frankfurt School and the Institute of Social Research 1923–1950.* Boston: Little, Brown.

Kincheloe, J., & McLaren, P. (1994). Rethinking critical theory and qualitative research. In N. Denzin & Y. Lincoln (Eds.), *Handbook of qualitative research* (pp. 138–157). Thousand Oaks, CA: Sage.

Knoblach, C., & Brannon, L. (1993). *Critical teaching and the idea of literacy.* Portsmouth, NH: Boyton/Cook.

Lankshear, C., & McLaren, P. (Eds.). (1993). *Critical literacy: Politics, praxis, and the postmodern.* Albany: State University of New York Press.

Luke, A. (1989). *Literacy, textbooks, and ideology: Postwar literacy instruction and the mythology of Dick and Jane.* London: Falmer.

Luke, A. (1991). The political economy of reading instruction. In C. Baker & A. Luke (Eds.), *Towards a critical sociology of reading pedagogy* (pp. 3–25). Amsterdam: John Benjamins.

Luke, A. (1995). Text and discourse in education: An introduction to critical discourse analysis. In M. Apple (Ed.), *Review of research in education* (Vol. 21, pp. 3–48). Washington, DC: American Educational Research Association.

Luke, A., & Freebody, P. (1997a). Critical literacy and the question of normativity: An introduction. In S. Muspratt, A. Luke, & P. Freebody (Eds.), *Constructing critical literacies: Teaching and learning textual practice* (pp. 1–18). Cresskill, NJ: Hampton Press.

Luke, A., & Freebody, P. (1997b). The social practices of reading. In S. Muspratt, A. Luke, & P. Freebody (Eds.), *Constructing critical literacies: Teaching and learning textual practice* (pp. 185–225). Cresskill, NJ: Hampton Press.

Luke, C., & Gore, J. (Eds.). (1992). *Feminisms and critical pedagogy.* New York: Routledge.

Mitchell, C., & Weiler, K. (Eds.). (1991). *Rewriting literacy: Culture and the discourse of the other.* New York: Bergin & Garvey.

Noffke, S. (1997). Professional, personal, and political dimensions of action research. In M. Apple (Ed.), *Review of research in education* (Vol. 22, pp. 305–343). Washington, DC: American Educational Research Association.

Pearson, P. D., Barr, R., Kamil, M., & Mosenthal, P. (Eds.). (1984). *Handbook of reading research* (Vol. 1). New York: Longman.

Popkewitz, T. (1990). Whose future? Whose past? Notes on critical theory and methodology. In E. Guba (Ed.), *The paradigm dialog* (pp. 46–66). Newbury Park, CA: Sage.

Popkewitz, T., & Brennan, M. (1998). Introduction. In T. Popkewitz & M. Brennan (Eds.), *Foucault's challenge: Discourse, knowledge, and power in education* (pp. 3–35). New York: Teachers College Press.

Quantz, R. (1992). On critical ethnography (with some postmodern considerations). In M. LeCompte, W. Millroy, & J. Preissle (Eds.), *The handbook of qualitative research in education* (pp. 447–505). San Diego: Academic Press.

Shannon, P. (1989). *Broken promises: Reading instruction in twentieth-century America.* Granby, MA: Bergin & Garvey.

Shannon, P. (1991). Politics, policy, and reading research. In R. Barr, M. Kamil, P. Mosenthal, & P. D. Pearson (Eds.), *Handbook of reading research* (Vol. 2, pp. 147–168). New York: Longman.

Shannon, P. (1996). Critical issues: Literacy and educational policy. Part two (Poverty, literacy, and politics: Living in the USA). *Journal of Literacy Research, 28*(3), 429–449.

Simon, R., & Dippo, D. (1986). On critical ethnographic work. *Anthropology and Education Quarterly, 17,* 195–202.

Street, B. (1984). *Literacy in theory and practice.* Cambridge: Cambridge University Press.

Venezky, R. (1984). The history of reading research. In P. D. Pearson (Ed.), *Handbook of reading research* (Vol. 1, pp. 3–38). New York: Longman.

Venezky, R. (1991). The development of literacy in the industrialized nations of the west. In R. Barr, M. Kamil, P. Mosenthal, & P. D. Pearson (Eds.), *Handbook of reading research* (Vol. 2, pp. 46–67). New York: Longman.

Walsh, C. (Ed.). (1991a). *Literacy as praxis: Culture, language, and pedagogy.* Norwood, NJ: Ablex.

Walsh, C. (1991b). *Pedagogy and the struggle for voice.* New York: Bergin & Garvey.

Weiler, K. (1991). Freire and a feminist pedagogy of difference. *Harvard Educational Review, 61*(4), 449–474.

Wexler, P. (1976). *The sociology of education: Beyond equality.* Indianapolis, IN: Bobbs-Merrill.

Wexler, P. (1987). *Social analysis of education: After the new sociology.* London: Routledge & Kegan Paul.

Wigfield, A., & Asher, S. (1984). Social and motivational influences on reading. In P. D. Pearson (Ed.), *Handbook of reading research* (Vol. 1, pp. 423–452). New York: Longman.

Willinsky, J. (1990). *The new literacy.* New York: Routledge.

Willis, P. (1977). *Learning to labor.* Westmead, England: Saxon House.

Young, M. F. D. (Ed.). (1971). *Knowledge and control.* London: Collier-Macmillan.

CHAPTER 11

Ethnographic Approaches to Literacy Research

Susan Florio-Ruane
Michigan State University
Mary McVee
University of Nevada, Reno

ETHNOGRAPHY OLD AND NEW:
UNDERSTANDING LANGUAGE, CULTURE, AND EDUCATION

When the first *Handbook of Reading Research* was published in 1984, it included a chapter on ethnography by Larry F. Guthrie and William S. Hall. Joining a related chapter on sociolinguistics (by David Bloome and Judith Green), the chapter reviewed the interpretive study of literacy education in U.S. schools. Shortly thereafter, related reviews were published in the third edition of the *Handbook of Research on Teaching* (1986), including a chapter on qualitative research (by Frederick Erickson) and one on classroom discourse (by Courtney Cazden). Ethnography dominated educators' interest in interpretive research. Noting that by 1984 ethnography was fast "approaching the status of a catchword" (p. 91), Guthrie and Hall reviewed its contributions to literacy research. In this, the second chapter on ethnography, we examine some of the ways in which the approach continues to inform research on language, culture, and education.

Although ethnography was new to many educational researchers in the early 1980s, it has a long history. Literally "a picture of the people," ethnography is the study of culture. It offers a holistic theoretical perspective from which to view education, an array of accessible research tools, and a narrative genre for research reporting. Shirley Brice Heath instructed educational researchers that an understanding of ethnography "depends on linking it to its traditional disciplinary base in anthropology and its role in the anthropologist's study of human behavior in cross-cultural perspective" (1982, p. 33). Heath's comment underscores the disciplinary roots of ethnography in *studies of culture* and the importance of *comparison and contrast across cultures* as a part of such study.

Human beings have been studying culture more or less systematically as long as they have been traveling. Using observation, participation, comparison, and contrast, people have exploited their visits to unfamiliar places to learn about others' ways of life and to reflect on their own. Ethnography was born out of our curiosity about different ways of behaving and making sense. Hymes noted in this regard that:

> If one traces the history of ethnography where it leads, one goes back centuries, indeed, to the ancient Mediterranean world, ... Herodotus being its most famous, but not only exemplar. With regard to just the Americas, one can trace a fairly continuous history of the ethnographic reports, interacting with the posing of ethnological questions, from the first discovery of the New World.... If ethnography is new to some in education, certainly it is not new to the world. (1982, p. 21)

Yet, despite its long history and disciplinary pedigree, two related problems have complicated the application of ethnography to contemporary research on literacy education in the United States:

1. The definition of culture, and hence the clarification of ethnography's purposes, method, and texts, is under transformation within anthropology (Behar & Gordon, 1995; Clifford & Marcus, 1986; Rosaldo, 1989).
2. The field of anthropology lacks, in Hymes's words, "a unified conception of ethnography in relation to the study of institutions in our own society, such as education" (1982, p. 21).

Anthropologists were grappling with these issues as their ways of working came to the attention of the educational research community in the mid 20th century. The cross-fertilization of ethnography with questions of educational policy and practice has advanced work in both domains.

In colonial times, ethnographers considered culture to be a static state, isomorphic with bounded ethnic or language groups. In the postcolonial world, however, culture has taken on kaleidoscopic complexity. Certainly cultural contact and transformation have always been present in human society, but their dynamics are more starkly visible in the 20th century's global, economic interdependence and technologies for rapid travel and communication. "Triangulating" cultural identity, people cross borders of all kinds as a part of their daily life (Florio-Ruane, 1997; Hoffman, 1989). The following vignette illustrates this.

In the early 1980s, one of the authors of this chapter (Florio-Ruane) traveled to rural Alaska shortly after the completion of the Alaska pipeline. She arrived on a frigid November evening, invited by the Teacher Corps at the University of Alaska in Fairbanks to offer a workshop on writing instruction for teacher educators. Working in a pilot field-based program, these young men and women crisscrossed Alaska to instruct and supervise native Alaskans learning to teach in their home villages. For the Athabaskans who lived in the interior, this would be the first generation of native school teachers, yet another aspect of the 20th-century cultural transformation they experienced as they abandoned nomadic life and became literate in English.

Stepping off the small plane in Fort Yukon, a village north of the Arctic Circle, Florio-Ruane was whisked into the frigid night on a dogsled. Although dogsleds were rapidly being replaced by snow mobiles, they were still in use, especially for treating visitors to an authentic Alaskan experience. (The next day, however, she would mount a Ski-doo when invited to check hand-made rabbit traps on the arctic tundra.) Florio-Ruane was delivered to a rustic cabin on the outskirts of town and greeted warmly by its owners. Their children barely looked away from the television set to acknowledge their guest's arrival. They were engrossed in watching a tight-trousered John Travolta strut down a New York street to the disco rhythms of the Bee Gees, a popular Australian band.

Contemporary anthropologists can no longer afford to engage exclusively in the description and comparison of "cultures" as static systems. In James Clifford's words, "people and things are increasingly out of place" (1988, p. 6). This forces a shift in the focus of cultural inquiry to what Bhabha calls those "in between spaces" where the self is elaborated as people engage with one another (1994, pp. 1–2). Just at the point when U.S. educational researchers were beginning to employ the cultural lens, the very idea of "culture" was under transformation. Eisenhart commented that in our time, "older views of culture as a group's distinct pattern of behaviors, or coherent 'way-of-life,' lost ground to an interpretive view of culture as 'webs of significance,' or meanings partially shared and manipulated by those who knew them" (Eisenhart, in press, p. 2).

Thus anthropologists found themselves addressing education as a process that not only transmits culture but also transforms it as diverse people come together within the institutions of complex society (Eisenhart, 1995). Yet, coming newly to ethnography, educational researchers did not immediately to grasp this shift in thinking about culture or its significance for research on teaching and learning. Some early ethnographic studies of education presumed a relatively static model of culture (Eisenhart, in press). Others, perhaps uninspired by the flatness of such a model, disregarded culture altogether and drew from ethnography only its narrative-style data collection and reporting techniques. But, as educational researchers first encountered it, ethnography was old—and it was new. Ethnography was emerging as a way of seeing that might be usefully applied to studying education in the complex institutions of our own society and in others worldwide. Concomitantly, this application would contribute to the ferment within anthropology around the concept of culture or the function of education as cultural praxis.

THE ETHNOGRAPHIC STUDY OF EDUCATION AS CULTURAL PRAXIS

Educational anthropology gathered itself into a field of study in the United States in the 1960s. It formalized that process with the establishment of the Council on Anthropology and Education (CAE) in 1970. From the outset, the blending of anthropology and education pushed the limits of theory and method in both fields. This was especially the case in ethnographic research on the teaching and learning of literacy. Reading, writing, and oral language were viewed by cultural anthropologists as a constellation of communicative tools and practices essential to the reflexive process of constructing culture by participating in it. To study literacy education as cultural praxis required interpretive, field-based methods of data collection, analysis, and reporting.

This shift in research question and method captured the attention of literacy researchers in the 1960s and 1970s but was anticipated as early as 1936. In that year, Bradislaw Malinowski, a pioneer of modern ethnography, urged anthropologists who wanted to study language and its acquisition to go to the people. He reasoned that if we want to understand how language is learned and used, we should, as participant observers, study and describe "living speech in its actual context of situation" (Malinowski, 1936, cited in Hymes, 1964, p. 63, and Florio-Ruane, 1987, p. 187). Malinowski's dictum was striking in its advancement of three key ideas:

1. Language, although rule governed, is living and, as such, is subject to improvisation, negotiation, and change—it has a history, a present, and a future.
2. People use language (both oral and written) to communicate within activities, settings, and relationships.
3. Meaning resides in the relationship of language forms to the functions they serve in those activities, settings, and relationships.

More than a half century later, these features of language and culture continue to inform research on literacy education.

By the 1970s, educational researchers had devised a robust method for studying the effects of teaching on the learning of students. According to Koehler (1978), this method, known as "process-product," described "which teaching processes are effective in relation to desired outcomes such as student achievement" (cited in Cazden, 1986, p. 432). Yet powerful as this method is for testing the outcomes of instructional interventions, it is limited in its ability "to define or describe the process" by which the outcomes are achieved (Koehler, 1978, cited in Cazden, 1986, p. 432). To theorize about the dynamic processes of teaching and learning, researchers needed to know more about the "hidden dimensions" of what Erickson called, "taught cognitive learning" in both its immediate and wider sociocultural contexts (Erickson, 1982).

For contemporary literacy researchers, the ethnographic turn brought new ways to think about their work. Literacy could be thought of not only as a constellation of school subjects (reading, writing, speaking, and listening) or a private intellectual achievement, but as observable practices, learned and used within communities and constituent of social and cultural identity (Bauman & Sherzer, 1974; Gee, 1989). In this spirit, literacy is studied within an "ecology" that is cultural, social, historical, and psychological (Barton, 1994). Researchers look at the role of written language in the "total communicative economy" of a society (Basso, 1974). They analyze the multiple and situated "literacies" individuals learn and practice (e.g., Scribner, 1984; Scribner & Cole, 1981), and describe the forms and functions of those literate practices as well as their distribution across status, role, activity, situation, and community (e.g., Heath, 1983).

Since the late 1970s, we have seen ethnographic studies of school structuring and classroom social organization as these shape literacy teaching and learning; case studies and cross-case comparisons of literate practices taught and learned within schools, families, and communities; studies of differential treatment and access to knowledge among literacy learners from diverse social and linguistic backgrounds; and studies of text-related discourse, both oral and written, as the social construction of knowledge among members of a community (see reviews by Bloome, 1991; Cazden, 1987; Erickson, 1986; Florio-Ruane, 1994; Jacob & Jordan, 1987; and Raphael & Brock, 1997). Throughout, ethnographic research on education has retained an interest in cross-cultural comparison, focusing primarily on differential treatment and access to knowledge within the schools of a society characterized by diversity in race, language, ethnicity, and social class (Hess, 1998). These have been important issues for applied research because, as Scribner (1984) noted, how we think about literacy profoundly informs the policies (both explicit and implicit) that guide formal education. In her words:

> The definitional controversy has more than academic significance. Each formulation of an answer to the question, 'What is literacy?' leads to a different evaluation of the scope of the problem (i.e., the extent of *il* literacy) and to different objectives for programs aimed at the formation of a literate citizenry. Definitions of literacy shape our perceptions of individuals who fall on either side of the standard (what a 'literate' or 'nonliterate' is like) and thus in a deep way affect both the substance and style of educational programs. (p. 6, parentheses and emphasis in original)

DEVELOPMENTS IN ETHNOGRAPHIC RESEARCH ON LITERACY EDUCATION

In 1982, Dell Hymes challenged anthropologists and educational researchers to work together not simply to apply or import research techniques from anthropology to education, but to create a field, an *educational* anthropology. As we prepared this chapter, we considered various ways to illustrate developments in educational anthropology. We noted that, in 1984, one literacy researcher, Kathryn Au, was noted by Guthrie and

Hall for her "studies of reading as a social activity" (p. 102). As such, Au's work had three important characteristics: It applied ethnography to investigating educational practice; it undertook comparative analysis by considering the mismatch of norms for literate practices across pupils' home and school experiences; and it applied insights about language use in diverse cultural contexts to the improvement of teaching and learning within classrooms.

We returned to Au's work as we drafted this chapter in 1998. In addition to reading or rereading many of her writings, we asked her to reflect on her work and the field in terms of the following important developments in educational ethnography since the last *Handbook* chapter was published:

1. Research in the context of reform, especially instructional research grounded in thoughtful ethnography.
2. Ethnographic studies of literacy in relation to social historical theory.
3. The influence of postmodern thought in educational ethnography, especially feminism, which emphasizes the transactional nature of research and teaching. We close our chapter by looking at these three issues with particular reference to Au's research and commentary.

ETHNOGRAPHICALLY GROUNDED INSTRUCTIONAL RESEARCH IN THE CONTEXT OF REFORM

Like her contemporaries (several of whom were cited in 1984 by Guthrie and Hall), Au's early research focused on comparisons of literacy and learning at home and at school. Well-known ethnographic research among Hawaiian youngsters (e.g., Boggs, 1972; Watson-Gegeo & Boggs, 1977) had documented differences in narrative practices across these settings. Informed by this body of research, Au worked with teachers and children in the Kamehameha Early Education Program (KEEP) to study approaches to literacy instruction that might more effectively support the school literacy learning of Hawaiian youngsters (e.g., Au, 1980).

From the outset, however, Au was less than sanguine about the contributions to education of a theoretical frame that presumed a static conception of culture. An experienced teacher and teacher educator, she found no easy instructional "matches" for what had allegedly been "mismatched" as children made the transition into school and its literate practices. Recognizing that neither children's cultural experiences nor the practice of teaching were that discretely simple, Au and Mason wrote that while the idea that

> culturally congruent elements in lessons given to minority children may help to prevent damaging conflicts between teacher and students ... has much intuitive appeal, ... we have very little evidence to support the notion that the presence of school situations resembling those in the home leads to improved academic achievement by minority children (1981, p. 150)

In the ensuing years, Au and her colleagues sought to move beyond descriptions of home and school as isolated places whose borders diverse children crossed at their peril. Instead, focusing on culturally responsive educational practice, Au engaged in a program of research to create, document and evaluated transactional ways of teaching that might enhance the learning of low-achieving young readers (e.g., Au & Carroll, 1997). For Au, the most important test of a method is the consequences of what can be learned by using it for the benefit of those studied. Thus, although descriptive studies are interesting, Au told us recently that educational ethnographers need to continue to ask of their work: *What is educational about educational anthropology?*

Trying to take from ethnography useful constructs for education, Au trained her gaze on the points of contact between teachers and young readers and writers. These encounters are viewed as not only points of contact among people whose prior cultural experiences may differ, but as occasions that are cultural in their own right—places of learning and transformation. Au has said in this regard that as we consider contexts (e.g., language use, cultural practices) for learning, we must examine instruction. Her ethnographically informed instructional research has been directly applied to the improvement of teaching and teacher education, both preservice education within the university and in-service education in the profession at large (Au, 1995).

In 1981, Au lamented (with Cathie Jordan) that research on cultural differences had not "substantially changed the situation for minority culture children" (p. 139). Au told us that in the 1980s she found it "very discouraging how little impact research has had on policy and teacher education." She noted that by using ethnography we "can further refine our understandings and descriptions" of the processes by which literacy is learned. But there is a danger that our descriptions will not inform subsequent practice. In her words, "it is more critical at this juncture for us to be reform minded" (interview, February, 1998).

Au is one of a number of educational ethnographers whose descriptive studies of the discontinuity between learning at home and at school, especially for economically disadvantaged and/or ethnic minority children, have given way to research in sites of their own and others' reform-oriented practice (Hess, 1998). Ray McDermott, whose research was also described in Guthrie and Hall's chapter, recently wrote (with Shelley Goldman) of the proliferation of applied studies by educational ethnographers, that "good theory and successfully changing the world do not have to be completely overlapping, but we cannot afford to let them be antithetical" (McDermott & Goldman, 1998, p. 126).

Ethnographic Research on Literacy, Culture, and Thought

Au's work exemplifies another development of ethnography since the mid 1980s, that of the integration of social historical theory (Vygotsky, 1978) with educational anthropology. Researchers from a hybrid of traditions including anthropology and psychology have probed how literacy as both cultural tool and cultural practice is influenced by social and historical factors as well as the micro-politics of face to face interaction (e.g., Scribner & Cole, 1981; Moll, 1992). Au's work has been influenced by this exploration. Yet as we merge the study of culture with the study of individuals' learning in dialogue with one another, Au believed there remains a need to "take adequate account of differences in ethnicity, primary language, and social class that may affect students' school literacy learning" (1998, p. 306). This statement echoes the commitment that Au and her colleagues held when they conducted their work at KEEP in the 1980s. However, Au's reading of social historical theory led her to a more complex understanding of culture as a process of identification of self in and by means of contact with others.

Au fears that when educators hear the phrase "literacy as a cultural tool," they may tend to think of "culture" and "tools" as static. Given the history of research in the field, it is easy to make this assumption and to disregard the possibility that new forms of literacy can and do happen as a part of teaching and learning (see, e.g., New London Group, 1996). During an interview with Au preparatory to the writing of this chapter, she stressed the idea that tools for communication are human creations that arise out of the "hybrid culture" of interactions among people. This is true in both within and outside the classroom. In this sense, a classroom can become a cultural setting in which participants develop common expressive ground as they undertake meaningful activities in support of learning.

Looking back on Au's earlier research, it is notable that teachers adopted and adapted not perfect "matches" of ways of talking about text at home to ways of talking about text at school, but hybrid forms of text-based talk that drew on the meanings, intentions, and prior knowledge of both teachers and pupils. Learning about Hawaiian children's entering knowledge of "talk-story" gave teachers insight into the meaning that youngsters were making of oral response to narrative selections read in school. This insight can be thought of as transforming the relationship between teacher and learner (and among learners) as teachers found ways of conversationally calling up appropriate and familiar ways of speaking to support the further development of school-based cognitive skills. To this end, teachers were initially learners not unlike ethnographic field workers. It was their responsibility to understand youngsters' understandings, especially their prior knowledge and experience with text-based talk. Their pedagogical task was to engage in relationships with youngsters and around stories by "mutual participation" (Au & Jordan, 1981, p. 146). Ultimately, the teachers made these transactions educational as they interwove the threads of school literacy into the fabric of youngsters' prior, informal learning.

Viewed this way, culturally responsive instruction involves identifying features of both teachers' and students' experiences that can be drawn on and transformed to create educationally productive dialogue. Its purpose is not to give teachers a recipe or set of rules that might further separate them from meaningful encounters with youngsters and text, but to help them think from observant participation toward more educational ways to engage with youngsters around text. To respond to another is not simply to match one person's behavior to another's, but to construct ways of behaving and making sense together. This insight parallels changes in anthropology moving toward the webs of meaning that people weave, rather than the cultural boxes they inhabit. In that spirit, Au currently works with teachers to transform instruction by exploring their own cultural identities and those of their students, in particular, around issues of "ethnicity and primary language" (Au, 1996).

Other Voices: Cultural Study and Literacy Education in a New Key

A third issue related to the fusion of theoretical and practical work described earlier is the movement to address the transactional aspects of ethnographic research—what Erickson (1996) referred to as "Eve's task." Citing the influence of feminism on ethnography, Erickson pointed out that 25 years earlier the anthropologist's professed aim was to describe others and their points of view. In Erickson's view, this naming function is akin to the Biblical imperative Adam was given by God to name and thus to claim dominion over the "others" in the Garden. A form of "Adam's task" was undertaken by ethnographers who sought to describe others and thereby gain some control over them—both literally, as ethnography served colonialism, and perhaps more insidiously today as descriptions of others can tend to freeze or stereotype their realities, rendering them voiceless in the creation of those descriptions.

Cultural description was considered novel, even controversial, as social research in the first part of this century. It has since become a valued and familiar part of the educational research landscape. As such, its biases and limitations are exposed along with its contributions to knowledge. Ethnography is vulnerable to critique. New controversies have arisen about the very presumption that ethnographer can or should speak for and about others. Of this Erickson said,

> ethnographic realism is no longer credible to many of us within ethnography itself. We have come to realize that the so-called "participant observer" is only minimally participating, and is mostly outside the social gravity within which the "observed" live. (1996, p. 7)

To redress this problem, educational ethnographers have begun trying to add "Eve's task" to their work. Moving from participant observer to "observant participant," ethnographers are beginning to acknowledge that the work of understanding and describing others' lives is inevitably mediated by our own autobiographies. Ruth Behar makes this point in her ethnographic study, *Translated Woman* (1993), where the "story" of her key informant, a Mexican woman named Esperanza, is jointly constructed by and serves the authorial purposes of both Esperanza and Ruth. Behar further notes that although this idea may be a new one to contemporary ethnographers, it is not new to feminists, for whom Eve's task has been a long-standing, if undervalued, one in their scholarship (Behar & Gordon, 1995).

In exploring how researchers and informants construct meaning in relationship with one another, Au and other ethnographic researchers working in literacy education (e.g., Florio-Ruane, Raphael, Glazier, McVee, & Wallace, 1997; Brock, 1997) are examining the "self–other dialogue" (Tedlock, 1991) foundational to both research and teaching. About this effort, Au recently wrote that "educators' recognition of the inequities possible in a given educational situation depends on an understanding of their own cultural identities as well as the cultural identities of their students" (1998, p. 308).

Using literacy activities such as writing workshop, mini-lessons, individual conferences, author's chair, personal literacy portfolios, and publication, Au encourages her own students' exploration of the cultural foundations of their literate practices. As her students write and rework narratives relating to their past, Au does the same. Thus Au's pedagogy and research exemplify the weaving of "Adam's task" of description with "Eve's task" of revealing the ways self and other are entwined in education and research. Especially in literacy education, the idea that teachers as well as students bring to communication knowledge, beliefs and values that are culturally acquired is fundamental. This idea underscores language use and language learning as living processes with a past, present, and certainly a future. As such, they are appropriately studied ethnographically.

REFERENCES

Au, K. H. (1980). Participation structures in a reading lesson with Hawaiian children: Analysis of a culturally appropriate instructional event. *Anthropology and Education Quarterly, 11*(2), 91–115.

Au, K. H. (1995). Multicultural perspectives on literacy research. *Journal of Reading Behavior, 27*(1), 85–100.

Au, K. H. (1996, November). *Personal narratives, literacy portfolios, and cultural identity.* Paper presented at the meetings of the American Anthropological Association, Washington, DC.

Au, K. H. (1998). Social constructivism and the school literacy learning of students of diverse cultural backgrounds. *Journal of Literacy Research, 30*(2), 297–319.

Au, K. H., & Carroll, J. H. (1997). Improving literacy achievement through a constructivist approach: The KEEP demonstration classroom project. *Elementary School Journal, 97*(3), 203–221.

Au, K. H., & Jordan, C. (1981). Teaching reading to Hawaiian children: Finding a culturally appropriate solution. In H. T. Trueba, G. P. Guthrie, & K. H. Au (Eds.), *Culture and the bilingual classroom: Studies in classroom ethnography* (pp. 139–152). Rowley, MA: Newbury House.

Au, K. H., & Mason, J. M. (1981). Social organizational factors in learning to read: The balance of rights hypothesis. *Reading Research Quarterly, 17*(1), 115–152.

Barton, D. (1994). *Literacy: An introduction to the ecology of written language.* Oxford: Blackwell.

Basso, K. (1974). The ethnography of writing. In R. Bauman & J. Sherzer (Eds.), *Explorations in the ethnography of speaking* (pp. 425–432). Cambridge: Cambridge University Press.

Bauman, R., & Sherzer, J. (Eds.). (1974). *Explorations in the ethnography of speaking.* Cambridge: Cambridge University Press.

Behar, R. (1993). *Translated woman: Crossing the border with Esperanza's story.* Boston: Beacon Press.

Behar, R., & Gordon, D. A. (Eds.). (1995). *Women writing culture.* Berkeley: University of California Press.

Bhabha, H. K. (1994). *The location of culture.* London: Routledge.

Bloome, D. (1991). Anthropology and research on teaching the English language arts. In J. Flood, J. M. Jensen, D. Lapp, & J. Squire (Eds.), *Handbook of research on teaching the English language arts* (pp. 46–56). New York: Macmillan.

Bloome, D., & Green, J. (1984). Directions in the sociolinguistic study of reading. In P. D. Pearson, R. Barr, M. L. Kamil, & P. Mosenthal (Eds.), *Handbook of reading research* (1st ed. pp. 395–421). New York: Longman.

Boggs, S. T. (1972). The meaning of questions and narratives to Hawaiian children. In C. B. Cazden, V. P. John, & D. Hymes (Eds.), *Functions of language in the classroom* (pp. 299–327). New York: Teachers College Press.

Brock, C. (1997). *Exploring a second language student's literacy learning opportunities: A collaborative case study analysis.* Unpublished doctoral dissertation, Michigan State University, East Lansing.

Cazden, C. B. (1986). Classroom discourse. In M. C. Wittrock (Ed.), *Handbook of research on teaching* (3rd ed., pp. 432–463). New York: Macmillan.

Cazden, C. B. (1987). *Classroom discourse: The language of teaching and learning.* Portsmouth, NH: Heinemann.

Clifford, J. (1988). *The predicament of culture: Twentieth-Century Ethnography, Literature, and Art.* Cambridge: Harvard University Press.

Clifford, J., & Marcus, G. E. (1986). *Writing culture: The poetics and politics of ethnography.* Berkeley: University of California Press.

Eisenhart, M. (1995). The fax, the jazz player, and the self-story teller: How do people organize culture? *Anthropology and Education Quarterly, 26*(1), 3–26.

Eisenhart, M. (in press). Changing conceptions of culture and ethnographic methodology: Recent thematic shifts and their implications of research on teaching. In V. Richardson (Ed.), *Handbook of research on teaching* (4th ed.). New York: Macmillan.

Erickson, F. (1986). Qualitative methods in research on teaching. In M. C. Wittrock (Ed.), *Handbook of research on teaching* (3rd ed., pp. 119–161). New York: Macmillan.

Erickson, F. (1996). On the evolution of qualitative approaches in educational research: From Adam's task to Eve's. *Australian Educational Researcher, 23*(2), 1–15.

Erickson, F. (1982). Taught cognitive learning in its immediate environments: A neglected topic in the anthropology of educators. *Anthropology and Education Quarterly, 13*(2), 149–180.

Florio-Ruane, S. (1987). Sociolinguistics for educational researchers. *American Educational Research Journal, 24*(2), 185–197.

Florio-Ruane, S. (1994). Anthropological study of classroom culture and social organization. In T. Hussein & T. N. Postlethwaite (Eds.), *The international encyclopedia of education* (2nd ed., pp. 796–803). Oxford: Pergamon.

Florio-Ruane, S. (1997). To tell a new story: Reinventing narratives of culture, identity and education. *Anthropology and Education Quarterly, 28*(2), 152–162.

Florio-Ruane, S., Raphael, T. E., Glazier, J., McVee, M., & Wallace, S. (1997). Discovering culture in discussion of autobiographical literature: Transforming the education of literacy teachers. In C. K. Kinzer, K. A. Hinchman, & D. J. Leu (Eds.), *Inquiries in literacy theory and practice: Forty-sixth Yearbook of the National Reading Conference* (pp. 452–464). Chicago: National Reading Conference.

Gee, J. P. (1989). *What is literacy?* Brookline, MA: The Literacies Institute, Educational Development Corporation.

Guthrie, L. F. & Hall, W. S. (1984). Ethnographic approaches to reading research. In P. D. Pearson, R. Barr, M. L. Kamil, & P. Mosenthal (Eds.), *Handbook of reading research* (1st ed., pp. 91–109). New York: Longman. 91–109.

Heath, S. B. (1983). *Ways with words: Language, life and work in communities and classrooms.* New York: Cambridge University Press.

Heath, S. B. (1982). Ethnography in education: Defining the essentials. In P. Gilmore & A. A. Glatthorn (Eds.), *Children in and out of school: Ethnography and education* (pp. 33–55). Washington, DC: Center for Applied Linguistics.

Hess, G. A. (1998, December). *Keeping educational anthropology relevant: Asking good questions rather than trivial ones.* Presidential address to the Council on Anthropology and Education, Meetings of the American Anthropological Association, Philadelphia.

Hoffman, E. (1989). *Lost in translation: A new life in a new language.* New York: Penguin.

Hymes, D. (1964). *Language in culture and society.* New York: Harper and Row.

Hymes, D. (1982). What is ethnography? In P. Gilmore & A. A. Glatthorn (Eds.), *Children in and out of school: Ethnography and education* (pp. 21–32). Washington, DC: Center for Applied Linguistics.

Jacob, E., & Jordan, C. (Eds.). (1987). Explaining the school performance of minority students. *Anthropology and Education Quarterly, 18*(4).

Koehler, V. (1978). Classroom process research: Present and future. *Journal of Classroom Interaction, 13*(2), 3–11.

McDermott, R., & Goldman, S. (1998). Review of *Constructing School Success*: The consequences of untracking low-achieving students. *Anthropology and Education Quarterly, 29*(1), 125–127.

Moll, L. (1992). Bilingual classroom studies and community analysis. *Educational Researcher, 21*(2), 20–24.

New London Group. (1996). A pedagogy of multiple literacies: Designing social futures. *Harvard Educational Review, 66*(1), 60–92.

Raphael, T. E., & Brock, C. H. (1997). Instructional research in literacy: Changing paradigms. In C. K. Kinzer, K. A. Hinchman, & D. J. Leu (Eds.), *Inquiries in literacy theory and practice: Forty-sixth Yearbook of the National Reading Conference* (pp. 13–36). Chicago: National Reading Conferences.

Rosaldo, R. (1989). *Culture and truth: The remaking of social analysis.* Boston: Beacon Press.

Scribner, S. (1984, November). Literacy in three metaphors. *American Journal of Education,* (pp. 6–21).

Scribner, S., & Cole, M. (1981). *The psychology of literacy.* Cambridge, MA: Harvard University Press.

Tedlock, B. (1991). From participant observation to the observation of participation: The emergence of narrative ethnography. *Journal of Anthropological Research, 47,* 69–94.

Vygotsky, L. (1978). *Mind in society: The development of higher psychological processes.* Cambridge, MA: Harvard University Press.

Watson-Gegeo, K. A., & Boggs, S. T. (1977). From verbal play to talk story: The role of routine in speech events among Hawaiian children. In S. Ervin-Tripp & C. Mitchell-Kernan (Eds.), *Child discourse* (pp. 67–90). New York: Academic Press.

CHAPTER 12

Verbal Reports and Protocol Analysis

Peter Afflerbach
University of Maryland at College Park

Protocol analysis offers the opportunity to gather detailed understandings of reading and reading-related phenomena. The ongoing evolution of theories of mind and reading combined with the suitability of the verbal report methodology contribute to the considerable popularity of protocol analysis (Ericsson & Simon, 1984/1993; Kucan & Beck, 1997; Pressley & Afflerbach, 1995). The convergence of theory and method offers rich opportunities for reading researchers. This chapter provides an overview of the history of use of verbal reports and protocol analysis in reading research, a discussion of current understandings and uses of verbal reports and protocol analysis, and an examination of ongoing challenges and future directions for protocol research.

A BRIEF HISTORY OF VERBAL REPORTS AND PROTOCOL ANALYSIS

Verbal reports and subsequent protocols have been elicited and analyzed for centuries. The question "What's on your mind?" and the offer "A penny for your thoughts" both reflect an abiding interest in understanding how and what people think. In this sense, verbal reports and protocol analysis represent one evolution of the human habit of asking people to share their thoughts into a useful form of scientific inquiry. Evidence of interest in people's thinking exists in the works of Aristotle and Plato, both of whom encouraged colleagues to discuss the things they thought about. Thousands of years later, James (1890) used subjects' reports of their thinking to inform his theories of psychology. Reviews of introspection (Boring, 1953; Pritchard, 1990a) demonstrate that asking people to discuss and describe their thoughts has been a continuous, if sporadic, general methodology in psychology. The increasing permanence of records of scientific inquiry and the emergence of the expectation that the methods of this inquiry be described in detail contribute to our understanding of the legacy and promise of protocol analysis. It is probable that verbal report and protocol analysis will continue as a popular methodology to describe cognitive, affective, and social aspects of reading.

The use of protocol analysis is marked by a fair amount of controversy. The first half of the 20th century is notable for the tension between behaviorists and those interested in describing processes of reading. Researchers examining the workings of the mind needed methodologies that could describe mental processes. One result was the use of introspection at the turn of the century (Marbe, 1901/1964; Titchener, 1912a, 1912b) and its application in reading inquiry (Huey, 1908). However, the early and mid 20th century saw protocol analysis relegated to occasional use, as introspection was challenged by behaviorists. Behaviorism dictated that peoples' verbalizations were not theoretically important (Watson, 1913, 1920). Verbal reports and protocol analysis were suspect as behaviorists doubted the veridicality of introspective reports and challenged the notion that individuals mediate their mental processes. Methodology that sought subjects' reports of thinking was consigned to relatively dusty shelves, and protocol analysis saw only limited use. Yet inquiry using verbal reports did continue. For example, McAllister (1930) described the difficulties in identifying readers' processes through inferences based on products, such as reading test scores, readers' retellings of text, or their answers to comprehension questions. Protocol analysis provided a new class of data that changed the inferential path, and allowed for hypothesizing about reading processes from more process-oriented data. Detailed accounts of reading processes, specifically cognition and response, have become one grail of users of protocol analysis (Afflerbach & Johnston, 1984).

A sample of research published during (and in spite of) the reign of behaviorism emphasized the dynamic nature of reading. This work focused on readers' difficulty with content-area learning and responses to questions (McAllister, 1930); readers' use of context to develop word meanings and vocabulary understanding (Werner & Kaplan, 1950); and readers' responses to texts (Piekarz, 1954). Concurrent with the relatively spare use of protocol analysis in reading was protocol-based research investigating a range of thinking tasks and situations, including medical problem solving (Duncker, 1945), mathematical problem solving (Polya, 1954a, 1954b), and chess (de Groot, 1965). These inquiries served as both demonstration and reminder for once and future reading researchers. They demonstrated the suitability of the methodology for revealing thinking and problem solving, mental processes that figure largely in reading. They reminded that under appropriate conditions, verbal reports yield rich and compelling protocol data. Kucan and Beck (1997) noted that the occasional use of protocol analysis during the reign of behaviorism was crucial not only for keeping verbal reports on the radar screen, but for shaping their use. That is, findings from verbal report studies helped demonstrate that foundational work was needed in theory building to accommodate and logically organize the processes and responses revealed by protocol analysis. Subjects' utterances could not be interpreted as reports of cognitive processes or responses until theories of cognition and response were more fully developed. Accompanying the nascent cognitive revolution was the increasing realization that understanding reading required the detailed descriptions of reading processes that protocol analysis could provide.

Increasing interest in the use of protocol analysis was supported by detailed characterizations of human problem solving (Newell & Simon, 1972), which in turn supported research that conceptualized reading as strategic problem solving. An example is the work of Olshavsky (1976–1977), conducted on the cusp of the cognitive revolution as it applied to reading. Olshavsky's findings demonstrated that reading is clearly strategic, as well as the need for detailed accounts of the nature of reading strategies. Her work demonstrated that the complexity of reading demanded research designs that accommodate both a breadth and depth of examination. It also hinted that the cognitive strategy use of accomplished readers was accompanied by response and engagement. The strong conceptualization of reading as cognition and the strong defense of protocol analysis as a means to investigate reading contributed to initial investigations of readers' strategies including inferences (Collins, Brown, & Larkin, 1980), summarization (Brown & Day, 1983), and general cognitive strategy use while reading (Garner, 1982; Hare, 1981). Critical analysis of the methodology of verbal reports and protocol analysis was provided by Ericsson and Simon (1980, 1984/1993). Their work continues to influence the conceptualization and use of protocol analysis related to information processing and cognition, and the authors present a compelling case for protocol analysis as a methodology with flexibility of application that can help describe the breadth of cognition. Ericsson and Simon provided strong evidence of the prospective validity of protocol analysis, and they proffered specific methodological recommendations for using protocol analysis.

The increasing use of verbal reports and protocol analysis in reading research led to a state of the methodological art summary (Afflerbach & Johnston, 1984) that described their potential advantages. First, they provide access to the constructive and responsive processes that comprise reading. This information is accretive to our understanding of the complex constructs of cognition and response that might otherwise be investigated in an indirect manner. Second, protocol analysis allows for the examination of important but often neglected reader characteristics, including motivation and affect. Moreover, protocol analysis may explain the relationships and interactions of motivation and affect with cognitive processes and responses. Third, protocol analysis allows for the examination of the influence of contextual variables (e.g., text, task, setting, reader ability) on the act of reading. Finally, protocol analysis provides valuable information on a range of processes related to reading, such as instruction, assessment, discussion, and teacher decisionmaking. Fairly regular reviews of the intersection of reading research and protocol analysis critically examine the accomplishments and challenges related to the methodology and reading research (Deffner, 1988; Ericsson, 1988; Kucan & Beck, 1997; Pressley & Afflerbach, 1995; Pritchard, 1990a; Waern, 1988).

The historical path to contemporary applications of protocol analysis and current conceptualizations of readers' thoughts and actions is continually marked by symbiosis. Protocol analysis continues to influence the very constructs it is used to investigate, in the "bootstrap operation" first alluded to by Ericsson and Simon (1980). That is, protocol analysis may first contribute to the initial building of theories that represent progress in the understanding of reading. These theories help us chart a course of the work that remains to fill the gaps in this understanding, and protocol analysis serves ably in the second role of focused research tool. The last two decades have witnessed burgeoning use of protocol analysis to investigate acts of cognition, response, and reading related phenomena. In turn, the refinement of cognitive theory (Anderson & Pearson, 1984; van Dijk & Kintsch, 1983) and literary theory (Beach & Hynds, 1991; Eco, 1990) have helped steer protocol analyses to positions in which it can both refine existing theory and break ground for new theory. Although protocol analysis provides compelling evidence that constructive cognition is central to reading, it also proves that reading is more than cognition. The symbiotic relationship of the methodology and the aspects of reading it investigates should continue.

The history of verbal reports and protocol analysis is marked by controversy over the veridicality of the data provided. There are numerous challenges to the validity and use of verbal reports and protocol analysis. These challenges are ably addressed in theory, whereas in practice they receive intermittent attention. Less attention is paid to the caveats that are provided by both users and skeptics of the methodology (cf. Afflerbach & Johnston, 1984; Nisbett & Wilson, 1977; Pressley & Afflerbach, 1995), all of whom insist that integrity of method influences quality of data. Although behaviorism posed a major obstacle to the acceptance and use of protocol analysis, there are more recent claims against the validity of verbal reports and protocol analysis (Nisbett & Wilson, 1977). The increasing use of protocol analysis within reading research indicates a general acceptance of the methodology, but inappropriate use of verbal reports and protocol analysis can quickly revive claims against validity. The diminution of claims for protocol analysis will not stem from the lack of a theory of how verbal reports and protocol analysis provide legitimate data. Rather, it may result from a lack of attention to the details of appropriate use of the methodology.

WHAT VERBAL REPORTS AND PROTOCOL ANALYSIS TELL US ABOUT READING

The close relationship between protocol analysis and the investigation of readers' cognition and response leads to both predictable and novel applications of the methodology in reading research. The suitability of the method to different areas of inquiry within the broad discipline of reading has provided rich accounts of reading (Pressley & Afflerbach, 1995). At the same time, the broad range of reading research that uses protocol analysis defies easy categorization. There are several prominent themes that emerge from this research, including the investigation and description of a predetermined and relatively finite aspect of reading (e.g., a cognitive strategy), and the exploration of the complexity of cognition, social meaning construction, and response within situated acts of reading (e.g., reading a newspaper article on a controversial topic). The use of protocol analysis to investigate single phenomena, be it process or strategy, reflects the close relationship of protocol analysis with cognitive psychology. Protocol research within cognitive psychology often focused on relatively simple problems. This served to constrain subjects' thoughts and verbalizations and allowed researchers to focus on the cognitive aspects of human-task interactions within small and well-defined problem spaces (Newell & Simon, 1972). Because the nature of readers' thoughts and actions is often complex, a focus on single aspects of reading may contribute detailed accounts of aspects of reading. Examples of studies with a single focus within reading research (a focus that is often expanded, based on the consideration of the richness of a set of protocol data) include determining main ideas (Afflerbach, 1990a; Johnston & Afflerbach, 1985), generating inferences (Collins et al., 1980; Magliano & Graesser, 1993; Phillips, 1988), hypothesizing and predicting the contents of texts (Afflerbach, 1990b; Bruce & Rubin, 1984), summarizing texts (Brown & Day, 1983), searching for information (Guthrie, Britten, & Barker, 1991), demonstrating awareness of text cohesion (Bridge & Winograd, 1982), and the monitoring of cognition (Garner & Reis, 1981; Lundeberg, 1987; Lytle, 1982). These studies demonstrate that protocol analysis can focus on particular reader process and strategy, and they often include research designs that provide the means to quantify reader strategy use. Often, the research involves manipulations of independent variables such as readers' prior knowledge (Afflerbach, 1990a) or text genre (Olson, Mack, & Duffy, 1981). I note that many of these studies evolve to adopt a dual focus, as it is determined that the original focus strategy (e.g., summarization) is situated in the rich context that is described by serendipitous verbal reports of what else is going on in the reader's head. It is often the case that reports of these studies combine both quantitative and qualitative (descriptive) data. Many single-focus reading studies supplement and complement researchers' initial hypothesis testing with protocol data that serve exploratory, discovery, and descriptive purposes that help situate a reading strategy or reading stance, continuing the bootstrap operation (Ericsson & Simon, 1980).

The majority of research that is conceptualized with a single focus demonstrates that protocol analysis was suitable for describing the reading strategies that are selected a priori by researchers and that are encouraged through manipulation of text, reader, context, and instructions. These studies also demonstrate that the target reading processes and strategies occur as situated in complex problem spaces. Increasingly, the interrelationships and interdependencies of strategy, skill, response, motivation, and affect must be more fully understood. Although we possess a fairly comprehensive catalog of the strategies that good readers use, by no means do we have complete understanding of the strategic, responsive, and social reader.

A second body of work focuses on reading writ more broad, related to what Earthman (1992) calls the "concert" of readers orchestrating complex strategies of cognition, knowledge construction, and response within acts of reading. This work is anticipated by cognitive psychology (Schoenfeld, 1983) and literary criticism (Rosenblatt, 1978). Protocol analysis tells more than the story of cognitive strategies. Changing the investigative lens, it can describe the influence of contextual variables on strategy and process use. The study of interrelationships and interdependencies of strategies, skills, stances, goals, and reader affect and motivation proves challenging for practitioners of protocol analysis: The problem spaces within which readers work are broad and ill-defined. Numerous inquiries focus on acts of reading (as opposed to isolate factors within an act of reading). These inquiries attempt to describe the totality of the reading task and seek protocols from which case accounts of reading can be constructed (Schmalhofer & Boschert, 1988; Schwegler & Shamoon, 1991). Studies focus on acts of reading such as reading to evaluate legal texts (Neutelings & Maat, 1997), physicists reading professional journal articles (Bazerman, 1985), biologists reading a divisive article of evolutionary biology (Charney, 1993), professors and students reading primary source texts in history (Leinhardt & Young, 1996; Wineburg, 1991, 1998; Young & Leinhardt, 1998), and social science professors reading professional articles in their fields of specialization (Wyatt et al., 1993). The results of such studies help describe the complex thought and action that characterize accomplished reading. In general, these studies honor a cognitive heritage but increasingly describe critical noncognitive aspects of acts of reading (Smagorinsky, 1998).

The cognitive focus in research using protocol analysis is complemented by work from the literary tradition. Literary theory has a long history of describing the possible relationships between the text and the reader. For example, new criticism (Ransom, 1979, pp. 12–33; Wimsatt & Beardsley, 1954) and reader response (Fish, 1980; Rosenblatt, 1978) propose significantly different stances between the reader and the text. Protocol analysis provides data that help describe and gauge the legitimacy of these proposed stances. In a manner similar to Olshavsky's (1976–1977) pursuit of the strategic reader, Squire (1964) conducted research that helped set the stage for future investigations of the responsive reader. His investigation of short-story reading demonstrated both the richness of readers' literary responses and the need for conceptualizations of reading that might describe and accommodate these responses. Subsequent protocol analysis studies described readers' interactions and transactions with literary texts, including reading and discussing poems (Beach, 1972; Kintgen, 1983; Peskin, 1998), the construction of meaning within the genre of short story (Earthman, 1992; Rogers, 1991), and describing narratives in relation to excerpts from novels (Graves & Frederiksen, 1991). There are several important outcomes from these studies. First, the response and transactions that readers have with literature are varied and often intensely individualistic. As important is the demonstration that there is no response to literature without cognition (Langer, 1990), just as research focused on expository and informational text demonstrates that there is no cognition without response.

Pressley and Afflerbach (1995) synthesized the results of reading research that utilized think-aloud protocols to describe constructively responsive reading. Their work emanates from the realization that within and across research paradigms and traditions of cognition and response there is a corpus of work that shares both the verbal reporting methodology and a focus on readers' thoughts and actions. These investigations involve complex variables and their interactions, including text types, reader characteristics, and reading situations and tasks. The corpus of work demonstrates that competent readers report similar strategies and responses, regardless of the paradigms undergirding a particular research study, the focus of research, the reading text or task, or the particular directions given to subjects. Thus, protocol analysis studies from both the cognitive and literary response traditions, and studies with both broad and narrow foci yield verbal reports with often strikingly similar contents. Lacking, however, is a "common language" (Rich, 1974) to describe core aspects of competent reading that are based on data from protocol analysis. Pressley and Afflerbach believed that readers' verbal reports can be central to the development of both a common language and reading theory. Their meta-analysis of extant protocol studies involved the categorization and sorting of readers' verbalizations across studies and paradigms, and allowed for the concatenation of strategies and responses as reported in studies with foundations in cognitive psychology and literary response. From this synthesis of readers' verbal reports came the model of constructively responsive reading: constructive as knowledge is constructive, and responsive as readers respond to the texts that they read in relation to the contexts in which reading occurs. Pressley and Afflerbach's portrait of the constructively responsive reader offered a comprehensive list of what readers do, grouped under three general categories of strategy and response. Accomplished readers identify and remember important information, they monitor their reading, and they evaluate their reading. Further, Pressley and Afflerbach determined that constructively responsive reading is marked by four characteristics. Readers seek to identify the overall meaning of the text by actively searching, reflecting on, and responding to text in pursuit of main ideas. Readers respond to text with predictions and hypotheses that reflect their prior knowledge. Readers are passionate in their responses to text. Readers' prior knowledge predicts their comprehension and responses to texts.

Pressley and Afflerbach's (1995) synthesis was informed both by the results of individual studies that used verbal reports and by existing models of reading. Thus, the theory of constructively responsive reading incorporates critical aspects of previous text processing theories. For example, readers' verbalizations describe the processing of text information that helps readers construct micro and macro text structures through the use of corresponding text-processing strategies (van Dijk & Kintsch, 1983). The top-down aspects of text processing and the importance of prior knowledge as described in schema theory (Anderson & Pearson, 1984) are present in many verbal reports and are both accommodated in constructively responsive reading. The transaction between reader and text and the stance that a reader takes toward a text, both conceptualizations of literary theorists (Beach & Hynds, 1991; Rosenblatt, 1978), are part of constructively responsive reading. So is readers' comprehension monitoring and metacognition (Baker & Brown, 1984), constructs most often associated with cognitive theorists. The massive amounts of inferencing that occur in reading (Graesser & Bower, 1990) are a hallmark of constructively responsive reading, as is reader awareness of the social space in which reading and meaning-making are situated (Geisler, 1991; Smagorinsky, 1998). Constructively responsive reading is based on the detailed descriptions of the things that talented readers do when reading different texts for different purposes. In addition to providing the initial attempt to describe competent reading as revealed by aggregate think-aloud protocol data, Pressley and Afflerbach demonstrated the suitability of verbal reports for describing complex acts of reading, the relationship of the research traditions of cognitive psychology and literary response, and the usefulness of verbal reports for theory building.

The majority of protocol analysis research focuses on talented readers. This is of practical and theoretical importance. Practically, better readers are often more verbal, make better use of their limited working memory, and may better verbalize the things they do in a think-aloud. These readers may be more sophisticated, diverse, and successful in the application of reading strategies and in responding to what they read.

Implicit in much of the protocol-based research is the notion that the detailed description of talented readers can inform our efforts to teach less expert readers. The detailed descriptions of talented reading can provide the detailed information that can be incorporated into instruction in the strategies, skills, and other knowledge that developing readers need to become expert. Bruner (1985) noted that there is not a well-defined path from novice to expert, because we lack a theory of what each one is, and how one progresses from novice to expert. It may be that our understanding of the nature of reading and reading instruction, critically informed by protocol analysis, can help describe that path. That is, verbal reports may serve as a means of helping teach the very strategies they have helped describe. This idea is addressed in a recent review of think-aloud protocols by Kucan and Beck (1997), which describes the relationship of verbal reports and protocol analysis to reading comprehension instruction. Their review serves as an indicator of progress from the prolegomenon for identifying, specifying, and teaching reading strategies provided by Collins and Smith (1982). One result of research using protocol analysis is the provision of detailed and explicit accounts of reading processes and strategies. This fine-grained detail can inform instruction and external modeling of competent strategy use, which eventually becomes internalized as a student's reading routine. This use of verbal report data with scaffolded instruction and work across zones of proximal development derives from the work of Vygotsky (1978), and it fits well with the notion of the development of cognitive strategy use and the incremental differences between novice and expert performance (Palincsar & Brown, 1984; Paris, Lipson, & Wixson, 1983).

The detailed accounting of readers' strategies, motivations, and mindsets that is provided by protocol analysis may prove as valuable for determining the detail and focus of reading instruction as it is for building models of reading (Pearson & Fielding, 1991). These instructional efforts follow from earlier work that sought to describe and teach reading strategies using explicit instruction (e.g., Bereiter and Bird, 1985; Palincsar & Brown, 1984; Pressley, Harris, & Marks, 1992). For example, verbal reports are used in efforts to help students better comprehend text (Loxterman, Beck, & McKeown, 1994) and participate in discussions of authors and texts (Trabasso & Magliano, 1996). A result is that verbal reports and protocol analysis have influenced thinking about what to teach (the strategies and responses revealed in expert readers' protocols) and how to teach (the verbal description and explicit modeling of strategy instruction derived, in part, from think-aloud protocols). An additional value of thinking aloud is that it encourages children to spend time with their thinking. The promise of this aspect of verbal reports and protocol analysis is that they may provide the opportunity for readers to better mediate their learning by becoming better acquainted with it. An intriguing possibility is that classroom discussions can provide models of thinking and social interaction (Kucan & Beck, 1997). This suggestion adds to the conceptualization of verbal reports as aides for learning, and returns to the notion that verbal reports are closely related to inner speech (Vygotsky, 1978). As such, verbal reporting may serve an important regulatory function in learning (Feuerstein, 1980) as learners situate themselves in relation to a particular reading and learning task (Wertsch, 1991). The classroom discussions and social interactions can be considered verbal reports that provide models for students who are keyed into the critical features of such phenomena (Gambrell & Almasi, 1996).

Protocol analysis can also help us better understand the diverse strategies and processes which may ultimately impact students' reading achievement. Understanding the detail and focus of student thought during instruction (Peterson, Swing, Braverman, & Buss, 1982), the differences in how teachers and students determine main ideas (Schellings & Van Hout Walters, 1995), teachers' evolving understanding of writing processes (Afflerbach et al., 1988), the procedural and declarative knowledge that teachers use to evaluate and grade students' literacy achievement (Afflerbach &

Johnston, 1993), and the manner in which students reason their way through test items (DuBois, 1998; Norris, 1990, 1992; Nuthall & Alton-Lee, 1995) have all been investigated using think-aloud protocols. Results from these studies may contribute to optimizing the processes and strategies that support successful reading instruction. In addition, these studies demonstrate the flexibility and suitability of the verbal report methodology for investigating reading related phenomena. Future investigations may use protocol analysis to examine the social contexts of reading and the situated nature of reading and tasks related to reading (Greeno, Pearson, & Schoenfeld, 1996). Such inquiry should contribute to a more complete understanding of acts, strategies, and responses within the culture of reading (Bruner, 1996). The research findings yielded through the use of protocol analysis continue to demonstrate the accuracy of Huey's (1908) claim that reading well is one of the most compelling human accomplishments.

ONGOING CHALLENGES TO THE USE OF PROTOCOL ANALYSIS TO STUDY AND DESCRIBE READING AND READING-RELATED PHENOMENA

Protocol analysis helps describe strategies for understanding words (Werner & Kaplan, 1950), paragraphs (Afflerbach, 1990a; Collins et al., 1980), textbook excerpts (Haas & Flower, 1988), legal documents (Deegan, 1995; Lundeberg, 1987), historical documents (Wineburg, 1991), the subtexts of teachers' and children's history texts (Afflerbach & VanSledright, 1999), professional articles (Wyatt et al., 1993), and the intertextuality between texts (Hartmann, 1995). Protocol analysis also has informed our understanding of reading poems (Beach, 1972; Kintgen, 1983), short stories (Rogers, 1991; Squire, 1964), and excerpts from novels (Graves & Frederiksen, 1991). The past and present use of protocol analysis helps describe the promise and challenge of their future use. The worth of verbal reports and protocol analysis for investigating reading and reading-related phenomena will be demonstrated through both methodological rigor and flexible use. The movement from a developing to a mature protocol analysis methodology is fueled, in part, by the ability to identify and anticipate strengths and weaknesses of the methodology and to design research that reflects this knowledge.

As verbal reports and protocol analysis are utilized, several methodological concerns demand close attention. These include full disclosure of the nature of the use of the verbal reporting methodology, the triangulation of verbal protocol data, the distinction between concurrent and retrospective reports, and the intimate nature of think-aloud protocols. The lack of complete reporting of the details of the verbal report and protocol analysis methodology represents a lost opportunity to build knowledge of the method—especially as it is increasingly applied to the complex problem spaces that are replete with the interactions of readers, tasks, texts, and intervening variables. The distinct lack of convention and comprehensiveness in many research accounts of the methodology is not surprising, as published accounts of research reflect different traditions of inquiry and the norms of different research communities. Protocol analysis is often treated as a mature methodology, as if everything about eliciting, collecting, and interpreting verbal reports has been learned. There is often a startling lack of detail provided in published research reports. The result is lack of further understanding of the intricacies of the method. Less than full disclosure of method thwarts critical evaluation of the reading research process and product. Scant accounting of the details of design, instructions to subjects, prompting, selection of tasks, coding of transcripts, and classification of phenomena influences the research consumer's ability to understand and accept or reject a researcher's claims. Concise descriptions provide a gloss for better understanding of researcher intent and method and of research results. A lack of detail of how the protocol analysis method is used creates questions that the accompanying research text cannot answer.

Consistent and detailed description of the methodology facilitates the examination of commonalties across investigations and across paradigms in reading research that uses protocol analysis (Pressley & Afflerbach, 1995). Researchers investigating readers' use of cognitive strategies as situated in reading a scientific text should be able to divine commonalities and differences in research on readers' literary responses. This should contribute to better understanding of the aggregate findings of reading research using the verbal reporting methodology. Attention also must be given to characteristics of every aspect of reader–text interaction to better understand what is revealed in verbal reports. A key tenet of Ericsson and Simon's (1980, 1984/1993) work is that people can self-report the contents of their working memory. This provides the "stuff" of think-aloud protocols, and it is critical to understand how contextual variables influence the availability of information to report and the process of reporting. Table 12.1 contains representative aspects of the verbal report methodology that demand comprehensive description, including the characteristics of subjects, texts, tasks, directions to subjects, the transcription of the verbal protocols, the selection of protocol excerpts and their representativeness, the categories used to score think-alouds, and the reliability of coding of protocol contents. Each is worthy of careful attention in the design and execution of research using protocol analysis.

The results of protocol analysis should be triangulated with information from complementary methodologies. Data from process measures, product measures, and comparisons of online performance can strengthen the claims made with verbal report

TABLE 12.1

**Aspects of the Verbal Reporting and Protocol Analysis Methodology
That Require Detailed Descriptions**

Aspect of Methodology	Representative Concerns
Subjects	Verbal ability Familiarity with the methodology Knowledge of text content and structure Relationship with researcher
Texts	Degree of intactness Difficulty or familiarity Mode of text presentation
Tasks	Influence of verbal reporting task on designated reading task Automatic or nonautomatic processing Novelty of task Amount of text available for previewing or rereading
Directions to subjects	Focus on specific or general reading strategies To read as one "normally would"
Transcription process	Faithfulness of print to tape Status of nonverbal utterances Treatment of pause time
Selection of protocol excerpts	Representativeness and typicality
Categories used to score think-alouds	Relationship to previous research and theory
Coding of protocol excerpts	Reliability

data. Magliano and Graesser (1993) suggested a three-pronged approach to drawing conclusions about cognitive aspects of text processing. The first involves theoretical analysis of the processing that might be expected of a particular reader of a particular text, as determined by expert consensus (e.g., van den Broek, Fletcher, & Risden, 1993). For example, accomplished readers identify portions of a poem that are expected to elicit a strong emotional response. The second prong is verbal reports and protocol analysis, with protocol data analyzed in relation to the triangulation measures. The third prong involves the collection of behavioral measures, such as reading time, objective memory of text, and readers' eye movements (e.g., Just & Carpenter, 1980). The greater the degree of alignment of all three measures, the greater confidence research producers and consumers may place in verbal report data. Pressley and Afflerbach (1995) noted that the weakest link in the aggregate of verbal report data and triangulation measures is the demonstrated correlations between objective measures of text processing and subjects' verbal reports (e.g., Wade, Trathen, & Schraw, 1990). Efforts to seek such a three-pronged alignment will do much to move protocol analysis to the status of mature methodology. Ericsson and Simon's (1984/1993) observations and recommendations are related to verbal reports of cognition: the processes and strategies readers use to comprehend text. The majority of reading research that uses protocol analysis has a cognitive focus. As reading research evolves and investigates acts of reading in which cognition is packaged with affect and motivation, and situated in diverse social contexts, participants may be viewed as readers, negotiators, and collaborators. It is necessary to examine these aspects of reading and their relationship to the verbal reporting methodology. As protocol analysis evolves to examine situated acts of reading (and their attendant social, affective, and motivational aspects), the type of data that can provide triangulation will change. For example, motivation that is present in a protocol might receive support from the triangulation provided by a motivation observation checklist, or readers' retrospective self-reports of motivation.

Future inquiry should carefully consider the delineation between concurrent verbal reports and other verbal reports within a protocol. A central argument of Ericsson and Simon (1980, 1984/1993) is that the contents of working memory are available for verbal report. Given the process and storage constraints that working memory places on reading (Britton, Glynn, & Smith, 1985), there is clear need to determine at what point a reader is accessing and reporting working memory contents and when the same reader is leaving working memory to access recent long-term memory. What is concurrent and what is retrospective? Theoretical descriptions clearly delineate between the two, and they revolve around the notion of the reportability of the contents of working (or short-term) memory. Concurrent reports are online accounts of the contents of working memory. Retrospective reports rely, in part, on subjects' long-term memory. However, in real time the differences blur. An online and concurrent verbal report can dodge in and out of retrospection based on the length of the verbalization, the instructions to subjects, and the nature of the task. If concurrent and retrospective reports are purported to be qualitatively different in theory, we need to better know their characteristics, interactions, and relationship as they may be embedded within a single verbal report transcript. This is especially critical in light of our increasing awareness of the cognitive, affective, and social aspects of reading, all of which can muddle the fine line between concurrent and other verbalizations. Promising work demonstrates that concurrent verbal reports and retrospective debriefing from subjects can enrich our understanding of complex phenomena. Thus, the two distinct types of verbal report may be mutually supportive (Haastrup, 1987; Lundeberg, 1987).

There is no more intimate reading research methodology than protocol analysis. It is typical for the array of verbal protocols collected from different readers in the same study to exhibit variance in terms of reader focus, strategies used, responses elicited, feelings emoted, and how the act of reading is situated in a social context. Verbal reports and protocol analysis reveal considerable individual differences in how people read. These differences may be masked or ignored if the purpose of the research is to quantify the use of a particular cognitive strategy or literary response. Although research has paid attention to the individual differences in reading that are revealed by protocol analysis, it has not adequately considered how the intimate nature of the method may influence the data gathered. Verbal reports depend on subjects' ability to verbalize what they are thinking. The verbalization may be influenced by the relationship between the participant and the researcher, gender differences between subject and researcher, cultural differences in reporting and using language, or differences in how the subject conceptualizes her or his role as a reporter of reading phenomena (Belenky, Clinchy, Goldberger, & Tarule, 1986; Smagorinsky, 1998). Individuals use language differently, and any comprehensive theory of the methodology of verbal reports must account for how individual language differences may influence the eliciting, giving, and subsequent analysis of verbal reports.

THE FUTURE FOCI OF PROTOCOL ANALYSIS
AND READING

Verbal reports and protocol analysis enrich our understanding of reading. They played a central role in developing detailed descriptions of cognition and response in reading. Future applications of protocol analysis will continue to provide information about reading as our understanding of reading and how to profitably apply protocol analysis evolve. An immediate application of protocol analysis will be to help describe reading at the intersection of cognition, response, and the social world of the reader. Situated cognition and situated response provide compelling protocol data. Protocol analysis should also help describe developing readers, and provide a contrast to the expert reader descriptions of reading that dominate.

Protocol analysis provides much information about how expert readers read. In fact, it is not a stretch to say that protocol analysis has contributed greatly to our understanding of how academics read texts within their areas of expertise. The focus on expert performance contributes to our understanding of talented reading. However, the resource of protocol analysis has not been fully realized in the investigation of the developmental nature of reading, the growth of ability to read, and the growth of ability to provide verbal reports. Reading inquiry using protocol analysis has generally been guided by the notion that less able readers will not provide useful verbal reports. This assumption needs careful examination. Less able readers are often less verbal, and their reports might be more unduly influenced by the burden of the task of reading and reporting. This could contribute to both qualitative and quantitative differences in the uses of strategies and responses. However, lacking protocol studies of how developing readers read, we forego the development of a potentially rich database that could inform our understanding of how children read, their nascent theories of reading, their lack of convention, and their creativity in approaching and overcoming reading challenges. The verbal reports of such readers may provide diagnostic information that describes the processing, comprehension, interpretation, and motivation challenges less able readers face.

The preeminent focus of verbal reports and protocol analysis remains cognition. Our understanding of readers' cognitive strategy use is rich but incomplete. Cognition has received the majority of attention from reading researchers using protocol analysis. An initial model of cognition, knowledge construction, and response (Pressley & Afflerbach, 1995) invites challenge and revision. Researchers should continue the rich cognitive tradition, and future research should more clearly delineate between the shared and unique aspects of cognition and response, and how each figures in particular reading situations.

Each investigation of reading strategies is socially situated. Thus, it is not surprising that subjects' verbal reports, which are most often directed to cognitive events, spill over into the realm of the context. In fact, readers' verbal reports related to the contextual factors of a reading act (even when they are not requested) serve as support for the veridicality or authenticity of the report, and the social nature of reading. The noncognitive aspects of reading are rarely the focus of think-aloud protocol directives. Yet, it is difficult to transcribe verbal protocols of reading without encountering affect and motivation, which are evinced by readers' exclamations, expletives, grunts, groans, and affirmations. In addition to proving difficult to transcribe to English, these interjections demonstrate above all that readers are more than cognitive in their reading. That considerable affect and motivation are revealed in verbal reports suggests that a systematic approach to their investigation and the systematic variation of instructions to subjects and requests for the focus of their reporting might contribute to new insights about reading.

As our understandings of curriculum, instruction, and learning evolve, so too should our research foci. There are rich opportunities for examining the interface of reading with traditional content learning areas. It will be beneficial to examine protocol studies in other domains: investigations of writing (Flower & Hayes, 1977), physics problem solving (Simon & Simon, 1978) and students' cognitions during instruction (Peterson et al., 1982) contributed to our understanding of theories of problem solving and cognition that may help frame inquiry in reading. As cognitive psychology maintains a strong paradigmatical position, we see the continued use of protocol analysis for inquiry of writing (Breetveldt, van den Bergh, & Rijlaarsdam, 1994), problem solving in physics (Slotta, Chi, & Joram, 1995), genetics (Smith, 1990), mathematics (Hall, Kibler, Wenger, & Truxaw, 1989; Miller & Stigler, 1991), and the programming of intelligent tutoring systems (Pirolli & Recker, 1994). These studies offer the opportunity to examine the relationship of reading to other cognitive, responsive, and constructive acts of mind. They may help inform the design and focus of future protocol studies of reading.

Future use of protocol analysis should also focus on the teaching and learning of reading. Verbal protocols have "the potential to reveal" (Kucan & Beck, 1997, p. 292) aspects of thinking and reading, including the development of self-awareness and metacognition. To the extent that verbal reports help developing readers better understand themselves, this form of encouraged inner speech should prove valuable. In addition to further specification of current models of reading, protocol analysis should help describe emerging realities of reading and literacy. Searching for information (Guthrie, Britten, & Barker, 1991) and interacting with hypertext (Reinking, 1992) are two examples of phenomena that are increasingly important to the literate individual, as are comprehending and responding to combinations of print and graphics. As curricular materials change, protocol analysis may help describe the benefits and challenges of this change for teachers and students. For example, Afflerbach and VanSledright (1999) investigated fifth graders reading of American history texts related to the Jamestown colony. They found that although nontraditional, primary source texts (e.g., excerpts from colonists' diaries, poems) proved captivating and motivating for some students, other students were significantly challenged by the unfamiliar syntax and archaic vocabulary found in the texts. VanSledright and Afflerbach (1999) also investigated the manner in which preservice teachers navigate revisionist history texts, with a focus on how future teachers reconcile existing historical knowledge with contradictory accounts, and how they approach teaching contentious historical topics to students.

Additional uses of verbal reports and protocol analysis may be found in the areas of teacher decision making, teachers' professional development, and reading assessment. Teacher decision making is a complex and rapid phenomenon, and verbal protocols may help us better understand how reading teachers make critical decisions. Teachers' professional development is critical to successful reading programs, and verbal protocols may also help describe the experiences, processes, and materials that contribute to this professional development. For example, knowing how teachers select, read, and use professional journals (Shearer, Coballes-Vega, & Lundeberg, 1993) may positively influence teachers' professional development, and ultimately student achievement. Reading assessment continues to evolve. A frequent criticism of many reading assessments is that they provide information about products, and not reading processes. Think-aloud protocols have been used to investigate the processes used by reading test-takers (Kavale & Schreiner, 1979; Norris, 1990, 1992; Pritchard, 1990b). New forms of reading assessment may help describe the reading and test-taking processes of students, but also the relationship of reading to performance in an assessment situation (DuBois, 1998).

Verbal reports and protocol analysis should continue to play a central role in defining the problem spaces within which it is used. The traditions of use of the methodology for inquiry in cognition (Pressley & Afflerbach, 1995) and literary response (Beach & Hynds, 1991) have been joined with inquiry that seeks to describe the teaching and learning of cognitive strategy and literary response (Kucan & Beck, 1997). The conceptualization of the nature of verbal reports and protocol analysis is continually debated (Ericsson & Simon, in press; Smagorinsky, 1998) and from this ongoing debate should evolve new areas of inquiry. In summary, verbal reports and protocol analysis prove valuable in describing reading and charting one course of reading research. The flexibility and suitability of the methodology are demonstrated by increasingly diverse applications in the study of reading. The appeal of verbal reports and protocol analysis must be complemented by careful attention to aspects of the methodology that either undergird or undermine the validity of verbal report data. Be it cognition and response, reading instruction and learning, or the socially situated nature of each, verbal reports and protocol analysis may serve the reading research enterprise well.

REFERENCES

Afflerbach, P. (1990a). The influence of prior knowledge on expert readers' main idea construction strategies. *Reading Research Quarterly, 25,* 31–46.

Afflerbach, P. (1990b). The influence of prior knowledge and text genre on readers' prediction strategies. *Journal of Reading Behavior, 22,* 131–148.

Afflerbach, P., Bass, L., Hoo, D., Smith, S., Weiss, L., & Williams, L. (1988). Pre-service teachers use think-aloud protocols to study writing. *Language Arts, 65,* 693–701.

Afflerbach, P., & Johnston, P. (1984). Research methodology: On the use of verbal reports in reading research. *Journal of Reading Behavior, 16,* 307–322.

Afflerbach, P., & Johnston, P. (1993). Eleven teachers composing language arts report cards: Conflicts in knowing and communicating. *Elementary School Journal, 94,* 73–86.

Afflerbach, P., & VanSledright, B. (1999). *The challenge of understanding the past. How do fifth graders construct meaning from diverse history texts?* Elva Knight Research Presentation, International Reading Association, San Diego, CA.

Anderson, R., & Pearson, P. (1984). A schema-theoretic view of basic processes in reading. In P. D. Pearson (Ed.), *Handbook of reading research* (pp. 225–291). New York: Longman.

Baker, L., & Brown, A. (1984). Metacognitive skills and reading. In P. D. Pearson, R. Barr, M. Kamil, & P. Mosenthal (Eds.), *Handbook of reading research* (pp. 353–394). New York: Longman.

Bazerman, C. (1985). Physicists reading physics: Schema-laden purposes and purpose-laden schema. *Written Communication, 2,* 3–24.

Beach, R. (1972). *The literary response process of college students while reading and discussing three poems.* Doctoral dissertation, University of Illinois. (Dissertation Abstracts International Order No. 73–17112)

Beach, R., & Hynds, S. (1991). Research on response to literature. In R. Barr, M. L. Kamil, P. B. Mosenthal, & P. D. Pearson (Eds.), *Handbook of reading research* (Vol. 2, pp. 453–489). New York: Longman.

Belenky, M., Clinchy, B., Goldberger, N., & Tarule, J. (1986). *Woman's ways of knowing: The development of self, voice, and mind.* New York: Basic Books.

Bereiter, C., & Bird, M. (1985). Use of thinking aloud in identification and teaching of reading comprehension strategies. *Cognition and Instruction, 2,* 131–156.

Boring, E. (1953). A history of introspection. *Psychological Bulletin, 50*, 169–189.

Breetveldt, I., van den Bergh, H., & Rijlaarsdam, G. (1994). Relations between writing processes and text quality: When and how? *Cognition and Instruction, 12*, 103–123.

Bridge, C., & Winograd, P. (1982). Readers' awareness of cohesive relationships during cloze comprehension. *Journal of Reading Behavior, 14*, 299–312.

Britton, B., Glynn, S., & Smith, E. (1985). Cognitive demands of processing expository text. In B. Britton & J. Black (Eds.) *Understanding expository text* (pp. 227–248). Hillsdale, NJ: Lawrence Erlbaum Associates.

Brown, A., & Day, J. (1983). Macrorules for summarizing strategies: The development of expertise. *Journal of Verbal Learning and Verbal Behavior, 22*, 1–14.

Bruce, B., & Rubin, A. (1984). Strategies for controlling hypothesis formation in reading. In J. Flood (Ed.), *Promoting reading comprehension* (pp. 97–112). Newark, DE: International Reading Association.

Bruner, J. (1985). Models of the learner. *Educational Researcher, 14*, 5–8.

Bruner, J. (1996). *The culture of education.* Cambridge, MA: Harvard University Press.

Charney, D. (1993). A study in rhetorical reading: How evolutionists read "The spandrels of San Marco." In J. Selzer (Eds.), *Understanding scientific prose* (pp. 203–231). Madison: University of Wisconsin Press.

Collins, A., Brown, J., & Larkin, K. (1980). Inferences in text understanding. In R J. Spiro, B. C. Bruce, & W. F. Brewer (Eds.), *Theoretical issues in reading comprehension* (pp. 385–407). Hillsdale, NJ: Lawrence Erlbaum Associates.

Collins, A., & Smith, E. (1982). Teaching the process of reading comprehension. In D. Detterman & R. Sternberg (Eds.), *How and how much can intelligence be increased?* (pp. 173–185). Norwood, NJ: Ablex.

Deegan, D. (1995). Exploring individual differences among novices reading in a specific domain: The case of law. *Reading Research Quarterly, 30*, 154–170.

Deffner, G. (1988). Concurrent thinking aloud: An on-line tool for studying representations used in text understanding. *Text, 8*, 351–367.

de Groot, A. (1965). *Thought and choice in chess.* The Hague, Netherlands: Mouton.

DuBois, P. (1998). Evaluating test items in AIR's cognitive survey lab. *Internet report: What's new.* Washington, DC: American Institutes for Research.

Duncker, K. (1945). On problem solving. *Psychological Monographs, 58*, 1–113 (whole no. 270).

Earthman, E. (1992). Creating the virtual work: Readers' processes in understanding literary texts. *Research in the Teaching of English, 26*, 351–384.

Eco, U. (1990). *The limits of interpretation.* Bloomington: Indiana University Press.

Ericsson, K. (1988). Concurrent verbal reports on text comprehension: A review. *Text, 8*, 295–325.

Ericsson, K., & Simon, H. (1980). Verbal reports as data. *Psychological Review, 87*, 215–253.

Ericsson, K., & Simon, H. (1993). *Protocol analysis: Verbal reports as data.* Cambridge, MA: MIT Press. (Original work published 1984)

Ericsson, K. & Simon, H. (in press). How to study thinking in everyday life: Contrasting think-aloud protocols with descriptions and explanations of thinking. *Mind, Culture, and Activity.*

Feuerstein, R. (1980). *The dynamic assessment of retarded performers: The learning potential assessment, device, theory, instrument, and techniques.* Baltimore, MD: University Park Press.

Fish, S. (1980). *Is there a text in this class? The authority of interpretive communities.* Cambridge, MA: Harvard University Press.

Flower, L., & Hayes, J. (1977). Problem-solving strategies and the writing process. *College English, 39*, 449–461.

Gambrell, L., & Almasi, J. (1996). *Lively discussions! Fostering engaged reading.* Newark, DE: International Reading Association.

Garner, R. (1982). Verbal report data on reading strategies. *Journal of Reading Behavior, 14*, 159–167.

Garner, R., & Reis, R. (1981). Monitoring and resolving comprehension obstacles: An investigation of spontaneous lookbacks among upper-grade good and poor comprehenders. *Reading Research Quarterly, 16*, 569–582.

Geisler, C. (1991). Toward a sociocognitive model of literacy: Constructing mental models in philosophical conversation. In C. Bazerman & J. Paradis (Eds.). *Textual dynamics of the professions* (pp. 171–190). Madison: University of Wisconsin Press.

Graesser, A., & Bower, G. (1990). *Inferences and text comprehension.* San Diego, CA: Academic Press.

Graves, B., & Frederiksen, C. (1991). Literary expertise in the description of fictional narrative. *Poetics, 20*, 1–26.

Greeno, J., Pearson, P., & Schoenfeld, A. (1996). *Implications for NAEP of research on learning and cognition. Report to the National Academy of Education.* Washington, DC: National Academy of Education.

Guthrie, J., Britten, T., & Barker, K. (1991). Roles of document structure, cognitive strategy, and awareness in searching for information. *Reading Research Quarterly, 26*, 300–324.

Haas, C., & Flower, L (1988). Rhetorical reading strategies and the construction of meaning, *College Composition and Communication, 39*, 167–183.

Haastrup, K. (1987). Using thinking aloud and retrospection to uncover learners' lexical inferencing procedures. In C. Faerch & G. Kasper (Eds.), *Introspection in second language research* (pp. 197–212). Philadelphia: Multilingual Matters, Ltd.

Hall, R., Kibler, D., Wenger, E., & Truxaw, C. (1989). Exploring the episodic structure of algebra story problem solving. *Cognition and Instruction, 6*, 223–283.

Hare, V. (1981). Readers' problems identification and problem solving strategies for high- and low-knowledge articles. *Journal of Reading Behavior, 13,* 359–365.

Hartmann, D. (1995). Eight readers reading: The intertextual links of proficient readers reading multiple passages. *Reading Research Quarterly, 30,* 520–561.

Huey, E. (1908). *The psychology and pedagogy of reading.* Cambridge, MA: MIT Press.

James, W. (1890). *The principles of psychology.* New York: Holt.

Johnston, P., & Afflerbach, P. (1985). The process of constructing main ideas from text. *Cognition and Instruction, 2,* 207–232.

Just, M., & Carpenter, P. (1980). A theory of reading: From eye fixations to comprehension. *Psychological Review, 87,* 329–354.

Kavale, K., & Schreiner, R. (1979). The reading process of above average and average readers: A comparison of the use of reasoning strategies in responding to standardized comprehension measures. *Reading Research Quarterly, 15,* 102–128.

Kintgen, E. (1983). *The perception of poetry.* Bloomington: Indiana University Press.

Kucan, L., & Beck, I. (1997). Thinking aloud and reading comprehension research: Inquiry, instruction, and social interaction. *Review of Educational Research, 67,* 271–299

Langer, J. (1990). The process of understanding: Reading for literary and informative purposes. *Research in the Teaching of English, 24 ,* 229–260.

Leinhardt, G., & Young, K. (1996). Two texts, three readers: Distance and expertise in reading history. *Cognition and Instruction, 14,* 441–486.

Loxterman, J., Beck, I., & McKeown, M. (1994). The effects of thinking aloud during reading on students' comprehension of more or less coherent text. *Reading Research Quarterly, 29,* 353–368.

Lundeberg, M. (1987). Metacognitive aspects of reading comprehension: Studying understanding in legal case analysis. *Reading Research Quarterly, 22,* 407–432.

Lytle, S. L (1982). *Exploring comprehension style: A study of twelfth-grade readers' transactions with texts.* Doctoral dissertation, University of Pennsylvania. (University Microfilms No. 82-27292)

Magliano, J., & Graesser, A. (1993). A three-pronged method for studying inference generation in literary text. *Poetics, 20,* 193–232.

Marbe, K. (1964). *Experimentell-psychologische: Untersuchungen uber das Urteil.* Reprinted and translated in J. Mandler & G. Mandler (Eds.). (1964). *Thinking: From association to gestalt* (pp. 143–148). New York: Wiley. (Original work published 1901)

McCallister, J. (1930). Reading difficulties in studying content subjects. *Elementary School Journal, 31,* 191–201.

Miller, K., & Stigler, J. (1991). Meanings of skill: Effects of abacus expertise on number representation. *Cognition and Instruction, 8,* 29–67.

Neutelings, R., & Maat, H. (1997). Investigating the processes of reading-to-assess among Dutch legislators. *Journal of Literacy Research, 29,* 47–71.

Newell, A., & Simon, H. (1972). *Human problem solving.* Englewood Cliffs, NJ: Prentice Hall.

Nisbett, R., & Wilson, T. (1977). Telling more than we can know: Verbal reports on mental processes. *Psychological Review, 84,* 231–259.

Norris, S. (1990). Effect of eliciting verbal reports of thinking on critical thinking test performance. *Journal of Educational Measurement, 27,* 41–58.

Norris, S. (1992). A demonstration of the use of verbal reports of thinking in multiple-choice critical thinking test design. *Alberta Journal of Educational Research, 38,* 153–176.

Nuthall, G., & Alton-Lee, A. (1995). Assessing classroom learning: How students use their knowledge and experience to answer classroom achievement text questions in science and social studies. *American Educational Research Journal, 32,* 185–223.

Olshavsky, J. (1976–1977). Reading as problem solving: An investigation of strategies. *Reading Research Quarterly, 12,* 654–674.

Olson, G., Mack, R., & Duffy, S. (1981). Cognitive aspects of genre. *Poetics, 10,* 283–315.

Palincsar, A., & Brown, A. (1984). Reciprocal teaching of comprehension-fostering and monitoring activities. *Cognition and Instruction, 1,* 117–175.

Paris, S., Lipson, M., & Wixson, K. (1983). Becoming a strategic reader. *Contemporary Educational Psychology, 8,* 293–316.

Pearson, P., & Fielding, L. (1991). Comprehension instruction. In R. Barr, M. L. Kamil, P. B. Mosenthal, & P. D. Pearson (Eds.), *Handbook of reading research* (Vol. II, pp. 815–860). New York: Longman.

Peskin, J. (1998). Constructing meaning when reading poetry: An expert-novice study. *Cognition and Instruction, 16,* 235–263.

Peterson, P., Swing, S., Braverman, M., & Buss, R. (1982). Students' aptitudes and their reports of cognitive processes during instruction. *Journal of Educational Psychology, 74,* 535–547.

Phillips, L. (1988). Young readers' inference strategies in reading comprehension. *Cognition and Instruction, 5,* 193–222.

Piekarz, J. (1954). *Individual responses in interpretive responses in reading.* Unpublished doctoral dissertation, University of Chicago.

Pirolli, P., & Recker, M. (1994). Learning strategies and transfer in the domain of programming. *Cognition and Instruction, 12,* 235–275.

Polya, G. (1954a). *Mathematics and plausible reasoning (a) Induction and analogy in mathematics.* Princeton, NJ: Princeton University Press.

Polya, G. (1954b). *Patterns of plausible inference.* Princeton, NJ: Princeton University Press.

Pressley, M., & Afflerbach, P. (1995). *Verbal protocols of reading: The nature of constructively responsive reading.* Hillsdale, NJ: Lawrence Erlbaum Associates.

Pressley, M., Harris, K., & Marks, M. (1992). But good strategy instructors are constructivists!! *Educational Psychology Review, 4,* 1–32.

Pritchard, R. (1990a). The evolution of introspective methodology and its implications for studying the reading process. *Reading Psychology: An International Quarterly, 11,* 1–13.

Pritchard, R. (1990b). The effects of cultural schemata on reading processing strategies. *Reading Research Quarterly, 25,* 273–295.

Ransom, J. (1979). *The new criticism.* Westport, CT: Greenwood Publishing.

Reinking, D. (1992). Differences between electronic and printed texts: An agenda for research. *Journal of Educational Multimedia and Hypermedia, 1,* 11–24.

Rich, A. (1974). *The dream of a common language.* New York: Norton.

Rogers, T. (1991). Students as literary critics: The interpretive experiences, beliefs, and processes of ninth-grade students. *Journal of Reading Behavior, 23,* 391–423.

Rosenblatt, L. (1978). *The reader, the text, the poem: The transactional theory of the literary work.* Carbondale, IL: Southern Illinois University Press.

Schellings, G., & Van Hout Walters, B. (1995). Main points in an instructional text, as identified by students and their teachers. *Reading Research Quarterly, 30,* 742–756.

Schmalhofer, F., & Boschert, S. (1988). Differences in verbalization during knowledge acquisition from texts and discovery learning from example situations. *Text, 8,* 369–393.

Schoenfeld, A. (1983). Beyond the purely cognitive: Belief systems, social cognitions and metacognitions as driving forces in intellectual performance. *Cognitive Science, 1,* 329–363.

Schwegler, R., & Shamoon, L. (1991). Meaning attribution in ambiguous texts in sociology. In C. Bazerman & J. Paradis (Eds.), *Textual dynamics of the professions* (pp. 216–233). Madison: University of Wisconsin Press.

Shearer, B., Coballes-Vega, C., & Lundeberg, M. (1993, December). *How do teachers who are professionally active select, read, and use professional journals?* Paper presented at the annual meeting of the National Reading Conference, Charleston, SC.

Simon, D., & Simon, H. (1978). Individual differences in solving physics problems. In R. Siegler (Ed.), *Children's thinking: What develops?* (pp. 325–348). Hillsdale, NJ: Lawrence Erlbaum Associates.

Slotta, J., Chi, M., & Joram, E. (1995). Assessing students' misclassifications of physics concepts: An ontological basis for conceptual change. *Cognition and Instruction, 12,* 373–400.

Smagorisnsky, P. (1998). Thinking and speech and protocol analysis. *Mind, Culture, and Activity, 5,* 157–177.

Smith, M. (1990). Knowledge structures and the nature of expertise in classical genetics. *Cognition and Instruction, 7,* 287–302.

Squire, J. (1964). *The responses of adolescents while reading four short stories.* Champaign, IL: National Council of Teachers of English.

Titchener, E. (1912a). Prolegomena to a study of introspection. *American Journal of Psychology, 23,* 427–448.

Titchener, E. (1912b). The schema of introspection. *American Journal of Psychology, 23,* 485–508.

Trabasso, T., & Magliano, J. (1996). How do children understand what they read and what can we do to help them? In M. Graves, P. van den Broek, & B. Taylor (Eds.), *The first r: A right of all children* (pp. 160–188). New York: Teachers College Press.

van den Broek, P., Fletcher, C., & Risden, K. (1993). Investigations of inferential processes in reading: A theoretical and methodological integration. *Discourse Processes, 16,* 169–180.

van Dijk, T., & Kintsch, W. (1983). *Strategies of discourse comprehension.* New York: Academic Press.

VanSledright, B., & Afflerbach, P. (1999). "But the pale faces knew it not": Using revisionist history texts to challenge traditional views of America's past. Paper submitted for publication.

Vygotsky, L. (1978). *Mind in society: The development of higher psychological processes.* Cambridge, MA: Harvard University Press.

Wade, S., Trathen, W., & Schraw, G. (1990). An analysis of spontaneous study strategies. *Reading Research Quarterly, 25,* 147–166.

Waern, Y. (1988). Thoughts on text in context: Applying the think-aloud method to text processing. *Text, 8,* 327–350.

Watson, J. (1913). Psychology as the behaviorist views it. *Psychological Review, 20,* 158–177.

Watson, J. (1920). Is thinking merely the action of language mechanisms? *British Journal of Psychology, 11,* 87–104.

Werner, H., & Kaplan, E. (1950). Development of word meaning through verbal context: An experimental study. *Journal of Psychology, 29,* 251–257.

Wertsch, J. (1991). *Voices of the mind: A sociocultural approach to mediated action.* Cambridge, MA: Harvard University Press.

Wimsatt, W., & Beardsley, M. (1954). *The verbal icon.* Lexington: University of Kentucky Press.

Wineburg, S. (1991). On the reading of historical texts: Notes on the breach between school and academy. *American Educational Research Journal, 28,* 495–520.

Wineburg, S. (1998). Reading Abraham Lincoln: An expert/expert study in the interpretation of historical texts. *Cognitive Science, 22*, 319–346.

Wyatt, D., Pressley, M., El-Dinary, P., Stein, S., Evans, P., & Brown, R. (1993). Reading behaviors of domain experts processing professional articles that are important to them: The critical role of worth and credibility monitoring. *Learning and Individual Differences, 5*, 49–72.

Young, K., & Leinhardt, G. (1998). Writing from primary documents: A way of knowing history. *Written Communication, 15*, 25–68.

CHAPTER 13

A Case for Single-Subject Experiments in Literacy Research

Susan B. Neuman
Temple University

Sandra McCormick
The Ohio State University

From the mid 1800s through the present, there have been cycles of interest in research methods used to explore literacy issues. For example, questions examining the efficacy of various literacy interventions have traditionally employed experimental group research designs, whereas questions focusing on process characteristics, the "hows" and "whys" of literacy research, have looked more toward qualitative methodologies. Noticeably absent from the research literature, however, have been studies based on a single subject, or $N = 1$ research designs. The purpose of this chapter, therefore, is to examine the utility of single-subject experimental design for literacy research. We begin by briefly describing its history and logic, then turn to its theoretical and practical advantages. We end by delineating both potential problems and possible solutions for future investigations pertaining to literacy development.

Single-subject design is an experimental technique where one subject or a small number of subjects is studied intensively. Unlike much traditional group-data analysis, these designs allow for the study of response changes in single individuals. Thus, although there may be any number of subjects in an investigation, the designation *single-subject* means that each subject's behaviors and outcomes are analyzed individually, not averaged with other members of an experimental or control group. In this respect, the method has something in common with case-study research. Unlike much case-study research, however, single-subject experimental studies allow the researcher to describe cause-and-effect relationships between independent and dependent variables.

In most cases, single-subject experimental studies are conducted in the context in which the behavior is practiced (i.e., the classroom), rather than in contrived laboratory settings. Here, the emphasis is on examining the *functional relationship* between an independent variable (the intervention) and a dependent variable (the outcome measure) for a particular individual. Typically, the dependent variable (or variables) focuses on behaviors that are measurable and practically important for student success (i.e., increase in number of inferential questions correctly identified). Consequently, whether or not the intervention is inferred to be successful is based on its educational (or social) relevance and importance rather than on statistically significant standards.

Single-subject experimental design has evolved over the last decades in response to a need to systematically examine the effects of instruction on student behavior. In the 1950s and 1960s, a number of investigators (Baer, Wolf, & Risley, 1968; Bellack & Chassan, 1964; Shapiro & Ravenette, 1959) in several subfields of psychology, such as psychotherapy, experimental personality research, psychopathology, and psychoanalysis, increasingly expressed concern about the lack of an approach to study behavior changes that was individualized and intensive, yet controlled. Although case study methodologies were extensively used, and regarded as useful for in-depth and personalized clinical work in these disciplines, researchers also wanted an experimental technology that could describe the functional relationships between interventions and outcomes. Although recognizing the merits of between-subject experimental studies to serve the latter aim, questions were raised concerning the incongruities seen in averaged group data with actual behaviors observed in individual clients participating in large-group studies. The result of these concerns were efforts that led to the evolution of single-subject experimental research.

Several investigators have been innovators and pacesetters in crafting the basic tenets and procedures of this research paradigm. Although as early as 1947 Thorne had suggested certain guidelines for single-case experiments, these had little impact until Shapiro and Ravenette (1959) presented a design model that formed the basis for a present, widely used analysis system in single-subject experimental research, the A-B-A-B design. The essential components of this design were a no-treatment phase (A) and a treatment (B), followed by the withdrawal of the treatment (A), and the reintroduction of treatment (B), the basic logic being that performance under baseline conditions predicts future performance if the treatment were not introduced. Shapiro (1961, 1966) also is credited with other important initial drives in developing the called-for methodology, such as definition, manipulation, and repeated administration of independent variables—with single cases. Sidman's now classic book, published in 1960, outlined other research designs appropriate for response analysis with single individuals, including the multi-element design. He also confronted the issue of generality in $N = 1$ studies, delineating several methods for replication of single-subject experiments within and across individuals for establishment of general hypotheses.

Shortly thereafter, and from a different disciplinary perspective, Campbell and Stanley (1963) suggested equivalent time-series designs for use in psychological and educational research, also a suitable means for experimental investigation of individual behaviors, and also involving basic principles of the A-B-A-B design. Bellack and Chassan's (1964) pharmacological work further advanced the A-B-A-B design prototype, and Chassan (1960, 1967) suggested appropriate statistics for extending single-subject analyses (for an update, see Kamil, 1995; Kratochwill & Levin, 1992). In 1968, Baer, Wolf, and Risley's introduction of the multiple-baseline design widened the analysis systems available for examining research questions with single individuals within an experimental framework. As this methodology has evolved over the last several decades, the literature has become replete with variants of the basic research designs, as well as principles for conducting robust studies and interpreting analyses.

THE LOGIC OF SINGLE-SUBJECT EXPERIMENTAL RESEARCH

Essentially, all single-subject experimental designs are considered to rest on a baseline logic. That is, the behavior of each subject during no-treatment conditions, or baseline, is compared with the subject's behavior during treatment conditions. It is assumed that performance under baseline predicts what would typically occur if the treatment were not introduced. In this respect, single-subject experimental research shares the same underlying assumption of group experimentation.

Although there are many variations in designs, several characteristics are central to all single-subject experimental research studies (see McCormick, 1995, for more detail). The first and foremost characteristic is *individual data analysis* (also called *personalized data analysis*). Because individual differences can be obscured when data are averaged across a group and reported as group mean, individual data analysis is undertaken because it is believed that the understanding of human variability is critical to the solution of specific problems. Thus, instead of attempting to control for variability through randomization and statistical procedures, the purpose of single-subject design strategy is to uncover and carefully examine variability.

A second characteristic is *direct manipulation of independent variables*; that is, here, the focus is on altering conditions, rather than on describing existing conditions. Therefore, a third earmark of single-subject experimental studies is the implementation of *planned and monitored interventions*. For example, it is standard procedure to systematically check the consistency with which the intervention is implemented to ensure that it is conducted as planned throughout the study. Based on frequent monitoring, data on the integrity of the independent variable, along with reliability coefficients for the dependent variable, are typically included in all data descriptions.

Differing from many well-established research models, single-subject experimental research does not rely on a single pretest to document pre-intervention behaviors. Instead, there is *data collection over several sessions to establish a baseline* to account for day-to-day variability in human responses. Furthermore, an important overriding practice is the *repeated, and frequent, measurement of variables during intervention*; again because of the possibility of day-to-day response variability, a single posttest at the end of an intervention is not considered a sufficient measure of behavior change. These intervention data are compared with a participant's own baseline responses. Comparison of every participant's own baseline data with their own specific responses during intervention is referred to as "using each subject as his or her own control." Once the intervention begins, there usually is *manipulation of only one independent variable at a time*. This is to provide assurance that the particular variable being studied is implicated in any changes of behavior that might occur. Throughout, *standardized measurement conditions* are maintained; the dependent variable is consistent across all phases of the study. Independent observers are often used to conduct checks throughout the study to ensure reliability of the observations or other data.

Most single-subject experimental studies include *maintenance assessments*, and *measure transfer of effects*. Although literacy researchers have been encouraged to include measures to assess maintenance of effects in research contextualized within other experimental paradigms, frequently this is not done. In contrast, it is a rare single-subject experiment that does not assess maintenance of the behavior after a relatively extended time has elapsed following termination of the study. Moreover, it is customary to evaluate reliability of both the dependent variable and the independent variable (i.e., providing measures of treatment integrity, as well as standard reliability coefficients).

With its emphasis on experimental control, single-subject research is considered to be strong with respect to internal validity because of the continuous measurement of responses over time, the use of subjects as their own controls, and the dual reliability assessments (Campbell & Stanley, 1963). Thus, single-subject research is known to use control procedures instead of control groups (McCormick, 1995). On the other hand, the issue of external validity—that is, the question of how generality can be established when the numbers of subjects are small (as also has been the case with qualitative studies)—is addressed through repeating the study to determine if an experimentally produced effect will occur another two, three, or more times. To establish external validity, single-subject researchers may undertake replications of the same experiment with other subjects, and/or replications in other settings. As Wixson has suggested (1993), "many replications of small studies may inform us as well as one large study that attempts to control so many factors that we have little 'ecology validity'" (p. 3; see Palincsar & Parecki, 1995, for a more detailed discussion).

Concerns for social validity (Tawney & Gast, 1984), as well, are often addressed in single-subject design research. That is, if a major change occurs as a result of an intervention, is it meaningful to the learner, and educationally significant? Social validity might address: What is the magnitude of the effect of improving one's ability to answer inferential questions, or to be able to assess one's writing? Does it impact classroom participation? Grades? Locus of control? Wolf (1978), for example, argued for the inclusion of subjective measures in studies to examine the student's view of the goals, procedures, and effects of an intervention. Given these concerns, more studies are beginning to include self-assessment measures, or debriefing interviews to determine student's perception of the benefits (and perhaps, costs) of an instructional intervention.

SELECTED TYPES OF DESIGNS

All of these procedures are carried out within certain designs that are specific to single-subject research. The most commonly used are three of those conceptualized during the early years of development of single-case experimental methodology, although over time these designs and their appropriate uses have been refined. These are the A-B-A-B reversal design, the alternating-treatments design (originally termed the multielement design), and the multiple-baseline design. The A-B-A-B reversal design (see Fig. 13.1) allows measurement of a baseline condition (condition A), the introduction of an intervention (condition B), return to the baseline condition (i.e., return to condition A), and reintroduction of the intervention (i.e., return to condition B). This design is based on the premise that if desired responses increase with the introduction of the intervention, diminish again with return to the baseline condition (i.e., temporary removal of the intervention), and increase once more with reinstatement of the intervention, this attests to the strength of that intervention. Had a study been terminated after the first A and B conditions only, threats to internal validity, such as maturational factors, would weaken conclusions about the effectiveness of the program being investigated. As can be seen for the hypothetical study represented by Fig. 13.1, an intervention involving use of word sorts to increase attention to orthographic features of words on spelling lists appears to be effective for Bob and Amy, but not for Rob. Because data have been maintained separately for these students, individual decisions can be made about their programs.

The multielement design, introduced almost four decades ago, is currently more commonly called the *alternating-treatments design* (Neuman, 1995). In 1979 Barlow and Hayes suggested the latter name as being more descriptive of its functions. With use of this analysis model, several interventions (most typically three) are randomly alternated for each subject, enabling the researcher to draw conclusions about which yields the most useful modifications in performance. Fig. 13.2 demonstrates use of this design with three participants. As can be noted in the hypothetical investigation, use of discussion through cooperative groups (condition 1) and through paired learning (condition 2) shows equally positive effects on Judy's understanding of cause-and-effect relationships, with both of these interventions leading to greater success than independent work (condition 3) in dealing with such questions. As can be seen in the figure, Anne, too, has improved achievement with these two interventions; however, for Anne cooperative group work clearly has the larger impact of the two. On the other hand, none of the arrangements appear to better than any other for Dan. Individual examination of the data portrays variability in student needs.

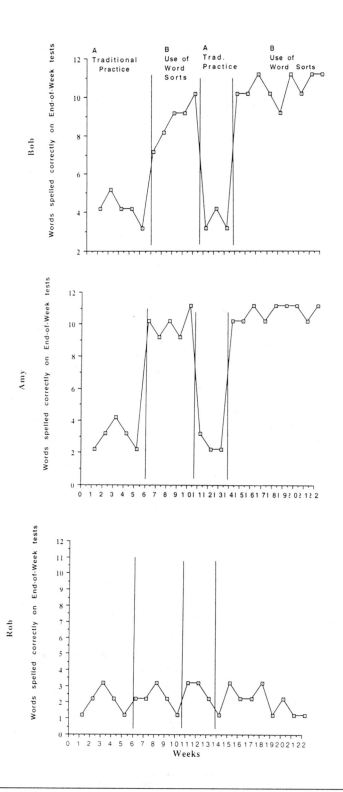

FIG. 13.1. Hypothetical example of a study employing an A–B–A–B design.

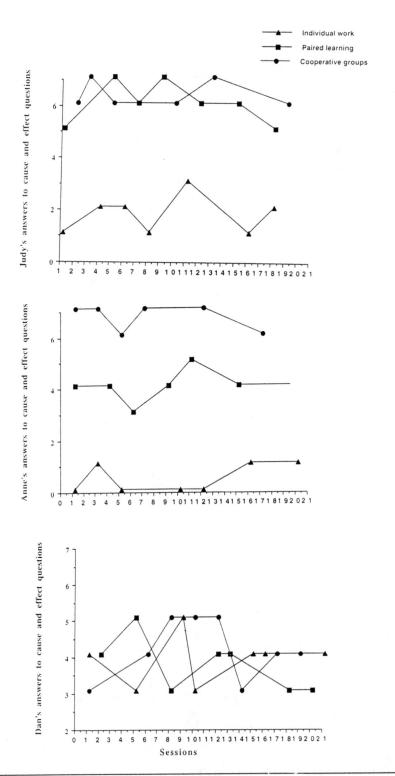

FIG. 13.2. Hypothetical example of use of an alternating treatments design with three subjects.

The third extensively used design is the *multiple-baseline design*. With this means of analysis, evaluations can be made across several subjects, several behaviors, or several settings. An example of the logic of the multiple-baseline design can be seen as applied to three subjects in Fig. 13.3. This example hypothetically examines the effect of use of study guides during independent reading of expository text. After baseline measurement, an intervention is initially introduced to one subject, but not to the others. Because a positive change in responses is seen with Diane, and is absent with those not yet receiving the intervention, this provides one confirmation of its effectiveness. Next, the intervention is applied with Jim. The change in response level for this subject, and again, its absence with Elaine, who is still in the baseline condition (i.e., not yet receiving the intervention), provides a replication of this confirmation. And, finally, when Elaine also demonstrates responsiveness to the intervention, an affirmation of its constructiveness is provided. The same logic is exercised when examining several interventions with a single individual, or one behavior across several settings.

As this discussion illustrates, it is critical for researchers to be in contact with their data to insure that students are truly benefiting from an intervention. Consequently, data are analyzed in these designs through visual analysis. Although statistical analyses of data are possible, visual analysis is the most frequent data analytic strategy. There are several reasons for analyzing the data in graphic form. First, it is a dynamic process; it provides continuous and concrete evidence of the impact of specific targeted instruction. Decisions about the efficacy of instruction for an individual can be determined; one can shorten or lengthen the intervention on the basis of whether the approach continues to be effective. Second, one can examine the effectiveness of the intervention across different types of learners, leading to better instruction designed for individual learners. For example, one approach may be most effective with one learner, but not with another, who might benefit from a different approach. And third, the visual analysis of data is a more conservative estimate of impact than statistical analysis (particularly with large sample sizes). Generally, if you can see it (i.e., changes in a target behavior), you can believe it. If the patterns show substantial differences as a result of an intervention, the findings are likely to be robust and reliable.

More comprehensive discussions of single-subject experimental designs and the analysis of graphic data are available in a number of texts (e.g., Barlow & Hersen, 1984; Cooper, Heron, & Heward, 1987; Johnston & Pennypacker, 1993; Kazdin, 1982; Kratochwill & Levin, 1992; Neuman & McCormick, 1995). For those interested in conducting well-controlled intervention research, these texts offer a rich resource of information on expanded descriptions of tenets, designs, and ways to conduct single-subject experimental studies.

WHY USE SINGLE-SUBJECT EXPERIMENTAL DESIGNS IN LITERACY RESEARCH?

Traditionally, single-subject design research has been most widely used to examine interventions in psychology-related fields and special education. More recently, however, these designs have attracted the attention of literacy researchers. For example, studies have been reported on a wide range of topics including the effects writing processes, story grammar instruction, spelling, study skills, story mapping, word identification strategies, sociodramatic play and language performance, methods of teacher cueing, context use, self-correction behaviors, comprehension, family literacy, reciprocal teaching, and oral reading (e.g., Bianco & McCormick, 1989; Danoff, Harris, & Graham, 1993; Gurney, Gersten, Dimino, & Carnine, 1990; Guza & McLaughlin, 1987; Idol & Croll, 1987; Lenz & Hughes, 1990; Levy, Wolfgang, & Koorland, 1992; McCormick & Cooper, 1991; Mudre & McCormick, 1989; Neuman & Gallagher, 1994; Newby,

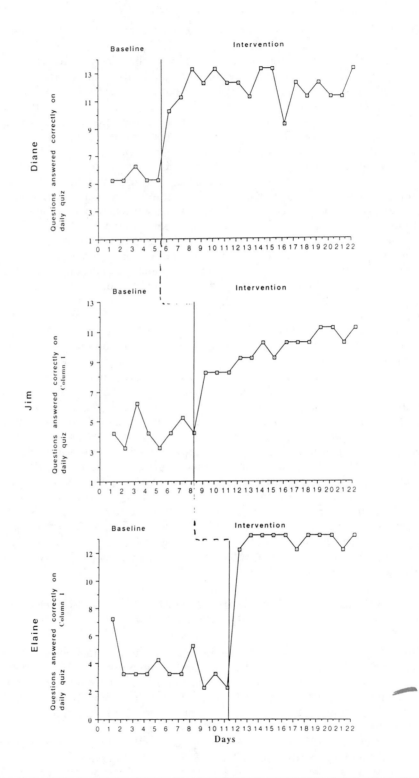

FIG. 13.3. Hypothetical study employing a multiple-baseline across-subject design.

Caldwell, & Recht, 1989; Palincsar & Brown, 1984; Rose & Beattie, 1986; Schumaker, Deshler, Alley, Warner, & Denton, 1982).

Why has single-subject experimental design become increasingly attractive to those of us studying literacy development? First, these designs have been constructed to investigate specific interventions and their effects in great detail. Carefully designing the measurement strategy, with each variable studied at length to determine its effects, allows researchers to systematically determine whether or not a particular intervention (or a part of an overall intervention) is most effective and for whom, since individual subjects may respond differently. As data from these studies accumulate, factors that do and do not influence reading can be addressed, bringing the profession closer to an understanding of how written language is learned for many students across ages. Eventually, it may even be possible to describe characteristics of learners for which specific interventions might be most effective. In this respect, single-subject experimental design can provide literacy researchers with a mechanism for examining the theoretical nature of reading.

Second, single-subject designs have many ecological factors that make them especially useful to literacy researchers. The alternating-treatments design for example, is both an experimentally sound and an efficient method to measure a particular student, or groups of students' performance on a target behavior in classrooms. Following a brief baseline, treatments are alternated randomly, and are continued until one treatment proves to be more effective than the others (or until it is clear than no method is superior to another). During the entire experiment, the learner's performance for each treatment is plotted on a graph, and the effects of the treatments can easily be discerned through visual analysis. These procedures control for many of the intervening threats to the internal validity of a study, such as differential selection of subjects as well as history effects. Yet, unlike many experimental studies where control conditions are required, these procedures are highly compatible with classroom instruction. They can be conducted in the context of instruction, can be targeted to individual learners and their needs, and can provide answers to critical instructional questions in a relatively short time. Further, procedurally, single-subject research is compatible with the aims and ecological variables of teacher research in classrooms (see, e.g., Braithwaite, 1995).

The third, and perhaps the most critical, reason for using single-subject design is the growing complexity of research issues in literacy. Where once a particular research method might have been sufficient to address a research issue, today's questions about literacy interventions often require combinations of designs. There are a number of studies, for example, that use standard group designs along with single-subject design, providing both power in terms of potential generalizability yet specificity in determining whether or not the intervention may be appropriate for different types of learners (see, e.g., Neuman & Gallagher, 1994; Palincsar & Brown, 1984). As systems for inquiry continue to advance, some researchers have suggested the advantages of combining single-subject designs with qualitative research (e.g., Bisesi & Raphael, 1995), as well as linkages to sophisticated statistical, nonparametric, and meta-analytic procedures (see Kamil, 1995; Kratochwill & Levin, 1992). Encompassing features of quantitative research and qualitative research, these combinations of methods help researchers not only to examine whether or not an intervention was successful, but why, how, and for whom.

TECHNICAL ADVANTAGES OF SINGLE-SUBJECT DESIGNS FOR LITERACY RESEARCH

There are a number of technical advantages for using single-subject methodology to explore a range of questions in literacy today. These include, but are certainly not limited to the following advantages.

Identifying Functional Relationships.   Functional relationships mean that the researcher or teacher has confidence (based on empirical verification) that the behavioral change is due to the intervention and not for other likely reasons (Tawney & Gast, 1984). Single-subject designs add a sophisticated methodology for establishing functional relationships by control over variability in behavior—a central goal of research design (Campbell & Stanley, 1963). Because the intervention (or phases of intervention) is introduced while other variables are held constant, one can isolate a particular phase to determine if it is responsible for changing behavior. This kind of a controlled experiment, therefore, not only can demonstrate that power of an intervention, but also what particular phase was most influential in determining change. For example, in their study of teenage mothers' interactions with their children, Neuman and Gallagher (1994) found that one of three phases—"contingent responsivity," a mother's ability to respond to her child's language request—was particularly influential in increasing the child's active engagement in storybook reading and play. Similarly, in a study designed to improve students' ability to assess their own writing, Marteski (1998) found that two of three phases of intervention (content and mechanics, but not sentence construction), were most responsible for students' writing improvement. Without such experimental control, therefore, we might make the mistake of attributing an improvement in behavior to a total intervention, when in reality the improvement occurred in a particular part of it. Single-subject experimental designs can help investigators avoid such errors.

Exploration of Intersubject Variability.   Another technical advantage of using single-subject designs is the capability to examine variability among subjects. It is long been recognized that children typically defined as "struggling readers" are hardly homogeneous. As teachers can clearly attest, there are differences in degree of difficulty and kind. However, variability among students or their sensitivity to particular types of instruction is rarely examined. Further, the results of intervention studies are based typically on statistically significant improvements for groups, even though some in the group might respond favorably to an intervention, whereas others may not benefit at all.

Single-subject designs circumvent this problem (or if used in combination with other designs, may respond to these concerns). That is, single-subject designs examine a functional relationship between an independent and dependent variable in a single subject, and replicate the experiment for a second, third and fourth time with other subjects. In Marteski's study (1998), for example, replications were conducted with below-average, average, and above-average learners. In each case, the results of self-assessment of content and analysis of writing mechanics showed improvement in writing, indicating that the intervention was effective for all three types of learners. In other cases, however, when variability is observed across replications, the researcher can seek out sources of variability among subjects. Examining the effects of a taped words treatment on reading proficiency, for example, Shapiro and McCurdy (1989) found that the intervention was effective for four of five students, suggesting a limitation for using the strategy more broadly. When such variability is found, the researcher might adjust the intervention and measure it against its previous effectiveness with other subjects, leading to a modified intervention. This type of flexibility may add a critical dimension to our analysis to examine literacy interventions among difference types of struggling readers that is difficult to accomplish in group experimental designs.

Exploration of Intrasubject Variability.   Essentially, single-subject designs involve time-series analyses of repeated measures for each individual subject (McReynolds & Thompson, 1986). Consequently, it allows us to understand the natural variability that occurs for individual students. For example, perhaps a simple intervention like asking students to reread the text before answering questions is highly effective in improving reading comprehension scores immediately. Yet over several weeks, the intervention becomes ineffective for one learner, but not for another. This might suggest that the once-useful strategy for the first student has become overautomaticized, curtailing its usefulness, whereas for another, it becomes more powerful over time.

This variability, readily observed with single-subject design, would not likely be noticed in group experimental designs. Most experimental designs involve only two measurement periods (before and after), and the data that are gathered are averaged across subjects. In contrast, because measurement is ongoing, and analyzed individually, instructional decisions regarding whether or not a particular intervention is effective are dependent on its educational utility, and not on a preconceived time period of how long the intervention should be administered.

Environment for Conducting Studies and Relation to Practice.   Single-subject research studies are best examined in the context in which the behavioral changes are likely to take place. For example, the researcher who is attempting to determine if prompting a child to use a metacognitive strategy, like predicting, might improve the child's comprehension would likely conduct the study in the classroom context, and in the course of guided reading activity rather than in a laboratory study with specialized text. Changes in the child's ability, therefore, would be directly related to the skills and strategies needed to accomplish successful reading in the classroom. Thus, single-subject studies potentially diminish two age-old problems in research: (a) translating research findings into practical settings, and (b) involving children in activity that may take time away from classroom instruction. Rather, single-subject research can be conducted during ongoing instruction, and can use materials for recording and scoring that need not be elaborate. Further, such ongoing assessment has been recommended as a strategy to help teachers better tailor instruction to meet children's individual needs.

PROBLEMS AND POTENTIAL SOLUTIONS IN USING SINGLE-SUBJECT DESIGNS IN LITERACY RESEARCH

Although single-subject design has many advantages for literacy research, there are some limitations. These include methodological problems in the research design and demonstration of experimental control, analysis and reliability of data, and generalization of results.

Research Design and Experimental Control

Experimental control, a key feature of single-subject research, is demonstrated by systematically and repeatedly establishing that changes in behavior covary with changes in an intervention. Consequently, interventions must have discriminatory power from other techniques in the classroom. For example, a special intervention that uses a particular spelling technique must be clearly differentiable from other writing activities that occur on a day-to-day basis, so that any changes in behavior may be attributable to the independent variable rather than to many other activities in the classroom. This suggests that the intervention must be potentially powerful enough to demonstrate reasonably immediate effects. For example, it would not be wise to examine the effects of sustained silent reading (SSR) versus strategic instruction on the percent of time spent reading because it may take multiple sessions before the investigator might observe real changes in the dependent variable on the basis of the treatment.

Further, literacy researchers must be concerned about carryover effect, which may limit the kinds of questions that can be answered using single-subject design research. Consider, for example, the case of contrasting the effects on comprehension recall of a guided visualization strategy with a verbal think-aloud approach during reading. Even with counterbalancing treatments, it may be obvious to the researcher that after several sessions, the guided visualization strategy is being used to organize how the individual might verbally think aloud. In this case, one treatment may ostensibly influence how the other treatment is being used.

These concerns suggest that the researcher who uses these designs carefully select independent variables to avoid contaminating the intervention with another or with ongoing instruction. This may be difficult in studies in which learned behaviors are specifically transferable to other behaviors. Thus, the kinds of questions that can be addressed must be suited to experimental control procedures. Some examples are:

- Effects of oral versus silent reading on reading fluency.
- The impact of a self-assessment strategy on a child's ability to examine strengths and weaknesses of writing.
- Effects of key word method on oral reading.

Analysis and Reliability of Data

Single-subject researchers must be able to provide an operational definition that is precise, exclusive, and clear, for each dependent variable. Because standardized assessments are often not used, reliability of dependent measures is crucial in these studies. Reliability requires that the definition of a dependent variable is targeted and specific to insure appropriate and concise coding of what may constitute a response. Ambiguity cannot exist.

Particularly in the area of literacy research, this may mean that an analysis of one dependent variable is not enough to make a case for an effective intervention. Reading is a construct. Thus, studies that attempt to influence a specific behavior such as comprehension, for example, might include multiple, dependent variables like prediction, recall, and inference that are independent from one another, and could be reliably measured by two or more independent observers. To insure that there is no overlap, however, it is critical to include definitions of variables, and methods used for establishing reliability in all studies, enhancing the confidence of the study results, as well as insuring the possibility of replication.

Generality of Results

Generalizing from a single study, whether it be a group or single-subject design, can be highly problematic. Even in the case of the traditional group experimental design where sampling strategies involve random assignment, findings may have limited generality to any particular individual within the population. Thus, concerns raised about generalizability of single-subject research studies may actually share much in common with other experimental approaches as well.

In practice, some single-subject researchers (see, e.g., Axelrod, 1983) argue that as an applied field, generalizability is not of crucial importance, because the goal is to improve effective teaching for individual students. Others, however, argue for direct, and systematic replications for establishing generalizability (see Palincsar & Parecki, 1995). Direct replication, most often used, involves repeating the intervention with new but similar subjects. To enhance generalization beyond direct replication to individuals who are dissimilar to those included in the original study, however, involves systematic replications. Here, we might involve students that are qualitatively different from those in the original study or in earlier replications, in different settings. This type of replication allows us to answer the question of generality simultaneously across settings and subjects.

The ability to generalize in single-subject research is directly related to the number of replications performed and to the specificity of methodology in the original study. Therefore, authors should be encouraged to incorporate many different replications, as well as to replicate earlier studies.

CONCLUSIONS

Since the 1960s, single-subject experimental research has migrated into a number of fields, including social work, medicine, and education. Articles reporting investigations have appeared in numerous social science journals, with its use seen in both basic and applied research. Still, this research analysis system has not been broadly embraced by the literacy field. There are, however, a number of reasons for considering incorporating single-subject experimental research into the methodological repertoires of literacy investigators because of (a) the efficacy of the methodology, (b) its close ties to practical applications, and (c) the consistency of the approach with current conceptualization about literacy learning and literacy study.

Single-subject experimental research is a sophisticated methodology that, alone or in combination with other methodologies, may address complex literacy issues. It is a research design grounded in scientific logic that can be used for investigation of a wide range of experimental questions. These designs allow us to empirically demonstrate causal relations, responding to the impact that a specific intervention may have on changes in behavior. When used appropriately, single-subject design may provide investigators with an additional methodological tool that is capable of generating new theory and practical application for literacy research.

REFERENCES

Baer, D. M., Wolf, M. M., & Risley, T. (1968). Current dimensions of applied behavior analysis. *Journal of Applied Behavior Analysis, 1,* 91–97.

Barlow, D. H., & Hayes, S. C. (1979). Alternating treatments design: One strategy for comparing the effects of two treatments in a single behavior. *Journal of Applied Behavior Analysis, 12,* 199–210.

Barlow, D. H., & Hersen, M. (1984). *Single case experimental designs* (2nd ed.). New York: Pergamon.

Bellack, L., & Chassan, J. B. (1964). An approach to the evaluation of drug effects during psychotherapy: A double-blind study of a single case. *Journal of Nervous and Mental Disease, 139,* 20–30.

Bianco, L., & McCormick, S. (1989). Analysis of effects of a reading study skill program for high school learning-disabled students. *Journal of Educational Research, 82,* 282–288.

Bisesi, T. L., & Raphael, T. E. (1995). Combining single-subject designs with qualitative research. In S. B. Neuman & S. McCormick (Eds.), *Single-subject experimental research: Applications for literacy* (pp. 104–119). Newark, DE: International Reading Association.

Braithwaite, J. A. (1995). Teachers using single-subject designs in the classroom. In S. B. Neuman & S. McCormick (Eds.), *Single-subject experimental research: Applications for literacy* (pp. 120–136). Newark, DE: International Reading Association.

Campbell, D. T., & Stanley, J. C. (1963). *Experimental and quasi-experimental designs for research.* Chicago: Rand-McNally.

Chassan, J. B. (1960). Statistical inference and the single case in clinical design. *Psychiatry, 23,* 173–184.

Chassan, J. B. (1967). *Research designs in clinical psychology and psychiatry.* New York: Appleton-Century-Crofts.

Cooper, J. O., Heron, T. E., & Heward, W. L. (1987). *Applied behavior analysis.* New York: Macmillan.

Danoff, B., Harris, K. R., & Graham, S. (1993). Incorporating strategy instruction within the writing process in the regular classroom: Effects on the writing of students with and without learning disabilities. *Journal of Reading Behavior, 25,* 295–322.

Gurney, D., Gersten, R., Dimino, J., & Carnine, D. (1990). Story grammar: Effective literature instruction for high school students with learning disabilities. *Journal of Learning Disabilities, 6,* 335–342, 348.

Guza, D. S., & McLaughlin, T. F. (1987). A comparison of daily and weekly testing on student spelling performance. *Journal of Educational Research, 80,* 373–376.

Idol, L., & Croll, V. J. (1987). Story-mapping training as a means of improving reading comprehension. *Learning Disability Quarterly, 10,* 214–229.

Johnston, J. M., & Pennypacker, H. S. (1993). *Strategies and tactics of behavioral research* (2nd ed.). Hillsdale, NJ: Lawrence Erlbaum Associates.

Kamil, M. L. (1995). Statistical analyses procedures for single-subject designs. In S. B. Neuman & S. McCormick (Eds.), *Single-subject experimental research: Applications for literacy* (pp. 84–103). Newark, DE: International Reading Association.

Kazdin, A. E. (1982). *Single-case research designs: Methods for clinical and applied settings.* New York: Oxford University Press.

Kratochwill, T. R., & Levin, J. R. (Eds.). (1992). *Single-case research designs and analysis: New directions for psychology and education.* Hillsdale, NJ: Lawrence Erlbaum Associates.

Kucera, J., & Axelrod, S. (1995). Multiple-baseline designs. In S. B. Neuman & S. McCormick (Eds.), *Single-subject experimental research: Applications for literacy* (pp. 47–63). Newark, DE: International Reading Association.

Lenz, B. K., & Hughes, C. A. (1990). A word identification strategy for adolescents with learning disabilities. *Journal of Learning Disabilities, 23,* 149–158, 160.

Levy, A., Wolfgang, C. H., & Koorland, M. A. (1992). Sociodramatic play as a method for enhancing the language performance of kindergarten age students. *Early Childhood Research Quarterly, 7,* 245–262.

Lipson, M. Y., & Wixson, K. K. (1986). Reading disability research: An interactionist perspective. *Review of Educational Research, 56,* 111–136.

Marteski, F. (1998). *Developing student ability to self assess.* Doctoral dissertation, Temple University, Philadelphia, PA.

McCormick, S. (1995). What is single-subject experimental research? In S. B. Neuman & S. McCormick (Eds.), *Single-subject experimental research* (pp. 1–31). Newark, DE: International Reading Association.

McCormick, S., & Cooper, J. O. (1991). Can SQ3R facilitate secondary learning disabled students' literal comprehension of expository text? *Reading Psychology, 12,* 239–271.

McReynolds, L., & Thompson, C. (1986). Flexibility of single-subject experimental designs. *Journal of Speech and Hearing Disorders, 51,* 194–203.

Mudre, L. H., & McCormick, S. (1989). Effects of meaning-focused cues on underachieving readers' context use, self-corrections, and literal comprehension. *Reading Research Quarterly, 24,* 89–113.

Neuman, S. B. (1995). Alternating-treatments designs. In S. B. Neuman & S. McCormick (Eds.), *Single-subject experimental research: Applications for literacy* (pp. 64–83). Newark, DE: International Reading Association.

Neuman, S. B., & Gallagher, P. (1994). Joining together in literacy learning: Teenage mothers and children. *Reading Research Quarterly, 29,* 383–401.

Neuman, S. B., & McCormick, S. (1995). *Single-subject experimental research: Applications for literacy.* Newark, DE: International Reading Association.

Newby, R. F., Caldwell, J., & Recht, D. (1989). Improving the reading comprehension of children with dysphonetic and dyseidetic dyslexia using story grammar. *Journal of Learning Disabilities, 22,* 373–379.

Palincsar, A. S., & Brown, A. L. (1984). Reciprocal teaching of comprehension-fostering and comprehension-monitoring activities. *Cognition & Instruction, 1,* 117–175.

Palincsar, A. S., & Parecki, A. D. (1995). Important issues related to single-subject experimental research. In S. B. Neuman & S. McCormick (Eds.), *Single-subject experimental research: Applications for literacy* (pp. 137–150). Newark, DE: International Reading Association.

Rose, T. L., & Beattie, J. R. (1986). Relative effects of teacher-directed and taped previewing on oral reading. *Learning Disability Quarterly, 7,* 39–44.

Schumaker, J. B., Deshler, D. D., Alley, G. R., Warner, M. M., & Denton, P. H. (1982). Multipass: A learning strategy for improving reading comprehension. *Learning Disability Quarterly, 5,* 295–311.

Shapiro, E. S., & McCurdy, B. R. (1989). Effects of a taped words treatment on reading proficiency. *Exceptional Children, 55,* 321–325.

Shapiro, M. B. (1961). The single case in fundamental clinical psychological research. *British Journal of Medical Psychology, 34,* 255–263.

Shapiro, M. B. (1966). The single case in clinical-psychological research. *Journal of General Psychology, 74,* 3–23.

Shapiro, M. B., & Ravenette, A. T. (1959). A preliminary experiment of paranoid delusions. *Journal of Mental Science, 105,* 295–312.

Sidman, M. (1960). *Tactics of scientific research: Evaluating scientific data in psychology.* New York: Basic Books.

Tawney, J., & Gast, D. (1984). *Single-subject research in special education.* Columbus, OH: Charles Merrill.

Thorne, F. C. (1947). The clinical method in science. *American Psychologist, 2,* 161–166.

Watson, J. B., & Rayner, R. (1920). Conditioned emotional reactions. *Journal of Experimental Psychology, 3,* 1–14.

Wixson, K. (1993, November). *A review of literacy studies using single-subject design.* Paper presented at the National Reading Conference, Austin, TX.

Wolcott, H. F. (1973). *The man in the principal's office: An ethnography.* Prospect Heights, IL: Waveland Press.

Wolf, M. (1978). Social validity: The case for subjective measurement or how applied behavior analysis is finding its heart. *Journal of Applied Behavior Analysis, 11,* 203–214.

Yaden, D. B. (1995). Reversal designs. In S. B. Neuman & S. McCormick (Eds.), *Single-subject experimental research: Applications for literacy* (pp. 32–46). Newark, DE: International Reading Association.

CHAPTER 14

Discourse and Sociocultural Studies in Reading

James Paul Gee
University of Wisconsin at Madison

This chapter develops an integrated perspective on language, literacy, and the human mind, a perspective that holds important implications for the nature of reading, both cognitively and socioculturally. I start with a brief discussion of the converging areas of study that constitute the background for discourse-based and sociocultural studies of language and literacy. Then, I turn to a particular view of the mind as social, cultural, and embedded in the world. This view of mind implies that meaning is always situated in specific sociocultural practices and experiences. After a discussion of how this notion of *situated meaning* applies to reading, I turn to a discussion of *cultural models*, that is, the often tacit and taken-for-granted, socioculturally specific "theories" through which people organize and understand their situated experiences of the world and of texts. I then discuss how humans enact different identities in distinct forms of spoken and written language conveying distinctive situated meanings and cultural models. I close with a brief discussion of some implications for literacy research and practice.

CONVERGING AREAS

One of the most important recent developments in the study of language and literacy is the way in which a variety of formerly discrete areas are beginning to converge around some central themes. These themes tend to undermine long-standing dichotomies in reading research: for example, dichotomies between cognition and context, skills and meaning, formal structures and communicational functions, and the individual and the social. Some of the converging areas I have in mind, beyond current work in reading research itself (for overviews on reading theory and practice, see, e.g., Adams, 1990; Reutzel & Cooter, 1996), are briefly discussed next:

Ethnomethodology and conversational analysis, with related work in *interactional sociolinguistics* (Duranti & Goodwin, 1992; Goffman, 1981; Goodwin, 1990; Mehan, 1979; Ochs, Schegloff, & Thompson, 1996; Schiffrin, 1994, chap. 4), has argued that social and institutional order is the product of the moment-by-moment intricacies of social and verbal interaction that produce and reproduce that order. "Knowing" is a matter of "knowing how to proceed" ("go on") in specific social interactions. Related work in discursive psychology (Billig, 1987; Edwards & Potter, 1992; Harre & Gillet, 1994; Harre & Stearns, 1995; Shotter, 1993) stressed the ways in which "mental" states (things like remembering, emotion, interpreting, and intending) are not just "in the head," but strategically constructed and negotiated in interaction.

The ethnography of speaking (Gumperz, 1982a, 1982b; Gumperz & Levinson, 1996; Hymes, 1974, 1996) has argued that language in use does not convey general and decontextualized meanings. Rather, participants in interaction use various lexical, structural, and prosodic "cues," in speech or writing, to infer just what context (or part of a context) is relevant and how this context gives words meanings specific to it. The form and meaning of these "contextualization cues" differ across different cultures, even among people from different social groups speaking the same language.

Sociohistorical psychology, following Vygotsky and later Bakhtin (Bakhtin, 1986; Cole, 1996; Engestrom, 1987, 1990; Scribner & Cole, 1981; Vygotsky, 1978, 1987; Wertsch, 1985, 1991, 1997), has argued that the human mind is "furnished" through a process of "internalizing" or "appropriating" images, patterns, and words from the social activities in which one has participated. Further, thinking is not "private," but almost always mediated by cultural tools, that is, artifacts, symbols, tools, technologies, and forms of language that have been historically and culturally shaped to carry out certain functions and carry certain meanings (cultural tools have certain "affordances," although people can transform them through using them in new settings).

Closely related work on *situated cognition* (Hutchins, 1995; Lave, 1988, 1996; Lave & Wenger, 1991; Rogoff, 1990; Rogoff & Lave, 1984; Tharp & Gallimore, 1988), also with an allegiance to Vygotsky, has argued that knowledge and intelligence reside not solely in heads, but rather are distributed across the social practices (including language practices) and the various tools, technologies, and semiotic systems that a given "community of practice" uses in order to carry out its characteristic activities (e.g., part of a physicist's knowledge is embedded and distributed across that person's colleagues, social practices, tools, equipment, and texts). Knowing is a matter of being able to participate centrally in practice, and learning is a matter of changing patterns of participation (with concomitant changes in identity).

Cultural models theory (D'Andrade, 1995; D'Andrade & Strauss, 1992; Holland & Quinn, 1987; Shore, 1996; Strauss & Quinn, 1998), a social version of schema theory, has argued that people make sense of their experiences by applying largely tacit "theories" or "cultural models" to them. Cultural models, which need not be complete or logically consistent, are simplified and prototypical arguments, images, "storylines," or metaphorical elaborations, shared within a culture or social group, that explain why and how things happen as they do and what they mean. These "theories" (which are embedded not just in heads, but in social practices, texts, and other media) guide action, inform judgments of self and others, and shape ways of talking and writing.

Cognitive linguistics (Lakoff, 1987; Lakoff & Johnson, 1980; Ungerer & Schmid, 1996) argues that all human languages are organized in terms of intricate, complex, intersecting, and overlapping systems of metaphors (and related figurative devices). These metaphors shape, in different ways in different cultures, how we interpret our experience and how we think about ourselves and the material, social, and cultural world. For example, in English we often think and talk about argument in ways shaped by how we talk about warfare ("I *defended* my argument and *destroyed* his case at the same time") or talk about minds as if they were enclosed spaces ("He just couldn't get it *into* his head").

The new science and technology studies (Bloor, 1991; Collins, 1992; Collins & Pinch, 1993; Latour, 1987, 1991; Latour & Woolgar, 1986; Mulkay, 1991; Pickering, 1992, 1995; Shapin, 1994; Shapin & Schaffer, 1985) have argued that scientific knowledge is rooted in scientists' day-to-day social practices and distributed across (and stored within) those practices and the characteristic spaces, tools, texts, symbols, and technologies that scientists use. Scientists' day-to-day practices are far more historically, technologically, socially, and culturally conditioned than appears from the "write-up" of their results in books and journals. Scientists' knowledge is a matter of "coordinating" and "getting coordinated by" (in mind and body) colleagues, objects, nature, texts, technologies, symbols, language, and social and instrumental practices.

Modern composition theory (Bazerman, 1989; Berkenkotter & Huckin, 1995; Bizzell, 1992; Faigley, 1992; Myers, 1990; Swales, 1990, 1998) has stressed the ways in which knowledge and meaning are situated within the characteristic talking, writing, acting, and interacting genres (patterns) of disciplines and other specialized domains. These (historically changing) genres create both the conditions for and the limits to what can be said and done in the discipline at a given time and place.

Sociocultural literacy studies (*"the new literacy studies"*: Barton & Hamilton 1998; Cazden, 1988; Cook-Gumperz, 1986; Gee, 1996; Heath, 1983; Kress, 1985; Scollon & Scollon, 1981; Street, 1984, 1995) have stressed that there are multiple literacies (many different ways of writing and reading connected to ways of speaking and listening), each embedded in specific sociocultural practices and each connected to a distinctive and "political" set of norms, values, and beliefs about language, literacy, and identity (*political* here means that things like power, status, and other social goods are at stake).

Work on *connectionism* (Churchland, 1995; Clark 1989, 1993, 1997; Elman et al., 1996; Gee, 1992; Karmiloff-Smith, 1992; Winograd & Flores, 1989) in cognitive science has argued that humans do not primarily think and act on the basis of mental representations that are general rules or logical propositions. Rather, thinking and acting are a matter of using, and adapting to current circumstances, stored patterns or images of our past experiences. These patterns or images are shaped (edited) by the social, cultural, and personal contexts of those experiences.

Modern sociology (Beck, Giddens, & Lash, 1994; Giddens, 1984, 1987) has stressed the ways in which human thinking, acting, and interaction are simultaneously structured by institutional forces and, in turn, give a specific order (structure, shape) to institutions such that it is impossible to say which comes first, institutions or the human social practices that continually enact and reproduce (and transform) them. Modern sociology has also stressed, as well, the ways in which this reciprocal exchange between human interaction and human institutions is being transformed by global economic and demographic changes such that the nature of time, space, human relationships, and communities is being radically transformed.

Finally, a good deal of so-called *poststructuralist* and *postmodernist* work (e.g., Bakhtin, 1986; Bourdieu, 1979/1984; Fairclough, 1992; Foucault, 1973, 1977), much of it earlier than the movements just discussed, has centered around the notion of *discourses*. Discourses are characteristic (socially and culturally formed, but historically changing) ways of talking and writing about, as well as acting with and toward, people and things (ways that are circulated and sustained within various texts, artifacts, images, social practices, and institutions, as well as in moment-to-moment social interactions) such that certain perspectives and states of affairs come to be taken as "normal" or "natural" and others come to be taken as "deviant" or "marginal" (e.g., what counts as a "normal" prisoner, hospital patient, or student, or a "normal" prison, hospital, or school, at a given time and place).

THE SOCIAL MIND

There are two ways in which the mind is *social*, two ways in which it "leaks" outside the head and into the world. Both have important consequences for reading research and practice. The first way is rooted in the nature of the mind itself. When confronted with data (experience), the human mind is not so much a *rule follower* as a powerful *pattern recognizer* (Clark, 1993, 1997; Gee, 1992). However, given that the world is full of potentially meaningful patterns, and the human mind is adept at finding patterns, something must guide the learner in selecting which patterns to focus on (Elman, 1993; Elman et al., 1996: chap. 6; Gee, 1994). This "guiding something" is the site at which the role of the teacher and "more expert peers," as well as of the curriculum itself, is being redefined in many contemporary reform-based pedagogies (Greeno, 1997).

The second way in which the mind is social is that human thinking is often distributed across other people and various symbols, tools, objects, and technologies. In navigating a large ship, for example, each sailor's cognition is attached to the knowledge of others (who have different sorts of interlocking expertise) and to the "cognition" built into charts, instruments, and technologies. Knowledge is distributed throughout the "system" (Hutchins, 1995). It is not fully coherent or useful if viewed from the perspective of any one decontextualized part of the system. Readers and written texts can often usefully be seen as parts of larger systems, often composed of other people and other sorts of language, symbols, and tools, across which "cognition" is distributed (both in terms of knowledge and values). Such a distributed view of knowledge is at the base of current reform-based classroom "learning communities" (Brown & Campione, 1994; Brown, Collins, & Dugid, 1989).

To say that the mind is a "pattern recognizer" is to say first and foremost that it operates primarily with (flexibly transformable) *patterns* extracted from experience, not with highly general or decontextualized *rules* (Churchland, 1995; Margolis, 1987). It is crucial to note, however, that the patterns most important to human thinking and action follow a sort of "Goldilocks Principle": They are not too general and not too specific. They are *mid-level generalizations* between these two extremes (Barsalou, 1992).

Think about recognizing faces. If you see your friend when she is sick as a different person than when she is well, your knowledge is too specific. If, on the other hand, you see all your female friends as the same, your knowledge is too general. The level at which knowledge is most useful for practice is the level at which you see your friend's many appearances as one person, although different from other people like her. So, too, there is little you can do in physics, if you can only recognize specific refraction patterns: Your knowledge is too specific. There is also little you can effectively do, beyond passing school tests, if all you can do is recite the general theory of electromagnetism: Your knowledge is too general.

Really effective knowledge, then, is being able to recognize, work on, transform, and talk about mid-level generalizations such as, to continue the physics example, "light as a bundle of light waves of different wave lengths combinable in certain specific ways" or "light as particles (photons) with various special properties in specific circumstances" or "light as a beam that can be directed in specific ways for various specific purposes (e.g., lasers)" or "light as colors that mix in certain specific ways with certain specific results." Note the mix of the general and the specific in these patterns.

And it is not just in technical areas like physics that mid-level generalizations are crucial. In everyday life as well, they are the basis of thinking for practice. For example, the word (concept) *coffee* is primarily meaningful as a set of mid-level generalizations that simultaneously define and are triggered by experience: dark-liquid-in-a-certain-type-of-cup; beans-in-a-certain-type-of-bag; grains-in-a-certain-sort-of-tin; berries-on-a-certain-type-of-tree; flavoring-in-certain-type-of-food (Clark, 1989).

Let me call such mid-level generalizations *situated meanings* (later I call them *world-building situated meanings* to distinguish them from other sorts of situated meanings, because they are concerned with *content*). What I have said so far about situated meanings can, however, be misleading. Situated meanings are not static, and they are not definitions (though they are the primary way in which words have meanings in use). Rather, they are flexibly transformable patterns that come out of experience and, in turn, construct experience as meaningful in certain ways and not others. They are always, in fact, adapted (contextualized) to experience in practice (activity).

To see the dynamic nature of situated meanings, imagine the situated meaning (mid-level generalization) you have for a *bedroom* (Clark, 1989; Rumelhart, McClelland, & PDP Research Group, 1986). You conjure up an image that connects various objects and features in a typical bedroom, relative, of course, to your sociocultural experience of bedrooms and homes. Now I tell you to imagine that the bedroom has a refrigerator in it. At once you transform your situated meaning for a bedroom, keeping parts of it, deleting parts of it, and adding, perhaps, things like a desk and a college student.

You can even make up (assemble) situated meanings de novo. For example, say that I tell you to form a meaning for the phrase (concept) *things you would save first in a fire* (Barsalou, 1991). You have no trouble putting together a pattern—again based on your sociocultural experiences—of things like children, pets, important documents, expensive or irreplaceable items, and so forth. You have just invented a mid-level generalization suitable for action, a new concept, one we could even assign a word to, but a concept tied intimately to your sociocultural experiences in the world.

The moral is this: Thinking and using language is an active matter of assembling the situated meanings that you need for action in the world (Barsalou, 1992; Bruner, 1996; Clark, 1996). This assembly is always relative to your socioculturally defined experiences in the world and, more or less, routinized ("normed") by the sociocultural groups to which you belong and with whom you share practices (Gee, 1992). The assembly processes for *coffee* (in "everyday life") and *light* (in physics) are fairly routinized, but even here the situated meanings are adapted each time to the specific contexts they are used in and are open to transformations from new experiences. The situated meanings behind words (concepts) like *democracy, honesty, literacy,* or *masculine* are, of course, less routinized.

SITUATED MEANINGS IN READING

The theoretical notion of situated meanings is a dynamic (connectionist-inspired) and contextualized version of *schemas* (D'Andrade, 1995), a notion that has, for many years now, played a major role in reading research, theory, and practice (Anderson & Pearson, 1984; Rumelhart, 1980). The idea of situated meanings is highly consequential when applied not just to social practices generally, but to the specific social practices in which written texts play a major role. Let me give two examples. The first is relevant to the current worldwide controversy over *genre* in theory and pedagogical practice (Cope & Kalantzis, 1993; Hasan & Williams, 1996).

The names of genres—just like the word *light*—have a spurious generality. We do not operate (effectively) at the (overly) general level of *report, explanation, argument, essay, narrative,* and so forth. Rather, we operate at the "next level down," so to speak (a level at which we have no simple labels). For example, in certain academic fields, things like *an essay review, a theoretical piece, a research-based journal article,* and *an overview of the literature (a review article)* are the situated meanings of genre labels. The "real" genres we work with exist between overly general labels like *article* or *essay* and specific concrete instantiations of writing. Furthermore, genres, as situated meanings, must be flexibly fit to and transformed by the actual contexts in which they are used (remember the bedroom example earlier).

The same is true of the writing and reading that children do at all levels of schooling. Children (like all writers and readers) operate at the next level down from things like *narrative in general* or *reports in general*. They need to operate with mid-level instantiations of types-of-narratives-(or reports)-for-types-of-contexts-for-types-of-purposes, whether these have "official" labels or not. They need to be exposed to multiple examples of these, examples that display the sorts of variations that occur even within a "type" for the purposes of "best fit" to context and purpose (remember our *bedroom* example, again). Children need, as well, overt guidance to focus on the features of language and context that help them recognize and produce the "right" situated meanings (mid-level patterns)—that is, those shared by the community of practice to which they are being "apprenticed."

My second example comes from a study by Lowry Hemphill (1992) investigating how high school students from different socioeconomic backgrounds read various canonical works of literature. In the case I consider here, the students were reading Robert Frost's poem "Acquainted With the Night." One girl, whom I call Maria, responded to the line *I have passed by the watchman on his beat* as follows:

> I think he's trying to say that though he [has] like seen the sadder situations. And the watchman meaning I would think a cop was on his daily routine. The watchman still couldn't stop the situation that was happening. Which was probably something bad. Or you know dishonest. But he still was able to see what was going on.

And then to the line *And dropped my eyes unwillingly to explain*:

> Oh well this line's making me think that well the watchman caught him. And he was ashamed of what he was doing. And he didn't want to explain his reasons for his own actions to the watchman. Cause he was so ashamed.

Another girl, whom I call Mary, responded to her reading of the poem, in an essay, as follows (I cite only parts of the essay):

> Figuratively, Frost is describing his life....
>
> In the third stanza, he says "I have stood still...." Maybe he has stopped during his walk of life and heard people with different paths or lives calling him but he later finds they were not calling him after all.
>
> There is a slight undertone of death in the last two or three lines. The clock symbolizing the time he has left. The clock telling him that he can't die yet however much he may want to.
>
> ... the reader, if he looks closely can see past the words on the paper and into Robert Frost's soul.

In reading, we recognize situated meanings (mid-level generalizations/patterns/inferences) that lie between the "literal" specifics of the text and general themes that organize the text as a whole. These situated meanings actually mediate between these two levels. In the Frost poem, Maria uses (recognizes) situated meanings like "Something bad is happening and an authority figure can't stop it," "One avoids authority figures if and when one has done something bad," "An authority figure catches one doing something bad and one is ashamed." Mary uses (recognizes) situated meanings like "Choosing among different paths through a landscape is like making different decisions in one's life" or "Time passing as shown by things like clocks is like the passing of time in a life as one ages."

Maria and Mary have seen different patterns in Frost's poem, in terms of which they situate its meanings. We see later, too, that the girls are reading out of different "theories" of reading and different "theories" of literature. These "theories" are constructed out of the different sorts of situated meanings the girls find and, in turn, these theories lead them to find these situated meanings in the text.

CULTURAL MODELS

Confronted with situated meanings, it is natural to ask why words (concepts), like *light* or *coffee*, seem to us, in fact, to have much more general meanings. Part of the answer is simply the fact that a single word exists, and we are misled by this to think that a single, general meaning exists. But another and more important part of the answer is that words are tied to "cultural models," "storylines," or "theories" that "belong" to socioculturally defined groups of people (Bruner, 1996; D'Andrade & Strauss, 1992; Holland & Quinn, 1987; Strauss & Quinn, 1998). These cultural models, storylines, or theories "explain" (relative to the standards of the sociocultural group) why the features in the mid-level patterns "hang together" in the way they do (Gee, 1994). Furthermore, these cultural models, storylines, or theories are usually not stored in any one person's head, but are distributed across the different sorts of "expertise" and viewpoints found in the sociocultural group (Shore, 1996).

The storyline connected to *coffee* for some of us is something like: Berries are picked and then prepared as beans or grain to be made later into a drink, as well as into flavorings for other foods. Different types of coffee, drunk in different ways, have different social and cultural implications, for example, in terms of status. This is about all of the storyline I know—the rest of it (I trust) is distributed elsewhere in the society should I need it. The storyline for *light* in physics is a formal theory, a theory distributed across physicists of different sorts, as well as across written texts and instruments (and it is quite different from the cultural model of light that many people use in their everyday lives).

Cultural models, storylines, and theories organize the thinking and work of sociocultural groups (or "communities of practice"). They "rationalize" the situated meanings and practices that people in those groups use. They are part (but only part) of what defines the group in the first place.

Consider Maria and Mary again. They operate with different cultural models (theories) of what it is to read Frost's text, models tied to the allegiances they have (or are forming) to specific "communities of practice" (Cranny-Francis, 1996; Martin, 1996; Wenger, 1999). Maria appears to operate with a cultural model of reading (at least in this situation) that finds significance in relating the words of the text to situated meanings (patterns) that she finds in her "everyday" life, keeping in mind that what counts as "everyday life" differs for different sociocultural groups of people. In her world, if people are out late at night and avoiding contact with authority figures, they are, in all likelihood, in trouble. Her cultural model of reading seems also to stress social contacts and relationships between people. Maria reads from her own experience to the words and back again to her social experience.

Mary appears to operate with a cultural model of reading (in this situation) that finds significance in treating concrete details and actions as "correlates" for more universal emotions and themes. Patterns in the world (e.g., paths through landscapes, clocks telling time) are correlated with emotions or themes. Mary's "theory of reading," of course, was quite explicitly delineated by people like T. S. Eliot and William Carlos Williams, among other canonical (Anglo) modernists (Perkins, 1976). Hemphill (1992) found that students like Maria fared less well than students like Mary in English classes, although, in fact, both ways of reading (one out of narrative schemas and the other out of figurative schemas) have been celebrated in the reading literature (Reutzel & Cooter, 1996).

The pedagogical bite of all this discussion about situated meanings and cultural models is this: Any efficacious pedagogy must be a judicious mixture of *immersion* in a community of practice (Lave, 1996) and *overt focusing* and scaffolding from "masters" or "more advanced peers" (Vygotsky, 1987) who focus learners on the most fruitful sorts of patterns in their experience ("fruitful" for developing the cultural models that are used by the community of practice to which the learner is being "apprenticed"). Just what constitutes a "judicious mixture," in different settings, is a cutting-edge topic for research (Cazden, 1992). Fights over "rich immersion (e.g., whole language) as against "overt instruction" (e.g., phonics) are, as dichotomies, irrelevant and meaningless (other than politically).

WHO AND WHAT: FURTHER SITUATED MEANINGS

So far I have argued that language is given meaning-in-use through its association with situated meanings, cultural models, and the sociocultural groups that socialize learners into these. But there are two other sorts of situated meanings that language always involves just as much as the "world-building" ones we have discussed thus far.

In addition to "world-building situated meanings" (content), any utterance communicates what I call a *who* and a *what* (Wieder & Pratt, 1990; see also Edwards & Potter, 1992; Harre & Gillett, 1994; Shotter, 1993). What I mean by a *who* is a socially situated place (position) from which the utterance is "authorized" and issued (and these are not always the same). With written texts, this *who* may or may not be a person or, at least, a single person (it may, for instance, be an institution). What I mean by a *what* is a socially situated activity or practice that the utterance helps (with other nonlanguage "stuff") to constitute.

To understand the meaning of any piece of language, written or oral, then, we must grasp the situated world-building, *who*, and *what* meanings the language communicates. In turn, we "grasp" these situated meanings (if we do) because we have participated in worldly and sociocultural experiences from which they emerge and which they, in turn, define and transform (Duranti & Goodwin, 1992; Gumperz & Levinson, 1996; Hanks, 1995; Scribner & Cole, 1981; Wertsch, 1991).

Let me give a specific example. Biologists and other scientists write differently in professional journals than they do in popular science magazines, and these different ways of writing construct different worlds, accomplish different activities (social practices), and display different identities. It is in understanding these that we come to understand the texts. Consider, then, the two extracts that follow, the first from a professional journal, the second from a popular science magazine, both written by the same biologist on the same topic (examples from Myers, 1990):

> Experiments show that *Heliconius* butterflies are less likely to oviposit on host plants that possess eggs or egg-like structures. These egg-mimics are an unambiguous example of a plant trait evolved in response to a host-restricted group of insect herbivores. (professional journal, p. 150)

> *Heliconius* butterflies lay their eggs on *Passiflora* vines. In defense the vines seem to have evolved fake eggs that make it look to the butterflies as if eggs have already been laid on them. (popular science, p. 150)

The first extract, from a professional scientific journal, is about the conceptual structure of a specific theory within the scientific discipline of biology. The subject of the initial sentence is *experiments*, a methodological tool in natural science. The subject of the next sentence is *these egg-mimics*: Note how plant parts are named, not in terms of the plant itself, but, rather, in terms of the role they play in a particular *theory* of natural selection and evolution, namely, "coevolution" of predator and prey (i.e., the theory that predator and prey evolve together by shaping each other). Note also, in this regard, the earlier *host plants* in the preceding sentence, rather than the "vines" of the popular passage.

In the second sentence, the butterflies are referred to as *a host-restricted group of insect herbivores*, which points simultaneously to an aspect of scientific methodology (like *experiments* did) and to the logic of a theory (like *egg-mimics* did). Any scientist arguing for the theory of coevolution faces the difficulty of demonstrating a causal connection between a particular plant characteristic and a particular predator when most plants have so many different sorts of animals attacking them. A central methodological technique to overcome this problem is to study plant groups (like *Passiflora* vines) that are preyed on by only one or a few predators (in this case, *Heliconius* butterflies). *Host-restricted group of insect herbivores* then refers both to the relationship between plant and insect that is at the heart of the theory of coevolution and to the methodological technique of picking plants and insects that are restricted to each other so as to "control" for other sorts of interactions.

The first passage is concerned with scientific methodology and a particular theoretical perspective on evolution. On the other hand, the second extract, from a popular science magazine, is not about methodology and theory, but about *animals* in *nature*. The butterflies are the subject of the first sentence and the vine is the subject of the second. Further, the butterflies and the vine are labeled as such, not in terms of their role in a particular theory.

The second passage is a story about the struggles of insects and plants that are transparently open to the trained gaze of the scientist. Further, the plant and insect become "intentional" actors in the drama: the plants act in their own "defense" and things "look" a certain way to the insects; they are "deceived" by appearances as humans sometimes are.

These two examples replicate in the present what, in fact, is a historical difference. In the history of biology, the scientist's relationship with nature gradually changed from telling stories about direct observations (seeing) of nature to carrying out complex experiments to test complex theories (Bazerman, 1989) and manage uncertainty (Myers, 1990). This change was caused, in part, by the fact that mounting "observations" of nature led scientists not to consensus but to growing disagreements as to how to describe and explain such observations (Shapin & Schaffer, 1985). "Seeing" became more and more mediated by theory and technology. This problem led, in turn, to the need to convince the public that such uncertainty did not damage the scientist's claim to be able to "see" and know the world in some relatively direct way, a job now carried out by much "popular science" writing.

This example tells us two things: First, texts (and language generally) are always connected to different *worlds* (here the "nature-as-lab" vs. "nature as open to the gaze"), different *whos* (here the experimenter/theoretician vs. the careful observer of nature), and different *whats* (the professional contribution to science and the popularization of it). Second, such worlds ("content"), *whos*, and *whats* are licensed by specific socially and historically shaped practices representing the *values* and *interests* of distinctive groups of people. To be able to read (and write) such worlds, *whos*, and *whats* requires one to understand such practices with their concomitant values and interests. If we can use the term *politics* to mean any place where social interests and social goods are at stake, then all reading (and writing) is political in a quite straightforward sense (Fairclough, 1995; Gee, 1996).

In texts (and, indeed, in all social activity) particular patterns of world-building, *whos*, and *whats* become recognizable as betokening a particular sociocultural group or *community of practice*. People (as speakers/listeners and as writers/readers) coordinate their words, deeds, values, and feelings with those of other people, as well as with the "affordances" of various spaces, objects, symbols, tools, and technologies, to create a kind of socioculturally meaningful "dance" (Latour, 1991). A particular coordination becomes the "dance" of certain types of (but not all) biologists or gang members or "greens" or elementary school students or students of history or teachers or Native Americans or executives or lawyers, and so on and so forth through a nearly endless list.

I have elsewhere (Gee, 1992, 1996, 1999) called these socioculturally meaningful "dances" (recognizable coordinations of people, places, objects, tools, technologies, and ways of speaking, listening, writing, reading, feeling, valuing, believing, etc.) *Discourses* (with a capital D; *discourse* with a little d just stands for language in use). In terms of our earlier example, thanks to the workings of history, "popular science" is a somewhat different "dance" (though with some, but not all, of the same people, places, and tools) than "professional science."

For those interested in reading and writing, it is important to note, as well, that the very form of language is always an important part of Discourses. The form of the language in the professional passage about butterflies above differs in a systematic way from the form of the language in the popular passage: for example, abstract versus concrete subjects (e.g., *experiments* vs. *butterflies*), technical versus nontechnical terms (e.g., *oviposit* vs. *lay*), complex noun phrases versus simple noun phrase (e.g., *host-restricted group of insect herbivores* vs. Heliconius *butterflies*), nominalizations versus nonderived noun phrases (e.g., *egg-mimics* vs. *fake eggs*), copulative verbs versus more contentful verbs (e.g., *are* vs. *lay*), and so forth.

These formal differences, rather then being random, "hang together" (or "co-relate") with each other to form a pattern that instantiates a particular *function*, that is, the communication of specific sorts of worlds, *whos*, and *whats*. For historical, social, linguistic, and cognitive reasons, a given co-related set of forms (like the partial list for "professional science" given earlier), is apt for this function, and this function is "married" to this set of forms (Halliday & Martin, 1993; Kress, 1996; Kress & van Leeuwen, 1996, pp. 5–12; Olson, 1996). To appreciate this "aptness" and this "marriage" is the heart and soul of acquiring the "code" in reading and writing, at all levels, from phonics to genre to Discourse (Adams, 1990).

IMPLICATIONS

A Discourse-based, situated, and sociocultural view of literacy demands that we see reading (and writing and speaking) as not one thing, but many: many different socioculturally situated reading (writing, speaking) practices. It demands that we see meaning in the world and in texts as situated in learners' experiences, experiences that, if they are to be useful, must give rise to mid-level situated meanings through which learners can recognize and act on the world in specific ways. At the same time, these experiences must be normed and scaffolded by "masters" and "more advanced peers" within a Discourse, and such norming and scaffolding must lead "apprentices" to build the "right" sorts of situated meanings based on shared experiences and shared cultural models. Minus the presence of masters of the Discourse, such norming and scaffolding is impossible. Such "sharing" is always, of course, ripe with ideological and power effects, and, it leads us always to ask of any school-based Discourse: In what sense is this Discourse *authentic*, that is, how and where does it relate to Discourses outside school (e.g., science, work, communities)? In the end, *to read* is to be able to actively assemble situated meanings in one or more specific "literate" Discourses. There is no "reading in general," at least none that leads to thought and action in the world.

REFERENCES

Adams, M. J. (1990). *Learning to read: Thinking and learning about print.* Cambridge, MA: MIT Press.
Anderson, R. C., & Pearson, P. D. (1984). A schema-theoretic view of basic processes in reading. In P. D. Pearson (Ed.), *Handbook of reading research*, (pp. 255–291). New York: Longman.
Bakhtin, M. M. (1986). Speech genres and other essays. Austin: University of Texas.

Barsalou, L. W. (1991). Deriving categories to achieve goals. In G. H. Bower (Ed.), *The psychology of learning and motivation: Advances in research and theory* (Vol. 27, pp. 1–64). New York: Academic Press.

Barsalou, L. W. (1992). *Cognitive psychology: An overview for cognitive scientists.* Hillsdale, NJ: Lawrence Erlbaum Associates.

Barton, D., & Hamilton, M. (1998). *Local literacies: Reading and writing in one community.* London: Routledge.

Bazerman, C. (1989). *Shaping written knowledge.* Madison: University of Wisconsin Press.

Beck, U., Giddens, A., & Lash, S. (1994). *Reflexive modernization: Politics, traditions and aesthetics in the modern social order.* Stanford, CA: Stanford University Press.

Berkenkotter, C., & Huckin, T. N. (Eds.). (1995). *Genre knowledge in disciplinary communication.* Hillsdale, N J: Lawrence Erlbaum Associates.

Billig, M. (1987). *Arguing and thinking: A rhetorical approach to social psychology.* Cambridge: Cambridge University Press.

Bizzell, P. (1992). *Academic discourse and critical consciousness.* Pittsburgh: University of Pittsburgh Press.

Bloor, D. (1991). *Knowledge and social imagery* (2nd ed.). Chicago: University of Chicago Press.

Bourdieu, P. (1984). *Distinction: A social critique of the judgement of taste.* Cambridge, MA: Harvard University Press. (Original work published 1979)

Brown, A. L., & Campione, J. C. (1994). Guided discovery in a community of learners. In K. McGilly (Ed.), *Classroom lessons: Integrating cognitive theory and classroom practice* (pp. 229–270). Cambridge, MA: MIT Press.

Brown, A. L., Collins, A., & Dugid, P. (1989). Situated cognition and the culture of learning. *Educational Researcher, 18,* 32–42.

Bruner, J. (1996). Frames for thinking: Ways of making meaning. In D. Olson & N. Torrance (Eds.). *Modes of thought: Explorations in culture and cognition* (pp. 93–105). Cambridge: Cambridge University Press.

Cazden, C. (1988). *Classroom discourse: The language of teaching and learning.* Portsmouth, NH: Heinemann.

Cazden, C. (1992). *Whole language plus: Essays on literacy in the United States and New Zealand.* New York: Teachers College Press.

Churchland, P. M. (1995). *The engine of reason, the seat of the soul.* Cambridge, MA: MIT Press.

Clark, A. (1989). *Microcognition: Philosophy, cognitive science, and parallel distributed processing.* Cambridge, MA: MIT Press.

Clark, A. (1993). *Associative engines: Connectionism, concepts, and representational change.* Cambridge: Cambridge University Press.

Clark, A. (1997). *Being there: Putting brain, body, and world together again.* Cambridge, MA: MIT Press.

Clark, H. H. (1996). *Using language.* Cambridge: Cambridge University Press.

Cole, M. (1996). *Culture in mind.* Cambridge, MA: Harvard University Press.

Collins, H., & Pinch, T. (1993). *The golem: What everyone should know about science.* Cambridge: Cambridge University Press.

Collins, H. M. (1992). *Changing order: Replication and induction in scientific practice* (2nd ed.). Chicago: University of Chicago Press.

Cook-Gumperz, J. (Ed.). (1986). *The social construction of literacy.* Cambridge: Cambridge University Press.

Cope, B., & Kalantzis, M. (Eds.). (1993). *The powers of literacy: A genre approach to teaching writing.* Pittsburgh: University of Pittsburgh Press.

Cranny-Francis, A. (1996). Technology and/or weapon: The discipline of reading in the secondary English classroom. In R. Hasan & G. Williams (Eds.), *Literacy in society* (pp. 172–190). London: Longman.

D'Andrade, R. (1995). *The development of cognitive anthropology.* Cambridge: Cambridge University Press.

D'Andrade, R., & Strauss, C. (Eds.). (1992). *Human motives and cultural models.* Cambridge: Cambridge University Press.

Duranti, A., & Goodwin, C. (Eds.). (1992). *Rethinking context: Language as an interactive phenomenon.* Cambridge: Cambridge University Press.

Edwards, D., & Potter, J. (1992). *Discursive psychology.* London: Sage.

Elman, J. L. (1993). Learning and development in neural networks: The importance of starting small. *Cognition, 48,* 71–99.

Elman, J. L., Bates, E. A., Johnson, M. H., Karmiloff-Smith, A., Parisi, D., & Plunkett, K. (1996). *Rethinking innateness: A connectionist perspective on development.* Cambridge, MA: MIT Press.

Engestrom, Y. (1987). *Learning by expanding: An activity-theoretical approach to developmental research.* Helsinki: Orienta-Konsultit.

Engestrom, Y. (1990). *Learning, working and imagining: Twelve studies in activity theory.* Helsinki: Orienta-Konsultit.

Faigley, L. (1992). *Fragments of rationality: Postmodernity and the subject of composition.* Pittsburgh: University of Pittsburgh Press.

Fairclough, N. (1992). *Discourse and social change.* Cambridge: Polity Press.

Fairclough, N. (1995). *Critical discourse analysis.* London: Longman.

Foucault, M. (1973). *The birth of the clinic: An archaeology of medical perception.* New York: Vintage.

Foucault, M. (1977). *Discipline and punish: The birth of the prison.* New York: Pantheon.

Gee, J. P. (1992). *The social mind: Language, ideology, and social practice.* New York: Bergin & Garvey.

Gee, J. P. (1994). First language acquisition as a guide for theories of learning and pedagogy. *Linguistics and Education, 6,* 331–354.

Gee, J. P. (1996). *Social linguistics and literacies: Ideology in Discourses* (2nd ed.). London: Taylor & Francis.

Gee, J. P. (1999). *An introduction to discourse analysis: Theory and method.* London: Routledge.

Giddens, A. (1984). *The constitution of society: Outline of the theory of structuration.* Cambridge: Polity Press.

Giddens, A. (1987). *Social theory and modern sociology.* Stanford, CA: Stanford University Press.

Goffman, I. (1981). *Forms of talk.* Philadelphia: University of Pennsylvania Press.

Goodwin, M. H. (1990). *He-said-she-said: Talk as social organization among black children.* Bloomington: Indiana University Press.

Greeno, J. G. (1997). Response: On claims that answer the wrong questions, *Educational Researcher, 26,* 5–17.

Gumperz, J. J. (1982a). *Discourse strategies.* Cambridge: Cambridge University Press.

Gumperz, J. J. (Ed.). (1982b). *Language and social identity.* Cambridge: Cambridge University Press.

Gumperz, J. J., & Levinson, S. C. (Eds.). (1996). *Rethinking linguistic relativity.* Cambridge: Cambridge University Press.

Halliday, M. A. K., & Martin, J. R. (1993). *Writing science: Literacy and discursive power.* Pittsburgh: University of Pittsburgh Press.

Hanks, W. F. (1995). *Language and communicative practices.* Bolder, CO: Westview Press.

Harre, R., & Gillett, G. (1994). *The discursive mind.* Thousand Oaks, CA: Sage.

Harre, R., & Stearns, P. (Eds.). (1995). *Discursive psychology in practice.* London: Sage.

Hasan, R., & Williams, G. (Eds.). (1996). *Literacy in society.* London: Longman.

Heath, S. B. (1983). *Ways with words: Language, life and work in communities and classrooms.* Cambridge: Cambridge University Press.

Hemphill L. (1992, September). *Codeswitching and literary response.* Paper presented at the conference on literacy and identity, Carlisle, MA: Carlisle Education Center.

Holland, D., & Quinn, N. (Eds.). (1987). *Cultural models in language and thought.* Cambridge: Cambridge University Press.

Hutchins, E. (1995). *Cognition in the wild.* Cambridge, MA: MIT Press.

Hymes, D. (1974). *Foundations in sociolinguistics: An ethnographic approach.* Philadelphia: University of Pennsylvania Press.

Hymes, D. (1996). *Ethnography, linguistics, narrative inequality: Towards an understanding of voice.* London: Taylor & Francis.

Karmiloff-Smith, A. (1992). *Beyond modularity: A developmental perspective on cognitive science.* Cambridge, MA: MIT Press.

Kress, G. (1985). *Linguistic processes in sociocultural practice.* Oxford: Oxford University Press.

Kress, G. (1996). *Before writing: Rethinking paths into literacy.* London: Routledge.

Kress, G., & van Leeuwen, T. (1996). *Reading images: The grammar of visual design.* London: Routledge.

Lakoff, G. (1987). *Women, fire, and dangerous things.* Chicago: University of Chicago Press.

Lakoff, G., & Johnson, M. (1980). *Metaphors we live by.* Chicago: University of Chicago Press.

Latour, B. (1987). *Science in action.* Cambridge, MA: Harvard University Press.

Latour, B. (1991). *We have never been modern.* Cambridge, MA: Harvard University Press.

Latour, B., & Woolgar, S. (1979). *Laboratory life.* London: Sage.

Lave, J. (1988). *Cognition in practice.* Cambridge: Cambridge University Press.

Lave, J. (1996). Teaching, as learning, in practice. *Mind, Culture, and Activity, 3,* 149–164.

Lave, J., & Wenger, E. (1991). *Situated learning: Legitimate peripheral participation.* Cambridge: Cambridge University Press.

Margolis, H. (1987). *Patterns, thinking, and cognition: A theory of judgment.* Chicago: University of Chicago Press.

Martin, J. R. (1996). Evaluating disruption: Symbolizing theme in junior secondary narrative. In R. Hasan & G. Williams (Eds.), *Literacy in society* (pp. 124–171). London: Longman.

Mehan, H. (1979). *Learning lessons.* Cambridge, MA: Harvard University Press.

Mulkay, M. (1991). *Sociology of science: A sociological pilgrimage.* Bloomington: Indiana University Press.

Myers, G. (1990). *Writing biology: Texts in the social construction of scientific knowledge.* Madison: University of Wisconsin Press.

Ochs, E., Schegloff, E. A., & Thompson, S. A. (Eds.). (1996). *Interaction and grammar.* Cambridge: Cambridge University Press.

Olson, D. (1996). Literate mentalities: Literacy, consciousness of language, and modes of thought. In D. Olson & N. Torrance (Eds.), *Modes of thought: Explorations in culture and cognition* (pp. 141–151). Cambridge: Cambridge University Press.

Perkins, D. (1976). *A history of modern poetry: From the 1880s to the high modernist mode.* Cambridge, MA: Harvard University Press.

Pickering, A. (Ed.). (1992). *Science as practice and culture.* Chicago: University of Chicago Press.

Pickering, A. (1995). *The mangle of practice: Time, agency, and science.* Chicago: University of Chicago Press.

Reutzel, D. R., & Cooter, R. B., Jr., (1996). *Teaching children to read: From basals to books* (2nd ed.). Englewood Cliffs, NJ: Prentice Hall.

Rogoff, B. (1990). *Apprenticeship in thinking: Cognitive development in social context*. New York: Oxford University Press.

Rogoff, B., & Lave, J. (Eds.). (1984). *Everyday cognition: Its development in social context*. Cambridge, MA: Harvard University Press.

Rumelhart, D. E. (1980). Schemata: The building blocks of cognition. In R. Spiro, B. Bruce, & W. Brewer (Eds.), *Theoretical issues in reading comprehension* (pp. 33–58). Hillsdale, NJ: Lawrence Erlbaum Associates.

Rumelhart, D. E., McClelland, J. L., & PDP Research Group (1986). *Parallel distributed processing: Explorations in the microstructure of cognition (Vol. 1): Foundations*. Cambridge, MA: MIT Press.

Schiffrin, D. (1994). *Approaches to discourse*. Chicago: University of Chicago Press.

Scollon, R., & Scollon, S. B. K. (1981). *Narrative, literacy, and face in interethnic communication*. Norwood, NJ: Ablex.

Scribner, S., & Cole, M. (1981). *The psychology of literacy*. Cambridge, MA: Harvard University Press.

Shapin, S. (1994). *A social history of truth: Civility and scient in seventeenth-century England*. Chicago: University of Chicago Press.

Shapin, S., & Schaffer, S. (1985). *Leviathan and the air-pump: Hobbes, Boyle and the experimental life*. Princeton, NJ: Princeton University Press.

Shore, B. (1996). *Culture in mind: Cognition, culture, and the problem of meaning*. New York: Oxford University Press.

Shotter, J. (1993). *Cultural politics of everyday life*. Toronto: University of Toronto Press.

Strauss, C., & Quinn, N. (1998). *A cognitive theory of cultural meaning*. Cambridge: Cambridge University Press.

Street, B. (1984). *Literacy in theory and practice*. Cambridge: Cambridge University Press.

Street, B. (1995). *Social literacies: Critical approaches to literacy development, ethnography, and education*. London: Longman.

Swales, J. M. (1990). *Genre analysis: English in academic and research settings*. Cambridge: Cambridge University Press.

Swales, J. M. (1998). Textography: Toward a contextualization of written academic discourse. *Research on Language and Social Interaction, 31*, 109–121.

Tharp, R., & Gallimore, R. (1988). *Rousing minds to life: Teaching, learning, and schooling in social context*. Cambridge: Cambridge University Press.

Ungerer, F., & Schmid, H.-J. (1996). *An introduction to cognitive linguistics*. London: Longman.

Vygotsky, L. S. (1978). *Mind in society: The development of higher psychological processes*. Cambridge, MA: Harvard University Press.

Vygotsky, L. S. (1987). *The collected works of L. S. Vygotsky (Vol. 1): Problems of general psychology. Including the volume Thinking and speech*. (R. W. Rieber & A. S. Carton, Eds.). New York: Plenum Press.

Wenger, E. (1999). *Communities of practice: Learning, meaning, and identity*. Cambridge: Cambridge University Press.

Wertsch, J. V. (1985). *Vygotsky and the social formation of mind*. Cambridge, MA: Harvard University Press.

Wertsch, J. V. (1991). *Voices of the mind: A sociocultural approach to mediated action*. Cambridge, MA: Harvard University Press.

Wertsch, J. V. (1997). *Mind as action*. Oxford: Oxford University Press.

Wieder, D. L., & Pratt, S. (1990). On being a recognizable Indian among Indians. In D. Carbaugh (Ed.), *Cultural communication and intercultural contact* (pp. 45–64). Hillsdale, NJ: Lawrence Erlbaum Associates.

Winograd, T., & Flores, F. (1989). *Understanding computers and cognition*. Reading, MA: Addison-Wesley.

CHAPTER 15

Research Synthesis: Making Sense of the Accumulation of Knowledge in Reading

Timothy Shanahan
University of Illinois at Chicago

Research synthesis has a long and distinguished history in reading research, although formal methods for conducting such inquiry have been formulated only recently. Perhaps no research paradigm is perceived to be as immediately applicable to policy and practice, nor is as widely misunderstood, as synthesis research. This chapter provides a brief history of synthesis research in reading, and a sketch of some of its basic methodological techniques and interpretive issues.

The term *research synthesis*, as well as its synonyms *integrative review, research integration,* and *literature review,* refer to those methods of inquiry used to derive generalizations from the collective findings of a body of existing studies. A fundamental notion of scientific inquiry is that knowledge accumulates. No single investigation is sufficient for creating a full understanding of any complex phenomena, and we thus need systematic ways for constructing insights and understandings from the findings of a multiplicity of studies. Synthesis methodology allows for a systematic and replicable analysis of extant research studies. By pooling the results of a collection of investigations, we can draw more reliable conclusions, resolve discrepancies and contradictions, and become more fully cognizant of the contexts that influence the phenomena of interest. Research synthesis is an essential part to knowledge building within the research process, and it is fundamental to the idea of applying research to issues of practice and policy.

Literature reviews tend to be of two very different types, and the confusion of these often leads to misunderstandings. The first type of review serves as an adjunct to empirical studies, such as the background sections of published research or the second chapters of doctoral and master's theses. Thesis reviews tend to be more comprehensive than the background sections of published studies, but their purposes are the same. These reviews place the author's investigation within the context of relevant findings and methods, and the reviews are subordinate to the empirical studies that they accompany. This kind of review helps make the case for a study or method, but rarely relies on systematic methods or concludes with independent research findings.

A second type of literature review sets out to test hypotheses or to formulate new generalizations for policy, practice, or research. It is these reviews that are the focus of this chapter. Such reviews are published in research journals devoted solely to research synthesis, such as *Review of Educational Research, Psychological Bulletin,* and *Review of Research in Education,* or in various research handbooks and encyclopedias of educational research including the *Handbooks of Reading Research, Handbook of Research on Teaching Literacy Through Communicative and Visual Arts* (Flood, Heath, & Lapp, 1997), and the *Handbook of Research on Teaching the English Language Arts* (Flood, Jensen, Lapp, & Squire, 1991). They also might appear as books, or in research journals that publish a wider variety of studies, such as *Reading Research Quarterly.* Such reviews are best thought of as independent research efforts, and are not simply rhetorical adjuncts to new empirical efforts. These reviews are research studies in that they systematically collect, analyze, and evaluate data in order to determine answers to the researchers' questions. The data that must be collected and analyzed for synthesis research consists of the universe of relevant studies that have already been conducted. Research syntheses, as independent research studies, are held to the same evaluative standards used with other forms of research.

Another important distinction should be made, this one between qualitative and quantitative research reviews. Quantitative reviews pool data from the original or primary studies and statistically analyze the effects of contextual factors and confounds on the dependent measures of interest. Because of their reliance on rigorously documented and standardized procedures, quantitative reviews are replicable. Conversely, qualitative or narrative reviews provide a more intuitive description and analysis of research findings, and are more dependent on researchers' judgment and insight than on a well-defined collection of analytic techniques. Throughout the history of the study of reading, research integration has been a qualitative pursuit. At their best, narrative reviews have been perceptive and useful, but such efforts are being supplanted or supplemented by more organized and explicitly defined quantitative techniques such as meta-analysis, as well as by more rigorous qualitative approaches. Quantitative or meta-analytic approaches are less likely than narrative reviews to miss subtle, but key, relationships (Cooper, Door, & Bettencourt, 1995; Cooper & Rosenthal, 1980). The term *integrative* review is probably more often applied to quantitative than qualitative reviews, but this is not consistent, probably because both types of review are ultimately integrative in nature. Many of the more recent research integration efforts published in reading have tended to use quantitative analysis or some combination of quantitative and qualitative techniques.

HISTORY OF RESEARCH SYNTHESIS IN READING

Empirical research studies in reading date back to the 1870s with the eye movement investigations of Javal (1879), mental measurements studies of Cattell (1886), and studies of reading disability (Morgan, 1896). By 1908, enough information had accumulated so that Edmund Burke Huey found it useful to review the studies. There were so few up to that time (fewer than 40) that Huey was able to carry out a nearly comprehensive analysis of existing research (Huey, 1908/1968).

By the 1920s, William S. Gray began to guide the future accumulation of research studies in reading with the first publication of *Summary of Investigations Relating to Reading* (1925). This work, not much more than an annotated list of 436 studies, first appeared as a monograph issued by the University of Chicago Press. Subsequently, it was released annually by the *Elementary School Journal* (1926–1932), the *Journal of Educational Research* (1933–1960), the *Reading Teacher* (1961–1964), *Reading Research Quarterly* (1965–1979), and finally as a monograph again, this time from the International Reading Association (1980–1997). The later summaries were compiled by Helen M. Robinson and Samuel Weintraub, and they included information on approximately 1,000 new reports on reading each year. The summaries were of great significance to research synthesis as they made accessible the findings of a diverse collection of works relevant to reading, including those drawn from physiology and psychology, sociology, and education. The usefulness of the Gray collection was eventually superceded by the advent, beginning in 1966, of the Educational Resources Information Clearinghouse (*ERIC*), an index of articles, books, and unpublished papers on a wide variety of educational topics. Once *ERIC*, along with several other indexing services, were computerized, allowing greater and more systematic access to the accumulation of research, subscriptions to the *Summary of Investigations Relating to Reading* dwindled, and it was eventually brought to an end.

Gray also published several literature reviews himself. Like Huey before him, Gray's summaries attempted to make sense of the entire scope of research on reading, rather than emphasizing a particular topic or issue. These works—for example, his landmark review "Reading" that appeared in the *Encyclopedia of Educational Research* (1941/1984)—were more like compendia or summaries of disparate studies than critical integrative analyses. Still, as Guthrie (p. vii) wrote in the preface to the republication of that review, "Gray anticipated the trend for research synthesis as a basis of research generalization."

Also significant in the history of reading instruction were the several volumes of reviews prepared by the National Society for the Study of Education (NSSE). The NSSE yearbooks, particularly volumes 20 (Whipple, 1921), 24 (Whipple, 1925), 36 (Gray, 1937), 47 (Henry, 1948), 48 (Henry, 1949), 60 (Henry, 1961), and 67 (Robinson, 1968), were widely distributed and were influential of practice and research in reading. The syntheses published in these volumes were often cited in the teacher preparation textbooks and journals of the time, and guided contemporary research efforts. A later volume on reading instruction (Purves & Niles, 1984) seems to have been less influential, probably due to the availability of other syntheses. NSSE also published literacy-relevant reviews on the teaching of English (Brown, 1906), composition (Hudelson, 1923), adult reading (Henry, 1956), the teaching of English (Squire, 1977), linguistics (Marckwardt, 1970), writing (Petrosky & Bartholomae, 1986), and reading-writing relationships (Nelson & Calfee, 1998).

The early reliance on syntheses of research in education is interesting. The 24th volume of the NSSE yearbooks is a case in point. It was prepared not by NSSE, but by a National Committee on Reading that emerged from a 1922 meeting of school superintendents. The synthesis was to provide "recommendations concerning debatable issues in the field of reading, based on experimental evidence, as far as possible, and on expert opinion when evidence was lacking" (Whipple, 1925, p. v). Not only did this report provide 12 specific research-based recommendations for instruction, but it raised 38 research questions that it indicated to be "in urgent need of investigation." The 47th NSSE yearbook was undertaken, similarly, in response to a letter from William S. Gray that "suggested that changing conceptions of the role of reading ... indicate the need of a yearbook providing an authoritative interpretation of the significance of new knowledge and of emerging problems in the area" (Henry, 1949, p. v). These efforts, especially that of 1922, appear to prefigure the recent synthesis panels formed by the National Research Council (Snow, Burns, & Griffin, 1998) and the U.S. Congress (http://www.nationalreadingpanel.org).

To a great extent, the *Handbooks of Reading Research* (Barr, Kamil, Mosenthal, & Pearson, 1991; Pearson, Barr, Kamil, & Mosenthal, 1984), of which this chapter is an entry in volume 3, have replaced the NSSE yearbooks as a widely used source of "authoritative interpretation" of research on reading. After examining the substantial accumulation of research studies in reading, Robert Dykstra (1984, p. xix), in his forward to the first volume of the *Handbook*, wrote, "What has been lacking, however, is a comprehensive analysis and interpretation of this rich cumulative data base. The *Handbook of Reading Research* fills this void admirably."

One final source of useful research syntheses in reading should be noted. The National Reading Conference selects a researcher to conduct and report a topical review of research at its annual meeting. These reviews have considered metacognition, reading–writing connections, social organization of reading instruction, and a number of other issues and have been published annually in the *NRC Yearbook* since 1989.

Since the earliest reviews by Huey and Gray, many research reviews in reading have been published. These syntheses have been more focused, integrative, and analytic than those earlier inventories. Nevertheless, as in other fields (Dunkin, 1996), the value of existing literature reviews has sometimes been undercut by subjective and biased procedures. It is due to the recognition of such limitations that synthesists are increasingly adopting more systematic procedures. This is not to say that no worthwhile syntheses preceded the recent formulation of such methods. Table 15.1 provides a summary list of 25 particularly influential literature reviews in reading. To compile

TABLE 15.1

Twenty-Five Influential Research Syntheses in Literacy

Adams, M. J. (1990). *Beginning to read*. Cambridge, MA: MIT Press.

Anderson, R. (1996). Research foundations to support wide reading. In V. Greaney (Ed.), *Promoting reading in developing countries* (pp. 55–77). Newark, DE: International Reading Association.

Anderson, R., Hiebert, E. Scott, J. A., & Wilkinson, I. A. G. (1985). *Becoming a nation of readers: The report of the Commission on Reading*. Washington, DC: National Institute of Education.

Barr, R. (1997). Reading teacher education. *Handbook of research on teaching* (4th ed.). Washington, DC: American Educational Research Association.

Carver, R. (1990). *Reading rate*. San Diego, CA: Academic Press.

Chall, J. S. (1967). *Learning to read: The great debate*. New York: McGraw-Hill.

Clay, M. (1991). *Becoming literate: The construction of inner control*. Portsmouth, NH: Heinemann.

Corder, R. (1971). *The information base for reading: A critical review of the information base for current assumptions regarding the status of instruction and achievement in reading in the United States.* Berkeley, CA: ETS. (ED 054 922)

Curtis, M. E. (1997). Teaching reading to children, adolescents, and adults: Similarities and differences. In L. R. Putnam (Ed.), *Readings in language and literacy: Essays in honor of Jeanne S. Chall* (pp. 37–54). Cambridge, MA: Brookline Books.

Davis, F. B. (1971). *The literature of research in reading with emphasis on models*. New Brunswick, NJ: Rutgers University Press.

Hiebert, E., & Raphael, T. (1996). In D. C. Berliner & R. C. Calfee (Eds.), *Handbook of educational psychology* (pp. 550–602). New York: Macmillan.

Hillocks, G., Jr. (1987). *Research on written composition*. Urbana, IL: National Conference on Research in English.

Hoetker, J., & Ahlbrand, W. P., Jr. (1969). The persistence of recitation. *American Educational Research Journal, 6, 145–167.*

Klare, G. M. (1963). *The measurement of readability*. Ames: Iowa State University Press.

(Continues)

TABLE 15.1 (Continued)

Lysynchuk, L. M., Pressley, M., d'Ailly, H., Smith, M., & Cake, H. (1989). A methodological analysis of experimental studies of comprehension strategy instruction. *Reading Research Quarterly, 24,* 458–470.

Moore, D. (1996). Contexts for literacy in secondary schools. In D. J. Leu, C. K. Kinzer, & K. A. Hinchman (Eds.), *Literacies for the 21st century: Research and practice. Forty-fifth Yearbook of the National Reading Conference* (pp. 15–46). Chicago: National Reading Conference.

Rosenshine, B., & Merstir, C. (1994). Reciprocal teaching: A review of the research. *Review of Educational Research, 64,* 479–530.

Shanahan, T., & Barr, R. (1995). Reading Recovery: An independent evaluation of the effects of an early instructional intervention for at-risk learners. *Reading Research Quarterly, 30,* 958–997.

Singer, H., & Ruddell, R. (1976). *Theoretical models and processes of reading* (2nd ed.). Newark, DE: International Reading Association. (The 1st, 3rd, and 4th editions were also frequently cited).

Stahl, S. A., & Miller, P. D. (1989). Whole language and language experience approaches for beginning reading: A quantitative research synthesis. *Review of Educational Research, 59,* 87–116.

Stanovich, K. E. (1986). Matthew effects in reading: Some consequences of individual differences in the development of reading fluency. *Reading Research Quarterly, 21,* 360–406.

Sticht, T. G., Beck, L. J., & Hauke, R. N. (1974). *Auding and reading: A developmental model.* Alexandria, VA: Human Resources Research Organization.

Vellutino, F. R. (1979). *Dyslexia: Theory and research.* Cambridge, MA: MIT Press.

Wade, S. (1983). A synthesis of the research for improving reading in the social studies. *Review of Educational Research, 53,* 461–497.

Wagner, R. K., & Torgesen, J. K. (1987). The nature of phonology: Processing. *Psychological Bulletin, 101,* 192–212.

these, I invited the members of the Reading Hall of Fame to nominate reviews that they thought to be particularly excellent or significant in the history of reading. From these nominations, I culled a representative list, omitting the many mentions of the NSSE yearbooks and *Handbooks of Reading Research.* Another listing of 41 exemplary literature reviews in reading has been developed on the basis of citation frequency (Guthrie, Seifert, & Mosberg, 1983). The use of formal, systematic methods of review and analysis should increase the probability of producing syntheses that are this useful.

CONDUCTING SYNTHESIS RESEARCH

The fundamental idea behind modern research synthesis is that the review should rise above authoritative opinion. That is, synthesis research strives for clear selection standards in the identification of relevant research, explicit criteria for judgments, operational definitions, and replicability of methods. Research syntheses, in other words, should be conducted and reported in the fashion of other empirical studies as they are empirical studies in their own right. The need for unbiased approaches is possibly even more important with synthesis studies, as it has been found that scholars use or cite them at substantially higher rates than they do other empirical works (Garfield, 1989). It has also been found that reading research syntheses accomplish higher citation rates than other reviews of educational research (Guthrie et al., 1983).

The following four sections provide a brief synopsis of the fundamental procedures and issues of conducting a literature synthesis with regard to identification and selection of studies; description and classification of study characteristics; analysis of the findings of the primary studies; and reporting the results. For a more complete treatment of all of these topics, as well as several other related issues, readers are encouraged to turn to *The Handbook of Research Synthesis* (Cooper & Hedges, 1994) and *Meta-Analysis in Social Research* (Glass, McGaw, & Smith, 1981).

Identification and Selection of Studies

The validity or trustworthiness of any study is highly dependent on the soundness of the procedures used to construct the data. When a researcher collects too little data to allow reasonable generalizations, or collects data in a manner that biases the results, we have little trouble rejecting the findings of the work. Synthesis studies should be held to the same standards of research practice, although evidence suggests that this often has not been the case (Cooper, 1995; Dunkin, 1996; Jackson, 1980; Sohn, 1995). The "data" collected and analyzed in research synthesis are the characteristics and findings of the studies being synthesized, and from these data, generalizations to the population of all studies of that phenomenon are made. Integrative reviews that fail to consider key studies or that systematically bias the outcomes toward particular results will mislead practice and policy decisions.

Fortunately, over the past two decades, a number of search strategies and tools have emerged that can increase the systematicity, thoroughness, and replicability of literature reviews, and the use of these strategies is on the increase (White, 1994). These approaches can be summarized under the categories of formulating questions, identifying key terms, conducting a systematic search, and selecting studies for analysis.

Formulating Questions.   Light and Pillemer (1984) stressed the importance of formulating research questions that have sufficient precision to structure the search and to guide the eventual synthesis of results. The researcher must initially decide whether the questions are to be general (What do we know about phonemic awareness?), or specific (What is the average effect of teaching comprehension strategies on reading achievement?). If the questions are to be general, then it is essential that a wide net be cast initially, to ensure the identification of appropriate materials; it seems particularly advisable to search both within and across disciplines. Green (1992), for instance, described how researchers in pursuit of information about "communicative competence" found relevant studies within four disciplines: anthropology/ethnography of communication, child language/psycholinguistics, social psychology, and sociology. At times, even with more specific and constraining questions, a researcher might profitably draw information from more than one discipline, although the specificity of the questions is likely to reduce the need for this to some extent.

The specificity of the original questions will depend on what the researcher already knows, but as the process proceeds the nature of the questions will often change, depending on what information is in the literature. Researchers may begin with fairly global or general questions about a phenomenon, but as they proceed through the literature, they will often uncover more specific questions. This seems especially likely when a graduate student is conducting an initial review on a topic, or when a more experienced scholar is branching out into a new area of interest. For example, in a synthesis on Reading Recovery (Shanahan & Barr, 1995), we began with questions about program effectiveness, but added questions about the differences in that program between New Zealand and the United States. We also became sensitive to the issues of program cost that had been raised in a number of papers, and developed questions on this aspect of the program as well.

Rarely does a scholar write a review in an area in which he or she has not already developed substantial knowledge and even conducted his or her own empirical work. Some exceptions to this are invited reviews or the reviews conducted by graduate students. However, even in the more typical case in which the scholar has substantial prior knowledge, it is wise for the researcher to go beyond his or her own individual perspective by considering the state of knowledge in the field as described in extant authoritative summations. This aids the refinement of the synthesis questions, and can be essential in the next stages of the search, particularly in identifying key terms that will allow for a systematic search. As White (1994) aptly stated, "The point is not to track down every paper that is somehow related to the topic.... The point is *to avoid missing a useful paper that lies outside one's regular channel purview,* thereby ensuring that one's habitual channels of communication will not bias the results of studies obtained by the search" (p. 44). It is reasonable to use what one knows, but our research approaches help us to get beyond our own narrow perspectives.

Reading is particularly fortunate as a scholarly field in that it has a rich collection of authoritative summations that can be used as a jumping-off point for literature reviews. Some key resources are *The Handbooks of Reading Research, The Literacy Dictionary* (Harris & Hodges, 1995), *The Encyclopedia of English Studies and Language Arts* (Purves, 1994), and the *Handbook of Research on Teaching the English Language Arts* (Flood et al., 1991). There are various encyclopedias and handbooks of research in the areas of curriculum, education, teaching, and teacher education that also contain review chapters on reading. The researcher should also seek out previous reviews that have been written on the topic of interest. Jackson (1980) highlighted the importance of building on existing reviews, and was critical of how often integrative reviews neglect such information. I recently wrote a review on tutoring in reading, and was surprised to find that 11 published reviews already existed on this topic, many from the field of special education—a literature that I do not examine regularly (Shanahan, 1998). There were also reviews on reading tutoring that predated my own interest in the topic, as well as those that focused on tutoring of other subjects that I found to be helpful. The availability of these syntheses saved me a lot of time, and helped focus the questions that I set out to answer.

Identifying Key Terms.   Some search strategies, such as looking through the journals to which you subscribe, do not require the identification of key terms. The researchers, in such a case, know what they want and can adjust the boundaries of the search to include whatever they choose. Unfortunately, such haphazard approaches will be biased and unreplicable. Truly systematic approaches, on the other hand, require that the researcher identify key terms—terms that other researchers could use—to find the relevant work. The identification and use of key terms within reading education is, at this time, still more art than science, as consistency of use and match of terms with constructs are not as precise as in some fields of study. Are *phonemic awareness* and *phonological awareness* the same? What about *auditory discrimination*? Does *critical reading* include *inferencing,* or is that a separate construct? What is the term that is used to describe classroom organizations in which students stay with one teacher over multiple years?

The value of examining previous reviews and other summative materials has already been considered. Additionally, there are various indices for identifying key terms in research. The most useful of these sources for those in reading are likely to be the *Thesaurus of ERIC Descriptors, Thesaurus of Psychological Index,* and *Thesaurus of Sociological Indexing.* These not only help to identify subject terms that are used to organize the information contained in the computerized databases, but they also show relationships among terms and provide historical information about the use of terms. For example, the *ERIC* system did not begin to use the term *reading–writing relationships* until 1982. To identify studies of the integration of reading and writing completed prior to that time will require different search terms or strategies. Finally, it is useful to identify two or three studies early on that are exactly what you seek. These can be found through prior knowledge, access to the "invisible college" (i.e., an informal network of researchers doing work on a particular topic), informal analysis of journals, or by conducting a preliminary computer search. Once these locator studies have been identified, locate them in the indexing sources to find out what key terms were used to place them within the information systems; the use of these terms should sharpen the search strategy.

The use of these indexing terms to conduct subject searches can be problematic, however. The system of indexing is fallible, highly dependent on the judgment of a reference librarian who might not adequately understand the contents of a given study or the study author who might lack a complete grasp of potential indexing terms. Given this limitation, subject searching alone will fail to uncover many potentially valuable studies. To guard against this, the researcher can conduct *keyword searches* or natural language searches, in which all studies are identified that use particular terms in the title or abstract or even in the entire document, no matter how the document itself is indexed in the system. These procedures overcome the noted indexing problems and increase comprehensiveness, but they give up a great deal of precision and add to the cost of the synthesis in terms of researcher time.

Most computerized information systems, such as *PsycINFO* or *ERIC*, are capable of carrying out Boolean searches. This means that the researcher can use terms such as *or*, *and*, and *not* to identify intersections and unions among various research terms and to thereby refine the search. So, for example, if researchers want to identify all studies of either *word analysis* or *phonics*, they would search for: *word analysis OR phonics*. The use of *or* in this context will find all studies indexed under either term, but it will only find a single instance of the doubles, a real time saver for the researcher. Or, if the search descriptors were *reading comprehension AND vocabulary*, the search would result only in those studies that had used both of these terms, and would omit any study that focused only on reading comprehension or only on vocabulary. Increasingly, various search tools provide electronic interfaces that can make these Boolean searches easier and more transparent. A search of *word analysis*, for example, in the *Ovid* system will result in a listing of related terms that the researcher can check off if they are to be added to the search. The current list for *word analysis* includes *reading instruction, oral reading, phonemes*, and *phonics*, and allows me to choose to search for *word analysis* as a keyword rather than a subject. In this case, I neither have to know all of the related terms already nor is it necessary for me to type in a bunch of *or* terms between the choices.

However, at least for now, it is essential that the researcher understand the logic of Boolean searches, as current search aids are still pretty primitive. A researcher might be interested in only examining studies of *word analysis* that have been conducted with particular age or grade levels or types of populations; these delimiters will not come up automatically in the newer systems, but still can be used to narrow down the population of potential studies. Terms such as *preschool, teacher education, adolescents*, and *immigrants* can be used to refine our search even though none of these are obviously related to *word analysis* or hundreds of other topics in reading. The use of this approach can also help a researcher to overcome the limitations of the *ERIC* system, which does not focus entirely on research. *ERIC* often includes curriculum guides and other materials that are not the result of empirical study. When searching *ERIC* for research studies, it can be helpful to use the word *research* or *reading research* as a subject to limit the numbers of nonrelevant items identified. This strategy cannot profitably be used with other major indexes, as those tend to include few items that are not empirical studies.

Conducting a Systematic Search.   "Every past study does not have an equal chance of being retrieved by the reviewer" (Light & Pillemer, 1984, p. 295). Systematic search techniques can help to prevent the bias caused by unequal access to various studies. Given the goal of accurately representing the research, it is essential that the synthesis analyze a representative collection of pertinent studies. As has been noted, representativeness is even more important than comprehensiveness, although obviously the more comprehensive a search, the less possibility there is that it could be nonrepresentative (Jackson, 1980). Still, it is possible to miss key information, even with a thorough search. Kamil and colleagues (Kamil & Intrator, 1999; Kamil & Lane, 1998) in studying the technology and reading literature found that many relevant studies had been omitted systematically by the electronic search tools. A large number of the studies on this topic had appeared in newer journals not yet represented in the databases, and these tools also omitted recent publications as it takes time for indexing. They used hand searching to supplement their electronic search to compensate for such omissions.

The lack of any clear way to specify a complete population of studies has plagued, and will continue to plague, synthesis research. As Jackson (1980, p. 444) indicated, "There is no way of ascertaining whether a set of *located* studies is representative of the full set of *existing* studies on the topic." There are many reasons for this. In an applied field like reading, it can be difficult to know which disciplines to search within, although even when confined to a single discipline there will be no complete list of all of the published works, not to mention the unpublished ones. ERIC includes contents from approximately 700 journals, but even this listing omits several relevant research journals.

A more serious concern, and one that has received much attention, is the so-called *file drawer problem* (Rosenthal, 1979). Not every piece of research is published, and unpublished studies have been found to be systematically different than published ones. Generally, published studies are of somewhat higher quality, but they also have a greater tendency toward statistical significance. That this is a form of bias is pointedly illustrated by Greenwald (1975), who found that about 50% of researchers would submit their work for publication if they found statistically significant results, but only about 6% would do so if the results were nonsignificant. A comparison of published studies with unpublished doctoral dissertations found a substantially greater tendency (a difference of about one-third standard deviation) for journal articles to report significant differences (Glass et al., 1981). Thus, it is not surprising that some experts would reason that "the likelihood of the Type I error [the error of concluding significant differences when no such differences exist] is inestimably greater in the case of the literature review than in the case of the empirical study" (Sohn, 1995, p. 109).

Because of this bias toward significance, it is usually advisable to synthesize more than published research. Because the ERIC system includes unpublished technical reports and conference papers—including documents produced by the various national centers for research on reading, writing, and adult literacy—it can be a good source for expanding the search pool. *PsycINFO* is also a useful resource in this regard as it includes non-English-language studies and unpublished doctoral dissertations. The latter are best examined through *Dissertation Abstracts International*, which includes a broad collection of dissertation studies from fields such as engineering, natural sciences, and divinity, each of which, surprisingly, includes reading studies. The inclusion of a more representative sample of studies, including those with findings of nonsignificant differences, will lead to sounder conclusions and more specific understandings of the relationships under examination. However, when only published studies are to be reviewed, it is essential that the researcher explicitly note the bias inherent in the sampling procedure as a potential limitation of the synthesis.

White (1994) described five major modes of searching: searches in subject searchers, footnote chasing, consultation, browsing or hand searching, and citation searches. Each of these strategies has wide use (Cooper, 1995), and each presents particular problems for the researcher trying to avoid bias. Given the differences in the various approaches, a combination of strategies will be most powerful. Combined approaches are more likely to lead to a more comprehensive and representative population of research studies.

The use of various subject searchers, especially electronic ones, is particularly powerful. A large number of journal entries and other documents have been indexed since 1966, and *ERIC, PsycINFO, Wilson Social Science Abstracts*, and similar databases have made it possible for the researcher to sort through tens of thousands of documents in a matter of minutes. As of June 1999, *ERIC* listed 134,538 documents on reading, writing, and literacy, and *PsycINFO* included an overlapping set of 43,222 (different entry points—CD-ROM, various Internet connections to the electronic systems—can result in different numbers of references). Often a researcher relies on only a single searcher. This can be a mistake. Even though there is redundancy among the searchers, each retrieves a different pattern of data. This variation is partly due to the fact that each database references a different list of sources. However, differences also result because of variations in terminology or precision of terminology usage. In any event, searches in different databases lead to different results. For instance, the term *reciprocal teaching* results in 134 documents in *ERIC*, and 88 in *PsycINFO; expository writing* leads to 1,322 hits in *ERIC* and 53 in *PsycINFO;* and *readability* results in 2,517 and 713 hits, respectively. It is not just that the numbers of documents differ either, as the overlap among these searches varies and is sometimes quite low (Glass et al., 1981). Other searchers tend to have even less overlap, and their use can lead to the location of items that might be missed with a single searcher.

But what of "fugitive," or hard to find, literature? As has been noted, *ERIC* includes unpublished work, and *Dissertations Abstracts International* is a good source for doctoral dissertations. Other sources can help identify research presented at conferences. The *Cambridge Scientific Abstracts* provides listings of conference program presentations since 1973, and the *Index to Social Sciences and Humanities Proceedings* is a guide to published conference proceedings (this latter source provides an indexed listing of the studies published in *National Reading Conference Yearbook*, but it does not include papers presented at the International Reading Association or American Educational Research Association as neither publishes proceedings). When conference papers of this type are found it is usually necessary to contact the scholars who produced the work to obtain a copy. Studies—even published ones—that predate the development of computerized search tools are becoming a form of fugitive literature. The *Educational Index*, a noncomputerized database, is available for searching educational research by topic or author as far back as 1929. Finally, research published in book or chapter form should not be neglected either, so a Library of Congress search of books will be helpful at least in some cases. Other sources for finding fugitive literature are detailed in Rosenthal (1994).

Once a computerized search has been conducted, and the relevant studies have been found, what White (1994) has labeled "footnote chasing" becomes possible. A researcher should comb the references in these studies to identify additional sources. This allows the researcher to uncover a variety of citation networks, extends the search back in time, and helps locate unpublished materials. A researcher can carry such a search back as many "generations" as seems to have value. Cooper (1982) claims that such tracking has a tendency to favor the identification of published work, and that it is used infrequently by researchers (Cooper, 1995) despite its effectiveness.

Researchers develop networks of contact among various parts of the scholarly community. The reliance on these networks can help identify work that might be unobtainable in any other way, but it can also be a source of bias. Novice researchers are more likely to use computerized databases and, consequently, their syntheses tend to be more comprehensive, whereas senior scholars rely more extensively on the narrower information drawn from their networks of colleagues (Cooper, 1995). It is not that senior researchers should avoid using the "invisible college," only that they should do so in less biased and more replicable ways. The search strategies already noted should result in the identification of relevant research articles and the names of key researchers. It is useful to consult with these key researchers, to obtain copies of their unpublished materials and to request any related bibliographies that they may have developed. Although making such contacts can be forbidding to the novice, researchers usually comply with such requests (Garvey & Griffith, 1979).

Studies can also be found by browsing journals and books. Researchers do this with the journals that they subscribe to or read regularly. Green and Hall (1984) recommend a more systematic browsing that requires going through the "best" journals, year by year, page by page, to find relevant materials. There is always a certain amount of lag time between publication and inclusion of a study in the various indexes, so browsing can identify especially recent materials that might be neglected if only a computerized index were used. Browsing is reasonable, however, only when there is a chance "to find a relatively high concentration of things one is looking for" (Wilson, 1992, p. 51). For instance, in one review, we examined the reference lists of all articles and chapters in the most highly cited journals and books in reading and writing, including all of the journals published by major professional organizations (Shanahan & Kamil, 1994). Such an approach can expand the comprehensiveness of the search, and can be repeated by other researchers. The examination of books that have been grouped together by the Library of Congress can similarly help identify relevant materials (White, 1994).

Finally, citation searches are useful under certain circumstances. Although researchers rarely examine the *Social Science Citation Index (SSCI)* in their integrative searches (Cooper, 1995), these can pull in a vast array of material. Unlike the footnote or reference tracking approaches noted earlier in which the researcher traces the reference lists for previous studies, here the researcher works in the opposite direction. If I know, for instance, that someone has conducted an earlier study, *SSCI* allows me to seek articles and chapters conducted since that time that have cited this study. Citation searches only work when there is a primary research study to begin from. Citation searches tend to end up with a lot of "noise"—that is, they identify many irrelevant items as various researchers might cite an article for different purposes. Such searches are most helpful when you can only identify one or two key studies, or when you have reason to believe that the other search strategies will fail to identify key work.

Selecting Studies for Inclusion.   Not all of the studies that are identified will necessarily be included in the final synthesis. Arguments about inclusion usually turn on two issues: quality and relevance (Wortman, 1994). The quality issue concerns whether studies can suffer from flaws so fundamental that their inclusion in a synthesis will mislead more than enlighten. Slavin (1986) argues for "best evidence syntheses" in which only studies of high quality are included to ensure valid conclusions. By this method the researcher systematically sets aside results obtained from badly flawed studies, and draws conclusions based on only the best evidence. This seems reasonable, unless the selection procedures systematically excludes results that run counter to the synthesist's perspective.

Glass has probably been the most vocal proponent of including all identified studies in a review: "To make these decisions *a priori* may inject arbitrariness and bias into the conclusions" (Glass et al., 1981, p. 67). Glass is not unaware of the problems posed by the differential quality of various studies. However, he believes that the most serious problems in past literature reviews have been due to bias, and such qualitative judgment is an easy way to introduce such bias. The researcher who claims to have selected only the best studies might be, surreptitiously or unconsciously, choosing those conducted from a particular perspective or with a particular outcome. Instead of making unstudied judgments of this type, Glass proposes that such limitations be coded and treated as measurable sources of variation in study outcomes. Rather than throwing out particular studies due to their limitations, we should try to use these studies to figure out if an intervention appears to do better when the treatment is kept brief or when there was no pretest. Methods for such analysis are described in the next section of this chapter.

An examination of recent reviews suggests that most reviewers are more selective than Glass recommends. In any event, contemporaneous reviews are more *systematically* selective than older ones. Increasingly, they include descriptions of the decision rules or procedures for selection. Usually the synthesizer establishes standards that specify essential reporting features or research procedures. If these standards are not met, then the study is excluded. Standards might require that the report include certain statistics (i.e., numbers of participants, lengths of treatment, means and standard deviations), or that certain research characteristics be apparent (i.e., pre- and posttest measures, control group, random assignment). As long as care is taken not to use such procedures to omit studies with discrepant results, these approaches seem quite reasonable. In my analysis of studies of tutoring in reading (Shanahan, 1998), I wanted to focus only on studies that reported group means and standard deviations. The tutoring literature includes many studies that used single-subject designs, however, and they report outcomes differently than what I had envisioned analyzing. Under these circumstances, it was essential that I analyze these studies separately to determine whether they had a different pattern of results. I could not omit these studies until I had determined that both types of research were in agreement about the effectiveness of tutoring. If they disagreed, then I would have needed to report the discrepancy and try to explain it. I should not just define the difference away through my selection criteria, however.

Light and Pillemer (1984) suggested that another valid approach to the selection of appropriate studies is to use a panel of experts to make the selection. This has been common in medical synthesis or for integrative studies conducted by the General Accounting Office, and it is now beginning to appear in syntheses of reading (Snow et al., 1998). Such an approach seems sound, if it accomplishes a reliable result from a panel that accurately reflects the various competing perspectives. The idea of using more than a single selector of studies, and providing some numerical estimate of interevaluator agreement, would go a long way to protecting the findings against arbitrariness (Wanous, Sullivan, & Malinak, 1989). Whatever approach is taken, it is important that clear selection criteria be used, and that these be established prior to the examination of the data (Light & Pillemer, 1984).

Given the techniques that have been recommended here, a word of caution should be noted. When seeking literature in multiple places, the researcher will often find multiple studies by the same author. Care must be taken when selecting from these, to ensure that the same data are not being counted again and again (Dunkin, 1996). Such double counting increases the influence of these data in a manner that reduces the validity of the report. When there is a question about the separability of data from different analyses, the author of the original reports should be contacted.

A final note on the selection of studies has to do with the relevance criteria. Everyone agrees that only relevant studies should be reviewed. Unfortunately, educational research is undermined by its reliance on an imprecise lexicon. What is comprehension? How do you distinguish emergent literacy and beginning reading? No matter how certain your answers to such questions, be assured that at least some of your colleagues will differ in their use of these terms. This is especially true with regard to operational definitions of abstract terms; for instance, can we combine the results of reading comprehension studies that measure improvements on cloze tests and summarization, or are these different? Because of this, it is possible for researchers to disagree about the relevance of certain types of studies.

Qualitative researchers (Green, 1992; Masterman, 1970) have developed rigorous analytic procedures that are useful for determining the similarities and differences in the use of lexical terms. By carefully noting each use or operationalization of a term by a given researcher, and by conducting a semantic feature analysis of these usages, it is possible to determine whether various measures or definitions reflect the same underlying ideas. Such charts or maps can then be used in the selection process itself, or in the coding processes that are next described. The use of such procedures within meta-analytic syntheses would go a long way to meeting the criticisms that such approaches often combine apples and oranges.

Description and Classification of Study Characteristics

Meta-analysis, "the statistical analysis of the summary findings of many empirical studies" (Glass et al., 1981, p. 21), is the most thorough and systematic of integrative review techniques in its consideration of the influence of study characteristics on outcomes. However, it is fair to say that all literature reviews provide at least some consideration of the influence of such factors, although they tend to do so more subjectively. No matter what approach is used to analyze the data, the researcher should develop a rigorous system for describing and classifying the characteristics of studies under review so that relationships among key variables can be determined.

"A well-designed coding scheme is more likely if the synthesizer knows both the research domain and research integration methods, because this knowledge provides the basis for making critical choices" (Stock, 1994, p. 126). Stock recommends the use of seven categories for classifying study features: *report identification* (e.g., author, country, year, source of publication, coder of study); *setting* (e.g., scope of sampling, involvement of special populations, climate characteristics, subject matter); *subjects* (e.g., demographics, cognitive abilities); *methodology* (e.g., subject assignment, source of data, treatment of missing data); *treatment* (e.g., theoretical orientation, components of the treatment, nature of control groups, duration of treatment, check of fidelity); *process* (e.g., confidence of coding, how missing information is handled); and *effect size* (e.g., outcome measures, sample size). This scheme includes three types of information: variables that are substantively related to the phenomena of interest, variables related to how the phenomena have been studied, and variables that reveal the procedures and judgments of the synthesizer. The researcher should decide on a key set of coding variables, and summarize each study as it is read and analyzed. Wortman (1994) provided an example of a partial coding form that might be the basis for such work.

Coding is a time-consuming aspect of synthesis, and it can pose threats to validity (Orwin, 1994). Complications often arise because studies can be deficient in their reporting as they may omit key information needed by the synthesizer. It is also possible that the way information is reported in a study fails to match well with the coding scheme. Studies, for instance, will sometimes only report aggregate results, even though it would be possible to parcel the variance across various groupings, or they may provide such breakdowns with no aggregate results; either approach can be problematic depending on the synthesis strategy. When the data have been separated by the primary researcher, judgments must be made whether to treat each outcome as a separate study, to take an average of the outcomes, or to select a single representative indicator from each (Lipsey, 1994).

Coding errors are also possible, even when the primary research is well reported; studies are complex and it is easy to miss things. Several ways to reduce coding errors have been proposed. Researchers should, when there are questions about the primary studies, contact the original investigators or turn to external sources for filling in missing information (Orwin, 1994). There are detailed statistical procedures for making missing data decisions (Piggot, 1994). More than one coder should be employed so that independent coding can take place, and interrater agreement can be evaluated (Wanous et al., 1989). Orwin (1994) described how to train coders, pilot the coding protocol, assess reliability, and provide confidence estimates on the various judgments inherent in coding. Nevertheless, this remains one of the less studied, and least understood, aspects of research synthesis.

Analysis of the Findings

Traditional narrative literature reviews tend to rely on subjective determinations of the effects or so-called "box score" or "vote counting" methods, in which the researcher simply counts the number or proportion of studies that arrived at a particular result. These approaches have been criticized because of their failure to take account of the strengths of the effects found in the primary studies, and their inability to account for differences in numbers of participating subjects. Nonparametric analyses of the numbers of studies reporting statistical differences, such as sign tests, suffer from the same weaknesses, and do not actually offer greater precision of analysis.

Methods have been proposed for overcoming these problems, and aggregating the statistical significance across studies (Becker, 1994; Rosenthal, 1978). Each of these methods suffers from various interpretive problems, and none has achieved wide use in reading research.

The preferred method for synthesizing research findings is to calculate effect sizes based on the numbers of participants and the sizes of relationships or differences evident in the primary studies. The effect size statistic was originally formulated for combining the results from experimental studies. Thus, an effect size is the standardized mean difference between experimental and control groups, divided by within-group standard deviation, or $ES = (X_E - X_C)/s_x$. There are now methods for estimating effect sizes from studies using factorial designs, studies without control groups, studies with dichotomous variables, correlational data, and significance tests (Glass et al., 1981; Rosenthal, 1994).

The benefit of the various effect size statistics is that they permit unbiased estimates of the differences and relationships found in the primary studies, and allow these to be compared and combined across studies. Effect size estimates have proven valuable for their ability to identify subtle differences ignored or missed by narrative approaches. Effect sizes are reasonably easy to interpret, too. In an experimental study, a positive effect size indicates that the experimental treatment is successful, whereas a negative effect would mean that the control group had been superior. An effect size of 1.0 means that the treatment led to a 1 standard deviation improvement in outcome. For example, Stahl and Fairbanks (1986) found that the impact on reading comprehension of vocabulary instruction had an effect size of .30. "This indicates that students at the 50th percentile of the instructed groups scored as well as children at the 62nd percentile of the control groups on the global reading comprehension measures" (p. 94).

However, effect sizes have different meanings at different points of the sampling distribution. For example, a treatment with a 1.0 effect size would be expected to move average students, those initially at the 50th percentile, up to the 85th percentile, but it would only be expected to take those who began at the 3rd percentile up to the 16th. This is because standard deviation units vary in size. For the purposes of comparison, a 1 standard deviation difference in terms of elementary reading scores on a standardized test would typically be comparable to a 1-year gain in reading. So if a treatment that lasted for 3 months were associated with an effect size of 1.0, we could assume the students who received this treatment raised their scores about one standard deviation (from whatever point they began) or made about a 1-year gain in reading ability.

Although the statistical interpretation of effect sizes is generally rather simple, they can easily be misunderstood when they have been derived from very different studies.

For instance, I found similar effect sizes for various types of tutoring, including tutoring provided by highly trained teachers, tutoring provided by adult volunteers with minimum training, and peer tutoring arrangements where elementary students taught each other (Shanahan, 1998). The similar effect sizes could be misinterpreted as meaning that the use of highly trained teachers is a waste of resources, as even elementary school students are as effective. However, in the tutoring studies that I examined, highly trained teachers were used only when those being tutored were in need of long-term educational support because of their extensive deficiencies in reading, and peer tutoring was usually used with normal learners for brief periods of time. The effects were roughly equal, but the conditions under which they were derived require different interpretations.

Another problem with effect sizes is that they can offer a sense of greater precision or accuracy than they actually possess (Cook & Leviton, 1980). This is not much a problem if the researcher has identified a comprehensive or nearly comprehensive collection of studies, if the studies are truly representative of relevant research (meaning that error will be randomized), or if sources of bias are identified and analyzed. However, if this kind of care has not been taken, then effect size calculations can make the findings appear to be more scientific than they deserve.

In traditional reviews, synthesizers would hope to find a collection of studies with reasonably homogeneous findings. They would strive to select studies with similar outcomes, although this would introduce error and arbitrariness. In contrast, meta-analysis depends on variation (Light & Pillemer, 1984). By using the varied effect sizes calculated for each of the primary studies as the dependent measure, it becomes possible for the researcher, subjectively or through multiple regression analysis, to parcel out the variance. This allows the researcher to examine reasons for the differences in effect sizes. It becomes possible to search for publication bias (do studies in special education journals attribute greater effectiveness to phonics instruction than do those in reading journals?), to determine whether population estimates change over time (are recent studies more or less likely to find significant improvement from study skills programs than older studies?), or to connect variation with a variety of substantive independent variables.

Effect size is only useful for making sense of quantitative results, of course, and it is not applicable with most case studies, ethnographies, or single-subject designs. As these more qualitative approaches seem to be on the increase in reading research, this is a serious limitation. It is important that the synthesizer find ways to summarize both kinds of information. Light and Pillemer (1984) give many reasons why qualitative research should be used to help explain, interpret, and amplify the statistical or quantitative results. Qualitative information allows for the documentation of process differences. It can help with interpretation when critical outcomes or conditions are difficult to measure quantitatively, when there are multiple levels of impact, and when subtle differences exist between conditions that have received the same label. Qualitative information can help to qualify consistent findings, and to help in the interpretation of inconsistent ones.

Reporting the Results

Various reporting criteria have been proposed for research synthesis (Becker, 1991; Bem, 1995; Ellis, 1991; Jackson, 1980). Bem pointed out that reviews are difficult to write, because they can turn into "mind-numbing lists of citations and findings that resemble a phone book—impressive cast, lots of numbers, but not much plot" (p. 172). Most editorial problems with research syntheses appear to focus on clarity, and the various guidelines suggest several ways to enhance clarity of purpose, problem definition, arguments, and conclusions. For example, they recommend that authors not allow subpoints or the analysis of needless literatures to overwhelm the major findings of the synthesis, and they highlight the importance of providing clear-cut conclusions.

Bem (1995) went on to suggest that although there is no one way to organize a review, conceptual clarity is most likely when the synthesis adopts a plan built around a guiding theory, a set of competing models, or a particular point of view. This is in marked contrast to advice that traditional empirical study format (introduction, method, results, implications) be used with synthesis research (Cooper, 1982). Examples of both conceptual and traditional empirical organizational strategies are evident in the reading research literature, and both can be effective.

Unlike style issues, there is no disagreement among research synthesizers about the need for explicitness in reporting the variety of judgements underlying the study. "A widely held precept in all the sciences is that reports of research ought to include enough information about the study that the reader can critically examine the evidence. This precept should probably also apply to integrative reviews, since such reviews are a form of research" (Jackson, 1980, p. 456).

Research syntheses should clearly specify the search strategies used. This means that the review should include statements that specify all sources used (including which computerized databases), all subject headings and other descriptors including a specification of how these were used singly and in combination, and selection principles (Dunkin, 1996). Unexplained selectivity undermines the validity of the synthesis; studies that fall within the scope of the review can only be excluded when the reviewer explains or justifies the exclusion. This kind of detailed explanation of decisions and judgments allows others to identify systematic bias that might be influencing the conclusions of the synthesis, and it provides the basis for future replication and extension. It is essential that a list of the studies reviewed be included in the report.

In terms of summarizing the primary studies, there is a need for balance between the demands of clarity and interesting reporting on the one hand, and the demand for scientific thoroughness and explicitness on the other. Rather than providing narrative summaries of all studies included, it is usually best to provide essential coding and reference information in tabular form. Key studies can then be used to illustrate the major findings of the synthesis.

CONCLUSIONS

Ultimately, no matter what methodological choices are made, synthesis research is about arriving at valid descriptions of or generalizations about the accumulation of knowledge. Thus, the synthesis researcher is engaged in the enterprise of determining the nature of intellectual progress in the field (Mosenthal & Kamil, 1991). Synthesis, more than any other empirical approach, tends to convey the sense that it is arriving at some immutable and complete conception of truth because of its rhetorical power in describing what we have found out collectively and what still needs to be understood. However, like any empirical method, its purchase on "truth" is tied directly to the theoretical perspectives and methodological approaches used to generate its findings.

REFERENCES

Barr, R., Kamil, M. L., Mosenthal, P., & Pearson, P. D. (Eds.). (1991). *Handbook of reading research* (Vol. 2). New York: Longman.

Becker, B. J. (1994). Combining significance levels. In H. Cooper & L. V. Hedges (Eds.), *The handbook of research synthesis* (pp. 215–230). New York: Russell Sage Foundation.

Becker, B. J. (1991). The quality and credibility of research reviews: What the editors say. *Personality and Social Psychology Bulletin, 17,* 267–272.

Bem, D. J. (1995). Writing a review article for *Psychological Bulletin. Psychological Bulletin, 118,* 172–177.

Brown, G. P. (1906). *On the teaching of English. Fifth Yearbook of the National Society for the Study of Education* (Part 1). Bloomington, IN: NSSE.

Cattell, J. M. (1886). The time it takes to name and see objects. *Mind, 11*, 63–65.

Cook, T. D., & Leviton, L. C. (1980). Reviewing the literature: A comparison of traditional methods with meta-analysis. *Journal of Personality, 48*, 449–472.

Cooper, H. M. (1982). Scientific guidelines for conducting integrative research reviews. *Review of Educational Research, 52*, 291–302.

Cooper, H. M. (1995). Literature searching strategies of integrative research reviews. *American Psychologist, 40*, 1267–1269.

Cooper, H. M., Door, N., & Bettencourt, B. A. (1995). Putting to rest some old notions about social science. *American Psychologist, 50*, 111–112.

Cooper, H. M., & Rosenthal, R. (1980). Statistical versus traditional procedures for summarizing research findings. *Psychological Bulletin, 87*, 442–449.

Cooper, H. M., & Hedges, L. V. (Eds.). (1994). *The handbook of research synthesis.* New York: Russell Sage Foundation.

Dunkin, M. J. (1996). Types of errors in synthesizing research in education. *Review of Educational Research, 66*, 87–97.

Dykstra, R. (1984). Foreword. In P. D. Pearson, R. Barr, M. L. Kamil, & P. Mosenthal (Eds.), *Handbook of reading research* (pp. xix–xx). New York: Longman.

Ellis, M. V. (1981). Conducting and reporting integrative research reviews: Accumulating scientific knowledge. *Counselor Education and Supervision, 30*, 225–237.

Flood, J., Heath, S. B., & Lapp, D. (1997). *Handbook of research on teaching literacy through communicative and visual arts.* New York: Macmillan.

Flood, J., Jensen, J. M., Lapp, D., & Squire, J. R. (Eds.). (1991). *Handbook of research on teaching the English language arts.* New York: Macmillan.

Garfield, E. (1989). Reviewing review literature. *Essays of an information scientist 10*, 113–122). Philadelphia: ISI Press.

Garvey, W. D., & Griffith, B. C. (1979). Scientific communication as a social system. In W. D. Garvey (Ed.), *Communication: The essence of science* (pp. 148–164). Oxford, England: Pergamon Press.

Glass, G. V., McGaw, B., & Smith, M. L. (1981). *Meta-analysis in social research.* Beverly Hills, CA: Sage.

Gray, W. S. (1925). *Summary of investigations relating to reading.* Chicago: University of Chicago Press.

Gray, W. S. (1937). *The teaching of reading.* Thirty-sixth Yearbook of the National Society for the Study of Education (Part 1). Chicago: NSSE.

Gray, W. S. (1984). *Reading* (J. T. Guthrie, Ed.). Newark, DE: International Reading Association. (Original work published 1941)

Green, B. F., & Hall, J. A. (1984). Quantitative methods for literature reviews. *Annual Review of Psychology, 35*, 37–53.

Green, J. L. (1992). Multiple perspectives: Issues and directions. In R. Beach, J. L., Green, M. L. Kamil, & T. Shanahan (Eds.), *Multidisciplinary perspectives on literacy research* (pp. 19–33). Urbana, IL: National Conference on Research in English.

Greenwald, A. G. (1975). Consequences of prejudice against the null hypothesis. *Psychological Bulletin, 82*, 10–12.

Guthrie, J. T., Seifert, M., & Mosberg, L. (1983). Research synthesis in reading: Topics, audiences, and citation rates. *Reading Research Quarterly, 19*, 16–27.

Harris, T. L., & Hodges, R. E. (1995). *The literacy dictionary.* Newark, DE: International Reading Association.

Henry, N. B. (1956). *Adult reading. Fifty-sixth yearbook of the National Society for the Study of Education* (Part 2). Chicago: NSSE.

Henry, N. B. (1961). *Development in and through reading: Sixtieth yearbook of the National Society for the Study of Education* (Part 1). Chicago: NSSE.

Henry, N. B. (1949). *Reading in the elementary school: Forty-eighth yearbook of the National Society for the Study of Education* (Part 2). Chicago: NSSE.

Henry, N. B. (1948). *Reading in the high school and college: Forty-seventh yearbook of the National Society for the Study of Education* (Part 2). Chicago: NSSE.

Hudelson, E. (1923). *English composition: Its aims, methods, and measurement: Twenty-second yearbook of the National Society for the Study of Education.* Bloomington, IL: NSSE.

Huey, E. B. (1968). *The psychology and pedagogy of reading.* Cambridge, MA: MIT Press. (Original work published 1908)

Jackson, G. B. (1980). Methods for integrative reviews. *Review of Educational Research, 50*, 438–460.

Javal, E. (1879). Essai sur la physiologie de la lecture. *Annales d'Oculsitique, 82*, 242–253.

Kamil, M. L., & Intrator, S. M. (1999). Quantitative trends in publication of research on technology and reading, writing, and literacy. *National Reading Conference Yearbook, 47*, 385–396.

Kamil, M. L., & Lane, D. M. (1998). Researching the relationship between technology and literacy: An agenda for the 21st century. In D. Reinking, M. McKenna, L. Labbo, & R. Kieffer (Eds.), *Handbook of literacy and technology: transformations in a post-typographic world* (pp. 323–342). Mahwah, NJ: Lawrence Erlbaum Associates.

Light, R. J., & Pillemer, D. B. (1984). *Summing up: The science of reviewing research.* Cambridge, MA: Harvard University Press.

Lipsey, M. W. (1994). Identifying potentially interesting variables and analysis opportunities. In H. Cooper & L. V. Hedges (Eds.), *The handbook of research synthesis* (pp. 111–124). New York: Russell Sage Foundation.

Marckwardt, A. H. (Ed.). (1970). *Linguistics in school programs. Sixty-ninth yearbook of the National Society for the Study of Education* (Part 2). Chicago: NSSE.

Masterman, M. (1970). The nature of paradigm. In I. Lakatos & A. Musgrave (Eds.), *Criticism and the growth of knowledge* (pp. 59–89). London: Cambridge University Press.

Morgan, W. P. (1896). A case of congenital word-blindness. *British Medical Journal, 2,* 1612–1614.

Mosenthal, P. B., & Kamil, M. L. (1991). Epilogue: Understanding progress in reading research. In R. Barr, M. L. Kamil, P. Mosenthal, & P. D. Pearson (Eds.), *Handbook of reading research* (Vol. 2, pp. 1013–1046). New York: Longman.

Nelson, N., & Calfee, R. (1998). *The reading-writing connection: Ninety-seventh yearbook of the National Society for the Study of Education* (Part 2). Chicago: NSSE.

Orwin, R. G. (1994). Evaluating coding decisions. In H. Cooper & L. V. Hedges (Eds.), *The handbook of research synthesis* (pp. 139–162). New York: Russell Sage Foundation.

Pearson, P. D., Barr, R., Kamil, M. L., & Mosenthal, P. (Eds.). (1984). *Handbook of reading research.* New York: Longman.

Petrosky, A. R., & Bartholomae, D. (1986). *The teaching of writing: Eighty-fifth yearbook of the National Society for the Study of Education* (Part 2). Chicago: NSSE.

Piggot, T. D. (1994). Methods for handling missing data in research synthesis. In H. Cooper & L. V. Hedges (Eds.), *The handbook of research synthesis* (pp. 163–176). New York: Russell Sage Foundation.

Purves, A. C. (1994). *Encyclopedia of English studies and language arts.* New York: Scholastic.

Purves, A. C., & Niles, O. (1984). *Becoming readers in a complex society: Eighty-third yearbook of the National Society for the Study of Education* (Part 1). Chicago: NSSE.

Robinson, H. M. (1968). *Innovation and change in reading instruction: Sixty-seventh yearbook of the National Society for the Study of Education* (Part 2). Chicago: NSSE.

Rosenthal, R. (1978). Combining results of independent studies. *Psychological Bulletin, 85,* 185–193.

Rosenthal, R. (1979). The "file drawer problem" and tolerance for null results. *Psychological Bulletin, 85,* 185–193.

Rosenthal, R. (1994). Parametric measures of effect size. In H. Cooper & L. V. Hedges (Eds.), *The handbook of research synthesis* (pp. 231–244). New York: Russell Sage Foundation.

Shanahan, T. (1998). On the effectiveness and limitations of tutoring in reading. In P. D. Pearson & A. Iran-Nejad (Eds.), *Review of Research in Education, 23,* 217–234. Washington, DC: American Educational Research Association.

Shanahan, T., & Barr, R. (1995). Reading Recovery: An independent evaluation of the effects of an early instructional intervention for at risk learners. *Reading Research Quarterly, 30,* 958–997.

Shanahan, T., & Kamil, M. L. (1994). *Academic libraries and research in the teaching of English.* Champaign, IL: Center for the Study of Reading.

Slavin, R. E. (1986). Best evidence synthesis: An alternative to meta-analytic and traditional reviews. *Educational Researcher, 15*(9), 5–11.

Snow, C. E., Burns, M. S., & Griffin, P. (1998). *Preventing reading difficulties in young children.* Washington, DC: National Academy Press.

Sohn, D. (1995). Meta-analysis as a means of discovery. *American Psychologist, 50,* 108–110.

Squire, J. R. (1977). *The teaching of English: Seventy-sixth yearbook of the National Society for the Study of Education* (Part 1). Chicago: NSSE.

Stahl, S. A., & Fairbanks, M. M. (1986). The effects of vocabulary instruction: A model-based meta-analysis. *Review of Educational Research, 56,* 72–110.

Stock, W. A. (1994). Systematic coding for research synthesis. In H. Cooper & L. V. Hedges (Eds.), *The handbook of research synthesis* (pp. 125–138). New York: Russell Sage Foundation.

Wanous, J. P., Sullivan, S. E., & Malinak, J. (1989). The role of judgment calls in meta-analysis. *Journal of Applied Psychology, 74,* 259–264.

Whipple, G. M. (1921). *Factors affecting results in silent reading, and exercises for making reading function: Twentieth yearbook of the National Society for the Study of Education* (Part 2). Bloomington, IL: NSSE.

Whipple, G. M. (1925). *Report of the National Committee on Reading: Twenty-fourth yearbook of the National Society for the Study of Education.* Bloomington, IL: NSSE.

White, H. D. (1994). Scientific communication and literature retrieval. In H. Cooper & L. V. Hedges (Eds.), *The handbook of research synthesis* (pp. 41–56). New York: Russell Sage Foundation.

Wilson, P. (1992). Searching: Strategies and evaluation. In H. D. White, M. J. Bates, & P. Wilson (Eds.), *For information specialists: Interpretations of reference and bibliographic work* (pp. 153–181). Philadelphia: ISI Press.

Wortman, P. M. (1994). Judging research quality. In H. Cooper & L. V. Hedges (Eds.), *The handbook of research synthesis* (pp. 97–110). New York: Russell Sage Foundation.

PART III

Literacy Processes

CHAPTER 16

The Neurobiology of Reading and Reading Disability (Dyslexia)

Bennett A. Shaywitz
Yale University School of Medicine

Kenneth R. Pugh
Yale University School of Medicine
Haskins Laboratories, New Haven, Connecticut

Annette R. Jenner
Robert K. Fulbright
Yale University School of Medicine

Jack M. Fletcher
University of Texas Medical Center–Houston

John C. Gore
Sally E. Shaywitz
Yale University School of Medicine

THE COGNITIVE BASIS OF DYSLEXIA

Speech enables its users to create an indefinitely large number of words by combining and permuting a small number of phonologic segments, the consonants and vowels that serve as the natural constituents of the biologic specialization for language. An alphabetic transcription brings this same ability to readers, but only as they connect its arbitrary characters (letters) to the phonologic segments they represent. Making that connection requires an awareness that all words, in fact, can be decomposed into phonologic segments. It is this awareness that allows the reader to connect the letter strings (the orthography) to the corresponding units of speech (phonologic constituents) they represent. As numerous studies have shown, however, such awareness is largely missing in dyslexic children and adults (Brady & Shankweiler, 1991; Bruck, 1992; Fletcher et al., 1994; Rieben & Perfetti, 1991; Shankweiler et al., 1995; Stanovich & Siegel, 1994). As for why dyslexic readers should have exceptional difficulty developing phonologic awareness, there is support for the notion that the difficulty resides in the phonologic component of the larger specialization for language (Liberman, 1996, 1998; Liberman, Shankweiler, & Liberman, 1989). If that component is imperfect, its representations will be less than ideally distinct, and therefore harder to bring to conscious awareness. There is now overwhelming evidence that phonologic awareness is characteristically lacking (or deficient) in dyslexic readers, who therefore have difficulty mapping the alphabetic characters onto the spoken word.

With the elucidation of the cognitive deficit in dyslexia, the stage was set to delineate the neural mechanisms underlying the deficit in phonologic awareness. In the remainder of this chapter we review the evidence from anatomic, morphometric, and functional imaging studies that now allow investigators to begin to understand the neurobiologic underpinnings of dyslexia. We have chosen to emphasize functional imaging studies, that is, those studies directed at understanding the functional organization of the brain as dyslexic readers engage in tasks tapping the component processes of reading. Other sorts of evidence, for example, anatomic and morphometric studies, are reviewed briefly. Electrophysiologic methods are touched on even more briefly.

NEUROANATOMIC STUDIES IN DYSLEXIA

Historically, the first kinds of studies attempting to determine the cerebral localization of a particular cognitive function exploited the postmortem examination of the brain in individuals with a deficit in the cognitive function in question. The classic example is, of course, Broca's description of the localization of expressive language (Young, 1990). Such studies are rare in dyslexia because fortunately individuals with dyslexia do not die as a result of their reading disability. In the early 1980s the brains of four individuals with a history of dyslexia were made available for study by the Orton Dyslexia Association brain bank. These postmortem studies focused on cortical structure, and based on findings in the brains of seven adults with purported reading problems as children, Galaburda and his associates (Galaburda & Kemper, 1979; Galaburda, Sherman, Rosen, Aboitiz, & Geschwind, 1985; Humphreys, Kaufmann, & Galaburda, 1990) reported a number of differences between the brains of dyslexic readers and nonimpaired individuals. One finding involved the planum temporale, the transverse superior surface of the posterior superior temporal gyrus, a region of cortex long believed to subserve language. In nonimpaired individuals there was a trend toward leftward asymmetry of the planum temporale. The size of the planum temporale in dyslexics, however, was found to be equal between hemispheres in all brains examined. Galaburda and his associates suggested that this symmetry results from an increase in the size of the right planum and not a reduction in the normally larger left planum.

Microscopic examination of the cerebral cortex revealed minor focal malformations (Galaburda & Kemper, 1979; Galaburda et al., 1985; Humphreys et al., 1990). The most common of these in male dyslexics were "ectopias," small collections of neurons in the molecular layer (layer I) of the cortex with underlying dysplasias or laminar disruptions. Dysplasias in their mildest form consist of focal disorganization in the laminar structure of the cortex, resulting in cortex that does not have easily defined layers. In more severe forms, however, dysplasias result in microgyria, infoldings of the cortex, which cause fused laminae and an absence of columnar organization. It has been hypothesized that these anomalies are formed sometime during the middle of gestation, before neuronal migration is complete. Although similar anomalies have been seen in other developmental disorders, they differ slightly in their morphology in the developmental dyslexic population. The location of these ectopias, primarily in the left perisylvian and inferior prefrontal cortices, areas implicated in language function, suggests that they may be playing a role in the language difficulties dyslexics often experience. In addition to cortical anomalies, more recent investigations have revealed differences in subcortical structures, specifically in the thalamus (Galaburda, 1994; Livingstone, Rosen, Drislane, & Galaburda, 1991). Examination of the lateral geniculate nucleus (LGN), the area of the thalamus responsible for the initial processing of visual information, has revealed disorganization of the laminar structure similar to that seen in the cortex. In addition, these studies reveal differences between reading groups in the size of neurons in these thalamic nuclei. In sum, these postmortem studies have found anomalies in the brains of dyslexics at both the cortical and subcortical level. However, the number of brains that have been examined at this point is small (n = 10), and educational histories and information of physical characteristic (i.e. handedness) are often difficult to obtain.

STRUCTURAL BRAIN IMAGING WITH CT AND MRI

Not only is it very rare that the brains of individuals with dyslexia are available for study, but in addition, significant methodologic limitations (e.g., the often inadequate documentation of a reading difficulty in the subjects in question) (Hynd & Semrud-Clikeman, 1989) are imposed on such postmortem studies. The development of structural neuroimaging procedures, first computerized tomography (CT) and for the last two decades magnetic resonance imagery (MRI), provided new methodologies with which to examine neuroanatomic correlates of dyslexia. Based on the anatomic studies described earlier, investigators have used CT and MRI to compare brain images in dyslexic individuals and controls. Given that current MRI methodology is still not sensitive enough to detect the presence of small heterotopias, the focus of most studies has been on the comparison of structures that could be easily identified, for example, the determination of brain symmetry in cerebral hemispheres (particularly temporal lobe regions) and the size of specific regions of the corpus callosum. Differences in the relative size of the posterior compared to the anterior regions may provide a clue to the relative sizes of the cerebral hemisphere regions linked by the corpus callosum. Posterior regions of the corpus callosum (splenium and perhaps isthmus) may reflect pathways influencing verbal performance, whereas those more anterior portions of the corpus callosum contain fibers influencing visuospatial performance (Hines, Chiu, McAdams, Bentler, & Lipcamon, 1992). Neuroimaging studies carried out prior to 1987 have been critically reviewed by Hynd and Semrud-Clikeman (1989) and more recent studies are reviewed by Filipek (1996). Although early CT studies seemed to confirm a reversed or lack of the normal asymmetry in dyslexic individuals (Hier, LeMay, Rosenberger, & Perlo, 1978; LeMay, 1981; Leisman & Ashkenazi, 1980; Rosenberger & Hier, 1980; Rumsey et al., 1986), later reports failed to confirm any differences (Denckla, LeMay, & Chapman, 1985; Haslam, Dalby, Johns, & Rademaker, 1981; Parkins, Roberts, Reinarz, & Varney, 1987) and more recent MRI reports have not clarified the controversy (Duara et al., 1991; Hynd, Semrud-Clikeman, Lorys, Novey, & Eliopulos, 1990; Jernigan, Hesselink, Sowell, & Tallal, 1991; Larsen Høien, Lundberg, & Ødegaard, 1990; Leonard et al., 1993). As noted by us (Schultz et al., 1994) and more recently by Filipek (1996), the lack of consistent results across studies might be explained by differences in subject characteristics (e.g., wide variations in subjects' age, sex, handedness, and diagnostic criteria used to define dyslexia), as well as methodologic variations in measurement of anatomic regions of interest, such as the planum temporale.

FUNCTIONAL BRAIN IMAGING

Rather than being limited to examining the brain in an autopsy specimen, or measuring the size of brain regions using static morphometric indices based on CT or MRI, functional imaging offers the possibility of examining brain function during performance of a cognitive task. One approach uses electrophysiological methods, for example, event-related potentials. Older studies were detailed by Hughes (1977), and more recent ones are reviewed by Dool, Steimack, and Rourke (1993). Methodological reviews of progress and newer electrographic technologies are provided in reviews by Swick, Kutas, and Neville (1994), Thatcher (1996), and Wood, Garrett, Hart, Flowers, and Absher (1996). One of the most recent studies of this kind (Salmelin, Service, Kiesila, Uutela, & Salonen, 1996) used magnetoencephalography (MEG) and found that in contrast to normals, dyslexics failed to activate the left inferior temporo-occipital region (including Wernicke's area) while reading real words.

General Principles of Functional Brain Imaging

Although MEG is useful for determining the time course of cognitive processes, it is not nearly as precise as the imaging modalities for localizing where in brain these processes occur. In principle, functional imaging is quite simple. When an individual is asked to perform a discrete cognitive task, that task places processing demands on particular neural systems in the brain. To meet those demands requires activation of neural systems in specific brain regions, and those changes in neural activity are, in turn, reflected by changes in brain metabolic activity, which in turn are reflected by cerebral blood flow and in the cerebral utilization of metabolic substrates such as glucose. Functional imaging makes it possible to measure those changes in metabolic activity and blood flow in specific brain regions while subjects are engaged in cognitive tasks.

Cerebral Blood Flow Using Xenon

The first studies of this kind used xenon-133 single-photon emission computed tomography (SPECT) to measure cerebral blood flow at baseline rather than during any reading task (Lou, Henriksen, & Bruhn, 1984, 1990) In three children, one boy and two girls, with what the authors refer to as severe phonologic–syntactic dysphasia, a reduced blood flow was found in left central perisylvian regions. It is difficult to interpret this study of just three subjects; not only were there no blood flow studies during reading or any activation task, but diagnostic criteria for what the authors meant by phonologic–syntactic dysphasia were never specified.

In a series of experiments, Wood and Flowers used xenon-133 to measure cerebral blood flow in dyslexia (Flowers, Wood, & Naylor, 1991; Wood, Flowers, Buchsbaum, & Tallal, 1991). In the first study (Flowers et al., 1991), a normal sample of 69 subjects (39 men, 30 women), performed an orthographic analysis (spelling) task; that is, they listened to highly imageable common concrete nouns and responded to a four-letter word. Task accuracy was correlated with cerebral blood flow during task performance in two brain regions, the inferior frontal gyrus (Broca's area, IFG) and the superior temporal gyrus (Wernicke's area, STG). In these normal readers, task accuracy was correlated with cerebral blood flow in the left STG but not at other sites. In the second study, the same measure was used in adult dyslexics referred from the Orton Reading Center. Subjects were classified as dyslexic ($n = 33$), borderline ($n = 27$), or nondisabled ($n = 23$) on the basis of testing as children and current adult reading scores. The correlation between cerebral blood flow and task performance was significant at the left STG (Wernicke's area) for all subjects from the Orton group, and the authors concluded that activation in the left posterior language area is correlated with spelling performance in disabled as well as normal readers. In the third study, Wood and Flowers addressed phonemic processing rather than spelling. The task was to respond to the target syllable *da* presented auditorally within a string of syllables, such as *da, ba, pa, ga, ka, ta*. Here, normal readers showed reduced cerebral blood flow at the left STG whereas dyslexic readers showed a *trend* toward greater left temporal flow. Furthermore, poorer childhood readers had greater flow at the site immediately posterior to the left STG, although this high temporoparietal flow that characterized poor childhood readers was not related to adult reading outcome.

Positron Emission Tomography

A number of studies have used positron emission tomography (PET). In practice, PET requires intraarterial or intravenous administration of a radioactive isotope to the subject so that cerebral blood flow or cerebral utilization of glucose can be determined while the subject is performing the task. Positron-emitting isotopes of nuclei of biological interest have very short biological half-lives and are synthesized in a cyclotron immediately prior to testing, a factor that mandates that the time course of the experiment conform to the short half-life of the radioisotope.

In one of the first PET studies of dyslexia, Gross-Glenn et al. (1991) used F-18 fluorodeoxyglucose (FDG) to compare 11 men, most college graduates, all of whom had a history of reading and spelling problems in childhood, to 14 men without a history of reading problems. The task required the subjects to pronounce aloud high-frequency nouns that appeared on a screen. Effects were complex, but dyslexics appeared to demonstrate reduction in glucose metabolism in right frontal regions. Another more serious concern is that the task used, reading simple real words, does not maximize demands on phonology (see later discussion).

Hagman et al. (1992) used PET and measured F-18 FDG while 10 dyslexics, (9 men, 1 woman) matched to 10 nondisabled subjects identified a target syllable *da* during auditory presentation of a string of syllables. Behaviorally, dyslexics identified syllables more poorly than normals, and on PET, dyslexics demonstrated significantly higher metabolism in medial temporal lobe regions.

Rumsey et al. (1992) used PET and measured cerebral blood flow using O-15 in 14 dyslexic subjects; their task was to respond if binaurally presented real words rhymed. Dyslexics failed to activate the left parietal and left middle temporal regions. In a second report, Rumsey et al. again used O-15 PET and studied 15 dyslexic men and 20 matched controls. Their task was a semantic judgement, that is, to listen to sentence pairs and respond if the meaning of both sentences was the same. Both normal and dyslexic readers increased cerebral blood flow in the middle temporal regions during the task; no significant differences were observed between normal and dyslexic readers.

Paulesu et al. (1996) used PET to compare five university male students with histories of reading problems but who were currently reading in the average range and five similarly aged subjects without a history of reading problems; one task required subjects to rhyme single letters and a companion task involved short-term memory for single letters. Dyslexics activated Broca's area during the single-letter rhyme task and Wernicke's area during the memory task, but, in contrast to controls, both language regions were not activated in concert in either task. The authors attribute the problem to a disconnection between the anterior and posterior language regions, a theory supported by their finding of underactivation in the insula in this group of compensated dyslexics.

In a recent report, Rumsey et al. (1997) used PET to study 17 dyslexic men and 14 male controls. Subjects performed two pronunciation tasks (low-frequency real words and pseudowords) and two lexical decision tasks (orthographic and phonologic).

Compared to controls, dyslexic readers demonstrated reduced blood flow in temporal cortex and inferior parietal cortex, especially on the left, during both pronunciation and decision making.

Functional Magnetic Resonance Imaging (fMRI)

Functional magnetic resonance imaging (fMRI) promises to surpass other methods for its ability to map the individual brain's response to specific cognitive stimuli. Because it is noninvasive and safe, it can be used repeatedly, properties that make it ideal for studying humans, especially children. In principle, the signal used to construct MRI images changes, by a small amount (typically of the order 1%–5%), in regions that are activated by a stimulus or task. The increase in signal results from the combined effects of increases in the tissue blood flow, volume, and oxygenation, although the precise contributions of each of these is still somewhat uncertain. MR image intensity increases when deoxygenated blood is replaced by oxygenated blood. A variety of methods can be used to record the changes that occur, but one preferred approach makes use of ultrafast imaging, such as echo planar imaging (EPI), in which complete images are acquired in times substantially shorter than a second. Echo planar imaging can provide images at a rate fast enough to capture the time course of the hemodynamic response to neural activation and to permit a wide variety of imaging paradigms over large volumes of the brain. Details of fMRI are reviewed in Anderson and Gore (1997).

RECENT PROGRESS USING FUNCTIONAL MRI
TO STUDY READING

Functional MRI and Visual Processing

Eden et al. (1996)and Demb, Boynton, and Heeger (1998) have used fMRI to study the role of visual processing in dyslexia. Eden et al. (1996) studied six dyslexic and eight controls, a subset of men from Rumsey's subjects. Presentation of a moving stimuli activated higher order visual regions (MT/V5) in controls but not in dyslexics, whereas presentation of a stationary visual task activated this region in both controls and dyslexics. Demb et al. (1998) studied brain activation during a visual speed discrimination task in three dyslexic men and two dyslexic women. Compared to controls, dyslexics showed reduced brain activity in primary visual cortex and several extrastriate regions (e.g., MT). Neither of these studies used reading tasks and the implications for reading in dyslexia are uncertain. The reader is referred to recent reviews (Eden et al., 1996; Stein & Walsh, 1997) for a more detailed discussion of how visual processing deficits might relate to dyslexia.

Functional MRI and Phonological Processing

Our research group has used fMRI to examine the functional organization of the brain for reading and reading disability. Initial studies focused on the identification of those cortical sites associated with various subcomponent operations in reading in nonimpaired readers; included in these studies was an examination of the relationship between brain organization and reading strategies. We next examined how the brain activation patterns of individuals with dyslexia differed from nonimpaired readers. Most recently we have examined differences in the functional connectivity between dyslexic and nonimpaired readers. Before describing some of these results in more detail we first review the rationale for the tasks we have used and the strategy employed to analyze the results of these measures.

THEORETICAL ISSUES IN TASK DESIGN

Most functional imaging studies, whether PET or functional MRI, use a subtraction methodology in attempting to isolate brain/cognitive function relations (Friston, Frith, Liddle, & Frackowiak, 1993; Petersen & Fiez, 1993; Sergent, 1994). Reading can be considered as involving three component processes: orthographic, phonological, and lexical–semantic processing. Accordingly, the tasks should be able to isolate orthographic, phonological, and lexical–semantic foci. In addition, we use a variety of subtractions in order to converge on a conclusion about the relative function of a given cortical region. Thus, we have built into the tasks a consistent means of validity checking, and in principle, we can put the logic of the hierarchical design to a careful test.

A typical series of tasks is illustrated in Table 16.1. Both the decision and response components of the tasks were comparable; in each instance the subject viewed two simultaneously presented stimulus displays, one above the other, and was asked to make a same/different judgment by pressing a response button if the displays matched on a given cognitive dimension: line orientation judgment; letter case judgment; single letter rhyme; nonword rhyme; and category judgment. The five tasks are ordered hierarchically; at the lowest level, the line orientation (L) judgment task (e.g., Do [\\\/] and [\\\/] match?) taps visual–spatial processing, but makes no orthographic demands. Next, the letter case judgment task (e.g., Do [bbBb] and [bbBb] match in the pattern of upper and lower case letters?) adds an orthographic processing demand, but makes no phonologic demands, because the stimulus items, which consist entirely of consonant strings, are therefore phonotactically impermissible. The third task, single letter rhyme (SLR) (e.g., Do the letters [T] and [V] rhyme?), although orthographically more simple than C, adds a phonologic processing demand, requir-

TABLE 16.1
Tasks and Subtractions

Task	Stimuli	Processes Engaged
Line	/ / \ / / / \ /	Visual-spatial
Case	bbBb BbBb	Visual-spatial + Orthographic
Single letter rhyme	T v V	Visual-spatial + Orthographic + Phonological
Nonword rhyme	LETE JEAT	Visual-spatial + Orthographic + Phonological
Category	CORN RICE	Visual-spatial + Orthographic + Phonological + Semantic
Subtractions		*Processes Isolated*
Case – Line		Orthographic
Rhyme – Line		Orthographic + Phonological
Rhyme – Case		Phonological
Category – Line		Orthographic + Phonological + Semantic
Category – Rhyme		Semantic
Category – Case		Phonological + Semantic

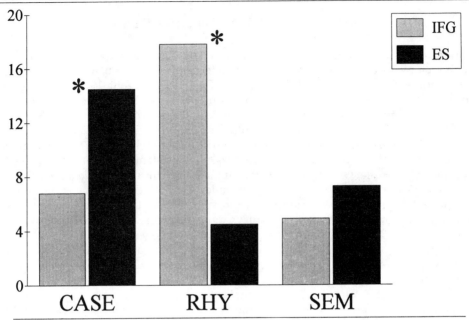

FIG. 16.1. Ordinate represents mean activations for case, rhyme, and semantic subtractions in the inferior frontal gyrus (IFG, gray bars) and extrastriate (ES, black bars) regions, respectively. In the IFG region, rhyme significantly differed from both case and semantic. In the extrastriate region, case significantly differed from both rhyme and semantic.

ing the transcoding of the letters (orthography) into phonologic structures, and then a phonologic analysis of those structures sufficient to determine that they do or do not rhyme; the fourth task, nonword rhyme (NWR) (e.g., Do [leat] and [jete] rhyme?), requires analysis of more complex structures. The final task, semantic category (SC) judgment (e.g., Are [corn] and [rice] in the same category?), also makes substantial demands on transcoding from print to phonology (Lukatela & Turvey, 1994; Van Orden, Pennington, & Stone, 1990), but requires in addition that the printed stimulus items activate particular word representations in the reader's lexicon to arrive at the word's meaning. A common baseline subtraction condition is used in analysis: C, SLR, NWR, and SC tasks contrasted with the nonlanguage line orientation judgement (L) baseline condition.

Our initial series of investigations examined normal readers, 19 neurologically normal right-handed men and 19 women. Figure 16.1 illustrates activations in three subtraction conditions (representing orthographic, phonological, and semantic processing) in two regions of interest (inferior frontal gyrus, IFG, and extrastriate, ES). In the IFG, activations during phonological processing were significantly greater than activations during either orthographic or semantic processing. These findings are consonant with previous functional imaging studies that show activation in this region in speech production tasks (Petersen, Fox, Posner, Mintun, & Raichle, 1989), in complex discriminations of speech tokens (Demonet et al., 1992; Demonet, Price, Wise, & Frackowiak, 1994; Zatorre, Evans, Meyer, & Gjedde, 1992) in phonological judgments on visually presented single letter displays (Sergent, Zuck, Levesque, & MacDonald, 1992) and word/nonword discriminations on visual stimuli (Price et al., 1993). Our findings are also consonant with studies of patients with lesions in this region who show evidence of problems with phonetic discriminations (Blumstein, Baker, & Goodglass, 1977). In contrast, in ES, activations on orthographic subtractions were significantly greater than during either phonological or semantic processing. This finding that orthographic processing makes maximum demands on extrastriate sites is consistent with claims made by Petersen and his colleagues (Petersen & Fiez, 1993; Petersen et al., 1989) using different tasks in several PET studies.

Activations during phonological processing were also observed at sites in both the superior temporal gyrus and middle temporal gyrus, areas that fall within traditional language regions. However, semantic processing activated both of these areas significantly more strongly than did phonological processing, suggesting that these regions subserved both phonological and lexical semantic processing. The most natural conclusion is that the temporal sites examined are multifunctional, relevant for both phonological and lexical semantic processing, an interpretation supported by previous PET studies (Demonet et al., 1992; Petersen et al., 1989; Wise et al., 1991) as well as a previous fMRI study by us (Shaywitz et al., 1995). Further, lesion studies have suggested that damage to temporal and temporoparietal sites results in semantic deficits (Hart & Gordon, 1990).

SEX DIFFERENCES

Of particular interest were differences in brain activation during phonological processing in men compared to women. This is illustrated in Fig. 16.2 which shows activations during phonological processing for each hemisphere and sex. For comparison, two regions of interest are shown. In the extrastriate region, no significant hemisphere differences in activations are seen for either men or women. In contrast, in the IFG, although in women activations are similar for right and left hemispheres, in men phono-

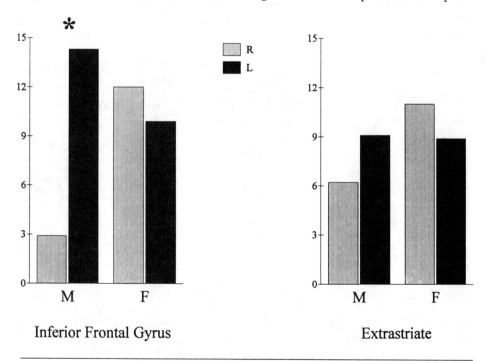

FIG. 16.2. Ordinate represents mean activations for males and females, across tasks, in the inferior frontal gyrus (IFG, gray bars) and extrastriate (ES, black bars) regions, respectively. In the extrastriate region, no significant hemisphere differences in activations are seen for either men or women. In contrast, in the IFG, although in women activations are similar for right and left hemispheres, in men phonological processing results in significantly more activation in the left hemisphere.

logical processing results in significantly more activation in the left hemisphere. This pattern of activation is further illustrated in Fig. 16.3, which demonstrates that activation during phonological processing in men was more lateralized to the left IFG; in contrast, activation during this same task in women resulted in a more bilateral pattern of activation of this region. These findings provide the first clear evidence of sex differences in the functional organization of the brain for language and indicate that these differences exist primarily at the level of phonological processing. At one level, they support and extend a long-held hypothesis that suggests that language functions are more likely to be highly lateralized in males but represented in both cerebral hemispheres in females (Halpern, 1992; Witelson & Kigar, 1992).

Since this initial finding of sex differences in functional activation within IFG, we have obtained three replications of the same basic sex by hemisphere pattern. In one study (Pugh et al., 1996b) we obtained this two-way interaction during a speech discrimination task performed under different levels of demand on selective attention. Additionally, in a recent report examining nonimpaired and dyslexic adult readers on our hierarchically organized reading tasks (Shaywitz et al., 1998, see later for detailed discussion) we obtained the sex by hemisphere finding in IFG as well. Importantly, this two way interaction was not qualified by reading group; both nonimpaired and dyslexic samples showed the sex differentiation within IFG Fig. 16.4. It should be noted that although the basic sex difference in hemispheric activation in IFG appears statistically robust across investigations using large numbers of subjects, it is clear that there is much overlap between the distributions as well. For example, this effect has been recently replicated using different language processing tasks (Jaeger et al., 1998), yet other imaging experiments have not observed robust sex differences in lateralization (Price, Moore, & Friston, 1996). As with analogous sex differences in lateralization using visual-hemifield or binaural presentation conditions in language processing tasks,

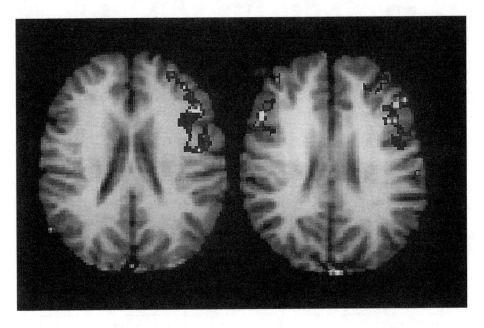

FIG. 16.3. Composite brain activations in 19 men (left) and 19 women (right). During rhyming, men activate the left inferior frontal gyrus. In contrast, women activate both left and right inferior frontal gyrus during the same task. Both men and women performed the task equally accurately.

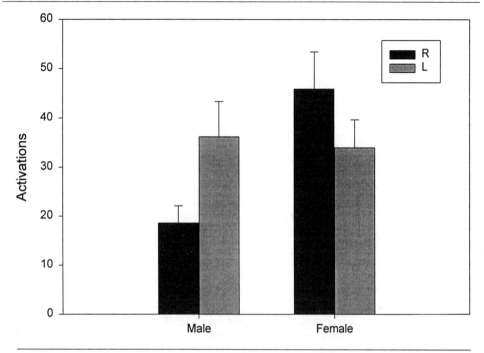

FIG. 16.4. Ordinate represents mean activations in the right (black bars) compared to the left (gray bars) inferior frontal gyrus for males and females as each were performing nonword rhyme. Increased activation in the left compared to right is noted for males but not for females. This two way interaction was not qualified by reading group; both nonimpaired and dyslexic samples showed the sex differentiation within IFG.

given the large overlap in distribution (see Geary, 1998, for discussion) the basic effect may not be expected to attain significance in each and every sample and for all language processing manipulations. In sum, the evidence from several imaging experiments seems clear—the modal pattern at the IFG indicates relatively greater right hemisphere involvement for females than for males at IFG.

The critical question raised by findings such as these is what, if anything, do these general sex differences in laterality imply about differences at the level of cognitive performance during reading and language processing tasks? Do these differences at the level of brain activation patterns in IFG, a phonologically relevant brain region, imply differences in code utilization at the cognitive level of analysis between left-lateralized and bilateral readers? We have examined this issue by using activation data to predict sensitivity to phonological factors in reading performance measured outside the magnet (Pugh et al., 1997). The variable of interest in our efforts to link processes in word identification with brain physiology is the regularity effect in the lexical decision experiment. The presence or absence of regularity effects, defined as longer latencies (or higher error rates) to exception words (PINT) than to regular words (MILL), may indicate whether lexical access is more or less reliant on a type of fine-grained grapheme-to-phoneme assembly process for a given reader or a given reading group (Bruck, 1992; Pugh, Rexer, & Katz, 1994; Share, 1995; Stanovich & Siegel, 1994; Waters, Seidenberg, & Bruck, 1984).

The computational basis of this "reliance" varies depending on the model of word recognition in which the regularity effects are being interpreted, but often the regularity effect is interpreted in the context of dual-coding models of reading. In such models (Coltheart, 1978; Coltheart, Curtis, Atkins, & Haller, 1993; Paap, McDonald,

Schvaneveldt, & Noel, 1987; Paap & Noel, 1991), two routes to word identification are posited, a phonologically mediated route and an orthographic, or direct access, route. The phonological route consists of two stages. The first stage converts orthographic characters into appropriate phonological representations (the output from this mapping is commonly referred to as assembled phonology). In a second stage, these phonological representations are matched to their appropriate entries in the reader's speech lexicon. The alternative direct access route is, by some accounts (e.g., Share, 1995), thought to develop later as a consequence of extensive exposure to print; it is viewed as involving a more or less direct mapping from orthographic representations to lexical entries. Phonological information becomes available upon lexical access, and the lexically derived phonological coding is referred to as addressed phonology. Thus, a phonological representation of a printed word can come about in at least two ways and, in the case of some words, those representations can be different. For exception words, the assembled phonological system generates a regularized output (e.g., PINT to rhyme with MINT), whereas the direct orthographic system is lexically influenced and yields an irregular, but correct, phonological output (e.g., the correct pronunciation of PINT). Resolution of the conflict between these two competing processes putatively causes delays in responses to exception words relative to regular words, for which no such conflict arises (Paap & Noel, 1991).

In the lexical decision phase of this brain/behavior study the standard regularity × frequency interaction was obtained (longer latencies for low-frequency exception words than for low-frequency regular words). However, we observed considerable variation among subjects with respect to their sensitivity to this regularity effect. We found that individual differences in the magnitude of regularity effects were strongly correlated with individual differences in relative lateralization of activation in IFG (IFG; B.A. 44/45), the same site where sex differences were initially obtained. Relative lateralization was computed for each subject by the formula RH proportion = RH activation/RH activation + LH activation, where RH indicates right hemisphere and LH indicates left hemisphere. A significant interaction between regularity and RH proportion was obtained, $F(1,29) = 16.27, p < .001$. Additionally, regression analyses revealed that brain activation measures accounted for 62% of the variance among subjects in the magnitude of regularity effects in the lexical decision task.

We found that readers who activate IFG in a bihemispheric manner (high RH proportion) were sensitive to regularity on word latencies, whereas readers who activate IFG in strongly LH-dominant manner (low RH proportion) were not sensitive to regularity. These results indicate that individual differences in laterality at IFG, differences that in general discriminate males and females, in addition account for differences in code utilization in reading tasks measured independently. Recently we have replicated this RH proportion × regularity relationship in adult dyslexic readers. That this same brain/behavior continuum is found in dyslexic as well as nonimpaired readers suggests that laterality differences, although important with respect to sex difference research, are somewhat orthogonal to critical reading group differences that predict disability. We turn next to that topic.

fMRI IN DYSLEXIC READERS

As reviewed earlier, previous efforts using functional imaging methods to examine brain organization in dyslexia have been inconclusive (Eden et al., 1996; Flowers et al., 1991; Gross-Glenn et al., 1991; Paulesu et al., 1996; Rumsey et al., 1992, 1997; Salmelin et al., 1996), largely, we think, because the experimental tasks tapped several aspects of the reading process in somewhat unsystematic ways. Our aim, therefore, was to develop a set of hierarchically structured tasks that control the kind of language-relevant coding required, including especially the demand on phonologic analysis, and then to compare the performance and brain activation patterns (as measured by fMRI) of dyslexic (DYS) and nonimpaired (NI) readers. Thus, proceeding from the base of the hierarchy to the top, the tasks made demands on visual-spatial processing, orthographic processing, simple phonologic analysis, complex phonologic analysis, and lexical-semantic judgment. We hypothesized that differences in brain activation patterns would emerge as DYS and NI readers were asked to perform tasks that make progressively greater demands on phonologic analysis. These tasks were described previously and are shown in Table 16.1.

We studied 61 right-handed subjects, 29 DYS readers (14 men, 15 women, ages 16–54 years) and 32 NI readers (16 men, 16 women, ages 18–63 years). Both groups were in the average range for IQ; DYS readers had a full-scale IQ (mean ± SEM) of 91 ± 2.3 and NI readers had an IQ of 115 ± 2.2. Other than requiring that all subjects have an IQ in the average range (80 or above), we elected not to match subjects on IQ so as not to bias our sample selection in favor of less impaired readers because in adults IQ is known to be influenced by reading ability. One of the 29 DYS and none of the NI readers met *Diagnostic and Statistical Manual of Mental Disorders* (4th ed.; *DSM–IV*) criteria for attention- deficit/hyperactivity disorder (ADHD).

Reading performance in the DYS subjects was significantly impaired: the mean standard score on a measure of nonword reading (27) was 81 ± 1.9 (mean ± SEM) in DYS readers compared to 114 ± 1.5 in NI readers, with no overlap between groups. Similarly, error patterns on the fMRI tasks revealed that DYS differed from NI most strikingly on the NWR task. Nonword reading is perhaps the clearest indication of decoding ability because familiarity with the letter pattern cannot influence the individual's response.

We focused on 17 brain regions of interest (ROI) that previous research had implicated in reading and language (Demonet et al., 1994; Henderson, 1986; Petersen, Fox, Snyder, & Raichle, 1990; Pugh et al., 1996a) and examined these for evidence of differences between the two reading groups in patterns of activation across the series of tasks. Previous investigators have assumed the existence of a posterior cortical system adapted for reading, a system including Wernicke's area, the angular gyrus, extrastriate cortex, and striate cortex (Benson, 1994; Black & Behrmann, 1994; Geschwind, 1965). As shown in Fig. 16.5 (top panels) and Fig. 16.6, we found differences between DYS and NI readers in the patterns of activation in several critical components of this system: posterior STG (Wernicke's area), BA 39 (angular gyrus), and BA 17 (striate cortex). The pattern of group differences was similar at each of these sites: NI subjects show a systematic increase in activation in going from C to SLR to NWR, that is, as orthographic to phonologic coding demands increase, whereas DYS readers fail to show such systematic modulation in their activation patterns in response to the same task demands. In addition, an anterior region, IFG, demonstrates significant differences in the pattern of activation between NI and DYS readers (Fig. 16.5, bottom panel, and Fig. 16.6). However, here, in contrast to findings in the posterior system, DYS compared to NI readers demonstrate greater activation in response to increasing phonologic decoding demands.

Hemispheric differences between NI and DYS readers have long been suspected (Galaburda et al., 1985; Geschwind, 1985; Rumsey et al., 1992; Salmelin et al., 1996), and these were found in two regions: the angular gyrus and BA 37. In each case, activations in NI readers were greater in the left hemisphere, and in contrast, in DYS readers activations in these regions were greater in the right hemisphere. This pattern was observed across all tasks. Based on our earlier work (Shaywitz et al., 1995) we examined for hemispheric differences between males and females. In the IFG a significant sex difference was found. During NWR, men showed significantly greater activation in the left hemisphere compared to right, whereas women showed relatively greater right-hemisphere activation, consistent with previous observations.

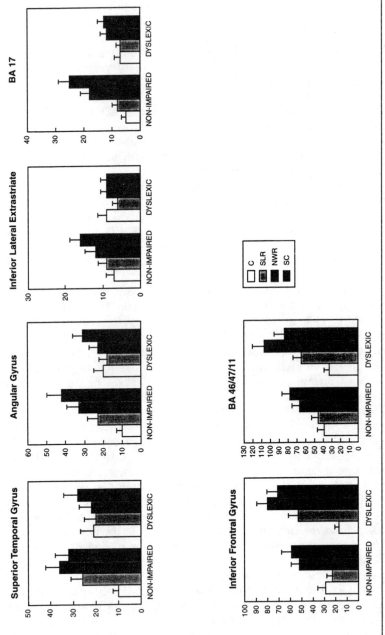

FIG. 16.5. Mean number of activated pixels for brain regions where activation patterns across tasks differ significantly between NI and DYS readers. Mean activations ± SEM are shown on ordinate, tasks on abscissa. We found differences between DYS and NI readers in the patterns of activation in several critical components of this system: posterior STG (Wernicke's area), BA 39 (angular gyrus), and BA 17 (striate cortex). The pattern of group differences was similar at each of these sites: NI subjects show a systematic increase in activation in going from C to SLR to NWR, that is, as orthographic to phonologic coding demands increase, whereas DYS readers fail to show such systematic modulation in their activation patterns in response to the same task demands. In addition, an anterior region, IFG, demonstrates significant differences in the pattern of activation between NI and DYS readers. However, here, in contrast to findings in the posterior system, DYS compared to NI readers demonstrate greater activation in response to increasing phonologic decoding demands.

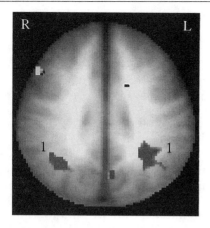 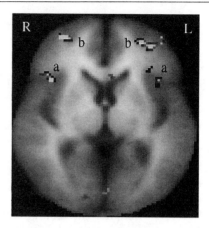

FIG. 16.6. Composite activation maps in dyslexic and nonimpaired readers during phonologic processing. These maps were generated from a general linear model based on a randomization of statistical parametric maps and show activations at $p = .01$. During phonologic processing, dyslexic readers demonstrated more activation than nonimpaired readers anteriorly in the inferior frontal gyrus bilaterally (a) and the middle frontal gyrus (b). In contrast, nonimpaired but not dyslexic readers activated a large area in the posterior region, the angular gyrus (1).

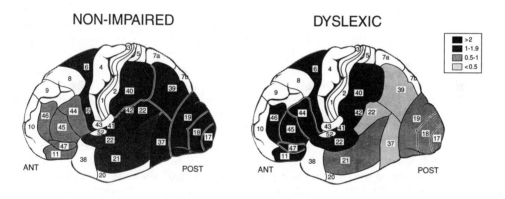

FIG. 16.7. Relative increase in activation during phonologic compared to orthographic coding in different brain regions in NI and DYS readers. As shown in the inset key, the shadings represent the relative magnitude of the increase in activation (mean pixel counts) for a given region of interest (ROI) calculated as: [(NWR – Line) – (Case – Line)]/(Case – Line). In posterior regions (e.g., posterior BA 22 [STG] and BA 39 [angular gyrus]) the relative change in activation is large (> 2, shown in black) in NI readers but very small in DYS readers (< 0.5, shown as lightest gray). A contrasting pattern is shown in anterior regions, for example, in BA 44 and 45 (IFG), where NI readers demonstrate an increase in activation (0.5–1) and DYS readers demonstrate an even greater increase (> 2). There are regions where NI and DYS readers show similar increases in activation, for example, BA 6 and anterior STG (BA 41, BA 42, anterior BA 22). Brain regions shown in white were not part of the 17 ROIs examined; numbers represent Brodmann's areas (BA).

In this study we found significant differences in brain activation patterns between DYS and NI readers, differences that emerged during tasks that made progressive demands on phonologic analysis. These findings relate the cognitive/behavioral deficit characterizing DYS readers to anomalous activation patterns in both posterior and anterior brain regions (Fig. 16.7). Thus, within a large posterior cortical system including

Wernicke's area, the angular gyrus, and the extrastriate and striate cortex, DYS readers fail to systematically increase activation as the difficulty of mapping print onto phonologic structures increases. In contrast, in anterior regions including the IFG and BA 46/47/11, dyslexic readers show a pattern of overactivation in response to even the simplest phonologic task (SLR) (Fig. 16.5). For NI readers these data provide functional evidence of a widely distributed computational system for reading characterized by specialization and reciprocity: Within the system, task-specific responses vary from region to region. For example, in the IFG only the complex phonologic task (NWR) produced a significant increase in activation relative to the orthographic (C) task, suggesting that this region is engaged in letter-to-sound transcoding; in Wernicke's area both simple (SLR) and more complex (NWR) phonologic tasks produced significant increases in activation relative to the orthographic task, implying that this region processes information in a more abstract phonological form (Fig. 16.5).

What is particularly interesting is that the findings from this most recent functional imaging study of dyslexia now help reconcile the seemingly contradictory findings of previous imaging studies of dyslexia, some of which involved anomalous findings in the visual system (Eden et al., 1996) whereas others indicated abnormal activation within components of the language system (Flowers et al., 1991; Gross-Glenn et al., 1991; Paulesu et al., 1996; Rumsey et al., 1992, 1997; Salmelin et al., 1996). These data indicate that dyslexic readers demonstrate a functional disruption in an extensive system in posterior cortex encompassing both traditional visual and traditional language regions as well as a portion of association cortex. The involvement of this latter region centered about the angular gyrus is of particular interest because this portion of association cortex is considered pivotal in carrying out those cross-modal integrations necessary for reading (i.e., mapping the visual percept of the print onto the phonologic structures of the language; Benson, 1994; Black & Behrmann, 1994; Geschwind, 1965) Consistent with this study of developmental dyslexia, a large literature on acquired inability to read (alexia) describes neuroanatomic lesions most prominently centered about the angular gyrus (Damasio, 1983; Dejerine, 1891; Friedman, Ween, & Albert, 1993). It should not be surprising that both the acquired and the developmental disorders affecting reading have in common a disruption within the neural systems serving to link the visual representations of the letters to the phonologic structures they represent. Although reading difficulty is the primary symptom in both acquired alexia and developmental dyslexia, associated symptoms and findings in the two disorders would be expected to differ somewhat, reflecting the differences between an acquired and a developmental disorder. In acquired alexia, a structural lesion resulting from an insult (e.g., stroke, tumor) disrupts a component of an already functioning neural system, and the lesion may extend to involve other brain regions and systems. In developmental dyslexia, as a result of a constitutionally based functional disruption, the system never develops normally, so that the symptoms reflect the emanative effects of an early disruption to the phonologic system. In either case the disruption is within the same neuroanatomic system.

For dyslexic readers, these brain activation patterns provide evidence of an imperfectly functioning system for segmenting words into their phonologic constituents; accordingly, this disruption is evident when dyslexic readers are asked to respond to increasing demands on phonologic analysis. These findings now add neurobiologic support for previous cognitive/behavioral data pointing to the critical role of phonologic analysis, and its impairment, in dyslexia. The pattern of relative underactivation in posterior brain regions contrasted with relative overactivation in anterior regions may provide a neural signature for the phonologic difficulties characterizing dyslexia.

FUNCTIONAL CONNECTIVITY IN READING

Although most of the extant neuroimaging studies have sought to identify specific brain regions where activation patterns discriminate DYS from NI readers (e.g., the angular gyrus), a deeper understanding of the neurobiology of developmental dyslexia requires that we consider relations between distinct brain regions that function cooperatively to process information during reading; we can refer to this issue as one of functional connectivity (Friston, Frith, & Frackowiak, 1994; Horwitz, 1994; McIntosh & Gonzalez-Lima, 1994). Our observation that the angular gyrus, along with Wernicke's area in the superior temporal gyrus, and striate and extrastriate sites, all parts of this putative posterior network that serves reading, showed anomalous activation in DYS readers only during tasks that engaged phonological processing led us to speculate that these regions fail to act as a system for decoding print into phonological structures (Shaywitz et al., 1998).

Evidence consistent with the notion of a breakdown in functional connectivity within the posterior reading system in DYS readers has been recently reported by Horwitz, Rumsey, and Donohue (1998) using activation data from the Rumsey et al. (1997) positron emission tomography (PET) study. These authors examined correlations (within task/between subject) between activation levels in the left hemisphere (LH) angular gyrus and other brain sites during two reading aloud tasks (exception word and nonword naming). Correlations between the LH angular gyrus and occipital and temporal lobe sites were strong and significant in NI readers and weak in DYS readers. Such a result suggests a breakdown in functional connectivity across the major components of the posterior reading system. We also examined functional connectivity between the angular gyrus and occipital and temporal lobe sites using our hierarchical tasks; tasks that systematically varied demands made on phonological assembly (Pugh et al., 2000). Preliminary results indicated that although for DYS readers LH functional connectivity was indeed weak on word and nonword reading tasks as suggested by Horwitz et al. (1998), there appeared to be no dysfunction in the tasks that tap metaphonological judgments only (SLR), or complex visual–orthographic coding only (C). The results are most consistent with a specific phonological deficit hypothesis: A breakdown in LH posterior systems manifests only when orthographic to phonological assembly is required. Moreover, we found that even on word and nonword tasks that right-hemisphere homologues appeared to function in a potentially compensatory manner for DYS readers; correlations were strong and stable in this hemisphere for both reading groups.

CONCLUSIONS AND IMPLICATIONS

Within the last two decades overwhelming evidence from many laboratories has converged to indicate the cognitive basis for dyslexia: Dyslexia represents a disorder within the language system and more specifically within a particular subcomponent of that system, phonological processing. Recent advances in imaging technology and the development of tasks that sharply isolate the subcomponent processes of reading now allow the localization of phonological processing in brain and, as a result, provide for the first time the potential for elucidating a biological signature for reading and reading disability. The discovery of a neuroanatomic locus unique to phonologic processing has significant implications. At the most fundamental level, it is now possible to investigate specific hypotheses regarding the neural substrate of dyslexia, and to verify, reject, or modify suggested cognitive models. From a more clinical perspective, the isolation of phonological processing in brain, and with it, a potential biological signature for dyslexia, offers the promise for more precise identification and diagnosis of dyslexia in children, adolescents, and adults.

ACKNOWLEDGMENT

The authors are supported by grants from the National Institute of Child Health and Human Development (PO1 HD21888 and P50 HD25802. Portions of this chapter appeared in *The Neuroscientist*, Swaiman, PNAS, and are reprinted with permission. All figures are the property of Sally E. Shaywitz and may not be reproduced without permission.

REFERENCES

Anderson, A., & Gore, J. (1997). The physical basis of neuroimaging techniques. In M. Lewis & B. Peterson (Eds.), *Child and adolescent psychiatric clinics of North America* (Vol. 6, pp. 213–264). Philadelphia; PA: W. B. Saunders.

Benson, D. F. (1994). *The neurology of thinking*. New York: Oxford University Press.

Black, S. E., & Behrmann, M. (1994). Localization in alexia. In A. Kertesz (Ed.), *Localization and neuroimaging in neuropsychology* (pp. 331–376). New York: Academic Press.

Blumstein, S. E., Baker, E., & Goodglass, Y. (1977). Phonological factors in auditory comprehension in aphasia. *Neuropsychologia, 15,* 19–30.

Brady, S. A., & Shankweiler, D. P. (Eds.). (1991). *Phonological processes in literacy: A tribute to Isabelle Y. Liberman.* Hillsdale, NJ: Lawrence Erlbaum Associates.

Bruck, M. (1992). Persistence of dyslexics' phonological awareness deficits. *Developmental Psychology, 28*(5), 874–886.

Coltheart, M. (1978). Lexical access in simple reading tasks. In G. Underwood (Ed.), *Strategies of information processing* (pp. 151–216). New York: Academic Press.

Coltheart, M., Curtis, B., Atkins, P., & Haller, M. (1993). Models of reading aloud: Dual-route and parallel-distributed-processing approaches. *Psychological Review, 100,* 589–608.

Damasio, A. R. (1983). Pure alexia. *Trends in Neurosciences, 6*(3), 93–96.

Dejerine, J. (1891). Sur un cas de cécité verbale avec agraphie, suivi d'autopsie. *Compte Render de la Société du Biologie, 43,* 197–201.

Demb, J., Boynton, G., & Heeger, D. (1998). Functional magnetic resonance imaging of early visual pathways in dyslexia. *Journal of Neuroscience, 18,* 6939–6951.

Demonet, J. F., Chollet, F., Ramsey, S., Cardebat, D., Nespoulous, J. L., Wise, R., Rascol, A., & Frackowiak, R. (1992). The anatomy of phonological and semantic processing in normal subjects. *Brain, 115,* 1753–1768.

Demonet, J. F., Price, C., Wise, R., & Frackowiak, R. S. J. (1994). A PET study of cognitive strategies in normal subjects during language tasks: Influence of phonetic ambiguity and sequence processing on phoneme monitoring. *Brain, 117,* 671–682.

Denckla, M. B., LeMay, M., & Chapman, C. A. (1985). Few CT scan abnormalities found even in neurologically impaired learning disabled children. *Journal of Learning Disabilities, 18*(3), 132–135.

Dool, C. B., Steimack, R. M., & Rourke, B. P. (1993). Event-related potentials in children with learning disabilities. *Journal of Clinical Child Psychology, 22*(3), 387–398.

Duara, R., Kushch, A., Gross-Glenn, K., Barker, W., Jallad, B., Pascal, S., Loewenstein, D. A., Sheldon, J., Rabin, M., Levin, B., & Lubs, H. (1991). Neuroanatomic differences between dyslexic and normal readers on magnetic resonance imaging scans. *Archives of Neurology, 48*(4), 410–416.

Eden, G. F., VanMeter, J. W., Rumsey, J. M., Maisog, J. M., Woods, R. P., & Zeffiro, T. A. (1996). Abnormal processing of visual motion in dyslexia revealed by functional brain imaging. *Nature, 382,* 66–69.

Filipek, P. (1996). Structural variations in measures in the developmental disorders. In R. Thatcher, G. Lyon, J. Rumsey, & N. Krasnegor (Eds.), *Developmental neuroimaging: Mapping the development of brain and behavior* (pp. 169–186). San Diego, CA: Academic Press.

Fletcher, J. M., Shaywitz, S. E., Shankweiler, D. P., Katz, L., Liberman, I. Y., Stuebing, K. K., Francis, D. J., Fowler, A. E., & Shaywitz, B. A. (1994). Cognitive profiles of reading disability: Comparisons of discrepancy and low achievement definitions. *Journal of Educational Psychology, 86*(1), 6–23.

Flowers, D. L., Wood, F. B., & Naylor, C. E. (1991). Regional cerebral blood flow correlates of language processes in reading disability. *Archives of Neurology, 48,* 637–643.

Friedman, R. F., Ween, J. E., & Albert, M. L. (1993). Alexia. In K. M. Heilman & E. Valenstein (Eds.), *Clinical neuropsychology* (3rd ed., pp. 37–62). New York: Oxford University Press.

Friston, K. J., Frith, C. D., & Frackowiak, R. S. J. (1994). *Human Brain Mapping, 1,* 69–79.

Friston, K. J., Frith, C. D., Liddle, P. F., & Frackowiak, R. S. J. (1993). Functional connectivity: The principal-component analysis of large (PET) data sets. *Journal of Cerebral Blood Flow and Metabolism, 13,* 5–14.

Galaburda, A. M. (1994). Developmental dyslexia and animal studies: At the interface between cognition and neurology. *Cognition, 50,* 133–149.

Galaburda, A. M., & Kemper, T. L. (1979). Cytoarchitectonic abnormalities in developmental dyslexia: A case study. *Annals of Neurology, 6,* 94–100.

Galaburda, A. M., Sherman, G. F., Rosen, G. D., Aboitiz, F., & Geschwind, N. (1985). Developmental dyslexia: Four consecutive patients with cortical anomalies. *Annals of Neurology, 18*(2), 222–233.

Geary, D. (1998). *Male, female: The evolution of human sex differences*. Washington, DC: American Psychological Association.

Geschwind, N. (1965). Disconnection syndromes in animals and man. *Brain, 88*, 237–294.

Geschwind, N. (1985). Biological foundations of reading. In F. H. Duffy & N. Geschwind (Eds.), *Dyslexia: A neuroscientific approach to clinical evaluation* (pp. 195–211). Boston, MA: Little, Brown.

Gross-Glenn, K., Duara, R., Barker, W. W., Loewenstein, D., Chang, J.-Y., Yoshii, F., Apicella, A. M., Pascal, S., Boothe, T., Sevush, S., Jallad, B. J., Novoa, L., & Lubs, H. A. (1991). Positron emission tomographic studies during serial word-reading by normal and dyslexic adults. *Journal of Clinical and Experimental Neuropsychology, 13*(4), 531–544.

Hagman, J. O., Wood, F., Buchsbaum, M. S., Tallal, P., Flowers, L., & Katz, W. (1992). Cerebral brain metabolism in adult dyslexic subjects assessed with positron emission tomography during performance of an auditory task. *Archives of Neurology, 49*, 734–739.

Halpern, D. F. (1992). *Sex differences in cognitive abilities* (2nd ed.). Hillsdale, NJ: Lawrence Erlbaum Associates.

Hart, J., & Gordon, B. (1990). Delineation of single-word semantic comprehension deficits in aphasia, with anatomical correlation. *Annals of Neurology, 27*, 226–231.

Haslam, R. H. A., Dalby, J. T., Johns, R. D., & Rademaker, A. W. (1981). Cerebral asymmetry in developmental dyslexia. *Archives of Neurology, 38*, 679–682.

Henderson, V. W. (1986). Anatomy of posterior pathways in reading: A reassessment. *Brain and Language, 29*, 119–133.

Hier, D. B., LeMay, M., Rosenberger, P. B., & Perlo, V. P. (1978). Developmental dyslexia: Evidence for a subgroup with a reversal of cerebral asymmetry. *Archives of Neurology, 35*, 90–92.

Hines, M., Chiu, L., McAdams, L. A., Bentler, P. M., & Lipcamon, J. (1992). Cognition and the corpus callosum: Verbal fluency, visuospatial ability, and language lateralization related to midsagittal surface areas of callosal subregions. *Behavioral Neuroscience, 106*, 1, 3–14.

Horwitz, B. (1994). Data analysis paradigms for metabolic-flow data: Combining neural modeling and functional neuroimaging. *Human Brain Mapping, 2*, 112–122.

Horwitz, B., Rumsey, J., & Donohue, B. (1998). Functional connectivity of the angular gyrus in normal reading and dyslexia. *Proceedings of the National Academy of Science, 95*, 8939–8944.

Hughes, J. R. (1977). Electroencephalographic and neurophysiological studies in dyslexia. In A. L. Benton & D. Pearl (Eds.), *Dyslexia: An appraisal of current knowledge* (pp. 205–240). New York: Oxford University Press.

Humphreys, P., Kaufmann, W. E., & Galaburda, A. M. (1990). Developmental dyslexia in women: Neuropathological findings in three patients. *Annals of Neurology, 28*, 727–738.

Hynd, G. W., & Semrud-Clikeman, M. (1989). Dyslexia and brain morphology. *Psychological Bulletin, 106*(3), 447–482.

Hynd, G. W., Semrud-Clikeman, M., Lorys, A. R., Novey, E. S., & Eliopulos, D. (1990). Brain morphology in developmental dyslexia and attention deficit disorder/hyperactivity. *Archives of Neurology, 47*, 919–926.

Jaeger, J., Lockwood, A., Vanvalin, R., Kemmerer, D., Murphy, B., & Wack, D. (1998). Sex differences in brain regions activated by grammatical and reading tasks. *Neuroreport, 9*, 2803–2807.

Jernigan, T. L., Hesselink, J. R., Sowell, E., & Tallal, P. A. (1991). Cerebral structure on magnetic resonance imaging in language- and learning-impaired children. *Archives of Neurology, 48*, 539–545.

Larsen, J. P., Høien, T., Lundberg, I., & Ødegaard, H. (1990). MRI evaluation of the size and symmetry of the planum temporale in adolescents with developmental dyslexia. *Brain and Language, 39*(2), 289–301.

Leisman, G., & Ashkenazi, M. (1980). Aetiological factors in dyslexia: IV. Cerebral hemispheres are functionally equivalent. *Neuroscience and Biobehavioral Review, 11*, 157–164.

LeMay, M. (1981). Are there radiological changes in the brains of individuals with dyslexia? *Bulletin of the Orton Society, 31*, 135–141.

Leonard, D., Voeller, K., Lombardino, L., Morris, M., Hynd, G., Alexander, A., Andersen, H., Garofalakis, M., Honeyman, J., Mao, J., et al. (1993). Anomalous cerebral structure in dyslexia revealed with magnetic resonance imaging. *Archives of Neurology, 50*, 461–469.

Liberman, A. (1996). *Speech: A special code*. Cambridge, MA: MIT Press.

Liberman, A. (1998). *Reading and spelling: Development and disorders*. Mahwah, NJ: Lawrence Erlbaum Associates.

Liberman, I. Y., Shankweiler, D., & Liberman, A. M. (1989). The alphabetic principle and learning to read. In D. Shankweiler & I. Y. Liberman (Eds.), *Phonology and reading disability: Solving the reading puzzle* (pp. 1–33). Ann Arbor, MI: University of Michigan Press.

Livingstone, M. S., Rosen, G. D., Drislane, F. W., & Galaburda, A. M. (1991). Physiological and anatomical evidence for a magnocellular defect in developmental dyslexia. *Proceedings of the National Academy of Sciences, USA, 88*(18), 7943–7947.

Lou, H. C., Henriksen, L., & Bruhn, P. (1984). Focal cerebral hypoperfusion in children with dysphasia and/or attention deficit disorder. *Archives of Neurology, 42*, 825–829.

Lou, H. C., Henriksen, L., & Bruhn, P. (1990). Focal cerebral dysfunction in developmental learning disabilities. *Lancet, 335*, 8–11.

Lukatela, G., & Turvey, M. T. (1994). Visual lexical access is initially phonological: 2. Evidence from phonological priming by homophones and pseudohomophones. *Journal of Experimental Psychology: General, 123*(4), 331–353.

McIntosh, A. R., & Gonzalez-Lima, F. (1992). The application of structural modeling to metabolic mapping of functional neural systems. In F. Gonzalez-Lima, Th Finkenstadt, and H. Scheich (Eds.), *Advances in metabolic mapping techniques for brain imaging of behavioral and learning functions* (pp. 219–255). Dordrecht, The Netherlands: Kluwer Academic Publishers.

Paap, K., McDonald, J., Schvaneveldt, R., & Noel, R. (1987). Frequency and pronounceability in visually presented naming and lexical decision tasks. In M. Coltheart (Ed.), *Attention and performance XII: The psychology of reading* (pp. 221–243). Hillsdale, NJ: Lawrence Erlbaum Associates.

Paap, K. R., & Noel, R. W. (1991). Dual-route models of print to sound: Still a good horse race. *Psychological Research, 53*, 13–24.

Parkins, R., Roberts, R. J., Reinarz, S. J., & Varney, N. R. (1987, January). *CT asymmetries in adult developmental dyslexics.* Paper presented at the annual convention of the International Neuropsychological Society, Washington, DC.

Paulesu, E., Frith, U., Snowling, M., Gallagher, A., Morton, J., Frackowiak, R. S. J., & Frith, C. D. (1996). Is developmental dyslexia a disconnection syndrome? Evidence from PET scanning. *Brain, 119*, 143–157.

Petersen, S. E., & Fiez, J. A. (1993). The processing of single words studied with positron emission tomography. *Annual Review of Neuroscience, 16*, 509–530.

Petersen, S. E., Fox, P. T., Posner, M. I., Mintun, M., & Raichle, M. E. (1989). Positron emission tomographic studies of the processing of single words. *Journal of Cognitive Neuroscience, 1*(2), 153–170.

Petersen, S. E., Fox, P. T., Snyder, A. Z., & Raichle, M. E. (1990). Activation of extrastriate and frontal cortical areas by visual words and word-like stimuli. *Science, 249*, 1041–1044.

Price, C., Moore, C., & Friston, K. (1996). Getting sex into perspective. *Neuroimage, 3*, S586.

Price, C., Wise, R., Howard, D., Patterson, K., Watson, J., & Frackowiak, R. S. J. (1993). The brain regions involved in the recognition of visually presented words. *Journal of Cerebral Blood Flow and Metabolism, 13*(1), s501.

Pugh, K., Mencl, W., Shaywitz, B., Shaywitz, S., Fulbright, R., Skudlarski, P., Constable, R., Marchione, K., Jenner, A., Shankweiler, D., Katz, L., Fletcher, J., Lacadie, C., & Gore, J. (2000). The angular gyrus in developmental dyslexia: Task-specific differences in functional connectivity in posterior cortex. *Psychological Science, 11*, 51–56.

Pugh, K., Rexer, K., & Katz, L. (1994). Evidence for flexible coding in visual word recognition. *Journal of Experimental Psychology, HPP20*, 807–825.

Pugh, K. R., Shaywitz, B. A., Shaywitz, S. E., Constable, T. R., Skudlarski, P., Fulbright, R. K., Bronen, R. A., Shankweiler, D. P., Katz, L., Fletcher, J. M., & Gore, J. C. (1996a). Cerebral organization of component processes in reading. *Brain, 119*, 1221–1238.

Pugh, K. R., Shaywitz, B. A., Shaywitz, S. E., Fulbright, R. K., Byrd, D., Skudlarski, P., Shankweiler, D. P., Katz, L., Constable, R. T., Fletcher, J., Lacadie, C., Marchione, K., & Gore, J. C. (1996b). Auditory selective attention: An fMRI investigation. *Neuroimage, 4*, 159–173.

Pugh, K. R., Shaywitz, B. A., Shaywitz, S. E., Shankweiler, D. P., Katz, L., Fletcher, J. M., Skudlarski, P., Fulbright, R. K., Constable, R. T., Bronen, R. A., Lacadie, C., & Gore, J. C. (1997). Predicting reading performance from neuroimaging profiles: The cerebral basis of phonological effects in printed word identification. *Journal of Experimental Psychology: Human Perception and Performance, 23*(2), 299–318.

Rieben, L., & Perfetti, C. A. (1991). *Learning to read: Basic research and its implications.* Hillsdale, NJ: Lawrence Erlbaum Associates.

Rosenberger, P., & Hier, D. (1980). Cerebral asymmetry and verbal intellectual deficits. *Annals of Neurology, 8*, 300–304.

Rumsey, J. M., Andreason, P., Zametkin, A. J., Aquino, T., King, C., Hamburber, S. D., Pikus, A., Rapoport, J. L., & Cohen, R. M. (1992). Failure to activate the left temporoparietal cortex in dyslexia. *Archives of Neurology, 49*, 527–534.

Rumsey, J. M., Dorwart, R., Vermess, M., Denckla, M. B., Kruesi, M. J. P., & Rapoport, J. L. (1986). Magnetic resonance imaging of brain anatomy in severe developmental dyslexia. *Archives of Neurology, 43*, 1045–1046.

Rumsey, J. M., Nace, K., Donohue, B., Wise, D., Maisog, J. M., & Andreason, P. (1997). A positron emission tomographic study of impaired word recognition and phonological processing in dyslexic men. *Archives of Neurology, 54*, 562–573.

Rumsey, J. M., Zametkin, A. J., Andreason, P., Hanahan, A. P., Hamburger, S. D., Aquino, T., King, C., Pikus, A., & Cohen, R. M. (1994). Normal activation of frontotemporal language cortex in dyslexia, as measured with oxygen 15 positron emission tomography. *Archives of Neurology, 51*, 27–38.

Salmelin, R., Service, E., Kiesila, P., Uutela, K., & Salonen, O. (1996). Impaired visual word processing in dyslexia revealed with magnetoencephalography. *Annals of Neurology, 40*, 157–162.

Schultz, R. T., Cho, N. K., Staib, L. H., Kier, L. E., Fletcher, J. M., Shaywitz, S. E., Shankweiler, D. P., Katz, L., Gore, J. C., Duncan, J. S., & Shaywitz, B. A. (1994). Brain morphology in normal and dyslexic children: The influence of sex and age. *Annals of Neurology, 35*(6), 732–743.

Sergent, J. (1994). Brain-imaging studies of cognitive function. *Trends in Neurosciences, 17*, 221–227.

Sergent, J., Zuck, E., Levesque, M., & MacDonald, B. (1992). Positron emission tomography study of letter and object processing: Empirical findings and methodological considerations. *Cerebral Cortex, 2*(1), 68–80.

Shankweiler, D., Crain, S., Katz, L., Fowler, A. E., Liberman, A. M., Brady, S. A., Thornton, R., Lundquist, E., Dreyer, L., Fletcher, J. M., Stuebing, K. K., Shaywitz, S. E., & Shaywitz, B. A. (1995). Cognitive profiles of reading-disabled children: Comparison of language skills in phonology, morphology, and syntax. *Psychological Science, 6*(3), 149–156.

Share, D. L. (1995). Phonological recoding and self-teaching: Sine qua non of reading acquisition. *Cognition, 55*, 151–218.

Shaywitz, B. A., Shaywitz, S. E., Pugh, K. R., Constable, R. T., Skudlarski, P., Fulbright, R. K., Bronen, R. A. Fletcher, J. M., Shankweiler, D. P., Katz, L., & Gore, J. C. (1995). Sex differences in the functional organization of the brain for language. *Nature, 373*, 607–609.

Shaywitz, B. A., Shaywitz, S. E., Pugh, K. R., Skudlarski, P., Fulbright, R. K., Constable, R. T., Fletcher, J. M., Liberman, A. M., Shankweiler, D. P., Katz, L., Bronen, R. A., Marchione, K. E., Lacadie, C. & Gore, J. C. (1996). The functional organization of brain for reading and reading disability (dyslexia). *The Neuroscientist, 2*, 245–255.

Shaywitz, S. E., & Shaywitz, B. A. (1999). Dyslexia. In K. F. Swaiman & S. Ashwal (Eds.), *Pediatric neurology: Principles and practice* (3rd ed., Vol. 1, pp. 576–584). St. Louis, MO: Mosby.

Shaywitz, S. E., Shaywitz, B. A., Pugh, K. R., Fulbright, R. K., Constable, R. T., Mencl, W. E., Shankweiler, D. P., Liberman, A. M., Skudlarski, P., Fletcher, J. M., Katz, L., Marchione, K. E., Lacadie, C., Gatenby, C. & Gore, J. C. (1998). Functional disruption in the organization of the brain for reading in dyslexia. *Proc. Natl. Acad. Science USA, 95*, 2636–2641.

Stanovich, K. E., & Siegel, L. S. (1994). Phenotypic performance profile of children with reading disabilities: A regression-based test of the phonological-core variable-difference model. *Journal of Educational Psychology, 86*(1), 24–53.

Stein, J., & Walsh, V. (1997). To see but not to read: The magnocellular theory of dyslexia. *Trends in Neurosciences, 20*(4), 147–152.

Swick, D., Kutas, M., & Neville, H. J. (1994). Localizing the neural genetics of event-related brain potentials. In A. Kertesz (Ed.), *Localization and neuroimaging in neuropsychology* (pp. 73–121). New York: Academic Press.

Thatcher, R. W. (1996). Neuroimaging of cyclic cortical reorganization during human development. In R. W. Thatcher, G. R. Lyon, J. Rumsey, & N. Krasnegor (Eds.), *Developmental neuroimaging: Mapping the development of brain and behavior* (pp. 91–106). New York: Academic Press.

Van Orden, G. C., Pennington, B. F., & Stone, G. O. (1990). Word identification in reading and the promise of subsymbolic psycholinguistics. *Psychological Review, 97*(4), 488–522.

Waters, G., Seidenberg, M. S., & Bruck, M. (1984). Children's and adults' use of spelling-sound information in three reading tasks. *Memory and Cognition, 12*, 293–305.

Wise, R., Chollet, F., Hadar, U., Friston, K., Hoffner, E., & Frackowiak, R. (1991). Distribution of cortical neural networks involved in word comprehension and word retrieval. *Brain, 114*, 1803–1817.

Witelson, S. F., & Kigar, D. L. (1992). Sylvian fissure morphology and asymmetry in men and women: Bilateral differences in relation to handedness in men. *Journal of Comparative Neurology, 323*, 326–340.

Wood, F., Flowers, L., Buchsbaum, M., & Tallal, P. (1991). Investigation of abnormal left temporal functioning in dyslexia through rCBF, auditory evoked potentials, and positron emission tomography. *Reading and Writing: An Interdisciplinary Journal, 3*(379–393), 191–205.

Wood, F. B., Garrett, A. S., Hart, L. A., Flowers, D. L., & Absher, J. R. (1996). Event related potential correlates of glucose metabolism in normal adults during a cognitive activation task. In R. W. Thatcher, G. R. Lyon, J. Rumsey, & N. Krasnegor (Eds.), *Developmental neuroimaging: Mapping the development of brain and behavior* (pp. 197–206). New York: Academic Press.

Young, R. (1990). *Mind, brain and adaptation in the nineteenth century.* Oxford: Oxford University Press.

Zatorre, R. J., Evans, A. C., Meyer, E., & Gjedde, A. (1992). Lateralization of phonetic and pitch discrimination in speech processing. *Science, 256*(5058), 846–849.

CHAPTER 17

Phonological and Lexical Processes

Usha Goswami
Institute of Child Health,
University College London

A child's awareness of the phonology of his or her language is now known to be one of the most important predictors of that child's progress in learning to read and to spell. Phonological awareness is measured by tasks that require a child to reflect on the component *sounds* of spoken words, rather than on their meanings. Possible relationships between the child's lexical development, phonological development, and reading have received much less attention. However, lexical development and phonological development show some interesting parallels, with recent research suggesting that phonological development may be intimately connected to lexical development. This research increasingly indicates that phonological awareness is tied to the *quality* of the representations of words that children have in their mental lexicons. In particular, the quality of these representations at the phonological (speech-based) level seems to be critical for reading development. Children whose lexical development has precluded the establishment of high-quality phonological representations of speech seem to be those who are most likely to show poor phonological awareness, and consequently to have difficulties in learning to read and to spell.

PHONOLOGICAL PROCESSES

Levels of Phonological Awareness

Children's awareness of the phonological structure of their language can be measured at a number of different levels. There are at least three levels of phonological structure that are important for reading development. These are the level of the syllable, the level of onsets and rimes, and the level of the phoneme. Tasks that measure *syllabic awareness* assess children's ability to detect constituent syllables in words. For example, a word like *alphabet* has three syllables, and a word like *reading* has two. Tasks that measure *onset-rime awareness* assess children's ability to detect two units within the syllable, the *onset*, which corresponds to any phonemes before the vowel, and the *rime*, which corresponds to the vowel sound and to any following phonemes. In a word like *spring*, the onset corresponds to the sound made by the spelling unit *spr*, and the rime corresponds to the sound made by the spelling unit *ing*. *Phonemes* are the smallest sounds that change the meanings of words: *pit* and *sit* differ by a single phoneme (the initial phoneme), and so do *pit* and *pat* (the medial phoneme). Onset-rime awareness and phoneme awareness do not always correspond to separate levels of phonological structure, however. Many English words have single-phoneme onsets (as in *pit, sit,* and *pat*). A number of English words have single-phoneme rimes (examples are *go, zoo,* and *tree*).

The Sequence of Phonological Development

A wide range of tasks, usually involving oral administration, has been devised in order to measure the development of phonological knowledge at these three levels. Examples include sound deletion tasks, same/different judgment tasks, and segment counting tasks. These tasks make a variety of other cognitive demands on children, so it is most useful to use the same task to compare the development of phonological awareness at the different levels. Unfortunately, many research studies have used different tasks to assess phonological ability at the three different levels, limiting the conclusions that can be drawn.

In this review, I focus on studies that have used the same task to measure at least two levels of phonological knowledge. Representative studies have used the *tapping* task, in which children are given a wooden dowel and required to tap out the number of sounds in words at different phonological levels; the *oddity* task, in which children have to listen to a group of spoken words and then select the word that has a different sound from the others; and the *same–different judgment* task, in which children listen to pairs of words and have to judge whether they share a sound or not.

The *tapping* task was originally devised by Isabelle Liberman and her colleagues, who used it at the syllable and phoneme levels (Liberman, Shankweiler, Fischer, & Carter, 1974). The task was based on words that had either one syllable or phoneme (*dog, I*), two syllables or phonemes (*dinner, my*), or three syllables or phonemes (*president, book*). Four- to 6-year-old children were asked to tap once for each of the syllables or phonemes in the words. Liberman et al. found that 46% of the 4-year-olds reached their criterion (of six consecutive correct responses) in the syllable task, compared to 0% for phonemes. For the 5-year-olds, 48% of children reached criterion in the syllable task, compared to 17% for phonemes. The 6-year-olds were the only group to show success in the phoneme task. Seventy percent of this age group could segment the stimuli into phonemes, and 90% succeeded in the syllable task. It is notable that these children had been learning to read for about a year (the mean age of this group was 6 years 11 months). This suggests that syllable awareness develops prior to phoneme awareness, and that the development of phoneme awareness is partly dependent on being taught to read.

The *oddity* task was devised by Bradley and Bryant (1983), who used it to measure the development of onset and rime awareness versus phoneme awareness (Kirtley, Bryant, MacLean, & Bradley, 1989). The children's task was to spot the "odd word out" in groups of three or four words that differed in terms of either their initial sounds (bus, bun, *rug*), their medial sounds (*pin*, bun, gun), or their final sounds (*doll*, hop, top). Bradley and Bryant found that 4- and 5-year-olds were very proficient at spotting the odd word out, performing at above-chance levels in all three versions of the task, although the rime awareness (middle and end sound different) tasks were easier than the onset awareness (initial sound different) task. Although these word triples differed in terms of single phonemes, too, further work confirmed that the oddity judgments were being made on the basis of shared onsets or shared rimes (Kirtley et al., 1989).

When word triples like *top, rail, hop,* where the odd word out could be chosen on the basis of the whole rime, were compared to triples like *mop, lead, whip,* where the odd word out had to be selected on the basis of the final phoneme, 4-, 5-, and 6-year-old children showed a selective deficit in the phoneme version of the task. Kirtley et al. argued that onset-rime awareness develops prior to phoneme awareness.

The *same–different judgment* task has been used extensively by Treiman and her research group. Treiman and Zukowski (1991) measured the development of phonological awareness at all three levels (syllable, onset-rime, and phoneme) by asking children to say whether pairs of spoken words shared a sound at either the beginning or the end. The children were aged 4, 5, and 6 years. In the beginning version of the task, the shared sound was either the initial syllable (*hammer, hammock*), the onset (*broom, brand*), or the initial phoneme (*steak, sponge*). In the end version of the task the shared sound was either the final syllable (*compete, repeat*), the rime (*spit, wit*), or the final phoneme (*smoke, tack*). Treiman and Zukowski found that criterion on the syllable tasks (six consecutive correct responses) was reached by 100% of the 4-year-olds, 90% of the 5-year-olds, and 100% of the 6-year-olds. Criterion on the onset-rime tasks was reached by 56% of the 4-year-olds, 74% of the 5-year-olds, and 100% of the 6-year-olds. In contrast, criterion on the phoneme tasks was reached by only 25% of the 4-year-olds, 39% of the 5-year-olds, and 100% of the 6-year-olds. The 6-year-olds had been learning to read for about a year, and they were the only group to show equivalent levels of performance at the three phonological levels. Treiman and Zukowski's data are thus consistent with the developmental patterns reported by researchers using the tapping and oddity tasks (see also Treiman & Zukowski, 1996). Syllable and onset-rime awareness develop prior to phoneme awareness, and are present in preschoolers. Phoneme awareness largely develops when children go to school and begin being taught to read (and to spell).

The general conclusion to be drawn from these (and many other) studies is that the development of phonological awareness progresses from the syllable level and the onset-rime level to the phoneme level (see Goswami & Bryant, 1990, for a review). However, the fact that onsets and rimes and phonemes are not always distinct levels of phonological structure suggests that the development of onset-rime awareness and the development of phonemic awareness may be partly interdependent. For example, in words with single-phoneme onsets, onset awareness and phoneme awareness are the same. Thus onset awareness supports the development of phonemic awareness. Further, Snowling and her colleagues have shown that the degree of phonemic similarity between words affects children's ability to make judgments about shared rimes. It is more difficult to pick the odd word out in the triple *job, rob, nod* than in the triple *job, rob, knock,* as *d* (*-od*) is phonemically closer to *b* (*-ob*) than *k* (*-ock*) (Snowling, Hulme, Smith, & Thomas, 1994). Thus onset-rime awareness can be affected by phonemic similarity.

Linking Phonological Awareness to Reading

Children's phonological skills play a crucial role in their reading development. A large number of correlational and training studies support the existence of a causal link between a child's phonological awareness and his or her progress in learning to read (e.g., Bradley & Bryant, 1983; Cossu, Shankweiler, Liberman, Katz, & Tola, 1988; Cunningham, 1990; Fox & Routh, 1975; Gough & Tunmer, 1986; Juel, 1988; Juel, Griffith, & Gough, 1986; Lundberg, Frost, & Petersen, 1988; Lundberg, Olofsson, & Wall, 1980; Mann, 1993; Morais, Alegria, & Content, 1987; Naslund & Schneider, 1991; Perfetti, Beck, Bell, & Hughes, 1987; Snowling, 1980; Stanovich, Cunningham, & Cramer, 1984; Tunmer & Nesdale, 1985; Vellutino & Scanlon, 1987; Wagner, 1988; Wagner, Torgeson, & Rashotte, 1994). An important question for educators, however, is whether there are *specific* links between the different levels of phonological awareness and children's reading development. We have already seen that being taught to read and spell has an impact on the development of phonemic awareness. We can also ask whether the early-developing forms of phonological awareness, namely, syllable and onset-rime awareness, have their own impact on reading development. As these skills develop prior to school entry and prior to formal tuition in reading and spelling, it is important to know whether the levels of phonological awareness that children bring with them to the task of learning to read have important links with reading development.

Links at the Onset-Rime Level.   A number of studies have suggested that there is indeed a special link between early onset-rime awareness and reading development in English. For example, Bradley and Bryant (1983) gave around 400 children in England the oddity rhyme task when they were 4 and 5 years of age, and followed up 368 of them 3–4 years later, measuring their progress in reading and spelling when the children were 8 and 9 years old. They found a strong predictive relationship between early rhyming and later reading. Children with good rhyming skills prior to school entry tended to become better readers and spellers, and this relationship held even after other variables, including IQ, vocabulary, and memory, were taken into account. The relationship with rhyme was also specific to reading: No predictive relationship was found between rhyming ability and progress in mathematics. This showed that the connection between rhyme and learning to read was not a reflection of general cognitive ability. Other studies with English-speaking children have reported a similar specific connection (Bryant, Maclean, Bradley, & Crossland, 1990; Cronin & Carver, 1998; Ellis & Large, 1987; Maclean, Bryant, & Bradley, 1987; Walton, 1995). Studies of children who are learning to read more orthographically transparent languages report much weaker connections between rhyming and reading (Hoien, Lundberg, Stanovich, & Bjaalid, 1995; Wimmer, Landerl, & Schneider, 1994).

Further, children who have reading difficulties are known to have difficulties in onset-rime tasks. For example, Bradley and Bryant (1978) gave the oddity task to 10-year-old backward readers reading at the 7-year level, and compared their performance in choosing the odd word out to that of normally developing 7-year-old readers. This *reading level match design* holds reading level constant and varies age, rather than vice versa. Bradley and Bryant found that the backward readers were much worse in all versions of the oddity task than the younger controls. Given that the backward readers had higher mental ages than the control children as well as more years of general experience in taking tests, their deficit in rhyme is a particularly striking one. A rhyming deficit in dyslexia has since been found in other studies conducted in English using the stringent reading level match design (e.g., Bowey, Cain, & Ryan, 1992; Holligan & Johnston, 1988).

Finally, training children's rhyming skills has a significant impact on their reading progress. As part of their longitudinal study, Bradley and Bryant (1983) took the 60 children in their cohort of 400 who had performed most poorly in the oddity task and gave some of them 2 years of intensive training in grouping words on the basis of onsets rhymes and phonemes. Training was based on a picture sorting task, in which the children were taught to group words by phonological category (e.g., placing pictures of a *hat*, a *rat*, a *mat*, and a *bat* together). A control group learned to sort the same pictures by semantic category (e.g., placing pictures of a *rat*, a *pig*, and a *cow* together for the category "farmyard animals").

Half of the experimental group then spent the second year of the study learning how the shared phonological segment in words like *hat*, *rat*, and *mat* was reflected in shared spelling. The children were given plastic letters for this task, and were taught, for example, that a word like *hat* could be changed into a word like *rat* by discarding the onset and retaining the rime. The other half of the experimental group continued to receive phonological training only. At the end of the second year of the study, the children in the experimental group who had had plastic letters training were 8 months further on in reading than the children in the semantic control group, and a year further on in spelling. Compared to children who had spent the intervening period in an additional unseen control group, they were an astonishing 2 years further on in spelling, and 12 months in reading. The gains made by the children in the experimental group who had continued to receive phonological training only were less impressive, but still notable. This study suggests that there is a clear connection between training children in how the alphabet is used to represent onsets and rimes, and reading and spelling development. On the basis of results such as these, Goswami and Bryant (1990) suggested that a connection between awareness of rime and alliteration and later progress in reading and spelling was an important causal factor in reading development in English.

Links at the Phonemic Level.   Agreement on the importance of phoneme awareness for reading development is universal. It is probably true to say that every study that has measured the relationship between phonemic awareness and progress in reading has found a positive connection (e.g., Fox & Routh, 1975; Hoien et al., 1995; Juel, 1988; Juel et al., 1986; Lundberg et al., 1980; Mann, 1993; Perfetti et al., 1987; Snowling, 1980; Stanovich et al., 1984; Tunmer & Nesdale, 1985; Vellutino & Scanlon, 1987; Wagner, 1988; Wagner et al., 1994), and training studies have confirmed the existence of a causal link. As phonemic awareness, phonemic training, and reading development are discussed extensively later in this book (see Blachman's chapter), only one example is given here. Torgeson, Wagner, and colleagues consistently found a significant relationship between reading development and their measures of analytic and synthetic phoneme awareness in studies using subjects from first to fourth grade (these tasks require children to identify each phoneme in a word or to blend together a sequence of phonemes, respectively). They also established that training analytic and synthetic phoneme awareness has an impact on reading development (e.g., Torgeson, Morgan, & Davis, 1992; Wagner et al., 1994). Like Bradley and Bryant, this research group has managed to study relatively large groups of children.

The Role of Onset-Rime and Phonemic Levels of Awareness in Reading Development

This survey of research studies (see also Blachman's chapter, this volume) makes it clear that both onset-rime awareness and phonemic awareness play important roles in reading development. One useful way of thinking about the relationships between reading development and rhyme versus phoneme awareness is to think about phonological knowledge as a continuum. For example, Stanovich (1992) made a distinction between *shallow phonological sensitivity*, which is measured by tasks such as the oddity task, and *deep phonological sensitivity*, which is measured by tasks such as phoneme segmentation. Stanovich suggested that whereas shallow phonological sensitivity is a prerequisite for the acquisition of alphabetic literacy, deep phonological sensitivity is itself fostered by the analytic attitude developed during the child's initial learning of an alphabetic orthography. Variations of this position have been proposed by a number of researchers in the field (e.g., Hansen & Bowey, 1994; Goswami & Bryant, 1990; Stahl & Murray, 1994).

A number of experimental studies support this theoretical description. For example, Stahl and Murray (1994) reported a strong connection between early reading and the ability to separate an onset from a rime in CVC (consonant–vowel–consonant) stimuli in a sample of 113 kindergarten and first-grade children, but a much weaker relationship between separating rimes into phonemes and reading. They concluded that onset-rime awareness was one of the first steps in acquiring the alphabetic principle. Hansen and Bowey (1994) measured both onset-rime knowledge and phonemic knowledge in 77 second-grade children using the oddity task. Using a multiple-regression procedure, they found that onset-rime awareness predicted significant independent variance in word attack skills even after controlling for phonemic awareness. The reverse was not true. McClure, Ferreira, and Bisanz (1996) found that blending onsets and rimes into CCVC words was easier than blending phonemes for kindergarten children. They suggested that onset-rime units should be emphasized in early reading instruction.

Recently, however, the importance of rhyme for reading development in English has been questioned by Hulme and his colleagues (Muter, Hulme, Snowling, & Taylor, 1997; Nation & Hulme, 1997). Muter et al. followed 38 4-year-olds for a period of 2 years. Tests of onset-rime awareness (rhyme oddity, rhyme production, onset deletion) and phoneme awareness (final phoneme identification) were given at 4 years, and reading was measured at 5 and 6 years. They reported that a composite "phonemic" measure (derived by adding onset deletion and final phoneme identification scores, and thereby confounding onset and phonemic knowledge) was a significant predictor of reading, whereas a composite "rhyme" measure (derived by adding the rhyme oddity and the rhyme production scores) was not. Muter et al. concluded that early rhyming skills were not a determinant of early reading skills (p. 391). More recently, Muter et al. discovered significant scoring errors in their data set, and published an Erratum (Muter, Hulme, Snowling, & Taylor, 1998). Bryant reanalyzed their data without these errors and using a different procedure for scoring onset-rime awareness, and found that phonological awareness was described by a single factor encompassing both the onset-rime and phoneme measures (Bryant, 1998). This single factor was highly predictive of reading in the Muter et al. sample.

Nation and Hulme carried out a study analogous to that of Hansen and Bowey (1994) using a group of similar size but spanning a much larger age range (from first to fourth grade). Using a multiple regression procedure, they found that phonemic segmentation predicted significant independent variance in reading, whereas onset-rime segmentation did not. This result, which differs from that reported by Hansen and Bowey, is probably explained by the lack of variance in their onset-rime segmentation measure. In each grade, the children segmented approximately 60% of the nonsense word stimuli (e.g., *sloob*, *skreft*) correctly. Consistent with the findings of other researchers, however, the first graders in this study found onset-rime segmentation easier than phoneme segmentation (55% correct vs. 24% correct). This was not true of the fourth graders (60% correct vs. 75% correct). The good phonemic segmentation shown by these children is probably explained by the fact that they were being taught to read by a method that emphasized the phoneme. The negative conclusions about the importance of rhyme in early reading reached by Hulme, Snowling, and colleagues thus seem premature.

The Representation of Phonological Knowledge

A theory of metalinguistic development that links the representation of phonological knowledge to general cognitive mechanisms for the representation and re-representation of knowledge was put forward by Gombert (1992). Following Karmiloff-Smith's (1992) theory of representational redescription, Gombert argued that linguistic knowledge is initially represented procedurally, and is embedded in motor commands and actions. Linguistic knowledge at this level consists of correspondences between particular linguistic forms and the pragmatic contexts in which they are used. This knowledge is then rerepresented, so that it is accessible to other parts of the mind, although the child has *no* explicit awareness of this accessibility. Linguistic knowledge becomes *epilinguistic* and is used for the cognitive control of linguistic behavior, although it is not yet accessible to conscious inspection. Epilinguistic knowledge is syllable and rime knowledge. Finally, this linguistic knowledge is rerepresented again, leading to the acquisition of *metalinguistic control* over phonological structures. The need to achieve metalinguistic control is driven by external factors, such as tuition in literacy. It is only at this final point that the child can manipulate phonology in the way required by most phonological awareness tasks.

With respect to reading, Gombert suggested that the precociously developing ("epilinguistic") sensitivity to rimes at the implicit level is used by the cognitive system as soon as reading begins. However, at the explicit level (meaning the level of formal tuition), most beginning readers learn about grapheme–phoneme correspondences, so phonemic awareness is used by the cognitive system to support reading development at a conscious level. Tuition in grapheme–phoneme correspondences means that metalinguistic control at the phonemic level will emerge prior to metalinguistic control at the onset-rime level. This view suggests that a consideration of both the tasks that are used to measure onset-rime and phoneme awareness and the methods used for teaching reading may be very important for interpreting apparent discrepancies in research findings in the phonological awareness literature (see Goswami & East, in press). Tasks that tap phonological awareness at the epilinguistic level may lead to rather different patterns of findings from tasks that tap awareness at the metalinguistic level (see Duncan, Seymour, & Hill, 1997; Seymour & Evans, 1994; Yopp, 1988). Similarly, programs of reading instruction that emphasize onsets and rimes may lead to earlier explicit metalinguistic control at this level.

Phonological Memory

Phonological memory or verbal working memory is another area of phonological processing that is closely related to reading development. Phonological memory is usually measured via the digit span task, in which children are given increasingly long sequences of digits to repeat back to the experimenter following a short delay. Associations between digit span and reading have been reported in a number of studies (e.g., Brady, 1991; Johnston, Rugg, & Scott, 1987; Jorm & Share, 1983; Mann, Liberman, & Shankweiler, 1980; Swanson, Cochrane, & Ewers, 1989; Torgeson, Wagner, Simmons, & Laughton, 1990), although the relationships found were reviewed by Hansen and Bowey (1994) and were characterized as being somewhat weak and inconsistent. Hansen and Bowey argued that the nonsense word repetition measure of phonological memory developed by Gathercole and Baddeley (1989), in which children are given nonsense words of increasing length to report back to the experimenter (e.g., *ballop*, *thickery*), may be a more suitable measure of phonological memory for researchers interested in reading development. Associations between nonsense word repetition and reading development have been reported by Hansen and Bowey (1994), and by Stone and Brady (1995).

A critical issue for those interested in the relationships between phonological memory and reading, however, is whether phonological memory tasks and phonological awareness tasks have *independent* predictive relationships with reading. An alternative possibility is that both kinds of task derive their predictive success from a single underlying factor that determines phonological processing. Recent studies attempting to distinguish between these two alternatives suggest that phonological memory does not make an independent contribution to reading development once phonological awareness is taken into account. For example, Gottardo, Stanovich, and Siegal (1997) reported that phonological sensitivity (measured by the Rosner Auditory Analysis Test) accounted for 24.6% of unique variance in single word reading in third-grade children after controlling for verbal working memory (measured by a sentence memory task) and syntactic processing. Verbal working memory accounted for only 1.3% of unique variance in single word reading after controlling for phonological sensitivity and syntactic processing. Gottardo et al. concluded that the variance in reading explained by verbal working memory was largely variance that was shared with phonological sensitivity and syntactic processing.

A similar conclusion was reached by Hansen and Bowey (1994) in the study discussed earlier. They used oddity tasks at the onset-rime and phoneme levels to measure phonological awareness, and nonsense word repetition, digit span, sentence imitation, rehearsal rate (measured in words per second), and word span tasks to measure phonological memory. They found that significant variation in reading scores was accounted for by the phonological memory measures after phonological awareness was controlled in a set of hierarchical multiple regressions, and vice versa. However, they also noted that there was substantial overlap in the variance in reading scores accounted for by the two sets of measures.

What kind of single underlying phonological processing factor could affect both phonological awareness and phonological memory? A number of authors (e.g., Bowey & Hansen, 1994; Elbro, 1996; Fowler, 1991; Metsala, 1997; Snowling, Goulandris, Bowlby & Howell, 1986; Swan & Goswami, 1997a, 1997b) argued that the quality or clarity of the child's phonological representations of speech are a plausible candidate. This *phonological representations hypothesis* means that the quality of children's phonological representations of speech should affect their reading development, with lexical processes and phonological processes being developmentally entwined.

LEXICAL PROCESSES

The Relationship Between Lexical Development and Phonological Processing

There is growing evidence that lexical processes and phonological processes are indeed entwined. We can certainly discern a lexical contribution to performance in the nonsense word repetition measure of phonological memory. As noted by a number of authors (e.g., Snowling, Chiat, & Hulme, 1991), many of the nonsense word items used in this task either contain real lexical items (e.g., *ball* in *ballop*, *thick* in *thickery*), or contain segments of real lexical items (e.g., the segment *allop* in *ballop* is found in real words like *gallop*). Children with these lexical items in their vocabularies are therefore at an advantage when it comes to forming and retaining representations of these nonsense words. Rather than having to construct brand new representations, they can assemble the nonsense words from parts of lexically familiar representations. The relationship between this measure of phonological processing and lexical development would seem to be a fairly direct one. Consistent with this view, vocabulary development and performance in the nonsense word repetition task are known to be linked (e.g., Gathercole & Baddeley, 1989).

It can also be proposed that there is a lexical contribution to performance in phonological awareness tasks. A recent Finnish study found that there was a connection between lexical development at age 1 (measured by the number of mappings of meanings to speech units that each child had at 1 year) and phonological awareness at age 4 (measured by the oddity task; see Silven, Niemi, & Voeten,1998). There are a number of theoretical explanations for this kind of connection. One popular one is that lexical restructuring occurs with development, so that representations of lexical units change from being fairly holistic in phonological terms to being segmentally organized at the phonological level (Fowler, 1991; Metsala, 1997; Walley, 1993). This restructuring is gradual, so that increasingly smaller phonological segments are represented over time. Restructuring is thought to be driven by the number of lexical items in the child's lexicon. As this number increases, there is a need to discriminate between words both quickly and accurately, and this acts as a catalyst for the emergence of more fine-grained sublexical units of organization. This organization appears to narrow from the level of the syllable, to the intrasyllabic levels of onset and rime, and finally to the level of the phoneme at all serial positions in the word (Fowler, 1991; Goswami, in press; Menyuk & Menn, 1979; Studdert-Kennedy, 1987; Walley, 1993). Lexical restructuring is also hypothesized to vary with word frequency. Highly familiar lexical items should have representations that are more likely to become fully specified and complete in their segmental organization, as they will be required more frequently. This theoretical view has clear implications for phonological processing. As the emergence of segmental organization appears to follow the same developmental pattern as the emergence of phonological awareness skills (from syllable to onset-rime to phoneme), the development of phonological awareness may be at least partly dependent on lexical development.

Lexical Development and Reading: Testing the Phonological Representations Hypothesis

The important general point about this account is that it predicts that the degree to which lexical restructuring has taken place will determine the level of phonological awareness shown by the child, and consequently the ease with which he or she learns to read (see Elbro, 1996). So far, however, little empirical data is available to test this claim. A pure test of the lexical restructuring hypothesis is difficult, as the restructuring process must be item specific, driven by vocabulary size and word frequency. Nevertheless, two experimental approaches can be identified. One seeks evidence for lexical restructuring, and the other seeks a direct link between the specificity of a child's phonological representations and the child's phonological awareness.

Evidence for Lexical Restructuring.   One way to test the lexical restructuring hypothesis is to see whether words that demand the most discrimination (high-frequency words with many similar-sounding neighbors) show earlier evidence of segmental organization. Metsala (1997) used a "gating" paradigm for this test. The gating task presents the listener with increasing amounts of acoustic–phonetic information from word onset over a series of trials. The listener has to try to identify the target after each "gate." Identification on the basis of a small amount of acoustic–phonetic information suggests segmental organization. Metsala found that even the youngest children (7-year-olds) were able to recognize high-frequency words that shared a lot of phonological similarity with other words (words in dense "neighborhoods") on the basis of very little acoustic–phonetic information. As age increased, less acoustic–phonetic information was also needed to recognize high-frequency words that shared little phonological similarity to other words (words in sparse neighborhoods) and low-frequency words in both sparse and dense neighborhoods. Metsala argued that this was evidence for lexical restructuring, as it showed that the children were learning to represent the segmental distinctions that were necessary for discriminating between lexical alternatives, and that this process occurred first for the words that demanded the most discrimination.

Evidence for Links Between Representational Quality and Phonological Awareness.   In order to see whether the quality of children's phonological representations was linked to their phonological awareness skills, Swan and Goswami (1997b) examined whether children performed differently in phonological awareness tasks that were based on words that had precise versus imprecise phonological representations. They assumed that picture naming provided a reasonable measure of representational adequacy. When a child correctly identifies a picture name on demand, an accurate phonetic code must have been generated from a well-specified phonological representation. It has long been known that children who have reading difficulties have picture naming difficulties as well (e.g., Snowling, von Wagtendonk, & Stafford, 1988; Swan & Goswami, 1997a; Wolf, 1991). Swan and Goswami therefore examined the possibility that there was a specific connection between the representational adequacy of individual lexical items and performance in phonological awareness tasks.

Their study included a group of 11-year-old dyslexic readers, a group of 11-year-old normally reading children, and a group of 9-year-old reading level controls. Phonological awareness was measured at the three levels of syllable, onset-rime, and phoneme using a set of picture-based tasks. Prior to the phonological testing, the children were asked to name all of the pictures being used in order to gain a measure of the quality of each child's phonological representations for each lexical item. Performance in the phonological awareness tasks was then compared both before taking picture naming performance into account, and after adjusting performance for the representational adequacy of each item (scored by eliminating the lexical items causing naming difficulties for each child at each phonological level).

Prior to taking picture naming performance into account, Swan and Goswami found phonological deficits in the dyslexic group compared to controls at each phonological level. However, after adjustments for individual picture naming performance, the phonological deficits at the syllable and onset-rime level disappeared in comparison to both the chronological age controls and the reading level controls. The deficit at the phoneme level remained significant in comparison to both control groups.

Swan and Goswami's findings imply that there is a very close relationship between lexical development, reading development, and the development of phonological awareness. Levels of phonological awareness that do not depend on reading experience (syllable and onset-rime awareness) appear to have developed to the same extent in dyslexic children as in normally reading children of the same age once lexical development is taken into account. Levels of phonological awareness that do depend on reading experience (phoneme awareness) have not. These data are consistent with the view that performance in phonological awareness tasks depends to some extent on the quality of a child's phonological representations of speech. At the syllable and onset-rime levels, the dependence of phonological awareness on representational quality is almost entirely word specific. At the phoneme level, dyslexic children have difficulties even when the representational quality of specific words is adequate for output. These findings are consistent with Gombert's (1992) framework. Representation of syllables and rimes—epilinguistic knowledge—seems to develop automatically once a good phonological representation is achieved. Phoneme knowledge, which depends on external factors such as being taught to read, does not. Such conclusions must remain tentative, however, as picture naming may not be the best index of representational adequacy.

Phonological Processes, Lexical Processes, and Reading: The Role of Orthographic Analogies

A rather different connection between lexical development and reading concerns children's use of analogies in learning to read. Although analogizing has traditionally been linked to phonological development, it can be shown that both phonological and lexical processes play a role in this process. Making an analogy in reading depends on using the spelling-sound information in one word, such as *light*, to read a new word that shares the same spelling pattern, such as *fight*. A child who realizes that *light* can be used as a clue for reading *fight* is making the prediction that the new word (*fight*) will rhyme with the known word (*light*) because it shares the spelling pattern for the rime. This prediction requires phonological knowledge at the level of the rime. However, as originally noted by Goswami (1986), another factor that governs the development of children's analogizing is the number of words in the child's mental lexicon from which analogies can be made.

Phonological Development and Orthographic Analogies in Reading.   Early research into analogies in reading development examined whether an analogy mechanism was available to beginning readers. This research compared 6-year-old children's ability to make analogies between clue words like *beak* and new words like *bean* (which shares the initial three letters with *beak*) and *peak* (which shares the final three letters with *beak*). The clue word paradigm is shown in Fig. 17.1. The clue word analogy studies showed that analogies between spelling sequences at the ends of words (e.g., *beak–peak*) were made more frequently than analogies between spelling sequences at the beginnings of words (e.g., *beak–bean*), and occurred earlier developmentally (Goswami, 1986, 1988). This suggested that onset-rime knowledge was involved in analogies in reading. Further experiments showed that this was indeed the case (Goswami, 1990a, 1991, 1993). The rime effect was not due to phonological priming, as analogy levels were reduced or disappeared when the clue and test words shared a rhyming sound but differed in orthography (as in *head* and *said*, or *most* and *toast*; Goswami, 1990b).

Further research showed that analogies that depended on spelling units corresponding to the onset and part of the rime, as in *beak → bean*, were strongly linked to an awareness of phonemes (Goswami & Mead, 1992). These beginning analogies emerged later than rime analogies in the clue word task, by a reading age of around 6 years 10 months (Goswami, 1993), and analogies that depended on single phonemes that did not correspond to either onset or rime units, such as analogies between vowel digraphs in single-syllable words (*beak → heap*), emerged at around the same time. This pattern is consistent with the sequence of phonological development discussed previously. Onset-rime awareness emerges prior to phoneme awareness, and rime analogies are used before analogies requiring phonemic knowledge. Another way of

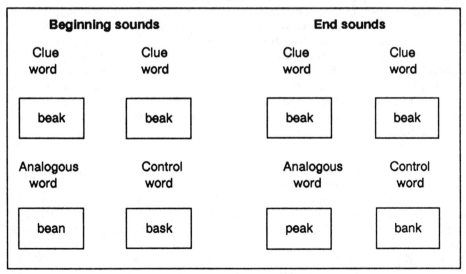

FIG. 17.1. The clue word task. From Goswami and Bryant (1990), with permission.

describing these results is to say that early analogy use depends on epilinguistic knowledge (i.e., about rime). As children are taught grapheme–phoneme relations and gain metalinguistic control over phonological structures, later analogies can exploit phoneme-level correspondences.

There is now quite a lot of independent evidence that children do use analogies in reading, and that even beginning readers have analogy strategies available (e.g., Ehri & Robbins, 1992; Moustafa, 1995; Muter, Snowling, & Taylor, 1994; Walton, 1995). Training beginning readers to use rime analogies has also been shown to have beneficial short-term effects on reading (e.g., Bruck & Treiman, 1992; Peterson & Haines, 1992; Wise, Olson, & Treiman, 1990), and dyslexic readers benefit from an analogy-based approach (Greaney & Tunmer, 1996; Greaney, Tunmer, & Chapman, 1997). Even beginning readers can benefit from literacy tuition in rhyme and analogy (Goswami & East, in press). Finally, recent connectionist simulation models of reading have shown that the rime plays an important role in reading acquisition in English, with networks given the facility for onset-rime mappings showing faster acquisition of the associations between print and sound (e.g., Zorzi, Houghton, & Butterworth, 1998).

Lexical Development and Orthographic Analogies in Reading.   Children's spontaneous use of analogies in reading (in the absence of clue words) increases as their reading vocabularies grow larger (Bowey & Hansen, 1994; Bowey & Underwood, 1996; Leslie & Calhoon, 1995; Treiman, Goswami, & Bruck, 1990). This shows that lexical development plays a role in the analogy process. Although the primary form of lexical acquisition is learning new words in speech, once children begin learning to read they begin another form of lexical acquisition, the development of the visual lexicon. This is the store of words that have orthographic entries. The visual lexicon corresponds to the reading vocabulary of the child. As the number of items in the child's reading vocabulary increases, more and more words are available to serve as a basis for analogies to new words, providing a mechanism for expanding the visual lexicon further.

A number of research studies have shown that there is a link between the size of the mental lexicon and children's use of rime analogies. This link is usually measured indirectly, for example, by comparing the use of rime analogies for frequent versus infrequent orthographic rime correspondences (defined in terms of the number of one-syllable words with the same rime), or by measuring the relationship between reading proficiency and the use of orthographic rime correspondences (e.g., Hansen & Bowey, 1994; Bowey & Underwood, 1997; Leslie & Calhoon, 1995; Treiman et al., 1990). Such studies show a clear relationship between rime "neighborhood size" and reading skill. For example, Leslie and Calhoon (1995) showed that rimes from large rime neighborhoods were read more accurately by first- and second-grade readers than rimes from moderate or small rime neighborhoods, and that more skilled readers showed larger differences than less skilled readers. They concluded that reading instruction should include tuition in reading by analogy, and that words containing rimes from large neighborhoods should be introduced first (see also Goswami, 1996).

The Spelling System of English.   The question of whether reading proficiency itself can be promoted by teaching children to think about spelling units that correspond to rimes is an important one. Gombert's (1992) theory predicts that it should be, as direct tuition in rime-level correspondences would lead to metalinguistic control over rime structures, enabling the strategic rather than implicit (epilinguistic) use of analogy. A recent statistical analysis of the English orthography carried out by Treiman, Mullennix, Bijeljac-Babic, and Richmond-Welty (1995) also suggests that it should be. This analysis showed that one of the spelling units that offers the most consistent mappings to phonology in English reflects the rime.

Treiman et al. calculated how many times individual letters had the same pronunciations when they occurred in the same positions across different words for all the monosyllabic words of English with a consonant–vowel–consonant (CVC) phonological structure (e.g., c in *cat, cup, coat*, etc., p in *cup, top, shape*, etc.). The CVC words in this analysis included words spelled with vowel digraphs, like *rain* and *beak*, and words with "rule of e" spellings, like *cake* and *lane*. Treiman et al. found that the pronunciation of vowels was very inconsistent across different words (51%), whereas the pronunciation of initial and final consonants was reasonably consistent ($C_1 = 96\%$, $C_2 = 91\%$). An analysis of the spelling–sound consistency of the larger spelling units in the words, namely, the onset-vowel (C_1V) and rime (VC_2) units, showed a clear advantage for the rime. Although only 52% of CVC words sharing a C_1V spelling had a consistent pronunciation (e.g., *bea* in *beak* and *bean*), 77% of CVC words sharing a VC_2 spelling had a consistent pronunciation (e.g., *eak* in *peak* and *weak*).

This statistical analysis of the properties of the English orthography shows that the spelling–sound consistency of written English is greatest for initial consonants (onsets), final consonants, and rimes. The finding that the orthographic structure of English confers a special status on spelling units that correspond to rimes suggests a reason for the strong and specific link between rhyme and reading in English that was discussed earlier. Phonological skills at the onset-rime level may help children to become aware of the functional importance of rime units in the orthography. A long-term training study that investigates the role of tuition in rhyme and analogy on reading development has yet to be carried out, however.

CONCLUSIONS REGARDING PHONOLOGICAL AND LEXICAL PROCESSES IN READING: TOWARD A THEORETICAL FRAMEWORK

In order to organize the information that has been discussed in this chapter into an explanatory framework, Gombert's (1992) theory of metalinguistic development can be integrated with Goswami and Bryant's (1990) theory about important causal connections in reading. A decade ago, Goswami and Bryant (1990) suggested three causal connections that were important for reading development. These were a connection between preschool awareness of rhyme and alliteration and later progress in reading and spelling, a connection between tuition at the level of the phoneme and the development of phonemic awareness (which was suggested to be rapid following such tuition and to operate in parallel with the first connection), and a connection between progress in spelling and progress in reading (and vice versa). Concerning the first of these connections, it was suggested that the link between early rhyme awareness and later progress in reading and spelling could be at least partly explained by children's use of analogies in reading. As onset-rime awareness is present at school entry, it was suggested that analogy was used as soon as children were introduced to literacy, even though the small size of their reading vocabularies constrained its use. It was noted that children's analogical inferences were rather few at the beginning and were often unsuccessful, and the role of development was thus emphasized. It was suggested that a great deal of reading development consisted of children getting gradually better at strategies that they used right from the start.

The evidence reviewed in this chapter has not questioned the importance of these three connections. However, Gombert's (1992) theory enables a deeper understanding of how they exert their causal influences. The connection between preschool awareness of rime and alliteration and later progress in reading and spelling can be understood as a connection between phonological awareness at the epilinguistic level and reading development. The connection between tuition at the level of the phoneme and the development of phonemic awareness can be understood as part of a more general connection between the teaching methods employed in the classroom and the emergence of metalinguistic control over phonological structures at the level of both onset-rime and phoneme. The connection between spelling and reading can also be understood in terms of metalinguistic control, as learning to spell requires the explicit representation of phonological knowledge.

Finally, the evidence reviewed here suggests that a new causal connection needs to be added to Goswami and Bryant's original framework. This new connection concerns the quality of a child's phonological representations of speech. This connection is causally primary in terms of the other proposed causal connections, and emphasizes the important role of lexical development in phonological development and reading. A child's linguistic experience from infancy onward will affect the child's lexical development and consequently the development of epilinguistic and metalinguistic awareness and the ability to benefit from reading and spelling tuition. Factors such as the quality of the child's linguistic environment (e.g., clarity and frequency of speech of caretaking adults) and the efficiency of the child's linguistic processing (which could be affected by factors such as the frequency of ear infections in early childhood) might all be expected to play their own roles in this important connection.

REFERENCES

Bowey, J. A., Cain, M. T., & Ryan, S. M. (1992). A reading-level design study of phonological skills underlying fourth grade children's word reading difficulties. *Child Development, 63,* 999–1011.

Bowey, J. A., & Hansen, J.(1994). The development of orthographic rimes as units of word recognition. *Journal of Experimental Child Psychology, 58,* 465–488.

Bowey, J. A., & Underwood, N. (1996). Further evidence that orthographic rime usage in nonword reading increases with word-level reading proficiency. *Journal of Experimental Child Psychology, 63,* 526–562.

Brady, S. A. (1991). The role of working memory in reading disability. In S. A. Brady & D. Shankweiler (Eds.), *Phonological Processes in Literacy: A tribute to Isabelle Y. Liberman* (pp. 129–151). Hillsdale, NJ: Lawrence Erlbaum Associates.

Bradley, L., & Bryant, P. E. (1978). Difficulties in auditory organisation as a possible cause of reading backwardness. *Nature, 271,* 746–747.

Bradley, L., & Bryant, P. E. (1983). Categorising sounds and learning to read: A causal connection. *Nature, 310,* 419–421.

Bruck, M., & Treiman, R. (1992). Learning to pronounce words: The limitations of analogies. *Reading Research Quarterly, 27*(4), 374–389.

Bryant, P.E. (1998). Sensitivity to onset and rime does predict young children's reading: A comment on Muter, Hulme, Snowling and Taylor (1997). *Journal of Experimental Child Psychology, 71,* 29–37.

Bryant, P. E., Maclean, M., Bradley, L., & Crossland, J. (1990). Rhyme, alliteration, phoneme detection, and learning to read. *Developmental Psychology, 26,* 429–438.

Cossu, G., Shankweiler, D., Liberman, I. Y., Katz, L., & Tola, G. (1988). Awareness of phonological segments and reading ability in Italian children. *Applied Psycholinguistics, 9,* 1–16.

Cronin, V. & Carver, P. (1998). Phonological sensitivity, rapid naming and beginning reading. *Applied Psycholinguistics, 19,* 447–461.

Cunningham, A. E. (1990). Implicit vs. explicit instruction in phonemic awareness. *Journal of Experimental Child Psychology, 50,* 429–444.

Duncan, L. G., Seymour, P. H. K., & Hill, S. (1997). How important are rhyme and analogy in beginning reading? *Cognition, 63,* 171–208.

Ehri, L. C., & Robbins, C. (1992). Beginners need some decoding skill to read words by analogy. *Reading Research Quarterly, 27*(1), 12–28.

Elbro, C. (1996). Early linguistic abilities and reading development: A review and a hypothesis. *Reading and Writing, 8,* 453–485.

Ellis, N. C., & Large, B. (1987). The development of reading: As you seek, so shall ye find. *British Journal of Psychology, 78,* 1–28.

Fowler, A. (1991). How early phonological development might set the stage for phoneme awareness. In S. Brady and D. Shankweiler (Eds.) *Phonological processes in literacy* (pp. 97–117). Hillsdale, NJ: Lawrence Erlbaum Associates.

Fox, B., & Routh, D. K. (1975). Analysing spoken language into words, syllables and phonemes: A developmental study. *Journal of Psycholinguistic Research, 4,* 331–342.

Gathercole, S. E., & Baddeley, A. (1989). Evaluation of the role of phonological STM in the development of vocabulary in children: A longitudinal study. *Journal of Memory and Language, 28,* 200–213.

Gombert, J. E. (1992). *Metalinguistic development.* Hemel Hempstead, Herts.: Havester Wheatsheaf.

Goswami, U. (1986). Children's use of analogy in learning to read: A developmental study. *Journal of Experimental Child Psychology, 42*, 73–83.

Goswami, U. (1988). Orthographic analogies and reading development. *Quarterly Journal of Experimental Psychology, 40A*, 239–268.

Goswami, U. (1990a). A special link between rhyming skills and the use of orthographic analogies by beginning readers. *Journal of Child Psychology and Psychiatry, 31*, 301–311.

Goswami, U. (1990b). Phonological priming and orthographic analogies in reading. *Journal of Experimental Child Psychology, 49*, 323–340.

Goswami, U. (1991). Learning about spelling sequences: The role of onsets and rimes in analogies in reading. *Child Development, 62*, 1110–1123.

Goswami, U. (1993). Toward an interactive analogy model of reading development: Decoding vowel graphemes in beginning reading. *Journal of Experimental Child Psychology, 56*, 443–475.

Goswami, U. (in press). Phonological representations, reading development and dyslexia: Toward a cross-linguistic theoretical framework. *Dyslexia.*

Goswami, U. C. (1996). *The Oxford Reading Tree rhyme and analogy programme.* Oxford, UK: Oxford University Press.

Goswami, U., & Bryant, P. E. (1990). *Phonological skills and learning to read.* Hillsdale, NJ: Lawrence Erlbaum Associates.

Goswami, U., & East, M. (in press). Rhyme and analogy in beginning Reading: Conceptual and Methodological Issues. *Applied Psycholinguistics.*

Goswami, U., & Mead, F. (1992). Onset and rime awareness and analogies in reading. *Reading Research Quarterly, 27*(2), 152–162.

Gottardo, A., Stanovich, K. E., & Siegal, L. S. (1997). The relationships between phonological sensitivity, syntactic processing and verbal working memory in the reading performance of third-grade children. *Journal of Experimental Child Psychology, 63*, 563–582.

Gough, P. H., & Tunmer, W. E. (1986). Decoding, reading and reading disability. *Remedial and Special Education, 7*, 6–10.

Greaney, K. T., & Tunmer, W. E. (1996). Onset/rime sensitivity and orthographic analogies in normal and poor readers. *Applied Psycholinguistics, 17*, 15–40.

Greaney, K. T., Tunmer, W. E., & Chapman, J. W. (1997). Effects of rime-based orthographic analogy training on the word recognition skills of children with reading disability. *Journal of Educational Psychology, 89*, 645–651.

Hansen, J., & Bowey, J. A. (1994a). Phonological analysis skills, verbal working memory and reading ability in second grade children. *Child Development, 65*, 938–950.

Hoien, T., Lundberg, L., Stanovich, K. E., & Bjaalid, I. K. (1995). Components of phonological awareness. *Reading & Writing, 7*, 171–188.

Holligan, C., & Johnston, R. S. (1988). The use of phonological information by good and poor readers in memory and reading tasks. *Memory & Cognition, 16*, 522–532.

Johnston, R. S., Rugg, M. D., & Scott, T. (1987). Phonological similarity effects, memory span and developmental reading disorders: The nature of the relationship. *British Journal of Psychology, 78*, 205–211.

Jorm, A. F., & Share, D. L. (1983). Phonological recoding and reading acquisition. *Applied Psycholinguistics, 4*, 103–147.

Juel, C. (1988). Learning to read and write: A longitudinal study of 54 children from first through fourth grades. *Journal of Educational Psychology, 80*, 437–447.

Juel, C., Griffith, P., & Gough, P. (1986). Acquisition of literacy: A longitudinal study of children in first and second grade. *Journal of Educational Psychology, 78*, 243–255.

Karmiloff-Smith, A. (1992). *Beyond modularity: A developmental perspective on cognitive science.* Cambridge, MA: MIT Press/Bradford Books.

Kirtley, C., Bryant, P., MacLean, M. & Bradley, L. (1989). Rhyme, rime and the onset of reading. *Journal of Experimental Child Psychology, 48*, 224–245.

Leslie, L., & Calhoon, A. (1995). Factors affecting children's reading of rimes: Reading ability, word frequency and rime neighbourhood size. *Journal of Educational Psychology, 87*, 576–586.

Liberman, I. Y., Shankweiler, D., Fischer, F. W., & Carter, B. (1974). Explicit syllable and phoneme segmentation in the young child. *Journal of Experimental Child Psychology, 18*, 201–212.

Lundberg, I., Frost, J., & Petersen, O. (1988). Effects of an extensive programme for stimulating phonological awareness in pre-school children. *Reading Research Quarterly, 23*, 163–284.

Lundberg, I., Olofsson, A., & Wall, S. (1980). Reading and spelling skills in the first school years predicted from phonemic awareness skills in kindergarten. *Scandanavian Journal of Psychology, 21*, 159–173.

MacLean, M., Bryant, P. E., & Bradley, L. (1987). Rhymes, nursery rhymes and reading in early childhood. *Merrill-Palmer Quarterly, 33*, 255–282.

Mann, V. A. (1986). Phonological awareness: The role of early reading experience. *Cognition, 24*, 65–92.

Mann, V. A. (1993). Phoneme awareness and future reading ability. *Journal of Learning Disabilities, 26*, 259–269.

Mann, V. A., Liberman, I., & Shankweiler, D. (1980). Children's memory for sentences and word strings in relation to reading ability. *Memory & Cognition, 8*, 329–335.

McClure, K. K., Ferreira, F., & Bisanz, G. L. (1996). Effects of grade, syllable segmentation and speed of presentation on children's word blending ability. *Journal of Educational Psychology, 88*, 670–681.

Menyuk, P., & Menn, L. (1979). Early strategies for the perception and production of words and sounds. In P. Fletcher & M. Garman (Eds.), *Language acquisition* (pp. 49–70). Cambridge: Cambridge University Press.

Metsala, J. L. (1997). An examination of word frequency and neighbourhood density in the development of spoken word recognition. *Memory & Cognition, 25*, 47–56.

Morais, J., Alegria, J., & Content, A. (1987). The relationship between segmental analysis and alphabetic literacy: An interactive view. *Cahiers de Psychologie Cognitive, 7*, 415–38.

Moustafa, M. (1995). Children's productive phonological recoding. *Reading Research Quarterly, 30*, 464–475.

Muter, V., Hulme, C., Snowling, M., & Taylor, S. (1997). Segmentation, not rhyming, predicts early progress in learning to read. *Journal of Experimental Child Psychology, 65*, 370–396.

Muter, V., Hulme, C., Snowling, M., & Taylor, S. (1998). Segmentation, not rhyming, predicts early progress in learning to read: Erratum. *Journal of Experimental Child Psychology, 71*, 1–28.

Muter, V., Snowling, M., & Taylor, S. (1994). Orthographic analogies and phonological awareness: Their role and significance in early reading development. *Journal of Child Psychology & Psychiatry, 35*, 293–310.

Naslund, J. C., & Schneider, W. (1991). Longitudinal effects of verbal ability, memory capacity and phonological awareness on reading performance. *European Journal of Psychology of Education, 6*(4), 375–392.

Nation, K., & Hulme, C. (1997). Phonemic segmentation, not onset-rime segmentation, predicts early reading and spelling skills. *Reading Research Quarterly, 32*, 154–167.

Perfetti, C., Beck, I., Bell, L., & Hughes, C. (1987). Phonemic knowledge and learning to read are reciprocal: A longitudinal study of first grade children. *Merrill Palmer Quarterly, 33*, 283–319.

Peterson, M. E., & Haines, L. P. (1992). Orthographic analogy training with kindergarten children: Effects on analogy use, phonemic segmentation, and letter–sound knowledge. *Journal of Reading Behaviour, 24*, 109–127.

Seymour, P. H. K., & Evans, H. M. (1994). Levels of phonological awareness and learning to read. *Reading & Writing, 6*, 221–250.

Silven, M., Niemi, P., & Voeten, M. (1998). *Do early interaction and language predict phonological awareness of 3- to 4-year-olds?* Manuscript submitted for publication.

Snowling, M. J. (1980). The development of grapheme-phoneme correspondence in normal and dyslexic readers. *Journal of Experimental Child Psychology, 29*, 294–305.

Snowling, M., Chiat, S., & Hulme, C. (1991). Words, nonwords and phonological processes. Some comments on Gathercole, Willis, Emslie and Baddeley. *Applied Psycholinguistics, 12*, 369–373.

Snowling, M. J., Goulandris, N., Bowlby, M., & Howell, P. (1986). Segmentation and speech perception in relation to reading skill: A developmental analysis. *Journal of Experimental Child Psychology, 41*, 489–507.

Snowling, M. J., Hulme, C., Smith, A., & Thomas, J. (1994). The effects of phonemic similarity and list length on children's sound categorisation performance. *Journal of Experimental Child Psychology, 58*, 160–180.

Snowling, M., van Wagtendonk, B., & Stafford, C. (1988). Object-naming deficits in developmental dyslexia. *Journal of Research in Reading, 11*, 67–85.

Stahl, S. A., & Murray, B. A. (1994). Defining phonological awareness and its relationship to early reading. *Journal of Educational Psychology, 86*, 221–234.

Stanovich, K. E. (1992). Speculations on the causes and consequences of individual differences in early reading acquisition. In P. B. Gough, L. C. Ehri, & R. Treiman (Eds.), *Reading acquisition* (pp. 307–342). Hillsdale, NJ: Lawrence Erlbaum Associates.

Stanovich, K. E., Cunningham, A. E., & Cramer, B. R. (1984). Assessing phonological awareness in kindergarten: Issues of task comparability. *Journal of Experimental Child Psychology, 38*, 175–190.

Stone, B., & Brady, S. A. (1995). Evidence for deficits in basic phonological processes in less-skilled readers. *Annals of Dyslexia, 45*, 51–78.

Studdert-Kennedy, M. (1987). The phoneme as a perceptuomotor structure. In A. Allport, D. Mackay, W. Prinz, & E. Scheerer (Eds.), *Language perception and production: Relationships between listening, speaking, reading and writing* (pp. 67–84). Orlando, FL: Academic Press.

Swan, D., & Goswami, U. (1997a). Picture naming deficits in developmental dyslexia: The phonological representations hypothesis. *Brain & Language, 56*, 334–353.

Swan, D., & Goswami, U. (1997b). Phonological awareness deficits in developmental dyslexia and the phonological representations hypothesis. *Journal of Experimental Child Psychology, 66*, 18–41.

Swanson, H. L., Cochrane, K. F., & Ewers, C. A. (1989). Working memory in skilled and less skilled readers. *Journal of Abnormal Child Psychology, 17*, 145–156.

Torgeson, J. K., Morgan, S., & Davis, C. (1992). The effects of two types of phonological awareness training on word learning in kindergarten children. *Journal of Educational Psychology, 84*, 364–370.

Torgeson, J. K., Wagner, R. K., Simmons, K., & Laughton, P. (1990). Identifying phonological coding problems in disabled readers: Naming, counting, or span measures? *Learning Disability Quarterly, 13*, 236–243.

Treiman, R., Goswami, U., & Bruck, M. (1990). Not all nonwords are alike: Implications for reading development and theory. *Memory and Cognition, 18*, 559–567.

Treiman, R., Mullennix, J., Bijeljac-Babic, R., & Richmond-Welty, E. D. (1995). The special role of rimes in the description, use and acquisition of English orthography. *Journal of Experimental Psychology, General, 124*, 107–136.

Treiman, R., & Zukowski, A. (1991). Levels of phonological awareness. In S. Brady & D. Shankweiler (Eds.), *Phonological processes in literacy* (pp. 67–83). Hillsdale, NJ: Lawrence Erlbaum Associates.

Treiman, R., & Zukowski, A. (1996). Children's sensitivity to syllables, onsets, rimes and phonemes. *Journal of Experimental Child Psychology, 61*, 193–215

Tunmer, W. E., & Nesdale, A. R. (1985). Phonemic segmentation skill and beginning reading. *Journal of Educational Psychology, 77*, 417–527.

Vellutino, F. R., & Scanlon, D. M. (1987). Phonological coding, phonological awareness and reading ability: Evidence from a longitudinal and experimental study. *Merrill-Palmer Quarterly, 33*, 321–363.

Wagner, R. K. (1988). Causal relations between the development of phonological processing abilities and the acquisition of reading skills: A meta-analysis. *Merrill-Palmer Quarterly, 34*, 261–279.

Wagner, R. K., Torgeson, J. K., & Rashotte, C. A. (1994). The development of reading-related phonological processing abilities: New evidence of bi-directional causality from a latent variable longitudinal study. *Developmental Psychology, 30*, 73–87.

Walley, A. (1993). The role of vocabulary development in children's spoken word recognition and segmentation ability. *Developmental Review, 13*, 286–350.

Walton, P. D. (1995). Rhyming ability, phoneme identity, letter-sound knowledge and the use of orthographic analogy by prereaders. *Journal of Educational Psychology, 87*, 587–597.

Wimmer, H., Landerl, K., & Schneider, W. (1994). The role of rhyme awareness in learning to read a regular orthography. *British Journal of Developmental Psychology, 12*, 469–484.

Wise, B. W., Olson, D. K., & Treiman, R. (1990). Subsyllabic units as aids in beginning readers' word learning: Onset-rime versus post-vowel segmentation. *Journal of Experimental Child Psychology, 49*, 1–19.

Wolf, M. (1991). Naming speed and reading: The contribution of the cognitive neurosciences. *Reading Research Quarterly, 26*, 123–141.

Yopp, H. K. (1988). The validity and reliability of phonemic awareness tests. *Reading Research Quarterly, 21*, 253–266.

Zorzi, M., Houghton, G., & Butterworth, B. (1998). The development of spelling-sound relationships in a model of phonological reading. *Language & Cognitive Processes, 13*, 337–371.

CHAPTER 18

Vocabulary Processes

William E. Nagy
Seattle Pacific University

Judith A. Scott
University of California, Santa Cruz

This chapter is about vocabulary processes and, in particular, vocabulary acquisition processes. Our focus is on how school children add words to their reading and writing vocabularies and how they learn the meanings of new words. The chapter on vocabulary instruction by Blachowicz and Fisher in this volume addresses methods and activities that promote vocabulary learning in the classroom. Other important word-level processes in reading are addressed in chapters on lexical and phonemic processes, word identification, and spelling.

There continues to be a strong, if not increasing, interest in vocabulary among reading researchers, according to extensive reviews of recent research provided by Beck and McKeown (1991) in the previous volume of the *Handbook*, as well as by Baumann and Kameenui (1991) and Ruddell (1994). A similar concern for vocabulary among second-language researchers is evidenced by several recent books (e.g., Coady & Huckin 1997; Schmitt & McCarthy, 1997). This interest in vocabulary stems in part from the long-standing recognition that vocabulary knowledge strongly influences reading comprehension (Davis, 1944; Anderson & Freebody, 1981). Among practitioners, on the other hand, interest in vocabulary has varied and is currently not especially high. For the last 2 years, the International Reading Association reported on a survey of "hot topics" in literacy research (Cassidy & Wenrich, 1997, 1998). In both years, vocabulary was rated as "cold," the bottom category. This low level of interest reflects an emphasis on instruction that is authentic, meaningful, and integrated, which stands in stark contrast to most traditional practices associated with vocabulary. To many, the word *vocabulary* may suggest a reductionist perspective in which words are learned by memorizing short definitions and sentences are understood in a strictly bottom-up fashion by putting together the meanings of individual words—a picture inconsistent with our current understanding of the reading process.

This chapter counters a reductionist perspective on vocabulary in two ways. In the first section of the chapter we discuss the complexity of word knowledge. In the second section we discuss how children gain information about words from context, word parts, and definitions, noting the limitations as well as the potential of each of these sources, and emphasizing the role of metalinguistic awareness in vocabulary learning.

THE COMPLEXITY OF WORD KNOWLEDGE

Any attempt to understand the processes by which children's vocabularies grow must be based on a recognition of the complexity of word knowledge. Five aspects of this complexity that have long been recognized by vocabulary researchers are: (a) incrementality—knowing a word is a matter of degrees, not all-or-nothing; (b) multidimensionality—word knowledge consists of several qualitatively different types of knowledge; (c) polysemy—words often have multiple meanings; (d) interrelatedness—one's knowledge of any given word is not independent of one's knowledge of other words; and (e) heterogeneity—what it means to know a word differs substantially depending on the kind of word. We consider these in turn.

Incrementality

Word learning is incremental—it takes place in many steps. In her classic research on early childhood language development, Eve Clark (1973, 1993) provided a detailed picture of how children's knowledge of word meanings is often initially incomplete but, over time, gradually approximates the adult understanding. Likewise, Susan Carey's (1978) seminal work on children's word learning distinguished between quick mapping (i.e., the initial establishment of a partial representation of a word meaning, sometimes on the basis of a single encounter) and extended mapping (i.e., the process of progressive refinement of word knowledge).

The incremental nature of word learning has sometimes been expressed in terms of a linear scale with several points. Dale (1965) proposed four stages: (1) never saw it before; (2) heard it but doesn't know what it means; (3) recognizes it in context as having something to do with ...; and (4) knows it well. A recent variation by Paribakht and Wesche (1997) is similar, but adds a fifth point: (5) I can use this word in a sentence.

Although such scales are a great improvement over an all-or-nothing picture of word knowledge, and serve as a useful basis for more sensitive assessments of word knowledge (Paribakht & Wesche, 1997), they are not intended to imply that there are only four or five discrete levels of word knowledge. In a series of experiments, Durso and Shore (1991) found that college undergraduates were able to distinguish between correct and incorrect uses of words, at a rate significantly greater than chance, even for words that they had previously judged not to be real English words at all. These results suggest that even at the lowest levels of word knowledge, within Dale's stage 1, there are measurable differences in word knowledge. At the other end of the scale, in a series of studies of high-quality vocabulary instruction, Beck, McKeown, and their colleagues (Beck, Perfetti, & McKeown, 1982; McKeown, Beck, Omanson, & Perfetti, 1983; McKeown, Beck, Omanson, & Pople, 1985) found that up to 40 instructional encounters with a word (and high-quality instruction at that) do not bring students to a ceiling.

An incremental view of word learning helps explain how a great deal of vocabulary knowledge can be gained incidentally from context, even when individual encounters with words in context are not particularly informative (Schatz & Baldwin, 1986). Several studies have used tests representing multiple levels of word knowledge to measure the amount of word knowledge readers gain when encountering words in natural context (Nagy, Herman, & Anderson, 1985; Schwanenflugel, Stahl, & McFalls, 1997; Stallman, 1991). If incidental learning from context could lead to only vague knowledge of words, one would expect the benefits of reading to be strongest for the most lenient criteria of word knowledge, and weaker or absent for more stringent criteria.

However, in all three of these studies, the amount of word learning observed was not significantly different for different levels of word knowledge.

The research is clear in showing that word learning *can* be incremental—that one's knowledge of a word can grow on the basis of almost infinitesimally small steps. Less is known about the extent to which word learning is *necessarily* incremental—that is, what limits may exist on the amount or type of knowledge that a learner can gain about a word on the basis of any single encounter. Although good instruction is unquestionably more efficient than chance incidental encounters for learning a specific set of words, there is still good reason to believe that there are practical, if not theoretical, limits to how much an individual can learn about a word on any given occasion. Even four instructional encounters of high quality do not lead to a level of word knowledge adequate to measurably improve comprehension of text containing the instructed word (McKeown et al., 1985). Other research on word learning (e.g., Gildea, Miller, & Wurtenberg, 1990) suggests that there are significant limitations on learners' ability to integrate information from multiple sources on any given occasion.

Polysemy

Words often have more than one meaning, and the more frequent a word is in the language, the more meanings it is likely to have. The simple fact that a word can have two or more unrelated meanings (e.g., *bear* meaning animal and *bear* meaning carry) adds substantial cognitive complexity to the task of using a dictionary (Miller & Gildea, 1987). Even more troublesome, at least to the theoretician, is the fact that the multiple meanings of words range from being completely unrelated to being so close that the shade of meaning separating the two may exist only in the mind of a compulsive lexicographer (Anderson & Nagy, 1991). In fact, word meanings are inherently flexible, and always nuanced in some way by the context in which they occur (Green, 1989; Nagy, 1997). The meaning of a word one encounters must be inferred from context, even if the word is already familiar, as in the phrase "a soft distant symphony of rushing wind" (Polacco, 1996, p. 25). In many cases, the required inferences are easy and natural, but figurative language is certainly not without its pitfalls for students (Ortony, Reynolds, & Arter, 1978; Winner, Engel, & Gardner, 1980). If vocabulary instruction is to address this aspect of the complexity of word knowledge, students must not only be taught to choose effectively among the multiple meanings of a word offered in dictionaries, but to expect words to be used with novel shades of meanings.

Multidimensionality

Discussions of the incremental nature of word learning sometimes appear to assume that word knowledge can be expressed in terms of a single dimension. For some purposes, it may be useful to conceptualize word knowledge in terms of a continuum ranging from "none" to "complete." However, it has long been recognized that word knowledge consists of multiple dimensions (Calfee & Drum, 1986; Cronbach, 1942; Kameenui, Dixon, & Carnine 1987; Richards, 1976). Nation (1990) offered eight aspects of word knowledge: knowledge of the word's spoken form, written form, grammatical behavior, collocational behavior (what other words does this word commonly occur with?), frequency, stylistic register, conceptual meaning, and associations with others words. Other versions of such a list (e.g., Laufer, 1998) distinguish among different types of relationships between words, such as morphological relationships (prefixation and suffixation) and semantic relationships (antonyms, synonyms), and further subcategorize meaning into referential (denotative) and affective (connotative). Graves (1986) distinguished different kinds of word learning tasks—learning new concepts, learning new labels for known concepts, and bringing words into students' productive vocabularies.

Various aspects of word knowledge might be reducible to a single continuum if one could show that there were strong implicational relations between them. However, it is unlikely that there are any absolute constraints governing the order in which different aspects of word knowledge are acquired. Everyday observation suggests that different facets of word knowledge are relatively independent: One student might know the definition for a word but not be able to use it properly in a sentence; another may use the word in seemingly appropriate ways and yet have a misunderstanding of its meaning. One person may recognize a word and yet have no understanding at all of what it means, whereas others (as was demonstrated by Durso and Shore, 1991) may not recall having ever seen a word before and yet have a partial understanding of its meaning.

In a recent study of learners of English as a second language, Schmitt (1998) found that one could not predict on the basis of one aspect of word knowledge what the learner's knowledge of another aspect would be. Thus, word knowledge must be characterized in terms of a number of different aspects which are at least partially independent. Furthermore, each of these is itself likely to be best characterized as a matter of degree.

Interrelatedness

Words are often taught and tested as if they were essentially isolated units of knowledge. Clearly such practice is inconsistent with a constructivist understanding of knowledge that emphasizes the importance of linking what is learned to familiar words and concepts. How well a person knows the meaning of *whale* depends in part on their understanding of *mammal*. A person who already knows the words *hot*, *cold*, and *cool* has already acquired some of the components of the word *warm*, even if the word *warm* has not yet been encountered.

The potential extent of interconnectedness in vocabulary knowledge is underscored by the Landauer and Dumais (1997) simulation of word learning from context. In their simulation, the input was 4.6 million words of text (in samples each about 150 words in length) from an electronic encyclopedia. A multidimensional vector was calculated for each word on the basis of its co-occurrence with other words in the sample texts. The simulation was evaluated by using the knowledge represented in these vectors to take a test of 80 items from the *Test of English as a Foreign Language* (TOEFL), a test commonly used to measure the English proficiency of international students studying in the United States. Interestingly, the Landauer and Dumais model got a score almost identical to the mean of a large sample of applicants to U.S. colleges from non-English-speaking countries.

One of the most striking findings of this study is the fact that as much as three fourths of the learning that resulted from the input of a segment of text was for words that were not even contained in that segment. At first glance, this finding seems counterintuitive. On the other hand, in the case of words obviously related in meaning, it is not difficult to understand how exposure to a text can contribute to one's knowledge of words not in the text. For example, reading a text about weaving might well increase one's understanding of the words *warp* and *woof* even if these words did not occur in the text. In the Landauer and Dumais (1997) simulation, computationally equivalent to a connectionist network, the information about any given word is represented throughout the entire network, and input about any single word can potentially change the configuration of relationships throughout the network. Although one must be cautious in extrapolating from this simulation to human learning, at very least it raises the possibility that the interconnectedness among words in human memory may be far greater than is commonly assumed, and certainly far greater than is represented in dictionary definitions.

Heterogeneity

Another type of complexity in word knowledge is the fact that what it means to know a word depends on what kind of word one is talking about. For example, knowing function words such as *the* or *if* is quite different from knowing terms such as *hypotenuse* or *ion*. The fact that the different dimensions of word knowledge are at least partially independent of each other also means that the same word can require different types of learning from different types of students, depending on what they already know about a word.

Implications of the Complexity of Word Knowledge

The complex picture of word knowledge we have outlined stands in sharp contrast to some of the traditional vocabulary instruction practices still being used in schools, although most of the points we have made have been acknowledged by vocabulary researchers for decades (e.g., Calfee & Drum, 1986; Cronbach, 1942; Richards, 1976). The knowledge that students have for many words is far more complex than could be attained through instruction that relies primarily on definitions. Not only are there too many words to teach them all to students one by one; there is too much to learn about each word to be covered by anything but exceptionally rich and multifaceted instruction. Hence, the complexity of word knowledge further bolsters the argument that much of students' vocabulary knowledge must be gained through means other than explicit vocabulary instruction. In those cases when students are dependent on instruction to learn a word, if they are to truly gain ownership of that word, the instruction must provide multiple and varied encounters with that word (Stahl & Fairbanks, 1986).

Although we believe it is important to recognize that only a small proportion of words that students learn can be covered in explicit vocabulary instruction, we want to stress an even more basic point: that knowing a word cannot be identified with knowing a definition. This point was argued at length by Anderson and Nagy (1991) in Volume II of the *Handbook*. Here we want to emphasize the point that word knowledge is primarily procedural rather than declarative, a matter of "knowing how" rather than "knowing that." Admittedly, there is a declarative component to at least some types of vocabulary knowledge. This seems especially true in the realm of technical or content-specific vocabulary; for example, if someone is not able to explain what *carbon dioxide* is, it is questionable that he or she knows the meaning of the word. On the other hand, for much nontechnical vocabulary, it may be more useful to conceptualize word knowledge as being primarily procedural. That is, knowing a word means being able to do things with it: To recognize it in connected speech or in print, to access its meaning, to pronounce it—and to be able to do these things within a fraction of a second. None of these processes is anything like remembering a verbal definition. In most cases, knowing a word is more like knowing how to use a tool than it is like being able to state a fact. Word knowledge is applied knowledge: A person who knows a word can recognize it, and use it, in novel contexts, and uses knowledge of the word, in combination with other types of knowledge, to construct a meaning for a text.

METALINGUISTIC DEMANDS OF WORD LEARNING

In traditional vocabulary instruction, students spend much of their time learning definitions (Watts, 1995). Such instruction is inconsistent with current understandings of the learning process. In the previous section of this chapter, we have outlined the dimensions of word knowledge that are rarely conveyed adequately in definitions. Another problem with memorizing definitions is the passive nature of the role it assigns to students. Teaching students new words by giving them definitions is the antithesis of a constructivist approach to learning.

If students are to take an active role in word learning, and assume increasing responsibility for their own vocabulary growth, they need at least some information about the nature of word knowledge and the processes by which it is acquired. That is, they need metacognitive and metalinguistic ability in the realm of word learning. In this section of the chapter, we describe some of the specific types of metalinguistic abilities that contribute to word learning.

Metalinguistic ability is the ability to reflect on and manipulate the structural features of language (Tunmer, Herriman, & Nesdale, 1988). It can be understood as a subcategory of metacognition, that is, the awareness of and control over one's cognitive processes. Recently, much attention has been devoted to a particular kind of metalinguistic ability, phonemic awareness (i.e., the ability to reflect on and manipulate phonemes, the individual units of sound out of which spoken words are constructed). However, other types of metalinguistic awareness, such as morphological awareness and syntactic awareness, are also believed to play an important role in reading (Carlisle, 1995; Tunmer et al., 1988; Tunmer, Nesdale, & Wright, 1987; Warren-Leubecker, 1987; Willows & Ryan, 1986).

A number of vocabulary researchers (e.g., Anderson & Nagy, 1992; Baumann & Kameenui, 1991; Graves, 1986) have held up the idea of "word awareness" or "word consciousness" as an important goal of vocabulary instruction. However, the exact nature of such awareness has seldom been explicated. We believe that word awareness, like word knowledge, is a complex and multifaceted construct, and that there are many ways in which students' awareness of language impacts their word learning. Understanding the metalinguistic demands of the vocabulary-related tasks students encounter in school provides insight into the surprising difficulties students often experience with these tasks.

Metalinguistic Awareness and Word Parts

The importance of phonemic awareness has been highlighted in a growing body of research on learning to read (see Blachman's chapter in this volume). In an alphabetic language like English, in which letters generally map onto phonemes, it is crucial that children are able to segment spoken words into phonemes and learn the mappings between these phonemes and the letters that represent them.

Recently, however, the contribution of morphological awareness to reading has drawn the attention of some researchers. Morphemes are meaningful word parts; for example, the word *walks* can be divided into two morphemes, *walk* and *s*. In those places where English orthography deviates from the phonemic principle, it is often in the direction of giving consistent representations to morphemes. For example, *ed* is pronounced differently in the words *helped, poured,* and *pleaded.* The less regular relationship between spelling and sound allows for a more consistent link from spelling to meaning. Only by noticing the shared morpheme in *sign* and *signature* can one make any sense of the spelling of the former. The fact that many of the apparent irregularities in English spelling are motivated by morphological relationships suggests that awareness of these relationships may contribute to spelling and reading ability. And, in fact, it has been found that morphological awareness makes a significant contribution to reading ability, even when phonemic awareness has been taken into account (Carlisle, 1995; Carlisle & Nomanbhoy, 1993). Knowledge of morphology is likewise correlated with reading ability into high school (Nagy, Diakidoy, & Anderson, 1993).

It is hard to overstate the importance of morphology in vocabulary growth. Nagy and Anderson (1984) estimated that about 60% of the new words a student encounters in reading are analyzable into parts that give substantial help in figuring out their meaning. Anglin's (1993) study of children's vocabulary growth showed that between first and fifth grade, the number of root words known by children in his study increased by around 4,000 words. In the same time period, the number of derived (prefixed or suffixed) words known by students increases by about 14,000 words. There is a veritable explosion in children's knowledge of derived words, especially between third and fifth grades. As Anglin noted, the bulk of this increase appears to reflect morphological problem solving, that is, interpreting new words by breaking them down into their component morphemes.

There is reason to believe that effective use of morphology in word learning depends on metalinguistic sophistication that continues to develop through high school. Most children presumably achieve the basic morphological insight—that longer words can often be broken down into shorter words or pieces that give clues to their meanings—before fourth grade (Anglin, 1993; Tyler & Nagy, 1989). However, word structure in English is complex, and there is development in children's knowledge of word formation processes at least through high school (Nagy et al., 1993; Nagy & Scott, 1990; Tyler & Nagy, 1989)

English and Spanish share many cognates—word pairs such as English *tranquil* and Spanish *tranquilo* that are similar in spelling, pronunciation, and meaning. Recognizing such relationships must depend on abilities similar to those required to recognize morphological relationships in English. Many pairs of morphologically related words in English likewise involve changes in spelling and pronunciation as well as shifts in meaning—for example, *divide/division, sane/sanity, combine/combination, respond/responsible*. Hancin-Bhatt and Nagy (1994) found that Spanish–English bilingual students' ability to recognize such relations increased far more dramatically between fourth and eighth grade than did their vocabulary knowledge in either Spanish or English. These results suggest that the ability to see morphological relationships that are partially obscured by changes in spelling and pronunciation may depend on metalinguistic sensitivities that develop, or at least increase substantially, after fourth grade.

It should also be noted that some aspects of morphological knowledge are closely related to syntactic awareness. In particular, learning the meanings of derivational suffixes (e.g., *-tion, -ness, -ly*) requires reflecting on the syntactic role of the suffixed word in the sentence (see Nagy et al., 1993).

Not surprisingly, there are differences of opinion about the contribution of morphological knowledge to reading and vocabulary growth. Some (e.g., Nation, 1990) note the irregularities of English morphology (what does *casualty* have to do with *casual*, or *emergency* with *emerge*?) and suggest that students should only consider morphological clues after they have first used context to make a hypothesis about the meaning of a word. However, the vast majority of words composed of more than one morpheme are semantically transparent—that is, their meanings are largely predictable on the basis of the meanings of their parts (Nagy & Anderson, 1984). The fact that some words (like *casualty*) are irregular indicates, not that word parts are useless as clues, but that readers must be strategic and flexible in their use of potential sources of information about words.

Metalinguistic Awareness and Use of Context

Context and morphology (word parts) are the two major sources of information immediately available to a reader who comes across a new word. Effective use of context, like effective use of morphology, requires some level of metalinguistic awareness.

Tunmer and his colleagues (Gough & Tunmer, 1986; Tunmer, 1990; Tunmer et al., 1988) argued that syntactic awareness (i.e., the ability to reflect on and manipulate the order of words in a sentence) contributes to reading ability in at least two ways. First of all, developing one's reading vocabulary depends on both phonological recoding and context, because phonological recoding alone cannot always uniquely determine the pronunciation of a word; context is sometimes necessary to determine which of several possible sounds a letter may represent. Effective use of context is, in turn, hypothesized to rely on syntactic awareness. Second, syntactic awareness may help the reader monitor comprehension.

Gottardo, Stanovich, and Siegel (1996), on the other hand, claimed that syntactic awareness does not make an independent contribution to reading, above and beyond the contribution represented by short-term, phonological memory. That is, correlations between reading difficulty and deficient syntactic awareness may arise as epiphenomena of deficiencies in phonological processing (p. 563). Although not denying the importance of phonological processing in reading difficulties, we believe that several types of evidence suggest a direct link between syntactic awareness and reading comprehension.

First of all, syntactic awareness training has been shown to improve reading comprehension (Kennedy & Weener, 1974; Weaver, 1979). Likewise, training studies in the use of context (e.g., Buikema & Graves, 1993; Jenkins, Matlock, & Slocum, 1989; see Kuhn & Stahl, 1998 for a review) have resulted in increases in children's ability to learn words. The relative brevity of most such interventions makes it likely that the benefits reflect increased metalinguistic and metacognitive awareness rather than gains in short-term phonological memory.

Second, it could be argued that the verbal working memory task used by Gottardo et al. (1996) includes a component of metalinguistic awareness. Subjects were asked to make true–false judgments about simple statements (e.g., fish swim in the sky), and their score on these judgments was incorporated into the verbal working memory score. After listening to a set of sentences, they were asked to recall the final word of each sentence in the set. To do this, subjects must pay attention to the surface form of the sentence, rather than its meaning, a task that requires conscious attention to word order, that is, syntactic awareness.

Third, there is evidence that the contribution of syntactic awareness and other components of metalinguistic awareness to reading comprehension, relative to that of phonological awareness, increases with grade level (Roth, Speece, Cooper, & De la Paz, 1996).

The most convincing evidence that syntactic awareness contributes to effective use of context comes from examining the protocols of students attempting to infer the meanings of novel words from context. In Werner and Kaplan's (1952) classic study of inferring word meanings from context, children were given a series of sentences containing a nonsense word and asked to infer its meaning. Here are the responses from an 11-year-old boy (p. 16; the word *hudray* was intended to mean "grow" or "increase"):

Sentence 1: If you eat well and sleep well you will hudray.
Response: Feel good.
Sentence 2: Mrs. Smith wanted to hudray her family.
Response: Mrs. Smith wanted to make her family feel good.
Sentence 3: Jane had to hudray the cloth so that the dress would fit Mary.
Response: Jane makes the dress good to fit Mary so Mary feels good.

These responses show that this child is willing to ignore the syntactic structure of the sentences (especially sentence 3) in order to maintain his original hypothesis about the word's meaning. McKeown's (1985) study of high- and low-ability readers learning from context likewise included examples of responses that appear to reflect lack of attention to the syntactic role of the target word in the sentence.

Does use of context to learn the meanings of new words always require metalinguistic awareness? Presumably not; the rapid vocabulary acquisition of very young children takes place at an age when many aspects of metalinguistic awareness are not measurably present. However, a distinction must be made between incidental learning of word meanings from context and deriving word meanings. The latter process is usually examined by asking students to come up with, or select, an appropriate meaning for an unfamiliar word with the context available. Such a task is likely to be more metacognitively and metalinguistically demanding than incidental word learning. This may account for the fact that studies of truly incidental word learning have often found no significant effects of verbal ability (e.g., Nagy, Anderson, & Herman, 1987; Nagy et al., 1985; Stahl, 1989; Stallman, 1991), whereas studies of deriving word meaning have generally found large ability effects (e.g., Jenkins, Stein, & Wysocki, 1984; Daneman & Green, 1986; McKeown, 1985; Sternberg & Powell, 1983).

The research on learning words from context clearly documents the fact that chances of learning very much about a word from any single encounter with that word in natural context are very slim (Beck, McKeown, & McCaslin, 1983; Nagy et al., 1987; Schatz & Baldwin, 1986). It is extremely important for teachers to recognize that although context may be a "natural" means of word learning, it is not especially effective in the short run. Likewise, it is important for students to have realistic expectations about the amount of information they can gain from context. Training students on artificially helpful contexts may actually decrease their effectiveness at using the contextual clues available in natural text (Kranzer, 1988).

Metalinguistic Awareness and the Use of Definitions

The chief strength of definitions is that they provide explicit information about word meanings that is normally only implicit in context. If you want a student to know what a particular word means, explaining it is unquestionably more effective than waiting for the student to encounter it numerous times in context.

One of the chief weaknesses of definitions is their failure to provide information about usage that is accessible to school children. Miller and Gildea (1987) studied sentences children generated when given definitions of unfamiliar words, and concluded that this widely used task, although it reveals interesting things about children's processing of definitions, is pedagogically useless. Children's difficulty with this task may stem in part from the often convoluted language of definitions, but even clearly written definitions do not guarantee success. McKeown (1993) carefully revised definitions to make them both more accurate and more clear to students and found that the revised definitions were significantly superior to their original dictionary counterparts in terms of students' ability to apply knowledge of their meanings. There was also an effect on usage: Only 25% of the sentences generated from the original definitions were judged acceptable, whereas 50% of the sentences generated from the revised definitions were acceptable. This is a substantial increase, but it is also a striking demonstration of the fact that even definitions of very high quality are often inadequate as sources of information on usage.

Students sometimes have trouble extracting even a general idea of the meaning of a word from a definition (Scott & Nagy, 1997). Some of the difficulty may stem from lack of familiarity with the conventions of traditional definitions, but changing the format and style of definitions does not necessarily increase their usefulness to students (Fischer, 1990, 1994; Scott & Nagy, 1997). A bigger problem appears to be the metacognitive and metalinguistic demands of using definitions.

Scott and Nagy (1997), following up on Miller and Gildea's (1987) study, found that the difficulty experienced by children in interpreting definitions was primarily due to their failure to take the syntax, or structure, of definitions into account. Their errors could be best characterized as selecting a salient fragment of the definition as representing the meaning of the whole word.

There are two metalinguistic dimensions to these errors. One is a lack of sensitivity to syntactic structure. In analyzing think-aloud protocols of children attempting to integrate information from definitions with sentences containing the word defined, Scott (1991) found a common problem was failure to take part of speech into account. It wasn't clear whether the failure was in the analysis of the sentence, or in the analysis of the definition, but lack of attention to syntax was obviously a major factor.

Another aspect of metalinguistic awareness involved in children's understanding of definitions has to do with their concept of definition. Fischer's (1990; 1994) investigation of German high school students use of bilingual dictionary definitions suggested that the students approached the task with the expectation of finding simple synonyms. It may be natural for students of a second language as similar to their first as English is to German to expect one-to-one mappings between words. Language instruction may contribute to such expectations. However, true synonyms are rare, both within and between languages.

The Concept of Word

We have just described some of the ways that metalinguistic awareness contributes to students' independent word learning—their use of word parts, context, and definitions. However, metalinguistic awareness contributes to vocabulary learning at an even more fundamental level. Almost any conceivable vocabulary activity requires children to talk and think about words and their meanings; that is, it presupposes the metalinguistic concept of word. This concept is more complex and more problematic than is commonly recognized. In fact, research on the acquisition of this concept suggests that, even in the middle elementary grades, it cannot be taken completely for granted.

Roberts (1992) documented the gradual nature of children's development of the concept of *word*. Five-year-old preschoolers have trouble dissociating a word from its referent; when asked which is the bigger word, *caterpillar* or *dog*, they will usually answer *dog*. In Roberts's study, even third-grade students were not all at ceiling in her measures of their understanding of the concept of word.

Bowey and Tunmer (1984) pointed out that there are three requirements for full awareness of the concept of word: (a) awareness of the word as a unit of language, (b) awareness of the word as an arbitrary phonological label, and (c) comprehension of the metalinguistic term *word*. In a review of research on metalinguistic awareness, Gombert (1992) argued that there is no clear evidence for the existence of these abilities before the age of 7 years (p. 80). Likewise, there is evidence that some of these requirements are not fully present in children up to the age of at least 10. Piaget (1926) claimed that children did not recognize words as a simple sign (i.e., as an arbitrary label) until the age of 9 or 10. Berthoud-Papandropolou (1980; cited in Gombert, 1992), investigating children's ability to segment sentences into words, concluded that children younger than 11 did not consistently reach 100% accuracy.

Understanding the Function of Vocabulary in Decontextualized Language

The language young children most commonly experience is contextualized—that is, it is language about, and embedded in, a shared context. In a face-to-face conversation, the speakers share a physical context, use gesture and intonation, and make many assumptions about shared knowledge, experiences, and beliefs. They are able to communicate effectively in words that would not necessarily be understood by someone who had access only to a transcript of the conversation. Written language—and especially language written for an audience not present and not personally known to the writer—tends to be decontextualized; that is, the success of the communication relies more heavily on the language itself, and less on shared knowledge or context (Snow, 1991, 1994). What contextualized language accomplishes through gesture, intonation, and allusions to shared knowledge and experiences, decontextualized language must accomplish primarily through precision in choice of words (Chafe & Danielewicz, 1987). This is one of the reasons why written language, which is typically decontextualized, tends to use a far richer vocabulary than oral language, which is typically contextualized (Hayes, 1988).

Not all oral language is contextualized. Storytellers use language to create a world distinct from the here-and-now context, in which the language alone carries most of the communicative burden. But many children, especially if they have not been read to very much, may come to school having had relatively little experience with decontextualized language. Not surprisingly, facility with decontextualized language is related to children's reading ability (Snow, 1991, 1994; Snow, Cancino, Gonzales, & Shriberg, 1989).

Because decontextualized language contains richer vocabulary, exposure to such language is important for children's vocabulary growth. However, we would like to suggest that children's vocabulary growth is benefited not just by exposure to decontextualized language, but by an appreciation of the role that vocabulary plays in such language. Precision of word choice is seldom crucial in everyday conversation, but it is the primary communicative tool of the writer. The motivation to learn the richer vocabulary of decontextualized language may depend on a student's feel for the difference between the communicative strategies of speakers and writers. Scott, working with a group of teacher-researchers, found that conscious attention to words and word choice helped students' writing, led to critical analysis of authors' writing, and changed the way teachers taught both reading and writing (Scott, Asselin, Henry, & Butler, 1997; Scott, Blackstone, Cross, Jones, Skobel, Wells, & Jensen, 1996; Scott, Butler, & Asselin, 1996; Scott & Wells, 1998). Research on the long-term impact of such instruction on students' vocabulary growth is still needed.

CONCLUSION

Any type of learning, if examined closely enough, looks so complex that one wonders how children can do it at all. In this chapter, we have tried to convey some of the complexity of the processes involved in vocabulary acquisition.

For many children, of course, vocabulary growth appears to proceed with astonishing ease and rapidity. Beck and McKeown (1991), comparing previously published figures, estimated that average children learn words at a rate of something like 2,500 to 3,000 words a year. More conservative accounts put the figure at 1,000 words a year (Goulden, Nation, & Read, 1990; D'Anna, Zechmeister, & Hall, 1991). We have argued elsewhere at length (Anderson & Nagy, 1992; Nagy, 1998) why we consider these latter estimates unrealistically low. Anglin (1993) conducted a major study of children's vocabulary growth between first and fifth grade that helped clarify the nature of the differences between conflicting estimates. Given a conservative definition of vocabulary—counting only root words—Anglin found a rate of growth identical to that reported by Goulden et al. (1990) and D'Anna et al. (1991). However, using a more inclusive concept of "psychologically basic vocabulary"—including, for example, idioms and derived words for which there was no evidence that children used morphological analysis—Anglin (1993) arrived at an estimate in the range suggested by Beck and McKeown (1991). In their commentary on Anglin's work, Miller and Wakefield (1993) argued that Anglin's figures should be doubled.

Regardless of exactly where the truth lies within this range of estimates, we are left with a paradox. At least some children learn 2,000 or more new words per year, most of these apart from explicit instruction. Is the complexity and difficulty of the vocabulary acquisition processes presented in this chapter illusory?

We believe not. The high rates of vocabulary growth seen in many children occur only through immersion in massive amounts of rich written and oral language. Students who need help most in the area of vocabulary—those whose home experience has not given them a substantial foundation in the vocabulary of literate and academic English—need to acquire words at a pace even faster than that of their peers, but by no means do they always find this process easy or automatic.

Vocabulary researchers concerned with second language learning have argued that "natural" vocabulary acquisition is simply not efficient enough to produce the desired rates of learning. Natural context is not an especially rich source of information about word meanings. If there are particular words one wants a student to learn, free reading is perhaps the least effective means available. However, presenting students with more concentrated information about words introduces another set of difficulties. We have outlined two major categories of such difficulties in this chapter. The first is the complexity of word meanings. Definitions, the traditional means of offering concentrated information about words to students, do not contain the quantity or quality of information that constitutes true word knowledge. Students can gain some word knowledge from definitions, but generally only if they are given other types of information about the word (e.g., examples of how it is used) and opportunities to apply this information in meaningful tasks (Stahl, 1986; Stahl & Fairbanks, 1986). Some types of words (e.g., verbs and abstract nouns) may be more difficult to learn from definitions than others (e.g., concrete nouns).

A second major type of difficulty is the metalinguistic sophistication that is presupposed by most vocabulary-related school tasks. Vocabulary activities at every grade level require metalinguistic abilities and awareness that cannot be taken for granted on the part of students. In the early elementary grades, even fundamental concepts about words as units of form and meaning are still in the process of being consolidated. Independent word learning strategies rely on metalinguistic knowledge that is still developing during the upper elementary grades.

A recent study on the development of phonemic awareness (Scarborough, Ehri, Olson, & Fowler, 1998) shows that this aspect of metalinguistic awareness, which impacts the earliest stages of formal reading instruction, does not appear to reach a ceiling among college students. Given the complex nature of word knowledge, we feel safe in predicting that the various aspects of metalinguistic awareness involved in word learning will not be fully present even in many adults.

We believe that the role of metalinguistic awareness in vocabulary growth offers a promising area for future research. Although there is substantial research support for the broad outlines of the picture of vocabulary processes that we have drawn in this chapter, there are also large areas of uncharted territory. Roberts's (1992) article on children's development of the concept of word is one of the few examples of research explicitly addressing the metalinguistic foundations of vocabulary learning in the literature on literacy research. No one, to our knowledge, has addressed the effects of varying levels of metalinguistic awareness on children's ability to profit from different types of vocabulary instruction or from different types of information about words. There is also need for research examining the effects of instruction that fosters word consciousness on students' vocabulary growth.

If students are to become active and independent learners in the area of vocabulary, they need to have some understanding of the territory that they are operating in. Such an understanding depends on explanations by teachers who themselves have some grasp of the complexity of word knowledge. Students' understanding of words and of the word learning process also depends on the type of vocabulary instruction they experience. A diet of synonyms and short glossary definitions runs the danger of failing to produce usable knowledge of those words, and creates simplistic beliefs that can interfere with future word learning. The quality of vocabulary instruction must therefore be judged, not just on whether it produces immediate gains in students' understanding of specific words, but also on whether it communicates an accurate picture of the nature of word knowledge and reasonable expectations about the word learning process.

REFERENCES

Anderson, R. C., & Freebody, P. (1981). Vocabulary knowledge. In J. Guthrie (Ed.), *Comprehension and teaching: Research reviews* (pp. 77–117). Newark, DE: International Reading Association.

Anderson, R. C., & Nagy, W. (1991). Word meanings. In R. Barr, M. Kamil, P. Mosenthal, & P. D. Pearson (Eds.), *Handbook of reading research* (Vol. II, pp. 690–724). White Plains, NY: Longman.

Anderson, R. C., & Nagy, W. (1992). The vocabulary conundrum. *American Educator, 16,* 14–18, 44–47.

Anglin, J. M. (1993). Vocabulary development: A morphological analysis. *Monographs for the Society of Research in Child Development,* Serial No. 238, Vol. 58, No. 10.

Baumann, J. F., & Kameenui, E. J. (1991). Research on vocabulary: Ode to Voltaire. In J. Flood, J. Jensen, D. Lapp, & J. Squire (Eds.), *Handbook of research on teaching the English language arts* (pp. 604–632). New York: Macmillan.

Beck, I., & McKeown, M. (1991). Conditions of vocabulary acquisition. In R. Barr, M. Kamil, P. Mosenthal, & P. D. Pearson (Eds.), *Handbook of reading research* (Vol. II, pp. 789–814). White Plains, NY: Longman.

Beck, I., McKeown, M., & McCaslin, E. (1983). All contexts are not created equal. *Elementary School Journal, 83,* 177–181.

Beck, I., Perfetti, C., & McKeown, M. (1982). Effects of long-term vocabulary instruction on lexical access and reading comprehension. *Journal of Educational Psychology, 74,* 506–521.

Bowey, J., & Tunmer, W. E. (1984). Development of children's understanding of the metalinguistic term word. *Journal of Educational Psychology, 76*(3), 500–512.

Buikema, J., & Graves, M. (1993). Teaching students to use context cues to infer word meanings. *Journal of Reading, 36,* 450–457.

Calfee, R. C., & Drum, P. (1986). Research on teaching reading. In M. C. Wittrock (Ed.), *Handbook of research on teaching* (pp. 804–849). New York: Macmillan.

Carey, S. (1978). The child as word learner. In M. Halle, J. Bresnan, & G. Miller (Eds.), *Linguistic theory and psychological reality* (pp. 264–293). Cambridge, MA: MIT Press.

Carlisle, J. (1995). Morphological awareness and early reading achievement. In L. Feldman (Ed.), *Morphological aspects of language processing* (pp. 189–209) Hillsdale, NJ: Lawrence Erlbaum Associates.

Carlisle, J., & Nomanbhoy, D. (1993). Phonological and morphological awareness in first graders. *Applied Psycholinguistics, 14,* 177–195.

Cassidy, J., & Wenrich, J. (1997). What's hot, what's not for 1997. *Reading Today, 14*(4), 34.

Cassidy, J., & Wenrich, J. (1998). What's hot, what's not for 1998. *Reading Today, 15*(4), 1, 28.

Chafe, W., & Danielewicz, J. (1987). Properties of spoken and written language. In R. Horowitz & S. J. Samuels (Eds.), *Comprehending oral and written language* (pp. 83–113). San Diego, CA: Academic Press.

Clark, E. V. (1973). What's in a word? On the child's acquisition of semantics in his first language. In T. E. Moore (Ed.), *Cognitive development and the acquisition of language* (pp. 65–110.) New York: Academic Press.

Clark, E. V. (1993). *The lexicon in acquisition.* Cambridge: Cambridge University Press.

Coady, J., & Huckin, T. (1997). *Second language vocabulary acquisition.* Cambridge: Cambridge University Press.

Cronbach, L. J. (1942). An analysis of techniques for diagnostic vocabulary testing. *Journal of Educational Research, 36,* 206–217.

D'Anna, C. A., Zechmeister, E. B., & Hall, J. W. (1991). Toward a meaningful definition of vocabulary size. *Journal of Reading Behavior, 23,* 109–122.

Dale, E. (1965). Vocabulary measurement: Techniques and major findings. *Elementary English, 42,* 82–88.

Daneman, M., & Green, I. (1986). Individual differences in comprehending and producing words in context. *Journal of Memory and Language, 25,* 1–18.

Davis, F. B. (1944). Fundamental factors in reading comprehension. *Psychometrika, 9,* 185–197.

Durso, F. T., & Shore, W. J. (1991). Partial knowledge of word meanings. *Journal of Experimental Psychology: General, 120,* 190–202.

Fischer, U. (1990). *How students learn words from a dictionary and in context.* Unpublished doctoral dissertation, Princeton University.

Fischer, U. (1994). Learning words from context and dictionaries: An experimental comparison. *Applied Psycholinguistics, 15,* 551–574.

Gildea, P., Miller, G. & Wurtenberg, C. (1990). Contextual enrichment by videodisk. In D. Nix & R. Spiro (Eds.), *Cognition, education, and multimedia: Exploring ideas in high technology* (pp. 1–29). Hillsdale, NJ: Lawrence Erlbaum Associates.

Gombert, J. (1992). *Metalinguistic development.* Chicago, University of Chicago Press.

Gottardo, A., Stanovich, K., & Siegel, L. (1996). The relationships between phonological sensitivity, syntactic processing, and verbal working memory in the reading performance of third grade children. *Journal of Experimental Child Psychology, 63,* 563–582.

Gough, P., & Tunmer, W. E. (1986). Decoding, reading, and reading ability. *Remedial and Special Education, 7,* 6–10.

Goulden, R., Nation, P., & Read, J. (1990). How large can a receptive vocabulary be? *Applied Linguistics, 11,* 341–363.

Graves, M. F. (1986). Vocabulary learning and instruction. In E. Z. Rothkopf & L.C. Ehri (Eds.), *Review of research in education* (Vol. 13, pp. 49–89). Washington, DC: American Educational Research Association.

Green, G. M. (1989). *Pragmatics and natural language understanding.* Hillsdale, NJ: Lawrence Erlbaum Associates.

Hancin-Bhatt, B., & Nagy, W. (1994) Lexical transfer and second language morphological development. *Applied Psycholinguistics 15,* 289–310.

Hayes, D. (1988). Speaking and writing: Distinct patterns of word choice. *Journal of Memory and Language, 27,* 572–585.

Jenkins, J. R., Matlock, B., & Slocum, T. A. (1989). Two approaches to vocabulary instruction: The teaching of individual word meanings and practice in deriving word meaning from context. *Reading Research Quarterly, 24,* 215–235.

Jenkins, J. R., Stein, M. L., & Wysocki, K. (1984). Learning vocabulary through reading. *American Educational Research Journal, 21,* 767–787.

Kameenui, E. J., Dixon, D. W., & Carnine, R. C. (1987). Issues in the design of vocabulary instruction. In M. G. McKeown & M. E. Curtis (Eds.), *The nature of vocabulary acquisition* (pp. 129–145). Hillsdale, NJ: Lawrence Erlbaum Associates.

Kennedy, D., & Weener, P. (1974). Visual and auditory training with the cloze procedure to improve reading and listening comprehension. *Reading Research Quarterly, 8,* 524–541.

Kranzer, K. G. (1988). *A study of the effects of instruction on incidental word learning and on the ability to derive word meaning from context.* Unpublished doctoral dissertation, University of Delaware.

Kuhn, M., & Stahl, S. (1998). Teaching children to learn word meanings from context: A synthesis and some questions. *Journal of Literacy Research, 30,* 119–138.

Landauer, T., & Dumais, S. (1997). A solution to Plato's problem: The Latent Semantic Analysis theory of acquisition, induction, and representation of knowledge. *Psychological Review, 104,* 211–240.

Laufer, B. (1998). What's in a word that makes it hard or easy: Some intralexical factors that affect the learning of words. In N. Schmitt & M. McCarthy (Eds.), *Vocabulary: Description, acquisition and pedagogy* (pp. 140–155). Cambridge: Cambridge University Press.

McKeown, M. (1985). The acquisition of word meaning from context by children of high and low ability. *Reading Research Quarterly, 20,* 482–496.

McKeown, M. (1993). Creating definitions for young word learners. *Reading Research Quarterly, 28,* 16–33.

McKeown, M., Beck, I., Omanson, R., & Perfetti, C. (1983). The effects of long-term vocabulary instruction on reading comprehension: A replication. *Journal of Reading Behavior, 15,* 3–18.

McKeown, M., Beck., I., Omanson, R., & Pople, M. (1985). Some effects of the nature and frequency of vocabulary instruction on the knowledge and use of words. *Reading Research Quarterly, 20,* 522–535.

Miller, G., & Gildea, P. (1987). How children learn words. *Scientific American, 257,* 94–99.

Miller, G., & Wakefield, P. (1993). On Anglin's analysis of vocabulary growth. *Monographs of the Society for Research in Child Development,* Serial No. 238, Vol. 58, pp. 167–175.

Nagy, W. (1997). On the role of context in first- and second-language vocabulary learning. In N. Schmitt & M. McCarthy (Eds.), *Vocabulary: Description, acquisition and pedagogy* (pp. 64–83). Cambridge: Cambridge University Press.

Nagy, W., & Anderson, R. C. (1984). How many words are there in printed school English? *Reading Research Quarterly, 19,* 304–330.

Nagy, W., Anderson, R. C., & Herman, P. (1987). Learning word meanings from context during normal reading. *American Educational Research Journal, 24,* 237–270.

Nagy, W., Diakidoy, I. & Anderson, R. C. (1993). The acquisition of morphology: Learning the contribution of suffixes to the meanings of derivatives. *Journal of Reading Behavior, 25,* 155–170.

Nagy, W., García, G. E., Durgunoglu, A., & Hancin-Bhatt, B. (1993). Spanish-English bilingual students' use of cognates in English reading. *Journal of Reading Behavior, 25,* 241–259.

Nagy, W., Herman, P., & Anderson, R. (1985). Learning words from context. *Reading Research Quarterly, 20,* 233–253.

Nagy, W. E., & Scott, J. A. (1990). Word schemas: Expectations about the form and meaning of new words. *Cognition and Instruction, 7,* 105–127.

Nation, I. S. P. (1990). *Teaching and learning vocabulary.* New York: Newbury House.

Ortony, A., Reynolds, R., & Arter, J. (1978). Metaphor: Theoretical and empirical research. *Psychological Bulletin, 85,* 919–943.

Paribakht, T. S., & Wesche, M. (1997). Vocabulary enhancement activities and reading for meaning in second language vocabulary acquisition. In J. Coady & T. Huckin (Eds.), *Second language vocabulary acquisition* (pp. 174–200). Cambridge: Cambridge University Press.

Piaget, J. (1926). *The language and thought of the child* (M. Worden, Trans.). New York: Harcourt, Brace, & World.

Polacco, P. (1996). *I can hear the sun: A modern myth.* New York: Philomel.

Richards, J. (1976). The role of vocabulary teaching. *TESOL Quarterly, 10,* 77–89.

Roberts, B. (1992). The evolution of the young child's concept of word as a unit of spoken and written language. *Reading Research Quarterly, 27,* 124–138

Roth, F., Speece, D., Cooper, D., & De la Paz, S. (1996). Unresolved mysteries: How do metalinguistic and narrative skills connect with early reading? *Journal of Special Education, 30,* 257–277.

Ruddell, M. R. (1994). Vocabulary knowledge and comprehension: A comprehension-process view of complex literary relationships. In R. Ruddell, M. R. Ruddell, & H. Singer (Eds.), *Theoretical models and processes of reading* (4th ed., pp. 414–447). Newark, DE: International Reading Association.

Scarborough, H., Ehri, L., Olson, R., & Fowler, A. (1998). The fate of phonemic awareness beyond the elementary school years. *Scientific Studies of Reading, 2,* 115–142.

Schatz, E. K., & Baldwin, R. S. (1986). Context clues are unreliable predictors of word meanings. *Reading Research Quarterly, 21,* 439–453.

Schmitt, N. (1998). Tracking the incremental acquisition of second language vocabulary: A longitudinal study. *Language Learning, 48*(2), 281–317.

Schmitt, N. & McCarthy, M. (Eds.). (1997). *Vocabulary: Description, acquisition, and pedagogy.* Cambridge: Cambridge University Press.

Schwanenflugel, P., Stahl, S., & McFalls, E. (1997). Partial word knowledge and vocabulary growth during reading comprehension. *Journal of Literacy Research, 29,* 531–553.

Scott, J. (1991). *Using definitions to understand new words.* Unpublished doctoral dissertation, University of Illinois at Urbana-Champaign.

Scott, J., Asselin, M., Henry, S., & Butler, C. (1997, June). *Making rich language visible: Reports from a multi-dimensional study on word learning.* Paper presented at the annual meeting of the Canadian Society for the Study of Education, Newfoundland.

Scott, J., Blackstone, T., Cross, S., Jones, A., Skobel, B., Wells, J., & Jensen, Y. (1996, May). *The power of language: Creating contexts which enrich children's understanding and use of words.* A micro-workshop presented at the 41st annual convention of the International Reading Association, New Orleans, LA.

Scott, J., Butler, C., & Asselin, M. (1996, December). *The effect of mediated assistance in word learning.* Paper presented at the 46th annual meeting of the National Reading Conference, Charleston, SC.

Scott, J., & Nagy, W. (1997). Understanding the definitions of unfamiliar verbs. *Reading Research Quarterly, 32,* 184–200.

Scott, J., & Wells, J. (1998). Readers take responsibility: Literature circles and the growth of critical thinking. In K. Beers & B. Samuels (Eds.), *Into focus: Middle school readers* (pp. 177–197). Norwood, MA: Christopher-Gordon.

Snow, C. (1991). The theoretical basis for relationships between language and literacy development. *Journal of Research in Childhood Education, 6,* 5–10.

Snow, C. (1994). What is so hard about learning to read? A pragmatic analysis. In J. Duchan, L. Hewitt, & R. Sonnenmeier (Eds.), *Pragmatics: From theory to practice* (pp. 164–184). Englewood Cliffs, NJ: Prentice Hall.

Snow, C., Cancino, H., Gonzales, P., & Shriberg, E. (1989). Giving formal definitions: An oral language correlate of school literacy. In D. Bloome (Ed.), *Literacy in classrooms* (pp. 233–249). Norwood, NJ: Ablex.

Stahl, S. (1986). Three principles of effective vocabulary instruction. *Journal of Reading, 29,* 662–668.

Stahl, S. (1989). Task variations and prior knowledge in learning word meanings from context. In S. McCormick & J. Zutell (Eds.), *Cognitive and social perspectives for literacy research and instruction. Thirty-eighth yearbook of the National Reading conference* (pp. 197–204). Chicago: National Reading Conference.

Stahl, S., & Fairbanks, M. (1986). The effects of vocabulary instruction: A model-based meta-analysis. *Review of Educational Research, 56,* 72–110.

Stallman, A. (1991). *Learning vocabulary from context: Effects of focusing attention on individual words during reading.* Unpublished doctoral dissertation, University of Illinois at Urbana-Champaign.

Sternberg, R., & Powell, J. S. (1983). Comprehending verbal comprehension *American Psychologist, 38,* 878–893.

Tunmer, W. E. (1990). The role of language prediction skills in beginning reading. *New Zealand Journal of Educational Studies, 25,* 95–114.

Tunmer, W. E., Herriman, M., & Nesdale, A. (1988). Metalinguistic abilities and beginning reading. *Reading Research Quarterly, 23,* 134–158.

Tunmer, W. E., Nesdale, A. R., & Wright, A. D. (1987). Syntactic awareness and reading acquisition. *British Journal of Developmental Psychology, 5,* 25–34.

Tyler, A., & Nagy, W. (1989). The acquisition of English derivational morphology. *Journal of Verbal Learning and Verbal Behavior, 14,* 638–647.

Warren-Leubecker, A. (1987). Competence and performance factors in word order awareness and early reading. *Journal of Experimental Child Psychology, 43*(1), 62–80.

Watts, S. M. (1995). Vocabulary instruction during reading lessons in six classrooms. *Journal of Reading Behavior, 27*, 399–424.

Weaver, P. (1979). Improving reading instruction: Effects of sentence organization instruction. *Reading Research Quarterly, 15*, 127–146.

Werner, H., & Kaplan, E. (1952). The acquisition of word meanings: A developmental study. *Monographs of the Society of Research in Child Development*, Vol. 15, Serial 51(1).

Willows, D., & Ryan, E. B. (1986). The development of grammatical sensitivity and its relationship to early reading achievement. *Reading Research Quarterly, 21*, 253–266.

Winner, E., Engel, M., & Gardner, H. (1980). Misunderstanding metaphor: What's the problem? *Journal of Experimental Child Psychology, 30*, 22–32.

CHAPTER 19

Learning From Text: A Multidimensional and Developmental Perspective

Patricia A. Alexander
University of Maryland

Tamara L. Jetton
James Madison University

Three students, preparing to read and discuss a chapter from Mark Twain's The Adventures of Huckleberry Finn, sit in a literature circle and hope that their attempts to learn from this novel prove successful. One of the students, Ralph, has been struggling because the world of Huck Finn seems alien to him. He does not understand why Huck Finn finds the river a place of escape and freedom because he knows rivers only from glimpses from the family car. He also finds the language of the runaway slave, Jim, strange. Despite these impediments, Ralph is fascinated with the character of Huck Finn and the interesting predicaments that Huck faces. Because of this interest, Ralph is determined to learn more about Huck's adventures.

Clare faces other challenges than Ralph. She has already read several of Mark Twain's short stories and The Adventures of Tom Sawyer in junior high school. Through these previous exposures, Clare has an adequate understanding of Twain's satiric style. She is also aware of his interest in exploring the psyche of young male characters striving for adventure. She has also learned to read the dialect aloud to get the meaning. However, Clare does not find Huckleberry Finn interesting. She cannot relate to the mostly male characters, and she does not find the raft adventure very exciting. Despite the ease with which she can read the novel, she finds it difficult to stay involved in the story.

The third student, Kim, confronts other obstacles in her reading. She has been wearing the shameful badge of "poor reader" since elementary school. Although she can read the words on the page, she rarely understands them, and she avoids reading whenever possible. Consequently, she has had few opportunities to practice the strategies that could improve her comprehension. Thus, she faces every reading event with dread and resignation.

The three students we just met—Ralph, Clare, and Kim—paint a picture of the reading process that takes place daily in classrooms, and they remind us how complex learning from text can be. That is, these students struggling to learn from text are, indeed, diverse and have variable lessons to teach. For decades, researchers have attempted to capture this complex picture of text-based learning. In 1979, Jenkins articulated what he called his "Problem Pyramid" or "Theorist's Tetrahedron," a model that he envisioned as a useful heuristic for capturing the inherent complexity and multidimensionality of learning and memory. This "two-decade-old" model also serves as a poignant reminder that current concerns for the complexity and situativity of learning, including learning from text, are not new. Rather, the roots of such notions reach deeply into the history of educational literature. For instance, we can point to these themes in the philosophical writings of James (1890), Dewey (1913), Vygotsky (1934/1986), and others.

We do not intend to suggest that there is nothing new about text-based learning. To be sure, the conditions under which students learn and teachers instruct have been transformed in the decades since Jenkins first forwarded his multifaceted model. These changes have had a significant impact not only on the very conception of text, but also on what it means to *learn* from text. In this chapter, we explore the forces that independently and collectively influence how and what students learn from text. Our goal is to achieve a multidimensional portrayal of learning from text, and to examine how such learning changes and develops as students progress in their schooling.

THE MULTIDIMENSIONAL NATURE
OF LEARNING FROM TEXT

The extensiveness of this volume alludes to the vast array of factors that insinuate themselves into the process of learning from text. For instance, text-based learning cannot be restricted to classrooms or even to schools, but also must encompasses societal contexts (Cole, 1990; Rogoff & Lave, 1984). Thus, we survey certain macrolevel forces shaping text-based learning in today's postindustrial society. Then, we take a more microlevel view by considering how the interplay of text characteristics and learner attributes transfigure text-based learning.

Context: Situating Text-Based Learning
in a PostIndustrial Society

Before we investigate specific textual and learner factors, we need a view of learning from text in today's world. Within this panorama, we weigh the impact of living in a society where information is an ever-present, essential commodity, and we consider how technology has complicated the process of learning from text, for better or for worse. Finally, we reflect on the diversification of society and the concomitant changes that this brings to text-based learning.

Text-Based Learning in an Information Age

In the past, this chapter would have focused on what students must do to decipher the contents of their textbooks and to commit that information to memory. However, learning from text today is far more complex than developing a repertoire of study skills suitable for subject-specific textbooks. For one thing, it is evident that we are faced with a knowledge explosion (diSessa, 1988), where the creation and flow of information is endless and, often, unmanageable. From personal interactions to television, from books to billboards, this flood of information is characteristic of contemporary living. Consequently, long before children ever enter school, they have participated in millions of information interchanges. But what, if anything, have they learned from those exposures?

It might be argued, for instance, that today's students are becoming desensitized to information, as a way of coping with the continual assaults to their senses (Postman, 1995). As our research suggests, there is also the dilemma that so much information within one's everyday environment will make it more difficult to discern important from unimportant content or relevant from irrelevant, and even misleading, information (e.g., Alexander, Kulikowich, & Schulze, 1994a; Garner, Alexander, Gillingham, Kulikowich, & Brown, 1991). At the same time, students' attentions and interests are consistently drawn to content that is trivial or tangential to the overall message being conveyed, but "seductive" in its treatment of such themes as death, illness, money, or sex (e.g., Garner, Gillingham, & White, 1989; Schank, 1979; Wade, 1992).

Neither the dilemma just described, nor its solution, rests solely with the learner. Teachers, along with instructional and assessment materials commonplace in schools, often exacerbate the problem. Over two decades ago, Durkin (1978–1979) published her classic study on comprehension instruction. In this study, she determined that there was a great deal of *mentioning* going on in classrooms, but little explicit instruction on comprehension. There is no reason to assume that the instructional conditions that Durkin reported then are markedly different in classrooms today. (e.g., Beck, McKeown, & Gromoll, 1989; Sinatra, Beck, & McKeown, 1992). Consequently, it is even more vital to provide students, especially those who are less knowledgeable or less experienced, with the guidance needed to separate the message from the noise surrounding it. Alexander, Murphy, and Woods (1996) offered several guidelines for teaching in an information-rich society that inform this discussion of text-based learning.

Seek Principled Understanding.   Becoming educated demands much more than the simple accumulation of information. It requires the development of a rich body of knowledge organized around pivotal concepts or principles—what Gelman and Greeno (1989) termed *principled understanding*. Students with a principled base of knowledge not only have faster and greater access to learned content, but they also have the edge in future learning. This is what Stanovich (1986) conveyed in his concept of the Matthew effect, based on the biblical adage that the "rich get richer." Regrettably, disjointed or piecemeal instruction, which may be all too common in today's classrooms (Whitehead, 1929/1957), is apt to contribute to a knowledge base that is correspondingly disjointed and piecemeal.

Teach More About Less.   Along with making thoughtful decisions about what information to stress, teachers must orchestrate learning opportunities that permit students to explore these concepts more deeply and fully. This is what diSessa (1988) envisioned when he called on educators to teach more about less. Some successful instructional programs share the characteristic that students are given ample time, incentive, and opportunity to explore a theme or idea in depth (CSILE: Scardamalia, Bereiter, & Lamon, 1994; Schools for Thought: Cognition and Technology Group at Vanderbilt, 1996). Not only do students find the experience personally enriching, but they also acquire a body of principled knowledge that does not lie dormant or fallow, as much of school learning can do.

Aim for Rooted Relevance.   It is rare to pick up a volume on literacy without encountering the words *authentic, meaningful,* or *personally relevant*. However, it is important to reflect on what we mean by such terms and their implication for text-based learning in today's society. As indicated, there is more information to be learned today than yesterday. Optimal learning is more apt to result when the content is not only relevant to students, but also serves to build principled understanding in academic domains (e.g., Ball, 1993; Bereiter, 1994; Guthrie, McGough, Bennett, & Rice, 1996). Bruner (1960) called this being "intellectually honest."

Technology and Its Influence on Learning From Text

We would be remiss in our exploration of the context for text-based learning if we did not consider the impact that technology is having on the very nature of learning. These new technologies have increased the quantity and form of information encountered in schools and out, and have the potential to alter the way we learn, what we learn about, and the way we teach (Goldman, 1997). As Postman (1993) stated, "new technology does not add or subtract something. It changes everything" (p. 18). Nevertheless, the question remains whether such innovative activities have resulted in a better product. Can we assume that the knowledge that students gain through such online or on-screen encounters with text is better than the knowledge they might have acquired otherwise? Other chapters in this volume explore the relationship between technology and reading in far more depth than we intend to do here. Some researchers encourage us to embrace these new technologies and to harness the potential they hold for improving learning and teaching (Hawley & Jackson, 1995). Others express caution and doubt as to the true merits of technological advances (Cuban, 1993). However, it is evident that educators cannot simply sit back and wait to see what happens. Today's students are already learning *with* and *from* these technologies (Alexander, Kulikowich, & Jetton, 1994).

The Sociocultural Nature of Learning from Text

More than at any other time in its history, the reading community recognizes that learning from text is a sociocultural activity continuously shaped by the environment in which it occurs (e.g., Alexander, 1998a; Cole & Engeström, 1993; Resnick, Levine, & Teasley, 1991; Rogoff, 1990). One need only compare the chapters in this volume to those of the previous *Handbooks* (Barr, Kamil, Mosenthal, & Pearson, 1991; Pearson, Barr, Kamil, & Mosenthal, 1984) to find evidence of this fact. The bottom line is that schools are sociocultural institutions, and the learning that occurs there concerns the transmission of content valued by society (Perret-Claremont, Perret, & Bell, 1980; Radziszewska & Rogoff, 1988). Further, the students who attend those schools come from diverse sociocultural communities that may or may not have access to the literacies of the dominant culture reflected in classrooms (Cole, 1990). The recent debates in the popular and scholarly presses relative to the "canon" of schools (e.g., Schwab, 1962) amplify yet another issue pertinent to this discussion. Specifically, the texts we place in schools, the ideas contained in them, and the perspectives or interpretations offered on textual concepts reflect the current sociocultural climate.

Whether we have come very far in our efforts to offer a more balanced ecumenical view of academic content remains to be seen. Still, we have witnessed steps toward expanding the content in texts beyond the eurocentric perspective that has dominated American education since the days of the Psalter (Hawley & Jackson, 1995). For example, the availability of the Internet and the World Wide Web has given students of all ages greater access to people and writings that they would not otherwise have encountered (Bereiter & Scardamalia, 1989). However, we often do not need to look beyond the walls of our neighborhood schools to realize how diverse classroom communities are becoming. The question is not whether diversity exists, but rather whether diversity is addressed effectively in the learning process (Alexander & Knight, 1993).

One of the obvious effects of the growing sensitivity toward sociocultural influences can be seen in the collaborative learning activities ongoing in classrooms (Wade & Moje, this volume). In these situations, students are in constant contact with peers who affect their learning. A plethora of new approaches have appeared, including reciprocal teaching (Palincsar & Brown, 1984), anchored instruction (Cognition and

Technology Group at Vanderbilt, 1990), and Jigsaw (Aronson, 1978; Brown & Campione, 1996).

Texts: Their Nature, Quality, and Form

In addition to considering how the diverse and multicultural milieu of schools and society are part of text learning, we must also weigh the nature of the texts as they relate to learning. Specifically, we view texts as dual in nature, reflecting both public and private worlds. We also consider those elements that characterize quality texts. Lastly, we analyze the text types that are central to the research on text-based learning.

The Nature of Texts.   Given their purposes and structures, texts possess a dual nature in that they are both *individual* and *social, permanent* and *dynamic*. The individual nature of text is illustrated through the voice of the authors, whose goal is to convey their feelings and thoughts through language, printed or oral. When authors construct text, they seek to externalize deeply held ideas or sensations. However, authors' thoughts do not exist in a vacuum. Much of the understanding they possess comes from other voices, other authors (Bazerman, 1995). For example, authors might quote, paraphrase, or summarize others' writings as they develop their own ideas. Texts are, therefore, both private and public in that the ideas, expressions, and language come through both an individual author and a social world (Brandt, 1990, 1992).

Texts also have a dual nature with regard to stability. On the one hand, traditional texts are permanent, static artifacts that sit on shelves in homes, schools, and libraries. On the other hand, the dynamism of texts results when humans construct and interact with them. As authors construct texts, and their voices intertwine with other voices, a common thread binds the needs of the writer with the needs of the greater society. As a result, texts are dynamic, changing over time as they are constructed anew by society (Berkenkotter & Huckin, 1995). Texts are also dynamic with respect to the interactions among writers, the words on the page, and the readers. According to Nystrand (1986, 1989), the meaning of texts evolves as readers, who possess their own sociocultural ideals, interact with the text in unique ways. This view is consistent with other theories in reading and communication (Bakhtin, 1981; Fish, 1980).

Quality of Text.   Linguistic quality is another critical factor in readers' ability to learn from text. Texts constructed to facilitate readers' attempts to learn have been called "considerate," whereas texts that cause readers to expend large amounts of cognitive effort to offset their poor construction are characterized as "inconsiderate" (Armbruster, 1984). The issue of text quality has been a perplexing one since Plato's time. One reason so many theorists vary in their views on text quality is because such judgments are based on individual and societal value systems (Kellogg, 1994). However, those investigating writing quality have reached some agreement on certain general characteristics. For one, quality depends on how effectively a text communicates its purpose or aim. Kinneavy (1997) outlined the basic purposes of composition, in which he acknowledged the role of the writer, the reader, the signal or the linguistic product, and the reality. As each of these components becomes the focus of the discourse, a particular purpose or aim evolves. When the main emphasis is on the writer, the aim becomes *expressive*, intending to convey emotions, individuality, and aspirations. When the focus is on the reader, the aim becomes *persuasive*, seeking to elicit a particular stance or reaction from the reader. The emphasis on the signal results in a *literary* purpose, aiming for an appreciation of the language of the text. Lastly, when reality is dominant, a *referential* aim evolves. Examples of the referential aim include exploratory, informative, and scientific texts. These aims are not orthogonal, however. Thus, one text can include several aims, with one predominant.

Not only does a quality text include a clear purpose, but it is also considerate of its audience. T. Anderson and Armbruster (1984) referred to this trait as *audience appropriateness*. Writers must consider the prior knowledge of their audience, and include sufficient relevant information, few and well-defined technical terms, and referents for any figurative language. Further, writers must consider whether this single or plural audience has particular interests or expectations, certain positions on the topic, or would view them as credible sources (Rafoth, 1988). Another trait associated with text quality concerns a writer's ability to convey and maintain the purpose or aim throughout the text. This has been described as *unity* or *focus* (Beason, 1993). Other rhetorical devices that assist writers in achieving quality include organization or structure, development/support, stylistic expression, and mechanics (Purves, 1992). In order to achieve organization, a writer must address two concerns. First, the content must include both a macrostructure (i.e., a network of main ideas) and a microstructure (i.e., supporting details) that provide a foundation for the main ideas (Kintsch & van Dijk, 1978; Meyer & Rice, 1991). Second, the ideas cast in the form of words, sentences, and paragraphs should be cohesive or well linked (Beck & McKeown, 1989).

Writers typically achieve development by providing sufficient explanation, depth, and proof, often in the form of primary or secondary sources that include anecdotes, quotations, observations, and philosophical principles. Moreover, in developing a text, writers must consider how much detail to include as support for the reader and how information can be summarized. Choices of this nature are often difficult to make because they are highly dependent on the knowledge of the reader (Beck, Omanson, & McKeown, 1982; Langer, 1981). Quality texts are also concerned with the stylistic expression evident in the clarity, variation, and uniqueness of words, phrases, and clauses (Bazerman, 1995). Stylistic expression should be appropriate for the desired aim or purpose of the text. That is, texts that are more referential in aim may include less emotionally charged words. Also, stylistic considerations include decisions about whether a word is commonly known, how concrete or abstract the language should be, and about the use of a variety of sentence types and patterns. Another indicator not often identified with text quality is validity, pertaining to the truth or accuracy of the writer's ideas (Beason, 1993). This factor appears to be a critical consideration where students are learning information from their textbooks or undergoing conceptual change. Lastly, text quality can be indicated by surface features of the text, such as the standard conventions of language usage (Elbow, 1981). In our opening scenario, Ralph's struggle to understand Jim's dialect is illustrative of this problem.

Text Genres.   Two general categories of text that are the subject of numerous investigations are linear and nonlinear texts. The descriptor *linear* designates written discourse for which decisions relative to processing are typically left to the reader (Alexander, Kulikowich, & Jetton, 1994). *Nonlinear* texts are connected discourse accompanied by a database management system that guides or prompts readers to reaccess or extend the main text through associative computer-based links to other informational screens (Gillingham, Young, & Kulikowich, 1994). Research on learning focused on linear texts in particular *genres*, which are recognizable forms of communication, distinguished by their purposes, structure, and content (Jetton & Alexander, 1998; Swales, 1990). The three genres garnering attention in the research are narrative, expository, and mixed texts. Narratives, such as myths and novels, are expressions of actual or fictitious, event-based experiences (Graesser, Golding, & Long, 1991). In contrast, expository texts (e.g., newspapers, encyclopedias) inform readers by presenting information that explains principles and general behavioral patterns (Axelrod & Cooper, 1996). A mixed text, by comparison, possesses properties of both narration and exposition, as when textbooks incorporate personally involving information about central figures (Pearson, Gallagher, Goudvis, & Johnson, 1990). Biography is one of the most common examples of mixed text.

One reason genres are important is because they appear to elicit varied processing. This pattern is evident in the research on interest and importance (Schellings, van Hout-Wolters, & Vermunt, 1996). This research specifically concerns *situational* or *text-based* interest, which is a temporal and short-lived state of arousal evoked by the text (Hidi, 1990; Schiefele, 1991). Importance falls into three categories, *author-determined* or *structural importance*, *reader-determined* or *constructed importance*, and *teacher-determined* or *instructional importance* (Alexander & Jetton, 1996). Structural importance pertains to the hierarchical structure of information in text (Kintsch & van Dijk, 1978; Meyer, 1975), whereas reader-determined importance entails one's personal judgment of importance based on internal criteria (Goodman & Goodman, 1979; Rosenblatt, 1978). Instructional importance refers to students' determination of importance based on the value system in the classroom (Jetton & Alexander, 1997). That is, students' energies are directed toward discerning what teachers value and what will be the basis of teacher-made assessments.

Researchers are now investigating how interest and importance play out in classroom communities. For example, several studies support the contention that, although they appear nonstrategic at determining structural importance, students are relatively facile at ascertaining what textual content their teachers value (Jetton, 1994). These studies investigated how teachers conveyed interest and important through their questions, discussions, and assessments. Interestingly, Jetton (1994) found that teachers' questions often target seductive details or personally involving information as much as the structurally important information in the text. Jetton and Alexander (1997) also determined that the level of teachers' subject-matter knowledge and their pedagogical abilities were significant factors in what they stress from students' readings. They found that content and pedagogical knowledge needed to work in tandem in order for optimal instruction to be achieved.

Knowledge: The Scaffold for Text-Based Learning

Of all the factors considered in this exploration, none exerts more influence on what students understand and remember than the knowledge they possess (Alexander, 1996; Stanovich, 1986). This was certainly evident for Ralph in our opening vignette, who struggled to read *Huckleberry Finn* because he lacked sufficient background knowledge. In essence, "existing knowledge serves as the foundation of all future learning by guiding organization and representations, by serving as a basis of association with new information, and by coloring and filtering all new experiences" (Alexander & Murphy, 1998, p. 28). The power of knowledge is seen in many quarters of literacy research. For instance, readers' prior knowledge affects both their perspective on content (R. Anderson, Reynolds, Schallert, & Goetz, 1977; Pichert & Anderson, 1977; Pritchard, 1990), and the attention they allocate (e.g., R. Anderson, Pichert, & Shirey, 1983; Reynolds & Shirey, 1988). Additionally, knowledge is tied to students' interests (Schraw & Dennison, 1994) and their judgments of importance (Alexander & Jetton, 1996).

Much of contemporary understanding of knowledge and its relation to text-based learning was sparked by information-processing research of the 1970s and 1980s (e.g., R. Anderson, 1977; Chi, Feltovich, & Glaser, 1981). As research on knowledge matured, and as information-processing theory gave way to alternative theories of learning and development, views on the nature and role of knowledge transformed. These changes are clearly reflected in the chapters of this volume. For instance, we realize more than ever that knowledge is not a singular entity, but consists of many diverse forms and dimensions (Paris, Lipson, & Wixson, 1983; Prawat, 1989; Ryle, 1949). There is also a growing awareness that what one knows is as likely to come from everyday, out-of-school experiences as from formal learning, and can sometimes result in resistant, constrained or distorted understandings (Gardner, 1991). In addition, researchers and practitioners have come to recognize that learning from text is inevitably and understandably a social and a cultural activity (Yinger & Hendricks-Lee, 1993).

The Many Faces of Knowledge

One way to understand the complexity of knowledge is to consider its many forms and dimensions. In 1991, Alexander, Schallert, and Hare undertook the ambitious task of describing and configuring the multitude of knowledge terms that were part of the lexicon within literacy. This exploration was extended and refined by others (e.g., Greene & Ackerman, 1995). For the purpose of this discussion, we overview three categories, linguistic knowledge, schooled and unschooled knowledge, and subject-matter knowledge, concentrating on the latter.

Linguistic Knowledge.   It seems intuitive to say that access to a message coded in written or oral language is a first step toward interpreting and learning from that message. Not only must learners decipher the textual content graphophonemically, but they must also do so fluidly and rather effortlessly (Adams, 1991; Stanovich, 1980). It is also conceivable that linguistic elements (e.g., vocabulary knowledge and an awareness of text genres and structures) grow in importance over the course of schooling, as students encounter more demanding and specialized texts (Britton, 1981; Jetton, Rupley, & Willson, 1995). The relationship between learning from text and individuals' knowledge of text genres and structures is exemplified by the work of Goldman and colleagues (e.g., chap. 20, this volume; Goldman & Varma, 1995). Specifically, Goldman (1997) argued that learning requires a personal but coherent interpretation of the text guided by "genre-specific, global organizational schemes to generate the 'hierarchical connections'" (p. 367). For example, these organizational schemes permit readers to recognize paragraph structures that typify informational texts (e.g., descriptive or cause/effect; Armbruster, 1984) or claim–warrant–evidence patterns indicative of persuasive text (Chambliss, 1995). In short, knowledge of text genres and structures allows readers to access information more readily and accurately, as they construct their personal interpretations of the text.

Schooled and Unschooled Knowledge.   Before students step foot into a school or a classroom, they have amassed an extensive body of conceptual knowledge. Everyday life is indeed a potent teacher. As Vygotsky (1934/1986) and others suggested (e.g., Alexander, 1992), the character of spontaneous concepts (i.e., unschooled or informal knowledge) can be quite different from the understandings that individuals attain during their formal education (i.e., scientific or schooled knowledge). For one, it seems that unschooled knowledge may be less accessible for reflection, because it is often more tacit than explicit in nature (Prawat, 1989). Thus, as they are reading along, constructing an interpretation of a given text, students may be blissfully unaware that the understanding they form is colored or shaped by deeply held perceptions grounded in their everyday experiences. For another, some students appear to have limited regard for much of what they learn in schools (Alexander & Dochy, 1995; Cognition and Technology Group at Vanderbilt, 1990; Gardner, 1991). The result is that students' formal knowledge often becomes *inert* or dormant knowledge (Whitehead, 1929/1957) that seemingly plays no significant role in learners' thoughts or deeds.

Another reason for the power of unschooled knowledge may relate to the fact that everyday understandings frequently have a concrete, personal referent that much of schooled knowledge lacks. This situation may help to explain why some everyday conceptions are so resistant to change (e.g., Alexander, 1998b; Guzzetti & Hynd, 1998; Vosniadou, 1994). Studies of learning in physics are especially noteworthy, because day-to-day observations, which can unwittingly foster erroneous interpretations, can cloud or misdirect students' efforts to learn from text (Alexander & Kulikowich, 1994). Even when students seem to be "getting it," they can easily revert to more primitive interpretations when the tasks are varied or when students leave the confines of their academic environments (e.g., Alvermann, Smith, & Readence, 1985). Yet, resistance to change is not the sole dominion of science or mathematics. It can permeate students' learning from text in any domain or with any topic, as the literature on persuasion demonstrates (e.g., Garner & Hansis, 1994). Whatever the explanation, schools are not the sole source (or perhaps even the most influential source) of students' knowledge base. Thus, the more educators understand about the interplay between schooled and unschooled knowledge, and about everyday cognition, the more effectively they can guide students to richer, more meaningful interpretations of text (e.g., Carraher, Carraher, & Schliemann, 1985; Saxe, 1992).

Subject-Matter Knowledge.   In the context of schools, the notion of formal knowledge is typically associated with particular courses or fields of study. The term *subject-matter knowledge* marks this class of formal knowledge (Alexander, Jetton, & Kulikowich, 1995). We can identify at least two forms of subject-matter knowledge talked about in the literacy research, domain and topic knowledge. *Domain knowledge* can be thought of as the breadth of one's knowledge about any chosen field of study, such as physics or biology (e.g., Stahl, Hynd, Glynn, & Carr, 1996). It is a particularized case of a learner's prior knowledge, in that it is more often associated with "studied" areas and is, therefore, largely formally acquired. *Topic knowledge,* in contrast, signifies the depth of one's knowledge relative to certain domain-related concepts (Alexander, Kulikowich, & Schulze, 1994b). Within the text processing literature, topic knowledge frequently describes the readers' background knowledge relative to the subject of a particular selection of text and to the concepts included in that text (Alexander et al., 1991). For the most part, the more topic knowledge students have in a given field, then the more domain knowledge they are also likely to have (e.g., Alexander, 1998a). However, this is not always the case. For example, when examining undergraduates' performance in astrophysics, Alexander, Kulikowich, and Schulze (1994b) found that certain students with relatively high levels of domain knowledge knew relatively little about particular concepts in text (e.g., event horizons or singularities). Conversely, some students evidenced prior exposure to various concepts (e.g., black holes or origins of the universe) but scored low on a more global measure of astrophysics knowledge.

One additional point about subject-matter knowledge that is particularly relevant to this discussion deals with the nature of subject-matter domains (Spiro, Coulson, Feltovich, & Anderson, 1994; Spiro & Jehng, 1990). Specifically, academic domains have varied characters that have a direct bearing on the texts created to represent them and on the way teachers use these texts to convey content knowledge (Alexander, 1998a; Phillips, 1987). When we use the term *domain* in this manner, we are referring to a highly abstracted body of knowledge aligned with a designated area of study. Further, academic domains are, for the most part, sociocultural constructions, although the degree to which this is so is a matter of debate in the literature (Ball, 1993; Bereiter, 1994; von Glaserfeld, 1991). At least in theory, domains consist of bodies of conceptual knowledge organized around concepts and principles judged by experts as core to that field (Matthews, 1994; West & Pines, 1985). This knowledge is also reified and legitimized through social practice (Stahl et al., 1996; VanSledright, 1996).

However constructed, domains present themselves differently and these differences translate into variations in text learning. Anyone who has opened a mathematics book or read a literature anthology recognizes how authors variably portray these domains. Such differences are largely reflections of the way societies regard these academic domains, as well as the beliefs teachers and learners hold about them (Anders & Evans, 1994; Garner & Alexander, 1994). Such differences also pertain to the inscriptions most associated with that domain (e.g., linguistic or mathematical). Building on these factors, and using history and mathematics as exemplars, we can thus contrast domains along two dimensions, structuredness and knowledge inscription. The notion of structuredness is based on Frederiksen's (1984) work on problem solving where he distinguished well-structured from ill-structured problems. *Well-structured* problems are those for which the information required for solution is clearly specified, the solution strategy is evident and typically algorithmic in nature, and expected outcomes are generally agreed upon. *Ill-structured* problems are complex, "fuzzy" problems for which all requisite information is not or cannot be presented, the solution paths are many, and "acceptable" outcomes are numerous.

Although oversimplified, we can make similar comparisons to academic domains. For instance, mathematics, as taught in schools, can be considered a rather well-structured domain, because its prototypic problems frequently require algorithmic solution and have "expected" responses. Its knowledge base is also highly procedural or rule based (Stewart, 1987). This is one reason that students and teachers often think in terms of "doing" mathematics (Lampert, 1990; Putnam, Heaton, Prawat, & Remillard, 1992). History, on the other hand, focuses on content that is more conceptual and less rule driven (VanSledright, 1996). The "problems" presented to students in history cannot be resolved through the application of certain algorithms and rarely have one agreed-on answer or response. In addition, it is likely that questions about what it means to know mathematics versus history or what is required to do well in mathematics versus history would result in varied responses (Matthews, 1994; Wineburg, 1996).

Perhaps some of the variability in the way society construes academic domains is linked to the mode of inscription commonly chosen to represent the domain in text (Cole & Engeström, 1993; Nolen, Johnson-Crowley, & Wineburg, 1994). When students open their mathematics books, for example, they encounter an interspersion of mathematical symbols and linguistic information. History texts, by comparison, are often filled with more connected discourse punctuated with pictorial or graphic displays. This means that students' ability to learn in such fields as mathematics is somewhat analogous to reading in two languages and code shifting between them (Alexander & Kulikowich, 1994). Other researchers have conveyed the dilemmas of learning from text in more conceptually laden fields such as history, where authors rarely have the time or inclination to explain the plethora of abstract notions sprinkled throughout (McKeown, Beck, Sinatra, & Loxterman, 1992). Part of the problem is in the assumptions made about what readers know. Another problem is that students move through their educational experience with only minimum instruction in *how* to decipher the messages embedded within the words and symbols in the text (Bean, this volume; Nist & Simpson, this volume).

Strategies: Tools for Regulating and Enhancing Learning from Text

Research on strategic processing and its relationship to text-based learning has had a long, albeit somewhat controversial, history. This point was made apparent at two national symposia (Graves, 1997; McKeachie, 1996) in which participants hotly debated the evidence that strategies make a difference in learning. What also became evident during these lively discussions was that the emphasis on strategic processing has waxed and waned over the last 25 years. Nonetheless, what has remained consistent is the realization that all learning, and certainly the process of learning from text, demands a reader who is *strategically* engaged in the construction of meaning (American Psychological Association Presidential Task Force on Psychology in Education, 1993; Learner-Centered Principles Revision Work Group, 1995). As evidenced in the case of Kim, who lacked the procedural tools to unravel the meaning of *Huckleberry Finn*, the absence of strategic processing can cause readers to approach tasks with fear and resignation.

What are Strategies?   Surprisingly, although the term *strategy* is common in the educational literature, there has been little effort to unpack its meaning (Alexander et al., 1991; Dole, Duffy, Roehler, & Pearson, 1991). Based on a review of the literature, Alexander, Graham, and Harris (1998) identified six attributes that seemingly marked strategies from other forms of human action. Specifically, they stated that strategies are *procedural, purposeful, effortful, willful, essential,* and *facilitative* in nature. At its simplest, a strategy can be understood as a specialized instance of *procedural* knowledge (Alexander et al., 1991)—essentially the "how to" knowledge (J. Anderson, 1987; Ryle, 1949). Strategies can take the form of *algorithms,* step-by-step procedures that should result in the expected solution to a given problem. Or, they can take the form of *heuristics,* broad guidelines that presumably contribute to but cannot guarantee better performance. Strategies can also be quite general (i.e., widely applicable) or bound to specific domains or tasks, or they can deal with the oversight or regulation of thought and action (Winne, 1995; Zimmerman, 1995).

Moreover, the reader must *purposefully* or intentionally or willfully invoke strategies (Alexander & Judy, 1988; Snow, Corno, & Jackson, 1996). Others cannot dictate that an individual should operate strategically. Precisely because strategies signify planful engagement in one's learning, they require a commitment of time and mental energy (Garner, 1987); thus, they are *effortful* procedures. Further, strategies are *essential* tools in learning. It is unfathomable to expect meaningful learning from text to occur without some evidence of strategic processing (Weinstein, Goetz, & Alexander, 1988; Weinstein & Mayer, 1986). Likewise, when readers employ strategies efficiently and effectively, these procedures are *facilitative,* promoting deeper and better understanding (Pressley, Goodchild, Fleet, Zajchowski, & Evans, 1989).

Distinguishing Skills From Strategies.   During the 1970s, when it first dotted the reading landscape, the term *strategies* signified a form of mental processing that deviated from traditional skills-based reading. However, any distinctions between skills and strategies that seemed apparent then have begun to fade, leaving many to wonder where skills end and strategies begin. As a way to unearth those contrasts, we propose two differences between skillful and strategic processing relevant to text-based learning: automaticity and intentionality (Alexander, Graham, & Harris, 1998). Habits, according to James (1890), are typical behaviors—so typical, in fact that they occur in mind*less* fashion. Skills are, in essence, essential academic habits. They are the routinized, automatic procedures we employ when we engage in any nontrivial task. Thus, skilled readers, like skilled cooks or skilled accountants, have honed essential domain procedures to a level of automaticity.

One laudable goal of reading instruction is to enable students to become skillful readers. Because skilled readers have internalized effective procedures, they have more resources available when these typical behaviors prove inadequate or unsuited to the task at hand (Britton, 1981)—as they will. At such times, students must be cognizant of their performance limitations, intentionally weigh their options, and willfully execute compensatory procedures. They must become, in effect, strategic. Viewed in this way, the same procedures (e.g., finding main idea) can fit under both the skill and strategy categories. The appropriate label rests on whether that the reader consciously evokes the procedure or is simply functioning in a typical, automatic way.

Strategies for Learning From Nonlinear Text.   Even though space only permits us to mention the issue, we want to draw special attention to the nature of strategic processing required in nonlinear, technology-based environments (e.g., navigation). Whether you believe that technology is changing the face of learning or not, its presence is undeniable, and stands in sharp contrast to the little we understand about nonlinear text processing (Scardamalia, Bereiter, McLean, Swallow, & Woodruff, 1989). Today's students are literally growing up in front of computer screens. For them, searching the web, e-mailing, or online "chats" are commonplace (Garner & Gillingham, 1996; Kamil & Lane, 1998). Still, our knowledge of how students learn *with* and *in* nonlinear environments is sadly limited (Alexander, Kulikowich, & Jetton, 1994; Kamil & Intrator, 1998). As Salomon (Salomon & Globerson, 1989; Salomon, Perkins, & Globerson, 1991) and others (e.g., Bolter, 1991; Garner & Gillingham, 1996; Goldman, 1996) suggested, we must begin to rethink the very concepts of learning, memory, and strategies in light of new technologies. The chapters in this (Kamil & Intrator; Leu) and other volumes (e.g., Reinking, McKenna, Labbo, & Kieffer, 1998) devoted to technology and literacy clearly signal an important trend in text-based learning.

For example, in their review of research dealing with technology and reading or writing, Kamil and Intrator (1998) found that the quantity of published articles in this area remained rather consistent during the past 11 years, despite the expanding presence of technology. Further, they determined that most of this research was not published in mainstream journals. It is not surprising, therefore, that current knowledge of the navigation strategies that learners of varying knowledge, interests, and goals *do* or *should* employ in these nontraditional learning environments is too limited to guide practice. The bottom line is that we are clearly behind the curve in understanding the promises and potentials that nonlinear text pose for learning.

Readers' Goals and Interests: Driving Forces in Text-Based Learning

Increasingly, educators are forging intricate relationships between the realms of cognition and motivation in order to understand learning and development better (Alexander, 1996; Pintrich, 1994). The reason for this new alliance is unmistakable. Learning from text is inevitably a synthesis of *skill*, *will*, and *thrill* (Garner & Alexander, 1991). Few would argue with the premise that readers need to be skilled. Yet, learning from text cannot take place in any deep or meaningful fashion without the learner's commitment (i.e., will). Nor will the pursuit of knowledge continue unless the reader realizes some personal gratification or internal reward from this engagement (i.e., thrill).

Although reading researchers and practitioners have been aware of motivation for decades, they have only recently moved beyond discussions of global traits (e.g., intrinsic and extrinsic motivation) to studies of more particular constructs (e.g., self-efficacy). Faced with the mounting evidence that students do not always read often or well, they have turned to noncognitive determiners as plausible explanatory factors. Consequently, discussions of such motivational constructs as will (Corno & Rohrkemper, 1985), expectancies (Eccles, Wigfield, & Schiefele, 1998), and goals (Ames, 1992; Dweck & Leggett, 1988) have appeared with increasing regularity in the text literature. In this chapter, we have chosen to highlight the research on goals and interest. Of course, we recognize that these are only two of many motivational constructs. Thankfully, other excellent reviews complement and extend our discussion (e.g., Oldfather & Wigfield, 1996; Wigfield & Guthrie, this volume).

Goals and Goal Orientations

Students engage in text processing for many reasons (Schunk, 1991; Wigfield & Eccles, 1992; Wigfield & Harold, 1992), and these reasons or goals have a great deal to do with what they ultimately learn from that text. *Goals* can be thought of as the particular reasons, intentions, or motives that persons have for their actions (Pintrich & Schunk, 1996). When the three students in our opening vignette read *Huckleberry Finn*, they probably had particular goals in mind (e.g., get a good grade, answer homework questions, or learn more about Mark Twain). Individuals also have a general disposition toward academic tasks or learning that carries over, to a certain extent, from one situation to the next, and from one task to the next (Ames, 1992). This disposition is what is referred to as a *goal orientation* (e.g., Dweck & Leggett, 1988). Kim's reluctance to engage in the reading of *Huck Finn* may reflect such an orientation to text-based learning. We can extract three categories of goal orientations from the literature that speak directly to text-based learning: performance, learning, and work-avoidant goals.

When some readers embark on the task of learning from text, they may seek to accomplish the task to get a good grade, to look smart, or to please their teachers or others in authority (Wentzel, 1991, 1993). The label *performance goal* (Dweck & Leggett, 1988) captures this particular orientation. For students with performance goals, the task and what it gets them become, in effect, their instructional ends. Other individuals have the tendency to approach an academic task with the primary objective of gaining knowledge or skills from it; that is, of "mastering" the content (Meece, Blumenfeld, & Hoyle, 1988). Researchers use the term *learning* or *mastery goal* to characterize this orientation (Nicholls, 1984, 1989). The task, in essence, becomes a means to an end, and not the end itself. It is held that students with a learning goal orientation are more likely to achieve academically because they engage deeply in the task, are willing to take risks, and or sustain their initiative when faced with academic difficulty. There is support for such a position in several studies (Alexander & Murphy, 1999; Murphy, 1998). Meece and Holt (1993) also identified a somewhat less laudable orientation toward academic tasks referred to as *work-avoidant goals*. Students who manifest this orientation have one principal objective in mind—get the task done with a minimum amount of cognitive effort. Students who hold this orientation tend to benefit very little from text-based learning tasks, and likely feel little self-gratification or excitement for their efforts.

Interest

As was apparent in the case of Ralph, the student who faced obstacles in his reading of *Huck Finn*, some students persist in their pursuit of understanding when others, under similar circumstances, would simply close their books and walk away. Interest, like that voiced by Ralph, can be a powerful catalyst for such persistence. The relationship between interest and learning has a long history in the literature (Dewey, 1913; James, 1890). Although research on interest lay dormant for some years, it is currently enjoying a renaissance (Renninger, Hidi, & Krapp, 1992). Much of credit for this resurgence goes to literacy researchers who have explored the relationship between interest and text processing. In general, when individuals show positive or negative feelings toward any particular person, object, or activity, we say that they are interested (Schiefele, 1991). Although interest has importance in its own right, it connects to other relevant constructs in the literature. For example, the attention readers pay to particular elements of the text is associated with interest (Reynolds, 1992; Reynolds & Shirey, 1988; Shirey, 1992), as is students' involvement in reading (Reed & Schallert, 1993; Reed, Schallert, & Goetz, 1993), and their academic engagement (Almasi, McKeown, & Beck, 1996; Guthrie, Van Meter, et al., 1996). Like goal orientations, there are various categories and conceptions of interest. Unlike goal orientations, however, the research on interest has a distinctively domain-specific or task-specific quality. In other words, when we refer to our interests, we are typically talking about affective responses to particular persons, objects, or activities (e.g., "I find that story interesting"; "I am interested in the Civil War").

Motivating From Without and From Within.   In 1980, Kintsch described two forms of interest, emotional interest and cognitive interest. According to Kintsch, emotional interest is the affective impact that text can create, and results from the inherent qualities or personal relatedness of the text or from the reader's identification with the character in the case of narrative and mixed texts. Cognitive interest, by comparison, results when the text captures the reader's mind or thoughts. The background of the reader, style of the text, and novelty of the content are factors that contribute to cognitive interest. In many ways, Kintsch's (1980) distinction between emotional and cognitive interest harkens back to Dewey (1913, 1916/1944) and his admonition regarding interest and effort in education. Dewey's message, reiterated in many contemporary works on interest and learning, was simple but powerful. Educators can exert effort in the learning environment to *make* something they teach interesting to their students, what we have called "motivating from without" (Jetton, Alexander, & White, 1992). Or, they can help students discover the value or interest that the knowledge or the task holds in and of itself. This is what we have described as "motivating from within" (Jetton et al., 1992).

Recently, our research (e.g., Alexander, Jetton, & Kulikowich, 1995; Alexander, Murphy, Woods, Duhon, & Parker, 1997), and that of others (Hidi, 1990; Schiefele, 1991) has concentrated on two alternative characterizations of interest—situational and individual or personal interest. Situational interest is centered in the immediate environment and is typically regarded as transitory or fleeting (Alexander, 1997b; Hidi & Anderson, 1992). Because situational interest entails getting learners' attention and keeping them excited or enthused, it can be a positive influence in students' text-based learning. We can easily imagine the negative consequences of learning in an environment where the teachers are unstimulating, the texts are bland, and the tasks are boring (Mitchell, 1997). Of course, we would caution that the nature of the content stressed in these classrooms is also an important factor in students' learning. Students and teachers can spend quite a bit of instructional time excited and enthused about tangential information (Schellings & van Hout-Wolters, 1995). Moreover, situational interest is only one aspect of motivation, and certainly not the most important one (Dewey, 1916/1944).

In contrast to the fleeting and bounded nature of situational interest, individual or personal interest is enduring and reaches deeply into an individual's cognitive and affective nature (Alexander, 1997b; Alexander, Kulikowich, & Schulze, 1994a). Individuals' vocations and avocations are indicative of their personal interests (Mitchell, 1993). Further, these deep-seated interests are strongly associated with self-concepts and self-schemata (Alexander, 1997a; Pintrich, 1994), and may be triggers for learning goals (e.g., Meece & Holt, 1993). Thus, individual interests can serve as catalysts for the active pursuit of experiences, knowledge, and skills associated with those interests. Alexander (1997a) referred to this as *knowledge seeking*. In the following section, our intention is to explore changes in text-based learning that transpire over time. As part of that examination, we consider how students' individual interests become strongly tied to their knowledge, their goals, and their strategic processing.

A DEVELOPMENTAL VIEW
OF LEARNING FROM TEXT

Despite all we have discovered about learning from text through the decades, there is one obvious gap in our knowledge base. We lack a clear picture of the way learning from text changes over the course of one's education. To address this limitation, we offer such a developmental perspective and frame discussion around two guiding questions:

- How does text-based learning change as students become more educated?
- In what way should environments adjust to changes in students' text-based learning?

The model we use as our scaffold charts student progress from acclimation through competence and, potentially, to proficiency or expertise, the highest level of learning in any field of study.

Acclimated Learners

Alexander (1997b) chose the label *acclimated* for the first stage in students' academic development to emphasize the orientation and adaptation characteristic of this period. In effect, acclimated learners are seeking to understand the terrain of an unfamiliar domain. Yet, several conditions complicate this process for acclimated students. First, these individuals possess little knowledge about the domain or topics covered in the text, and what knowledge they do possess is apt to be fragmented and unprincipled (Gelman & Greeno, 1989). When they encounter a concept such as "taxation without representation" in their history chapter, for instance, they must not only wrestle with its specific intent and import, but must also try to position that concept within the constellation of related terms.

As this suggests, much of these readers' energies is directed toward building a relevant base of conceptual knowledge (Spiro et al., 1994). Because background knowledge is an essential variable in *what* and *how* readers learn, acclimated learners are disadvantaged in their initial attempts to make sense of domain-related texts. This is particularly true when the texts do not provide adequate explanation or elaboration of key ideas (Sinatra et al., 1992). These novice learners show the effects of these knowledge disadvantages as they struggle to distinguish between relevant and irrelevant content and more and less important concepts (Alexander, Pate, Kulikowich, Farrell, & Wright, 1989; Wade, 1992).

Further, because acclimated students have little principled knowledge, they are unlikely to have any deep-seated interest in the content of the text (Garner et al., 1991). Therefore, any interest that comes from the text or its processing is probably more situational in form. For example, Garner et al. (1991) found that low-knowledge students performed better when reading a text containing "personally involving" content (i.e., fascinating or intriguing information about individuals or events)—a factor not evidenced for high-knowledge readers. In addition, Garner et al. (1991) found that students lowest in subject-matter knowledge were more likely to remember the low-importance/high-interest text segments at the expense of those ideas that were high in importance but much less captivating. Based on the literature, we would speculate that acclimated students must rely heavily on general cognitive, metacognitive, and self-regulatory strategies to construct meaning (McCutchen, 1986; Zimmerman & Martinez-Pons, 1992). However, when subject-matter knowledge is limited, students appear to apply strategies in somewhat less efficient and effective ways (Alexander & Judy, 1988).

This pattern of strategic processing may be partly attributable to students' performance goals (Ames, 1992; Wentzel, 1993)—that is, their efforts to complete the task for external reasons, such as grades or recognition. Until students begin to see the value in the domain or its content, their sights may be set more on *doing* the reading rather than *mastering* the content in the text. Further, when students are struggling to learn in a novel domain, they may be less secure about their competence or their ability to become knowledgeable, and, therefore, less willing to employ strategies required to process text deeply (Palmer & Goetz, 1988). Of course, as Brown and Campione (1990) suggested, there are always those *intelligent novices* who come to an unfamiliar domain with a history of academic success and a repertoire of effective strategies. These intelligent novices are better equipped to discern the content within challenging text that is structurally more important and to organize the information in memory. For such reasons, this class of acclimated learners may progress rather rapidly toward competence in a domain.

Competent Learners

All readers must experience the phenomenon of acclimation at some point in their academic careers. However, many will develop the level of knowledge, strategic capability, and the motivational interest and goals required to reach competence. Competence entails a qualitative and quantitative transformation in the students' subject-matter knowledge and in their strategic processing. These learners also have more of an investment (i.e., individual interest) in the domain, and a greater likelihood of espousing learning goals. Students who are competent in a domain have the advantage of a richer framework of subject-matter knowledge that can guide their text learning. In addition, they come to the text with subject-matter knowledge that is more cohesively structured. In effect, competent learners begin to think or perform as a member of the domain community (Shulman & Quinlan, 1996). In recent studies, we have witnessed the advantages afforded students who were reading in domains in which they were more competent than their peers (e.g., Alexander & Murphy, 1999). These more knowledgeable students are also more interested in the textual content than their acclimated peers, and they can better address the conceptual gaps inherent in many school texts (McKeown et al., 1992). Thus, although an acclimated reader misses the significance of the concept "taxation without representation" in her history text, a more competent history student uses her sense of this concept to understand the conflicts between American colonists and British loyalists.

As with subject-matter knowledge, strategic processing undergoes transformation when individuals reach competence (Harris & Graham, 1996). Specifically, when learning from text occurs in domains of competence, readers encounter fewer surface-level barriers to their comprehension. For this reason, there should be less need for the employment of lower level text processing strategies (e.g., altering rate of reading). On the other hand, because readers can delve more deeply into the meaning of the text, a rise in certain higher order processing and reasoning strategies should occur. This is the outcome that Alexander, Murphy, Woods, Duhon, and Parker (1997) documented in their study of undergraduates' text processing in educational psychology.

Alexander and Murphy (1999) amplified the critical role that strategies play in the movement from acclimation to competence in their study of learner profiles. These profiles were based on knowledge, strategy use, and interest data acquired when undergraduates began and concluded a course in educational psychology. The largest cluster of students at pretest was the Low Profile group composed of students low in knowledge, strategic processing, text recall, and interest. By course end, this one cluster was replaced by two groups of less successful students. The larger of these, NonStrategic Readers, were students seemingly unwilling or unable to acquire subject-matter knowledge from demanding domain-related texts. Without this ability, it is doubtful whether these acclimated students will achieve competence. The second unsuccessful group, Effortful Processors, consisted of students who reported the highest level of strategy use at posttest. However, these students were unable to convert such effort into achievement. Thus, strategy use alone cannot ensure competent performance.

Despite the significant role that subject-matter knowledge and strategic processing play in distinguishing more from less successful students, knowledge alone did not predict the highest achievement in the Alexander and Murphy study. To the contrary, it was a strong interest in the domain and a willingness to pursue understanding that separated highly successful learners from those who were only somewhat successful. Specifically, Strong Knowledge students actually began the course with relatively more knowledge than any of the other profiles. However, these students reported a lower level of interest in the domain and demonstrated an unwillingness to exert effort after meaning. By contrast, Learning-Oriented students were not quite as advantaged as their Strong Knowledge peers in domain knowledge at the outset of the semester. By posttest, however, the initial advantage that the Strong Knowledge group had over the Learning-Oriented students disappeared. By the end of the semester, the Learning-Oriented students had the highest means not only for interest and recall, but also subject-matter knowledge. They also reported the greatest use of higher order strategies compared with other clusters. In many ways, this Learning-Oriented cluster highlights the interplay of knowledge, strategic processing, and motivation that might be anticipated in readers who are approaching competence in an academic domain.

Proficiency or Expertise

It is quite likely that a number of you reading this chapter come to the task with a wealth of knowledge about the domain of reading and the topic of learning from text. Further, you engage in this reading with an abiding interest in the domain and with the goal of exploring this topic at a rather deep level. Thus, your investment in understanding our message is highly personal and goal directed. Moreover, your ability to apply a rich repertoire of strategies, efficiently and effectively, enhances your chances of achieving this learning goal. Because much of the processing of this chapter can be carried out automatically and effortlessly, you can analyze the arguments we forward or posit counter arguments or elaborations. This unique combination of extensive subject-matter knowledge, strategic sophistication, and deep personal interest in the domain and the topic marks you as an expert.

Alexander (1997b) argued that few who set out on the road toward expertise ever achieve this laudable end, because demands on knowledge, strategic ability, *and* motivation are so great. Relatively few students have the desire or the ability to meet such demands in specific academic domains. Even highly skilled readers, who find themselves confronting extremely novel and complex texts in a domain, can appreciate the time, effort, and experience it takes to reach proficiency in such domains as history, physics, literature, or mathematics. Regrettably, few students experience the sensation of processing text as domain experts. One reason is that schools typically require students to devote themselves to text-based learning in areas for which they are acclimated. They are given little time to explore a well-known topic in any depth. When students are constantly reading about topics they know little about and care little about, the stress placed on their strategic processing and on performance goals is understandable. In addition, school-aged learners rarely have much say in what they choose to read, whereas experts are often reading texts of choice. Such autonomy alone can alter learning outcomes by stimulating creativity or higher level processing (Deci, Valleran, Pelletier, & Ryan, 1991; Ryan, 1992).

Implications for Instructional Practice

What do these stages of domain learning have to say to the way that learning from text transpires in schools? To answer this question, we focus on three aspects of classrooms: instructional support, instructional materials, and learner autonomy.

Instructional Support.   Within the literature, there is a recurring debate over how directed learning should be (Alexander & Knight, 1993). Should teachers explicate for students what they need to know or be able to do, or should students be set free to discover such information on their own? As is often the case in such debates, the answer lies between the extremes, and would seem partly dependent on the reader's expertise relative to the content. Acclimated learners, as noted, come to the text with limited and fragmented knowledge, low personal interest, and with an amalgamation of strategies they often haltingly apply. Thus, acclimated learners are quite vulnerable when it comes to discerning relevant from irrelevant content and more from less important information. They therefore require clear scaffolding that aids them in building a meaningful base of content knowledge and the seeds of personal interest (Mitchell, 1993; Pearson, 1984). As students progress toward competence, however, the level of scaffolding required should logically diminish. Of course, teachers need to be vigilant and sensitive to occasions when competent students confront troublesome texts or concepts or may benefit from the modeling of strategies. Further, students should be afforded contexts that foster expertise. One characteristic of these contexts is the opportunity to pursue a certain topic or domain in depth.

Instructional Materials.   One consistent finding of the research of Garner et al. (1991) and Goldman and Varma (1995) is that the quality of text becomes differentially important depending on the reader's stage of academic development. In short, competent and proficient learners are better equipped to deal with vagueness, incoherence, or other inconsiderate characteristics of domain-related texts than are acclimated learners. Consequently, it is more essential that the materials intended to convey fundamental information to novices be extremely well crafted, directing readers' attention to key ideas that are amply described. The paradox is that many texts read by students trying to build a foundation of knowledge and interest are weak treatments of that domain or its related concepts. Moreover, texts containing seductive details may detract readers from the main ideas, especially if they are at the acclimated stage. Thus, acclimated readers often find themselves at the mercy of these inconsiderate texts (T. Anderson & Armbruster, 1984).

But texts are only one element in the constellation of instructional materials that educators must carefully evaluate in light of students' stage of academic achievement. Teachers' own words and the assessment they create are critical pieces in the instructional puzzle, as we have seen (Jetton & Alexander, 1997). Teachers who do not provide students with clear explanations, when such explanations are warranted, or who do not allow students to engage in meaningful dialogue around substantive ideas can exacerbate students' learning problems. Likewise, the questions that teachers pose in discussions or incorporate on their tests are highly influential in guiding students' learning (Alexander, Jetton, Kulikowich, & Woehler, 1994; Schellings & van Hout-Wolters, 1995). Yet, their impact is likely greater for students who are not already grounded in the domain or topic being studied but are seeking to master the content.

Learner Autonomy.   According to Deci and Ryan (1991), autonomy involves learner choice, and is, therefore, a manifestation of self-determination. Intrinsic motivation for learning and creativity are linked with learner autonomy (Amabile, 1990). Acclimated learners are much less likely than competent and proficient students to experience the type of autonomy or self-determination that Deci and Ryan (1991) describe. Moreover, if acclimated learners spend their instructional time responding to external mandates (e.g., reading the texts that others choose and for reasons that others dictate), they are unlikely to realize the full benefits of any text-based learning task. The implication for educators is that all readers, whether acclimated, competent, or proficient, should have the opportunity to make choices. These choices can extend to the materials read, the purposes for that reading, or the methods of evaluation.

This is not to suggest that learners, especially acclimated students, need free rein in the classroom. Selecting between carefully chosen options still allows for some level of autonomy. Thus, a teacher can present acclimated students with several suitable texts or performance options so that they feel greater ownership of their learning. Of course, as students become increasingly more competent, they are more capable of self-determination and self-direction. Competent and proficient learners also tend to create their own opportunities for autonomy, as when they reframe a given task in terms of their own internal goals or seek knowledge beyond that required of them. Still, one hallmark of successful instructional programs such as Jigsaw (Aronson, 1978; Brown & Campione, 1990, 1994) and CORI (Guthrie, Van Meter et al., 1996) is their provision for student choice and self-determination in some measure.

POSTSCRIPT

In this examination of text-based learning, we have highlighted past and current research addressing the themes of context, text, and learner (i.e., knowledge, strategic processing, and motivations). In effect, we have followed Jenkins's (1979) admonition to view learning through a multidimensional lens. Further, we have extended this exploration by considering how the very nature of text-based learning can be transformed, as students continue their journey from acclimation to academic competence or proficiency. As an afterthought, however, we wish to forward several predictions about the future of research on text-based learning. Specifically, we speculate on the contents of this chapter as it will appear in Volume IV of the *Handbook on Reading Research*.

We would anticipate (and hope for) three significant changes in that content. First, we would expect that knowledge of text-based learning in alternative, nonlinear environments would be greatly expanded. As noted, we are already years behind in our understanding of learning under such nontraditional and nonlinear conditions. Second, far more research on the developmental nature of learning from text will occur and will find its way into future reviews of this topic. Despite the richness of the literature relevant to learning from text, the scope of our vision is sorely constrained by the paucity of longitudinal research on this critical subject. Finally, the next installment in this legacy will speak not only to our knowledge about text-based learning, but also to the powerful impact that the beliefs of researchers, teachers, and students play in the very nature of this process. These are our predictions. We await the future edition of this important volume to confirm or disconfirm the merits of our foresight.

REFERENCES

Adams, M. J. (1991). *Beginning to read*. Cambridge, MA: MIT Press.

Alexander, P. A. (1992). Domain knowledge: Evolving themes and emerging concerns. *Educational Psychologist, 27*, 33–51.

Alexander, P. A. (1996). The past, present, and future of knowledge research: A reexamination of the role of knowledge in learning and instruction. [Editor's notes]. *Educational Psychologist, 31*, 89–92.

Alexander, P. A. (1997a). Knowledge seeking and self-schema: A case for the motivational dimensions of exposition. *Educational Psychologist, 32*, 83–94.

Alexander, P. A. (1997b). Mapping the multidimensional nature of domain learning: The interplay of cognitive, motivational, and strategic forces. In P. R. Pintrich & M. L. Maehr (Eds.), *Advances in motivation and achievement* (Vol. 10, pp. 213–150). Greenwich, CT: JAI Press.

Alexander, P. A. (1998a). Knowledge and literacy: A transgenerational perspective. In T. Shanahan & F. Rodriguez-Brown (Eds.), *Forty-Seventh Yearbook of the National Reading Conference* (pp. 167–181). Chicago, IL: National Reading Conference.

Alexander, P. A. (1998b). The nature of disciplinary and domain learning: The knowledge, interest, and strategic dimensions of learning from subject-matter text. In C. Hynd (Ed.), *Learning from text across conceptual domains* (pp. 263–287). Mahwah, NJ: Lawrence Erlbaum Associates.

Alexander, P. A. (1998c). Positioning conceptual change within a model of domain literacy. In B. Guzzetti & C. Hynd (Eds.), *Theoretical perspectives on conceptual change* (pp. 55–76). Mahwah, NJ: Lawrence Erlbaum Associates.

Alexander, P. A., & Dochy, F. J. R. C. (1995). Conceptions of knowledge and beliefs: A comparison across varying cultural and educational communities. *American Educational Research Journal, 32*, 413–442.

Alexander, P. A., Graham, S., & Harris, K. R. (1998). A perspective on strategy research: Progress and prospects. *Educational Psychology Review, 10*, 129–154..

Alexander, P. A., & Jetton, T. L. (1996). The role of importance and interest in the processing of text. *Educational Psychology Review, 8*(1), 89–122.

Alexander, P. A., Jetton, T. L., & Kulikowich, J. M. (1995). Interrelationship of knowledge, interest, and recall: Assessing a model of domain learning. *Journal of Educational Psychology, 87*, 559–575.

Alexander, P. A., Jetton, T. L., Kulikowich, J. M., & Woehler, C. (1994). Contrasting instructional and structural importance: The seductive effect of teacher questions. *Journal of Reading Behavior, 26*, 19–45.

Alexander, P. A., & Judy, J. E. (1988). The interaction of domain-specific and strategic knowledge in academic performance. *Review of Educational Research, 58*, 375–404.

Alexander, P. A., & Knight, S. L. (1993). Dimensions of the interplay between learning and teaching. *Educational Forum, 57*, 232–245.

Alexander, P. A., & Kulikowich, J. M. (1994). Learning from physics text: A synthesis of recent research. *Journal of Research in Science Teaching* [Special Issue on Print Based Language Arts and Science Learning], *31*, 895–911.

Alexander, P. A., Kulikowich, J. M., & Jetton, T. L. (1994). The role of subject-matter knowledge and interest in the processing of linear and nonlinear texts. *Review of Educational Research, 64*, 201–252.

Alexander, P. A., Kulikowich, J. M., & Schulze, S. K. (1994a). How subject-matter knowledge affects recall and interest on the comprehension of scientific exposition. *American Educational Research Journal, 31*, 313–337.

Alexander, P. A., Kulikowich, J. M., & Schulze, S. K. (1994b). The influence of topic knowledge, domain knowledge, and interest on the comprehension of scientific exposition. *Learning and Individual Differences, 6*, 379–397.

Alexander, P. A., & Murphy, P. K. (1998). The research base for APA's learner-centered principles. In N. M. Lambert & B. L. McCombs (Eds.), *Issues in school reform: A sampler of psychological perspectives on learner-centered school* (pp. 25–60). Washington, DC: American Psychological Association.

Alexander, P. A., & Murphy, P. K. (1999). Learner profiles: Valuing individual differences within classroom communities. In P. L. Ackerman, P. C. Kyllonen, & P. D. Roberts (Eds.), *Learning and individual differences: Processes, traits, and content determinants* (pp. 412–432). Washington, DC: American Psychological Association.

Alexander, P. A., Murphy, P. K., & Woods, B. S. (1996). Of squalls and fathoms: Navigating the seas of educational innovation. *Educational Researcher, 25*(3), 31–36, 39.

Alexander, P. A., Murphy, P. K., Woods, B. S., Duhon, K. E., & Parker, D. (1997). College instruction and concomitant changes in students' knowledge, interest, and strategy use: A study of domain learning. *Contemporary Educational Psychology, 22*, 125–146.

Alexander, P. A., Pate, P. E., Kulikowich, J. M., Farrell, D. M., & Wright, N. L. (1989). Domain-specific and strategic knowledge: Effects of training on students of differing ages or competence levels. *Learning and Individual Differences, 1*, 283–325.

Alexander, P. A., Schallert, D. L., & Hare, V. C. (1991). Coming to terms: How researchers in learning and literacy talk about knowledge. *Review of Educational Research, 61*, 315–343.

Almasi, J. F., McKeown, M. G., & Beck, I. L. (1996). The nature of engaged reading in classroom discussions of literature. *Journal of Literacy Research, 28*, 107–146.

Alvermann, D. E., Smith, L. C., & Readence, J. E. (1985). Prior knowledge activation and the comprehension of compatible and incompatible text. *Reading Research Quarterly, 20*, 420–436.

Amabile, T. M. (1990). With you, without you: The social psychology of creativity, and beyond. In M. A. Runco & R. S. Albert (Eds.), *Theories of creativity* (pp. 61–91). Newbury Park, CA: Sage.

American Psychological Association Presidential Task Force on Psychology in Education. (1993). *Learner-centered psychological principles: Guidelines for school redesign and reform.* Washington, DC: American Psychological Association.

Ames, C. (1992). Classrooms: Goals, structures, and student motivation. *Journal of Educational Psychology, 84*, 261–271.

Anders, P. L., & Evans, K. S. (1994). Relationship between teachers' beliefs and their instructional practice in reading. In R. Garner & P. A. Alexander (Eds.), *Beliefs and text and instruction with text* (pp. 137–153). Hillsdale, NJ: Lawrence Erlbaum Associates.

Anderson, J. (1987). Skill acquisition: Compilation of weak-method problem solutions. *Psychological Review, 94*, 192–210.

Anderson, R. C. (1977). The notion of schemata and the educational enterprise. In R. C. Anderson, R. J. Spiro, & W. E. Montague (Eds.), *Schooling and the acquisition of knowledge* (pp. 415–431). Hillsdale, NJ: Lawrence Erlbaum Associates.

Anderson, R. C., Pichert, J. W., & Shirey, L. L. (1983). Effects of reader's schema at different points in time. *Journal of Educational Psychology, 75,* 271–279.

Anderson, R. C., Reynolds, R. E., Schallert, D. L., & Goetz, E. T. (1977). Frameworks for comprehending discourse. *American Educational Research Journal, 14,* 367–381.

Anderson, T. H., & Armbruster, B. B. (1984). Content area textbooks. In R. C. Anderson, J. Osborn, & R. J. Tierney (Eds.), *Learning to read in American schools* (pp. 193–224). Hillsdale, NJ: Lawrence Erlbaum Associates.

Armbruster, B. B. (1984). The problem of "inconsiderate texts." In G. G. Duffy, L. R. Roehler, & J. Mason (Eds.), *Theoretical issues in reading comprehension* (pp. 202–217). New York: Longman.

Aronson, E. (1978). *The Jigsaw classroom.* Beverly Hills, CA: Sage.

Axelrod, R. B., & Cooper, C. R. (1996). *The concise guide to writing.* New York: St. Martin's Press.

Bakhtin, M. M. (1981). *The dialogic imagination.* Austin, TX: University of Texas Press.

Ball, D. L. (1993). With an eye on the mathematical horizon: Dilemmas of teaching elementary school mathematics. *Elementary School Journal, 93,* 373–397.

Barr, R., Kamil, M. L., Mosenthal, P., & Pearson, P. D. (1991). *Handbook of reading research: Vol. II.* New York: Longman.

Bazerman, C. (1995). *The informed writer* (2nd ed.). Boston: Houghton Mifflin.

Beason, L. (1993). Feedback and revision in writing across the curriculum classes. *Research in the Teaching of English, 27,* 395–422.

Beck, I. L., & McKeown, M. G. (1989). Expository text for young readers: The issue of coherence. In L. B. Resnick (Ed.), *Learning to read in American schools* (pp. 47–66). Hillsdale, NJ: Lawrence Erlbaum Associates.

Beck, I. L., McKeown, M. G., & Gromoll, E. W. (1989). Learning from social studies texts. *Cognition and Instruction, 6,* 99–158.

Beck, I. L., Omanson, R. C., & McKeown, M. G. (1982). An instructional redesign of reading lessons: Effects on comprehension. *Reading Research Quarterly, 17,* 462–481.

Bereiter, C. (1994). Constructivism, socioculturalism, and Popper's World 3. *Educational Researcher, 23*(7), 21–23.

Bereiter, C., & Scardamalia, M. (1989). Intentional learning as a goal of instruction. In L. B. Resnick (Ed.), *Knowing, learning, and instruction: Essays in honor of Robert Glaser* (pp. 361–392). Hillsdale, NJ: Lawrence Erlbaum Associates.

Berkenkotter, C., & Huckin, T. N. (1995). *Genre knowledge in disciplinary communication.* Hillsdale, NJ: Lawrence Erlbaum Associates.

Bolter, J. D. (1991). *Writing space: The computer, hypertext, and the history of writing.* Hillsdale, NJ: Lawrence Erlbaum Associates.

Brandt, D. (1990). *Literacy as involvement: The acts of writers, readers, and texts.* Carbondale, IL: Southern Illinois University Press.

Brandt, D. (1992). The cognitive as the social: An ethnomethodological approach to writing process research. *Written Communication, 9,* 315–355.

Britton, B. K. (1981, April). *Use of cognitive capacity in reading.* Paper presented at the annual meeting of the American Educational Research Association, Los Angeles.

Brown, A. L., & Campione, J. C. (1990). Communities of learning and thinking: Or, a context by any other name. *Human Development, 21,* 108–125.

Brown, A. L., & Campione, J. C. (1994). Guided discovery in a community of learners. In K. McGilly (Ed.), *Classroom lessons: Integrating cognitive theory and classroom practice* (pp. 229–272). Cambridge, MA: MIT Press.

Brown, A. L., & Campione, J. C. (1996). Psychological theory and the design of innovative learning environments: On procedures, principles, and systems. In L. Schauble & R. Glaser (Eds.), *Innovations in learning: New environments for education* (pp. 289–325). Mahwah, NJ: Lawrence Erlbaum Associates.

Bruner, J. S. (1960). *The process of education.* Cambridge, MA: Harvard University Press.

Carraher, T. N., Carraher, D. W., & Schliemann, A. D. (1985). Mathematics in the streets and in schools. *British Journal of Developmental Psychology, 3,* 21–29.

Chambliss, M. (1995). Text cues and strategies successful readers use to construct the gist of lengthy written arguments. *Reading Researcher Quarterly, 30,* 778–807.

Chi, M. T. H., Feltovich, P., & Glaser, R. (1981). Categorization and representation of physics problems by experts and novices. *Cognitive Science, 5,* 121–152.

Cognition and Technology Group at Vanderbilt. (1990). Anchored instruction and its relationship to situated cognition. *Educational Researcher, 19*(6), 2–10.

Cognition and Technology Group at Vanderbilt. (1996). Looking at technology in context: A framework for understanding technology and education research. In D. C. Berliner & R. C. Calfee (Eds.), *Handbook of educational psychology* (pp. 807–840). New York: Macmillan.

Cole, M. (1990). Cognitive development and formal schooling: The evidence from cross-cultural research. In L. C. Moll (Eds.), *Vygotsky and education* (pp. 89–110). Cambridge: Cambridge University Press.

Cole, M., & Engeström, Y. (1993). A cultural-historical approach to distributed cognition. In G. Salomon (Ed.), *Distributed cognition: Psychological and educational considerations* (pp. 1–46). Cambridge: Cambridge University Press.

Corno, L., & Rohrkemper, M. (1985). The intrinsic motivation to learn in classrooms. In C. Ames & R. Ames (Eds.), *Research on motivation in education: The classroom milieu* (Vol. 2, pp. 53–84). New York: Academic Press.

Cuban, L. (1993). *How teachers taught: Constancy and change in American classrooms, 1890–1980.* New York: Teachers College Press.

Deci, E. L., & Ryan, R. M. (1991). A motivational approach to self: Integration in personality. In R. Dienstbier (Ed.), *Nebraska Symposium on motivation: Perspectives on motivation* (Vol. 38, pp. 237–288). Lincoln, NE: University of Nebraska Press.

Deci, E. L., Valleran, R. J., Pelletier, L. G., & Ryan, R. M. (1991). Motivation and education: The self-determination perspective. *Educational Psychologist, 26,* 325–346.

Dewey, J. (1913). *Interest and effort in education.* Boston: Riverside.

Dewey, J. (1944). *Democracy and education.* New York: Macmillan. (Original work published 1916).

diSessa, A. A. (1988). What will it mean to be "educated" in 2020? In R. S. Nickerson & P. P. Zodhiates (Eds.), *Technology in education: Looking toward 2020* (pp. 43–66). Hillsdale, NJ: Lawrence Erlbaum Associates.

Dole, J. A., Duffy, G. G., Roehler, L. R., & Pearson, P. D. (1991). Moving from the old to the new: Research on reading comprehension instruction. *Review of Educational Research, 61,* 239–264.

Durkin, D. (1978–1979). What classroom observations reveal about reading comprehension instruction. *Reading Research Quarterly, 14,* 481–533.

Dweck, C. S., & Leggett, E. L. (1988). A social-cognitive approach to motivation and personality. *Psychological Review, 95,* 256–273.

Eccles, J. S., Wigfield, A., & Schiefele, U. (1998). Motivation to succeed. In N. Eisenberg (Vol. Ed.), *Handbook of child psychology: Vol. 3, Social, emotional and personality development* (5th ed., pp. 1017–1095). New York: Wiley.

Elbow, P. (1981). *Writing with power.* New York: Oxford University Press.

Fish, S. (1980). *Is there a text in this class? The authority of interpretive communities.* Cambridge, MA: Harvard University Press.

Frederiksen, N. (1984). Implications of cognitive theory for instruction in problem solving. *Review of Educational Research, 54,* 363–407.

Gardner, H. (1991). *The unschooled mind.* New York: Basic Books.

Garner, R. (1987). *Metacognition and reading comprehension.* Norwood, NJ: Ablex.

Garner, R., & Alexander, P. A. (1991, April). *Skill will and thrill: The role of interest in text comprehension.* Paper presented at the annual meeting of the American Educational Research Association, Chicago.

Garner, R., & Alexander, P. A. (Eds.). (1994). *Beliefs about text and about instruction with text.* Hillsdale, NJ: Lawrence Erlbaum Associates.

Garner, R., Alexander, P. A., Gillingham, M. G., Kulikowich, J. M., & Brown, R. (1991). Interest and learning from text. *American Educational Research Journal, 28,* 643–659.

Garner, R., & Gillingham, M. G. (1996). *Conversations across time, space, and culture.* Mahwah, NJ: Lawrence Erlbaum Associates.

Garner, R., Gillingham, M. G., & White, C. S. (1989). Effects of "seductive details" on macroprocessing and microprocessing in adults and children. *Cognition and Instruction, 6,* 41–57.

Garner, R., & Hansis, R. (1994). Literacy practices outside of school: Adults' beliefs and their responses to "street texts." In R. Garner & P. A. Alexander (Eds.), *Beliefs and text and instruction with text* (pp. 57–73). Hillsdale, NJ: Lawrence Erlbaum Associates.

Gelman, R. & Greeno, J. G. (1989). On the nature of competence: Principles for understanding in a domain. In L. B. Resnick (Ed.), *Knowing, learning, and instruction: Essays in honor of Robert Glaser* (pp. 125–186). Hillsdale, NJ: Lawrence Erlbaum Associates.

Gillingham, M. G., Young, M. F., & Kulikowich, J. M. (1994). Do teachers consider nonlinear text to be text? In R. Garner & P. A. Alexander (Eds.), *Beliefs about text and instruction with text* (pp. 201–219). Hillsdale, NJ: Lawrence Erlbaum Associates.

Goldman, S. R. (1996). Reading, writing, and learning in hypermedia environments. In H. Van Oostendorp & S. de Mui (Eds.), *Cognitive aspects of electronic text processing* (pp. 7–42). Norwood, NJ: Ablex.

Goldman, S. R. (1997). Learning from text: Reflections on the past and suggestions for the future. *Discourse Processes, 23,* 357–397.

Goldman, S. R., & Varma, S. (1995). CAPing the construction-integration model of discourse comprehension. In C. Weaver, S. Mannes, & C. Fletcher (Eds.), *Discourse comprehension: Essays in honor of Walter Kintsch* (pp. 337–358). Hillsdale, NJ: Lawrence Erlbaum Associates.

Goodman, K. S., & Goodman, Y. M. (1979). Learning to read is natural. In L. B. Resnick & P. A. Weaver (Eds.), *Theory and practice of early reading* (Vol. 1, pp. 137–154). Hillsdale, NJ: Lawrence Erlbaum Associates.

Graesser, A. C., Golding, J. M., & Long, D. L. (1991). Narrative representation and comprehension. In R. Barr, M. L. Kamil, P. B. Mosenthal, & P. D. Pearson (Eds.), *Handbook of Reading Research* (Vol. II, pp. 171–205). White Plains, NY: Longman.

Graves, M. F. (1997, March). *What sort of comprehension strategy instruction should schools provide?* Symposium presented at the annual meeting of the American Educational Research Association, Chicago.

Greene, S., & Ackerman, J. M. (1995). Expanding the constructivist metaphor: A rhetorical perspective on literacy research and practice. *Review of Educational Research, 65,* 383–420.

Guthrie, J. T., McGough, K., Bennett, L., & Rice, M. E. (1996). Concept-oriented reading instruction: An integrated curriculum to develop motivations and strategies for reading. In L. Baker, P. Afflerbach, & D. Reinking (Eds.), *Developing engaged readers in school and home community* (pp. 165–190). Mahwah, NJ: Lawrence Erlbaum Associates.

Guthrie, J. T., Van Meter, P., McCann, A., Wigfield, A., Bennett, L., Poundstone, C., Rice, M. E., Faibisch, F., Hunt, B., & Mitchell, A. (1996). Growth of literacy engagement: Changes in motivations and strategies during concept-oriented reading instruction. *Reading Research Quarterly, 31,* 306–332.

Guzzetti, B., & Hynd, C. (1998). *Theoretical perspectives on conceptual change.* Mahwah, NJ: Lawrence Erlbaum Associates.

Harris, K. R., & Graham, S. (1996). *Making the writing process work: Strategies for composition and self-regulation.* Cambridge, MA: Brookline.

Hawley, W. D., & Jackson, A. W. (Eds.). (1995). *Toward a common destiny: Improving race relations in America.* San Francisco: Jossey-Bass.

Hidi, S. (1990). Interest and its contribution as a mental resource for learning. *Review of Educational Research, 60,* 549–571.

Hidi, S., & Anderson, V. (1992). Situational interest and its impact on reading and expository writing. In K. A. Renninger, S. Hidi, & A. Krapp (Eds.), *The role of interest in learning and development* (pp. 215–238). Hillsdale, NJ: Lawrence Erlbaum Associates.

James, W. (1890). *Principles of psychology* (Vols. 1 & 2). New York: Holt.

Jenkins, J. J. (1979). Four point to remember: A tetrahedral model of memory experiments. In L. S. Cermak & F. I. M. Craik (Eds.), *Levels of processing in human memory* (pp. 429–446). Hillsdale, NJ: Lawrence Erlbaum Associates.

Jetton, T.L. (1994). *Teachers' and students' understanding of scientific exposition: How importance and interest influence what is accessed and what is discussed.* Unpublished doctoral dissertation, Texas A & M University.

Jetton, T. L., & Alexander, P. A. (1997). Instructional importance: What teachers value and what students learn. *Reading Research Quarterly, 32,* 290–308.

Jetton, T. L., & Alexander, P. A. (1998, April). *Teachers' views of discussions: Issues of control, time, and ability.* Paper presented at the American Educational Research Conference, San Diego.

Jetton, T. L., Alexander, P. A., & White, S. H. (1992, December). *Motivating from without: The effect of including personally-involving information in content area texts.* Paper presented at the annual meeting of the National Reading Conference, San Antonio, TX.

Jetton, T. L., Rupley, W. H., & Willson, V. L. (1995). Comprehension of narrative and expository texts: The role of content, topic, discourse, and strategy knowledge. In K. A. Hinchman, D. J. Leu, & C. K. Kinzer (Eds.), Perspectives on literacy research and practice (pp. 197–204). Chicago, IL: National Reading Conference.

Kamil, M. L., & Intrator, S. (1998). Trends in publication of research on technology and reading, writing, and literacy. In T. Shanahan & F. V. Rodriguez-Brown (Eds.), *Yearbook of the National Reading Conference* (pp. 385–396). Chicago, IL: National Reading Conference.

Kamil, M. L., & Lane, D. (1998). Researching the relationship between technology and literacy: An agenda for the 21st century. In D. Reinking, M. C. McKenna, L. Labbo, & R. Kieffer (Eds.), *Handbook of literacy and technology: Transformations in a post-typographic world* (pp. 323–341). Mahwah, NJ: Lawrence Erlbaum Associates.

Kellogg, R. T. (1994). *The psychology of writing.* New York: Oxford University Press.

Kinneavy, J. E. (1997). The basic aims of discourse. In V. Villanueva Jr. (Ed.), *Cross-talk in comp theory* (pp.107–117), Urbana, IL: National Council of Teachers of English.

Kintsch, W. (1980). Learning from text, levels of comprehension, or: Why anyone would read a story anyway. *Poetics, 9,* 87–89.

Kintsch, W., & van Dijk, T. A. (1978). Toward a model of text comprehension and production. *Psychological Review, 85,* 363–394.

Lampert, M. (1990). What the problem is not the question and the solution is not the answer: Mathematical knowing and teaching. *American Educational Research Journal, 27,* 29–64.

Langer, J. A. (1981). From theory to practice: A prereading plan. *Journal of Reading, 25,* 152–156a.

Learner-Centered Principles Revision Work Group. (1995). *Learner-centered psychological principles: A framework for school redesign and reform.* Unpublished document. Washington, DC: American Psychological Association.

Matthews, M. R. (1994). *Science teaching: The role of history and philosophy of science.* New York: Routledge.

McCutchen, D. (1986). Domain knowledge and linguistic knowledge in the development of writing ability. *Journal of Memory and Language, 25,* 431–444.

McKeachie, W. J. (1996, April). *The state of strategy research: Is this old territory or are there new frontiers?* Symposium presented at the annual meeting of the American Educational Research Association.

McKeown, M. G., Beck, I. L., Sinatra, G. M., & Loxterman, J. A. (1992). The contribution of prior knowledge and coherent text to comprehension. *Reading Research Quarterly, 27,* 79–93.

Meece, J. L., Blumenfeld, P. C., & Hoyle, R. H. (1988). Students' goal orientations and cognitive engagement in classroom activities. *Journal of Educational Psychology, 80,* 514–523.

Meece, J. L., & Holt, K. (1993). A pattern analysis of students' achievement goals. *Journal of Educational Psychology, 85,* 582–590.

Meyer, B. J. F. (1975). *The organization of prose and its effects on memory.* Amsterdam: North-Holland.

Meyer, B. J. F., & Rice, E. (1991). The structure of text. In R. Barr, M. L. Kamil, & P. Mosenthal (Eds.), *Handbook of reading research* (pp. 319–351). White Plains, NY: Longman.

Mitchell, M. (1993). Situational interest: Its multifaceted structure in the secondary school mathematics classroom. *Journal of Educational Psychology, 85,* 424–436.

Mitchell, M. (1997, April). *Interest and anxiety in mathematics.* Paper presented at the annual meeting of the American Educational Research Association, Chicago.

Murphy, P. K. (1998). *Toward a multifaceted model of persuasion: Exploring textual and learner interactions.* Unpublished doctoral dissertation. College Park, MD: College of Education, University of Maryland.

Nicholls, J. G. (1984). Achievement motivation: Conceptions of ability, subjective experience, task choice, and performance. *Psychological Review, 91,* 328–346.

Nicholls, J. G. (1989). *The competitive ethos and democratic education.* Cambridge, MA: Harvard University Press.

Nolen, S. B., Johnson-Crowley, N., & Wineburg, S. S. (1994). Who is this "I" person, anyway? The presence of a visible author in statistical text. In R. Garner & P. A. Alexander (Eds.), *Beliefs and text and instruction with text* (pp. 41–55). Hillsdale, NJ: Lawrence Erlbaum Associates.

Nystrand, M. (1986). *The structure of written composition: Studies in reciprocity between writers and readers.* London: Academic Press.

Nystrand, M. (1989). A social-interactive model of writing. *Written Communication, 6,* 66–85.

Oldfather, P., & Wigfield, A. (1996). Children's motivations to read. In L. Baker, P. Afflerbach, & D. Reinking (Eds.), *Developing engaged readers in school and home communities* (pp. 89–113). Mahwah, NJ: Lawrence Erlbaum Associates.

Palincsar, A. S., & Brown, A. L. (1984). Reciprocal teaching of comprehension-fostering and monitoring activities. *Cognition and Instruction, 1,* 117–175.

Palmer, D. J., & Goetz, E. T. (1988). Selection and use of study strategies: The role of the studier's beliefs about self and strategies. In C. Weinstein, E. T. Goetz, & P. A. Alexander (Eds.), *Learning and study strategies: Issues in assessment, instruction, and evaluation* (pp. 77–100). San Diego, CA: Academic Press.

Paris, S. G., Lipson, M. Y., & Wixson, K. K. (1983). Becoming a strategic reader. *Contemporary Educational Psychology, 8,* 293–316.

Pearson, P. D. (1984). Direct explicit teaching of reading comprehension. In G. G. Duffy, L. R. Roehler, & J. Mason (Eds.), *Comprehension instruction: Perspectives and suggestions* (pp. 222–233). New York: Longman.

Pearson, P. D., Barr, R., Kamil, M. L., & Mosenthal, P. (Eds.). (1984). *Handbook of reading research.* New York: Longman.

Pearson, P. D., Gallagher, M. Y., Goudvis, A., & Johnston, P. (1981, December). *What kinds of expository materials occur in elementary school children's textbooks?* Paper presented at the annual meeting of the National Reading Conference, Dallas, TX.

Perret-Claremont, A., Perret, J., & Bell, N. (1980). The social construction of meaning and cognitive activity in elementary school children. In L. B. Resnick, J. M. Levine, & S. D. Teasley (Eds.), *Perspectives on socially shared cognition* (pp. 41–62). Washington, DC: American Psychological Association.

Phillips, D. C. (1987). *Philosophy, science, and social inquiry.* Oxford, UK: Pergamon Press.

Pichert, J. W., & Anderson, R. C. (1977). Taking different perspectives on a story. *Journal of Educational Psychology, 69,* 309–315.

Pintrich, P. R. (1994). Continuities and discontinuities: Future directions for research in educational psychology. *Educational Psychologist, 29,* 137–148.

Pintrich, P. R., & Schunk, D. H. (1996). *Motivation in education.* Englewood Cliffs, NJ: Prentice Hall.

Postman, N. (1993). *Technopoly.* New York: Vintage Books.

Postman, N. (1995). *The end of education: Redefining the value of school.* New York: Alfred A. Knopf.

Prawat, R. S. (1989). Promoting access to knowledge, strategy, and disposition in students: A research synthesis. *Review of Educational Research, 59,* 1–41.

Pressley, M., Goodchild, F., Fleet, J., Zajchowski, R., & Evans, E. D. (1989). The challenges of classroom strategy instruction. *Elementary School Journal, 89,* 301–342.

Pritchard, R. (1990). The effects of cultural schemata on reading processing strategies. *Reading Research Quarterly, 25,* 273–295.

Purves, A. C. (1992). Reflections on research and assessment in written composition. *Research in the Teaching of English, 26,* 108–122.

Putnam, R. T., Heaton, R. M., Prawat, R. S., & Remillard, J. (1992). Teaching mathematics for understanding: Discussing case studies of four fifth-grade teachers. *Elementary School Journal, 93,* 213–228.

Radziszewska, B., & Rogoff, B. (1988). Influence of adult and peer collaboration on children's planning skills. *Developmental Psychology, 24,* 840–848.

Rafoth, B. A. (1988). Discourse community: Where writers, readers, and texts come together. In B. A. Rafoth & D. L. Rubin (Eds.), *The social construction of written communication* (pp. 131–146). New York: Oxford University Press.

Reed, J. H., & Schallert, D. L. (1993). The nature of involvement in academic discourse. *Journal of Educational Psychology, 85,* 253–266.

Reed, J. H., Schallert, D. L., & Goetz, E. T. (1993, April). *Interest happens but involvement takes effort: Distinguishing between two constructs in academic discourse tasks.* Paper presented at the annual meeting of the American Educational Research Association, Atlanta, GA.

Reinking, D., McKenna, M. C., Labbo, L., & Kieffer, R. (1998). *Handbook of literacy and technology: Transformations in a post-typographic world*. Mahwah, NJ: Lawrence Erlbaum Associates.

Renninger, K. A., Hidi, S., & Krapp, A. (1992). *The role of interest in learning and development*. Hillsdale, NJ: Lawrence Erlbaum Associates.

Resnick, L. B., Levine, J. M., & Teasley, S. D. (1991). *Perspectives on socially shared cognition*. Washington, DC: American Psychological Association.

Reynolds, R. E. (1992). Learning important information from text: The role of selective attention. *Review of Educational Psychology, 4*, 345–391.

Reynolds, R. E., & Shirey, L. L. (1988). The role of attention in studying and learning. In C. E. Weinstein, E. T. Goetz, & P. A. Alexander (Eds.), *Learning and study strategies: Issues in assessment, instruction, and evaluation* (pp. 77–100). San Diego, CA: Academic Press.

Rogoff, B. (1990). *Apprenticeship in thinking: Cognitive development in social context*. New York: Oxford University Press.

Rogoff, B., & Lave, J. (1984). *Everyday cognition*. Cambridge, MA: Harvard University Press.

Rosenblatt, L. (1978). *The reader, the text, and the poem: The transactional theory of the literary work*. Carbondale, IL: Southern Illinois University Press.

Ryan, R. M. (1992). Agency and organization: Intrinsic motivation, autonomy, and the self in psychological development. In J. Jacobs (Ed.), *Nebraska symposium on motivation* (Vol. 40). Lincoln, NE: University of Nebraska Press.

Ryle, G. (1949). *The concept of mind*. London: Hutchinson.

Salomon, G., & Globerson, T. (1987). Skill may not be enough: The role of mindfulness in learning and transfer. *International Journal of Educational Research, 11*, 623–637.

Salomon, G., Perkins, D. N., & Globerson, T. (1991). Partners in cognition: Extending human intelligence with intelligent technologies. *Educational Researcher, 20*(3), 2–9.

Saxe, G. B. (1992). Studying children's learning in context: Problems and prospects. *Journal of the Learning Sciences, 2*, 215–234.

Scardamalia, M., Bereiter, C., & Lamon, M. (1994). The CSILE project: Trying to bring the classroom in world 3. In K. McGilly (Ed.), *Classroom lessons: Integrating cognitive theory and classroom practice* (pp. 201–228). Cambridge, MA: MIT Press.

Scardamalia, M., Bereiter, C., McLean, R. S., Swallow, J., & Woodruff, E. (1989). Computer-supported intentional learning environments. *Journal of Educational Computing Research, 5*, 51–68.

Schank, R. C. (1979). Interestingness: Controlling variables. *Artificial Intelligence, 12*, 273–297.

Schellings, G. L. M., & van Hout-Wolters, B. H. A. M. (1995). Main points in an instructional text, as identified by students and their teachers. *Reading Research Quarterly, 30*, 742–756.

Schellings, G. L. M., van Hout-Wolters, B. H. A. M., & Vermunt, J. D. (1996). Selection of main points in instructional texts: Influences of task demands. *Journal of Literacy Research, 28*, 355–378.

Schiefele, U. (1991). Interest, learning, and motivation. *Educational Psychologist, 26*, 229–323.

Schraw, G., & Dennison, R. S. (1994). The effect of reader purpose on interest and recall. *Journal of Reading Behavior, 26*, 1–18.

Schunk, D. (1991). Self-efficacy and academic motivation. *Educational Psychologist, 26*, 207–231.

Schwab, J. J. (1962). The concept of the structure of a discipline. *Educational Record, 43*, 197–205.

Shirey, L. L. (1992). Importance, interest, and selective attention. K. A. Renninger, S. Hidi, & A. Krapp (Eds.), *The role of interest in learning and development* (pp. 281–296). Hillsdale, NJ: Lawrence Erlbaum Associates.

Shulman, L. S., & Quinlan, K. M. (1996). The comparative psychology of school subjects. In R. Calfee & D. Berliner (Eds.), *The handbook of educational psychology* (pp. 399–422). New York: Macmillan.

Sinatra, G. M., Beck, I. L., & McKeown, M. G. (1992). A longitudinal characterization of young students' knowledge of their country's government. *American Educational Research Journal, 29*, 633–662.

Snow, R. E., Corno, L., & Jackson, D. III. (1996). Individual differences in affective and conative functions. In D. C. Berliner & R. C. Calfee (Eds.), *Handbook of educational psychology* (pp. 243–310). New York: Macmillan.

Spiro, R. J., Coulson, R. L., Feltovich, P. J., & Anderson, D. K. (1994). Cognitive flexibility theory: Advance knowledge acquisition in ill-structured domains. In R. B. Ruddell, M. R. Ruddell, & H. Singer (Eds.), *Theoretical models and processes of reading* (pp. 602–615). Newark, DE: International Reading Association.

Spiro, R. J., & Jehng, J. C. (1990). Cognitive flexibility and hypertext: Theory and technology for the nonlinear and multidimensional traversal of complex subject matter. In D. Nix & R. J. Spiro (Eds.), *Cognition, education, and multimedia* (pp. 163–205). Hillsdale, NJ: Lawrence Erlbaum Associates.

Stahl, S. A., Hynd, C. R, Glynn, S. M., & Carr, M. (1996). Beyond reading to learn: Developing content and disciplinary knowledge through texts. In L. Baker, P. Afflerbach, & D. Reinking (Eds.), *Developing engaged readers in school and home community* (pp. 139–163). Mahwah, NJ: Lawrence Erlbaum Associates.

Stanovich, K. E. (1980). Toward an interactive-compensatory model of individual differences in the development of reading fluency. *Reading Research Quarterly, 16*, 32–71.

Stanovich, K. E. (1986). Matthew effects in reading: Some consequences of individual differences in the acquisition of literacy. *Reading Research Quarterly, 21*, 360–407.

Stewart, I. (1987). *The problem of mathematics*. New York: Oxford University Press.

Swales, J. M. (1990). *Genre analysis: English in academic and research settings*. New York: Cambridge University Press.

VanSledright, B A. (1996). Closing the gap between school and disciplinary history? Historian as high school history teacher. In J. Brophy (Ed.), *Advances in research on teaching* (Vol. 6, pp. 257–289) Greenwich, CT: JAI Press.

von Glaserfeld, E. (1991). *Radical constructivism in mathematics education*. Dordrecht, the Netherlands: Kluwer.

Vosniadou, S. (1994). Capturing and modeling the process of conceptual change. *Learning and Instruction, 4,* 45–69.

Vygotsky, L. (1986). *Thought and language* (A. Kozulin, Trans.). Cambridge, MA: MIT Press. (Original work published 1934)

Wade, S. E. (1992). How interest affects learning from text. In K. A. Renninger, S. Hidi, & A. Krapp (Eds.), *The role of interest in learning and development* (pp. 255–277). Hillsdale, NJ: Lawrence Erlbaum Associates.

Weinstein, C. E., Goetz, E. T., & Alexander, P. A. (1988). *Learning and study strategies: Issues in assessment, instruction, and evaluation*. San Diego: Academic Press.

Weinstein, C. E., & Mayer, R. E. (1986). The teaching of learning strategies. In M. C. Wittrock (Ed.), *Handbook of research on teaching* (3rd ed., pp. 315–327). New York: Macmillan.

Wentzel, K. R. (1991). Relations between social competence and academic achievement in early adolescence. *Child Development, 62,* 1066–1078.

Wentzel, K. R. (1993). Social and academic goals at school: Motivation and achievement in early adolescence. *Journal of Early Adolescence, 13,* 4–20.

West, L. H. T., & Pines, A. L. (1985). *Cognitive structures and conceptual change*. New York: Academic Press.

Whitehead, A. N. (1957). *The aims of education and other essays*. New York: Macmillan. (Original work published 1929)

Wigfield, A., & Eccles, J. (1992). The development of achievement task values: A theoretical analysis. *Developmental Review, 12,* 265–310.

Wigfield, A., & Harold, R. D. (1992). Teacher beliefs and children's achievement self-perceptions: A developmental perspective. In D. H. Schunk & J. L. Meece (Eds.), *Student perceptions in the classroom* (pp. 95–121). Hillsdale, NJ: Lawrence Erlbaum Associates.

Wineburg, S. S. (1996). The psychology of learning and teaching history. In D. C. Berliner & R. C. Calfee (Eds.), *The handbook of educational psychology* (pp. 423–437). New York: Macmillan

Winne, P. H. (1995). Inherent details in self-regulated learning. *Educational Psychologist, 30,* 173–187.

Yinger, R. J., & Hendricks-Lee, M. S. (1993). An ecological conception of teaching. *Learning and Individual Differences, 4,* 269–281.

Zimmerman, B. J. (1995). Self-regulation involves more than metacognition: A social cognitive perspective. *Educational Psychologist, 30,* 217–221.

Zimmerman, B. J., & Martinez-Pons, M. (1992). Perceptions of efficacy and strategy use in the self-regulation of learning. In D. H. Schunk & J. L. Meece (Eds.), *Student perceptions in the classroom* (pp. 185–207). Hillsdale, NJ: Lawrence Erlbaum Associates.

CHAPTER 20

Structural Aspects of Constructing Meaning From Text

Susan R. Goldman
John A. Rakestraw, Jr.
Vanderbilt University

The ability to acquire information from print is a hallmark of literacy. However, literate people often take for granted their ability to understand the meaning of what they read. Understanding involves building coherent mental representations of information. It means processing the meaning of individual words and phrases in the text as well as how these individual words and phrases relate to one another, both within the text and within a larger, preexisting knowledge base. To accomplish this, readers rely on both text-driven and knowledge-driven processes.

There are structural aspects of both text-driven and knowledge-driven processing. Typically, structural aspects of reading are associated with surface structure features of the text. In this chapter, we expand the consideration of structural aspects of reading to include those associated with prior knowledge of the structure of different discourse genre, rhetorical devices for cueing various genre structures, and generic structures of sentences and paragraphs within a text. In the first section of the chapter we provide a general overview and comparison of text-driven and knowledge-driven processing. We then consider the empirical research on structural aspects of text-driven and knowledge-driven processing. In the third section, we examine structural issues in the context of electronic text. Electronic text provides new sets of text-structural conventions (e.g., the idea that underlining signifies the presence of a link to some other information); at the same time, electronic text renders other structural cues obsolete or alters their value (e.g., location of text on a page).

Our review focuses on structural aspects of reading text. We have had to exclude other facets of reading in which structure plays a role. Specifically, we do not deal with learning the orthographic system, word recognition, and decoding and can only briefly mention structural aspects of sentence processing. Finally, we have not been able to discuss structural aspects of affective, aesthetic, and evaluative responses to literature.[1]

---

[1]The processes associated with these aspects of reading seem to be based more on responses to what has been read and represented rather than on construction of a representation. There is, of course, the possibility that various aspects of the structure of a text facilitate or encourage particular aesthetic responses. This is certainly the case in poetry, where various genres have canonical structural forms. However, we have neither the expertise nor industry to tackle these structural aspects of reading.

Historically, previous accounts of structural aspects of reading have focused solely on elements of the surface structure of the text. By elements we mean specific words or phrases that signal the organization of the information, such as *In summary*, or *because*. Structural aspects of text have also included the physical manifestation of the text on the page, including typography and paragraphing. Two noteworthy treatments of these issues are reviews by Lorch (1989) and Waller (1991). They each discussed the effects on comprehension and memory of several types of structural cues. Our treatment of structure departs from the traditional in two important ways. First, we approach the issue of structure from the perspective of an integrated theory of text processing and knowledge acquisition, described in the next section. We are not so much interested in whether, or which, structural cues improve memory or processing as in understanding why such facilitation occurs and the constraints on it. Second, consistent with our theory-based assumptions about the interactive nature of processing, representation, and memory, we are concerned with the knowledge of structure that readers bring *to* the text and how that knowledge enhances or constrains the construction of meaning. As we illustrate, this perspective locates the impact of structural aspects of text in the meaning construction process, a process that reflects a complex of interactions among the reader and the text in the context of the reading task and situation.

TEXT-DRIVEN AND KNOWLEDGE-DRIVEN PROCESSING: OVERVIEW AND COMPARISON

Readers rely on text-driven and knowledge-driven processing as they attempt to construct meaningful mental representations of what they are reading. Our assumptions about this general process are consistent with a variety of theories of text comprehension (e.g., Gernsbacher, 1990; Graesser, Gernsbacher, & Goldman, 1997; Graesser, Singer, & Trabasso, 1994; Kintsch, 1988, 1998; van Dijk & Kintsch, 1983; see also edited volumes by Britton & Graesser, 1996; Lorch & O'Brien, 1995; and van Oostendorp & Goldman, 1999). We assume that readers parse the input text into concepts and their relationships, representing these in some form of associative network of nodes and links among those nodes. At the same time, prior knowledge related to text information contributes to the network. In building the network, readers strive to maintain local and global coherence. That is, they attempt to link successive input with concept nodes and structures that are emerging in the representation. If readers cannot find a way to create a connection, there is a "break" in continuity or coherence. When "breaks" in coherence occur, readers may resolve them by establishing a new structure in the representation (Gernsbacher, 1997), by making inferences that allow the seemingly inconsistent information to fit within the established representation (e.g., Graesser, Singer, & Trabasso, 1994; van Dijk & Kintsch, 1983), or by rereading, reinterpreting, and reorganizing previously represented information (e.g., Goldman & Saul, 1990). These activities for establishing and maintaining local and global coherence involve text-driven and knowledge-driven processing.

Text-driven processing refers to the use of the content and organization of the text as a basis for the construction of mental representations. *Content* refers to specific words or text segments and the meaning relationships among them (e.g., reference, presupposition, cause–effect) (cf. Graesser, 1981; Graesser & Clark, 1985). *Organization*, or structural aspects, of text refers to the ordering of words in sentences and sentences in the text, as well as rhetorical and graphic devices that mark the functions of specific sentences and the organization of the text as a whole (e.g., Goldman, 1996; Lorch, 1989; Meyer, 1975). For example, at the sentence level, placing information first signals that the reader should regard it as the topic of the sentence (Halliday & Hasan, 1976). At the paragraph or passage level, enumerators such as *first* and *last* mark items in a list.

Phrases such as *in summary* and *briefly* convey information about the function of the sentences they introduce. Other phrases signal particular structures associated with a specific discourse genre. For example, *Once upon a time* marks the beginning of a fictional story. Graphic devices are also used to indicate the organization of a text, such as, marking items in a list by bullets, indenting paragraphs, and centering headings (e.g., Bond & Hayes, 1984; Waller, 1991). This chapter focuses on structural aspects of the text. We discuss text *content* in so far as it interacts with structural aspects of processing.

Knowledge-driven processing refers to the important role that prior knowledge plays in the ways readers use what they already know to construct mental representations of what they read. There are ample evidence and discussion of the effects of prior *content* knowledge on what people understand and learn from reading (e.g., McNamara, Kintsch, Songer, & Kintsch, 1996; Spilich, Vesonder, Chiesi, & Voss, 1979). Here our emphasis is on *structural* aspects of prior knowledge, by which we mean readers' knowledge of the organization of words in sentences (syntax), the organization of sentences within paragraphs, and the organization of different discourse genre and rhetorical structures. Such knowledge includes knowledge of the kinds of information that ought to occur in particular genre and rhetorical devices for cueing particular genre structures such as fairy tales, persuasive essays, and the like (Meyer, 1985; Weaver & Kintsch, 1991).

In normal reading situations, representation construction reflects the interaction of text-driven and knowledge-driven processing. The relative reliance on one or the other in a particular reading situation depends on how much readers know about the domain or topic, about the discourse genre, and about how to interpret the surface structure of the material being read. Generally, in situations of high content knowledge, readers will be less reliant on structural aspects of the text than in low content knowledge situations because they can draw on preexisting information to create accurate and coherent mental representations. In low content knowledge situations, processing may be more text driven, with readers relying on cues in the text to organize and relate the information and achieve the intended meanings (Beck & Dole, 1992; Beck, McKeown, Sinatra, & Loxterman, 1991; Britton & Gülgöz, 1991; Coté, Goldman, & Saul, 1998; Goldman & Durán, 1988; McNamara et al., 1996; McNamara & Kintsch, 1996; Olhausen & Roller, 1988; Roller, 1990).

In addition to the relationship to prior content knowledge, readers' abilities to use the cues present in the surface text depend on having prior knowledge of the structures of texts and how to use them in the understanding process. Structural cues in the text cannot be effective if readers lack the prior knowledge needed to recognize and interpret these cues. Hence, structural aspects of the surface text are only *potential* processing instructions to the reader; their effectiveness depends on readers having the prior knowledge of how to accurately interpret and use them (Gernsbacher, 1997; Gernsbacher & Faust, 1991; Givón, 1992; Goldman, 1997; Goldman & Murray, 1992; Perfetti, 1998; Zwaan & Radvansky, 1998).

STRUCTURAL ASPECTS OF TEXT-DRIVEN PROCESSING: TYPES OF CUES AND EMPIRICAL FINDINGS

The surface structure of a text provides potential processing instructions for constructing the intended connections among concepts. Such cues to conceptual connection can facilitate the resolution of seeming inconsistencies or even prevent the appearance of an inconsistency (Zwaan, Magliano, & Graesser, 1995; Zwaan & Radvansky, 1998). Some of these processing instructions are in the ordered sequence of linguistic units (e.g., words, phrases, sentences, paragraphs, and chapters). Other kinds of processing instructions are more explicit. These more explicit cues include specific words or phrases (e.g., *first, because,* and *in contrast*), as well as graphic and typographical cues (e.g., layout and font style). For example, connective phrases that specify temporal (*after, at the same time*) or spatial information (*in another part of the house*) can cue readers to the structural organization that best conveys the relationship between two events in a narrative. Without connectors, the resulting representation may or may not reflect the author's intended meaning or communicative intent. For expository text as compared to narrative, readers often have less knowledge on which to rely, and the lack of explicit cues in the surface code may lead to great variability in representations constructed by different individuals (Goldman, Coté, & Saul, 1995; Sanders, 1997; Sanders, Spooren, & Noordman, 1992; Spooren, 1997).

Types of Structural Cues in Text

Surface Structure Order

In the English language, word order conveys meaning-relevant information. For example, the difference in meaning between the sentences *John hit Mary* and *Mary hit John* is conveyed only by the order of the words in the sentence. There are no cues to the roles of each actor other than the default assumption in English that the first-mentioned noun corresponds to the agent of the action, unless otherwise marked. In spoken and written discourse, we make assumptions about meaning based on the order of words within utterances/sentences and on the order of utterances/sentences within a larger discourse. A recent analysis of the pragmatic and communicative levels of language (Graesser, Millis, & Zwaan, 1997) indicates that order-related principles play a prominent role in accounting for interpretations and meanings of both written and oral messages.

Explicit Cues to Relations Among Text Elements

In addition to word order, texts may contain both linguistic and graphic cues to the organization and logical relations among text elements. Linguistic and graphic cues have in common the potential to guide readers' processing of the underlying coherence relations expressed in the text. For the potential to be realized, readers must be aware of the relevance of the cue and make use of the organizational information conveyed by the cue in constructing their mental representations (Goldman et al., 1995; Lorch, 1989).

Linguistic Cues.   Linguistic cues, sometimes referred to as discourse markers, have been analyzed from a number of perspectives. For example, Bateman and Rondhuis (1997) recently provided an excellent review and analysis of three theories of coherence relations that typify formal, linguistic analyses of discourse.[2] Of specific relevance to understanding meaning from reading is a taxonomy of coherence relations developed by Sanders et al. (1992). They defined coherence relations as the "aspect of meaning of two or more discourse segments that cannot be described in terms of the meaning of the segments in isolation. In other words, it is because of this coherence relation that the meaning of two discourse segments is more than the sum of its parts" (p. 2). A specific class of discourse markers called connectives express, signal, or cue the

---

[2]The three theories they review are Lascarides and Asher's (1991) and Asher's (1993) "Segmented Discourse Representation Theory"; Martin's (1992) "Conjunctive Relations"; and Mann and Thompson's (1988) "Rhetorical Structure Theory."

underlying conceptual coherence relations. Examples of connectives are *because, furthermore,* and *however*. Earlier proposals (Halliday & Hasan, 1976) delineated four fundamental connective relations: temporal, additive, causal, and adversative.[3] Connectives such as these most frequently cue local coherence relations, that is, relations among information in sentences occurring relatively close together in the text.

Other rhetorical devices specify structure at more global levels, including how paragraphs relate to the overall theme of a discourse, how sentences relate across paragraphs, and how the structure supports the recognition of the most important information (Lorch, 1989). Calling them signaling devices, Lorch (1989) distinguished these devices from those aspects of a text that communicate the semantic content: Signals emphasize particular aspects of content or structure, but they do not add content (Lorch, 1989). Lorch provided a list of signaling devices used in expository prose that included titles, headings, and subheadings; repetition of content to emphasize, preview, or summarize; function indicators (pointer words like *thus*, pointer phrases like *in summary*, pointer sentences like *let me summarize what has been said*); relevance indicators (*let me stress that*); enumeration devices; and typographical cues (underlining, boldface, and spatial layout such as indenting, centering).

The different types of signaling devices provide different information to readers (Lorch, 1989). Function and relevance indicators help readers pick out what to selectively attend to. A summary indicator causes readers to read the signaled content more slowly than they otherwise would (Lorch & Lorch, 1986). Enumeration devices (e.g., *first, second, finally*) provide information about the relationship of the specific information to the global organization of the text and support readers' efforts to monitor their comprehension (Goldman & Saul, 1990). Other signaling devices alert the reader to the overall topic and structure of the text. For example, titles, headings, and subheadings identify topics and subtopics. Headings and subheadings occur throughout a text. As a whole they provide a potential retrieval plan based on the structure they convey. Headings and subheadings are also useful in guiding searches for selected information (Goldman & Durán, 1988; Guthrie, 1988).

The signaling devices discussed by Lorch (1989) cue the overall rhetorical structure of the discourse. Meyer (1985) proposed a set of five "top-level" rhetorical structures in an attempt to systematize the structures of the major genre of expository texts. These were collection or list, description, causal, comparative, and problem/solution. These rhetorical structures may be signaled by particular words or phrases but do not have to be. Weaver and Kintsch (1991) discussed a similar set of rhetorical schemata for expository text. In addition, there are many other categories of text genre that differ with respect to their structure. For example, the structure of a story is different from that of a persuasive essay; the structure of a news story is different from that of an editorial (Graesser et al., 1997). Finally, it is likely that the overall rhetorical or genre structure interacts with more local structural components. For example, a persuasive essay may make the structure of evidence more important whereas an informational description essay may emphasize a more taxonomic organization.

---

[3]Sanders et al. (1992) did not include temporal connectives among their taxonomy of cues to conceptual coherence. They claimed that these are not coherence relations in the same sense as causal and additive connectives. However, in making the time dimension explicit, temporal connectives do foreground time and differentially affect the availability of the preceding information (Bestgen & Vonk, 1995; Zwaan & Radvansky, 1998). A series of actions connected by the connective *and* is more available than a series whose temporal order is explicitly marked. For example, the second of two actions connected by an *and* (e.g., *He opened the door and went inside*) was more available than the second of two actions connected by a *then* (e.g., *He opened the door then went inside*) (Bestgen & Vonk, 1995). The explicit temporal connective places the two actions in different temporal periods and hence situations (Zwaan & Radvansky, 1998), making the first action less available than the second. Gernsbacher (1997) suggested that the connector *then* cues a need to switch to a new substructure in the mental representation being constructed.

Graphic Cues.   The distinctive graphic properties associated with titles, head-ings, subheadings, and paragraph spacing highlight the overall structure of the text for the reader. Other forms of graphic cueing rely on distinct font style (e.g., boldface, ital-ics, underlining) to mark a word, phrase, or a sentence as special in some way. These kinds of cues can be used in different ways, depending on the conventions adopted by a particular author. They may indicate important concepts readers should attend to, mark terms that are defined in a glossary, or add emphasis to the term. For graphical cueing to be effective, a text needs to have a relatively low proportion of graphically cued to noncued information (Lorch, 1989).

Evidence for the Importance of Structure in Text-Driven Processing

There is ample sentence-level and discourse-level evidence that structural aspects of the surface text are important in the comprehension process. In the present context we mention the sentence-level evidence but devote discussion to the discourse level. At the sentence level, two robust phenomena illustrate readers' reliance on word order in comprehending sentences: the Advantage of First Mention (Gernsbacher & Hargreaves, 1988) and Garden Path sentences (Frazier, 1987). (See Gernsbacher, 1995, 1997 for further information.)

Discourse-Level Effects

At the discourse level, research on narrative and on expository text demonstrates the importance of text-based structure to processing, memory, and importance judg-ments. We discuss the empirical support and theoretical explanations for three major conclusions:

Conclusion 1. Structural cues can improve identification of main or important ideas and their memorability.

Conclusion 2. Parallelisms between the surface structure text and the underlying conceptual structure of the information facilitate comprehension. The corollary to this generalization is that comprehension is ham-pered when the two are not aligned.

Conclusion 3. Making the structure of the text more salient improves comprehen-sion and learning.

Conclusion 1. Structural Cues can Improve Identification of Main or Impor-tant Ideas and Their Memorability.   Text structure is one way that readers iden-tify the main points and important ideas in a text (Alexander & Jetton, 1996; Meyers, 1975; van Hout-Wolters, 1986). There is a variety of evidence in support of this conclu-sion.

- Readers are generally more adept at identifying a main idea that appears at the beginning of a paragraph than when it is embedded in the text (Baumann, 1986; Taylor & Williams, 1983). Readers appear to have a default rule that the main idea will be the first sentence of a paragraph. If it is not in the first sentence, they need to reformulate or construct the main idea (Hare & Chesla, 1986; Kieras, 1982, 1985).
- Sentences that occur early in the passage and first in paragraphs are given more weight as measured by longer reading times and more frequent reinspections

compared to other sentences. (Goldman, 1988; Goldman & Saul, 1990; Kieras, 1980; Lorch, 1989; Lorch & Chen, 1986; Lorch & Lorch, 1986; Meyer, 1975).

- The first sentence in a paragraph or story episode is a better cue for later occurring sentences than other sentences in the paragraph (e.g., Cirilo, 1981; Cirilo & Foss, 1980; Haberlandt, 1980, 1984; Haberlandt, Berian, & Sandson, 1980; Kieras, 1978; Mandler & Goodman, 1982).
- Ideas marked by typographical features such as bolding or italicizing, or by the occurrence of signal words and phrases, are processed longer and recalled better than unsignaled information (e.g., Golding & Fowler, 1992; Goldman, 1988; Goldman & Saul, 1990; Kieras, 1980; Lorch, 1989; Lorch & Chen, 1986; Lorch & Lorch, 1986; Meyer, 1975).
- The presence of paragraph indentation increases the likelihood of a consensus regarding the main points of the passage (Stark, 1988).

The effects of structural cuing on main idea identification are so well established that at least one reading researcher (Garner, 1992) suggested that writers of texts for children should put explicit statements in texts that particular ideas are important and make these ideas appear in the first sentences of paragraphs. Care must be exercised in considering Garner's (1992) recommendation because the effects of structural cueing are to improve memory for the signaled content but to not affect or to even inhibit memory for the unsignaled (Glynn, Britton, & Tillman, 1985; Lorch, 1989).

Explanations for Structure Effects on Main Idea Identification and Memory

There are three related theoretical frameworks that offer explanations for the effects of structure on main idea identification and memory. One of the initial explanations derives from text processing research, in which it was assumed that readers created a hierarchical representation of the information in the text. Hierarchical representations were assumed to be generated through a process that placed heavy emphasis on the order in which sentences were read (W. Kintsch & van Dijk, 1978; Meyer, 1975). The title and first several sentences of a passage usually established concepts that were subsequently repeated throughout the passage as more information about them was provided. The incoming information "attached" to the initially established concepts, usually in a subordinate or supporting relation. Sentences that had many subsequent sentences connected to them took on more superordinate, thematic status in the passage (e.g., W. Kintsch & van Dijk, 1978; Meyer, 1975). Research indicated that level in the hierarchy did indeed predict recall, with statements high in a text hierarchy recalled more frequently than those low in the hierarchy (Black & Bower, 1980; Cirilo & Foss, 1980; W. Kintsch & Keenan, 1973; W. Kintsch & van Dijk, 1978; Meyer, 1975; Meyer & McConkie, 1973; Rumelhart, 1975).

The second account is Gernsbacher's (1990, 1997) Structure Building Framework. It provides a generalized account of the hierarchical "levels effect." According to the Structure Building Framework, comprehenders build representations in a three-phase process: (a) lay foundations, (b) develop by mapping on new information to previous information; and (c) if new information does not map, shift and build a new structure. Concepts that are mentioned first in a sentence or discourse serve as the foundation or "higher order" organizers for the structure, as in the Advantage of First Mention effect mentioned earlier. Because this information is necessary for further structure building, memory for these concepts is enhanced. Later concepts are mapped onto the initial concepts and are attached "lower down" in the structure. When concepts are no longer needed for building the representation, they are suppressed. Gernsbacher has shown that the Structure Building Framework accounts for a variety of phenomena at the sentence and paragraph level, including anaphoric resolution, the superior cue value of the first versus the second of two nouns in a sentence, and the effects of changes in time and place on narrative processing (for a review see Gernsbacher, 1997). The Structure Building Framework is also consistent with a variety of sentence parsing strategies.

The third class of explanations for order effects, activation-based theories,[4] are consistent with but do not depend on assumptions about hierarchical structure or the building of specific structures. Activation-based network theories are based on accrual of activation by a concept or idea represented as a node in a network representation (Goldman & Varma, 1995; Goldman, Varma, & Coté, 1996; W. Kintsch, 1988, 1998; Langston & Trabasso, 1999; van den Broek, Risden, Fletcher, & Thurlow, 1996; van den Broek, Young, Tzeng, & Linderholm, 1999). According to this class of explanations, concepts and ideas that occur early in a sentence or discourse enjoy a high degree of initial activation. This high level of activation makes it more likely that they will be carried over or remain active into later processing cycles and have an opportunity to form connections with incoming information. Concepts and ideas that have more connections, comparatively speaking, take on a more central role in the representation and are remembered better. Network-based activation explanations have applicability to a wide variety of sentence- and discourse-level phenomena (W. Kintsch, 1998; Langston & Trabasso, 1999; van den Broek et al., 1999). Text-based structural cues other than order of mention are important to activation-based networks in that they can provide explicit pointers to relations among concepts and ideas. These cues act as processing instructions that may bias which concepts are linked together and the kinds of links that are constructed. The cues may also alter the amount of activation allocated to particular concepts when they are processed, with greater allocations resulting in a concept being accessible longer thereby providing more opportunities to link with other incoming information (for discussion see Goldman et al., 1996).

Conclusion 2. Parallelisms Between the Surface Structure Text and the Underlying Conceptual Structure of the Information Facilitate Comprehension. When the Two are not Aligned, Comprehension is Hampered.   Evidence suggests that comprehension is facilitated if there is congruence between the structure of the text and the structure of the situation or conceptual domain (Zwaan & Radvansky, 1998). For example, when the actual temporal order of events matches their description in a text, performance is better on comprehension questions (Ohtsuka & Brewer, 1992), chronological order of recall, and processing speed (Bestgen & Vonk, 1995; Zwaan & Whitten, 1998). Furthermore, when the surface text structure and the underlying conceptual structure are parallel, that is when they match, texts are more considerate of the reader (Anderson & Armbruster, 1984; Armbruster, 1984; Armbruster & Gudbrandsen, 1986). "Simplifying" texts by removing these structural cues and making shorter sentences can make the texts harder to understand because these techniques remove the links that provide parallel surface and conceptual meaning. The result is that coherence is reduced (Anderson, Hiebert, Scott, & Wilkinson, 1985; Beck & Dole, 1992; Beck & McKeown, 1989; Beck, McKeown, & Gromoll, 1989; Davison, 1984).

---

[4]Resonance theory is closely related to the activation-based network models discussed in this section. Resonance theory is based on the idea that incoming information is linked with information already in memory on the basis of overlapping semantic and contextual features (Myers & O'Brien, 1998; O'Brien & Myers, 1999). According to resonance theory, when a new concept is processed, it sets off an activation-based reverberation throughout the memory system, essentially looking for a feature-based match. Concepts that have high featural overlap are linked. The theory has been most consistently applied to problems of resolving coreference relations.

An additional aspect of parallelism concerns matches across structure at different levels of discourse. Hoover (1997) showed that structure at the global level, that is, the theme of the discourse, impacted processing at the sentence level. If the theme of the discourse and the theme of the sentence matched there was a decrease in the time to read the passive sentence. Perfetti and Goldman (1975) showed a similar phenomenon for the value of a noun as a cue: Thematized nouns in passive sentences were better cues for sentence recall than nonthematized nouns.

Evidence for the importance of parallelism also comes from studies in which that parallelism is disrupted. For example, when sentences within paragraphs and paragraphs within passages are scrambled it takes readers longer to read them as compared to the unscrambled versions (W. Kintsch, Mandel, & Kozminsky, 1977; Taylor & Samuels, 1983). Disruption of order disrupts both local and global coherence, and memory for the material suffers in comparison to correctly ordered passages (Kieras, 1978; W. Kintsch & Greene, 1978; Mandler & Johnson, 1977; Stein & Nezworski, 1978; Thorndyke, 1977; Vauras, von Wright, & Kinnunen, 1991).

Parallelism has also been examined in the context of main point identification. When the surface structure cue and the underlying semantic content point to the same information as the main point, readers are best able to identify it (Stark, 1988). If the surface structure cue points to a semantically inappropriate main point, readers tend to rely more on the content in making their choice (Kieras, 1980). Furthermore, Goldman et al. (1995) found that when both paragraphing cues and content converged on the same information, readers processed text differently than when the paragraphing cued a semantically inappropriate sentence. Specifically, when structural cues and the content identified the same sentences as main points, readers looked at these sentences more frequently, spent more time reading them, and recalled them better than they did sentences that were elaborations of the main points. In contrast, when the structural and conceptual conflicted (elaboration sentences were paragraph initial), readers looked at the elaborations more frequently but they still spent more time reading the main points and recalled them better than the elaborations. Apparently, the effect of the surface structure "miscue" was to momentarily mislead the readers to look at elaborations rather than main points. However, readers quickly recognized that these elaborations were less important semantically and moved on to reading other, more important sentences.

Finally, research indicates that the importance of parallelism between the surface structure and the content structure depends on readers' prior knowledge about the topic of the text they are reading. When readers are less familiar with and have little knowledge in the content domain, they are more dependent on surface structure cueing. For example, Goldman et al. (1995) found that readers spent more time processing elaboration information that was "miscued" as main points if the content was less familiar to them. The miscueing did not affect processing time in more familiar content areas.

Conclusion 3. Making the Structure of the Text More Salient Improves Comprehension and Learning. This Effect Interacts With Prior Knowledge of the Content Discussed in the Text.   Investigations of the impact of making the structure of the text more salient can be divided into two phases of research. In the first phase, researchers concentrated on making explicit the organization of the information in the text without regard for differences in content knowledge among readers. Lorch (1989) reviewed many of these studies and concluded that information that is highlighted through typographical mechanisms such as special font or underlining tends to be remembered better than when it is not highlighted. Devices such as number signals (enumerated lists) make readers more aware of the organization of the text and provide a retrieval plan that supports better recall (Lorch, 1985; Lorch & Chen, 1986). The inclusion of sentences that explicitly relate disparate parts of the text (e.g., *Recall that previously we discussed ...*) enhance memory for the information as well as the coherence of the organization (Glover et al., 1988). Other studies indicate that signaling devices can be useful in directing readers' processing strategies so that they focus on the topics and their organization (Lorch, Lorch, & Inman, 1993) or the major concepts and their relations (Loman & Mayer, 1983; Mayer, Dyck, & Cook, 1984).

The foregoing manipulations to the surface text can be used to create greater parallelism between the surface text and the underlying conceptual structure, thereby making it easier for students to identify the structure. For example, in a recent study, Rickards, Fayen, Sullivan, and Gillespie (1997) manipulated the presence of topic sentences that signaled the role of the subsequent information in the conceptual structure of a variety of science passages. The presence of signals led to significant increases in the amount of notetaking during lecture and a higher incidence of notes on the high-level, signaled material. Notes of the students who had heard the versions without signaling were lists of facts.

In the second phase of research, the interaction of surface structure and prior knowledge in conceptual domains has been examined. There are many situations where readers know little and are attempting to acquire content knowledge. However, low knowledge in a domain sets constraints on the potential utility of surface structure cues; indeed, sometimes even the presence of surface structure cues is insufficient to overcome gaps in content knowledge (Noordman & Vonk, 1992). Noordman and Vonk (1992) found that adults who read informational text in which causal relations were explicitly cued by the connector *because* made inferences only at the level of the surface text, not at the level of the conceptual model of the situation. Noordman and Vonk (1992) concluded that these readers "accept the conjunction *because* as a signal of coherence ... but they do not work out what the relation between the events and states is during reading.... So the concepts in the sentence are only related by the textual signals" (p. 387).

However, other research suggests that it is quite possible to make changes to the surface structure of a text and facilitate the learning performance of low knowledge individuals. For example, McNamara et al. (Experiment 2, 1996) compared highly cohesive texts with those that required readers to supply a number of key inferences. Differences between the more versus less cohesive texts were the inclusion in the more cohesive texts of sentence connectives, phrases that explicitly linked ideas together, topic headings, and topic sentences that made explicit the relationship of the paragraph to the overall topic of the text. The performance of low-knowledge readers on the more cohesive texts was superior to their performance on the less cohesive ones on measures of literal and inferential comprehension as well as on problem-solving questions.

Research by Voss and Silfies (1996) also suggests that changes to the surface structure of the text that make more explicit the underlying causal structure can compensate for lack of content knowledge. Voss and Silfies (1996) compared comprehension of history texts about fictional countries that varied in terms of the explicitness of the underlying causal structure. For questions about information that was contained in both the expanded (explicit) and unexpanded texts, performance on the expanded text was predicted by reading skill but performance on the unexpanded text was predicted by prior knowledge. These correlations illustrate that when all the information is in the text the impact of prior knowledge is lessened. Voss and Silfies (1996) discussed their findings in relation to the distinction between the representation of the text and the representation of the situation described by the text (Kintsch, 1988).[5]

---

[5]Findings such as these suggest that a categorical distinction between representations of the text and of the situation are not that useful. Conceiving of these in terms of continua seems more appropriate (Coté et al., 1998; Goldman & Van Oostendorp, 1999; W. Kintsch, 1998).

Summary

Our review of structural aspects of text-driven processing indicates that such information can have a powerful effect on online processing as well as on the mental representations that result. Structural aspects of the text are particularly important when readers know little about what they are reading. There are two important connections between structural aspects of text-driven processing and structural aspects of prior knowledge. First, the effects of structural aspects of the text depend on whether readers can supply the structure themselves and thus do not need the cues in the text. Second, if readers cannot supply the structure themselves, they need to have sufficient knowledge of structure cues in text to allow them to interpret and use information to construct coherent and appropriately structured mental representations of the information.

STRUCTURAL ASPECTS OF KNOWLEDGE-DRIVEN PROCESSING: EMPIRICAL FINDINGS

As readers attempt to build mental representations of information they are reading, they rely on their expectations about how particular linguistic forms are supposed to be structured. These expectations are based on readers' knowledge about the structure of multiple levels of language, including words, sentences, paragraphs, and different text genre, (e.g., biographies, stories, persuasive essays, informational essays). For example, if readers know how paragraphing and various rhetorical devices can be used to mark the global discourse organization and main ideas, these structural aspects of the text can impact the meaning relationships readers understand and represent (e.g., Goldman et al., 1995; Goldman & Murray, 1992; Meyer, Brandt, & Bluth, 1980; Spooren, 1997). The research literature indicates three important conclusions about knowledge of structure:

Conclusion 1. Readers use their knowledge of structure in processing text. When an expected structure is violated, comprehension is impaired.

Conclusion 2. Knowledge of structural forms of text develops with experiences with different genre, and is correlated with age/time in school.

Conclusion 3. Making readers more aware of genre structure improves learning.

Conclusion 1. Readers Use Their Knowledge of Structure in Processing Text. When an Expected Structure is Violated, Comprehension is Impaired.   The impact of readers' knowledge of text structures is often evident in their text processing and memory. For example, readers expect stories to conform to an episodic structure organized around the goals and needs of particular protagonists (Mandler & Johnson, 1977; Stein & Glenn, 1979; Stein & Policastro, 1984; Trabasso & van den Broek, 1985). Readers construct mental representations of stories that include the goals plus several other dimensions of the situation described in the story, including the story context (e.g., time and space), and the local causal relations among events (Haenggi, Gernsbacher, & Bollinger, 1993; Zwaan, Langston, & Graesser, 1995; Zwaan, Magliano, & Graesser, 1995). Explicit time and space markers act as cues to the appropriate episodic structure of a developing situation model (Bestgen & Vonk, 1995; Zwaan & Radvansky, 1998).

Readers actively monitor the dimensions of situations, and changes in them, because such changes reflect episode boundaries and serve as cues for the creation of new parts of the mental representation (Gernsbacher, 1990, 1997; Zwaan, 1996; Zwaan, Langston, & Graesser, 1995; Zwaan, Magliano, & Graesser, 1995; Zwaan & Radvansky,

1998). Similarly, readers use their expectations about the structure of nonnarrative texts to guide the structure of their mental representations. However these expectations are more variable than for narratives because, as discussed earlier, there are many more rhetorical structures for expository genre (Goldman et al., 1995; Lorch, 1995; Meyer, 1985; Weaver & Kintsch, 1991). At a minimum, readers monitor for changes in theme or topic in an expository text (e.g., Hyönä, 1991; Lorch, Lorch, & Matthews, 1985).

The need to "shift" structures in the mental representation creates increased processing demands on the reader. These increased demands are manifest in longer reading times on information that conveys the shift (Haberlandt, 1980; Hyönä, 1990; Kieras, 1981; Lorch, Lorch, Gretter, & Horn, 1987; Lorch et al., 1985; Lorch, Lorch, & Morgan, 1987). Children as well as adults manifest the shift effect. For example, Hyönä (1994) investigated whether 10- and 11-year-old students showed the shift effect in narratives and expository texts. He found that 11-year-olds and adults behaved similarly and allocated more processing time to sentences introducing a new episode in a narrative than to sentences continuing an already initiated episode. For expository texts, Hyönä (1994) found that 10-year-olds and adults showed a reliable topic shift effect, paying more attention to a sentence that changed the theme than to one that continued an established theme.

Furthermore, Hyönä (1995) provided evidence that the shift effect reflects time needed to create new structures and substructures in the mental representation. Using eye movement data, Hyönä compared first- and second-pass reading times. On first-pass reading, extra processing time was allocated to topic shift sentences but not to sentences that continued a topic. On subsequent passes, there was no difference in the processing time allocated to topic shift and nonshift sentences. These data suggest that the increased processing time on the first pass reflects time needed to create new structures in the mental representation. On the second pass, these structures are already part of the representation.[6]

There is an interesting difference between the behavior of the shift effect in narrative and expository text. In expository text it is possible to reduce the severity of the shift effect by cueing topic shifts with transition questions presented immediately prior to each shift (Lorch et al., 1987). On the other hand, the presence of explicit temporal connectors does not reduce the shift effect in stories (Zwaan, 1996).

Memory for text is also affected by readers' knowledge of text structure. Children and adults who demonstrate (directly or indirectly) knowledge of text structure show strong recall performance for well-organized texts (e.g., Carrell, 1992; Englert & Hiebert, 1984; Garner et al., 1986; Hague, 1988; McGee, 1982). For example, Meyer et al. (1980) looked at recall by ninth-grade, good and poor readers of passages in which the top-level structure was either signaled or not. When the structure was not signaled, only the recalls of the good readers used the same type of top-level structure as the author of the passage had. The poorer readers did not use it. Similarly, Carrell (1992) found that the use of one's knowledge of text structures during reading and recall improved the quality of the written recalls. Taylor and Samuels (1983) gave fifth- and sixth-grade students passages in which the sentences were in their normal order or in which they had been scrambled. Students who reported awareness of the structure of the passages (28% of the sample) recalled more from the normally ordered than from the scrambled passages. For those who were unaware of the structure, there was no difference in recall.

---

[6]Interestingly, despite the fact that processing time was similar for topic-shift and continuing-topic sentences, Hyönä (1995) did find more regressive fixations on the topic shift sentences. He interpreted these as reflecting efforts to integrate parts of the mental representation.

Evidence for readers' use of their knowledge of structure also comes from research that intentionally violates structural expectations by scrambling, miscueing, or somehow reorganizing the text so that it does not conform to the expected structure. When these structural expectations are violated (e.g., by reordering events or interleaving episodes), comprehension and memory are more difficult (W. Kintsch et al., 1977; Mandler & DeForest, 1979; Stein & Nezworski, 1978). We already mentioned some of this research in our discussion of the importance of parallelism between text structure and conceptual structure.

Other researchers have looked at more specific violations of genre expectations. Vauras, Hyönä, and Niemi (1992) examined the effects of reordering information in a history text on processing and memory. College students read history texts that followed a normal and coherent goal–attempt–outcome organizational sequence as compared to one that reordered the expected sequence to attempt–outcome–goal. Reading time was longer on the reordered version than on the coherent one. In the reordered texts, the longest times were spent on goal sentences. Eye movement data allowed Vauras et al. (1992) to examine first-pass fixations and regressions. The longest times on first-pass reading were on sentences initiating the reordered sequence. There were also more regressions on reordered texts to the start of the reordered sequence, but overall more time was spent on goal sentences. Furthermore, in the coherent text, time spent processing predicted recall; in the reordered it did not. Vauras et al. (1992) concluded that the readers of the reordered texts were expending time identifying the importance or "place" of the information in the hierarchical text structure. Once that was figured out, that structure governed the recall. In the reordered version it took longer to figure out the structure. This pattern of processing is similar to the pattern observed when paragraphs are miscued (e.g., Goldman et al., 1995).

Knowledge of structure is clearly important in efficient and strategic processing of text. How and when is that knowledge acquired, and what we might expect children to know about discourse structure?

Conclusion 2. Knowledge of the Structure of Different Text Genre Develops With Experiences With Different Forms of Text, Correlated With Age/Time in School.   Investigations of students' knowledge of different genre indicate that expectations about narrative structure appear early relative to knowledge of other genre (e.g., Goldman & Varnhagen, 1982; Stein & Policastro, 1984). Several studies indicate that children's knowledge of expository structures increases with age, a correlate of experience with diverse text forms. In an early study, Danner (1976) compared awareness of expository structure in students in Grades 2, 4, and 6 and found that overt awareness of the differences in passage organization increased with age. Garner et al. (1986) examined children's knowledge of three aspects of expository text structure: paragraph identification, differentiation of main ideas from elaborations, and topic relevance. Comparing students in Grades 3, 5, and 7, Garner et al. (1986) found that all students accurately identified paragraphs but third and fifth graders most frequently explained their choices based on graphic cues. In contrast, seventh graders talked about meaning relations as the basis for their decisions. There was moderate success in all age groups at distinguishing main ideas from elaborations and using the main ideas in paragraph initial position. On the differentiation task, everyone picked out those sentences that were topically related but the seventh graders also were able to exclude the ones that were topically unrelated. An important conclusion from this work is that seventh graders were markedly different from younger students in their knowledge of structure and their heuristic use of it, as evidenced in their use of meaning rather than the graphic signal in defining paragraphs and in their exclusion of topically unrelated sentences.

Other researchers have examined changes in knowledge of specific rhetorical structures of expository text. For example, Yochum (1991) compared attribution and causation structures. Children answered comprehension questions and provided free recalls. Performance was somewhat better for the causative structure as compared to the attributive. Comparing fifth-, seventh-, and ninth-grade students to adults, Olhausen and Roller (1988) found that text structure and content structure were used to identify main idea sentences. However, they noted that ninth-graders and adults more actively used the content structure than the younger students did.

Research with adolescents indicates that knowledge of the structure of expository genre is far from complete by the end of high school. Chambliss (1995) looked at upper level high school students' awareness of argument structures in texts. Specifically, she examined high school students' facility with the claim–evidence–warrant argument structure introduced by Toulmin (1958). Chambliss found that claims and evidence were easier for students to recognize than warrants. These two parts of the structure constitute a simplified form of the full argument structure. They were also the parts emphasized by the teacher.

Generally speaking, readers appear to have rather incomplete knowledge of the rhetorical structures of expository genre by the end of high school. This suggests the need to examine the impact of explicit instruction in genre structure on students' acquisition of useable knowledge about these structures.

Conclusion 3. Making Readers More Aware of Genre Structure Improves Learning.   In our previous discussion of text-driven processing we noted that attempts to increase the salience of structure *in the text* frequently facilitated reading comprehension. In this section we consider efforts to make *readers* more aware of structure in text. A variety of intervention techniques are effective in making readers more knowledgeable about structure and improving comprehension and memory (Alverman & Moore, 1991; Pearson & Fielding, 1991). Attention to structure can be increased by teaching readers to follow the text structure used by the author (e.g., Bartlett, 1978; Meyer et al., 1980), to employ adjunct aids to highlight that structure (e.g., Robinson & Kiewra, 1996; Slater, Graves, & Piche, 1985), or to create visual representations of the text structure (Richgels & McGee, 1989; Richgels, McGee, Lomax, & Sheard, 1987). These techniques have been used to instruct students on a variety of text structures including causation, compare/contrast, and problem/solution (Armbruster, Anderson, & Ostertag, 1987; Richgels & McGee, 1989; Richgels et al., 1987).

College students also benefit from explicit genre-structure instruction. Samuels, Tennyson, Sax, Mulcahy, Schermer, and Hajovy (1988) provided instruction on the structure of scientific journal articles, a genre with which college students were unfamiliar. Instruction focused on the categories of information as well as the organization of that information. On subsequent recall of scientific articles that either conformed or did not conform to the standard organization, the instructed group performed significantly better than the control group on both types of passages. The advantage was particularly striking for the article that conformed to the standard organization, with the instructed group recalling five times as much as the control group.

Training on text structure may be particularly important in low- or moderate-knowledge situations (Afflerbach, 1986), as illustrated in a study of high school students. Weisberg and Balajthy (1989) had high school students use graphic organizers and summaries to understand the comparisons and contrasts expressed in a series of passages that discussed topics of differing degrees of familiarity. Immediately after the intervention, the instructed group performed better than a control group on a graphic organizer task but there were no differences on a comprehension test. On a comprehension transfer test 1 month later, experimental students were better able to identify comparisons and contrasts in a new set of passages than were control students. This was true for topics of moderate and low familiarity.

Interventions that focus on genre structure indicate that instruction that improves readers' awareness of how to identify different genre structures can be effective in improving memory and learning of text content. The benefits may be particularly helpful for situations in which readers have little knowledge in the content domain of the text.

Summary of Text-Driven and Knowledge-Driven Processing

Readers need to know enough about text structure and content to make use of whatever cues are in the surface text, yet not too much lest they think they know everything in the text and therefore do not need to pay attention to the material at all. When readers are in low-knowledge circumstances they need assistance in constructing a representation of the information in the knowledge domain. This is the more likely situation for informational text than for narrative text. In low-knowledge situations it is very important that surface text cues be aligned with the underlying conceptual or situational models. Surface structural cues to organization and main idea identification can assist readers in learning in a new domain if readers know how to interpret these cues.

STRUCTURE AND ELECTRONIC HYPERTEXTS

In the final section of this chapter we consider implications for electronic hypertexts of findings regarding structure in traditional text. Structural aspects of traditional text and hypertext have different capabilities or functionalities, making it problematic to generalize from traditional studies of text structure to hypertext (cf. Mayer, 1997). Rather, first we consider structural differences and similarities between traditional text and electronic hypertexts. We examine potential implications for text- and knowledge-driven processing, as well as some of the empirical literature that has begun to explore the functionalities afforded by hypertext. More general reviews of issues of technology and literacy are discussed in two other chapters in this volume (Kamil, Intrator, & Kim, chap. 40, this volume; Leu, chap. 39, this volume), as well as in other edited volumes that focus on technology, hypertext, hypermedia, and literacy (e.g., Flood, Heath, & Flood, 1997; Reinking, McKenna, Labbo, & Kieffer, 1998; Rouet, Levonen, Dillon, & Spiro, 1996; van Oostendorp & de Mul, 1996).

Electronic Hypertexts and Structural Aspects of Processing

Hypertexts differ from traditional texts in that hypertexts have embedded in them explicit connections to other texts. These embedded links allow readers to "jump" easily to other texts. However, as in traditional text, whether readers take advantage of the possibilities the links afford depends on their knowledge of whether and how following such links will facilitate their meaning construction activities (Kamil, 1998; Kamil & Lane, 1998). The efficacy of hypertext for learning probably relies on alignment of the hypertext environment, readers' goals, and their interests (Alexander, Kulikowich, & Jetton, 1994; Goldman, 1996; Kamil et al., this volume; Leu, this volume). This is similar to the effect of interests and goals on learning from traditional texts.

In what follows, we discuss several recent studies in order to identify aspects of what we are calling *hypertext-enabled structures* that have significant implications for comprehension. These are structures that take advantage of the dynamic linking capability and graphic display properties of hypertext. First, we consider several studies of different hypertext-enabled structures that identify advantages and disadvantages of these different structures. These studies compare the overall effectiveness of these structures to each other and also to traditional linear text. We then discuss studies that investigate the impact of task and content domain on readers' use of hyper-text-enabled structures.

Relative Advantages of Different Hypertext-Enabled Structures

Whether hypertext is superior to linear text is a topic fraught with conflicting opinions and results. Some have claimed that the branching capacity of hypertext allows the reader to "transcend the linear, bounded and fixed qualities of traditional linear text" (Delaney & Landow, quoted in McHoul & Roe, 1996, p. 348). However, McHoul and Roe (1996) contended that linear text is not nearly so bounded and fixed in that readers can move from place to place in a text depending on their goals, interests, and assess-ment of what they still need to find out. Moreover, many structural aspects of text-driven processing (e.g., sentence and word order and the structure of paragraphs) are consistent across hypertext and traditional text.

These similarities notwithstanding, what differs is that the linear structure of tradi-tional text controls the amount of information the reader needs to structure and orga-nize. In hypertext systems, readers have to choose what they read next. These choices permit the "restructuring" of a text. The question is whether and under what circum-stances this restructuring facilitates text comprehension and learning.

One capability of hypertext is being able to provide a graphic overview of the struc-ture of the text from which readers can access specific parts of the text. Dee-Lucas and Larkin (1995) compared the effects of just such a structured overview with that of an unstructured text overview (alphabetical list of topics) and of a text presented linearly in a hypertext system. Both overviews provided hypertext entries into the text content. The researchers concluded that the major advantage of the structured overview was that readers developed a more extensive text representation that included more main points, topic headings, and their relationships. The major disadvantage of the unstruc-tured overview was that readers were not able to integrate the various main ideas.

In contrast to the advantages that Dee-Lucas and Larkin (1995) found for the struc-tured overview as compared to the linear hypertext system, Shapiro (1998) did not find an advantage of her hierarchical system over a linearly ordered one on the quality of readers' essays or on assessments of their factual knowledge. This was also true in comparing the linear to a third hypertext system in which the links present in the hier-archical system were available but in alphabetical order. However, the hierarchical and alphabetic systems resulted in readers including significantly more items in their con-cept maps than did the linear system. Surprisingly, the alphabetical system produced better quality essays than the hierarchical.

In explaining her findings, Shapiro (1998) suggested that readers of the alphabetic system had to struggle to find associations among different concepts. As a result, they developed a better understanding of the relationships among these concepts than did readers of the hierarchical system where the relationships were more explicit. This is similar to McNamara's (McNamara et al., 1996; McNamara & W. Kintsch, 1996) find-ings for high-knowledge subjects reading less coherent texts. One problem with this analogy is that Shapiro's (1998) readers had little knowledge in the domain. For McNamara et al. (1996), low-knowledge readers needed more explicit text. It is possi-ble that the alphabetic system provided sufficient support for the low-knowledge readers to attempt to find relationships among the concepts and build a coherent rep-resentation. However, the hierarchical system made readers believe that they under-stood the relationships, even though their representations did not go much beyond the presented information, reminiscent of the findings reported by Noordman and Vonk (1992). Shapiro's study suggests that potential advantages of hypertext can be realized only if hypertext links are designed so as to encourage users to reflect and operate on relationships expressed in links.

Research by Lehto, Zhu, and Carpenter (1995) also suggests that there are advantages to more structured hypertext. Lehto et al. (1995 experiment 2) had students answer reference questions using either a structured hypertext version of a college text in which hyperlinks replicated the text author's index and table of contents, or a hypertext that incorporated a computer-generated full-text index. Students using the more structured version answered reference questions more quickly and reference and recall questions more accurately than those using the version with full-text indexing. These results suggest that the structure imposed by the careful selection of terms to be electronically linked facilitates learning more effectively than the freedom of full-text links.

These studies of hypertext-enabled structures suggest some of the issues that arise when evaluating these systems. One issue will only be resolved as use of hypertext systems becomes more ubiquitous. That is, currently readers are more accustomed to reading from linear text than from hypertext and may need to acquire new strategies for reading in hypertext environments (Leu, this volume). The greater familiarity with reading from traditional text makes it difficult to interpret results of studies that show limited utility of hypertext-enabled structures. Other issues that currently *can* be addressed concern the alignment of the requirements of the task being done with the system, the structure or organization of the hypertext system itself, and the structure of the knowledge domain. If these are not compatible, we should not expect benefits.

Task Effects on Results for Hypertext-Enabled Structures

Task effects in hypertext systems have been noted by a number of researchers (e.g., Chen & Rada, 1996; Jonassen, 1993; Rada & Murphy, 1992). Here we are concerned specifically with the interaction of task effects and structure manipulations. Dee-Lucas and Larkin (1995, Experiment 2) replicated their first experiment but made one change: They told readers to integrate the material by focusing on the main ideas in order to summarize the material. Differences among the three groups that had been present in recall were not present in the written summaries. Thus, students using the unstructured overview recalled more of the main ideas than they had in the first experiment. Dee-Lucas and Larkin (1995) concluded that providing subjects with the explicit goal of integrating the content enabled readers to overcome some of the inadequacies of the unstructured overview.

It could be argued that there is no reason to expect hypertext-enabled structures to be superior to linear text in the Dee-Lucas and Larkin (1995) experiments because sequentially reading the text ought to provide a good basis for summary and recall tasks (Goldman, 1996). However, hypertext-enabled structures seem particularly well-suited to supporting information search tasks. Lehto et al. (1995, Experiment 1) compared a reading-to-do search task to a reading-to-learn task done with either a printed book that included the standard author and subject indices or a hypertext version that included these same indices plus a full-text search capability. Users of the hypertext system completed the reading-to-do tasks more quickly and accurately and gave up less frequently than subjects using the printed book. However, these results were reversed for the reading-to-learn task in which hypertext users provided fewer correct responses than did the users of the book. Thus, hypertext-enabled systems may be quite useful for some tasks but not terribly much better than linear text for others.

In a somewhat different approach to the issue of task demands, Wenger and Payne (1996) examined whether reading hypertext required more working memory resources, a claim based on the fact that hypertext involves processing both node titles and their contents. Readers were given a second task to do concurrently with reading the hypertext system. Two findings are important in the present context. First, measures taken during reading indicated that hypertext did not place a higher demand on limited-capacity memory than linear text. Second, results for the secondary tasks indicated that hypertext induced more relational processing, a finding that was also reflected in the recall data.

Content Domain Issues

Hypertext-enabled structures may be particularly advantageous for learning in ill-structured and complex domains (Spiro, Feltovich, Jacobson, & Coulson, 1995; Spiro & Jehng, 1990; see also Jacobson & Spiro, 1995). If a knowledge domain is sufficiently complex, then gaining a rich understanding of it requires accessing it from a variety of intellectual perspectives (Spiro et al., 1991). Jacobson and Spiro suggested that hypertext-enabled learning environments are particularly well suited to presenting a complex domain's complexity without oversimplifying it. Indeed, Spiro et al. (1991) found that "criss-crossing the landscape" is beneficial at the *upper levels* of expertise in a domain. However, novices benefit more from a linear, singular perspective, at least the first time they are introduced to particular concepts and ideas.

CONCLUSIONS AND FUTURE DIRECTIONS

We have argued that structural aspects of text-driven and of knowledge-driven processing make important contributions to the meaning construction process. This claim may appear to fly in the face of recent computational models that pay little or no attention to structure (Landauer & Dumais, 1996, 1997; Landauer, Laham, Rehder, & Schreiner, 1997; Lund & Burgess, 1996). For example, Latent Semantic Analysis (LSA) is an automatic mathematical and statistical technique that accounts for meaning by relying on the co-occurrences of words across a range of documents (Landauer, Foltz, & Laham, 1998). Despite the lack of attention to word order, empirical work indicates that LSA does a reliable job of representing and evaluating meaning, coherence, and domain knowledge (Foltz, Kintsch, & Landauer, 1998; Rehder et al., 1998). Does this work imply that we should no longer be concerned about the role of structure in reading? We think not. Structure provides us with processing instructions that can guide meaning construction (Givón, 1992). It seems highly improbable that human readers would ignore this guidance. On the other hand, it has proven extremely complex for computational models to take advantage of structural guidance, especially when there is more than ample computing power for deriving meaning spaces from word co-occurrence patterns over large numbers of documents. Human readers capitalize on the guidance afforded in the structure and organization of words in sentences, sentences in paragraphs, and paragraphs in longer discourses. Doing so requires knowledge of the meaning implications of those structures at both local and global coherence levels.

Structure-guided meaning construction appears to be particularly important for learning situations in which readers have little or no prior content knowledge (Goldman et al., 1995; Voss & Silfies, 1996). The cues assist readers in making the appropriate connections among concepts and events in text. However, it is also possible for text or hypertext to be structured too much—that is, to be overly explicit so that readers think they do not have to bring much to the meaning construction process (E. Kintsch, 1990; Shapiro, 1998). When local coherence is provided in the text, processing to deeper levels of underlying conceptual coherence may actually be impeded by overly explicit text or hypertext systems. This is especially true for readers who are reasonably well informed about the content contained in a text (e.g., McNamara & Kintsch, 1996). For those with prior knowledge of the domain, learning benefits come from taking multiple intellectual perspectives on the content domain (Spiro et al., 1991).

Finally, readers' active involvement in creating representations of text appears to be critical for useful and useable knowledge (e.g., Goldman, 1996; Mannes & Kintsch, 1987; Scardamalia & Bereiter, 1991; Scardamalia, Bereiter, McLean, Swallow, & Woodruff, 1989). Overly explicit structure in the text may mislead readers into adopting a less active stance with respect to the text or hypertext. Indeed, work on the design of hypertext systems (Lehrer, 1993) suggests that it is the active generation of the system that has powerful effects on learning. However, active involvement can be limited by lack of relevant content knowledge. Under these circumstances, structural aspects of text and hypertext have the potential to scaffold readers sufficiently so that they can participate in active meaning construction. Fruitful avenues of research on structural aspects of constructing meaning from text need to deal with trade-offs and balances among what is explicit in the text and what the reader has to infer. Such research will need to explore ways to assess knowledge in content domains, as well as knowledge of structural aspects of text, its acquisition, and the appropriate use of it as readers engage with information presented in either text or hypertext environments.

REFERENCES

Afflerbach, P. (1986). The influence of prior knowledge on expert readers' importance assignment processes. In J. A. Niles (Ed.), *Solving problems in literacy: Learners, teachers, and researchers* (pp. 30–40). Chicago: National Reading Conference.

Alexander, P. A., & Jetton, T. L. (1996). The role of importance and interest in the processing of text. *Educational Psychology Review, 8,* 89–121.

Alexander, P. A., Kulikowich, J. M., & Jetton, T. L. (1994). The role of subject-matter knowledge and interest in the processing of linear and nonlinear texts. *Review of Educational Research, 64,* 201–252.

Alverman, D. E., & Moore, D. W. (1991). Secondary school reading. In R. Barr, M. L. Kamil, P. Mosenthal, & P. D. Pearson (Eds.), *Handbook of reading research* (Vol. 2, pp. 951–983). New York: Longman.

Anderson, T. H., & Armbruster, B. B. (1984). Content area textbooks. In R. C. Anderson, J. Osborn, & R. J. Tierney (Eds.), *Learning to read in American schools: Basal readers and content texts* (pp. 193–226). Hillsdale, NJ: Lawrence Erlbaum Associates.

Anderson, R. C., Hiebert, E. H., Scott, J. A., & Wilkinson, I. A. G. (1985). *Becoming a nation of readers. The report of the Commission on Reading.* Washington, DC: National Institute of Education.

Armbruster, B. B. (1984). The problem of "inconsiderate text." In G. G. Duffy, L. R. Roehler, & J. Mason (Eds.), *Comprehension instruction* (pp. 202–217). New York: Longman.

Armbruster, B. B., Anderson, T. H., & Ostertag, J. (1987). Does text structure/summarization instruction facilitate learning from expository text? *Reading Research Quarterly, 22,* 331–346.

Armbruster, B. B., & Gudbrandsen, B. (1986). Reading comprehension instruction in social studies programs. *Reading Research Quarterly, 21,* 36–48.

Asher, N. (1993). *Reference to abstract objects in discourse.* Dordrecht: Kluwer.

Bartlett, B. J. (1978). *Top-level structure as an organizational strategy for recall of classroom text.* Unpublished doctoral dissertation, Arizona State University, Tempe.

Bateman, J. A., & Rondhuis, J. K. (1997). Coherence relations: Towards a general specification. *Discourse Processes, 24,* 3–49.

Baumann, J. F. (1986). Effect of rewritten content textbook passages on middle grade students' comprehension of main ideas: Making the inconsiderate considerate. *Journal of Reading Behavior, 18,* 1–21.

Beck, I. L., & Dole, J. A. (1992). Reading and thinking with history and science text. In C. Collins & J. M. Mangieri (Eds.), *Teaching thinking: An agenda for the twenty-first century* (pp. 1–22). Hillsdale, NJ: Lawrence Erlbaum Associates.

Beck, I. L., & McKeown, M. G. (1989). Expository text for young readers: The issue of coherence. In L. B. Resnick (Ed.), *Knowing, learning, and instruction: Essays in honor of Robert Glaser* (pp. 47–66). Hillsdale, NJ: Lawrence Erlbaum Associates.

Beck, I. L., McKeown, M. G., & Gromoll, E. W. (1989). Learning from social studies. *Cognition and Instruction, 6,* 99–158.

Beck, I. L., McKeown, M. G., Sinatra, G. M., & Loxterman, J. A. (1991). Revising social studies text from a text-processing perspective: Evidence of improved comprehensibility. *Reading Research Quarterly, 26,* 251–276.

Bestgen, Y., & Vonk, W. (1995). The role of temporal segmentation markers in discourse processing. *Discourse Processes, 19,* 385–406.

Black, J. B., & Bower, G. H. (1980). Story understanding as problem-solving. *Poetics, 9,* 223–250.

Bond, S. J., & Hayes, J. R. (1984). Cues people use to paragraph text. *Research in the Teaching of English, 18,* 147–168.

Britton, B. K., & Graesser, A. C. (Eds.). (1996). *Models of text comprehension.* Hillsdale, NJ: Lawrence Erlbaum Associates.

Britton, B. K., & Gülgöz, S. (1991). Using Kintsch's computational model to improve instructional text: Effects of repairing inference calls on recall and cognitive structures. *Journal of Educational Psychology, 83,* 329–345.

Carrell, P. L. (1992). Awareness of text structure—Effects on recall. *Language Learning, 42,* 1–20.

Chambliss, M. (1995). Text cues and strategies successful readers use to construct the gist of lengthy written arguments. *Reading Research Quarterly, 30,* 778–807.

Chen, C. & Rada, R. (1996). Interacting with hypertext: A meta analysis of experimental studies. *Human-Computer Interaction, 11,* 125–156.

Cirilo, R. K. (1981). Referential coherence and test structure in story comprehension. *Journal of Verbal Learning and Verbal Behavior, 20,* 358–367.

Cirilo, R. K., & Foss, D. J. (1980). Text structure and reading time for sentences. *Journal of Verbal Learning and Verbal Behavior, 19,* 96–109.

Coté, N., Goldman, S. R., & Saul, E. U. (1998). Students making sense of informational text: Relations between processing and representation. *Discourse Processes, 25,* 1–53.

Danner, F. W. (1976). Children's understanding of intersentence organization in the recall of short descriptive passages. *Journal of Educational Psychology, 68,* 174–183.

Davison, A. (1984). Readability formulas and comprehension. In G. G. Duffy, L. R. Roehler, & J. Mason (Eds.), *Comprehension instruction* (pp. 128–144). New York: Longman.

Dee-Lucas, D., & Larkin, J. H. (1995). Learning from electronic texts: Effects of interactive overviews for information access. *Cognition & Instruction, 13,* 431–468.

Englert, C. S., & Hiebert, E. H. (1984). Children's developing awareness of text structures in expository materials. *Journal of Educational Psychology, 76,* 65–74.

Flood, J., Heath, S. B., & Flood, D. (Eds.), *Handbook of research on teaching literacy through the communicative and visual arts.* New York: Simon & Schuster Macmillan.

Foltz, P. W., Kintsch, W., & Landauer, T. K. (1998). The measurement of textual coherence with latent semantic analysis. *Discourse Processes, 25,* 285–307.

Frazier, L. (1987). Sentence processing: A tutorial review. In M. Coltheart (Ed.), *Attention and performance: The psychology of reading* (Vol. XII, pp. 559–586). Hillsdale, NJ: Lawrence Erlbaum Associates.

Garner, R. (1992). Learning from school texts. *Educational Psychologist, 27,* 53–63.

Garner, R., Alexander, P., Slater, W., Hare, V. C., Smith, T., & Reis, R. (1986). Children's knowledge of structural properties of expository text. *Journal of Educational Psychology, 78,* 411–416.

Gernsbacher, M. A. (1990). *Language comprehension as structure building.* Hillsdale, NJ: Lawrence Erlbaum Associates.

Gernsbacher, M. A. (1995). The structure building framework: What it is, what it might also be, and why. In B. K. Britton & A. C. Graesser (Eds.), *Models of text understanding* (pp. 289–311). Hillsdale, NJ: Lawrence Erlbaum Associates.

Gernsbacher, M. A. (1997). Two decades of structure building. *Discourse Processes, 23,* 265–304.

Gernsbacher, M. A., & Faust, M. E. (1991). The mechanism of suppression—A component of general comprehension skill. *Journal of Experimental Psychology–Learning, Memory, and Cognition, 17,* 245–262.

Gernsbacher, M. A., & Hargreaves, D. J. (1988). Accessing sentence participants: The advantage of first mention. *Journal of Memory and Language, 27,* 699–717.

Givón, T. (1992). The grammar of referential coherence as mental processing instructions. *Linguistics, 30,* 5–55.

Glover, J. A., Dinnel, D. L., Halpain, D. R., McKee, T. K., Corkill, A. H., & Wise, S. L. (1988). Effects of across-chapter signals on recall of text. *Journal of Educational Psychology, 80,* 3–15.

Glynn, S. M., Birtton, B. K., & Tillman, M. H. (1985). Typographic cues in text: Management of the reader's attention. In D. Jonassen (Ed.), *The technology of text* (Vol. 2, pp. 192–209). Englewood Cliffs, NJ: Educational Technology Publications.

Golding, J. M., & Fowler, S. B. (1992). The limited facilitative effect of typographical signals. *Contemporary Educational Psychology, 17,* 99–113.

Goldman, S. R. (1988, November). *Strategies for understanding information organization in discourse.* Paper presented at the Psychonomics Society Convention, Chicago.

Goldman, S. R. (1996). Reading, writing, and learning in hypermedia environments. In H. Van Oostendorp & S. de Mul (Eds.), *Cognitive aspects of electronic text processing* (pp. 7–42). Norwood, NJ: Ablex.

Goldman, S. R. (1997). Learning from text: Reflections on the past and suggestions for the future. *Discourse Process, 23,* 357–398.

Goldman, S. R., Coté, N. C., & Saul, E. U. (1995). Paragraphing, reader, and task effects on discourse comprehension. *Discourse Processes, 20,* 273–305.

Goldman, S. R., & Durán, R. P. (1988). Answering questions from oceanography texts: Learner, task and text characteristics. *Discourse Processes, 11,* 373–412.

Goldman, S. R., & Murray, J. D. (1992). Knowledge of connectors as cohesion devices in text: A comparative study of native-English and English-as-a-second-language speakers. *Journal of Educational Psychology, 84,* 504–519.

Goldman, S. R., & Saul, E. U. (1990). Flexibility in text processing: A strategy competition model. *Learning and Individual Differences, 2,* 181–219.

Goldman, S. R., & Van Oostendorp, H. (1999). Conclusions, conundrums and challenges for the future. In H. Van Oostendorp & S. R. Goldman (Eds.), *The construction of mental representations during reading* (pp. 367–376). Mahwah, NJ: Lawrence Erlbaum Associates.

Goldman, S. R., & Varma, S. (1995). CAPping the construction-integration model of discourse comprehension. In C. Weaver, S. Mannes, & C. Fletcher (Eds.), *Discourse comprehension: Essays in honor of Walter Kintsch* (pp. 337–358). Hillsdale, NJ: Lawrence Erlbaum Associates.

Goldman, S. R., Varma, S., & Coté, N. (1996). Extending capacity-constrained construction integration: Toward "smarter" and flexible models of text comprehension. In B. K. Britton & A. C. Graesser (Eds.), *Models of text comprehension* (pp.73–113). Hillsdale, NJ: Lawrence Erlbaum Associates.

Goldman, S. R., & Varnhagen, C. K. (1983). Comprehension of stories with no-obstacle and obstacle endings. *Child Development, 54,* 980–992.

Graesser, A. C. (1981). *Prose comprehension beyond the word.* New York: Springer-Verlag.

Graesser, A. C., & Clark, L. F. (1985). *Structures and procedures of implicit knowledge* (pp. 245–295). Norwood, NJ: Ablex.

Graesser, A. C., Gernsbacher, M. A., & Goldman, S. R. (1997). *Cognition.* In T. A. van Dijk (Ed.), *Discourse as structure and process. Discourse studies: A multidisciplinary introduction* (Vol. 1, pp. 292–319). London: Sage.

Graesser, A. C., Millis, K. K., & Zwaan, R. A. (1997). Discourse comprehension. *Annual Review of Psychology, 48,* 163–189.

Graesser, A. C., Singer, M., & Trabasso, T. (1994). Constructing inferences during narrative text comprehension. *Psychological Review, 101,* 371–395.

Guthrie, J. T. (1988). Locating information in documents: Examination of a cognitive model. *Reading Research Quarterly, 23,* 178–199.

Haberlandt, K. (1980). Story grammar and reading time of story constituent. *Poetics, 9,* 99–118.

Haberlandt, K. (1984). Components of sentence and word reading times. In D. E. Kieras & M. A. Just (Eds.), *New methods in reading comprehension research* (pp. 219–252). Hillsdale, NJ: Lawrence Erlbaum Associates.

Haberlandt, K., Berian, C., & Sandson, J. (1980). The episode schema in story processing. *Journal of Verbal Learning and Verbal Behavior, 19,* 635–650.

Haenggi, D., Gernsbacher, M. A., & Bolliger, C. M. (1993). Individual differences in situation-based inferencing during narrative text comprehension. In H. van Oostendorp & R. A. Zwaan (Eds.), *Naturalistic text comprehension: Advances in discourse processing* (pp. 79–96). Norwood, NJ: Ablex.

Hague, S. (1988, December). *Awareness of text structure: The question of transfer from L1 to L2.* Paper presented at the meeting of the National Reading Conference, Tucson, AZ.

Halliday, M. A. K., & Hasan, R. (1976). *Cohesion in English.* London: Longman.

Hare, V. C., & Chesla, L. G. (1986). When main idea identification fails. In J. A. Niles & R. V. Lalik (Eds.), *Solving problems in literacy: Learners, teachers, and researchers* (pp 316–325). Chicago: National Reading Conference.

Hoover, M. L. (1997). Effects of textual and cohesive structure on discourse processing. *Discourse Processes, 23,* 193–220.

Hyönä, J. (1990). Text structure, repetition and eye movements. In Ö. Dahl & K. Fraurud (Eds.), *Proceedings of the Second Scandinavian Conference on Text Comprehension in Man and Machine* (pp. 45–55). Stockholm: University of Stockholm.

Hyönä, J. (1994). Processing of topic shifts by adults and children. *Reading Research Quarterly, 29,* 77–90.

Hyönä, J. (1995). An eye movement analysis of topic-shift effect during repeated reading. *Journal of Experimental Psychology: Learning, Memory, and Cognition, 21,* 1365–1373.

Jacobson, M. J., & Spiro, R. J. (1995). Hypertext learning environments, cognitive flexibility, and the transfer of complex knowledge: An empirical investigation. *Journal of Educational Computing Research, 12,* 301–333.

Jonassen, D. H. (1993). Acquiring structural knowledge from semantically structured hypertext. *Journal of Computer-Based instruction, 20,* 1–8.

Kamil, M. L., (1998, December). *A taxonomy of hypertext links.* Paper presented at the National Reading Conference, Austin, TX.

Kamil, M. L., & Lane, D. M. (1998). Researching the relationship between technology and literacy? An agenda for the 21st century. In D. Reinking, M. McKenna, L. D. Labbo, & Kieffer, R. (Eds.), *Handbook of literacy and technology: Transformations in a post-typographic world* (pp. 323–342). Mahwah, NJ: Lawrence Erlbaum Associates.

Kieras, D. E. (1978). Good and bad structure in simple paragraphs: Effects on apparent theme, reading time, and recall. *Journal of Verbal Learning and Verbal Behavior, 17,* 13–28.

Kieras, D. E. (1980). Initial mention as a signal to thematic content in technical passages. *Memory and Cognition, 8,* 345–353.

Kieras, D. E. (1981). The role of major referents and sentence topics in the construction of passage macrostructure. *Discourse Processes, 4,* 1–15.

Kieras, D. E. (1982). A model of reader strategy for abstracting main ideas from simple technical prose. *Text*, 2(1–3), 47–81.

Kieras, D. (1985). Thematic processes in the comprehension of technical prose. In B. K. Britton & J. B. Black (Eds.), *Understanding expository text: A theoretical and practical handbook for analyzing explanatory text* (pp. 89–107). Hillsdale, NJ: Lawrence Erlbaum Associates.

Kintsch, E. (1990). Macroprocesses and microprocesses in the development of summarization skill. *Cognition and Instruction*, 7, 161–195.

Kintsch, W. (1988). The role of knowledge in discourse comprehension: A construction-integration model. *Psychological Review*, 95, 163–182.

Kintsch, W. (1998). *Comprehension: A paradigm for cognition*. New York: Cambridge University Press.

Kintsch, W., & Greene, E. (1978). The role of culture specific schemata in the comprehension and recall of stories. *Discourse Processes*, 1, 1–15.

Kintsch, W., & Keenan, J. (1973). Reading rate and retention as a function of the number of propositions in the base structure of sentences. *Cognitive Psychology*, 5, 257–274.

Kintsch, W., Mandel, T. S., & Kozminsky, E. (1977). Summarizing scrambled stories. *Memory and Cognition*, 5, 547–552.

Kintsch, W., & van Dijk, T. A. (1978). Toward a model of text comprehension and production. *Psychological Review*, 85, 363–394.

Landauer, T. K., & Dumais, S. T. (1996). How come you know so much? From practical problems to new memory theory. In D. J. Herrmann, C. McEvoy, C. Hertzog, P. Hertel, & M. K. Johnson (Eds.), *Basic and applied memory research: Vol. 1. Theory in context* (pp. 105–126). Mahwah, NJ: Lawrence Erlbaum Associates.

Landauer, T. K., & Dumais, S. T. (1997, April). A solution to Plato's problem: The latent semantic analysis theory of acquisition, induction, and representation of knowledge. *Psychological Review*, 104, 211–240.

Landauer, T. K., Foltz, P. W., & Laham, D. (1998). Latent semantic analysis: An introduction to latent semantic analysis. *Discourse Processes*, 25, 259–284.

Landauer, T. K., Laham, D., Rehder, B., & Schreiner, M. E. (1997). How well can passage meaning be derived without using word order? A comparison of latent semantic analysis and humans. In M. G. Shafto & P. Langley (Eds.), *Proceedings of the 19th Annual Conference of the Cognitive Science Society* (pp. 412–417). Mahwah, NJ: Lawrence Erlbaum Associates.

Langston, M., & Trabasso, T. (1999). Modeling causal integration and availability of information during comprehension of narrative texts. In H. van Oostendorp & S. R. Goldman (Eds.), *The construction of mental representations during reading* (pp. 29–69). Mahwah, NJ: Lawrence Erlbaum Associates.

Lascarides, A., & Asher, N. (1991). Discourse relations and defeasible knowledge. In *Proceedings of the 29th Annual Meeting of the Association for Computational Linguistics* (pp. 55–63). Morristown, NJ: Association for Computational Linguistics.

Lehrer, R. (1993). Authors of knowledge: Patterns of hypermedia design. In S. P. Lajoie & S. J. Derry (Eds.), *Computers as cognitive tools* (pp. 197–227). Hillsdale, NJ: Lawrence Erlbaum Associates.

Lehto, M. R., Zhu, W., & Carpenter, B. (1995). The relative effectiveness of hypertext and text. *International Journal of Human-Computer Interaction*, 7, 293–313.

Loman, N. L., & Mayer, R. E. (1983). Signaling techniques that increase the understandability of expository prose. *Journal of Educational Psychology*, 75, 402–412.

Lorch, R. F., Jr. (1985). Effects on recall of signals to text organization. *Bulletin of the Psychonomic Society*, 23, 374–376.

Lorch, R. F., Jr. (1989). Text signaling devices and their effects on reading and memory processes. *Educational psychology review*, 1, 209–234.

Lorch, R. F., Jr. (1995). Integration of topic information during reading. In R. F. Lorch, Jr. & E. J. O'Brien (Eds.), *Sources of coherence in reading* (pp. 279–294). Hillsdale, NJ: Lawrence Erlbaum Associates.

Lorch, R. F., & Chen, A. H. (1986). Effects of number signals on reading and recall. *Journal of Educational Psychology*, 78, 263–270.

Lorch, R. F., & Lorch, E. P. (1986). On-line processing of summary and importance signals in reading. *Discourse Processes*, 9, 489–496.

Lorch, E. P., Lorch, R. F., Jr., Gretter, M. L., & Horn, D. G. (1987). On-line processing of topic structure by children and adults. *Journal of Experimental Child Psychology*, 43, 81–95.

Lorch, R. F., Jr., Lorch, E. P., & Inman, W. E. (1993). Effects of signaling topic structure on text recall. *Journal of Educational Psychology*, 85, 281–290.

Lorch, R. F., Jr., Lorch, E. P., & Matthews, P. D. (1985). On-line processing of the topic structure of a text. *Journal of Memory and Language*, 24, 350–362.

Lorch, R. F., Jr., Lorch, E. P., & Mogan, A. M. (1987). Task effects and individual differences in on-line processing of the topic structure of a text. *Discourse Processes*, 10, 63–80.

Lorch, R. F., & O'Brien, E. J. (Eds.). (1995). *Sources of coherence in reading*. Hillsdale, NJ: Lawrence Erlbaum Associates.

Lund, K., & Burgess, C. (1996). Producing high-dimensional semantic spaces from lexical co-occurrence. *Behavior Research Methods, Instruments and Computers*, 28, 203–208.

Mandler, J. M., & DeForest, M. (1979). Is there more than one way to recall a story? *Child Development*, 50, 886–889.

Mandler, J. M., & Goodman, M. S. (1982). On the psychological validity of story structure. *Journal of Verbal Learning & Verbal Behavior, 21*, 507–523.

Mandler, J. M., & Johnson, N. J. (1977). Remembrance of things parsed: Story structure and recall. *Cognitive Psychology, 9*, 111–151.

Mann, W. C., & Thompson, S. A. (1988). Rhetorical structure theory: Toward a functional theory of text organization. *Text, 8*, 243–281.

Mannes, S. M., & Kintsch, W. (1987). Knowledge organization and text organization. *Cognition and Instruction, 4*, 91–115.

Martin, J. R. (1992). *English text: Systems and structure.* Amsterdam: Benjamins.

Mayer, R. E. (1997). Multimedia learning: Are we asking the right questions? *Educational Psychologist, 32*, 1–19.

Mayer, R. E., Dyck, J. L., & Cook, L. K. (1984). Techniques that help readers build mental models from scientific text: Definitions pretraining and signaling. *Journal of Educational Psychology, 76*, 1089–1105.

McGee, L. M. (1982). Awareness of text structure: Effects on children's recall of expository texts. *Reading Research Quarterly, 17*, 581–590.

McHoul, A., & Roe, P. (1996). Hypertext and reading cognition. In G. E. Stelmach & P. A. Vroon (Series Eds.) & B. Gorayska & J. L. Mey (Eds.), *Advances in psychology. Cognitive technology: In search of a humane interface* (Vol. 113, pp. 347–359). New York: Elsevier.

McNamara, D. S., & Kintsch, W. (1996). Learning from texts: Effects of prior knowledge and text coherence. *Discourse Processes, 22*, 247–288.

McNamara, D. S., Kintsch, E., Songer, N. B., & Kintsch, W. (1996). Are good texts always better? Interactions of text coherence, background knowledge, and levels of understanding in learning from text. *Cognition and Instruction, 14*, 1–43.

Meyer, B. J. F. (1975). *The organization of prose and its effects on memory.* Amsterdam: North-Holland.

Meyer, B. J. F. (1985). Prose analysis: Purposes, procedures, and problems. In B. K. Britton & J. B. Back (Eds.). *Understanding expository text* (pp. 11–64). Hillsdale, NJ: Lawrence Erlbaum Associates.

Meyer, B. J. F., Brandt, D. M., & Bluth, G. J. (1980). Use of top-level structure in text: Key for reading comprehension of ninth-grade students. *Reading Research Quarterly, 16*, 72–103.

Meyer, B. J. F., & McConkie, G. W. (1973). What is recalled after hearing a passage? *Journal of Educational Psychology, 65*, 109–117.

Myers, J. L., & O'Brien, E. J. (1998). Accessing the discourse representation during reading. *Discourse Processes, 26*, 131–157

Noordman, L. G. M., & Vonk, W. (1992). Readers' knowledge and the control of inferences in reading. *Language and Cognitive Processes, 7*, 373–391.

O'Brien, E. J., & Myers, J. L. (1999). Text comprehension: A view from the bottom up. In S. R. Goldman, A. C. Graesser, & P. van den Broek (Eds.), *Narrative comprehension, causality, and coherence: Essays in honor of Tom Trabasso* (pp. 35–54). Mahwah, NJ: Lawrence Erlbaum Associates.

Ohtsuka, K., & Brewer, W. F. (1992). Discourse organization in the comprehension of temporal order in narrative texts. *Discourse Processes, 15*, 317–336.

Olhausen, M. M., & Roller, C. M. (1988). The operation of text structure and content schemata in isolation and in interaction. *Reading Research Quarterly, 23*, 70–88.

Pearson, P. D., & Fielding, L. (1991). Comprehension instruction. In R. Barr, M. L. Kamil, P. Mosenthal, & P. D. Pearson (Eds.), *Handbook of reading research* (Vol. II, pp. 815–860). New York: Longman.

Perfetti, C. A. (1998). The limits of co-occurrence: Tools and theories in language research. *Discourse Processes, 25*, 363–377.

Perfetti, C. A., & Goldman, S. R. (1975). Discourse functions of thematization and topicalization. *Journal of Psycholinguistic Research, 4*, 257–272.

Rada, R., & Murphy, C. (1992). Searching versus browsing in hypertext. *Hypermedia, 4*, 1–30.

Rehder, B., Schreiner, M. E., Wolfe, M. B. W., Laham, D., Landauer, T. K., & Kintsch, W. (1998). Using latent semantic analysis to assess knowledge: Some technical considerations. *Discourse Processes, 25*, 337–354.

Reinking, D., McKenna, M., Labbo, L. D., & Kieffer, R. (Eds.). (1988). *Handbook of literacy and technology: Transformations in a post-typographic world.* Mahwah, NJ: Lawrence Erlbaum Associates.

Richgels, D. J., McGee, L. M., Lomax, R. G., & Sheard, C. (1987). Awareness of four text structures: Effects in recall of expository text. *Reading Research Quarterly, 22*, 177–196.

Richgels, D. L., & McGee, L. M. (1989). Instruction in awareness of causation and compare/contrast text structure. In S. McCormick & J. Zutell (Eds.), *Cognitive and social perspectives for literacy research and instruction: Thirty-eighth yearbook of the National Reading Conference* (pp. 301–309). Chicago: National Reading Conference.

Rickards, J. P., Fayen, B. R., Sullivan, J. F., & Gillespie, G. (1997). Signaling, notetaking, and field independence–dependence in text comprehension and recall. *Journal of Educational Psychology, 89*, 508–517.

Robinson, D. H., & Kiewra, K. A. (1996). Visual argument: Graphic organizers are superior to outlines in improving learning from text. *Journal of Educational Psychology, 87*, 455–467.

Roller, C. M. (1990). The interaction between knowledge and structure variables in the processing of expository prose. *Reading Research Quarterly, 25*, 78–89.

Rouet, J., Levonen, J., Dillon, A., & Spiro, R. (Eds.). (1996). *Hypertext and cognition.* Mahwah, NJ: Lawrence Erlbaum Associates.

Rumelhart, D. E. (1975). Notes on a schema for stories. In D. G. Bobrow & A. Collins (Eds.), *Representation and understanding: Studies in cognitive science* (pp. 211–236). New York: Academic Press.

Samuels, S. J., Tennyson, S. P., Mulcahy, N., L., Schermer, N., & Hajovy, H. (1988). Adults' use of text structure in the recall of a scientific journal article. *Journal of Educational Research, 81,* 171–174.

Sanders, T. (1997). Semantic and pragmatic sources of coherence: On the categorization of coherence relations in context. *Discourse Processes, 24,* 119–147.

Sanders, T. J. M., Spooren, W. P. M., & Noordman, L. G. M. (1992). Toward a taxonomy of coherence relations. *Discourse Processes, 15,* 1–35.

Scardamalia, M., & Bereiter, C. (1991). Higher levels of agency for children in knowledge building: A challenge for the design of new knowledge media. *Journal of the Learning Sciences, 1,* 37–68.

Scardamalia, M., Bereiter, C., McLean, R. S., Swallow, J., & Woodruff, E. (1989). Computer-supported intentional learning environments. *Journal of Educational Computing Research, 5,* 51–68.

Shapiro, A. M. (1998). Promoting active learning: The role of system structure in learning from hypertext. *Human-Computer Interaction, 13*(1), 1–36.

Slater, W. H., Graves, M. F., & Piche, G. L. (1985). Effects of structural organizers on ninth-grade students' comprehension and recall of four patterns of expository text. *Reading Research Quarterly, 20,* 189–202.

Spilich, G. J., Vesonder, G. T., Chiesi, H. L., & Voss, J. F. (1979). Text processing of domain-related information for individuals with high and low domain knowledge. *Journal of Verbal Learning and Verbal Behavior, 18,* 275–290.

Spiro, R. J., Feltovich, P. L., Jacobson, M. J., & Coulson, R. L. (1991). Cognitive flexibility, constructivism, and hypertext: Random access instruction for advanced knowledge acquisition in ill-structured domains. *Educational Technology, 31*(5), 24–33.

Spiro, R. J., Feltovich, P. J., Jacobson, M. J., & Coulson, R. L. (1995). Cognitive flexibility, constructivism, and hypertext: Random access instruction for advanced knowledge acquisition in ill-structured domains. In L. P. Steffe & J. Gale (Eds.), *Constructivism in education* (pp. 85–107). Hillsdale, NJ: Lawrence Erlbaum Associates.

Spiro, R. J., & Jehng, J. C. (1990). Cognitive flexibility and hypertext: Theory and technology for the nonlinear and multidimensional traversal of complex subject matter. In D. Nix & R. J. Spiro (Eds.), *Cognition, education, and multimedia: Exploring ideas in high technology* (pp. 163–205). Hillsdale, NJ: Lawrence Erlbaum Associates.

Spooren, W. (1997). The processing of underspecified coherence relations. *Discourse Processes, 24,* 149–168.

Stark, H. A. (1988). What do paragraph markings do? *Discourse Processes, 11,* 275–303.

Stein, N. L., & Glenn, C. F. (1979). An analysis of story comprehension in elementary school children. In R. O. Freedle (Ed.), *New directions in discourse processing: Vol. 2. Advances in discourse processes* (pp. 53–120). Norwood, NJ: Ablex.

Stein, N. L., & Nezworski, T. (1978). The effects of organization and instructional set on story memory. *Discourse Processes, 1,* 177–193.

Stein, N. L., & Policastro, M. (1984). The concept of a story: A comparison between children's and teachers' viewpoints. In H. Mandl, N. L. Stein, & T. Trabasso (Eds.), *Learning and comprehension of text* (pp. 113–155). Hillsdale, NJ: Lawrence Erlbaum Associates.

Taylor, B. M., & Samuels, S. J. (1983). Children's use of text structure in the recall of expository material. *American Educational Research Journal, 40,* 517–528.

Taylor, M. B., & Williams, J. P. (1983). Comprehension of learning-disabled readers: Task and text variations. *Journal of Educational Psychology, 75,* 743–751.

Thorndyke, P. W. (1977). Cognitive structures in comprehension and memory of narrative discourse. *Cognitive Psychology, 9,* 77–110.

Toulmin, S. (1958). *The uses of argument.* Cambridge, MA: Cambridge University Press.

Trabasso, T., & van den Broek, P. (1985). Causal thinking and the representation of narrative events. *Journal of Memory and Language, 24,* 612–630.

van den Broek, P., Risden, K., Fletcher, C. R., & Thurlow, R. (1996). A "landscape" view of reading: Fluctuating patterns of activation and the construction of a stable memory representation. In B. K. Britton & A. C. Graesser (Eds.), *Models of understanding text* (pp. 165–187). Mahwah, NJ: Lawrence Erlbaum Associates.

van den Broek, P., Young, M., Tzeng, Y., & Linderholm, T. (1999). The landscape model of reading: Inferences and the on-line construction of a memory representation. In H. van Oostendorp & S. R. Goldman (Eds.), *The construction of mental representations during reading* (pp. 71–98). Mahwah, NJ: Lawrence Erlbaum Associates.

van Dijk, T. A., & Kintsch, W. (1983). *Strategies of discourse comprehension.* New York: Academic Press.

van Hout-Wolters, B. H. A. M. (1986). *Markeren van kerngedeelten in studieteksten: Een proces-produkt benadering* [Cueing key phrases in instructional texts: A process-product approach]. Lisse, The Netherlands: Swets & Zeitlinger.

van Oostendorp, H., & Goldman, S. R. (Eds.). (1999). *The construction of mental representations during reading.* Mahwah, NJ: Lawrence Erlbaum Associates.

van Oostendorp, H., & de Mul, S. (Eds.). (1996). *Cognitive aspects of electronic text processing.* Norwood, NJ: Ablex.

Vauras, M., Hyönä, J., & Niemi, P. (1992). Comprehending coherent and incoherent texts: Evidence from eye movement patterns and recall performance. *Journal of Research in Reading, 15*(1), 39–54.

Vauras, M., von Wright, J., & Kinnunen, R. (1991). Learning of differently structured expository texts. In M. Vauras (Ed.), *Text learning strategies in school-aged students.* Annales Academiae Scientiarum Fennicae, Dissertationes Humanarum Litterarum 59. Helsinki: Academia Scientiarum Fennica.

Voss, J. F., & Silfies, L. N. (1996). Learning from history text: The interaction of knowledge and comprehension skill with text structure. *Cognition and Instruction, 14,* 45–68.

Waller, R. (1991). Typography and discourse. In R. Barr, M. L. Kamil, P. Mosenthal, & P. D. Pearson (Eds.), *Handbook of reading research* (Vol. II, pp. 341–380). New York: Longman.

Weaver, C. A. III, & Kintsch, W. (1991). Expository text. In R. Barr, M. L. Kamil, P. Mosenthal, & P. D. Pearson (Eds.), *Handbook of reading research* (Vol. II, pp. 230–243). New York: Longman.

Weisberg, R., & Balajthy, E. (1989). Transfer effects of instructing poor readers to recognize expository text structure. In S. McCormick & J. Zutell (Eds.), *Cognitive and social perspectives for literacy research and instruction: Thirty-eighth yearbook of the National Reading Conference* (pp. 279–285). Chicago: National Reading Conference.

Wenger, M. J., & Payne, D. G. (1996). Comprehension and retention of nonlinear text: Considerations of working memory and material-appropriate processing. *American Journal of Psychology, 109,* 93–130.

Yochum, N. (1991). Children's learning from informational text: The relationship between prior knowledge and text structure. *Journal of Reading Behavior, 23,* 87–108.

Zwaan, R. A. (1996). Processing narrative time shifts. *Journal of Experimental Psychology: Learning, Memory, and Cognition, 22,* 1196–1207.

Zwaan, R. A., Langston, M. C., & Graesser, A. C. (1995). The construction of situation models in narrative comprehension: An event-indexing model. *Psychological Science, 6,* 292–297.

Zwaan, R. A., Magliano, J. P., & Graesser, A. C. (1995). Dimensions of situation model construction in narrative comprehension. *Journal of Experimental Psychology: Learning, Memory and Cognition, 21,* 386–397.

Zwaan, R. A., & Radvansky, G. A. (1998). Situation models in language comprehension and memory. *Psychological Bulletin, 123,* 162–185.

Zwaan, R. A., & Whitten, S. N. (1998). *Effects of temporal markers and discourse order on situation model construction.* Manuscript submitted for publication.

CHAPTER 21

Classroom Language and Literacy Learning

Louise C. Wilkinson
Rutgers, The State University of New Jersey

Elaine R. Silliman
University of South Florida, Tampa

To a great extent within classrooms, the language used by teachers and students determines what is learned and how learning takes place. The classroom is a unique context for learning and exerts a profound effect on students' development of language and literacy skills, particularly in the early years. Some have argued strongly that students should have significant opportunities for the integration of oral and written language in the classroom, because these experiences both support and encourage the development of literate cognition (Corson, 1984; Wells, 1990).

Three decades ago, sociolinguistic studies launched a new direction for inquiry into language and literacy learning; these studies focused on the use of oral language in classrooms. Since the publication of *Functions of Language in the Classroom* (Cazden, John, & Hymes, 1972), a considerable body of empirical research, from that perspective and others, has been generated. This chapter reviews that legacy of research on classroom language, including implications for understanding how children learn literacy. The historical roots of research on classroom language are examined, including the early sociolinguistic studies, which focused on language function, communicative demands of classrooms, and individual differences among students' language usage. Vygotsky's social constructivist theory, with the view learning is both socially-based and integrated, has played a major role in guiding research for the past three decades. Assumptions about classroom language and literacy learning are:

1. Learning is a *social activity*—interpersonal behaviors, both observed and enacted in the classroom, are the basis for new conceptual understandings in cognition and communication.
2. Learning is *integrated*—strong interrelationships exist between oral and written language learning.

3. *Learning requires active student engagement in classroom activities and interac-tion*—engaged students are motivated for literacy learning and have the best chance of achieving full communicative competence across the broad spectrum of language and literacy skills.

Because learning occurs in particular social contexts, research on actual classroom language, specifically, instructional conversations, is reviewed, along with work on emergent literacy and ability-based reading and writing groups. Finally, implications of research on classroom language for educational practice, policies, and students' learning are discussed.

SOCIOLINGUISTIC ORIGINS OF CLASSROOM LANGUAGE RESEARCH

The sociolinguistic approach to classroom language originated in the early 1970s, emphasizing descriptions of students' and teachers' actual language in classrooms; the goal was understanding classroom life, revealing the communicative competence of students, the diversity of students and their language, and the complexity of classroom communication (Cazden et al., 1972). These descriptions served as reference points for the improvement and/or evaluation of specific educational programs and as a source of new ideas for investigating the processes of teaching and learning (Wilkinson, 1982a).

Twenty-eight years have elapsed since the publication of the first volume on sociolinguistic research on classroom communication. Numerous studies were stimulated in a relatively short period of time and published in widely circulated, peer-reviewed journals in education, communication sciences and disorders, psychology, special education, linguistics, anthropology, and sociology. Several reviews of selected research in this area have already appeared (e.g., Brown, 1992; Cazden, 1988; Green & Smith, 1983; Rosenshine & Meister, 1994; Stone, 1998), including volumes that have synthesized work across disciplines (e.g., Speece & Keogh, 1996; Wilkinson, 1990).

The Early Descriptive Studies

The first sociolinguistic studies concentrated on the communication of school-age children and their teachers in a variety of classroom situations, including some that attempted to mimic those "real" situations in more restricted, experimental ones (e.g., Cohen, 1984; Cooper, Marquis, & Ayers-Lopez, 1982). Because sociolinguistic research has been generated within a variety of disciplines, generalizations about guiding theoretical assumptions and consequent methodological practices are somewhat problematical. For example, (a) psychologists investigated individual differences in language use and communication (e.g., Cooper et al., 1982; Wilkinson & Calculator, 1982; Wilkinson & Spinelli, 1983); (b) linguists studied the development of communicative functions of some primary school children (e.g., Griffin & Shuy, 1978); (c) sociologists examined the regulation of social order in the classroom through communicative processes, such as turn taking and attentional norms (e.g., Eder, 1982; Merritt, 1982); (d) educators described the organization of formal activities, such as lessons (e.g., Bloome & Knott, 1985; Green & Wallat, 1981; Goldenberg & Patthey-Chavez, 1995; Mehan, 1979, 1994); (e) specialists in communication sciences and disorders and special educators examined the organization of clinical and classroom discourse and learning styles of children having language-learning disabilities (e.g., Donahue, 1994; Kovarksy & Duchan, 1997; Prutting, Bagshaw, Goldstein, Juskowitz, & Umen, 1978; Silliman,

1984); and (f) anthropologists investigated verbal and nonverbal aspects of communication within and between cultural groups (e.g., Erickson & Shultz, 1982; Florio & Shultz, 1979).

Common Assumptions

Sociolinguists held common assumptions; for example, differences in oral communication were marked by social variables, such as gender, ethnicity, social class, and age as a social role. The following assumptions defined sociolinguistic research on classroom language (Wilkinson, 1982b):

- Communicative competence in school involved knowing about the structure, content, and uses of everyday language, as well as the functions of language in classrooms.
- Classrooms were unique communicative contexts that made unique demands on the purposes and uses of language.
- Students differed in their communicative competencies and in how they used language appropriately and effectively in classrooms.
- The most appropriate methodological approaches were the careful descriptions of the language actually used by students and teachers in classrooms.

Knowledge of Language Structure, Content, and Functions.   When children enter school, they have a basic system of oral communication, which consists of language structure (sound structure, inflections, syntax), content (meaning), and use (purposes of appropriate communication). Due to the influences of schooling, knowledge about meanings, language functions (pragmatics), different discourse genres, and more complex syntax (Scott, 1995) continue to develop during the school years and into adulthood. Mehan (1979) eloquently stated the interactional competencies that students needed to develop for success in school:

> [Students] must know with whom, when and where they can speak and act, and they must provide the speech and behavior that are appropriate for given classroom situations. Students must also be able to relate behavior, both academic and social, to varying classroom situations by interpreting implicit classroom rules. (p. 133)

Classroom communicative competence was seen as an end in itself—rules to be learned by students so that they could understand and participate in classrooms. Communicative competence was viewed as a means of attaining other educational objectives, such as literacy acquisition.

The Communicative Demands of Classrooms.   Classrooms are unique contexts, with requirements regarding the way language is used to communicate effectively. The effects of students' not knowing the "rules of the game," the standard ways of communicating in the classroom, are not limited to the obvious problems that these students face in their unsuccessful communications with students and teachers. Further, if some children do not understand the classroom and its unique communicative demands, then they may learn little from classroom experiences. Accurate assessment of their achievement is unlikely, because access to their knowledge is predicated on optimal communicative performance. The lack of participation of some students may present them with problems and interfere with their overall adjustment to school and subsequent academic achievement.

Continuity between language use in school and home is an issue for preparing children to enter school. Most of the research on emergent literacy has been conducted with children from high-print homes that identify with the dominant culture, which is school oriented, and where parent–child interactions in the home provide experiences that are similar to classroom interactions. Schools facilitate students' acquisition of academic information; similarly, in homes with a great deal of printed materials, early parent–child communication typically involves information exchange (e.g., Cherry, 1979; Ervin-Tripp, 1977). A difference between the high-print home and school interactions is that teachers typically evaluate students' responses, which is not often the case at home (Cherry, 1978). Through motivation to learn about print, children learn about literacy events, functions, artifacts, forms (e.g., sound and letter names), and conventions before they ever learn to read and write (Morrow, 1993; van Kleeck, 1990, 1995; 1998; van Kleeck & Schuele, 1987; Whitehurst & Lonigan, 1998).

Students Differ in Communicative Competencies.   Because prior school experiences are combined with home interactions, some children enter school knowing about how to use language for a variety of "school-like" purposes. They have expectations about classrooms. Because not all students learn the "rules of the game" of mainstream education, some have difficulty knowing how to participate appropriately. They may also have less experience with a variety of literacy functions and forms. Students' participation in school activities, such as reading aloud, question and answer exchanges with teachers, and receiving evaluation of their discourse contributions from teachers, determines their access to learning. The educational failure of some students may be caused in part by differences in the communicative patterns between students and teachers who come from different cultural backgrounds.

During the past decade, diversity among learners dominated sociolinguistic research. This was fueled partly by the changes in the demographics of American classrooms, which were due both to federal laws for special education and to waves of new immigrants. As classroom composition changed substantially during the last decade of the 20th century, the focus of research questions changed to reflect: (a) aspects of second language acquisition and their impact on literacy learning (e.g., August & Hakuta, 1997, 1998; Gutierrez-Clellen, 1998); (b) African American dialect differences and effects of variations on reading, writing, and classroom participation (e.g., Delpit, 1988; 1992; Scott & Rogers, 1996; Seymour, Bland-Stewart, & Green, 1998; Seymour & Roeper, 1999; Tharp, 1994); and (c) promoting literacy learning in children and youth with atypical language development (e.g., Palincsar & Klenk, 1992, 1993; Palincsar, Parecki, & McPhail, 1995; Wallach & Butler, 1994), including second-language learners with atypical language development (e.g., Ruiz, 1995).

One example of cultural differences between students and their teachers is found in the work of Michaels (1986), who investigated narrative production during "sharing time" in African American and White children in an elementary classroom. Sharing time is a classroom activity during which teachers call on students to share stories with the class. Michaels found that African American and White children differed in the style of topical development of their stories, and, as a result, their narratives were differentially evaluated by teachers. White children produced more literate, topic-centered narratives, which focused on a single object or event, whereas African American children tended to produce more oral, episodic narratives, which centered simultaneously on multiple objects and events. Stories of African American students were more likely to be negatively evaluated by their teachers. However, recent research challenges Michaels' distinction between topic-centered and episodic narratives in African American children (Champion, 1998; Champion, Katz, Muldrow, & Dail, 1999; Champion, Seymour, & Camarata, 1995; Hester, 1996; Hicks, 1991). Urban African American children acquire a flexible repertoire of narrative styles; the style chosen depends on the nature of the task demand, among other variables. Sharing time may elicit a more oral style, because of the familiar topic and experience (Hester,

1996). Identifying the range of normal variation in narrative styles requires understanding the nature of the cultural and social practices that individual African American children bring to school and express in their narratives (Champion et al., 1999).

To minimize mistaking differences in discourse styles and dialect use as cognitive and linguistic problems, teachers and other educational professionals need to pool their collective expertise. Students' development of identities as competent learners and communicators requires understanding discourse and dialect differences, and the social and cultural practices that children from culturally/linguistically diverse groups bring to school.

Descriptive Methodologies.   Sociolinguistic studies are descriptive, where observers obtain a verbatim account of the actual language used, along with a detailed description of the context. The research focus is often a process and/or a pattern of behavior, such as the initiation–response–evaluation (IRE) pattern (Cherry, 1978).

Early sociolinguistic research typically recorded everyday language, accompanied by additional symbol systems, such as graphic symbols, to capture accompanying nonverbal behaviors (e.g., Erickson, 1982). Because the early studies typically used audio and video recordings, the written records of recordings and subsequent analyses of these transcriptions occurred retrospectively, not online. Retrospective analyses permitted the researcher to catch patterns and sequences of talk that may have occurred very rapidly in real time and eluded perceptive observers. Recordings and transcriptions allow for infinite retrievability of actual talk as it occurs in real time. When using transcription and recording, multiple analyses are possible. Observers can analyze how different aspects of the language system may interact—for example, how children's choices of particular syntax or vocabulary interact with their production of narratives.

These early sociolinguistic studies catalyzed research on oral language and literacy for three decades. Additionally, Vygotsky's social constructivist theory and the assumption that all learning is both socially based and integrated played a major role in shaping the research agenda. Vygotsky's work is the starting point for the discussion of major themes and research trends in classroom language research and the relationship to literacy learning.

INTEGRATING CLASSROOM COMMUNICATION, ORAL LANGUAGE, AND LITERACY LEARNING

Vygotsky: Learning is a Socially Based Activity

Vygotsky is the leading proponent for the view that learning is primarily socially based. Webb and Palincsar (1996) identified Vygotsky's most general statement about the social origins of learning:

> Any function in the child's cultural development appears twice, or on two planes. First it appears between people as an interpsychological category. This is equally true with regard to voluntary attention, logical memory, the formation of concepts, and the development of volition.... Internalization transforms the process itself and changes its structure and functions. Social relationships or relationships among people genetically underlie all high functions and their relationships. (Vygotsky, 1981, p. 163)

In the past decade, theorists elaborated Vygotsky's theory in three ways: *mediated action, voice,* and *appropriation.*

Mediated Action.   One elaboration concerned dynamic human actions as central units of analysis. For Wertsch (1990, 1991, 1995, 1998), human activity is contextualized because it is shaped by cultural tools that mediate and transform mental actions into new patterns of knowing and doing (Wertsch, 1995). Mental functioning is "defined by the mediational means it employs to carry out a task" (Wertsch, 1991, pp. 14–15). How individuals act, alone or with others, cannot be separated from their cultural tools, which mediate interaction. These tools may be as diverse as computers, language, numbers, reading, writing, textbooks, maps, diagrams, the physical configuration of a classroom, or sports equipment (Cole, 1998; Wertsch, 1991, 1998). Activities and cultural tools are inseparable (Rogoff, 1995; Rogoff, Radziszewska, & Masiello, 1995; Wertsch, 1998) because "Culture is exteriorized mind; mind is interiorized culture" (Cole, 1998, p. 292).

Voice.   Bakhtin's (1986) view was that communication is a powerful cultural tool for shaping how individuals engage in mental activity, because mental activity is situated in sociocultural contexts, which are inherently communicative (Wertsch, 1991). Beyond sounds, words, and sentences used, the goal of communication is to understand another's perspective about ideas, feelings, or attitudes to achieve shared understanding. Perspective in speaking and writing is referred to as *voice*, the communication of the self's identity to others and the role of the self in particular participation structures (Cazden, 1993). Because interpretative frameworks are culturally embedded, perspectives conflict. Thus, understanding of others' perspectives always involves fusing one's own multiple voices with the many, and frequently contradictory, voices of others as mediated through participation a variety of discourse genres, including instructional discourse (Cole, 1998; Wertsch, 1991).

Appropriation.   A third elaboration concerns internalization, which implies a dichotomy between the social (external) and mental (internal) world, and a separation between the activities in which people engage and the social context of those activities (Rogoff, 1995; Wertsch, 1998). Wertsch recast the concept of internalization within the mediated action framework, whereas Rogoff redefined internalization as participatory appropriation.

Wertsch suggested that one meaning of mastery meaning is *skill*—knowing how to apply a cultural tool for particular cognitive and social purposes, which is lacking in students who have not mastered reading as a mediational means. Consequently, students cannot participate appropriately in discussions about written texts. When teachers support their learning, students learn how to participate in the dialogue and, ultimately, learn the "skill" of reading. Skill development, then, emerges from mastery of particular cultural tools suggesting that performance supports competence.

A richer view of internalization is *appropriation* of mediational means, referring to students' making tools "their own and spontaneously employing them" (Wertsch, 1998, p. 137; Palincsar et al., 1995) for learning how to learn. Students have now appropriated the teaching voice to self-direct their learning.

Rogoff's (1995) view of *appropriation* stressed the central role of discourse processes. Through dialogic participation "individuals transform their understanding of and responsibility for activities [and] in the process become prepared to engage in subsequent similar activities" (Rogoff, 1995, p. 150). For both Wertsch and Rogoff, *appropriation* accounts for the transfer of responsibility for learning because "cultural tool kits" (Wertsch, 1991, p. 93) are transformed for new purposes.

How do the concepts of mediated action, voice, and appropriation apply to the classroom? The content and processes of learning are grounded in the social activities organized and mediated through cultural tool kits, which are made available through the dialogue *scaffolds* of teaching and learning.

Scaffolds for Learning.   Vygotsky's notion of scaffolds for learning has played a critical role in the development of theory and research on language and literacy learning. Cazden (1988) extended scaffolding to describe teacher–student interactions, but this type of supported learning may also be referred to as assisted performance (Cazden, 1988; Gallimore & Tharp, 1990), guided participation (Rogoff, 1990, 1995), or guided discovery (Brown & Campione, 1994). Although the meanings of these alternate descriptions are all rooted in Vygotskian theory, they are not necessarily interchangeable with the concept of scaffolding (Stone, 1998).

A scaffold is an external structure that braces another structure being built. As a metaphor (Pressley & McCormick, 1995), scaffolding functions as an interactional mechanism for learning and development. Through dialogic and associated nonverbal interactions, more capable teachers provide graduated assistance to novice learners to achieve higher levels of conceptual and communicative competence. With scaffolding, the learner can experiment with new concepts and strategies in ways that normally would not be possible without assistance (Cazden, 1988; Silliman & Wilkinson, 1991, 1994a). An effective scaffold provides "support at the edge of a child's competence" (Gaskins et al., 1997, p. 45), defining children's zones of proximal development or their potential for new learning (Stone, 1993; Vygotsky, 1962). Proximal development refers to the assumption that skills the child can display with assistance are partially developed, but cannot be employed yet without support (Pressley & McCormick, 1995). The wider the zone, the more capable are children to perform tasks; conversely, the narrower the zone, the less capable they are to benefit from assistance (Campione & Brown, 1987). The zone of proximal development is activated through dynamic connections to scaffolding; however, these concepts do not explain specific mechanisms and outcomes of learning and development (Stone, 1993, 1998). Instead, their appeal is descriptive power, conveying culturally mediated activities that constitute the social and communicative contexts of interaction (Palincsar, 1998).

Ideally, this guidance provided by teachers to students takes the form of classroom discussions and "grand conversations." In practice, teacher–student dialogues are likely to be "gentle inquisitions" (Eeds & Wells, 1989). The use of scaffolds in both regular and special education classrooms reflects a continuum from interrogation sequences to instructional conversations (Tharp & Gallimore, 1988). The type and quality of scaffolding arrayed along the continuum of directive to supportive convey expectations to learners about their overlapping communicative roles as listeners, speakers, readers and writers, and influences their self-definitions as learners (Silliman & Wilkinson, 1994a). As Tharp (1994) noted: "The critical form of assisting learners is through dialogue, through the questioning and sharing of ideas and knowledge that happens in instructional conversations.... To truly teach, one must converse, to converse is to teach" (p. 156).

Silliman and Wilkinson (1994a) identified two types of scaffolds in regular and special education classrooms: *directive* and *supportive*. Each has its own structure of social interaction as patterned by the discourse of teaching. Both provide assistance to students in language and literacy learning, but the functions and forms of assistance vary and differentially influence students' understanding of the purposes, meaning, and possibilities for learning (Mehan, 1994).

Directive Scaffolds.   From an instructional viewpoint, the most formal organizational unit of classroom interaction, and by far the most prevalent, is the *directive scaffold* (Mehan, 1994; Silliman & Wilkinson, 1994a). In a larger sense, the directive scaffold parallels the direct instruction or skills-emphasis model of instruction (Pressley, 1998; Pressley & McCormick, 1995).

From a structural viewpoint, directive scaffolds are defined by the predominance of teacher control mechanisms, designed to assess students' content knowledge in accord with a predetermined standard for acceptable participation (Gallimore & Tharp, 1990). Acceptable participation is typically defined by how teachers evaluate the manner and accuracy of responses. One powerful control mechanism is the initiation–response–evaluation (IRE) conversational sequence, exemplified by question–answer–evaluation, the most well known and studied of directive scaffolds (Becker & Silverstein, 1984; Cherry, 1978; Durkin, 1978–1979; Lemke, 1985; Mehan, 1979; Panagos & Bliss, 1990; Ripich & Panagos, 1985; Silliman & Wilkinson, 1991; Spinelli & Ripich, 1985). As a scripted format, directive scaffolds represent a default pattern (Cazden, 1988) in their presumption that the teacher's primary function is knowledge transmission and assessment. IRE sequences of interaction consist of an initiation (I) by the teacher, a response (R) by the student, and an evaluation by the teacher (E). Outcomes of traditional instructional discourse include a passive orientation to learning, an emphasis on the reproduction of information, and the understanding that evaluation is the exclusive responsibility of teachers (Silliman & Wilkinson, 1994a).

Because teachers and others seldom question the cultural and institutional belief that the critical function of instruction is knowledge transmission (Mehan, 1994), the common tendency is for them to fall back on the IRE pattern. Even when teachers shift toward literature-based reading instruction, the preference for "gentle inquisitions" continues (Bergeron, 1993; Scharer & Peters, 1996). Because classroom discourse reflects larger sociocultural values and practices (Cole, 1998), an important question is the teaching voice conveyed to children through IRE dialogues (Palincsar, Brown, & Campione, 1993). Mehan (1994) asked whether students who are taught to conform to adult authority through passive participation can become active participants in a democratic society and the workplace.

Wells (1993) was the leading proponent for the view that a role exists for the IRE sequence in classroom teaching, particularly if the last element, "E," is recognized as a responsive follow-up, and not just the opportunity for the teacher to provide an evaluation for the student's response. Responsive follow-up serves to provide explicit and positive information to students as a means for guiding them on how they can improve their subsequent contributions (Gallimore & Tharp, 1990; Roehler & Cantlon, 1997; Tharp, 1994). Gavelek and Raphael (1996) expanded on Wells's position: "What matters greatly are the ways these different language opportunities connect among each other, the ways teachers mine these opportunities for their instructional potential, and the ways students come to understand that language is one of the most important tools of our culture" (p. 191) (see also, Collins, 1992; Palincsar, Brown, & Campione, 1993).

Supportive Scaffolds.   Supportive scaffolds more directly mirror Vygotsky's views. Contemporary instructional applications primarily derive from the initial work of Palincsar and Brown (1984) on reciprocal teaching with Grade 7 readers who had good decoding skills, but problems with text comprehension. Reciprocal teaching, a dialogue-based, active learning approach, focused on four comprehension strategies as the tools for gaining meaning from texts.

Supportive scaffolds are consistent with current recommendations for the design of learning contexts that are learner centered, value learning as the search for understanding, provide opportunities for dynamic assessment and responsive feedback, and view the educational process as consisting of a community of learners (Bransford, Brown, & Cocking, 1999). Supportive scaffolds allow integration of dynamic assessment with teaching as the means for engaging in the on-line evaluation of students' comprehension needs and modifying the level and type of support "on the spot" (Pressley & Woloshyn, 1995).

From a developmental perspective, supportive scaffolds are considered as a process for the appropriation of cultural tools that mediate how to understand, remember, and express one's perspectives in more literate ways. Responsibility is gradually transferred from adults to students for task planning, strategy choices and selection, monitoring of effectiveness, self-correction, and the evaluation of task outcomes. These functions define the flexible and reflective self-regulation that is engaged in strategic problem solving. (Brown & Campione, 1994; Brown & Palincsar, 1987; Diaz, Neal, & Amaya-Williams, 1990). Well-developed, reflective self-regulation goes beyond strategy mastery. The critical component is knowing when and where particular strategies should be used (Bransford et al., 1999; Pressley & Woloshyn, 1995).

Tharp (1993, 1994) identified four critical features of supportive scaffolding for language and literacy development:

- Competence in instructional language is a "metagoal" of all instructional activities.
- Instructional practices are grounded in culturally meaningful experiences that assist students in transferring classroom learning to other settings, such as the home, community, and workplace (Brown & Campione, 1994; Bransford et al., 1999; Pressley, Wharton-McDonald, & Mistretta, 1998).
- Effective teaching and learning occur in collaborative activities with teachers and peers. Active learning contexts create classrooms where individual differences are respected due to the construction of "multiple zones of proximal development ... through which participants can navigate via different routes and at different rates" (Brown & Campione, 1994, p. 236). Collaboration as a process of inquiry also enhances the motivation to learn (Tracey & Morrow, 1998).
- The basic form of teaching is dialogue through instructional conversations. These dialogues integrate listening, speaking, reading, and writing as tools of inquiry serving multiple communicative purposes. Instructional conversations, when organized by thematic units and the activation of background knowledge (Goldenberg & Patthey-Chavez, 1995), function as formats for supporting the development of new conceptual understandings that have educational value (Roehler & Cantlon, 1997). Through such collaboration, students invest in their own learning, seeking out challenging concepts in order to "form, express, and exchange ideas in speech and writing" (Tharp & Gallimore, 1988, p. 23).

Researchers have studied instructional conversations as central mechanisms for supporting active, strategic learning in language and literacy, for example, with African American and bilingual students at risk for literacy failure (e.g., Brown & Campione, 1994; Goldenberg, 1996). Other studies focused on children with learning disabilities who were also at high risk for failure in literacy learning (e.g., Echevarria, 1995; Englert, Tarrant, Mariage, & Oxer, 1994; Graham & Harris, 1996, 1997, 1999; Gaskins et al., 1997; Palincsar & Klenk, 1992, 1993; Palincsar et al., 1995). Still others were concerned with the prevention of reading failure (Pressley, 1998). These studies showed significant variations in their scope, specific purposes, designs, and types of data. Few routinely assessed children's oral language comprehension or production or considered these aspects as variables accounting for individual differences in responsiveness to strategy learning in reading, writing, and spelling through the mechanism of instructional conversations. Finally, few studies conducted detailed discourse analyses to determine similarities and differences among teachers in their applications of scaffolded instruction. Despite variations among studies and their limitations, compelling evidence has accumulated for the contributions of Vygotskian theory and the concept of supportive scaffolding to constructivist teaching practices with diverse learners in language and literacy.

Qualifications.   Stone (1998) described the limitations of scaffolding for instructional purposes, particularly with children at risk for literacy failure. The efficacy of the scaffolding metaphor depends on explaining the discourse dynamics regulating transfer of responsibility. Because the discourse dynamics underlying instructional conversations are "the heart of successful scaffolding of children's learning" (Stone, 1998, p. 361), their explanation directly affects the reality of Cazden's (1988) assumption that a scaffold "self-destructs ... as the need lessens and the student's competence grows" (p. 104).

Stone proposed that scaffolding sequences are cycles of communication challenges and inferences. These sequences are the mechanism by which students come to understand the teaching perspective. Through creating the instructional conversation, the expert adult presents students with a challenge (new information or a new way of thinking), creating a discrepancy to be resolved. The teacher mediates through many dialogic forms, adjusting the type and level of assistance to students' comprehension requirements, which leads students to infer what the activity means in the particular setting, how to go about implementing it, and, eventually, appropriating the tools of the instructional conversation as their own.

Four types of scaffolding sequences have been identified from classroom-based instructional conversations (Roehler & Cantlon, 1997):

- *Explicit modeling:* Through verbal example, the teacher demonstrates how to "work through" a specific strategy, including reasons for selection, specifying steps, or providing guiding clues. Students are encouraged to adopt similar schemas in resolving the task. Examples include think-alouds, where comprehension is shown to be an emerging process of understanding, and talk-alouds, where the teacher demonstrates how to ask relevant questions and formulate semantically contingent comments (Roehler & Cantlon, 1997).
- *Direct explanations and reexplanations:* Explicit statements tailored to assist students in understanding the underlying concept, the relevance of applying the concept in particular situations, or how concepts are used (Pressley & McCormick, 1995; Roehler & Cantlon, 1997), such as: "It is a good idea to analyze what you have to do before you begin doing it" (Pressley & Woloshyn, 1995, p. 90).
- *Invitations to participate in the conversation:* Participation is encouraged through such devices as eliciting students' reasoning to support a statement or position (e.g., "What makes you think that?" "How do you know?") (Goldenberg & Patthey-Chavez, 1995, p. 61) or creating opportunities for more complex language expression through invitations to expand in meaningful ways (e.g., "Tell us more about that" "What do you mean?") (Goldenberg & Patthey-Chavez, 1995, p. 61).
- *Verifying and clarifying student understanding:* Explicit and positive feedback is intended to guide students on learning how to evaluate the creation of a shared perspective or self-revise when misunderstandings occur. When a student's statement or response conveys emerging understanding, the relevance of the contribution to the topics is verified, such as by saying "We hadn't talked about that. That's important, isn't it. To show that we enjoyed it" (Roehler & Cantlon, 1997, p. 19). When misunderstanding happens, students are guided to repair the breakdown through the asking of appropriate and relevant questions.

For transfer of responsibility to take place, students must eventually be capable of sharing teachers' perspectives about the purposes and goals of scaffolding sequences within activities (Palincsar, 1998; Smagorinsky, 1998). A major issue, then, is that developmental variability in students' inferencing capacities may explain individual differences in the outcomes of scaffolded instruction for literacy learning (Bishop, 1997; Donahue & Lopez-Reyna, 1998; Westby, 1999).

Oral Language and Literacy Learning Are Integrated

Speaking, listening, reading, and writing are integrated, because all are primarily communicative processes (Silliman & Wilkinson, 1994a). Literacy is a continuum transcending oral and written mediums of communication, with different discourse styles overlapping both (Biber, 1988; Horowitz & Samuels, 1987; Scott, 1988; Spiro & Taylor, 1987; Wallach, 1990). Literacy confers on individuals' social identities as full participants in the larger sociocultural community and serves as an essential metacognitive tool for communication, because written language transcends immediate temporal and spatial constraints.

Emergent Literacy.   The research on emergent literacy presents a clear case for the integration of language and literacy learning. There is ample evidence of interrelationships among reading, writing, and oral language among young children. The traditional one-way view of literacy is that it begins when children begin formal schooling because children must be "ready" to learn to read and write (Terrell, 1994). Emergent literacy, in contrast, refers to knowledge children acquire about relationships among oral language, reading, and writing before entering school (Morrow & Smith, 1990).

Learning to read and write is not a matter of readiness, but is integrated with and naturally embedded in the many routine social interactions with literate adults encountered from infancy onwards (Heath, 1982; Stallman & Pearson, 1990; Whitehurst & Lonigan, 1998). Adults reading books to young children is a compelling example of how many young children are taught a literate perspective, even before they learn to read. Young children are exposed to the routinized forms and formats of literacy as they participate in book reading with caregivers, and these experiences centered on book reading events provide them with increasingly complex meanings, and some familiarity with letter shapes and names. These recurrent events may even lead some children to discover on their own that words consist of small sound segments (phonemes), which, in print, are represented by letters (Kamhi & Catts, 1999). The fact that most children do not discover this alphabetic insight on their own has lead to heated controversy over the best way to teach children to read.

Based on a substantial body of research over the past 25 years, the strong consensus is that the prevention of reading failure is linked to explicit instruction in word recognition for all children (Snow, Burns, & Griffin, 1998): "Getting started in alphabetic reading depends critically on mapping the letters and spellings of words into the speech units that they represent; failure to master word recognition can impede text comprehension" (p. 6). Instability of word recognition skills also significantly affects accurate spelling (Bruck, Treiman, Caravolas, Genesee, & Cassar, 1998; Ehri, 1997). The importance of *balanced instruction* in learning how to read resides in knowing about differences between recognizing words as a listener (oral word recognition) and recognizing words as a reader (print word recognition). Five points are pertinent (Kamhi & Catts, 1999):

- For oral word recognition, only the phonological route activates meaning from what is being said. This unconscious process involves assigning features of sound (phonological structure) and features of meaning from the "mental lexicon." Young children are not necessarily aware that words consist of discrete segments of sounds or phonemes and tend to process phrases in more wholistic ways, such as "Did you know?" as chunks or whole words, for example, "Didjano." Moreover, the alphabet does not convey that phonemes are represented in letters (Blachman, 1994).

- To recognize print words, children must move from a wholistic orientation toward words to an analytical orientation toward the sound segments, referred to as *phonological awareness*, which develops slowly over the preschool years. Ultimately, phonological awareness involves the ability to think more consciously about the phonemic segments symbolized by letters. Letter-sound knowledge and phonological awareness are interrelated (Treiman, Tincoff, Rodriquez, Mouzaki, & Francis, 1998). The biggest barrier for many children to overcome in learning to read is gaining the insight that "letters in words stand for little segments of sound" (Nicholson, 1997, p. 392; Wilkinson & Silliman, 1994). Two routes are possible for eventually learning to read with meaning (Kamhi & Catts, 1999), which is predicated, in part, on rapid and accurate word recognition (Adams, 1990).

- The phonological route to meaning is indirect. Children must acquire knowledge of phoneme–letter correspondences. With this knowledge, they can then recode visual features of letters into their phoneme counterparts. This ability allows the novice readers to recognize words that exist in their mental lexicons but that are unfamiliar when printed. With the phonological route, children must attend to letter sequences (spellings). With increased skill in managing letter sequences, children can recognize words by "sight," no longer needing the phonological route to construct meaning unless an unfamiliar word is encountered (Kamhi & Catts, 1999).

- The second route for accessing meaning is direct. Children match the visual configurations of letters to their meanings in order to recognize words by "sight"; however, a major problem is the large number of unfamiliar words that children routinely encounter that are not possible to figure out by relying on context (Kamhi & Catts, 1999). Poor readers tend to rely on context more than good readers because those with reading difficulties, by definition, have problems with activating the phonological route (Share & Stanovich, 1995; Snow et al., 1998).

- The single best predictor of reading achievement is children's performance on phonological awareness tasks in kindergarten and first grade (Adams, 1990; Blachman, 1994; Kamhi & Catts, 1999; Snow et al., 1998). This finding has fundamental implications for the selection of tests that should be administered in kindergarten and first grade (Torgesen, 1999).

The need for explicit instruction in phonological awareness is not identical to teaching phonics, which focuses solely on sound–letter correspondences. A balanced approach to reading, writing, and spelling creates active learning contexts. It also integrates formal attention to phonological awareness as a developmental process with the construction and expression of meaning through good literature and authentic writing experiences (e.g., Gaskins, Ehri, Cress, O'Hara, & Donnelly, 1996–1997; Pressley, 1998; Tracey & Morrow, 1998).

Schooled Literacy.   For most children, classrooms are the first formal environment for schooled literacy. Reading and writing are presented as a set of decontextualized discrete skills to be mastered separately from other curricular areas (Zubrick, 1987). However, research indicates that both elementary and middle-grade readers' knowledge of oral-written language relationships is enriched by talking informally with peers and with student-dominated discussions. Almasi and Gambrell's (1994) study of fourth-grade students provided evidence that students learned more in peer-led literature discussion groups than those led by teachers. Eeds and Wells (1989) demonstrated that, in a fifth-grade classroom, the teacher and students "built meaning by working together" in literature discussion groups by discussing key points and negotiating meaning through conversation. Children also construct meaning when they converse without the presence of an adult (Hepler & Hickman, 1982) and as they write, read, select books, and respond to books through drama and art (Guice, 1992).

Alvermann's (1999) study of high school students' discussion of texts in content area classes reveals some of the conditions that make discussion worthwhile, including task construction, shared expectations among group members, and the size of the group. Langer (1990) believed that secondary school students' interpretations of books are best enriched when they are supported in discussions reflecting real questions about books that have been modeled by knowledgeable teachers. This seems to be true of middle-grade students who benefit from learning different interpretive literary models. Temple and Collins (1992) found that a variety of classroom activities provided middle school students with both the time and place to use oral language for new purposes in their discussions of books with peers and through their participation in literature discussion groups.

For some elementary school students, the ability to use reading as a comprehension tool for critical thinking is linked to the scope of children's linguistic, discourse, and real-world knowledge (Catts, Fey, Zhang, & Tomblin, in press; Kamhi & Catts, 1999; Wallach & Butler, 1994). Good readers are superior to poor readers in their vocabulary knowledge (Fry, Johnson, & Muehl, 1970; Nippold, 1998), comprehension and use of syntactic complexity (Clay, 1972; Goodman & Goodman, 1977; Scott, 1995), discourse processing strategies (Bishop, 1997; Pressley, 1998; Westby, 1999), and understanding of the language of instruction (Francis, 1973). Stahl and Pagnucco (1996) studied first-grade students in two types of reading programs, the traditional basal approach and one based on the process, whole-language model. They found that children's writing was influenced by their reading achievement. Reading and writing skills grew in tandem, and the sophistication of children's writing more often was related to their reading level than to the type of instructional experiences they experienced in writing (see also Shanahan & Tierney, 1991).

The Engagement Perspective on Classroom Language and Literacy Learning

The engagement perspective highlights the importance of motivation in learning to read and underscores the social basis of classroom learning (Guthrie & Alvermann, 1999; Guthrie et al., 1996). Importantly, language learning is linked with both motivation and strategies in learning to read. From this viewpoint, classroom activities should be designed to motivate students for reading and writing and to provide them with opportunities to use oral language for meaningful communicative purposes. Guthrie and Anderson (1999) defined two essential features of the engagement perspective:

1. Classrooms are social, providing opportunities for students to learn particular content and contributing to their motivation to learn.
2. Social interaction influences reading strategies.

Classrooms Are Social: Opportunities to Learn and Be Motivated.   A m e r i-can classrooms are organized around activities and content. Engaged readers interact with each other as they work to master knowledge (Almasi & McKeown, 1996). Morrow and Asbury's (1999) series of studies showed that classroom settings that invite collaboration among elementary students are likely to engage students. Both effort and attention remained at a high level. The most avid students were eager to practice literacy skills in literacy centers, where there was an ample supply of books and the opportunity to interact with peers; they talked with other students about books, shared their writing, and discussed homework. This positive effect was true for poor readers as well. Madden (1988) showed that attitudes of poor readers improved when they learned in cooperative and collaborative reading activities. However, for students with language-based reading and writing problems in inclusion programs, beyond the improved social competence associated with cooperative learning, specific outcomes for their word recognition and reading comprehension remain unknown (Silliman, Ford, Beasman, & Evans, 1999).

Social Interaction Influences Reading Strategies.   Social interaction patterns can enhance the development of strategies for reading. Students' prior levels of knowledge and motivation determine how much learning will occur, and the content of learning depends on the quantity and quality of social interactions around learning topics. "What they learn from each other and the teacher is dependent upon and interacts with motivation, strategy use, existing knowledge, and the context and quality of the interaction" (Guthrie & Anderson, 1999, p. 56).

Almasi and Gambrell (1994) showed that particular forms of social interaction during literature discussion in elementary school classrooms foster the growth of literary interpretation strategies. When teachers encouraged students to listen closely to each other, entertain multiple interpretations of text, and recognize alternative perspectives, the students gained; that is, students responded to and challenged each other, interpreted the textual meaning, challenged authors' style, and shared opinions and questions. When students can talk to each other about their writing, they learn an acute sense of audience and authorship. Strategies for reading and writing are influenced by the social structure of peer interactions within the classroom.

The Alvermann et al. (1996) study showed high school students preferred studying and working in small groups with other students who held similar beliefs and that social exchange facilitated learning. Open-ended tasks resulted in the most discussion, compared with tasks that could be completed alone or shared with only one other student. Similar to the results of Almasi and Gambrell (1994), students achieved more in student-directed, versus teacher-directed, groups.

Most of the research on book discussions in classrooms has been conducted with literary texts. However, Meloth and Deering (1994) revealed that discussion of informational books can lead to the learning and practice of critical skills as well. Students studying science looked for explanations as they read texts; they developed learning strategies, such as collecting evidence, evaluating information, and drawing conclusions.

Peer Learning in the Classroom.   How peers influence students' learning has been the focus of much research during the past three decades. Webb and Palincsar (1996) provided a comprehensive overview of contemporary approaches to peer learning in the classroom. Most of these approaches allowed extensive opportunities for students to use oral discussion in connection with their literacy learning. Examples of engagement approaches include: (a) *cooperative groups* for reading and for writing (e.g., Bramlett, 1994; Deering & Meloth, 1993; Jenkins et al., 1994; Kamps, Leonard, Potucek, & Garrison-Harrell, 1995); (b) *conversational discussion groups* (e.g., Koskinen

& O'Flahavan, 1995; Leal, 1992); (c) *KEEP-experience text relationship* (Au, 1979; Au & Carroll, 1997; Gallego, 1992); (d) *questioning the author* (Almasi & McKeown, 1996; McCarthy, Hoffman, & Galda, 1999); and (e) *literature discussions* (Eeds & Wells, 1989; Lewis, 1997; Nystrand, Gamoran, & Heck, 1993; Scharer & Peters, 1996; Villaume & Worden, 1993). Other engagement approaches that integrate reading and writing through student inquiry include *Book Club* (McCarthy et al., 1999; Raphael & McMahon, 1994), *Reading Recovery* (e.g., Gaffney & Anderson, 1991), and Gallego's (1992) adaption of *interactive semantic mapping*.

The role of oral language in facilitating literacy-learning is highlighted in the special case of *ability-based reading and writing groups*, which are common in American elementary schools (e.g., Grant & Rothenberg, 1986). Groups are both teacher directed and student directed. Grouping students according to their ability for teacher-led instruction may be beneficial because it raises students' attentiveness and gives them more individualized instruction (Wilkinson, 1990b). An example is when grouping students allows teachers to instruct small groups of students that are homogeneous with respect to students' aptitude and their preparation for the academic material to be taught. All-student groups that are not led by the teacher are also found in American classrooms. Research (e.g., Alvermann et al., 1996) shows these learning formats, too, can be beneficial to students' learning.

Both elementary and secondary students of varying ability levels (heterogeneous groups) benefit from learning opportunities in small all-student groups (Webb, 1989, 1991; Wilkinson, 1990b). However, the small-group processes that promote positive effects for learning are not well understood. Prior research and theory suggest a central role for social factors, as manifested in group processes through verbal communication. There have been several studies examining all-student interaction in heterogeneous ability level groups, which have primarily concerned mathematics instruction (e.g., Webb, 1991). Overall, the data from the elementary and secondary school studies are remarkably consistent. Under certain circumstances, low-ability students seem to achieve at higher than expected levels after placement in small, heterogeneous ability groups (Wilkinson, 1990b). If low-achieving students are regarded as low status, their achievement is less than that obtained by high-status, high-ability students in the same group (Cohen, 1984). A series of related studies of elementary reading and mathematics groups provided evidence that low-ability students remain low achievers throughout the school year and show a lack of skill at requesting and providing needed information during seatwork (Wilkinson & Calculator, 1982; Wilkinson & Spinelli, 1983). Indeed, all-student heterogeneous groups may serve to maintain the status quo among students in their status and consequent opportunities to engage in the rich verbal interactions that are deemed crucial for learning, unless teachers intervene to alter the interactional processes.

Achievement is enhanced by verbal interaction in other content areas, as well. Webb (1989), in reviewing 19 published studies on learning mathematics and computer science in small all-student groups, reported that verbal behavior seemed to influence learning, rather than being dependent on achievement level. Although Webb's earlier work linked the special behaviors of giving and receiving help with learning, she concluded that a more comprehensive analysis of students' questions, errors, and responses may help to identify causal relationships.

Also important are the *cooperative learning* studies. Given the opportunity, students successfully form partnerships, and small teams, in both regular education and special education populations (e.g., Kamps et al., 1995; Madden, 1988). Goals of the individuals in groups determine, to a large extent, the quantity and quality of social interaction. Johnson, Johnson, and Stanne (1989) demonstrated that when the goals were shared, group collaboration and communication increased. Equity was also a critical feature. When students on a team equally contributed, communication was most likely to be more motivating, resulting in students' learning. When students in a small-group activity believe that they can trust other students to listen and accept their suggestions, they personally invest in the group's activity (Alvermann et al., 1996).

FUTURE EMPHASES

The future of language and literacy instruction in American schools will be influenced by the strong policy environment created by the educational reform movement. In recent years, the topic of educational reform has received national attention in the United States as exemplified by enactment of three federal laws: the 1990 Americans with Disabilities Act, the 1993 Improving America's Schools, also known as National Goals 2000, and the 1997 reauthorization of the Individuals with Disabilities Education Act (IDEA). The common theme of these three laws is attaining equality of opportunity in all areas, including education, for all Americans. To achieve equal opportunity in education, high standards of accomplishment are expected for all students, including those with disabilities. Specifically, the new reform emphasizes the following key points:

- All students will meet high standards in mastering the core curriculum for language and literacy.
- Accountability must include standards for processes and outcomes of language and literacy learning.
- Inclusion remains an option to meet the needs of students who are at risk for failure to master language and literacy skills that are necessary for academic success in school; however, to achieve success, optional inclusion requires true collaboration among general and special educators and clear criteria for which students can best profit from inclusion.
- Integrated curricula that balance content and strategy learning and emphasize problem solving and active learning should be implemented in classrooms; to reduce the incidence of reading failure, a balanced approach is warranted that incorporates contextualized instruction in phonological awareness and the alphabetic principle with learning how to comprehend texts.

The combined effects of the new laws with the emphasis on standards and assessments and the increasing diversity of the school population have changed American classrooms substantially, and therefore significantly affect teachers' work with children. Several competencies are essential for teachers to develop, including new instructional techniques and alternative assessments.

Teachers should be encouraged to adopt the *engagement perspective*, which emphasizes students' active learning and the integration of language with literacy learning across the curriculum. The future suggests the importance of a broader view of language and literacy learning: The engagement perspective, integrating the use of both oral and written language learning, emphasizes contextualized uses of language. Because the engagement perspective focuses on the motivation for reading, successful programs enable all students to succeed and become motivated, strategic, and competent readers. Just as the vision of reading differs significantly between the engagement perspective and the old view of reading as a collection of skills, so do the visions for the kinds of instructional practices, curricula, and assessments as key to reading mastery. Adopting an engagement perspective as the educational vision for reading competence mandates particular instructional practices in the classroom. Furthermore, the curriculum should be able to support these pedagogical practices optimally, and the use of alternative assessments is a necessity, because the mastery of certain aspects of reading can be revealed only by rich qualitative data.

One of the challenges remaining is: How are instructional conversations actually used in literacy instruction, and how do they affect the motivation of individual students to read and write for a variety of communicative purposes? Teachers and other educational staff should be encouraged to implement more classroom *discussion-based activities*, such as debating, questioning, clarifying, and elaborating, which can be initiated by the teacher or the student. All employ instructional conversations to varying degrees, which assist students to develop effective strategies for comprehension and expression as tools of inquiry (Englert et al., 1994; Goldenberg & Patthey-Chavez, 1995; Oyler, 1996; Roehler & Cantlon, 1997; Scharer & Peters, 1996). Hynde (1999) suggested the following:

- Optimal tasks for group discussion are those that are open ended and subject to multiple interpretations.
- Optimal groups for discussion are those that are friendly and motivated by the topic.
- Optimal motivation for students includes their ideas for topics of discussion.
- Middle and high school students should have the opportunity to evaluate their work.
- Teachers may need to guide the discussion (themselves or via students) if they have a specific direction they want the discussion to take.

Alternative assessment is one of the key new competencies that teachers must master. Particularly important is the use of observational methods to reveal students' literacy competencies and the critical importance of interdisciplinary collaboration for assessment, so that a full picture of students' developmental strengths and educational needs may emerge. Teachers are faced with the challenge of variability among students in their language and literacy skills and how best to assess and promote the development of these skills. Teachers, along with special educators, speech-language pathologists, reading specialists, and others, are looking for alternatives to standardized tests, which are limited in the information provided, particularly about the progress of individual students.

Teachers require adequate means for assessing students' progress. The approach of Silliman and Wilkinson (1994b), the *observational lens model*, is a qualitative one in which the actual language and literacy behaviors of students are described over time, and the progress of individual students is documented. This method, which is consistent with portfolio assessment (Paratore, 1995), emphasizes the need for careful and frequent monitoring of the instructional process and its influence on individual student outcomes. Ongoing language assessment must include the collection of actual samples of students' linguistic and discourse patterns as found in the oral domain and in reading, writing, and spelling. Meaningful assessment must also include other components, such as systematic observations of classroom interactions, interviews with students, teachers, and families, and the interpretation of outcomes through the prism of the cultural and social practices that frame home and school values.

Finally, the *engagement perspective* requires educators to change their instructional practices significantly, adopting a student-centered classroom and implementing the instructional principles that Hynde (1999) described. Reading lessons should be designed to motivate students to want to read, and to provide them with opportunities to develop their literacy skills, knowledge, and social competencies. Activities, such as debating and discussion, having students serve as teachers, and using portfolios as a primary method of assessment, are typical of engaged classrooms and should be incorporated as hallmarks of American classrooms.

REFERENCES

Adams, M. (1990). *Beginning to read*. Cambridge, MA: MIT Press.

Almasi, J., & Gambrell, L. (1994). *Sociocognitive conflict in peer-led and teacher-led discussions of literature* (Rep. No. 12). University of Maryland and University of Georgia, National Reading Research Center: University of Georgia

Almasi, J., & McKeown, M. (1996). The nature of engaged reading in classroom discussions of literature. *Journal of Literacy Research, 28*(1), 107–146.

Alvermann, D., Young, J., Weaver, D., Hinchman, K., Moore, D., Phelps, Thrash, S., & Zalewkis, E. (1996). Middle and high school students' perceptions of how they experience text-based discussions: A multicase study. *Reading Research Quarterly, 31*, 244–267.

Alvermann, D. (1999). Modes of inquiry into studying engaged reading. In J. Guthrie & D. Alvermann (Eds.), *Engaged reading: Processes, practices, and policy implications* (pp. 134–149). New York: Teachers College Press.

Au, K. H. (1979). Using the experience-text-relationship method with minority children. *Reading Teacher, 32*, 677–679.

Au, K., & Carroll, J. (1997). Improving literacy achievement through a constructivist approach: The KEEP demonstration classroom project. *Elementary School Journal, 97*, 203–221.

August, D., & Hakuta, K. (1997). *Improving schooling for language-minority children: A research agenda*. Washington, DC: National Academy Press.

August, D., & Hakuta, K. (1998). *Educating language-minority children*. Washington, DC: National Academy Press.

Bakhtin, M. M. (1986). *Speech genres and other late essays* (Caryl Emerson & Michael Holquist, Eds.; V. W. McGee, Trans.). Austin: University of Texas Press.

Beck, I., McKeown, M., Sandora, C., Kucan, L., & Worthy, J. (1996). Questioning the author: A year-long classroom implementation to engage students with text. *Elementary School Journal, 96*, 385–414.

Becker, L. B., & Silverstein, J. E. (1984). Clinician-child discourse: A replication study. *Journal of Speech and Hearing Disorders, 49*, 104–106.

Bergeron, B. (1993). Power and classroom discourse. *Journal of Classroom Interaction, 28*(2), 1–6.

Biber, D. (1988). *Variation across speech and writing*. New York: Cambridge University Press.

Bishop, D. V. M. (1997). *Uncommon understanding: Development and disorders of language comprehension in children*. East Sussex, UK: Psychology Press.

Blachman, B. A. (1994). Early literacy acquisition: The role of phonological awareness. In G. P. Wallach & K. G. Butler (Eds.), *Language learning disabilities in school-age children and adolescents: Some principles and applications* (pp. 253–274). Boston: Allyn & Bacon.

Bloome, D., & Knott, G. (1985). Teacher-student discourse. In D. N. Ripich & F. M. Spinelli (Eds.), *School discourse problems* (pp. 53–76). Boston: College-Hill Press.

Bramlett, R. (1994). Implementing cooperative learning: A field study evaluating issues for school-based consultants. *Journal of School Psychology, 32*(1), 67–84.

Bransford, J. D., Brown, A. L., & Cocking, R. R. (1999). *How people learn: Brain, mind, experience, and school*. Washington, DC: National Academy Press.

Brown, A. L. (1992). Design experiments: Theoretical and methodological challenges in creating complex interventions in classroom settings. *Journal of the Learning Sciences, 2*, 141–178.

Brown, A. L., & Campione, J. C. (1994). Guided discovery in a community of learners. In K. McGilly (Ed.), *Classroom lessons: Integrating cognitive theory and classroom practice* (pp. 229–270). Cambridge, MA: MIT Press.

Brown, A. L., & Palincsar, A. S. (1987). Reciprocal teaching of comprehension strategies. In J. D. Day & J. G. Borkowski (Eds.), *Intelligence and exceptionality: New directions for theory, assessment, and instructional practice* (pp. 81–132). Norwood, NJ: Ablex.

Bruck, M., Treiman, R., Caravolas, M., Genesee, F., & Cassar, M. (1998). Spelling skills of children in whole language and phonics classrooms. *Applied Psycholinguistics, 19*, 669–684.

Campione, J. C., & Brown, A. L. (1987). Linking dynamic assessment with school achievement. In C. S. Lidz (Ed.), *Dynamic assessment: An integrated approach to evaluating learning potential* (pp. 82–115). New York: Guilford Press.

Catts, H. W., Fey, M. E., Zhang, X., & Tomblin, J. B. (in press). Language basis of reading and reading disabilities: Evidence from a longitudinal investigation. *Scientific Studies of Reading*.

Cazden, C. B. (1988). *Classroom discourse: The language of teaching and learning*. Portsmouth, NH: Heinemann.

Cazden, C. B. (1993). Vygotsky, Hymes, and Bakhtin: From word to utterance and voice. In E. A. Forman, N. Minick, & C. A. Stone (Eds.), *Contexts for learning: Sociocultural dynamics in children's development* (pp. 197–212). New York: Oxford University Press.

Cazden, C. B., John, V., & Hymes, D. (Eds.). (1972). *Functions of language in the classroom*. New York: Teachers College Press.

Champion, T. (1998). "Tell me somethin' good": A description of narrative structures among African American children. *Linguistics and Education, 9*, 251–286.

Champion, T. B., Katz, L., Muldrow, R., & Dail, R. (1999). Storytelling and storymaking in an urban preschool classroom: Building bridges from home to school culture. *Topics in Language Disorders, 19*(3), 52>@150>67.

Champion, T., Seymour, H., & Camarata, S. (1995). Narrative discourse of African American children. *Journal of Narrative and Life History, 5,* 333–352.

Cherry, L. (1978). Teacher-student interaction and teacher expectations of students' communicative competence. In R. Shuy & P. Griffin (Eds.), *The study of children's functional language and education in the early years* (Final report to the Carnegie Corporation) New York & Arlington, VA: Center for Applied Linguistics.

Cherry, L. (1979). The role of adults' requests for clarification in the language development of children. In R. Freedle (Ed.), *New directions in discourse processing* (pp. 273–286). Norwood, NJ: Ablex.

Clay, M. M. (1972). Reading: The patterning of complex behaviour. Auckland: Heinemann.

Cohen, E. (1984). Talking and working together: Status, interaction and learning. In P. Peterson, L. Wilkinson, & M. Hallinan (Eds.), *The social context of instruction* (pp. 171–189). Orlando, FL: Academic Press.

Cole, M. (1998). Can cultural psychology help us think about diversity? *Mind, Culture, and Activity, 5,* 291–304.

Collins, C. (1992). Improving reading and thinking: From teaching or not teaching skills to interactive interventions. In M. Pressley, K. Harris, & J. Guthrie (Eds.), *Promoting academic competence and literacy in schools* (pp. 149–167). San Diego, CA: Academic Press.

Cooper, C., Marquis, A., & Ayers-Lopez, S. (1982). Peer learning in the classrooms: Tracing developmental patterns and consequences of children's spontaneous interactions. In L. C. Wilkinson (Ed.), *Communicating in the classroom* (pp. 69–84). New York: Academic, Press.

Corson, D. (1984). The case for oral language in schooling. *Elementary School Journal, 81,* 458–467.

Deering, P., & Meloth, M. (1993). A descriptive study of naturally occurring discussions in cooperative learning groups. *Journal of Classroom Interaction, 28*(2), 7–13.

Delpit, L. D. (1988). The silenced dialogue: Power and pedagogy in educating other people's children. *Harvard Educational Review, 58,* 280–298.

Delpit, L. D. (1992). Acquisition of literate discourse: Bowing before the master? *Theory Into Practice, 21,* 296–302.

Diaz, R. M., Neal, C. J., & Amaya-Williams, M. (1990). The social origin of self-regulation. In L.C. Moll (Ed.), *Vygotsky and education: Instructional implications and applications of sociohistorical psychology* (pp. 127–154). New York: Cambridge University Press.

Donahue, M. L. (1994). Differences in classroom discourse styles of students with learning disabilities. In D. N. Ripich & N. A. Creaghead (Eds.), *School discourse problems* (2nd ed., pp. 229–261). San Diego, CA: Singular Publishing.

Donahue, M. L., & Lopez-Reyna, N. A. (1998). Conversational maxims and scaffolded learning in children with learning disabilities: Is the flying buttress a better metaphor? *Journal of Learning Disabilities, 31,* 398–403.

Durkin, D. (1978–1979). What classroom observations reveal about reading comprehension instruction. *Reading Research Quarterly, 15,* 481–533.

Echevarria, J. (1995). Interactive reading instruction: A comparison of proximal and distal effects of instructional conversations. *Exceptional Children, 61*(6), 536–552.

Eder, D. (1982). Differences in communicative styles across ability groups. In L. C. Wilkinson (Ed.), *Communicating in the classroom* (pp. 245–264). New York: Academic Press.

Eeds, M., & Wells, D. (1989). Grand conversations: An exploration of meaning construction in literature study groups. *Research in the Teaching of English, 23*(1), 4–29.

Ehri, L. C. (1997). Learning to read and learning to spell are one and the same, almost. In C. A. Perfetti, L. Rieben, & M. Fayol (Eds.), *Learning to spell: Research, theory, and practice across languages* (pp. 237–269). Mahwah, NJ: Lawrence Erlbaum Associates.

Englert, C. S., Tarrant, K. L., Mariage, T. V., & Oxer, T. (1994). Lesson talk as the work of reading groups: The effectiveness of two interventions. *Journal of Learning Disabilities, 27*(3), 165–185.

Erickson, F. (1982). Classroom discourse as improvisation: Relationships between academic task structure and social participation structure in lessons. In L. C. Wilkinson (Ed.), *Communicating in the classroom* (pp. 153–182). New York: Academic Press.

Erickson, F., & Schultz, J. (1982). *The counselor as gatekeeper: Social interaction in interviews.* New York: Academic Press.

Ervin-Tripp, S. (1977). Wait for me roller-skate. In S. Ervin-Tripp & C. Mitchell-Kernan (Eds.), *Child discourse* (pp. 165–188). New York: Academic.

Florio, S., & Shultz, J. (1979). Social competence at home and at school. *Theory Into Practice, 18,* 234–243.

Francis, H. (1973). Children's experience of reading and notions of units in language. *British Journal of Educational Psychology, 43,* 17–23.

Fry, M. A., Johnson, C. S., & Muehl, S. (1970). Oral language production in relation to reading achievement among select second graders. In D. J. Bakker & P. Staz (Eds.), *Specific reading disability.* Rotterdam: Rotterdam University Press.

Gaffney, J., & Anderson, R. (1991). Two tiered scaffolding: Congruent process of teaching and learning. In E. Hiebert (Ed.), *Literacy for a diverse society: Perspectives, practices, and policies* (pp. 184–198). New York: Teachers College Press.

Gallego, M. (1992). Collaborative instruction for reading comprehension: The role of discourse and discussion. In M. Pressley, K. Harris, & J. Guthrie (Eds.), *Promoting academic competence and literacy in schools* (pp. 223–242). San Diego, CA: Academic Press.

Gallimore, R., & Tharp, R. (1990). Teaching mind in society: Teaching, schooling, and literate discourse. In L. C. Moll (Ed.), *Vygotsky and education: Instructional implications and applications of sociohistorical psychology* (pp. 175–205). New York: Cambridge University Press.

Gambrell, L., & Almasi, J. (Eds.). (1996). *Lively discussions: Fostering engaged reading*. Newark, DE: International Reading Association.

Gaskins, I. W., Ehri, L. C., Cress, C., O'Hara, C., & Donnelly, K. (1996–1997). Procedures for word learning: Making discoveries about words. *Reading Teacher, 50,* 312–327.

Gaskins, I. W., Rauch, S., Gensemer, E., Cunicelli, E., O'Hara, C., Six, L., & Scott, T. (1997). Scaffolding the development of intelligence among children who are delayed in learning to read. In K. Hogan & M. Pressley (Eds.), *Scaffolding student learning: Instructional approaches and issues* (pp. 43–73). Cambridge, MA: Brookline.

Gavelek, J., & Raphael, T. (1996). Changing talk about text: New roles for teachers and students. *Language Arts, 73,* 182–192.

Goldenberg, C. (1996). Latin American immigration and U. S. schools. *Social Policy Report of the Society for Research in Child Development, 10*(1), 1–29.

Goldenberg, C., & Patthey-Chavez, C. (1995). Discourse processes in instructional conversations: Interactions between teacher and transition readers. *Discourse Processes, 19,* 57–73.

Goodman, K. S., & Goodman, Y. M. (1977). Learning about psycholinguistic processes by analyzing oral reading. *Harvard Educational Review, 47,* 317–333.

Graham, S., & Harris, K. R. (1996). Self-regulation and strategy instruction for students who find writing and learning challenging. In M. Levy & S. Ransdell (Eds.), *The science of writing: Theories, methods, individual differences, and applications* (pp. 347–360). Mahwah, NJ: Lawrence Erlbaum Associates.

Graham, S., & Harris, K. R. (1997). It can be taught, but it does not develop naturally: Myths and realities in writing instruction. *School Psychology Review, 26,* 414–424.

Graham, S., & Harris, K. R. (1999). Assessment and intervention in overcoming writing difficulties: An illustration from the self-regulated strategy development model. *Language, Speech, and Hearing Services in Schools, 30,* 225–264.

Grant, L., & Rothenberg, J. (1986). The social enhancement of ability differences: Teacher-student interactions in first- and second-grade reading groups. *Elementary School Journal 87*(1), 29–49.

Green, J., & Smith, D. (1983). Teaching and learning: A linguistic perspective. *Elementary School Journal, 83,* 353–391.

Green, J., & Wallat, C. (1981). Mapping instructional conversations—A sociolinguistic ethnography. In J. Green & C. Wallat (Eds.), *Ethnography and language in educational setting* (pp. 161–205). Norwood, NJ: Ablex.

Griffin, M., & Shuy, R. (Eds.). (1978). *The Study of Children's Functional Language in the Early Years.* Final Report to the Carnegie Corporation of New York. New York: Center for Applied Linguistics.

Guice, S. (1992, December). *Readers, texts, and contexts in a sixth-grade community of readers.* Paper presented at the annual meeting of the National Reading Conference, San Antonio, TX.

Guthrie, J., & Alvermann, D. (Eds.). (1999). *Engaged reading: Processes, practices, and policy implications*, New York: Teachers College Press.

Guthrie, J., & Anderson, E. (1999). Engagement in reading: Processes of motivated strategic, knowledgeable, social readers. In J. Guthrie & D. Alvermann (Eds.), *Engaged reading: Processes, practices, and policy implications* (pp 17–46). New York: Teachers College Press.

Guthrie, J., Van Meter, P. ,McCann, A., Wigfield, A., Bennett, L., Poundstone, C., Rice, M., Faibisch, F., Hunt, B., & Mitchell, A. (1996). Growth of literacy engagement: Changes in motivations and strategies during concept-oriented reading instruction. *Reading Research Quarterly, 31,* 306–325.

Gutierrez-Clellen, V. F. (1998). Syntactic skills of Spanish speaking children with low school achievement. *Language, Speech, and Hearing Services in Schools, 29,* 207–215.

Heath, S. B. (1982). What no bedtime story means: Narrative skills at home and school. *Language in Society, 11,* 49–76.

Hepler, S., & Hickman, J. (1982). "The book was okay. I love you"—Social aspects of response to literature. *Theory Into Practice, 21,* 278–283.

Hester, E. J. (1996). Narratives of young African American children. In A. G. Kamhi, K. E. Pollack, & J. L. Harris (Eds.), *Communication development and disorders in African American children: Research, assessment, and intervention* (pp. 227–245). Baltimore, MD: Paul H. Brookes.

Hicks, D. (1991). Kinds of narratives: Genre skills among first graders from two communities. In A. McCabe & C. Peterson (Eds.), *Developing narrative structure* (pp. 55–87). Hillsdale, NJ: Lawrence Erlbaum Associates.

Horowitz, R., & Samuels, S. J. (1987). Comprehending oral and written language: Critical contrasts for literacy and schooling. In R. Horowitz & S. J. Samuels (Eds.), *Comprehending oral and written language* (pp. 1–52). New York: Academic Press.

Hynde, C. (1999). Instructional considerations in middle and secondary schools. In J. Guthrie & D. Alvermann (Eds.), *Engaged reading: Processes, practices, and policy implications* (pp. 81–104). New York: Teachers College Press.

Jenkins, J., Jewell, M., Leicester, N., O'Connor, R., Jenkins, L., & Troutner, N. (1994). Accommodations for individual differences without classroom ability groups: An experiment in school restructuring. *Exceptional Children, 60,* 344–358.

Johnson, D., Johnson, R., & Stanne, M. (1989). Impact of goal and resource interindependence on problem-solving success. *Journal of Social Psychology, 129*(5), 621–629.

Kamhi, A. G., & Catts, H. W. (1999). Language and reading: Convergence and divergence. In H. W. Catts & A. G. Kamhi (Eds.), *Language and reading disabilities* (pp. 1–24). Needham Heights, MA: Allyn & Bacon.

Kamps, D., Leonard, B., Potucek, J., & Garrison-Harrell, L. (1995). Cooperative learning groups in reading: An integration strategy for students with autism and general classroom peers. *Behavioral Disorders, 21*(1), 89–109.

Koskinen, P., & O'Flahavan, J. (1995). Teacher role options in peer discussions about literature, *Reading Teacher, 48,* 354–356.

Kovarsky, D., & Duchan, J. F. (1997). The interactional dimensions of language therapy. *Language, Speech, and Hearing Services in Schools, 28,* 297–307.

Langer, J. A. (1990). Understanding literature. *Language Arts, 67,* 812–816.

Leal, D. (1992). The nature of talk about three types of text during peer group discussions. *Journal of Reading Behavior, 24*(3), 313–338.

Lemke, J. L. (1985). Using language in the classroom knowledge: Reading lessons. *Curriculum Inquiry, 15,* 247–279.

Lewis, C. (1997). The social drama of literature discussions in 5th/6th grade. *Research in the Teaching of English, 31*(2), 163–204

Madden, L. (1988, December) Improve reading attitudes of poor readers through cooperative reading teams. *Reading Teacher,* pp. 194–199.

McCarthy, S., Hoffman, L., & Galda, J. (1999). Readers in elementary classrooms: Learning goals and instructional principles. In J. Guthrie & D. Alvermann (Eds.), *Engaged Reading* (pp. 46–80). New York: Teachers College.

Mehan, H. (1979). *Learning lessons: Social organization in the classroom.* Cambridge, MA: Harvard University Press.

Mehan, H. (1994). The role of discourse in learning, schooling, and reform. In B. McLeod (Ed.), *Language and learning: Educating linguistically diverse students* (pp. 71–96). Albany: State University of New York Press.

Meloth, M., & Deering, P. (1994). Task talk and task awareness under different cooperative learning conditions. *American Education Research Journal, 31*(1), 138–165.

Merritt, M. (1982). Distributing and directing attention in primary classrooms. In L. C. Wilkinson (Ed.), *Communicating in the classroom* (pp. 223–244). New York: Academic Press.

Michaels, S. (1986). Narrative presentations: An oral preparation for literacy with first grade. In J. Cook-Gumperz (Ed.), *The social construction of literacy,* (pp. 94–116). New York: Cambridge University Press.

Morrow, L., & Asbury, E. (1999). Best practices for a balanced early literacy program. In L. Gambrell, L. Morrow, S. Neuman & M. Pressley (Eds.), *Best practices in literacy instruction* (pp. 49–67). New York: Guilford.

Morrow, L. M. (1993). *Literacy development in the early years: Helping children read and write* (2nd ed.). Boston: Allyn & Bacon.

Morrow, L. M., & Smith, J. K. (1990). Introduction. In L. M. Morrow & J. K. Smith (Eds.), *Assessment for instruction in early literacy* (pp. 1–6). Englewood Cliffs, NJ: Prentice Hall.

Nicholson, T. (1997). Closing the gap on reading failure: Social background, phonemic awareness, and learning to read. In B. Blachman (Ed.), *Foundations of reading acquisition and dyslexia: Implications for early intervention* (pp. 381–407). Mahwah, NJ: Lawrence Erlbaum Associates.

Nippold, M. A. (1998). *Later language development: The school-age and adolescent years* (2nd ed.). Austin, TX: Pro-Ed.

Nystrand, M., Gamoran, A., & Heck, M. (1993). Using small groups for response to and thinking about literature. *English Journal, 82*(1), 14–22.

Oyler, C. (1996). Sharing authority: Student initiations during teacher-led read-alouds of information books. *Teaching and Teacher Education, 12*(2), 149–160.

Palincsar, A. S. (1998). Keeping the metaphor of scaffolding fresh—A response to C. Addison Stone's "The metaphor of scaffolding: It's utility for the field of learning disabilities." *Journal of Learning Disabilities, 31,* 370–373.

Palincsar, A. S., & Brown, A. L. (1984). Reciprocal teaching of comprehension-fostering and comprehension-monitoring activities. *Cognition and Instruction, 1,* 117–175.

Palincsar, A. S., Brown, A. L., & Campione, J. C. (1993). First grade dialogues for knowledge acquisition and use. In E. A. Forman, N. Minick, & C. A. Stone (Eds.), *Contexts for learning: Sociocultural dynamics in children's development* (pp. 43–57). New York: Oxford University Press.

Palincsar, A. S., & Klenk, L. (1992). Fostering literacy learning in supportive contexts. *Journal of Learning Disabilities, 25*, 211–225, 229.

Palincsar, A. S., & Klenk, L. (1993). Broader visions encompassing literacy, learners, and contexts. *Remedial and Special Education, 14*, 19–29.

Palincsar, A. S., Parecki, A. D., & McPhail, J. C. (1995). Friendship and literacy through literature. *Journal of Learning Disabilities, 28*, 503–510, 522.

Panagos, J. M., & Bliss, L. S. (1990). Clinical presuppositions for speech therapy lessons. *Journal of Childhood Communication Disorders, 13*, 19–28.

Paratore, J. R. (1995). Assessing literacy: Establishing common standards in portfolio assessment. *Topics in Language Disorders, 16*(1), 67–82.

Pressley, M. (1998). *Reading instruction that works: The case for balanced teaching.* New York: Guilford Press.

Pressley, M., & McCormick, C. (1995). *Cognition, teaching, and assessment.* New York: HarperCollins.

Pressley, M., Wharton-McDonald, R., & Mistretta, J. (1998). Effective beginning literacy instruction: Dialectical, scaffolded, and contextualized. In J. L. Metsala & L. C. Ehri (Eds.), *Word recognition in beginning literacy* (pp. 357–373). Mahwah, NJ: Lawrence Erlbaum Associates.

Pressley, M., & Woloshyn, V. (Eds.). (1995). *Cognitive strategy instruction that really improves children's academic performance* (2nd ed.). Cambridge, MA: Brookline.

Prutting, C. A., Bagshaw, N., Goldstein, H., Juskowitz, S., & Umen, L. (1978). Clinician-child discourse: Some preliminary questions. *Journal of Speech and Hearing Disorders, 43*, 123–139.

Raphael, T. & McMahon, S. (1994). Book Club: An alternative framework for reading instruction. *Reading Teacher, 48*(2), 102–116.

Ripich, D. N., & Panagos, J. M. (1985). Accessing children's knowledge of sociolinguistic rules for speech therapy lessons. *Journal of Speech and Hearing Disorders, 50*, 335–346.

Roehler, L. R., & Cantlon, D. J. (1997). Scaffolding: A powerful tool in social constructivist classrooms. In K. Hogan & M. Pressley (Eds.), *Scaffolding student learning: Instructional approaches and issues* (pp. 6–42). Cambridge, MA: Brookline.

Rogoff, B. (1990). *Apprenticeship in thinking: Cognitive development in social context.* New York: Oxford University Press.

Rogoff, B. (1995). Observing sociocultural activity on three planes: participatory appropriation, guided participation, and apprenticeship. In J. V. Wertsch, P. Del Rio, & A. Alvarez, (Eds), *Sociocultural studies of mind* (pp. 139–164). New York: Cambridge University Press.

Rogoff, B., Radziszewska, B., & Masiello, T. (1995). Analysis of developmental processes in sociocultural activity. In L. Martin, K. Nelson, & E. Tobach (Eds.), *Sociocultural psychology: Theory and practice of doing and knowing* (pp. 125–149). New York: Cambridge University Press.

Rosenshine, B., & Meister, C. (1994). Reciprocal teaching: A review of research. *Review of Educational Research, 64*, 479–530.

Ruiz, N. T. (1995). The social construction of ability and disability: II. Optimal and at-risk lessons in a bilingual special education classroom. *Journal of Learning Disabilities, 28*, 491–502.

Scharer, P., & Peters, D. (1996). An exploration of literature discussions conducted by two teachers moving toward literature-based instruction, *Reading Research and Instruction, 36*(1), 33–50.

Scott, C. M. (1988). Spoken and written syntax. In M. Nippold (Ed.), *Later language development: Ages nine through nineteen* (pp. 49–95). Boston: College-Hill.

Scott, C. (1995). Syntax for school-age children: A discourse perspective. In M. Fey, J. Windsor, & S. Warren (Eds.), *Language intervention: Preschool through the elementary years* (pp. 107–141). Baltimore, MD: Paul H. Brookes.

Scott, C. M., & Rogers, L. M. (1996). Written language abilities of African American children and youth. In A. G. Kamhi, K. E. Pollack, & J. L. Harris (Eds.), *Communication development and disorders in African American children: Research, assessment, and intervention* (pp. 307–332). Baltimore, MD: Paul H. Brookes.

Seymour, H. N., Bland-Stewart, L., & Green, L. J. (1998). Difference versus deficit in child African American English. *Language, Speech, and Hearing Services in Schools, 29*, 96–108.

Seymour, H. N., & Roeper, T. (1999). Grammatical acquisition of African American English. In O. L. Taylor & L. B. Leonard (Eds.), *Language acquisition across North American: Cross-cultural and cross-linguistic perspectives* (pp. 109–153). San Diego, CA: Singular.

Shanahan, T., & Tierney, R. (1991). Research on the reading-writing relationship: Interactions, transactions, and outcomes. In R. Barr, M. Kamil, P. Mosenthal, & P. D. Pearson (Eds.), *Handbook of reading research* (Vol. II, pp. 246–280). New York: Longman.

Share, D., & Stanovich, K. (1995). Cognitive processes in early reading development: Accommodating individual differences into a model of acquisition. *Issues in Education, 1*, 1–57.

Silliman, E. R. (1984). Interactional competencies in the instructional context: The role of teaching discourse in learning. In G. P. Wallach & K. G. Butler (Eds.), *Language learning disabilities in school-age children* (pp. 288–317). Baltimore, MD: Williams & Wilkins.

Silliman, E. R., Ford, C., Beasman, J., & Evans, D. (1999). An inclusion model for children with language learning disabilities: Building classroom partnerships. *Topics in Language Disorders, 19*(3), 1–18.

Silliman, E. R., & Wilkinson, L. C. (1991). *Communicating for learning: Classroom observation and collaboration.* Gaithersburg, MD: Aspen.

Silliman, E. R., & Wilkinson, L. C. (1994a). Discourse scaffolds for classroom intervention. In G. P. Wallach & K. G. Butler (Eds.), *Language learning disabilities in school-age children and adolescents* (pp. 27–54). Boston: Allyn & Bacon.

Silliman, E. R., & Wilkinson, L. C. (1994b). Observation is more than looking: Assessing progress in classroom language. In G. P. Wallach & K. G. Butler (Eds.), *Language learning disabilities in school-age children and adolescents* (pp. 145–173). Boston: Allyn & Bacon.

Smagorinsky, P. (1998). Thinking and speech and protocol analysis. *Mind, Culture, and Activity, 5,* 157–177.

Smith, D. (1987). Talking with young children about their reading. *Australian Journal of Reading, 10*(2), 120–122.

Snow, C. E., Burns, M. S., & Griffin, P. (Eds.). (1998). *Preventing reading difficulties in young children.* Washington, DC: National Academy Press.

Speece, D. L., & Keogh, B. K. (Eds.). (1996). *Research on classroom ecologies: Implications for inclusion of children with learning disabilities.* Mahwah, NJ: Lawrence Erlbaum Associates.

Spinelli, F. M. & Ripich, D. N. (1985). A comparison of classroom and clinical discourse. In D. N. Ripich & J. M. Spinelli (Eds.), *School discourse problems* (pp. 179–196). San Diego, CA: College-Hill.

Spiro, R. J., & Taylor, B. M. (1987). On investigating children's transition from narrative to expository discourse: The multidimensional nature of psychological text classification. In J. Tierney, P. L. Anders, & J. N. Mitchell (Eds.), *Understanding readers' understanding* (pp. 77–93). Hillsdale, NJ: Lawrence Erlbaum Associates.

Stahl, S., & Pagnucco, J. (1996). First graders reading and writing instruction in traditional and process-oriented classes. *Journal of Educational Research, 89*(3), 131–144.

Stallman, A. C., & Pearson, P. D. (1990). Formal measures of early literacy. In L. M. Morrow & J. K. Smith (Eds.), *Assessment for instruction in early literacy* (pp. 7–44). Englewood Cliffs, NJ: Prentice Hall.

Stone, C. A. (1993). What is missing in the metaphor of scaffolding? In E. A. Forman, N. Minick, & C. A. Stone (Eds.), *Contexts for learning: Sociocultural dynamics in children's development* (pp. 169–183). New York: Oxford University Press.

Stone, C. A. (1998). The metaphor of scaffolding: Its utility for the field of learning disabilities. *Journal of Learning Disabilities, 31,* 344–364.

Temple, C., & Collins, P. (1992). *Stories and readers: New perspectives on literature in the elementary classroom.* Norwood, MA: Christopher-Gordon.

Terrell, B. Y. (1994). Emergent literacy: In the beginning there was reading and writing. In D. N. Ripich & N. A. Creaghead (Eds.), *School discourse problems* (2nd ed., pp. 9–28). San Diego, CA: Singular.

Tharp, R. (1993). Institutional and social context of educational practice and reform. In E. A. Forman, N. Minick, & C. A. Stone (Eds.), *Contexts for learning: Sociocultural dynamics in children's development* (pp. 269–282). New York: Oxford University Press.

Tharp, R. (1994). Research knowledge and policy issues in cultural diversity and education. In B. McLeod (Ed.), *Language and learning: Educating linguistically diverse students* (pp. 129–167). Albany: State University of New York Press.

Tharp, R. G., & Gallimore, R. (1988). *Rousing minds to life: Teaching, learning, and schooling in social context.* Cambridge, England: Cambridge University Press.

Torgesen, J. K. (1999). Assessment and instruction for phonemic awareness and word recognition skills. In H. W. Catts & A. G. Kamhi (Eds.), *Language and reading disability* (pp. 128–153). Needham Heights, MA: Allyn & Bacon.

Tracey, D. H., & Morrow, L. M. (1998). Motivating contexts for young children's literacy development: Implications for word recognition. In J. L. Metsala & L. C. Ehri (Eds.), *Word recognition in beginning literacy* (pp. 341–356). Mahwah, NJ: Lawrence Erlbaum Associates.

Treiman, R., Tincoff, R., Rodriguez, K., Mouzaki, A., & Francis, D. J. (1998). The foundations of literacy: Learning the sounds of letters. *Child Development, 69,* 1524–1540.

van Kleeck, A. (1990). Emergent literacy: Learning about print before learning to read. *Topics in Language Disorders, 10*(2), 25–45.

van Kleeck, A. (1995). Emphasizing form and meaning separately in prereading and early reading instruction. *Topics in Language Disorders, 16*(1), 27–49.

van Kleeck, A. (1998). Preliteracy domains and stages: Laying the foundations for beginning reading. *Journal of Children's Communication Development, 20,* 33–51.

van Kleeck, A., & Schuele, C. M. (1987). Precursors to literacy: Normal development. *Topics in Language Disorders, 7*(2), 13–31.

Villaume, S., & Worden, T. (1993, October). Developing literate voices: The challenge of whole language, *Language Arts, 70,* 462–468.

Vygotsky, L. S. (1962). *Thought and language.* Cambridge, MA: MIT Press.

Vygotsky, L. S. (1981). The genesis of higher mental functions. In J. V. Wertsch (Ed.), *The concept of activity in psychology* (pp. 144–188). Armonk, NY: M. E. Sharpe.

Wallach, G. (1990). Magic buries Celtics: Looking for broader interpretations of language learning and literacy. *Topics in Language Disorders. 10*(2), 63–80.

Wallach, G. P., & Butler, K. G. (1994). Creating communication, literacy, and classroom success. In G. P. Wallach & K. G. Butler (Eds.), *Language learning disabilities in school-age children and adolescents* (pp. 2–26). Boston: Allyn & Bacon.

Webb, N. M. (1989). Peer interaction and learning in small groups. *International Journal of Educational Research, 13*, 21–39.

Webb, N. (1991). Task-related verbal interaction and mathematics learning in small groups. *Journal for Research in Mathematics Education, 22*, 366–389.

Webb, N., & Palincsar, A. (1996). Group processes in the classroom. In D. C. Berliner & R. C. Calfee (Eds.), *Handbook of educational psychology* (pp. 841–873). New York: Simon & Schuster Macmillan.

Wells, G. (1990). Talk about text. *Curriculum Inquiry, 20*, 369–404.

Wells, G. (1993). Reevaluating the IRF sequence: A proposal for the articulation of theories of activity and discourse for the analysis of teaching and learning in the classroom. *Linguistics and Education, 5*, 1–37.

Wertsch, J. V. (1990). The voice of rationality in a sociocultural approach to mind. In L. C. Moll (Ed.), *Vygotsky and education: Instructional implications and applications of sociohistorical psychology* (pp. 111–126). New York: Cambridge University Press.

Wertsch, J. V. (1991). *Voices of the mind: A sociocultural approach to mediated action.* Cambridge, MA: Harvard University Press.

Wertsch, J. V. (1995). The need for action in sociocultural research. In J. V. Wertsch, P. Del Rio, & A. Alvarez (Eds.), *Sociocultural studies of mind* (pp. 56–74). New York: Cambridge University Press.

Wertsch, J. V. (1998). *Mind as action.* New York: Oxford University Press.

Westby, C. E. (1999). Assessing and facilitating text comprehension problems. In H. W. Catts & A. G. Kamhi (Eds.), *Language and reading disabilities* (pp. 154–223). Needham Heights, MA: Allyn & Bacon.

Whitehurst, G., & Lonigan, C. (1998). Child development and emergent literacy. *Child Development, 69*, 848–872.

Wilkinson, L. C. (1982a). A sociolinguistic approach to communicating in the classroom. In L. C. Wilkinson (Ed.), *Communicating in the classroom* (pp. 3–12). New York: Academic Press.

Wilkinson, L. C. (Ed.). (1982b). *Communicating in the classroom.* New York: Academic Press.

Wilkinson, L. (1990a). Sociolinguistic studies of classroom communication. In L. Morrow & J. Smith (Eds.), *Assessment for instruction in early literacy,* (pp. 184–204). Englewood Cliffs, NJ: Prentice Hall.

Wilkinson, L. (1990b). Grouping children for learning: Implications for kindergarten education. In E. Rothkoph (Ed.), *Review of research in education* (pp. 203–223). Washington, DC: American Educational Research Association.

Wilkinson, L. (1998). Current issues and future directions in teaching and learning language. In J. Flood, D. Lapp, & S. Heath (Eds.), *Handbook for literacy educators: Research on teaching the language and visual arts* (pp. 617–625). New York: Macmillan.

Wilkinson, L. (1999). Reading engagement and school reform: Challenges for leadership in literacy education. In J. Guthrie & D. Alvermann (Eds.), *Engaged reading: Processes, practices and policy implications* (pp. 150–168). New York: Teachers College Press.

Wilkinson, L. C., & Calculator, S. (1982). Requests and responses in peer-directed readings groups. *American Education Research Journal, 19*, 107–122.

Wilkinson, L., & Silliman, E. (1997). Alternative assessment, literacy education and school reform. In J. Flood & D. Lapp (Eds.), *Handbook for literacy educators* (pp. 6–76). New York: International Reading Association and Macmillan.

Wilkinson, L. C., & Spinelli, F. (1983). Using requests effectively in peer directed instructional groups. *American Educational Research Journal, 20*, 479–501.

Wilkinson, L. C., & Silliman, E. R. (1994). Assessing students' progress in language and literacy. In L. Morrow, L. Wilkinson, & J. Smith (Eds.), *Integrated language arts: Controversy to consensus* (pp. 241–270). Needham Heights, MA: Allyn & Bacon.

Zubrick, A. (1987). So nervous about noise. *Australian Journal of Reading, 10*(2), 97–99.

CHAPTER 22

Children's Literature

Lee Galda
University of Minnesota

Gwynne Ellen Ash
University of Georgia

Bernice E. Cullinan
New York University

This volume of the *Handbook of Reading Research* marks the first time that a chapter on children's literature has been included; thus, there are no previous chapters on which to ground a current review. However, there is certainly not space enough for a review of all research on children's literature. We begin, therefore, with a description of the mutidisciplinary nature of children's literature, present a definition of and suggest an organizing principle for research on children's literature, and then move to a discussion of research in three major areas: texts, readers, and contexts. Each section begins with a brief description of the history of that type of research, but primarily we describe research efforts that exemplify important directions in the field, focusing on important or representative work rather than attempting a comprehensive review.

As interest in children's literature grew during the literature-based curriculum movement of the 1980s and 1990s, research interest in children's literature flourished as well. From the early research to current efforts there is a developing sense of the complexity of the constructs of literature, readers, and contexts for reading, as well as the interaction among readers, texts, and contexts for reading. The questions posed, the methodologies employed, and the theoretical arguments used in this research reflect this complicating of the idea of what it means to do research on children's literature. Questions that had, initially, seemed simple and straightforward are now regarded as multifaceted and complex, as our understanding of the transactional nature of literary response (Rosenblatt 1978, 1995), our view of reading (Pearson, 1986) and learning (Vygotsky, 1978), and the influence of contexts on the nature of the reading transaction (R. Beach, 1993) have informed our thinking about children's literature. Readers interested in more thorough reviews of early research will find the reviews of Galda and Cullinan (1991), Martinez and Roser (1991), Monson and Peltola (1976), Monson and Sebesta (1991), Morrow (1991), Purves and Beach (1972), Hearne (1988), and Short (1995) of interest.

THE MULTIDISCIPLINARY NATURE
OF CHILDREN'S LITERATURE

The field of children's literature is quite diverse in its orientation. Children's literature courses at major universities might be offered in an English department, a school of library science, or in a college of education. Research on children's literature reflects this diversity. Although it has been the case that scholars from one domain remained somewhat unaware of scholarship in others, both professional organizations and technological innovations have worked to break down barriers and increase communication across fields of inquiry. Scholarship today reflects an increasing awareness of the multiple ways to examine the phenomenon "children's literature." This examination may focus on children's literature as text, either through literary analysis or an analysis of content. Other efforts reflect an interest in how children read and respond to children's literature, what children like to read, the effects of children's literature on its readers, or the contexts that support children's engagement with literature.

RESEARCH ON CHILDREN'S LITERATURE

Children's literature research is diverse in focus and in methodology, ranging from close textual analysis to large reading interest surveys, from statistical studies with literature as a treatment variable to case studies of individual readers. Research on children's literature also overlaps with research in other areas, such as research on emergent literacy, literature-based instruction, reading comprehension, reading motivation and attitudes, and response to literature. Generally, we have selected studies for this chapter that focus on the texts of children's literature or on children's literary understandings. The studies reviewed in this volume by Gavelek, Raphael, Biondo, and Wang, by Morrow and Gambrell, and by Marshall, complement and extend those reviewed here. In this chapter, we define research on children's literature as any systematic inquiry into the nature of children's literature, the developing interests and literary understandings of its readers, and the implications of literary study in classrooms.

These three strands—texts, readers, and contexts—are, of course, interdependent, as the transactional (Rosenblatt, 1978, 1995) theory of literary reading and responding reminds us. Nevertheless, they are a useful way to organize the various studies of children's literature.

Research on Children's Literature as Text

Research on children's literature as text consists of two broad strands, literary analyses and content analyses, each containing considerable variation. Literary analyses examine individual texts or genres to describe what the authors do, looking, for example, at narrative patterns, character development, symbolism, intertextuality, or the function of the setting. These analyses may be historical accounts of changes in the field, may focus on one text or many, within or across genres, or may focus on the work of individual authors. Content analyses examine what texts are about, considering the content from a particular perspective such as sociohistorical, gender, culture, or thematic studies.

Literary analyses consider children's literature as an object of literary criticism and analysis. As Beckett (1997) pointed out in her introduction to *Reflections of Change: Children's Literature Since 1945*, the body of literary research in children's literature has been increasing steadily since 1970 and the founding of the International Research Society for Children's Literature. "Already one of the most exciting and vibrant fields of literary research in much of the Western world, children's literature theory and criticism are now emerging rapidly in many other parts of the world as … scholars from around the world have increasing opportunity to exchange ideas" (p. x). As books for children have become central to both pedagogy and marketplace, and with the additional influence of postmodernism, literary and other textual studies of children's literature have burgeoned in recent years. Current literary analyses often explore illustration, genre characteristics, or stylistic devices within and across books from a postmodern perspective.

As scholars were writing increasingly sophisticated and theoretically grounded literary analyses, other scholars were producing increasingly sophisticated studies of the content of children's literature texts. Many early studies were quantitative, featuring simple "counts" of content markers. Questions about the images of ethnic, socioeconomic, and gender groups portrayed in children's literature and the social and cultural values portrayed were answered by identifying specific criteria for analysis, then simply counting items that met those criteria in the selected sample of texts.

The content focus of children's literature research reflects the interests of the times. During the 1960s and 1970s, many researchers examined the presence and image of African Americans in children's books (e.g., Broderick, 1973; Chall, Radwin, French, & Hall, 1979; Larrick, 1965). Others conducted content analyses that sought to discover the social and cultural values portrayed in children's books. Other content analyses examined the portrayal of phenomena as diverse as social relationships, violence, war, gender roles, and teachers. Still other studies compared the content of children's books to the content of television programs for children, or the language used on children's television programs with the language used in children's books. (See Monson and Peltola, 1976, for an annotated bibliography of studies from 1960 to 1974.) Although interesting, these early quantitative content analyses rarely considered the social and cultural forces that shaped content, or the possible implications of the consideration of that content by child readers.

More recent research on children's literature as text has been informed by more complex theoretical positions and more extensive qualitative research methodologies. Current studies are based on an understanding of texts and, sometimes, the readings of those texts as nested in the social, cultural, and political contexts in which they are created. Current content analyses explore culture, gender, or other social issues in children's literature, often through the lens of critical theory, focusing on particular texts or a group of texts, and sometimes taking an historical perspective. (See Short, 1995, for an annotated bibliography of studies from 1985 to 1993.)

Content Analyses.   One of the first contemporary studies to discuss the content of children's books as historically situated and complex was Taxel's (1983, 1984) study of children's books written about the American Revolution. Working within the framework of critical theory, he undertook a structural analysis of the form and an historiographic analysis of the content of 32 children's novels about the American Revolution published between 1899 and 1976. This analysis revealed that the majority of the books, especially those published in the period from post World War I to the end of World War II, presented simplistic, conservative interpretations of the Revolution, reflecting a "hegemonic, selective tradition" (p. 27). However, in the books written during the Vietnam era the portrayal of the Revolution was influenced by a definite antiwar sentiment. Taxel then linked the corresponding decline of the importance of values, the fracture of family and family relationships, and an increasing focus on individual perceptions of and implications from the Revolution, to historical, socioeconomic changes occurring as the books were being written. Most notable in this study is Taxel's attempt to describe both content and form, and their interrelationship, through his carefully articulated coding system, and to suggest explanations that are grounded in theory and cultural history.

A number of contemporary content analyses have explored gender issues, such as Mowder's (1992) study of the Little House books from a sociocultural perspective, Agee's(1993) look at gender-role socialization in two award-winning novels for children, Christian-Smith's (1987) exploration of the adolescent romance novel as gender text, and Dougherty and Engel's (1987) look at equality in Caldecott books. Other studies have focused on a wide range of topics: death and dying (Harvey & Dowd, 1993), the image of home (Stott & Francis, 1993) and school (Greenway, 1993), and the portrayal of the Vietnam conflict (Johannessen, 1993). Many current studies of text focus on questions related to cultural diversity.

The magnitude of interest in cultural diversity has influenced the field of children's literature research in many ways, one of which is a rapidly growing body of work examining texts as cultural products. Sims Bishop's content analysis of contemporary realistic children's fiction about African Americans published between 1965 and 1979 (Sims, 1982) is a landmark study as she not only described the content, but situated her findings in the larger, political context. Sims Bishop proposed four major categories of books about African Americans: (a) books with a social conscience, (b) melting pot books, (c) culturally conscious books, and (d) image-making books. Her categories have influenced many contemporary studies of cultural diversity in literature for children.

The influence of the Sims Bishop and the Taxel studies can be seen in Trousdale's (1990) analytic study of four prize-winning children's books about the African American experience. Using Black Christian religious beliefs as a template, Trousdale examined the theology and values of three books written by White authors and one book written by a Black author. She concluded that there are marked differences between the books written by White authors and that written by the Black author, and called for a more critical perspective on books written from outside the culture portrayed.

Several other recent studies examine the portrayal of ethnic groups in children's literature, either from a historical perspective or emphasizing current trends and important authors and illustrators. Johnson-Feelings's *Telling Tales: The Power and Pedagogy of African American Literature for Youth* (1991) is a scholarly analysis of the history of this literature. Harris (1990, 1993, 1997) is concerned with both the past (1990) and the contemporary portrayal of Blacks in literature for children. Her research makes clear the changes in the literature: In recent years we have witnessed more "culturally conscious" literature, and that literature has become an established part of the marketplace and the literary community. Moreover, writers from the Black tradition are beginning to take artistic risks (Harris, 1997, p. 51).

Other researchers have built on the model of textual scholarship presented by Sims Bishop and Harris to look at the portrayal of parallel cultures. Studies such as Nieto's (1997) exploration of the image of Puerto Ricans in children's books, Barrera and de Cortes's (1997) examination of Mexican American children's literature, and Reese and Caldwell-Wood's (1997) analysis of the image of Native Americans in children's literature reflect an increasing sensitivity to the problem of aggregating quite varied ethnic experiences as if they were not distinctly different. Thus a study of, for example, Native Americans in children's literature would have to include careful consideration of the varied cultures from the many Indian Nations that comprise Native Americans. Unfortunately, studies of the portrayal of Native Americans in children's literature indicate that oversimplified generalizations dominate the literature (Hirschfelder, 1982; McCann, 1993; Slapin & Seale, 1992). However, current sensibilities and some careful and committed new artists, many of whom are Native American, are beginning to alter this situation. This trend toward more culturally conscious literature, although slight, seems to be evident across most literature about parallel cultures.

Analyses that consider authorial perspectives (see Cai, 1995, 1997, Harris, 1994, Reese & Caldwell-Wood, 1997, and Sims, 1984, for a discussion of this issue) are part of an important and often controversial strand of research in children's literature as cultural text. Unfortunately, many studies do not acknowledge, much less account for, the importance of the reader in the creation of meaning, assuming, instead, that meaning resides in the text alone. Thus the researcher's reading becomes the reading, and the transactional nature of the literary experience is ignored. This limitation applies to many literary analyses as well.

Literary Analysis. The literary analysis of children's literature has evolved from the field of literary criticism. As literary criticism has developed, so, too, has the criticism of children's literature. Today we find literary analyses of children's texts from a variety of perspectives: structuralist criticism, semiotics, feminist and critical theory, archetypal or mythic criticism, narrative theory, genre criticism, rhetorical criticism, reader-response criticism, historical criticism, and literary biography. Many of these analyses are published in journals such as the *Children's Literature Association Quarterly, Children's Literature in Education, The Lion and the Unicorn, Signal,* and in collected proceedings from conferences such as the International Research Society for Children's Literature. Most of these studies rely on a formalist, close reading of children's texts in order to examine literary and artistic devices within single texts, across an author's work, or within a genre or subgenre. Other than reader-response criticism, most literary analyses ignore the reader, and the assumption that the meaning, however defined and analyzed, lies in the text itself underlies the analysis. Little attention is paid to child readers and classroom use. Nevertheless, literary analysis has been central to the elevation of children's literature as a serious field of literary scholarship and the development of children's literature theory (Beckett, 1997).

Because there are so many diverse literary analyses of children's texts, we focus here on a few notable studies and then briefly review some current scholarship. Interested readers might want to consult the summer issues of *Children's Literature Association Quarterly* or *Children's Literature Abstracts* for their extensive listings of recent scholarship in this area.

A fascinating piece of scholarship, Neumeyer's (1994) *The Annotated Charlotte's Web* is a close reading of the manuscript and revisions of a beloved children's story. Neumeyer provided four types of annotations: information about the writing process from White's eight drafts; cross-references to White's other writings; stylistic commentary; and comments that refer to the conventions and traditions within which White was working (pp. xvii–xviii), as well as critical commentary on reviews of the book. The text is historically and biographically interesting, as well as a superb example of textual analysis.

In *Words About Pictures: The Narrative Art of Children's Picture Books,* Nodelman (1988) offered a semiotic analysis of how the verbal and visual aspects of picture books work together to convey a narrative. This analysis of this genre peculiar to children's literature is one of the seminal studies in children's literature, combining, as it does, semiotic analysis, narrative theory, and reader-response theory with close and compelling examples drawn from varied, acclaimed examples of the picture book genre.

Arguing that children's literature is "pervaded by ideological presuppositions," as is all discourse, Stephens (1992) used methodologies from critical linguistics and narrative theory to explore narrative fiction written for children. He demonstrated how texts work in terms of both story and discourse to situate child readers within both the implicit and explicit ideologies (Hollindale, 1988) operating within a text. His discussion of the genres of realism and fantasy contrasted the metaphoric ideological representation operating in fantasy with the metonymic mode of realism. Probably the most thorough semiotic examination of children's literature as ideological text, Stephens's work exemplifies the increasing complexity and sophistication of such research.

Other studies include critical analyses of an author or illustrator's work such as Keyser's *Whispers in the Dark: The Fiction of Louisa May Alcott* (1993), Trites's (1995) exploration of voicelessness in selected novels of Patricia MacLachlan, May's (1995) examination of Jane Yolen's literary fairy tales, and Larry's (1995) study of Nancy Ekholm Burkert's illustrations for "Snow White." These and the myriad other literary analyses published each year are augmented by a number of historical studies of children's literature such as Hollindale's (1995) examination of the development of young adult literature, and Nikolajeva's (1995) semiotic study of the history of children's literature. Other literary analyses, such as Nikola-Lisa's (1995) exploration of the representations of African American language in picture books, represent a wide range of theoretical perspectives and analytic foci. Some of these contemporary studies, like Nodelman (1988) and Stephens (1992), represent a new trend in that they are concerned not only with texts, but with the texts as read by children. How children read and respond to their literature represents the second major strand of research in children's literature.

Research on Children Reading Children's Literature

Children, the primary readers of children's literature, are the focus of a rapidly increasing number of studies. Early research consisted of primarily preference and interest studies, and this line of research is still pursued today, albeit with increased sophistication. Research on children's responses to what they read was not common until the 1980s. The reading interests and preferences of children and young adults have been the subject of many studies, the first of which was conducted in 1897 (see Monson & Sebesta, 1991, and Purves & Beach, 1972, for a review of early research). Although methodologically marred, many of these early studies supported broad generalizations about interests and preferences that are still used to select books for children: age affects interests, fiction is preferred over nonfiction, and boys and girls prefer different kinds of books (Zimet, 1966), with boys preferring adventure, girls stories about family and school life, and no one enjoying moralistic, didactic stories.

Some early studies of reading interests examined the content, genres, and literary devices that children enjoy. Generalizations from these studies include a preference for narrative forms with lively action, humor, and nonsense (Purves & Beach, 1972). Preference for fantasy or realism is less clear, with studies reporting varied results (Consuelo, 1967; Nelson, 1966; Smith, 1926). The reading interests of boys and girls diverge in upper elementary school, with boys beginning to develop an interest in adventure and girls an interest in realistic fiction (Landy, 1977; Lynch-Brown, 1977; Wolfson, Manning, & Manning, 1984). Young adolescents of both sexes develop an increased interest in nonfiction, mystery, biography, contemporary realism, and historical fiction (Carlsen, 1967; Coomer & Tessmer, 1986; Gallo, 1983), whereas girls prefer romance and career stories and boys prefer science fiction, adventure, and sports stories (Guthrie & Greaney, 1991; Monson & Sebesta, 1991). Generally, boys prefer stories about boys, and girls' gender preferences are less pronounced (Bleakley, Westerberg, & Hopkins, 1988). Adolescents prefer books in which the central problem is resolved, rather than those with no resolutions, and boys' preference for male protagonists increases, whereas girls' preference for female protagonists decreases from Grades 7 to 11 (Beyard-Tyler & Sullivan, 1980).

These studies employed a variety of strategies to determine children's interests, including questionnaires, interviews, checklists, paired comparisons, reading records, student ratings, free response measures, and semantic differential formats (Monson & Sebesta, 1991). Broad consistencies across studies, despite methodological differences, seem robust.

Broad consistencies and individual differences also describe much of the research in children's response to what they read. Published reviews of research in response, including Marshall in this volume, Beach (1993), and Martinez and Roser (1991), indicate again and again that reading and responding to literature is marked by both individual abilities and interests and by cultural and social influences.

In the early 1970s, Britton's *Language and Learning* (1970) triggered attention to developmental factors in readers. He found that although a child's responses to literature may be naive and unsophisticated, they are really the beginnings of more sophisticated responses. Studies that explored reader factors such as cognitive development began in the 1960s and continued to develop through the 1970s and 1980s, with a focus on elementary children emerging in the early 1980s (Galda, 1982; Hickman, 1981). A number of studies explored how stance influences the meaning readers make (Langer, 1991; Many & Cox, 1992), and how it is enacted in the classroom. A recent focus of research in response combines an interest in multicultural literature, critical theory, and response.

Research on Reading Interests and Preferences.

The terms *reading interests* and *reading preferences* have been used fairly indiscriminately in the research literature, although, as Summers and Lukasevich (1983) and Monson and Sebesta (1991) pointed out, they are different constructs. *Preferences* indicate what readers *might like* to read, whereas *interests* indicate what they *actually* are selecting to read.

It is difficult to determine whether or not preferences and interests have changed over the years. Broad patterns have been obtained from the very beginning of research on interests, but over the years more details have been added to these patterns, affording greater specificity. Detailed or broad, however, most of this research is only descriptive, telling us what children's preferences and interests are, but not truly unraveling the complexity of determining just why and how aspects of any given piece of literature will appeal to a young reader. Preference and interest are highly individual phenomena that change from reader to reader and book to book, but at the same time are embedded in sociocultural norms and expectations. There have been a few, but nonetheless notable, analytic studies that try to explain how and why readers' preferences and interests develop.

Favat's (1977) *Child and Tale: The Origins of Interest* is a "classic" reading interest study. Favat took as a given the young child's interest in fairy tales, basing this assumption on the work of children's literature scholars and early reading interest studies. He concluded that there is a "curve of reading preference" for fairy tales, beginning during the preschool years, peaking between the ages of 6 and 8, and gradually declining thereafter until loss of interest around age 10 (p. 5). He then used analytic tools developed by Propp and a Piagetian theoretical framework to discuss the tales, comparing their content and structures to children's psychological and moral development as described by Piaget. Similarities between tale and child, he argued, drive the interest. One of the implications that he drew is that early iterations of response theory problematize the notion that adults can know, a priori, what child readers will discover in the books they read. Thus although proposing psychological similarities across children, he also acknowledged individual differences in the construction of meaning.

In their study of preferences in intermediate-grade Canadian children, Summers and Lukasevich (1983) used a theme-based reading preference inventory to survey over 1,000 children in Grades 5, 6, and 7, from three different communities, and found significant age, gender, and community interactions. They concluded that

> reading preference is highly variable and that children can be expected to exhibit different preferences by community, fluctuate by grade, and exhibit the most stable differences in terms of specific likes and dislikes for males and females.... The best approach for the teacher is to treat "norms" lightly and analyze preferences for a particular class, within a specific school and community. (p. 358)

Taking as a starting point the implication of Summers and Lukasevich (1983) that reading interests are always in the process of being constructed by readers, Dressman (1997a, 1997b) observed one third-grade class in each of three elementary school libraries as they used the school library, and interviewed each librarian and focal groups of children three times (including a book sorting task). He concluded that social class and gender are enacted by readers as they act on their preferences. Dressman's complication of a simplistic notion of preference by defining preference as performance scrutinizes not only generally accepted conceptions of what preference is but also the effect of what educators do with what they think they know about preference.

Two studies actually compared what children liked with what adults honored. Nilsen, Peterson, and Searfoss (1980) found a definite negative correlation between books that received critical acclaim by adults and books that were popular with children, which implies that a book, no matter how high its literary quality, must be engaging to children to be read. A later study in the same vein examined the International Reading Association's Children's Choices awards that were also finalists or winners of the John Newbery Medal or the Boston Globe Horn Book Award from 1975 to 1985 and compared them to award-winning novels that were not Children's Choices (Lehman, 1989). Lehman found that there were differences between what children and adults valued in books, most notably in style and structure, with children preferring optimistic texts that were action oriented, well paced, and offered clear resolutions of conflict.

Preference and interest studies across the years point to broad patterns of preference that relate especially to age and gender. Contemporary studies complicate this notion by viewing it through the lens of critical theory and social constructivism. So, too, have contemporary studies complicated the notion of response.

Research on Children Responding to Literature.   Research on response has moved toward examining how culture influences both reading and writing literature. This is apparent not only in text studies, but also in the increased interest in children's response to the multicultural literature they read. Several recent studies have examined whether and how children resist what they read, especially when the values operating in the texts conflict with the values operating in readers' lives.

Stephens (1992) argued that children's literature is permeated by social and ethical ideologies, and researchers are beginning to explore what happens when the ideologies of the text meet the ideologies of a reader. Early response studies described readers rejecting a text when their expectations and preferences were violated (Galda, 1982), often discussing this rejection in terms of cognitive and moral development. This notion of resistance is at the center of some of the most exciting contemporary studies of response (Beach, 1997; Enciso, 1997; Rogers, 1997). For example, Beach (1997) explored the multiple ways in which students resist texts that challenge their value systems, especially those that relate to cultural privilege. Enciso (1997) details how a small group of fourth- and fifth-grade students struggled with ideas of difference encountered in their reading of Spinelli's (1990) *Maniac Magee*, and how they "talked back" to the text and to each other as they constructed their meanings of difference. These and other studies that closely examine responses through both reader response and cultural theories enlarge our understanding of the complicated nature of literary response.

For many years researchers have sought to "prove" that reading literature influenced the attitudes and values of its readers. Recent studies by McGinley and Kamberelis (1996; McGinley et al., 1997) have brought greater rigor and depth to the study of how stories can influence readers' lives. McGinley and colleagues gathered data in a series of ethnographic studies of classrooms in which children were engaged in various reading and literature-related activities. They examined discussions, written products, and informal interview transcripts in an attempt to understand how their reading experiences functioned in the lives of the children in those classrooms. They found that children's reading allowed them to

> envision and explore possible selves, roles, and responsibilities through the lives of story characters, both real and fictional; to describe or remember personal experiences or interests in their lives; and to objectify and reflect upon certain problematic emotions and circumstances as they related to important moral and ethical dilemmas in their lives. (McGinley et al.,1997, pp. 55–56)

These functions of literature in the lives of children echo findings in many early studies of response. Additionally, McGinley and Kamberelis (1996) described the social functions that reading literature served:

> providing children with a means to understand, affirm, or negotiate social relationships among peers, family members, and community members, as well as to raise and develop their awareness of significant social issues and social problems. (p. 56)

Their research, influenced by narrative theory and transactional theory, and embedded within a social constructivist notion of reading in classrooms, reaches beyond the realm of reader response, encompasses cultural and social issues, and is thoroughly grounded in the classroom. This reflects our ever-increasing awareness of the complexity of understanding readers, the texts they read, and the contexts in which they read.

Contexts That Support Children's Engagement With Literature

The contexts that support children's engagement with literature are the third major strand of research on children's literature. This strand includes inquiries about literary studies in the classroom, including literary discussions, about effects of teachers reading aloud from children's books, and about teacher beliefs and practices regarding children's literature.

Some early researchers attempted to assess the effects of using literature as a program treatment variable. Researchers looked at the effects of literature on a variety of variables including attitude toward reading, the effects of bibliotherapy using children's books, the effects of children's books on international understanding, and the effect of reading books with Black characters on the racial preferences of white children. Other research pointed out that hearing children's literature read aloud positively influences children's attitudes toward reading. (See Monson & Peltola, 1976, for a review of these early studies.) Many studies have examined the use of children's literature as an instructional tool in the teaching of reading, writing, and the development of oral language. And many researchers have pointed out that reading literature increases children's knowledge of the world (Steffensen, Jaog-Dev, & Anderson, 1979) and of text patterns (Pappas, 1991). Current studies in these areas are reviewed in this volume in chapter 31 by Morrow and Gambrell and chapter 32 by Gavelek et al.

These early studies formed the basis for an extensive line of research that examined the educational uses of children's literature just as the use of children's literature as an educational tool began to sweep the nation.

Research on Literary Instruction.   A review of the last two volumes of the *Handbook of Reading Research* (Barr, Kamil, Mosenthal, & Pearson, 1991; Pearson, Barr, & Kamil, 1984) would give the impression that children's literature is used in the classroom for the sole function of reading instruction. This might indicate that teachers are not engaging in literature instruction using children's literature; in fact, Langer(1990) feared that literary research has lagged behind research on reading and writing processes. Fortunately, that is not entirely the case.

Although some argue that the purpose of children's literature in the classroom is still undecided (J. D. Beach, 1992), recommendations for the use of children's literature range from the development of literary classrooms (Hade, 1991) to instruction in literary movements such as postmodernism (Stevenson, 1994). Nevertheless, most research has focused on children's ability to recognize literary elements or to use those elements in their speech or writing.

Theme as an aspect of literary instruction with children's literature was explored by Lehr (1988) in her study of sense of theme across kindergarten, second, and fourth grade. Using children who had high or low exposure to literature, Lehr found that kindergarten students were able to identify and match theme between books at an accuracy rate of 80% for realistic fiction and 35% for folktales, indicating that children have the ability to identify and discuss theme even at an early age; further, there was a developmental trend of increase in ability to identify theme.

Au's (1992) research supports the argument that theme should be a central aspect of the use of children's literature in the classroom. Using a piece of children's literature in a basal reader, Au found that three of the seven students involved in the multiday lesson identified at least two themes (a teacher-initiated and a student-initiated theme) in the story, two identified one theme, and only two students did not make any theme-related statements during the discussion.

In a larger study of the effects of a literature-based classroom on the literacy achievement, use of literature, and attitudes of children from minority backgrounds, Morrow (1992) discovered that students involved in both the school-based and home- and school-based literature programs outperformed the control group (which was instructed homogeneously through a basal and its accompanying workbook) on overall retelling of a story as well as identification and use of story elements such as theme and plot.

Theme is not, however the only literary aspect of a piece of children's literature. Smolkin (1997) investigated fifth-grade students' understanding of conversationally cooperative and noncooperative dialogue in a play. Arguing that dialogue is a literary aspect found truly only in plays, Smolkin found that children did not understand the function of interruptive dialogue, preferring to supply cooperative dialogue when given an interruption point and asked to predict the upcoming lines.

The ability to identify and focus on literary elements after a reading appears to be enhanced by the stance the reader takes at the time of the reading (Many, 1991). Fourth, sixth, and eighth graders read the same three stories and then responded in writing. Students asked to take an aesthetic stance prior to reading were more likely to identify literary elements in their response than those given an efferent stance, and this ability increased with age. This finding was supported by Many and Wiseman's (1992) research in which students given a literary experience presentation performed better on a measure of identifying literary elements than did students given a literary analysis presentation or no presentation prior to reading. However, further study by Wiseman, Many, and Altieri (1992) found that when a literary experience approach was followed by a literary analysis approach, students in this group outperformed a student-led discussion group on a similar measure. (See Many & Cox, 1992, for an extended discussion of stance and literary understanding.)

Research has also demonstrated that children use what they have learned about the literary aspects of children's literature in their writing and their speech, a development that seems to necessitate the sharing of quality literature for a quality result. Dressel (1990) found that children who were read higher quality literature were more likely to reflect aspects of its literary elements (character development, plot development, integral setting, style and mood) as a whole, as well as genre consistency, than were students exposed to works of lesser quality, regardless of reading ability. Lancia (1997) had similar findings in a second-grade classroom. The language, or style, of stories was also the subject of a study by Pappas and Brown (1987). Studying the development of literary register in a kindergarten student, they found that across three readings of a text, the child's language grew closer to that of the literary register in her retellings. That is, she became more familiar with the register of literature and was able to imitate it. Further, Hade (1988) found that children read stories aloud adopted the syntactic, and possibly semantic, structure of the text in their retellings.

However, it appears that reading less than quality literature does not interfere with students' abilities to appreciate the literary qualities of recommended literature (Greenlee, Monson, & Taylor, 1996). When interviewed, 11- and 12-year-old students liked the recommended texts (texts that are award winners or that teachers recommend) just as much as series texts (e.g., Goosebumps, Babysitters' Club); unfortunately, they were, for the most part, unable to render literary judgments about the relative qualities of the texts. Further, there was some indication that they needed help selecting recommended texts that fit their interests.

Research on Reading Children's Literature Aloud.   Since the beginning of the 20th century, both theorists and practitioners have argued that reading to children helps prepare them for literacy and to develop literacy skills, develops interest in reading, promotes language development, increases reading achievement, positively influences their writing, and provides opportunities for social interaction. (See Galda & Cullinan, 1991, for a review of this research.) Overwhelmingly, children enjoy having adults read to them (Mendoza, 1985); however, where the reading takes place, what texts are read, how often texts are read, and how the texts are read can influence children's reading and literary development. Contemporary studies of reading aloud from children's literature look closely at factors that influence it, ranging from group size, to genre and style, to frequency, to reading style.

Morrow (1988, 1990) and Morrow and Smith (1990) have done extensive research on the effects of group size on children's comprehension and responses to literature. They concluded that although both small-group and one-to-one readings created a larger volume of questions and comments than whole-class readings, small-group settings seemed to offer as many opportunities for interaction as individual settings, and led to better comprehension. This interaction pattern was replicated in a kindergarten classroom by Klesius and Griffith (1996).

Beginning research grounded in earlier work (Feitelson, Kita, & Goldstein, 1986), Rosenhouse, Feitelson, Kita, and Goldstein (1997) investigated if the type of book that was read would affect children's comprehension and independent reading. Comparing the reading of a series of books by one author in which characters continued through the text, a series of varied texts by one author, a series of varied texts by many authors, and a traditional nonreading curriculum (worksheets, art, etc.) in Israeli first graders produced positive effects in decoding, reading comprehension, and story retelling for all of the read-aloud groups. Further, the continued series group showed an increase in reading for pleasure and trade books purchased.

Not just style of book but also genre can influence a book's effect in a read-aloud experience. In an investigation into the read alouds of books other than stories, Oyler and Barry (1996) found that information books could also benefit children's reading. Interactive reading of the informational texts produced increased incidences of intertextual references by the students as the year progressed. Referenced texts would then become shared texts, so all students could make the same connections.

The number of times a book is read greatly affects its impact on students as well. Although the comprehension and fluency benefits of students' own repeated readings of a text have been well documented (see Dowhower, 1994, for a review of the literature), investigations (Dowhower, 1987; Rasinski, 1990) have also found that modeling, such as teachers' repeated read-alouds of favorite storybooks, is an important aspect of developing children's understanding of literature. Martinez and Roser (1985) discovered that repeated exposures to a text increased the amount, the form, and the focus of student talk about a text, and the depth of processing of a text in preschoolers who had been repeatedly read a storytime text. These findings were supported by Morrow (1988), who found that repeated reading resulted in responses with greater amounts of interpretation.

Beyond repeated readings, storybook reading style can vary (Dickinson & Keebler, 1989; Martinez & Teale, 1993). Specifically, Martinez and Teale (1993) argued that it varies according to three criteria: focus of teacher talk, information shared during the reading, and strategies used by the teacher. All of these aspects tended to coalesce into a single, repeated style for the teacher. Unfortunately, the influence of a singular approach to reading as a model for the children listening is unknown. Further research is necessary to determine how these variations in style might affect students' developing literacy.

Research on Discussing Children's Literature.   Early research that focused on oral language and children's literature either ignored the role of oral language in literary growth, looked at the effects of literature on oral language, or categorized and counted conversations or classroom discourse to obtain a picture of broad patterns. (See Pinnell & Jaggar, 1991 for a review of this early research.) Like other aspects of research in children's literature, recent research on discussing children's literature reflects the trend toward complicating and contextualizing our notions of literary discussions and how they operate to increase literary understanding, allow children to explore issues and meaning, and socialize children into ways of talking about books.

Although discussion has been shown to be excellent activity for helping students construct meaning with the children's literature they have read (Eeds & Wells, 1989), it is clear that students who are left to wander into discussion unaided, untrained, and unarmed might as well sit alone and ponder the meaning of their text (Wollman-Bonilla, 1994). How discussions of reading are structured depends on the who, what, and why: Who controls the discussion, what type of book is being discussed, and why is discussion an engaging social interaction for the students?

In their classic study, Eeds and Wells (1989) turned the control of the conversations over to the students with the teacher as a participant rather than inquisitor, so that they might have "grand conversations." When discussing four children's novels, the students were able to shape their own meaning based on their initial interpretation and the interpretation of others. Further, they connected the stories to personal events in their lives, made and evaluated predictions about outcomes in the stories, and learned both to evaluate and value children's literature as literature.

McGee (1992) investigated the "grand conversations" of first graders. After reading books aloud, the discussion leaders followed the pattern of the "grand conversation," but ended the session by asking an interpretive question. Over one third of all comments made by the students in the discussion were classified as interpretive, and more than two-thirds of the comments after the question could be so classified.

Literature study circles (LSCs) were a natural outcome of "grand conversations" that emphasized student-led discussion of authentic, unabridged children's literature in small groups (Short & Pierce, 1990). Open-ended student-led discussions were the instructional activity, resulting in critical thinking and self-reflection on the text and higher student engagement with the text. LSCs have also been used with multicultural/diverse learners (Samway & Whang, 1996) and learners with special needs with similar effectiveness (Gilles, 1990).

Raphael and McMahon (1994) studied a student-led discussion group with more structure provided by the teacher, a Book Club. Although retaining many aspects of student choice (such as book selection), the Book Club used a set intervention structure: reading, writing, discussion, and instruction. In the discussion, students used talk to share their responses, to clarify confusing points, to talk about the main idea, to relate the text to other texts, to critique the author's craft and purposes, to discuss their personal response, and to relate their reading to their own prior knowledge (Raphael et al., 1992).

In addition to the organization of the discussion, Leal (1992)investigated the effect of the type of text on the talk in which first-, third-, and fifth-grade students engage. Comparing the talk about a storybook, an informational book, and an informational storybook, Leal found that when discussing the informational storybook students were more likely to stay on task, twice as likely to make predictions and inferences, more likely to use peer input, and more likely to discuss related topics that went beyond the scope of the text. Further, older students were more likely to engage in sophisticated talk about books, working together in longer conversations that relied heavily on peer input.

Researchers (Nystrand & Gamoran, 1991) have found that student engagement in the literature setting is strongly connected to authentic questions and the incorporation of students' responses in the discussion. Commeyras and Sumner (1995) reported similar findings in their study of second graders' discussions of children's literature. Although the crux of the study was that it was difficult for the teachers to allow children's questioning, especially when the questions seemed to them to be less than valuable, Commeyras and Sumner also concluded that students were able to pose questions of educational value if they as teachers would only recognize them as such and allow the students to engage in discussion with such questions. Likewise, Simpson (1996) also grew to value the questions developed by her students in critical text analysis discussions. [*Why don't teachers value?*]

Beyond the teacher, there were other factors that shaped students' engagement in reading and discussing children's literature. After observing fourth-grade students, Almasi and McKeown (1996) concluded that the context of the literacy act and the culture of the classroom were significant in shaping students' engaged reading. Literary text featured influenced engagement, as did the ability to engage in shared, reflective, and challenging discussion of the texts. As these researchers (Almasi & McKeown, 1996; Commeyras & Sumner, 1995; Simpson, 1996) demonstrated, discussion is often dominated by extratextual as well as textual factors.

Research on Teachers' Beliefs and Practices.   Before teachers are able to gain knowledge and make decisions about the use of children's literature in their classroom, they must confront the fact that what they see and enjoy in children's literature may not be the same as the view through a child's mind. Some believe that children's literature will never truly be children's literature, as long as adults write, publish, review, and select it—that it will constantly inhabit the role of other (Nodelman, 1992). In order to bridge the potential gap between adult as critic and child as critic, studies have sought to compare and integrate adults' and childrens' experiences with childrens' literature. [*if true there will be never children's lit?*]

Similarly, Allen, Freeman, Lehman, and Scharer (1995) studied teachers' interpretations of a child's picture storybook, *Amos and Boris* (Steig, 1971), in order to evaluate teachers' decisions about using literature with children, their own literary literacy, and their beliefs about what makes a quality picture storybook. Overall, teachers believed they should use children's literature to develop literacy skills, based on the frameworks provided in most basal readers, but most teachers did not comment on the overall literary merit of the work (which the authors indicated might be a consequence of the basalization of children's literature). Further, there was little focus on the literary skill that could be learned from the text.

In survey-based evaluations (Lehman, Freeman, & Allen, 1994; Scharer, Freeman, Lehman, & Allen, 1993) of children's literature, teachers expressed the belief that children's literature should be the primary component of a language arts program. Not surprisingly, however, there was little evidence that children's literature was being used for literary as well as literacy instruction (Lehman, Freeman, & Allen, 1994; Scharer et al., 1993).

Selection of children's literature is another area where teachers' beliefs and practices have been studied. In an extensive survey, Smith, Greenlaw, and Scott (1987) found that ethnic minorities, the elderly, women, and the physically challenged are underrepresented in teacher's selections of favorite read-alouds, and often they are only presented in a negative light. It is not argued that this selection is a representation of the teachers' beliefs, but rather a lack of critical examination of the texts as read. Four years later, however, Jipson and Paley (1991) found similar patterns in their survey conducted in different parts of the country, indicating perhaps that teachers need to establish selection criteria that include not only literary quality and children's interests (Lehman, Freeman, & Allen, 1994), but also issues of diversity and representation.

Teachers' beliefs and practices regarding the assessment of the use of children's literature in their classes have also been studied. Notably, assessment was one of the biggest areas of conflict for teachers between their beliefs and practices (Johnston, Guice, Baker, Malone, & Michelson, 1995). Further, detailed assessment knowledge was key to higher levels of awareness of children' literature. However, most assessment decisions made by these teachers appeared to be based on literacy rather than literary evaluation (Johnston et al., 1995), a trend supported by other studies (Lehman, Freeman, & Allen, 1994; Scharer, 1992). Finally, although the teachers had strong beliefs about using authentic assessments, most still used some objective measures of literacy achievement (Johnston et al., 1995; Lehman, Freeman, & Allen, 1994; Scharer, 1992).

Recent research on contexts that support children's engagement with literature points to the complexity of examining those contexts. What is read, how it is read, whether and how it is discussed, and the teacher's beliefs about reading, learning, and literature all influence the experience of a child with a text.

WHERE DO WE GO FROM HERE?

We began this review with a description of the multidisciplinary nature of children's literature as a field of study and of research in children's literature as encompassing a diverse set of methodologies and theoretical perspectives. As interest in children's literature has grown, the scope of research in children's literature has enlarged as well; it now is an integral part of many reading programs and, as such, has become enmeshed in the greater body of reading research. Indeed, the major task in this review has been to select appropriate pieces—pieces that are children's literature research rather than reading research—from the very diverse and immense body of research that touches on children's literature.

The ubiquity of children's literature is at once its strength and its weakness. Literature is present in many studies of literature-based classrooms or of reading comprehension, but often not attended to. Comprehension is of text rather than particular text, and literature-based instruction is seen as a set of generic strategies rather than related to particular readers and particular texts. Literature is present, but often treated as invisible.

Yet it is those studies that explore particular readers and particular texts in particular contexts that are the most exciting and enlightening. Whether a textual analysis, a study of response, or a study of literary instruction, research that explores the complexities of children reading books is the research that informs us. We need more studies that are grounded in theory, whether it be sociocultural, transactional, narrative, or critical, and that use articulated strategies for a close and careful analysis. We need more studies that cross the boundaries among us, that allow us to speak to one another across schools of library science, colleges of education, and departments of English. Today we have many ways of looking at the complex issues that surround children's literature. Scholarship can benefit from hearing from multiple, informed voices.

REFERENCES

Agee, J. (1993). Mothers and daughters: Gender-role socialization in two Newbery award books. *Children's Literature in Education, 24*(3), 165–183.

Allen, V. G., Freeman, E. B., Lehman, B. A., & Scharer, P. L. (1995). *Amos and Boris*: A window on teachers' thinking about the use of literature in their classrooms. *Reading Teacher, 48,* 384–390.

Almasi, J. F., & McKeown, M. G. (1996). The nature of engaged reading in classroom discussions of literature. *Journal of Literacy Research, 28,* 107–146.

Au, K. H. (1992). Constructing the theme of a story. *Language Arts, 69,* 106–111.

Barr, R., Kamil, M. L., Mosenthal, P., & Pearson, P. D. (Eds.). (1991). *Handbook of reading research* (Vol. II). New York: Longman.

Beach, J. D. (1992). New trends in historical perspective: Literature's place in language arts education. *Language Arts, 69,* 550–556.

Beach, R. (1993). *A teacher's introduction to reader-response theories.* Urbana, IL: National Council of Teachers of English.

Beach, R. (1997). Students' resistance to engagement with multicultural literature. In T. Rogers & A. Soter (Eds.), *Reading across cultures* (pp. 69–96). New York: TCP.

Beckett, S. L. (1997). Introduction: Reflections of change. In S. L. Beckett, *Reflections of change: Children's literature since 1945* (pp. ix–xi). Westport, CT: Greenwood.

Beyard-Tyler, K. C., & Sullivan, H. J. (1980). Adolescent reading preferences for type of theme and sex of character. *Reading Research Quarterly, 16,* 104–120.

Bleakley, M., Westerberg, V., & Hopkins, K. (1988). The effect of character sex on story interest and comprehension in children. *American Educational Research Journal, 25,* 145–155.

Britton, J. (1970). *Language and learning.* London: Penguin.

Broderick, D. (1973). *The image of the Black in children's literature.* New York: Bowker.

Cai, M. (1995). Can we fly across cultural gaps on the wings of imagination? Ethnicity, experience, and cultural identity. *The New Advocate, 8*(1), 1–17.

Cai, M. (1997). Reader-response theory and the politics of multicultural literature. In T. Rogers & A. Soter (Eds.), *Reading across cultures* (pp. 199–212). New York: Teachers College Press.

Carlsen, G. (1967). *Books and the teen-age reader.* New York: Harper and Row.

Chall, J., Radwin, E., French, V., & Hall, C. (1979). Blacks in the world of children's books. *Reading Teacher, 32,* 527–533.

Christian-Smith, L. (1987). Gender, popular culture, and curriculum: Adolescent romance novels as gender texts. *Curriculum Inquiry, 17*(4), 365–406.

Commeyras, M., & Sumner, G. (1995). *Questions children want to discuss about literature: What teachers and students learned in a second-grade classroom* (Research Rep. No. 47). Athens, GA, and College Park, MD: Universities of Maryland and Georgia, National Reading Research Center.

Consuelo, R. M. (1967). What do first graders like to read? *Catholic School Journal, 67,* 42–43.

Coomer, J. W., & Tessmer, K. M. (1986). 1986 Books for Young Adults poll. *English Journal, 75,* 58–61.

Dickinson, D., & Keebler, R. (1989). Variations in preschool teachers' storybook reading styles. *Discourse Processes, 12,* 353–376.

Dougherty, W., & Engel, R. (1987). An 80s look for sex equality in Caldecott winners and honor books. *Reading Teacher, 40*(4), 394–398.

Dowhower, S. L. (1987). Effects of repeated reading on second-grade transitional reader's fluency and comprehension. *Reading Research Quarterly, 22,* 389–406.

Dowhower, S. L. (1994). Repeated reading revisited: Research into practice. *Reading and Writing Quarterly: Overcoming Learning Difficulties, 10,* 343–358.

Dressel, J. H. (1990). The effects of listening to and discussing different qualities of children's literature on the narrative writing of fifth graders. *Research in the Teaching of English, 24,* 397–444.

Dressman, M. (1997a). *Literacy in the library: Negotiating the spaces between order and desire.* Westport, CT: Bergin & Garvey.

Dressman, M. (1997b). Preference as performance: Doing social class and gender in three school libraries. *Journal of Literacy Research, 29,* 319–361.

Eeds, M., & Wells, D. (1989). Grand conversations: An exploration of meaning construction in literature study groups. *Research in the Teaching of English, 23*(10), 4–29.

Enciso, P. (1997). Negotiating the meaning of difference: Talking back to multicultural literature. In T. Rogers & A. Soter (Eds.), *Reading across cultures* (pp. 13–41). New York: Teachers College Press.

Favat, F. A. (1977). *Child and tale: The origins of interest*, (National Council of Teachers of English Research Rep. No. 19). Urbana, IL: National Council of Teachers of English.

Feitelson, D., Kita, B., & Goldstein, Z. (1986). Effects of listening to series stories on first graders' comprehension and use of language. *Research in the Teaching of English, 20*, 339–356.

Galda, L. (1982). Assuming the spectator stance: An examination of the responses of young readers. *Research in the Teaching of English, 16*(1), 1–20.

Galda, L., & Cullinan, B. E. (1991). Literature for literacy: What research says about the benefits of using trade books in the classroom. In J. Flood, J. M. Jensen, D. Lapp, & J. R. Squire (Eds.), *Handbook of research on teaching the English language arts* (pp. 529–535). New York: Macmillan.

Gallo, D. R. (1983, June 14). *Students' reading interests—A report of a Connecticut survey*. Paper presented at the Spring Conference of the Educational Paperback Association, New York, NY. (ERIC Document Reproduction Service No. ED232 143)

Gilles, C. (1990). Collaborative literacy strategies: "We don't need a circle to have a group." In K. G. Short & K. M. Pierce (Eds.), *Talking about books: Creating literate communities* (pp. 55–68). Portsmouth, NH: Heinemann.

Greenlee, A. A., Monson, D. L., & Taylor, B. M. (1996). The lure of series books: Does it affect appreciation for recommended literature? *Reading Teacher, 50*, 216–225.

Greenway, B. (1993). "Creeping like a snail unwillingly to school": Negative images of school in children's literature. *The New Advocate, 6*(2), 105–114.

Guthrie, J., & Greaney, V. (1991). Literacy acts. In R. Barr, M. L. Kamil, P. Mosenthal, & P. D. Pearson (Eds.), *Handbook of reading research* (Vol. II, pp. 68–96). New York: Longman.

Hade, D. D. (1988). Children, stories, and narrative transformations. *Research in the Teaching of English, 22*, 1988.

Hade, D. D. (1991). Being literary in a literature-based classroom. *Children's Literature in Education, 22*(1), 1–17.

Harris, V. J. (1990). African-Americans in children's literature: The first one hundred years. *Journal of Negro Education, 59*, 540–555.

Harris, V. J. (1993). Contemporary griots: African-American writers of children's literature. In V. J. Harris (Ed.), Teaching multicultural literature in grades K–8 (pp. 55–108). Norwood, MA: Christopher Gordon.

Harris, V. J. (1994). Multiculturalism and children's literature: An evaluation of ideology, publishing, curricula, and research. In C. K. Kinzer & D. J. Leu (Eds.), *Multidimensional aspects of literacy research, theory, and practice: Forty-third yearbook of the National Reading Conference* (pp. 15–27). Chicago: National Reading Conference.

Harris, V. J. (1997). Children's literature depicting Blacks. In V. J. Harris (Ed.), *Using multiethnic literature in the K–8 classroom* (pp. 21–58). Norwood, MA: Christopher Gordon.

Harvey, C. & Dowd, F. S. (1993). Death and dying in young adult fiction. *Journal of Youth Services in Libraries, 6*(2), 141–154.

Hearne, B. (1988). Problems and possibilities: U.S. research in children's literature. *School Library Journal, 43*(11), 27–31.

Hickman, J. (1981). A new perspective on response to literature: Research in an elementary school setting. *Research in the Teaching of English, 15*, 343–354.

Hirschfelder, A. (1982). *American Indian stereotypes in the world of children: A reader and bibliography*. Metuchen, NJ: Scarecrow.

Hollindale, P. (1988). Ideology and the children's book. *Signal, 55*, 3–22.

Hollindale, P. (1995). The adolescent novel of ideas. *Children's Literature in Education, 26*(1), 83–95.

Jipson, J., & Paley, N. (1991). The selective tradition in teachers' choice of children's literature: Does it exist in the elementary classroom? *English Education, 23*, 148–159.

Johannessen, L. R. (1993). Young adult literature and the Vietnam War. *English Journal, 82*(5), 43–49.

Johnson-Feelings, D. (1991). *Telling tales: The power and pedagogy of African American literature for youth*. Westport, CT: Greenwood.

Johnston, P., Guice, S., Baker, K., Malone, J., & Michelson, N. (1995). Assessment of teaching and learning in "literature-based" classrooms. *Teaching and Teacher Education, 11*, 359–371.

Keyser, E. L. (1993). *Whispers in the dark: The fiction of Louisa May Alcott*. Knoxville, TN: University of Tennessee Press.

Klesius, J. P., & Griffith, P. L. (1996). Interactive storybook reading for at-risk learners. *Reading Teacher, 49*, 552–560.

Lancia, P. J. (1997). Literary borrowing: The effects of literature on children's writing. *Reading Teacher, 50*, 470–475.

Landy, S. (1977). Why Johnny can read ... but doesn't. *Canadian Library Journal, 34*, 379–387.

Langer, J. A. (1990). Understanding literature. *Language Arts, 67*, 812–816.

Langer, J. A. (1991). The process of understanding: Reading for literary and informative purposes. *Research in the Teaching of English, 24*(3), 229–257.

Larrick, N. (1965, September 11). The all-white world of children's books. *Saturday Review*, (pp. 63–65).

Larry, C. E. (1995). The art of tradition: Nancy Ekholm Burkert's illustration for *Snow White and the Seven Dwarfs. Journal of Children's Literature*, 21(2), 20–26.

Leal, D. J. (1992). The nature of talk about three types of text during peer group discussions. *Journal of Reading Behavior*, 24, 313–338.

Lehman, B. A. (1989). Child reader and literary work: Children's literature merges two perspectives. *Children's Literature Association Quarterly*, 14(3), 123–128.

Lehman, B. A., Freeman. E. B., & Allen, V. G. (1994). Children's literature and literacy instruction: "Literature-based" elementary teachers' belief and practices. *Reading Horizons*, 35, 3–23.

Lehr, S. (1988). The child's developing sense of theme as a response to literature. *Reading Research Quarterly*, 23, 337–357.

Lynch-Brown, C. (1977). Procedures for determining children's book choices: Comparison and criticism. *Reading Horizons*, 17, 243–250.

Many, J. E. (1991). The effects of stance and age level on children's literary responses. *Journal of Reading Behavior*, 23, 61–85.

Many, J. & Cox, C. (Eds.). (1992). *Reader stance and literary understanding*. Norwood, NJ: Ablex.

Many, J. E., & Wiseman, D. L. (1992). The effect of teaching approach on third grade students' response to literature. *Journal of Reading Behavior*, 24, 265–287.

Martinez, M., & Roser, N. (1985). Read it again: The value of repeated readings during storytime. *Reading Teacher*, 38, 782–786.

Martinez, M. G., & Roser, N. L. (1991). Children's responses to literature. In J. Flood, J. M. Jensen, D. Lapp, & J. R. Squire (Eds.), *Handbook of research on teaching the English language arts* (pp. 643–654). New York: Macmillan.

Martinez, M. G., & Teale, W. H. (1993). Teacher storybook reading style: A comparison of six teachers. *Research in the Teaching of English*, 27, 175–199.

May, J. P. (1995). Jane Yolen's literary fairy tales: Legends, folktales, and myths remade. *Journal of Children's Literature*, 21(1), 74–78.

McCann, D. (1993). Native Americans in books for the young. In V. J. Harris (Ed.), *Teaching multicultural literature in grades K–8* (pp. 139–169). Norwood, MA: Christopher Gordon.

McGee, L. (1992). An exploration of meaning construction in first graders' grand conversations. In C. K. Kinzer & D. J. Leu (Eds.), *Literacy research, theory, and practice: Views from many perspectives: Forty-first yearbook of the National Reading Conference* (pp. 177–186). Chicago: National Reading Conference.

McGinley, W., & Kamberelis, G. (1996). Maniac Magee and Ragtime Tumpie: Children negotiating self and world through reading and writing. *Research in the Teaching of English*, 30, 75–113.

McGinley, W., Kamberelis, G., Mahoney, T., Madigan, D., Rybicki, V., & Oliver, J.(1997). Visioning reading and teaching literature through the lens of narrative theory. In T. Rogers & A. Soter (Eds.), *Reading across cultures* (pp. 42–68). New York: Teachers College Press.

Mendoza, A. (1985). Reading to children: Their preferences. *Reading Teacher*, 38, 522–527.

Monson, D. L., & Peltola, B. J. (1976). *Research in children's literature: An annotated bibliography*. Newark, DE: International Reading Association.

Monson, D. L. & Sebesta, S. L. (1991). Reading preferences. In J. Flood, J. M. Jensen, D. Lapp, & J. R. Squire (Eds.), *Handbook of research on teaching the English language arts* (pp. 664–673). New York: Macmillan.

Morrow, L. M. (1988). Young children's responses to one-to-one story readings in school settings. *Reading Research Quarterly*, 23, 89–107.

Morrow, L. M. (1990). Small group story readings: The effects on children's comprehension and responses to literature. *Reading Research and Instruction*, 29(4), 1–17.

Morrow, L. M. (1991). Promoting voluntary reading. In J. Flood, J. M. Jensen, D. Lapp, & J. R. Squire (Eds.), *Handbook of research on teaching the English language arts* (pp. 681–690). New York: Macmillan.

Morrow, L. M. (1992). The impact of a literature-based program on the literacy achievement, use of literature, and attitudes of children from minority backgrounds. *Reading Research Quarterly*, 27, 251–275.

Morrow, L. M., & Smith, J. K. (1990). The effects of group size on interactive storybook reading. *Reading Research Quarterly*, 25, 213–231.

Mowder, L. (1992). Domestication of desire: Gender, language, and landscape in the Little House books. *Children's Literature Association Quarterly*, 17(1), 15–18.

Nelson, R. C. (1994). Children's poetry preferences. *Elementary English*, 43, 247–251.

Neumeyer, P. F. (1994). *The Annotated Charlotte's Web*. New York: HarperCollins.

Nieto, S. (1997). We have stories to tell: Puerto-Ricans in children's books. In V. J. Harris (Ed.), *Using multi-ethnic literature in the K–8 classroom* (pp. 59–94). Norwood, MA: Christopher Gordon.

Nikolajeva, M. (1995). Children's literature as a cultural code: A semiotic approach to history. In M. Nikolajeva (Ed.), *Aspects and issues in the history of children's literature* (pp. 39–48). Westport, CT: Greenwood.

Nikola-Lisa, W. (1995). Varied voices: Representations of African-American language in children's picture books. *The New Advocate*, 8(4), 223–242.

Nilsen, A. P., Peterson, R., & Searfoss, L. W. (1980). The adult as critic vs. the child as critic. *Language Arts*, 57, 530–539.

Nodelman, P. (1988). *Words about pictures: The narrative art of children's picture books*. Athens, GA: University of Georgia Press.

Nodelman, P. (1992). The other: Orientalism, colonialism, and children's literature. *Children's Literature Association Quarterly, 17*(1), 31–35.

Nystrand, M., & Gamoran, A. (1991). Instructional discourse, student engagement, and literature achievement. *Research in the Teaching of English, 25*, 261–290.

Oyler, C., & Barry, A. (1996). Intertextual connections in read-alouds of information books. *Language Arts, 73*, 324–329.

Pappas, C. C. (1991). Young children's strategies in learning the "book language" of informational books. *Discourse Processes, 14*, 203–225.

Pappas, C. C., & Brown, E. (1987). Learning to read by reading: Learning how to extend the functional potential of language. *Research in the Teaching of English, 21*, 160–177.

Pearson, P. D. (1986). Twenty years of research in reading comprehension. In T. E. Raphael (Ed.), *Contexts for school-based literacy* (pp. 43–62). New York: Random House.

Pearson, P. D., Barr, R., & Kamil, M. L. (Eds.). (1984). *Handbook of reading research* (Vol. I). New York: Longman.

Pinnell, G. S., & Jaggar, A. M. (1991). Oral language: Speaking and listening in the classroom. In J. Flood, J. M. Jensen, D. Lapp, & J. R. Squire (Eds.), *Handbook on research in teaching the English language arts* (pp. 691–720). New York: Macmillan.

Purves, A. C. & Beach, R. (1972). *Literature and the reader: Research in response to literature, reading interests, and the teaching of literature.* Urbana, IL: National Council of Teachers of English.

Raphael, T. E., & McMahon, S. I. (1994). Book Club: An alternative framework for reading instruction. *Reading Teacher, 48*, 102–116.

Raphael, T. E., McMahon, S. I. , Goatley, V. J., Boyd, F. B., Pardo, L. S., & Woodman, D. A. (1992). Research directions: Literature and discussion in the reading program. *Language Arts, 69*, 54–61.

Rasinski, T. V. (1990). Effects of repeated reading and listening-while-reading on reading fluency. *Journal of Educational Research, 83*, 147–150.

Reese, D., & Caldwell-Wood, N. (1997). Native Americans in children's literature. In V. J. Harris (Ed.), *Using multi-ethnic literature in the K–8 classroom* (pp. 155–192). Norwood, MA: Christopher Gordon.

Rogers, T. (1997). No imagined peaceful place: A story of community, texts, and cultural conversations in one urban high school English classroom. In T. Rogers & A. Soter (Eds.), *Reading across cultures* (pp. 95–115). New York: Teachers College Press

Rosenblatt, L. M. (1978). *The reader, the text, the poem: The transactional theory of the literary work.* Carbondale, IL: Southern Illinois University Press.

Rosenblatt, L. M. (1995). *Literature as exploration.* New York: Modern Language Association.

Rosenhouse, J., Feitelson, D., Kita, B., & Goldstein, Z. (1997). Interactive reading aloud to Israeli first graders: Its contribution to literacy development. *Reading Research Quarterly, 32*, 168–183.

Samway, K. D., & Whang, G. (1996). *Literature study circles in a multicultural classroom.* York, ME: Stenhouse.

Scharer, P. L. (1992). Teachers in transition: An exploration of changes in teachers and classrooms during implementation of literature-based reading instruction. *Research in the Teaching of English, 26*, 408–445.

Scharer, P. L., Freeman, E. B., Lehman, B. A., & Allen, V. G. (1993). Literacy and literature in elementary classrooms: teacher's beliefs and practices. In D. J. Leu & C. K. Kinzer (Eds.), *Examining central issues in literacy research, theory, and practice* (42nd yearbook of the National Reading Conference) (pp. 359–366). Chicago: National Reading Conference.

Short, K. G. (1995). Research and professional resources in children's literature: *Piecing a patchwork quilt.* Newark, DE: International Reading Association.

Short, K. G., & Pierce, K. M. (Eds.). (1990). *Talking about books: Creating literate communities.* Portsmouth, NH: Heinemann.

Simpson, A. (1996). Critical questions: Whose questions? *Reading Teacher, 50*, 118–127.

Sims, R. (1982). *Shadow and substance.* Urbana, IL: National Council of Teachers of English.

Sims, R. (1984). Point of view: A question of perspective III. *The Advocate, 4*, 21–23.

Slapin, B., & Seale, D. (1992). *Through Indian eyes: The native experience in books for children.* Philadelphia: New Society.

Smith, N. B. (1926). An investigation in children's interests in different types of stories. *Detroit Educational Bulletin, 9*, 3–4.

Smith, N. J., Greenlaw, M. J., & Scott, C. J. (1987). Making the literate environment equitable. *Reading Teacher, 40*, 400–407.

Smolkin, L. B. (1997). Dealing with dialogue: Fifth graders' responses to reading a play. *Research in the Teaching of English, 31*, 240–266.

Spinelli, J. (1990). *Maniac Magee.* New York: Little, Brown.

Steffensen, M. S., Joag-Dev, Z. C., & Anderson, R. C. (1979). A cross-cultural perspective on reading comprehension. *Reading Research Quarterly, 15*(1), 10–29.

Steig, W. (1971). *Amos and Boris.* New York: Farrar, Straus and Giroux.

Stephens, J. (1992). *Language and ideology in children's fiction.* New York: Longman.

Stevenson, D. (1994). "If you read this last sentence, it won't tell you anything": Postmodernism, self-referentiality, and *The Stinky Cheese Man. Children's Literature Association Quarterly, 19*, 32–34.

Stott, J. C., & Francis, C. D. (1993). "Home" and "not home" in children's stories: Getting there and being worth it. *Children's Literature in Education, 24*(4), 158–166.

Summers, E. G., & Lukasevich, A. (1983). Reading preferences of intermediate-grade children in relation to sex, community, and maturation (grade level): A Canadian perspective. *Reading Research Quarterly, 18*(3), 347–360.

Taxel, J. A. (1983). The American revolution in children's fiction. *Research in the Teaching of English, 17*(1), 61–83.

Taxel, J. A. (1984). The American revolution in children's fiction: An analysis of historical meaning and narrative structure. *Curriculum Inquiry, 14*(1), 7–55.

Trites, R. S. (1995). Is flying extraordinary? Patricia MacLachlan's use of aporia. *Children's Literature, 23,* 202–220.

Trousdale, A. M. (1990). A submission theology for Black Americans: Religion and social action in prize-winning books about the Black experience in America. *Research in the Teaching of English, 24,* 117–140.

Vygotsky, L. S. (1978). *Thought and language* (A. Kozulin, Trans.). Cambridge, MA: MIT Press.

Wiseman, D. L., Many, J. E., & Altieri, J. (1992). Enabling complex aesthetic responses: An examination of three literary discussion approaches. In D. J. Leu & C. K. Kinzer (Eds.), *Literacy research, theory, and practice: Views from many perspectives,* (41st Yearbook of the National Reading Conference) (pp. 283–290). Chicago: National Reading Conference.

Wolfson, B. J., Manning, G., & Manning, M. (1984). Revisiting what children say their reading interests are. *Reading World, 24,* 4–10.

Wollman-Bonilla, J. E. (1994). Why don't they "just speak?" Attempting literature discussion with more and less able readers. *Research in the Teaching of English, 28,* 231–258.

Zimet, S. F. (1966). Children's interest and story preferences. *Elementary School Journal, 67,* 122–133.

CHAPTER 23

Research on Response to Literature

James Marshall
University of Iowa

If we were to subject this chapter's title to a close reading—still a primary critical practice and teaching strategy in the study of literature (Applebee, 1993; Rabinowitz, 1992)—we would begin to uncover some of the tensions and difficulties the chapter itself will attempt to explore. Consider the title's major terms.

Research, for instance, has been for the last quarter century such a contested term that its meaning can probably only be retrieved in very specific rhetorical contexts. What counts as appropriate method (quantitative vs. qualitative) or persuasive data (statistical or ethnographic) are well-rehearsed topics across the social sciences, whereas the question of who can most appropriately and helpfully conduct research in classrooms (university-based scholars or school-based teachers) remains unresolved. But because the subject of *research* is, in this case, *response to literature*, the boundaries of a working definition must extend beyond the social sciences and beyond educational venues. At the very least, a full review of research on response to literature would include the wide array of scholarly and critical practices undertaken by literary experts in their attempts to understand texts (research in bibliography, history, culture, biography, theory)—research that follows its own conventions of argument and cites from its own traditions of scholarship. A full review might also include the more publicly reported forms of research that provide the evidence for policymakers (average SAT verbal scores, National Assessment of Education Progress [NAEP] reports on literacy, popular newspaper polls showing what Americans are reading) and that are employed regularly by politicians and public intellectuals in their arguments for educational reform. The word *research*, in other words, has many different owners, and we may limit what we see if we eliminate too quickly some of those who claim the term as theirs.

The word *response* in the title is no less slippery. Depending on context, it can refer to a tradition of empirical research (e.g., Odell & Cooper, 1976; Purves & Rippere, 1968; Squire, 1964), to a school of literary theory (e.g., Bleich, 1975; Fish, 1980; Tompkins, 1980), or to an approach to teaching literature (e.g., Probst, 1991; Rosenblatt, 1938). No matter who uses the term, however, it carries with it at least three difficulties.

First, the word implies a passivity on the part of the responder, locating initial agency in the text responded to. The text acts on the reader, in this view, and the reader "responds" in some describable way. But such a view of reading has little in common with the largely constructivist theory that has framed reading research since the mid 1970s; moreover, it has little in common with the claims that those who argue for "response approaches" would themselves make about teaching or literary understanding. The reader, in these arguments, is conceived as an active maker of meaning rather than a passive receiver, and the word *response* fails to carry the message of agency.

Second, and perhaps just as problematic, any response to literature, whether viewed as passive or active, will remain largely invisible to those studying it until it is represented by the reader in some verbal or material form. A reader's response to literature, in other words, is never directly accessible: It is always mediated by the mode of representation to which the reader has access (e.g., talk, writing, drawing). As Robert DeMaria (1997) recently argued in his study of Samuel Johnson's reading life, "A writer is known through his writing, so a reader should be known through his reading. But the act of reading leaves no traces, and writing about reading is writing" (p. xii). One reader's response to literature, then, can never be studied apart from the medium in which it appears, and the response itself must be understood as shaped by the conventions of that medium, and by the reader's familiarity and skill with those conventions.

Third, the word *response* is troubling because it is difficult to say what it should include. Certainly we mean more than simple comprehension (the ability to say back what happened), but what is that something more? Emotional response? Autobiographical connection? Interpretive insight? Delight in the act of reading itself ? Or can we include an understanding of the text's context, of the author's intentions, of the critical tradition that has framed discussion about the text? Almost anything we do or say during or after the act of reading literature can be construed as a response, and thus the task of mapping the possible seems immensely large.

Finally, the word *literature* itself is contested, by now in such familiar ways that we can simply gesture at the arguments. Terry Eagleton (1983) perhaps provided the most succinct overview of the issues in his frequently cited chapter in *Literary Theory*, but the debate was also taken up by Rosenblatt (1938, 1978), Britton (1970), and Fish (1980), all of whom argued, with significant variations, that literature is not intrinsically a kind of text, but becomes itself, that is, becomes literature, only when it is read *as* literature. We can read texts conventionally considered literature in nonliterary ways, in other words, and we can read texts conventionally considered nonliterary in literary ways. All of which means, then, that the word *literature*, like the words *research* and *response*, is notoriously unstable, and thus provides little guidance about what kinds of *research on response to literature* ought to be included in a chapter with such a title.

This review attempts to bring into one conversation three traditions of thought about readers' responses to literature. These traditions—the political, the critical, and the empirical—are distinct from one another not only because they engage different questions about response, but also because they address different audiences and point toward different bodies of intertextual reference for their evidence and authority. Although the scholarship across these traditions is interrelated in potentially important ways, work within any one has often ignored or remained silent about the work in those adjacent to it. The absence of discussion across traditions has probably impoverished all three, but more important for the purposes of this review, such absence has left researchers with an underdrawn, underconceptualized landscape for studying readers' responses to literature. This review attempts to redraw that landscape and encourage discussion across all three traditions.

THE POLITICAL TRADITION

The political tradition of thought about response to literature concerns itself primarily with the moral dimensions of reading literature for individuals and communities, and thus by extension examines the relationships between literature and the political, religious, or cultural well-being of those who read it. Work in this tradition tends to be conducted by public intellectuals working in public forums, and finds its most visible origins in Plato's *Republic* (1962), where Socrates warns his students that most of the stories available to children in his time would have to be rejected in his proposed utopia because "[the stories] are quite untrue" and focus on "wars and plots and battles among the gods" (p. 123). Only stories especially chosen for their moral value will be taught to prospective guardians of the republic for "opinions formed (in childhood) are usually difficult to eradicate or change; it is therefore of the utmost importance that the first stories they hear shall aim at producing the right moral effect."

The proposition that reading can and should have "the right moral effect" on those who read was a central premise for those reformation scholars who first translated the Bible into vernacular languages (Manguel, 1996; Olson, 1977; Ong, 1982), and played a large role in the expansion of literacy (Graff, 1982) and the wider availability of printed material—especially material of a religious nature—during the early modern period (Eisenstein, 1980; Ong, 1982). Learning to read the Bible for oneself, in one's own tongue, unmediated by priestly commentary and Latinate instruction, was a driving force of Reformation thought, and provided an extraordinarily strong motive for the expansion of education—especially education in reading.

But although religion provided the original motivation for the expansion of reading in Western Europe and, later, colonial America (Davidson, 1989), the kinds of texts available soon extended beyond the religious. (Eisenstein, 1980; Kaestle, 1991) More critically, traditional religion itself, by the mid 19th century, had become less powerful as an organizing force in communities and in the lives of individuals. That is how Matthew Arnold viewed his cultural situation, and it is with him that discussions of the moral and political dimensions of reading literature take their modern shape.

Arnold was not only a poet, literary critic, and Oxford professor; he was also, for most of his adult life, an inspector of public schools (Arnold, 1961; Willinsky, 1990), and it is from that perspective that he perceived the need for a replacement for religion. "The masses are losing the Bible and its religion," he argued in *Literature and Dogma* (cited in Willinsky, 1990, p. 352), and he saw poetry, and more generally great literature, as a force powerful enough to heal the moral and spiritual decay that would follow from that loss. As a school inspector and public intellectual, he was positioned to argue for the teaching of great literature in schools for "the best literature has the quality of being in itself formative" and that "it is destined to [add to itself] the religious idea of devout energy, to transform, and to govern" (cited in Willinsky, 1990, p. 352). Reading great literature is not just a practice to be privately enjoyed, in other words, it can become the basis for humane and generous cultural norms that will organize the moral and political life of a nation and provide "a moral salve, a spiritual balm, for the sickened souls of the times" (Willinsky, 1990, p. 350).

Arnold's legacy is visible in two contemporary, interrelated, and very public debates about the reading of literature, each shaped in part by Arnold's insistence on literature's moral and political influences and each shaping, in turn, current discussions of how readers can and do respond to literature.

The first debate centers on the now familiar arguments about the power and legitimacy of the traditional western literary canon—the selection of texts and authors that extends, in its usual formulation, from Homer to the high moderns of the 20th century (Woolf, Joyce, Eliot). On the one hand are those who argue that the canon has been established on primarily aesthetic grounds—that the texts located there are of proven literary value—and should be studied because they represent, in Arnold's phrase, "the best that has been thought and said" (e.g., Bloom, 1994; Denby, 1996). On the other hand are those who argue that the canon represents an elitist, highly selective group of texts that grossly underrepresents those who have traditionally been without political or cultural visibility (primarily women and minorities) and that serves best those with already established economic and political power (primarily white men) (Gates 1992; Graff, 1992; Nelson, 1997; Ohmann, 1976). The debate has generated a good deal of serious historical research about the origins of the canon (e.g., Guillory, 1992; Shumway, 1994), but it has also at times devolved into ridicule and passionate attack (e.g., D'Souza, 1991; Hughes, 1993). Although the discussion has taken many permutations, at least two general observations seem possible.

First, the arguments on both sides are not about what individuals should read (this is not, in other words, a debate about censorship); the arguments focus, rather, on what texts should be taught and studied in school. The attention to what students are to read again recalls Arnold's insistence that literature not only belongs in classrooms, but has the power to instill particular values and to forge particular kinds of communities when placed there. Those who argue for the viability of the canon (e.g., Bloom, 1994; Hirsch, 1987) insist that it provides students with a sense of their cultural heritage and that it further provides a common body of knowledge and a common vocabulary of reference without which a coherent political community would be endangered. Those who argue against the traditional canon and for the inclusion of a much wider variety of texts and authors (e.g., Nelson, 1997; Ohmann, 1976) insist that providing such a cultural heritage for students has often rendered invisible a large portion of the community's population and effectively neutralized the wide variation in tradition and belief present in any group, even if it calls itself a community.

Second, although the subject of the debate is literature and although participants are often literary scholars, those participants often see their efforts in the debate in primarily political terms—that is, as a struggle for power, as an attempt to affect change in the world (D'Souza, 1989; Fish, 1995; Nelson; 1997). Although the debate is always mediated by discussion of particular kinds of texts, and usually examines whether those texts should be read in school, the goal is always the formation of a particular kind of community—a community defined by the literary texts it chooses to privilege or, conversely, by the literary texts it chooses to ignore. Such efforts are grounded by a consistent belief in the power of literature to shape the political well-being of communities (Coles, 1989) in ways that both Plato and Arnold might understand.

The second public conversation about the reading of literature, deeply related to the first, concerns the much more specifically ethical effects of reading literature on individuals: Can reading particular texts, in other words, be bad for you—or good for you? On the one hand, this conversation includes arguments about censorship, again usually in school (e.g., Moffett, 1988) and centers most often on issues of violence or explicit sexuality. These arguments can sometimes intersect with arguments about the literary canon because contemporary texts often excluded from the canon may contain more explicit representations of these matters. On the other hand, this conversation has generated a highly successful effort to sponsor the reading of particular texts because the texts will have a salutary moral effect on the children who read them. William Bennett, in an ongoing series of collected stories (e.g., *The Book of Virtues*, 1993), has argued for literature's power to instill a "moral literacy" in children—a literacy that will provide them with a vocabulary of traditional values analogous, in many ways, to the vocabulary of traditional cultural knowledge represented in the canon and in Hirsch's arguments for "cultural literacy." Bennett's arguments in favor of reading particular kinds of texts, like those against the reading of other texts, rest on the assumption that individual character can be powerfully affected by literature and that a culture ignores at its peril the kinds of texts children are given to read.

But what if children and adults read almost nothing at all? As a final turn in this overview of the political tradition in response to literature, we should consider ongoing discussions about the value of reading literature—almost any literature—and about the disappearance of such reading as a social practice in contemporary culture. McLuhan (1962) provided forceful arguments about how and why reading practices would change in light of new media, but his philosophical acceptance of these changes is counterbalanced by more recent and sometimes elegiac mediations of what the disappearance might mean (Birkerts, 1994; Fiedler, 1982; Kernan, 1990; Pennac, 1994; Schwartz, 1996). Such arguments are captured in the titles of several books (e.g., *Literature Lost, What Was Literature, The Death of Literature, The Gutenberg Elegies*) and, in brief, argue that the act of reading itself, as much as the particular literature that one reads, can be a social good worth celebrating and preserving. As Birkerts put it, "Literature holds meaning not as a content that can be abstracted and summarized, but as experience. It is a participatory area. Through the process of reading we slip out of our customary time orientation marked by distractedness and superficiality, into the realm of duration. Only in this state are we prepared … to question our origins and destinations and to conceive of ourselves as souls" (p. 32).

Such language would be recognizable to Plato, but his concerns about the dangers of reading literature on the spiritual growth of citizens have been replaced by a comparable concern about the dangers of not reading literature. What connects the arguments, of course, is a fundamental belief that reading literature is serious and powerful in its effects, and that political and moral consequences of reading must be examined carefully in a society that hopes to endure. Such beliefs play a more-or-less visible role in other traditions of thought about response to literature, but they are seldom addressed as clearly as in the political tradition I have tried to outline here. That political tradition has helped shape other conversations about reading, and should be accounted for when those other conversations are considered.

THE CRITICAL TRADITION

[handwritten: Analyzing the research]

Although work in the political tradition is usually conducted by public intellectuals addressing a largely lay audience of concerned citizens, work in the critical tradition is conducted mostly by literary scholars, is usually called literary theory or, more specifically, reader response theory, and is addressed most often to academic peers through university presses and specialized journals. And if the political tradition finds its origins in Plato, the critical tradition of thought about literary response finds its clearest antecedents in Aristotle, whose description in the *Poetics* of the effects of tragedy on an audience may be one of the first attempts in Western thought to explain the nature of literary response.

[handwritten margin notes: interactions w/ text and literature, student & text, response, literacy scholars, theoretical framework of response]

Work in the critical tradition has been thoughtfully reviewed several times (e.g., Beach, 1993; Eagleton, 1983; Freund 1987; Mailloux, 1982). Although different reviewers have mapped the terrain of reader response theory in varying ways (Mailloux, for instance, finds three major categories of theorists—Psychological, Phenomenological, and Structural—whereas Beach finds five—Textual, Experiential, Psychological, Social, and Cultural), most reviews locate the beginnings of contemporary response theory in the work of I. A. Richards (1929) and Louise Rosenblatt (1938).

They make an unlikely pair. Richards's contribution was in many ways empirical. As he said in his introduction to *Practical Criticism* (1929), he hoped in his work to "provide a new technique for those who wish to discover for themselves what they think and feel about poetry" (p. 3). In brief, Richards asked his Cambridge students to "respond freely" to poetry they were assigned. He then did an elementary content analysis of their responses, categorizing them by their reliance on sentimentality, doctrinal adhesions, technical presuppositions, or stock responses, among others (pp. 14–15). Although Richards was largely critical of his students for their limitations, and although he maintained largely text-centered assumptions about the location of literary meaning, his study clearly made the case that "the personal situation of the reader inevitably (and within limits rightly) affects his reading" (quoted in Beach, 1993, p. 16). Richards's empirical approach to the study of response—the content analysis of particular written responses—became in the 1960s and 1970s a standard procedure for researchers interested in the factors that help shape readers' responses to literature (e.g., Purves & Rippere, 1968; Squire, 1964).

In some ways, Rosenblatt's contribution in *Literature as Exploration* (1938) was much more obviously theoretical (Richards's categories of responses were atheoretic, built from the bottom up) and much more obviously concerned with students and schools. Her book opened with an observation about the social condition contemporary students are facing ("In a turbulent age, our schools and colleges must prepare the student to meet unprecedented and unpredictable problems," p. 3) and was itself sponsored by the Commission on Human Relations, a group associated with the Progressive Education Association (Willinsky, 1991). Progressive assumptions about education were present throughout her book, where she argued not only that readers play an important role in the construction of literary meaning, but that "Books are a means of getting outside the particularly limited cultural group into which the individual (is) born" and that literature itself "can play an important part in the process through which the individual becomes assimilated into the cultural pattern" (Willinsky, 1991, p. 119).

Rosenblatt was to extend and in important ways revise these ideas in her later work (1978), but what is important about her early contributions to reader response theory is how widely they have been ignored by most of those working in the critical tradition. Richards, both because of *Practical Criticism* and because of the stature he established through his other critical work (e.g., *Principles of Literary Criticism*), has consistently been cited as an important early influence in the development of reader response theory (e.g., Eagleton, 1983; Graff, 1989). But although Rosenblatt enjoys an extraordinarily wide audience among educators (e.g, Clifford, 1991) and although she is frequently cited in the empirical literature on literary response, she is almost invisible among literary theorists working in university English departments through university presses and academic journals. She is not discussed or even cited, for instance, in Terry Eagleton's overview of 20th-century literary theory (1983), in Gerald Graff's history of university literature teaching (1989), or even in Jane Tompkins's more specific collection of essays on reader response criticism (1980). As I show in the next section of this review, her influence has been widely felt, but not visibly within the tradition of critical thought to which she made her earliest contributions.

Although Richards and Rosenblatt developed their ideas on literary response relatively early in the century (1929 and 1938), reader response theory as a whole remained largely undeveloped until about 40 years later—until, that is, the critical assumptions that had supported the all-but-imperial new criticism began to unravel (Marshall, Smagorinsky, & Smith, 1995; McCormick, 1994). As Beach (1993) and McCormick (1994) argued, reader response theory found adherents, mostly in the United States, during the 1970s and 1980s, mostly in reaction to the formalist criticism that had achieved dominance in the 1940s through the 1960s (Graff, 1989; Ohmann, 1976). In brief, formalist critics had insisted on the study of texts for their internal tensions and organic structures, and had labeled as an "affective fallacy" any attention to the effects of a text on particular readers (Beach, 1993). As McCormick (1994) pointed out, however, the kind of close reading associated with the new critical tradition was itself developed out of political anxieties engendered by industrialization and the rapid advance of consumerism and mass advertising. The close reading of great literature would help preserve, the argument went, an Arnoldian sense of culture in the face of a society that was becoming increasingly, in Arnold's view, "anarchic" (Willinsky, 1991, p. 34). As F. R. Leavis, one of the most important champions of close reading, put it, "There is a necessary relationship between the quality of the individual's response to art and his general fitness for a humane existence" (quoted in Willinsky, 1991, p. 34). And thus the teacher's goal, through an insistence on closer reading of the formal structures in a text, was to help develop particular, socially valuable kinds of response.

But such assumptions became increasingly suspect as structural and then poststructural arguments about literary meaning became widely current and as the political environment of universities and the political assumptions of university faculty began to shift (Eagleton, 1983; Graff, 1989; Tompkins, 1985). It was at this moment, from the early 1970s to the early 1980s, that reader response theory was most widely discussed and most fully developed. The theorists working in this tradition can be generally divided into three groups, each of which, although attending carefully to readers' responses to literature, locates the most powerful influences on those responses in different sources.

The first group finds the source of literary meaning in the psychological identity and autobiographical history of readers themselves. Thus in Holland's (1975) proposal for a "transactive" criticism, readers read so as to "replicate" their identity. In highly detailed case studies of five readers' responses to Faulkner's "A Rose for Emily," Holland demonstrated how different readers will have "different ways of making the text into an experience with a coherence and significance that satisfies" (quoted in Mailloux, 1982, p. 24). David Bleich (1975, 1978) made a comparable kind of argument, although he identified the source of response not as an identity theme in readers but as a "subjective reconstruction" (Mailloux, 1982, p. 30) of the text that rests on the emotional effects that were experienced during reading and on the psychological predispositions of readers themselves. Although Bleich's later work (1988), drawing on the sociocultural perspectives of Vygotsky and Bahktin, placed such psychological sources within a larger cultural context, he continued to argue, like Holland, that the meanings that readers take away from texts will always reflect readers' own psychological orientations more than intentions embedded by authors in the texts themselves.

The second group of reader response theorists places the source of literary meaning in a set of conventions for reading shared by authors and readers—conventions that shape and limit, but do not determine absolutely what kinds of meaning can be taken from a particular reading. Thus Jonathan Culler (1975) uses the analogy of Chomskian linguistics to argue that literary communication is rule governed and relies on an audience of "competent" readers who know and can apply those rules in particular reading circumstances. Wolfgang Iser (1978) argued that a literary text "contains intersubjectively verifiable instructions for meaning production" (p. 25) and that competent readers will be able to follow those instructions and assemble the meanings intended, filling in the "gaps" left by the author in ways that make or a coherent and satisfying reading. The early work of Stanley Fish (1970) likewise posited the importance of nimble, attentive, ideal readers who can both follow the moves of an author and at the same time carefully monitor their own responses—for those responses are, ultimately, the meaning that the author probably intended. And Louise Rosenblatt, writing some 30 years after the appearance of *Literature as Exploration*, argued in *The Reader, the Text, the Poem* (1978) for a transactional view of literary response. Such a view holds that literature demands a particular kind of reading—aesthetic reading—in which the reader attends to the experience being undergone, and not to the knowledge or meanings that can be carried way—a kind of reading she called *efferent*. To read efferently those texts that were meant to be read aesthetically is to impoverish the reading experience and undermine a fully developed understanding of the responses made possible by the text.

The third group of reader response theories—a group that includes the later work of those theorists (Bleich, 1988; Fish, 1980) whose early work focused more exclusively on individual response—locates a powerful source of readers' responses in the sociocultural context in which they are reading. Thus Fish (1980) argued for the centrality of the "interpretive communities" to which readers belong—communities that shape the strategies and assumptions of individual readers, even determining what gets counted as literature and thus what gets read in literary ways. Such an argument resonates with Bakhtin's (1981) insistence on a dialogic perspective—one in which individual articulations of meaning are always in answer to other response—and, in turn, must always be answered. Far from being individually, even solipsistically determined by psychological materials, responses in this view are socially constructed, made up of interwoven assumptions and linguistic formulations that have histories in particular cultures and that carry those histories with them when they are spoken by particular readers.

Once the argument is made that individual responses are shaped by social and cultural assumptions, of course, it becomes possible to investigate the political dimensions of response, that is; the ways in which particular literary meanings or responses are formulated as "natural" or "obvious" to those in power and the ways in which such "natural" responses can be resisted by those who have been traditionally marginalized. Thus, feminist critics (e.g., Fetterley, 1978; Millet, 1970; Showalter, 1985) demonstrated how gender politics has influenced the construction of the literary canon and naturalized particular ways of reading. Other reader response theorist historicized the investigation of response (e.g., Levine, 1988; McCormick, 1994; Tompkins, 1985; Travis, 1998), showing how the assumptions governing reading and literary value have shifted over time, changing the kinds of responses that were likely, or even possible, in historically specific cultural situations.

Even this relatively rough categorization of reader response theory suggests that important differences are present among theorists, and that if these differences are ignored, the usefulness of work in illuminating the various aspects of response can be undermined. To name Holland (1975), Rosenblatt (1978), and Fish (1980) all as reader response theorists when arguing for particular kinds of pedagogy, for instance (e.g., Rouse, 1991), is to lose distinctions and to misrepresent the implications of various kinds of reader response theory for work in classrooms. Locating the source of response in individual readers' psychology is a very different matter from locating it in the cultural context in which those readers' find themselves, and different pedagogies will follow.

Unless, that is, one accepts the assumptions of a sociocultural perspectives (e.g., Bahktin, 1981; Vygotsky, 1978; Wertsch, 1991)—at which point individual psychology, even Holland's identity themes, will be seen as shaped in large measure by the vocabulary of values and norms made available to readers by culture at particular moments in time. There is a way in which reader response theory must always account not only for readers' responses but also for its own reading of those readers' responses. As Culler (1980) argued in his criticism of Holland, once we locate interpretive authority in readers, the readers of readers must themselves be examined, and a virtually infinite regress of readerly inquiry becomes possible.

In spite of the possibilities for inquiry, there has been, perhaps surprisingly, very little empirical work examining readers' responses within the critical tradition. This is not to say that there has been no empirical work on readers' responses; that, in fact, is the subject of the next section of this review. It is to say, rather, that the critical tradition has argued from premise, assumption, and exemplary demonstration more often than from the investigation of particulars. Except for Richards's originating work, Holland's elaborately detailed psychiatric case studies, and Bleich's close readings of individual readers' "response statements," the critical tradition has generated very little data about how individual readers construct responses to literature. So removed from empirical scholarship has this tradition remained, in fact, that a recent study of reception history and reader response refers to Janice Radway's *Reading the Romance* (1984) as "one of the rare empirical studies of literary reading" (Travis, 1998, p. 7). That such an observation could be written, reviewed, and published within the venues of the critical tradition suggests how clearly the boundaries are marked that separate one tradition from another in the research on readers' response to literature.

THE EMPIRICAL TRADITION

[handwritten marginalia: researchers • practical application how it is being used, why variations in responses]

Although work in the critical tradition has been conducted largely by literary scholars from university departments of English, work in the empirical tradition has usually been conducted by researchers whose interests are more closely associated with teachers, students, and schools—researchers, that is, from schools of education or related fields with backgrounds in the social sciences as well as the humanities. The research methods of the empirical tradition, in fact, have been largely derived from the social sciences, shifting over time with changing research paradigms, borrowing early on from psychometric models, and more recently from anthropology (Athanases & Heath, 1995; Bloome & Egan-Robertson, 1993). Yet, although the research methods have changed, the challenge for empirical researchers has remained the same—how to describe and account for responses to literature that are, as noted earlier, largely invisible in themselves. Such responses cannot be studied except as represented in some form of discourse (e.g., speech, writing, drawing) that mediates them and helps determine their content.

The review that follows concentrates most heavily on recent studies. Previous research in this tradition has been reviewed many times (e.g., Applebee, 1977; Beach & Hynds, 1991; Cooper, 1976; Petrosky, 1977; Purves & Beach, 1972).

Richards's (1929) originating study of his students' responses to literature provided a durable model of content analysis for researchers who followed, although the categories used to sort responses changed over time and with the interests and theoretic perspective of researchers (see Beach & Hynds, 1991, for a comprehensive listing of category systems). In general, the kinds of categories fall within two major types. On the one hand are those, following Richards, that attempt to describe kinds of response, often looking for similarities and differences among many responses, working from the bottom up toward descriptive generalizations. Thus Richards (1929) coded his students' responses for their "inhibition," their "doctrinal adhesions," or their "stock responses," among others. Squire (1964) categorized responses as "associational" or for "self-involvement," among other characteristics. Purves and Rippere (1968), in probably the most widely used category system (Applebee, 1977), coded responses for "engagement," "perception," "interpretation," "evaluation," and "miscellaneous." More recent work has categorized responses as "information-driven," "story-driven," or "point-driven" (Vipond & Hunt, 1984) or as marked by "insight," "empathy," and "imagery vividness" among other qualities (Miall & Kuiken, 1995). A second type of category system, on the other hand, attempts to code responses for quality of thinking or depth of response, using a pre-existing framework for determining levels of performance. Thus Applebee's (1978) study of children's developing responses to literature distinguishes among "narration," "summarization," "analysis," and "generalization." A National Assessment of Education Progress study (1981) scored response as "egocentric" at the low end to "analysis superficial" and "analysis elaborated" at the high end. And classroom studies have categorized responses as moving from simple to more complex (Hillocks & Ludlow, 1984) or as undeveloped to more fully elaborated (Marshall, 1987).

As sophisticated and widely employed as some of these systems have been in helping to understand the nature, content, or quality of literary response, they have been most often used in the service of another, perhaps more difficult question: Because readers' responses to literature obviously vary widely (thus the category systems), why do they vary? What, in other words, are the causes of variation in readers' response to literature? The answers, of course, like the responses themselves, cover a range of possibilities, but they can be discussed in three general groups: those that locate the source of variation in the literary *text* being read, in the *reader* doing the reading, or in the *context* in which the reading is taking place.

The Text

Although researchers in the empirical tradition often focus primarily on the reader or the reading context in their analysis of literary response, the text always remains a critical element. Not only does the text provide the occasion for whatever responses are developed (Rabinowitz & Smith, 1997), it shapes those responses at the most basic level as soon as it is identified as "literature." Whether a particular text is called literature because of its formal conventions (Eagleton, 1983; Rabinowitz, 1987) or because of the interpretive conventions of the community in which it is read (Fish, 1980), once it is so named it usually triggers specialized ways of reading that differ in describable ways from ways of reading nonliterary texts. Thus Rosenblatt distinguished between aesthetic reading, which focuses on the lived-through nature of the literary experience, from efferent reading, which focuses on the information that can be carried away from the reading. And Langer (1995), although interested primarily in how readers develop an "envisionment" of a literary text, examined such development only after the text has been identified as literary. How readers read nonliterary texts, she argued, is quite different.

Literature has been found, however, to serve more than aesthetic instructional ends. In a study of fifth graders, for instance, Dressel (1990) found that fifth graders who heard and discussed high-quality stories wrote essays that were scored higher than those of peers who heard and discussed stories of lower quality. Another study (Jones, Coombs, & McKenney, 1994) found that sixth graders who read literature about Mexico scored better on posttests than peers who read textbooks covering the same material. Literature, in other words, has at times been found to have positive effects on nonliterary aspects of student achievement.

The term *literature*, however, is often too broad a category to be of much help in understanding particular responses: The genre, subject, and difficulty of the literature may all play a role in shaping response. Thus Radway (1984), in her now classic study of women romance readers, found that these readers had very specific expectations about what romance novels were to include (modest but attractive heroines, somewhat dangerous but tame-able heroes, happy endings) and exclude (violent rape, unattractive, selfish main characters, unhappy endings). A replication of Radway's study with seventh-grade students found similar patterns (Willinsky & Hunniford, 1986).

In a different kind of argument about the role of texts in readers' responses, Trousdale (1990) observed that in four prizewinning books featuring African American characters, the three written by White authors ascribed to Black characters a "theology of racial submission." Such thematic features, she argued, have a great deal to do with whether teachers are comfortable with books featuring minorities and thus whether the books get taught in schools.

Perhaps the most active current line of research on the role of texts in literacy response include those studies that investigate the effects of multicultural literature on readers' social attitudes and beliefs, especially those attitudes toward minority cultures represented in the literature read. Although earlier studies focused on such matters as well (e.g., Licheter & Johnson, 1973), the interest has grown rapidly in recent years, (e.g., Bishop, 1987; Hynds & Appleman, 1997), in many ways paralleling ongoing discussions within the political tradition about canon formation and the inclusion within classrooms of previously marginalized authors, texts, and cultures. Thus Bishop (1987) argued that "Educators and parents alike maintain a strong belief in the power of literature to affect the minds of hearts of its readers" and that "multicultural literature is one of the most powerful components of a multicultural education curriculum, the underlying purpose of which is to help to make the society a more equitable one" (p. 40).

Although there is significant support for such arguments among educators (e.g., Rogers & Soter, 1997), the empirical record is somewhat mixed, probably because it is so difficult to reliably measure shifts in social attitude. Wham, Barnhart, and Cook (1996) found positive gains in elementary students' attitudes toward multicultural diversity following home and classroom reading of multicultural storybooks. And Athanases (1996), in a study of tenth-grade students' responses to a texts featuring gay and lesbian experiences, found that under the right instructional circumstances students can be brought to a deeper understanding of identities and oppression. On the other hand, several researchers identified multiple sources of student resistance to multicultural literature (Beach, 1997; Rogers, 1997), whereas others have described the instructional tensions that arise when multicultural literature is grafted onto reader-response frameworks for teaching (e.g, Hines, 1993).

That the effects of multicultural literature on students seem uneven or that problems sometimes arise when multicultural literature is brought into classrooms should not be surprising because the study of such literature is itself so new and appropriate pedagogies are still under development. Still, it seems plain that more sophisticated measures of the social and political attitudes of readers will have to be constructed before a full empirical case can be made for the influence of these texts on readers' ways of viewing the world.

The Reader

Earlier empirical research on the role of the reader in literary response focused on issues of the reader's developmental level (e.g, Applebee, 1978; Culliman, Galda, & Harwood, 1983); the reader's personality (e.g, Bleich, 1975; Holland, 1975); the reader's orientation to the text (e.g., Dillon, 1982; Hunt & Vipond, 1985); and the reader's reading skill—a construct that includes background knowledge and genre familiarity (e.g., Beach & Wendler, 1987; Lehr, 1988).

All of these factors, not surprisingly, have been shown to have dramatic influence on the nature of readers' responses to literature. Developmental studies, for example, have shown that younger readers usually engage in perception whereas older readers show more evidence of interpretation and indicate a wider range of responses (Applebee, 1977). Beach and Wendler (1987), in a study comparing 8th graders, 11th graders, college freshmen, and college juniors, found that the college students were much more likely to focus on the psychological aspects of characters, whereas younger readers were more likely to focus on action in the story. Work focusing on the personality of readers has found that readers are likely to recreate literary works in accord with their own psychological predispositions or "identity themes." Factors such as ego development (Trimble, 1984), tolerance for ambiguity (Peters & Blues, 1978), and self-actualization (Ebersole & DeVogler-Ebersole, 1984) have been related to the responses of readers. Hunt and Vipond's work on readers' orientation to the text found differences among "information-driven," "story-driven," and "point-driven" stances with regard to particular texts (Hunt & Vipond, 1985), whereas Flynn (1986) distinguished among "dominant," "submissive," and "integrated" response in a study of male and female readers. And studies focusing on readers' skill have found that readers with more exposure to literature were more likely to make thematic statements (Lehr, 1988) and that young children were more likely to make complex responses to familiar stories than to unfamiliar stories (Martinez & Roser, 1985).

More recent research has tended to focus less on the factors affecting readers' responses and more on the actual process of response itself. Drawing on her study of middle school students' reading of literary works, for instance, Langer (1995) described four stages of a reader's developing "envisionment:" "stepping into an envisionment" in which readers attempt to orient themselves to the text's world; "being in and moving through" an envisionment, where readers call on previous knowledge to question and make sense of the text; "stepping out and rethinking what one knows," a stage where readers make connections between the text and their own understanding of the world; and "stepping out and objectifying the experience," when readers analytically focus on the form and theme of the text itself, making judgments of its value and connections to other texts.

Several studies have examined the ways in which proficient readers respond to texts, and how those responses differ from those of less readers. Hartman (1995), for example, used the think-aloud protocols of eight proficient readers to study the intertextual links that the readers made as they read five separate passages. He found that the readers made two types of such connections: (a) links among ideas, events, and people; and (b) social, political, and historical connections. His evidence led him to argue that models of reading literature have been unnecessarily narrow and that proficient readers employ a plurality of ways to read, even when reading the same passage. In a related study, Garrison and Hynds (1991) found that proficient readers integrated textual cues and prior knowledge in the process of reflecting about stories, whereas less proficient readers approached texts in a linear way. Earthman (1992), also using think-aloud protocols, found that more experienced readers—in this case, graduate students—were more likely to attend to difficult gaps in literary texts (Iser, 1978) and that less experienced readers (college freshmen) were more likely to retain their initial view of a work, whereas graduate students assumed varying perspectives. Many (1991) found that the use of the aesthetic stance—a construct derived from Rosenblatt (1978)—was associated with higher levels of personal understanding.

The case study maintained its favored position as a research method in recent work. Smith (1991), for example, in case studies of ninth-grade readers, found that they were more engaged in story-driven and association-driven responses than in point-driven responses, whereas Hancock (1993) in a case study of 10 sixth-grade readers found that each exhibited a unique response profile, and Rogers (1991), in a study of students' interpretive processes, found that students could process texts at an interpretive level but that their interpretations were largely textual. In larger and longer studies, Vine and Faust (1993) and Sullivan (1995) found comparably wide amounts of variation in students' responses, although Sullivan, with a significantly larger group, was able to identify several essential elements characterizing adolescents' aesthetic engagement with literature.

Perhaps one of the most interesting and provocative lines of research on the role of the reader in literary response is that which focuses on gender. Building on theoretical work of feminist critics (e.g., Christian-Smith, 1993; Fetterley, 1977; Millet, 1970), empirical work examined how the social, economic, and political position of women readers has influenced how and what and why they read. Janice Radway (1984), for instance, found in her study of women who read a great deal of romance fiction that the plot of the romance, in which the heroine transforms the usually distant and dangerous male hero into a loving companion, reinforced the women readers' role as wives and mothers. Flynn (1986) found that males and females differed in their characteristic responses, with males attempting to dominate the text or distance themselves from it, whereas women readers were able to maintain a more balanced approach. Hansen (1986) found that male readers responded more to the formal elements in poems about violence, and females attended more to the poems' messages.

Not only ways of reading, but kind and amount of reading vary with gender as well. Johnson, Peer, and Baldwin (1984), for instance, found in a study of young readers' reading preferences that the importance of male protagonists decreases for males and increases for females, and Moffitt and Wartella (1992) found in a survey of leisure reading among adolescents that 85% of females reported reading for pleasure but only 65% of males did so.

Such gender-based differences in reading practices have led some educators (e.g., Cherland, 1994; Simpson, 1996) to observe a "sexual division of literacy" (Luke, 1994)—a division enforced, directly and indirectly, both by the marketing practices of publishers and by the cultural conventions of schooling. In this view, females are more amply and visibly rewarded for becoming strong readers of fiction, with its emphasis on personal feelings and relationships, whereas males move more flexibly among a range of informational texts, with their emphasis on facts and ideas. As Simpson (1996) and Luke (1994) argued, it is familiarity and skill with informational, nonliterary texts (not familiarity and skill with literature) that lead most directly to educational success and economic power—especially as students move into the argumentative discourses of the academy. The study of readers' responses to literature, in other words, leads almost inevitably beyond a focus on individual readers and individual texts to an examination of the cultural contexts in which reading takes place.

Context

Empirical research that explores the contexts in which readers' responses take shape often builds on two sets of related assumptions. First, the research assumes that the conventions of schooling have an enormous influence on the kinds of literary response that students will come to see as appropriate and even natural. These conventions specify and privilege particular ways of talking (e.g., Cazden, 1988; Mehan, 1979) and writing (Applebee, 1981, 1984), and almost always include the demand for evaluation of particular students' performance (Purves, 1981). Schools are a primary vehicle for the introduction of a culture's literature to students (Applebee, 1973; Scholes & Kellog, 1968), and thus occupy a powerful position in introducing a culture's preferred modes of literary response (Purves, 1973). The second set of assumptions, somewhat broader than the first, and drawn from well-developed social-cultural theory (e.g., Vygotsky, 1978; Wertsch, 1991), holds that individual responses to literature will always be influenced by the norms, values, and preoccupations of a reader's cultural context, that these are internalized by readers and become the intellectual tools with which responses are built. A reader's culture, in other words, is both outside and, in some ways, inside the reader, and thus constitutes the material of which responses themselves are made.

One line of research in this area has examined what teachers believe about appropriate forms of literary response, how they themselves respond, and how those beliefs are translated into classroom practice. Grossman (1991) for instance, building on her earlier study of teaching practice and teacher education (1990), found in a case study that a teacher who was strongly text oriented planned her teaching around close textual analysis, whereas a teacher with a strong reader-response orientation planned her lessons around the evocation of students' various literary responses. In a related study, Zancanella (1991) found that teachers largely shared a personal approach in their own reading of literature, but that many returned to a "school approach" when they entered the classroom, emphasizing, like Grossman's text-oriented teacher, close reading, the identification of literary terms, and the analysis of themes and images. Comparable results were found in a survey study conducted by Protherough and Atkinson (1992) in England and Wales and by Clift (1987, 1991) in studies of beginning teachers of English. Such patterns seem particularly resistant to change, although Scharer (1992), in a study of elementary teachers moving toward literature-based reading instruction, found that teachers could be persuaded to allow more student choice of books and more use of informal assessment in literature instruction. And Wedman and Moutray (1991) found that preservice teachers' questioning practices could be influenced by training and practice.

Another line of research examining the role of context in shaping response has more closely studied the literature curriculum in schools and the classroom practices that enact it. Recent national surveys of frequently taught books (Applebee, 1993; Applebee & Purves, 1992), for instance, suggested that the standard literature curriculum remains extraordinarily stable, with *Romeo & Juliet*, *Julius Caesar*, *The Great Gatsby*, and *To Kill a Mockingbird* maintaining a privileged position among the books assigned in secondary schools, even amid widespread shifts in literary theory and widely heard calls for the inclusion of more contemporary, multicultural literature (e.g., Bishop, 1993; Gates, 1992). At the elementary level, however, more literature and more different kinds of literature have begun to appear in classrooms, where teachers are sometimes blending work in basal readers with literature trade books (Hoffman, Roser, & Battle, 1993).

Studies of classroom practice in the teaching of literature have focused on a fairly wide range of issues, from the teaching of irony (Smith, 1989), to the role of writing in students' understanding of literature (Marshall, 1987), to the role of nonverbal sign systems in helping readers formulate responses (Whiten, 1996). Dressel (1990) found that stories written by children who had heard high-quality literature were scored higher than those written by children who had heard lower quality literature. Lee (1993), in a study that encouraged African American students to draw on their knowledge about the discourse of "signifying," found that students who had been given the opportunity to reflect on the meaning of signifying scripts made gains in their understanding of literacy texts. Wiseman and Many (1992) found that efferent teaching led college students to focus on the shared significance of literary works within their community whereas aesthetic teaching encouraged students to consider the work's personal significance. Gerla (1996), in a study of at-risk students, found that 16-year-olds moved from almost total avoidance of literature to more active engagement through an immersion program of reading and writing. And Wilhelm (1997), also working with at-risk students, found that dramatic and artistic interventions could powerfully affect the level of students' engagement with literature and the quality and range of their responses.

At the same time, Peter Smagorinsky, in an ongoing series of studies (e.g., Smagorinsky, 1997; Smagorinsky & Coppock, 1995; Smagorinsky & O'Donnell-Allen, 1998), explored how different cultural tools (drawing, dance, drama) provide a medium for expressing response to literature while at the same time providing a medium for reflection about the response. Smagorinsky found that different response media evoke different kinds of insight and different levels of understanding (Smagorinsky & O'Donnell-Allen, 1998).

That such classroom studies, useful though they are, are so widely dispersed in topic and approach supports Applebee's contention (1996) that the field of literacy education lacks a powerful and coherent framework that would structure teachers' work and make visible the connections among its various parts. Some categories of research into classroom practice have achieved a kind of critical mass, however, and among these are studies that examine classroom discourse about literature.

Building on earlier work that explored the more general conventions of classroom talk (e.g., Barnes, 1969; Sinclair & Coulthard, 1975), research in this area has focused on the patterns of talk that characterize life in English classrooms and has examined the results of those patterns on students' responses and understanding of the literature they are asked to read. In a study of elementary teachers, for instance, Scharer and Peters (1996) found that teachers were aware of the importance of discussions for their students as readers, but such awareness was insufficient for teachers to alter their practice over time. Marshall et al. (1995) found comparable patterns in their studies of secondary teachers where teachers articulated one set of beliefs about the classroom talk they valued, but were often constrained in their ability to enact those beliefs and usually orchestrated discussions that looked much different from those they themselves hoped for. In a study of more and less able sixth graders, Wollman-Bonilla (1994) found that the more able readers constructed a conversation in which group members actively participated, whereas the less able students constructed a more teacher-dominated activity in which there was little voluntary participation. Eeds and Wells (1989), on the other hand, found that students of mixed ability who chose their books were capable in discussion of sharing personal stories inspired by the reading and valuing and evaluating the text as literature.

Perhaps the largest and most ambitious series of studies of literature discussions have been those undertaken by Nystrand and Gamoran (1991, 1997). In their research on many different classroom discussions, the researchers identified substantive engagement as including (a) authentic, open-ended questions (to which there is no predetermined answer); (b) the use of "uptake"—teachers' response to student contributions that incorporate the students' words and ideas; and (c) teacher evaluations that not only comment favorably on students' responses but also use those responses as the occasion to move the discussion forward. As might be expected, such substantive engagement was somewhat rare in most discussions of literature, but where it was found it was associated with significantly higher achievement in written assessments.

Very different patterns of talk characterized discussions of literature outside of school. In studies of adult-book clubs, for instance, Smith (1995, 1996) found that participants in the clubs were more likely than students in classrooms to relate personal experiences, talk about important ethical issues, and share their experience of reading. They felt free to offer tentative ideas and to disagree with one another—all of which, perhaps ironically, brought them closer together. Literature in these clubs serves a social as much as an educational agenda: It is the occasion for bringing people together for thoughtful talk.

Nystrand and Gamoran, especially in their most recent work (1997), drew quite explicitly on sociocultural perspectives to explain their interest in readers as members of groups—groups that have enormous influence on how and when and why individual readers respond as they do. It is this explicit interest in situated reading, in seeing the reader as always contextualized within particular cultural frameworks, that characterizes perhaps the most promising line of empirical work on response to literature. Some of this work has examined life in classrooms, not with an eye to student achievement or exemplary teaching practice, but to the cultural patterns that are taken for granted there. In a seminal study of intertextuality in a first-grade classroom, for instance, Bloome and Egan-Robertson (1993) argued that the most appropriate unit of analysis in the study of reading is not the individual, but the "interaction of a group of people"—"people," they go on, "are the context for each other" (p. 309). Responses are made by people, but always by people in particular circumstances that are governed by rules about linguistic register, about sequences of speaker turns, and about the coherence that must be maintained with other speakers' interests. In a related study that draws on performance theory (e.g., Bauman, 1977; Bauman & Briggs, 1990; Goffman, 1981) as a lens, Lewis (1997) explored the positions that students assumed during discussions—positions that were themselves the result of social and interpretive expectations within the classroom and that shifted as students moved from peer-led to teacher-led discussions. And Finders (1997), in her study of the "underground literacies" of adolescent girls, traced the ways in which the cultural expectations surrounding age, gender, and social class shape the kinds of reading and writing students do inside and outside of classrooms. As Finders argued, to say that students are freely choosing what to read and how to respond, even in the absence of teachers, is to underconceptualize the complexity of literacy as a social practice and to underestimate the power of cultural norms in shaping the kinds of responses that we regularly make to literature.

CONCLUSION

The three traditions of thought about response to literature—the political, the critical, the empirical—have separately made significant contributions to our understanding of how and why readers read as they do. Drawing on different assumptions, asking different questions, and citing different sources of authority, these traditions have sustained different kinds of scholarly conversations over time, and only rarely has one conversation been interrupted by the concerns of another.

But that situation seems to be changing rapidly. As work in the empirical tradition, for instance, concerns itself increasingly with the cultural contexts in which reading takes place (how is reading valued in particular situations? who has power to say how it will be valued?), it will need to address the long-standing concerns of the political tradition. And as the discussions within the political tradition become increasingly practical (what should students read? what evidence do we have about the effects of reading literature?), they will need to draw on the kinds of evidence that research in the empirical tradition can provide.

New research that finds a way to blend the three traditions can address a range of unanswered questions. These include:

1. What are the most common classroom practices in the teaching of literature at the university level? What texts are most often taught there? What purposes shape the teachers' instruction? Although we have numerous studies of literature teaching in secondary schools (e.g., Applebee, 1993), we have virtually no empirical studies of literature teaching at the postsecondary level (Marshall, in press). The absence of empirical work in this area is ironic because studies of teachers' sources of knowledge (e.g., Grossman, 1990) and years of anecdotal teacher reports suggest that the literature instruction teachers receive in college—the texts that are taught, the discussions that are held, the writing that is assigned—profoundly affects the instruction they provide when they begin teaching. Literature teaching at the university level probably does more to shape literature teaching in secondary settings than any other single influence, and yet we have had virtually no systematic studies of how literature teaching at the university proceeds.

2. What should be the relationship between the study of literature at the university level and the study of literature in K–12 settings? At least since the report of the Committee of Ten in 1892 (Marshall & Smith, 1997), literature instruction at the secondary level has been defined, in part, by the goal of preparing students for university-level instruction. And yet new developments in the critical tradition at the university level (e.g., cultural studies, deconstruction, new historicism) raise the question of whether secondary schools, given their more pressing agendas, can or should take preparation for such critical practices as a legitimate goal. As the university curriculum in literature becomes ever more specialized (Graff, 1987; Shumway, 1994), it becomes possible to ask if the university and the secondary schools are increasingly divided in their reasons for teaching literature and in the classroom practices that might follow from those reasons.

3 What classroom practices should follow from new developments in literary theory? For almost 50 years, there has been fairly widespread agreement that the teaching of literature should include practice in the close reading of texts, amplified by large-group discussions and formally argued writing. But such practices were deeply associated with the formalist, new critical scholarship that has now been all but abandoned at the university. With the advent of new literary theory, perhaps especially reader response theory, it seems important to design new pedagogies that more clearly reflect the theoretical frames and instructional purposes guiding the teaching of literature.

4. What pedagogical implications should follow from the development of multicultural curricula in secondary schools and universities? If texts are selected for reading in class because they are in some way relevant to students' cultural situation or current interests, then it makes sense to incorporate a range of reader response approaches in our classroom (e.g., How are these characters or situations like ones you have known? How can you use what you already know to make sense of the world of the text?). But if texts are selected for instruction precisely because they may represent worlds, cultures, values, and beliefs that are significantly different from what students already know (as in much recent African American, Caribbean, Latino/a, and Asian American literature), then new pedagogies seem called for. Teachers and students, in such a context, cannot rely on a process of identification with characters or situations (these characters are *like* me and therefore I can identify with them). Instead, students must work through a more difficult and possibly more austere relationship with the text—and this will require a very different kind of classroom practice.

None of these questions can be fully addressed without reference to the three traditions that I have attempted to describe in this chapter. Empirical studies of classroom practice at the university level, for instance, will be shaped by the participants' sense of what literature is for (from the political tradition) and by their beliefs about how it can be most productively read (from the critical tradition). Likewise, discussions of relationships between schools and universities or between literary theory and classroom practice will have to draw from empirical data about what actually occurs in the literature classroom as well as from informed exploration of why literature is important to study and how students make sense of what they read. The three traditions, while driven by different purposes, working from different histories, and addressing different audiences, can, when taken together, provide a powerful base from which to begin new, even more challenging research initiatives in the reading and teaching of literature.

ACKNOWLEDGMENTS

I thank Deborah Appleman, Pamela Grossman, Michael Smith, and Peter Smagorinsky for their very thoughtful and helpful responses to an earlier version of this chapter.

REFERENCES

Applebee, A. N. (1973). *Tradition and reform in the teaching of English.* Urbana, IL: National Council of Teachers of English.

Applebee, A. N. (1977). The elements of response to a literary work: What have we learned? *Research in the Teaching of English, 11*, 255–71.

Applebee, A. N. (1978). *The child's concept of story.* Chicago: University of Chicago Press.

Applebee, A. N. (1981). *Writing in the secondary school.* Urbana, IL: National Council of Teachers of English.

Applebee, A. N. (1984). *Contexts for learning to write.* Norwood, NJ: Ablex.

Applebee, A. N. (1993). *Literature in the secondary school: Studies of curriculum and instruction in the United States* (NCTE Research Rep. No. 25). Urbana, IL: National Council of Teachers of English.

Applebee, A. N. (1996). *Curriculum as conversation.* Chicago: University of Chicago Press.

Applebee, A., Langer, J., & Mullis, I. V. (1987). *Learning to be literate in America: Reading, writing, and reasoning.* National Assessment of Educational Progress. Princeton, NJ: Educational Testing Service.

Applebee, A. N., & Purves, A. C. (1992). Literature and the English language arts. In P. W. Jackson (Ed.), *Handbook of research on curriculum* (pp. –). New York: Macmillan.

Arnold, M. (1961). *Poetry and criticism of Matthew Arnold.* Boston: Houghton Mifflin.

Athanases, S. (1996). A gay-themed lesson in an ethnic literature curriculum: Tenth-graders' responses to "Dear Anita." *Harvard Educational Review, 66,* 231–255.

Athanases, S. Z., & Heath, S. G. (1995). Ethnography in the study of the teaching and learning of English. *Research in the Teaching of English, 29,* 287.

Bakhtin, M. (1981). *The dialogic imagination.* Austin: University of Texas Press.

Barnes, D. (1976). *From communication to curriculum.* Middlesex, England: Penguin Books.

Bauman, R. (1977). *Verbal art as performance.* Prospect Heights, IL: Waveland Press.

Bauman, R., & Briggs, C. (1990). Poetics and performance as critical perspectives on language and social life. *Annual Review of Anthropology, 19,* 59–88.

Beach, R. (1993). *A teacher's introduction to reader response theories.* Urbana, IL: National Council of Teachers of English.

Beach, R. (1997). Students' resistance to engagement with multicultural literature. In T. Rogers & A. Soter (Eds.), *Reading across cultures.* New York: Teachers College Press.

Beach, R., & Hynds, S. (1991). Research on response to literature. In R. Barr, M. L. Kamil, P. Mosenthal, & P. D. Pearson (Eds.), *Handbook of reading research* (Vol. II, pp. 453–489). New York: Longman.

Beach, R., & Wendler, L. (1987). Developmental differences in response to a story. *Research in the Teaching of English, 21,* 286–297.

Bennett, W. (1993). *The book of virtues.* New York: Simon & Schuster.

Birkerts, S. (1994). *The Gutenberg elegies.* Boston: Faber & Faber.

Bishop, R. S. (1987). Extending multicultural understanding through children's books. In B. E. Cullinan (Ed.), *Children's literature in the reading program* (p. 60–67). Newark, DE: International Reading Association.

Bishop, R. S. (1993). Multicultural literature for children: Making informed choices. In V. Harris (Ed.), *Teaching multicultural literature in grades K–8.* Norwood, NJ: Ablex.

Bleich, D. (1975). *Readings and feelings: An introduction to subjective criticism.* Urbana, IL: National Council of Teachers of English.

Bleich, D. (1978). *Subjective criticism.* Baltimore, MD: Johns Hopkins University Press.

Bleich, D. (1988). *The double perspective: Language, literacy, and social relations.* New York: Oxford University Press.

Bloom, H. (1994). *The Western canon.* New York: Harcourt, Brace.

Bloome, D., & Egan-Robertson, A. (1993). The social construction of intertextuality in classroom reading and writing lessons. *Reading Research Quarterly, 28,* 305–333.

Cazden, C. (1988). *Classroom discourse: The language of teaching and learning.* Portsmouth, NH: Heinemann.

Cherland, M. R. (1994). *Private practices: Girls reading fiction and constructing identity.* London: Taylor & Francis.

Christian-Smith, L. (1993). *Texts of desire: Essays on fiction, femininity, and schooling.* London: Falmer Press.

Clifford, J. (Ed.). (1991). *The experience of reading: Louise Rosenblatt and reader response theory.* Portsmouth, NH: Heinemann.

Clift, R. T. (1987). English teacher or English major: Epistemological differences in the teaching of English. *English Education, 19,* 229–236.

Clift, R. T. (1991). Learning to teach English-maybe: A study of knowledge development. *Journal of Teacher Education, 42,* 357–372.

Coles, R. (1989). *The call of stories.* Boston: Houghton Mifflin

Cooper, C. (1976). Empirical studies of response to literature. *Journal of Aesthetic Education, 10,* 77–93.

Cooper, C. R. (Ed.). (1985). *Researching response to literature and the teaching of literature.* Norwood, NJ: Ablex.

Culler, J. (1975). *Structuralist poetics: Structuralism, linguistics, and the study of literature.* London: Routledge and Kegan Paul.

Culler, J. (1980). Literary competence. In J. Tompkins (Ed.), *Reader-response criticism* (p. 101–117). Baltimore, MD: Johns Hopkins University Press.

Culliman, R., Galda, L., & Harwood, K. (1983). The readers and the story: Comprehension and response. *Journal of Research and Development in Education, 16*(3), 29–38.

Davidson, C. (Ed.). (1989). *Reading in America.* Baltimore, MD: Johns Hopkins University Press.

DeMaria, R. (1997). *Samuel Johnson and the life of reading.* Baltimore, MD: Johns Hopkins University Press.

Denby, D. (1996). *Great books.* New York: Simon & Schuster.

Dillon, C. (1982). Styles of reading. *Poetics Today, 5,* 77–88.

Dressel, J. H. (1990). The effects of listening to and discussing different qualities of children's literature on the narrative writing of fifth-graders. *Research in the Teaching of English, 24,* 397–414.

D'Souza, D. (1991). *Illiberal education: The politics of race and sex on campus.* New York: The Free Press.

Eagleton, T. (1983). *Literary theory.* Minneapolis: University of Minnesota Press.

Ebersole, P., & DeVogler-Ebersole, K. (1984). Depth of meaning in life and literary preferences. *Psychology, 22,* 28–30.

Eeds, M. & Wells, D. (1989). Grand conversations: An exploration of meaning construction in literature study groups. *Research in the Teaching of English, 23,* 4–29.

Eisenstein, E. (1980). *The printing press as an agent of change.* Cambridge: Cambridge University Press.

Ellis, J. (1997). *Literature lost.* New Haven, CT: Yale University Press.

Fetterley, J. (1978). *The resisting reader: A feminist approach to American fiction.* Bloomington, IN: Indiana University Press.

Fiedler, L. (1982). *What was literature?* New York: Simon & Schuster.

Finders, M. (1997). *Just girls.* New York: Teachers College Press.

Fish, S. (1980). *Is there a text in this class? The authority of interpretive communities.* Cambridge: Cambridge University Press.

Fish, S. (1995). *Professional correctness: Literary studies and political change.* Oxford: Oxford University Press.

Flynn, E. (1986). Gender and reading. In E. Flynn & P. Schweichart (Eds.), *Gender and reading* (p. 267–289). Baltimore, MD: Johns Hopkins University Press.

Fox, D. L. (1995). From English major to English teacher: Two case studies. *English Journal, 84*(2), 17–25.

Freund, E. (1987). *The return of the reader: Reader response criticism.* London: Meuthen.

Garrison, B. M., & Hynds, S. (1991). Evocation and reflection in the reading transaction: A comparison of proficient and less proficient readers. *Journal of Reading Behavior, 23,* 259–280.

Gates, H. L. (1992). *Loose canons.* New York: Oxford University Press.

Gee, J. P. (1988). The legacies of literacy: From Plato to Freire through Harvey Graff. *Harvard Educational Review, 58,* 195–212.

Gerla, J. P. (1996). Response-based instruction: At-risk students engaging in literature. *Reading and Writing Quarterly, 12,* 149–169.

Graff, G. (1987). *Professing literature.* Chicago: University of Chicago Press.

Graff, G. (1992). *Beyond the culture wars: How teaching the conflicts can revitalize American education.* New York: W. W. Norton.

Graff, H. (1982). The legacies of literacy. *Journal of Communication, 32,* 12–26.

Grossman, P. L. (1990). *The making of a teacher: Teacher knowledge and teacher education.* New York: Teachers College Press.

Grossman, P. L. (1991). What are we talking about anyhow? Subject matter knowledge of secondary English teachers. In J. Brophy (Ed.), *Advances in research on teaching, vol. 2: Subject matter knowledge* (pp. –). Greenwich, CT: JAI Press.

Guillory, J. (1992). *Cultural capital: The problem of literary canon formation.* Chicago: University of Chicago Press.

Hancock, M. R. (1993). Exploring the meaning-making process through the context of literature response journals: A case study investigation. *Research in the Teaching of English, 27,* 335–368.

Hansen, E. (1986). *Emotional processes engendered by poetry and prose reading.* Stockholm: Almquist & Wiksell.

Hartman, D. K. (1995). 8 Readers reading: The intertextual links of proficient readers reading multiple passages. *Reading Research Quarterly, 30,* 220–261.

Hillocks, G., & Ludlow, L. (1984). A taxonomy of skills in reading and interpreting fiction. *American Educational Research Journal, 21,* 7–24.

Hines, M. B. (1993). Multiplicity and difference in literary inquiry: Toward a conceptual framework for reader-centered cultural criticism. In T. Rogers & A. Soter (Eds.), *Reading across cultures.* New York: Teachers College Press.

Hirsch, E. D. (1987). *Cultural literacy: What every American needs to know.* Boston: Houghton Mifflin.

Hoffman, J. V., Roser, N. L., & Battle, J. (1993). Reading aloud in classrooms: From the modal to a "model." *The Reading Teacher, 46,* 496–505.

Holland, N. (1975). *Five readers reading.* New Haven, CT: Yale University Press.

Hughes, R. (1993). *Culture of complaint.* New York: Warner Books.

Hunt, R., & Vipond, D. (1985). Crash-testing a transactional model of literary response. *Reader, 14,* 23–39.

Hunt, R., & Vipond, D. (1986). Evaluations in literary reading. *Text, 6,* 53–71.

Hynds, S., & Appleman, D. (1997). Walking our talk: Between response and responsibility in the literature classroom. *English Education, 29,* 272–297.

Iser, W. (1978). *The act of reading: A theory of aesthetic response.* Baltimore, MD: Johns Hopkins University Press.

Johnson, D., Peer, G., & Baldwin, R. S. (1984). Protagonist preferences among juvenile and adolescent readers. *Journal of Educational Research, 77,* 147–150.

Jones, H. J., Coombs, W. T., & McKenney, C. W. (1994). A themed literature unit versus a textbook: A comparison of the effects on content acquisition and attitudes in elementary social studies. *Reading Research and Instruction, 34,* 85–96.

Kaestle, C. F. (1991). *Literacy in the United States.* New Haven, CT: Yale University Press.

Kernan, A. (1990). *The death of literature.* New Haven, CT: Yale University Press.

Langer, J. A. (1995). *Envisioning literature: Literary understanding and literature instruction.* New York: Teachers College Press.

Lee, C. D. (1993). *Signifying as a scaffold for literary interpretation: The pedagogical implications of an African-American discourse genre* (NCTE Research Rep. No. 26). Urbana, IL: National Council of Teachers of English.

Lehr, S. (1988). The child's developing sense of theme as a response to literature. *Reading Research Quarterly, 23,* 337–357.

Levine, L. (1988). *Highbrow/lowbrow: The emergence of cultural hierarchy in America.* Cambridge, MA: Harvard University Press.

Lewis, C. (1997). The social drama of literature discussions in 5th/6th grade classroom. *Research in the Teaching of English, 31*(2), 163–204.

Licheter, J. H., & Johnson, D. (1973). Changes in attitude toward Negroes by White elementary students after the use of multiethnic readers. *Journal of Educational Research, 65,* 295–299.

Luke, A. (1994). On reading and the sexual division of literacy. *Journal of Curriculum Studies, 26*, 361–381.

Mailloux, S. (1982). *Interpretive conventions: The reader in the study of American fiction*. Ithaca, NY: Cornell University Press.

Manguel, A. (1996). *A history of reading*. New York: Viking Press.

Many, J. E. (1991). The effects of stance and age-level on children's literary responses. *Journal of Reading Behavior, 23*, 61–85.

Many, J. E. & Wiseman, D. L. (1992). The effect of teaching approach on third grade students' response to literature. *Journal of Reading Behavior, 24*, 265–287.

Marshall, J. (1987). The effects of writing on students understanding of literary texts. *Research in the Teaching of English, 21*, 30–63.

Marshall, J. (in press). Closely reading ourselves: Teaching English and the education of teachers. In P. Franklin (Ed.), *Preparing a nation's teachers: Models for English and foreign language*. New York: Modern Language Association.

Marshall, J., & Smith, J. (1997). Teaching as we're taught: The role of universities in the education of English teachers. *English Education, 29*, 246–267.

Marshall, J. D., Smagorinsky, P., & Smith, M. W. (1995). *The language of interpretation: Patterns of discourse in discussions of literature* (NCTE Research Rep. No. 27). Urbana, IL: National Council of Teachers of English.

Martinez, M. G., & Roser, N. L. (1991). Children's responses to literature. In J. Flood, J. M. Jensen, D. Lapp, & J. R. Squire (Eds.), *Handbook of research on teaching the English language arts* (pp. 643–654). New York: Macmillan.

McCormick, K. (1994). *The culture of reading and the teaching of English*. Manchester: Manchester University Press.

McLuhan, M. (1962). *Gutenberg galaxy: The making of typographic man*. Toronto: University of Toronto Press.

Mehan, H. (1979). *Learning lessons*. Cambridge, MA: Harvard University Press.

Miall, D. S., & Kuiken, D. (1995). Aspects of literary response: A new questionnaire. *Research in the Teaching of English, 29*, 37–58.

Millet, K. (1970). *Sexual politics*. Garden City, NY: Doubleday.

Moffett, J. (1988). *Storm in the mountains*. Carbondale, IL: Southern Illinois University Press.

Moffitt, M. A., & Wartella, E. (1992). Youth and reading: A survey of leisure reading pursuits of female and male adolescents. *Reading Research and Instruction, 31*, 1–17.

National Assessment of Educational Progress (1981). *Reading, thinking, and writing: Results from the 1979–1981 assessment of reading and literature*. Denver: National Assessment of Educational Progress.

Nelson, C. (1997). *Manifesto of a tenured radical*. New York: New York University Press.

Nystrand, M., & Gamoran, A. (1991). Instructional discourse, student engagement, and literature achievement. *Research in the Teaching of English, 25*, 261–290.

Nystrand, M., & Gamoran, A. (1997). *Opening dialogue: Understanding the dynamics of language and learning in the English classroom*. New York: Teachers College Press.

Odell, L., & Cooper, C. (1976). Describing responses to works of fiction. *Research in the Teaching of English, 10*, 203–225.

Ohmann, R. (1976). *English in America*. New York: Oxford University Press.

Olson, D. (1977). From utterance to text. The bias of language in speech and writing. *Harvard Education Review, 47*, 257–281.

Ong, W. J. (1982). *Orality and literacy*. New York: Methuen.

Pennac, D. (1994). *Better than life*. Toronto: Coach House Press.

Peters, W., & Blues, A. (1978). Teacher intellectual disposition as it relates to student openness in written response to literature. *Research in the Teaching of Literature, 12*, 120–136.

Petrosky, A. (1977). Response to literature. *English Journal, 66*, 86–88.

Plato. (1997). *The republic*, 237–238. Indianapolis: Hackett Publishing Company.

Protherough, R., & Atkinson, J. (1992). How English teachers see English teaching. *Research in the Teaching of English, 26*, 385–407.

Probst, R. (1991). Response to literature. In J. Flood, J. M. Jensen, D. Lapp, & J. R. Squire (Eds.), *Handbook of research on teaching the English language arts* (pp. 655–663). New York: Macmillan.

Purves, A. (1973). *Literature education in ten countries: An empirical study*. New York: Wiley Press.

Purves, A. (1981). *Reading and literature: American achievement in international perspective*. Urbana, IL: National Council of Teachers of English.

Purves, A., & Beach, R. (1972). *Literature and the reader: Research on response to literature, reading interests, and the teaching of literature*. Urbana, IL: National Council of Teachers of English.

Purves, A., & Rippere, V. (1968). *Elements of writing about a literary work: A study of response to literature*. Urbana, IL: National Council of Teachers of English.

Rabinowitz, P. (1987). *Before reading*. Ithaca, NY: Cornell University Press.

Rabinowitz, P. (1992). Against close reading. In M. Kecht (Ed.), *Pedagogy is politics. Theory and critical teaching*. Champaign: University of Illinois Press.

Rabinowitz, P., & Smith, M. W. (1998). *Authorizing readers: Resistance and respect in the teaching of literature*. New York: Teachers College Press.

Radway, J. (1984). *Reading the romance: Women, patriarchy, and popular literature*. Chapel Hill, NC: University of North Carolina Press.

Richards, I. A. (1929). *Practical criticism*. New York: Harcourt, Brace.

Rogers, T. (1991). Students as literary critics: The interpretive experiences, beliefs, and processes of ninth-grade students. *Journal of Reading Behavior, 23*, 391–423.

Rogers, T. (1993). No imagined peaceful place: A story of community, texts, and cultural conversations in one urban high school. In T. Rogers & A. Soter (Eds.), *Reading across cultures*. New York: Teachers College Press.

Robert, T., & Soter, A. (1997). *Reading across cultures: Teaching literature in a diverse society*. New York: Teachers College Press.

Rosenblatt, L. (1938). *Literature as exploration*. New York: Modern Language Association.

Rosenblatt, L. (1978). *The reader, the text, the poem*. Carbondale, IL: Southern Illinois University Press.

Rouse, J. (1991). A transactional affair. In J. Clifford (Ed.), *The experience of reading: Louise Rosenblatt and reader response theory* (pp. 197–208). Portsmouth, NH: Heinemann.

Scharer, P. L. (1992). Teachers in transition: An exploration of changes in teachers and classrooms during implementation of literature-based reading instruction. *Research in the Teaching of English, 26*, 408–443.

Scharer, P. L., & Peters, D. (1996). An exploration of literature discussions conducted by two teachers moving toward literature-based instruction. *Reading Research and Instruction, 36*, 33–50.

Schwartz, L. S (1996). *Ruined by reading*. Boston: Beacon Press.

Showalter, E. (1985). *New feminist criticism: Essays on women literature and theory*. New York: Pantheon.

Shumway, D. (1994). *Creating American civilization: A genealogy of American literature as a academic discipline*. Minneapolis: University of Minnesota Press.

Sims, R. (1983). Strong black girls: A ten-year-old responds to fiction about Afro-Americans. *Journal of Research and Development, 16*, 21–28.

Simpson, A. (1996). Fictions and facts: An investigation of the reading practices of girls and boys. *English Education, 28*(4), 268–279.

Sinclair, J., & Coulthard, R. (1975). *Towards an analysis of discourse: The English used by teachers and pupils*. London: Oxford University Press.

Squire, J. (1968). *The responses of adolescents while reading four short stories* (NCTE Research Rep. No. 2). Urbana, IL: National Council of Teachers of English.

Smagorinsky, P. (1997). Artistic composing as representational process. *Journal of Applied Developmental Psychology, 18*, 87–105.

Smagorinsky, P., & Coppock, J. (1994). Cultural tools and the classroom context: A exploration of alternative response to literature. *Written Communication, 11*, 283–310.

Smagorinksy, P., & Coppock, J. (1995). The readers, the text, the context: An exploration of a choreographed response to literature. *Journal of Reading Behavior, 27*, 271–298.

Smagorinsky, P., & O'Donnell-Allen, A. (1998). Reading as mediated and mediating action: Composing meaning for literature through multimedia interpretive texts. *Reading Research Quarterly, 33* .

Smith, M. W. (1989). Teaching the interpretation of irony in poetry. *Research in the Teaching of English, 23*, 254–272.

Smith, M. W. (1991). Constructing meaning from text: An analysis of ninth-grade reading responses. *Journal of Educational Research, 84*, 263–271.

Smith, M. W. (1995). Adult book-club discussions: Toward an understanding of the culture of practice. In J. Marshall, P. Smagorinsky, & M. Smith (Eds.), *The language of interpretation: Patterns of discourse in discussions of literature* (pp. –). Urbana, IL: National Council of Teachers of English.

Smith, M. W. (1996). Conversations about literature outside classrooms: How adults talk about books in their book clubs. *Journal of Adolescent and Adult Literacy, 40*, 180–186.

Sullivan, M. A. (1995). Reader response, contemporary aesthetics, and the adolescent reader. *Journal of Aesthetic Education, 29*. 79–95.

Tompkins, J. (1980). *Reader response criticism*. Baltimore, MD: Johns Hopkins University Press.

Tompkins, J. (1985). *Sensational designs*. New York: Oxford Press.

Travis, M. (1998). *Reading cultures: The construction of readers in the twentieth century*. Carbondale, IL: Southern Illinois University Press.

Trimble, C. (1984). The relationship among fairly tales, ego development, grade level, and sex (Doctoral dissertation, University of Alabama). *Dissertation Abstracts International, 46*, 04A.

Trousdale, A. M. (1990). A submission theology in prize-winning children's books about the black experience in America. *Research in the Teaching of English, 24*, 117–140.

Vine, H., & Faust, M. A. (1993). *Situating reading: Students making meaning of literature*. Urbana, IL: National Council of Teachers of English.

Vipond, D., & Hunt, R. (1984). Point-driven understanding: Pragmatic and cognitive dimensions of literary reading. *Poetics, 13*, 261–277.

Vygotsky, L. (1978). *Mind in society*. Cambridge, MA: Harvard University Press.

Wedman, J. M., & Moutray, C. (1991). The effect of training on the questions preservice teachers ask during literature discussions. *Reading Research and Instruction, 30*, 62–76.

Wertsch, J. (1991). *Voices of the mind: A sociocultural approach to mediated action*. Cambridge, MA: Harvard University Press.

Wham, M. A., Barnhart, J., & Cook, G. (1996). Enhancing multicultural awareness through the storybook reading experience. *Journal of Research and Development in Education, 30*, 1–9.

Whiten, P. E. (1991). Exploring visual response to literature. *Research in the Teaching of English, 30*, 114–140.

Wilhelm, J. D. (1997). *You gotta be the book*. New York: Teachers College Press.

Willinsky, J. (1990). Matthew Arnold's legacy: The powers of literature. *Research in the Teaching of English, 24*, 343–361.

Willinsky, J. (1991). *The triumph of literature: The fate of literacy*. New York: Teachers College Press.

Willinsky, J., & Hunniford, R. M. (1986). Reading the romance younger: The mirrors and fears of preparatory literature. *Reading-Canada-Lecture, 4*, 16–31.

Wiseman, D. C., & Many, J. E. (1992). The effects of aesthetic and efferent teaching approaches on undergraduate students' responses to literature. *Reading Research and Instruction, 31*, 66–83.

Wollman-Bonilla, J. E. (1994). Why don't they "just speak?" Attempting literature discussions with more and less able readers. *Research in the Teaching of English, 28*, 231–258.

Zancanella, D. (1991). Teachers reading/Readers teaching: Five teachers' personal approaches to literature and their teaching of literature. *Research in the Teaching of English, 25*, 5–32.

CHAPTER 24

Engagement and Motivation in Reading

John T. Guthrie
Allan Wigfield
University of Maryland

Within a given school at a given time, some students are intent on reading and writing to understand. They focus on text meaning and avoid distractions. These engaged readers exchange ideas and interpretations of text with peers. Their devotion to reading spans across time, transfers to a variety of genre, and culminates in valued learning outcomes. In contrast, disengaged readers are inactive and inert. They tend to avoid reading and minimize effort. Rarely do they enjoy reading during free time or become absorbed in literature. In this chapter, we discuss work on engaged reading and its consequences, with a particular focus on how children's motivation contributes to engagement. We also discuss how various instructional processes can facilitate reading engagement and motivation.

Researchers have referred to different aspects of engaged reading. In her work on literacy, Au (1997) referred to children's ownership as their sense of self-confidence and command of reading and writing. These are related to engagement. Oldfather and Dahl (1994) and Turner (1995) portrayed students' intrinsic motivation, referring to their enjoyment in reading for its own sake, which is essential to engaged reading. Likewise, Csikszentmihalyi (1991) described engaged reading as a state of total absorption or "flow." Quite often, researchers describe learners as "engaged" based on their on-task behavior, which is also relevant (Berliner & Biddle, 1995; Tobin, 1984).

The viewpoints just discussed focused on certain motivational aspects of engagement. Other authors provide more comprehensive views. Cambourne (1995) referred to engagement in literacy as a merger of multiple qualities. He argued that engagement entails holding a purpose, seeking to understand, believing in one's own capability, and taking responsibility for learning. Guthrie, McGough, Bennett, and Rice (1996) described engaged readers as *motivated* to read for a variety of personal goals, *strategic* in using multiple approaches to comprehend, *knowledgeable* in their construction of new understanding from text, and *socially interactive* in their approach to literacy.

Despite their wide range of terminology, these investigators concur that readers are decision makers whose affects as well as their language and cognition play a role in their reading practices. A point of agreement among the diverse depictions of engaged reading is that the reader has wants and intentions that enable reading processes to occur. That is, a person reads a word or comprehends a text not only because she can do it, but because she is motivated to do it.

As Guthrie et al. (1996) noted, engaged reading is strategic and conceptual as well as motivated and intentional. The cognitive side of engagement emphasizes that effective readers are deliberately making choices within a context and selecting strategies for comprehending text content. For example, Almasi, McKeown, and Beck (1996) illustrated that engaged readers seek conceptual understanding. They question the author and each other in dialogue, collectively constructing a meaning that incorporates information from multiple perspectives of different readers. In these efforts to gain conceptual understanding, engaged readers are strategic. As Duffy et al. (1987) and Pressley, Schuder, Bergman, and El-Dinary (1992) found, readers decide when and how to apply their strategies conditionally (Paris, Wasik, & Turner, 1991). Such strategic reading results in conceptual understanding (Beck, McKeown, Worthy, Sandora, & Kucan, 1996) and advanced knowledge acquisition (Alexander, Jetton, & Kulikowich, 1996). This new knowledge may be used in more extended inquiry into broader literary themes (Harste, 1994) or science topics (Roth & Bowen, 1995). As Guthrie, Van Meter, Hancock, McCann, Anderson, and Alao (1998) suggested, "engagement in reading refers to the motivated use of strategies to gain conceptual knowledge during reading" (p. 261). In addition, within many classrooms, engaged readers are interacting with peers socially to construct meanings of literary works (Almasi, 1995) and participate in communities of discourse as a natural part of schooling (Gee & Green, 1998). Although the cognitive and social dimensions of engaged reading are distinguishable from the motivational dimension, engagement cannot occur without all three. We therefore propose that *engaged readers in the classroom or elsewhere coordinate their strategies and knowledge (cognition) within a community of literacy (social) in order to fulfill their personal goals, desires, and intentions (motivation).*

ENGAGED READING IS RELATED TO ACHIEVEMENT

Engaged reading is strongly associated with reading achievement. Students who read actively and frequently improve their comprehension of text as a consequence (Cipielewski & Stanovich, 1992). However, it is also likely that students who are capable of understanding a wide range of texts choose to read independently for their own enjoyment. This connection between engagement and achievement, measured as the ability to understand narrative and expository text, was shown in a national sample of students (Campbell, Voelkl, & Donahue, 1997). At all three ages studied (9, 13, and 17 years), the more highly engaged readers showed higher achievement than the less engaged readers. The cross age comparisons were remarkable. The 13-year-old students with higher reading engagement were higher in achievement than the 17-year-old students who were less reading engaged. In other words, middle school students who were engaged in reading achieved as highly as students who were less engaged in reading but had 4 more years of schooling. As students become engaged readers, they provide themselves with self-generated learning opportunities that are equivalent to several years of education.

Engagement in reading may substantially compensate for low family income and educational background. In the same national data, engaged readers from low income/education families were higher in achievement than less engaged readers from high income/education backgrounds. Of course, the highest achievement in text comprehension was found among students who were both more engaged and enjoyed a family background with economic and educational opportunity. Further, although girls exceed boys in overall reading achievement, boys who were more engaged in reading had substantially higher text comprehension than girls who were less engaged readers (Guthrie & Schafer, 1998). In sum, engaged readers can overcome obstacles to achievement, and they become agents of their own reading growth.

The pattern of engagement and achievement in the previous paragraph is consistent with the Matthew effect, in which the high achievers improve more rapidly than low achievers over time in school (Stanovich, 1986). As relatively good readers tend to read more, they increase their competence, which increases their reading ability. We suggest that motivation mediates this Matthew effect. That is, increasing competence is motivating, and increasing motivation leads to more reading (Guthrie, Wigfield, Metsala, & Cox, 1999). Motivation is the link between frequent reading and reading achievement. This link sustains the upward (and downward) spiral of achievement (Guthrie, Wigfield et al., 1999). In this perspective, motivation is the foundational process for reading engagement and is a major contributor, when things go awry, to disengagement from reading. Consequently, the remainder of this chapter addresses motivation for reading.

MOTIVATION, RELATED CONSTRUCTS, AND HISTORICAL PERSPECTIVE

Current motivation theorists focus on individuals' goals, values, and beliefs (Deci & Ryan, 1992; Eccles, Wigfield, & Schiefele, 1998; Schunk & Zimmerman, 1997; Wigfield, 1997). Consistent with these theories, we suggest that *reading motivation is the individual's personal goals, values, and beliefs with regard to the topics, processes, and outcomes of reading.* Under this rubric, we include motivational goals, intrinsic motivation, extrinsic motivation, self-efficacy, and social motivation, which we discuss more fully later. These aspects of motivation are distinct from several affective and belief attributes of students studied by reading researchers. First, motivation is distinct from attitude (McKenna, Kear, & Ellsworth, 1995), which refers to liking for a task. For instance, students may report high self-efficacy without liking to read, as witnessed by students who reported that they are good at doing it, but do not like to read (Oldfather & McLaughlin, 1993). Motivation is also distinct from interest. In the research literature, interest is usually associated with a topic, such as outer space, dinosaurs, or Civil War history (Alexander et al., 1996; Schiefele, 1996; Schraw, 1997). In comparison, motivational attributes are more general. The intrinsically motivated reader is disposed to read a wide range of topics and genres. Third, readers' beliefs may also be distinguished from their motivation. Schraw and Bruning (1999) showed that readers with transactional beliefs expect that their construction of meaning is related to their own knowledge, interests, and experiences as well as the information in a text. Although these beliefs are correlated with intrinsic motivation (e.g., learning goals), these beliefs are distinct from the motivations themselves (Schraw & Bruning, 1999). Thus, the motivation constructs we are discussing can be distinguished from other affectively oriented constructs in the reading literature.

From a historical perspective, our framework on reading motivation can be related to Deweyan principles of inquiry. Dewey's emphasis on active inquiry is highly compatible with our engagement orientation (see Mosenthal, 1999). In Dewey's view the learner is problem centered, being guided and motivated by a question or interest of personal significance. Collective thinking about a given topic in history or science is provoked by doubt, which leads to new learning and reflection. Dewey assumed that authentic learning depended on intrinsic motivation, self-efficacy, and socially constructed meaning, although he did not use this language or collect any data to investigate his assumptions. William S. Gray (Gray & Monroe, 1929) investigated reading motivation more directly than Dewey. He explored the reading interests and purposes of adult readers in many walks of life. Through extensive interviewing, he described a spectrum of reading purposes, concluding that the wider the range and the higher the intensity of these reading purposes, the more dedicated was the individual to societal causes and self-improvement.

Reading motivation has received some attention from current reading researchers. Wigfield and Asher (1984) contributed a chapter on motivation to the first edition of this *Handbook*. They reviewed research on theories of achievement motivation and the development of attitudes and interest in reading, and noted that these areas were disparate. They called for an integration of these research areas, so that models of reading motivation could be formulated. Athey (1985) and Matthewson (1991) presented theoretical frameworks for studying affective variables related to reading, and discussed how these variables have motivational properties. Until the 1990s, sustained research on reading motivation has been relatively rare. However, in 1992 the National Reading Research Center (NRRC) was funded partly to investigate engagement and motivation. Investigators attempted to build an initial bridge between reading as a language and cognitive endeavor and reading as a motivated act expressive of personal values and beliefs (Guthrie & Alvermann, 1999). We turn next to a review of research on reading motivation.

THE NATURE OF READING MOTIVATION

In discussing motivation we begin with the point that motivation is crucial for the activation of behavior, and then discuss current views on the multifaceted nature of motivation in general and reading motivation in particular. We then discuss how motivation guides cognitive activity, and consider how children's motivation changes across the school years.

Motivation as Activating

Motivation is crucial to engagement because motivation is what activates behavior. A less motivated reader spends less time reading, exerts lower cognitive effort, and is less dedicated to full comprehension than a more highly motivated reader. The ways in which theorists have conceptualized this activation have changed over the years, however. In early conceptualizations, motivation was characterized as a unidimensional quality of which more is better and less is worse for learning and performing school tasks (see Weiner, 1992). In this view, motivation is a temporary, task-specific source of energy for cognitive and language activity, including reading. However, in the past 30 years, researchers have discovered that motivation is multifaceted. In this view, all aspects of motivation are activating, but within an individual some aspects of motivation will be stronger than others.

Motivation as Multifaceted

To investigate a diverse array of motivations for reading, but not knowing which particular forms would emerge, we conducted interviews and focus groups with elementary school students (Guthrie, Van Meter et al., 1996). We drew on these interviews and on current motivation theory to form questionnaires assessing goals for reading, intrinsic motivation and extrinsic reading motivation, self-efficacy, and social motivation. Subsequent work showed that these aspects of motivation appeared in different age groups and populations (Baker & Wigfield, in press; Wigfield & Guthrie, 1997). We next define these aspects more fully.

Goals for reading concern the purposes individuals have for engaging in activities such as reading (Ames, 1992; Blumenfeld, 1992). In the motivation literature, researchers have focused primarily on two broad goal orientations individuals have for learning. Individuals with a learning goal orientation seek to improve their skills and accept new challenges in activities such as reading (Ames, 1992; Ames & Archer, 1988; Dweck & Leggett, 1988; Nicholls, 1979; Nicholls, Cheung, Lauer, & Patashnick, 1989). Some researchers use the phrase *mastery orientation* almost synonymously with learning goal orientation. Both phrases refer to student dedication to content understanding and learning flexible skills, not to a behaviorist mastery learning paradigm.

Individuals with a performance or ego orientation attempt to outperform others and maximize favorable evaluations of their ability (see Thorkildsen & Nicholls, 1998, for further discussion of these goal orientations, and Skaalvik, 1997, for discussion of two kinds of performance goal orientations). Each goal orientation has implications for motivation, and most motivation researchers believe that the learning goal orientation is more likely to foster long-term engagement and learning (see Ames, 1992; Maehr & Midgley, 1996). Thus, engaged readers likely will have a learning orientation toward reading, seeking to improve their knowledge and conceptual understanding as they read.

Intrinsic reading motivation refers to an individual's enjoyment of reading activities that are performed for their own sake (Deci, 1992) and pursued during free time (Morrow, 1996). Intrinsic motivation is also characterized by a disposition to perform the activities (Ryan, Connell, & Grolnick, 1992). Deci (1992) suggested that intrinsically motivated activity has an *experiential* component, which consists of excitement, interest, and enjoyment in participating in an activity. Further, intrinsic motivation has a *dispositional* component, which refers to the "desire to interact with those activities" (p. 49). Intrinsic motivation refers to the dual qualities of enjoyment or interest in performing an activity, such as reading, and the disposition or intention to participate in the activity when it is appropriate.

Wigfield and Guthrie (1997) distinguished different aspects of intrinsic motivation for reading, including curiosity, involvement, and preference for challenge. Curiosity is the child's participation in activities that fulfill a desire to learn and understand the world around them. Involvement refers to the child's enjoyment of immersion or absorption in a text. This is often referred to as "getting lost in a book." Preference for challenge is the desire to figure out complicated literature or understand complex ideas in text. These motivational facets are independent. A child may be relatively high on one (e.g., involvement) and low on another (e.g., preference for challenge), although these aspects of motivation often cluster together (Baker & Wigfield, in press; Wigfield & Guthrie, 1997).

Extrinsic motivation for reading is the desire to receive external recognition, rewards, or incentives (Deci, Vallerand, Pelletier, & Ryan, 1991). Incentive programs that provide pizza or school recognition for book reading rely on and probably strengthen extrinsic motivation. Extrinsic motivation is not simply the opposite of intrinsic motivation. In fact, they are moderately and positively correlated (Miller & Meece, 1997; Wigfield & Guthrie, 1997). Both predict children's reading amount and frequency. However, extrinsic motivation is usually associated with the use of surface strategies for reading and the desire to complete a task rather than to understand or enjoy a text or a task (Meece & Miller, 1999). Further, extrinsic motivation can produce self-terminating behavior. When children win the incentive (e.g., the pizza) their reading often ceases. Extrinsic incentives often lead students increasingly to become dependent on rewards and recognition to energize their reading (Barrett & Boggiano, 1988).

Self-efficacy is another aspect of motivation. Bandura (1986, 1997) defined self-efficacy as "people's judgments of their capabilities to organize and execute courses of action required to attain designated types of performances" (1986, p. 391). Applying this concept to reading, Schunk and Rice (1993) showed that providing clear goals for reading tasks and feedback on progress toward success increased self-efficacy and strategies for text comprehension. Schunk and Zimmerman (1997) reviewed research showing that students with high self-efficacy see difficult reading tasks as challenging and work diligently to master them, using their cognitive strategies productively.

Social motivation for reading relates to children's interpersonal and community activities. Children who like to share books with peers (Morrow, 1996) and participate responsibly in a community of learners by completing needed tasks are likely to be intrinsically motivated readers (Wentzel & Wigfield, 1998). Social motivation leads to increased amount of reading (Guthrie, Schafer, Wang, & Afflerbach, 1995) and high achievement in reading (Wentzel, 1996).

Motivation Guides Cognition and Language Use

Students with high intrinsic motivation, a learning goal orientation, and high self-efficacy are relatively active readers and high achievers (Guthrie, Wigfield et al., 1999). Why should this be? It is likely that motivational processes are the foundation for coordinating cognitive goals and strategies in reading. For example, if a person is intrinsically motivated to read and believes she is a capable reader, the person will persist in reading difficult texts and exert effort in resolving conflicts and integrating text with prior knowledge. However, if a text is not fulfilling intrinsic motivational goals, such as involvement, the person will terminate or minimize the cognitive activity of reading that material. A learner with high involvement motivation will seek books known to provide that satisfaction. The cognitive abilities needed to find books, avoid distraction while reading, and assimilate new ideas are activated if the text is fulfilling goals of involvement. This is consistent with both a cognitive science of reading (Lorch & van den Broek, 1997) and a situated account of the acquisition of expertise (Greeno et al., 1998), as well as the development of intrinsic motivation (Deci, 1992). In sum, becoming an excellent, active reader involves attunement of motivational processes with cognitive and language processes in reading.

Reading Motivation Shifts Over Time

Researchers studying the development of children's motivation have found that motivation changes in important ways across the middle childhood and early adolescent years (see Eccles et al., 1998, for detailed discussion). In brief, children's competence beliefs, values, and intrinsic motivation for learning tend to decline across the elementary school years, although the pattern of this change varies some across different activity areas. Children's extrinsic motivation tends to increase, as does their focus on performance goals. Children's competence and efficacy beliefs become more closely tied to indicators of their performance. Although this brief summary portrays a pattern of change for the population, individual children may vary. Some show overall increases in their motivation, whereas others show overall declines (Harter, Whitesell, & Kowalski, 1992).

Changes in children's motivation have been explained in two main ways. One explanation focuses on children's increasing capacity to understand their own performance. Children become much more sophisticated at processing the evaluative feedback they receive. For some children this leads to a growing realization that they are not as capable as other children, thereby reducing their motivation. A second explanation focuses on how instructional practices may contribute to a decline in some children's motivation. Practices that focus on social comparison between children, with too much competition between them, can lead to declines in competence beliefs, learning goals, and intrinsic motivation. Simultaneously, these practices tend to increase extrinsic motivation and performance goals (see Eccles et al., 1998; Wigfield, Eccles, & Pintrich, 1996). Instructional practices facilitating self-efficacy, intrinsic motivation, and learning goals are discussed later.

Do the declines in general motivation occur for reading motivation? Several researchers have observed decreases in different aspects of motivation for reading. Wigfield et al. (1997) reported that children's competence beliefs and interest in reading declined across the elementary school years, they also found that the decline in reading interest was greatest across Grades 1 to 4. Meece and Miller (1999) found decreases in learning goals and increases in performance goals for reading and writing in Grades 3–5. In a national study of how much elementary school-aged children liked recreational and school reading, McKenna et al. (1995) found that children's liking of both kinds of reading was higher among younger than older children.

Further declines in interest and competence beliefs regarding reading occur in children's transition to junior high school (Wigfield, Eccles, MacIver, Reuman, & Midgley, 1991). Oldfather and colleagues (Oldfather & Dahl, 1994; Oldfather & McLaughlin, 1993) found that students' intrinsic motivation to read declined as they went into junior high school. They attributed the change in motivation to changes in classroom conditions. Children in their study moved from a self-contained, responsive classroom that honored students' voices and had no grades, to a teacher-centered environment in which students had fewer opportunities for self-expression and little opportunity for negotiating with teachers about their learning.

Other researchers have found fewer age differences in reading motivation. Gottfried (1990) did not find age differences in 7- to 9-year-old children's intrinsic motivation for reading. Wigfield and Guthrie (1997) and Baker and Wigfield (in press) found relatively few differences in the different aspects of children's reading motivation for fourth- through sixth-grade students. The somewhat conflicting results may be due to the different ages of children in these studies. The largest decreases in intrinsic reading motivation seem to occur at two points: during the early to middle elementary school years, and then into middle or junior high school. Observed differences also may be tied to differences in instructional practices in reading. Some instructional practices foster motivation and others do not; we discuss this issue next.

INSTRUCTIONAL PROCESSES INFLUENCE READING MOTIVATION

Instructional processes and context surround the engagement processes and reading outcomes. We depict these processes in a circle at the outside of Fig. 24.1. These instructional processes have been shown through empirical and theoretical arguments to impact engagement processes and learning outcomes (see Guthrie & Alao, 1997; Guthrie, Cox, Anderson, Harris, Mazonni, & Rach, 1998). They include learning and knowledge goals, real-world interactions, autonomy support, interesting texts, strategy instruction, praise and rewards, evaluation, teacher involvement, and coherence of instructional processes.

Learning and Knowledge Goals

These goals refer to core learning goals that are co-developed by the teacher and the students in conjunction with external requirements from the school. These goals are tied to the learning and performance goal orientations discussed earlier. Roeser, Midgley, and Urdan (1996) showed that teachers' learning-goal orientation in the

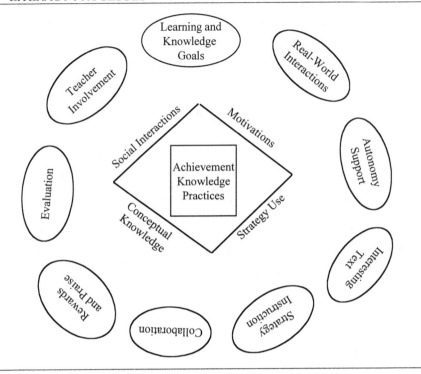

FIG. 24.1. Engagement model of reading development.

classroom contributed to their students' self-efficacy. When students believed that teachers thought that understanding the work was more important than just getting right answers, students were likely to believe in their capacity to do the hardest work. Students who were learning-goal oriented (e.g., dedicated to understanding content, using strategies effectively, and linking their new knowledge to previous experiences) were likely to be more highly engaged than other students. In contrast, when students' goals are dominated by the performance orientation of seeking to outperform others or demonstrate their competence or a procedural emphasis (e.g., completing a complex series of steps correctly (Meece, Blumenfeld, & Hoyle, 1988), they will be less engaged in learning.

Real-World Interactions

These interactions refer to connections between the academic curriculum and the personal experiences of the learners. Real-world interactions are enjoyable, immediately interesting activities that can provide motivation for reading and learning from text (Brophy, 1998; Csikszentmihalyi, 1991). If students are learning from text as they role-play in an historical drama, they are demonstrating that this merger can occur. An intrinsically motivating activity can induce reading, and reading can be optimized in an intrinsically motivating scenario. Zahorik (1996) found that both elementary and secondary teachers frequently reported that they attempt to motivate students with "hands-on" activities, such as using manipulatives in mathematics, participating in simulations and drama, or growing seedlings in science. Confirming and extending this line of inquiry, Hootstein (1995) interviewed eighth-grade teachers about the strategies they use to motivate students to learn U.S. history. Teachers emphasized the following: (a) having students role play historical text characters, (b) organizing projects that result in the creation of products, (c) relating history to current events or to students' lives, (d) showing historical videos and films, and (e) providing small-scale, hands-on experiences such as inspecting historical artifacts. All these activities were perceived by the teachers as immediately enjoyable to learners and could be used to initiate historical understanding. Teachers believe that reading motivation can be increased when texts and books are connected to stimulating activities (Nolen & Nichols, 1994), related to learning events (Guthrie, Alao, & Rinehart, 1997), or connected to personally significant projects (McCombs & Whistler, 1997). Teachers who report using variety, diversity, and high-interest tasks are providing intrinsically motivating, learning activities (Pressley, Rankin, & Yokoi, 1996; Stipek, 1996).

Real-world experiences are intrinsically motivating. They are designed to, and usually do, evoke keen attention and a sense of wonder. For example, when elementary students see a native North American in original dress in a social studies unit or observe a monarch butterfly hatch in a life science activity, they are excited and brimming with questions. Ross (1988) confirmed these effects in an extensive meta-analysis of literature. He found that "hands-on" science activities aroused attention, questions, and active learning. Guthrie, Van Meter et al. (1998) found that reading instruction embedded within an intrinsically motivating, "hands-on" science curriculum increased reading comprehension, strategy use, and problem solving in Grade 3 and 5 students. Confirming this, Romance and Vitale (1992) reported the results of an integrated curriculum that combined reading and "hands-on" activities in science. In a quasi-experimental comparison, students in the integrated curriculum scored higher on measures of reading achievement and science knowledge than students in a traditional form of instruction. To explain these effects, Anderson (1998) reasoned that hands-on science activities would motivate students to read deeply and thus increase their conceptual learning from text. She found that students who read texts in association with hands-on activities (live crabs and turtles in the classroom) had higher comprehension and conceptual knowledge gain than students who read the same texts without the intrinsically motivating context. Further, a year-long intervention study showed that reading engagement initially learned with intrinsically motivating activities in one knowledge domain transferred flexibly to a new knowledge domain (Guthrie, Anderson, Alao, & Rinehart, 1999).

Autonomy Support

Autonomy support is the teacher's guidance in making choices among meaningful alternatives relevant to the knowledge and learning goals. Studies confirm the conventional wisdom that choice is motivating. Providing choices is a prominent practice among reading teachers (Baumann, Hoffman, Moon, & Duffy-Hexter, 1998). Researchers studying elementary school teachers' beliefs about motivation in general (Nolen & Nichols, 1994) and reading specifically (Sweet, Guthrie, & Ng, 1998) have found that teachers believe that children need choice to develop independence. Turner (1995) found that teachers who develop reputations as highly motivating often provide a myriad of choices during a lesson. Teachers often promote student choice by giving them input into which books will be read, whether students will participate in reading aloud or silently, and what sequence of activities will be undertaken (Pressley et al., 1996). Choice is motivating because it affords student control. Children seek to be in command of their environment, rather than being manipulated by powerful others. This need for self-direction can be met in reading instruction through well-designed choices.

Evidence for the benefits of autonomy support on intrinsic motivation has been shown in many investigations (Cordova & Lepper, 1996; Deci et al., 1991). For example, Deci, Schwartz, Sheinman, and Ryan (1981) reported that teachers who enabled students to make choices about their learning and participation in instructional decisions created a classroom environment in which students were intrinsically motivated to learn the content and contributed actively to classroom activities. Specific to reading, Grolnick and Ryan (1987) showed that an autonomy-supportive context increased motivation and comprehension in reading. Students who read social studies texts to answer their own personally formulated questions showed higher comprehension than groups of students who were instructed to memorize the content or to read without direction. Legitimating the students' questions as purposes for reading increased student control and autonomy in the text reading situation. A recent study with college students in which limited text choice is provided in a single task showed no effects of choice on cognitive engagement (Schraw, Flowerday, & Reisetter, 1998). It is likely that increased engagement requires a sustained experience of autonomy support over a series of many activities and extended time.

Autonomy support and student motivation appear to be reciprocal. As students perceive that teachers respect them enough to provide genuine choices, students increase their effort and commitment to learning. When teachers see that students are taking responsibility for their learning, initiating productive reading activities, and gaining self-confidence, teachers reward students with increased responsibility and opportunity for self-directed learning. This synergism evolves during the course of the year (Skinner & Belmont, 1993). Occasionally, conflicts occur between the motivational orientation of some students and the classroom motivational emphasis. For example, extrinsically motivated students are not initially comfortable in a classroom in which learning goal orientation is dominant. These students need teacher support for becoming self-directed learners (Lehtinen, Vauras, Salonen, Olkinuora, & Kinnunen, 1995). In other words, the flow of motivational influence is from student to teacher as well as from teacher to student (Skinner & Belmont, 1993).

Teachers' beliefs about effective strategies for motivating students are remarkably consistent with self-determination theory of motivational development (Deci & Ryan, 1992). Self-determination theory describes the development of intrinsic motivation in terms of environmental support for the individual's needs for autonomy, relatedness, and competence (Deci & Ryan, 1985). Need for autonomy is met through support for self-directed learning. Need for relatedness is addressed in collaborative classroom activities. Need for self-perceived competence is partially fulfilled in evaluation that supports progress toward goals and reward for effort in learning. When these needs are fulfilled, students become intrinsically motivated and gain cognitive expertise in reading. Consistent with this framework, teachers provide choice (autonomy support), social interaction (relatedness support), and activity connections (competence support) to students who they think need motivational development. Simultaneously, teachers often permit intrinsically motivated students to direct their own reading and learning (Sweet et al., 1998).

Interesting Texts for Instruction

Many teachers, parents, and administrators expect that students are motivated by interesting texts. The logic is that students will devote effort, attention, and persistence to reading about topics that they find enjoyable or intriguing. Here the phrase *interesting texts* refers to single-authored works in which the text matches the topic interest and cognitive competency of the reader. If a book is personally significant and easy to comprehend, it is likely to be rated as interesting (Schraw, Bruning, & Svoboda , 1995). One benefit is that students spend more time reading personally interesting texts than uninteresting texts (McLoyd, 1979). Another benefit is that students learn relatively more content from interesting texts even after accounting for their relatively high prior knowledge for the content of these texts (Schiefele, 1996). Providing an abundance of high-interest texts in the classroom enables teachers to adapt their reading instruction to the preexisting motivations of students. Such adaptation may explain the relatively high association between the size of a classroom library and student reading achievement, which has been documented across multiple nations (Elley, 1992).

Providing interesting texts for instruction can adapt the instructional materials to students' preexisting preferences for content or genre, although administrative forces often oppose it (Allington & Guice, 1997). Once given interesting texts, students need ample time to read (Morrow, 1996). A profusion of trade books in a classroom has little benefit on motivation or achievement unless it is accompanied by sufficient time designated for text interaction (Elley, 1992). Using interesting texts, furthermore, is compatible with focused instruction on word recognition and word fluency development (Cunningham & Stanovich, 1997), provided the texts are matched to student reading level. Although the number of interesting books in classrooms often is not very substantial, students in book-rich classrooms fare well. Au and Asam (1996) reported that student ownership of literacy, which is closely linked to intrinsic motivation or reading, was increased in the KEEP program, in which a diversity of books was provided. In her integrated reading and writing program, Morrow (1992) found that students who read interesting texts in a physically appealing classroom corner increased their frequency and time spent reading in free-time activities.

Strategy Instruction

Strategy instruction consists of teachers' direct instruction, scaffolding, and guided practice in learning from text. Development of intrinsic motivation is strongly dependent on students' competence (Deci et al., 1991). If students are able to complete the reading tasks in their classroom, and are aware of their abilities and limitations, they will be more motivated than if they are less capable or less aware (J. Harter, 1982; S. Harter, 1981). Consequently, strategy instruction in reading, in forms that are either direct or implicit, is likely to be empowering and motivating. Strategies for reading and writing are difficult to learn and use. Many investigators report that strategies require long-term teaching (Gaskins & Elliot, 1991), and once learned, strategies may not be frequently used (Brown, 1992). Consequently, students must be intentional (Bereiter & Scardamalia, 1989), wanting to learn the content for which the strategies will be useful. In reading, intrinsic motivations are vital to strategy learning. Guthrie, Van Meter, et al. (1996) found that all students (100%) who increased in intrinsic motivation during a year increased in reading strategy use. However, only 50% of the students who were stable or declined in intrinsic motivation increased in reading strategy use. Possession of strategies and the motivation for using them are likely to be mutually enhancing.

Strategies that are likely to increase self-efficacy in elementary and middle school students include using prior knowledge (Anderson & Pearson, 1984), searching for information (Guthrie, McGough et al., 1996), comprehending informational text (Dole, Duffy, Roehler & Pearson, 1991), interpreting literary text (Graesser, Singer, & Trabasso, 1994), and self-monitoring (Baker & Brown, 1984; Zimmerman, 1989). Coaching students in these strategies may include appraising students' strategy knowledge level, and providing modeling, small group discussion, peer modeling, and individual feedback on progress. Initial evidence suggests that such reading strategy instruction increases reading self-efficacy (Schunk & Zimmerman, 1997).

Collaboration

Collaboration is the social discourse among students in a learning community that enables them to see perspectives and to socially construct knowledge from text. Many teachers use collaboration to activate and maintain intrinsic motivation. Teachers believe that social collaboration in the classroom will increase interest in the content of learning (Hootstein, 1995; Zahorik, 1996) and maintain active learning over an extended period of time (Nolen & Nichols, 1994). Teachers also believe that collaboration enables students to be disposed to read more independently in the future (Morrow, 1996).

Students' intrinsic motivation for reading and learning is closely connected to their feeling of social support in the classroom. When students have a caring teacher and a sense of belonging in the classroom (Wentzel, 1997), they are likely to be motivated for reading. Among students from sixth to eighth grade, intrinsic reading motivation and reading self-efficacy were highly correlated with students' adoption of prosocial goals. Prosocial students volunteer to help classmates who need assistance and are responsible in fulfilling social norms in their teams or classrooms (Wentzel, 1996). These findings are consistent with qualitative inquiries. Oldfather and Dahl (1994) showed that students who felt that they were recognized, accepted, and affirmed as individuals in the classroom social structure were motivated to read, write, and express themselves forthrightly. Despite these highly provocative patterns of association for motivation and perceived social support, intervention studies comparing more and less socially supportive contexts that permit an inference of causality for the effects of collaboration on motivation are relatively rare. This is an important area for research.

Praise and Rewards

Perhaps the most pervasive strategy for encouraging effort and attention is providing praise and rewards. Effective teachers can be seen to provide informative compliments that make learners feel a sense of accomplishment and pride in work. Brophy (1981) reviewed the literature on the effects of praise. Effective praise is given contingently on effort and achievement, specifies the particulars of the accomplishment, shows spontaneity, orients students toward better appreciation of their own work, attributes success to effort, and fosters appreciation of task relevant strategies. Wlodkowski (1985) suggested that praise should be "3S–3P" which stands for praise that is sincere, specific, sufficient, and properly given for praiseworthy success in the manner preferred by the learner.

Teachers' attempts at effective praise are not always successful. If students interpret praise to be manipulative, their motivation may decline because they feel they are being treated as objects (Flink, Boggiano, Main, Barrett, & Katz, 1992). However, when praise is sincerely given and interpreted as recognition of achievement, it can increase students' self-perceived competence and motivation. Beginning teachers are especially inclined to emphasize praise and punishment as their primary motivational strategies. Newby (1991) found that first-year teachers used praise and punishment more than 75% of the time as their motivational strategy. Considerable experience and professional development are needed to learn to merge other principles of motivational support with reward and praise.

Abundant evidence supports the proposition that giving rewards and positive incentives for book reading increases the time and effort in book reading activities. Further, reading incentive programs are quite common in elementary schools (Gambrell & Marniak, 1997). As young children (K–2) acquire competence in reading, they experience an increase in self-efficacy for reading (Chapman & Tunmer, 1997; Gaa, 1973), that spurs future achievement. Teachers of primary students can foster self-efficacy by helping students set goals, see their progress, and become aware of their growing competence (Baker, in press).

Giving rewards, such as praise, points in a contest, gold stars, or self-selected books, is relatively simple. Should not this solve the problem of reading motivation? Unfortunately not, because rewards and incentives have a paradoxical effect. Rewards can increase short-term attention on specific activities, but students who experience an environment in which extrinsic rewards are dominant will become increasingly ex-trinsically motivated and focused on performance goals (Flink et al., 1992). Such stu-dents become more committed to high grades, correct answers, and task completion (Anderman & Young, 1994), and less dedicated to comprehending content, gaining valuable reading skills, or enjoying reading and learning content (Maehr & Midgley, 1996).

There are several consequences of a strong extrinsic orientation and focus on perfor-mance goals. Students with performance goals frequently rely on memorizing, guess-ing, and other surface learning strategies for reading. They attempt to avoid challenging tasks and give up easily when frustrated. These students are not cognitively engaged in reading and frequently adopt work-avoidant goals, attempting to meet their performance goals with minimal effort (Meece & Holt, 1993). Thus, these patterns of motivation activate behavior that do not promote long-term engagement, and ultimately can undermine the life of a literate, learning community.

Evaluation

Classroom instruction that fosters motivation, strategic development, knowledge gains, and social growth can be undermined by evaluation that contradicts these in-structional purposes. Evaluation activities can be placed on a continuum from (a) highly objective and standardized (examples are standardized tests), to (b) highly stu-dent-centered and personalized (such as portfolios). Those toward the standardized end are easy to administer, score, and report to administrators, but they fail to reflect student ownership, motivation, and reading practices. Those toward the personalized end of the continuum will more readily support student motivation, but are more diffi-cult to administer and report. A combination is likely to be optimal for the administra-tive school needs and the educational needs of students, although there is precious little research evidence available to document this sensible approach.

Several classroom characteristics are necessary for student-centered evaluation. Teachers must provide ample time for students to think, plan, write, and revise (Oldfather & McLaughlin, 1993). Writing activities that invite a wide range of alterna-tive genres and topics are more motivating than activities that are highly defined and constrained (Turner, 1995), but they are more time-consuming. However, if students are empowered to be self-expressive, they will develop the view that all knowledge is contextual, experience themselves as creators of knowledge, and value both subjective and objective strategies for knowing (Belenky, Clinchy, Goldberger, & Tarule, 1986; McCombs & Whistler, 1997).

Teachers who are known to be able to spark and sustain their students' attention and interest in reading often report that they evaluate effort and progress rather than absolute skill or comparative advantage (Stipek, 1996). These teachers encourage stu-dents to believe that effort will yield success and enjoyment (Nolen & Nichols, 1994). The use of classroom portfolios (Au & Asam, 1996) or project-based exhibits from ex-tended projects (Afflerbach, 1996) provides a structure and materials base for evaluat-ing students via their progress in a meaningful activity. Such evaluation provides feedback on progress, which increases self-efficacy (Schunk & Zimmerman, 1997) and affords students opportunities for establishing a belief in their own competence, which is necessary for intrinsic motivation (Deci et al., 1991).

Teacher Involvement

This represents the teacher's knowledge of individual learners, caring about their progress, and pedagogical understanding of how to foster their active participation. Ellen Skinner and her colleagues investigated the roles of teacher involvement on engagement (Skinner, Wellborn, & Connell, 1990). The involved teacher knows about the students' personal interests, cares about each student's learning, and holds realistic but positive goals for their effort and learning. Skinner and Belmont (1993) found that when students perceived teachers to be involved (i.e., interested in their progress) and autonomy supportive (i.e., providing students some control of learning), students were engaged in the classroom (e.g., participating in class discussions, actively learning, and appearing happy). Highly engaged students were relatively high achievers as indicated by school grades and achievement test scores across all school subjects, including reading, math, and science. Noteworthy was the finding that teacher involvement did not directly influence outcomes, but involvement had a significant benefit on engagement, which then appeared to lead to positive student outcomes. Skinner and Belmont (1993) showed in addition that the influences were reciprocal. Student engagement impacted teacher involvement as much as teacher involvement influenced student engagement.

Coherence of Instructional Processes

We have discussed each of the instructional processes in isolation. There can be important connections across them, and we use the term *coherence* to refer to these interconnections. For example, when real-world interactions are closely aligned with interesting texts, coherence is increased. When students' engagement in reading is being enhanced by coordination among instructional processes, coherence in the classroom is occurring at a high level. When strategy instruction is linked to central knowledge goals, collaboration is forged with autonomy support, and teacher involvement is evident in evaluation, then coherence among the instructional processes is present (see Guthrie & Cox, 1998, for teaching guidelines). In addition to fusing the pedagogical approaches, coherent instruction links reading, writing, and rich knowledge domains. In coherent instruction, student engagement is increased (Guthrie, Van Meter, et al., 1998), conceptual learning from text is facilitated (Anderson, 1998), reading achievement is fostered (Romance & Vitale, 1992), and reading within content areas can be sustained (Gaskins et al., 1994; Santa, 1997). However, full investigations of the complex interactions among these instructional practices have been rare.

HOW READING ENGAGEMENT MEDIATES THE EFFECTS OF CLASSROOM CONTEXT ON STUDENT OUTCOMES

We have reviewed here research showing that characteristics of the classroom influence reading engagement and motivation. We also reviewed work showing that student engagement yields positive reading achievement outcomes and desirable reading practices, such as electing to read frequently and sharing books in a literate community. Ellen Skinner and her colleagues (Deci et al., 1991; Skinner et al., 1990) initially proposed this link between engagement and outcomes. Their model, which also examined context effects, had a profound impact on subsequent thinking and research. In the mid 1990s, several investigators synthesized research and proposed related models in which effects of classroom context on students outcomes are *mediated* by engagement (Pintrich, Marx, & Boyle, 1993; Pintrich & Schrauben, 1992). That is, classroom context does not directly affect student outcomes. Rather, the effects of the classroom context depend on the level of student engagement. This mediated engagement model offers a useful heuristic for understanding the relationships of context, engagement, and outcomes in reading.

Our conceptualization of the mediated engagement model specific to reading is graphically presented in Fig. 24.1. In this model we include the different constructs and instructional processes contained in the research and theory reviewed in this chapter. At the center of the figure is a diamond referring to engagement processes of the reader. One facet of the diamond represents *motivation*, which includes the multifaceted aspects of motivation we have discussed: goals, intrinsic and extrinsic motivation, self-efficacy, and social motivation. These motivational aspects of the reader propel students to choose to read and use cognitive strategies to comprehend. The *strategy* facet of the diamond refers to students' multiple cognitive processes of comprehending, self-monitoring, and constructing their understanding and beliefs during reading. The *conceptual knowledge* facet of the diamond refers to the research base showing that reading is knowledge-driven. That reading is a social endeavor is represented by the *social interaction* facet of the diamond. This includes collaborative practices in a community and the social goals of helping other students or cooperating with a teacher.

At the center of the figure is a square containing achievement, knowledge, and reading practices. Achievement may be represented by standardized test scores, teacher assigned grades, or performance assessments of literacy. Knowledge acquisition may be indicated through portfolios or standardized measurements. Reading practices may be reflected in amount of independent reading, composite indicators of engagement in reading, or beliefs and preferences about reading. Although we believe that engagement in reading increases the occurrence of reading outcomes (e.g., achievement, knowledge, and practices), we also expect that the relationships are reciprocal.

Desired outcomes of teaching, such as text comprehension ability, knowledge acquisition from text, and sustainable reading practices, do not result automatically in response to instruction. These outcomes rely on engagement as a mediating process. When engagement is sustained, outcomes will be positive. Instructional processes as presented in the previous section, then, impact outcomes indirectly by building and sustaining engagement in reading. Engagement in this depiction is a *mediator* for instructional processes. Engagement is the avenue through which instruction impacts outcomes. Students grow in achievement, knowledge, and practices as a result of their increasing engagement. And students' growing engagement flows from their continual experience of the instructional processes presented here. Engaged reading and learning take time. They do not immediately arise in a limited task or situation. Sustained experience and perception of motivation-enhancing contexts are necessary for reader engagement.

NOW AND FUTURE RESEARCH

At least four major aspects of reading engagement and motivation call for deeper inquiry. First, we need richer characterizations of engaged and motivated readers. Extended interviews, observational studies, or longitudinal case studies would complement the existing literature. These studies are especially needed in young readers from age 3 to 8 years. Second, we need contextualized observations or measures that would be most responsive to classroom, environmental, or interpersonal events, although such contextualization may have the cost of being less predictive of engagement in different settings or future times. Third, we need empirical investigations of the emerging reading engagement model shown in Fig. 24.1. We expect that every individual link in the outer ring in Fig. 24.1 could have an interactive relationship with each other link. Measuring each of the constructs shown in Fig. 24.1 and then modeling their relationships using structural equation modeling would be one promising approach. Fourth, we should use multiple methodologies to understand and portray schools that are winning the battle against disengagement from reading. The complexities of a school-wide inquiry into reading engagement call for qualitative methods such as case studies with interviewing, observing, and videotaping. We recommend coordinating qualitative approaches with quantitative studies that examine the relations among multiple variables with such statistical techniques as structural equation modeling, or hierarchical linear modeling. To portray school effects fully, statistical methods can complement the rich descriptions that flow from qualitative inquiries.

REFERENCES

Alexander, P. A., Jetton, T. L., & Kulikowich, J. M. (1996). Interrelationship of knowledge, interest, and recall: Assessing a model of domain learning. *Journal of Educational Psychology, 87,* 559–575.

Afflerbach, P. (1996). Engaged assessment of engaged reading. In L. Baker, P. Afflerbach, & D. Reinking (Eds.), *Developing engaged readers in school and home communities* (pp. 191–214). Hillsdale, NJ: Lawrence Erlbaum Associates.

Allington, R. L., & Guice, S. (1997). Literature curriculum: Issues of definition and control. In J. Flood, S. B. Heath, & D. Lapp (Eds.), *Research on teaching literacy through communicative and visual arts* (pp. 727–735). New York: Macmillan.

Almasi, J. F. (1995). The nature of fourth graders' sociocognitive conflicts in peer-led and teacher-led discussions of literature. *Reading Research Quarterly, 30,* 314–351.

Almasi, J. F., McKeown, M. G., & Beck, I. L. (1996). The nature of engaged reading in classroom discussions of literature. *Journal of Literacy Research, 28,* 107–147.

Ames, C. (1992). Classrooms: Goal, structures, and student motivation. *Journal of Educational Psychology, 84,* 261–271.

Ames, C., & Archer, J. (1988). Achievement goals in the classroom: Students' learning strategies and motivational processes. *Journal of Educational Psychology, 80,* 260–267.

Anderman, E. M., & Young, A. J. (1994). Motivation and strategy use in science: Individual differences and classroom effects. *Journal of Research in Science Teaching, 31,* 811–831.

Anderson, E. (1998). *Motivational and cognitive influences on conceptual knowledge acquisition: The combination of science observation and interesting texts.* Unpublished doctoral dissertation, University of Maryland, College Park.

Anderson, R. C., & Pearson, P. D. (1984). A schema-theoretic view of basic processes in reading. In P. D. Pearson, R. Barr, M. L. Kamil, & P. Mosenthal (Eds.), *Handbook of reading research* (pp. 255–291). New York: Longman.

Athey, I. (1985). Reading research in the affective domain. In H. Singer & R. Ruddell (Eds.), *Theoretical models and processes of reading* (pp. 527–558). Newark, DE: International Reading Association.

Au, K. H. (1997). Ownership, literacy achievement, and students of diverse cultural backgrounds. In J. T. Guthrie & A. Wigfield (Eds.), *Reading engagement: Motivating readers through integrated instruction* (pp. 168–182). Newark, DE: International Reading Association.

Au, K. H., & Asam, C. L. (1996). Improving the literacy achievement of low-income students of diverse backgrounds. In M. F. Graves, P. van den Broek, & B. M. Taylor (Eds.), *The first R: Every child's right to read* (pp. 199–223). New York: Teachers College Press.

Baker, L. (in press). Engaging children in word recognition instruction. In L. Baker, J. Dreher, & J. T. Guthrie (Eds.) *Engaging young readers.* New York: Guilford Publications.

Baker, L., & Brown, A. L. (1984). Metacognitive skills and reading. In P. D. Pearson, R. Barr, M. L. Kamil, & P. Mosenthal (Eds.), *Handbook of reading research* (pp. 353–395). New York: Longman.

Baker, L., & Wigfield, A. (in press). Dimensions of children's motivation for reading and their relations to reading activity and reading achievement. *Reading Research Quarterly.*

Bandura, A. (1986). *Social foundations of thought and action: A social cognitive theory.* Englewood Cliffs, NJ: Prentice Hall.

Bandura, A. (1997). *Self-efficacy: The exercise of control.* New York: W. H. Freeman.

Barrett, M., & Boggiano, A. K. (1988). Fostering extrinsic orientations: Use of reward strategies to motivate children. *Journal of Social and Clinical Psychology, 6,* 293–309.

Baumann, J., Hoffman, J., Moon, J. & Duffy-Hexter, A. M. (1998). Where are teachers' voices in the phonics/whole language debate? Results from a survey of U. S. elementary teachers. *The Reading Teacher, 51,* 636–652.

Beck, I. L., McKeown, M. G. Worthy, J., Sandora, C. A., & Kucan, L. (1996). Questioning the author: A year-long classroom implementation to engage students with text. *The Elementary School Journal, 96,* 385–414.

Belenky, M., Clinchy, B., Goldberger, N., & Tarule, J. (1986). *Women's ways of knowing: The development of self, voice, and mind.* New York: Basic Books.

Bereiter, C., & Scardamalia, M. (1989). Intentional learning as a goal of instruction. In L. B. Resnick (Ed.), *Knowing, learning, and instruction: Essays in honor of Robert Glaser* (pp. 361–392). Hillsdale, NJ: Lawrence Erlbaum Associates.

Berliner, D. C., & Biddle, B. J. (1995). *The manufactured crisis: Myths, fraud, and the attack on American public schools.* Reading, MA: Addison Wesley.

Blumenfeld, P. C. (1992). Classroom learning and motivation: Clarifying and expanding goal theory. *Journal of Educational Psychology, 84,* 272–281.

Brophy, J. (1981). Teacher praise: A functional analysis. *Review of Educational Research, 51,* 5–32.

Brophy, J. (1998). *Motivating students to learn.* Boston: McGraw-Hill.

Brown, A. L. (1992). Design experiments: Theoretical and methodological challenges in creating complex interventions in classroom settings. *Journal of the Learning Sciences, 2,* 141–178.

Cambourne, B. (1995). Toward an educationally relevant theory of literacy learning: Twenty years of inquiry. *The Reading Teacher, 49,* 182–192.

Campbell, J. R., Voelkl, K. E., & Donahue, P. L. (1997). *NAEP 1996 trends in academic progress* (NCES Publication No. 97–985). Washington, DC: U.S. Department of Education.

Chapman, J. W., & Tunmer, W. E. (1997). A longitudinal study of beginning reading achievement and reading self-concept. *British Journal of Educational Psychology, 67,* 279–291.

Cipielewski, J., & Stanovich, K. E. (1992). Predicting growth in reading ability from children's exposure to print. *Journal of Experimental Child Psychology, 54,* 74–89.

Cordova, D. I., & Lepper, M. R. (1996). Intrinsic motivation and the process of learning: Beneficial effects of contextualization, personalization, and choice. *Journal of Educational Psychology, 88*(4), 715–730.

Csikszentmihalyi, M. (1991). Literacy and intrinsic motivation. In S. R. Graubard (Ed.), *Literacy* (pp. 115–140). New York: Noonday.

Cunningham, A. E., & Stanovich, K. E. (1997). Early reading acquisition and its relation to reading experience and ability 10 years later. *Developmental Psychology, 33*(6), 934–945.

Deci, E. L. (1992). The relation of interest to the motivation of behavior: A self-determination theory perspective. In A. Renninger, S. Hidi, & A. Krapp (Eds.), *The role of interest in learning and development* (pp. 43–70). Hillsdale, NJ: Lawrence Erlbaum Associates.

Deci, E. L., & Ryan, R .M. (1985). *Intrinsic motivation and self-determination in human behavior.* New York: Plenum Press.

Deci, E. L., & Ryan, R .M. (1992). The initiation and regulation of intrinsically motivated learning and achievement. In A. K. Boggiano & T. S. Pittman (Eds.), *Achievement and motivation: A social developmental perspective* (pp. 3–36). Toronto: Cambridge University Press.

Deci, E. L., Schwartz, A. J., Sheinman, L., & Ryan, R. M. (1981). An instrument to assess adults' orientations toward control versus autonomy with children: Reflections on intrinsic motivation and perceived competence. *Journal of Educational Psychology, 73*(5), 642–650.

Deci, E. L., Vallerand, R. J., Pelletier, L. G., & Ryan, R. M. (1991). Motivation and education: The self-determination perspective. *Educational Psychologist, 26,* 325–346.

Dole, J. A., Duffy, G. G., Roehler, L. R., & Pearson, P. D. (1991). Moving from the old to the new: Research on reading comprehension instruction. *Review of Educational Research, 61,* 239–264.

Duffy, G. G., Roehler, L., Sivan, E., Rackliffe, G., Book, C., Meloth, M., Vaurus, L., Wesselman, R., Putnam, J., & Bassir, D. (1987). Effects of explaining the reasoning associated with using reading strategies. *Reading Research Quarterly, 22*(3), 347–368.

Dweck, C. S., & Leggett, B. (1988). A social-cognitive approach to motivation and personality. *Psychological Review, 95,* 256–273.

Eccles, J. S., Wigfield, A., & Schiefele, U. (1998). Motivation to succeed. In W. Damon (Series Ed.) and N. Eisenberg (Ed.), *Handbook of child psychology: (Vol. 3) Social, emotional, and personality development* (5th ed.). New York: Wiley.

Elley, W. B. (1992). *How in the world do students read?* Hamburg: International Reading Association.

Flink, C., Boggiano, A. K., Main, D. S., Barrett, M., & Katz, P. A. (1992). Children's achievement-related behaviors: The role of extrinsic and intrinsic motivational orientations. In A. K. Boggiano & T. S. Pittman (Eds.), *Achievement and motivation: A social-developmental perspective* (pp. 189–214). New York: Cambridge University Press.

Gaa, J. P. (1973). Effects of individual goal setting conferences on achievement, attitudes, and goal-setting behavior. *Journal of Experimental Education, 42,* 22–28.

Gambrell, L. & Marniak, B. (1997). In J. T. Guthrie & A. Wigfield (Eds.), *Reading engagement: Motivating readers through integrated instruction* (pp. 205–217). Newark, DE: International Reading Association.

Gaskins, I., & Elliot, T. (Eds.). (1991). *Implementing cognitive strategy training across the school: The benchmark manual for teachers.* Cambridge, MA: Brookline Books.

Gaskins, I., Guthrie, J. T., Satlow, E., Ostertag, F., Six, L., Byrne, J., & Conner, B., (1994). Integrating instruction of science and reading, and writing: Goals, teacher development, and assessment. Journal of Research in Science Teaching, *31,* 1039–1056.

Gee, J. P., & Green, J. L. (1998). Discourse analysis, learning and social practice: A methodological study. *Review of Research in Education, 23,* 119–171.

Gottfried, A. E. (1990). Academic intrinsic motivation in young elementary school children. *Journal of Educational Psychology, 82*(3), 525–538.

Graesser, A. C., Singer, M., & Trabasso, T. (1994). Constructing inferences during narrative text comprehension. *Psychological Review, 101,* 371–395.

Gray, W. S., & Monroe, R., (1929). *The reading interests and habits of adults: a preliminary report.* New York: Macmillan.

Greeno, J. G., & the Middle School Mathematics Through Applications Project Group. (1998). The situativity of knowing, learning, and research. *American Psychologist, 53*(1), 5–26.

Grolnick, W. S., & Ryan, R. M. (1987). Autonomy in children's learning: An experimental and individual difference investigation. *Journal of Personality and Social Psychology, 52,* 273–288.

Guthrie, J. T., & Alao, S. (1997). Designing contexts to increase motivations for reading. *Educational Psychologist, 32,* 95–107.

Guthrie, J. T., Alao, S., & Rinehart, J. M. (1997). Engagement in reading for young adolescents. *Journal of Adolescent & Adult Literacy, 40,* 438–446.

Guthrie, J. T., & Alvermann, D. A. (Eds.). (1999). *Engaged reading: Processes, practices and policy implications.* New York: Teachers College Press.

Guthrie, J. T., Anderson, E., Alao, S. & Rinehart, J. (1999). Influences of Concept-Oriented Reading Instruction on strategy use and conceptual learning from text. *Elementary School Journal 99*(4), 343–366..

Guthrie, J. T., & Cox, K. (1998). Portrait of an engaging classroom: Principles of Concept-Oriented Reading Instruction for diverse students. In K. Harris (Ed.), *Teaching every child every day: Learning in diverse schools and classrooms* (pp. 70–130). Cambridge, MA: Brookline.

Guthrie, J. T., Cox, K., Anderson, E., Harris, K., Mazonni, S., & Rach, L. (1998). Principles of integrated instruction for engagement in reading. *Educational Psychology Review, 10*(2), 177–199.

Guthrie, J. T., McGough, K., Bennett, L., & Rice, M. E. (1996). Concept-Oriented Reading Instruction: An integrated curriculum to develop motivations and strategies for reading. In L. Baker, P. Afflerbach, & D. Reinking (Eds.), *Developing engaged readers in school and home communities* (pp. 165–190). Mahwah, NJ: Lawrence Erlbaum Associates.

Guthrie, J. T., & Schafer, W. (1998, November 30). *Effects of integrated instruction and reading time on reading achievement in middle school: A policy analysis of NAEP data.* Submitted to National Center for Educational Statistics, Washington, DC.

Guthrie, J. T., Schafer, W. D., Wang, Y. Y., & Afflerbach, P. (1995). Relationships of instruction of reading: An exploration of social, cognitive, and instructional connections. *Reading Research Quarterly, 30*(1), 8–25.

Guthrie, J. T., Van Meter, P., Hancock, G. R., McCann, A., Anderson, E., & Alao, S. (1998). Does Concept-Oriented Reading Instruction increase strategy-use and conceptual learning from text? *Journal of Educational Psychology, 90*(2), 261–278.

Guthrie, J. T., Van Meter, P., McCann, A. D., Wigfield, A., Bennett, L., Poundstone, C. C., Rice, M. E., Faibisch, F. M., Hunt, B., & Mitchell, A. M. (1996). Growth of literacy engagement: Changes in motivations and strategies during concept-oriented reading instruction. *Reading Research Quarterly, 31,* 306–332.

Guthrie, J. T., Wigfield, A., Metsala, J. L., & Cox, K. E. (1999). Motivational and cognitive predictors of text comprehension and reading amount. *Scientific Studies of Reading, 3*(3), 231–256.

Harste, J. C. (1994). Multiple ways of knowing. *Language Arts, 71,* 337–349.

Harter, J. (1982). The perceived competence scale for children. *Child Development, 53,* 87–97.

Harter, S. (1981). A new self-report scale of intrinsic versus extrinsic orientation in the classroom: Motivational and informational components. *Development Psychology, 17,* 300–312.

Harter, S., Whitesell, N. R., & Kowalski, P. (1992). Individual differences in the effects of educational transitions on young adolescents' perceptions of competence and motivational orientation. *American Educational Research Journal, 29,* 777–808.

Hootstein, H. (1995). Motivational strategies of middle school social studies teachers. *Social Education, 59,* 23–26.

Lehtinen, E., Vauras, M., Salonen, P., Olkinuora, E., & Kinnunen, R. (1995). Long-term development of learning activity: Motivational, cognitive, and social interaction. *Educational Psychologist, 30,* 21–35.

Lorch, R. F., & van den Broek, R. (1997). Understanding reading comprehension: Current and future contributions of cognitive science. *Contemporary Educational Psychology, 22*(4), 213–247.

Maehr, M., & Midgley, C. (1996). *Transforming school cultures.* Boulder, CO: Westview Press.

Matthewson, G. C. (1991). Model of attitude influence upon reading and learning to read. In R. B. Ruddell, M. R. Ruddell, & H. Singer (Eds.), *Theoretical models and processes of reading* (pp. 1131–1161). Newark, DE: International Reading Association.

McCombs, B. L., & Whistler, J. S. (1997). The learner-centered classroom and school: Strategies for increasing student motivation and achievement. In B. L. McCombs & J. S. Whistler (Eds.), *The learner-centered classroom* (pp. 63–101). San Francisco: Jossey-Bass.

McKenna, M. C., Kear, D. J., & Ellsworth, R. A. (1995). Children's attitudes toward reading: A national survey. *Reading Research Quarterly, 30,* 934–956.

McLoyd, V. (1979). The effects on extrinsic rewards of differential value on high and low intrinsic interest. *Child Development, 50,* 1010–1019.

Meece, J. L., Blumenfeld, P. C., & Hoyle, R. H. (1988). Students' goal orientations and cognitive engagement in classroom activities. *Journal of Educational Psychology, 80*(4), 514–523.

Meece, J. L., & Holt, K. (1993). A pattern analysis of students' achievement goals. *Journal of Educational Psychology, 85,* 582–590.

Meece, J. L., & Miller, S. D. (1999). Changes in elementary school children's achievement goals for reading and writing: Results of a longitudinal and an intervention study. *Scientific Studies of Reading, 3*(3), 207–230.

Miller, S. D., & Meece, J. L. (1997). Enhancing elementary students' motivation to read and write: A classroom intervention study. *Journal of Educational Research, 90,* 286–301.

Morrow, L. M. (1992). The impact of a literature-based program on literacy achievement, use of literature and attitudes of children from minority backgrounds. *Reading Research Quarterly, 27,* 250–275.

Morrow, L. M. (1996). *Motivating reading and writing in diverse classrooms* (NCTE Research Rep. No. 28). Urbana, IL: National Council of Teachers of English.

Mosenthal, P. B. (1999). Understanding engagement: Historical and political contexts. In J. T. Guthrie & D. E. Alvermann (Eds.), *Engaged reading: Processes, practices and policy implications* (pp. 1–16). New York: Teachers College Press.

Newby, T. J. (1991). Classroom motivation: Strategies of first-year teachers. *Journal of Educational Psychology, 83,* 187–194.

Nicholls, J. G. (1979). Quality and equality in intellectual development: The role of motivation in education. *American Psychologist, 34,* 1071–1084.

Nicholls, J. G., Cheung, P., Lauer, J., & Patashnick, M. (1989). Individual differences in academic motivation: Perceived ability, goals, beliefs, and values. *Learning and Individual Differences, 1,* 63–84.

Nolen, S. B., & Nichols, J. G. (1994). A place to begin (again) in research on student motivation: Teachers' beliefs. *Teaching and Teacher Education, 10,* 57–69.

Oldfather, P., & Dahl, K. (1994). Toward a social constructivist reconceptualization of intrinsic motivation for literacy learning. *Journal of Reading Behavior, 26,* 139–158.

Oldfather, P., & McLaughlin, H. J. (1993). Gaining and losing voice: A longitudinal study of students' continuing impulse to learn across elementary and middle school contexts. *Research in Middle Level Education, 3,* 1–25.

Paris, S. G., Wasik, B. A., & Turner, J. C. (1991). The development of strategies readers. In R. Barr, M. L. Kamil, P. Mosenthal, & P. D. Pearson (Eds.), *Handbook of reading research* (pp. 609–640). New York: Longman.

Pintrich, P. R., Marx, R. W., & Boyle, R. A. (1993). Beyond cold conceptual change: The role of motivational beliefs and classroom contextual factors in the process of conceptual change. *Review of Educational Research, 63,* 167–199.

Pintrich, P. R., & Schrauben B. (1992). Students' motivational beliefs and their cognitive engagement in classroom academic tasks. In D. H. Schunk & J. L. Meese (Eds.), *Student perceptions in the classroom* (pp. 149–184). Hillsdale, NJ: Lawrence Erlbaum Associates.

Pressley, M., Schuder, T., Bergman, J. L., & El-Dinary, P. B. (1992). Teachers in the students achieving independent learning program: A researcher-educator collaborative interview study of transactional comprehension strategies instruction. *Journal of Educational Psychology, 84,* 231–246.

Pressley, M., Rankin, J., & Yokoi, L. (1996). A survey of instructional practices of primary teachers nominated as effective in promoting literacy. *Elementary School Journal, 96*(4), 363–383.

Roeser, R. W., Midgley, C., & Urdan, T. C. (1996). Perceptions of the school psychological environment and early adolescents' psychological and behavioral functioning in school: The mediating role of goals and belonging. *Journal of Educational Psychology, 88*(3), 408–422.

Romance, N. R., & Vitale, M. R. (1992). A curriculum strategy that expands time for in-depth elementary science instruction by using science-based reading strategies: Effects of a year-long study in grade four. *Journal of Research in Science Teaching, 29,* 545–554.

Ross, J. A. (1988). Controlling variables: A meta-analysis of training studies. *Review of Educational Research, 58,* 405–437.

Roth, W., & Bowen, G. M. (1995). Knowing and interacting: A case study of culture, practices and resources in a grade 8 open-inquiry science classroom guided by a cognitive apprenticeship metaphor. *Cognitive and Instruction, 13,* 73–128.

Ryan, R. M., Connell, J. P., & Grolnick, W. S. (1992). When achievement is not intrinsically motivated: A theory of internalization and self-regulation in school. In A. K. Boggiano & T. S. Pittman (Eds.), *Achievement and motivation: A social developmental perspective* (pp. 167–188). Toronto: Cambridge University Press.

Santa, C. (1997). School change and literacy engagement. In J. T. Guthrie & A. Wigfield (Eds.), *Reading engagement: Motivating readers through integrated instruction* (pp. 218–235). Newark, DE: International Reading Association.

Schiefele, U. (1996). Topic interest, text representation, and quality of experience. *Contemporary Educational Psychology, 21,* 3–18.

Schraw, G. (1997). Situational interest in literary text. *Contemporary Educational Psychology, 22*(4), 436–456.

Schraw, G., Bruning, R., & Svoboda, C. (1995). Source of situational interest. *Journal of Reading Behavior, 27,* 1–17.

Schraw, G., & Bruning, R. (1999). How implicit models of reading affect motivation to read and reading engagement. *Scientific Studies of Reading, 3*(3), 281–302.

Schraw, G., Flowerday, T., & Reisetter, M. F. (1998). The role of choice in reader engagement. *Journal of Educational Psychology, 90,* 705–714.

Schunk, D. H., & Rice, J. M. (1993). Strategy fading and progress feedback: Effects on self-efficacy and comprehension among students receiving remedial reading services. *Journal of Special Education, 27,* 257–276.

Schunk, D. H., & Zimmerman, B. J. (1997). Developing self-efficacious readers and writers: The role of social and self-regulatory processes. In J. T. Guthrie & A. Wigfield (Eds.), *Reading engagement: Motivating readers through integrated instruction* (pp. 34–50). Newark, DE: International Reading Association.

Skaalvik, E. (1997). Self-enhancing and self-defeating ego orientation: Relations with task and avoidance orientation, achievement, self-perceptions, and anxiety. *Journal of Educational Psychology, 89,* 71–81.

Skinner, E. A., & Belmont, M. J. (1993). Motivation in the classroom: Reciprocal effects of teacher behavior and student engagement across the school year. *Journal of Educational Psychology, 85,* 571–581.

Skinner, E. A., Wellborn, J. G., & Connell, J. P. (1990). What it takes to do well in school and whether I've got it: A process model of perceived control and children's engagement and achievement in school. *Journal of Educational Psychology, 82*(1), 22–32.

Stanovich, K. E. (1986). Matthew effects in reading: Some consequences of individual differences in the acquisition of literacy. *Reading Research Quarterly, 21,* 360–407.

Stipek, D. (1996). Motivation and instruction. In D. C. Berliner & R. C. Calfee (Eds.), *Handbook of educational psychology* (pp. 85–113). New York: Macmillan.

Sweet, A., Guthrie, J. T., & Ng, M. (1998). Teachers' perceptions and students reading motivations. *Journal of Educational Psychology, 90*(2), 210–223.

Thorkildsen, T., & Nicholls, J. G. (1998). Fifth graders' achievement orientations and beliefs: Individual and classroom differences. *Journal of Educational Psychology, 90,* 179–202.

Tobin, K. (1984). Student task involvement in activity oriented science. *Journal of Research in Science Teaching, 21,* 469–482.

Turner, J. C. (1995). The influence of classroom contexts on young children's motivation for literacy. *Reading Research Quarterly, 30,* 410–441.

Weiner, B. (1992). *Human motivation: Metaphors, theories, and research.* Newbury Park, CA: Sage.

Wentzel, K. R. (1996). Social and academic motivation in middle school: Concurrent and long-term relations to academic effort. *Journal of Early Adolescence, 16,* 390–406.

Wentzel, K. R. (1997). Student motivation in middle school: The role of perceived pedagogical caring. *Journal of Educational Psychology, 89*(3), 411–419.

Wentzel, K. R., & Wigfield, A. (1998). Academic and social motivational influences on students' academic performance. *Educational Psychology Review, 10,* 155–175.

Wigfield, A. (1997). Children's motivations for reading and reading engagement. In J. T. Guthrie & A. Wigfield (Eds.), *Reading engagement: Motivating readers through integrated instruction* (pp. 14–33). Newark, DE: International Reading Association.

Wigfield, A., & Asher, S. R. (1984). Social and motivational influences on reading. In P. D. Pearson (Ed.), *Handbook of reading research* (pp. 423–452). New York: Longman.

Wigfield, A., Eccles, J. S., MacIver, D., Reuman, D., & Midgley, C. (1991). Transitions at early adolescence: Changes in children's domain-specific self-perceptions and general self-esteem across the transition to junior high school. *Developmental Psychology, 27,* 52–565.

Wigfield, A., Eccles, J. S., & Pintrich, P. R. (1996). Development between the ages of 11 and 25. In D. C. Berliner & R. C. Calfee (Eds.). *Handbook of educational psychology* (pp. 148–185). New York: Simon & Schuster Macmillan.

Wigfield, A., Eccles, J. S., Yoon, K. S., Harold, R. D., Arbreton, A. J. A., Freedman-Doan, C., & Blumenfeld, P. C. (1997). Change in children's competence beliefs and subjective task values across the elementary school years: A 3-year study. *Journal of Educational Psychology, 89*(3), 451–469.

Wigfield, A., & Guthrie, J. T. (1997). Relations of children's motivation for reading to the amount and breadth of their reading. *Journal of Educational Psychology, 89,* 420–432.

Wlodkowski, R. (1985). *Enhancing adult motivation to learn.* San Francisco: Jossey Bass.

Zahorik, J. (1996). Elementary and secondary teachers' reports of how they make learning interesting. *Elementary School Journal, 96,* 551–564.

Zimmerman, B. J. (1989). A social cognitive view of self-regulated learning. *Journal of Educational Psychology, 81,* 329–339.

PART IV

Literacy Practices

CHAPTER 25

Emergent Literacy: A Matter (Polyphony) of Perspectives

David B. Yaden, Jr.
Rossier School of Education, University of Southern California/CIERA

Deborah W. Rowe
Peabody College, Vanderbilt University

Laurie MacGillivray
Rossier School of Education, University of Southern California/CIERA

BACKGROUND PERSPECTIVES AND ISSUES OF DEFINITION

What is Emergent Literacy Research?

To those outside the field of education, it must seem like an unnecessary splitting of hairs to debate whether young children's first encounters with print should be called *prereading, reading readiness, emergent literacy,* or *early literacy.* However, our view from within the field suggests that shifting terminology reflects more than just a proliferation of new terms for the same concept. Instead, when new terms take hold, we can usually also identify significant shifts in theory, research, and educational practice. The increasing use of the term *emergent literacy,* beginning in the 1980s, reflects such a shift. As Teale and Sulzby (1986) noted in the introduction to their influential volume *Emergent Literacy: Writing and Reading,* the adoption of a new term—"emergent literacy"—signaled a break with the theoretical concept of "reading readiness," particularly with the notions that young children needed to be taught a series of prerequisite skills prior to reading, and that writing should be delayed until children were reading conventionally. Although there was by no means unanimous agreement among re-searchers on the nature of literacy-learning processes, there was general excitement in the field concerning the possibility of uncovering the planfulness behind young children's unconventional scribbles and their early attempts at reading.

Further, there was intense interest in looking at the continuities between early literacy behaviors and conventional reading and writing. "These behaviors and knowledges are not pre-anything," Teale and Sulzby (1986) wrote. "It is not reasonable to point to a time in a child's life when literacy begins. Rather … we see children in the process of becoming literate, as the term emergent indicates" (p. xix). Discontinuities between adults' and children's literacy behaviors were recognized, but within a developmental frame that highlighted children's active construction of increasingly more sophisticated and conventional literacy strategies.

Historically, then, the term *emergent literacy* can be seen as implying a broad theoretical stance about literacy learning (developmental and constructivist), an age group (birth to age 5–6 years), and a focus on informal learning in holistic activities at home, preschool, or kindergarten. Although this view of emergent literacy is still important in the field, we find, at the time of this review, that researchers are less unified in their perspectives and approaches to studying early literacy learning. Perhaps not surprisingly, since the publication of the last *Handbook* chapter by Sulzby and Teale (1991), both the term *emergent literacy* and those using it have come to represent a broad spectrum of ontological, epistemological, and methodological stances (see Crawford, 1995; Hiebert & Raphael, 1998; Whitehurst & Lonigan, 1998, for recent comparisons).

Delimiting the Field

Faced with this diversity, we have debated the various features that we might use to make decisions about whether a study should be included in this chapter. As we reviewed the literature and talked informally with colleagues and teachers in the field, we found that age level remains a crucial defining characteristic of emergent literacy research (cf. Sulzby, 1991). When educators write or talk about emergent literacy, they are most often referring to children from birth through kindergarten. A second assumption is that emergent literacy research somehow tracks children's literacy knowledge and processes as they move from unconventional to conventional literacy during holistic literacy events such as storybook reading or play.

Thus, in this chapter, we have used the characteristics of age and research focus to guide (though not strictly limit) our choice of studies to be reviewed. As we have selected studies, we have generally adhered to earlier definitions (cf. Sulzby, 1991; Sulzby & Teale, 1991; Teale, 1987; Teale & Sulzby, 1986) and more recent ones (see McGee & Purcell-Gates, 1997) that suggest the importance of focusing on the "unconventionality" of children's early literacy behaviors and their development in informal settings at home and at school prior to beginning formal literacy instruction. For example, we share the view of McGee and Purcell-Gates (1997, p. 312) that systematic training in phoneme awareness tasks during the preschool years does not constitute the study of "emergent" literacy behaviors, nor do studies during the primary grades where formal literacy instruction and/or interventions are introduced and conducted quasi-experimentally. These types of studies are dealt with thoroughly elsewhere in this volume (see chapters on beginning reading and phoneme awareness). The following review, then, is primarily restricted to research with preschool children in either home, day-care, or kindergarten environments where systematic and explicit attempts to teach the children specific "skills" thought necessary for reading and writing were not taking place.

CONSTRUCTING A FRAMEWORK FOR THE REVIEW

Developing an Organizational Scheme

In order to get a sense of the structure we might employ in describing our research pool, we asked several questions during the reading of each article. For example, what is the purpose of the research? What are the research questions asked? What is the theory claimed? Who are the researched? What instruments are used and how? What is the research design? What is the nature of the data and how is it treated? What actually gets reported? What is concluded? As a result of this analysis, we decided that the most manageable way to present the last decade's research in emergent literacy was to organize the major sections first by the field or domain in which research has been most frequently conducted, and then, second, to differentiate within fields (using subheadings) by specific research focus. Hence, the following review shares some similarity with our predecessors' chapter (cf. Sulzby & Teale, 1991) in that storybook reading, emergent writing, home literacy influences, and metalinguistic awareness remain major areas of research activity in emergent literacy since the publication of the last *Handbook*. We also have devoted another major section to the effects of sociodramatic play upon emergent literacy, because research inquiry in this area has dramatically intensified during the last 10 years. Finally, in regard to major divisions, we have chosen to highlight early literacy research with children designated as having special learning needs as well as studies of comprehensive emergent literacy programs, because investigations in these areas have continued to noticeably grow in number.

In addition to the "content" divisions just discussed, we have chosen to add a third dimension of differentiation in the narrative itself that we believe distinguishes the purpose (conscious or otherwise) of the research epistemologically. Therefore, we have described the research in each section as either being *outcome-based, process-oriented*, or *developmental* in nature. These distinctions are discussed briefly in the next section.

Epistemological Perspectives

The following three categories mentioned earlier represented to us reasonably clear epistemological (as opposed to more narrow methodological) distinctions in the body of emergent literacy research that can further be placed within major groupings of either positivist or post-positivist inquiry (see Cunningham & Fitzgerald, 1996, for a comprehensive treatment of epistemologies in reading research; see also Denzin & Lincoln, 1994).

In the present chapter, we describe as *outcome-based* investigations that favor a positivist orientation and frame the constructs of literacy as more "componential," able to be stably indexed, and communicated pedagogically. The general purpose of such research is primarily to *verify* relations between emergent literacy variables and those considered more representative of conventional literacy. In addition, these inquiries are usually conducted according to quasi-experimental design criteria.

On the other hand, studies that we view as representing postpositivist assumptions fall into two groups. Research that we deem as more *process-oriented* tends to adhere more to qualitative or interpretivist principles (Erickson, 1990). Investigators pursuing these types of studies emphasize the ongoing simultaneity of inputs into the child's literacy experience and tend to use terms like *transaction, reorganization*, and *mediation* to describe the relation between the many, multifaceted layers of sociocultural and cognitive processes thought to be involved in the growth of reading and writing in young children.

Our final category of *developmental* research reflects interpretivist assumptions as well, but emphasizes the "moment-by-moment," evolutionary, systemic nature of literacy growth, unlike the descriptions of earlier developmentally oriented research in reading readiness and early literacy, which had a tendency to focus on the sequential development of discrete stages from a positivist perspective. As opposed to step- or stage-like literacy growth, we have characterized this movement as more *homeorhetic* (see Piaget, 1985, p. 4), in other words, being a somewhat "stabilized flow," increasing with spurts and hesitations rather than uniformity (cf. also definitions of *punctuated equilibrium* as in Gould and Eldredge, 1993).

STORYBOOK READING

Although storybook reading has continued to remain a major area of research over the last decade, questions about its actual efficacy for later literacy achievement have arisen more and more. Two widely quoted, recent reviews of the effects of joint storybook reading on subsequent reading achievement illustrate the current tension in the field regarding this once highly acclaimed practice. For example, after conducting a quantitative meta-analysis of 31 experimental studies of storybook reading over three decades, Bus, van Ijzendoorn, and Pelligrini (1995) asserted that "book reading is as strong a predictor of reading achievement as phoneme awareness" (p. 17). On the other hand, Scarborough and Dobrich (1994), having reviewed many of the same studies, concluded that "for now we think some parents would be reassured to know that there is no clear indication that literacy development depends crucially on shared reading experiences in the preschool years" (p. 295). Interestingly, both teams of researchers reported that storybook reading between parents and preschool children accounted for 8% of the variance of subsequent reading measures. Perhaps it is because of this existing tension that we notice a growing trend in the current storybook reading literature toward outcome-based, quasi-experimental research rather than the descriptive, qualitative inquiry that has generally characterized earlier studies.

Assessing the Language and Literacy Outcomes of Storybook Reading

Most of the studies in this subsection employ experimental interventions using some variation of a shared or big book treatment. For example, Mautte (1990) found that repeated big-book sessions weekly over 5 months produced significant differences in the language development between experimental and control groups of 66 4-year-old children deemed at risk. Similarly, Valdez-Menchaca and Whitehurst (1992) found differences between experimental and control groups of 20 low-income, Spanish-speaking 2-year-olds on a language performance measure when comparing "dialogic" storybook reading to traditional readiness instruction. In a further series of studies by Whitehurst and colleagues (Arnold, Lonigan, Whitehurst, & Epstein, 1994; Whitehurst, Epstein, Angell, Payne, Crone, & Fishel, 1994), groups of 2- to 4-year-old children read to "dialogically" by preschool teachers—as well as their mothers—significantly improved their scores on language, print concepts, and writing measures over their peers who were read to regularly but not engaged actively during the reading.

In one of the longest series of experimental studies conducted regarding the effect of shared book reading, Phillips, Norris, and Mason (1996) followed groups of Canadian kindergartners initially exposed in 1988 to a reading intervention program called Little Books (McCormick & Mason, 1990) and reported that the treatment groups' early literacy knowledge growth during their year of kindergarten was responsible for significant performance advantages over control groups in reading achievement throughout

Grades 1 to 4. And in another set of planned interventions, Feitelson and colleagues (Feitelson, Goldstein, Iraqi, & Share, 1993; Rosenhouse, Feitelson, Kita, & Goldstein, 1997) experimentally demonstrated in two studies that a 6-month intervention of daily "interactive reading" of storybooks in either Arabic or Hebrew to kindergartners and first graders produced significant performance differences over control groups on measures of listening comprehension, picture storytelling, decoding, and language use.

Other experimental investigations of storybook reading documenting either language or literacy outcomes include Morrow's (1989) finding that once-a-week story reading over 11 weeks with small groups of low-income children was more effective than traditional readiness activities in increasing their verbal participation, language complexity, and print concepts. Further, Neuman and Soundy (1991) compared "cooperative storybook reading" partnerships among low and high kindergarten achievers with groups engaged in sustained silent reading (SSR) and found that over a 6-week period, the children in the partnerships produced more story elements in retellings based on a picture-sequencing activity. In addition, Otto (1993) compared two groups of kindergartners exposed to a 14-week program of traditional, trade storybooks versus commercially prepared beginning readers and reported that children in the latter group were less able to interact with the complex text of traditional storybooks and scored at a lower level on Sulzby's (1985) emergent reading scale. Thus, despite disagreements as to "effect size," experimental investigations of storybook reading have continued to verify both its short- and long-term positive impact on language and literacy development (for an alternative view based upon correlational results, see Meyer, Wardrop, Stahl, & Linn, 1994).

Adult Storybook Reading Styles

Numerous descriptive and correlational studies (e.g., Dickinson & Keebler, 1989; Teale, Martinez, & Glass, 1989) suggested that the manner of parents' and teachers' read-alouds differentially impacts children's understanding of literacy. Subsequently, several researchers during the last decade, following outcome-based assumptions, either attempted to experimentally manipulate style variables in order to determine the precise effect of adults' mediation during storybook reading or used multivariate, correlational methods to determine relationships between adults' and childrens' behaviors.

In general, these more current studies have continued to find variation in measures of literacy performance or children's interactive, dialogic behaviors, which, in turn, can be related to differences in adults' manner of storybook reading. However, in our view, there has been no real convergence of findings upon any particular set of styles, despite statements to the contrary (see Dickinson & Smith, 1994, p. 116). Since the Sulzby and Teale (1991) review, at least a dozen new styles have been identified in the literature by studies using experimental designs (Nielsen, 1993), employing cluster analysis and other correlational methods (Allison & Watson, 1994; Dickinson & Smith, 1994; Haden, Reese & Fivush, 1996; Morrow, Rand, & Smith 1995), as well as qualitative, process-oriented techniques (De Temple & Tabors, 1995; Martinez & Teale, 1993). Given the styles identified in previous research, nearly 20 distinct descriptors of adult storybook reading behavior have now been introduced in the past two decades (e.g., analytic, coconstructive, collaborators, comprehenders, co-responders, describers, didactic-interactional, directors, gesture-eliciting, informer-monitors, label-eliciting, labeling, literary, nonreaders, performance-oriented, recitation readers, standard active readers, and straight readers).

We believe that the most pressing need for research in this area is to *synthesize* both the extant styles identified and the numerous analytic discourse coding schemes that have been used to generate them. Such a synthesis may help resolve a dispute in this area as to whether there may be, indeed, "an overwhelming number of styles" as suggested by Martinez and Teale (1993, p. 197) or, on the other hand, "only a limited set of approaches to reading books typically used by preschool teachers," as concluded by Dickinson and Smith (1994, p. 116).

Gender, Genre, and Individual Differences in Storybook Reading

Although research on adult behavior as a major source of variability within storybook reading has significantly grown over past 10 years, several other aspects of the storybook reading experience have also been studied. These studies tend to fall into the "process-oriented" or "developmental" categories because their goal is to closely describe the nature of the interaction itself, and rather *infer* (as opposed to *predict*) what the long-term effects on storyreading of these variables might be. The studies that we reviewed in this area had several foci, the main emphases being on aspects of text structure, book familiarity due to repeated readings, and individual characteristics of either the parent or child reader.

Text Structure and Familiarity.   Continuing an important line of work in this area (see Pappas, 1991), Pappas (1993) examined the emergent reading of narrative stories and information books by 16 kindergartners over 4 months and found that children were equally able to negotiate complex text structure differences (e.g., co-referentiality vs. coclassification) between narrative and information books. Additionally, looking at particular types of text format *within* genres that may have a differential effect on children's responses to storybooks. Yaden, Smolkin and colleagues (Smolkin, Yaden, Brown & Hofius, 1992; Yaden, 1993; Yaden, Smolkin, & MacGillivray, 1993) found that certain features of alphabet books (in particular, certain types of illustrations, and print that has been made "salient" in some way, e.g., speech balloons, labels in pictures, etc.) change the nature of the children's and parents' responses toward more discussion about the graphic nature of text and conventions of print (see also Greenewald & Kulig, 1995). Finally, extending earlier findings regarding the benefits to children when storybooks are reread, Elster and Walker (1992) discovered that low-income, 4- and 5-year-old children's ability to infer cause/effect relationships and make predictions was significantly enhanced with repeated readings of predictable texts.

Adult/Child Characteristics.   Extending their previous work with middle income families, Bus and van Ijzendoorn (1992, 1995) used discriminant function analysis to find that the level of attachment security between mother and child predicted the frequency of storybook reading in the home, leading the researchers to conclude that literacy experiences for children may be heavily dependent on the parent's own childhood history of attachment security. Further, Rowe (1994) noted in a year-long ethnography that her own implicit assumptions about what constituted a literacy event led to both subtle and overt attempts to redefine reading and writing events that the children had taken in another direction.

In related work focusing on children's behaviors, Martens (1996) described her 3-year-old daughter's learning as embedded within multiple meaning systems such as art, movement, play, and oral language. Similarly, in a process-oriented study exploring individual differences in approaches to shared book reading among peers, MacGillivray (1997) identified four "role-sets" (e.g., coworkers, fellow artists, teacher/student, boss/employee) that strongly framed the types of literacy interactions that took place and determined whether literacy knowledge was shared versus used as leverage to dominate.

Emergent Reading

Current investigations into the phenomenon of independent re-enactments of stories by young children generally confirm Sulzby's (1985) earlier suggestions that these reading demonstrations have developmental properties and indicate that early on children demonstrate knowledge of the written register (see also Cox, Fang, & Otto, 1997). Continuing research on emergent reading by Sulzby (1994; Sulzby & Zecker, 1991) and other investigators such as Elster (1994, 1995, 1998), McIntyre (1990), and MacGillivray (1997) showed that the levels themselves are highly fluid and subject to a number of external influences, including personal and background factors, prior knowledge, exposure to other texts, and exposure to adult storybook reading styles. Given that the system of emergent reading levels identified by Sulzby (1985, 1994) is one of the few analytic systems available for assessing comprehension prior to word reading (E. Sulzby, personal communication, April 25, 1999), we believe that the above studies provide important information for researchers to consider when using those levels as outcome measures to determine various aspects of literacy growth (cf. Allison & Watson, 1994, for example).

Storybook Reading and the Deaf

Studies of storybook reading with deaf children encompass a range of methodological approaches and, in many cases, focus on comparisons between deaf preschoolers and their hearing counterparts regarding parental reading strategies, children's responses, and other benefits accrued by children during storybook reading under normal conditions. In this particular literature, we noted a discrepancy between those studies that investigated only parents' behaviors during storybook reading (e.g., Lartz, 1993; Lartz & McCollum, 1990) and those investigating children's actual responses (see Gillespie & Twardosz, 1997; Williams, 1994; Williams & McLean, 1997). The latter investigations indicate that deaf and hard-of-hearing preschool children are clearly capable of exhibiting responses characteristic of their hearing peers when engaged in dialogic, interactive reading during storybook reading sessions. Indeed, the finding that parents simplify their reading style to accommodate their children's perceived language delay stands in contrast to the observation that deaf children have the capability to understand but are not given as many chances to prove it.

EMERGENT LITERACY AND SOCIODRAMATIC PLAY

The play–literacy connection has been one of the most heavily researched areas of early literacy learning and instruction in the last decade. Although other types of play exist, dramatic play—also called symbolic, sociodramatic, pretend, imaginative, or make-believe play—has been of most interest to literacy researchers. A central characteristic of this type of play is that children use make-believe transformations of objects and their own identities to act out scripts that they invent (Christie, 1991). Although seminal psychological studies in some lines of play–literacy research were published in the mid to late 1980s, the refinement of this work and its extension by educators into additional areas represents a new focus for early literacy research in the 1990s.

Global Links Between Dramatic Play and Literacy Learning

Although quite different, Piaget's (1962) and Vygotsky's (1978) theories concerning the role of dramatic play in cognitive development provided important impetus for research on the play-literacy connection (Pellegrini & Galda, 1993). This line of work is based on the general premise that dramatic play is an arena for developing general representational skills that are eventually applied in other domains, including reading and writing (Pellegrini & Galda, 1991). Outcome-based research designs have involved correlating play measures at Time 1 with measures of emergent reading and writing at Time 2 to establish which aspects of children's dramatic play predicted later reading and writing.

In general, this research offers a positive view of play as providing opportunities to build important cognitive and linguistic skills needed by emergent readers and writers. It also suggests that different aspects of play may be important in emergent reading and writing. Both correlational studies (Dickinson & Beals, 1994; Pellegrini & Galda, 1991) and experimental studies (Pellegrini & Galda, 1982; Silvern, Williamson, & Waters, 1983) have found that metaplay (i.e., oral language where children talk with peers about play) predicts later reading performance, whereas symbolic transformations are the best predictor of emergent writing (Pellegrini & Galda, 1991).

It should be noted here that, by their choice of measures, these studies primarily assess children's metalinguistic skills and their movement toward conventional decoding and writing. They do not investigate possible relationships between play and children's ability to comprehend texts or produce coherent written products.

Book-Related Play Events: Incorporating Book Themes Into Play

A second group of studies has investigated the direct connections between play and literacy that occur when children incorporate book plots, themes, characters, or information into their play scripts. Outcome-based studies have usually experimentally tested the effects of one or more types of play training on measures of story comprehension—most often immediate and delayed retellings of stories or multiple-choice recall tests. In general, the premise behind these studies has been that dramatic story reenactments provide opportunities for mental reconstructions of story events and the development of story schemas, both of which are posited to increase story comprehension (Williamson & Silvern, 1991).

Christie's review (1991) of the results of early play-training research concludes that these interventions have facilitative effects on a variety of literacy-related variables such as story production and comprehension. More recently, researchers have attempted to increase their understanding of the mechanism by which these results were obtained by designing experimental studies to explore the effect of different types of adult interventions and developmental changes in the relation between play and comprehension.

Effects of Adult Intervention.   With regard to adult intervention, results indicate that adult assistance is generally helpful in story reenactment tasks, whether adult roles are directive or facilitative (Pellegrini, 1984; Williamson & Silvern, 1991). Second, children may not need intensive adult help to engage in valuable story-related play (Pellegrini & Galda, 1993)—especially with familiar stories. In child-directed play settings, adult intervention may be less positive, and may, in fact, inhibit children's use of elaborated language (Pellegrini & Galda, 1993). Evidently, when adults are present they do most of the work, requiring children to engage in less negotiation with peers.

Developmental Patterns.   Developmental studies suggest that play training may be differentially effective for children of different ages. Pellegrini and Galda's (1993) review of these studies concludes that symbolic play had a positive effect on kindergarten and first-grade children's story comprehension but was less facilitative for older primary grades children. Williamson and Silvern (1991), however, found dramatic story reenactments to be helpful for older students who were below-average comprehenders. Although these results might be interpreted as suggesting that children need chances to talk about language rather than to play, Williamson and Silvern (1991) noted that children must be engaged in play to produce talk about play. Further, it seems that particular features of dramatic play (such as the presence of peers who have friendship relationships, Pellegrini, Galda, & Flor, in press) increase the likelihood that children will use the elaborated, cohesive language, and metalinguistic verbs valued in school talk.

Range of Play Behaviors.   More recent process-oriented studies have widened the range of story-related play studied. Building on informal observations of children's spontaneous book-to-play connections, several researchers have conducted long-term, naturalistic observations of young children's play in literacy-rich home and preschool settings. Findings indicate that children initiated book-related play not only in dramatic play events (Goodman, 1990; Rowe, 1998; Wolf & Heath, 1992) but also in other social contexts including informal book-reading events with peers and adults (Fassler, 1998; Rowe, 1998, in press; Wolf & Heath, 1992) and negotiations of social rules with parents (Wolf & Heath, 1992). Comprehension of story events was only one of several observed purposes for children's spontaneous book-related play. Children also used play for making personal responses to books, participating in book-reading events, creating a lived-through experience of the book, and furthering personal inquiries into questions about the world (Rowe, 1998, in press; Wolf & Heath, 1992). However, because most of the participants in the naturalistic studies reviewed here were from mainstream homes with many book experiences, future studies need to address questions concerning variation in book-related play across social and cultural contexts (see e.g., Martinez, Cheyney, & Teale, 1991).

Literacy-Enriched Play Centers: Incorporating Literate Roles in Dramatic Play

Naturalistic observations (Neuman & Roskos, 1991) of children's spontaneous dramatic play have indicated that children often incorporate literate behaviors as part of the play scripts they invent. However, as Morrow (1991) found in her study of 35 middle-class kindergarten classrooms, many school settings in the early 1990s were not well designed to facilitate literacy behaviors. In her sample, few literacy materials were easily available for children's use, and teachers did little to promote voluntary literacy activities during play. Taken together, these findings evoked considerable interest on the part of educational researchers in developing literacy-enriched play centers by adding general literacy materials such as pencils and paper, as well as theme-related literacy props (e.g. stamps, envelopes, appointment books, and phone books for an "office" play center; see also Neuman & Roskos, 1990, 1991, 1992). A major premise underlying this work is that play interventions can have a direct impact on written language development by providing opportunities for children to read and write in contextualized situations (Hall, 1991; Christie, 1991).

Although the designs of studies investigating literacy-enriched play centers have differed (see Christie's 1991 review for an extensive discussion of the methodology used), as a group they address four major questions: First, what patterns of child and adult interactions are observed in literacy-enriched play centers? Second, do these centers increase the amount of literacy-related play? Third, does adult mediation impact the amount and type of play? And fourth, do literacy-enriched play centers affect children's performance on measures of emergent reading and writing?

Child and Adult Interaction Patterns.   Process-oriented studies of literacy-enriched play centers demonstrate that there is considerable variation in the nature of play (Stone & Christie, 1996; Neuman & Roskos, 1993) as themes, materials, and adult intervention change. Play centers are not a single consistent intervention day after day, but instead are complex ecological niches where the context of play activity is socially constructed by participants in face to face interaction. Neuman and Roskos's (1997) analyses suggest that these play centers provide support for literacy learning through (a) the presence of people who share expertise and provide assistance, (b) feedback from others, (c) access to literacy tools and related supplies, (d) multiple options for activity, and (e) problem-solving situations.

Naturalistic observation of children's play in literacy-enriched play centers indicates that children display considerable knowledge of literacy functions and strategies (Neuman & Roskos, 1993, 1997; Schrader, 1991; Stone & Christie, 1996). Children's use of functional knowledge and strategies is impacted, however, by factors such as age (Stone & Christie, 1996), the familiarity and complexity of the literacy routines being played out (Neuman & Roskos, 1997), and the specific roles taken by peers (Stone & Christie, 1996; Vukelich, 1993) and adults (Neuman & Roskos, 1993).

Researchers have described several different facets of adults' interactions during play, including their social roles in play events (Roskos & Neuman, 1993) and the interactive strategies used to support and extend children's literacy activities (Neuman & Roskos, 1993). Findings show that adults adopt multiple roles in the course of these events, rather than operating within a single interaction style (Roskos & Neuman, 1993; Schrader, 1991). Effective mediation appears to require adults to match their strategies to the child's intentions and knowledge (Schrader, 1991), and to phase in and out of more and less directive roles (Roskos & Neuman, 1993). Although not analyzed directly in any of these studies, there is some indication that there is cultural variation in the language and actions adults use to operationalize intervention strategies (Neuman & Roskos, 1993). Although there has been less attention paid to peer interactions, initial studies (Neuman & Roskos, 1991; Stone & Christie, 1996) suggest that peers also help each other with such tasks as naming literate objects and negotiating literate roles and routines.

Frequency of Literacy-Related Play. In addition to process-oriented investigations of adult and child behaviors, there has been considerable attention in outcome-oriented studies to determine whether the addition of themed literacy materials actually increases the amount of literacy-related play. The answer to this question is a resounding "Yes!" The inclusion of literacy-enriched play centers increases—often dramatically—the amount of literacy-related activities children engage in during play (Christie & Enz, 1992; Morrow & Rand, 1991; Neuman & Roskos, 1991, 1992, 1993; Vukelich, 1991b). Literacy-related play in intervention groups has been found to be more complex than that produced by control subjects, to incorporate more explicit oral communication, to use literacy objects in more functional ways, and to produce more object transformations (Neuman & Roskos, 1992). These effects appear to be sustained over time after the novelty of new materials wears off (Neuman & Roskos, 1992, 1993). Types of literacy materials inserted in the play centers also appear to impact patterns of play (Morrow & Rand, 1991).

Effects of Adult Mediation. The answer to the third question concerning whether adult mediation increases the amount of literacy-related play is also a clear "Yes." When "materials only" and "materials plus adult scaffolding" interventions were compared, children engaged in significantly more literacy-related play when adults were present (Morrow & Rand, 1991; Vukelich, 1991a). Christie and Enz (1992) suggested that, in addition to direct effects of adult attempts to encourage literacy-related play, adult presence may have the indirect effects such as maintaining children's interest in dramatic play.

Effects on Measures of Emergent Reading.   The fourth question concerning the impact of literacy-enriched play centers on measures of emergent reading and writing is less easily answered. To date, the four studies investigating the question have obtained mixed results. Although Neuman and Roskos (1990) found that a literacy-enriched play center intervention increased children's print awareness scores, other researchers (Christie & Enz, 1992; Vukelich, 1991b) failed to find significant increases. When children's understanding of the functions of writing was measured, Vukelich (1991b) found significant increases for one treatment group, whereas Neuman and Roskos (1993) found none. In the latter study, however, the researchers found significantly higher scores on measures of environmental print reading when children played in literacy-enriched play centers where adults offered suggestions and took roles in the play. It is likely that these contradictory findings are, in part, the result of the kinds of treatment groups that were compared. Several of these studies were designed without a no-treatment control group, making it difficult to determine whether each of the alternate treatments was equally effective or none of the treatments impacted literacy learning in important ways. More controlled research is needed to address this question.

EMERGENT WRITING

Research on emergent writing has a relatively short history. The field was launched in the early 1970s by several influential studies (e.g., Clay 1975; Read, 1975) that focused attention on the planfulness of children's initial, and mostly unconventional, attempts at writing. During the 1980s, the volume of emergent writing research increased substantially, with researchers focusing on emergent writing forms and the developmental sequences leading children from scribbling to conventional writing (Sulzby & Teale, 1991). Interestingly, in the 1990s, there has been a decrease in the amount of research on emergent writing as compared with the previous decade. We expect this trend reflects the fact that researchers began the 1990s with a relatively well-developed research base describing children's emergent writing behaviors. Although some researchers continue to advance the field by focusing on cognitive aspects of children's writing processes, others have adopted theoretical stances that introduce intriguing new questions about the influence of social interaction, culturally based literacy practices, and the integration of multiple sign systems.

Theoretical Issues

Our review identified five theoretical issues related to children's literacy learning processes that have generated a good deal of discussion over the last decade. The first question is whether emergent writing development is best viewed as a psychogenetic progression through a series of stages (Besse, 1996) or the social construction of literacy hypotheses based on the child's personal experiences (Rowe, 1994; Sulzby, 1996). Both explanations continue to be used by researchers to explain patterns in children's emergent writing.

A second theoretical question that continues to be of interest is the relation between writing and oral language. Although there has been a tendency to analyze emergent writing as an independent phenomenon, Pontecorvo and Morani (1996) cautioned against simple dichotomies between oral and written language. Their work with French children suggested that writing emerges from oral practices of the child's culture—a hypothesis also advanced by researchers working with children from the United States (e.g., Cox et al., 1997; Dyson, 1993; Sulzby, 1996).

A third theoretical question considers the relation between emergent writing and reading. Of particular interest in outcome-based studies have been questions concerning the role of invented spelling in beginning reading. Richgels (1995b), for example, used a causal comparative design to demonstrate that good invented spellers learned to read phonetically simplified words better than poor invented spellers. We take studies of this sort as another indicator of the maturing of the field because they replace the implicit assumption that emergent writing supports literacy learning with theoretical understanding of the ways that emergent writing interacts with other aspects of literacy learning.

The fourth theoretical question concerns the sociocognitive and sociocultural dimensions of children's literacy learning. It is these questions that have experienced the greatest increase in attention for process-oriented researchers. Researchers working within a sociocognitive frame work have moved beyond the individual to examine the role other people play in children's emergent writing. Researchers working within a sociocultural frame work have examined how emergent writing grows from the cultural practices of classrooms and homes. This work has challenged the notion that there is a single "literacy" or one universal pattern of literacy learning. Further, this work has broadened the focus of emergent literacy research to include the power relationships that impact how children's writing is valued in different contexts.

A final theoretical issue receiving increased attention in process-oriented research is the relation between emergent writing and other sign systems such as drawing, constructive art, and drama. Several researchers (e.g., Dyson, 1995; Gallas, 1994; Leland & Harste, 1994; Rowe, 1994, 1998) have argued that emergent literacy should be broadly conceptualized as the ways children make meaning in a variety of sign systems. Although the multimodal nature of emergent writing is not a new area of study, Kress (1997) argued that it is now more important because of the advent of new communication technologies where written language is less central—a point underscored by Labbo's (1996a) description of the multimodal texts generated by emergent writers on the computer.

Forms of Emergent Writing

During the decade covered by this review, researchers have continued to add descriptions of the forms of children's emergent writing to the literature, but at a much slower pace than the work of the 1970s and 1980s. Methodologically, there is a mix of naturalistic and controlled observations, with some researchers recording students' writing during their regular classroom instruction and others observing responses to researcher-designed writing prompts and clinical interviews.

Developmental case studies (Branscombe & Taylor, 1996; Martens, 1996; Olson & Sulzby, 1991; Schickedanz, 1990) focusing on young children's hypotheses for writing words have largely confirmed patterns described earlier by researchers such as Clay (1975) and Sulzby (1989). A number of process-oriented studies have focused on describing sentence- and text-level patterns in children's writing more fully. Aspects studied include punctuation (Martens, 1996; Martens & Goodman, 1996), genre of children's texts (Chapman, 1996; Pontecorvo & Morani, 1996), children's use of quoted speech (Sulzby, 1996), and integration of multiple sign systems (Gallas, 1994; Kress, 1997; Rowe, 1994).

Emergent Writing as a Social Event

Although many of the studies reviewed in the previous section have acknowledged the role of other people in children's construction of written texts, their focus remains largely on the individual child and his or her text. The studies reviewed in this section focus on the ways social interaction impacts emergent writing.

Peer Interaction.   Several process-oriented studies (Labbo, 1996b; Rowe, 1994; Troyer, 1991) used naturalistic techniques to describe interactions that occur naturally between peers as they gather in classrooms to write texts of their own choosing. In general, researchers reported that peer interactions have provided needed support for writing (Labbo, 1996a; Rowe, 1994; Troyer, 1991). It also appears that interaction patterns vary and are affected both by individual factors such as the child's personal style, age, and familiarity of the task at hand (Zucchermaglio & Scheuer, 1996), and by social factors such as the nature of the task, norms for writing developed in the particular classroom (MacGillivray, 1994), and the particular roles taken by adults and children in the event (Burns & Casbergue, 1992; DeBaryshe, Buell, & Binder, 1996; Power, 1991; Rowe, 1994; Zucchermaglio & Scheuer, 1996).

Social Demonstrations.   Children's writing processes and strategies also appear to be impacted by the social demonstrations they encounter (Rowe, 1994). Researchers working from a sociocognitive perspective have described the ways that the genre (Ballenger, 1996; Chapman, 1996) and content (Rowe, 1994) of children's texts are affected by the books they read, their observations of other authors in the process of writing, and their interactions with others about their writing. Several process-oriented studies also report that social relationships of friendship and family are a major motivator for learning about print and using it (Ballenger, 1996; MacGillivray, 1994; Rowe, 1994).

Social Context.   Sociocultural studies of emergent writing provide a somewhat different lens for understanding the social nature of emergent writing. They have investigated how classroom interactions and literacy strategies are tied, explicitly or implicitly, to culturally held definitions of literacy, power relationships, and values (MacGillivray & Martinez, 1998; Power, 1991; Purcell-Gates, 1995). Other process-oriented studies have documented how children's literacy knowledge is related to social features of particular classroom events (i.e., Kantor, Miller, & Fernie, 1992; MacGillivray, 1994). Drawing on a series of naturalistic studies of kindergarten and early primary grade writers in school settings, Dyson (1992, 1993) concluded that writing is a sociocultural process in that written texts position authors in particular ways in the social life of the classroom, reflect the ways different types of literacy are valued by groups within the classroom, and represent a way of engaging in a particular kind of social dialogue with particular others. Together, these studies highlight the cultural and interactive basis for how children define and use literacy—an observation that helps to explain the variation in emergent literacy patterns reported earlier. Further, these studies raise a number of complex issues concerning societal values and definitions of literacy, clashes of culture between home and school, and differential valuing of the cultural capital children bring to school.

EMERGENT LITERACY AND THE HOME

Since the last *Handbook,* there has been more research in homes where traditional literacy activities (e.g., storybook reading) rarely occur. Following a trend begun in the 1980s, more research has moved beyond parent surveys and self-reports to include observations within homes, and studies with mixed designs using qualitative and quantitative techniques have been conducted more frequently. Foci vary, but particular attention has been paid to literacy as a complex process. Ever since Heath's (1983) seminal report, simple explanations such as socioeconomic status are no longer acceptable for explaining a child's literacy failure or success (see also Taylor & Dorsey-Gaines, 1988) and research in the last decade has attempted more precisely to figure out what does offer a strong literacy foundation (see the chapter on home literacy, this volume, for additional research on intergenerational literacy activities and family intervention programs).

Parents' Perceptions of Literacy Learning and Practices

The research on parents' perceptions is primarily process oriented, and the studies we reviewed used different means for gathering data, including observation (Goldenberg, Reece, & Gallimore, 1992), interviews (Fitzgerald, Spiegel, and Cunningham, 1991), focus groups (Neuman, Hagedorn, Celano, & Daly, 1995), and questionnaires (Hiebert & Adams, 1987; Snow, Barnes, Chandler, Goodman, & Hemphill, 1991). In addition, studies attend to both parental perceptions of how literacy is *acquired* as well as to parents' perceptions of literacy *uses* and *functions* in general.

Views on How Literacy Is Used.   Examples of this latter focus are reports from the Baltimore Early Childhood Project (see Baker, Sonnenschein, & Serpell, 1994; Serpell, 1997; Sonnenschein, Brody, Munsterman, 1996), where three differing themes were noted: (a) Literacy is a source of entertainment; (b) literacy is a set of skills to be deliberately cultivated; and (c) literacy is an integral ingredient of everyday life. Further, in a study of Icelandic families, Ronald Taylor (1995) found that leisure was the most observed and reported purpose of reading for both urban and nonurban families, despite differences in the mothers' educational level. Also, Leseman and De Jong (1989) conducted an investigation of families with 4-year-olds living in inner cities in the Netherlands and noted that literacy interactions were more related to cultural lifestyle (i.e., Dutch, immigrant Surinamese, and immigrant Turkish) and religious practices than to socioeconomic status.

Views on How Literacy Is Acquired.   Most of the studies on parents' perceptions of literacy acquisition have reported results by cultural groups without further differentiation as regards to individual ability or other factors (an exception is Fitzgerald et al., 1991, who distinguished parents by "high and low" level literacy). Even so, considerable variation has been found both within and across the populations studied.

In an oft-cited study, Goldenberg, Reese, and Gallimore (1992) asserted that most of the Hispanic mothers of their 10, working-class Spanish-speaking kindergartners viewed learning to read as a process that started with learning letters and sounds (see also Madrigal, Cubillas, Yaden, Tam & Brassell, 1999). Additionally, Anderson's (1995) examination of perceptions of literacy acquisition with three cultural groups in Canada showed that although most of the parents supported some tenets of emergent literacy theory, they differed on critical issues such as whether children "learned to read holistically" (p. 266). Similarly, Neuman et al. (1995) found a range of views on literacy learning within a group of African American adolescent parents.

The Relationship Between Home Factors and School Achievement

The research on home factors as related to literacy development builds on earlier work (e.g., Taylor & Dorsey-Gaines, 1988) and further documents that economic levels alone do not determine school success or failure. Nonetheless, a wide range in the quantity and nature of literacy practices across socioeconomic groups has been documented (see, e.g., Beals & DeTemple, 1993; Purcell-Gates, 1996; Shapiro, 1995). For example, Snow and her colleagues (Snow et al., 1991) in the Home-School Study of Language and Literacy Development found that the type of talk during mealtimes, particularly talk about things "not immediately present," related positively to the literacy-related language skills of the young children from low socioeconomic areas (cf. also Dickinson & Tabors, 1991). Further, in a multiyear study with all middle-class children, Scarborough, Dobrich, and Hager (1991) showed that preschoolers who became poor readers by second grade had less frequent early literacy-related experiences than those who became better readers. Finally, in another longitudinal study, Smith (1997) measured children's emergent literacy knowledge at the time of entering preschool and found a strong positive relationship to their reading ability 5 years later.

Although Smith's (1997) study focused on measuring entering abilities and Scarborough et al. (1991) attended to initial experiences with print, both longitudinal studies offer insight into the difficult process of sorting out the complexities of the impact early literacy experiences on later achievement. What does seem to be the case, however, is that the more literacy knowledge children bring to school, the better they will do in schools as they are currently conceived.

The Dynamics of Family Literacy Practices

Most studies looking at home literacy practices choose to focus closely on a few families, using process-oriented, case study methodology. Building on the work of Heath (1983), the studies described next offer new insights into the specifics of family life, focusing on aspects of culture, ethnicity, and gender.

In a widely cited ethnography, Purcell-Gates (1995) documented the literacy development of an urban Appalachian mother and her son, and stressed the importance of one's initiation and introduction into the world of print by others. Even print-rich environments provide less opportunities for literacy growth if children do not know how to interact with the print artifacts within them. In other case study research, Mulhern (1997; in press) detailed the life of three Mexican immigrant kindergartners and captured the way children negotiated the various expectations of adults, siblings, and peers during their interactions with print. Like Neuman et al. (1995), Mulhern revealed the diversity within what could be viewed as a homogenous group. Finally, Solsken's (1993) research situated literacy learning as a continual process of self-definition, arguing that through literate acts young learners also construct identities related to gender and work. In summary, these descriptive studies of children's early navigation of literacy learning offer critical information into the rich and complex processes of understanding how they make sense of the world as it is mediated by the world of print and others' attitudes toward using it.

Environmental Print

Although Yetta Goodman (1986; see also Orellana & Hernandez, 1999) identified the exposure to environmental print as one of the main "roots" of literacy, other studies—operating with outcome-based assumptions—have been unable to find strong relationships between environmental print recognition and conventional reading ability. In one of the few experimental studies, for example, Stahl and Murray (1993) found that children's exposure to logos did not facilitate their word recognition ability. Further, a study by Shaffer and McNinch (1995) highlighted the variation in ability between academically at-risk preschool children and their academically advantaged peers in giving meaningful responses to logographic stimuli. Additionally, Purcell-Gates (1996) wrote that "children are better served by observing and experiencing the reading and writing of connected discourse decontextualized from physical (such as signs and containers) and pictorial contexts" (p. 426) because she discovered an average of less than one instance of actual reading and writing per hour in 20 low-income families.

METALINGUISTIC AWARENESS
AND EMERGENT LITERACY GROWTH

In reviewing literature regarding metalinguistic awareness and early reading 10 years ago, Sulzby and Teale (1991) focused exclusively on the development of and instruction in phoneme awareness, partly to draw attention to the important but neglected link between emergent reading and writing, and conventional literacy behaviors. Since then, their observations that (a) children can be trained in phoneme awareness prior to formal instruction provided that they have a modicum of letter knowledge and (b) phoneme awareness is linked to later reading and spelling achievement have been confirmed repeatedly in research throughout the last decade (see Blachman, this volume, for a comprehensive summary). They further alluded to three other issues that were raised again recently by McGee and Purcell-Gates (1997). First of all, what are the differences, if any, between phoneme awareness that develops informally and that which is instilled by training, and what is the impact of those differences on learning to read and write? A second issue has to do with quality or, perhaps, amount of knowledge that is needed to exhibit conventional behaviors. And lastly, there is the concern about who profits from training and who does not. Because Blachman's chapter (this volume) offers thorough coverage of the development of phoneme awareness in particular, we focus on the broader aspects of metalinguistic and metacognitive knowledge as well as those studies addressing the issues raised earlier.

The Emergence of Metalinguistic Awareness
Through Storybook Reading

Goodman (1986), in particular, argued that children acquire both metalanguage terms (e.g., word, letter, story, etc.) and conscious awareness about written language through storybook reading events. That children spontaneously talk about aspects of letters, words, and texts during storybook reading has been documented by Yaden and colleagues (Yaden, 1993; Yaden, Smolkin, & Conlon, 1989; Yaden et al., 1993) in process-oriented and developmentally oriented studies using both longitudinal and single-subject designs. This research indicates that metalinguistic awareness about written and spoken language emerges developmentally (cf. Roberts, 1992) from tacit awarenesses about texts initially focused on elements of meaning to more explicit reflections concerning the conventions of books, and aspects of letters and words themselves. In an experimental study using genre as a treatment variable, Murray, Stahl, and Ivey (1996) demonstrated that children reading alphabet books with accompanying examples of words illustrating the various sounds had significantly higher levels of phoneme awareness than children reading traditional storybooks or alphabet books without accompanying examples. Murray et al. (1996) pointed out, however, that all groups of children reading different types of alphabet and storybooks advanced in phoneme awareness and in concepts about print and letter knowledge.

Evidence of Metalinguistic Awareness
During Invented Spelling

The work of Richgels and colleagues (Burns & Richgels, 1989; Richgels, 1995a, 1995b; Richgels, Poremba, & McGee, 1996) has done much to differentiate between different types of metalinguistic knowledge and their correlational relations to spelling and later reading achievement. In addition to noting that many 4-year-olds are capable of spelling phonetically, Burns and Richgels (1989) found that, among inventive spellers as a group—all of whom were able to segment words by sounds and had a substantial amount of letter/sound knowledge—only a portion of them could read words proficiently, thus calling into question the widely held view (cf. Share & Stanovich, 1995) that any amount of segmentation ability directly enables word reading ability. Further, Richgels (1995b) also demonstrated that kindergartners with no formal instruction in phoneme awareness who were also classified as good inventive spellers were better able to learn phonetically simplified words than poor inventive spellers, thus strengthening the connection between higher levels of naturally developing spelling ability and later word learning.

Forms of Metalinguistic Awareness During Dictation and Writing Tasks

All of the studies reviewed next posit developmental trends in children's demonstration of both written and oral language awareness. For example, Pontecorvo and ZuccTemaglio (1989), hypothesizing that children can engage in decontextualized communication prior to writing themselves, studied 6-year-old children's dictation to adults over a year and a half and found increases in narrative sophistication, use of connectives and anaphoric references, and pace of dictation (i.e., signaling clause segmentation by pausing for the scribe). Further, in a multivariate, correlational study, Roberts (1992) found that children demonstrated *tacit* awareness of spoken and written language first, followed by *explicit* awareness of written forms, and only later reflective knowledge about spoken language.

More recently, in a developmentally oriented study charting the emergence of word segmentation ability in Hebrew and Spanish with groups of preschool through second graders, Tolchinsky and Teberosky (1998) found distinct differences between languages in that Hebrew children pronounced dramatically more consonants in isolation, whereas Spanish children engaged in substantially more oral spelling. Although Tolchinsky and Teberosky (1998) concluded that the syllable was the preferred unit of segmentation in both languages, they stressed that any relationship between phonological segmentation and writing must take into account both the orthography and the acoustic properties of the language being learned.

Evidence of Metalinguistic Ability During Classroom Reading and Writing Events

In this final subsection, we review research that attempts to capture children's metalinguistic abilities as they are exhibited in more general classroom settings and observed as youngsters engaged in a variety of forms of communication with peers as well as adults. Through an observational study in which children were observed over 2 years in their classrooms in various reading and writing situations, Dahl (1993) documented five categories of "spontaneous" (not in response to questions or probes) metacognitive and metalinguistic statements that children made about aspects of written language, including its form, function, and their rule systems for reading and writing it. Similarly, drawing on data gathered in primary classrooms comparing whole-language and skills-based instruction (Dahl & Freppon, 1995; Purcell-Gates & Dahl, 1991), McIntyre and Freppon (1994) observed children both using and talking about several dimensions of alphabetic knowledge in both instructional settings. Their study, in particular, shows that despite the specific approach to teaching employed, children experiment with oral and written language forms, take the initiative in learning how to use it even beyond classroom applications, and make judgments about the larger purposes and functions of written language in a social context.

As to the issues raised at the beginning of this section, we discovered no studies that compared the quality of metalinguistic abilities learned informally versus by direct training, although there are any number of studies concerning each group separately. Further, we could not identify a specific level of tacit or conscious metalinguistic beyond the standard descriptions of "good versus poor," "high versus low," or "experienced versus inexperienced," which could be used as some sort of criterion threshold for determining when there is "enough" metalinguistic knowledge to make a difference in a child's momentum toward conventional literacy. Lastly, the suggestion from the research is that those who benefit from training are those children who *already* have an incipient foundation of knowledge and experience to build on, levels of socioeconomic status notwithstanding. The later this foundation is built, the slower is the growth.

EMERGENT LITERACY GROWTH
IN CHILDREN WITH SPECIAL NEEDS

Notably within the last 10 years, there has been an increase in the number of studies examining the presence of emergent literacy abilities in children with a variety of learning disabilities, language impairments as well as visual and hearing losses. Unfortunately, given the space limitations of this chapter, it was simply not possible to discuss all of the research we found dealing with emerging literacy in, for example, the variety of children designated as autistic, learning-disabled, hearing impaired, and visually impaired (e.g., Craig, 1996; Kavims & Pierce, 1995). Suffice it to say the general tenor of this body of work suggests that emergent literacy assumptions are particularly applicable in explaining how children with special learning requirements acquire knowledge of reading and writing.

The investigations that we did review more closely, examining emergent literacy assumptions and techniques with hearing-impaired and deaf children (Rottenberg & Searfoss, 1992; Williams, 1994), children with language delays (Sulzby & Kaderavek, 1996), and those prenatally exposed to crack cocaine (Barone, 1994, 1997), found that these children grew in literacy knowledge similarly to populations of normally developing children. In addition, Barone's (1997) 4-year study of children prenatally exposed to crack cocaine has shown that, given equal opportunity in homes and classrooms to actively engage with written materials and literate others, these children are equally capable of both normal learning in school and excelling. Also, the findings with hearing-impaired children (see Rottenberg & Searfoss, 1992; Williams, 1994, discussed earlier) that early written language learning can proceed normally without extensive oral language support is an important consideration in developing models of early literacy learning (cf., e.g., Share & Stanovich, 1995), which have a tendency to assume the primacy of an oral language component.

COMPREHENSIVE EMERGENT
LITERACY PROGRAMS

This final section reviews instructional programs or investigations targeting preschool or kindergarten children that attempt to incorporate all aspects of an emergent literacy program (see Labbo & Teale, 1998, for a comprehensive description of the underpinnings of an emergent literacy curriculum design) rather than assessing the value of only a single component such as storybook reading, story extension activities (Labbo, 1996b), or emergent writing (e.g., Richgels, 1995a).

The overall findings from the reviewed studies (see Englert et al., 1995; Nielsen & Monson, 1996; Sulzby, Branz, & Buhle, 1993) decidedly confirm the recent statement of

Labbo and Teale (1998) that "no matter what the age or previous experience of the children, an emergent literacy approach is appropriate" (p. 250). For example, implementing multiple emergent literacy activities over 2 years, Englert et al. (1995) reported that second-year students in their project outperformed both first-year students and a control group of Project READ children on selected measures of writing, reading comprehension, and metacognitive knowledge. Although not attributing students' knowledge gains to any one facet of the program, the authors stressed that the holistic nature of the learning experiences, the teachers' "ownership" over time of the projects' principles and curriculum, and the sense that a "literate community" was established between students, teachers, and wider community were crucial components in making it a success.

In two international applications of emergent literacy principles, Kriegler, Ramarumo, Van der Ryst, Van Niekerk, and Winer (1994) describe a 23-week emergent literacy program implemented in 19 nursery schools in rural South Africa where over half of the adults in the community had received no formal schooling. Despite the fact that the intervention last only 6 months, Kriegler et al. (1994) reported that a treatment group of 21 nursery school children, even though 8 months younger, increased in their knowledge of book handling, word recognition, and print conventions over two control groups not participating in the project. Similarly, in Finland where children normally learn to read following analytic and synthetic phonic approaches, Korkeamaki and Dreher (1995, 1996) reported the success of an emergent literacy program for kindergarten and primary grade children.

Contrary to the controversial stance of late (see Foorman, Francis, Fletcher, Schatschneider, & Mehta, 1998) that kindergarten children designated at-risk or primary grade children identified with reading difficulties need primarily structured phonics activities and phonemic awareness training, the research we examined promotes the observation that children with an astounding range of cognitive abilities, physical or language learning complications, environmental circumstances, or prior experience with print (or lack of, as the case may be) respond, for the most part, very positively to emergent literacy programs. Key features shared by all of these programs include (a) drawing children in as socially competent partners, (b) allowing them to experiment without undue duress, (c) providing them with a variety of adult- and peer-mediated dialogue about literature and ways to read and write, and (d) creating any number of opportunities for them to practice their unconventional, yet emerging skills.

FUTURE REFLECTIONS

In this brief review, we have attempted to present an "aerial" view, so to speak, of the topographical features that comprise the field we know as emergent literacy. As in any view, however, we recognize that ours too is value-laden and subject to certain assumptions that lead us to see one thing as opposed to another. However, the advantage for educators, we think, of taking ownership of one's own perspective is that it forces us to recognize, understand, and, hopefully, appreciate why others see things differently. Taking a step back from this present work, then, we are struck by the forceful movement in emergent literacy studies toward both complexity and contextualization, yet at the same time, a "balkanization," as it were, of the points of view brought to bear during discussions of this complexity. This is a matter we address shortly.

Our overall interpretation of the research during this past decade is that it impels the research community to recognize that simple answers to basic questions—Is it good to read to children? How do forms of emergent writing change as children develop as writers? What is the role of the home in preparing children for successful literacy learning?—are unlikely to easily account for the diversity of children's literacy behaviors. Instead, we see the need for both initial research questions and subsequent findings to be increasingly situated within a web of other, related questions: Which children? Where? With whom? Under what circumstances? To us, it now seems incumbent on researchers to define and study literacy in more contextualized frames.

Our review suggests to us, however, that although the last decade has brought more diversity in the posing of research questions, more variety in the populations under investigation, and much greater depth in certain areas of inquiry, the research community investing time in the study of young children's literacy growth may still be laboring with limited epistemologies that are unable to account for the growing complexity that is evident (see Yaden, 1999, for a discussion of "complexity" theories and reading acquisition). We would like to close this review with our own "take" on how these tensions between the complexity of the phenomenon under study—emergent literacy, in our case—and economy of research interpretation have affected the nature of early literacy research and, finally, offer some suggestions as to how these tensions might be lessened, albeit never resolved. In keeping with our earlier metaphor of topology, we would like to frame the following discussion by describing three major crossroads that we feel have to be negotiated in order to move the field ahead in the 21st century.

A Theoretical Crossroad

The first crossroad is theoretical. Although over the years models of early literacy acquisition have been posed (cf. Goodman, 1986; Mason, 1984; Lomax & McGee, 1987; Share & Stanovich, 1995; Wells & Chang-Wells, 1992; Whitehurst & Epstein et al., 1994), none has received very wide acceptance—not at least in comparison to models of adult reading (cf. Stanovich, 1980). However, with the increasing tendency toward the intersection of complex cognitive, social, and cultural explanations of emergent literacy learning, the absence of a theoretical model against which these ideas might be tested leaves the field, as pointed out by Mason (1984) some years ago, without direction in explaining individual differences or in designing "what early reading instruction to provide and when to provide it" (p. 532), if indeed it should be provided at all—as Sulzby and Teale (1991, p. 749) mused at the beginning of this decade.

Although in our perusal of studies we found ubiquitous references to either Piaget or Vygotsky—and sometimes both—in most of the studies we reviewed, regardless of whether they were outcome-based, process-oriented, or developmental, no one was seriously addressing the question that Teale (1987) raised more than 10 years ago of "how to deal with the compatible, yet conflicting, theories of Vygotsky and Piaget when it comes to literacy development" (p. 67). In our view, passing references to the "zone of proximal development" or parenthetical citations only to the standard works of either theorist are not sufficient grounds on which to launch an investigation with any theoretical integrity. Nor are mere connections to previous investigations on similar topics that may themselves be theoretically suspect.

Thus, in our view, serious theoretical work remains to be done. We concur wholeheartedly with the statement of McGee and Purcell-Gates (1997) that "as researchers we need to focus on articulating a theoretical model [or models, we might add] that synthesizes what our findings have revealed to this point" (p. 317). We believe that whether these models are refinements of those already in existence or to be built anew, researchers in emergent literacy must pay closer attention to examining the deeper connections between sociocognitive studies, which seem especially promising for adding new insights into issues of variation and similarity in children's learning patterns, and sociocultural perspectives, which situate emergent literacy within the social and cultural practices of classrooms and families. Although we welcome the diversity of view points that we see in the past decade's research, at the same time it remains fundamentally important that researchers look for theoretical and methodological connections between perspectives. We also suggest that researchers, in their individual investigations, avoid the seductive tendency of our own editorial guidelines toward proliferating parenthetical citations and spend more space discussing only the studies most germane to their work and carefully delineating the constructs of what they are examining and how their approach to inquiry offers promise in explaining or describing the topic under study.

A Definitional Crossroad

The second crossroad is definitional. The great diversity of questions studied (and proposed for study) under the aegis of *emergent literacy* in the 1990s is a testament to the acceptance of this construct in the field of literacy research. At the same time, however, this diversity raises questions concerning the meaning and usefulness of the term itself. As we have read and discussed among ourselves and colleagues the broad array of studies reviewed in this chapter, one of the most troubling issues has been deciding whether there is, or should be, a unified theoretical, methodological, or curricular perspective that underlies emergent literacy research.

Our analyses suggest that emergent literacy represents an identifiable, though changing theoretical stance. As in the 1980s, key tenets of an emergent literacy perspective today include (a) an optimistic view of children's ability to learn and forward trajectory from unconventional to conventional literacy; (b) a positive view of children as constructors of their own literacy knowledge; and (c) a belief that emergent literacy learning occurs "informally" (following Teale's 1978 definition of this term) in holistic, meaning-driven reading and writing events. Simultaneously, however, each of these tenets has been recast in some ways as the field has matured.

First of all, although the value of emergent literacy behaviors and their relation to later conventional reading and writing continues to be "assumed" in many developmental and process-oriented studies, a number of researchers are now designing investigations that attempt to empirically document the impact of early unconventional literacy behaviors on later reading and writing, a trend that nearly every reviewer in the last 15 years in this field has remarked should happen. We suggest, though, in the pursuit to "verify" the importance of these nascent abilities, that present and future researchers would do well to keep in mind the caution about "conventionality" laid out succinctly by Mason and Allen (1986) a number of years ago, which is worth quoting at length again:

> Children's movement into reading is not marked by a clear boundary between readers and nonreaders. Very young children may know where there is something to read but be unable to read it. Somewhat older children may be able to read isolated words in context, but not in isolation. Still older children may be able to read isolated words by storing partial letter–sound associations in memory, but they may not be able to read isolated words by decoding the letters into sounds. Which are we to consider readers and which are nonreaders? … Reading acquisition is better conceptualized as a developmental continuum rather than the all-or-none phenomenon. (p. 18)

The point that we would like to reiterate here is that children can hold *both* unconventional and conventional notions about reading and writing at the same time. If this is the case, then it becomes extremely difficult to "verify" that certain early behaviors predict others (or are "orthogonal" to them) because they are inextricably connected, in the first place, developmentally—a point made much more powerfully by Vygotsky (1987) over 60 years ago in response to psychologists attempting to bifurcate language into either its acoustic or semantic properties in order to emphasize one over the other. In the case of emergent literacy research, scholars working within paradigms supporting positivistic assumptions of "objective verification" or, as the case is more often, postpositivist notions of "confirmability," cannot do either if "fragmentation" is the result.

A related point in this definitional recasting is that although emergent literacy research in the 1990s remains primarily "verbocentric," we believe there is much to be gained from defining literacy more broadly to include both linguistic and nonlinguistic forms of communication. We concur with Kress's (1997) prediction that children will increasingly be exposed to communication tools and situations that are multimodal rather than exclusively linguistic. Because emergent writers have, from the beginning, been shown to combine writing, drawing, talk, and gesture, it seems that future emergent literacy research is already poised to investigate this broader view of literacy and literacy learning. Particularly when considering the research in storybook reading with the hearing impaired and visually impaired and other children with out-of-the-ordinary learning capabilities, the exploration of the uniqueness of and similarities between different semiotic systems is paramount if comprehensive models of literacy are ever to be constructed.

Methodological Crossroads

A final crossroads we see is methodological. As theoretical perspectives and definitions of literacy change, so must research questions, designs, and reporting. First, as we adopt a more contextualized view of literacy, researchers can no longer assume generalizability (or "transferability" of findings) for all students. This suggests that we must seek a broader array of research participants so that a wider range of social, political, economic, and cultural understandings of literacy is represented in the literature. However, simple dichotomous comparisons between low and high, disadvantaged and advantaged, inexperienced and experienced, or unsuccessful and successful are not illuminative if the purpose is simply to point out who has the knowledge and who does not. Rather, what we see as needed are studies that make a concerted attempt to reveal the strengths, factors of resilience, and ways in which students from underrepresented populations can be successful in school. Unlike current diagnoses of reading disability (cf. Semrud-Clikeman, 1996), which continue to put the onus of failure on individuals' inadequacies to the complete absolvement of instructional inequities, we would like to see more insightful recommendations for early literacy instruction that take into consideration population-specific characteristics (cf. Moll, 1992, and the concept of "funds of knowledge") and the realization that the institution of schooling, as has been previously noted (see Serpell, 1997), is more than a little responsible for whether children succeed or not.

Second, as theoretical perspectives, topics of inquiry, and descriptive category systems proliferate, we believe there is much to be gained by careful discussion of conceptual and methodological connections between studies. Although it is customary for researchers to justify the significance of their research questions in relation to the findings (or lack thereof) in previous research, these justifications must go far beyond the standard formula of setting up a few (or many) studies as "straw men," and then adding the frequent but out-worn phrase of "little is known, then, about ...," because as we found in this review, the latter statement is seldom accurate. We therefore urge researchers (and the publishers of their work) to be assiduous in providing more complete, comparative analyses of theory, methods, and findings in their research reporting.

Finally, we believe that if research into emergent literacy abilities is ever going to converge on plausible syntheses or the "whole picture" of emergent literacy (cf. McGee & Purcell-Gates, 1997, p. 315), then up-front discussions about differing epistemological perspectives must happen. As Cunningham and Fitzgerald (1996) observed, "If any agreement between camps is possible, it may result only from epistemological discussions rather than discussions of reading theory or practice" (p. 39). From our review, one barrier we see being constructed rapidly in this field actually emanates from researchers following suggestions in the literature to incorporate mixed designs in approaching emergent literacy topics. As we noted earlier, however, "outcome-based" investigations adhere to assumptions that normally conflict with the central tenets of what we understand to represent an emergent literacy perspective. Even so, the problem we see is not so much rooted in being "experimental" (see, e.g., the volume by Neuman & McCormick, 1995, on single-subject experimental research in literacy) or attempting to find plausible connections between elements of early and late literacy experiences, but rather in the inappropriate use of early literacy assessment tools without full appreciation of the developmental properties of the constructs underlying them or the possible differences in performance that may be introduced by alternative versions of the same index.

As we suggested earlier, it is important for researchers to heed Sulzby's (1994) admonition that the "stage-like" appearance of emergent storybook reading is deceptive. Additionally, environmental print measures vary from collecting children's responses in actual community contexts with intact print artifacts to drawn objects on index cards or either black and white or color photographs (cf. Smith, 1997). However, given the extensive literature on the complexity of children's learning about two-dimensional space (Willows & Houghton, 1987) in various illustrative formats, we do not see that these tasks are simply interchangeable. This situation may, in part, explain the current empirical disconnect between Goodman's (1986) theoretical premise of the importance of print in situational contexts to young children's literacy learning and the failure of outcome-based studies to conclusively verify it.

What we are primarily asking emergent literacy researchers to understand and what Cunningham and Fitzgerald (1996, p. 55) have urged the larger reading community to consider much more seriously is the epistemological parameters of their work (cf. also Mosenthal, 1995). What constitutes or counts as knowledge? Where is knowledge located? How is knowledge attained? Further research maturity in the field of emergent literacy studies will come only, we think, by grappling continuously—and honestly—with these questions.

ACKNOWLEDGMENTS

A portion of the work reported herein was supported under the Educational Research and Development Centers Program, PR/Award Number R305R7004, as administered by the Office of Educational Research and Improvement, U.S. Department of Education. However, the comments do not necessarily represent the positions or policies of the National Institute of Student Achievement, Curriculum, or Assessment, or the National Institute of Early Childhood Development, or the U.S. Department of Education, and you should not assume endorsement by the federal government.

CIERA is the acronym for the Center for the Improvement of Early Reading Achievement in which David Yaden and Laurie MacGillivray are principal investigators.

REFERENCES

Allison, D. T., & Watson, J. A. (1994). The significance of adult storybook reading styles on the development of young children's emergent reading. *Reading Research and Instruction, 34*, 57–72.

Anderson, J. (1995). How parents perceive literacy acquisition: A cross-cultural study. In W. Linek & E. Sturdevant (Eds.), *Generations of literacy: The Seventeenth Yearbook of the College Reading Association* (pp. 262–277). Harrisburg, VA: College Reading Association.

Arnold, D. H., Lonigan, C. J., Whitehurst, G. J., & Epstein, J. N. (1994). Accelerating language development through picture book reading: Replication and extension to a videotape training format. *Journal of Educational Psychology, 86*, 235–243.

Baker, L., Sonnenschein, S., & Serpell, R. (1994, December). Children's emergent literacy experiences in the sociocultural contexts of home and school. *NRRC News: A Newsletter of the National Reading Research Center, l*, 4–5.

Ballenger, C. (1996). Learning the ABS's in a Haitian preschool: A teacher's story. *Language Arts, 73*, 317–323.

Barone, D. (1994). The importance of classroom context: Literacy development of children prenatally exposed to crack-cocaine—Year two. *Research in the Teaching of English, 28*, 286–312.

Barone, D. (1997). Changing perceptions: The literacy development of children prenatally exposed to crack or cocaine. *Journal of Literacy Research, 29*, 183–219.

Beals, D. E., & DeTemple, J. M. (1993). Home contributions to early language and literacy development. In D. Leu & C. Kinzer (Eds.), *Examining central issues in literacy research, theory and practice: Forty-second yearbook of the National Reading Conference* (pp. 207–216). Chicago: National Reading Conference.

Besse, J. (1996). An approach to writing in the kindergarten. In C. Pontecorvo, M. Orsolini, B. Burge, & L. Resnick (Eds.), *Children's early text construction* (pp. 127–144). Mahwah, NJ: Lawrence Erlbaum Associates.

Branscombe, N., & Taylor, J. (1996). The development of Scrap's understanding of written language. *Childhood Education, 72*, 278–284.

Burns, S. M., & Casbergue, R. (1992). Parent-child interaction in a letter-writing context. *Journal of Reading Behavior, 24*, 289–312.

Burns, J. M., & Richgels, D. J. (1989). An investigation of task requirements associated with invented spellings of 4-year-olds with above average intelligence. *Journal of Reading Behavior, 21*, 1–14.

Bus, A. G., & van Ijzendoorn, M. H. (1992). Patterns of attachment in frequently and infrequently reading mother-child dyads. *Journal of Genetic Psychology, 153*, 395–403.

Bus, A. G., van Ijzendoorn, M. H. (1995). Mothers reading to their 3-year-olds: The role of mother–child attachment security in becoming literate. *Reading Research Quarterly, 30*, 998–1015.

Bus, A. G., van Ijzendoorn, M. H., & Pellegrini, A. D. (1995). Joint book reading makes for success in learning to read: A meta-analysis on intergenerational transmission of literacy. *Review of Educational Research, 65*, 1–21.

Chapman, M. L. (1996). More than spelling: Widening the lens on emergent writing. *Reading Horizons, 36*, 317–339.

Christie, J. F. (1991). Psychological research on play: Connections with early literacy development. In J. Christie (Ed.), *Play and early literacy development* (pp. 27–43). Albany: State University of New York Press.

Christie, J. F., & Enz, B. J. (1992). The effects of literacy play interventions on preschoolers' play patterns and literacy development. *Early Education and Development, 3*, 205–220.

Clay, M. M. (1975). *What did I write?* Auckland, NZ: Heinemann.

Cox, B. E., Fang, Z., & Otto, B. W. (1997). Preschoolers' developing ownership of the literate register. *Reading Research Quarterly, 32*, 34–53.

Craig, C. (1996, May–June). Family support of the emergent literacy of children with visual impairments. *Journal of Visual Impairment and Blindness*, May–June pp. 194–200.

Crawford, P. A. (1995). Early literacy: Emerging perspectives. *Journal of Research in Early Childhood Education, 10*, 71–86.

Cunningham, J. W., & Fitzgerald, J. (1996). Epistemology and reading. *Reading Research Quarterly, 31*, 36–61.

Dahl, K. L. (1993). Children's spontaneous utterances during early reading and writing instruction in whole language classrooms. *Journal of Reading Behavior, 25*, 279–294.

Dahl, K. L., & Freppon, P. (1995). A comparison of innercity children's interpretations of reading and writing instruction in the early grades in skills-based and whole language classrooms. *Reading Research Quarterly, 30*, 50–75.

DeBaryshe, B. D., Buell, & Binder, J. (1996). What a parent brings to the table: Young children writing with and without parental assistance. *Journal of Literacy Research, 28*, 71–90.

Denzin, N., & Lincoln, Y. (Eds.). (1994). *Handbook of qualitative research*. Thousand Oaks, CA: Sage.

De Temple, J. M., & Tabors, P. O. (1995). Styles of interaction during a book reading task: Implications for literacy intervention with low-income families. In K. A. Hinchman, D. J. Leu, & C. K. Kinzer (Eds.), *Perspectives on literacy: Research and Practice: Forty-fourth yearbook of the National Reading Conference* (pp. 265–271). Chicago: National Reading Conference.

Dickinson, D., & Beals, D. (1994). Not by print alone: Oral language supports for early literacy development. In D. F. Lancy (Ed.), *Children's emergent literacy: From research to practice* (pp. 29–40). Westport, CT: Praeger.

Dickinson, D., & Keebler, R. (1989). Variation in preschool teachers' styles of reading books. *Discourse Processes, 12*, 353–375.

Dickinson, D. K., & Smith, M. W. (1994). Long-term effects of preschool teachers' book readings on low income children's vocabulary and story comprehension. *Reading Research Quarterly, 29*, 104–122.

Dickinson, D. K., & Tabors, P. O. (1991). Early literacy: Linkages between home, school and literacy achievement at five. *Journal of Research in Childhood Education, 6*, 30–46.

Dyson, A. H. (1992). Whistles for Willie, lost puppies, and cartoon dogs: The sociocultural dimensions of young children's composing. *Journal of Reading Behavior, 24*, 433–462.

Dyson, A. H. (1993). From invention to social action in early childhood literacy: A reconceptualization through dialogue about difference. *Early Childhood Research Quarterly, 8*, 409–425.

Dyson, A. H. (1995). Writing children: Reinventing the development of childhood literacy. *Written Communication, 12,* 4–46.

Elster, C. (1994). Patterns within preschoolers' emergent readings. *Reading Research Quarterly, 29,* 402–418.

Elster, C. (1995). Importations in preschooler's emergent readings. *Journal of Reading Behavior, 27,* 65–84.

Elster, C. (1998). Influences of text and pictures on shared and emergent readings. *Research in the Teaching of English, 32,* 43–78.

Elster, C., & Walker, C. A. (1992). Flexible scaffolds: Shared reading and rereading of story books in Head Start classrooms. In C. K. Kinzer & D. J. Leu (Eds.), *Literacy research and practice: Views from many perspectives: Forty-first yearbook of the National Reading Conference* (pp. 445–452). Chicago: National Reading Conference.

Englert, C. S., Garmon, A., Mariage, T., & Rozendal, M., Turrant, K., & Urba, J. (1995). The Early Literacy Project: Connecting across the literacy curriculum. *Learning Disability Quarterly, 18,* 253–275.

Erickson, F. (1990). Qualitative methods. In M. Wittrock (Ed.), *Research in teaching and learning* (Vol. 2, pp. 77–194). New York: Macmillan.

Fassler, R. (1998). "Let's do it again!" Peer collaboration in an ESL kindergarten. *Language Arts, 75,* 202–210.

Feitelson, D. Goldstein, Z., Iraqi, J., & Share, D. L. (1993). Effects of listening to story reading on aspects of literacy acquisition in a diglossic situation. *Reading Research Quarterly, 28,* 71–79.

Fitzgerald, J., Spiegel, D. L., & Cunningham, J. W. (1991). The relationship between parental literacy level and perceptions of emergent literacy. *Journal of Reading Behavior, 23,* 191–213.

Foorman, B. R., Francis, D. J., Fletcher, J. M., Schatschneider, C., & Mehta, P. (1998). The role of instruction in learning to read: Preventing reading failure in at-risk children. *Journal of Educational Psychology, 90,* 37–55.

Gallas, K. (1994). *The languages of learning: How children talk, write, dance, draw and sing their understanding of the world.* New York: Teachers College Press.

Gillespie, C. W., & Twardosz, S. (1997, December). *A bedtime storybook reading intervention with deaf children.* Paper presented at the Annual Meeting of the National Reading Conference, Scottsdale, AZ.

Goldenberg, C., Reese, L., & Gallimore, R. (1992). Effects of literacy materials from school on Latino children's home experiences and reading achievement. *American Journal of Education, 100,* 497–537.

Goodman, J. R. (1990). *A naturalistic study of the relationship between literacy development and dramatic play in 5-year-old children.* Unpublished doctoral dissertation, Vanderbilt University, Nashville, TN.

Goodman, Y. (1986). Children coming to know literacy. In W. H. Teale & E. Sulzby (Eds.), *Emergent literacy: Writing and reading* (pp. 1–14). Norwood, NJ: Ablex.

Gould, S. J., & Eldredge, N. (1993). Punctuated equilibrium comes of age. *Nature, 366,* 223–237.

Greenewald, M. J., & Kulig, R. (1995). Effects of repeated readings of alphabet books on kindergartners' letter recognition. In K. A. Hinchman, D. J. Leu, & C. K. Kinzer (Eds.), *Perspectives on literacy: Research and Practice: Forty-fourth yearbook of the National Reading Conference* (pp. 231–234). Chicago: National Reading Conference.

Haden, C. A., Reese, E., & Fivush, R. (1996). Mothers' extratextual comments during storybook reading: Stylistic differences over time and across texts. *Discourse Processes, 89,* 259–271.

Hall, N. (1991). Play and the emergence of literacy. In J. Christie (Ed.), *Play and early literacy development* (pp. 3–25). Albany: State University of New York Press.

Heath, S. B. (1983). *Ways with words: Language, life and work in communities and classrooms.* Cambridge: Cambridge University Press.

Hiebert, E. H., & Adams, C. S. (1987). Fathers' and mothers' perceptions of their preschool children's emergent literacy. *Journal of Experimental Child Psychology, 44,* 25–37.

Hiebert, E. H., & Raphael, T. E. (1998). *Early literacy instruction.* Fort Worth, TX: Harcourt Brace.

Kantor, R., Miller, S., & Fernie, D. (1992). Diverse paths to literacy in a preschool classroom: A sociocultural perspective. *Reading Research Quarterly, 27,* 185–201.

Kavims, D. S., & Pierce, P. L. (1995). Literacy-rich environments and the transition of young children with special needs. *Topics in Early Childhood Special Education, 15,* 219–234

Korkeamaki, R. L., & Dreher, M. J. (1995). Meaning-based reading instruction in a Finnish kindergarten. In K. A. Hinchman, D. J. Leu, & C. K. Kinzer (Eds.), *Perspectives on literacy: Research and practice: Forty-fourth yearbook of the National Reading Conference* (pp. 235–242). Chicago: National Reading Conference.

Korkeamaki, R. L., & Dreher, M. J. (1996). Trying something new: Meaning-based reading instruction in a Finnish first grade classroom. *Journal of Literacy Research, 28,* 9–34.

Kress, G. (1997). Before writing. *Rethinking the paths to literacy.* London: Routledge.

Kriegler, S, Ramarumo, M., Van der Ryst, M., Van Niekerk, K., & Winer, Y. (1994). Supporting emergent literacy in print bereft rural communities. *School Psychology International, 15,* 23–37.

Labbo, L. D. (1996a). A semiotic analysis of young children's symbol making in a classroom computer center. *Reading Research Quarterly, 31,* 356–385.

Labbo, L. D. (1996b). Beyond storytime: A sociopsychological perspective on young children's opportunities for literacy development during story extension time. *Journal of Literacy Research, 28,* 405–428.

Labbo, L. D., & Teale, W. H. (1998). An emergent literacy perspective on reading instruction in kindergarten. In S. Stahl & D. Hayes (Eds.), *Instructional reading models* (pp. 249–281). Hillsdale, NJ: Lawrence Erlbaum Associates.

Lartz, M. N. (1993). A description of mothers' questions to their young deaf children during storybook reading. *American Annals of the Deaf, 138,* 322–330.

Lartz, M. N., & McCollum, J. (1990). Maternal questions while reading to deaf and hearing twins: A case study. *American Annals of the Deaf, 135,* 235–240.

Leland, C. H., & Harste, J. C. (1994). Multiple ways of knowing: Curriculum in a new key. *Language Arts, 71*(5), 337–345.

Leseman, P. P. M., & De Jong, P. F.(1998). Home literacy: Opportunity, instruction, cooperation, and social emotional quality predicting early reading achievement. *Reading Research Quarterly, 33,* 294–313.

Lomax, R. G., & McGee, L. M. (1987). Young children's concepts about print and reading. Toward a model of word reading acquisition. *Reading Research Quarterly, 22,* 237–256.

MacGillivray, L. (1994). Tacit shared understandings of a first grade writing community. *Journal of Reading Behavior, 26,* 245–266.

MacGillivray, L. (1997). "I've seen you read": Reading strategies in a first-grade classroom. *Journal of Research in Childhood Education, 11*(2), 135–151.

MacGillivray, L., & Martinez, A. (1998). Princesses who commit suicide: Primary children writing within and against gender stereotypes. *Journal of Literacy Research, 30,* 53–84.

Madrigal, P., Cubillas, D., Yaden, D., Tam, A., & Brassell, D. (1999). *Creating a book loan program for inner-city Latino parents—A story* (Tech. Rep. No. 2-003). Ann Arbor, MI: University of Michigan School of Education, Center for the Improvement of Early Reading Achievement.

Martens, P. (1996). *I already know how to read. A child's view of literacy.* Portsmouth, NH: Heinemann.

Martens, P. & Goodman, Y. (1996). Invented punctuation. In N. Hall & A. Robinson (Eds.), *Learning about punctuation* (pp. 37–53). Portsmouth, NH: Heinemann.

Martinez, M. G., & Teale, W. H. (1993). Teacher storybook reading style: A comparison of six teachers. *Research in the Teaching of English, 27,* 175–199.

Martinez, M., Cheyney, M., & Teale, W. (1991). Classroom literature activities and kindergartners' dramatic story reenactments. In J. Christie (Ed.), *Play and early literacy development* (pp. 119–140). Albany: State University of New York Press.

Mason, J. M. (1984). Early reading from a developmental perspective. In P. D. Pearson, R. Barr, M. L. Kamil, & P. Mosenthal (Eds.), *Handbook of reading research* (Vol. I, pp. 505–543). New York: Longman.

Mason, J. M., & Allen, J. (1986). A review of emergent literacy with implications for research and practice in reading. *Review of Research in Education* (Vol. 13, pp. 3–38). Washington, DC: American Educational Research Association.

Mautte, L. A. (1990). The effects of adult interactive behaviors within the context of repeated storybook readings upon the language development and selected prereading skills of prekindergarten at-risk students. *Florida Educational Research Council Research Bulletin, 22,* 9–32.

McCormick, C., & Mason, J. M. (1990). *Little books.* Glenview, IL: Scott Foresman.

McGee, L. M., & Purcell-Gates, V. (1997). Conversations: So what's going on in research in emergent literacy? *Reading Research Quarterly, 32,* 310–318.

McIntyre, E. (1990). Young children's reading strategies as they read self-selected books in school. *Early Childhood Research Quarterly, 5,* 265–277.

McIntyre, E., & Freppon, P. (1994). A comparison of children's development of alphabetic knowledge in a skills-based and whole language classroom. *Research in the Teaching of English, 28,* 391–417.

Meyer, L. A., Wardrop, J. L. Stahl, S. A., & Linn, R. L. (1994). Effects of reading storybooks aloud to children. *Journal of Educational Research, 88,* 69–85.

Moll, L. (1992). Literacy research in community classrooms: A socio-cultural approach. In B. R. Beach, J. L. Green, M. S. Kamil, & T. Shanahan (Eds.), *Multidisciplinary perspectives on literacy research* (pp. 211–244). Urbana, IL: National Council of Teachers of English.

Morrow, L. M. (1989). The effect of small group story reading on children's questions and comments. In S. McCormick & J. Zutell, (Eds.), *Cognitive and social perspectives for literacy research and instruction: Thirty-eighth yearbook of the National Reading Conference* (pp. 77–86). Chicago: National Reading Conference.

Morrow, L. M. (1991). Relationships among physical design of play centers, teachers' on literacy in play, and children's literacy behaviors during play. In J. Zutell & S. McCormick (Eds.), *Learner factors/teacher factors: Issues in literacy research and instruction: Fortieth yearbook of the National Reading Conference* (pp. 127–140). Chicago: National Reading Conference.

Morrow, L. M., & Rand, M. (1991). Promoting literacy during play by designing early childhood classroom environments. *Reading Teacher, 44,* 396–402.

Morrow, L. M., Rand, M., & Smith, J. (1995). Reading aloud to children: Relationships between teacher and student behaviors. *Reading Research and Instruction, 35,* 85–101.

Mosenthal, P. B. (1995). Why there are no dialogues among the divided: The problem of solipsistic agendas in literacy research. *Reading Research Quarterly, 30,* 574–577.

Mulhern, M. M. (1997). Doing his own thing: A Mexican-American kindergartner becomes literate at home and school. *Language Arts, 74,* 468–476.

Mulhern, M. M. (in press). *Esperanza, Ruben and Yesenia: The emergent literacy of three Mexican immigrant children.* Albany: State University of New York Press.

Murray, B. A., Stahl, S. A., & Ivey, M. G. (1996). Developing phoneme awareness through alphabet books. *Reading and Writing: An Interdisciplinary Journal, 8,* 307–322.

Neuman, S. B., & McCormick, S. (1995). *Single-subject experimental research: Applications for literacy.* Newark, DE: International Research Association.

Neuman, S., & Roskos, K. (1990). Play, print, and purpose. Enriching play environments for literacy development. *Reading Teacher, 44,* 214–221.

Neuman, S., & Roskos, K. (1991). The influence of literacy-enriched play centers on preschoolers' conceptions of the functions of print. In J. Christie (Ed.), *Play and early literacy development* (pp. 167–187). Albany: State University of New York Press.

Neuman, S., & Roskos, K. (1992). Literacy objects as cultural tools: Effects on children's literacy behaviors in play. *Reading Research Quarterly, 27,* 203–225.

Neuman, S., & Roskos, K. (1993). Access to print for children of poverty: Differential effects of adult mediation and literacy-enriched play settings on environmental and functional print tasks. *American Educational Research Journal, 30,* 95–122.

Neuman, S., & Roskos, K. (1997). Literacy knowledge in practice: Contexts of participation for young writers and readers. *Reading Research Quarterly, 32,* 10–32.

Neuman, S. B., Soundy, C. (1991). The effects of "storybook partnerships" on young children's conception of stories. In J. Zutell & S. McCormick (Eds.), *Learner factors/teacher factors: Issues in literacy research and instruction: Fortieth yearbook of the National Reading Conference* (pp. 141–148). Chicago: National Reading Conference.

Neuman, S. B., Hagedorn, T., Celano, D., & Daly, P. (1995). Toward a collaborative approach to parent involvement in early education: A study of teenage mothers in an African-American community. *American Educational Research Journal, 32,* 801–827

Nielsen, D. C. (1993). The effects of four models of group interaction with storybooks on the literacy growth of low-achieving kindergarten children. In D. J. Leu & C. K. Kinzer (Eds.), *Examining central issues in literacy research, theory and practice: Forty-second yearbook of the National Reading Conference* (pp. 279–288). Chicago: National Reading Conference.

Nielsen, D. C., & Monson, D. L. (1996). Effects of literacy environment on literacy development of kindergarten children. *Journal of Educational Research, 89,* 259–271.

Olson, K., & Sulzby, E. (1991). The computer as a social/physical environment in emergent literacy. In J. Zutell & S. McCormick (Eds.), *Learner factors/teacher factors: Issues in literacy research and instruction: Fortieth yearbook of the National Reading Conference* (pp. 111–118). Chicago: National Reading Conference.

Orellana, M. F., & Hernandez, A. (1999). Talking the walk: Children reading urban environmental print. *The Reading Teacher, 52*(6), 2–10.

Otto, B. W. (1993). Signs of emergent literacy among inner-city kindergartners in a storybook reading program. *Reading and Writing Quarterly: Overcoming Learning Difficulties, 9,* 151–162.

Pappas, C. C. (1991). Young children's strategies in learning the "book language" of information books. *Discourse Processes, 14,* 203–225.

Pappas, C. C. (1993). Is narrative primary? Some insights from kindergartners pretend readings of stories and information books. *Journal of Reading Behavior, 25,* 97–129.

Pellegrini, A. D. (1984). Identifying causal elements in the thematic-fantasy play paradigm. *American Educational Research Journal, 21,* 691–701.

Pellegrini, A. D., & Galda, L. (1982). The effects of thematic-fantasy play training on the development of children's story comprehension. *American Educational Research Journal, 19,* 443–452.

Pellegrini, A. D., & Galda, L. (1991). Longitudinal relations among preschoolers symbolic play, metalinguistic verbs, and emergent literacy. In J. Christie (Ed.), *Play and early literacy development* (pp. 47–67). Albany: State University of New York Press.

Pellegrini, A. D., & Galda, L. (1993). Ten years after: A reexamination of symbolic play and literacy research. *Reading Research Quarterly, 28,* 162–175.

Pellegrini, A. D., Galda, L., and Flor, D. (in press). Relationships, individual differences, and children's uses of literate language. *British Journal of Educational Psychology.*

Phillips, L. M., Norris, S. P., & Mason, J. M. (1996). Longitudinal effects of early literacy concepts on reading achievement: A kindergarten intervention and five-year follow-up. *Journal of Literacy Research, 28,* 173–195.

Piaget, J. (1962). *Play, dreams and imitations.* New York: Norton.

Piaget, J. (1985). *The equilibration of cognitive structures: The central problem of intellectual development* (T. Brown & K. Thampy, Trans.). Chicago: University of Chicago Press.

Pontecorvo, C., & Morani, R. (1996). Looking for stylistic features in children's composing of stories: Products and processes. In C. Pontecorvo, M. Orsolini, B. Burge, & L. Resnick (Eds.), *Children's early text construction* (pp. 229–258). Mahwah, NJ: Lawrence Erlbaum Associates.

Pontecorvo, C., & Zucchermaglio, C. (1989). From oral to written language: Preschool children dictating stories. *Journal of Reading Behavior, 21,* 109–126.

Power, B. P. (1991). Pop ups: The rise and fall of one convention in a first grade writing workshop. *Journal of Research in Childhood Education, 6,* 54–66.

Purcell-Gates, V. (1995). *Other people's words: The cycle of low literacy.* Cambridge, MA: Harvard University Press.

Purcell-Gates, V. (1996). Stories, coupons, and the *TV Guide*: Relationships between home literacy experiences and emergent literacy knowledge. *Reading Research Quarterly, 31,* 406–429.

Purcell-Gates, V. P., & Dahl, K. (1991). Low SES children's success and failure at early literacy learning in skills-based classrooms. *Journal of Reading Behavior, 23,* 1–34.

Read, C. (1975). *Children's categorizations of speech sounds in English* (NCTE Research Rep. No. 17). Urbana, IL: National Council of Teachers of English.

Richgels, D. (1995a). A kindergarten sign-in procedure: A routine in support of written language learning. In K. A. Hinchman, D. J. Leu, & C. K. Kinzer (Eds.), *Perspectives on literacy: Research and practice: Forty-fourth yearbook of the National Reading Conference* (pp. 243–254). Chicago: National Reading Conference.

Richgels, D. (1995b). Invented spelling ability and printed word learning in kindergarten. *Reading Research Quarterly, 30*, 96–109.

Richgels, D., Poremba, K. J., & McGee, L. M. (1996). Kindergartners talk about print: Phonemic awareness in meaningful contexts. *Reading Teacher, 49*, 632–642.

Roberts, B. (1992). The evolution of the young child's concept of word as a unit of spoken and written language. *Reading Research Quarterly, 27*, 124–139.

Rosenhouse, J., Feitelson, D., Kita, B., & Goldstein, Z. (1997). Interactive reading aloud to Israeli first graders: Its contribution to literacy development. *Reading Research Quarterly, 32*, 168–183.

Roskos, K., & Neuman, S. (1993). Descriptive observations of adults' facilitation of literacy in young children's play. *Early Childhood Research Quarterly, 8*, 77–97.

Rottenberg, C. J., & Searfoss, L. W. (1992). Becoming literate in a preschool class: Literacy development of hearing-impaired children. *Journal of Reading Behavior, 24*, 463–479.

Rowe, D. (1994). *Preschoolers as authors: Literacy learning in the social world of the preschool.* Cresskill, NH: Hampton Press.

Rowe, D. (1998). The literate potentials of book-related dramatic play. *Reading Research Quarterly, 33*, 10–35.

Rowe, D. (in press). Bringing books to life: The role of book-related dramatic play in young children's literacy learning. In K. Roskos & J. Christie (Eds.), *Literacy and play in the early years: Cognitive, ecological and sociocultural perspectives.* Mahwah, NJ: Lawrence Erlbaum Associates.

Scarborough, H. S., & Dobrich, W. (1994). On the efficacy of reading to preschoolers. *Developmental Review, 14*, 245–302.

Scarborough, H. S., Dobrich, W., & Hager, M. (1991). Preschool literacy experience and later reading achievement. *Journal of Learning Disabilities, 24*, 508–511.

Schickedanz, J. (1990). *Adam's righting revolutions: One child's literacy development from infancy through grade one.* Portsmouth, NH: Heinemann.

Schrader, C. (1991). Symbolic play: A source of meaningful engagements with writing and reading. In J. Christie (Ed.), *Play and early literacy development* (pp. 189–213). Albany: State University of New York Press.

Semrud-Clikeman, M. (1996). Neuropsychological evidence for subtypes in developmental dyslexia. In E. Putnam (Ed.), *How to become a better reading teacher* (pp. 43–52). Englewood Cliffs, NJ: Prentice Hall.

Serpell, R. (1997). Critical issues: Literacy connections between school and home: How should we evaluate them? *Journal of Literacy Research, 29*, 587–616.

Shaffer, G. L. & McNinch, G. H. (1995). Parents' perceptions of young children's print awareness of environmental print. In W. Linek & E. Sturtevant (Eds.), *Generations of literacy: Seventeenth yearbook of the College Reading Association* (pp. 278–286). Harrisonburg, VA: College Reading Association.

Shapiro, J. (1995). Home literacy environment and young children's literacy knowledge and behavior. In W. Linek & E. Sturtevant (Eds.), *Generations of literacy: Seventeenth yearbook of the College Reading Association* (pp. 288–300). Harrisonburg, VA: College Reading Association.

Share, D. L., & Stanovich, K. E. (1995). Cognitive processes in early reading development: Accommodating individual differences into a model of acquisition. *Issues in Education: Contributions from Educational Psychology, 1*, 1–58.

Silvern, S. Williamson, P., & Waters, B. (1983). Play as a mediator of comprehension: An alternative to play training. *Educational Research Quarterly, 7*, 16–21.

Smith, S. S. (1997). A longitudinal study: The literacy development of 57 children. In C. Kinzer, K. A. Hinchman, & D. J. Leu (Eds.), *Inquiries in literacy: Theory and practice: Forty-sixth yearbook of the National Reading Conference* (pp. 250–264). Chicago: National Reading Conference.

Smolkin, L. B., Yaden, D. B., Brown, L., & Hofius, B. (1992). The effects of genre, visual design choices, and discourse structure on preschoolers' responses to picture books during parent-child read-alouds. In C. K. Kinzer & D. J. Leu (Eds.), *Literacy research, theory and practice: Views from many perspectives: Forty-first yearbook of the National Reading Conference* (pp. 291–302). Chicago: National Reading Conference.

Snow, C. E., Barnes, W. E., Chandler, J., Goodman, I. F., & Hemphill, L. (1991). *Unfulfilled expectations: Home and school influences on literacy.* Cambridge, MA: Harvard University Press.

Solsken, J. W. (1993). *Literacy, gender and work: Gender work in families and school.* Norwood, NJ: Ablex.

Sonnenschein, S., Brody, G., & Munsterman, K. (1996). The influence of family beliefs and practices on children's early reading development. In L. Baker, P. Afflerbach, & D. Reinking (Eds.), *Developing engaged readers in school and home communities* (pp. 3–20). Mahwah, NJ: Lawrence Erlbaum Associates.

Stahl, S. A., & Murray, B. A. (1993). Environmental print, phonemic awareness, letter recognition and word recognition. In D. Leu & Kinzer, C. (Eds.) *Examining central issues in literacy, research, theory and practice: Forty-second yearbook of the National Reading Conference* (pp. 227–234). Chicago: National Reading Conference.

Stanovich, K. E. (1980). Toward an interactive-compensatory model of individual differences in the development of reading fluency. *Reading Research Quarterly, 16*, 32–71.

Stone, S., & Christie, J. (1996). Collaborative literacy learning during socio-dramatic play in a multiage (K–2) primary classroom. *Journal of Research in Childhood Education, 10,* 123–133.

Sulzby, E. (1985). Children's emergent reading of favorite storybooks. A developmental study. *Reading Research Quarterly, 20,* 458–479.

Sulzby, E. (1989). Assessment of writing and children's language while writing. In L. Morrow & J. Smith (Eds.), *The role of assessment and measurement in early literacy instruction* (pp. 83–109). Englewood Cliffs, NJ: Prentice Hall.

Sulzby, E. (1991). The development of the young child and the emergence of literacy. In J. Flood, J. M. Jensen, D. Lapp, & J. R. Squire (Eds.), *Handbook of research on teaching the language arts* (pp. 273–285). New York: Macmillan.

Sulzby, E. (1996). Roles of oral and written language as children approach conventional literacy. In C. Pontecorvo, M. Orsolini, B. Burge, & L. Resnick (Eds.), *Children's early text construction* (pp. 25–46). Mahwah, NJ: Lawrence Erlbaum Associates.

Sulzby, E., Branz, C. M., & Buhle, R. (1993). Repeated readings of literature and low socioeconomic Black kindergarten and first graders. *Reading and Writing Quarterly: Overcoming Learning Disabilities, 9,* 183–196.

Sulzby, E., & Kaderavek, J. N. (1996). Parent-child language during storybook reading and toy play contexts: Case studies of normally developing and specific language impaired (SLI) children. In D. J. Leu, C. Kinzer, & K. A. Hinchman (Eds.), *Literacies for the 21st century: Research and practice: Forty-fifth yearbook of the National Reading Conference* (pp. 257–269). Chicago: National Reading Conference.

Sulzby, E., & Teale, W. (1991). Emergent literacy. In R. Barr, M. Kamil, P. Mosenthal, & P. D. Pearson (Eds.), *Handbook of reading research* (Vol. II, pp. 727–757). New York: Longman.

Taylor, R. L. (1995). Functional uses of reading and shared literacy activities in Icelandic homes: A monograph in family literacy. *Reading Research Quarterly, 30,* 194–219.

Taylor, D., & Dorsey-Gaines, C. (1988). *Growing up literate: Learning from inner-city families.* Portsmouth, NH: Heinemann.

Teale, W. H. (1978). Positive environments for learning to read: What studies of early readers tell us. *Language Arts, 55,* 922–932.

Teale, W. H. (1987). Emergent literacy: Reading and writing development in early childhood. In J. Readence & R. S. Baldwin, (Eds.), *Research in literacy: Merging perspectives: Thirty-sixth yearbook of the National Reading Conference* (pp. 45–74). Rochester, NY: National Reading Conference.

Teale, W. H., Martinez, W. G., & Glass, W. L. (1989). Describing classroom storybook reading. In D. Bloome (Ed.), *Classrooms and literacy* (pp. 158–188). Norwood, NJ: Ablex.

Teale, W. H., & Sulzby, E. (1986). *Emergent literacy: Writing and reading.* Norwood, NJ: Ablex.

Tolchinsky, L., & Teberosky, A. (1998). The development of word segmentation and writing in two scripts. *Cognitive Development, 13,* 1–24.

Troyer, C. R. (1991). From emergent literacy to emergent pedagogy: Learning from children learning together. In J. Zutell & S. McCormick (Eds.), *Learner factors/teacher factors: Issues in literacy research and instruction: Fortieth Yearbook of the National Reading Conference* (pp. 119–126). Chicago: National Reading Conference.

Valdez-Menchaca, M. C., & Whitehurst, G. J. (1992). Accelerating language development through picture book reading: A systematic extension to Mexican day care. *Developmental Psychology, 28,* 1106–1114.

Vukelich, C. (1991a). Materials and modeling: Promoting literacy during play. In J. Christie (Ed.), *Play and early literacy development* (pp. 215–231). Albany: State University of New York Press.

Vukelich, C. (1991b, December). *Learning about the functions of writing: The effects of three play interventions on children's development and knowledge about writing.* Paper presented at the National Reading Conference, Palm Springs, CA.

Vukelich, C. (1993). Play: A context for exploring the functions, features, and meaning of writing with peers. *Language Arts, 70,* 386–392.

Vygotsky, L. S. (1978). *Mind in society.* Cambridge, MA: Harvard University Press.

Vygotsky, L. S. (1987). Thinking and speech (N. Minick, Trans.). In R. Rieber & A. Carton (Eds.), *The collected works of L. S. Vygotsky* (pp. 39–285). New York: Plenum Press.

Wells, G., & Chang-Wells, G. L. (1992). *Constructing knowledge together: Classrooms as centers of inquiry and literacy.* Portsmouth, NH: Heinemann.

Whitehurst, G. J., Arnold, D. S., Epstein, J. N., Angell, A. L., Smith, M., & Fischel, J. E. (1994). A picture book reading intervention in day care and home for children from low income families. *Developmental Psychology, 30,* 679–689.

Whitehurst, G. J., Epstein, J. N., Angell, A. L., Payne, A. C., Crone, D. A., & Fischel, J. E. (1994). Outcomes of an emergent literacy intervention in Head Start. *Journal of Educational Psychology, 86,* 542–555.

Whitehurst, G. L., & Lonigan, C. J. (1998). Child development and emergent literacy. *Child Development, 69*(3), 848–872.

Williams, C. L. (1994). The language and literacy worlds of three profoundly deaf preschool children. *Reading Research Quarterly, 29,* 124–155.

Williams, C. L., & McLean, M. M. (1997). Young deaf children's response to picture book reading in a preschool setting. *Research in the Teaching of English, 31,* 337–366.

Williamson, P. A., & Silvern, S. B. (1991). Thematic-fantasy play and story comprehension. In J. Christie (Ed.), *Play and early literacy development* (pp. 69–90). Albany: State University of New York Press.

Willows, H. A., & Houghton, D. M. (1987). *The psychology of illustration: Volume 1: Basic research.* New York: Springer-Verlag.

Wolf, S., & Heath, S. B. (1992). *The braid of literature: Children's worlds of reading.* Cambridge, MA: Harvard University Press.

Yaden, D. B. (1993). Evaluating early literacy knowledge by analyzing children's responses to storybooks during home read-alouds. In A. Carrasquillo & C. Hedley (Eds.), *Whole language and the bilingual learner* (pp. 132–150). Norwood, NJ: Ablex.

Yaden, D. B. (1999). Reading disability and dynamical systems: When predictability implies pathology. In P. Mosenthal & D. Evensen (Eds.), *Reconsidering the role of the reading clinic in a new age of literacy: Vol. 6. Advances in reading/language research* (pp. 293–323). Greenwich, CT: JAI Press.

Yaden, D. B., Smolkin, L. B., & Conlon, A. (1989). Preschoolers' questions about pictures, print conventions, and story text during reading aloud at home. *Reading Research Quarterly, 24,* 188–214.

Yaden, D. B., Smolkin, L. B., & MacGillivray, L. (1993). A psychogenetic perspective on children's understanding about letter associations during alphabet book readings. *Journal of Reading Behavior, 25,* 43–68.

Zucchermaglio, C., & Scheuer, N. (1996). Children dictating a story: Is together better? In C. Pontecorvo, M. Orsolini, B. Burge, & L. Resnick (Eds.), *Children's early text construction* (pp. 83–98). Mahwah, NJ: Lawrence Erlbaum Associates.

CHAPTER 26

Beginning Reading Instruction: Research on Early Interventions

Elfrieda H. Hiebert
CIERA/University of Michigan

Barbara M. Taylor
CIERA/University of Minnesota

Interest in beginning reading is currently intense—the source of mandates by legislators and debates among scholars. A new twist has developed in the form of mandates by federal and state legislators for "research-proven" programs (U.S. Congress, 1998). Even with generous definitions of what constitutes research, investigations of beginning reading instruction from the early 1980s, when Barr (1984) summarized the topic in the first volume of the *Handbook of Reading Research*, to the early 1990s were limited in number. The second volume of the *Handbook of Reading Research* (Barr, Kamil, Mosenthal, & Pearson, 1991) saw little attention to beginning reading instruction. It was with Adams's (1990) review of research on beginning reading acquisition, the growing popularity of Reading Recovery (Clay, 1985, 1993), actions in legislatures, and discussions in the media that beginning reading instruction became a focus of researchers' attention.

Our aim was to survey new developments in research on beginning reading instruction since Barr's review (1984). Consequently, we have not reviewed studies that juxtapose one method against another method, despite the recent publicity surrounding one study of this type—that of Foorman, Francis, Fletcher, Schatschneider, and Mehta (1998). Barr (1984) concluded her review with the statement that the quest for the best method "neither answers the practical question of which program is more effective because outcomes are not simply a reflection of method conditions nor does it increase our understanding of the complexities of classroom instruction of which reading method is a part" (p. 574). Despite including a method that was not part of the studies reviewed by Barr (1984)—whole language—Foorman et al.'s global categorization of methods and aggregating of students (e.g., Grade 1 and 2 readers) has generated rhetoric but few answers for classroom teachers (Taylor, Anderson, Au, & Raphael, in press).

Another set of studies that represents a new development since the 1984 *Handbook* consists of analyses of children's learning processes and instructional tasks (e.g., Fisher & Hiebert, 1990; Purcell-Gates & Dahl, 1991). These studies make useful distinctions in the instruction and tasks of classrooms, including those where teachers profess different philosophies, but are less forthcoming on how differences in instruction and tasks affect children's reading achievement.

It is a group of instructional projects that aim to prevent reading difficulties among the most challenged beginning readers that we believe represents a new direction in research on early reading instruction. The aim of these studies is to build instruction on knowledge of fundamental reading processes, rather than on particular reading instructional techniques. Since these programs take a preventive rather than a remedial perspective, they have been called interventions. The only reference for *intervention* in the first volume of the *Handbook of Reading Research* was to the preschool efforts of the Follow-Through Studies, and there were no such references in the second volume.

EARLY READING INTERVENTIONS: AN OVERVIEW

Early reading interventions focus on the attainment of a particular goal or set of goals by a particular group of children over a particular period of time. Even though the phrase *reading intervention* has become common only during the 1990s, the proliferation of intervention projects and the space constraints of this review made it necessary for us to be representative, rather than comprehensive, in choosing intervention projects. For each of the three grade levels of kindergarten, first grade, and second grade, we have identified four projects that represent intervention efforts at that level.

Our need to limit studies means that readers who are interested solely in tutoring should refer to other sources (Wasik, 1998; Wasik & Slavin, 1993). Further, despite the congressional endorsement of schoolwide programs, we did not include the two reading programs on the current list of 24 schoolwide demonstration models (American Research Institutes, 1999). Not only have the two reading-specific efforts on this list—Distar and Success for All—been analyzed and reanalyzed (see, e.g., Pogrow, 1998; Stallings, 1975) but it is likely that attention to schoolwide projects diverts attention from schoolwide reading programs, which are characteristic of high-poverty schools where challenged readers do well (Taylor, Pearson, Clark, & Walpole, 1999).

Two questions guided our review of interventions:

1. How well have children learned to read and what have they learned? and
2. What are the primary features of curriculum, instruction, and professional development that characterize interventions in which this growth has occurred?

After studying the report(s) on each intervention, we summarized the information on achievement and on characteristics for all the interventions at a grade level in tabular form. We used the information in the tables to compare and contrast the effectiveness and characteristics of the interventions at each grade level.

In addressing the question of how well children have learned to read as a result of each intervention, we wanted to use as common a metric as possible. Whenever possible, effect sizes for outcomes were established. Some of the 12 interventions, however, did not include comparison groups. In other projects, comparison groups were not equivalent in composition. We have provided the available indicators of achievement for each project but we make no claims that these indicators are equivalent. We have attempted, to the degree possible with the existing data sets, to establish the influence of interventions on children's reading acquisition.

The components of curriculum, instruction, and professional development in the second question reflect the typical emphases within pedagogical and research literatures (Good & Brophy, 1990). While components share foci across grade levels, their content differs across the three grades. For example, while the curricular goal of letter naming is germane to kindergarten projects, first- and second-grade interventions attended to goals of word recognition and comprehension. Because all three components have been manipulated in most of the interventions, we cannot isolate the contributions of one component relative to another. The complexities of classrooms and the small budgets available to reading researchers preclude investigations of all of the permutations of these variables. A conclusion of this review is that, within successful interventions, all three factors have been adapted considerably.

Kindergarten Interventions

The literature on kindergarten interventions is disparate, reflecting varying interpretations of what constitutes appropriate experiences for young children. One way of parsing the kindergarten studies is by the scope of their efforts: comprehensive restructuring of the entire literacy program or changes to part of the literacy program. We included two projects of each type for this review.

In a 2-year literacy program that spanned preschool through kindergarten, Durkin restructured instructional activities to make them consonant with the home experiences of early readers (Durkin, 1966): (a) incorporating a conversation period that included reading stories aloud; (b) writing and posting children's special words, such as their names and those of family members and pets; and (c) talking about letter/sound relationships of key words as children learned to print letters (e.g., *dinosaur, Danny* when learning *d*).

Hanson and Farrell (1995) revisited some of the school districts that had implemented the Beginning Reading Program (BRP), a reading program that was delivered to 15% of children enrolled in kindergarten during the early 1970s. The BRP consisted of activities around a set of 52 stories, which were read aloud and used in lessons, read by children individually, and read by children at home. The vocabulary in these books was used to teach sight words and decoding skills. The last page of each of the booklets offered questions for parents and teachers to ask as they interacted with their children. Hanson and Farrell claim that technical reports published through the Southwest Regional Laboratory two decades ago showed that a majority of kindergartners learned to read from 20–30 minutes of daily instruction. This pattern held regardless of socioeconomic background, although Hanson and Farrell admit that children from at-risk backgrounds required more instructional time on the first several units of the program. In revisiting the school districts where BRP had been used, Hanson and Farrell were interested in determining whether effects of the kindergarten intervention remained as students prepared to graduate from high school. Their study reports on assessments of high school seniors who had had BRP as kindergartners and those who had not, with no subsequent interventions in the interim.

Many investigations that have examined the effects of supplemental phonemic awareness training in kindergarten curriculum have relied on members of the research team to provide the instruction (e.g., Ball & Blachman, 1991; Torgeson, Morgan, & Davis, 1992). Because this review attends to changes in classroom instruction, we chose interventions on a particular aspect of the literacy curriculum where classroom teachers delivered the instruction themselves. In the first, Ayres (1993, 1998) compared phonemic awareness development and subsequent reading acquisition through direct and indirect instruction of phonemic awareness. Direct instruction of phoneme awareness involved activities with puppets, word games, and magnetic letters, and was either followed or preceded by story mapping and retelling activities. Indirect instruction of phoneme awareness used poems and books, often with rhyme and alliteration, to direct children to sounds, words, syllables, and sentences, and was either preceded or followed by a combination of the direct and indirect approaches. In all approaches, invented spelling was encouraged at a writing center where letter stamps, paper, and writing implements were available.

In the second such intervention, Phillips, Norris, and Mason (1996) supplemented existing kindergarten programs with a set of 24 story booklets—texts with familiar content, a close fit between illustrations and text, and repetitive phrases and sentences. The three treatment groups involved children with the books in different contexts: (a) home—children were given a new booklet at the beginning of each week to take home; (b) school—a different booklet was used in the classroom each week for 10 to 15 minutes a day; and (c) school and home—the intervention procedures for the school treatment were followed, with the booklet taken home on Fridays.

How Successful Were Projects in Supporting Children's Reading Development?   The first conclusion from the achievement data in Table 26.1 is that participating as kindergartners in literacy-oriented activities such as book reading and chanting poems aids in subsequent reading development. Of the three studies reporting kindergarten reading outcomes, only Durkin (1974–1975) provides word recognition measures. We provided raw scores for word recognition, rather than effect sizes, because of the discrepancy between the intervention and comparison children: The former identified almost 10 times more words than the latter. Even when children have not learned to read conventionally, kindergarten participants in the interventions have better success at reading acquisition in Grade 1, as indicated by the sizes of effects at the end of Grade 1: .73 (Ayres's indirect/combination phonemic awareness training) and .62 (Phillips et al.'s school book group). The effect of the kindergarten intervention remains robust through the end of Grade 2: .60 (Durkin, 1974–1975) and .68 (Phillips et al.'s school book group). While Hansen and Farrell (1995)'s analysis shows that the effects can be long-lasting, the size of the effect drops after Grade 2.

What Features of Curriculum, Instruction, and Professional Development Characterized Successful Interventions?   A first conclusion from the summary of the project components in Table 26.2 is that the kindergarten interventions were intended to develop underlying concepts about reading and writing, not conventional reading and writing skills per se. One exception to this pattern is Hanson and Farrell's (1995) project, which attended to the development of sight vocabulary and decoding skills. The other three projects were oriented to foundational aspects of reading and writing—Durkin (1974–1975) to literacy concepts overall; Phillips et al. (1996) to book concepts; and Ayres (1993) to phonemic awareness. Although these three projects emphasized underlying literacy concepts rather than literacy per se, the reading achievement of children in subsequent grades showed that they positively affected children's reading success in Grades 1 and beyond.

The different foci of the four projects are reflected in the list of instructional elements, summarized in Table 26.2. Increased literacy awareness that extends into primary-grade reading achievement can be achieved through a variety of activities, including handling of books (Hanson & Farrell, 1995; Phillips et al., 1996) and shared reading by the teacher and writing activities (Ayres, 1993, 1998; Durkin, 1974–1975). For children such as those in Ayres's project who had not had extensive involvement with literacy, some experience with books and writing seems to facilitate subsequent acquisition of specific information about phonemes and letter-sound relations more than instruction that provided information on the phonemes and letter-sound relations directly.

These projects also demonstrate that a solid foundation can be laid in kindergarten through restructuring class activities as a whole, rather than by implementing intensive one-on-one instruction. All of the projects used small group and whole class expe-

TABLE 26.1

Achievement Patterns of Kindergarten Interventions

	Ayers (1993, 1998)				Durkin (1974–1975)	Hanson and Farrell (1995)	Phillips et al. (1996)		
Sample	Intact half-day kindergarten classes in middle-class, ethnically diverse suburban neighborhood.				Two classes within the same school in small town with majority upper range of low-SES families.	3,959 high-school seniors, 1/3 of whom attended kindergartens that implemented BRP; range of SES included, with at-risk over-represented.	Children came from schools where fourth graders had, in previous cohorts, scored approximately a decile below the national median.		
Project groups	Direct/ Story	Indirect/ Combination	Combination/ Indirect	Story/ Direct	• Intervention for ages 4 and 5 • Comparison: kindergarten only	• Intervention: BRP as kindergartners • Comparison group	Home	School	School–Home
Performances at end of intervention	.22	1.75	.15	.71	Letters: 58 IQ: .52 Words^a: Intervention: 124.84 (SD = 42.57) Comparison: 16.91 (SD = 14.43)	(Data not provided)	MAT: .01 CIRCUS: .10	MAT: .16 CIRCUS: .01	MAT: .32 CIRCUS: .08
Post-intervention	Standardized reading achievement tests: End of Grade 1				Standardized reading tests (2 in Gr. 4 and IQ test in Gr. 3)	Academic Instructional Measurement System; Reading Vocabulary Test; Reading Biographer	Canadian Test of Basic Skills (grade-appropriate)		
	-.60	.73	-.71	.45	Gr. 1: .86 Gr. 2: .60 Gr. 3: .35 Gr. 3, IQ: -.23 Gr. 4: .50, .41	Reading comprehension^b: .60^c Reading vocabulary^b: .40^c Illiteracy rate^b: -.06^c Remediation rate^b: -.22^c	Gr1: .16 Gr2: .32 Gr3: .01 Gr4: .24	Gr1: .62 Gr2: .68 Gr3: .36 Gr4: .29	Gr1: .47 Gr2: .53 Gr3: .13 Gr4: .32

^{a}Group averages for word measure

^{b}Mean difference, not effect size, between BRP kindergarten and No BRP kindergarten groups

^{c}Indicates a significant difference

TABLE 26.2

Instructional Components of Kindergarten Interventions

Goals	Ayres (1993, 1998)	Durkin (1974–1975)	Hansen and Farrell (1995)	Phillips et al. (1996)
•Concepts such as directionality, book handling	•Indirectly, depending on treatment	•Yes—language and literacy concepts were central	•Not specified	•In context of books: tracking print, directionality
•Letter naming	•Not specified	•Yes	•Not specified	•Not specified
•Phonemic awareness	•Directly and indirectly, depending on treatment	•Indirectly through writing	•Not specified	•In context of books: sounds of letters heard in words in books
•Book expertise	•Yes, differing by degree with treatment	•Yes	•Yes, central to project	•Yes
•Word reading	•Not specified	•Yes	•Yes: sight vocabulary and decoding skills	•In context of books
•Word writing	•All treatments had a writing center where invented spelling was encouraged	•Yes	•Not specified	•Writing of books is mentioned but not emphasized

(Continues)

TABLE 26.2 (Continued)

Instructional Elements	Ayres (1993, 1998)	Durkin (1974–1975)	Hansen and Farrell (1995)	Phillips et al. (1996)
•Teacher–student ratio	•Whole-class lessons, followed by individual activities and small groups working at writing center	•Whole class and individual	•Whole-class lessons, followed by individual readings of books at school and home	•Whole-class lessons, small group lessons, and individual readings in school-home treatment; book taken home in take-home treatment
•Time	•2 treatments of 10 weeks in ½ day kindergartens	•2-year intervention during language arts period of half-day preschool and kindergarten	•52 lessons over kindergarten	•24 weeks of half-day kindergartens
•Assessments by teachers	•Not specified (other than those of researcher)	•Not specified (other than those of researcher)	•Assessments at end of every 5 lessons	•Project staff shared assessments monthly with teachers
•Learning activities, specifically:				
•Reading of books	•Reading of texts chosen for phonemic characteristics (e.g., alliteration) in indirect but not direct treatment	•Daily conversation period that included read-aloud by teacher	•52 specially written booklets, ending with discussion questions	•Following along during repeated reading and independent rereading

(Continues)

TABLE 26.2 (Continued)

	Ayres (1993, 1998)	Durkin (1974–1975)	Hansen and Farrell (1995)	Phillips et al. (1996)
•Writing	•Writing center present in all forms and phases of intervention	•Forming letters and writing words was emphasized	•Not specified	•Writing activities that extended books
•Word recognition activities	•"Word games" are mentioned but recognition of words was not an explicit goal	•Class- and individual-selected words (e.g., holiday words)	•Words selected according to phonics patterns and frequency	•Not specified
•Games	•Rhyming games with puppets and stuffed animals, and "word games"	•Not specified	•Letter-sound games	•Not specified
Professional Context	•2 teachers were guided by teacher/researcher who designed and assisted with activities	•2 teachers interacted with researcher who directed the design and implementation of activities	•Teachers went through a prepackaged presentation that included audiovisuals, followed by discussions	•Teachers were introduced to strategies through a workshop that included a videotaped instructional episode. Follow-up meetings provided guidelines on various aspects of project (e.g., lesson components). Teachers could reach researchers by phone at any time; monthly visits by project staff included monthly reports on observations and student progress.

riences. Individual interactions with teachers occurred (such as the support around special words in Durkin's project) but not in one-on-one tutoring formats.

With regard to professional development, all but the Hanson and Farrell (1995) project were experimental in nature. The professional development components of Durkin and Ayres were especially labor-intensive, with researchers working with a handful of teachers. Pflaum, Walberg, Karegianes, and Rasher (1980) argued that results wane after the first year of a treatment, likely because the novelty and time investment decrease for teachers and researchers. By contrast, the achievement patterns reported by Hanson and Farrell resulted from large-scale professional development, several generations after the field tests. The staff developers were provided with substantial amounts of guidance that also had been field tested. In all of these projects, professional development consisted of information on beginning reading acquisition and instruction, not a course on reading pedagogy across the elementary grades.

First-Grade Interventions

The four Grade 1 reading interventions chosen for this review share goals and instructional strategies for supporting the reading acquisition of initially low-performing first graders but vary in the teacher-student ratios employed in the interventions. The first two projects (Pinnell, Lyons, DeFord, Bryk, & Seltzer, 1994; Vellutino, Scanlon, Sipay, Small, Pratt, Chen, & Denckla, 1996) focus on one-to-one tutoring as the central treatment but differ in the amounts of professional development and in content of the treatment, while the second set of projects (Hiebert, Colt, Catto, & Gury, 1992; Hiebert & Colt, 1994; Taylor, Short, Frye, & Shearer, 1992; Taylor, Short, Shearer, & Frye, 1995) attend to small group instruction. The two projects in our sample differ in the number of children in the small groups—six to seven (Taylor et al., 1995) and three (Hiebert et al., 1992)—and in the instructional context—classroom teachers teaching small groups during classroom periods (Taylor et al., 1992) and Title I teachers teaching small groups outside the classroom (Hiebert et al., 1992).

Although Pinnell et al. purported to compare the effectiveness of Reading Recovery with different lessons (another tutorial approach), different teacher-student ratios (small group instruction), and differences in teacher training (2-week intensive with videotapes rather than the year-long Reading Recovery graduate course with behind the glass observations), we chose to report only on the results of the Reading Recovery group from Pinnell et al. (1994). We concur with Rasinski (1995) that variables such as teacher expertise, training opportunities (in the treatments where training was presumably held constant), and time students spent with a teacher were confounded in the treatments, making conclusions about the treatments other than Reading Recovery difficult. The implementation of Reading Recovery, however, appears to have been rigorous with teachers in at least their third year of implementing Reading Recovery.

Reading Recovery, based on the work of Marie Clay in New Zealand (Clay, 1993), is a one-on-one tutoring program for first-grade children from the lowest 20% of their class on emergent reading measures. Children leave their classroom for a daily 30-minute session for 12–15 weeks with a Reading Recovery teacher. The daily routine includes rereading two to three familiar stories, reading a story from the previous day while the teacher takes a running record, engaging in word analysis, writing a message, and discussing and reading a new book. Lessons end with children identifying materials to read at home.

In Vellutino et al.'s (1996) project, children received 30 minutes of daily one-on-one tutoring for 15 weeks on average. Sessions were tailored to children's individual needs with about 15 minutes spent on reading connected text and 15 minutes on word identification activities. Typically, activities included fostering children's deliberate use of word identification strategies while reading, practicing sight words, developing pho-

nemic awareness and an understanding of the alphabetic principle, working on phonetic decoding, and writing.

Hiebert et al. (1992) restructured a Title I program by having teachers and their aides
work with first graders in groups of three daily for at least a semester. Books were chosen to complement the word identification strategies in lessons such as *The Cake That
Mack Ate* (Robart, 1986) for a lesson on words with "ake." Lessons consisted of reading
familiar and unfamiliar books, writing rhyming words and journal writing, and instruction in letter-sound and word patterns. During the last component, children
might find *cake* in the book they have just read and then write and reread the word and
other words with the same pattern. Children took a familiar book home daily for rereading.

Early Intervention in Reading (EIR) is a supplemental intervention program in
which the classroom teacher provides 20 minutes of extra instruction daily to a group
of six to seven struggling readers (Taylor et al., 1992, 1995). The texts used in this program start out short and increase in length. At the beginning of Grade 1, a three-day cycle of activities includes repeated reading of a new story, phonemic awareness training
or making word activities, and guided writing. During reading, the teacher stresses
strategies for word recognition and independence on the part of the children. In addition to the daily group instruction, the children read a familiar or current story to an
aide, volunteer, or older student. By spring of first grade, teachers shift to working
with dyads of children as they read unfamiliar books.

*How Successful Were Projects in Supporting Children's Reading Develop-
ment?*   The results that are summarized in Table 26.3 indicate that, in all four projects, the group receiving the intervention did better than the comparison group. The
data on percentile ranks reported by Vellutino et al. suggest that gains from the intervention are fairly robust. Except for the very low-achieving students in the intervention group, percentile ranks in the year following the intervention remain fairly stable.
Although effect sizes for text reading by the Reading Recovery group decreased by
half from the end of Grade 1 to 2 (Pinnell et al., 1994), students made better progress
than counterparts who did not receive the intervention. The data on the comparison
groups for all of the interventions indicate that the long-term prognosis for students'
reading without an intervention is not good. In a follow-up of the cohort reported in
Hiebert et al. (1992), Hiebert and Colt (1994) found that 24% of the comparison group
as compared to 2% of the intervention group were excluded from test taking as third
graders because of special needs.

Information on the absolute performances of intervention students in two projects
(Hiebert & Colt, 1994; Vellutino et al., 1996) provide additional insight into the effects
of first-grade interventions. Both investigations used 45 percentile or national curve
equivalent (NCE) ranks as an indicator of facile reading. While the students were assessed at different points in time, the percentages of students who attained this level
are similar across the two projects: 48% of the third graders (Hiebert & Colt, 1994) and
45% of the first graders (Vellutino et al., 1996).

Data from these two reports on the performances of the range of classmates relative
to intervention students shed additional light on the effects of interventions. Prior to
the Vellutino et al. intervention that began in the middle of Grade 1, the normal readers' group had a mean percentile rank of 72, compared to 22 (very good), 19 (good), 14
(low), and 9 (very low) for the four initially poor reader groups. Gains were substantial
for all four groups of initially poor readers with gain scores of 41, 31, 15, and 11, respectively. Only a fourth of the intervention group, however, were within a standard deviation of the normal readers. Similarly, while intervention students in the Hiebert et al.
project were able to read at a similar level of text as average students in their classes,
approximately 40% of their classmates were already fluent with second-grade text.

TABLE 26.3
Achievement Patterns of First-Grade Interventions

	Hiebert et al. (1992)	Pinnell et al. (1994)	Taylor et al. (1992)	Vellutino et al. (1996)
Sample	First graders in Title I schools who scored < 25 NCE on a standardized reading readiness test; 53 in structured program and 66 in regular program	RR programs had existed at sites for at least 2 years. Comparison group came from same school: each school identified lowest 10 first graders, 4 of whom were randomly assigned to RR and the rest to comparison group	30 lowest achieving first graders in 6 first grade classes of a large metropolitan district received intervention; 30 children of comparable entry levels in 6 different first grade classrooms in same districts formed comparison group	74 children who received the intervention and 42 children (comparison) who received Title I as tutorials or in small groups represented 9% of the total cohort of first graders in 6 middle- to upper-middle-class school districts. All scored initially at or below 15th percentile on either Word Identification or Word attack subtests of Woodcock Reading Mastery Tests—Revised
Performances at end of intervention[c]	Word Rec: 1.39[a] Text: 1.16 CTBS Reading: 1.29 CTBS Language: 1.14	Text: 1.50 GM: .51 Woodcock: .49	Standardized reading test: .48[b]	Percentiles on Woodcock

Group	≤15[c]	16–30	31–45	> 45
Comparison	26%	14%	31%	29%
Intervention	15%	17%	22%	45%

(*Continues*)

TABLE 26.3 (Continued)

	Hiebert et al. (1992)	Taylor et al. (1992)	Pinnell et al. (1994)	Vellutino et al. (1996)
End of Grade 1 performances relative to classmates:	Quintile 1: 2.61[c] (.83) Quintile 2: 1.75 (.84) Quintile 3: 1.14 (.96) Quintile 4: .60 (.54) Intervention/Quintile 5: 1.22 (.92)	(Not available)	(Not available)	Average: 72.21 (16.68) Intervention: Very Good: 62.63 (11.99) Good: 47.83 (9.78) Low: 29.11 (8.31) Very Low: 19.84 (12.47)
Post-intervention	CTBS (end Gr. 2): Groups <35[d] 35–44 ≥45 Intervention 20 30 48 Comparison 42 13 21	(Not available)	GM (end Gr. 1): .19 Text (beg. Gr. 2): .75	Woodcock Reading Mastery Tests (end Gr. 2): Average: 74.62 (20.57) Intervention: Very Good: 63.79 (15.08) Good: 43.50 (16.83) Low: 27.56 (12.12) Very Low: 14.37 (16.66)

[a]Except for Pinnell et al. where intervention period was a term, performances are for end of Grade 1

[b]From Shanahan and Barr (1995, Table 7)

[c]Percentile rankings on the Basic Skills Cluster of the Woodcock Reading Mastery Tests—Revised

[d]From Hiebert and Colt (1994); 2% of the Intervention group and 24% of the Comparison group were excluded from taking standardized tests

The finding that children who receive the innovative method in a reading research project outperform the children who receive the status quo instruction follows a long-standing pattern in reading research (Pflaum et al., 1980). Unlike studies of the past where instructional approaches were compared in global ways, this group of studies provides specific answers to the question, What exactly makes the difference?

What Features of Curriculum, Instruction, and Professional Development Characterized the Interventions?   The summary of components in the first-grade interventions in Table 26.4 show that all emphasize reading words in text quickly and fluently. This goal of fluent reading of text is viewed developmentally, with knowledge of the alphabetic principle as the basis for decoding ability. In projects such as Taylor et al.'s (1992, 1995), decoding ability is developed through a progression of strategies, sequential in nature: acquiring letter-sound knowledge, engaging in sequential decoding, decoding by recognizing word patterns, developing accuracy in word recognition, and developing automaticity and fluency in word recognition. Although comprehension is not ignored in any project, comprehension activities were not the sole focus at any point in their instructional routines. However, on the comprehension components of standardized tests and on the comprehension questions that accompany the oral reading of texts, children's performances appear to keep pace with the development of their fluency.

All first-grade projects emphasize reading many different texts and rereading these texts to attain high levels of fluency. For these reading and rereading activities, all of the projects stress the importance of specifying the texts that children read. The projects differ, however, in the specific features emphasized in selecting the books. In one project (Hiebert et al., 1992), books are chosen to highlight words with particular letter-sound patterns. In the other projects, books are chosen for the strength of their stories (Taylor et al., 1992) or the presence of features such as naturalness of language, number of pages, and usefulness of illustrations (Pinnell et al., 1994). Whatever the criteria for selecting text, one distinction of these projects relative to typical textbook programs (Hiebert, 1999) is the use of several different books over a week's lessons rather than a single book (Hiebert et al., 1992; Pinnell et al., 1994, Vellutino et al., 1996). When a single book does provide the week's instructional focus, occasions for seeing the words from a book in several contexts such as charts and little books are provided (Taylor et al., 1992).

The first-grade projects differ from the kindergarten and second-grade projects in their integration of findings from various cognitive science and literacy literatures. In particular, research on metacognition (Palincsar & Brown, 1984) is emphasized in the instructional routines of Reading Recovery (Pinnell et al., 1994) and EIR (Taylor et al., 1992). Children are guided in self-monitoring for word recognition errors and in using various word recognition strategies to figure out unfamiliar words. The strategies cover the range from semantic, syntactic, visual, and phonic information while reading for meaning. The projects also integrate research on writing, especially as a source for developing phonemic awareness and subsequent phonics skill. Projects differ in the units of writing, ranging from sentences related to books that have been read (Pinnell et al., 1994; Taylor et al., 1992) to words with common patterns (Hiebert et al., 1992).

The first-grade interventions also draw heavily on work from instructional psychology (Good & Brophy, 1990). All four first-grade interventions attend to teachers' delivery of lessons, providing an instructional routine of reading text, writing and spelling words and texts, and word recognition activities. Regular assessment of progress is also evident in the first-grade interventions, with teachers using assessment to plan instruction (Pinnell et al., 1994; Vellutino et al., 1996), to reflect on students' progress (Taylor et al., 1992), and to identify appropriate books for students (Hiebert et al., 1992).

TABLE 26.4

Instructional Components of First-Grade Interventions

	Hiebert et al. (1992)	Pinnell et al. (1994)	Taylor et al. (1995)	Vellutino et al. (1996)
Goals				
•Ensuring a phonemic foundation	•Not specified	•Yes	•Yes	•Yes
•Letter naming	•Not specified	•Yes	•Not specified	•Not specified
•Attending to phonics (letter-sound patterns, sequential decoding, word patterns)	•Yes (word patterns)	•Yes (letter-sound patterns)	•Yes (sequential decoding)	•Yes (letter-sound patterns, followed by sequential decoding)
•Developing a strategic stance to written language systems	•Yes	•Yes	•Yes	•Yes
•Developing fluency in reading, including focus on high-frequency words	•Yes	•Indirectly through repeated reading	•Indirectly through repeated reading	•Not specified
•Comprehension	•Indirectly through writing and book talk	•Indirectly through "reading for meaning"	•Not specified	•Indirectly through "reading for meaning"
Instructional Elements				
•Teacher:student ratio	•1:3	•1:1	•1:6–7	•1:1
•Time allocation	•30 min. daily/entire year	•30 min. daily/12–16 weeks	•20 min. daily/entire year	•30 min. daily/15 weeks
•Text of appropriate difficulty	•Yes	•Yes	•Not specified	•Yes

(Continues)

TABLE 26.4 (Continued)

	Hiebert et al. (1992)	Pinnell et al. (1994)	Taylor et al. (1995)	Vellutino et al. (1996)
Instructional Elements				
• Writing to promote phonemic awareness and word recognition	• Yes	• Yes	• Yes	• Yes
• Discussions to foster comprehension	• Not specified	• Yes	• Indirectly through writing sentence summary of story	• Not specified
Professional Context	• Initial 2-day workshop and monthly meetings which included videotapes of teachers. Also, observations by project staff were conducted	• Weekly 2.5 hour session over 2 terms with demonstration teaching "behind the glass" and discussion	• Initial half-day workshop and monthly meetings with videotapes of teachers. Also classroom visits by mentors were made	• Thirty-hour seminar was supplemented by individual reading of materials. Tutoring sessions were audiotaped, 10% (randomly selected) of which were reviewed by a program developer. Supervisors discussed these tapes with individual tutors. Also biweekly meetings of all tutors and supervisors were held

There are simply too many vagaries in the projects to make definitive conclusions about the teacher-student ratio. Since the effect size reported for the one project where groups numbered six to seven children (Taylor et al., 1992) is sufficiently less than those for the other first-grade projects, one conclusion might be that groups that are too large for teachers to monitor responses may not be the most conducive context for early interventions. But, since many students may require support (such as the students in Quintiles 3 and 4 who fell below the Quintile 5 students who received the intervention), the issue is to determine which students benefit most from which contexts at particular points in time rather than to identify a single context for all forms of first-grade interventions.

The projects all include professional development opportunities for teachers, but these opportunities vary considerably. Three of the projects (Hiebert et al., 1992; Taylor et al., 1992; Vellutino et al., 1996) provided monthly or bimonthly meetings. In contrast, Reading Recovery involves teachers in a weekly graduate course over their first year which includes "behind-the-glass" observation of one teacher teaching, while the other teachers discuss children's responses and teachers' decisions. The evidence in Table 26.3, however, suggests that changes in the reading achievement of a substantial portion of a first-grade cohort can be accomplished with focused professional development that is less intensive than the graduate course of Reading Recovery (Hiebert et al., 1992; Taylor et al., 1992; Vellutino et al., 1996).

Second-Grade Interventions

The second-grade interventions allow for comparisons and contrasts across a variety of instructional contexts. Two interventions involved tutoring students: one with specialists in a Reading Recovery adaptation (Hatcher, Hulme, & Ellis, 1994) and the other with volunteers (Morris, Shaw, & Perney, 1990). The last two interventions involved restructuring of the classroom reading program (Eldredge, Reutzel, & Hollingsworth, 1996; Stahl, Heubach, & Cramond, 1997).

Hatcher et al. (1994) adapted the Reading Recovery tutorial in two ways: (a) an inclusion of phonology training (as compared to the typical tutorial, which they described as "reading only" and a "reading and phonology" treatment), and (b) a focus on second-grade children (third year of infant school in Great Britain). In the Morris et al. (1990) effort, volunteer tutors from the community who were supervised by a reading specialist worked with children in two one-hour sessions weekly where they read familiar and unfamiliar texts, did word recognition activities, and wrote. Although second graders were the targeted group, about a third of the sample consisted of third graders who, like the second graders, were reading at a first-grade level or lower when they began the tutoring.

Although the second set of interventions was aimed at entire classes, the activities were not implemented uniformly across all of the students in a class. Stahl et al. worked with teachers in reorganizing their reading programs to emphasize three components: a reading lesson that stressed repeated reading and partner reading, an independent reading period daily where children chose books to read, and a home reading program. Eldredge et al. (1996) compared children's fluency, vocabulary acquisition, and reading comprehension as a function of participating in shared book reading relative to conventional round-robin reading. Both contexts involved opportunities to discuss text and participate in rereading text in independent or partner settings. Round-robin reading involved substantially more correction of children's oral reading and emphasized individual readings of texts within small groups of like-ability peers and the teacher. The shared book reading treatment provided occasions for children to read together and for the teacher to lead and model oral reading of particular parts of the text (especially those that might be difficult). Children read texts independently, with a peer, or with audiotaped versions of the book.

How Successful Were Projects in Supporting Children's Reading Development?   As the achievement patterns in Table 26.5 show, the pattern for second grade is similar to that of first-grade interventions: Participation in an intervention positively affects second graders' reading achievement. The efficacy of second-grade efforts relative to kindergarten or first grade is difficult to establish since only Hatcher et al. reported post-intervention results and these were soon after the treatment. Several conclusions are possible, however, about the achievement patterns of interventions for second graders.

First, the interventions are more effective for some students than for others. The profiles provided from Stahl et al. (1997) in Table 26.5 show that second graders who were able to read at least primer-level text when the school year began learned to read quite well, while children below primer level did not catch up as a result of the intervention. These children made progress, but they entered third grade unable to proficiently read third-grade text.

Second, the achievement levels of the average students, presented in Table 26.5, raise questions about the adequacy of "third-grade" reading for success in the middle grades. Even in high-poverty schools, many of the children are reading texts several levels above the third-grade level. Facility with third-grade text as a goal for children by the end of third grade begs the question of what level text the average third grader is able to read and the level of materials textbook publishers (and subsequently teachers) expect children to read. While progress has been made by the children most at risk in the current projects, it is unclear whether children are able to function adequately in subsequent grades. As Morris et al. note, while 50% of students in their project made a full year's reading gain, these gains are likely insufficient to ensure children's success in school.

Third, the results of Eldredge et al. (1996) support the construct of connections among components of reading. While the Eldredge et al. project addressed oral reading of text, the effect for comprehension was almost as substantial as the effect for vocabulary and fluency, providing further confirmation for a strong relation between fluency and comprehension (Lesgold, Resnick, & Hammond, 1985), at least for primary-level readers. Further, the Hatcher et al. project corroborates the finding of Ayres's (1993, 1998) with kindergartners: There are differences in children's achievement as a function of the kinds of activities in which they participate. It is to the nature of these activities that we turn our attention next.

What Features of Curriculum, Instruction, and Professional Context Characterized Successful Interventions?   As is evident in Table 26.6, there is commonality in the content of second-grade interventions, and this focus differs from first-grade interventions. The second-grade interventions are focused on the development of automaticity in word recognition, rather than simply on word recognition. The content of the activities and the inclusion of measures indicate that this attention to automaticity did not reflect a narrow view of accuracy and fluency in proficient reading. Rather, the view was that comprehension depends on automatic word recognition. To accomplish this goal, all of the projects, with the exception of the Hatcher et al. phonology-only treatment, increased the amount of time that children spent with a *model of proficient reading*. When phonology practice was emphasized to the detriment of reading texts, children did not do as well. Extensive reading and a model of expert reading—whether through a whole class read-along, an older student, a teacher/tutor, or an adult on a taperecording—benefits children's comprehension as well as their oral reading.

As with the first-grade interventions, conclusions about the role of particular teacher-student ratios in intervening with poor readers in second grade cannot be drawn. The two projects in which tutorials were the medium of instruction targeted

TABLE 26.5

Achievement Patterns of Second-Grade Interventions

	Eldredge et al. (1995)	Hatcher et al. (1996)			Morris et al. (1990)	Stahl et al. (1997)		
						Entry level	Exit level: Cohort 1 (4 classes)	Exit level: Cohort 2 (9 classes)
Sample	Schools had 50% low-income students	Seven year olds who were designated as having a reading difficulty			Second and third graders reading at first-grade level	Schools with high concentrations of low-income students		
Performances at end of intervention	Word analysis: 1.24 Comprehension: .49 Vocabulary: .51 Fluency: .69	Reading + Phonology	Reading	Phonology	Basal word recognition: .61 Oral passage reading: 1.07	Below	2.5[b]	2.25
		Accuracy: .60	.09	.19	Text Levels[a] (Intervention/Comparison): ≤ First grade: 20/29 Second grade: 7/1 Third grade: 3/0	Primer	3.5	3.00
		Comp: .70	.16	.08		Gr. 1	4	4
		Spell: .39				Gr. 2	5.5	4.5
		Arithmetic: -.08				Gr. 3	6.5	5.5
						Gr. 4	6.5	6.5
Postintervention:	(None)	Accuracy: .45 Comprehension: .66 Spelling: .35			(None)	(None)		

[a]Number of students able to read particular text levels

[b]Average Reading Level, not effect sizes, of students who had begun with particular entry levels

TABLE 26.6

Instructional Components of Second-Grade Interventions

	Eldredge et al. (1996)[a]	Hatcher et al. (1990)[b]	Morris et al. (1990)	Stahl et al. (1997)
Goals				
• Word recognition	• Word features were discussed as part of follow-up readings of texts	Phonology Only: Tasks at 9 levels of difficulty, beginning with identifying and supplying rhyming words to transposing sounds within words	• Automaticity with one-syllable spelling patterns in English	• Aim was to move from accuracy-driven decoding to fluency and automaticity
• Fluency (rate and accuracy) and automaticity	• Rereading for fluency one of primary goals of project	Reading Only: Reading Recovery teaching format but without explicit reference to phonology	• Portion of each lesson is devoted to easy contextual reading to strengthen fluency	• Strong emphasis
• Comprehension	• Discussion and retelling of story was critical to lessons	Reading + Phonology: Reading Recovery teaching format was supplemented with phonological activities, including writing	• Priority on reading and comprehending interesting stories	• Even with emphasis on fluent reading, lessons were described as "comprehension-oriented"
Instructional Elements				
• Time allocation	• 30 min. daily for 4 months	• 30 min. twice weekly over 20 weeks	• Two 1-hour sessions weekly	• 30 min. daily for 7 weeks plus 25 min., biweekly cross-age tutoring

(Continues)

473

TABLE 26.6 (Continued)

	Eldredge et al. (1996)[a]	Hatcher et al. (1990)[b]	Morris et al. (1990)	Stahl et al. (1997)
Instructional Elements				
• Teacher:student ratio	• Whole class plus independent, buddy, and audiotaped settings	• 1:1	• 1:1	• Small group led by teacher; fourth graders as tutors
• Materials	• Trade books	• Set of 73 books graded in difficulty	• "Natural" stories	• Texts of classroom, including trade books and textbooks
• Assessment	• No assessments by teachers	• Assessments were conducted by research staff before, after, and 9 months following intervention	• Members of research staff give pretest and posttests consisting of informal reading and spelling measures	• Assessments conducted periodically by research team and shared with teachers; teachers conducted running records, though not consistently
• Instructional activities specifically:				
• Increased reading of appropriate text	• Strong emphasis	• Reading from books as part of twice weekly lessons	• Substantial increases in amount of time spent reading	• Substantial increase in amount of reading
• Writing to promote phonemic awareness and word recognition	• Not as part of project	• Yes	• Approximately 1/4 of sessions spent on writing	• Journal writing was done consistently and used for story discussions

(Continues)

TABLE 26.6 (Continued)

	Eldredge et al. (1996)[a]	Hatcher et al. (1990)[b]	Morris et al. (1990)	Stahl et al. (1997)
•Comprehension	•Strong emphasis	•Not specified	•Premium is placed on stories that interest students; sessions end with tutor reading literature	•Strongly emphasized in all contexts
•Word Study	•As part of follow-up story activities	•Emphasized with a section on reading and writing words and looking at and writing letters	•1/8–1/6 of session: Word categorization activities and games with word families	•No new components of word study initiated as part of project
Professional Context	•Teachers (treatment and comparison) individually given in-service sessions; teachers were provided with daily lessons for entire project; teachers observed three times weekly, with suggestions offered at the end of the observation	•Teacher/tutors received release time; 3 days of training prior to treatment; fidelity of implementation was monitored by research staff; teachers also completed records for each session	•Various adults from community; supervised by a reading specialist who prepared tutoring lessons; on the job training guidance given to tutors	•In first year, teachers designed activities with research team prior to school year, with weekly meetings subsequently. Second group did not design program; nature of support and inservice for second year teachers uncertain

[a]Components of Shared Reading Experience are described as the treatment since Round-Robin Reading represented status quo instruction
[b]Instructional elements for Hatcher et al. pertain to the Reading + Phonology treatment

the lowest students. The two projects that restructured classroom programs included the range of students. The lowest students in the classrooms of the Stahl et al. intervention were likely as challenged in their reading as the students in the two tutorial projects. But, without equivalent allocations of learning time and measures across projects, claims cannot be made for the efficacy of one context over another.

Although none of the second-grade projects provided the level of professional development in the Reading Recovery training (including Hatcher et al.'s replication of Reading Recovery), the support that teachers and tutors received was specific to the lessons that they taught. Such specificity contrasts with mandates from states and districts that often require courses or workshops on reading pedagogy in the elementary grades.

EARLY READING INTERVENTIONS: CONCLUSIONS AND QUESTIONS

Reviews of literature in education often conclude with a call for further research. We, too, will raise issues that require further attention if educators are to support more children in learning to read well. But there is also a need to take stock of where we are and to view our results within theoretical perspectives.

Conclusions From Current Research

The limited number of projects that could be included in this review means that conclusions should be viewed as exploratory. However, the consistency across the findings and their consistency with the conclusions of earlier reviews of related literatures (Stahl & Miller, 1989), with initial data on the reading programs of schools that beat the odds (Taylor et al., 1999), and with theoretical perspectives on reading acquisition permit five observations about instruction that supports reading acquisition.

- *Receiving well-designed and focused instruction during the primary grades leads to higher levels of reading proficiency among a significant portion of an age cohort—a group which typically does not do well in status quo instruction.* When the effect sizes are averaged across interventions, the average effect size for kindergarten and first-grade interventions is the same—.92—and for second-grade, .74. Raising the achievement of initially low-achieving students by almost one standard deviation means that many more children in the bottom quartile have skills that allow them to participate more fully in school contexts. The distributions provided by Hiebert et al. (1992) suggest that approximately 75% of children in the bottom quartile can be brought within range of their average peers when taught in groups of three, while Taylor et al. (1992) provide evidence that approximately two thirds of this population can attain this level in small groups of six or seven. In technical reports on Reading Recovery (Reading Recovery Staff at Ohio State University, 1992, 1993), 85% or more of tutees are reported as successful readers as a result of the intervention. While questions remain about the comparability of samples across interventions (Hiebert, 1994), the percentages reported across various interventions indicate that a much more substantial portion of children in the bottom quartile can be taught to read than is the case in status quo instruction.
- *The foundation gained from early interventions is necessary but not sufficient to be successful in the tasks of the middle grades.* While a substantial portion of a cohort are likely to be more prepared for third-grade reading as a result of an intervention,

these children are "not out of the woods yet." Data from the four projects in this review that provided data on children's attainment of an absolute achievement level (Hiebert et al., 1992; Morris et al., 1990; Stahl et al., 1997; Vellutino et al., 1996) indicate that, while intervention recipients are doing considerably better than their counterparts who did not receive interventions, many are not reading as well as their peers in the top half of the cohort. For example, although intervention recipients in the Hiebert et al. (1992) study were able to read first-grade text, approximately 40% of their classmates left first grade able to read second-grade text proficiently. There can be no argument that the interventions have positive outcomes. The sufficiency of interventions at a single grade level, however, can be argued. We found no reports of efforts that linked effective kindergarten interventions with effective first-grade interventions which, in turn, were linked to second-grade interventions. A typical stance among researchers is to emphasize an intervention at a particular grade level. For children who enter school with low levels of literacy, the ability to attain standards of highly proficient reading may depend on a series of differentiated interventions across the primary grades.

The waning effects of the primary-level interventions as children move into third and fourth grades provide further evidence that, while these interventions are necessary for a particular group of children to attain an even basic level of reading proficiency, the early reading interventions by themselves are not sufficient to guarantee success with the tasks of the middle grades. When subsequent instruction fails to attend to what children continue to need, the successes of the early grades—while real at the time—wane.

- *Starting early—at least when the activities and expectations of the interventions are developmentally appropriate—seems to be effective.* Interventions in kindergarten can be effective in developing fundamental knowledge about reading and writing through activities around books, writing, and rhyming games—knowledge that apparently becomes the foundation for subsequent facility in learning to read. The trace of the kindergarten intervention appears to be as resilient as the one for an intensive first-grade intervention such as Reading Recovery, for which an effect size of .25 is reported at third grade (Wasik & Slavin, 1993, Table 4). In the Durkin project, the effect sizes at Grade 4 are .50 and .41, and in the school-based groups of Phillips et al., .29 and .32.

It is uncertain whether there are critical points at which the strategies of the kindergarten interventions such as the ones reviewed in this chapter are most effective. First-grade interventions were more systematic in their presentation of content and strategies than kindergarten interventions. Does this direction in the first-grade interventions reflect the expectations of schools and families or the needs of children? Might the stance of the kindergarten interventions be appropriate for a portion of a first-grade cohort—particularly those for whom the first-grade interventions have not been highly effective? To date, researchers have not examined this question (as discussed below). Another question raised by Durkin's (1974–1975) project is whether the strategies of the kindergarten interventions might have even greater effects if they were integrated into preschool and Head Start programs. What can be concluded with confidence from the available evidence is that involving kindergartners in rich literacy experiences has positive outcomes over an extended period of time.

- *A small portion of a cohort is still not reading sufficiently well to participate in classroom activities in grade two or beyond, as a result of participating in the reading interventions.* Approximately the lowest 10% of the entire population appears to require even further support beyond these early interventions. This conclusion is not meant to diminish the importance of the interventions. Without such interventions, a much more substantial portion of students leaves grade one or grade two without the reading proficiency that will permit them to participate in tasks required in the next grade—even nominally. Further, the achievements of the children in the lowest 10% may be even poorer without participation in the intervention. Even with interventions, however, a portion of the lowest students have not become literate. Some of this group likely have neurological processing problems that make learning to read difficult. But this group likely accounts for 3%–4% of a cohort (as cited by Snow, Burns, & Griffin, 1998), rather than 10% or more. For the children in the lowest 10% of the achievement distribution, interventions will need to be attentive to factors we have only begun to fathom: more time for some, different materials for others, and different instructional procedures for still others.

- *Opportunities for teachers to learn are an essential part of any project where patterns of reading acquisition move more children to proficient reading levels.* While these projects indicate that teachers benefit from professional development, conclusions about the level and length of these experiences are difficult to make from these reports. In 10 of the 12 interventions, the professional development efforts were "first-generation." Research teams did not teach students but they invested considerable amounts of time in supporting teachers in numerous ways, including providing materials and lesson plans and giving and interpreting assessments. For the initiation of reform in schools that are challenged by community poverty, facilitators in such first-generation projects may be critical for initiating reform (LeFevre & Richardson, 1999).

    The professional development efforts in the two projects where these efforts had gone beyond a field test (Pinnell et al., 1994; Hanson & Farrell, 1995) differ from one another. The training received by the Reading Recovery tutors in Pinnell et al. (1994) was both intensive and extensive. Hanson and Farrell's (1995) intervention provided teachers with workshops in which content and instructional activities were presented in a consistent but concentrated format. The large-scale implementation of the BRP with positive results suggests that focused professional development can reap substantial benefits for students. Although the level, content, and length of professional development remains unclear from these reports, the performances of the status quo groups indicate that opportunities for expanding teachers' learning about beginning reading instruction are needed to initiate changes in the profiles of struggling beginning readers.

Nature and Foci of Future Research

Considered from the perspective of current legislation for reading programs that ties funding to research proof, the quantity and quality of research on beginning reading programs over the past two decades is meager. Considered from the perspective of investments of foundation and federal dollars into research on model beginning reading practices, the presence of even a small number of projects is to be applauded. Within the multibillion dollar Title I budget, research funds are directed at evaluation efforts conducted by Department of Education personnel (Office of Policy & Planning, 1993), not at innovative instruction. Although grants are available for technology initiatives and schoolwide programs from the Department of Education, funds for the study of reading acquisition and reading instruction have been limited to an omnibus federal center. While the current center is directed at practices of early reading, the scope of work that bidders needed to satisfy covered seven topics (Federal Register, 1997). Research and development activities on the efficacy of early reading instructional practices was only one of these seven topics. Further, this topic included instruction involving the use of technology. None of the research initiatives on exemplary reading programs compare with the research programs for science and mathematics instruction within the National Science Foundation, or for bilingual or special education students within the Office of Special Education and Rehabilitation Services.

Of the 12 projects reviewed here, 7 were conducted on minimal budgets, typically as part of a faculty member's research commitment within his or her university. With few exceptions (e.g., Vellutino et al.'s [1996] funding through the National Institute for Child Health and Human Development), the investments in research on reading interventions have been modest. While the quality of reading interventions has been criticized by policy analysts (Cohen, Ball, & Rowan, 1998), funding for the evaluation efforts of interventions within the Department of Education is several times the combined funding of all the projects in this review (e.g., Stringfield, Milsap, & Herman, 1997).

We propose two responses to the current state of affairs. First, the influence and coherence of research on early interventions depends on research that is driven by an integrated model of reading instruction and reading acquisition. We have models of reading acquisition (Adams, 1990; Ehri, 1991; Juel, 1991). We also have models of learning in school settings, such as Vygotsky's (1978) elegant description of the distinction between learning to read in a school setting and learning to speak one's first language in homes and communities. The efforts to construct a model of reading acquisition in school settings have begun (see Snow et al., 1998). While in an embryonic state, such an integrated model of reading instruction and acquisition recognizes the adaptation of goals and activities at different developmental levels.

A strong model that attends to reading acquisition in the context of school instruction is the foundation for the second response: rigorous proposals to federal, state, and private agencies for the funding of critical and as yet unanswered questions about children's reading acquisition within school settings. We will describe two of the issues that require attention: expectations regarding long-term effects and the relationship between the profiles of schools and the capacity of interventions.

Long-Term Effects on Children's Learning.   The evidence points to an immediate effect for early reading interventions that steadily decreases in subsequent years. When confronted with this evidence, scholars tend to question the viability of an intervention that fails to exhibit a sustaining effect several years after the intervention. However, models of reading acquisition and of development suggest that they have raised the wrong question. Although early reading interventions support children in gaining basic reading fluency, neither theory or empirical evidence indicate that children will develop a strategic stance from a single first-grade intervention that carries over to the variety of texts and reading and writing tasks with those texts in subsequent years. Research on a strategic reading of informational text, especially among children who may be vulnerable to failure in school, indicates that such a stance depends on substantial amounts of reading and ambitious instruction (Palincsar & Brown, 1984).

The appropriate question that should be raised about the long-term effects of the early reading interventions is: How can the "jump start" from these interventions be parlayed into success in middle-grade reading? Although fluency in recognizing words may not ensure a strategic stance for new texts, the new levels of fluency developed from the interventions could become the basis for subsequent instructional treatments that focus on the developmental tasks that face middle-grade readers. To date, while efforts to redesign classroom instruction of children who have been successful in early interventions have been reported at conferences (e.g., Hiebert & Colt,

1994), such efforts have not been reported in the archival literature. Current knowledge of the development of reading proficiency suggests that attention to such treatments has a stronger conceptual foundation and prospect for supporting higher levels of literacy than interventions that are aimed only at the initial stages of reading acquisition.

Profiles of Schools and the Capacity of Interventions.   Children attained similar levels of reading in the interventions, regardless of the teacher-student ratio. Teacher-student ratio does influence, however, the number of children who can be expected to reach particular levels of reading as a result of an intervention—in other words, capacity. Levels of success within an intervention need to be considered along with the number of children who benefit from the allocation of resources in the decision-making of schools as they redesign their reading programs. The likely solutions for many schools with majority low-income populations lie in a combination of teacher-student contexts that occur at different points in children's reading acquisition. Vellutino et al.'s tutoring occurred in the last term of first grade and first term of second grade. Since the predictive validity of reading assessments is low until children are reading at least some words, small group interventions (see, e.g., Hiebert et al., 1992; Taylor et al., 1992) during the first term of first grade could ensure that the resources of one-to-one tutoring are brought to bear on children who are unlikely to learn to read well without such concentrated attention.

A question to be addressed in future research is the degree to which early interventions should serve as models of classroom instruction. Conflicting messages from scholars, teachers, and educators have left many kindergarten teachers confused about what constitutes appropriate literacy experiences for young children. Similarly, conflicting messages have left many first-grade teachers confused about the appropriateness of small group experiences or the use of books that attend to particular vocabularies. A first item of business in schools where many children are challenged in learning to read is an assessment of the degree to which the needs for specialized interventions can be alleviated through well-designed classroom instruction and activities. The first-grade interventions shared the use of an instructional routine—a characteristic of nationally identified expert first-grade teachers (Wharton-MacDonald, Pressley, & Hampston, 1998). The routines of these interventions may be particularly useful for the many new teachers who will teach the next generation of children (Darling-Hammond, 1997).

This discussion of long-term effects and the capacity of interventions relative to school profiles indicates that critical questions remain to be addressed. The current state of research on early interventions is spotty, at best. The assumption that a one-time intervention can solve the reading challenges faced by children in high-poverty schools is not supported by the current research or by any theoretical models of reading. Early reading interventions have been useful in broadening the conversation about effective beginning reading instruction, especially for children who find learning to read difficult, through their validation of effective program components. Traditionally, debates have raged about whether a code versus meaning or phonics versus whole language approach is best in first grade. The early reading interventions have been instrumental in turning educators' conversations to different issues. In particular, the current wave of early interventions has shown that proficient reading requires support on a set of processes simultaneously rather than on a single process. In this regard, these interventions represent an important departure from many of the studies of the past which focused on a single instructional component, most typically explicit decoding instruction.

ACKNOWLEDGMENTS

The contributions of both authors were supported under the Educational Research and Development Centers Program, PR/Award R305R70004, as administered by the Office of Educational Research and Improvement, U.S. Department of Education. However, the comments do not necessarily represent the positions or policies of the National Institute of Student Achievement, Curriculum, and Assessment or the National Institute on Early Childhood Development, or the U.S. Department of Education, and you should not assume endorsement by the federal government.

REFERENCES

Adams, M. J. (1990). *Beginning to read: Thinking and learning about print.* Cambridge, MA: MIT Press.

American Research Institutes. (1999). *An educators' guide to schoolwide reform.* Arlington, VA: Educational Research Service.

Ayres, L. R. (1993). *The efficacy of three training conditions on phonological awareness of kindergarten children and the longitudinal effect of each on later reading acquisition.* Unpublished doctoral dissertation, Oakland University.

Ayres, L. R. (1998). Phonological awareness training of kindergarten children: Three treatments and their effects. In C. Weaver (Ed.), *Reconsidering a balanced approach to reading* (pp. 209–255). Urbana, IL: National Council of Teachers of English.

Ball, E. W., & Blachman, B. A. (1991). Does phoneme awareness training in kindergarten make a difference in early word recognition and developmental spelling? *Reading Research Quarterly, 26*(1), 49–66.

Barr, R. (1984). Beginning reading instruction: From debate to reformation. In P. D. Pearson, R. Barr, M. Kamil, & P. Mosenthal (Eds.), *Handbook of reading research* (Vol. 1, pp. 545–582). New York: Longman.

Barr, R., Kamil, M. L., Mosenthal, P., & Pearson, P. D. (Eds.). (1991). *Handbook of reading research* (Vol. 2). New York: Longman.

Clay, M. M. (1985). *The early detection of complex reading behavior.* Portsmouth, NH: Heinemann.

Clay, M. M. (1993). *Reading Recovery: A guidebook for teachers in training.* Portsmouth, NH: Heinemann.

Cohen, D. K., Ball, D. L., & Rowan, B. (1998, October). *Studying reform efforts in elementary schools.* Symposium given at the University of Michigan.

Darling-Hammond, L. (1997). The quality of teaching matters most: What teachers know and can do makes the most difference in what children learn. *Journal of Staff Development, 18*, 38–44.

Durkin, D. (1966). *Children who read early: Two longitudinal studies.* New York: Teachers College Press.

Durkin, D. (1974–1975). A six-year study of children who learned to read in school at the age of four. *Reading Research Quarterly, 1*, 9–61.

Ehri, L. C. (1991). Development of the ability to read words. In R. Barr, M. L. Kamil, P. B. Mosenthal, & P. D. Pearson (Eds.), *Handbook of Reading Research* (Vol. 2, pp. 383–417). New York: Longman.

Eldredge, J. L., Reutzel, D. R., & Hollingsworth, P. M. (1996). Comparing the effectiveness of two oral reading practices: Round-robin reading and the shared book experience. *Journal of Literacy Research, 28*, 201–225.

Federal Register. (1997). *Catalog of federal domestic assistance No. 84.305R.* Washington, DC: U.S. Government Printing Office.

Fisher, C. W., & Hiebert, E. H. (1990). Characteristics of tasks in two literacy programs. *Elementary School Journal, 91*, 6–13.

Foorman, B. R., Francis, D. J., Fletcher, J. M., Schatschneider, C., & Mehta, P. (1998). The role of instruction in learning to read: Preventing reading failure in at-risk children. *Journal of Educational Psychology, 90*, 37–55.

Good, T. L., & Brophy, J. E. (1990). *Educational psychology: A realistic approach.* White Plains, NY: Longman.

Hanson, R. A., & Farrell, D. (1995). The long-term effects on high school seniors of learning to read in kindergarten. *Reading Research Quarterly, 30*, 908–933.

Hatcher, P. J., Hulme, C., & Ellis, A. W. (1994). Ameliorating early reading failure by integrating the teaching of reading and phonological skills: The phonological linkage hypothesis. *Child Development, 65*, 41–57.

Hiebert, E. H. (1994). Reading Recovery in the United States: What difference does it make to an age cohort? *Educational Researcher, 23*, 15–25.

Hiebert, E. H. (1999). Text matters in learning to read (Distinguished Educators Series). *Reading Teacher, 52*, 552–568. (Also CIERA Rep. No. 1–001. Ann Arbor: CIERA/University of Michigan.)

Hiebert, E. H., & Colt, J. M. (1994, April). *Extending instruction for children in an early literacy intervention.* Paper presented at the annual meeting of the American Educational Research Association, San Francisco, CA.

Hiebert, E. H., Colt, J. M., Catto, S., & Gury, E. (1992). Reading and writing of first-grade students in a restructured Chapter 1 program. *American Educational Research Journal, 29*, 545–572.

Juel, C. (1991). Beginning reading. In R. Barr, M. L. Kamil, P. B. Mosenthal, & P. D. Pearson (Eds.), *Handbook of reading research* (Vol. 2, pp. 759–788). New York: Longman.

LeFevre, D., & Richardson, V. (1999, April). *The role of the facilitator in school change in reading instruction*. Paper presented at the annual meeting of the American Educational Research Association, Montreal, QB.

Lesgold, A. M., Resnick, L. B., & Hammond, K. (1985). Learning to read: A longitudinal study of word skill development in two curricula. In G. E. MacKinnon & T. G. Waller (Eds.), *Reading research: Advances in theory and practice* (Vol. 4, pp. 107–138). New York: Academic Press.

Morris, D., Shaw, B., & Perney, J. (1990). Helping low readers in grade 2 and 3: An after-school volunteer tutoring program. *Elementary School Journal, 91*, 132–150.

Office of Policy and Planning. (1993). *Reinventing Chapter 1: The current Chapter 1 program and new directions.* Washington, DC: U.S. Department of Education.

Palincsar, A. S., & Brown, A. L. (1984). Reciprocal teaching of comprehension-fostering and comprehension-monitoring activities. *Cognition and Instruction, 1*, 117–175.

Pflaum, S. W., Walberg, H. J., Karegianes, M. L., & Rasher, S. P. (1980). Reading instruction: A quantitative analysis. *Educational Researcher, 9*, 12–18.

Phillips, L. M., Norris, S. P., & Mason, J. M. (1996). Longitudinal effects of early literacy concepts on reading achievement: A kindergarten intervention and five-year follow-up. *Journal of Literacy Research, 28*, 173–195.

Pinnell, G. S., Lyons, C. A., DeFord, D. E., Bryk, A. S., & Seltzer, M. (1994). Comparing instructional models for the literacy education of high-risk first graders. *Reading Research Quarterly, 29*, 8–39.

Pogrow, S. (1998). What is an exemplary program, and why should anyone care? A reaction to Slavin & Klein. *Educational Researcher, 27*, 22–29.

Purcell-Gates, V., & Dahl, K. (1991). Low-SES children's success and failure at early literacy learning in skills-based classrooms. *Journal of Reading Behavior, 23*, 1–34.

Rasinski, T. (1995). Commentary: On the effects of Reading Recovery: A response to Pinnell, Lyons, DeFord, Bryk, and Seltzer. *Reading Research Quarterly, 30*, 264–271.

Reading Recovery Staff at Ohio State University. (1992). *National Diffusion Network Executive Summary: Reading Recovery 1984–1991*. Columbus: Ohio State University.

Reading Recovery Staff at Ohio State University. (1993). *National Diffusion Network Executive Summary: Reading Recovery 1984–1992*. Columbus: Ohio State University.

Robart, R. (1986). *The cake that Mack ate*. Boston: Atlantic Monthly Press.

Shanahan, T., & Barr, R. (1995). Reading Recovery: An independent evaluation of the effects of an early instructional intervention for at-risk learners. *Reading Research Quarterly, 30*, 958–997.

Snow, C. E., Burns, M. S., & Griffin, P. (Eds.). (1998). *Preventing reading difficulties in young children*. Washington, DC: National Academy Press.

Stahl, S. A., Heubach, K., & Cramond, B. (1997). *Fluency-oriented reading instruction* (Reading Research Rep. No. 79). Athens, GA, and College Park, MD: Universities of Georgia and Maryland, National Reading Research Center.

Stahl, S. A., & Miller, P. D. (1989). Whole language and language experience approaches for beginning reading: A quantitative research synthesis. *Review of Educational Research, 59*, 87–116.

Stallings, J. (1975). Implementation and child effects of teaching practices in Follow Through classrooms. *Monographs of the Society for Research in Child Development, 40* (entire issue).

Stringfield, S., Milsap, M. A., & Herman, R. (1997). *Urban and suburban/rural strategies for educating disadvantaged children*. Washington, DC: Planning & Evaluation, U.S. Department of Education.

Taylor, B. M., Anderson, R. C., Au, K. H., & Raphael, T. E. (in press). Discretion in the translation of research to policy: A case from beginning reading. *Educational Researcher*.

Taylor, B. M., Pearson, P. D., Clark, K. F., & Walpole, S. (1999). *Beating the odds in teaching all children to read* (CIERA Rep. No. 2.006). Ann Arbor: CIERA/University of Michigan.

Taylor, B. M., Short, R. A., Frye, B. J., & Shearer, B. A. (1992). Classroom teachers prevent reading failure among low-achieving first-grade students. *Reading Teacher, 45*, 592–597.

Taylor, B. M., Short, R. S., Shearer, B., & Frye, B. (1995). First grade teachers provide early reading intervention in the classroom. In R. L. Allington & S. A. Walmsley (Eds.), *No quick fix: Rethinking literacy programs in America's elementary schools* (pp. 159–176). New York: Teachers College Press.

Torgeson, J. K., Morgan, S. T., & Davis, C. E. (1992). Effects of two types of phonological awareness training on word learning in kindergarten children. *Journal of Educational Psychology, 84*, 364–370.

U.S. Congress. (1998). *Title VIII: Reading Excellence Act*. Washington, DC: Congressional Record.

Vellutino, F. R., Scanlon, D. M., Sipay, E. R., Small, S. G., Pratt, A., Chen, R., & Denckla, M. B. (1996). Cognitive profiles of difficult-to-remediate and readily remediated poor readers: Early intervention as a vehicle for distinguishing between cognitive and experiential deficits as basic causes of special reading disability. *Journal of Educational Psychology, 88*, 601–638.

Vygotsky, L. S. (1978). *Mind in society*. Cambridge, MA: Harvard University Press.

Wasik, B. A. (1998). Volunteer tutoring programs in reading: A review. *Reading Research Quarterly, 33*, 266–284.

Wasik, B. A., & Slavin, R. E. (1993). Preventing early reading failure with one-to-one tutoring: A review of five programs. *Reading Research Quarterly, 28*, 179–200.

Wharton-MacDonald, R., Pressley, M., & Hampston, J. M. (1998). Literacy achievement in nine first-grade classrooms: Teacher characteristics and student achievement. *Elementary School Journal, 99*, 101–128.

CHAPTER 27

Phonological Awareness

Benita A. Blachman
Syracuse University

Research evidence from a variety of disciplines provides unequivocal support for the critical role of phonological processes in learning to read (Adams, 1990; Blachman, 1997a; Brady & Shankweiler, 1991; Goswami & Bryant, 1990; Rieben & Perfetti, 1991; Shankweiler & I. Y. Liberman, 1989; Share, 1995; Shaywitz, 1996; Stanovich, 1988, 1992; Wagner & Torgesen, 1987). One area of phonological processing, phonological awareness, has been systematically studied for almost 30 years and has gained particular prominence because of its unique contribution to successful reading acquisition and its part in reading failure (see Blachman 1994a, 1997b, for reviews). What is *phonological awareness* and what role does it play in learning to read? The purpose of this chapter is to address these questions.

Phonological awareness, simply stated, is an awareness of the phonological segments in speech—the segments that are more or less represented by an alphabetic orthography. This awareness develops gradually over time and has a causal reciprocal relationship to reading. Researchers have asked children and adults to demonstrate phonological awareness by, for example, categorizing spoken words on the basis of shared sounds (e.g., *hen* and *hot* go together because they both start with /h/), segmenting words into their constituent phonemes, and deleting phonemes (e.g., say *sat* without the /s/). What these tasks have in common is the requirement that the child focus on the underlying phonological structure of the spoken word, not the word's meaning. Interestingly enough, researchers have found that children who are successful on these types of tasks learn to read and spell words with greater ease than children who are unsuccessful. Why should a child's awareness of the internal structure of spoken words give us insight into that child's future achievement in reading words? In order to explain this phenomenon, it is important to explore the relationship between speech and the alphabet.

SPEECH AND THE ALPHABET

As literate adults, we have been conditioned by our long-standing familiarity with an alphabetic writing system to appreciate that graphic symbols more or less represent the sounds of speech. It cannot be taken for granted, however, that the young child, who has not yet learned to read, recognizes that speech can be segmented into phonemes and that these sublexical units are the segments of speech transcribed by an alphabet. It has been observed that "the mere fact that a child understands what is said to him tells us little about what speech segments he perceives" (Savin, 1972, p. 321). There is nothing inherent in becoming an adequate speaker-hearer of English that illuminates for the child the specific linguistic units represented in our alphabetic script. Yet, as Isabelle Liberman pointed out over 25 years ago, one of the fundamental tasks facing the beginning reader is recognizing that speech can be segmented and that these segmented units can be represented by printed forms (I. Y. Liberman, 1971).

The work of A. M. Liberman and his colleagues at Haskins Laboratories (A. M. Liberman, 1970; A. M. Liberman, Cooper, Shankweiler, & Studdert-Kennedy, 1967), illustrating the complex nature of the speech code, helped explain why it can be difficult for the young child to gain access to the phonemic segments represented by an alphabetic orthography. When a speaker produces the word "bag," for example, information about each segment is actually transmitted simultaneously. The vowel /æ/ exerts influence over the entire syllable, and the pronunciation of each phoneme is dependent on the context in which it occurs. Although the three segments of the written word *bag* can be easily identified, the individual phonemes that they represent are coarticulated during speech production (the consonants are folded into the vowels), creating a "merged" (A. M. Liberman et al., 1967; I. Y. Liberman, 1971) or "shingled" (Gleitman & Rozin, 1973) effect. The result is that we hear a single acoustic unit—the syllable. As I. Y. Liberman and Shankweiler (1991) later explained:

> The advantageous result of such coarticulation of speech sounds is that speech can proceed at a satisfactory pace—at a pace indeed at which it can be understood (Liberman, Cooper, Shankweiler, & Studdert-Kennedy, 1967). Can you imagine trying to understand speech if it were spelled out to you letter by painful letter? So coarticulation is certainly advantageous for the perception of speech. But a further result of coarticulation, and a much less advantageous one for the would-be reader, is that there is, inevitably, no neat correspondence between the underlying phonological structure and the sound that comes to the ears. Thus, though the word "bag," for example, has three phonological units, and, correspondingly, three letters in print, it has only one pulse of sound: The three elements of the underlying phonological structure—the three phonemes—have been thoroughly overlapped and merged into that one sound—"bag." ... [Beginning readers] can understand, and properly take advantage of, the fact that the printed word *bag* has three letters, only if they are aware that the spoken word "bag," with which they are already quite familiar, is divisible into three segments. They will probably not know that spontaneously, because, ... there is only one segment of sound, not three, and because the processes of speech perception that recover the phonological structure are automatic and quite unconscious. (1991, pp. 5–6)

Consequently, although an awareness of the phonemic segments in spoken words will make it easier for a child to understand how an alphabetic orthography transcribes speech, this awareness does not come naturally for many beginning readers. Researchers have pointed out that "sometimes children have trouble learning to decode because they are completely unaware of the fact that spoken language is segmented—into sentences, into syllables, and into phonemes" (Williams, 1987, pp. 25–26). Strong support for Williams's observation comes, for example, from Juel's (1988, 1994) longitudinal study of the reading development of 54 children from Grade 1 to Grade 4. Juel found that the fourth-grade poor readers entered first grade with limited phonological awareness. This lack of understanding of the internal structure of words contributed to their slowness in learning letter–sound correspondences and decoding. Indeed, at the end of Grade 4, the decoding of the poor readers was not yet equivalent to that of the average and good readers at the beginning of Grade 2. Unfortunately, the poor decoders were the ones who disliked reading and did less of it, losing valuable opportunities for vocabulary growth and exposure to new concepts and ideas, contributing to a cycle of failure described eloquently by Stanovich (1986) that can begin with failure to develop phonological awareness and spelling-to-sound mappings.

DEVELOPMENTAL AND CORRELATIONAL STUDIES

Some of the earliest investigations of phonological awareness explored the developmental nature of these skills. During the early 1970s, for example, several investigators found that the ability to analyze the spoken word into syllables or phonemes follows a developmental pattern (Bruce, 1964; Fox & Routh, 1975; Gleitman & Rozin, 1973; I. Y. Liberman, Shankweiler, Fischer, & Carter, 1974; Rosner & Simon, 1971; Savin, 1972; Zhurova, 1973). The relative ease of syllable segmentation compared to phoneme segmentation was confirmed using a variety of experimental tasks (Blachman, 1983, 1984; Fox & Routh, 1975; Goldstein, 1976; Leong & Haines, 1978; I. Y. Liberman et al., 1974; Treiman & Baron, 1981; Zifcak, 1981), while more recent work has investigated the intermediary role played by onsets and rimes (e.g., in the syllable *trip*, the onset is *tr* and the rime is *ip*) (Treiman, 1985; Treiman & Zukowski, 1991, 1996).

In addition to the developmental studies, researchers in the 1970s began to explore the relationship between phonological awareness and beginning reading (Calfee, Lindamood, & Lindamood, 1973; Fox & Routh, 1976; Goldstein, 1976; Helfgott, 1976; Rosner & Simon, 1971; Zifcak, 1981) and, despite the use of a variety of tasks to measure phonological awareness, the relationship was robust. Liberman and her colleagues were particularly interested in the 30% of first graders in their study (I. Y. Liberman et al., 1974) who could not segment words into phonemes at the end of first grade. In second grade, they found that half of the children in the lowest third of the class on a measure of word recognition had been unable to analyze words into phonemes on a segmentation task the previous year. However, no children in the upper third of the class had failed the segmentation test in first grade (I. Y. Liberman, 1973). In a cross-sectional study by Calfee, Lindamood, and Lindamood (1973), phonological awareness and word recognition and spelling were assessed in students from kindergarten through 12th grade. Substantial correlations were found at each grade level between the phoneme manipulation skills assessed in this study and a combined reading and spelling score.

Since these early studies, we have accumulated extensive evidence that how children perform on measures of phonological awareness is a powerful predictor of future reading achievement. It has been found repeatedly that children who lack this linguistic insight are likely to be among our poorest readers (Blachman, 1984; Blachman & James, 1985; Bradley & Bryant, 1983; Byrne & Fielding-Barnsley, 1993; Cardoso-Martins, 1995; Fletcher et al., 1994; Hoien, Lundberg, Stanovich, & Bjaalid, 1995; Iversen & Tunmer, 1993; Juel, 1988; Lundberg, Olofsson, & Wall, 1980; Mann & I. Y. Liberman, 1984; Share, Jorm, Maclean, & Matthews, 1984; Snowling, Goulandris, Defty, 1996; Stanovich, Cunningham, & Cramer, 1984; Torgesen & Burgess, 1998; Vellutino & Scanlon, 1987; Vellutino et al., 1996; Wagner, Torgesen, & Rashotte, 1994; Wagner et al., 1997). Several studies have demonstrated that even when phonological awareness is measured in very young preschool children it remains a robust predictor of early reading achievement (Bryant, Bradley, Maclean, & Crossland, 1989; Bryant, Maclean, Bradley, & Crossland, 1990; Maclean, Bryant, & Bradley, 1987; Scarborough, 1990, 1998) and that problems in phonological awareness persist for poor readers through the teenage years (Fawcett & Nicolson, 1995) and into adulthood (Pennington, Van Orden, Smith, Green, & Haith, 1990), even among adults with childhood diagnoses of dyslexia who nevertheless have acquired relatively high levels of word recognition (Bruck, 1992, 1993; Gallagher, Laxon, Armstrong, & Frith, 1996; Pratt & Brady, 1988).

A reciprocal relationship between early phonological awareness and early literacy acquisition has been confirmed by a number of investigators (Ehri, 1979; I. Y. Liberman, A. M. Liberman, Mattingly, & Shankweiler, 1980; Lundberg, 1991; Morais, 1987; Perfetti, 1985; Perfetti, Beck, Bell, & Hughes, 1987; Stuart & Coltheart, 1988; Vandervelden & Siegel, 1995). As Perfetti and his colleagues were able to demonstrate in their longitudinal study (Perfetti et al., 1987):

> The reciprocity hypothesis (i.e., that reflective phonemic knowledge and reading competence develop in mutual support) is not a denial of a causal role for phonemic awareness. It is instead a suggestion that the causal connection is only half the picture. The other half is that advancement in reading promotes increased reflective phonemic awareness, which in turn promotes further gains in reading. (p. 41)

Exploration of the exact nature of the reciprocal interplay between phonological awareness and word recognition is still in the early stages. It has been proposed, for example, that phonological sensitivity to rhyme and alliteration might initially facilitate the earliest stages of alphabetic literacy (although reciprocity may also be operating here), while more complete and explicit segmental analysis at the phonemic level may be triggered for many children by more formal reading instruction (Morais, 1987; Stanovich, 1991; Torgesen & Davis, 1996; and see Stahl & Murray, 1998, for a proposed model). The reciprocal nature of the relationship does not deny the fact that children who begin their reading instruction with deeper levels of phonological awareness have a "powerful bootstrapping mechanism to reading progress" (Stanovich, 1992).

INTERVENTION STUDIES

Another question that has been the subject of intense scrutiny is whether phonological awareness can be heightened in young children and, if so, whether increased phonological awareness has a positive impact on reading ability. A host of early studies demonstrated that indeed phonological awareness could be improved by direct instructional activities (Content, Kolinsky, Morais, & Bertelson, 1986; Elkonin, 1963, 1973; Fox & Routh, 1976; Helfgott, 1976; Kattke, 1978; Lewkowicz, 1980; Lewkowicz & Low, 1979; Marsh & Mineo, 1977; Olofsson & Lundberg, 1983; Rosner, 1974; Skjelfjord, 1976; Zhurova, 1973). Numerous studies have also shown that heightening the preschool, kindergarten, and first-grade child's awareness of the phonological structure of speech facilitates early reading and spelling acquisition (e.g., Ball & Blachman, 1991; Blachman, Ball, Black, & Tangel, 1994; Bradley & Bryant, 1983; Byrne & Fielding-Barnsley, 1991, 1993, 1995; Castle, Riach, & Nicholson, 1994; Cunningham, 1990; Fox & Routh, 1984; Iversen & Tunmer, 1993; Lie, 1991; Lundberg, Frost, & Petersen, 1988; O'Connor, Notari-Syverson, Vadasy, 1996; Rosner, 1971; Treiman & Baron, 1983). Instruction is even more effective when combined with instruction that connects the phonological segments to letters. With poor readers in Grades 1 and 2 and at-risk children selected in kindergarten and treated through Grade 2, there is strong evidence of a positive effect on reading with intervention that combines phonological awareness instruction and explicit, systematic instruction in reading (Hatcher, Hulme, & Ellis, 1994; Iversen & Tunmer, 1993; Torgesen, Wagner, & Rashotte, 1997; Vellutino et al., 1996). Several studies with somewhat older severely learning disabled children (ranging in age from 7 to 13 years) have also found that a treatment that emphasizes both phonological awareness and word recognition/decoding facilitates reading acquisition (Alexander, Anderson, Heilman, Voeller, & Torgesen, 1991; Lovett et al., 1994; Williams, 1980).

Manipulating Program Components

In the groundswell of phonological awareness intervention studies that have been conducted over the past 15 years, various program components have been manipulated (e.g., length of intervention, intensity, size of group). An important manipulation from a theoretical point of view is whether phonological awareness instruction is combined with instruction that links the phonological segments and the letters of the alphabet. By choosing to develop phonological awareness without also instructing children in the connections between the phonological segments and letters, Lundberg, Frost, and Petersen (1988) were able to demonstrate, for example, that phonological awareness can be heightened outside the context of literacy instruction. More important, they were able to challenge the idea that phonological awareness is only a consequence of reading instruction. In the Lundberg et al. study of 235 nonreading Danish kindergarten children, classroom teachers provided 8 months of training to the entire group of 15 to 20 in each classroom. Children began with listening and rhyming activities and by the fifth month were learning to segment two-phoneme words and then moved on to more complex items.

After the intervention, the children who had participated in the phonological awareness activities demonstrated superior skill on measures of phonological awareness, but not on end-of-kindergarten reading. At the end of first grade, however, the treatment children significantly outperformed the control children in spelling and by the end of second grade the treatment children were superior on both reading and spelling measures. Thus, once the children were exposed to formal reading and spelling instruction in Grades 1 and 2, the children who had participated in the phonological awareness intervention in kindergarten appeared to be better prepared to take advantage of that instruction than the control children. Because sound–symbol instruction is not part of the Danish kindergarten curriculum, Lundberg and his colleagues were able to isolate the effect of phonological awareness instruction uncontaminated by concurrent reading instruction, and in so doing answer an important theoretical question. They confirmed that phonological awareness is not simply a consequence of learning to read and spell. It is important to note that although the kindergarten program emphasized games, the authors had learned from earlier research (Olofsson & Lundberg, 1983) that structure was a critical variable in the success of the program. In their 1983 study, these researchers had varied structure across treatment conditions. Children in the most structured condition participated in three to four lessons per week for 15 to 30 minutes; children in the least structured condition participated in phoneme awareness activities that their teachers introduced spontaneously during normal play activities. Only the most structured group showed improvement on the posttest.

Connecting Sound Segments to Print

Despite evidence that one can develop phonological awareness outside the context of literacy instruction, there is considerable evidence that this instruction is enhanced when the connections to print are made explicit. In what is now a landmark longitudinal and experimental training study, Bradley and Bryant (1983, 1985) established a causal relationship between phonological awareness and reading and demonstrated the additional benefit of making explicit connections between sound segments and letters. In their large longitudinal study, Bradley and Bryant established a significant relationship between the phoneme awareness of 4- and 5-year-olds ($n = 368$) and their reading and spelling achievement 3 years later. During the second year of the study, 65 of the children with the lowest pretest scores on sound categorization (their measure of phoneme awareness) were assigned to one of four groups matched on IQ, age, sex, and sound categorization. Children in the first group learned to categorize pictures on the basis of shared sounds (e.g., *hen* and *hot* go together because they share the same initial sound). Children in the second group practiced categorizing the same pictures, but they also learned to represent the shared sounds with plastic letters. A third group categorized the same pictures on the basis of semantic features (e.g., *hen* and *dog* go together because they are both animals), whereas a fourth group received no instruction. Children in the first three groups received 40 individual, 10-minute lessons spread over 2 years. Results indicated that the children trained in sound categorization scored somewhat higher than untrained children. Children who received instruction in sound categorization and who were taught to connect the shared sounds to letters, however, had significantly higher scores in both reading and spelling than children in the two control groups and had significantly higher spelling scores than children in the sound categorization only group. In a follow-up study 4 years after the original study ended, Bradley (1988) located 63 of the original 65 children and found that the children who participated in the sound categorization group that also learned to represent the shared sounds with letters maintained their superior position in reading and spelling. Thus, Bradley and Bryant, as well as others (see also Hohn & Ehri, 1983), have demonstrated that explicit instruction in connecting the sound segments to print enhances instruction in phonological awareness.

Sound categorization, modified and referred to as phoneme identity in studies by the Australian researchers Byrne and Fielding-Barnsley (1991, 1993, 1995), has also been taught successfully to 4-year-old preschoolers. In this series of studies, jingles and poems were used to teach specific sounds in either the initial or final position. Next, large colored posters that depicted objects that either begin or end with the target sound were introduced and children were asked to identify pictures that begin or end with the target sound. Children also learned to recognize the letters that represent each target phoneme. Control children used the same materials, but they were taught to categorize the pictures on the basis of semantic categories. Both groups participated in twelve 20- to 30-minute sessions over a 12-week period. At the end of these sessions, treatment children showed greater gains in phoneme identity and had significantly higher scores than controls on a forced choice word recognition test (e.g., "does this [*sat*, for example] say '*sat*' or '*mat*'?" [p. 452]). Three years after this intervention to train preschoolers in phoneme identity and recognition of the letters that represent the target phonemes, the trained children demonstrated a significant advantage in reading comprehension and pseudoword decoding (Byrne & Fielding-Barnsley, 1995). Byrne and Fielding-Barnsley (1991) concluded, as have others (e.g., Gough & Walsh, 1991), that in order to understand the alphabetic principle, children need both phonological awareness and knowledge of how the sounds are represented in print.

A question not answered by the studies reviewed thus far is whether increased letter–sound knowledge alone could account for the significant advantage in reading among treated children. Ball and Blachman (1988, 1991) addressed this question in a kindergarten study, randomly assigning 90 nonreading children to one of three groups. Children in the first group received instruction in phoneme awareness and also instruction in making connections between the sounds and their written representations. The children in the second group used the identical materials and spent the same amount of time as the children in the first group learning sound–symbol associations, but they did not practice the phoneme awareness activities. Instead they engaged in a variety of language activities (e.g., listening to stories, vocabulary development). Children in both treatment groups had 28 instructional sessions over a 7-week period, meeting in groups of 4 or 5 for 15- to 20-minute sessions. A third group received no special instruction.

The children in the phoneme awareness plus letter sound group participated in a structured three-part lesson. Each lesson began with an activity to teach phoneme segmentation called *say-it-and-move-it* (adapted from Elkonin, 1963, 1973). Using a variety of manipulatives, such as disks, tiles, or blocks, the children were taught to move the appropriate number of disks to represent the sounds in one-, two-, and three-phoneme items. Initially, children represented one sound with one disk, followed by one sound repeated ("Show me /i/ /i/"). Next two-phoneme (e.g., /up/) and eventually three-phoneme (e.g., /sun/) words were introduced, being careful initially to select three-phoneme words that begin with continuous sounds (sounds that can be held with a minimum of distortion, such as /s/, /l/, /f/). After pronouncing the word slowly and moving disks to represent the sounds, children pronounced the word in a normal blended fashion. After the third week of phoneme segmentation activities, a limited number of letters that had been mastered by the children were added to the blank tiles. Each item to be segmented during that lesson contained only one of the letter tiles. Children were always given the option of segmenting the word using all blank tiles or using one letter tile combined with blank tiles to represent the sound segments. A second activity in every lesson provided reinforcement of phonological awareness through a variety of games. For example, some lessons included a sound categorization game adapted from Bradley and Bryant (1983, 1985), in which children would select the one picture from a set of four that didn't belong with the group because it didn't share the same rhyming segment or the same first, last, or middle sound. On other days children had an opportunity to practice blending activities by correcting "mistakes" made by a puppet who told stories and sometimes mispronounced key words by segmenting them. The third activity in each lesson emphasized letter names and letter sounds. The letters *a, m, t, i, s, r, u, b, f* were introduced using illustrations (e.g., the *r* card depicted a *red rooster* in *red running* shoes) and a variety of games for reinforcement.

Prior to the intervention, the three groups of children did not differ on age, sex, race, socioeconomic status (SES), phoneme segmentation, letter name knowledge, letter sound knowledge, or word recognition. After the intervention, the group trained in phoneme awareness plus letter sounds significantly outperformed the other two groups on measures of phoneme segmentation, word identification, and developmental spelling. Of particular importance is the fact that after the intervention the phoneme segmentation group and the language activities group did not differ from each other on letter sound knowledge (both groups had engaged in identical instruction in letter sounds), but both groups differed significantly from the untrained control group on this measure. Despite the enhanced letter sound knowledge of the language activities group, this group did not differ from the no-treatment control group on phoneme awareness, word recognition, or developmental spelling. Improvement in letter sound knowledge alone did not boost early reading and spelling skill. Based on these results and the work of others (see also Ehri & Wilce, 1987), it appears to be the *combination* of instruction in phoneme awareness and learning to connect the sound segments to letters that makes a difference.

The effectiveness of this program with kindergarten children prompted a new project (Blachman, Ball, Black, & Tangel, 1994) to evaluate the influence on reading of a phoneme awareness program carried out by kindergarten teachers and their teaching assistants. In previous studies (e.g., Ball & Blachman, 1991; Bradley & Bryant, 1983), the intervention was often conducted outside the regular classroom by specially trained teachers brought to the school by the researchers. Although such studies have demonstrated the value of an emphasis on phonological awareness, studies conducted outside the regular classroom may not be as convincing to the teachers being asked to implement phonological awareness programs in their classrooms. In the new study, the nonreading kindergarten children were drawn from four, demographically comparable, low-achieving and low-income, inner-city schools in upstate New York. The children attended 4 of the 5 lowest achieving schools among the 21 elementary schools in this urban district, and 85% of the children received free or supported lunch. The 84 treatment children and 75 control children attended different schools, but prior to the intervention the two groups of children did not differ on age, sex, race, SES level, Peabody Picture Vocabulary Test–Revised (PPVT–R) scores, phoneme awareness, letter name and letter sound knowledge, or word recognition. The children, as a whole, were in the low average range in receptive vocabulary and had limited knowledge of the alphabet as indicated by the fact that the children knew, on average, only two letter sounds in January of kindergarten (prior to the beginning of the intervention), despite the fact that the district's kindergarten program included letter name and letter sound instruction. In the spring of the kindergarten year, the treatment children participated in 41 phonological awareness lessons, each lasting 15 to 20 minutes (adapted from the shorter, 28-lesson program used in Ball & Blachman, 1991), delivered over an 11-week period to small, heterogeneous groups of four or five children. All lessons were conducted by classroom teachers and their teaching assistants (provided by the school district to all kindergarten teachers). All lessons followed the same three part lesson described earlier: (a) say-it-and-move-it, a phoneme segmentation activity; (b) a phoneme awareness related practice activity, such as grouping pictures on the basis of shared sounds; and (c) one of a variety of games to teach the names and sounds of eight letters.

After completion of these lessons, treatment children significantly outperformed the control children on measures of phoneme segmentation, letter name and letter sound knowledge, reading phonetically regular real words and pseudowords, and developmental spelling (see Tangel & Blachman, 1992, for a detailed analysis of kindergarten spelling). Although treatment children entered the study with the same low literacy skills as the control children, after 10 to 11 hours of instruction in phonological awareness and the connections between the sound segments and letters, the treatment children demonstrated superior knowledge of the internal structure of words. They demonstrated this knowledge not only on measures of phonological segmentation and letter sounds, but in their beginning ability to read words that conform to phonetically regular patterns and in the developmental sophistication of their invented spellings. These early invented spellings provide insight into how young children perceive the sound system of their language (see Read, 1986, and Templeton & Morris, this volume, for detailed discussions). Previous research had indicated that the level of sophistication of a child's invented spelling is related to the child's first-grade reading success (Ferroli & Shanahan, 1987; Mann, Tobin, & Wilson, 1987; Morris & Perney, 1984). The Blachman et al. study suggests that a child's invented spellings are positively influenced by instruction that heightens phonological awareness and connects the sound segments to print.

Children in this classroom-based phonological awareness study were followed until the end of second grade (Blachman, Tangel, Ball, Black, & McGraw, 1999). For the treatment children, their kindergarten phoneme awareness program was followed by 30 minutes of group reading instruction in Grade 1 (and continued in Grade 2 for some children) that built on the kindergarten phoneme awareness instruction and emphasized explicit, systematic instruction in the alphabetic code. In contrast, the control children had 30 minutes of group reading instruction using a traditional basal reader and workbook and used a phonics workbook at another time during the day. Both groups used the same phonetically based spelling program mandated by the school district. At the end of Grade 1, the treatment children significantly outperformed the control children on measures of phoneme segmentation, letter name and letter sound knowledge, and three of four measures of word recognition. By the end of Grade 2, the treatment children were significantly superior on all four measures of word recognition, including a standardized measure of phonetically regular word and nonword reading and a standardized measure of word identification based on words that appear frequently in basal reading programs. In spelling, treatment children demonstrated significantly higher scores on the developmental spelling measure and a standardized measure administered at the end of Grade 1 (see Tangel & Blachman, 1995, for a detailed analysis of Grade 1 spelling). One year later, however, there were no significant differences on the standardized measure of spelling (the only spelling measure administered at the end of Grade 2). An analysis that included only the children in the lowest quartile of the sample in spelling at the end of Grade 2 revealed striking differences favoring the treatment children on the standardized measure of spelling when partial credit was given for phonetically correct spelling, such as writing *lite* for *light*, and significant differences also favoring the treatment children on all four measures of word identification. Blachman and her colleagues attribute the lack of differences in spelling for the groups as a whole at the end of second grade to the fact that both groups had the benefit of the same phonetically based spelling program in Grades 1 and 2. Although by the end of second grade the control children had reached a level of spelling that was equivalent to that of the treatment children, their improved spelling did not appear to transfer to reading words. Specifically, the treatment children who had the benefit of phonological awareness instruction in kindergarten and a phonetic approach for both reading and spelling remained significantly ahead of the control children in reading words and nonwords at the end of second grade.

Comparing Phonological Awareness Tasks

In addition to asking whether phonological awareness training has an impact on reading, researchers have also attempted to refine the phonological awareness instruction by asking whether some tasks are more beneficial than others and whether one or another level of linguistic analysis has the most pedagogical value. For example, Torgesen, Morgan, and Davis (1992) compared the effectiveness of training nonreading kindergarten children who scored below the 50th percentile on a phonological awareness pretest in either blending or in blending and segmenting, whereas a third group (control group) participated in language experience activities (e.g., listened to stories, discussed pictures and events) but had no phonological training. Compared to the controls, both treatment groups gained more in blending, but only the group that had blending and segmenting training gained more than the controls on both the blending and segmenting tasks. Of perhaps greater importance is the finding that only the children who had training in both segmenting and blending performed better on a reading analog task than the untrained controls (see also Fox & Routh, 1984). Torgesen et al. (1992) concluded that "exposure to both kinds of tasks appears to provide a richer awareness of the phonological structure of words, one that is more easily accessible when faced with the challenge of learning to read new words" (p. 369).

More recently, O'Connor, Jenkins, and Slocum (1995) examined the effect on phonological awareness and word learning of training nonreading, kindergarten children—those with phonological pretest scores below the 30th percentile—in either segmenting and blending or in a more global array of phonological awareness tasks, while others were randomly assigned to a letter-sound training control group. The researchers also included an interesting untreated comparison group—a group of children who scored *above* the 50th percentile on the phonological awareness pretest and who were nonreaders. Results indicate that children in both phonological awareness conditions significantly outperformed children in the letter-sound training control condition on measures of blending and segmenting, as well as on a transfer task that assessed a broader array of phonological manipulations. Somewhat to the surprise of the researchers, who had originally hypothesized that the more global treatment condition would enable children to excel on a greater variety of phonological awareness tasks, the two phonological awareness conditions did not differ significantly from each other on these phonological awareness posttests. Not only was the blending and segmenting condition as effective in terms of transfer to other phonological awareness tasks, but children in the blending and segmenting condition (but not children in the more global condition) learned to read words in the reading analog tasks in significantly fewer trials than the children in the control condition. Given these results, the researchers emphasized the importance of including both blending and segmenting in instruction of children with low levels of phonological awareness. O'Connor et al. also noted that their untreated high-skilled comparison group (i.e., skilled in phonological awareness) continued to make progress in phonological awareness without specific intervention, whereas the untreated low-skilled children (those in the letter-sound control group) showed very little progress in phoneme analysis during the 5-month interval between the pretest and posttest. Thus, during the kindergarten year, the gap continued to grow between the untreated kindergarten children who scored above the 50th percentile on the phonological awareness pretest and the untreated children who scored below the 30th percentile on the same measure. In contrast, the children who scored below the 30th percentile on the pretest, but who participated in the phonological awareness intervention, ended the year with phonological awareness skills that were equivalent to those of the high-skilled group. In a similar vein, McBride-Chang, Wagner, and Chang (1997) found in a longitudinal study of nonreading kindergarten children followed over a 15-month period that those who began the study with higher levels of phonological awareness continued to develop this awareness at much faster rates than those who began the study with low levels of phonological awareness. McBride-Chang and his colleagues pointed out that "Matthew effects," as described by Stanovich (1986), in which "the rich get richer" in reading while others fall behind, are applicable to their data regarding phonological awareness.

In another study that evaluated different versions of phonological awareness programs (Cary & Verhaeghe, 1994), researchers compared the benefits to metaphonological development of intervention programs that focused on different levels of linguistic analysis. In their first study, one of the training programs focused on only rhymes and syllables, while the second program emphasized rhymes, syllables, and phonemes. In a second study, the intervention emphasized either syllable awareness or phoneme awareness, while a third program emphasized visual analysis of nonlinguistic stimuli. A major finding in both studies was that training that included phonemic analysis was the most beneficial. Explicit instruction in phonemic analysis generalized to rhyming and syllable tasks, but instruction in rhyme manipulation and syllabic analysis did not generalize to tasks involving analysis at the level of the phoneme. Other sources of data also indicate that phonemic analysis appears to play a greater role in reading acquisition than other levels of analysis. In a large study ($n = 1,509$) of the factor structure underlying six phonological awareness tasks (Hoien et al., 1995), three separable components were identified (i.e., syllable awareness, rhyme awareness, and phoneme awareness). Of significance here is the fact that the phoneme awareness factor made the greatest contribution to the prediction of reading (see also Nation & Hulme, 1997, who found that phoneme segmentation, but not segmentation of onset-rime units, is an excellent predictor of both reading and spelling). Thus, data from both treatment and prediction studies suggest that explicit instruction at the level of the phoneme may be particularly beneficial. Learning to recognize and produce rhyming words, activities that are commonplace in kindergarten curriculum guides, are probably inadequate by themselves to bring children to the level of awareness of the phonological structure of words needed for maximum benefit when learning to read and spell. Some as yet undetermined threshold level of phonemic awareness, as opposed to more global phonological awareness, may be necessary to help children take optimal advantage of early reading and spelling instruction.

RELATIONSHIPS AMONG PHONOLOGICAL PROCESSING ABILITIES

It is important to point out that phonological awareness cannot be adequately addressed without also considering what we know about the relationships among different components of phonological processing—especially, phonological awareness, verbal memory, and naming—all of which are critical to reading acquisition (I. Y. Liberman & Shankweiler, 1985; Wagner & Torgesen, 1987). With regard to verbal memory, for example, poor readers appear to form less accurate and less stable phonological representations in working memory. The consequence is that it is more difficult to hold onto information in working memory—creating processing limitations that contribute both to poor decoding and poor sentence comprehension (Brady, 1997; Perfetti, 1985; Shankweiler, 1989; Shankweiler & Crain, 1986). Another pervasive problem among poor readers is difficulty in the retrieval of phonological information. This difficulty has been demonstrated repeatedly by the word-finding errors and slowness on rapid naming tasks that are so characteristic of poor readers (Blachman, 1984; Bowers & Swanson, 1991; Denckla & Rudel, 1976; Felton, Naylor, & Wood, 1990; Wolf, 1986, 1991, 1997). These problems interfere with the development of accurate and fluent word recognition, and there is ample evidence that without accuracy and fluency at the level of the word, there will always be constraints on comprehension (Adams, 1990; Adams & Bruck, 1995; Beck & Juel, 1995; Chall, 1989; Ehri, 1991, 1997; Rieben & Perfetti, 1991; Vellutino, 1991; Vellutino, Scanlon, & Tanzman, 1994; Williams, 1979, 1985, 1994).

These phonological processing problems are also implicated in recent work on the subtypes of dyslexia, clearly pointing to a phonological core deficit (Fletcher et al., 1994, 1997; Stanovich, 1988). A common factor among four of the five specific reading disabled subtypes that Fletcher and his colleagues identified was a deficit in phonological awareness, with variation among the groups on whether or not subjects were also slower in naming speed and impaired in verbal short-term memory. These three components of phonological processing have also been monitored in the first in-depth look at the characteristics of children resistant to treatment. Vellutino and his colleagues (Vellutino et al., 1996; Vellutino, Scanlon, & Sipay, 1997) found that the small percentage of children who were the hardest to remediate in reading during up to two semesters of individual tutoring provided in Grades 1 and 2 differed from normal readers before the intervention began on phonologically based skills, including phoneme awareness, rapid naming, and verbal memory tasks. Children who made the most growth during the tutoring experience performed more like the normal readers on these preintervention tasks. As we learn more about this group of children, we should be able to more effectively tailor treatments to meet their needs. It may be that phonologically based interventions that are longer, more intense, and more explicit (Blachman, 1994b; Torgesen & Burgess, 1998) and structured to help children move "beyond accuracy to a higher level of speed, automaticity, and flexibility" (Olson, Wise, Johnson, & Ring, 1997, p. 322) are needed to facilitate fluent word recognition in children with the most severe reading disabilities.

Wagner and his colleagues (Wagner et al., 1997) have shown in a longitudinal study that included measures of phonological awareness, verbal memory, and naming, that phonological processing is remarkably stable through fourth grade. They reported that:

> The present results add to a growing body of evidence in favor of viewing phonological processing abilities as stable and coherent individual difference variables akin to other cognitive abilities, as opposed to more ephemeral by-products of reading instruction that might vary considerably from year to year. (p. 476)

Of particular importance in this study is the evidence that individual differences in phonological awareness substantially influenced subsequent individual differences in word-level reading at each time period examined.

SOME UNRESOLVED ISSUES

This brings us to a number of important questions. How good do you have to be, as measured by which task, to get the maximum advantage during reading instruction from insights about the phonological structure of words? Some awareness of phonemes, demonstrated, for example, by performance on simple phoneme identity and segmentation tasks and coupled with knowledge of how the sound segments are represented by letters, appears to give children an edge when more formal alphabetic reading instruction begins. Children who are phonologically aware, either because they have had explicit instruction or because they have been able to develop this awareness from early family and preschool literacy experiences, such as language play and being read to, appear to have this early reading and spelling advantage (Byrne & Fielding-Barnsley, 1993). As seen in the Juel (1994) study, for example, children who entered Grade 1 with more phonological awareness had an early reading experience that was much more positive than those who lacked these insights about the internal structure of words.

Is there an advantage to being able to perform more complex manipulations? Although we don't have adequate data to answer this question, it is likely that more complex manipulation of phonemes, such as is required in the deletion and rearrangement of phonemes in a spoken word, is actually the result of learning to read and spell. The reciprocal relationship between phonological awareness and reading is well documented (Ehri, 1979; I. Y. Liberman et al., 1980; Morais, 1987; Perfetti, 1985; Perfetti, Beck, Bell, & Hughes, 1987; Stuart & Coltheart, 1988; Vandervelden & Siegel, 1995), and we know that knowledge of the phonological structure of words becomes more sophisticated as children become readers and spellers. Being able to visualize the orthographic structure of a word most likely makes it easier to perform complex phonological judgments (Adams, 1990; Ball, 1997; Bruck, 1992; Ehri, 1989, 1991; Wagner et al., 1994). The question is whether children should spend time outside the context of learning to read and spell words learning to make more complex judgements about the phonological structure of spoken words. Wagner et al. (1997) suggest that although some children may need training in phonological awareness that goes beyond the kindergarten and first-grade year, "rather than providing this training in the context of oral language activities that might be appropriate for kindergarten and Grade 1, a more efficient approach might involve code-oriented reading instruction in which the connections between print and speech are made explicit" (p. 476).

There are also questions regarding the measurement and assessment of phonological awareness. Although there is consensus that phonological awareness changes over time (perhaps best described by Stanovich, 1992, in terms of *shallow* and *deep* levels of phonological sensitivity), we lack agreed-on guidelines for the assessment of the changing nature of this construct (Stahl & Murray, 1994), and the components of the construct, especially the role played by speech perception (McBride-Chang, 1995; McBride-Chang, Wagner, Chang, 1997), are still under investigation. There is a need for more research-based information about the essential characteristics (e.g., memory load) of different tasks (Vellutino et al., 1994), and a need for more attention to be paid to the linguistic complexity of items within and across tasks (Stahl & Murray, 1994; Treiman, 1992). Studies of task comparability provide some insight into task difficulty (Chafouleas, Lewandowski, Smith, & Blachman, 1997; Stanovich et al., 1984; Yopp, 1988) and have generally found tasks measuring rhyme sensitivity to be the easiest and tasks measuring phoneme manipulations, such as deletions and reversals, to be the most difficult, with phoneme counting and segmenting falling in between (see Adams, 1990, for a discussion of task complexity; see Snider, 1995, and Torgesen & Mathes, 1998, for research-based, clinical suggestions). Documenting systematic changes in a young child's invented spelling may be one of the most sensitive methods for monitoring changes in a child's awareness of the phonological structure of words (Ehri, 1989; Mann et al., 1987; Stage & Wagner, 1992; Stahl & Murray, 1994; Tangel & Blachman, 1992, 1995; Torgesen & Davis, 1996; Treiman, 1993) but, as Treiman (1997) pointed out, this is still a relatively untapped source of information.

A relatively recent and intensely debated question is how phonological awareness (and other aspects of phonological processing) may be influenced by the changing nature of the child's underlying phonological representations. As explained by Fowler (1991), "the child's early vocabulary may originally be represented at a more holistic level, with organization in terms of phonemic segments emerging only gradually in early childhood" (p. 97). It is easy to imagine that the demonstration of phonological awareness would be difficult for the child whose underlying representations are not yet segmentally structured. Fowler traced the parallels between the child's developing phonological awareness and the changes that occur as stored lexical items become more segmental, and suggested that we look more closely at the interplay between the two (see also Metsala & Walley, 1998, for a similar position referred to as the *lexical restructuring hypothesis*). An alternative, but not necessarily incompatible hypothesis, related to the nature of the underlying phonological representations, has been proposed by Elbro and his colleagues (Elbro, 1996; Elbro, Borstrøm, & Petersen, 1998) in their *distinctness hypothesis*. Elbro proposed that phonological awareness and other phonological processing abilities might be constrained by the quality of the underlying representations (Fowler, 1991; Katz, 1986), specifically their distinctness. In a recent investigation of this hypothesis, Elbro et al. (1998) found that their measure of distinctness ("based on the quality of the pronunciation of unstressed vowels in phonologically complex words," p. 53), together with measures of phoneme awareness and letter knowledge, contributed significantly to the prediction of dyslexia. In addition, the distinctness measure contributed to the development of phoneme awareness in Grade 2, even after controlling for articulation, expressive vocabulary, and early phoneme awareness measured in kindergarten. As pointed out by Brady (1997), "understanding how the phonological representations of poor readers differ, whether less segmentally (Fowler, 1991), less distinctly (Elbro, 1996), or both, stands as an important challenge. Attaining this knowledge may be central to fully explaining, and addressing, the phonological deficits of disabled readers" (p. 42).

CONCLUSIONS

Our understanding of phonological processing in general, and phonological awareness specifically, in relation to reading acquisition has brought theoretical coherence to a large body of research that can be used to inform practice. Although phonological processing is not the only place to look for answers to the mysteries inherent in reading acquisition, it has been one of the most productive areas of inquiry to date in terms of advancing our scientific understanding of the reading process. Research, grounded in a common theoretical framework, now provides evidence that instruction that heightens phonological awareness and that emphasizes the connections to the alphabetic code promotes greater skill in word recognition—a skill essential to becoming a proficient reader (Adams, 1990; Beck & Juel, 1995; Chall, 1989; I. Y. Liberman & A. M. Liberman, 1990; Ehri, 1991; Metsala & Ehri, 1998; Rack, Hulme, Snowling, & Wightman, 1994; Share & Stanovich, 1995; Stanovich, 1986, 1992; Vellutino, 1991; Vellutino et al., 1994).

An important implication of the research reviewed in this chapter is that teachers need to understand and provide for the individual differences in phonological awareness (I. Y. Liberman & Shankweiler, 1991) that they will encounter in their classrooms, especially in kindergarten and first grade. Although not every child needs an explicit program in phonological awareness, every teacher of young beginning readers should know why such instruction is important and how and when to provide it. All children need to learn about the segmental nature of speech and how the sound segments are represented in print. Although many children appear to make these discoveries on their own, by playing oral language games, by connecting speech and print when being read to (see, e.g., Murray, Stahl, & Ivey, 1996), and by opportunities to write, many other children will not be so fortunate. Some children will not have the necessary preschool exposure to language play and early literacy experiences that trigger these associations. Other children, because of differences or deficiencies in phonological ability, will not discover the connections between print and speech on their own, even if they have the important preschool literacy experiences and opportunities to play with oral language. Especially for these two groups of children, explicit instruction in phonological awareness and the connections between the sound segments and letters may help to close the ever-widening gap that exists between those beginning readers who lack insight into the phonological structure of spoken words and those who seem to acquire this awareness effortlessly.

REFERENCES

Adams, M. J. (1990). *Beginning to read: Thinking and learning about print*. Cambridge, MA: MIT Press.

Adams, M. J., & Bruck, M. (1995). Resolving the "Great Debate." *American Educator, 19*(2), 7, 10–20.

Alexander, A. W., Anderson, H. G., Heilman, P. C., Voeller, K. K. S., & Torgesen, J. K. (1991). Phonological awareness training and remediation of analytic decoding deficits in a group of severe dyslexics. *Annals of Dyslexia, 41*, 193–206.

Ball, E. W. (1997). Phonological awareness: Implications for whole language and emergent literacy programs. *Topics in Language Disorders, 17*(3), 14–26.

Ball, E. W., & Blachman, B. A. (1988). Phoneme segmentation training: Effect on reading readiness. *Annals of Dyslexia, 38*, 208–225.

Ball, E. W., & Blachman, B. A. (1991). Does phoneme awareness training in kindergarten make a difference in early word recognition and developmental spelling? *Reading Research Quarterly, 26*(1) 49–66.

Beck, I. L., & Juel, C. (1995). The role of decoding in learning to read. *American Educator, 19*(2), 8, 21–25, 39–42.

Blachman, B. A. (1983). Are we assessing the linguistic factors critical in early reading? *Annals of Dyslexia, 33*, 91–109.

Blachman, B. A. (1984). Relationship of rapid naming ability and language analysis skill to kindergarten and first grade reading achievement. *Journal of Educational Psychology, 76*, 610–622.

Blachman, B. A. (1994a). Early literacy acquisition: The role of phonological awareness. In G. Wallach & K. Butler (Eds.), *Language learning disabilities in school-age children and adolescents: Some underlying principles and applications* (pp. 253–274). Columbus, OH: Merrill/Macmillan.

Blachman, B. A. (1994b). What we have learned from longitudinal studies of phonological processing and reading, *and* some unanswered questions: A response to Torgesen, Wagner, and Rashotte. *Journal of Learning Disabilities, 27*, 287–291.

Blachman, B. A. (Ed.). (1997a). *Foundations of reading acquisition and dyslexia: Implications for early intervention*. Mahwah, NJ: Lawrence Erlbaum Associates.

Blachman, B. A. (1997b). Early intervention and phonological awareness: A cautionary tale. In B. A. Blachman (Ed.), *Foundations of reading acquisition and dyslexia: Implications for early intervention* (pp. 409–430). Mahwah, NJ: Lawrence Erlbaum Associates.

Blachman, B. A., Ball, E. W., Black, R., & Tangel, D. (1994). Kindergarten teachers develop phoneme awareness in low-income, inner-city classrooms: Does it make a difference? *Reading and Writing: An Interdisciplinary Journal, 6*, 1–17.

Blachman, B. A., & James, S. L. (1985). Metalinguistic abilities and reading achievement in first-grade children. In J. A. Niles & R. V. Lalik (Eds.), *Issues in literacy: A research perspective: Thirty-fourth yearbook of the National Reading Conference* (pp. 280–286). Rochester, NY: National Reading Conference.

Blachman, B. A., Tangel, D. M., Ball, E., Black, R., & McGraw, C. K. (1999). Developing phonological awareness and word recognition skills: A two-year intervention with low-income, inner-city children. *Reading and Writing: An Interdisciplinary Journal, 11*, 239–273.

Bowers, P. G., & Swanson, L. B. (1991). Naming speed deficits in reading disability: Multiple measures of a singular process. *Journal of Experimental Child Psychology, 51,* 195–219.

Bradley, L. (1988). Making connections in learning to read and spell. *Applied Cognitive Psychology, 2,* 3–18.

Bradley, L., & Bryant, P. (1983). Categorizing sounds and learning to read: A causal connection. *Nature, 30,* 419–421.

Bradley, L., & Bryant, P. (1985). *Rhyme and reason in reading and spelling.* International Academy for Research in Learning Disabilities Monograph Series, No. 1. Ann Arbor: University of Michigan Press.

Brady, S. (1997). Ability to encode phonological representations: An underlying difficulty of poor readers. In B. A. Blachman (Ed.), *Foundations of reading acquisition and dyslexia: Implications for early intervention* (pp. 21–47). Mahwah, NJ: Lawrence Erlbaum Associates.

Brady, S., & Shankweiler, D. (Eds.). (1991). *Phonological processes in literacy: A tribute to Isabelle Y. Liberman.* Hillsdale, NJ: Lawrence Erlbaum Associates.

Bruce, L. J. (1964). The analysis of word sounds by young children. *British Journal of Educational Psychology, 34,* 158–170.

Bruck, M. (1992). Persistence of dyslexics' phonological awareness deficits. *Developmental Psychology, 28,* 874–886.

Bruck, M. (1993). Word recognition and component phonological processing skills of adults with childhood diagnosis of dyslexia. *Developmental Review, 13,* 258–268.

Bryant, P. E., Bradley, L., Maclean, M., & Crossland, J. (1989). Nursery rhymes, phonological skills and reading. *Journal of Child Language, 16,* 407–428.

Bryant, P. E., Maclean, M., Bradley, L. L., & Crossland, J. (1990). Rhyme and alliteration, phoneme detection, and learning to read. *Developmental Psychology, 26,* 429–438.

Byrne, B., & Fielding-Barnsley, R. (1991). Evaluation of a program to teach phonemic awareness to young children. *Journal of Educational Psychology, 83,* 451–455.

Byrne, B., & Fielding-Barnsley, R. (1993). Evaluation of a program to teach phonemic awareness to young children: A 1-year follow-up. *Journal of Educational Psychology, 85,* 104–111.

Byrne, B., & Fielding-Barnsley, R. (1995). Evaluation of a program to teach phonemic awareness to young children: A 2- and 3-year follow-up and a new preschool trial. *Journal of Educational Psychology, 87,* 488–503.

Calfee, R. C., Lindamood, P., & Lindamood, C. (1973). Acoustic-phonetic skills and reading—Kindergarten through 12th grade. *Journal of Educational Psychology, 64,* 293–298.

Cardoso-Martins, C. (1995). Sensitivity to rhymes, syllables, and phonemes in literacy acquisition in Portuguese. *Reading Research Quarterly, 30*(4), 808–828.

Cary, L., & Verhaeghe, A. (1994). Promoting phonemic analysis ability among kindergartners: Effects of different training programs. *Reading and Writing: An Interdisciplinary Journal, 6,* 251–278.

Castle, J. M., Riach, J., & Nicholson, T. (1994). Getting off to a better start in reading and spelling: The effects of phonemic awareness instruction within a whole language program. *Journal of Educational Psychology, 86,* 350–359.

Chafouleas, S. M., Lewandowski, L. J., Smith, C. R., & Blachman, B. A. (1997). Phonological awareness skills in children: Examining performance across tasks and ages. *Journal of Psychoeducational Assessment, 15,* 334–347.

Chall, J. S. (1989). Learning to read: The great debate 20 years later: A response to "Debunking the great phonics myth." *Phi Delta Kappan, 70,* 521–538.

Content, A., Kolinsky, R., Morais, J., & Bertelson, P. (1986). Phonetic segmentation in prereaders: Effect of corrective information. *Journal of Experimental Psychology, 42,* 49–72.

Cunningham, A. E. (1990). Explicit versus implicit instruction in phonemic awareness. *Journal of Experimental Child Psychology, 50,* 429–444.

Denckla, M. B., & Rudel, R. G. (1976). Rapid "automatized" naming (R.A.N.): Dyslexia differentiated from other learning disabilities. *Neuropsychologia, 14,* 471–479.

Ehri, L. C. (1979). Linguistic insight: Threshold of reading acquisition. In T. G. Waller & G. E. MacKinnon (Eds.), *Reading research: Advances in theory and practice* (Vol. 1, pp. 63–144). New York: Academic Press.

Ehri, L. C. (1989). Development of spelling knowledge and its role in reading acquisition and reading disabilities. *Journal of Learning Disabilities, 22,* 356–365.

Ehri, L. C. (1991). Learning to read and spell words. In L. Rieben & C. A. Perfetti (Eds.), *Learning to read: Basic research and its implications* (pp. 57–73). Hillsdale, NJ: Lawrence Erlbaum Associates.

Ehri, L. C. (1997). Sight word learning in normal readers and dyslexics. In B. Blachman (Ed.), *Foundations of reading acquisition and dyslexia: Implications for early intervention* (pp. 163–189). Mahwah, NJ: Lawrence Erlbaum Associates.

Ehri, L. C., & Wilce, L. (1987). The influence of spellings on speech: Are alveolar flaps /d/ or /t/? In D. Yaden & S. Templeton (Eds.), *Metalinguistic awareness and beginning literacy: Conceptualizing what it means to read and write* (pp. 101–114). Portsmouth, NH: Heinemann.

Elbro, C. (1996). Early linguistic abilities and reading development: A review and a hypothesis about distinctness of phonological representations. *Reading and Writing: An Interdisciplinary Journal, 8,* 453–485.

Elbro, C., Borstrøm, I., & Petersen, D. K. (1998). Predicting dyslexia from kindergarten: The importance of distinctness of phonological representations of lexical items. *Reading Research Quarterly, 33*(1) 36–60.

Elkonin, D. B. (1963). The psychology of mastering the elements of reading. In B. Simon & J. Simon (Eds.), *Educational psychology in the U.S.S.R.* (pp. 165–179). London: Routledge & Kegan Paul.

Elkonin, D. B. (1973). U.S.S.R. In J. Downing (Ed.), *Comparative reading* (pp. 551–580). New York: Macmillan.

Fawcett, A. J., & Nicolson, R. I. (1995). Persistence of phonological awareness deficits in older children with dyslexia. *Reading and Writing: An Interdisciplinary Journal, 7*(4), 361–376.

Felton, R. H., Naylor, C. E., & Wood, F. B. (1990). Neuropsychological profile of adult dyslexics. *Brain and Language, 39,* 485–497.

Ferroli, L., & Shanahan, T. (1987). Kindergarten spelling: Explaining its relationship to first-grade reading. In J. E. Readence & R. S. Baldwin (Eds.), *Research in literacy: Merging perspectives: Thirty-sixth yearbook of the National Reading Conference* (pp. 93–99). Rochester, NY: National Reading Conference.

Fletcher, J. M., Morris, R., Lyon, G. R., Stuebing, K. K., Shaywitz, S. E., Shankweiler, D. P., Katz, L., & Shaywitz, B. A. (1997). Subtypes of dyslexia: An old problem revisited. In B. A. Blachman (Ed.), *Foundations of reading acquisition and dyslexia: Implications for early intervention* (pp. 95–114). Mahwah, NJ: Lawrence Erlbaum Associates.

Fletcher, J. M., Shaywitz, S. E., Shankweiler, D. P., Katz, L., Liberman, I. Y., Stuebing, K. K., Francis, D. J., Fowler, A. E., & Shaywitz, B. A. (1994). Cognitive profiles of reading disability: Comparisons of discrepancy and low achievement definitions. *Journal of Educational Psychology, 86,* 6–23.

Fowler, A. E. (1991). How early phonological development might set the stage for phoneme awareness. In S. A. Brady & D. P. Shankweiler (Eds.), *Phonological processes in literacy: A tribute to Isabelle Y. Liberman* (pp. 97–117). Hillsdale, NJ: Lawrence Erlbaum Associates.

Fox, B., & Routh, D. K. (1975). Analyzing spoken language into words, syllables, and phonemes: A developmental study. *Journal of Psycholinguistic Research, 4,* 331–342.

Fox, B., & Routh, D. K. (1976). Phonemic analysis and synthesis as word-attack skills. *Journal of Educational Psychology, 68,* 70–74.

Fox, B., & Routh, D. K. (1984). Phonemic analysis and synthesis as word-attack skills: Revisited. *Journal of Educational Psychology, 76,* 1059–1061.

Gallagher, A. M., Laxon, V., Armstrong, E., & Frith, U. (1996). Phonological difficulties in high-functioning dyslexics. *Reading and Writing: An Interdisciplinary Journal, 8,* 499–509.

Gleitman, L. R., & Rozin, P. (1973). Teaching reading by use of a syllabary. *Reading Research Quarterly, 8,* 447–483.

Goldstein, D. M. (1976). Cognitive-linguistic functioning and learning to read in preschoolers. *Journal of Educational Psychology, 68,* 680–688.

Goswami, U., & Bryant, P. (1990). *Phonological skills and learning to read.* Hillsdale, NJ: Lawrence Erlbaum Associates.

Gough, P. B. & Walsh, M. (1991). Chinese, Phoenicians, and the orthographic cipher of English. In S. A. Brady & D. P. Shankweiler (Eds.), *Phonological processes in literacy: A tribute to Isabelle Y. Liberman* (pp. 199–209). Hillsdale, NJ: Lawrence Erlbaum Associates.

Hatcher, P. J., Hulme, C., & Ellis, A. W. (1994). Ameliorating early reading failure by integrating the teaching of reading and phonological skills: The phonological linkage hypothesis. *Child Development, 65,* 41–57.

Helfgott, J. (1976). Phonemic segmentation and blending skills of kindergarten children: Implications for beginning reading acquisition. *Contemporary Educational Psychology, 1,* 157–169.

Hohn, W., & Ehri, L. (1983). Do alphabet letters help prereaders acquire phonemic segmentation skills? *Journal of Educational Psychology, 75,* 752–762.

Hoien, T., Lundberg, I., Stanovich, K. E., & Bjaalid, I. (1995). Components of phonological awareness. *Reading and Writing: An Interdisciplinary Journal, 7,* 171–188.

Iversen, S., & Tunmer, W. (1993). Phonological processing skills and the Reading Recovery Program. *Journal of Educational Psychology, 85,* 112–126.

Juel, C. (1988). Learning to read and write: A longitudinal study of 54 children from first through fourth grades. *Journal of Educational Psychology, 80*(4), 437–447.

Juel, C. (1994). *Learning to read and write in one elementary school.* New York: Springer-Verlag.

Kattke, M. L. (1978). The ability of kindergarten children to analyze 2-phoneme words (Doctoral dissertation, Columbia University Teachers College). *Dissertation Abstracts International, 39,* 3472A. (University Microfilms No. 78-22, 058)

Katz, R. (1986). Phonological deficiencies in children with reading disability: Evidence from an object-naming task. *Cognition, 22,* 225–257.

Leong, C. K., & Haines, C. F. (1978). Beginning readers' analysis of words and sentences. *Journal of Reading Behavior, 10,* 393–407.

Lewkowicz, N. K. (1980). Phonemic awareness training: What to teach and how to teach it. *Journal of Educational Psychology, 72,* 686–700.

Lewkowicz, N. K., & Low, L. Y. (1979). Effects of visual aids and word structure on phonemic segmentation. *Contemporary Educational Psychology, 4,* 238–252.

Liberman, A. M. (1970). The grammars of speech and language. *Cognitive Psychology, 1,* 301–323.

Liberman, A. M., Cooper, F. S., Shankweiler, D., & Studdert-Kennedy, M. (1967). Perception of the speech code. *Psychological Review, 74,* 731–761.

Liberman, I. Y. (1971). Basic research in speech and lateralization of language: Some implications for reading disability. *Bulletin of the Orton Society, 21,* 72–87.

Liberman, I. Y. (1973). Segmentation of the spoken word and reading acquisition. *Bulletin of the Orton Society*, 23, 65–67.

Liberman, I. Y., & Liberman, A. M. (1990). Whole language vs. code emphasis: Underlying assumptions and their implications for reading instruction. *Annals of Dyslexia, 40*, 51–76.

Liberman, I. Y., Liberman, A. M., Mattingly, I. G., & Shankweiler, D. (1980). Orthography and the beginning reader. In J. Kavanagh & R. Venezky (Eds.), *Orthography, reading and dyslexia* (pp. 137–153). Baltimore, MD: University Park Press.

Liberman, I. Y., & Shankweiler, D. (1985). Phonology and the problems of learning to read and write. *Remedial and Special Education, 6*, 8–17.

Liberman, I. Y., & Shankweiler, D. (1991). Phonology and beginning reading: A tutorial. In L. Rieben & C. A. Perfetti (Eds.), *Learning to read: Basic research and its implications* (pp. 3–17). Hillsdale, NJ: Lawrence Erlbaum Associates.

Liberman, I. Y., Shankweiler, D., Fischer, F. W., & Carter, B. (1974). Explicit syllable and phoneme segmentation in the young child. *Journal of Experimental Child Psychology, 18*, 201–212.

Lie, A. (1991). Effects of a training program for stimulating skills in word analysis in first-grade children. *Reading Research Quarterly, 26*(3), 234–250.

Lovett, M. W., Borden, S. L., DeLuca, T., Lacerenza, L., Benson, N. J., & Brackstone, D. (1994). Treating the core deficits of developmental dyslexia: Evidence of transfer of learning after phonologically- and strategy-based reading training programs. *Developmental Psychology, 30*, 805–822.

Lundberg, I. (1991). Phonemic awareness can be developed without reading instruction. In S. A. Brady & D. P. Shankweiler (Eds.), *Phonological processes in literacy: A tribute to Isabelle Y. Liberman* (pp. 47–53). Hillsdale, NJ: Lawrence Erlbaum Associates.

Lundberg, I., Frost, J., & Petersen, O. (1988). Effects of an extensive program for stimulating phonological awareness in preschool children. *Reading Research Quarterly, 23*(3), 263–284.

Lundberg, I., Olofsson, A., & Wall, S. (1980). Reading and spelling skill in the first school years predicted from phonemic awareness skills in kindergarten. *Scandinavian Journal of Psychology, 21*, 159–173.

Maclean, M., Bryant, P., & Bradley, L. (1987). Rhymes, nursery rhymes, and reading in early childhood. *Merrill-Palmer Quarterly, 33*, 255–281.

Mann, V. A., & Liberman, I. Y. (1984). Phonological awareness and verbal short-term memory: Can they presage early reading problems? *Journal of Learning Disabilities, 17*, 592–599.

Mann, V., Tobin, P., & Wilson, R. (1987). Measuring phonological awareness through the invented spellings of kindergarten children. *Merrill-Palmer Quarterly, 33*, 365–391.

Marsh, G., & Mineo, R. J. (1977). Training preschool children to recognize phonemes in words. *Journal of Educational Psychology, 69*, 748–753.

McBride-Chang, C. (1995). What is phonological awareness? *Journal of Educational Psychology, 87*, 179–192.

McBride-Chang, C., Wagner, R. K., & Chang, L. (1997). Growth modeling of phonological awareness. *Journal of Educational Psychology, 89*, 621–630.

Metsala, J. L., & Ehri, L. C. (Eds.). (1998). *Word recognition in beginning literacy*. Mahwah, NJ: Lawrence Erlbaum Associates.

Metsala, J. L., & Walley, A. C. (1998). Spoken vocabulary growth and the segmental restructuring of lexical representations: Precursors to phonemic awareness and early reading ability. In J. L. Metsala & L. C. Ehri (Eds.), *Word recognition in beginning literacy* (pp. 89–120). Mahwah, NJ: Lawrence Erlbaum Associates.

Morais, J., (1987). Phonetic awareness and reading acquisition. *Psychological Research, 49*, 147–152.

Morris, D., & Perney, J. (1984). Developmental spelling as a predictor of first-grade reading achievement. *Elementary School Journal, 84*, 441–457.

Murray, B. A., Stahl, S. A., & Ivey, M. G. (1996). Developing phoneme awareness through alphabet books. *Reading and Writing: An Interdisciplinary Journal, 8*, 307–322.

Nation, K, & Hulme, C. (1997). Phonemic segmentation, not onset-rime segmentation, predicts early reading and spelling skills. *Reading Research Quarterly, 32*, 154–167.

O'Connor, R. E., Jenkins, J. R., & Slocum, T. A. (1995). Transfer among phonological tasks in kindergarten: Essential instructional content. *Journal of Educational Psychology, 87*, 202–217.

O'Connor, R. E., Notari-Syverson, A., & Vadasy, P. F. (1996). Ladders to literacy: The effects of teacher-led phonological activities for kindergarten children with and without disabilities. *Exceptional Children, 63*(1), 117–130.

Olofsson, A., & Lundberg, I. (1983). Can phonemic awareness be trained in kindergarten? *Scandinavian Journal of Psychology, 24*, 35–44.

Olson, R. K., Wise, B., Johnson, M. C., & Ring, J. (1997). The etiology and remediation of phonologically based word recognition and spelling disabilities: Are phonological deficits the "hole" story? In B. A. Blachman (Ed.), *Foundations of reading acquisition and dyslexia: Implications for early intervention* (pp. 305–326). Mahwah, NJ: Lawrence Erlbaum Associates.

Pennington, B. F., Van Orden, G. C., Smith, S. D., Green, P. A., & Haith, M. M. (1990). Phonological processing skills and deficits in adult dyslexics. *Child Development, 61*, 1753–1778.

Perfetti, C. A. (1985). *Reading ability*. New York: Oxford University Press.

Perfetti, C. A., Beck, I., Bell, L., & Hughes, C. (1987). Phonemic knowledge and learning to read are reciprocal: A longitudinal study of first grade children. In K. Stanovich (Ed.), *Children's reading and the development of phonological awareness* [Special issue]. *Merrill-Palmer Quarterly, 33*(3), 283–320.

Pratt, A. C., & Brady, S. (1988). Relation of phonological awareness to reading disability in children and adults. *Journal of Educational Psychology, 80*, 319–323.

Rack, J., Hulme, C., Snowling, M., & Wightman, J. (1994). The role of phonology in young children learning to read words: The direct mapping hypothesis. *Journal of Experimental Child Psychology, 57*, 42–71.

Read, C. (1986). *Children's creative spellings.* London: Routledge & Kegan Paul.

Rieben, L., & Perfetti, C. A. (Eds.). (1991). *Learning to read: Basic research and its implications.* Hillsdale, NJ: Lawrence Erlbaum Associates.

Rosner, J. (1971). *Phonic analysis training and beginning reading skills.* Pittsburgh: University of Pittsburgh Learning Research and Development Center. (ERIC Document Reproduction Service No. ED 059–029)

Rosner, J. (1974). Auditory analysis training with prereaders. *The Reading Teacher, 27*, 379–384.

Rosner, J., & Simon, D. (1971). The auditory analysis test: An initial report. *Journal of Learning Disabilities, 4*, 40–48.

Savin, H. B. (1972). What the child knows about speech when he starts to learn to read. In J. F. Kavanagh & I. G. Mattingly (Eds.), *Language by ear and by eye: The relationships between speech and reading* (pp. 319–326). Cambridge, MA: MIT Press.

Scarborough, H. S. (1990). Very early language deficits in dyslexic children. *Child Development, 61*, 1728–1743.

Scarborough, H. S. (1998). Early identification of children at risk for reading disabilities: Phonological awareness and some other promising predictors. In P. Accardo, A. Capute, & B. Shapiro (Eds.), *Specific reading disability: A view of the spectrum* (pp. 75–119). Timonium, MD: York Press.

Shankweiler, D. P. (1989). How problems of comprehension are related to difficulties in decoding. In D. Shankweiler & I. Y. Liberman (Eds.), *Phonology and reading disability: Solving the puzzle* (pp. 1–33). Ann Arbor: University of Michigan Press.

Shankweiler, D., & Crain, S. (1986). Language mechanisms and reading disorders: A modular approach. *Cognition, 24*, 139–168.

Shankweiler, D., & Liberman, I. Y. (Eds.). (1989). *Phonology and reading disability: Solving the reading puzzle.* Ann Arbor: University of Michigan Press.

Share, D. L. (1995). Phonological recoding and self-teaching: Sine qua non of reading acquisition. *Cognition, 55*, 151–218.

Share, D. L., Jorm, A. F., Maclean, R., & Matthews, R. (1984). Sources of individual differences in reading achievement. *Journal of Educational Psychology, 76*(6), 1309–1324.

Share, D. L., & Stanovich, K. E. (1995). Cognitive processes in early reading development: Accommodating individual differences into a model of acquisition. *Issues in Education, 1*, 1–57.

Shaywitz, S. E. (1996). Dyslexia. *Scientific American, 275*(5), 98–104.

Skjelfjord, V. J. (1976). Teaching children to segment spoken words as an aid in learning to read. *Journal of Learning Disabilities, 9*, 297–306.

Snider, V. (1995). A primer on phonemic awareness: What it is, why it's important, and how to teach it. *School Psychology Review, 24*, 443–455.

Snowling, M. J., Goulandris, N., & Defty, N. (1996). A longitudinal study of reading development in dyslexic children. *Journal of Educational Psychology, 88*(4), 653–669.

Stage, S., & Wagner, R. (1992). Development of young children's phonological and orthographic knowledge as revealed by their spellings. *Developmental Psychology, 28*, 287–296.

Stahl, S. A., & Murray, B. A. (1994). Defining phonological awareness and its relationship to early reading. *Journal of Educational Psychology, 86*, 221–234.

Stahl, S. A., & Murray, B. A. (1998). Issues involved in defining phonological awareness and its relation to early reading. In J. L. Metsala & L. C. Ehri (Eds.), *Word recognition in beginning literacy* (pp. 65–87). Mahwah, NJ: Lawrence Erlbaum Associates.

Stanovich, K. E. (1986). Matthew effects in reading: Some consequences of individual differences in the acquisition of literacy. *Reading Research Quarterly, 21*, 360–407.

Stanovich, K. E. (1988). Explaining the differences between the dyslexic and the garden-variety poor reader: The phonological-core variable-difference model. *Journal of Learning Disabilities, 21*, 590–612.

Stanovich, K. E. (1991). Changing models of reading and reading acquisition. In L. Rieben & C. A. Perfetti (Eds.), *Learning to read: Basic research and its implications* (pp. 19–31). Hillsdale, NJ: Lawrence Erlbaum Associates.

Stanovich, K. E. (1992). Speculations on the causes and consequences of individual differences in early reading acquisition. In P. B. Gough, L. C. Ehri, & R. Treiman (Eds.), *Reading acquisition* (pp. 307–342). Hillsdale, NJ: Lawrence Erlbaum Associates.

Stanovich, K. E., Cunningham, A. E., & Cramer, B. B. (1984). Assessing phonological awareness in kindergarten children: Issues of task comparability. *Journal of Experimental Child Psychology, 38*, 175–190.

Stuart, M., & Coltheart, M. (1988). Does reading develop in a sequence of stages? *Cognition, 30*, 139–181.

Tangel, D. M., & Blachman, B. A. (1992). Effect of phoneme awareness instruction on kindergarten children's invented spelling. *Journal of Reading Behavior, 24*, 233–261.

Tangel, D. M., & Blachman, B. A. (1995). Effect of phoneme awareness instruction on the invented spelling of first grade children: A one year follow-up. *Journal of Reading Behavior, 27*, 153–185.

Torgesen, J. K., & Burgess, S. R. (1998). Consistency of reading-related phonological processes throughout early childhood: Evidence from longitudinal, correlational and instructional studies. In J. Metsala & L. Ehri (Eds.), *Word recognition in beginning literacy* (pp. 161–188). Mahwah, NJ: Lawrence Erlbaum Associates.

Torgesen, J. K., & Davis, C. (1996). Individual difference variables that predict response to training in phonological awareness. *Journal of Experimental Child Psychology, 63,* 1–21.

Torgesen, J. K., & Mathes, P. G. (1998). *What every teacher should know about phonological awareness* (Technical Assistance Report No. ESE9872). Florida Department of Education, Tallahassee.

Torgesen, J. K., Morgan, S. T., & Davis, C. (1992). Effects of two types of phonological awareness training on word learning in kindergarten children. *Journal of Educational Psychology, 84,* 364–370.

Torgesen, J. K., Wagner, R. K., & Rashotte, C. A. (1997). Prevention and remediation of severe reading disabilities: Keeping the end in mind. *Scientific Studies of Reading, 1*(3), 217–234.

Treiman, R. (1985). Onsets and rimes as units of spoken syllables: Evidence from children. *Journal of Experimental Child Psychology, 39,* 161–181.

Treiman, R. (1992). The role of intrasyllabic units in learning to read and spell. In P. B. Gough, L. C. Ehri, & R. Treiman (Eds.), *Reading acquisition* (pp. 65–106). Hillsdale, NJ: Lawrence Erlbaum Associates.

Treiman, R. (1993). *Beginning to spell.* New York: Oxford University Press.

Treiman, R. (1997). Spelling in normal children and dyslexics. In B. A. Blachman (Ed.), *Foundations of reading acquisition and dyslexia: Implications for early intervention* (pp. 191–218). Mahwah, NJ: Lawrence Erlbaum Associates.

Treiman, R., & Baron, J. (1981). Segmental analysis ability: Development and relation to reading ability. In G. E. MacKinnon & T. G. Waller (Eds.), *Reading research: Advances in theory and practice* (Vol. 3, pp. 159–198). New York: Academic Press.

Treiman, R., & Baron, J. (1983). Phonemic-analysis training helps children benefit from spelling-sound rules. *Memory & Cognition, 11,* 382–389.

Treiman, R., & Zukowski, A. (1991). Levels of phonological awareness. In S. A. Brady & D. P. Shankweiler (Eds.), *Phonological processes in literacy: A tribute to Isabelle Y. Liberman* (pp. 67–83). Hillsdale, NJ: Lawrence Erlbaum Associates.

Treiman, R., & Zukowski, A. (1996). Children's sensitivity to syllables, onsets, rimes, and phonemes. *Journal of Experimental Child Psychology, 61,* 193–215.

Vandervelden, M. C., & Siegel, L. S. (1995). Phonological recoding and phoneme awareness in early literacy: A developmental approach. *Reading Research Quarterly, 30*(4), 854–875.

Vellutino, F. R. (1991). Introduction to three studies on reading acquisition: Convergent findings on theoretical foundations of code-oriented versus whole-language approaches to reading instruction. *Journal of Educational Psychology, 83,* 437–443.

Vellutino, F. R., & Scanlon, D. M. (1987). Phonological coding, phonological awareness, and reading ability: Evidence from a longitudinal and experimental study. *Merrill-Palmer Quarterly, 33*(3), 321–363.

Vellutino, F. R., Scanlon, D. M., & Sipay, E. R. (1997). Toward distinguishing between cognitive and experiential deficits as primary sources of difficulty in learning to read: The importance of early intervention in diagnosing specific reading disability. In B. A. Blachman (Ed.), *Foundations of reading acquisition and dyslexia: Implications for early intervention* (pp. 347–379). Mahwah, NJ: Lawrence Erlbaum Associates.

Vellutino, F. R., Scanlon, D. M., Sipay, E. R., Small, S. G., Pratt, A., Chen, R. S., & Denckla, M. B. (1996). Cognitive profiles of difficult to remediate and readily remediated poor readers: Early intervention as a vehicle for distinguishing between cognitive and experiential deficits as basic causes of specific reading disability. *Journal of Educational Psychology, 88*(4), 607–638.

Vellutino, F. R., Scanlon, D. M., & Tanzman, M. S. (1994). Components of reading ability: Issues and problems in operationalizing word identification, phonological coding, and orthographic coding. In G. R. Lyon (Ed.), *Frames of reference for the assessment of learning disabilities: New views on measurement issues* (pp. 279–332). Baltimore, MD: Paul Brookes.

Wagner, R. K., & Torgesen, J. K. (1987). The nature of phonological processing and its causal role in the acquisition of reading skills. *Psychological Bulletin, 101,* 192–212.

Wagner, R. K., Torgesen, J. K., & Rashotte, C. A. (1994). The development of reading related phonological processing abilities: New evidence of bi-directional causality from a latent variable longitudinal study. *Developmental Psychology, 30,* 73–87.

Wagner, R. K., Torgesen, J. K., Rashotte, C. A., Hecht, S. A., Barker, T. A., Burgess, S. R., Donahue, J., & Garon, T. (1997). Changing relations between phonological processing abilities and word-level reading as children develop from beginning to skilled readers: A 5-year longitudinal study. *Developmental Psychology, 33,* 468–479.

Williams, J. P. (1979). The ABD's of reading: A program for the learning disabled. In L. B. Resnick & P. A. Weaver (Eds.), *Theory and practice of early reading* (Vol. 3, pp. 179–195). Hillsdale, NJ: Lawrence Erlbaum Associates.

Williams, J. P. (1980). Teaching decoding with an emphasis on phoneme analysis and phoneme blending. *Journal of Educational Psychology, 72,* 1–15.

Williams, J. P. (1985). The case for explicit decoding instruction. In J. Osborn, P. Wilson, & R. Anderson (Eds.), *Reading education: Foundations for a literate America* (pp. 205–213). Lexington, MA: Lexington Books.

Williams, J. P. (1987). Educational treatments for dyslexia at the elementary and secondary levels. In W. Ellis (Ed.), *Intimacy with language: A forgotten basic in teacher education* (pp. 24–32). Baltimore, MD: Orton Dyslexia Society.

Williams, J. P. (1994). Twenty years of research on reading: Answers and questions. In F. Lehr & J. Osborn (Eds.), *Reading, language, and literacy: Instruction for the twenty-first century* (pp. 59–73). Hillsdale, NJ: Lawrence Erlbaum Associates.

Wolf, M. (1986). Rapid alternating stimulus naming in the developmental dyslexias. *Brain and Language, 27,* 360–379.

Wolf, M. (1991). Naming speed and reading: The contribution of the cognitive neurosciences. *Reading Research Quarterly, 26,* 123–141.

Wolf, M. (1997). A provisional, integrative account of phonological and naming-speed deficits in dyslexia: Implications for diagnosis and intervention. In B. A. Blachman (Ed.), *Foundations of reading acquisition and dyslexia: Implications for early intervention* (pp. 67–92). Mahwah, NJ: Lawrence Erlbaum Associates.

Yopp, H. K. (1988). The validity and reliability of phonemic awareness tests. *Reading Research Quarterly, 23,* 159–177.

Zhurova, L. Y. (1973). The development of analysis of words into their sounds by preschool children. In C. A. Ferguson & D. I. Slobin (Eds.), *Studies of child language development.* New York: Holt, Rinehart & Winston.

Zifcak, M. (1981). Phonological awareness and reading acquisition. *Contemporary Educational Psychology, 6,* 117–126.

CHAPTER 28

Vocabulary Instruction

Camille L. Z. Blachowicz
Peter Fisher
National Louis University

The history of research on vocabulary instruction is rich and complex. A topic of great interest in the early decades of educational research, particularly with the work of E. L. Thorndike and his students, it waned as a subject of investigation in the 1950s. Surveys of educational practice (Dale, Razik, & Petty, 1973; Petty, Herold, & Stoll, 1967) suggested that vocabulary instruction through the early 1970s was little informed by prior research and that many classroom questions were unaddressed. In the mid 1970s, a review of reading research (Calfee & Drum, 1978) called vocabulary research a "vanishing species." Indeed, the first *Handbook of Reading Research* (Pearson, 1984) devoted only a few pages to vocabulary research.

However, the 1970s and 1980s saw a remarkable resurgence in work in this area. Becker (1977), in the *Harvard Educational Review*, published an article that posed the notion that a major factor in the school failure of disadvantaged children was inadequate vocabulary knowledge. His argument stimulated a dialogue with counterformulations of vocabulary size and subsequent theorization about vocabulary development and its growth. This well-documented dialogue continues as a rich debate today (Cunningham & Stanovich, 1998; Nagy & Scott, this volume; Zechmeister et al., 1995).

Related to this dialogue, numerous instructional investigations took place that were well summarized in the second *Handbook of Reading Research* (Barr, Kamil, Mosenthal, & Pearson, 1991), which contained two chapters on vocabulary, one dealing with vocabulary processes (Anderson & Nagy, 1991) and a second with vocabulary development (Beck & McKeown, 1991). The same topic was also addressed in the *Handbook of Teaching the English Language Arts* (Baumann & Kameenui, 1991), in the revised *Handbook of Research on Teaching* (Calfee & Drum, 1986), and in other excellent and comprehensive reviews (Baker, Simmons, & Kameenui, 1995a, 1995b; Graves, 1986; McKeown & Curtis, 1987; Ruddell, 1994), meta-analyses (Mezynski, 1983; Stahl & Fairbanks, 1986), and application volumes on instruction (Blachowicz & Fisher, 1996; Dale & O'Rourke, 1976; Irvin, 1990; Johnson & Pearson, 1984; Nagy, 1988; Nation, 1990). In addition, many articles on vocabulary have been published in instructional journals and more than 400 dissertations with relation to vocabulary have been abstracted in *Dissertation Abstracts* since the 1960s.

Given the plethora of reviews, analyses, and pedagogical applications cited above, one might ask, "What else is there to say?" And, indeed, this question presented itself to us as we began to struggle with how to deliver information about new research in the frameworks that have been previously developed. Guided by the fact that the title of this chapter is "Vocabulary Instruction" rather than "Vocabulary Processes," which are discussed by Nagy and Scott in this volume, or "Vocabulary Development," which has been well addressed in other volumes, we focus this chapter on research dealing exclusively with classroom instruction.

GOALS FOR THE CHAPTER

Our first goal for this chapter was to lay out the implications from the research that we feel represent shared insights for a "general theory" of vocabulary instruction. A second goal was to look at research examining practice and materials to see if these implications have impacted the classroom and if so, how. Third, we propose an alternative lens for viewing research-to-practice issues: a lens we call *adaptive practice*. Lastly, we focus on two special cases for adaptive practice in vocabulary instruction: (a) instruction in the content areas and (b) the instruction of students with differing characteristics (specifically English as a second language [ESL] students and poor readers).

SHARED INSIGHTS FROM TWO DECADES OF RESEARCH ON VOCABULARY

It would seem sensible to suggest that the nature of vocabulary instruction should vary according to the context of instruction and the nature of the words being taught and learned. However, guidelines for a "general theory" that has implications in a variety of situations have been suggested in many different forums by previous reviewers. Irvin (1990) promoted active learning and multiple exposures to words but then stressed independence and attitude to learning. Baumann and Kameenui (1991) developed 10 guidelines for decision making in vocabulary instruction as well as three overall objectives: (a) independence, (b) specific word learning, and (c) appreciation and enjoyment. Nagy (1988), Stahl (1986), and others gave guidelines for more specific instructional situations, whereas Pittelman, Heimlich, Berglund, and French (1991) and Heimlich and Pittelman (1986) included reviews for specific strategies. Collectively these reviews provide a comprehensive survey of the research prior to 1980, so we highlight research since that date in the following sections.

We believe that the research suggests four main principles to guide instruction:

1. That students should be active in developing their understanding of words and ways to learn them.
2. That students should personalize word learning.
3. That students should be immersed in words.
4. That students should build on multiple sources of information to learn words through repeated exposures.

Although it might be argued that these four principles could apply to all student learning, research on vocabulary instruction seems to support and extend them in relation to learning words in a variety of contexts.

Students as Active Learners

As in all teaching situations, having students become actively engaged in their own learning is a hallmark of good instruction (Wittrock, Marks, & Doctorow, 1975). We see this active engagement as being important in relation to two aspects of vocabulary instruction: learning the meanings of specific words (where it is important to make connections between and among words and concepts), and learning strategies to become independent word learners. The major focus of studies in the first area is on techniques that encourage students to see the semantic relatedness of words and concepts being studied (e.g., semantic mapping, semantic feature analysis). In the second area, most of the research concerns helping students to use context or morphology for effective word learning.

Involving students in grouping activities, or having them focus on semantic relatedness, encourages them to be active in their own learning. Research from the 1980s (Pittelman, Levin, & Johnson, 1985; Schewel, 1989) is conclusive in the benefit of semantic mapping for vocabulary learning. Semantic mapping is a technique that graphically represents the relationship between words. Finesilver (1994) found semantic mapping to be effective with junior high students in the context of regular classroom instruction. Semantic mapping requires students to identify and understand the relations between words, whereas semantic feature analysis is a graphic display that focuses on the features that distinguish words in a particular category, such as, various types of homes.

One particular form of semantic relatedness instruction is a concept of definition map (Schwartz & Raphael, 1985) in which categorical and semantic information of a word's definition are displayed along with examples. MacKinnon (1993), working with ninth-grade students, found concept of definition to be superior to other methods of instruction. Bos and Anders (1989, 1990, 1992) compared the effectiveness of three semantic relatedness techniques (mapping, semantic feature analysis, and semantic/syntactic feature analysis) to definitional instruction with students of various ages and abilities. All three interactive techniques were more effective than the definitional instruction for these students. Earlier research, reviewed in Pittelman et al. (1991), also supported the use of semantic feature analysis as an interactive instructional technique.

Some studies that focused on grouping words for instruction provided evidence that it is not just the relatedness of the words that is important but activities requiring students to recognize that relatedness. Durso and Coggins (1991) found that although a semantic organization of words for vocabulary instruction for college freshmen improved performance on comprehension tasks over use of an unorganized list, students' expressive vocabulary benefited only when they articulated the common theme, that is, became more active in their learning. Drum and Madison (1991, quoted in Stahl, Burdge, Machuga, & Stecyk, 1992) found mixed results when third- and fourth-grade teachers grouped words for presentation in semantically related sets but chose their own method of instruction using these sets. Stahl et al. (1992) investigated teaching words in semantically connected groups to fourth-grade students and found no benefit for doing so. On the other hand, they concluded that their results may have been due to the rich and varied instruction used with all the words with all the students. That is, the instruction involved active participation by students and so was effective for all groups. Simply grouping the words by semantic relatedness was not important in this context.

Although it seems generally agreed that helping students discover the semantic relatedness of words is an effective and active form of engaging them in deeper processing of the meaning, it is also important that students consciously develop strategies for active, independent word learning. We all use the context in which new words occur, either in oral or written language, to learn new words. Consequently, teaching students to consciously use context to become independent word learners is common in classrooms and instructional text. Yet, it has less emphatic support from the research. Some instructional studies (Buikema & Graves, 1993; Friedland, 1992; Gifford, 1993) suggest that teaching students to use context clues can be effective if the instruction is explicit, well scaffolded, and provides practice and feedback. What appears important from examining these studies with students of varying ages and ability levels is that a metacognitive component is included in the instruction. Stahl and Clark (1987), in their discussion of this issue, suggested that it is the anticipation of active learning that is central to the effectiveness of context instruction. Although no studies from this period were identified that showed context instruction to be ineffective, several studies (Baldwin & Schatz, 1985; Carver, 1994; Schatz & Baldwin, 1986) suggested that naturally occurring context does not always aid in word learning and may even be misleading.

A final strand of research that supports the idea of students' active engagement in their learning is from the area of clarifying misconceptions. Guzzetti, Snyder, Glass, and Gamas (1993) concluded from their meta-analysis that confronting students' misconceptions in some form is an effective way of changing them, especially when discussion or some other form of active examination of the misconception is included. Although this line of research is struggling with the nature of a misconception, which may be easier to identify in science and math than in other subject areas, the implications for misunderstanding specific word knowledge have yet to be fully explored.

Personalizing Word Learning

Research in vocabulary instruction supports the active engagement of students in making connections between and among words. Two slightly different forms of active engagement in word learning take place when students personalize word meanings in some way, such as through a mnemonic, or when they are active in choosing which words to learn as part of classroom instruction. Mnemonic strategies have a rich research history that has been extended by more recent studies. (Pressley, Levin, and Delaney [1982], Pressley, Levin, and McDaniel, [1987], and Levin [1993] provided extensive reviews of this topic.) In contrast, personalization through student self-selection of words for study has not been extensively investigated.

Mnemonic strategies have proven to very effective when students are engaged in learning new words for known concepts or when learning definitions. The keyword method has perhaps the strongest research support in this area. This strategy requires students to identify a keyword that is part of the target word and to link that keyword to the definition through the use of a visual image. Levin, Levin, Glasman, and Nordwall (1992) used a keyword method with third-, fourth-, seventh-, and eighth-grade students, working either individually or in small groups, in a comparison study with a sentence context method. They found superior performance for most groups not only on recall of definitions but on tests of sentence and story comprehension usage. McCarville (1993) found a positive effect using the keyword method with developmental college students. In contrast, Stahl, Richek and Vandevier (1991), also working with college students, found no advantage for a keyword over other methods, although here the means for all methods were approaching ceiling, so differences would be hard to demonstrate.

Earlier studies also supported the use of images (Carr & Mazur-Stewart, 1988) and acting out word meanings (Duffelmeyer, 1980). Other than Smith, Miller, Grossman, and Valeri-Gold (1994), who found the use of images effective with college developmental-studies students, there do not appear to have been any recent investigations that use these techniques in relation to vocabulary learning. Certainly, these ways of personalizing meaning can also be interpreted as using students' active participation in learning, as can the next strand of research, that is, giving them control over the words that they choose to learn.

Several studies have continued the work of Haggard (1982, 1985) in demonstrating the effectiveness of allowing students to select their own words to learn as part of classroom vocabulary instruction. Fisher, Blachowicz, and Smith (1991) examined the effects of allowing fourth-grade students in literature circles to select their own words for study. The students not only chose words that were at or above their grade level, but they retained knowledge of their meanings. A partial replication of this study at seventh grade (Blachowicz, Fisher, Costa, & Pozzi, 1993) found similar results. When students in fourth grade were allowed to choose their own words for vocabulary and spelling instruction, they learned the words more effectively, and remembered the meanings of the words they chose longer than words chosen by the teacher (Fisher & Danielsen, 1998). Dole, Sloan, and Trathen (1995) also found that allowing 10th graders in literature groups to select their own words was effective. On the other hand, the students who received instruction in a process showing them how to select words that were important for the selection learned more than those who did not. Undoubtedly, having students choose their own words for study appears effective in relation to reading literature, where the number of unknown words in a novel can be large, and the importance of any particular word is likely to be minimal. In the content areas, where it may be important to focus on particular words and concepts in a chapter, there is also some supporting evidence for student self-selection (which we discuss later in this chapter), although the picture is not definitive.

Reciprocal teaching is a related instructional technique in which students may learn vocabulary that they select themselves. One of the four components of reciprocal teaching involves students helping each other clarify parts of the text that they do not understand. This may involve the selection of vocabulary to study. Rosenshine and Meister (1994) reviewed the research in this area and found positive conclusions in relation to the effectiveness of the strategy for developing comprehension. Yet, they did not reach any conclusions in relation to vocabulary learning. It may be that students' control of their own learning in this situation is one part of its effectiveness. Further examination of instructional situations such as this, where students retain control over their learning in group settings, may be productive in refining our understanding of how and why student choice impacts on word learning.

Immersing Students in Words

Incidental word learning, through listening or reading, will always be part of students' general vocabulary development. Although the extent and nature of this learning are debated, the fact that it occurs is undisputed and the importance of a word-rich environment has been often demonstrated. Listening studies (Brett, Rothlein, & Hurley, 1996; Eller, Pappas, & Brown, 1988; Elley, 1988; Senechal & Cornell, 1993; Stahl, Richek & Vandevier, 1991), studies of family literacy (Beals & De Temple, 1993; Snow, 1991), studies of wide reading (Jenkins, Stein, & Wysocki, 1984; Krashen, 1989), and more focused studies of incidental word learning from context (Nagy, Herman, & Anderson, 1985; Parry, 1991; Shu, Anderson, & Zhang, 1995) all support the importance of exposing students to rich language environments. These studies with varying contexts and ages of learners all confirm that environments where language and word use are celebrated and noted encourage vocabulary learning. Scott and her colleagues conducted a series of studies (Scott & Butler, 1994a, 1994b; Scott, Asselin, Henry, & Butler, 1997; Scott, Butler, Asselin & Henry, 1996) examining the impact of word rich intermediate-grade classrooms that draw students' attention to the learning of words. Although there was no measurable impact using standardized measures of vocabulary, qualitative data overwhelmingly support the effectiveness of this rich environment on students' use of interesting words in their writing, and on students' awareness of and interest and attitude to words.

Learning Through Repeated Exposures

A "word-rich" environment supports general vocabulary development, but it may also provide a vehicle by which a student can build knowledge of a particular word through repeated exposures, and from multiple sources of information. Several studies compared definitional instruction with incidental word learning from context or with no-instruction control conditions and found that teaching definitions results in learning (Kameenui, Carnine, & Freschi, 1982; Pany & Jenkins, 1978; Stahl, 1983). On the other hand, instruction that combines definitional information with other active processing, such as adding contextual information (Stahl, 1983), writing (Duin & Graves, 1987), or rich manipulation of words (Beck & McKeown, 1983; Lansdown, 1991), is consistently more effective than definitional instruction alone. In contrast, Nist and Olejnik (1995), working with college students, did not find interactive effects for using both dictionary definitions and context. Their study did not provide students with instruction in context or dictionary use. Stahl and Fairbanks' meta-analysis (1986) concluded that methods that focus on providing students with multiple sources of information result in superior word learning.

Repeated exposures to a word can also be an important component of word learning. Stanley and Ginther (1991), working with sixth-grade students, supported earlier findings (Gipe, 1979–1980; McKeown, 1985) that exposing a word in differing contexts facilitates word learning. Results from a study of word frequency and word knowledge (Ryder & Slater, 1988) also support the importance of repeated exposures.

It could be argued that these four principles are only common sense in relation to vocabulary learning. Of course, letting students see and hear a word more than once and draw on multiple sources of meaning is likely to improve word learning. Surely encouraging and allowing students to be active in their learning and to personalize it should result in better learning. When common sense and research cross-check one another in this manner, the next question becomes one of looking at the ways in which these conclusions have affected instruction. Acknowledging the amount of energy and thinking that has already been devoted to this subject, one might expect to see research documentation of improved practice.

APPLICATIONS OF RESEARCH TO PRACTICE

Studies of teacher beliefs about vocabulary instruction, surveys of teacher reported practice, observational studies, and examinations of commercial instructional materials can all provide insights about the possible effects of vocabulary research on instruction. Self-report data suggest that teachers regularly allocate classroom time to vocabulary instruction (Johnson, Pittelman, Toms-Bronowski, & Levin, 1984; National Assessment of Educational Progress, 1990), and a significant majority of teachers indicate the importance of vocabulary instruction in their classrooms (Blachowicz, 1987; Blanton & Moorman, 1990; Johnson, Toms-Bronowski & Pittelman, 1982; Lloyd, 1995–1996; Scott & Butler, 1994a, 1994b), a conclusion that is supported by the volume of literature in teacher practice journals devoted to this topic.

Konopak and Williams (1994) suggest that strategies that teachers report to be usable for vocabulary instruction are derived from their general declared theoretical orientation toward instruction, either skills and text based (e.g., find a definition) or those implying more interactive learning (e.g., mapping, webbing). In more open-response surveys, teachers raise other contextual concerns to moderate their theoretical views, such as class size, reading level of materials, and demands of content instruction, as factors moving them to make changes in instruction (Bomkamp, 1995; Sable, 1992). Anders and Gallego (1989) suggested that this connection to theoretical orientation is also related to the amount of staff development available to teachers. The more teachers are engaged in staff development, the more their instructional practices reflect research-suggested strategies. So the picture on self-reported practices suggests a link to personal theory, a relation to staff development, and an awareness that contextual factors modify the application of theoretical principles. These issues are consistent with fine-grained examinations of wider classroom instruction in primary grades (Barr & Dreeben, 1983).

In looking at the observational studies detailing the way time is spent, results are less clear. Even though teachers espouse beliefs that vocabulary learning should be an expression of deep conceptual knowledge, teachers' classroom instruction often appears atomistic and skill based (Konopak & Williams, 1994). This type of instruction consists of using new words in context or paraphrasing sentences that contain new words (Scott & Butler, 1994a, 1994b). Watts (1995), in a more fine-grained look at six teachers during basal reading instruction, noted that instruction was primarily located in the prereading part of the lesson, where it was teacher directed and definitional. The same instruction was offered whether or not words were new to the students or already established. Further, it was directed toward understanding the specific passage rather than toward more generalized vocabulary learning strategies.

In lieu of individually developed perspectives, many teachers still depend heavily on commercially prepared instructional materials (Bomkamp, 1995; Sable, 1992). Examinations of vocabulary instruction in commercial materials also report a preponderance of simple, word/text-level instruction such as that noted earlier. When instruction is documented in commercial materials of the 1980s and earlier, the "best case" often involved little more than teacher presentation of a definition with worksheet follow-up. The "worst case" scenario was even more impoverished (Beck, McCaslin, & McKeown, 1980; Jenkins & Dixon, 1983), with no words being identified for instruction. More recent commercial materials (Ryder & Graves, 1994) appear more varied in approaches to vocabulary instruction and provide more research-suggested instructional practices, although these still remain predominantly localized as prereading activities. One concern raised by the research is that the words chosen for instruction in commercial anthologies might be ones that many students already know (Ryder & Graves, 1994; Stallman et al., 1990). When students are reading in instructional-level materials, the percentage of unknown words is estimated to be in the range of 1% to 5% (Betts, 1946). Further, when the words are complex or unknown, the instruction provided may not be sufficiently rich to impact comprehension, an issue raised by Gates (1962) several decades ago. This is also consistent with analyses of vocabulary selection and instruction in ESL instructional materials (Bernhardt, 1991; Nation, 1990).

It is interesting to note that, in preparing to review and report the research for this chapter, we surveyed a number of researchers whose work is well represented in this article and in the others already cited. Several who are parents of school-age children, or who are active in classrooms, answered the question as to how our research-informed knowledge has affected classroom practice, with the rueful answer of "Not much." So, we are left here with a surprising paradox. Even with an explosion of research and interest in vocabulary teaching over the last few decades, the research on classroom vocabulary instruction indicates that teachers seem to have a great interest in vocabulary but make inconsistent use of the research, a fact paralleled by examinations of materials prepared for instruction.

Other Lenses

Another direction from which to approach the larger question of the impact of research on vocabulary instruction is to examine the lenses through which the research has been viewed. In a compelling analysis of the ways in which literacy researchers have talked about "knowledge," Alexander, Schallert, and Hare (1991) noted that research often appears inconclusive, conflicting, or inapplicable because researchers are quite literally not talking about the same issues, often using the same term in considerably different ways. Even a cursory survey of the work on "method" in vocabulary instruction or of meta-analyses indicates that implications for vocabulary instruction are drawn from research with radically different theoretical and methodological bases. Some is research primarily relevant to the associational learning of new labels for established concepts, such as with the English as a Foreign Language (EFL) applications of the keyword method. Other research deals with the simultaneous learning of new concepts and new labels in content study (Balajthy & Weisberg, 1990). Still other research deals with the expanding of a general vocabulary in the wide reading of literature (Anderson, Wilson, & Fielding, 1988).

In their examination of how knowledge of the composing process and literary understanding is developed and used, Smagorinsky and Smith (1992) looked at the research in the composing process and noted that there are different perspectives from which to view research and how we know. One position is to look for general knowledge that can be applied across contexts. With respect to vocabulary instruction, this would imply faith in an assumption about a widespread applicability of a general theory about vocabulary instruction. In a sense, this has been the framework for much of the work in literacy, although summaries of research done in the fields of ESL and less able readers tend to take a more contextualized slant (Baker et al., 1995a; Huckin, Haynes, & Coady, 1993).

Smagorinsky and Smith (1992) suggested that an alternative goal for instructional research is to look for task-specific knowledge. Task-specific knowledge looks at different requirements for different instructional tasks and contexts and posits instruction relevant to that form. In terms of vocabulary instruction, this perspective may help to explain the minimal impact of research on instruction. Although research has provided us with some aspects of a general theory to help us advance in our thinking about vocabulary instruction, this general theory has not been found to be sufficiently productive for broad instructional impact or for the design of materials. We suggest, then, going beyond the general theory to a task-specific analysis of research, looking at vocabulary instruction as an adaptive process tailored for specific instructional tasks.

ADAPTIVE PROCESSES

In the following sections, we look at two specific tasks for vocabulary instruction that have been identified as critical by research on teacher needs and beliefs. Alvermann and Swafford (1989) and Swafford and Hague (1987) identified the teaching of content vocabulary as a central goal of school instruction. Teachers consistently struggle with the need to help students deal with new concepts and new vocabulary describing those concepts throughout the school year. A second critical vocabulary instruction task is making vocabulary accessible to learners of differing characteristics, such as those for whom English is not a first language (Carter & McCarthy, 1988; Maiguashca, 1993) or those who struggle with learning to read (Baker et al., 1995a).

Adapting Instruction for Content Vocabulary Learning

The Nature of the Task.   As students begin to learn vocabulary for the content areas, they are not only learning new words for familiar concepts, but they are also encountering words that are both new words and new concepts. In addition to this increase in new conceptual vocabulary learning, they face a complication in relation to what they already know, learning new meanings for familiar words used in a specialized way in a particular discipline. For example, a student may know the word *stage* in relation to a theater class but has to develop a second meaning when studying space probes to Mars and dealing with *rocket stage*.

Besides this increased load of new words, new concepts, and multiple meanings, another issue in content vocabulary learning relates to the differing instructional task. In learning vocabulary during reading instruction, students may only need a superficial knowledge of a word to read a text. For example, for the sentence, "He lay down to sleep on his pallet," the reader only needs to recognize that a pallet is some sort of bed; it is not necessary to differentiate a pallet from other types of beds. Also, it may not be important for the student to remember the meaning of pallet after reading to deal with a book or selection as a whole. The focus of this instruction is on the development of reading strategies.

In contrast, in content area instruction, specific meanings for words and concepts, and all they imply, are central to instruction. For example, it would be difficult for a student to understand a unit on light without a clear understanding, both receptive and expressive, of the term *refraction*. Further, in content learning, the terms must be remembered and are often the building blocks of later instruction. It would be difficult to deal with advanced geometry without a clear knowledge of the term *diameter*, which is taught at a much earlier level. Lastly, in content areas, students need many meanings for the same word, as the term *character* in early literature study is joined by *character development* in later study (Mallow, 1990). So, in sum, rather than dealing with vocabulary in a general manner as is done in elementary reading instruction, content vocabulary learning typically requires the learning of specific meanings, frequently of new concepts, in the context of specific units of study; requires the student to have receptive and expressive control of the key terms; and requires teaching to a level of retention (Cronbach, 1943).

These same issues emerge when one examines content vocabulary from the perspective of learner processes. In a series of studies looking at a vocabulary overview process to develop independent vocabulary learning strategies, Carr and her colleagues (Carr, 1985; Carr & Mazur-Stewart, 1988) identified the three main strategic processes students engage in when learning content vocabulary: Students need to develop independent selection strategies for identifying important words to be learned; students need to come to understand the words in the domain of study both receptively and expressively; and students need to retain the vocabulary and use it to scaffold later learning. To this, one might add the metacognitive process of evaluating one's own success in learning. These task process categories can serve as organizers for looking at the research on content vocabulary learning as well.

Students' Ability to Select Important Vocabulary for Learning.   A number of studies confirm the effect of difficult or specialized vocabulary on students' ability to identify important terms for study and the effect of this study on the comprehension of content area materials. Stahl, Jacobson, Davis, and Davis (1989) suggested that preparatory instruction of content area vocabulary, or development of prior knowledge before reading, affects the students' rating of importance of content vocabulary and associate terms. Roller (1985) found that students rated words as important when they were clearly related to a category identified by an important concept under study or were related to the students' perceived goals for study. However, work by Meyerson, Ford, Jones and Ward (1991) indicated that students asked to group vocabulary conceptually in science classes did not always group in science-related categories. This parallels earlier cited research suggesting that students working on biology study did not choose the same issues as important as did their teachers (Schellings & Van Hout-Wolters, 1995).

In further examining students' abilities to choose important vocabulary for study, Beyersdorfer (1992) found that middle-grade students working independently could use text-based cues, such as boldface and repetition of key terms, to aid in selection of vocabulary for study. However, low-achieving students relied more on prior knowledge and less on these text-based factors when selecting vocabulary for focus. She found that reading a second passage on the same topic that allowed students to cross-check their word choices increased the appropriateness of vocabulary selected for study as compared to teacher choices. Konopak's (1988a, 1988b) work with high school students also found an effect for ability as well as for text factors. Students' reading of texts revised for considerateness (proximity of vocabulary to defining terms, clarity of conceptions, explicitness, completeness) indicated that they were able to generate more accurate definitions for new terms having read revised texts. However, in relation to the metacognitive demands of self-selection and self-study, students had little awareness of when their learning was improved. Higher ability students performed better on providing both definitions and importance ratings of words for study.

As an aside, it may be important to remember that it is not only the content words of content learning that cause difficulty. Parry (1993), working with college-level ESL students, found that in content learning, vocabulary that causes difficulty was not only content words but "academic" words such as *unsubstantiated*, *crucial*, *meager*, and *repertoire*.

Viewed together, the studies just noted suggest that such scaffolds as teacher modeling of conceptual categorization and use of textual cuing along with instruction emphasizing the metacognitive aspects of self-selection and study may be necessary. These types of instruction extend to the procedural and conditional realms of word learning, rather than focusing solely on declarative knowledge of word meanings.

Students Coming to Understand the Words.   In an earlier part of this chapter, we dealt at length with research on semantic relatedness as a key for developing new conceptual vocabulary. The relating of new words to known linchpin concepts, and then extending the relationship outward, is a key type of content-area vocabulary instruction. Starting from the work of Taba (1967) and developed by Ausubel (1963) and Herber (1978), structured overviews and advance organizers provide formats for helping students organize vocabulary in relationship to the conceptual organization of a discipline (see Balajthy & Weisberg, 1990, for an excellent summary). Work with "possible sentences" (Stahl & Kapinus, 1991) suggests that more limited connections, such as those between pairs of words in a selection, can teach as well as more elaborate mapping strategies.

There are also numerous text factors that affect both the selection and learning of content vocabulary. Cuing, such as that done by typography (Waller, 1991), can aid students in identifying important vocabulary for study, and typography that signals relationships of greater or less importance is also useful (Garofalo, 1988). Konopak's (1988b) study of students' spontaneous learning of content vocabulary indicated that something as simple as underlining key concepts helps their learning and retention. The use of labels in illustrations is less clear. Levie and Lentz (1982) provided an overview of illustrations in text and indicated the lack of clarity in what we know about learning new concepts from illustrations. According to Levie and Lentz, pictures can assist the reader in determining whether or not attention should be allocated to learning a particular word. Pictures provide another set of cuing devices to help students recognize important vocabulary that should be chosen for study.

Retention and Use of Words.   The distinction between those strategies that aid students in coming to know words and in retaining them is not a clear one. A long tradition of teaching lore suggests that preteaching is essential for both vocabulary learning and retention. Further, we posited earlier in this chapter that the more students encounter and use the vocabulary they have come to understand, the better it will be retained. It is interesting to note that preteaching before reading, a widely used instructional strategy, has been subjected to very little research. That which exists suggests preteaching alone has little effect on subsequent learning of vocabulary as compared to other types of instruction (Mealey, 1990; Mealey & Konopak, 1990). Memory's work (1990) suggests that the location of instruction, before, during, or after, had little effect on the quality of definitions students produced. However, with respect to usage, Duin and Graves (1987) found teaching a set of related words to students before they write an essay in which those words might be used can improve the quality of their essays, when quality is measured on different writing scales, including one relating to use of new vocabulary.

For retention and usage, student manipulation of words in many contexts seems to be critical. We cited earlier Stahl and Vancil's study (1986), which highlights the importance of discussion in learning and retention of new vocabulary, and Stahl and Clark's work (1987), which implies that the expectation of discussion can also affect learning and retention. We cited this same finding with students who have learning difficulties, where Bos and Anders (1989) found that interactive instruction involving discussion and relating words was critical to the vocabulary retention of learning disabled students. Application studies representing teacher research also emphasize the manipulation of words in different context for learning, retention and usage. Laflamme (1997) compared a reading/writing strategy to a "study/memorize" strategy for high schoolers. His experimental students created dramatic and written situations embedding new vocabulary, engaged in activities that called on them to semantically relate words, and devised multiple ways to use words, all of which were superior to memorization and private study. The more personalization and use, the better was the retention and usage. Lansdown (1991) found similar results with middle school students. However, at issue in most of these studies is controlling for frequency of repetition.

In creating lasting links between words and meanings, besides many experiences and usages in differing situations, the creation of analogies seems to be an important tool (Tierney & Cunningham, 1984). Similarly, the creation of imagery (Smith et al., 1994) and visual elaboration are important for some learners in forming lasting links to meaning. The issue of mnemonics, discussed at length earlier in this chapter, is also significant.

Metacognitive Aspects of Word Learning.   With respect to students' control of their own learning, aside from selection strategies, it is clear, from studies of both bilingual and monolingual secondary school students, that students perceive the learning of vocabulary as a critical issue for their own learning (Alvermann et al., 1996; Jiminez, 1997). It is interesting that student at this level, according to Alvermann (Alvermann et al., 1996), prefer to identify and resolve unknown words themselves rather than have the teacher identify them and assign a method of learning. However, students are often hampered in answering the personal questions they raise about vocabulary by their inability to use the context or dictionary to answer these questions (Brady, cited in Rosenshine & Meister, 1994). So it would appear that, in developing strategies for the learning of content vocabulary, the form of instruction that may be most necessary involves teacher scaffolding and support in the selection process, in ensuring that students are engaged in active processing, and in giving instruction and feedback on using textual and outside aids to word learning.

Adapting Instruction for Students With Differing Characteristics

The Nature of the Task.   When instructing particular groups of students, teachers face the task of identifying the characteristics of the students that require adaptations of their teaching, in terms both of pedagogy and of curriculum content. In this section we examine the research in relation to two populations—ESL learners and poor readers. We are not suggesting that these populations have similar characteristics that require similar changes in instruction, nor that all poor readers or ESL learners are the same. With respect to process, Hatch and Brown (1995) enumerated five essential steps that ESL students must do to learn vocabulary (not dissimilar to the task analysis suggested above in relation to content reading). The steps are:

1. Having sources for encountering new words.
2. Getting a clear image, either visual or auditory or both, for the forms of new words.
3. Learning the meaning of the words.
4. Making a strong memory connection between the forms and meanings of the words.
5. Using the words.

An examination of the research suggests that these stages have not been isolated and examined in relation to instruction.

ESL Vocabulary Instruction.   Carter and McCarthy (1988) and Maiguashca (1993) provided historical views of the role of vocabulary teaching as part of instruction in second language learning. They noted the movement from controlled vocabulary lists in the late 1930s and 1940s, through structural approaches that emphasized the importance of teaching grammar, to the focus on a communicative approach, to a new emphasis on the teaching of vocabulary. There have been several recent books on the teaching of vocabulary to ESL learners (Carter & McCarthy, 1988; Hatch & Brown, 1995; Huckin et al., 1993; Nation, 1990; Taylor, 1990), and a series of annotated bibliographies (Meara, 1983, 1987, 1993), all of which demonstrate the renewed emphasis on the importance of vocabulary instruction in ESL.

One of the major debates in the area parallels that in first-language (L1) learning in relation to whether sufficient vocabulary can be acquired through wide reading, or whether teacher/instructor facilitation is required (Coady, 1993; Krashen, 1993; Nation, 1990). This debate on teaching word meanings occurs within the wider debate about comprehensible input (Krashen, 1982, 1989) as the most appropriate pedagogy for ESL instruction in general, and whether native-language strategies transfer to second-language learning or interfere with that learning (Bernhardt, 1991). Several studies examined and documented the contribution of L1 reading to L2 reading (Bernhardt & Kamil, 1995; Bossers, 1991; Brisbois, 1995; Carrell, 1991) and suggested that reading skills only transfer from L1 to L2 reading once a level of proficiency has been reached in L2 oral language. These studies are seen as evidence of Cummins's (1981) larger threshold and interdependence hypotheses—that although language skills will transfer, this is only possible after a threshold of L2 proficiency has been attained. As a result, Brisbois (1995) argued that L2 vocabulary knowledge is critical, particularly at the beginning levels of language study.

Nation (1990) and Coady, Magoto, Hubbard, Graney, and Mokhtari (1993) provided evidence that a second-language learner needs to know approximately 2,000 high-frequency words to understand about 85% of most text. They argued for the direct instruction of these words, and instruction in learning words from context to allow students to learn the less frequent words they need to understand text. Laufer (1992) suggested that lexical knowledge of at least 3,000 words is a better predictor of reading in L2 than a learner's general ability. However, Grabe (1991) and others cautioned that many academically oriented students need to know many of the less frequent words. Hazenburg and Hulstijn (1996) argued that a minimum of 10,000 basewords is needed for university studies. Coady (1993) pointed to the paradox that L2 learners encounter the less frequent words almost exclusively through reading and so must be able to read in order to learn these words, and yet commonly they do not know enough words to read well. In addition, as was found with lists compiled by members of the vocabulary control movement, such as West's (1936/1953) General Service List, each word form may represent several distinct meanings, and this suggests that a much larger vocabulary is in fact needed. However, most researchers appear to agree with Grabe (1991) that there needs to be a critical mass of knowledge, including word knowledge, for incidental word learning to occur. Studies of ESL word learning in context have proliferated as a result of the argument expounding incidental word learning. The volume edited by Huckin et al. (1993) contains many such examples. Taken together, these studies (Brown, 1993; Chern, 1993; Coady et al., 1993; Haynes & Baker, 1993; Huckin & Bloch, 1993; Parry 1993) suggest the importance of learning a core vocabulary in order to facilitate and supplement learning from context.

If instruction is important for developing a core vocabulary, does research suggest that certain techniques are more effective for teaching individual word meanings to ESL learners? The nature of the task is one of remembering, at least when words for familiar concepts are being learned in L2. Oxford and Crookall (1990) contrasted this with cognitive and compensation strategies, where alternative strategies for communicating are used in the context of second-language learning. First, then, techniques that help in remembering the translation are effective in these cases. Sanaoui (1995) documented the mnemonic devices that adult ESL learners actually used to learn vocabulary—writing, immediate repetition, spaced repetition, use in a sentence, contextual associations, lexical associations, talking with others, and imagery. This last device is most commonly associated with the keyword method, which is generally advocated for use in ESL instruction (Nation, 1990) and has an impressive body of research documenting its effectiveness (discussed earlier). A second suggestion was by Paribakht and Wesche (1996), who reviewed the literature on vocabulary acquisition and used it to construct a hierarchy of text-related exercise types from ESL instructional materials. This attempt to clarify which types of exercises for direct instruction are most useful in differing situations (related to the importance of the word and depth of word learning required) seems to us an important distinction that has been missing from the ESL literature. Third, various other forms of direct instruction that parallel techniques from L1 teaching have proved effective in various circumstances (James, 1996; Ossen, 1991; Mansaray, 1997; Zimmerman, 1994).

The majority of these research studies have been conducted with students who are literate in one language and learning another. There seem to be few, if any, studies of appropriate vocabulary instruction of students who are becoming literate in two languages simultaneously. There is considerable difference between becoming literate in a second language when only having oral fluency in the first language, and becoming literate in a second language when already literate in the first. Some studies, particularly in bilingual education, have begun to explore the instruction of nonnative speakers in relation to reading (Anderson & Roit, 1996; Carger, 1993; Gersten, Brengelman, & Jiminez, 1994; Perez, 1994, 1996), and often make reference to vocabulary instruction that is occurring. However, not much is known about the effectiveness of such instruction in relation to reading with this younger population, who may not yet have reached a threshold where learning from contextual reading is possible. Much more research is needed concerning the appropriate vocabulary instruction in relation to reading for these students who are becoming literate for the first time in second language.

Vocabulary Instruction for Poor Readers.   Attempting a task analysis of how poor readers learn (or don't learn) vocabulary is beyond the scope of this chapter. Clearly students who struggle with reading are at a disadvantage in terms of vocabulary learning. Their more able peers acquire knowledge of many new words through extensive reading, whereas they are more likely to experience reading material in school that is above their reading level, and that contains more words that they do not know (Pittelman et al., 1985). Not only are there more unfamiliar words, but the processing demands in such material leave little spare cognitive capacity for word learning. Research has demonstrated that these less able readers can be characterized as showing several deficiencies in relation to vocabulary knowledge and learning. Becker's review (1977) focused attention on vocabulary deficiencies as the primary cause of academic failure of disadvantaged students in Grades 3 through 12. Baker et al. (1995a), in a review of 16 primary and 7 secondary resources, noted that vocabulary knowledge differences between students is extensive, and that this gap begins early and grows during the school years. White, Graves, and Slater (1990), in their investigation of reading vocabulary size and growth in two low socioeconomic status (SES) schools and one middle SES school, demonstrated that even in first grade there were differences in the size of students vocabularies between schools, and that this difference was accentuated as students rose through the grades.

Given the nature of the problems that these readers face, what does research have to say about how best to address them? In their review, Baker et al. (1995b) argued that no one instructional method has proved better than any other, but that most interventions have proved effective in some settings. That is, some form of explicit instruction, either in specific word learning or of strategies for word learning, is generally more effective for these readers than incidental word learning from context or wide reading. Baker et al. suggested two principles for instruction: (a) Vocabulary instruction should be aligned with the depth of word knowledge required in any setting, and (b) interventions should move systematically toward ensuring that students become independent word learners. Marmolejo (1990), in a meta-analysis of 15 studies relating to specific word learning, found that direct instruction using semantic-based techniques was more effective for poor readers than instruction using definitions or definitions and context. An interesting comment from this research parallels our argument in relation to task analysis. Both papers commented on the difficulty of synthesizing results when so many different measures of word learning are used. The nature of these measures is related to the depth of word processing issue raised by Baker et al. (1995a). That is, the effectiveness of any particular method can only be evaluated in terms of the goals of the instruction and the depth of knowledge of the words in relation to those goals.

Although much of the research with poor readers fails to specify particular characteristics, most studies suggest that instruction that is effective for good readers is similarly appropriate for less able readers. One particular adaptation that shows promise is the use of computers to aid instruction. In general, computer-assisted instruction has been shown to have a differentially positive impact on the reading of students with mild disabilities (Marston, Deno, Kim, Diment, & Rogers, 1995; Montali & Lewandowski, 1996), and with learning-disabled (LD) students (MacArthur & Haynes, 1995). Reinking and Rickman (1990) found that poor readers, in particular, benefited from the highlighting of difficult words in computer-displayed stories with contextual definitions available for student access. With the clear motivational aspects of computer use for poor readers, it is surprising that there has not been more research related to the learning or word meanings, at least as a link to better comprehension.

Baker et al. (1995b) argued that teachers and researchers should be addressing how best to reduce the gap in word knowledge between good and poor readers. This is a laudable argument. In addition, if, as appears incontestable, some form of instruction is better than incidental learning for specific words, then perhaps we should be concerned with whether there is a corpus of words that would best benefit poor readers, much as ESL instruction has done. As we read the research just outlined, it became clear that further research into particular instructional techniques or strategies for students of differing characteristics seems redundant until issues of specificity of instruction, and how it plays out in classroom contexts, are addressed.

CONCLUSION

The issue of vocabulary instruction in the classroom has been a slippery one because it has both a simple and complex nature. On one side is the fact that all teachers are teachers of vocabulary. In each classroom, in every discipline, teachers struggle to put forth new concepts, new terms, or new uses for familiar terms. This has led teachers and researchers to look for the "one way," the "best way" to teach vocabulary, a quest that has teased and confused us since the work of Petty and his colleagues. On the other side is the realization that each discipline is different and that we teach vocabulary for many different purposes to students of increasing diversity. This reminds us that what may seem simple and universal is really multifaceted and bound by many differing teaching and learning contexts.

These realizations imply that teachers need to be knowledgeable about what they want students to know with respect to both the depth and breadth of learning and the kinds of connections to be made. Also, they must take into account the students' starting points. What do they already know that can help make the connection to new learning? What might conflict or confuse them? Teaching vocabulary becomes not a simple process of teaching words but one of teaching particular words to particular students for a particular purpose.

In this chapter, we have attempted to identify characteristics of shared knowledge resulting from the past few decades of intense concern with vocabulary development and instruction. We then attempted to look at the translation of that research into classroom instruction and materials design. This caused us to propose a more contextualized analysis and chunking of the research based on classroom tasks that teachers have identified as connected with vocabulary learning. We looked at two situations: the teaching of content-area vocabulary, and teaching students of differing characteristics. We can envision, and hope to see, many further analyses and clusterings of research on specific word learning tasks, perhaps making finer distinctions for differing contexts and students. This also suggests that future research must find more sensitive and detailed ways to examine the processes of word learning in the classroom and how learners take advantage of both instruction and of multiple contextual exposures.

Lastly, we would like to propose an anarchic direction for future analyses of instruction. In this diverse approach to vocabulary research we would like to see the lens of research both narrowed by having task- and variable-specific meta-analyses of research and research agendas, and broadened by beginning to research the procedural and conditional aspects of vocabulary instruction and learning. We envision not an elaboration of a single general theory but an explosion of a multiplicity of theories to match varying instructional contexts, so that the richness of research will reflect the complexity of the classrooms in which instruction takes place.

ACKNOWLEDGMENTS

Thanks to Susan Watts, Candace Boss, and Isabel Cavour for their helpful comments on this chapter.

REFERENCES

Alexander, P. A., Schallert, D. L., & Hare, V. C. (1991). Coming to terms: How researchers in learning and literacy talk about knowledge. *Review of Educational Research, 61,* 315–343.

Alvermann, D. E., Young, J. P., Weaver, D., Hinchman, K. A., Moore, D. W., Phelps, S. F., Thrash, E. C., & Zalewski, P. (1996). Middle and high school students' perceptions of how they experience text-based discussions: A multicase study. *Reading Research Quarterly, 31*, 244–267.

Alvermann, D. E., & Swafford, J. (1989). Do content area strategies have a research base? *Journal of Reading, 32*, 388–394.

Anders, P. L., & Gallego, M. A. (1989). Adoption of theoretically-linked vocabulary-reading comprehension practices. In S. McCormick & J. Zutell (Eds.), *Cognitive and social perspectives for literacy research and instruction: Thirty-eighth yearbook of the National Reading Conference* (pp.481–487). Chicago, IL: National Reading Conferences.

Anderson, R. C., & Nagy, W. E. (1991). Word meanings. In R. Barr, M. L. Kamil, P. B. Mosenthal, & P. D. Pearson (Eds.), *Handbook of reading research*, (Vol. II, pp. 690–724). New York: Longman.

Anderson, R. C., Wilson, P., & Fielding, L. (1988). Growth in reading and how children spend their time outside of school. *Reading Research Quarterly, 23*, 285–303.

Anderson, V., & Roit, M. (1996). Linking reading comprehension instruction to language development for language-minority students. *Elementary School Journal, 96*, 295–309.

Ausubel, D. P. (1963). *The psychology of meaningful verbal learning*. New York: Grune and Stratton.

Baker, S. K., Simmons, D. C., & Kameenui, E. J. (1995a). *Vocabulary acquisition: Synthesis of the research* (Tech. Rep. No. 13). National Center to Improve the Tools of Educators, University of Oregon, Eugene, OR.

Baker, S. K., Simmons, D. C., & Kameenui, E. J. (1995b). *Vocabulary acquisition: Curricular and instructional implications for diverse learners* (Tech. Rep. No. 14). National Center to Improve the Tools of Educators, University of Oregon, Eugene, OR.

Balajthy, E., & Weisberg, R. (1990). Transfer effects of prior knowledge and use of graphic organizers on college developmental readers' summarization and comprehension of expository text. In J. Zutell & S. McCormick (Eds.), *Literacy theory and research: Analyses from multiple paradigms: Thirty-ninth yearbook of the National Reading Conference* (pp. 339–346). Chicago: National Reading Conference.

Baldwin, R. S., & Schatz, E. I. (1985). Context clues are ineffective with low frequency words in naturally occurring prose. In J. A. Niles & R. V. Lalik (Eds.), *Issues in literacy: A research perspective: Thirty-fourth yearbook of the National Reading Conference* (pp. 132–135). Rochester, NY: National Reading Conference.

Barr, R., & Dreeben, R. (1983). *How schools work*. Chicago: University of Chicago Press.

Barr, R., Kamil, M. L., Mosenthal, P. B., & Pearson, P. D. (Eds.). (1991). *Handbook of reading research* (Vol. II). New York: Longman.

Baumann, J. F., & Kameenui, E. J. (1991). Research on vocabulary instruction: Ode to Voltaire. In J. Flood, J. M. Jensen, D. Lapp, & J. R. Squire (Eds.), *Handbook of research on teaching the English language arts* (pp. 604–632). New York: Macmillan.

Beals, D. E., & De Temple, J. M. (1993) Home contributions to early language and literacy development. In D. J. Leu & C. K. Kinzer (Eds.), *Examining central issues in literacy research, theory, and practice: Forty-second yearbook of the National Reading Conference* (pp. 207–215). Chicago, IL: National Reading Conference.

Beck, I. L., McCaslin, E. S., & McKeown, M. G. (1980). *The rationale and design of a program to teach vocabulary to fourth-grade students* (LRDC Publication 1980/25). Pittsburgh: University of Pittsburgh Learning Research and Development Center.

Beck, I. L., & McKeown, M.G. (1983). Learning words well—A program to enhance vocabulary and comprehension. *Reading Teacher, 36*, 622–625.

Beck, I. L., & McKeown, M. G. (1991). Conditions of vocabulary acquisition. In R. Barr, M. L. Kamil, P. B. Mosenthal, & P. D. Pearson (Eds.), *Handbook of reading research* (Vol. II, pp. 789–814). New York: Longman.

Becker, W. C. (1977). Teaching reading and language to the disadvantaged—What we have learned from field research. *Harvard Educational Review, 47*, 518–543.

Bernhardt, E. B. (1991). *Reading development in a second language: Theoretical, empirical and classroom perspectives*. Norwood, NJ: Ablex.

Bernhardt, E. B., & Kamil, M. L. (1995). Interpreting relationships between L1 and L2 reading: Consolidating the linguistic threshold and the linguistic interdependence hypotheses. *Applied Linguistics, 16*, 15–34.

Betts, E. A. (1946). *Foundations of reading instruction*. New York: American Books.

Beyersdorfer, J. M. (1991). *Middle school students' strategies for selection of vocabulary in science texts*. Unpublished doctoral dissertation, National-Louis University, Evanston, IL.

Blachowicz, C. L. Z. (1987). Vocabulary instruction: What goes on in the classroom? *Reading Teacher, 41*, 132–137.

Blachowicz, C., & Fisher, P. (1996). *Teaching vocabulary in all classrooms*. Columbus, OH: Prentice Hall.

Blachowicz, C. L. Z., Fisher, P. J. L., Costa, M., & Pozzi, M. (1993). *Researching vocabulary learning in middle school cooperative reading groups: A teacher-researcher collaboration*. Paper presented at the Tenth Great Lakes Regional Reading Conference, Chicago.

Blanton, W. E., & Moorman, G. B. (1990). The presentation of reading lessons. *Reading Research and Instruction, 29*(3), 35–55.

Bomkamp, E. M. (1995). Analyzing theories and practices of vocabulary instruction in elementary schools (Doctoral dissertation, Boston University, 1995). *Dissertation Abstracts International, 56*, 04A.

Bos, C. S., & Anders, P. L. (1989). *The effectiveness of interactive instructional practices on content area reading comprehension*. Office of Special Education and Rehabilitation Services. (ERIC Document Reproduction Service No. ED 329 935)

Bos, C. S., & Anders, P. L. (1990). Effects of interactive vocabulary instruction on the vocabulary learning and reading comprehension of junior-high learning disabled students. *Learning Disability Quarterly, 13,* 31–42.

Bos, C. S., & Anders, P. L. (1992). Using interactive teaching and learning strategies to promote text comprehension and content learning for students with learning disabilities. *International Journal of Disability, Development and Education, 39,* 225–238.

Bossers, B. (1991). On thresholds, ceilings and short circuits: The relation between L1 reading, L2 reading, and L1 knowledge. In J. Hulstijn & J. Metter (Eds.), *AILA Review, 8,* 45–60.

Brett, A., Rothlein, L., & Hurley, M. (1996). Vocabulary acquisition from listening to stories and explanations of target words. *Elementary School Journal, 96,* 415–422.

Brisbois, J. E. (1995). Connections between first- and second-language reading. *Journal of Reading Behavior, 27,* 565–584.

Brown, C. (1993). Factors affecting the acquisition of vocabulary: Frequency and saliency of words. In T. Huckin, M. Haynes, & J. Coady (Eds.), *Second language reading and vocabulary learning* (pp. 263–286). Norwood, NJ: Ablex.

Buikema, J. L., & Graves, M.F. (1993). Teaching students to use context clues to infer word meanings. *Journal of Reading, 36,* 450–457.

Calfee, R., & Drum, P. (1978). Learning to read: Theory, research and practice. *Curriculum Inquiry, 8,* 183–294.

Calfee, R., & Drum, P. (1986). Research on teaching reading. In M.C. Wittrock (Ed.), *Handbook of research on teaching* (3rd ed., pp. 804–849). New York: Macmillan.

Carger, C. L. (1993). Louie comes to life: Pretend reading with second language emergent readers. *Language Arts, 70,* 542–547.

Carr, E. M. (1985). The vocabulary overview guide: A metacognitive strategy to improve vocabulary comprehension and retention. *Journal of Reading, 28,* 684–689.

Carr, E. M. & Mazur-Stewart, M. (1988). The effects of the vocabulary overview guide on vocabulary comprehension and retention. *Journal of Reading Behavior, 20,* 43–62.

Carrell, P. L. (1991). Second language reading: Reading ability or language proficiency? *Applied Linguistics, 12,* 159–179.

Carter, R., & McCarthy, M. (1988). *Vocabulary and language teaching.* New York: Longman.

Carver, R. P. (1994). Percentage of unknown vocabulary words in text as a function of the relative difficulty of the text: Implications for instruction. *Journal of Reading Behavior, 26,* 413–437.

Chern, C. L. (1993). Chinese students' word-solving strategies in reading English. In T. Huckin, M. Haynes, & J. Coady (Eds.), *Second language reading and vocabulary learning* (pp. 67–85). Norwood, NJ: Ablex.

Coady, J. (1993). Research on ESL/EFL vocabulary acquisition: Putting it in context. In T. Huckin, M. Haynes, & J. Coady (Eds.), *Second language reading and vocabulary learning* (pp. 3–23). Norwood, NJ: Ablex.

Coady, J., Magoto, J., Hubbard, P., Graney, J., & Mokhtari, K. (1993). High frequency vocabulary and reading proficiency in ESL readers. In T. Huckin, M. Haynes, & J. Coady (Eds.), *Second language reading and vocabulary learning* (pp. 217–228). Norwood, NJ: Ablex.

Cronbach, L. J. (1943). Measuring knowledge of precise word meaning. *Journal of Educational Research, 36,* 528–534.

Cummins, J. (1981). *Bilingualism and minority-language children: Language and literacy series.* Toronto: Ontario Institute for Studies in Education. (ERIC Document Reproduction Service No. ED 215 557).

Cunningham, A. E., & Stanovich, K. E. (1998). What reading does for the mind. *American Educator, 22*(1 & 2) 8–15.

Dale, E., & O'Rourke, J. P. (1976). *The living word vocabulary.* Chicago: Field Enterprises.

Dale, E., Razik, T., & Petty, W. (1973). *Bibliography of vocabulary studies.* Columbus, OH: Ohio State University.

Dole, J. A., Sloan, C., & Trathen, W. (1995). Teaching vocabulary within the context of literature. *Journal of Reading, 38,* 452–460.

Duffelmeyer, F. A. (1980). The influence of experience-based vocabulary instruction on learning word meanings. *Journal of Reading, 24,* 35–40.

Duin, A. H., & Graves, M. F. (1987). Intensive vocabulary instruction as a prewriting technique. *Reading Research Quarterly, 22,* 311–330.

Durkin, D. D. (1978–1979). What classroom observations reveal about reading comprehension instruction. *Reading Research Quarterly, 14,* 481–533.

Durso, F. T., & Coggins, K. A. (1991). Organized instruction for the improvement of word knowledge skills. *Journal of Educational Psychology, 83,* 108–112.

Eller, G., Pappas, C. C., & Brown, E. (1988). The lexical development of kindergartners: Learning from written context. *Journal of Reading Behavior, 20,* 5–24.

Elley, W. B. (1988). Vocabulary acquisition from listening to stories. *Reading Research Quarterly, 24,* 174–187.

Finesilver, M. (1994). *An investigation of three methods to improve vocabulary learning at the middle school level.* Unpublished doctoral dissertation, National-Louis University, Evanston, IL.

Fisher, P. J. L., Blachowicz, C. L. Z., & Smith, J. C. (1991). Vocabulary learning in literature discussion groups. In J. Zutell & S. McCormick (Eds.), *Learner factors/teacher factors: Issues in literacy research and instruction: Fortieth yearbook of the National Reading Conference* pp. 201–209). Chicago: National Reading Conference.

Fisher, P. J. L., & Danielsen, D. (1998). When fourth-graders select their own words for spelling and vocabu-lary. In L. Wedwick & R. K. Moss (Eds.), *Conversations: Teacher research in literacy learning* (pp. 23–27). Bloomington: Illinois Reading Council.

Friedland, E. S. (1992). The effect of context instruction on the vocabulary acquisition of college students (Doctoral dissertation, State University of New York at Buffalo, 1992). *Dissertation Abstracts International, 53,* 11A.

Garofalo, K. M. (1988). Typographic cues as an aid to learning from textbooks. *Visible Language, 22,* 273–297.

Gates, A. I. (1962). The word recognition ability and the reading vocabulary of second and third grade chil-dren. *Reading Teacher, 15,* 443–448.

Gersten, R., Brengelman, S., & Jiminez, R. (1994). Effective instruction for culturally and linguistically di-verse students: A reconceptualization. *Focus on Exceptional Children, 27,* 1–16.

Gifford, A. P. (1993). An investigation of the effects of direct instruction in contextual clues on developmental reading students' ability to increase vocabulary and reading comprehension scores. (Doctoral disserta-tion, Southern Illinois University at Carbondale, IL, 1993). *Dissertation Abstracts International, 54,* 08A.

Gipe, J. P. (1979–1980). Investigating techniques for teaching word meanings. *Reading Research Quarterly, 14,* 624–645.

Grabe, W. (1991). Current developments in second language reading research. *TESOL Quarterly, 25,* 375–406.

Graves, M. F. (1986). Vocabulary learning and instruction. In E. Z. Rothkopf (Ed.), *Review of research in educa-tion* (Vol. 13, pp. 49–89). Washington, DC: American Educational Research Association.

Guzzetti, B. J., Snyder, T. E., Glass, G. V., & Gamas, W. S. (1993). Promoting conceptual change in science: A comparative meta-analysis of instructional interventions from reading education and science education. *Reading Research Quarterly, 28,* 116–159.

Haggard, M. R. (1982). The vocabulary self-selection strategy: An active approach to word learning. *Journal of Reading, 26,* 634–642.

Haggard, M. R. (1985). An interactive strategies approach to content reading. *Journal of Reading, 29,* 204–210.

Hatch, E., & Brown, C.(1995). *Vocabulary, semantics, and language education.* Cambridge, England: Cambridge University Press.

Haynes, M., & Baker, I. (1993). American and Chinese readers learning from lexical familiarization in Eng-lish text. In T. Huckin, M. Haynes, & J. Coady (Eds.), *Second language reading and vocabulary learning* (pp. 130–152). Norwood, NJ: Ablex.

Hazenburg, S., & Hulstijn, J. H. (1996). Defining a minimal receptive second-language vocabulary for non-native university students: An empirical investigation. *Applied Linguistics, 17,* 145–163.

Heimlich, J. E., & Pittelman, S. D. (1986). *Semantic mapping: Classroom applications.* Newark, DE: International Reading Association.

Herber, H. (1978). *Teaching reading in the content areas.* Englewood Cliffs, NJ: Prentice Hall.

Huckin, T., & Bloch, J. (1993). Strategies for inferring word-meanings in context: A cognitive model. In T. Huckin, M. Haynes, & J. Coady (Eds.), *Second language reading and vocabulary learning* (pp. 153–178). Norwood, NJ: Ablex.

Huckin, T., Haynes, M., & Coady, J. (Eds.). (1993). *Second language reading and vocabulary learning.* Norwood, NJ: Ablex.

Irvin, J. L. (1990). *Vocabulary knowledge: Guidelines for instruction.* Washington, DC: National Education Asso-ciation.

James, M. O. (1996). Improving second language reading comprehension: A computer assisted vocabulary development approach (Doctoral dissertation, University of Hawaii, Honolulu, 1996). *Dissertation Ab-stracts International, 57,* 05A.

Jenkins, J. R., & Dixon, R. (1983). Learning vocabulary. *Contemporary Educational Psychology, 8,* 237–260.

Jenkins, J. R., Stein, M. L., & Wysocki, K. (1984). Learning vocabulary through reading. *American Educational Research Journal, 21,* 767–787.

Jiminez, R. J. (1997). The strategic reading abilities and potential of five low-literacy Latina/o readers in mid-dle school. *Reading Research Quarterly, 32,* 224–243.

Johnson, D. D. & Pearson, P. D. (1984). *Teaching reading vocabulary* (2nd ed.). New York: Holt, Rinehart and Winston.

Johnson, D. D., Pittelman, S. D., Toms-Bronowski, S., & Levin, K. M. (1984). *An investigation of the effects of prior knowledge and vocabulary acquisition on passage comprehension* (Program Rep. No. 84-5). Madison: Wis-consin Center for Education Research, University of Wisconsin.

Johnson, D. D., Toms-Bronowski, S., & Pittelman, S. D. (1982). *An investigation of the effectiveness of semantic mapping and semantic feature analysis with intermediate grade level students* (Program Rep. No. 83-3). Madi-son: Wisconsin Center for Education Research, University of Wisconsin.

Kameenui, E. J., Carnine, D. W., & Freschi, R. (1982). Effects of text construction and instructional procedures for teaching word meanings on comprehension and recall. *Reading Research Quarterly, 17,* 367–388.

Konopak, B. C. (1988a). Effects of inconsiderate vs. considerate text on secondary students' vocabulary learning. *Journal of Reading Behavior, 20,* 25–41.

Konopak, B. C. (1988b). Eighth graders' vocabulary learning from inconsiderate and considerate text. *Read-ing Research and Instruction, 27,* 1–14.

Konopak, B., & Williams, N. L. (1994). Elementary teachers' beliefs and decisions about vocabulary learning and instruction. In C. K. Kinzer & D. J. Leu (Eds.), *Multidimensional aspects of literacy research, theory and practice: Forty-third yearbook of the National Reading Conference* (pp. 485–495). Chicago: National Reading Conference.

Krashen, S. (1982). *Principles and practice in second language learning.* Englewood Cliffs, NJ: Prentice Hall.

Krashen, S. (1989). We acquire vocabulary and spelling by reading: Additional evidence for the input hypothesis. *Modern Language Journal, 73,* 440–464.

Krashen, S. (1993). *The power of reading.* Englewood, CO: Libraries Unlimited.

Laflamme, J. G. (1997). The effect of the multiple exposure vocabulary method and the target reading/writing strategy on test scores. *Journal of Adolescent & Adult Literacy, 40,* 372–381.

Lansdown, S. H. (1991). Improving vocabulary knowledge using direct instruction, cooperative grouping, and reading in the junior high. *Illinois Reading Council Journal, 19*(4), 15–21.

Laufer, B. (1992). Reading in a foreign language: How does L2 lexical knowledge interact with the reader's general academic ability. *Journal of Research in Reading, 15,* 95–103.

Levie, W. H., & Lentz, R. (1982). Effects of text illustrations: A review of research. *Educational Communication and Technology, 30,* 195–232.

Levin, J. R. (1993). Mnemonic strategies and classroom learning: A twenty-year report card. *Elementary School Journal, 94,* 235–244.

Levin, J. R., Levin, M. E., Glasman, L. D. & Nordwall, M. B. (1992). Mnemonic vocabulary instruction: Additional effectiveness evidence. *Contemporary Educational Psychology, 17,* 156–174.

Lloyd, C. V. (1995–1996). How teachers teach reading comprehension: An examination of four categories of reading comprehension instruction. *Reading Research and Instruction, 35,* 171–185.

MacArthur, C. A., & Haynes, J. B. (1995). Student assistant for learning from text (SALT): A hypermedia reading aid. *Journal of Learning Disabilities, 28,* 150–159.

MacKinnon, J.. (1993). A comparison of three schema-based methods of vocabulary instruction (Doctoral dissertation, The Florida State University, Gainesville, 1993). *Dissertation Abstracts International, 54,* 07A.

Maiguashca, R. U. (1993). Teaching and learning vocabulary in a second language: Past, present, and future directions. *Canadian Modern Language Review, 50,* 83–99.

Mallow, J. V. (1991). Reading science. *Journal of Reading, 34,* 324–338.

Mansaray, H. A. (1997). The effects of vocabulary instruction on English-as-a-second-language and bilingual learners (Doctoral dissertation, Boston University, 1997). *Dissertation Abstracts International, 58,* 03A.

Marmolejo, A. (1990). The effects of vocabulary instruction with poor readers: A meta-analysis (Doctoral dissertation, Teachers College, Columbia University, New York, 1990). *Dissertation Abstracts International, 51,* 03A.

Marston, D., Deno, S. L., Kim, D., Diment, K., & Rogers, D. (1995). Comparison of reading intervention approaches for students with mild disabilities. *Exceptional Children, 62,* 20–37.

McCarville, K. B. (1993). Keyword mnemonic and vocabulary acquisition for developmental college students. *Journal of Developmental Education, 16*(3), 2–4, 6.

McKeown, M. G. (1985). The acquisition of word meaning from context by children of high and low ability. *Reading Research Quarterly, 20,* 482–496.

McKeown, M. G., & Curtis, M. E. (Eds.). (1987). *The nature of vocabulary acquisition.* Hillsdale, NJ: Lawrence Erlbaum Associates.

Mealey, D. L. (1990). An analysis of the value of preteaching content area vocabulary to college developmental readers. *Forum for Reading, 22*(1), 24–30.

Mealey, D., & Konopak, B. (1990). Content area vocabulary instruction: Is preteaching worth the effort? *Reading: Exploration and Discovery, 13*(1), 39–42.

Meara, P. (1983). *Vocabulary in a second language.* London: Center for Information on Language Teaching.

Meara, P. (1987). *Vocabulary in a second language* (Vol. 2). London: Center for Information on Language Teaching.

Meara, P. (1993). Vocabulary in a second language (Vol. 3) [Special issue]. *Reading in a Foreign Language, 9.*

Memory, D. M. (1990). Teaching technical vocabulary: Before, during, or after the reading assignment. *Journal of Reading Behavior, 22,* 39–53.

Mezynski, K. (1983). Issues concerning the acquisition of knowledge: Effects of vocabulary training and reading comprehension. *Review of Educational Research, 53,* 263–279.

Meyerson, M. J., Ford, M. S., Jones, W. P., & Ward, M. A. (1991). Science vocabulary knowledge of third and fifth grade students. *Science Education, 75,* 419–428.

Montali, J., & Lewandowski, L. (1996). Bimodal reading: Benefits of a talking computer for average and less skilled readers. *Journal of Learning Disabilities, 29,* 271–279.

Nagy, W. E. (1988). *Teaching vocabulary to improve reading comprehension.* Newark, DE: International Reading Association.

Nagy, W. E., Herman, P. A., & Anderson, R. C. (1985). Learning words from context. *Reading Research Quarterly, 20,* 233–253.

Nation, I. S. P. (1990). *Teaching and learning vocabulary.* Boston: Heinle & Heinle.

National Assessment of Educational Progress. (1990). *The reading report card: Trends from the nation's report card, 1971–1988* (Rep. No. 19-R-01). Princeton, NJ: Education Testing Service.

Nist, S. L., & Olejnik, S. (1995). The role of context and dictionary definitions on varying levels of word knowledge. *Reading Research Quarterly, 30,* 172–193.

Ossen, V. M. (1991). An examination of the effects of semantic mapping for improving vocabulary recognition and comprehension of scientific concepts for English and Spanish-speaking elementary school students (Doctoral dissertation, University of Lowell, Lowell, MA, 1991). *Dissertation Abstracts International, 51*, 12A.

Oxford, R., & Crookall, D. (1990). Vocabulary learning: A critical analysis of techniques. *TESL Canada Journal, 7*(2), 9–30.

Pany, D., & Jenkins, J. R. (1978). Learning word meanings: A comparison of instructional procedures and effects on measures of reading comprehension with learning disabled students. *Learning Disability Quarterly, 1*, 21–32.

Paribakht, T. S., & Wesche, M. (1996). Enhancing vocabulary acquisition through reading; A hierarchy of text-related exercise types. *Canadian Modern Language Review, 52*, 155–178.

Parry, K. (1991). Building a vocabulary through academic reading. *TESOL Quarterly, 25*, 629–653.

Parry, K. (1993). Too many words: Learning the vocabulary of an academic subject. In T. Huckin, M. Haynes, & J. Coady (Eds.), *Second language reading and vocabulary learning* (pp. 109–129). Norwood, NJ: Ablex.

Pearson, P. D. (Ed.). (1984). *Handbook of reading research.* New York: Longman.

Perez, B. (1994). Spanish literacy development: A descriptive study of four bilingual whole-language classrooms. *Journal of Reading Behavior, 26*, 75–94.

Perez, B. (1996). Instructional conversations as opportunities for English language acquisition for culturally and linguistically diverse students. *Language Arts, 73*, 173–181.

Petty, W., Herold, C., & Stoll, E. (1967). *The state of the knowledge about the teaching of vocabulary* (Cooperative Research Project No. 3128). Champaign, IL: National Council of Teachers of English. (ERIC Document Reproduction Service No. ED 012 395)

Pittelman, S. D., Heimlich, J. E., Berglund, R. L., & French, M. P. (1991). *Semantic feature analysis: Classroom applications.* Newark, DE: International Reading Association.

Pittelman, S. D., Levin, K. M., & Johnson, D. D. (1985). *An investigation of two instructional settings in the use of semantic mapping with poor readers* (Program Rep. No. 85-4). Madison: Wisconsin Center for Educational Research, University of Wisconsin.

Pressley, M., Levin, J. R., & Delaney, H. D. (1982). The mnemonic keyword method. *Review of Educational Research, 52*, 6–91.

Pressley, M., Levin, J. R., & McDaniel, M. A. (1987). Remembering versus inferring what a word means: Mnemonic and contextual approaches. In M. G. McKeown & M. E. Curtis (Eds.), *The nature of vocabulary acquisition* (pp. 107–127). Hillside, NJ: Lawrence Erlbaum Associates.

Reinking, D., & Rickman, S. S. (1990). The effects of computer-mediated texts on the vocabulary learning and comprehension of intermediate-grade readers. *Journal of Reading Behavior, 22*, 395–411.

Roller, C. M. (1985). The effects of reader- and text-based factors on writers' and readers' perceptions of the importance of information in expository prose. *Reading Research Quarterly, 20*, 437–457.

Rosenshine, B., & Meister, C. (1994). Reciprocal teaching: A review of the research. *Review of Educational Research, 64*, 478–530.

Ruddell, M. R. (1994). Vocabulary knowledge and comprehension: A comprehension-process view of complex literacy relationships. In R. B. Ruddell, M. R. Ruddell, & H. Singer (Eds.), *Theoretical models and processes of reading* (4th ed., pp. 414–447). Newark, DE: International Reading Association.

Ryder, R. J., & Slater, W. H. (1988). The relationship between word frequency and word knowledge. *Journal of Educational Research, 81*, 312–317.

Ryder, R. J., & Graves, M. F. (1994). Vocabulary instruction presented prior to reading in two basal readers. *Elementary School Journal, 95*, 139–153.

Sable, P. H. (1992). Vocabulary instruction in fourth and fifth grades: What teachers say they do (Doctoral dissertation, Harvard University, Boston, 1992). *Dissertation Abstracts International, 53*, 06A.

Sanaoui, R. (1995). Adult learners' approaches to learning vocabulary in a second language. *Modern Language Journal, 79*, 15–28.

Schellings, G. L. M., & Van Hout-Wolters, B. H. A. M. (1995). Main points in an instructional text as identified by students and by their teachers. *Reading Research Quarterly, 30*, 742–755.

Schatz, E. I., & Baldwin, R. S. (1986). Context clues are unreliable predictors of word meanings. *Reading Research Quarterly, 21*, 439–453.

Schewel, R. (1989). Semantic mapping: A study skills strategy. *Academic Therapy, 24*, 439–447.

Schwartz, R. M. & Raphael, T. E. (1985). Concept of definition: A key to improving students' vocabulary. *Reading Teacher, 39*, 198–205.

Scott, J. A., Asselin, M., Henry, S. K., & Butler, C. E. (1997). *Making rich language visible: Reports from a multi-dimensional study on word learning.* Paper presented at 1997 CSSE Meeting in Newfoundland, Canada.

Scott, J. A., & Butler, C. E. (1994a). *Patterns in language arts instruction: A survey of intermediate teachers.* Paper presented at the annual meeting of the Canadian Society for the Study of Education, Calgary, Canada.

Scott, J. A., & Butler, C. E. (1994b). *Language arts in the 1990s: A survey of general practices with an emphasis on the teaching of vocabulary in literature-based classrooms.* Paper presented at the annual meeting of the American Educational Research Association, New Orleans, LA.

Scott, J. A., Butler, C. E., Asselin, M. M., & Henry, S. K. (1996). *The effect of mediated assistance in word learning.* Paper presented at the annual meeting of the National Reading Conference, Charleston, SC.

Senechal, M., & Cornell, E. H. (1993). Vocabulary acquisition through shared reading experiences. *Reading Research Quarterly, 28*, 361–374.

Shu, H., Anderson, R. C., & Zhang, H. (1995). Incidental word learning of word meanings while reading: A Chinese and American cross-cultural study. *Reading Research Quarterly, 30*, 79–95.

Smagorinsky, P., & Smith, M. W. (1992). The nature of knowledge in composition and literary understanding: The question of specificity. *Review of Educational Research, 62*, 279–305.

Smith, B. D., Miller, C., Grossman, F., & Valeri-Gold, M. (1994). Vocabulary retention: Effects of using spatial imaging on hemispheric-preference thinkers. *Journal of Research and Development in Education, 27*, 244–252.

Snow, C. (1991). The theoretical basis of the Home-School Study of language and literacy development. *Journal of Research in Childhood Education, 6*, 5–10.

Stahl, S. (1983). Differential knowledge and reading comprehension. *Journal of Reading Behavior, 15*, 33–50.

Stahl, S. A. (1986). Three principles of effective vocabulary instruction. *Journal of Reading, 29*, 662–668.

Stahl, S. A., Burdge, J. L., Machuga, M. B., & Stecyk, S. (1992). The effects of semantic grouping on learning word meanings. *Reading Psychology, 13*, 19–35.

Stahl, S. A., & Clark, C. H. (1987). The effects of participatory expectations in classroom discussion on the learning of science vocabulary. *Reading Research and Instruction, 2*, 12–27.

Stahl, S. A., & Fairbanks, M. M. (1986). The effects of vocabulary instruction: A model-based meta-analysis. *Review of Educational Research, 56*, 72–110.

Stahl, S. A., Jacobson, M. G., Davis, C. E., & Davis, R. L. (1989). Prior knowledge and difficult vocabulary in the comprehension of unfamiliar text. *Reading Research Quarterly, 24*, 27–43.

Stahl, S. A., & Kapinus, B. A. (1991). Possible sentences: Predicting word meanings to teach content area vocabulary. *Reading Teacher, 45*, 36–43.

Stahl, S. A., Richek, M. A., & Vandevier, R. J. (1991). Learning meaning vocabulary through listening: A sixth-grade replication. In J. Zutell & S. McCormick (Eds.), *Learner factors/teacher factors: Issues in literacy research and instruction: Fortieth yearbook of the National Reading Conference* (pp. 185–192). Chicago: National Reading Conference

Stahl, S. & Vancil, S. (1986). Discussion is what makes semantic maps work in vocabulary instruction. *Reading Teacher, 40*, 62–69.

Stallman, A. C., Commeyras, M., Kerr, B., Reimer, K., Himenez, R., Hartman, D. K., & Pearson, P. D. (1990). Are "new" words really new? *Reading Research and Instruction, 29*(2), 12–29.

Stanley, P. D., & Ginther, D. W. (1991). The effects of purpose and frequency on vocabulary learning from written context of high and low ability reading comprehenders. *Reading Research and Instruction, 30*(4), 31–41.

Swafford, J., & Hague, S. (1987, October). *Content area reading strategies: Myth or reality?* Paper presented at the annual meeting of the College Reading Association, Baltimore, MD.

Taba, H. (1967). *Teachers' handbook for elementary social studies.* Reading, MA: Addison-Wesley.

Taylor, L. (1990). *Teaching and learning vocabulary.* New York: Prentice Hall.

Tierney, R. J., & Cunningham, J. W. (1991). Research on teaching reading comprehension. In R. Barr, M. L. Kamil, P. B. Mosenthal, & P. D. Pearson (Eds.), *Handbook of reading research* (Vol. 2, pp. 609–656). New York: Longman.

Waller, R. (1991). Typography and discourse. In R. Barr, M. L. Kamil, P. B. Mosenthal, & P. D. Pearson (Eds.), *Handbook of reading research* (Vol. 2, pp. 341–380). New York: Longman.

Watts, S. M. (1995). Vocabulary instruction during reading lessons in six classrooms. *Journal of Reading Behavior, 27*, 399–424.

White, T. G., Graves, M. F., & Slater, W. H. (1990). Growth of reading vocabulary in diverse elementary schools: Decoding and word meaning. *Journal of Educational Psychology, 82*, 281–290.

West, M. (1953). *A general service list of English words.* London: Longman. (Original work published 1936).

Wittrock, M. C., Marks, C. B., & Doctorow, M. J. (1975). Reading as a generative process. *Journal of Educational Psychology, 67*, 484–489.

Zechmeister, E. B., Chronis, A. M., Cull, W. L., D'Anna, C. A., & Healy, N. A. (1995). Growth of a functionally important lexicon. *Journal of Reading Behavior, 27*, 201–312.

Zimmerman, C. B. (1994). Self-selected reading and interactive vocabulary instruction: Knowledge and perceptions of word learning among L2 students (Doctoral dissertation, University of Southern California, San Diego, 1994). *Dissertation Abstracts International, 56*, 09A.

CHAPTER 29

Spelling

Shane Templeton
University of Nevada, Reno

Darrell Morris
Appalachian State University

Georgia Alexander, author of an elementary spelling text published in 1906, lamented how "We hammer at the child's brain as though it were so much cold steel, in the belief that if we hammer hard enough and long enough, some impression must be made" (p. v). Her observation reflected the widespread belief that English spelling is at best an imperfect attempt to represent sounds thus requiring pedagogical enforcement through brute memorization. The roots of this perception run deep historically. Spelling, the nature of the system and the nurture of its acquisition, has received considerable attention literally for centuries. The ways in which *spelling* has been conceptualized have evolved dramatically over the last few decades, from considering spelling as a tool for writing to recognizing that the ability to spell yields insight into the nature of individuals' lexicons. Similarly, the development of spelling knowledge has begun to be conceptualized as a process of *conceptual* learning rather than as a process of rote memorization. The field may now be at a more promising juncture at which both traditional and contemporary insights with respect to spelling may be merged. In reviewing the significant research and trends in spelling, the primary goal of this chapter is to attempt this synthesis. Although this possibility applies in the case of a number of written languages (e.g., Perfetti, Rieben, & Fayol, 1997), the present chapter focuses primarily on English.

In the attempt to provide a synthesis of traditional and contemporary insights, this chapter addresses the following: the nature of the English spelling system, the historical and contemporary context of spelling research and instruction, and the relationship between word knowledge in spelling and word knowledge in reading. The chapter closes with implications of research for instruction.

THE NATURE OF THE SYSTEM

With respect to the manner in which English words are written, there is a common folk wisdom about spelling, running something like the following: Spelling is inconsistent, illogical, and incomprehensible. What English spelling *should* do, according to this folk wisdom, is represent sounds consistently. Were this to be the case, then learning to read and write would be far easier and mastered earlier. As with most folk wisdom, spelling's reaches well back into history. Writing in 1617, Alexander Hume described spelling as leading to "uncertentie in our men's wryting" (cited in Venezky, in press). And as with most folk wisdom, there is some truth although probably more myth and misinformation. So many of the debates regarding learning to write and read English have raged, therefore, without an informed understanding of the English spelling system itself or of the nature of individuals' developing understanding of the system.

Folk wisdom was ascendant at the beginning of the 20th century. The manner of spelling English "wastes a large part of the time and effort given to the instruction of our children.... Moreover, the printing, typewriting, and handwriting of the useless letters which our spelling prescribes, and upon which its difficulty chiefly rests, wastes every year millions of dollars, and time and effort worth millions more" (Simplified Spelling Board, 1906, p. 7). Advanced by luminaries such as Theodore Roosevelt and George Bernard Shaw, as well as by a surprising number of linguists, there was significant support for modifying English spelling to make it more congruent with speech (Venezky, 1980). A number of *reformed* or *simplified spelling* systems were supported. Henry Bradley, one of the original editors of the *Oxford English Dictionary*, disagreed with the reformers and responded compellingly:

> Many of the advocates of spelling reform are in the habit of asserting, as if it were an axiom admitting of no dispute, that the sole function of writing is to represent sounds ... this is one of those spurious truisms ... which continue to be repeated because nobody takes the trouble to consider what they really mean. (Bradley, 1919, p. v)

Bradley described how written language can *visually* represent ideas or meaning, and that for mature readers and writers its function is ideographic. Linguists have long known that a spelling or *orthographic* system has to do more than simply record speech sounds. Ultimately, the written representation of a language is for the *eye* rather than for the *ear* (Craigie, 1927; Francis, 1958; Hockett, 1958; Scragg, 1974; Vachek, 1989), and this is particularly true for English spelling, which carries a rich linguistic heritage from a number of other languages, assimilated over the course of some 1,500 years. There is, in fact, a consistency to English spelling that belies the common folk wisdom: Although spelling should correspond at some level to the sound system or *phonology* of the language, it also represents the meaning or *semantic* system in the language. Cummings (1988) described these two types of correspondence in terms of a balance between a *phonetic demand* that "sounds be spelled consistently from word to word" and a *semantic demand* that "units of semantic content be spelled consistently from word to word" (p. 461).

In the second half of the 20th century there were two works that significantly affected psychologists' and educators' understanding of English spelling: Chomsky and Halle's *The Sound Pattern of English* (1968) and Venezky's *The Structure of English Orthography* (1970). Working at the time within the prevailing linguistic paradigm of transformational generative grammar, Noam Chomsky and Morris Halle (1968) proposed that English spelling was a "near optimal" system for representing the language (p. 49). They noted that a word's spelling contains only enough information in order for a native speaker of English to predict the pronunciation. In fact, Chomsky and Halle asserted that the spelling of a word corresponds quite closely to the representation of that word in the speaker's underlying mental lexicon. This allows, for example, a common lexical spelling of the base, *compet*, in the words *compete, competition,* and *competitive,* despite alternations in the pronunciation of the base. These alternating pronunciations, Chomsky and Halle argued, are predictable from other information in the phonological and syntactic components of language knowledge and therefore need not be represented in the lexicon—that is, need not be represented by more direct letter/sound correspondences, as they would be, for example, if they were spelled according to the International Phonetic Alphabet in which each sound has its own symbol:

kəmpiyt, kampətISən, kəmpɛtətlv.

Although Chomsky and Halle's theory suggested how a language user derives a surface phonetic representation of a word from its underlying lexical representation, Venezky's (1970) description of English spelling, in contrast, was precisely that—a straightforward description of how spelling corresponds to speech, without postulating how speakers of English might process this correspondence. His description clearly elucidated the *morphophonological* nature of English spelling: the meaning or structural characteristics of spelling that often play the predominant role in determining the spelling and the pronunciation of individual phonemes.

In an effort to clarify the description for educators, Henderson and Templeton (1986) explained the effects of the different functions of spelling features in terms of three *layers* of information that spelling represents—*alphabetic, pattern,* and *meaning*:

- The *alphabetic* layer matches letters and sounds in a left-to-right fashion. For example, in the word *tap*, the letter-sound matchup is obvious: < t > = /t/, < a > = /æ/, < p > = /p/.
- The *pattern* layer operates both within and between syllables: (a) *Within* single syllables, as with the vowel/consonant/silent *e* (VC*e*) pattern signaling a long vowel as in *tape* in contrast to the short vowel in *tap*. Included here as well are the more subtle orthographic features such as < ck > for /k/ (*back*) and < gh > for /g/ (*ghost*)—these features illustrate the principle that how certain sounds are spelled depends on their position in a syllable. (b) Between syllables, as with the vowel/consonant/consonant/vowel (VCCV) juncture pattern in *pillow* and the vowel/consonant/vowel (VCV) juncture pattern in *pilot*. This feature has wide applicability in English. When the vowel sound in an accented syllable is long, it is usually followed by a single consonant; if the vowel sound is not long, it is often followed by doubled consonants.
- The *meaning* layer reflects the fact that word parts that are related in meaning are usually spelled consistently, despite changes in pronunciation: *solemn/solemn*ity, *paradigm/paradigm*atic, *Canada/Canad*ian. Significantly, the meaning layer will very often override the other layers of information. For example, the short vowel sound in the second syllable of *competitive* is not followed by a doubled consonant, as might be predicted by the syllable pattern, because the spelling of the base is held constant with the semantically/morphologically related words *compete* and *competition*. Spelling also preserves the semantic or morphological core across words that on first consideration may not appear related, but that indeed share a common etymology and various *degrees* of relatedness (Nagy & Anderson, 1984; Templeton, 1989), for example, ex*hume*, *hum*us, *hum*anity, post*hum*ous. As we note later, this feature has important implications for vocabulary learning and instruction.

In summary, linguistic analyses of English spelling have revealed levels and consistency including although not limited to the representation of sound. Taken together, these analyses have demonstrated that the spelling system is not an illogical, fossilized remnant of the way English was once pronounced. The key to this insight requires breaking through the "sound" barrier, as it were, thus realizing the economy and consistency that pattern and meaning bring to the system. This insight, however, is not available automatically, and the nature of individuals' lexicons changes rather dramatically over time as individuals acquire competence in reading and writing (C. Chomsky, 1970). As we explore later in this chapter, research into the developmental nature of spelling knowledge supports the observation that, at the primary levels, students learn how to spell *sound*; at the intermediate levels and beyond, however, students learn how to spell *meaning*.

We turn now to a consideration of how researchers' and educators' changing conceptions of the English spelling system have influenced research throughout the 20th century.

HISTORICAL CONTEXT

In the United States, for much of the nation's history, spelling and reading were taught together (Henderson, 1990; Venezky, 1980). In the 20th century, they have been largely separated and have only recently once again begun to be merged. Spelling research and pedagogy have historically and unavoidably been based on assumptions about learners and the system to be learned. Until recently, however, assumptions about the system proceeded without informed linguistic analysis. Expressed simply, the prevailing paradigm held that learners were passive recipients and that the spelling system did not make sense.

In the introduction to his influential work *Teaching Spelling*, Edmund Henderson (1990) commented: "History has a remarkable way of repeating itself in new and better forms. This is certainly true for the teaching of spelling" (p. 1). Henderson was referring to the reemergence of interest among researchers and educators in a possible relationship between reading and spelling development. Up until the late 1800s, spelling and reading instruction were closely related. In the Alphabet Method of colonial times, children were first taught the alphabet letters and a short-vowel syllabarium (e.g., *ab*, *eb*, *ib*, *ob*, and *ub*); then they were taught to spell and read a basic sight vocabulary. Similarly, Webster's popular "Blue-backed Speller" of the 19th century combined systematic spelling drills with early reading lessons. In the first half of the 20th century, spelling continued to enjoy status as a school subject, although no longer was it thought to be integral to the teaching of reading. Spelling, instead, was viewed as an important element in written expression, a socially useful skill that, in part, defined an educated person.

Over the second half of the 20th century the importance of spelling instruction in the schools declined. Venezky (1980) was one of the first to address the issue:

> Neither spelling instruction nor spelling reform occupy central roles today in education or in public life. No major funding agency in the last 25 years has included among its highest priorities the improvement of spelling instruction or the development of a simplified spelling system.... The public schools exhibit limited enthusiasm for spelling. Some have no systematic spelling instruction at all while the average class offers perhaps two or three 15-minute periods for it each week. (p. 10)

In the 1980s and 1990s, many educators adopted a new conception of the role of spelling; instead of considering spelling as a form of orthographic knowledge or as an indicator of general literacy competence, these educators focused more narrowly on the role of spelling as a tool for writing (e.g., Calkins, 1996; Graves, 1983; Wilde, 1991). Spelling textbooks sales declined, and many teachers began to teach spelling as an adjunct or "add on" activity in the writing process.

In the last few years of the 20th century matters have changed, and spelling is once again a topic of interest and concern. This is in part due to the ever-shifting social and political winds, driven in part by lower standardized test scores. It is also due to the fact, however, that researchers (e.g. Adams, 1990; Ehri, 1997; Perfetti, 1993) have come to view spelling as a proxy for the orthographic knowledge that underlies efficient, automatic generation of words during *writing* and efficient, automatic perception of words during *reading*. Conceptualized in these orthographic terms, spelling as a developmental process assumes greater importance. In Henderson's terms, history *is* repeating itself. If it is to do so in "new and better forms," however, then spelling researchers and educators must address more than mere encoding; they must include a broad focus on word structure and meaning in a wide range of literacy activities.

Looking at spelling research throughout the 20th century, we suggest that there are three successive periods, each characterized by a distinct theoretical perspective that affected classroom instruction:

- Spelling is a process of rote memorization.
- Spelling is a process of abstracting regular sound/spelling patterns.
- Spelling is a developmental process.

Spelling Is a Process of Rote Memorization

In the 20th century, the earliest psychological and educational research investigating the learning of spelling was guided by a phonocentric view of the spelling system (English spelling is irregular) and a behavioral conception of the learner (Locke's *tabula rasa* on which the spellings of individual words were etched with essentially no organizational schema applied by the learner). Throughout much of the 20th century, theory and research reflected the perception that, because letter/sound representation is so variable, learning to spell is essentially a process of rote memorization and therefore instruction should emphasize primarily the development of *visual memory* for the spelling of words (Cahen et al., 1971; E. Horn, 1960; T. Horn, 1969). In fact, most of the empirical work on spelling instruction was carried out during this earlier period (e.g., see T. Horn, 1969, for a comprehensive review of this research). The focus was on identifying appropriate words for instruction, tabulating types of spelling errors in an effort to determine what makes particular words difficult to spell, and identifying effective instructional practices.

Selection of words for study was based on frequency counts of English (E. Horn, 1926; Thorndike, 1921); given the conceptualization of spelling as a tool for effective writing, it seemed logical to conclude that explicit instruction should focus on the most frequently occurring words. This focus in turn reinforced the strong instructional emphasis on memorization because of the "irregular" sound/symbol correspondences manifest in so many of these high-frequency words. Efforts to identify common spelling errors focused primarily on *sound*, and the errors that students made were analyzed primarily in terms of their correspondence to sound (Gates, 1937). Where structural features were the source of the error, as for example in the doubling of consonants, these features were tabulated as part of a single error category with no consideration of the underlying linguistic motivation for the feature. With the benefit of hindsight we can see the shortcomings of this level of analysis. Consider, for example, the increasing conceptual sophistication of consonant doubling in the following contexts: base word plus inflectional ending [*bat* + *ed* = *batted* vs. *rake* + *ed* = *raked*]; syllable juncture within monomorphemic words [*happen* vs. *pilot*]; doubling within assimilated prefixes [*ad* + *count* = *account*; *in* + *literate* = *illiterate*]).

Within the prevailing *spelling as rote memory* paradigm, studies that explored instructional practice supported the following:

- Presenting words in lists rather than in context (McKee, 1924).
- Administering a self-corrected pretest followed by study of list words—as opposed to study of list words followed by a posttest (E. Horn, 1960; T. Horn, 1946).
- Spending 60 to 75 minutes per week on spelling instruction (E. Horn, 1960).

Spelling Is a Process of Abstracting Regular Sound/Spelling Patterns

It was not until the second half of the 20th century that comprehensive analyses of the alphabetic, syllabic, and morphemic aspects of English spelling were undertaken (Chomsky & Halle, 1968; Cummings, 1988; Hanna, Hanna, Hodges, & Rudorf, 1966; Venezky, 1970, in press). The Stanford research (Hanna et al., 1966) was seminal because it demonstrated, for the first time, how a linguistic perspective can inform investigations into how students might learn to spell English. This research showed that English spelling is a logical, rule-based language system. By programming a computer to detect and learn regularities, Hanna et al. demonstrated that the system is far more regular than assumed when the focus is on *patterns* of letters and how they represent sound, as opposed to a strict one letter/one sound level of analysis. The researchers noted that how a particular sound is spelled very often depends on its position within a syllable, an assertion that was not merely theoretical but testable through the use of the computer. Although the computer spelled a majority of the words correctly, Hanna, Hodges, and Hanna (1971) observed that had morphemic information been available to the computer, the percentage would have been even higher. Although there has been debate about how Hanna et al. determined regularity, their basic finding remained: English spelling quite reliably represents the sounds of English when the *syllable* as opposed to the phoneme is the unit of analysis.

Thus, the variable of *pattern* was added to *frequency*. Although frequency of usage previously guided the selection of spelling words, frequency of usage *and* frequency of pattern occurrence now guided selection. This sequencing of patterns is reflected still in most contemporary spelling programs. Because Hanna and others such as Edgar Dale recognized the progressive complexity of the spelling system, they also emphasized the desirability of integrating spelling and morphology; this was a theme that later researchers and educators would also take up (Dale, O'Rourke, & Bamman, 1971; Hanna et al., 1971).

Spelling Is a Developmental Process

The result of Chomsky and Halle's and Venezky's analyses was a renaissance in linguistic insight that spelling can reliably represent meaning and sound when the morpheme is the unit of analysis. This renaissance affected research in word perception in reading and word generation in writing. In the latter instance, spelling came to be increasingly viewed as a *developmental* process.

The first groundbreaking investigations of young children's invented spelling (C. Chomsky, 1970; Read, 1971, 1975) were the motivation behind the conceptualization of spelling as a *developmental* process. Read's studies were undertaken in an effort in part to test the psychological reality of the phonological component of Chomsky's transformational generative grammar. The implications of this research were far-reaching, but perhaps most notably they led to the realization that young children are capable of constructing knowledge about the relationships between sounds and letters without explicit instruction. This realization supported the general conception of the child as a language learner who brings an innate psycholinguistic endowment to the task of language development (Chomsky, 1968; Lenneberg, 1967). In terms of literacy development in general and spelling development in particular, this realization also lent support to the perspective that learning to read and write was natural.

A number of studies over the last quarter century have elaborated on this developmental perspective (e.g., Ehri, 1993; Ellis, 1990; Frith, 1985; Ganske, 1994; Henderson & Beers, 1980; Hughes & Searle, 1997; Marsh, Friedman, Welch, & Desberg, 1980; Schlagal, 1992; Seymour, 1992; Templeton & Bear, 1992; Treiman, 1993; Wilde, 1991). Most of this work focuses on the early stages of development, but some researchers have explored word knowledge as manifested through spelling at later phases of literacy development (e.g., Derwing, Smith, & Wiebe, 1995; Fischer, Shankweiler, & Liberman, 1985; Fowler & Liberman, 1995; Marsh et al., 1980; Templeton, 1979; Templeton & Scarborough-Franks, 1985). A central tenet that has emerged from this line of research is that learners share a common developmental sequence of acquisition of orthographic knowledge, despite natural variation in their attention to printed language and their understanding of the relationships between print and speech.

Although there is considerable agreement regarding the characterization of spelling as a developmental process (Ehri, 1997; Hughes & Searle, 1997; Seymour, 1992; Templeton & Bear, 1992; Treiman, 1993), there is less agreement about how to describe and characterize this development over time and about the roles of explicit and implicit learning in this process. *Stage* or *phase* models are the primary vehicle for characterizing developmental growth, although more recently development has been investigated in terms of growth in *strategies* for problem solving (Varnhagen, 1995). Both stage models and strategy development models have drawn inferences about the nature of underlying knowledge of word structure at points along a developmental continuum.

Stage models emerged during the preeminence of Piagetian theory and characterized descriptions of language development (e.g., Brown, 1973). It was out of this context that the genesis of a stage model for spelling development emerged. The studies undertaken by Henderson and his students at the University of Virginia (Henderson & Beers, 1980; Templeton & Bear, 1992) grew out of Henderson's work as a reading clinician and later as director of the McGuffey Reading Center at the University of Virginia. This research was motivated by Henderson's hypothesis in the late 1960s that looking at how children *spell* words can provide insight into how they *read* words, or their lexical representation for words (Henderson, 1981). The Virginia work explored and refined developmental phases of orthographic knowledge that Henderson labeled *preliterate, letter name* or *alphabetic, within-word pattern, syllable juncture,* and *derivational constancy* (Barnes, 1982; Bear, 1982; C. Beers, 1978; J. Beers, 1974; Beers & Henderson; 1977; Gentry, 1977; C. Gill, 1980; J. T. Gill, 1992; Invernizzi, 1985; Morris, 1983, 1993; Morris, Nelson, & Perney, 1986; Schlagal, 1982; Stever, 1977; Temple, 1978; S. Templeton, 1976, 1979; Zutell, 1975). The labels reflect the salient orthographic features learners explore in both spelling and reading at each phase of development. These phases reflect a growth in sophistication of knowledge about letters and sounds, letter patterns and syllable patterns, and how meaning is directly represented through spelling (Schlagal, 1992).

In addition to the Virginia studies, a number of investigations explored in depth young children's invented spellings (e.g., Ellis & Cataldo, 1990; Hughes & Searle, 1997; Huxford, Terrell, & Bradley, 1992; Treiman, 1993). Children's semiphonetic/partial alphabetic and phonetic or full alphabetic spellings reflect the conception that the spelling system represents sounds in a predominately left-to-right fashion. For example, a child in the semiphonetic/partial alphabetic phase may spell *truck* as HRK; in the subsequent phonetic or full alphabetic phase the spellings may be, respectively, CHRIK, CHRUK, TRUK. In time, conventional representations for most short vowels are learned during the full alphabetic phase, although long vowel sounds may continue to be spelled with single letters. As children advance in their literacy skills, however, their invented spellings begin to include vowel markers—silent letters—which indicate that they are attending at some level to the *pattern* layer in English spelling; for example, BIEK (bike) and RANE (rain). They conceptualize *the vowel and what follows* within a word as an orthographic unit (Ehri, 1989; Invernizzi, 1992). This leads to the conceptualization that the spelling system is not a strictly linear left-to-right matchup of letters; through orthographic patterns, letters that themselves do not correspond to sound provide information about the pronunciation of other letters within the pattern. This level of spelling knowledge characterizes the within-word pattern phase. With further development, learners' spelling is characterized as *syllable juncture*; their spellings reveal closure on most vowel patterns in single-syllable words, and errors on stressed syllables of polysyllabic words reflect how these syllables would be spelled if they were single syllables, for example, PARAIDING (*parading*). In the syllable juncture stage, errors also occur at the conjoining of syllables, as for example ALOWED (*allowed*) and HAPEN (*happen*) (Bear, Templeton, & Warner, 1991; Ganske, 1994; Schlagal, 1992). Other errors characteristic of this phase are less frequent vowel patterns such as *-ough* in *though* and *enough*, and the schwa or reduced vowel in unstressed syllables, such as LOCLE (*local*) or PILAT (*pilot*).

As students encounter a greater number of words in their reading that reflect processes of derivational morphology, their errors at this level characterize the *derivational constancy* phase and reveal a conceptual readiness to explore how spelling preserves the semantic relationships across derivationally related words, as in SOLEM (*solemn*), CONFADENT (*confident*), and OPASITION (*opposition*). Just as it had been an impetus to the early work in invented spelling, the Chomskian revolution in linguistics spurred some of the earlier work investigating older students' knowledge of the spelling system (Templeton, 1979; Templeton & Scarborough-Franks, 1985). In fact, knowledge of some aspects of derivational morphology was more secure in students' spelling than in their pronunciation, leading Templeton (1979) and Templeton and Scarborough-Franks (1985) to suggest that students' productive knowledge of certain aspects of derivational morphology in orthography preceded and facilitated their productive knowledge of these processes in phonology. These studies supported Carol Chomsky's (1970) observation that:

> This process of internalization ... is no doubt facilitated in many cases by an awareness of how words are spelled.... Thus the underlying system which the child has constructed from evidence provided by the spoken language ... may itself by improved by his increased familiarity with the written language. (p. 298)

A number of researchers have explored the relationship between students' higher-level orthographic knowledge and other aspects of their literacy development (Marsh et al., 1980; Frith, 1985; Seymour, 1992). Taken together, this research has led to a more systematic exploration through instruction of the role that *morphology* plays in the spelling system. Developing and elaborating this knowledge may entail directing students' attention to the spelling/meaning relationships among derivationally related words; students who make errors such as SOLEM for *solemn* and CONFADENT for *confident* have the cognitive sophistication to conceptualize how the orthographic representation remains constant, despite changes in sound, in related words such as *solemn/solemnity* and *confide/confident* (Templeton, 1989; Zutell, 1979). While the research has been relatively sparse in this area, instructional suggestions along these lines have been offered for some time. Dale noted many years ago that "Organizing spelling lessons to coincide with the study of morphology gives the students a contextual structure for the study of spelling" (Dale et al., 1971, p. 172). More recently, the linguist Mark Aronoff noted that, "From a teacher's point of view, morphology is important for two major reasons: spelling and vocabulary.... Unfortunately, very little time is spent in school on systematic learning of morphology" (1994, pp. 820–821). For this reason, most students are not aware of the role that morphemic elements can play in the spelling of words (Derwing et al., 1995; Fowler & Liberman, 1995; Goulandris, 1994; Hughes & Searle, 1997; Templeton, 1989), nor, for that matter, are most adults (Fischer et al., 1985). Making this connection explicit for students may provide both a more productive strategy for spelling as well as a means of expanding vocabulary (Derwing et al., 1995; Templeton, 1992b).

If learning to spell is a developmental process, then it follows that individual students will progress at different rates and that spelling instruction may need to accommodate these individual differences. Morris and his colleagues have recently explored this issue of a *spelling instructional level*. In a year-long study of four third-grade classrooms in which all students were taught from a grade-level spelling book Morris, Blanton, Blanton, and Perney (1995) found that students varied greatly in year-end spelling achievement. Although two-thirds of the students scored 86% on a curriculum-based posttest, the bottom one third of students scored only 46% correct. In a separate follow-up study, Morris, Blanton, Blanton, Nowacek, and Perney (1995) manipulated spelling instructional level to see if low-spelling students (identified on a beginning-of-year pretest) would benefit from studying easier, more developmentally appropriate words. Over the course of a school year, 24 third-grade low spellers (intervention group) were taught from a second-grade spelling book, and a comparison group of 24 students were taught from a third-grade spelling book. End-of-year results showed that the intervention group scored significantly higher than the comparison group on a second-grade posttest and a third-grade transfer test. Moreover, the intervention group scored as high as the comparison group on a curriculum-based list of third-grade words that the comparison group (but not the intervention group) had been taught. Morris et al. explained these curious findings in terms of *instructional level* theory, arguing that, over the course of the year, the low spellers who were taught at the appropriate level (second grade, in this case) learned more about the spelling *system* than did the low spellers who were taught inappropriately ("over their head") at grade level. Although spelling authorities (e.g., Henderson, 1990; T. Horn, 1969) have long recommended that spelling instruction be differentiated in the classroom according to student ability level, the Morris et al. study is the first to provide empirical support for this position.

Recently, some researchers have explored students' metalinguistic reflections on their spelling as a function of spelling development (Hughes & Searle, 1997; Sabey, 1997). A consistent finding is that there is a lag between the sophistication of students' knowledge as evidenced in their spellings and their ability to reflect on their own strategies and knowledge. For example, within-word pattern spellers will eventually spell the inflectional ending -*ed* conventionally across its three possible pronunciations (e.g., clapp*ed* [/t/], climb*ed* [/d/], want*ed* [/Id/]), revealing a tacit sensitivity to visual and morphological features of the spelling system. They will explain their spellings, however, in terms of sound. Several researchers have suggested that these types of spellings reveal that even young children are sensitive to other features besides sound; for example, how meaning is directly represented visually (Read, 1994; Snowling, 1994; Treiman, 1993). Hughes and Searle's study (1997), in which students were interviewed about their developing conceptions of spelling, is notable because (a) it was longitudinal, following the spelling development of the same children over an 8-year period; and (b) it was conducted in classroom settings. For these reasons, this study is next examined more closely.

Hughes and Searle addressed a number of issues: the nature of spelling development over time, the relationship between spelling development and reading and writing development, and the role of spelling instruction specifically and literacy instruction in general in the development of spelling ability. The investigators selected two schools; one served a neighborhood of "urban professionals" and the other a "suburban community of nonprofessional" parents. For over half of the students in this second school, English was not the only language in the home. Based on developmental spelling research, Hughes and Searle constructed a spelling assessment list that was administered three times a year. Following each administration, students were interviewed one-to-one concerning how they approached their spelling of the words. At the completion of the study, 37 students had been followed over a 7-year period. Despite variation in the type and amount of spelling instruction over the years for the children in the study, Hughes and Searle were able to draw some conclusions about development and instruction:

- "Learning to spell [is] such a high-level, problem-solving, sense-making activity, so much like other processes of language learning" (p. 185).
- Across children there was a high "degree of consistency … in the patterns of learning to spell" and "a lot of commonality in the knowledge children used and how they used it" (p. 184).
- Significant amounts of reading and writing are critical if students are to advance in spelling ability.
- For all children in the early years of schooling, invented spelling should be encouraged. Once students begin to explore spelling on a regular basis, they should be encouraged to look for patterns; this reflects the importance of the *visual* comparison of words.
- It is highly desirable to ask questions that will serve to help children extend their sense of the "logics" of spelling.
- As children move into the higher grades, "Spelling instruction tends to become much more focussed on correcting and rewriting text. Ironically, this focus may come just at a time when many children are better able to handle approaches that encourage explicit analysis and generalization … we have to recognize [spelling's] complexity and give it more developmental time throughout a child's years at school" (p. 184).

The developmental perspective on spelling has been offered as an explanation for spelling acquisition in learning-disabled students (Moats, 1995; Worthy & Invernizzi, 1990) and nonliterate adults as well (Worthy & Viise, 1986). Although their rate of growth is slower, learning-disabled children seem to follow the same developmental benchmarks as other learners. Adults initially acquiring literacy follow the same trends as well; although they usually make fairly rapid progress through the alphabetic phase, the within-word pattern phase requires time and effort. This is where most adult literacy programs suffer their greatest attrition rate.

RECENT RESEARCH: SPELLING AND READING RELATIONSHIPS

The process and product of individuals' spelling have recently gained such intense interest largely because of a growing consensus within the research community that a common orthographic base underlies individuals' encoding of words through spelling and their decoding of words during reading. As has been noted, some of the developmental spelling research was motivated by the hypothesis that spelling and reading processes both draw on and reflect a common underlying base of orthographic knowledge. Recent research into the development of word knowledge lends support to this hypothesis (e.g., Ehri, 1997; Ganske, 1994; Gill, 1992; Invernizzi, 1992; Richgels, 1995; Zutell, 1992; Zutell & Rasinski, 1989). Asserting the central role of word knowledge in the reading process, several cognitive psychologists have suggested that the most effective means of determining the nature of individuals' lexical representations for specific words, as well as their lexical knowledge in general, is to administer a well-constructed spelling list (e.g., Ehri, 1997; Gill, 1992; Perfetti, 1993). Perfetti observed that "Spelling and reading use the same lexical representation. In fact, spelling is a good test of the quality of representation" (Perfetti, 1993, p. 170). Examining students' spelling can provide insights about the types of perceptual units engaged during word recognition in reading, the code that individuals use to access their lexical representations (Templeton, 1992b). In other words, if the full conventional orthographic representation of a word encountered during reading is *not* held in memory, then the way in which the reader spells that word may reveal the type of orthographic knowledge he or she is using to perceptually process the word.

Although the surface manifestations of reading words and spelling words appear to be asynchronous—that is, individuals can read words that they cannot spell conventionally—the general nature of individuals' orthographic or lexical knowledge is applied similarly to both processes (Ehri, 1997). Early writing helps to construct the lexical frame for words in early reading; in this regard, Frith (1985) commented that spelling is the pacemaker for reading at the early levels. Later, however, reading helps to construct, sketch, or fill in the space within that frame; reading becomes the pacemaker for spelling.

Henderson (1990) characterized Carol Chomsky's (1970) and Charles Read's (1971, 1975) early work with preschool and primary children's invented spelling as providing a "rosetta stone" for explaining the rationale that underlies early invented spelling (Henderson, 1981, 1990). For children who are emergent readers and writers, Ehri and Wilce (1987) found that the exercise of letter name knowledge through writing facilitates the development of phonemic awareness. Letters themselves can serve the function of concretizing sound, and although much of this process is implicit (e.g., Perfetti, 1992), it leads to children's conscious, reflective awareness of constituent sounds within words (Yaden & Templeton, 1986).

For most children, reflective awareness probably begins with the written representation of their name. In studies of kindergarten and first-grade readers, Morris (1983, 1993) found that a reciprocal relationship exists between developing awareness of sounds and the concept of a word in print. A stable concept of word in print is defined as awareness that a word is a series of letters bound by spaces at both ends; children evidence this awareness when they are able to point to the words in a line of text as they are reciting the text from memory. When children have a stable concept of the printed word, they have a stable mental representation that frames and sequences the sounds and letters within words. Indeed, knowing where printed words begin and end as well as that they correspond to spoken words sets the stage for the conscious awareness and manipulation of vowels as well as consonants. In tracing this phenomenon, Morris has supported the conception that the development of phonemic awareness is not an all-or-none affair; with respect to syllables and single-syllable words, children advance from beginning sounds to ending sounds to the medial sound, which is last to appear.

For the beginning reader who is an alphabetic speller, the effect of exposure to words and patterns not currently present in his or her spelling leads gradually to the appearance of silent letters in spelling. This builds the information within each lexical entry, moving it closer to convention and thus automaticity. For example, although *cape* may initially be read as /kæp/ by an alphabetic reader/writer, the feedback that *cape* is pronounced /keyp/ has the effect, over time, of directing the learner to look for reasons why: In this case, the presence of a word-final *e* emerges as the explanation, and together with similar information about other words, subsequently guides the reorganization of the lexicon so that long vowel sounds are distinguished from short vowel sounds in print by letters that themselves do not represent sounds. At this level, homophony may play an accompanying role in driving the lexicon forward; the child who spells both *cap* and *cape* as CAP similarly spells both *hat* and *hate* as HAT. This phenomenon, emerging first at a tacit level, causes the child to search for distinguishing alternatives.

Although not as much work has been done at the upper levels as at the lower to synthesize work in reading and spelling words, there are suggestive parallels to be drawn from studies that have investigated reading words at this level and those that have investigated spelling words. Templeton (1992b) suggested a parallel between the syllable juncture phase and derivational constancy phase in developmental spelling and the syllabic and morphemic layers of lexical decomposition described in several models of word recognition (e.g., Rayner & Pollatsek, 1995; Taft, 1991).

IMPLICATIONS OF RESEARCH FOR INSTRUCTION

At the close of a century that has seen a definite evolution in the way spelling is conceptualized, instructional implications have emerged that build on the twin foundations of developmental appropriateness and the basic logic of the spelling system of English. Our focus now must be on how best to interface what we understand about the learner with what we understand about the system; that is, configuring what classroom spelling instruction should look like in a developmental context. The developmental learner explores words, seeking after pattern. The particular type of pattern to be explored—alphabetic, within-word, or meaning—is a function of the developmental level of the learner.

Based on a review of the developmental research at the time, Read and Hodges (1982) concluded that a challenge to designers of spelling curriculum was to bring instruction more in line with a developmental perspective. Writing a decade after Read and Hodges's review, Zutell (1994) suggested that this was beginning to occur. Describing approaches to instruction in terms of *whole language* and *developmentalists*, Zutell held that the developmentalists had unified developmental research with some type of systematic instruction. This was in contrast to the whole-language perspective, which, although acknowledging a developmental progression, held that sufficient instruction included minilessons focused on specific spelling problems arising out of writing and direct instruction limited to the "few rules and patterns that have a high degree of utility" (p.1099).

As many educators have perceived the need for more focused exploration of words, the instructional literature has reflected the tenor of the implications from research (Bear, Invernizzi, & Templeton, 1995; Henderson, 1985, 1990; Henderson & Beers, 1980; Henry, 1996; Moats, 1995; Templeton & Bear, 1992). Instructional models range along a continuum from more explicit and deductive (e.g., Henry, 1996) to more implicit or inductive (e.g., Bear et al., 1995; Bear & Templeton, 1998; Hughes & Searle, 1997; Invernizzi, Abouzeid, & Gill, 1994). As described by Morris, Blanton, Blanton, Nowacek, and Perney (1995) and Zutell (1994), most of these approaches to instruction assume that learning to spell is a developmental process and that it requires direct facilitation and guidance, as opposed to assuming that spelling may be acquired on an "as needed" basis, at which time minilessons are conducted, usually in the context of writing. Although the latter practice clearly illustrates the importance of spelling and the appropriate application of spelling knowledge in the authentic context of writing, its possible shortcomings for most students are: (a) It depends on the teacher's knowledge base to present appropriate words that reflect the appropriate patterns, and (b) even if all teachers had this knowledge base readily available, such *incidental* instruction does not provide students the degree of exposure necessary for abstraction of appropriate spelling patterns. In the past, this latter issue has been discussed in terms of *time on task*; more recently, it has been addressed in terms of having a sufficient number of opportunities to examine and make connections across words to abstract patterns, thus strengthening pathways within and between lexical items—quite literally, establishing connections at the neurological level (Foorman, 1995).

The tenor of much recent research, therefore, reflects the conclusion that if systematic spelling instruction drives orthographic knowledge that is important to *both* spelling and word recognition—and indirectly, to comprehension (Perfetti, 1985; Stanovich & Cunningham, 1993)—then attention to spelling should not be left to an "as needed" basis. Toward this end, Templeton (1991) argued that spelling instruction ought to be reconceptualized: The purpose of instruction becomes more than simply mastering the conventional spellings of words, but more broadly *word study*, a means of looking at words from a variety of perspectives that serve reading, writing, and vocabulary development. Instruction can develop and reinforce specific orthographic patterns—the structural aspects of lexical knowledge and of individual lexical entries—and do so in an engaging fashion. Such instruction includes strategies for thinking about words and exercising word and conceptual knowledge through examining and exploring words from a variety of perspectives: word sorts/categorization, word-building activities, analogical reasoning with semantic and orthographic categories, and so forth (Cramer, 1998; Cunningham, 1995; Moats, 1995; Templeton, 1991). Exploration is based primarily although not exclusively on words that have been selected by the teacher so as to facilitate discovery of pattern (Bear et al., 1995; Invernizzi et al., 1994; Zutell, 1996). In the context of an inductive approach in which word sorting or categorizing was used as a means of developing sensitivity to patterns in spelling, Fresch and Wheaton (1992) and Sabey (1997) explored and emphasized "think-alouds" among their students. Although all students can benefit from such a broader approach to spelling or word study, students who have been classified as special education or learning disabled may require more deliberate, systematic, and deductive instruction (Gordon, Vaughn, & Schumm, 1993; Henry, 1994; Moats, 1995).

Given our understanding of the system to be learned and the nature of the learner, teachers need to assess their students' levels of spelling knowledge (Henderson, 1990; Morris, Nelson, & Perney, 1986; Morris, Blanton, Blanton, Nowacek, & Perney, 1995; Schlagal, 1992). With respect to learning about words, students are too often presented with new information about words before they have consolidated what they know about known words. Once students' developmental levels have been assessed, known words are examined to support conceptual development for spelling patterns; this pattern knowledge then can be extended to unknown words.

The implications of most of the preceding research is now being explored in the context of classrooms, addressing teacher attitudes and practices, student learning, development, and attitude, and the consequent instructional environment (Allal, 1997; Fresch & Wheaton, 1992; Hughes & Searle, 1997; Morris, Blanton, Blanton, & Perney, 1995; Sabey, 1997). Whether teachers teach with a published program of some type or not, there is a need to understand both the spelling system and the stages of the learner (Barone, 1992; Ganske, 1994; Gill & Scharer, 1996; Henry, 1989; Hughes & Searle, 1997; Morris et al., 1995). Teachers themselves often voice concerns about not being familiar enough with how best to teach spelling or with the nature of the spelling system itself (Gill & Scharer, 1996; Morris, Blanton, Blanton, Nowacek, & Perney, 1995). Although many teachers believe that spelling *patterns* should be emphasized, the teachers' knowledge of the nature and possible sequence of these patterns is limited. This uncertainty is particularly evident with respect to the morphological aspects of spelling (Moats & Smith, 1992). Based on their longitudinal investigation of spelling learning and instruction, Hughes and Searle (1997) concluded that:

> Many teachers themselves see spelling as more arbitrary than systematic; at least, they give that impression to their students. Even when that is not the case, it is likely that their

own knowledge of the spelling system is largely implicit or relatively poorly understood. For example, they may teach spelling as a solely sound-based system long after that is useful.... If we teachers do not believe that spelling has logical, negotiable patterns, how can we hope to help children develop that insight? (p. 133)

CONCLUSION

Throughout the 20th century, most researchers and educators have assumed that the task of learning to spell is a daunting one. Instructional efforts have ranged from attempting to teach all of the possible sound/symbol correspondences systematically to hoping that most learners would acquire necessary spelling knowledge as they developed their ability to read and write. Both of these extremes, and most points in between, have been influenced by what we characterized as a *phonocentric* view of English spelling. When researchers and educators assume that both decoding and encoding are based exclusively on mastering sound/symbol associations, then they inadvertently set students up for struggle and oftentimes frustration.

In a general evaluation of American spelling, Cummings (1988) referred to the "intricate simplicity" of the system: Its intricacies lie in the different levels on which it represents information from sound through meaning; its simplicity is the design and consistency with which it represents this information at each level (Templeton, 1992a). Educators' knowledge of this design and simplicity will better inform instruction, as well as the understanding of how students acquire knowledge of these influences. Learners' appreciation of the consistency and simplicity resonates with their advancing cognitive sophistication and knowledge. This knowledge in turn draws on an increasingly abstract conceptual domain reflected in the words students encounter in their reading.

With respect to specific instructional practice, it is hardly surprising that research does not unambiguously support a specific type of instructional activity or systematic program. Given the studies that have investigated the effect of examining words in the context of an active search for pattern, however, there are some general conclusions that are at least strongly suggested:

- For most students, an inductive or exploratory approach is appropriate; for severely struggling spellers who are working at an appropriate developmental level, a more deductive, systematic, and direct approach is preferred.
- An emphasis on the *interrelatedness* of spelling and phonics, morphology, and vocabulary. This emphasis includes the explicit presentation and discussion of how morphology is represented in the spelling system; this allows a significant merger of spelling and vocabulary instruction.
- An emphasis in teacher preparation and professional development programs on the need for developing teachers' knowledge base about word structure, thus being empowered to facilitate students' development of word knowledge.

Additional research is still needed in the following areas:

- Pacing spelling instruction to developmental level.
- "Intervention"-type instruction in the regular classroom, including investigations of students' application of spelling knowledge during the process of writing.
- Continuing work in exploring literacy development across spelling or orthographic knowledge, reading, and writing.

- Sustained investigation of effects of combining spelling and vocabulary instruction at the intermediate levels and beyond.
- More investigation of what students themselves believe they are doing as they apply spelling knowledge.
- The continued exploration of spelling development in native speakers of languages other than English as well as speakers acquiring English as a new language.

Although one may be tempted to disparage the narrower vision of spelling research and teaching throughout much of this century, each phase of the spelling research nevertheless made significant contributions to our understanding of the learning and teaching of spelling. Frequency studies, exploration of effects on memorization, developmental studies, and reconceptualizations of the role and nature of the spelling system have all provided essential underpinnings. There is now the potential for an important blend of traditional and contemporary aspects of instruction that promotes an appropriate synthesis of meaningful reading and writing experiences with developmentally paced word study.

REFERENCES

Adams, M. J. (1990). *Beginning to read: Thinking and learning about print.* Cambridge: MIT Press.

Alexander, G. (1906). *A spelling book.* New York: Longmans, Green.

Allal, L. (1997). Learning to spell in the classroom. In C. A. Perfetti, L. Rieben, & M. Fayol (Eds.), *Learning to spell: Research, theory, and practice across languages* (pp. 129–150). Mahwah, NJ: Lawrence Erlbaum Associates.

Aronoff, M. (1994). Morphology. In Purves, A. C., Papa, L., & Jordan, S. (Eds.), *Encyclopedia of English studies and language arts* (Vol. 2, pp. 820–821). New York: Scholastic.

Barnes, W. (1982). *The developmental acquisition of silent letters and orthographic images in English spelling.* Unpublished doctoral dissertation, University of Virginia, Charlottesville.

Barone, D. (1992). Whatever happened to spelling? The role of spelling instruction in process-centered classrooms. *Reading Psychology, 13*(1), 1–18.

Bear, D. R. (1982). *Patterns of oral reading across stages of word knowledge.* Unpublished doctoral dissertation, University of Virginia, Charlottesville.

Bear, D. R., Invernizzi, M., & Templeton, S. (1995). *Words their way: Word study for phonics, vocabulary, and spelling instruction.* Englewood Cliffs, NJ: Prentice Hall.

Bear, D. R., & Templeton, S. (1998). Explorations in developmental spelling: Foundation for teaching phonics, spelling, and vocabulary. *Reading Teacher, 52,* 222–242.

Bear, D. R., Templeton, S., & Warner, M. (1991). The development of a qualitative inventory of higher levels of orthographic knowledge. In J. Zutell & S. McCormick (Eds.), *Learner factors/teacher factors: Issues in literacy research and instruction, Fortieth yearbook of the National Reading Conference* (pp. 105–110). Chicago: National Reading Conference.

Beers, C. (1980). The relationship of cognitive development to spelling and reading abilities. In E. H. Henderson & J. W. Beers (Eds.), *Developmental and cognitive aspects of learning to spell* (pp. 74–84). Newark, DE: International Reading Association.

Beers, J. W. (1974). *First and second grade children's developing orthographic concepts of tense and lax vowels.* Unpublished doctoral dissertation, University of Virginia, Charlottesville.

Beers, J., & Henderson, E. (1977). A study of developing orthographic concepts among first graders. *Research in the Teaching of English, 11,* 133–148.

Bradley, H. (1919). *On the relations between spoken and written language.* Oxford, England: Clarendon Press.

Brown, R. (1973). *A first language.* Cambridge, MA: Harvard University Press.

Cahen, L. S., Craun, M. J., & Johnson, S. K. (1971). Spelling difficulty: A survey of the research. *Review of Educational Research, 41,* 281–301.

Calkins, L. (1996). *The art of teaching writing* (2nd ed.). Portsmouth, NH: Heinemann.

Chomsky, C. (1970). Invented spelling in the open classroom. *Word, 27,* 499–518.

Chomsky, N. (1968). *Language and mind.* New York: Harcourt Brace Jovanovich.

Chomsky, N., & Halle, M. (1968). *The sound pattern of English.* New York: Harper & Row.

Craigie, W. (1927). *English spelling: Its rules and reasons.* New York: F. S. Crofts.

Cramer, R. J. (1998). *The spelling connection: Integrating reading, writing, and spelling instruction.* New York: Guilford Press.

Cummings, D. W. (1988). *American English spelling*. Baltimore, MD: Johns Hopkins University Press.

Cunningham, P. (1995). *Phonics they use* (2nd ed.). New York: HarperCollins.

Dale, E., O'Rourke, J., & Bamman, H. (1971). *Techniques of teaching vocabulary*. Palo Alto, CA: Field Education Enterprises.

Derwing, B. L., Smith, M. L., & Wiebe, G. E. (1995). On the role of spelling in morpheme recognition: Experimental studies with children and adults. In L. B. Feldman (Ed.), *Morphological aspects of language processing* (pp. 3–27). Hillsdale, NJ: Lawrence Erlbaum Associates.

Ehri, L. C. (1989). The development of spelling knowledge and its role in reading acquisition and reading disability. *Journal of Learning Disabilities, 22*, 356–365.

Ehri, L. C. (1993). How English orthography influences phonological knowledge as children learn to read and spell. In R. J. Scales (Ed.), *Literacy and language analysis* (pp. 21–43). Hillsdale, NJ: Lawrence Erlbaum Associates.

Ehri, L. C. (1997). Learning to read and learning to spell are one and the same, almost. In C. A. Perfetti, L. Rieben, & M. Fayol (Eds.), *Learning to spell: Research, theory, and practice across languages* (pp. 237–269). Mahwah, NJ: Lawrence Erlbaum Associates.

Ehri, L., & Wilce, L. (1987). Does learning to spell help beginners learn to read words? *Reading Research Quarterly, 22*, 47–65.

Ellis, N., & Cataldo, S. (1990). The role of spelling in learning to read. *Language and Education, 4*, 1–28.

Fischer, F., Shankweiler, D., & Liberman, I. Y. (1985). Spelling proficiency and sensitivity to word structure. *Journal of Memory and Language, 24*, 423–441.

Foorman, B. R. (1995). Practiced connections of orthographic and phonological processing. In V. W. Berninger (Ed.), *The varieties of orthographic knowledge, Volume II: Relationships to phonology, reading and writing* (pp. 377–418). Boston: Kluwer.

Fowler, A. E., & Liberman, I. Y. (1995). The role of phonology and orthography in morphological awareness. In L. B. Feldman (Ed.), *Morphological aspects of language processing* (pp.157–188). Hillsdale, NJ: Lawrence Erlbaum Associates.

Francis, W. N. (1958). *The structure of American English*. New York: Ronald Press.

Fresch, M. J., & Wheaton, A. (1992, December). *Open word sorts: Helping third grade students become strategic spellers*. Paper presented at the 42nd annual meeting of the National Reading Conference, San Antonio, TX.

Frith, U. (1985). Beneath the surface of developmental dyslexia. In K. Patterson, J. Marshall, & M. Coltheart (Eds.), *Surface dyslexia* (pp. 301–330). London: Lawrence Erlbaum Associates.

Ganske, K. (1994). *Developmental spelling analysis: A diagnostic measure for instruction and research*. Unpublished doctoral dissertation, University of Virginia, Charlottesville.

Gates, A. I. (1937). *A list of spelling difficulties in 3876 words*. New York: Teachers College Press.

Gentry, J. R. (1977). A study of the orthographic strategies of beginning readers. *Dissertation Abstracts International, 39* (07A) 4017. (University Microfilms No. AAG7901152)

Gill, C. E. (1980). An analysis of spelling errors in French. *Dissertation Abstracts International, 41* (09A), 3924. (University Microfilms No. AAG8026641)

Gill, C. H., & Scharer, P. L. (1996). "Why do they get it on Friday and misspell it on Monday?" Teachers inquiring about their students as spellers. *Language Arts, 73*, 89–96.

Gill, J. T. (1992). The relationship between word recognition and spelling. In S. Templeton & D. R. Bear (Eds.), *Development of orthographic knowledge and the foundations of literacy: A memorial festschrift for Edmund H. Henderson* (pp. 79–104). Hillsdale, NJ: Lawrence Erlbaum Associates.

Gordon, J., Vaughn, S., & Schumm, J. S. (1993). Spelling interventions: A review of literature and implications for instruction for students with learning disabilities. *Learning Disabilities Research & Practice, 8*, 175–181.

Goulandris, N. (1994). Teaching spelling: Bridging theory and practice. In G. D. A. Brown & N. C. Ellis (Eds.), *Handbook of spelling: Theory, process, and intervention* (pp. 407–423). Chichester, England: John Wiley.

Graves, D. (1983). *Writing: Teachers and children at work*. Exeter, NH: Heinemann.

Hanna, P. R., Hanna, J. S., Hodges, R. E., & Ruforf, H. (1966). *Phoneme–grapheme correspondences as cues to spelling improvement*. Washington, DC: U.S. Office of Education Cooperative Research.

Hanna, P. Hodges, R. & Hanna, J. (1971). *Spelling: Structure and strategies*. Boston: Houghton Mifflin.

Henderson, E. H. (1981). *Learning to read and spell: The child's knowledge of words*. DeKalb, IL: Northern Illinois Press.

Henderson, E. H. (1985). *Teaching spelling*. Boston: Houghton Mifflin.

Henderson, E. H. (1990). *Teaching spelling* (2nd ed.). Boston: Houghton Mifflin.

Henderson, E. H., & Beers, J. (Eds.). (1980). *Developmental and cognitive aspects of learning to spell: A reflection of word knowledge*. Newark, DE: International Reading Association

Henderson, E. H., & Templeton, S. (1986). A developmental perspective of formal spelling instruction through alphabet, pattern, and meaning. *Elementary School Journal, 86*, 305–316.

Henry, M. K (1989). Children's word structure knowledge: Implications for decoding and spelling instruction. *Reading and Writing, 1*, 135–152.

Henry, M. K. (1996). *Words: Integrated decoding and spelling instruction based on word origin and word structure*. Austin, TX: Pro-Ed.

Hockett, C. (1958). *A course in modern linguistics*. New York: Macmillan.

Horn, E. (1926). *A basic vocabulary of 10,000 words most commonly used in writing.* Iowa City: University of Iowa.

Horn, E. (1960). Spelling. In C. W. Harris (Ed.), *Encyclopedia of educational research* (3rd ed., pp. 1337–1354). New York: Macmillan.

Horn, T. (1946). *The effect of the corrected test on learning to spell.* Unpublished master's thesis, University of Iowa, Iowa City.

Horn, T. (1969). Spelling. In R. L. Ebel (Ed.), *Encyclopedia of educational research* (4th ed., pp. 1282–1299). New York: Macmillan.

Hughes, M., & Searle, D. (1997). *The violent e and other tricky sounds: Learning to spell from kindergarten through grade 6.* York, ME: Stenhouse.

Huxford, L., Terrell, C., & Bradley, L. (1992). 'Invented' spelling and learning to read. In C. Sterling, & C. Robson (Eds.), *Psychology, spelling, and education* (pp. 159–167). Clevedon, UK: Multilingual Matters.

Invernizzi, M. (1985). A cross-sectional analysis of children's recognition and recall of word elements. *Dissertation Abstracts International, 47* (02A), 483. (University Microfilms No. AAG8526886)

Invernizzi, M. (1992). The vowel and what follows: A phonological frame for orthographic analysis. In S. Templeton, & D. R. Bear (Eds.), *Development of orthographic Knowledge and the foundations of literacy: A memorial festschrift for Edmund H. Henderson* (pp. 106–136). Hillsdale, NJ: Lawrence Erlbaum Associates.

Invernizzi, M., Abouzeid, M., & Gill, J. T. (1994). Using students' invented spellings as a guide for spelling instruction that emphasizes word study. *Elementary School Journal, 95,* 155–167.

Lenneberg, E. (1967). *The biological foundations of language.* New York: John Wiley & Sons.

Marsh, G., Friedman, M., Welch, V., & Desberg, P. (1980). The development of strategies in spelling. In U. Frith (Ed.), *Cognitive strategies in spelling* (pp. 339–353). New York: Academic Press.

McKee, P. (1924). *Teaching and testing spelling by column and context forms.* Unpublished doctoral dissertation, University of Iowa, Iowa City.

Moats, L. (1995). *Spelling: Development, disabilities, and instruction.* Baltimore, MD: York Press.

Moats, L., & Smith, C. (1992). Derivational morphology: Why it should be included in assessment and instruction. *Language, Speech, and Hearing in the Schools, 23,* 312–319.

Morris, D. (1983). Concept of word and phoneme awareness in the beginning reader. *Research in the Teaching of English, 17,* 359–373.

Morris, D. (1993). The relationship between children's concept of word in text and phoneme awareness in learning to read: A longitudinal study. *Research in the Teaching of English, 27,* 133–154.

Morris, D., Blanton, L., Blanton, W. E., Nowacek, J., & Perney, J. (1995). Teaching low-achieving spellers at their "instructional level." *Elementary School Journal, 96,* 163–178.

Morris, D., Blanton, L., Blanton, W., & Perney, J. (1995). Spelling instruction and achievement in six classrooms. *Elementary School Journal, 96,* 145–162.

Morris, D., Nelson, L., & Perney, J. (1986). Exploring the concept of "spelling instructional level" through the analysis of error-types. *Elementary School Journal, 87,* 181–200.

Nagy, W. E., & Anderson, R. C. (1984). How many words are there in printed school English? *Reading Research Quarterly, 19,* 304–330.

Perfetti, C. A. (1985). *Reading ability.* New York: Oxford University Press.

Perfetti, C. A. (1992). The representation problem in reading acquisition. In P. B. Gough, L. C. Ehri, & R. Treiman (Eds.), *Reading acquisition* (pp. 145–174). Hillsdale, NJ: Lawrence Erlbaum Associates.

Perfetti, C. A., Rieben, L., & M. Fayol (Eds.). (1997). *Learning to spell: Research, theory, and practice across languages.* Mahwah, NJ: Lawrence Erlbaum Associates.

Rayner, K., & Pollatsek, A. (1995). *The psychology of reading* (2nd ed.). Hillsdale, NJ: Lawrence Erlbaum Associates.

Read, C. (1971). Preschool children's knowledge of English phonology. *Harvard Educational Review, 41,* 1–34.

Read, C. (1975). *Children's categorizations of speech sounds in English.* Urbana, IL: National Council of Teachers of English.

Read, C. (1994). Teaching the lexicon to read and spell. Review of Shane Templeton and Donald R. Bear (Eds.), Development of Orthographic Knowledge and the Foundations of Literacy: A Memorial Festschrift for Edmund H. Henderson. *American Journal of Psychology, 107,* 471–476.

Read, C., & Hodges, R. (1982). Spelling. In H. Mitzel (Ed.), *Encyclopedia of educational research* (5th ed., pp. 1758–1767). New York: Macmillan.

Richgels, D. (1995). Invented spelling ability and printed word learning in kindergarten. *Reading Research Quarterly, 30,* 96–109.

Richgels, D. J. (1995). Invented spelling ability and printed word learning in kindergarten. *Reading Research Quarterly, 30,* 96–109.

Sabey, B. (1997). *Metacognitive responses of syllable juncture spellers while performing three literacy tasks.* Unpublished doctoral dissertation. University of Nevada, Reno.

Schlagal, R. C. (1982). A qualitative inventory of word knowledge: A developmental study of spelling, grades one through six. *Dissertation Abstracts International, 47* (03A), 915. (University Microfilms No. AAG8611798)

Schlagal, R. (1992). Patterns of orthographic development into the intermediate grades. In S. Templeton & D. R. Bear (Eds.), *Development of orthographic knowledge and the foundations of literacy: A memorial festschrift for Edmund H. Henderson* (pp. 31–52). Hillsdale, NJ: Lawrence Erlbaum Associates.

Scragg, D. G. (1974). *A history of English spelling.* New York: Barnes & Noble.

Seymour, P. (1992). Cognitive theories of spelling and implications for instruction. In C. M. Sterling & C. Robson (Eds.), *Psychology, spelling, and education* (pp. 50–70). Clevedon, UK: Multilingual Matters.

Simplified Spelling Board. (1906). *Simplified spelling.* Washington, DC: Government Printing Office.

Snowling, M. (1994). Towards a model of spelling acquisition: The development of some component skills. In G. D. A. Brown & N. C. Ellis (Eds.), *Handbook of spelling: Theory, process, and intervention* (pp. 111–128). Chichester, England: John Wiley and Sons.

Stanovich, K. E., & Cunningham, A. E. (1993). Where does knowledge come from? Specific associations between print exposure and information acquisition. *Journal of Educational Psychology, 85,* 211–229.

Stever, E. (1977). Dialectic and socioeconomic factors affecting the spelling strategies of second-grade students. *Dissertation Abstracts International, 37* (07A), 4120. (University Microfilms No. AAG7700149)

Taft, M. (1991). *Reading and the mental lexicon.* Hillsdale, NJ: Lawrence Erlbaum Associates.

Temple, C. A. (1978). An analysis of spelling errors in Spanish. *Dissertation Abstracts International, 40* (02A), 721. (University Microfilms No. AAG7916258)

Templeton, S.(1976, December). *The spelling of young children in relation to the logic of alphabetic orthography.* Paper presented at the 26th annual convention of the National Reading Conference, Atlanta, GA.

Templeton, S. (1979). Spelling first, sound later: The relationship between orthography and higher order phonological knowledge in older students. *Research in the Teaching of English, 13,* 255–264.

Templeton, S. (1989). Tacit and explicit knowledge of derivational morphology: Foundations for a unified approach to spelling and vocabulary development in the intermediate grades and beyond. *Reading Psychology, 10,* 233–253.

Templeton, S. (1991). Teaching and learning the English spelling system: Reconceptualizing method and purpose. *Elementary School Journal, 92,* 183–199.

Templeton, S. (1992a). New trends in an historical perspective: Old story, new resolution—Sound and meaning in spelling. *Language Arts, 69,* 454–463.

Templeton, S. (1992b). Theory, nature, and pedagogy of higher-order orthographic development in older students. In S. Templeton & D. R. Bear (Eds.), *Development of orthographic knowledge and the foundations of literacy: A memorial festschrift for Edmund H. Henderson* (pp. 253–277). Hillsdale, NJ: Lawrence Erlbaum Associates.

Templeton, S., & Bear, D. R. (Eds.). (1992). *Development of orthographic knowledge and the foundations of literacy: A memorial festschrift for Edmund H. Henderson.* Hillsdale, NJ: Lawrence Erlbaum Associates.

Templeton, S., & Scarborough-Franks, L. (1985). The spelling's the thing: Older students' knowledge of derivational morphology in phonology and orthography. *Applied Psycholinguistics, 6,* 371–389.

Templeton, W. S. (1976). An awareness of certain aspects of derivational morphology in phonology and orthography among sixth, eighth, and tenth-graders. *Dissertation Abstracts International, 37* (07A), 4190. (University Microfilms No. AAG7700209)

Thorndike, E. L. (1921). *The teacher's word book.* New York: Teachers College Press.

Treiman, R. (1993). *Beginning to spell.* New York: Oxford University Press.

Vachek, J. (1989). *Written language revisited.* Amsterdam: J. Benjamins.

Varnhagen, V. W. (1995). Children's spelling strategies. In V. W. Berninger (Ed.). *The varieties of orthographic knowledge. Volume II: Relationships to phonology, reading and writing* (pp. 251–290). Dordrecht, The Netherlands: Kluwer.

Venezky, R. L. (1970). *The structure of English orthography.* The Hague: Mouton.

Venezky, R. L. (1980). From Webster to Rice to Roosevelt: The formative years for spelling instruction and spelling reform in the U.S.A. In U. Frith (Ed.), *Cognitive processes in spelling* (pp. 9–30). London: Academic Press.

Venezky, R. L. (in press). *A treatise on English orthography.* New York: Guilford.

Wilde, S. (1991). *You Kan Red This!: Spelling and punctuation for whole language classrooms, K–6.* Portsmouth, NH: Heinemann.

Worthy, M. J., & Invernizzi, M. (1990). Spelling errors of normal and disabled students on achievement levels one through four: Instructional implications. *Annals of Dyslexia, 40* 138–151.

Worthy, J., & Viise, N. M. (1986). Morphological, phonological, and orthographic differences between the spelling of normally achieving children and basic literacy adults. *Reading and Writing: An Interdisciplinary Journal, 8,* 139–159.

Yaden, D., Jr., & Templeton, S. (Eds.). (1986). *Metalinguistic awareness and beginning literacy: Conceptualizing what it means to read and write.* Portsmouth, NH: Heinemann.

Zutell, J. (1975). Spelling strategies of primary school children and their relationship to the piagetian concept of decentration. *Dissertation Abstracts International, 36* (08A), 5030. (University Microfilms No. AAG7600018)

Zutell, J. (1979). Spelling strategies of primary school children and their relationship to Piaget's concept of decentration. *Research in the Teaching of English, 13*(1), 69–80.

Zutell, J. (1992). An integrated view of word knowledge: Correlational studies of the relationships among spelling, reading, and conceptual development. In S. Templeton & D. R. Bear (Eds.), *Development of orthographic knowledge and the foundations of literacy: A memorial festschrift for Edmund H. Henderson* (pp. 213–230). Hillsdale, NJ: Lawrence Erlbaum Associates.

Zutell, J. (1994). Spelling instruction. In A. C. Purves, L. Papa, & S. Jordan, (Eds.), *Encyclopedia of English studies and language arts* (Vol. 2, pp. 1098–1100). New York: Scholastic.

Zutell, J. (1996). The Directed Spelling Thinking Activity (DSTA): Providing an effective balance in word study instruction. *Reading Teacher, 50,* 98–108.

Zutell, J., & Rasinski, T. (1989). Reading and spelling connections in third and fifth grade students. *Reading Psychology, 10,* 137–155.

CHAPTER 30

What Should Comprehension Instruction Be the Instruction Of?

Michael Pressley
University of Notre Dame

Children are taught to read so that they can understand what is in text. Thus, most of what matters in reading instruction matters because ultimately it affects whether the student develops into a reader who can comprehend what is in text. Reading instruction is effective in stimulating student comprehension abilities to the extent that it stimulates students to process texts as good readers do. It is important to understand what those processes are, and thus, the first major section of this chapter is devoted to coverage of the ideas and research on effective comprehension that seems most relevant to consider in making recommendations about comprehension instruction. The discussion in the second section on instruction is explicitly informed by the review of effective comprehension in the first section.

As a preview of what is to come, this chapter differs from recent treatments on comprehension instruction (Pearson & Dole, 1991; Pearson & Fielding, 1987; Pressley, Johnson, Symons, McGoldrick, & Kurita, 1989), which have focused on strategy instruction to the exclusion of other approaches. I review in the first section of this chapter how the development of comprehension depends on word-level skills, background knowledge, and comprehension strategies. Hence, in the second section of the chapter, I make the case that instruction aimed at increasing comprehension abilities should be aimed at improving word-level competencies, building background knowledge, and promoting use of comprehension strategies.

I found it challenging to write an integrative, summary chapter on comprehension instruction, especially in light of the space constraints given to me. First, during the 20th century, there was a great deal of research that can be related to the naturalistic development of comprehension skills and development of comprehension abilities through instruction. Second, much of that work was fragmented, with the typical investigator interested in a particular aspect of comprehension or instruction, most often to the exclusion of others. Third, comprehension and comprehension instruction typically have been studied separately. Researchers interested in naturalistic comprehension often seem to have given little to no thought about the development of comprehension skills through instructional experiences. Typically, instructional researchers focused on the aspects of comprehension most relevant to the comprehension instruction they favored (e.g., strategy instructionalists were informed about readers' naturalistic use of comprehension strategies but not as much about word-level comprehension).

Despite the challenges, including the fragmented, large literature, I offer in the first section of this chapter a summary of the work on naturalistic comprehension that seems to me to be most pertinent to consider in thinking about instruction. What is emphasized in this section are ideas about naturalistic comprehension that have had some staying power, in that they are referenced often by the reading research community. Rather than exhaustive citation of research, I relate studies that have provided especially compelling evidence with respect to each of the points made about naturalistic comprehension. The second section is a list of instructional recommendations that make sense based on both work pertaining to naturalistic comprehension and research directly concerned with comprehension instruction.

WHAT IS KNOWN ABOUT THE DEVELOPMENT OF SKILLED COMPREHENSION

Comprehension involves a number of lower order (i.e., word-level) and higher order processes (i.e., processes above the word level) specific to reading. The review of efficient, naturalistic comprehension in this section proceeds from word-level processes to the higher order skills.

Word-Level Processes Affecting Comprehension

A useful way of thinking about word-level processes that affect comprehension is to consider those more affecting recognition of words (i.e., decoding) versus those more affecting understanding of words.

Decoding.   In recent years, there has been a great deal of work directed at how skilled readers are adept at sounding out words based on knowledge of graphemic–phonemic relationships and how children can be taught to blend graphemic–phonemic cues to read words (Ehri, 1991, 1992). Once sounded out, the child can recognize the word because all words in the books encountered by beginning readers are ones that have been in the speaking vocabularies of most children for years.

Thus, many researchers studying beginning reading assume that if children can decode words in the books that they are reading, they will understand them (Gough & Tunmer, 1986). An extension of this line of reasoning is that word-level decoding is a critical bottleneck in the comprehension process, that if the reader cannot decode a word, she or he cannot comprehend it (e.g., Adams, 1990; Metsala & Ehri, 1998; Pressley, 1998, Chap. 6).

There is increasing evidence that skilled decoders do not sound out letter by letter when they encounter an unfamiliar word, however, but rather recognize common letter chunks, such as the recurring blends (e.g., *sh-, br-*), prefixes, suffixes, Latin and Greek root words, and rimes (e.g., *-ight, -on, -ime, -ake*) of the language (e.g., Ehri, 1992). Thus, the fluent English reader would not sound out the nonsense word *dight*, but would recognize the *-ight* chunk automatically and blend its sound with the beginning *d* sound. The ability to recognize recurring word chunks and use them to sound out words is present to some extent even in a 4-year-old, that is, even in readers who are just learning to decode (Goswami, 1998).

With respect to comprehension of words, development of skill in recognizing word chunks should have a positive impact on the comprehension of words. This is because both recognizing and comprehending a word occur within short-term memory (i.e., consciousness), which is limited in its capacity (Miller, 1956). Hence, recognition and comprehension of a word compete for the short-term capacity available for processing of the word. Thus, the more effort required to decode a word, the less capacity is left over to comprehend it (LaBerge & Samuels, 1974). Hence, in general, the more automatic decoding processes are, the better is the understanding of the word. Reading of words boils down to decoding and comprehension, with word-level comprehension depending greatly on the efficiency of decoding (Gough & Tunmer, 1986).

One potential problem with this line of argument is that training children to read words to the point of automaticity has not always produced improved comprehension (e.g., Fleisher, Jenkins, & Pany, 1979; Samuels, Dahl, & Archwamety, 1974; Yuill & Oakhill, 1988, 1991). A recent analysis involving especially thorough training of word recognition, however, produced data more consistent with the conclusion that learning words to the point of rapid recognition improves reading comprehension (Tan & Nicholson, 1997).

The participants in Tan and Nicholson (1997) were 7- to-10-year-old weaker readers. In the critical training condition of the study, participants practiced recognizing target words until they could read each word without hesitation. This training condition also included brief training about the meaning of the trained words. In contrast, in the control condition, training consisted of discussions between the experimenter and the student about the meanings of target words, although the students did not see the words (i.e., the experimenter read the words to the students). Thus, the control condition was heavily oriented toward developing participants' understanding of the word with no attention to the development of word recognition.

Following training, the participants in Tan and Nicholson (1997) read a passage containing the target words, with 12 comprehension questions following the reading. Eight questions could be answered based on verbatim information in the text; four required making an inference based on combining pieces of information in the text. Although some of the questions tapped points in the passage relating directly to trained words, this was never the case for the majority of questions. (The exact number of questions based on target vocabulary varied from pupil to pupil because different training lists and passages were employed, depending on characteristics of the reader.) The most important result was that the trained participants answered more comprehension questions than did control participants, despite the fact, that if anything, the control condition developed understanding of the target words better than did the training condition. See Breznitz (1997a, 1997b) for another set of analyses confirming that more rapid decoding improves comprehension, probably by freeing up more short-term capacity for comprehension.

Researchers and educators who identify with whole-language philosophy and methods have rejected the validity of word recognition as being driven primarily by graphemic–phonemic analyses. Their perspective is that word recognition in the context of text involves three cuing systems: the graphemic–phonemic cues within a word, but also syntactic cues (i.e., information about the syntactic role of the word in the sentence) and semantic cues (i.e., meaning cues about the word in the text, including clues in illustrations accompanying the text). Most emphatically, the graphemic–phonemic cuing system is not primary in word decoding according to the whole-language perspective, with meaning cues considered much more critical (e.g., Goodman, 1993, 1996; Weaver, 1994).

Even though the scientific evidence favors the graphemic–phonemic cues as primary in skilled decoding (e.g., Nicholson, 1991; Nicholson, Bailey, & McArthur, 1991), skilled decoders recognize when they have misread a word because it does not make sense in the context being read (Gough, 1983, 1984; Isakson & Miller, 1976). That is why powerful approaches aimed at the improvement of beginning reading, such as Reading Recovery, teach students to pay attention to whether the word that has been sounded out makes sense in the context being read (Clay, 1991). Thus, powerful approaches to beginning reading encourage word comprehension in relation to the overall meaning of the text, and in doing so, provide feedback about the adequacy of decoding and whether there is the need to work additionally at decoding the word that was just processed.

Vocabulary.   The extent of a reader's vocabulary is related to the person's comprehension skills (e.g., Anderson & Freebody, 1981; Nagy, Anderson, & Herman, 1987). Particularly important here, there are experimental data making clear that a more extensive vocabulary promotes comprehension skill (Beck, Perfetti, & McKeown, 1982; McKeown, Beck, Omanson, & Perfetti, 1983; McKeown, Beck, Omanson, & Pople, 1985).

For example, in Beck et al. (1982), Grade 4 children were taught 104 new vocabulary words over a period of 5 months, with the students encountering the words often as part of the intervention and using the words in multiple ways as part of instruction. At the end of the study, comprehension tended to be better for students receiving the vocabulary intervention compared to control students, including on an analysis of pretest-to-posttest gain scores on a standardized comprehension test. Not all attempts to increase vocabulary have led to increases in comprehension skills, however. In reviewing the relevant studies, Beck and McKeown (1991; see also Durso & Coggins, 1991), concluded that when comprehension was not affected by vocabulary development, there tended to be superficial and rote learning of vocabulary–definition linkages. Vocabulary development–comprehension development linkages are more certain when students make deep and extensive connections between vocabulary words and their definitions—that is, when the teaching requires the students to use the words in multiple ways, over an extended period of time.

Although vocabulary can be taught, most vocabulary words are learned incidentally as a function of encounters in context (Sternberg, 1987). This is one reason why people who read a great deal have extensive vocabularies, with the lexical development stimulated by reading in turn empowering reading in the future (Stanovich, 1986). As will be elaborated in the next subsection, knowledge of all sorts potentially increases comprehension skills, although the impact of vocabulary knowledge is especially direct. If a word is not known to the reader, then the reader's understanding of it depends entirely on context clues, with the result uncertain understanding of the word. Readers often do not infer correctly the meaning of a word from context clues (Miller & Gildea, 1987). When a sentence or passage's comprehension depends critically on just that one word, the potential for lack of vocabulary knowledge undermining comprehension is obvious. Comprehension very much depends on word-level processing.

Summary.   Skilled decoding of words depends somewhat on comprehension (i.e., the meaning of a word as decoded is compared to the overall meaning of the text to determine if the word as decoded makes sense in the present context). Decoding also contributes to comprehension, however. The more skilled the decoding, the less conscious effort is required for it, and the more conscious capacity is left over for comprehension of the word, including in relation to contextual clues. If the word is not one in the reader's listening vocabulary, such context cues are critical in providing hints about the word's meaning. Although most vocabulary words are learned through contextual encounters, studies in which vocabulary have been taught explicitly have been especially revealing about the causal role of vocabulary knowledge in the development of comprehension skills.

Processes Above the Word Level Affecting Comprehension

As important as word-level processes are in comprehension, most comprehension researchers have focused on more integrative processes above the word level. The most prominent analyses in recent decades are taken up in this section.

Automatic Relating of Text Content to Prior Knowledge.   The mature reader knows much about the world. Such prior knowledge affects comprehension, with readers' schematic knowledge, in particular, and how schematic knowledge affected comprehension explored in detail in the 1970s and 1980s (e.g., Anderson & Pearson, 1984; Anderson, Reynolds, Schallert, & Goetz, 1977). A central premise of schema theory is that much of knowledge is stored in complex relational structures, schemata (schema is the singular, schemata the plural). Thus, the schema for a ship christening includes its purpose—to bless the ship. It includes information about where it is done (i.e., in dry dock), by whom (i.e., a celebrity), and when it occurs (i.e., just before launching of a new ship). The christening action is also represented (i.e., breaking a bottle of champagne that is suspended from a rope).

Schemata help people understand events easily. Thus, once some small part of the ship-christening schema is encountered, perhaps a picture of the bottle of champagne being held up to the ship, the activated schema causes reasonable inferences to be made about details of the event (e.g., as the bottle is seen breaking on the bow, the viewer might infer that there was a platform beside the ship with one or more persons on it, one of them a celebrity). Schematic processing is decidedly top-down in that activation of the higher order idea occurs first and affects thinking about the details of the situation.

Schematic processing affects comprehension from early in life. Katherine Nelson, Judith Hudson, Robyn Fivush, Patricia Bauer, and their colleagues determined that even very young children develop schematic representations for recurring events in their lives (Bauer & Fivush, 1992). Thus, children have schemata representing events such as dinner (both at home and at McDonald's!), bedtime, making cookies, birthday parties, and going to a museum (Hudson, 1990; Hudson & Nelson, 1983; Hudson & Shapiro, 1991; McCartney & Nelson, 1981; Nelson, 1978; Nelson & Gruendel, 1981). Such knowledge permits them to draw inferences from stories that include information related to their schematic knowledge (e.g., Hudson & Slackman, 1990). For example, when preschoolers are presented stories that are not quite right, in that they include information inconsistent with schemata stored by most children, what children do is to make inferences to "fix" the story to be consistent with their schemata (Hudson & Nelson, 1983). Of course, for schemata to affect text processing, the reader must have had the experiences permitting the schemata to develop. Thus, the richer a child's world experiences and vicarious experiences (e.g., through stories and high-quality television), the richer the child's schematic knowledge base.

Comprehension does not always occur vis-á-vis schemata. Sometimes understanding occurs from the bottom up (Graesser, 1981; Kintsch, 1974, 1982, 1983), with the reader processing many individual ideas in text (and sometimes referred to as propositions) and how the ideas are related to one another by the text to construct a general understanding of the text's meaning, with such summary meanings sometimes referred to as macropropositions (e.g., Kintsch, 1983; van Dijk & Kintsch, 1983). Knowledge from this perspective is most often conceived as networks of propositions and macropropositions. From this perspective, knowledge, in general, can be developed from reading broadly but also from other world experiences.

When readers encounter ideas in text that relate to knowledge encoded in their propositional networks, there is the possibility of activation of the directly relevant and associated prior knowledge, which is then used in comprehending the current text, for example, by permitting inferences based on the prior knowledge (e.g., Hayes-Roth & Thorndyke, 1979; Kintsch, 1988; van Dijk & Kintsch, 1983, chap. 6). One of the really important findings produced by those working within the propositional-theoretical tradition, however, is that skilled thinkers do not make inferences unless understanding of the text demands them (McKoon & Ratcliff, 1992). That is, when reading a text, there are many inferences that could be made based on prior knowledge, but are not made. Typically, good readers make prior knowledge-based inferences only when they are required to understand the ideas in text. In doing so, the readers relate only prior knowledge that is directly relevant to the ideas encoded in text. One of the ways that weak readers undermine their comprehension is by relating to texts they are reading prior knowledge that is not directly relevant to the most important ideas in the text, making unwarranted and unnecessary inferences as they do so (e.g., Williams, 1993).

In short, both schema and propositional theorists provide accountings about how long-term knowledge can affect processing and comprehension of new information, more or less automatically. Both theories specify that readers often relate their prior knowledge to ideas in text, when the ideas in text overlap to some extent the ideas in the long-term knowledge base. Such automatic use of prior knowledge to comprehend text is decidedly in contrast to the many reading processes that can be consciously controlled.

Conscious, Controllable Processing.   Peter Afflerbach and I (Pressley & Afflerbach, 1995) analyzed and summarized the 40+ think-aloud studies of reading that have been published. In each of these investigations, readers read texts and, as they did so, reported verbally what they were doing and/or thinking. The verbal protocol studies provided a great deal of information about readers' goals and how readers' goals influence text processing, as well as the articulation of online processing of text, inferences, and affective responses during reading. That is, the verbal protocols were especially informative about comprehension processes that are conscious and controllable.

Mature readers flexibly use a variety of processes as they read texts, including the following:

- Being aware of their purpose in reading, whether it be pleasure or to find critical information for some task (e.g., writing a paper, evaluating a political position).
- Overviewing the text to determine if it is really relevant to the reader's goal as well as to identify sections that might be particularly apt.
- Reading selectively, focusing on the portions of text most relevant to the reader's goal.
- Making associations to ideas presented in a text based on reader prior knowledge.
- Evaluating and revising hypotheses that arose during previewing or occurred in reaction to earlier parts of the text, revising hypotheses if that is in order.
- Revising prior knowledge that is inconsistent with ideas in the text, if the reader is convinced by the arguments in the text (alternatively, rejecting the ideas in the text, when they clash with prior knowledge).
- Figuring out the meanings of novel words in text, especially if the words seem important to the overall meaning of the text.
- Underlining, rereading, making notes, and/or paraphrasing in an attempt to remember some point made in the text.
- Interpreting text, perhaps to the point of having an imaginary conversation with the author.

- Evaluating the quality of the text.
- Reviewing the text after the reading is completed.
- Thinking about how to use the information in the text in the future.

Summary.   Words in text specify a large number of interrelated ideas, each of which can be thought of as a proposition. Readers can process interrelated propositions to construct summary understandings of what they read. The summary understandings that are produced depend in part, however, on the knowledge that the reader brings to the reading, with the knowledgeable reader possessing much knowledge that is schematic and can be used to understand text that is read. Whether a reader uses relevant schematic knowledge (i.e., prior knowledge) depends somewhat on unconscious and automatic processes of association but also on many conscious reading processes, ones that can occur before, during, and after reading.

Text comprehension begins with decoding of words, processing of those words in relation to one another to understand the many small ideas in the text, and then, both unconsciously and consciously, operating on the ideas in the text to construct the overall meaning encoded in the text. Of course, the meaning constructed by the reader is a function of the ideas explicitly represented in the text and the reader's response to those ideas, responses that often depend greatly on the prior knowledge of the reader (Anderson & Pearson, 1984; Rosenblatt, 1978). The many active processes of reading—prediction, construction of images during reading, monitoring of comprehension and rereading, summarization, and interpretation—depend greatly on prior knowledge, with skilled reading being an articulation of prior knowledge and these active reading processes. Because comprehension is complicated it requires a complicated educational strategy to meet the goal of improving readers' comprehension skills.

HOW TO DEVELOP COMPREHENSION ABILITIES THROUGH INSTRUCTION: RECOMMENDATIONS FOLLOWING FROM THE ANALYSIS OF COMPREHENSION

One implication of the analysis of comprehension just offered is that instruction aimed at promoting comprehension skills should be multicomponential. Another implication is that development of comprehension abilities is best thought of as a long-term developmental process. In particular, if the word-level processes are not mastered (i.e., recognition of most words is not automatic), it will be impossible to carry out the higher order processes that are summarized as reading comprehension strategies. Thus, for each of the recommendations that follow, I comment on the points in development when the recommendation makes most sense.

Teach Decoding Skills

There is much that is now known about promoting the development of decoding skills. The probability of success in early reading is promoted by teaching students the letter–sound relationships, with plenty of practice in sounding out words (Adams, 1990; Chall, 1967). There is increasing evidence that it also helps to teach the major word chunks in English (i.e., prefixes, suffixes, base words, blends, digraphs; Ehri & Robbins, 1992; Peterson & Haines, 1992). It is somewhat ironic that those who favor downplaying decoding instruction often do so by claiming that they want children to orient more to the meaning of the texts being read (e.g., Goodman, 1996; Weaver, 1994), for getting the meaning of the text is facilitated when the reader can easily recognize the individual words on the page (e.g., Juel, Griffith, & Gough, 1986; also see Tan &

Nicholson, 1997, reviewed earlier in this chapter). Not surprisingly, well-developed word recognition skills in the primary years also predict good comprehension in the later elementary grades (e.g., Juel, 1988). Thus, one way to develop comprehension abilities is to develop decoding skills during the primary years.

Encourage the Development of Sight Words

When less effort can be put into decoding during reading, there is more short-term capacity for comprehension of text. When words are recommended automatically, this maximizes the capacity available for understanding the word (LaBerge & Samuels, 1974). Demonstrations such as that of Tan and Nicholson (1997) go far in supporting the practice of drilling students on words they will frequently encounter and continue such drilling until words are recognized without hesitation. This is a practice that certainly makes sense during the early elementary years.

Teach Students to Use Semantic Context Cues to Evaluate Whether Decodings are Accurate

Although whole-language enthusiasts have urged that students be taught to use semantic context cues (i.e., picture cues, the emerging storyline) as primary in decoding per se (e.g., Goodman, 1993, 1996), there is little support for this recommendation (e.g., Nicholson, 1991; Nicholson et al., 1991). What good readers do, however, is catch themselves when they mis-decode by noticing that the word as decoded does not make sense in the present context (Isakson & Miller, 1976). Encouraging such monitoring and correction is decidedly consistent with what good readers do (Baker & Brown, 1984). In doing so, comprehension in general should be improved, for much more of the text will be correctly decoded. This is an important skill that can be developed as an integral part of primary reading instruction.

Teach Vocabulary Meanings

With respect to understanding the individual words, there is a substantial debate about whether it makes sense to attempt to teach vocabulary to students. One part of the argument invokes naturalistic vocabulary acquisition processes (Sternberg, 1987). Students learn most vocabulary in context, incidentally as a function of experiencing and reexperiencing vocabulary words in reading and speaking contexts, and vocabulary words so acquired are going to be better learned and understood than vocabulary taught through explicit instruction, because the learner will have been so active and constructive in developing the meaning of the word in the former compared to the latter situation. A second part of the argument is that there are so many vocabulary words that instruction has no hope of making much dent on comprehension (e.g., Nagy & Anderson, 1984). A counter is that those raising this objection overestimate the number of different words in English that need to be known in order to read well (e.g., d'Anna, Zechmeister, & Hall, 1991).

As an empiricist, however, I am impressed by demonstrations such as those provided by Beck and her colleagues that reading comprehension does improve when students are taught vocabulary that can be related to the readings they are doing (Beck et al., 1982; McKeown et al., 1983, 1985). I think there is more evidence in favor of teaching vocabulary than evidence against the practice. I know of no evidence that suggests such teaching should be limited to some particular age or grade level.

Encourage Extensive Reading

Being able to decode per se helps comprehension somewhat, but as long as decoding is effortful, decoding is a bottleneck, using up valuable capacity that could serve comprehension if reading of words was more fluent. The development of fluent, automatic word recognition depends on many encounters with words (LaBerge & Samuels, 1974), with the most natural way for that to occur through reading and lots of it. The more a reader reads and improves fluency, the more comprehension should improve by increasing the cognitive capacity available for comprehension.

Comprehension should be more certain as a consequence of extensive reading of and exposure to excellent literature and expository material for another reason, however. Literature exposure increases reader knowledge (Stanovich & Cunningham, 1993), for example, as reflected by the breadth of the reader's knowledge of vocabulary (e.g., Dickinson & Smith, 1994; Elley, 1989; Fleisher et al., 1979; Pellegrini, Galda, Perlmutter, & Jones, 1994; Robbins & Ehri, 1994; Rosenhouse, Feitelson, Kita, & Goldstein, 1997; Valdez-Menchaca & Whitehurst, 1992; Whitehurst et al., 1988). Thus, when children read books that include a great deal of information pertaining to beginning science, they know more science (Morrow, Pressley, Smith, & Smith, 1997), which should improve comprehension of related science content encountered in the future.

That there are multiple benefits from reading a great deal is why elementary students are so often advised to, "Read! Read! Read!" Encouraging extensive reading is possible throughout elementary schooling and for all students, for even the youngest and most immature readers can "read" picture books.

Encourage Students to Ask Themselves Why the Ideas Related in a Text Make Sense

Although readers often automatically relate what they know to ideas in text, they do not always do so when doing so might permit the reader to meet task demands. In particular, fact-filled text can be rendered much more memorable by encouraging students to consistently ask themselves why the facts in the text are sensible. Wood, Pressley, and Winne (1990, Experiment 2) provided a clear demonstration that children in Grades 4 through 8 can benefit from asking themselves why-questions about facts presented in connected text.

The children in Wood et al. (1990, Experiment 2) were asked to learn elementary science content pertaining to different types of animals. For each animal, they read a paragraph specifying the physical characteristics of the animal's home as well as its diet, sleeping habits, preferred habitat, and predators. Some students were instructed to ask themselves why each fact in the text made sense (e.g., for the facts related to skunks: "Why do skunks eat corn?" "Why do owls prey on skunks?" "Why is the skunk away from 3 a.m. until dawn?") and to attempt to answer such why questions based on prior knowledge as they read. These students remembered much more of what was presented in the text than control students, who read and studied the text as they normally would.

Why-questioning produces large effects on learning and can be used profitably by elementary and middle school students to learn material in factually dense text (Pressley, Wood, Woloshyn, Martin, King, & Menke, 1992). It does so by orienting readers to prior knowledge that can render the facts in a text more sensible, and hence, more comprehensible and memorable (Martin & Pressley, 1991). One way to think about teaching students to why-question themselves and answer such why-questions as they read factually dense text is to consider the approach a comprehension strategy.

I did not do so here because this approach has not been included in training programs to date that are intended to stimulate self-regulated use of comprehension strategies, taken up in the next subsection.

Teach Self-Regulated Use of Comprehension Strategies

Despite the improvements in fluency and knowledge permitted by extensive reading, the "read, read, read" approach does not lead to as active meaning construction during reading as occurs when students are taught explicitly to use and articulate comprehension strategies when they read. Teaching students to use comprehension strategies is sensible because self-regulated use of comprehension strategies is prominent in the reading of exceptionally skilled adult readers, as documented in the verbal protocol studies (Pressley & Afflerbach, 1995). That has not been the evidence compelling most scholars who advocate teaching of comprehension strategies, however.

What has compelled them is that comprehension instruction has consistently proven its worth in experimental evaluations of it. There have been two waves of important studies in my view.

The first wave occurred in the 1970s and early 1980s. There were a number of studies evaluating the teaching of individual comprehension strategies (for detailed reviews, see Haller, Child, & Walberg, 1988; Pearson & Dole, 1987; Pearson & Fielding, 1991; Pressley, Johnson, Symons, McGoldrick, & Kurita, 1989). In these studies, participants in the treatment condition were taught to use a particular strategy during reading, with control participants left to their own devices to process the text. (An assumption in all of these studies was that the participants, who typically were children, did not use the instructed strategy already.) Reading of text typically was followed by some type of objective test of understanding (e.g., multiple-choice items over literal and implied messages in text). If the strategy-trained students outperformed the control students on the test, there was support for the efficacy of the strategy.

Strategies that proved their worth in such studies included the following:(a) prior knowledge activation (e.g., Levin & Pressley, 1981), (b) question generation during reading (e.g., Rosenshine & Trapman, 1992), (c) construction of mental images representing the meanings expressed in text (e.g., Gambrell & Bales, 1986; Gambrell & Jawitz, 1993; Pressley, 1976), (d) summarization (e. g., Armbruster, Anderson, & Ostertag, 1987; Bean & Steenwyk, 1984; Berkowitz, 1986; Brown & Day, 1983; Brown, Day, & Jones, 1983; Taylor, 1982; Taylor & Beach, 1984), and (e) analyzing stories into story grammar components (Idol, 1987; Idol & Croll, 1987; Short & Ryan, 1984). That is, researchers succeeded in identifying strategies that readers could use before, during, and after they read, to understand and remember text (Levin & Pressley, 1981).

The second wave of studies followed the development of sophisticated models of thinking that specified that multiple strategies are articulated in sense making (e.g., Baron, 1985; Brown, Bransford, Ferrara, & Campione, 1983; Levin & Pressley, 1981; Nickerson, Perkins, & Smith, 1985). One of the most prominent of the efforts for teaching multiple comprehension strategies was *reciprocal teaching* (Palincsar & Brown, 1984). Four comprehension strategies were at the heart of the approach (i.e., prediction, questioning, seeking clarification when confused, summarization), with students taught over a fairly short period of time (e.g., 20 lessons) to use these strategies as they read text. Reciprocal teaching involved a rigid sequence of events. After a portion of text is read, the student leader of the group (one is appointed) poses a question for peers. The peers attempt to respond. Then the student leader proposes a summary. Only then are the other students in the group invited into the conversation, to seek clarifications by posing questions or make predictions about upcoming text, although a great deal of flexible discussion of text and issues in text can occur with this framework.

Across all of the studies of reciprocal teaching (Rosenshine & Meister, 1994), there were consistent, striking effects on cognitive process measures, such as those tapping summarization and self-questioning skills. With respect to standardized comprehension, however, the effects were less striking, with an average effect size of 0.3 SD. Reciprocal teaching was more successful when there was more direct teaching of the four comprehension strategies than when there was not, important in light of work by Duffy et al. (1987).

Roehler and Duffy (1984) hypothesized that comprehension strategies instruction should begin with teacher explanations of strategies and mental modeling of their use (i.e., showing students how to apply a strategy by thinking aloud; Duffy & Roehler, 1989). Then student practice of the strategies in the context of real reading makes sense. Such practice is monitored by the teacher, with additional explanations and modeling provided as needed. Feedback and instruction is reduced as students become more and more independent (i.e., instruction is scaffolded). Teachers encourage transfer of strategies by going over when and where the strategies being learned might be used. Teachers cue use of the new strategies when students encounter situations where the strategies might be applied profitably, regardless of when these occasions arise during the school day. Cuing and prompting continue until students autonomously apply the strategies they have been taught.

Duffy et al. (1987) evaluated the effects of direct explanation strategy instruction on Grade 3 reading over the course of an entire academic year. All of the skills typically taught in Grade 3 literacy instruction were taught as strategies. By the end of the year, students in the direct explanation condition outperformed control students on standardized measures of reading. These results had a profound effect on the reading education community, with direct explanation as Duffy et al. (1987) defined it subsequently being used by many educators to implement comprehension strategies instructions in their schools.

Additional evaluations of direct explanation approaches to the development of a strategic repertoire followed. The interventions that were evaluated were consistent with what is observed in classroom communities that have comprehension strategies instruction as a centerpiece of the literacy curriculum, with such communities very much influenced by the Roehler and Duffy (1984) model (Pressley, El-Dinary, Gaskins, Schuder, Bergman, Almasi, & Brown 1992). Such instruction came to be known as *transactional strategies instruction* (Pressley, El-Dinary, 1992), because it emphasized reader transactions with texts (Rosenblatt, 1978), interpretations constructed by readers thinking about text together (i.e., transacting; e.g., Hutchins, 1991), and teachers' and students' reactions to text affecting each other's individual thinking about text (i.e., interactions were transactional; e.g., Bell, 1968).

In brief, transactional strategies instruction involves direct explanations and teacher modeling of strategies, followed by guided practice of strategies, consistent with the Duffy et al. (1987) approach. Teacher assistance is provided on an as-needed basis (i.e., strategy instruction is "scaffolded"; Wood, Bruner, & Ross, 1976). There are lively interpretive discussions of texts, with students encouraged to interpret and respond to text as they are exposed to diverse reactions to text by their classmates. The flexibility of student discussion is great with the transactional strategies instruction approach (see Gaskins, Anderson, Pressley, Cunicelli, & Satlow, 1993). There are no restrictions on the order of strategies execution or when the particular members of the group can participate. The transactional strategies instructional approach succeeds in stimulating interpretive dialogues in which strategic processes are used as interpretive vehicles, with consistently high engagement by all group members.

One of the most striking aspects of transactional strategies instruction is that it takes a while, with instruction occurring over semesters and years. This contrasts substantially with the very brief comprehension strategies instruction that was evaluated in the early 1980s (e.g., Palincsar & Brown, 1984).

There have been three published experimental evaluations of long-term transactional strategies instruction: Brown, Pressley, Van Meter, and Schuder (1996) with Grade 2 students; Collins (1991) with Grades 5 and 6 students; and Anderson with middle school and high school students (1992; see also Anderson & Roit, 1993). Transactional strategies instruction produced better comprehension test scores and more interpretive readers in these studies, with the effects quite striking in all three of the evaluations.

In summary, in the past quarter century, there has been a great deal of evidence produced consistent with the general conclusion that comprehension strategies instruction improves understanding of text, especially when children are taught to use such strategies. Although the early studies were extremely limited in scope (i.e., single or a few strategies evaluated in short-term experiments), more recent work has evaluated credible instructional packages delivered over a semester to a year of instruction, consistent with the practices of many educators who are committed to developing strategic comprehension processing in their students through instruction followed by strategies practice.

That there was success in teaching comprehension strategies at the Grade 2 level in Brown et al. (1996) makes clear that such instruction is possible during the primary years. Indeed, I have observed the teaching of individual comprehension strategies at the Grade 1 level (Pressley, El-Dinary, et al, 1992). I have never observed the teaching of more than two strategies until the Grade 2 level, however.

SUMMARY AND CONCLUDING COMMENTS

Throughout the elementary years, it is possible to interact with children in ways to increase their comprehension skills. The beginning of comprehension is the decoding of individual words, and thus, instruction increasing the likelihood that students will become skilled decoders serves the development of comprehension competence. Once children can decode, they are empowered to read, read, and read, with greater fluency, vocabulary, and world knowledge by-products of such reading, all of which contribute to comprehension skill. Beyond incidental learning of vocabulary through reading, students also can be taught vocabulary, which positively affects comprehension. Finally, elementary students can be taught to be active as they read in the sense of using a variety of comprehension strategies to make sense of the meanings encoded in text. When they were taught strategies like the ones that excellent readers report as they read, comprehension, in fact, improved, dramatically in validation studies to date.

The development of comprehension skills is a long-term developmental process, which depends on rich world, language, and text experiences from early in life; learning how to decode; becoming fluent in decoding, in part, through the development of an extensive repertoire of sight words; learning the meanings of vocabulary words commonly encountered in texts; and learning how to abstract meaning from text using the comprehension processes used by skilled readers. The frequent admonition for children to "Read, read, read," makes sense in that extensive reading promotes fluency, vocabulary, and background knowledge (i.e., it promotes a number of competencies simultaneously). Immersion in reading alone, however, is unlikely to lead to maximally skilled comprehension. At the primary level, there is no compelling evidence that such immersion produces the skilled decoding that is important in permitting word-level recognition and comprehension, nor is there evidence that such immersion in the later elementary years results in the development of the many consciously articulated comprehension processes used by good readers.

The development of comprehension is multicomponential and developmental, and hence, teaching to stimulate the development of comprehension skills must be multi-componential and developmental. Thus, although it is defensible at the Grade 1 level to emphasize word-level skills in the service of the development of comprehension skills, it makes more sense for reading instruction in the middle elementary grades to emphasize the development of higher order comprehension strategies, although word-level instruction (e.g., teaching of vocabulary) and word-level development (e.g., increases in fluency with additional practice reading) continue. Comprehension instruction can be enhanced by long-term instruction that fosters development of the skills and knowledge articulated by very good readers as they read.

In closing, I recognize that one response to the list of points made in this chapter is that the list is unnecessary, that teachers know all of this already and are doing it. In fact, with the exception of encouraging students to read extensively, every one of the explicit instructional suggestions in this section is inconsistent with the most constructivist versions of whole language (e.g., Goodman, 1993, 1996; Weaver, 1994), which is the predominant philosophy in elementary language arts in many school districts in North America and abroad. Even the teaching of comprehension strategies, which has received consistent and strong endorsements from the reading research community, is not very common in elementary schools (Pressley, Wharton-McDonald, Hampson, & Echevarria, 1998). Comprehension instruction in elementary schools seems not to be what it could be. A reasonable hypothesis is that if elementary reading instruction were to be transformed so that children were taught the skills and knowledge reviewed in this section, children's comprehension would be better. This is a hypothesis worth testing in the immediate future.

REFERENCES

Adams, M. J. (1990). *Beginning to read*. Cambridge MA: Harvard University Press.

Anderson, R. C., & Freebody, P. (1981). Vocabulary knowledge. In J. T. Guthrie (Ed.), *Comprehension and teaching: Research reviews* (pp. 77–117). Newark, DE: International Reading Association.

Anderson, R. C., & Pearson, P. D. (1984). A schema-theoretic view of basic processes in reading. In P. D. Pearson, R. Barr, M. L. Kamil, & P. Mosenthal (Eds.), *Handbook of reading research* (pp. 255–291). New York: Longman.

Anderson, R. C., Reynolds, R. E., Schallert, D. L., & Goetz, E. T. (1977). Frameworks for comprehending discourse. *American Educational Research Journal, 14*, 367–382.

Anderson, V. (1992). A teacher development project in transactional strategy instruction for teachers of severely reading-disabled adolescents. *Teaching & Teacher Education, 8*, 391–403.

Anderson, V., & Roit, M. (1993). Planning and implementing collaborative strategy instruction for delayed readers in grades 6–10. *Elementary School Journal, 94*, 121–137.

Armbruster, B. B., Anderson, T. H., & Ostertag, J. (1987). Does text structure/summarization instruction facilitate learning from expository text? *Reading Research Quarterly, 22*, 331–346.

Baker, L., & Brown, A. L. (1984). Metacognitive skills and reading. In P. D. Pearson, R. Barr, M. Kamil, & P. Mosenthal (Eds.), *Handbook of reading research* (pp. 353–394). New York: Longman.

Baron, J. (1985). *Rationality and intelligence*. Cambridge, England: Cambridge University Press.

Bauer, P. J., & Fivush, R. (1992). Constructing event representations: Building on a foundation of variation and enabling relations. *Cognitive Development, 7*, 381–401.

Bean, T. W., & Steenwyk, F. L. (1984). The effect of three forms of summarization instruction on sixth graders' summary writing and comprehension. *Journal of Reading Behavior, 16*, 297–306.

Beck, I. L., & McKeown, M. (1991). Conditions of vocabulary acquisition. In R. Barr, M. L. Kamil, P. Mosenthal, & P. D. Pearson (Eds.), *Handbook of reading research* (Vol. II, pp. 789–814). New York: Longman.

Beck, I. L., Perfetti, C. A., &McKeown, M. G. (1982). Effects of long-term vocabulary instruction on lexical access and reading comprehension. *Journal of Educational Psychology, 74*, 506–521.

Bell, R. Q. (1968). A reinterpretation of the direction of effects in studies of socialization. *Psychological Review, 75*, 81–95.

Berkowitz, S. J. (1986). Effects of instruction in text organization on sixth-grade students' memory for expository reading. *Reading Research Quarterly, 21*, 161–178.

Breznitz, Z. (1997a). Effects of accelerated reading rate on memory for text among dyslexic readers. *Journal of Educational Psychology, 89,* 289–297.

Breznitz, Z. (1997b). Enhancing the reading of dyslexic children by reading acceleration and auditory masking. *Journal of Educational Psychology, 89,* 103–113.

Brown, A. L., Bransford, J. D., Ferrara, R. A., & Campione, J. C. (1983). Learning, remembering, and understanding. In J. H. Flavell & E. M. Markman (Eds.), *Handbook of child psychology, Vol. III, Cognitive development* (pp. 77–166). New York: Wiley.

Brown, A. L., & Day, J. D. (1983). Macrorules for summarizing texts: The development of expertise. *Journal of Verbal Learning and Verbal Behavior, 22,* 1–14.

Brown, A. L., Day, J. D., & Jones, R. S. (1983). The development of plans for summarizing texts. *Child Development, 54,* 968–979.

Brown, R., Pressley, M., Van Meter, P., & Schuder, T. (1996). A quasi-experimental validation of transactional strategies instruction with low-achieving second grade readers. *Journal of Educational Psychology, 88,* 18–37.

Chall, J. (1967). *Learning to read: The great debate.* New York: McGraw-Hill.

Clay, M. M. (1991). *Becoming literate: The construction of inner control.* Portsmouth, NH: Heinemann.

Collins, C. (1991). Reading instruction that increases thinking abilities. *Journal of Reading, 34,* 510–516.

d'Anna, C. A., Zechmeister, E. B., &Hall, J. W. (1991). Toward a meaningful definition of vocabulary size. *Journal of Reading Behavior, 23,* 109–122.

Dickinson, D. K., & Smith, M. W. (1994). Long-term effects of preschool teachers' book readings on low-income children's vocabulary and story comprehension. *Reading Research Quarterly, 29,* 104–122.

Duffy, G. G., & Roehler, L. R. (1989). Why strategy instruction is so difficult and what we need to do about it. In C. B. McCormick, G. Miller, & M. Pressley (Eds.), *Cognitive strategy research: From basic research to educational applications* (pp. 133–154). New York: Springer-Verlag.

Duffy, G. G., Roehler, L. R., Sivan, E., Rackliffe, G., Book, C., Meloth, M., Vavrus, L. G., Wesselman, R., Putnam, J., & Bassiri, D. (1987). Effects of explaining the reasoning associated with using reading strategies. *Reading Research Quarterly, 22,* 347–368.

Durso, F. T., & Coggins, K. A. (1991). Organized instruction for the improvement of word knowledge skills. *Journal of Educational Psychology, 83,* 109–112.

Ehri, L. C. (1991). Development of the ability to read words. In R. Barr, M. L. Kamil, P. B. Mosenthal, & P. D. Pearson (Eds.), *Handbook of reading research* (Vol. 2, pp. 383–417). New York: Longman.

Ehri, L. C. (1992). Reconceptualizing the development of sight word reading and its relationship to recoding. In P. B. Gough, L. C. Ehri, & R. Treiman (Eds.), *Reading acquisition* (pp. 107–143). Hillsdale NJ: Lawrence Erlbaum Associates.

Ehri, L. C., & Robbins, C. (1992). Beginners need some decoding skill to read words by analogy. *Reading Research Quarterly, 27,* 12–27.

Elley, W. B. (1989). Vocabulary acquisition from listening to stories. *Reading Research Quarterly, 24,* 174–187.

Feitelson, D., Kita, B., & Goldstein, Z. (1986). Effects of listening to series stories on first graders' comprehension and use of language. *Research in the Teaching of English, 20,* 339–356.

Fleisher, L., Jenkins, J., & Pany, D. (1979). Effects on poor readers' comprehension of training in rapid decoding. *Reading Research Quarterly, 15,* 30–48.

Gambrell, L. B., & Bales, R. J. (1986). Mental imagery and the comprehension-monitoring performance of fourth- and fifth-grade poor readers. *Reading Research Quarterly, 21,* 454–464.

Gambrell, L. B., & Jawitz, P. B. (1993). Mental imagery, text illustrations, and children's comprehension and recall. *Reading Research Quarterly, 28,* 264–273.

Gaskins, I. W., Anderson, R. C., Pressley, M., Cunicelli, E. A., & Satlow, E. (1993). Six teachers' dialogue during cognitive process instruction. *Elementary School Journal, 93,* 277–304.

Goodman, K. S. (1993). *Phonics phacts.* Portsmouth, NH: Heinemann.

Goodman, K. S. (1996). *On reading.* Portsmouth, NH: Heinemann.

Goswami, U. (1998). The role of analogies in the development of word recognition. In J. Metsala & L. Ehri (Eds.), *Word recognition in beginning reading* (pp. 41–63). Mahwah, NJ: Lawrence Erlbaum Associates.

Gough, P. D. (1983). Context, form, and interaction. In K. Rayner (Ed.), *Eye movements in reading* (pp. 203–211). New York: Academic Press.

Gough, P. B. (1984). Word recognition. In P. D. Pearson, R. Barr, M. L. Kamil, & P. Mosenthal (Eds.), *Handbook of reading research* (pp. 225–254). New York: Longman.

Gough, P. B., & Tunmer, W. E. (1986). Decoding, reading, and reading disability. *Remedial and Special Education, 7,* 6–10.

Graesser, A. C. (1981). *Prose comprehension beyond the word.* New York: Springer-Verlag.

Haller, E. P., Child, D. A., & Walberg, H. J. (1988). Can comprehension be taught? A quantitative synthesis of "metacognitive" studies. *Educational Researcher, 17*(9), 5–8.

Hayes-Roth. B., & Thorndyke, P. W. (1979). Integration of knowledge from text. *Journal of Verbal Learning and Verbal Behavior, 18,* 91–108.

Hudson, J. A. (1990). Constructive processing in children's event memory. *Developmental Psychology, 26,* 180–187.

Hudson, J., & Nelson, K. (1983). Effects of script structure on children's story recall. *Developmental Psychology, 19*, 625–635.

Hudson, J. A., & Shapiro, L. R. (1991). From knowing to telling: The development of children's scripts, stories, and personal narratives. In A. McCabe & C. Peterson (Eds.), *Developing narrative structure* (pp. 89–136). Hillsdale NJ: Lawrence Erlbaum Associates.

Hudson, J. A., & Slackman, E. A. (1990). Children's use of scripts in inferential text processing. *Discourse Processes, 13*, 375–385.

Hutchins, E. (1991). The social organization of distributed cognition. In L. Resnick, J. M. Levine, & S. D. Teasley (Eds.), *Perspectives on socially shared cognition* (pp. 283–307). Washington, DC: American Psychological Association.

Idol, L. (1987). Group story mapping: A comprehension strategy for both skilled and unskilled readers. *Journal of Learning Disabilities, 20*, 196–205.

Idol, L., & Croll, V. J. (1987). Story-mapping training as a means of improving reading comprehension. *Learning Disability Quarterly, 10*, 214–229.

Isakson, R. L., & Miller, J. W. (1976). Sensitivity to syntactic and semantic cues in good and poor comprehenders. *Journal of Educational Psychology, 68*, 787–792.

Juel, C. (1988). Learning to read and write: A longitudinal study of fifty-four children from first through fourth grade. *Journal of Educational Psychology, 80*, 437–447.

Juel, C., Griffith, P. L., & Gough, P. B. (1986). Acquisition of literacy: A longitudinal study of children in first and second grade. *Journal of Educational Psychology, 78*, 243–255.

Kintsch, W. (1974). *The representation of meaning in memory.* Hillsdale, NJ: Lawrence Erlbaum Associates.

Kintsch, W. (1982). Text representations. In W. Otto & S. White (Eds.), *Reading expository material* (pp. 87–102). New York: Academic Press.

Kintsch, W. (1983). Memory for text. In A. Flammer & W. Kintsch (Eds.), *Discourse processing* (pp. 186–204). Amsterdam: North-Holland.

Kintsch, W. (1988). The role of knowledge in discourse comprehension: A construction-integration model. *Psychological Review, 95*, 163–182.

LaBerge, D., & Samuels, S. J. (1974). Toward a theory of automatic information processing in reading. *Cognitive Psychology, 6*, 293–323.

Levin, J. R., & Pressley, M. (1981). Improving childrens' prose comprehension: Selected strategies that seem to succeed. In C. M. Santa & B. L. Hayes (Eds.), *Children's prose comprehension: Research and practice* (pp. 44–71). Newark, DE: International Reading Association.

Martin, V. L., & Pressley, M. (1991). Elaborative-interrogation effects depend on the nature of the question. *Journal of Educational Psychology, 83*, 113–119.

McCartney, K. A., & Nelson, K. (1981). Children's use of scripts in story recall. *Discourse Processes, 4*, 59–70.

McKeown, M. G., Beck, I. L., Omanson, R. C., & Perfetti, C. A. (1983). The effects of long-term vocabulary instruction on reading comprehension: A replication. *Journal of Reading Behavior, 15*, 3–18.

McKeown, M. G., Beck, I. L., Omanson, R. C., & Pople, M. T. (1985). Some effects of the nature and frequency of vocabulary instruction on the knowledge and use of words. *Reading Research Quarterly, 20*, 522–535.

McKoon, G., & Ratcliff, R. (1992). Inference during reading. *Psychological Review, 99*, 440–466.

Metsala, J., & Ehri, L. (Eds.). (1998). *Word recognition in beginning reading.* Mahwah, NJ: Lawrence Erlbaum Associates.

Miller, G. A. (1956). The magical number seven, plus-or-minus two: Some limits on our capacity for processing information. *Psychological Review, 63*, 81–97.

Miller, G. A., & Gildea, P. (1987). How children learn words. *Scientific American, 257*(3), 94–99.

Morrow, L. M., Pressley, M., Smith, J. K., & Smith, M. (1997). The effect of a literature-based program integrated into literacy and science instruction. *Reading Research Quarterly, 31*, 54–76.

Nagy, W., & Anderson, R. (1984). How many words are there in printed school English? *Reading Research Quarterly, 19*, 304–330.

Nagy, W., Anderson, R., & Herman, P. (1987). Learning word meanings from context during normal reading. *American Educational Research Journal, 24*, 237–270.

Nelson, K. (1978). How children represent their world in and out of language. In R. S. Siegler (Ed.), *Children's thinking: What develops?* (pp. 255–273). Hillsdale, NJ: Lawrence Erlbaum Associates.

Nelson, K., & Gruendel, J. (1981). Generalized event representations: Basic building blocks of cognitive development. In A. Brown & M. Lamb (Eds.), *Advances in developmental psychology* (Vol. 1, pp. 231–247). Hillsdale, NJ: Lawrence Erlbaum Associates.

Nicholson, T. (1991). Do children read words better in context or in lists? A classic study revisited. *Journal of Educational Psychology, 83*, 444–450.

Nicholson, T., Bailey, J., & McArthur, J. (1991). Context cues in reading: The gap between research and popular opinion. *Journal of Reading: Writing and Learning Disabilities, 7*, 33–41.

Nickerson, R. S., Perkins, D. N., & Smith, E. E. (1985). *The teaching of thinking.* Hillsdale, NJ: Lawrence Erlbaum Associates.

Palincsar, A. S., & Brown, A. L. (1984). Reciprocal teaching of comprehension-fostering and monitoring activities. *Cognition and Instruction, 1*, 117–175.

Pearson, P. D., & Dole, J. A. (1987). Explicit comprehension instruction: A review of research and a new conceptualization of instruction. *Elementary School Journal, 88*, 151–165.

Pearson, P. D., & Fielding, L. (1991). Comprehension instruction. In R. Barr, M. L. Kamil, P. B. Mosenthal, & P. D. Pearson (Eds.), *Handbook of reading research* (Vol. II, pp. 815–860). New York: Longman.

Pellegrini, A. D., Galda, L., Perlmutter, J., & Jones, I. (1994). *Joint reading between mothers and their head start children: Vocabulary development in two text formats* (Reading Research Rep. No. 13). Athens, GA, College Park, MD: National Reading Research Center.

Peterson, M. E., & Haines, L. P. (1992). Orthographic analogy training with kindergarten children: Effects of analogy use, phonemic segmentation, and letter-sound knowledge. *Journal of Reading Behavior, 24*, 109–127.

Pressley, G. M. (1976). Mental imagery helps eight-year-olds remember what they read. *Journal of Educational Psychology, 68*, 355–359.

Pressley, M. (1998). *Elementary reading instruction that works: Why balanced literacy instruction makes more sense than whole language or phonics and skills.* New York: Guilford Press.

Pressley, M., & Afflerbach, P. (1995). *Verbal protocols of reading: The nature of constructively responsive reading.* Hillsdale, NJ: Lawrence Erlbaum Associates.

Pressley, M., El-Dinary, P. B., Gaskins, I., Schuder, T., Bergman, J., Almasi, L., & Brown, R. (1992). Beyond direct explanation: Transactional instruction of reading comprehension strategies. *Elementary School Journal, 92*, 511–554.

Pressley, M., Johnson, C. J., Symons, S., McGoldrick, J. A., & Kurita, J. A. (1989). Strategies that improve children's memory and comprehension of text. *Elementary School Journal, 90*, 3–32.

Pressley, M., Wharton-McDonald, R., Hampson, J. M., & Echevarria, M. (1998). The nature of literacy instruction in ten grade-4/5 classrooms in upstate New York. *Scientific Studies of Reading, 2*, 159–194.

Pressley, M., Wood, E., Woloshyn, V. E., Martin, V., King, A., & Menke, D. (1992). Encouraging mindful use of prior knowledge: Attempting to construct explanatory answers facilitates learning. *Educational Psychologist, 27*, 91–110.

Robbins, C., & Ehri, L. C. (1994). Reading storybooks to kindergartners helps them learn new vocabulary words. *Journal of Educational Psychology, 86*, 54–64.

Roehler, L. R., & Duffy, G. G. (1984). Direct explanation of comprehension processes. In G. G. Duffy, L. R. Roehler, & J. Mason (Eds.), *Comprehension instruction: Perspectives and suggestions* (pp. 265–280). New York: Longman.

Rosenblatt, L. M. (1978). *The reader, the text, the poem: The transactional theory of the literary work.* Carbondale, IL: Southern Illinois University Press.

Rosenhouse, J., Feitelson, D., Kita, B., & Goldstein, Z. (1997). Interactive reading aloud to Israeli first graders: Its contribution to literacy development. *Reading Research Quarterly, 32*, 168–183.

Rosenshine, B., & Meister, C. (1994). Reciprocal teaching: A review of nineteen experimental studies. *Review of Educational Research, 64*, 479–530.

Rosenshine, B., & Trapman, S. (1992, April). *Teaching students to generate questions: A review of research.* Paper presented at the annual meeting of the American Educational Research Association, San Francisco.

Samuels, S. J., Dahl, P., & Archwamety, T. (1974). Effect of hypothesis/test training on reading skill. *Journal of Educational Psychology, 66*, 835–844.

Short, E. J., & Ryan, E. B. (1984). Metacognitive differences between skilled and less skilled readers: Remediating deficits through story grammar and attribution training. *Journal of Educational Psychology, 76*, 225–235.

Stanovich, K. (1986). Matthew effects in reading: Some consequences of individual differences in the acquisition of literacy. *Reading Research Quarterly, 21*, 360–407.

Stanovich, K. E., & Cunningham, A. E. (1993). Where does knowledge come from? Specific associations between print exposure and information acquisition. *Journal of Educational Psychology, 85*, 211–229.

Sternberg, R. J. (1987). Most vocabulary is learned from context. In M. G. McKeown & M. E. Curtis (Eds.), *The nature of vocabulary acquisition* (pp. 89–105). Hillsdale, NJ: Lawrence Erlbaum Associates.

Tan, A., & Nicholson, T. (1997). Flashcards revisited: Training poor readers to read words faster improves their comprehension of text. *Journal of Educational Psychology, 89*, 276–288.

Taylor, B. M. (1982). Text structure and children's comprehension and memory for expository material. *Journal of Educational Psychology, 74*, 323–340.

Taylor, B. M., & Beach, R. W. (1984). The effects of text structure instruction on middle-grade students' comprehension and production of expository text. *Reading Research Quarterly, 19*, 134–146.

Valdez-Menchaca, M. C., & Whitehurst, G. J. (1992). Accelerating language development through picture book reading: A systematic extension to Mexican day care. *Developmental Psychology, 28*, 1106–1114.

van Dijk, T. A., & Kintsch, W. (1983). *Strategies of discourse comprehension.* New York: Academic Press.

Weaver, C. (1994). *Understanding whole language: From principles to practice* (2nd ed.). Portsmouth, NH: Heinemann.

Whitehurst, G. J., Falco, F. L., Lonigan, C. J., Fischel, J. E., DeBaryshe, B. D., Valdez-Menchaca, M. C., & Caulfield, M. (1988). Accelerating language development through picturebook reading. *Developmental Psychology, 24*, 552–559.

Williams, J. P. (1993). Comprehension of students with and without learning disabilities: Identification of narrative themes and idiosyncratic text representations. *Journal of Educational Psychology, 85*, 631–641.

Wood, E., Pressley, M., & Winne, P. H. (1990). Elaborative interrogation effects on children's learning of factual content. *Journal of Educational Psychology, 82,* 741–748.

Wood, S. S., Bruner, J. S., & Ross, G. (1976). The role of tutoring in problem solving. *Journal of Child Psychology and Psychiatry, 17,* 89–100.

Yuill, N., & Oakhill, J. (1988). Effects of inference awareness training on poor comprehension. *Applied Cognitive Psychology, 2,* 23–45.

Yuill, N., & Oakhill, J. (1991). *Children's problems in reading comprehension.* Cambridge, England: Cambridge University Press.

CHAPTER 31

Literature-Based Reading Instruction

Lesley Mandel Morrow
Rutgers University

Linda B. Gambrell
Clemson University

Since the late 1980s there has been a dramatic increase in interest in literature-based reading instruction in elementary classrooms. There are a number of factors that have contributed to this shift toward inclusion of literature in the reading curriculum, including the availability of high-quality children's literature (Cullinan, 1989), the popularity of the whole-language movement (Fisher & Hiebert, 1990; Goodman, 1989), and the prominence of reader-response theory (Iser, 1980; Bleich, 1978; McGee, 1992; Rosenblatt, 1978). In this review of the research on literature-based reading instruction we first explore the historical roots of this movement, the predominant theory on which it is based, and descriptive features of literature-based instruction. We then examine research on literature-based reading instruction related to storybook reading with young children and literature-based instruction in classroom settings. We conclude with implications for theory, practice, policy, and future research.

The reading research of the 1980s was grounded in an active-constructive model of the reading process that emphasized the interaction between the reader and the text (Anderson & Pearson, 1984; Anderson, Hiebert, Scott, & Wilkinson, 1985). This research also provided important insights about the relationships between reading and writing. Most importantly, this research led us to rethink the reading curriculum and the materials that are used for instruction. It was during the 1980s, according to Barr (1992), that teachers began to move away from sole reliance on basal materials and experiment with alternative forms of literacy instruction.

HISTORICAL PERSPECTIVES
ON LITERATURE-BASED INSTRUCTION

Basal programs have been documented as the dominant reading materials used for instruction in American elementary classrooms from the 1940s through the 1990s (Koeller, 1988; Shannon, 1989). In 1958, according to Koeller (1988), 95% to 99% of teachers used basal programs, and in 1980, these figures were down slightly with 80% to 90% of the teachers reporting the use of basals for reading instruction.

In a survey conducted in 1980, Gambrell (1992) explored the programs, approaches, and materials used in the reading curriculum. The study was replicated in 1990 in an attempt to identify shifts or changes in the reading curriculum from 1980 to 1990. In the initial study conducted in 1980, the respondents were 93 teachers, kindergarten through sixth grade, from three eastern states and the District of Columbia. Each of the 93 teachers reported using a basal program as the primary basis for reading instruction. Only 5% of the teachers, primarily at the kindergarten level, reported that they supplemented basal instruction with other materials or approaches. The supplemental programs and materials were fairly evenly distributed among children's literature, language experience, and phonics programs. These results, which indicate almost sole reliance on the use of basal programs in the early 1980s, were not entirely unexpected. However, it was surprising that teachers reported so little use of supplementary materials in the reading curriculum.

The survey study was replicated in 1990 (Gambrell, 1992). The respondents were 84 teachers from seven Eastern states and the District of Columbia. Although 80% of the respondents reported that they used a basal program as the primary basis for reading instruction, over 50% of these teachers indicated they supplemented the basal program with children's literature, a significant increase from 1980. A small percentage of teachers (3%) reported that they supplemented the basal program with both children's literature and language experience. The most surprising finding was that the remaining 20% of the respondents reported using children's literature as the primary basis for their reading program. The results of the 1990 survey revealed that approximately half of the teachers using basals were incorporating children's literature into the reading curriculum and 20% of the teachers were using children's literature as the core of the reading curriculum (Gambrell, 1992).

Perhaps the most compelling evidence of widespread implementation of literature-based reading instruction comes from the findings of the 1992 National Assessment of Educational Progress (Mullis, Campbell, & Farstrup, 1993). The data from this national study revealed that approximately half of all fourth-grade teachers reported a "heavy" emphasis on literature-based reading, and that students of teachers reporting heavier emphases on literature-based reading instruction had higher levels of reading proficiency. In 1994, Strickland, Walmsley, Bronk, and Weiss interviewed teachers in eight states and found that 18% of the teachers reported using children's literature exclusively, whereas 80% used both basals and children's literature. Thus, it seems that the case is well made for the current popularity of literature-based reading instruction.

It should be noted, however, that the survey results described in these studies are based on teachers' and students' reports of reading programs rather than observations of actual practice. However, the findings of the survey studies (Gambrell, 1992; Strickland et al., 1994) are consistent with observational research conducted during the same time period (Barr, 1989; Durkin, 1978–1979; Gambrell, 1986; Morrow, 1983). Taken together, the survey studies and the observational studies provide convincing evidence of the heavy reliance on basal programs. Morrow (1983) , for example, found that the use of literature was limited in kindergarten through third grade classrooms and that most teachers did not set aside time for children to use trade books. Morrow's (1983) work also offered at least one explanation for the limited use of literature in the elementary reading curriculum. A survey conducted with parents, principals, and teachers revealed that reading for pleasure with children's literature was not a high priority and that the development of comprehension, word recognition, and study skills were ranked higher in importance by these groups.

More recently, Lehman, Freeman, and Allen (1994) conducted a survey study with 192 elementary teachers who enrolled in a one-day conference on literature-based reading instruction. Although this population is not a representative sample, the responses to the survey provide some interesting insights about teacher perceptions of the role of literature in the reading curriculum. In response to the survey, 94% of the teachers agreed that literature should be the primary component of the language arts program. When queried about their actual classroom practices, however, 45% reported using literature exclusively and 55% reported the use of basal programs for some instructional purposes. Clearly, the research to date on materials used for reading instruction documents the increasing significance of children's literature as we entered the decade of 1990 (Gambrell, 1992; Lehman et al., 1994; Morrow, 1997; Strickland et al., 1994).

During the 1990s many teachers made the transition from basal programs that are highly structured to literature-based programs that require extensive decision making with respect to materials, grouping practices, instruction, and assessment (Alexander, 1987; Cullinan, 1989; Scharer, 1992). With the increasing growth in the use of children's literature in the classroom, several concerns about the implementation of literature-based instruction began to emerge. Gardner (1988), for example, speculated that without significant staff development efforts, teachers would basalize literature by using instructional guides that have formats similar to basal manuals. Cullinan (1989) voiced the concern that few teachers keep current with respect to the field of children's literature and that teachers lack appropriate course work necessary for undertaking a literature based reading curriculum.

THEORETICAL UNDERPINNINGS OF LITERATURE-BASED READING INSTRUCTION

According to McGee (1992), one defining characteristic of the current literature-based reading movement that distinguishes the movement from others in the past is the grounding in reader response theory (Bleich, 1978; Iser, 1980; Rosenblatt, 1978). Reader response theory draws on literary criticism theory which attempts to explain how readers read and interpret literature (McGee, 1992; Tompkins & McGee, 1993). The basic notion of reader response theory is that readers play a central role in the construction of meaning. Rosenblatt (1978) used John Dewey's term, *transaction*, to emphasize the contribution of both reader and text to the reading process. Meaning, therefore, is a two-way process that resides in the transaction that occurs between the reader and text wherein the reader constructs a personal envisionment of meaning that is guided by the text. The transaction is a dynamic where readers shape text as they use their prior experiences to select images and feelings, while at the same time the text shapes readers by creating new experiences and orientations (McGee, 1992; Rosenblatt, 1978, 1991).

Rosenblatt (1978, 1991) distinguished between two stances that readers take, aesthetic and efferent, depending on their purposes for reading. The term *aesthetic* is derived from the Greek word meaning "to sense" or "to perceive." In taking an aesthetic stance in reading a story, a poem, or a play, for example, the reader's attention shifts inward and centers on what is being created during the actual reading: personal feelings, ideas, and attitudes. On the other hand, the term *efferent* is derived from the Latin word meaning "to carry away." In taking an efferent stance in reading informational text, such as a textbook, directions, or instructions, the readers' attention will narrow in order to build up the meanings and ideas to be retained. According to Rosenblatt (1991), it is the reader rather than the text that dictates the stance that is taken, and any text can be read either way. Readers may select a text because it suits their already chosen, efferent or aesthetic, purposes, or the reader may note cues in the text and adopt an appropriate stance. In keeping with reader response theory, Rosenblatt (1978) posited that when reading any one text , readers shift along a continuum from the aesthetic to the efferent stance (see Marshall in this volume).

Many researchers find Louise Rosenblatt's reader response theory to be both relevant and important in providing a foundation for literature-based reading instruction (e.g., Eeds & Wells, 1989; Galda, 1990; Langer, 1994; McGee, 1992). Recent research studies have explored literature-based reading instruction and children's responses to literature, motivation to read, and reading performance. These studies provide insights about new ways that teachers and researchers are conceptualizing reading instruction in literature-based classrooms (Allington, Guice, Michelson, Baker, & Li, 1996; McGee, 1992).

FEATURES OF LITERATURE-BASED INSTRUCTION

Literature refers to a wide range of materials including picture books, big books, predictable books, folktales, fables, myths, fantasy, science fiction, poetry, contemporary realistic fiction, historical fiction, nonfiction informational books, and biographies (Lehman et al., 1994; Routman, 1988). Current definitions of literature-based instruction emphasize the use of high-quality literacy works, usually trade books, as the core instructional materials used to support reading achievement (Harris & Hodges, 1995; Huck, 1977; Scharer, 1992).

According to Galda, Cullinan, and Strickland (1993), literature-based reading programs are characterized by the following: (a) a knowledgeable teacher who serves as an enthusiastic guide, (b) an environment that encourages social interaction about books, (c) a structure that allows students to make choices about what they will do with books, and (d) both the time and materials to allow students to read and respond to what they read. These characteristics are consistent with descriptions of literature-based language arts instruction in the research literature.

An observational study conducted by Fisher and Hiebert (1990) provided insights about operational definitions of literature-based instruction. They examined the types of tasks engaged in by elementary students in literature-based and skills-oriented classrooms. Videotapes, field notes, teacher interviews, and samples of student work were collected over five full days of instruction. Doyle's (1983) task framework was used to contrast the learning opportunities provided to students in classrooms using the two approaches to reading instruction. The analysis focused on seven aspects of tasks: subject-matter content, duration, cognitive complexity, product specification by student, product type, activity format, and task size. The findings of this study revealed substantial differences in the kind and number of literacy tasks in the literature-based and skills-oriented classrooms. Students in the literature-based classrooms spent more time in literacy activities, especially writing. The writing in the skills-oriented classrooms generally involved worksheets, whereas students in the literature based classrooms were usually involved in the generation of connected text. In addition, students in literature-based classrooms had more control over their literature activities. The activities were also more cognitively complex than those of the skills-oriented classrooms in that they required synthesis, integration, or generation of ideas, as opposed to recognition of facts or memory.

Reading aloud to students from children's literature is also frequently mentioned in the literature as a critical feature of literature based instruction. Many proponents of literature based programs emphasize the importance of reading aloud on a daily basis (Galda et al., 1993; Huck, Hepler, & Hickman, 1987; Routman, 1988; Tompkins & McGee, 1993). In a survey study that examined the read-aloud practices of kindergarten through third-grade teachers in 1980 with those of teachers in 1990, Chasen and Gambrell (1992) reported that in 1980, only 45% of the teachers reported reading aloud to their students on a daily basis, whereas in 1990 almost 75% of the teachers reported doing so. In a more recent survey study conducted by Lehman et al. (1994), 85% of elementary teachers reported reading aloud to their students at least once a day. Daily read-aloud has also been an important component of research studies exploring the effects of literature-based reading instruction (Morrow, 1992; Morrow, Pressley, Smith, & Smith, 1997; Scharer, 1992; Smith, 1993).

The literature-based perspective posits that the acquisition of literacy occurs in a book-rich context of purposeful communication where meaning is socially constructed (Cullinan, 1987). A number of authorities agree on the distinguishing features of a literature-based reading program (Cullinan, 1987; Galda et al., 1993; Tompkins & McGee, 1993). First, literature is used as an important vehicle for language arts instruction. Literature may be the sole or primary basis for reading instruction or it may be used as a supplement to basal programs, in which case the role of literature in the program is at least as important as the basal or other materials being used for instruction. Second, opportunities are provided for students to independently read books of their own choosing every day. Third, students are provided with sustained opportunities to read and write. These extended periods of time involve both independent and collaborative reading and writing activities. Fourth, social interaction among students is encouraged. Discussions of literature and related activities are commonplace in literature-based classrooms, as is collaboration on writing projects. Finally, an important characteristic of literature-based instruction is a strong read-aloud program, with teachers spending time reading high-quality literature aloud to their students on a regular basis, usually daily.

STORYBOOK READING WITH YOUNG CHILDREN

In early childhood, reading to children has always been the most common practice for implementing literature-based instruction with young children. Reading aloud to children has been advocated as a vital experience in literacy development both at home and in school. In 1985, the report of the National Institute of Education stated that "the single most important activity for building the knowledge required for eventual success in reading is reading aloud to children" (Anderson et al., 1985, p. 23).

Theoretical, correlational, case study, experimental designs, and anecdotal reports have reinforced accepted practices and perceptions by describing children's behavior and identifying direct relationships between being read to and aspects of literacy development. Clay (1979) and Smith (1978) discussed the positive effects of reading to children, suggesting that the activity helps youngsters to learn about features of written language. Children learn that written language is different from oral language, that print generates meaning, and that printed words on a page have sounds. Mason (1983) suggested that children who are read to develop a metacognitive knowledge about how to approach reading tasks. Metacognition is one's own awareness about how learning takes place in particular settings.

Correlational research has played a prominent role in identifying the relationship between literacy development and being read to by an adult. These studies have found that early readers and children who learned to read before coming to school came from homes where they were read to frequently (Clark, 1984; Durkin, 1966; Morrow, 1983; Sutton, 1964; Teale, 1978, 1981). Children who had a desire to learn to read, and subsequently became successful readers, were frequently read to by an adult in the home (Durkin, 1974–1975; Mason & Blanton 1971; Walker & Kuerbitz, 1979). Language development, specifically syntactic complexity and increased vocabulary, is also associated with early experiences of being read to frequently (Burroughs, 1972; Chomsky, 1972; Irwin, 1960; Templin, 1957).

Anecdotes and observations from case studies of children who have been read to frequently have described behaviors similar to those in the correlational investigations. Case studies by Baghban (1984), Doakes (1981), Hoffman (1982), and Rhodes (1979) indicate that young children who have been read to frequently know how to handle books, and can identify the front of a book, the print to be read, and the appropriate direction for reading the print.

The results of several studies using experimental designs investigated the effects of storybook reading as a regular classroom practice on children's achievement in various aspects of literacy development. In these investigations, the children in the experimental classrooms who were read to daily over long periods of time scored significantly better on measures of vocabulary, comprehension, and decoding ability than children in the control groups who were not read to by an adult (Bus, Ijzendoorn, & van, Pellegrini, 1995; Cohen, 1968; Dickinson & Smith, 1994; Elley, 1989; Feitelson, Goldstein, Iraqi, & Share, 1993; Feitelson, Kita, & Goldstein, 1986; Robbins & Ehri, 1994; Senechall & Cornell, 1993; Senechall, Thomas, & Monker, 1995).

How does being read to promote literacy development? Experimental investigations in school settings have tried to untangle specific elements of storybook readings that enhance literacy skills. Each of the studies has involved children in some type of active participation before, during, or after storybook reading. Qualitative studies, through observations and interviews, have documented how children and parents interact and participate together in reading storybooks in the home environment (Teale, 1987). Another group of studies has focused on the influence of the teacher when reading to a whole class in school. For example, some studies found that the reading style of the teacher affects children's comprehension of stories (Dunning & Mason, 1984; Green & Harker, 1982; Peterman, Dunning & Mason, 1985).

In experimental studies carried out in school settings where children participated with their teacher and peers in some part of the storybook reading experience, their comprehension and sense of story structure improved in comparison to children in the control groups. The treatments involved activities implemented *prior* to story reading, *during* story reading, and *after* story reading. Activities implemented prior to story reading included previewing the story through discussion, prediction, and setting a purpose for listening prior to the story being read. Activities implemented during the story reading focused on ideas related to the story that were spontaneously discussed at appropriate times. Activities implemented after the reading included discussing predictions, discussing purposes set, role playing stories, retelling stories, and reconstructing stories through pictures. Apparently, these activities enabled children to relate various parts of a story to each other and to integrate information across the entire story (Brown, 1975; Morrow, 1985; Pellegrini & Galda, 1982).

Ethnographic studies of read-aloud events, mostly in homes, illustrate that the events involve social interaction between parent and child in which the two participants actively construct meaning based on the text. The read-aloud event typically involves the child's independent practice of reading through a reenactment of the story reading event in which they model the parent–child interaction. The nature of the interaction between parent and child in story reading can influence the knowledge the child gains, as well as the attitudes toward reading and skills acquired for reading (Teale & Sulzby, 1987).

Meyer, Wardrop, Stahl, and Linn (1994) described negative effects on literacy development as a result of storybook reading. These authors suggested that reading stories is not a magical activity for literacy development; it is the quality of the interaction that occurs during reading that results in positive effects, rather than just storybook reading unto itself. They reported that storybook reading sessions in classrooms are often not of sufficient quality to engage students fully and to maximize literacy growth. Reading stories as an act in itself does not necessarily promote literacy; however, the research suggests that certain methods, environmental influences, attitudes, and interactive behaviors apparently enhance the potential of the read-aloud event for promoting literacy development.

The nature of the learning that occurs as a result of adults reading storybooks with young children is consistent in a number of literacy theories. Wittrock's (1974, 1981) model of generative learning supports the notion that the reader or listener understands prose by actively engaging in the construction of meaning and making connections with the textual information he or she hears or reads (Linden & Wittrock, 1981; Wittrock, 1974, 1981). According to Vygotsky's (1978) cultural-historical theory, literacy appears to develop from children's social interactions with others in specific environments of which reading, writing, and oral language are a part. The literacy activities and the interactions that are mediated by the adults determine the ideas about and skills acquired toward literacy development (Teale & Sulzby, 1987). Holdaway's (1979) model of developmental teaching, derived from observations of middle class homes, asserted that children benefit most when their earliest experiences with storybooks are mediated by an adult who interacts with the child in a problem-solving situation. The child is asked to respond, and the adult offers information as needed to sustain the activity. In such situations, children and adults interact to integrate, construct, and develop understandings of the printed text.

The primary goal of the read-aloud event, then, is the construction of meaning from the interactive process between adult and child (Vygotsky, 1978). During story reading, the adult helps the child understand and make sense of text by interpreting the written language based on experiences, background, and beliefs (Altwerger, Diehl-Faxon, & Dockstader-Anderson, 1985). Teale (1984) described the interaction as being interpsychological first, that is, negotiated between adult and child together; and intrapsychological next, when the child internalizes the interactions and can function independently.

Parent Interactive Behaviors During Story Readings

A parent or teacher rarely reads to a child without offering comments about the story, which in turn trigger responses and questions from the child. Likewise, children initiate discussion during a reading, which results in similar social interaction. Story reading appears to involve the cooperative construction of meaning between adult and child through negotiation and mediation in the verbal exchange about the story. Differences have been found in the way that individual parents interact with children in story readings. As story readings progress over time, parents tend to change the nature of their interactive style as children change the nature of their responses to the activity (Bloome, 1985; Heath, 1982; Ninio & Bruner, 1978; Taylor, 1986; Teale & Sulzby, 1987).

Researchers have identified a number of adult interactive behaviors that affect the qualitative aspects of read-aloud activities. They include questioning, scaffolding dialogue and responses, praise or positive feedback, offering or extending information, clarifying information, restating information, directing discussion, sharing personal reactions, and relating concepts to life experiences. Flood (1977), using a descriptive-correlational approach, described reading styles of parents during book reading sessions with pre-kindergarten children. He found the following variables combined as the best predictors of success on readiness scores: (a) total number of words spoken by children, (b) total number of questions answered by children, (c) number of preparatory questions asked by parents, (d) number of poststory evaluative questions asked by parents, (e) total number of questions asked by the child, and (f) positive reinforcement offered by the parent. Flood concluded that parents should be encouraged to talk about text with their children before, during, and after storybook reading.

Based on a careful analysis of a mother interacting with her child from the age of 8 to 18 months, Ninio and Bruner (1978) identified a four-step parent–child routine during the reading of picture books. This routine involved attention-getting dialogue, questions, labeling and scaffolding, then feedback. These researchers observed the scaffolding process in which the adult supplies all responses that the child cannot, preparing the child to do so later on. The adult scaffolds or gives responses to questions asked so that the child can discover what is expected and can experience success in later responses. As the child begins to make appropriate responses, parental scaffolding diminishes (Applebee & Langer, 1983; Ninio & Bruner, 1978).

Cochran-Smith (1984) observed storybook readings in school settings and concluded that the events were based on cooperative negotiation of textual meanings by the readers and listeners. Responses by the listeners influence the story reader's guidance and a mutual dependency arises. To be most useful, interactions must include "life to text" as well as "text to life" information. "Life to text" focuses on using the child's knowledge to make sense of information in the book. "Text to life" shows the child how the information in the book can be related to his or her life. The patterns reflect the Piagetian viewpoint of applying new ideas to existing schemata and accommodating new information. They also follow Ausubel's theory that learning becomes more meaningful as it is related to the child's present knowledge (Payton, 1984).

Shanahan and Hogan (1983) compared interactive behavior by adults during story reading with children's achievement on a test of print awareness. They determined that minutes of book reading per week, answering children's questions during readings, and references to children's own experiences were the best predictors of achievement on the print awareness measures.

Roser and Martinez (1985) described three roles that adults play during story readings at home and in school. As co-responders, adults initiate discussion in order to describe information, recount parts of a story, share personal reactions, relate experiences to real life, and invite children to share responses in the same ways. As informers/monitors, adults explain aspects of a story, provide information to broaden a child's knowledge, and assess a child's understanding of a story. As directors, adults introduce a story, announce conclusions, and assume leadership. As a child's participation in story readings increases, all three roles become interchangeable between adult and child.

According to Heath (1980), interactive language behaviors during story readings change as children get older. Initially, parents expect very young children to interrupt stories, and the parents accept dialogue and questioning from the children during the story reading event. By the age of 3 years, Heath observed, the child is expected by parents to listen to the story and learn information from it as in traditional school settings. The adult begins to question the child after a reading to determine content understanding and recall. Sulzby and Teale (1987) in their study of storybook reading behaviors of eight families found similar changes over time in the interactive patterns between parents and children.

Book reading behaviors differ with socioeconomic settings. Children in low socioeconomic communities tend to be read to infrequently or not at all. Differences in interactive behavior between participants in low socioeconomic status (SES) and those in high-SES homes are revealed in higher levels of vocabulary development for high-SES children (Ninio & Bruner, 1978). Heath (1980) found that in middle-class homes, "why" questions and affective comments were sought often; in lower SES settings, "when" and "what" questions were the rule. Children in the latter group were at a disadvantage when they met higher level thought questions at school.

Teacher Interactive Behaviors During Story Readings

Studies reported thus far have investigated the interactions during story reading events that involved one-to-one readings between parent and child at home. Studies focusing on teachers' interactive behaviors when reading to whole classes of children have documented the impact of teachers' reading style on children's comprehension of stories (Dunning & Mason, 1984; Green & Harker, 1982; Peterman et al., 1985).

A series of investigations was carried out in classrooms to determine children's comprehension of story in whole-class, small-group, and one-to-one settings (Morrow, 1987, 1988; Morrow & Smith, 1990). The interactions that occurred within these different settings were also studied . On a test of comprehension, children who heard stories in small-group settings performed significantly better than children who heard stories read one-to-one, who in turn performed significantly better than children who heard stories read to the whole class. In addition, children who heard stories read in a small-group or one-to-one setting generated significantly more comments and questions than children in the whole-class setting. Thus, reading to children in small groups offers as much interaction as one-to-one readings, and appears to lead to greater comprehension than whole-class or even one-to-one readings.

Children's Responses During Storybook Readings

Children's responses to read-aloud experiences, both in questions and in comments, are a critical aspect of the interactive process. Yaden (1985) pointed out that children's questions can aid their literacy development by providing a direct channel of information. When questions are asked and then answered, a child receives immediate feedback. The opportunity to question provides an environment for learning. Holdaway's (1979) model for literacy instruction advocates that children have the opportunity to regulate their own learning by questioning adults in literacy situations such as storybook reading. Cochran-Smith (1984) found that the types of questions and comments children make during story reading events help us gain insights into the way young children attempt to construct meaning and make sense of text.

Children's initial questions and comments during first storybook readings relate mainly to illustrations, as youngsters label or name items pictured or repeat and restate words said by the adult who is reading the story. Children also respond by answering questions posed by the adult (Bloome, 1985; Ninio & Bruner, 1978; Yaden, 1985). Questions and comments about story content or meaning become prevalent and more complex with time, eventually including narrational, evaluative, interpretive, associative, predictive, informative, and elaborative remarks (Roser & Martinez, 1985). One of the last things children ask about is the print itself. Few children, for instance, ask for speech equivalents of printed words, or for names of letter sounds. Children's responses most often reflect adult interactive behavior. The changes in children's responses over time indicate internalization of interactive behavior. As time goes by, children begin to control the story reading by taking more responsive roles during the activity.

Children often request that favorite stories be read aloud. This common practice of rereading favorite stories to children has attracted the attention of many scholars. Researchers have questioned whether lasting cognitive and affective benefits result from repeated readings of the same story. Investigators have sought to answer this question by studying the responses of children who have had the opportunity to hear repeated readings of the same story. Roser and Martinez (1985) and Yaden (1985) suggested that children's comments and questions increase and become more interpretive and evaluative when they have listened to repeated readings of the same story. Case study investigations (Snow, 1983; Snow & Goldfield, 1983) of repeated storybook readings found that in their comments and responses to the readings, children discussed more aspects of the text and discussed them in greater depth. Children also elaborated more often and interpreted issues in the story following repeated readings. Teale and Sulzby (1987) reported that with repeated readings, children internalized the interaction that occurred between parent and child. The child gradually took over conducting the story reading. Sulzby (1985) reported that the familiarity that comes with repeated readings enables children to reenact stories or attempt to read stories on their own.

These reenactments model the parent's storybook reading. Early attempts are governed by pictures; that is, the child reads the story by focusing on the illustration. At first, stories are not well formed, but the child's reenactments gradually take on the shape and sound of story reading. Eventually the child begins to attend to the print, combining reading and telling until actual reading is achieved. These reenactments play an important role in literacy learning (Teale & Sulzby, 1987). Reenactment could hardly occur without repeated readings of a story. Repeated readings seem to be an important component in reading stories. The familiarity gained through the experience provides children with frameworks of background information that enable them to deal with the text on a variety of levels.

LITERATURE-BASED INSTRUCTION IN CLASSROOM SETTINGS

Although there are relatively few empirical studies in the literature that directly compare literature-based reading instruction with alternative models, a number of studies provide evidence that evaluates the use of literature in the reading program. In this section we review a range of studies that explored the effects of literature-based reading instruction on elementary-age children's literacy development. Some of these studies compared whole-language or literature-based classrooms with skills-based classrooms. In the studies cited in this section the descriptions of whole-language classrooms emphasized the use of children's literature for reading and writing instruction. Other studies compared the effects of basal only control groups with basal plus literature-based reading instruction, where the basal instruction was supplemented with equal time devoted to literature-based reading instruction. In addition, a recent qualitative study by Baumann and Ivey (1997) explored the nature and efficacy of a combined literature/strategy-based instructional program on children's reading and writing development.

Comparisons of Literature-Based and Skills-Based Classrooms

A number of recent studies compared literature-based programs with skills-based reading and language arts instruction. In these studies, skills-based programs are typically defined as a traditional program characterized by the use of a commercial reading series emphasizing the introduction and practice of a hierarchy of reading skills ordered from basic to more complex. Literature-based programs are characterized as using children's literature as the basis for instruction, with a focus on meaningful reading and writing experiences and self-selected extension activities related to the literature. Studies of this type have demonstrated the positive effects of literature-based programs on the print awareness and word reading acquisition of kindergarten students (Reutzel, Oda, & Moore, 1989). At the elementary level, literature-based programs have been shown to positively influence students' knowledge of written language (Purcell-Gates, McIntyre, & Freppon, 1995), vocabulary (Reutzel & Cooter, 1990), and comprehension (Reutzel & Cooter, 1990; Richek & McTague, 1988). Other studies have found that students in a literature-based program were more strategic readers than those in a skills-based program (Dahl & Freppon, 1995; Freppon, 1991). In addition, students taught using a literature-based approach viewed reading as a meaning-making process and had higher levels of metacognitive awareness than students in the skills-based programs (Gambrell & Palmer, 1992; Freppon, 1991).

Studies Evaluating the Effects of Literature-Based Programs on Literacy Achievement

Two recent quasi-experimental studies investigated the effects of a combination approach consisting of equal time devoted to basals and children's literature as compared to control groups that used basals only (Morrow, 1992; Morrow et al., 1997). In a study conducted by Morrow (1992), second-grade classrooms were randomly assigned to one of three groups: (a) a literature-based reading and writing program that included literacy centers, teacher-directed literacy activities, and independent reading and writing periods as a complement to the existing basal reading program; (b) an identical group to the one described in (a), except for the addition of a component in which parents supported the literacy activities at home; or (c) a control group that used a basal-only program. In a second study, Morrow and her colleagues investigated the effects of a literature-based program integrated into science instruction (Morrow et al., 1997). The purpose of this study was to determine the impact of a literature-based program integrated into literacy and science instruction on achievement and use of literature. Third-grade classrooms were assigned to one of three groups: (a) literature-based reading and literature-based science instruction as a complement to the existing basal reading program; (b) literature-based reading instruction and textbook science instruction in addition to the existing basal reading program; or (c) basal reading instruction and traditional textbook-based science instruction. Both studies spanned an entire school year, and in both investigations a basal reader with workbook materials was used for reading instruction prior to the implementation of the study.

The literature component of both studies was designed to complement the existing basal reading instruction program; however, less time was spent with the basal in order to incorporate the emphasis on literature. Even so, the same amount of overall time was spent on reading instruction in both experimental and control groups. Also, in both studies children could not be randomly assigned to treatment conditions; therefore, intact classrooms were the unit of analysis, and the classroom mean was used for all measures.

The results of both studies were strikingly similar. Across both studies the performance of students in the literature treatment conditions was statistically superior to that of the control groups on the following measures: story retelling, story rewriting, and the writing of original stories. In addition, in the Morrow et al. (1997) study, the treatment group that received basal and literature-based reading instruction as well as science instruction using tradebooks (the most intensive literature treatment group) outperformed the basal and literature based-reading and science text group and the basal-only group on the California Test of Basic Skills (reading score and total language score). In addition, the literature and science tradebook group outperformed the comparison groups on two measures of science content, suggesting that the use of literature enhances content learning. Overall, the results of these studies suggest that the combination of literature-based instruction with traditional basal reading instruction is more powerful than traditional instruction alone. In addition, the Morrow et al. (1997) study confirms the findings of several recent quasi-experimental studies that have documented the positive effects of literature-based instruction on content area learning (Guzzetti, Kowalinski, & McGowan, 1992; Jones, Coombs, & McKinney, 1994; Smith, 1993).

Block (1993) investigated the effects of a literature-based reading program designed to teach reading and thinking strategies. In this study, second- and third-grade students were randomly assigned, by classrooms, to experimental or control conditions. In the literature-based classrooms, students received lessons twice weekly for 32 weeks. The lessons consisted of two parts: (a) teacher explanation and modeling of a thinking and reading comprehension strategy (e.g., decoding an unknown word, predicting) using written strategy application guides, and (b) student selection of literature and application of the previously taught cognitive strategy. In the control group, students received traditional instruction that did not emphasize strategy instruction. The results revealed that the strategy/literature-based group outperformed the control group on the reading comprehension, vocabulary, and total battery sections of the Iowa Test of Basic Skills. In addition, students in the strategy/literature-based group also outperformed controls in the ability to transfer cognitive strategies to out-of-school applications and on measures of self-esteem and critical and creative thinking.

Baumann and Ivey (1997) note that although Morrow's (1992) study explored the impact of a program of rich literature-based experiences on children's ability to respond and react to literary experiences, and Block's (1993) study investigated the effects of a systematic program of strategy instruction within a literature-based program, neither of these studies attempted to clarify the impact of a long-term, combined program of both contextualized skill and strategy instruction within a literature-based reading program. Baumann and Ivey (1997) conducted a year-long qualitative case study to explore what second-grade students learned about reading, writing, and literature in a program of strategy instruction integrated within a literature-based classroom environment. Baumann was the full-time teacher for the entire school year, and Ivey was a participant observer in the classroom. Data sources included personal journals kept by both investigators, individual student interviews and interviews with parents and caregivers, videotapes of regular classroom literacy activities, artifacts of students' reading and writing, assessments of student's literacy learning, and the teacher's daily plan book. A content analysis of the data sources revealed that students grew in overall reading performance and came to view reading as a natural component of the school experience. The students demonstrated high levels of engagement with books, developed skill in word identification, fluency, and comprehension, and grew in written composition abilities. This qualitative study provides support for the efficacy of teaching students reading and language arts strategies within a literature based framework. Baumann and Ivey (1997) concluded:

> that there is a bidirectional, mutually reinforcing relationship between the presence of literature environment and contextualized strategy instruction. The immersion in literature and the embedded strategy instruction created a kind of symbiotic, synergistic relationship in which each program characteristic contributed to and fed off the other. In other words, the literature enhanced students reading and writing fluency, and their developing literacy abilities promoted their literary knowledge and appreciation. (p. 272)

Literature Discussion Groups

The increase in the use of children's literature in the elementary classroom has drawn attention to the ways in which children respond to literature during discussion groups. The research studies that have focused on discussion groups used a variety of qualitative and quantitative methods to examine what happens when students engage in discussions about books they have read (Gambrell, 1996).

Literature discussion groups are typically described as involving small groups of children (from three to eight) who read a story or novel over a period of time. The underlying principle of literature discussion groups is that the teacher and students work together in order to construct and refine deeper meaning and understanding of the text. Researchers who have explored the cognitive processes that are necessary for higher level thinking agree that deep-level understanding occurs only through interactions with others (Almasi, 1995, 1996; Baker, 1979; Schallert & Kleiman, 1979). This finding is in keeping with the theories of Vygotsky (1978), which posit that social interaction is central to the development of language and thought. According to

Vygotskian theory, learning is facilitated through the assistance of more knowledgeable members of the community and higher level mental processes, such as those involved in language processes and academic discourse.

Several studies explored the effects of the book club format for literature discussion on reading development. The book club format typically consists of silent reading, writing in response to the reading, small-group discussion, and instruction (Goatley, Brock, & Raphael, 1995; Goatley & Raphael, 1992). A number of other studies have investigated the effects of peer-led literature discussion groups on reading comprehension and higher-level thinking (Almasi, 1995; Eeds & Wells, 1989; Goatley et al., 1995; Goatley & Raphael, 1992; Many & Wiseman, 1992; McGee, 1992).

There is quantitative and qualitative evidence that prior to instruction or experience with literature discussion groups, students' responses tend to be unelaborated and their discussions involve very limited interactions among students (Almasi, 1995; Gambrell, 1987; Goatley & Raphael, 1992). As a result of participation in literature discussion groups, however, students exhibited a wide range of behaviors that demonstrated comprehension and evaluation of the text as well as personal responses (Almasi, 1995; Eeds & Wells, 1989; Goatley, 1996). For example, Eeds and Wells (1989) found that even without direct questioning by the teacher there was evidence in students' discussions that they recalled text information, drew inferences, supported their inferences, and read critically. In some studies, students sometimes had difficulty making personal connections to text prior to the intervention of discussion groups; however, given opportunities to participate in discussions these same students quickly learned to respond personally to their reading (Gerla, 1996; Goatley, 1996).

Some researchers have reported that the collaborative nature of literature discussions appears to help students to construct meaning and clarify confusions (Almasi, 1995; Eeds & Wells, 1989; Goatley et al., 1995; Goatley & Raphael, 1992). Students in these studies were observed to orchestrate turn-taking, negotiate leadership, and to draw on a variety of sources to clarify or agree on text interpretation.

Many and Wiseman (1992) found that the quality of literature discussions was directly related to instructional approach. In the literary experience, group discussion focused on students' thoughts and personal reactions to the story; in the literary analysis group the emphasis was on literary elements such as character development, problems, and solutions. All the students in the study exhibited at least some level of personal response to the stories they read. The students in the literary experience group, however, appeared to clarify the story and their own experiences by making significant real-world connections to story events. The students who participated in a literary analysis group tended to focus more on literary elements such as character development or theme in their discussions.

The research on elementary-age students' discussions of children's literature suggests that young children are capable of producing elaborate and sophisticated responses to literature, especially when supported with instruction. Across these studies, children were able to construct meaning, share personal reactions, and demonstrate strategic reading behaviors such as hypothesizing, interpreting, predicting, confirming, generalizing, and evaluating. The research clearly indicates that reading and discussing children's literature offers students opportunities to explore interpretations of literature and respond at higher levels of abstract and critical thinking (McGee, 1992).

Literature-Based Reading Instruction in the Content Areas

The integrated language arts perspective (see Gavelek, Raphael, et al., this volume, chap. 32) is based on the belief that reading and writing are functional tools not to be mastered unto themselves, but to be situated within content area teaching (McGinley

& Tierney, 1989). In the integrated language arts approach, the use of children's literature is a major source of instruction materials in content area teaching. The literature provides the opportunity for children to engage in shared oral reading and writing experiences; the teacher uses literature in guided lessons; and there is time given for social interaction with peers during periods of independent reading of literature about subject areas (Edelsky, Altwerger, & Flores, 1991; Goodman, 1989; Harste, Woodward, & Burke, 1984; Wells, 1985).

When teaching science, math, and social studies, 95% of teachers use subject-specific texts 90% of the time (Ogens, 1990). Baker (1991) and Baker and Saul (1994) concluded that elementary science textbooks often require reasoning beyond the capabilities of students. Because one science text is typically used for all students in a class, mismatches occur between reading competence and reading demands for many children (American Association for the Advancement of Science, 1989; Chall, Conrad, & Harris-Sharples, 1991; Meyer, 1991). This is true in social studies and math as well.

Reliance on science and social studies textbooks tends to favor the accumulation of factual knowledge at the expense of activities that stimulate the process-oriented inquiry needed to deal with science- and social studies-related issues. The content of science and social studies textbooks is restricted to avoid controversy, and space limitations preclude attention to many topics. Children's literature that deals with these topics; however, has few restrictions and can provide the reader with insight beyond factual accounts. In addition, children's literature on content area topics provides a wide range of ideas that promote emotional responses, personal association, imagination, prediction, and evaluation (Ross, 1994; Smith, 1994).

The literature on integrating language arts with content area instruction yields many anecdotal reports that support this perspective and offer strategies for classroom practice. There are few investigations that involve empirical, controlled, experimental evaluation of the integration of language arts with other content areas. When investigating content integration in elementary classrooms, Schmidt et al. (1985) found that although teachers expressed belief in integration when interviewed, they spent a small percentage of their instructional time engaged in integrated language arts activities.

A number of studies have demonstrated that the use of children's literature enhances both literacy development and children's interest in reading (Hoffman, Roser, & Farest, 1988; Morrow, 1992; Morrow, O'Connor, & Smith, 1990; Morrow et al., 1997). It has been documented that students' understanding of difficult scientific concepts is enhanced through the use of literature (Moore & Moore, 1989). Careful selection of quality literature for the science curriculum could provide students with more interesting scientific reading than that found in science textbooks, thus stimulating students' interest in participating in science (Renninger, Hidi, & Krapp, 1992).

Several recent quasi-experimental studies investigated the efficacy of using children's literature for content area learning instead of traditional content area textbooks. Smith, Monson, and Dobson (1992) studied the effects of using historical novels in an integrated language arts approach to social studies and literacy instruction. The control group used basal readers and social studies texts whereas the treatment group used historical novels for reading and social studies instruction. Student's knowledge about U.S. history was assessed at the beginning and at the end of the school year using an oral free-recall measure. Students in the group using historical fiction novels in place of basal readers recalled significantly more details, main ideas, and total amount of historical information than the students using just the social studies text.

Guzzetti et al. (1992) compared a literature-based themed approach to a traditional textbook approach for a unit on China. On a multiple-choice concept test, statistically significant differences favored the literature-based group. The researchers concluded that students can acquire more social studies concepts and a greater understanding of those concepts through literature-based instruction.

Jones et al. (1994) compared a literature-based themed unit approach to a traditional textbook approach for learning about Mexico. During a 2-week period, two sixth-grade classes were taught a unit on Mexico. The results revealed that the literature-based group showed a statistically significant gain in achievement as compared to the textbook group on a test of content knowledge about Mexico (the instrument assessed only information that was common to both the literature and the textbooks).

Morrow et al. (1997) studied the impact of a literature-based program integrated into literacy and science instruction on achievement, use of literature, and attitudes toward the literacy and science program with third-grade children. Children in the literature/science group scored significantly better on standardized and informal written and oral tests used to determine growth in literacy and science.

Guthrie and his colleagues (Guthrie et al., 1996; Guthrie & McCann, 1997) described the positive outcomes of their research on Concept-Oriented Reading Instruction (CORI). In this interdisciplinary project, science was taught to enable students to gain conceptual understandings through real-life hands-on science activities and the use of concept-oriented children's literature. The interpretation of literary texts through discussions with the teacher and peers was an important part of the program. On performance assessment measures, students in the CORI classrooms did significantly better than the comparison group using basals and traditional textbooks in their ability to search and locate information, explain their understanding of science concepts, transfer concepts by writing solutions to problems, and engage in multiple strategies for literacy learning.

Additional research is needed to explore qualitative differences in the understanding of concepts learned through literature-based experiences and those acquired by traditional textbook presentations. The expectation is that literature-based experiences will lead to concepts being more meaningfully connected with related ideas, but we do not know this from studies reviewed.

There are important questions that have yet to be fully explored about the qualities of interaction that lead to improved learning (Cazden, 1986; Forman & Cazden, 1985; Slavin, 1983). Detailed analyses of literature based interactions have the potential to inform us about how students' prior knowledge is used during knowledge construction, as students discuss, question, and reflect on what they read (Jett-Simpson, 1989). Consistent with Vygotsky's (1978) theory, analyses of these academic interactions could help us better understand the development of thought, and distributed models of cognition.

The use of literature-based instruction integrated into content areas deserves careful analysis because it has been found to motivate children's interest in learning. We need to determine if student enthusiasm diminishes over time as a result of the novelty of the literature integration wearing off. This integration might make the relevance and importance of both content learning and literature-based instruction more obvious to the learner. If so, literature-based instruction integrated into the content areas could be a key ingredient in creating more motivating educational environments.

Using Literature-Based Instruction with Special Populations

Recent research provides insights about the value of using literature-based instruction with special populations. Several studies have specifically targeted adolescent special education students. In a pretest–posttest comparison study, Oberlin and Shugarman (1989) found that learning disabled middle school students who participated in a literature-based reading workshop demonstrated improved attitudes toward and increased levels of involvement with books. These 14 sixth-, seventh-, and eighth-grade students, who reported reading an average of only 1 book per year prior to the study, read an average of 20 books during the 18-week reading workshop.

Stewart, Paradis, Ross, and Lewis (1996) interviewed seventh and eighth graders at the conclusion of a literature-based developmental reading program. Ninety percent of the students indicated that they felt better about themselves as readers because they could read faster and more fluently, could remember and comprehend more of their reading, and were better able to complete reading assignments. Standardized test scores indicated that the students made academic gains commensurate with the gains of students in the previous, more traditional remedial program.

Using a case study approach, Worthy and Invernizzi (1995) reported on a 14-year-old, hyperlexic reader characterized as having well above average word recognition accompanied by severe deficits in reading comprehension. In this study, instruction that focused on meaningful reading of children's literature resulted in a gain in reading comprehension of more than 3 years over a period of three semesters. In addition, a written retelling indicated the student's improved sense of story structure as well as the ability to make inferences and use supporting details.

In a case study conducted by Jimenez and Gamez (1996), students speaking English as their second language began to think more strategically while using literature to learn about cognitive strategies. Three seventh graders made strategic and metacognitive comments that had not been noted in observations prior to the intervention. For example, the students mentioned such things as reading more in order to improve, reading being less difficult because it made more sense to them, picturing things in their heads as they read, and looking for clues when they encountered an unknown word.

Goatley and her colleagues (Goatley, 1996; Goatley et al., 1995; Goatley & Raphael, 1992) documented the positive benefits of literature discussion groups for special education students. Learning disabled and educable mentally retarded students in these studies participated actively and cooperatively, demonstrated text comprehension, and responded both aesthetically and efferently to literature. In one study, three 16-year-old boys were observed as they engaged in a program similar to a book club in which they read, wrote about, and discussed two novels over an 8-week period. These students, who avoided reading at the outset of the study, became not only willing but eager readers. They engaged in discussions about the literature, making personal connections and working together to construct an understanding of the stories.

Although the research on using literature based reading instruction with special populations is limited in scope, it appears that there are promising results with respect to promoting positive attitudes toward reading as well as increased reading proficiency. The interview and case studies reviewed here suggest that special populations can benefit from literature-based reading instruction; however, further research with special populations is warranted.

Literature-Based Instruction and Attitude Toward Reading

Understanding the role of attitude in reading development is important for a number of reasons (Guthrie, 1995; McKenna, Kear, et al., 1995). First, attitude may affect the level of ability that students ultimately attain because attitude influences factors such as engagement and amount of time spent reading. Second, poor attitude may cause students to choose not to read when other options exist (McKenna, Stratton, et al., 1995). There is considerable debate in the literature with respect to the motivational efficacy of literature-based and basal-based instruction; to date, the research on the effects of instructional approach on attitudes toward reading has yielded mixed results.

Stahl, McKenna, and Pagnucco (1994) conducted a review of the research comparing children's reading attitudes in literature-based and traditional programs using self-report attitude rating scales. They identified 14 studies, which revealed the following results: 2 favored literature based instruction, 1 favored traditional instruction, and 11 yielded no significant differences between literature-based and traditional programs with respect to attitudes toward reading.

Several large-scale studies by McKenna and his colleagues have focused on the effects of literature-based and basal-based reading instruction on students' attitudes toward reading. McKenna, Stratton, Grindler, and Jenkins (1995) conducted a series of three studies in Grades 1 to 5, investigating the differential effects of literature-based (whole language) and traditional (basal) instruction on reading attitudes. This large-scale study revealed no meaningful difference in attitude attributable to instructional approach.

In a national study of 18,185 elementary students from across the United States, McKenna, Kear, and Ellsworth (1995) investigated the effects of literature-based (whole language) and traditional (basal) instruction. In this study approximately 81% of the students were taught using basals as the primary instructional material, and only 3.6% were taught using literature as the primary instructional material. Approximately 12% of the students received instruction that was based on a combination of basal and other materials and approaches. The findings from this study supported McKenna, Stratton, Grindler, and Jenkins's (1995) finding that there were no meaningful differences in attitude due to instructional approach.

In a number of studies using a range of quantitative and qualitative methodologies, researchers have reported that literature-based programs positively affected children's attitudes toward reading (Gerla, 1996; Goatley & Raphael, 1992; Oberlin & Shugarman, 1989; Richek & McTague, 1988), and frequency of reading (Morrow, 1992; Morrow et al., 1997; Oberlin & Shugarman, 1989; Stewart et al., 1996). Students in literature-based programs were also found to be more persistent (Dahl & Freppon, 1995; Gerla, 1996) and demonstrated improved ability to work together (Dahl & Freppon, 1995; Goatley, 1996; Goatley et al., 1995).

Several other studies have investigated the effect of literature-based instruction on attitudes toward reading and content area learning. Guzzetti et al. (1992) investigated the learning and attitudes of sixth-grade students in a literature-based social studies program. Although they found differences in content acquisition favoring the experimental group, no differences were revealed between the groups on a survey designed to assess attitude toward reading and social studies. The students in the experimental group did not express a preference for social studies at the conclusion of the program. One possible explanation for this finding was revealed in the follow-up interviews. Students did not consider the unit they had completed as "social studies" because they had not used a "text."

Smith (1993) explored the attitudes of fifth graders using either historical fiction novels or a combination of basal readers and social studies textbooks. At the conclusion of the program, students in the literature-based group outperformed the comparison group on content knowledge, and survey responses revealed that students preferred using historical fiction novels rather than a basal reader and textbook to learn about history. In another study investigating sixth-grade students' attitudes toward literature and textbook instruction in social studies, Jones et al. (1994) found that students in the literature group outperformed the comparison group on achievement and desire to use literature in social studies.

Morrow et al. (1997) compared the reading and science achievement and the attitudes of students in three treatment conditions: (a) basal plus literature-based reading and literature-based science instruction, (b) basal plus literature-based reading instruction and textbook-based science instruction, and (c) basal reading instruction and textbook-based science instruction. The achievement scores across several measures of reading performance (retelling, probed recall, written stories, and a science test) favored the basal plus literature-based reading and science group. In addition, attitudes toward science were more positive for this group as compared with the other two groups.

Additional research is needed that will explore the effects of literature-based reading and content area instruction on students' attitudes and motivation to learn. Generally, the results of these studies are somewhat disappointing in that attitude has not been a major focus of well-controlled studies on literature-based reading instruction. Clearly, the question of the effect of instructional materials and approaches on attitudes toward reading is an important and complex one that calls for broad, program-level comparison studies that closely attend to program fidelity (McKenna, Kear, et al., 1995).

SUMMARY AND IMPLICATIONS FOR PRACTICE AND POLICYMAKING

Reading and language arts curriculum have shifted dramatically during the last decade with respect to increasing emphasis on literature-based instruction (Pearson, 1996, 1994). Given this dramatic shift, it is not surprising that the research on literature-based instruction does not provide adequate information on the nature of literature-based instruction and its impact on student literacy development (Allington et al., 1996). Two important limitations to the existing research on literature-based instruction have been identified by Allington and his colleagues. First, most studies focused on a single classroom or one school. Although there are examples of studies that used multiple classrooms (e.g., Mervar & Hiebert, 1989; Morrow, 1992; Reutzel & Cooter, 1990; Zarrillo, 1989), none were found that reported exploring the effects of literature-based instruction across a number of classrooms in a number of schools in multiple school districts. Second, only a few studies (e.g., Baumann, 1997; Morrow, 1992) reported on literature-based instruction in schools and districts serving large numbers of children from low-income families.

Although the research to date appears to support the efficacy of using the literature-based approach in the teaching of reading and in the content areas, there are many issues that are not clearly understood. For example, there is little agreement as to what constitutes a literature-based curriculum other than providing students with the opportunity to read high-quality children's literature (Allington et al., 1996). There are also many remaining questions about the effects of literature-based programs on the acquisition of early literacy skills and strategies. In particular, there has been increasing attention to the question of the appropriate role of children's literature in early literacy development as opposed to text that is more readable for young readers. The practices of the literature-based approach are currently being questioned by those favoring more direct instruction in beginning reading with an emphasis on phonemic awareness skills and phonics instruction (Foorman, Francis, Fletcher, & Schatschneider, 1998).

Although there are acknowledged limitations in the existing research on literature based instruction, the research does provide some clear implications for practice and policymaking. First, classrooms need to have classroom libraries that are rich in print materials of all types and genres. Research by Allington et al. (1996) revealed that few classrooms meet adequate standards for the number and range of reading materials available to students. Second, teacher knowledge of children's literature is basic to the success of a literature based program. Professional development opportunities for teachers are essential for developing the breadth of knowledge of literature that is needed for effective teaching. There needs to be a renewed emphasis on supporting the professional development of teachers if the implementation of literature based instruction is to provide the basis for a new, thoughtful literacy in our schools (Allington & Cunningham, 1996; Allington et al., 1996; Pearson, 1996).

Although a good deal of research related to literature-based instruction exists, a great deal remains to be done. Future research is needed to investigate the value of literature-based instruction as compared to the more direct models that are emerging. Clearly, we need research in this area that is rigorous, uses varied designs, and is of a qualitative and quantitative nature.

REFERENCES

Alexander, F. (1987). California reading initiative. In B. E. Cullinan (Ed.), *Children's literature in the reading program* (pp. 149–155). Newark, DE: International Reading Association.

Allington, R. L., & Cunningham, P. (1996). *Schools that work: All children readers and writers*. New York: HarperCollins.

Allington, R. L., Guice, S., Michelson, N., Baker, K., & Li, S. (1996). Literature-based curricula in high-poverty schools. In M. F. Graves, P. van den Broeck, & B. M. Taylor (Eds.), *The first "r": Every child's right to read* (pp. 73–96). New York: Teachers College Press.

Almasi, J. F. (1995). The nature of fourth graders' sociocognitive conflicts in peer-led and teacher-led discussions of literature. *Reading Research Quarterly, 30*(3), 314–351.

Almasi, J. G. (1996). A new view of discussion. In L. B. Gambrell & J. Almasi (Eds.), *Lively discussions!: Fostering engaged reading* (pp. 2–24). Newark, DE: International Reading Association.

Altwerger, A., Diehl-Faxon, J., & Dockstader-Anderson, K. (1985). Read-aloud events as meaning construction. *Language Arts, 62,* 476–484.

American Association for the Advancement of Science. (1989). *Science for all Americans: A Project 2061 report on literacy goals in science, mathematics, and technology.* Washington, DC: American Association for the Advancement of Science.

Anderson, R. C., Hiebert, E., Scott, J., & Wilkinson, I. (1985). *Becoming a Nation of Readers: The report of the Commission on Reading.* Washington, DC: National Institute of Education.

Anderson, R. C., & Pearson, P. D. (1984). A schema-theoretic view of basic processes in reading comprehension. In P. D. Pearson (Ed.), *Handbook of reading research* (pp. 255–292). New York: Longman.

Applebee, A. N., & Langer, J. A. (1983). Instructional scaffolding: Reading and writing as natural language activities. *Language Arts, 60,* 168–175.

Baghban, M. J. M. (1984). *Our daughter learns to read and write: A case study from birth to three.* Newark, DE: International Reading Association.

Baker, L. (1979). Comprehension monitoring: Identifying and coping with text confusions. *Journal of Reading Behavior, 11*(4), 366–374.

Baker, L. (1991). Textbooks and text comprehension. *Science Education, 75,* 359–367.

Baker, L., & Saul, W. (1994). Considering science and language arts connections: A study to teach cognition. *Journal of Research in Science Teaching, 31,* 1023–1037.

Barr, R. (1989). The social organization of literacy instruction. In S. McCormick & J. Zutell (Eds.), *Cognitive and social perspectives for literacy research and instruction: Thirty-eighth yearbook of the National Reading Conference* (pp. 19–33). Chicago: National Reading Conference.

Barr, R. (1992). Teachers, materials, and group composition in literacy instruction. In M. J. Dreher & W. H. Slater (Eds.), *Elementary school literacy: Critical issues* (pp. 27–51). Norwood, MA: Christopher-Gordon.

Baumann, J. F. (1997). The inside and outside of teacher research: Reflections on having one foot in both worlds. *Perspectives in Reading Research* (Rep. No. 11). Athens, GA: National Reading Research Center.

Baumann, J. F., & Ivey, G. (1997). Delicate balances: Striving for curricular and instructional equilibrium in a second-grade, literature/strategy-based classroom. *Reading Research Quarterly, 32*(3), 244–275.

Bleich, D. (1978). *Subjective criticism.* Baltimore, MD: Johns Hopkins University Press.

Block, C. C. (1993). Strategy instruction in a literature-based reading program. *Elementary School Journal, 94*(2), 139–151.

Bloome, D. (1985). Bedtime story reading as a social process. In J. A. Niles & R. V. Lalik (Eds.), *Issues in literacy: A research perspective* (pp. 287–294). Rochester, NY: National Reading Conference.

Brown, A. (1975). Recognition, reconstruction and recall of narrative sequences of preoperational children. *Child Development, 46,* 155–166.

Burroughs, M. (1972). *The stimulation of verbal behavior in culturally disadvantaged three-year-olds.* Unpublished doctoral dissertation, Michigan State University.

Bus, A .G., Ijzendoorn, M. H., & van Pellegrini, A. D. (1995). Joint book reading makes for success in learning to read: A meta-analysis on intergenerational transmission of literacy. *Review of Educational Research, 65,* 1–21.

Cazden, C .B. (1986). Classroom discourse. In M. C. Wittrock (Ed.), *The handbook of research in teaching* (3rd ed., pp. 432–463). New York: Macmillan.

Chall, J. S., Conrad, S. S., & Harris-Sharples, S. (1991). *Should textbooks challenge students? The case for easier and harder books.* New York: Teachers College Press.

Chasen, S. P., & Gambrell, L. B. (1992). A comparison of teacher read aloud practices and attitudes: 1980–1990. *Literacy: Issues and Practices, 9,* 29–32.

Chomsky, C. (1972). Stages in language development and reading exposure. *Harvard Educational Review, 42,* 1–33.

Clark, M. M. (1984). Literacy at home and at school: Insights from a study of young fluent readers. In J. Goelman, A. A. Oberg, & F. Smith (Eds.), *Awakening to literacy* (pp. 122–130). London: Heinemann.

Clay, M. M. (1979). *Reading: The patterning of complex behavior.* Auckland: Heinemann.

Cochran-Smith, M. (1984). *The making of a reader.* Norwood, NJ: Ablex.

Cohen, D. (1968). The effect of literature on vocabulary and reading achievement. *Elementary English, 45,* 209–213, 217.

Cullinan, B. E. (1987). *Children's literature in the reading program.* Newark, DE: International Reading Association.

Cullinan, B. E. (1989). Latching on to literature: Reading initiatives take hold. *School Library Journal, 35,* 27–31.

Dahl, K. L. & Freppon, P. A. (1995). A comparison of innercity children's interpretations of reading and writing instruction in the early grades in skills-based and whole language classrooms. *Reading Research Quarterly, 30*(1), 50–74.

Dickinson, D. K. & Smith, M. W. (1994). Long-term effects of preschool teachers' book readings on low-income children's vocabulary and story comprehension. *Reading Research Quarterly, 29,* 104–122.

Doakes, D. (1981). *Book experiences and emergent reading behavior in preschool children.* Unpublished doctoral dissertation, University of Alberta.

Doyle, W. (1983). Academic work. *Review of Educational Research, 53,* 159–199.

Dunning, D., & Mason, J. (1984, November). *An investigation of kindergarten children's expressions of story characters' intentions.* Paper presented at the 34th annual meeting of the National Reading Conference, St. Petersburg, FL.

Durkin, D. (1966). *Children who read early.* New York: Teachers College Press.

Durkin, D. (1974–1975). A six year study of children who learned to read in school at the age of four. *Reading Research Quarterly, 10,* 9–61.

Durkin, D. (1978–1979). What classroom observations reveal about reading comprehension instruction. *Reading Research Quarterly, 14,* 481–533.

Edelsky, C., Altwerger, B., & Flores, B. (1991). *Whole language: What's the difference?* Portsmouth, NH: Heinemann.

Eeds, M., & Wells, D. (1989). Grand conversations: An exploration of meaning construction in literature study groups. *Research in the Teaching of English, 23*(1), 4–29.

Elley, W. B. (1989). Vocabulary acquisition from listening to stories. *Reading Research Quarterly, 24,* 174–187.

Feitelson, D. Goldstein, Z., Iraqi, U., & Share, D. (1993). Effects of listening to story reading on aspects of literacy acquisition in a dialogic situation. *Reading Research Quarterly, 28.* 70–79.

Feitelson, D., Kita, B., & Goldstein, Z. (1986). Effects of listening to series stories on first graders' comprehension and use of language. *Research in the Teaching of English, 20,* 339–356.

Fisher, C. W., & Hiebert, E. H. (1990). Characteristics of tasks in two approaches to literacy instruction. *Elementary School Journal, 91*(1), 3–18.

Flood, J. (1977). Parental styles in reading episodes with young children. *Reading Teacher, 30,* 846–867.

Foorman, B. R., Fletcher, J. M., Francis, D. J., Schatschneider, C., & Mehta, P. (1998). The role of instruction in learning to read: Preventing reading failure in at-risk children. *Journal of Educational Psychology, 90*(1), 37–55.

Forman, E., & Cazden, C. B. (1985). Exploring Vygotskian perspectives in education: The cognitive value of peer interaction. In J. Wertsch (Ed.), *Culture, communication, and cognition: Vygotskian perspectives* (pp. 323–347). Cambridge, MA: Cambridge University Press.

Freppon, P. A. (1991). Children's concepts of the nature and purpose of reading in different instructional settings. *Journal of Reading Behavior, 23*(2), 139–163.

Galda, L. (1990). Children's literature as a language experience. *Advocate, 3*(4), 247–259.

Galda, L., Cullinan, B. E., & Strickland, D. S. (1993). *Language, literacy and the child.* New York: Harcourt Brace.

Gambrell, L. B. (1986). Reading in the primary grades: How often, how long? In M. R., Sampson (Ed.), *The pursuit of literacy* (pp. 102–107). Dubuque, IA: Kendall/Hunt.

Gambrell, L. B. (1987). Children's oral language during teacher-directed reading instruction. In J. E. Readence, & R. S. Baldwin (Eds.), *Research in literacy: Merging perspectives* (pp. 195–200). Rochester, NY: National Reading Conference.

Gambrell, L. B. (1992). Elementary school literacy instruction: Changes and challenges. In M. J. Dreher & W. H. Slater (Eds.), *Elementary school literacy: Critical issues* (pp. 227–239). Norwood, MA: Christopher-Gordon.

Gambrell, L. B. (1996). What research reveals about discussion. In L. B. Gambrell & J. F. Almasi (Eds.), *Lively discussions!: Fostering engaged reading* (pp. 25–38). Newark, DE: International Reading Association

Gambrell, L. B., & Palmer, B. (1992). Children's metacognitive knowledge about reading and writing in literature-based and conventional classrooms. In C. K. Kinzer & D. J. Leu (Eds.), *Literacy research, theory and practice; Views from many perspectives* (pp. 215–224). Chicago: National Reading Conference.

Gardner, M. (1988). An educator's concerns about the California Reading Initiative. *New Advocate, 1*, 250–253.

Gerla, J. P. (1996). Response-based instruction: At-risk students engaging in literature. *Reading & Writing Quarterly: Overcoming Learning Difficulties, 12*(2), 149–169.

Goatley, V. J. (1996). The participation of a student identified as learning disabled in a regular education book club: The case of Stark. *Reading & Writing Quarterly: Overcoming Learning Difficulties, 12*(2), 195–214.

Goatley, V. J., Brock, C. H., & Raphael, T. E. (1995). Diverse learners participating in regular education "Book Clubs." *Reading Research Quarterly, 30*(3), 352–380.

Goatley, V. J., & Raphael, T. E. (1992). *Non-traditional learners' written and dialogic response to literature: Fortieth yearbook of the National Reading Conference* (pp. 313–322). Chicago: National Reading Conference.

Goodman, Y. M. (1989). Roots of the whole language movement. *Elementary School Journal, 90*, 113–127.

Green, J. L., & Harker, J. O. (1982). Reading to children: A communicative process. In J. A. Langer & M. T. Smith-Burke (Eds.), *Reader meets author/Bridging the gap: A psycholinguistic and sociolinguistic perspective* (pp. 196–221). Newark, DE: International Reading Association.

Guthrie, J. T. (1995). Relationships of instruction to amount of reading: An exploration of social, cognitive, and instructional connections. *Reading Research Quarterly, 30*(1), 8–25.

Guthrie, J., & McCann D. A. (1997). Characteristics of classrooms that promote motivations and strategies for learning. In J. Guthrie & A. Wigfield (Eds.), *Reading engagement: Motivating readers through integrated instruction* (pp. 128–148). Newark, DE: International Reading Association.

Guthrie, J. T., Meter, P. V., McCann, A. D., Wigfield, A., Bennett, L., Poundstone, C. C., Rice, M. E., Faibisch, F. M., Hunt, B., & Mitchell, A. M. (1996). Growth of literacy engagement: Changes in motivations and strategies during concept-oriented reading instruction. *Reading Research Quarterly, 31*, 306–333.

Guzzetti, B. J., Kowalinski, B. J., & McGowan, T. (1992). Using a literature-based approach to teaching social studies. *Journal of Reading, 36*(2), 114–122:

Harris, T. L., & Hodges, R. E. (Eds.). (1995). *The literacy dictionary: The vocabulary of reading and writing*. Newark, DE: International Reading Association.

Harste, J., Woodward, V., & Burke, C. (1984). *Language stories and literacy lessons*. Portsmouth, NH: Heinemann.

Heath, S. B. (1980). The functions and uses of literacy. *Journal of Communication, 30*, 123–133.

Heath, S. B. (1982). What no bedtime story means: Narrative skills at home and school. *Language in Society, 11*, 49–76.

Hoffman, J. V., Roser, N. L., & Farest, C. (1988). Literature sharing strategies in classrooms serving students from economically disadvantaged and language different home environments. In J. E. Readence & R. S. Baldwin (Eds.), *Dialogues in literacy research: Thirty-seventh yearbook of the National Reading Conference* (pp. 331–338). Chicago: National Reading Conference.

Hoffman, S. J. (1982). *Preschool reading related behaviors: A parent diary*. Unpublished doctoral dissertation, University of Pennsylvania.

Holdaway, D. (1979). *The foundations of literacy*. Sydney: Ashton Scholastic.

Huck, C. (1977). Literature as the content of reading. *Theory Into Practice, 16*(5), 363–371.

Huck, C. S., Hepler, S., & Hickman, J. (1987). *Children's literature in the elementary school*. New York: Holt, Rinehart, and Winston.

Irwin, O. (1960). Infant speech: Effects of systematic reading of stories. *Journal of Speech and Hearing Research, 3*, 187–190.

Iser, W. (1980). The reading process: A phenomenological approach. In J. P. Tompkins (Ed.), *Reader response criticism: From formalism to poststructuralism* (pp. 50–69). Baltimore, MD: Johns Hopkins University Press.

Jett-Simpson, M. (1989). Creative drama and story comprehension. In J. W. Stewig & S. L. Sebesta (Eds.), *Using literature in the elementary classroom* (pp. 91–109). Urbana, IL: National Council of Teachers of English.

Jimenez, R. T., & Gamez, A. (1996). Literature-based cognitive strategy instruction for middle school Latina/o students. *Journal of Adolescent & Adult Literacy, 40*(2), 84–91.

Jones, H .J., Coombs, W .T., & McKinney, C. W. (1994). A themed literature unit versus a textbook: A comparison of the effects on content acquisition and attitudes in elementary social studies. *Reading Research and Instruction, 34*(2), 85–96.

Koeller, S. A. (1988). The child's voice: Literature conversations. *Children's Literature in Education, 19*(1), 3–16.

Langer, J. A. (1994). *A response-based approach to reading literature* (Report Series 6.7). Albany, NY: National Research Center on Literature Teaching and Learning.

Lehman, B. A., Freeman, E. V., & Allen, V. G. (1994). Children's literature and literacy instruction: "Literature-based" elementary teachers' belief and practices. *Reading Horizons, 35*(1), 3–29.

Linden, M., & Wittrock, M. C. (1981). The teaching of reading comprehension according to the model of generative learning. *Reading Research Quarterly, 17*, 44–57.

Many, J. E., & Wiseman, D. L. (1992). The effect of teaching approach on third-grade students' response to literature. *Journal of Reading Behavior, 24*(3), 265–287.

Mason, J. (1983, November). *Acquisition of knowledge about reading in the preschool period: An update and extension*. Paper presented at the Society for Research in Child Development Convention, Detroit.

Mason, G., & Blanton, W. (1971). Story content for beginning reading instruction. *Elementary English, 48*, 793–796.

McGee, L. M. (1992). Exploring the literature-based reading revolution (Focus on research). *Language Arts,* *69*(7), 529–537.

McGinley, W., & Tierney, R. J. (1989). Traversing the topical landscape: Reading and writing as ways of knowing. *Written Communication, 6,* 243–269.

McKenna, M. C., Kear, D. J., & Ellsworth, R. A. (1995). Children's attitudes toward reading: A national survey. *Reading Research Quarterly, 30*(4), 934–955.

McKenna, M. C., Stratton, B. D., Grindler, M. C., & Jenkins, S. J. (1995). Differential effects of whole language and traditional instruction on reading attitudes. *Journal of Reading Behavior, 27*(1), 19–44.

Mervar, K., & Hiebert, E. H. (1989). Literature-selection strategies and amount of reading in two literacy approaches. In S. McCormick & J. Zutell (Eds.), *Cognitive and social perspectives for literacy research and instruction: Thirty-eighth yearbook of the National Reading Conference* (pp. 529–535). Chicago: National Reading Conference.

Meyer, L., Wardrop, J. Stahl, S., & Linn, R. (1994) Effects of reading storybooks aloud to Children. *Journal of Educational Research, 88,* 69–85

Meyer, L. A. (1991). Are science textbooks considerate? In C. M. Santa & D. E. Alvermann (Eds.), *Science learning: Processes and applications* (pp. 28–37). Newark, DE: International Reading Association.

Moore, S., & Moore, D. (1989). Literacy through content: Content through literacy. *Reading Teacher, 42,* 170–171.

Morrow, L. M. (1983). Home and school correlates of early interest in literature. *Journal of Educational Research, 76,* 221–230.

Morrow, L. M. (1985). Retelling stories: A strategy for improving children's comprehension, concept of story structure and oral language complexity. *Elementary School Journal, 85,* 647–661.

Morrow, L. M. (1987). The effect of small group story reading on children's questions and comments. In S. McCormick & J. Zutell (Eds.), *Cognitive and social perspectives for literacy research and instruction: Thirty-seventh yearbook of the National Reading Conference* (pp. 77–86). Chicago: National Reading Conference.

Morrow, L. M. (1988). Young children's responses to one-to-one story readings in school settings. *Reading Research Quarterly, 23,* 89–107.

Morrow, L. M. (1992). The impact of a literature-based program on literacy achievement, use of literature, and attitudes of children from minority backgrounds. *Reading Research Quarterly, 27*(3), 251–275.

Morrow, L. M. (1997). *Literacy Development in the Early Years: Helping Children Read & Write* (3rd ed.). Needham Heights, MA: Allyn & Bacon.

Morrow, L. M., O'Connor, E., & Smith, J. (1990). Effects of a story reading program on the literacy development of at risk kindergarten children. *Journal of Reading Behavior, 22,* 255–275.

Morrow, L. M., Pressley, M., Smith, J. K., & Smith, M. (1997). The effect of a literature-based program integrated into literacy and science instruction with children from diverse backgrounds. *Reading Research Quarterly, 32*(1), 54–76.

Morrow, L. M., & Smith, J. K. (1990). The effects of group size on interactive storybook reading. *Reading Research Quarterly, 25,* 214–231.

Mullis, I., Campbell, J., & Farstrup, A. (1993). *NAEP 1991 reading report card for the nation and the states: Data from the national and trial state assessments.* Washington, DC: U.S. Government Printing Office.

Ninio, A., & Bruner, J. S. (1978). The achievement and antecedents of labeling. *Journal of Child Language, 5,* 1–15.

Oberlin, K. J., & Shugarman, S. L. (1989). Implementing the reading workshop with middle school LD readers. *Journal of Reading, 32*(8), 682–687.

Ogens, E. (1990). A review of science education: Past failures, future hopes. *American Biology Teacher, 53,* 199–203.

Payton, S. (1984). *Developing awareness of print: A young child's first steps toward literacy.* Unpublished master's thesis, University of Birmingham, England.

Pearson, P. D. (1994). Integrated language arts: Sources of controversy and seeds of consensus. In L. M. Morrow, J. K. Smith, & L. C. Wilkinson (Eds.), *Integrated language arts: Controversy to consensus* (pp. 11–32). Boston: Allyn & Bacon.

Pearson, P. D. (1996) Reclaiming the center. In M. F. Graves, P. van den Broeck, & B. M. Taylor (Eds.), *The first "r": Every child's right to read* (pp. 259–274). New York: Teachers College Press.

Pellegrini, A., & Galda, L. (1982). The effects of thematic-fantasy play training on the development of children's story comprehension. *American Educational Research Journal, 19,* 443–452.

Peterman, C. L., Dunning, D., & Mason, J. (1985, December). *A storybook reading event: How a teacher's presentation affects kindergarten children's subsequent attempts to read from the text.* Paper presented at the 35th annual meeting of the National Reading Conference, San Diego, CA.

Purcell-Gates, V., McIntyre, E., & Freppon, P. A. (1995). Learning written storybook language in school: A comparison of low-SES children in skills-based and whole language classrooms. *American Educational Research Journal, 32*(3), 659–685.

Renninger, K. A., Hidi, S., & Krapp, A. (1992). *The role of interest in learning and development.* Hillsdale, NJ: Lawrence Erlbaum Associates.

Reutzel, D. R., & Cooter, R .B. (1990). Whole language: Comparative effects on first-grade reading achievement. *Journal of Educational Research, 83*(5), 252–257.

Reutzel, D. R., Oda, L. K., & Moore, B. H. (1989). Developing print awareness: The effect of three instructional approaches on kindergartners' print awareness, reading readiness, and word reading. *Journal of Reaching Behavior, 21*(3), 197–217.

Rhodes, L. K. (1979, May). *Visible language acquisition: A case study.* Paper presented at the Twenty-Fourth Annual International Reading Association Convention, Atlanta, GA.

Richek, M. A., & McTague, B. K. (1988). The "Curious George" strategy for students with reading problems. *Reading Teacher, 42,* 220–226.

Robbins, C., & Ehri, L. C. (1994). Reading storybooks to kindergartners helps them learn new vocabulary words. *Journal of Educational Psychology, 86,* 54–64.

Rosenblatt, L. M. (1978). *The reader, the text, the poem: The transactional theory of the literary work.* Carbondale, IL: Southern Illinois University Press.

Rosenblatt, L. M. (1991). Literature—S.O.S. *Language Arts, 68*(6), 444–448.

Roser, N., & Martinez, M. (1985). Roles adults play in preschoolers' response to literature. *Language Arts, 62,* 485–490.

Ross, E. (1994). *Using children's literature across the curriculum.* Bloomington, IN: Phi Delta Kappa Educational Foundation.

Routman, R. (1988). *Transitions.* Portsmouth, NH: Heinemann.

Schallert, D. L., & Kleiman, G. M. (1979). *Some reasons why teachers are easier to understand than textbooks* (Reading Education Rep. No. 9). Cambridge, MA: Illinois University–Urbana, Center for the Study of Reading.

Scharer, P. L. (1992). Teachers in transition: An exploration of changes in teachers and classrooms during implementation of literature-based reading instruction. *Research in the Teaching of English, 26*(4), 408–445.

Schmidt, W. H., Roehler, L., Caul, J. L., Buchman, M., Diamond, B., Dolomon, D., & Cianciolo, P. (1985). The uses of curriculum integration in language arts instruction: A study of six classrooms. *Journal of Curriculum Studies, 17,* 305–320.

Senechall, M., & Cornell, E. H. (1993). Vocabulary acquisition through shared reading experiences. *Reading Research Quarter, 28,* 360–374.

Senechall, M., Thomas, E., & Monker, J. (1995) Individual differences in 4-year-old children's acquisition of vocabulary during storybook reading. *Journal of educational Psychology, 87,* 218–229.

Shanahan, T., & Hogan, V. (1983). Parent reading style and children's print awareness. In J. Niles (Ed.), *32nd Yearbook of the National Reading Conference* (pp. 212–217). Rochester, NY: National Reading Conference.

Shannon, P. (1989). *Broken promises.* Granley, MA: Bergin and Gavey.

Slavin, R. E. (1983). *Cooperative learning.* New York: Longman.

Smith, F. (1978). *Understanding reading* (2nd ed.). New York: Holt, Rinehart & Winston.

Smith, J. (1994). Models for implementing literature in content studies. *Reading Teacher, 48,* 198–209.

Smith, J. A. (1993). Content learning: A third reason for using literature in teaching reading. *Reading Research and Instruction, 32*(3), 64–71.

Smith, J. A., Monson, J. A., & Dobson, D. (1992). A case study on integrating history and reading instruction through literature. *Social Science Education, 56,* 370–375.

Snow, C. E. (1983). Literacy and language: Relationships during the preschool years. *Harvard Educational Review, 53,* 165–189.

Snow, C. E., & Goldfield, B. A. (1983). Turn the page, please: Situation specific language acquisition. *Journal of Child Language, 10,* 535–549.

Stahl, S. A., McKenna, M. C., & Pagnucco, J. R. (1994). The effects of whole-language instruction: An update and reappraisal. *Educational Psychologist, 29*(4), 175–185.

Stewart, R. A., Paradis, E. E., Ross, B. D., & Lewis, M. J. (1996). Student voices: What works in literature-based developmental reading. *Journal of Adolescent & Adult Literacy, 39*(6), 468–477.

Strickland, D., Walmsley, S., Bronk, G., & Weiss, K. (1994). *School book clubs and literacy development: A descriptive study* (Rep. No. 2.22). Albany, NY: State University of New York, National Research Center on Literature Teaching and Learning.

Sulzby, E. (1985). Children's emergent reading of favorite books: A developmental study. *Reading Research Quarterly, 20,* 458–481.

Sulzby, E., & Teale, W. H. (1987). *Young children's storybook reading: Hispanic and Anglo families and children* (Report to the Spencer Foundation). Ann Arbor, MI: University of Michigan.

Sutton, M. H. (1964). Readiness for reading at the kindergarten level. *Reading Teacher, 17,* 234–240.

Taylor, D. (1986). Creating family story: "Matthew, we're going to have a ride!" In W. H. Teale & E. Sulzby (Eds.), *Emergent literacy: Writing and reading* (pp. 139–155). Norwood, NJ: Ablex.

Teale, W. H. (1978). Positive environments for learning to read: What studies of early readers tell us. *Language Arts, 55,* 922–932.

Teale, W. H. (1981). Parents reading to their children. What we know and need to know. *Language Arts, 58,* 902–911.

Teale, W. H. (1984). Reading to young children: Its significance for literacy development. In H. Goelman, A. A. Oberg, & F. Smith (Eds.), *Awakening to literacy* (pp. 110–121). London: Heinemann.

Teale, W. H. (1987, December). *Emergent literacy: Reading and writing development in early childhood.* Paper presented at the 36th annual National Reading Conference, Austin, TX.

Teale, W. H., & Sulzby, E. (1987). Literacy acquisition in early childhood: The roles of access and mediation in storybook reading. In D. A. Wagner (Ed.), *The future of literacy in a changing world* (pp. 111–130). New York: Pergamon Press.

Templin, M. (1957). *Certain language skills in children.* Minneapolis: University of Minnesota Press.

Tompkins, G. E., & McGee, L. M. (1993). *Teaching reading with literature.* New York: Macmillan.

Vygotsky, L. S. (1978). *Mind in society: The development of psychological processes.* Cambridge, MA: Harvard University.

Walker, G. H., & Kuerbitz, I. E. (1979). Reading to preschoolers as an aid to successful beginning reading. *Reading Improvement, 16,* 149–154.

Wells, G. (1985). *The meaning makers.* London: Oxford University Press.

Wittrock, M. C. (1974). Learning as a generative process. *Educational Psychologist, 11,* 87–95.

Wittrock, M. C. (1981). Reading comprehension. In F. J. Pirozzolo & M. C. Wittrock (Eds.), *Neuropsychological and cognitive processes in reading* (pp. 229–259). New York: Academic Press.

Worthy, J., & Invernizzi, M. A. (1995). Linking reading with meaning: A case study of a hyperlexic reader. *Journal of Reading Behavior, 27*(4), 585–603.

Yaden, D. (1985, December). *Preschoolers' spontaneous inquiries about print and books.* Paper presented at the annual meeting of the National Reading Conference, San Diego, CA.

Zarrillo, J. (1989). Teachers' interpretations of literature-based reading. *Reading Teacher, 43*(1), 22–28.

CHAPTER 32

Integrated Literacy Instruction

James R. Gavelek
Taffy E. Raphael
Sandra M. Biondo
Danhua Wang
Oakland University

Deriving from Latin, *integrate* means to make whole or renew. Definitions from the 1996 *American Heritage Dictionary* include (a) to join so as to form a larger more comprehensive entity, and (b) to blend, harmonize, synthesize, arrange, incorporate, unify, coordinate, and orchestrate. By their very definition, integration and integrated approaches to literacy instruction are extremely appealing. Further, integrated instruction has been thought to address three needs in education: authenticity, meaningfulness, and efficiency. Integrated instruction is more *authentic*, being parallel to real-world tasks, not those developed solely for schooling. Integrated instruction is more *meaningful*—knowledge or information is rarely needed to answer isolated questions. Rather, knowledge construction is an integrative process. Third, integrated instruction is *efficient*, offering hope for greater curriculum coverage. Integrated instruction may be everyone's ideal, but it is the reality in few classrooms. Our literature review convinced us that integrated literacy instruction is one of our field's most multi-faceted and elusive constructs.[1]

Our chapter consists of four sections: (a) our process for generating the pool of writings for our review; (b) a brief historical treatment of integrated literacy instruction; (c) our analysis of the "state of research," and (d) a theoretical critique.

IDENTIFYING THE DATABASE

Assuming we could build on recent reviews, we began with three recent research handbooks (Barr, Kamil, Mosenthal, & Pearson, 1991; Flood, Jensen, Lapp, & Squire, 1991; Jackson, 1992). We found no chapters on integrated instruction, integrated cur-

---

[1]In our review, we distinguish our analyses of the construct of *integration* from analyses detailing specific *relationships between the language arts*. Excellent reviews of such relationships exist elsewhere (e.g., listening and reading reviewed by Sticht & James, 1984, and Sinatra, 1990; writing and reading by Langer & Allington, 1992; Shanahan & Lomax, 1988; Spivey & Calfee, 1998; Tierney & Shanahan, 1991).

riculum, or integrated literacy instruction; although several explored relationships between specific language processes (e.g., reading/writing by Tierney & Shanahan, 1991; speaking/listening by Pinnell & Jaggar, 1991) or reviewed language and the language arts (Marzano, 1991). Moreover, there were no index entries for integrated instruction in either the reading or language arts handbooks. When library searches (e.g., ERIC) of refereed journals between 1988 and 1998 revealed few entries for empirical studies on integration, we widened our "net" to include papers published from nonrefereed sources and did not restrict our time period. Bibliographic tracing led to writings from the late 1800s, although most studies were conducted in the 1980s and 1990s.

We met biweekly for 5 months to analyze the sources. Our first analysis focused on conceptually mapping what our field has meant by integrated literacy instruction and similar terms (e.g., integrated curriculum, interdisciplinary instruction). Our second, focused primarily on elementary grades (see Adler & Flihan, 1997, for a review of middle and high school research in this area), examined the research base for different types of integrated literacy instruction. To set a context, we begin historically.

A BRIEF HISTORY OF INTEGRATED LITERACY INSTRUCTION

As Langer and Allington (1992) discussed in detail, integrating school subjects was offered as a solution to various educational problems. For example, the National Education Association formed the Committee of Ten to examine students' college preparation. It determined students were underprepared in language skills and suggested that "There can be no more appropriate moment for a brief lesson in expression than the moment when the pupil has something which he is trying to express" (National Education Association, 1894, p. 87, as cited in Langer & Allington, 1992, p. 690). Others were concerned about the educational experiences of young learners. Scholars (Cremin, 1964) associated with the Progressive Education Movement emphasized a child-centered curriculum. This movement decried the factory-like efficiency models underlying school structures, and feared that learning had little meaning for the average child and little resemblance to the real world. This philosophy laid the groundwork for interdisciplinary approaches.

> Our whole policy of compensatory education rises or falls with our ability to make school life an interesting and absorbing experience to the child. In one sense there is no such thing as compulsory education. We can have compulsory physical attendance at school; but education comes only through willing attention to and participation in school activities. It follows that the teacher must select these activities with reference to the child's interest, powers, and capabilities. In no other way can she guarantee that the child will be present. (Dewey, 1913, p. ix)

To date, the most ambitious study undertaken to examine these beliefs in practice was the Eight Year Study conducted in the 1930s in 30 high schools across the country. With the cooperation of 300 colleges and universities who agreed to waive traditional subject-matter entrance examinations, the researchers were freed to develop a curriculum that focused on the personal and social needs of students. Courses were created that integrated across disciplinary boundaries, emphasizing learning experiences that mirrored real-world events.

Scores from standardized college-level tests of 1,475 matched pairs of students revealed that, generally, students from the progressive high schools outperformed peers in traditional programs. Progressive classroom students also were more active in extracurricular activities, suggesting their broader educational goals. However, despite this evidence, the study had little effect on redesigning instructional goals or organizing today's classrooms.

More recent iterations reflect continued influence of principles for integrated instruction, reflected in the progressive education movement. For example, the British infant school movement was grounded on principles of student-centered learning that emphasized language and language arts as central to the study of school subjects. The open school movement (Holt, 1967; Silberman, 1970) emphasized inquiry-driven activity across disciplines as students pursued questions they found intriguing. One philosophical base of whole language is integration—emphasizing what is "whole" about language and the study of school subjects (Goodman, 1989). Perhaps most recently, the influence of integrated approaches is visible in some current reform efforts (e.g., Coalition of Essential Schools, 1988; Sizer, 1984).

Although integrated approaches have a long history, those supporting them have not clearly delineated the construct. Integrated curricula are often based in life experiences, but it is not clear whether integrating experiences should be the basis for exploring curriculum content, or if the content itself should be presented as an integrated *fait accompli*. Across decades, our field has confounded these two orientations. Our first analysis focused on clarifying the construct.

Defining Integrated Instruction

In creating our conceptual map defining integrated literacy instruction, we noticed a lack of core citations and inconsistency in use of terms and definitions. Four decades ago, in his introduction to the *Yearbook of the National Society for the Study of Education* focused on integrated instruction, Dressel (1958, p. 8) wrote,

> In our day the term (integration) has come into such varied use as to be suspect.... The real difficulty with the word "integration" rests in the multiplicity of interrelated meanings which permit its use in reference to many and differing situations but which may also result in ambiguity that interferes with a reasoned discussion.

Four decades later, little has changed. Shoemaker (1991, p. 793) suggested there exist "an equal number of terms to describe the various ways [integrated instruction] might be approached." Editors of a National Council of Teachers of English Committee book on integrating the language arts note that "Integrated language arts learning takes many forms, some of which are controversial" (Busching & Schwartz, 1983, p. vii), but they neither critique nor define the term.

Some (e.g., Ellis & Fouts, 1993) equate terms such as interdisciplinary curriculum and integrated studies; others (e.g., Beane, 1995, 1997) distinguish between interdisciplinary and integrative curriculum. For some, "interdisciplinary" preserves disciplinary boundaries whereas "integrated" does not. Both Kain (1993) and Beane (1995) suggested that interdisciplinary studies may repackage or enhance discipline-based knowledge, but they are not integrated. In contrast, Petrie (1992) used interdisciplinary to characterize a blending of disciplines, and multidisciplinary to maintain boundaries across disciplines. These are but a few examples of the diverse ways in which integrated instruction and related terms have been characterized.

In discussing whole language, Bergeron (1990, p. 321) argued for the importance of shared definitions when promoting alternatives to current practice. She suggested "a common terminology for those ideas we wish to share.... Without a common terminology the differences between research and practice, and between innovation and instruction, will be difficult to reconcile." Integrated instruction reflects alternatives to current instructional practices, within the language arts, as well as between language arts and school subjects (e.g., general science) or disciplines (e.g., biology). The absence of shared definitions severely limits the usefulness of integrated instruction as a generative construct.

A Conceptual Map of Integrated Instruction

For some researchers describing curriculum integration, the referent is the curriculum (i.e., the "what"), whereas for others it is the processes that support integration (i.e., the "how"). In the former, teachers present a curriculum that has been integrated; in the latter, they teach processes for integrating across school subjects. In 1958, Dressel echoed this distinction when he suggested a difference between *integrated curriculum* and *integrating experience*. Building from Dressel (1958) and other scholars' conceptual schemes, we identified three categories that compose our conceptual map (see Fig. 32.1): integrated language arts, integrated curriculum, and integration in and out of school. Each denotes integration toward some purpose.

Integrated Language Arts.   When the language arts are brought together to achieve some end(s), we call this *integrated language arts*. Synonymous with *intradisciplinary* (Lipson, Valencia, Wixson, & Peters, 1993), *coordinated* (Grisham, 1995), and *topics-within-disciplines* (Shoemaker, 1993), some combination of reading, writing, listening, speaking, and viewing is taught together as students pursue interesting problems or topics. This is not simply using one of the language arts to support another (as in teaching text structures through writing to help children's reading), but the coordinated instruction of some combination of the major language processes as tools to achieve a learning goal.[2]

Many have emphasized the importance of the interrelationship among the language arts. Morrow, Pressley, Smith, and Smith (1997) argued that an integrated approach can help young children see that what they are learning in one domain can transfer to another. Walmsley and Walp (1990) suggested that written literacy can be a major vehicle for gaining access to, enlarging, and communicating knowledge. Wixson, Peter, and Potter (1996) characterized the base of intradisciplinary units as the

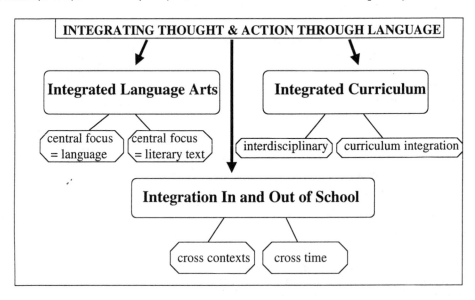

FIG. 32.1. A conceptual map of "integration."

---

[2]Integrated language arts has also been one of the primary tenets of whole-language approaches, although the two are not synonymous. In this review, we deliberately chose not to conflate the two terms. For a treatment of instructional research on whole language, see Raphael and Brock (1997). For the history of whole language, see Goodman (1989).

issues, themes, and problems within literature and other oral, visual, and written texts where students pursue important questions, enhancing the relevance of the language arts themselves. Within this category, the language processes may be applied directly to reading, interpreting, and responding to literature (e.g., a literary text, a collection of literature related by author or genre). Alternatively, language processes may be linked more generally to literary themes for understanding humanity (Galda, 1998), with instructional foci on developing students' understandings of these themes through activities grounded in using written and oral language and, more recently, viewing.

Integrated Curriculum.   The concept of *integrated curriculum*, highlights the integration of *content* by blending disciplines through "overlapping skills, concepts and attitudes" (Fogarty, 1991b, p. 64). One position—interdisciplinary curriculum—emphasizes connection between language arts and content area learning (e.g., Grisham, 1995; Roehler, 1983), or problem-centered, thematic pursuits (e.g., Anders & Pritchard, 1993; Powell, 1995). From this perspective, language and literacy are "functional tools, rather than curricular entities to be studied or mastered in their own right" (Pearson, 1994, p. 19). In these definitions, the presence of more than one discipline or school subject as part of the curricular unit is central—if not core—to integration.

Although associated with interdisciplinary approaches, Beane's (1993, 1997) view of curriculum integration fundamentally differs. Disciplines—especially as reflected in school subjects—represent what he calls the "hardening of the categories" (1997, p. 39). Placing curriculum integration within a collection of interdisciplinary approaches implies a continuum, where teachers moving from instruction in separate subject matters may first move toward connecting across disciplines, later to integration. Instead, Beane suggests that disciplinary boundaries be downplayed, not approached in terms of how they can each contribute to a particular line of inquiry or a project. The integrative activities within the curriculum use knowledge without regard to the school subject area or discipline with which it is associated.

Integration In and Out of School.   A conceptualization of integrated instruction emphasizes learning across contexts (e.g., home, school, community, work). This category is orthogonal and complementary to the previous two because integration across language processes or school subjects may occur within and beyond the school classroom.

Summary

Pearson (1994) highlighted the linguistic link between *integrity* and *integration*, and the irony that the notion of integrity is used to argue both for maintaining separation of the disciplines or school subjects and for promoting the integration of language processes, subject areas, disciplines, and disciplined inquiry. Definitions of integrated instruction leave open debate about what "counts" as integrated instruction. Is it sufficient to link more than one area of study? Can linked areas exist only within written literacy; within language and literacy; within language, literacy, and viewing; across language/literacy and disciplinary study? Must we see connections across units; or across grade levels and, hence, across classrooms and teachers? In the next section, we turn to our second analysis detailing the research base for integrating processes.

INTEGRATED INSTRUCTION: THE RESEARCH BASE

In our review, we discovered that despite a large body of writing on curriculum organization, "little of it reports research, if one defines 'research' as seeking to demonstrate or describe a relationship between ... some pattern of organization and such outcomes as the understanding of subject matter" (Goodlad & Su, 1992, p. 327). Referring to studies integrating social studies and literature, McGowan, Erickson and Neufeld (1996) concurred:

> The number of convincing arguments for social studies instruction based on literary sources far outweighs the amount of published research documenting the extent to which literature-based teaching promotes the knowledge, skills and values that constitute civic competence. Evidence seems limited, inconclusive, and concentrated on how trade books enhance students' knowledge acquisition. (p. 206)

Similarly, in describing integrated literacy instruction, Shanahan (1997, p. 15) wrote,

> given the long history and nearly universal acceptance of the idea of integration … there have been few empirical investigations of its effects.… I have been able to identify no study, in any field with any age level, that has clearly demonstrated more coherent or deeper understandings, or better applicability of learning as a result of integration.

In the sections that follow, we frame our review within the categories in Fig. 32.1. We first examine studies of language arts integration, then research on integrated curricula with the focus across disciplines. We end with studies that focus on integration in and out of school.

Integrated Language Arts

Some studies (e.g., Morrow, 1992; Walmsley & Walp, 1990) provide conceptual arguments for integration and insights into challenges and potential benefits for teachers and students. Some provide images of what integrated language arts instruction looks like in classrooms and how such experiences impact students across grade and ability levels (e.g., Baumann & Ivey, 1997; Block, 1993; Goatley, Brock, & Raphael, 1995; Raphael, Brock, & Wallace, 1998). Others (e.g., Meyer, Youga, & Flint-Ferguson, 1990; VanTassel-Baska, Johnson, Hughes, & Boyce, 1996) show positive effects of what is purported to be an integrated approach, but lack details about the nature of the intervention, and descriptions of the outcome measures make it difficult to determine what was integrated.

As conveyed in Fig. 32.1, studies of integrating the language arts tended to organize around either language processes or a literary selection. In the first instance, language processes are central; text selection tends to be incidental. Subject matter texts, a single literary text, or a text set related by theme or topic is chosen and used in the service of the language processes. The second form reverses figure and ground. Literary texts drive the language instruction, emphasizing language processes derived from those texts.

Walmsley and Walp's (1990) study illustrates integrated language arts research that takes written language as its central focus. With third- and fourth-grade teachers, they identified themes to guide unit construction, literature selection, and to-be-taught skills. The integrated language arts period included a teacher read-aloud, reading and writing instruction, and opportunity for students to present reading and writing projects. However, they noted separate times and activities for reading and writing, and the activities emphasized were traditional ones (e.g., directed reading activities, sustained silent reading). Although potentially integrative in focus, there was nothing inherent about the activities or organization to encourage integration. Assuming that teachers' guidance and framing questions underlying these units were integrative in nature, did this impact students' written language development? Because the authors noted that their project was aimed at solving specific problems in the elementary language arts curriculum rather than proving superiority of a method, they were cautious in claiming effectiveness. They did show that despite the challenges, data from vocabulary and comprehension subtest performance on a reading achievement test showed students performed at or above grade level. Further, a measure of the number of books from sustained silent reading for which students held conferences with their teacher revealed a substantial amount read at each grade level. However, we cannot know whether these measures would reflect differences had students been in a traditional program; nor is the form and nature of the integration students experienced clear from the description.

Morrow (1992) built on Walmsley and Walp's (1990) study, focusing directly on impact as she studied the effects of supplementing an existing basal reading program with literature in two second-grade classrooms. Although she did not explicitly define her intervention as an integrated language arts approach, the program shared many of those features: (a) emphasizing written and oral language processes in response to literature, (b) embedding skill-oriented literacy learning within literature reading, and (c) identifying key outcomes including comprehension, ability to create both oral and written stories, development of language complexity, vocabulary, and positive dispositions toward literacy and literature. When compared to similar children with neither literacy centers nor a literature emphasis, these children outperformed their control-group peers on virtually all measures. Students in the intervention group read more, had higher scores in story retellings, had higher comprehension scores, and created more original stories than did students in the control group, all with no cost to their performance on standardized tests.

Morrow's well-designed and carefully controlled experimental approach provided sufficient description of both the intervention and students' engagement to interpret findings. The study built a persuasive case for the value of, at the very least, systematically supplementing traditional commercial programs with literature. Although it would be easy to criticize the study for not clarifying "integrative" thinking results from such activity, it is important to remember that the study did not purport to be a model of integrated instruction.

In contrast, VanTassel-Baska and her colleagues (1996) purported to be investigating a model of integrated teaching, interweaving language processes. The researchers examined the impact on gifted and talented students' language arts development after students participated in what the researchers labeled as an "integrated curriculum model." Like Morrow, these researchers created an intervention—in this case a single unit called "Autobiographies: Personal Odysseys of Change"— and a control group for comparison purposes. Their goals included developing students' literary analysis and interpretive skills, persuasive writing skills, and linguistic competency. Participating schools were accepted if they could participate in the training (one to a few days) and provide a control group from the district. The study found that students in the experimental group outperformed those in the control groups in all three goal areas.

If we had more information, we might learn more from this research. Unfortunately, the unit was not described in terms of content, related activities, integrative lens, or planned length of participation. Researchers reported that some teachers made modifications (e.g., substituting literature if the packaged material was too difficult, dropping a research component for lack of time). However, changes were not discussed in terms of significance for unit integrity or relationship to unit goals. Unit effectiveness was judged in terms of traditional performance measures (e.g., describing the main idea of a literary selection, creating and justifying a title for a selection), not in terms of integrative abilities. One potentially integrative performance measure activity asked students to relate the concept of change to a selected literary passage. These problems make it challenging to know exactly what is integrative about this approach and how to interpret the findings that are favorable to students who participated in the researcher-developed unit. Studies such as this one may provide traditional "rigor" in testing one group's performance against another, but without information about the intervention, such findings beg the possibility of meaningful interpretations.

Although language was the central focus of the studies just described, others (e.g., Baumann & Ivey, 1997; Block, 1993; Goatley et al., 1995) have studied intradisciplinary integration by teaching language processes through integrative activities centered on the literature itself. Baumann and Ivey's (1997) study is characteristic of such research. The authors described their work as balancing literature study and skill/strategy instruction on the one hand, and balancing teacher-initiated and child-centered instruction on the other. Three kinds of activities—centered on the literature—were typical each day: (a) reading practice times, where students read connected text for 10 to 15 minutes; (b) strategy lessons focusing on word identification, vocabulary, comprehension, literature reading, and writing strategies; and (c) reading/language arts activities from teacher read-alouds to students writing related to the literature they were reading on their own. Baumann, as teacher, emphasized integrating strategy and skill instruction within the context of literature reading, writing, and discussion, and creating opportunities elsewhere in the curriculum to extend this integration.

Baumann and Ivey measured students' progress in literacy learning and attitudes through teacher and student reflections, students' work samples, videotapes of classroom literacy activities, and assessments, including anecdotal records, grades and progress reports, and an informal reading inventory. The researchers conducted cross-case analyses to provide insights into the breadth of children's learning, and two case studies to provide insights into students' depth of learning. They identified five areas of students' learning. Children became readers, engaged with literacy, developed strategic approaches to word identification, demonstrated they understood written texts, and learned to write about personal interests and experiences with a sense of audience.

These studies of intradisciplinary integration provide a small but encouraging base for the potential of integration to improve students' abilities to engage in literacy processes in meaningful ways and to do so within the context of reading, writing, and talking about literature and other resource materials. Initial studies point to the difficulties teachers face in creating such contexts and to the challenges of determining how these experiences affect students' literacy development.

Integrated Instruction: Interdisciplinarity and Curriculum Integration

According to curriculum scholars Goodlad and Su (1992, p. 330), an integrated curriculum "is intended to bring into close relationship such elements as concepts, skills, and values so that they are mutually reinforcing." Both empirical studies where disciplines are brought together to contribute to a common inquiry and studies where disciplinary boundaries are broken down in pursuit of a common problem are rare. Goodlad and Su suggest that such work may be more feasible in elementary schools, which lack constraints from separate curriculum specialists. However, school curriculum frameworks or standards establish such boundaries even when subjects are taught by the same teacher. Jacobs (1989a) cited two problems that plague curricula for interdisciplinary inquiry. The *potpourri problem* reflects lack of structures so that units become simply a sampling of knowledge from each discipline. The *polarity problem* underscores the territoriality that Goodlad and Su noted.

Where studies about interdisciplinary efforts do exist, they tend to preserve disciplinary boundaries. However, occasionally, an innovation will break down disciplinary boundaries (e.g., Bruner [1971] and colleagues' curriculum, *Man: A Course of Study*). The vast majority of "studies" of any type of interdisciplinary approach consisted of anecdotal cases written for practitioners promoting an integrated curriculum, usually where language and literacy processes are used in the practices associated with learning about school subjects (e.g., Casteel & Isom, 1994; Trepanier-Street, 1993). Further, the majority of these texts were simply "how-to" proposals, such as Fogarty's (1991) "Ten Ways to Integrate Curriculum" or descriptions such as Lapp and Flood's (1994) "Integrating the Curriculum: First Steps."

Interdisciplinary Research.   Research within this category centers on science, mathematics, and social studies. Interdisciplinary approaches centered on science tend to substitute literature and authentic resource materials for textbooks, and/or to make a conscious effort to teach domain-specific language arts skills and strategies within the context of learning a content area (e.g., Palincsar & Herrenkohl, 1999; Romance & Vitale, 1992, cited in Bristor, 1994; Morrow et al., 1997).

Bristor (1994) described results from the first 2 years of a 5-year study of science and language arts integration (see also Romance & Vitale, 1992). Motivated by efficiency and a desire to make content area literacy instruction more meaningful, researchers designed a program in which they drew on literacy research to build students' background knowledge prior to reading content texts. They linked relevant language arts curriculum objectives from their district guidelines to science activities. They drew on literature with science content from trade books and their basal reading program, and they engaged students in dramatic play related to the science themes. Based on subtests of standardized achievement texts, the researchers reported gains in the achievement in both reading and in science for students in the integrated program as compared to those in traditionally separate curriculum. Further, based on a 6-point scale inventory of affect, students in the integrated program showed more positive attitudes and greater self-confidence than comparable students in the separate curriculum.

Morrow et al. (1997) had similar findings. Students were in one of three treatment groups: literature/science, literature only, and control. The two experimental groups involved a literature-based intervention using trade books in both literacy and science programs, or only in the literacy programs. Control classrooms used commercially published basal readers and textbooks. Students were tested before and after the year-long intervention, using informal and standardized tests to evaluate their growth in literacy skills and science content knowledge. On almost all measures—from story retellings to standardized tests—findings favored the integration of literature into science instruction.

Winograd and Higgins (1995), former classroom teachers, described their approach to integrating language process instruction within their mathematics curriculum through student-generated story problems. Through a series of vignettes, they detailed the integration of mathematical reasoning, oral interactions through small-group discussions, and process writing activities. Further, they detailed how creating daily story problems led students to observe events outside the classroom as sources of story problems (e.g., one student interviewed his father about his job sanding streets after a snowfall). They suggest that such curriculum integration helps students move beyond surface features of a story problem to considering its meaning, and thus facilitates their ability to solve problems. Teachers invite students to write, and accompany that invitation with instruction in problem-writing and problem-solving skills and strategies.

Many researchers have examined interdisciplinary connections between social studies and literature or literacy. For example, Monson, Howe, and Greenlee (1989) surveyed middle elementary students to find out the questions they had about their counterparts in other countries, then examined literature and textbooks for information that could address students' questions. They found that children's questions could be answered more deeply in trade books than in textbooks, because trade books provided more depth in answering questions about the human condition than did comparable-age social studies books. Levstick's (1986, 1989, 1990) research with first-, fifth-, and sixth-grade students demonstrated that literature can be motivating to history learning. Children across age levels were very interested in the human condition, and literature served as a way of entering its study so that it was possible for the youngsters to make connections to their own lived experiences.

Smith and his colleagues (1993; Smith, Monson, & Dobson, 1992) found that children remembered more and had better conceptual understanding when literature and social studies were integrated. Smith pre- and posttested students using an oral free recall measure to determine their knowledge of U.S. history. The intervention used trade books dealing with U.S. history to supplement students' social studies instruction. The free-recall measure revealed that students in the literature–social studies group recalled 60% more information about U.S. history than did control-group students. Further, lack of difference on spring standardized scores indicated this advantage did not adversely affect performance in reading. Guzzetti, Kowalinski, and McGowan's (1992) comparison of sixth-grade students' learning about China through textbooks versus an integrated trade/textbook approach yielded similar findings.

Although these studies looked at how *literature* could be integrated with social studies, Beck and McKeown (1991; Beck, McKeown, Sandora, Kucan, & Worthy, 1996) examined how integrating *literacy instruction* with social studies impacted students' textbook comprehension. In a series of studies, they found that students' comprehension improved when they learned to consider the authors behind the textbooks, and to ask questions, metaphorically, of the author as they fill in gaps in their understanding.

Curriculum Integration.   In one of the few studies of curriculum integration, Sylvester (1994) documented teacher research he conducted with third graders as they created and participated in a classroom economy. Mathematics, literature, history, science, and other school subjects came together as students considered the real issues in the community's day-to-day operations. Drawing on his field notes and samples of students' work, Sylvester created three short case studies to illustrate the social and academic benefits students experienced. Students showed growth in self-esteem and motivation, interpersonal skills, sense of responsibility, and in "daydreaming new futures."

Sylvester suggested that, overall, students gained a great deal from the experience. First, he saw them engaged in meaningful drill, working on daily applications of math problems, and engaging in literacy for real purposes. Second, students saw themselves in new roles, as entrepreneurs with businesses to run; as government leaders; and as citizens with a voice in and responsibilities to the community. Third, they maintained a strong racial identity without it conflicting with attempts for academic success. Fourth, they learned to deal with power (e.g., their teacher) in proactive ways. Fifth, they came to see "reality" as something to question and analyze, not simply accept as "the way it is." These assertions seemed consistent with the descriptions of the classroom community, the neighborhood, and students' participation within them. However, to understand the potential of such innovations for students' literacy development, it would be useful to include thicker descriptions of students' use of literacy across contexts, and related changes in their literacy abilities.

Integration In and Out of School

Integration in and out of school merges classroom life with contexts beyond a classroom's walls. Attempts involve integration across school, home, and community (e.g., Edwards, 1996; Moll, 1992a, 1992b). These innovations reflect a shift in focus, from literacy as a set of skills to literacy as a set of cultural practices. In the former view, the job of school is simply to see that this set of skills is acquired by "organizing effective lessons ... diagnosing skills strength and deficits, providing appropriate exercises in developmentally felicitous sequences, motivating students to engage in these exercises, giving clear explanations and directions" (Resnick, 1990, p. 171). However, viewing literacy as a set of cultural practices underscores the importance of socializing students into the community or culture of literacy users (Moll, 1992a). Rethinking literacy in this way opens the door to connecting between students' cultural backgrounds and school experiences, the essence of integrating school literacy practices with those of home and community. A number of studies explored the meaning of such an approach for curriculum innovations and professional development.

Home–School Connections.   At one level, teachers create opportunities for students to share school language and literacy activities with their families (e.g., Morrow, 1992), or to draw on families to share home literacies and events in school (e.g., Edwards, 1996; Damkoehler, Gayle-Evans, Farrell-Stroyan, & Lockhart, 1996). Edwards (1996) provided one example of such home-school connections in her study of sharing time in two kindergarten classrooms, based on concerns about the discontinuity some children experience between home and school language patterns. Although Michaels (1981) attributed such discontinuity to students' ethnic backgrounds, teachers working with Edwards observed that "white children as well as black children failed to employ a topic-centered style during sharing time" (1996, p. 345). If students experience a discontinuity between home and school literacy practices, they lose opportunities to understand literacy as part of their cultural practices and connect from their lives to the work of school. The researchers thought students' difficulties might be helped by involving their families in decisions about what to share in school and practicing how to share it. Their approach was designed to make school language explicit and to provide a context for students to practice oral presentation, a major part of the kindergarten curriculum through "sharing time." Parents received guidance to help their children prepare for upcoming presentations. Teachers and researchers kept records of individual students' growth in oral language facility. As a result of participating in this daily activity, teachers believed their students became better listeners, developed an understanding of topic-centered presentation, and developed greater self-esteem. Field notes describing one child's progress traced his evolution from a shy child who typically mumbled so severely that he was inarticulate, to one who maintained eye contact with his peers, used complex sentences, and paused for questions, which he capably answered.

Similar attempts to connect to family stories have been made in later grades through studies of family histories (see, e.g., Damkoehler et al., 1996), although to date, little formal research has been conducted to indicate specific consequences for students' literacy learning. Within such studies, integration of oral and written language was important, but the integration of the child's home and school language experiences, and their developing understandings of themselves as cultural beings were equally crucial. Such experiences may serve as an important basis for students to later actually study the language, literacy, and culture in their homes and in the communities in which they live (Pearson, 1994, defined this as *integration into the community*).

School-Community Integration.   In "integration into the community" studies, integration occurs in two ways. First, language and literacy skills are applied as students gather information. In doing so, they have authentic reasons to engage in literate activity, and, we assume, are motivated because the subject of study is connected to their lives. Second, language and literacy skills are themselves the object of study, as students look across contexts to explore how language and literacy are used in different contexts, some of which may be unfamiliar.

Two well-known scholars in this area are Luis Moll and Shirley Brice Heath. In the 1970s, Heath (1982) conducted ethnographic research in North Carolina's Piedmont area, studying students and their families from three different cultural communities. She later applied what she had learned to collaborative work with teacher-researchers (Heath, 1983). She described a third-grade classroom with integrated written and oral language activities, as well as school activities integrated with students' home and community experiences. For example, speakers from the community were interviewed in the classroom. Students viewed themselves as "language detectives" uncovering differences in language use among working contexts: A grocer uses a lot of "politeness" terms and essentially asks "yes–no" questions, whereas guides from the nature museum talk in long paragraphs. Students also analyzed talk in their homes, beginning by recording the types of questions they heard asked, and later interviewing their parents about the types of reading, writing, and talking they engaged in at their jobs. Heath noted that by the end of the year, most students in this class were above grade level on reading tests, able to write stories and create paragraphs related to their content area study.

More recently, Moll (1992a, 1992b; Moll & González, 1994; Moll, Vélez-Ibáñez, & Greenberg, 1989), working collaboratively with teachers, explored "how literacy takes place in the broader social contexts of households and community life (in an) attempt to understand and forge relationships between these domains of study" (1992b, p. 211). One aspect of this work involved identifying the funds of knowledge in the community, then drawing on these funds to contribute in substantive ways to the classroom's intellectual life. This integration of classroom and community played out in several classroom-based projects. To date, Moll and his colleagues concentrated analyses on the impact of such approaches on teachers' professional development. Moll studied the curriculum practices teachers initiated, their understanding of literacy as cultural practice, and homes as important sites for literacy engagement and use for a wide range of purposes.

Moll illustrated how the interweavings of professional development initiatives in the form of a teacher study group and an after-school laboratory support students' literacy development (Moll et al., 1989) and contributed to teachers rethinking their literacy curriculum. For example, Ina A. created an interdisciplinary unit around the topic of construction, knowing that there were substantial resources she could draw on within the community, including parents of students in her class and other, unrelated adults. Students engaged in traditional forms of information gathering that invited practice of literacy skills, such as library research, creating models, and writing related essays in either Spanish or English, so they could emphasize their ideas without constraint. Community members in their study were invited to present to the classroom. Literacy routines in the classroom included research, oral presentations, and written presentations.

Teachers who participated with Ina A. described what Moll and González (1994) called the "transformative potential of viewing households from a funds of knowledge perspective" (p. 444). First, like teachers participating in Edwards (1996) study, they reported realizing as myth the notion that working-class parents of language minority students lacked experiences and knowledge to contribute to their students' literacy development. Second, they developed sophisticated notions of culture, moving from thinking of culture as a collection of personality traits, folk celebrations, and so forth to seeing culture as a collection of lived practices and knowledge (Moll, Amanti, Neff, & González, 1992).

One of the findings of Moll's line of research is the importance of teachers' own experiential learning. They developed their understanding of funds of knowledge and transformed their classrooms as a result. Other efforts explored paths from professional development to transforming curriculum. Tchudi and Lafer (1993) felt that among the challenges teachers face in teaching within integrated approaches is that they themselves have no experience in such methods. The researchers created a summer institute in which teachers could experience an interdisciplinary curriculum, grounded in the study of their local community's scientific, economic, literary, and cultural heritage. They described their work as existing within a language arts perspective of "reading and writing the culture" (p. 78), where participants read poetry, nonfiction, and fiction about the region; maintained journals; wrote imaginative texts across the curriculum drawing on their experiences studying the Truckee River of Nevada; met with local writers in workshops; and participated in a "chautauqua," a 19th-century tradition for a cultural exposition and tent show, including reenactments and lectures highlighting historical figures and events.

In their anecdotal report, the researchers traced the impact of participants' firsthand experience in an interdisciplinary approach on their subsequent site-based curriculum development. Tchudi and Lafer described four teachers who had substantial influence in changing their elementary school curriculum to an integrated approach developing a year-long theme of "communities." Their work in the elementary school eventually led to presentations at a regional conference and the publication of their curriculum by one of the state's professional organizations. Other participants revealed impact through revisions to courses they taught, implementation of new units, and providing support for other professionals in their teaching sites (e.g., compiling a bibliography on the desert/Nevada/water for young readers).

Challenges to Integration In and Out of School.   Goodlad and Su (1992) suggested what may be obvious from the lines of research just described: Teaching from an integrated perspective or creating an integrated curriculum is challenging, which helps us understand why, as Walmsley and Walp (1990) found, it is such a long-term process. Schmidt and his colleagues (1985) found that despite teachers' favoring integration and their belief that it is more efficient, integrated instruction of any kind (within the language arts and across disciplines) accounted for less than 10% of their instructional time during the academic year in which the study took place. Why do so few teachers move in this direction? Some researchers have documented specific challenges that inhibit integrated instruction. Both Pappas and Oyler (with Barry & Rassel, 1993) and Roskos and Neuman (1995) created case studies of teachers as they began planning and implementing integrated language arts units.

Pappas and Oyler (1993) presented case studies of two teachers as they began the process of integration. Their focus was initially intradisciplinary, but gradually moved toward cross-content area studies. Michael—a first-year, fifth-grade teacher—had established several features in his classroom characteristic of others studying integrated instruction. He had developed cross-disciplinary thematic units, integrating literacy instruction with science and social studies. He supplemented or replaced traditional textbook-driven curriculum, using materials with more potential to support integrative inquiry. For example, he received a grant to buy animals and informational books to support students' inquiry about the animals. He implemented alternative social structures in the classroom that gave students voice and some control over their learning, such as initiating literature response groups as part of the literacy program.

At the beginning of the following year, Michael discussed some of his goals. His comments suggest that such surface-level changes are not sufficient to insure integration. He said that one area he wanted to concentrate on was "content—I've just been bringing in books, but I don't think I was understanding that the books are to help us to understand and inquire about content" (Pappas & Oyler, 1993, p. 300). In other words, despite his incorporation of many of the features of an integrated classroom, he recognized that a key feature had been missing from his previous year's teaching—support for students to make the connections between the availability of new textual materials and engaging in language processes for the purposes of inquiry. Pappas and her colleagues suggested that changes in teaching practices involve more than simply "taking on new methods or techniques. At the root of their innovations is a different theory about knowledge and language" (Pappas & Oyler, 1993, p. 301). Further, as Lipson et al. (1993) noted, "this type of teaching requires a different view of the language arts within different organizational structures" (p. 254). In short, becoming effective integrative teachers requires fundamental changes in teachers' epistemological beliefs and the day-to-day practices of structuring their classroom.

In studying teacher planning, Roskos and Neuman (1995) provided insights into how fundamental changes in beliefs and practices play out in teachers' integrated unit planning, and in so doing, shed light on the demands such approaches place on teachers. They studied two kindergarten teachers as they planned topic-based units where students used language and literacy as tools for learning. Challenges to unit planning stemmed from two sources. First, there were multiple levels of planning, far more complex than they had experienced in more traditional lesson planning: metaplanning (i.e., planning the plan), topic and content planning, activity planning, environmental planning, and revision planning. Second, these layers of planning created demands on teachers' time, specificity of planning, knowledge, and level of work. There were greater demands for what Shulman (1986) termed *pedagogical content knowledge*. This type of knowledge requires that teachers be able to understand and interpret the subject matter that they plan to include, find ways to represent this knowledge for their students, and adapt it to their students' levels and their own classrooms. The teachers studied by Roskos and Neuman found that they were not simply adding new techniques, they were fundamentally changing the way they looked at their instruction.

One might wonder if teachers who do not have support for participating in experiential opportunities or mutual planning time can turn to commercially available materials to support their own integration attempts within their classrooms. A study of professional materials—teacher education texts, commercial reading and language arts programs—revealed discouraging information (Lipson et al., 1993). Researchers found that although the philosophy and rationale for integration may be clear from these resource materials, the discussion of how to effectively create and implement integrated units falls short of expectations. Similar findings emerged in their analysis of basal reading and supplementary materials (albeit from the early 1990s). Although superior to earlier editions, the series often lacked the focus and coherence needed to promote thematic learning. Supplementary materials were often collections of activities that led more to fragmentation than integration around coherent concepts.

Summary: Promises and Cautions.   Integrated instruction is hard work that involves crossing boundaries of the curriculum and the classroom/school, involves intensive planning, and involves well-developed knowledge. Moreover, it requires a theoretical framework to guide both curriculum construction and innovations in instruction. Without such a theory, there are risks. Social studies educators Alleman and Brophy (1993, 1994), recommended that educators "consider integration a potential tool that is feasible and desirable in some situations but not in all" (p. 66), because so many current recommendations for integrated practices lack any conceptual base. In their analysis of how integration played out in a social studies series, they noted activities irrelevant to learning social studies (e.g., using social studies content to focus on pluralizing nouns) or so time-consuming as to be questionable (e.g., artistic or construction work). Some activities distort social studies content (e.g., five steps to building a log cabin). Literacy educator Pearson, (1994, p. 25) saw similar problems from a literary perspective: "My fear is that if we view literature as a basis for contextualizing or applying specific language activities or strategies, we may end up doing violence to the very literature we selected so that these activities would be 'relevant and authentic.'"

More can be done to support teachers to ease constraints that mitigate against innovations. More can be done to create meaningful opportunities for teachers to experience such learning first hand. More can be made available in terms of professional resources. Certainly, more is needed in terms of both a theoretical and a research base as we consider not when or how to integrate the curriculum, but whether, for what purposes, and for whom.

A THEORETICAL CRITIQUE: INTEGRATED INSTRUCTION UNDERSTOOD TRANSACTIVELY

As editor of the National Society for the Study of Education yearbook devoted to integration, Dressel (1958) characterized it as "truly the central problem of education." Given this importance, we were surprised that among the many articles about integrated approaches, with few exceptions, there was little attempt to address integration theoretically. There were references to important theoretical lenses, but a theory conceptualizing the what, whys, and hows of integration was seldom in evidence. Typically, proponents emphasized authenticity, motivational value, and efficiency, which, although important, provide little rationale for thoughtful integration. What makes integration educative? And why?

Integration is multifaceted, referring to many distinct but related constructs. With no theoretical lens to guide research, policy, and practice, it is impossible to determine the relationship among these different facets of integration. Research questions to date may be too narrow, focused on whether or not integration is effective for organizing curricula. Instead of asking *whether* to integrate, we need a principled, contextual conception of integration to guide us in addressing *what to integrate with what, why, when, how,* and *for whom.*

In concluding our review, we briefly describe a transactional conception of integration, supported by recent developments in evolutionary biology (Levins & Lewontin, 1985; Maturana & Varela, 1980), neurophysiology (Varela, Thompson, & Rosch, 1991) and cognitive science (Winograd & Flores, 1986), as well as philosophy, psychology, and education (Dewey, 1896; Vygotsky, 1997). We stress two tenets derived from a transactional perspective: (a) the constitutive role of embodied language practices in mediating the relationship between individuals and their environment, and (b) the importance of understanding both the developmental history of learners and the cultural history of what they are to learn. We close with some ways in which a transactive conception of integration can lead to developing students' understanding of a critical disciplinarity.

A Transactional Conception of Knowing

Most work on integration seems predicated on an underlying dualism in which the individual and the environment are assumed to exist independent of each other. Arguing for a transactional conception of mind, Johnson (1987) suggested that this dualism leads to our asking, how are the two related, and which is responsible for the structure of the world? Idealist perspectives emphasize the contribution of the individual, whereas objectivist perspectives emphasize the contribution of the environment. Johnson (1987, p. 207) maintained that "it is a mistake to think of an organism and its environment as ... independent and unrelated entities; the organism does not exist ... apart from its environment." Contrary to idealism, individuals do not simply construct reality according to subjective desires and whims. Contrary to objectivism, individuals are not merely mirrors of nature that determine concepts in one and only one way. This dualism can result in *naive constructivism*, in which individuals are assumed to be free to draw relationships wherever they "see" them; or a *naive realism*, in which integration is judged against an individual's ability to accurately relate objects and events as they are assumed to exist objectively in the world. Instead, Johnson argued for a *transactional perspective of mind* such that

> our structured experience is an organism–environment interaction in which both poles are altered and transformed through an ongoing historical process. In other words the environment is structured in ways that limit the possibilities for our categorizations of it. But the structure of the environment by no means strictly determines the structure of our experience, which is to say, our understanding of our world. (Johnson, 1987, p. 207)

Thus, the locus of integrated knowledge is found in neither the eyes of the beholder nor the object beheld, but in the transactions between the two. When we speak of "experience," we mean our history, culture, language, institutions, and so on, not simply a set of mental representation of a static, already organized reality. Central to understanding the nature of these person–environment transactions is the role of embodied language practices.

The Constitutive Role of Embodied Language Practices

The belief that language represents or corresponds to an independently existing reality is deeply ingrained in our folk psychology and pedagogy. The role of language is often assumed to be transparent, merely a vehicle through which the already organized world is named and described. However, from a transactional perspective, "language [is] a means for social coordination and adaptation.... Describing how things are [is shorthand for] finding descriptions of reality that work more or less well given our purposes in framing descriptions of reality" (Johnson, 1987, p. 211).

Two implications follow when language is understood transactively. First, language helps us shape our knowledge, our "reality." Rather than mirroring what is in the world, language practices are constitutive of what we come to know. For language to realize this constitutive function, it must occur within the contexts of joint social activity where determinate meanings and their relationships are formed (e.g., literature discussions, project-based activities in subject areas).

Integration, the processes by which we come to know what goes with what, is a normative practice. It is discursive, but also grounded in practice. Language doesn't simply name already existing integrative relationships; it is constitutive in bringing these relationships into being. However, not anything goes; rather, established integrative relationships are based on a history of embodied social practices with a material and ideal world.

Many of the arguments for integration stem from notions of increased authenticity. This view of language offers a warrant for such a position. It argues for the kind of socially based activities within topics and themes characteristic of integrated instruction. Thus, teachers collaborating with Moll (1992a) used ethnographic techniques to describe how things were among students' households, and found that in doing so, they challenged the "reality" they had earlier created about the families' attitudes and resources. Students in Winograd and Higgins's (1995) study reconstructed their understandings of mathematical reasoning through the story problems they composed.

A second implication of a transactive conception of language follows from the first. Because language is not to be understood in terms of accuracy in representing or corresponding to an independently existing world, it is fundamentally underdetermined in its capacity for constructing, integrating, and communicating meanings. This is particularly problematic in schooling, where one goal is to convey society's common knowledge (Edwards & Mercer, 1987). This underscores the importance of creating discourse-based communities of practice (Brown, 1994; Swales, 1990; Wenger, 1998) that share a common lexicon, mechanisms for communication, and a critical mass of participants. Thus, a further warrant for integrated instruction, supported by a transactional perspective, is that such approaches build communities for engaging in embodied language practices as phenomena are explored. For example, Sylvester and his students tackled elusive concepts related to economics, government, and human rights. They did so using language that had shared meaning within the community. Rather than simply *talk* about these constructs, the students within this community *practiced* them.

The Developmental History of the Knower and Cultural History of the Known

We have seen that objects and events may be combined into larger wholes—they may be integrated—because individuals with particular developmental histories transact with school subjects with particular cultural histories. What goes with what is a function of the ongoing history of transaction between persons and their environment. Thus, a second insight of a transactive perspective concerns the importance of a joint emphasis on teachers' understanding the cultural history of that which is to be learned (e.g., disciplinary knowledge) and the developmental history of their students. It is only through genetic analyses of both knower and known that we can fully understand their present ongoing transactions. If teachers are to integrate the curriculum in a manner that their students are able to understand, they must coordinate their pedagogical transactions with these students in ways that are developmentally sensitive.

> The adult mind is so familiar with the notion of logically ordered facts that it does not recognize—it cannot realize—the amount of separating and reformulating which the facts of direct experience have to undergo before they can appear as a "study," or branch of learning. (Dewey, 1902/1956, p. 6)

The challenge of understanding and implementing integrated instruction from a transactive perspective thus requires that we simultaneously keep both the developing knower and known in our conceptual field of vision. Fostering the development of children in a changing world thus becomes the allegorical equivalent of building a ship while at sea. We must assist them in coming to understand the normative integrative meanings (e.g., subject matter knowledge) that have been culturally constructed, while at the same time understanding their origins in embodied discursive practices, practices that are likely to lead to newly integrated meanings. Such "binocular vision" is necessary if we are to foster their development of what we call a *critical disciplinarity*.

Fostering Students' Critical Disciplinarity

We believe that a critical disciplinarity rests on a critical literacy. Any conception of child development must recognize the central role of language in the development of mind and the development of the disciplines. Halliday (1993) suggested that "the distinctive characteristic of human learning is that it is a process of making meaning.... [T]he ontogenesis of language is at the same time the ontogenesis of learning." The challenge of fostering students' development of a critical disciplinarity involves the two-pronged task of assisting them in coming to understand the systematized meanings associated with disciplinary knowledge, while simultaneously encouraging an historical consciousness that reveals the constructed, discursive nature of such knowledge.

"Language is not a *domain* of human knowledge; language is the essential condition of knowing, the process by which experience *becomes* knowledge" (Halliday, 1993, p. 94). Several individuals have emphasized the developmental and epistemological primacy of narrative genres in the development of both the knower and the known. Scholes, a literary theorist, characterized narrative as "a major armature of thought" (1989, p. 4). Nelson (1996, p. 184) suggested that "narrative is the 'natural product' of language; it precedes and is the source of theoretical thinking." She maintained that "human cognition is basically formulated in terms of stories, and logic, classification, and rational inference are all in some sense derivative from storytelling." Similarly, Bruner (1996, p. 121) suggested that "it is very likely the case that the most natural and earliest way in which we organize our experience and knowledge is in terms of narrative form ... that the beginnings, the transitions, and the full grasp of ideas in the spiral curriculum depend upon embodying those ideas into a story or narrative form."

For example, the pedagogical use of well-chosen narrative histories of conceptual change across multiple school subjects has the potential to teach children not only about the disciplines, but the idea of (inter)disciplinarity itself—the discursive processes by which the disciplines are constructed, maintained, and permeated by other disciplines. Over and above their literary value, the principled integrative use of various narrative genres in elementary education has the ironic potential of leading to a deeper, more critical understanding of subject matter knowledge. One can imagine developmentally informed integrated literacy instruction that in the early elementary grades forefronts the storied, discursive nature of knowing, but in later elementary grades comes increasingly to emphasize the disciplined, systematic nature of organizing and understanding school subjects.

CONCLUDING STATEMENT

Integrated literacy instruction turned out to be a far more elusive and far more complex area than we had ever anticipated. In the process of this review, we found ourselves surprised at the small ratio of data-driven articles to overall papers on the subject and wondered if the push toward integration of any kind might be premature, or even ill-founded. We became increasingly convinced, however, by the albeit small number of studies, that integrative approaches are exciting ways of rethinking school curriculum within and beyond the language arts. Future research is required to provide the needed base for promoting integrated innovations. But we need more than just research. We need research driven by a strong, conceptual framework that helps us unpack the construct, consider its potential advantages, and find ways to address the very real challenges and drawbacks we cannot ignore.

REFERENCES

Adler, M., & Flihan, S. (1997). *The interdisciplinary continuum: Reconciling theory, research, and practice* (Report Series No. 2.36). National Research Center on English Learning & Achievement, University of Albany, State University of New York.

Alleman, J., & Brophy, J. (1993). Is curriculum integration a boon or a threat to social studies? *Social Education, 57*, 287–291.

Alleman, J., & Brophy, J. (1994). Trade-offs embedded in the literacy approach to early elementary social studies. *Social Studies and the Young Learner, 6*(3), 6–8.

Anders, P. L., & Pritchard, T. G. (1993). Integrated language curriculum and instruction for the middle grades. *Elementary School Journal, 93*(5), 611–624.

Barr, R., Kamil, M. L., Mosenthal, P. B., & Pearson, P. D. (Eds.). (1991). *Handbook of Reading Research.* New York: Longman.

Baumann, J. F., & Ivey, G. (1997). Delicate balances: Striving for curricular and instructional equilibrium in a second-grade, literature/strategy-based classroom. *Reading Research Quarterly, 32*(3), 244–275.

Beane, J. A. (1993). Problems and possibilities for an integrative curriculum. *Middle School Journal, 25*(1), 18–23.

Beane, J. A. (1995). Curriculum integration and the disciplines of knowledge. *Phi Delta Kappan, 76*(8), 616–622.

Beane, J. A. (1997). *Curriculum integration: Designing the core of democratic education.* New York: Teachers College Press.

Beck, I. L., & McKeown, M. G. (1991). Social studies texts are hard to understand: Mediating some of the difficulties (Research directions). *Language Arts, 68*(6), 482–490.

Beck, I. L., McKeown, M. G., Sandora, C., Kucan, L., & Worthy, J. (1996). Questioning the author: A yearlong classroom implementation to engage students with text. *Elementary School Journal, 96*(4), 385–414.

Bergeron, B. S. (1990). What does the term *whole language* mean? Constructing a definition from the literature. *Journal of Reading Behavior, 22*(4), 301–329.

Block, C. C. (1993). Strategy instruction in a literature-based reading program. *Elementary School Journal, 94*(2), 139–151.

Bristor, V. J. (1994). Combining reading and writing with science to enhance content area achievement and attitudes. *Reading Horizons, 35*(1), 31–43.

Brown, A. L. (1994). The advancement of learning. *Educational Researcher, 23*(8), 4–12.

Bruner, J. (1996). *The culture of education.* Cambridge, MD: Harvard University Press.

Bruner, J. (1971). *The relevance of education.* New York: W. W. Norton.

Busching, B. A., & Schwartz, J. I. (Eds.). (1983). *Integrating the language arts in the elementary school.* Urbana, IL: National Council of Teachers of English.

Casteel, C. P., & Isom, B. A. (1994). Reciprocal processes in science and literacy learning. *Reading Teacher, 47*(7), 538–545.

Coalition of Essential Schools. (1988). *The common principles of the Coalition of Essential Schools.* Providence, RI: Coalition of Essential Schools, Brown University.

Cremin, L. A. (1964). *The transformation of the school: Progressivism in American education 1876–1957.* New York: Random House.

Damkoehler, D., Gayle-Evans, G., Farrell-Stroyan, S., & Lockhart, M. (1996). Family histories: Collecting, connecting, celebrating. *Primary Voices K–6, 4*(2), 7–13.

Dewey, J. (1896). The reflex arc concept in psychology. *Psychological Review, III*(4), 357–370.

Dewey, J. (1956). *The child and the curriculum.* Chicago: University of Chicago Press. (Original work published 1902)

Dewey, J. (1913). *Interest and effort in education.* Boston: Houghton Mifflin.

Dressel, P. L. (1958). The meaning of significance of integration. In B. Henry (Ed.), *The integration of educational experiences: Fifty-seventh yearbook of the National Society for the Study of Education* (Part 3, pp. 3–25). Chicago: University of Chicago Press.

Dressel, P. L. (1958). Integration: An expanding concept. In B. Henry (Ed.), *The integration of educational experiences: Fifty-seventh yearbook of the National Society for the Study of Education* (Part 3, pp. 251–263). Chicago: University of Chicago Press.

Edwards, P. A. (1996). Creating sharing time conversations: Parents and teachers work together. *Language Arts, 73*(5), 344–349.

Edwards, D., & Mercer, N. (1987). *Common knowledge: The development of understanding in the classroom.* New York: Methuen.

Ellis, A., & Fouts, J. (1993). *Research on Educational Innovations.* Princeton, NJ: Eye on Education.

Flood, J., Jensen, J. M., Lapp, D., & Squire, J. R. (1991). *Handbook for research on teaching the English language arts.* New York: Macmillan.

Fogarty, R. (1991a). *How to integrate the curricula.* Palatine, IL: IRI/Skylight.

Fogarty, R. (1991b). Ten ways to integrate curriculum. *Educational Leadership, 49*(2), 61–65.

Galda, L. (1998). Mirrors and windows: Reading as transformation. In T. E. Raphael & K. H. Au (Eds.), *Literature-based instruction: Reshaping the curriculum* (pp. 1–11). Norwood, MA: Christopher-Gordon.

Goatley, V. J., Brock, C. H., & Raphael, T. E. (1995). Diverse learners participating in regular education "Book Clubs." *Reading Research Quarterly, 30*(3), 352–380.

Goodlad, J. I., & Su, Z. (1992). The organization of the curriculum. In P. W. Jackson (Ed.), *Handbook of research on curriculum* (pp. 327–344). New York: Macmillan.

Goodman, Y. M. (1989). Roots of the whole-language movement. *Elementary School Journal, 90*(2), 113–127.

Grisham, D. (1995). Exploring integrated curriculum. *Reading Psychology, 16,* 269–279.

Guzzetti, B. J., Kowalinski, B. J., & McGowan, T. (1992). Using a literature-based approach to teaching social studies. *Journal of Reading, 36*(2), 114–122.

Halliday, M. A. K. (1993). Towards a language-based theory of learning. *Linguistics and Education, 5,* 93–116.

Heath, S. B. (1982). Questioning at home and at school: A comparative study. In G. Spindler (Ed.), *Doing the ethnography of schooling* (pp. 102–131). New York: Holt, Rinehart, and Winston.

Heath, S. B. (1983). Research currents: A lot of talk about nothing. *Language Arts, 60*(8), 999–1007.

Holt, J. (1967). *How children learn.* New York: Pitman.

Jackson, P. (1992). *Handbook of research on curriculum.* New York: Macmillan.

Jacobs, H. H. (1989a). Design options for an integrated curriculum. In H. H. Jacobs (Ed.), *Interdisciplinary curriculum: Design and implementation* (pp. 13–22). Alexandria, VA: ASCD.

Johnson, M. (1987). *The body and the mind: The bodily basis of meaning, imagination, and reason.* Chicago: University of Chicago Press.

Kain, D. L. (1993). Cabbages-and-kings: Research direction in integrated/intradisciplinary curriculum. *Journal of Educational Thought, 27*(3), 312–331.

Langer, J. A., & Allington, R. L. (1992). Curriculum research in writing and reading. In P. W. Jackson (Ed.), *Handbook of research on curriculum* (pp. 687–725). New York: Macmillan.

Lapp, D., & Flood, J. (1994). Integrating the curriculum: First steps. *Reading Teacher, 47*(5), 416–419.

Levins, R., & Lewontin, R. C. (1985). *The dialectical biologist.* Cambridge, MA: Harvard University Press.

Levstick, L. S. (1986). The relationship between historical response and narrative in a sixth-grade classroom. *Theory and Research in Social Education, 14*, 1–15.

Levstick, L. (1989). Historical narrative and the young reader. *Theory into Practice, 28*(2), 114–119.

Levstick, L. S. (1990). Research directions: Mediating content through literary texts. *Language Arts, 67*, 848–853.

Lipson, M. Y., Valencia, S. W., Wixson, K. K., & Peters, C. W. (1993). Integration and thematic teaching: Integration to improve teaching and learning. *Language Arts, 70*, 252–263.

Marzano, R., J. (1991). Language, the language arts, and thinking. In J. Flood, J. M. Jensen, D. Lapp, & J. R. Squire (Eds.), *Handbook of research on teaching the English language arts* (pp. 559–586). New York: Macmillan.

Maturana, H. R., & Varela, F. J. (1980). *Autopoiesis and cognition.* London: D. Reidel.

McGowan, T. M., Erickson, L., & Neufeld, J. A. (1996). With reason and rhetoric: Building a case for the literature-social studies connection. *Social Education, 60*(4), 203–207.

Meyer, J., Youga, J., & Flint-Ferguson, J. (1990). Grammar in context: Why and how. *English Journal, 79*(1), 66–70.

Michaels, S. (1981). "Sharing time": Children's narrative styles and differential access to literacy. *Literacy in Society, 10*, 423–442.

Moll, L. C. (1992a). Bilingual classroom studies and community analysis. *Educational Researcher, 21*(2), 20–24.

Moll, L., C. (1992b). Literacy research in community and classrooms: A sociocultural approach. In R. Beach, J. Green, M. Kamil, & T. Shanahan (Eds.), *Multidisciplinary perspectives in community and classrooms* (pp. 211–244). Urbana, IL: National Council of Teachers of English.

Moll, L. C., Amanti, C., Neff, D., & González, N. (1992). Funds of knowledge for teaching: Using a qualitative approach to connect homes and classrooms. *Theory into Practice, 31*(2), 132–141.

Moll, L., & González, N. (1994). Critical issues: Lessons from research with language-minority children. *JRB: A Journal of Literacy, 26*(4), 439–456.

Moll, L. C., Vélez-Ibáñez, C., & Greenberg, J. (1989). *Year one progress report: Community knowledge and classroom practice: Combining resources for literacy instruction* (IARP Subcontract No. L-10). University of Arizona, College of Education and Bureau of Applied Research in Anthropology.

Monson, D. L., Howe, K., & Greenlee, A. (1989). Helping children develop cross-cultural understanding with children's books. *Early Child Development and Care, 48*, 3–8.

Morrow, L. M. (1992). The impact of a literature-based program on literacy achievement, use of literature, and attitudes of children from minority backgrounds. *Reading Research Quarterly, 27*(3), 251–275.

Morrow, L. M., Pressley, M., Smith, J. K., & Smith, M. (1997). The effect of a literature-based program integrated into literacy and science instruction with children from diverse backgrounds. *Reading Research Quarterly, 32*(1), 54–76.

Nelson, K. (1996). *Language in cognitive development.* Cambridge: Cambridge University Press.

Palincsar, A. S., & Herrenkohl, L. R. (1999). Designing collaborative contexts: Lessons from three research programs. In A. O'Donnell & A. King (Eds.), *Cognitive perspectives on peer learning* (pp. 151–178). Mahwah, NJ: Lawrence Erlbaum Associates.

Pappas, C. C., Oyler, C., with Barry, A., & Rassel, M. (1993). Focus on research: Collaborating with teachers developing integrated language arts programs in urban schools. *Language Arts, 70*, 297–303.

Pearson, P. D. (1994). Integrated language arts: Sources of controversy and seeds of consensus. In L. M. Morrow, J. K. Smith, & L. C. Wilkinson (Eds.), *Integrated language arts: Controversy to consensus* (pp. 11–31). Needham Heights, MA: Allyn & Bacon.

Petrie, H. (1992). Interdisciplinary education: Are we faced with insurmountable opportunities? In G. Grant (Ed.), *Review of Research in Education* (pp. 299–333). Washington, DC: American Educational Research Association.

Pinnell, G. S., & Jaggar, A. M. (1991). Oral language: Speaking and listening in the classroom. In J. Flood, J. M. Jensen, D. Lapp, & J. R. Squire (Eds.), *Handbook of research on teaching the English language arts* (pp. 691–720). New York: Macmillan.

Powell, R., & Skoog, G. (1995). Students' perspectives on integrative curricula: The case of Brown Barge Middle School. *Research in Middle Level Education Quarterly, 19*(1), 85–115.

Raphael, T. E., & Brock, C. H. (1997). Instructional research in literacy: Changing paradigms. In C. Kinzer, D. Leu, & K. Hinchman (Eds.), *Inquiries in literacy theory and practice* (pp. 13–36). Chicago: National Reading Conference.

Raphael, T. E., Brock, C. H., & Wallace, S. (1998). Encouraging quality peer talk with diverse students in mainstream classrooms: Learning from and with teachers. In J. R. Paratore & R. McCormack (Eds.), *Peer talk in the classroom: Learning from research* (pp. 176–206). Newark, DE: International Reading Association.

Resnick, L. B. (1990). Literacy in school and out. *Daedalus, 19*(2), 169–285.

Roehler, L. R. (1983). Ten ways to integrate language and subject matter. In B. A. Busching & J. I. Schwartz (Eds.), *Integrating the language arts in the elementary school* (pp. 28–34). Urbana, IL: National Council of Teachers of English.

Romance, N. R., & Vitale, M. R. (1992). A curriculum strategy that expands time for in-depth elementary science instruction by using science-based reading strategies: Effects of a year-long study in grade four. *Journal of Research in Science Teaching, 29*, 545–554.

Roskos, K., & Neuman, S. B. (1995). Two beginning kindergarten teachers' planning for integrated literacy instruction. *Elementary School Journal, 96*(2), 195–215.

Schmidt, W. H., Roehler, L., Caul, J. L., Buchman, M., Diamond, B., Solomon, D., & Cianciolo, P. (1985). The uses of curriculum integration in language arts instruction: A study of six classrooms. *Journal of Curriculum Studies, 17*(3), 305–320.

Scholes, R. (1989). *Protocols of reading.* New Haven, CT: Yale University Press.

Shanahan, T. (1997). Reading-writing relationships, thematic units, inquiry learning.... In pursuit of effective integrated literacy instruction. *Reading Teacher, 51*(1), 12–19.

Shanahan, T., & Lomax, R. G. (1988). A developmental comparison of three theoretical models of the reading and writing relationship. *Research in the Teaching of English, 22*, 196–212.

Shulman, L. (1986). Those who understand: Knowledge growth in teaching. *Educational Researcher, 15*(2), 4–14.

Shoemaker, B. J. E. (1991). Education 2000 integrated curriculum. *Phi Delta Kappan, 72*(10), 793–797.

Shoemaker, B. J. E. (1993). Two sides of the same coin. *Educational Leadership, 50*(8), 55–57.

Silberman, C. E. (1970). *Crisis in the classroom.* New York: Random House.

Sinatra, G. (1990). Convergence of listening and reading processing. *Reading Research Quarterly, 25*(2), 115–130.

Sizer, T. (1984). *Horace's compromise: The dilemma of the American high school.* Boston: Houghton Mifflin.

Smith, J. A. (1993). Content learning: A third reason for using literature in teaching reading. *Reading Research and Instruction, 32*(3), 64–71.

Smith, J. A., Monson, J. A., & Dobson, D. (1992). A case study on integrating history and reading instruction through literature. *Social Education, 56*(7), 370–375.

Spivey, N. N., & Calfee, R. C. (1998). The reading-writing connection, viewed historically. In N. Nelson & R. C. Calfee (Eds.), *Reading–writing connection: Ninety-seventh yearbook of the National Society for the Study of Education* (pp. 1–52). Chicago: University of Chicago Press.

Sticht, T. G., & James, J. H. (1984). Listening and reading. In P. D. Pearson, R. Barr, M. L. Kamil, & P. Mosenthal (Eds.), *Handbook of reading research* (Vol. 1, pp. 293–317). New York: Longman.

Swales, J. M. (1990). *Genre analysis: English in academic and research settings.* Cambridge: Cambridge University Press.

Sylvester, P. S. (1994). Teaching and practice: Elementary school curricula and urban transformation. *Harvard Educational Review, 64*(3), 309–331.

Tchudi, S., & Lafer, S. (1993). How dry is the desert: Nurturing interdisciplinary learning. *Educational Leadership, 51*, 76–79.

Tierney, R. J., & Shanahan, T. (1991). Research on the reading-writing relationship: Interactions, transactions, and outcomes. In R. Barr, M. L. Kamil, P. Mosenthal, & P. D. Pearson (Eds.), *Handbook of Reading Research, 2*, (246–280). Hillsdale, NJ: Lawrence Erlbaum Associates.

Trepanier-Street, M. (1993). What's so new about the project approach? *Childhood Education, 70*(1), 25–28.

VanTassel-Baska, J., Johnson, D. T., Hughes, C. E., & Boyce, L. N. (1996). A study of language arts curriculum effectiveness with gifted learners. *Journal for the Education of the Gifted, 19*(4), 461–480.

Varela, F. J., Thompson, E., & Rosch, E. (1991). *The embodied mind: Cognitive science and human experience.* Cambridge, MA: MIT Press.

Vygotsky, L. S. (1997). *The collected works of L. S. Vygotsky: Problems of the theory and history of psychology* (Vol. 3) (R. Van der Veer, Trans.). New York: Plenum.

Walmsley, S. A., & Walp, T. P. (1990). Integrating literature and composing into the language arts curriculum: Philosophy and practice. *Elementary School Journal, 90*(3), 251–274.

Wenger, E. (1998). *Communities of practice: Learning, meaning, and identity.* Cambridge: Cambridge University Press.

Winograd, T., & Flores, F. (1986). *Understanding computers and cognition:* Reading, MA.: Addison-Wesley.

Winograd, K., & Higgins, K. M. (1995). Writing, reading, and talking mathematics: One interdisciplinary possibility. *Reading Teacher, 48*(4), 310–318.

Wixson, K., Peter, C. W., & Potter, S. A. (1996). The case for integrated standards in English language arts. *Language Arts, 73*(1), 20–29.

CHAPTER 33

The Role of Text
in Classroom Learning

Suzanne E. Wade
University of Utah

Elizabeth B. Moje
University of Michigan

The title of this chapter, "The Role of Text in Classroom Learning," may evoke for many of our readers images of students sitting at desks or in groups reading published print texts such as basal readers and textbooks. These images may yield a number of questions about the role of text in classroom learning: What are these texts like? How are they being used in classrooms and for what purposes? In what ways do texts used in elementary classrooms differ from those used in secondary classrooms? How do students make sense of and learn with these texts? *What* are they learning? How do teachers use such texts as curriculum guides? Who controls the content and use of published texts? In this review, we address many of these questions about the uses of printed texts in classroom learning. In addition, we examine how other forms of printed text are used such as trade books, magazines, and newspapers. Further, we examine the written texts that teachers prepare for students' use, such as outlines of lecture notes, worksheets, and graphic organizers; written texts authored by students, such as essays, stories, and lecture notes; and electronic texts used and generated by students. This broadened conception of text also compels us to examine how teachers' and students' oral texts—lectures, recitations, discussions, and conversations—play a role in classroom learning. Finally, drawing from semiotic and other perspectives on text (Ackerman & Oates, 1996; Barthes, 1977/1996; Eco, 1983, 1992; Eisner, 1994; Hartman, 1997; Siegel, 1995), we include studies that analyze the texts derived from multiple forms of representation, such as drawings, paintings, musical renderings, and performances, and unsanctioned student texts such as notes to friends, comic books, popular magazines, and graffiti.

WHAT COUNTS AS TEXT?

The perspectives on text that guide this review are drawn from our analysis of five theoretical perspectives that examine text and how texts are used in teaching and learning. These perspectives include (a) cognitive and sociocognitive theories, (b) literary theories, (c) linguistic, sociolinguistic, and semiotic theories, (d) sociocultural theories, and (e) critical, feminist, and poststructural theories. After reviewing definitions of text held by representatives of those five perspectives, we concluded that to yield significant insights about teaching and learning our conception of text in this review should be broad and encompassing. Derrida (1976, 1982) counted as text any organized network of meaning, thus suggesting that text can be much more than print on a page. Bloome and Egan-Robertson (1993) argued that

> People textualize experience and the world in which they live, making those phenomena part of a language system (broadly defined). The result of textualizing experience can be a set of words, signs, representations, etc. But it might be other forms and products not usually associated with texts: architecture, rock formations, the stars in the sky, the wind, the ocean, emotion—these can all be texts, but their being texts depends on what people do. (p. 311)

Texts, then, are organized networks that people generate or use to make meaning either for themselves or for others. Texts can be formalized and permanent, reproduced as books or speeches and sold as commodities. Or, they can be informal and fleeting—written lists or notes that are scribbled out and quickly thrown away, or conversations and performances that are made permanent only as they are written or recorded by sound or video devices or passed on orally to other people. The level of formality or permanence of a text does not diminish its potential as a way of making meaning or its potential to be linked consciously or unconsciously to other, more or less formal types of texts. Different views of what counts as text—whether they are formal and informal; oral, written, enacted; permanent or fleeting—lead to different views of what counts as learning, and consequently expand or limit the opportunities students have to learn in classrooms.

Realizing that teachers, students, classroom contexts, and personal and institutional histories are unique, we undertake in this review the task of describing how different types of text, broadly defined, have been used in classrooms. We found that variations in text use reflected differences in pedagogical approach and in purpose (e.g., learning goals) but also differences in students, subject area, grade level, academic track or reading group level, systems of assessment and accountability, content and pedagogical knowledge of teachers, teachers' and students' beliefs about knowledge and appropriate uses of literacy, beliefs about the purpose of schooling, past school experiences, and home and community experiences. Together, these variables shape the sociocultural context in which teachers and students work (Moore, 1996), how they use text, and how they respond to reform efforts to restructure text use, curriculum, and schools.

Although each of the variables we have listed is critical in shaping how text is defined and used in classrooms, we have organized our analysis around two general categories of *pedagogical approach*—transmission approaches and participatory approaches. Because pedagogical approach is itself shaped by sociocultural and economic contexts, we describe the contexts of the classrooms studied as we discuss how the role of text varies in transmission and participatory approaches. In our discussion of the roles texts play in these two pedagogical approaches, we focus on two questions: (a) What counts as text, and (b) how are texts used by both teachers and students for the purpose of learning in classrooms?

We recognize that these pedagogical approaches are neither the only possible approaches nor are they pure categories. Although one approach will usually predominate in a classroom, elements of the others may be adapted to fit within it. Further, the pedagogies in some classrooms may best be thought of as hybrids. Although we wish to avoid the temptation to designate any approach as the "best" way, we do acknowledge that participatory approaches take a broad view of text—a view that we believe is beneficial for diverse groups of students in an increasingly technological and information-based world. Nevertheless, we have analyzed the strengths and limitations of how text and learning are viewed and put into practice in each approach—how each attempts to meet particular goals in teaching and learning, and not others, and how each focuses attention on certain attributes of texts and learners while ignoring others. Of course, the views that we have of teachers' and students' uses and perceptions of text are influenced by the theoretical perspectives of the researchers who described and evaluated them in published studies. Like Rex, Green, Dixon and the Santa Barbara Classroom Discourse Group (1998), who argued that the ways in which researchers define context influence the outcomes of their research, we assert that definitions of text and learning and the privileging and dismissal of different texts and ways of learning have ideological and material consequences for students, teachers, and society. Thus, the views provided of the role of text in classroom learning must be considered in light of particular theoretical perspectives on text and learning, which we endeavor to include in our discussion.

TEXT AND LEARNING IN THE TRANSMISSION APPROACH

Observational studies reveal that the transmission model has been the dominant pedagogical approach to teaching reading and subject-area content (Alvermann & Moore, 1991; Cuban, 1984, 1986; Durkin, 1978–1979; Goodlad, 1984, 1994; McNeil, 1986; Shannon, 1990; Stodolsky, 1988; Wildy & Wallace, 1995). The role of both the text and the teacher in the transmission approach is to transmit a large body of authorized, or "official," knowledge and skills to students—who are often thought of in generic terms without attention to race, class, or gender—to enable them to be successful in the meritocratic system that dominates schools and society (Apple, 1986, 1989; Shannon, 1990). Thus, instruction tends to be both content and teacher centered. Typically, the teacher initiates and controls the interaction toward the goal of achieving particular learning objectives—usually the mastery of discrete skills and the correct recall of information. The classroom structure is one of the teacher interacting with the whole class or working with small groups of students usually differentiated by ability, or of students working alone, monitored by the teacher. The teacher lectures, explains, asks questions, demonstrates, gives assignments or instructions, provides feedback, and assesses students' learning. Student participation consists of listening, responding, reading orally or silently, working alone on independent seatwork, and taking tests. The teacher is active and in control; students are (or are supposed to be) passive and compliant, generating texts to document their learning of information.

What Counts as Text Within the Transmission Approach

Critical researchers argue that just as knowledge in transmission classrooms is "official," so are the texts that dominate teacher and student discourse. These texts serve to establish boundaries as to what skills, topics, authors, and ideologies are considered legitimate and valued—that is, what counts as knowledge and as learning (Luke, de Castell, & Luke, 1989; Shannon, 1990). For elementary reading instruction, basal reading series are usually the primary, official texts. The 1992 National Assessment of Educational Progress (NEAP), which included a survey of reading instruction in Grade 4, found that for 36% of the fourth-grade students, teachers relied solely on basal readers for reading instruction, 49% were taught through a combination of both basal materials and trade books, and 15% were being taught without use of basal materials (Mullis, Campbell, & Farstrup, 1993). Fractor, Woodruff, Martinez, and Teale (1993) found that the number of elementary classrooms with library centers for trade books steadily decreased with grade level, from 75% of kindergarten classrooms that had libraries to only 26% of Grade 5 classrooms that did.

In response to criticisms by a number of reading researchers (Goodman, 1989; Goodman, Shannon, Freeman, & Murphy, 1988), basal series have changed over time, moving away from contrived stories with controlled vocabulary to the inclusion of published texts by authors of children's literature (Hoffman et al., 1994). As a result, many of the new basals represent an elementary-school anthology of literature from which teachers can draw, and a number of the literature-based series make extensive recommendations for the development of thematic units using diverse works of literature. Published basal series also have shifted from a focus on the drill and practice of discrete, sequenced reading skills to the teaching of context-based decoding and comprehension strategies and the eliciting of readers' responses. In making this shift, basal authors have provided teachers with pedagogical recommendations that are said to be less directive and prescriptive than former versions (Hoffman et al., 1994).

For subject-area instruction, the textbook has been the dominant form of official text within the transmission approach at both the elementary and secondary levels (Alvermann & Moore, 1991; Gottfried & Kyle, 1992; Yore, 1991). According to Alvermann and Moore (1991), a class set of a single textbook has been the main source of reading material in most content classrooms, and is rarely supplemented by library books, articles from magazines, or newspapers. Observational and interview studies indicate that this continues to be the case (cf. DiGisi & Willett, 1995; Jetton, 1994; Moje, 1996).

How Teachers and Students Use Published Texts in Transmission Classrooms

Although most elementary students regularly read from basal texts (Hoffman et al., 1994), the textbook appears to be used more by teachers than by students in subject-area classrooms (Alvermann & Moore, 1991; Armbruster et al., 1991; Hinchman, 1987; Smith & Feathers, 1983). Many teachers rely on textbooks to structure content, organize lessons, and provide suggestions and materials for teaching and assessment. Thus, as Tyson-Bernstein noted, "According to virtually all studies of the matter, textbooks have become the *de facto* curriculum of the public schools" (1988, p. 11). This reliance on the textbook as a curriculum guide tends to be most true of teachers with less knowledge of their subject area. For example, elementary teachers, who often feel underprepared in science, report a preference for structured science materials, including teachers' guides with suggestions about demonstrations, activities, and discussion/recitation questions (Lantz & Kass, 1987; Shymansky, Yore, & Good, 1991). At the secondary level, Jetton (1994) and Jetton and Alexander (1997) found that science teachers with low domain knowledge relied most on the textbook as the basic core of knowledge to transmit, whereas teachers with high domain knowledge relied on their prior knowledge and a variety of texts such as articles from science magazines. Carlsen (1991) also found that teacher's oral texts were more likely to follow the textbook when the teacher was less familiar with the topic. In lesson planning, for example, teachers with less domain knowledge asked questions that emphasized recall of material found in the textbook, whereas teachers with high domain knowledge asked questions that required students to synthesize content.

In addition to teachers' confidence (or lack of) in their subject-area expertise, certain institutional constraints and beliefs about the disciplines shape how much they rely on textbooks to structure their curriculum. Stodolsky and Grossman (1995) found that highly sequential and well-defined subject areas such as math and foreign languages allow for less curricular autonomy than less well-defined, less sequentially organized subjects such as English, science, and social studies. Also, state and district curriculum guidelines, assessment programs, and text adoption policies control what texts are selected, how they are used in classrooms, and what counts as learning. Thus, the perception of a need to sequence instruction and to meet state and district requirements compels teachers to place greater emphasize on coverage and therefore to rely on the content of official texts so that students are prepared for assessments and subsequent courses.

Although textbooks and their accompanying curriculum guides are used extensively by teachers to present content and to structure classroom learning activities, most studies have found that students engage in little reading of any kind of published text, either in class or as homework, other than basal texts used for reading instruction (Alvermann & Moore, 1991; Armbruster et al., 1991; DiGisi & Willett, 1995; Goodlad, 1984; Hinchman, 1987; Jetton, 1994; Smith & Feathers, 1983). In a study of fourth-grade teachers and students engaged in content-area lessons, Armbruster et al. (1991) found that even in lessons where the textbook was the focus of instruction, students did very little actual reading, and what they did do consisted of round-robin oral reading. At the secondary level, Alvermann and Moore (1991) found that "continuous reading in classrooms is rare" (p. 965). DiGisi and Willett (1995) found that only in basic biology classes was the textbook read in class, and then it was read orally by either the teacher or students to make sure the whole class heard the information—an oral rendering of the published text. Only in the most advanced level biology classes did teachers assign and expect students to use the textbook independently to learn information that they did not have time to cover in class. Stodolsky (1988) and Stodolsky, Salk, and Glaessner (1991) found that students, especially those having difficulty, viewed their mathematics textbooks as a source of problems assigned as homework rather than as a resource for new learning, relying on the teacher to explain and guide their learning; in fact, students ranked "hearing an explanation," "asking someone," and "being told what to do" as the best means for learning mathematics. In their review, Alvermann and Moore (1991) reported that in other content areas students often use the textbook only to skim for answers to end-of-the-chapter questions or to search for definitions of vocabulary words. These findings are supported by surveys conducted for the NEAP, which reported that approximately half of the students in the three grades tested (Grades 4, 8, and 12) reported reading 10 or fewer pages each day for school work across the curriculum (Langer, Applebee, Mullis, & Foertsch, 1990). Later NEAP reports confirmed these findings for students in Grade 12, but found that students in Grades 4 and 8 reported reading more each day in school and for homework in 1996 (Campbell, Voelkl, & Donahue, 1997). Other studies reported that when students realize they can rely exclusively on their teachers' lectures and recitations (oral texts) to learn the content, they see little need to read assigned pages (Hinchman & Zalewski, 1996; Moje, 1996).

Little text reading is assigned for several reasons. Some teachers are concerned that many students will not or cannot read assigned pages from textbooks, in part because the textbooks are too difficult or poorly written, or students lack the necessary background knowledge (Armbruster, 1984; Beck, McKeown, & Gromoll, 1989; Dole & Niederhauser, 1989; McKeown & Beck, 1990; McKeown, Beck, Sinatra, & Loxterman, 1992). Some teachers have questioned the value of reading about a topic as a tool for learning, especially in content areas such as science, advocating experience-based learning activities instead (Yore, 1991). Finally, many secondary teachers argue that they can cover vast amounts of content more quickly through other activities such as lectures and demonstrations (O'Brien, Stewart, & Moje, 1995).

The Role of Teacher-Generated Oral
and Written Text in Transmission Classrooms

Because subject-area teachers believe that students cannot or will not learn independently from textbooks and because they view their role as teaching content (rather than literacy), most teachers rely heavily on oral texts—whole-class lecture, explanation, demonstration, and recitation—considering them to be the most efficient way to deliver course content and to monitor learning (Davey, 1988; DiGisi & Willett, 1995; Goodlad, 1984; Hinchman, 1987; Jetton, 1994; Moje, 1996; Moje & Wade, 1997; O'Brien et al., 1995; Schumm, Vaughn, & Saumell, 1992; Stewart, 1990; Stodolsky, 1988). Sizer (1985) called this reliance on oral texts the "pedagogy of telling." As one biology teacher in DiGisi and Willett's study (1995, p. 131) stated, "I think the information should come first from the teachers and from labs and demonstrations ... the textbook should be almost secondary to what goes on in the classroom." In her study of six biology teachers, Jetton (1994) found that all of the teachers relied on the pedagogy of telling, aided by teacher-generated conceptual maps. These maps were presented on an overhead projector to guide students though the lectures, which were the dominant form of oral text. In addition, the teachers in this study created handouts of notes designed to simplify the information in the textbook.

Several studies have shown that secondary-school students place greater value on a combination of teacher-generated texts such as lectures, study guides, outlines, and conceptual maps—and on the texts they generate themselves in class such as lecture notes—than they do on official course texts (Dillon, O'Brien, Moje, & Stewart, 1994; Jetton, 1994; Moje, 1996). Thus, although findings of many studies that focus on printed texts indicate that students often use the textbook only to skim for answers to end-of-the-chapter questions or to search for definitions of vocabulary words, a number of studies illustrate that the other kinds of texts, especially those texts created in interactions between students and teachers, play a prominent role in classroom learning.

Among the forms of oral text that have been studied in transmission classrooms, researchers have given a good deal of attention to the ways that initiation–response–evaluation (IRE) formats such as recitation are used to monitor students' learning during lectures or their recall of information from assigned readings. IRE formats typically consist of a question posed by a teacher, answered by a student, and evaluated by the teacher (Bellack, Kliebard, Hyman, & Smith, 1966; Cazden, 1986; Dillon, 1984; Lemke, 1990; Sinclair & Coulthard, 1975). It is one of the most common patterns of verbal interaction in classrooms, serving the purpose of reviewing, drilling, and quizzing students about what they have learned (Alvermann & Moore, 1991), while also controlling student behaviors and the dissemination of knowledge (Lemke, 1990). A number of researchers (Alvermann & Hayes, 1989; Alvermann & Moore, 1991; Armbruster et al., 1991; Carlsen, 1991) found that almost all of the questions and answers during recitations are at the literal level, and that students tend to give brief and unelaborated answers. Not surprisingly, students rarely ask questions, question the teacher's interpretation, or offer alternative interpretations during recitations.

Researchers have also examined how the discourse during recitation and other forms of oral text contribute to the construction and reconstruction of particular assumptions about the nature of knowledge in the disciplines. For example, Moje's (1997) critical discourse analysis of the oral texts created by a high-school chemistry teacher, Ms. Landy, and her students illustrated how Landy emphasized objectivity in scientific observation, accurate and precise definitions and pronunciation of scientific terms, and rules and procedures. Furthermore, despite Landy's good intentions to teach her students to communicate in science ("to develop scientific literacy," in her words), her discourse of accuracy and precision positioned students as demonstrators of knowledge and positioned her as evaluator of their demonstrations.

Although written and oral texts may be viewed as quite separate in transmission classrooms, they seldom stand alone in any classroom, as we have seen. In most classrooms, oral and written texts are constructed and negotiated as teachers and student interact with one another. For example, Golden (1988) illustrated how print text meaning can change by showing how the same teacher leading two different small groups in a reading lesson segmented the same text in different ways and stressed different literacy elements. As a result, the text—and the concomitant learning—for the two groups of students was different (see also Cazden, 1985). In another study, Kamberelis and de la Luna (1996) illustrated how an African American fourth-grade teacher used the basal texts to challenge oppressive practices and structures while also helping students learn conventions of stories and processes for mainstream and alternative comprehension of texts. Thus, the criticism that texts serve as devices of control does not take into account how texts, even those that are standardized and formalized, are always reconstructed in interaction. How texts are reconstructed, however, depends on teachers' and students' ideological commitments, their content knowledge, and the social, cultural, and economic contexts in which their teaching and learning are embedded.

The Role of Student-Generated Texts

Student-Generated Oral Text.   Students' oral texts also play an important role in classroom learning. In a study of story-sharing time among young children in school, Michaels (1981) illustrated how the oral texts of mainstream and nonmainstream children were used to teach children the conventions of language and literacy. Although all children were invited to share stories, the texts they created were differentially valued. Michaels demonstrated that these oral sessions had an impact on children's developing sense of how to read and write stories. Through such sessions, norms for "appropriate" oral texts are often translated into similar norms for appropriateness in written text (see also Luke, 1993).

Studying the oral texts generated by students in peer-led discussions, Alvermann et al. (1996) found that talk was likely to be unrelated to the topic when students found the topic to be boring and meaningless or when the task was unchallenging and did not require debate or collaboration. For example, in one of the research sites—a 10th-grade college preparatory class in which the curriculum and final examination were controlled by state requirements—students divided the task up among group members to complete independently with minimal talk except to call out answers to other group members, even though students reported that they would have preferred meaningful discussions. A similar situation occurred in an 8th-grade language arts class in which discussion tasks consisted of questions and activities from the published resource book accompanying the literature textbook. Students in this class also rarely complied with the teacher's instructions to discuss tasks in groups because collaboration was not necessary. Both classrooms are interesting examples of how elements of participatory models, such as peer-led discussions that simply are added onto transmission approaches, are transformed by students to conform to the larger classroom context.

Student-Generated Written Text.   In transmission-oriented elementary school classrooms, language arts teachers often ask students to generate text as a way of assessing students' understanding of story structures, themes, and concepts or as a way of assessing their retention of information. In recent years, however, a number of elementary and middle school language arts teachers have incorporated journal writing and writer's workshop methods as a way of including student-generated texts in their curriculum (Dressman, 1993; Lensmire, 1994). We discuss these forms of text in more detail in the section on participatory pedagogies.

In most subject-area classes at both the elementary and secondary levels—especially in disciplines other than English composition—students have few opportunities to engage in the construction of written text, either in class or in homework assignments (Alvermann & Moore, 1991; Applebee, 1984; Jetton, 1994; Jetton & Alexander, 1997). In a national survey of secondary teachers and 259 observations of 9th- and 11th-grade classes in two schools, Applebee (1984) found that only 3% of class time was devoted to writing at least a paragraph in length. In addition, writing assignments that involved a paragraph or more were made only 3% of the time. Applebee also found that 32% of the teachers reported that they *never* assigned such writing, whereas only 31% (mostly English teachers) reported that they did so frequently. Similar findings have been reported over the years in NAEP surveys (Campbell et al., 1997). Most of the student-generated written text in subject-area classes is limited to multiple-choice and fill-in-the-blank exercises, short-answer responses requiring a sentence or two, copying from the blackboard, note taking, and math calculations (Alvermann & Moore, 1991; Applebee, 1984; Cohen & Ball, 1990; Jetton, 1994; Jetton & Alexander, 1997). The primary purposes of having students engage in this kind of writing were to review subject-area information and to test their recall of what had been taught. Almost all of this kind of writing was found to be at the literal level (Alvermann & Moore, 1991). Not surprisingly, the primary audience for such writing was the teacher in the role of examiner.

In summary, within transmission approaches, published print texts and teachers' oral texts have the role of transmitting information and controlling how that information is used in classroom learning, whereas student-generated texts have served primarily to document whether students have processed the information correctly. In addition, handouts, outlines, board notes, study guides, individualized question and answer sessions, informal conversations, and students' drawings constitute important texts that transmit and control, but also reconstruct, information and knowledge. Although it can be argued that teachers and students always textualize their classroom experiences in multiple ways in every kind of classroom, the primary role of texts within transmission approaches is to serve as repositories, transmitters, and guardians of information and knowledge.

However, reliance on transmission approaches alone may not accomplish the learning goals they espouse. Goldman (1997) criticized the outcomes of transmission approaches in three ways. First, knowledge acquired through transmission approaches has not been found to transfer to new situations. Second, performance on recognition and recall tests may suffer when learners go beyond surface-level processing and relate knowledge-to-be-learned to their prior knowledge and experience. Third, other types of learning that are deemed essential to success in the world, such as the ability to think critically and to collaborate with others in solving problems, have been ignored. Based on these critiques and on theories regarding the social construction of knowledge (Bloome & Green, 1984; Cole, 1985; Rogoff, 1990; Vygotsky, 1978, 1986; Wertsch, 1991), many restructuring efforts have focused on bringing learners together in collaborative and community-based problem-solving activities. In addition, cultural theories (Heath, 1983; McDermott & Varenne, 1995; Moll & Greenberg, 1990; Street, 1995) have prompted reformers to engage in pedagogical and school restructuring efforts designed to tap into students', families', and communities' ways of knowing. As a result, restructuring efforts have been underway in many schools and classrooms to create classroom learning environments that support these forms of learning, resulting in what a number of scholars refer to as "participatory approaches." In the next section, we examine the role of text in classroom learning by reviewing studies of participatory approaches.

TEXT AND LEARNING IN PARTICIPATORY APPROACHES

In recent years, educators have explored a number of alternatives to transmission approaches (e.g., Atwell, 1987; Calkins, 1994; Cummins, 1986; Marx, Blumenfeld,

Krajcik, & Soloway, 1997; Goldman, 1997; Goodman, 1986; Graves, 1983; Guthrie et al., 1996; Mercado, 1992; Moje, Willes & Fassio, in press; Moll & Gonzales, 1994; Moll, Tapia, & Whitmore, 1993; Rose, 1989; Warren, Rosebery, & Conant, 1989). Although these alternatives vary in many ways, we have identified two common features of each approach. First, whereas transmission approaches cast the teacher—and texts—as controllers of knowledge and learning, these alternative pedagogies invite students to *participate* in the construction of knowledge and in the construction of texts. Second, these participatory pedagogies view texts as *tools* for learning and constructing new knowledge rather than as repositories and guardians of information. Moll (1994) described participatory approaches in this way:

> These "participatory" approaches highlight children as active learners, using and applying literacy as a tool for communication and for thinking. The role of the teacher is to enable and guide activities that involve students as thoughtful learners in socially meaningful tasks. Of central concern is how the teacher facilitates the students' "taking over" or appropriating the learning activity. (p. 180)

We have identified two strands of these participatory approaches, those that focus on developing the individual student and those that focus on developing the individual as a member of social and cultural communities. Both approaches use texts as tools and rely on social interaction, but the individually focused approach is aimed at furthering each child's cognitive development as a result of peer interaction or interaction with a more knowledgeable other. In contrast, the socioculturally focused approach draws on students' social and cultural backgrounds and engages students in activities aimed at understanding, negotiating, and contributing to the classroom, school, or local community. As a result, the types of textual tools they use differ to some extent.

What Counts as Text Within Participatory Approaches

Participatory approaches rely on a wide range of texts, including published print materials such as textbooks, reference books, novels, journals, magazines ("'zines"), and comic books; student-generated writings, presentations, and notes; oral discourse constructed in discussions and conversations; electronic texts read and generated on the Internet and with hypermedia; television, radio, and film media; and visual and performance art. In addition, texts drawn from experiences in people's homes and communities—"funds of knowledge" (Moll & Greenberg, 1990; Vélez-Ibáñez, 1988)—are brought into play with those texts traditionally valued in school. Because participatory approaches are intertextual in nature, they do not lend themselves to categories that represent them as serving discrete roles in classroom learning. Consequently, in the following discussion, we divide our discussion of what these texts accomplish by looking at various types of participatory pedagogies and examining the interrelated roles and accomplishments of published print texts, oral texts, teacher- and student-generated texts, and texts drawn from media, home, and community used within these pedagogies.

How Teachers and Students Use Text
Within Participatory Approaches

In participatory approaches, teachers work with students to decode, comprehend, extract, and synthesize information from multiple texts, but they also encourage students to generate their own knowledge and to make their own interpretations of texts. Socioculturally situated approaches additionally encourage students to examine how they are members of communities and how their texts are connected to the texts of their classmates and community members. As Heath (1994) noted, the texts that students have access to are cultural tools that shape not only what people know, but how they know and learn. The purpose of text use and of learning from these perspectives, then, is to expand the cultural tools to which students have access, not by dismissing the texts (or tools) they bring to school, but by incorporating them into the curriculum and working with students to make connections among the various texts they explore. According to Moll and Gonzalez (1994), the emphasis in education should be on "students' novel use of cultural resources, including people, ideas, and technologies, to facilitate and direct their intellectual work" (p. 453).

Literature Discussions.   Many participatory classrooms ask students to read published literature texts and to create oral texts by discussing their interpretations with one another (Almasi, 1994; Evans, 1996; Many, 1991; McMahon & Raphael, 1997; Rogers, 1991; Santa Barbara Discourse Group, 1994). These approaches build on the idea that the role of literary texts in classroom discussions is dependent on very particular contexts, that the same text will be different from one class to another, and that the oral texts that are constructed around the published text are an important aspect of that difference. For example, the Santa Barbara Discourse Group (SBDG, 1994) illustrated that as various texts were used in a high school English classroom, different meanings and purposes were assigned to the particular texts being used. The SBDG gave the example of a class reading of *The Catcher in the Rye* (Salinger, 1951), which, because it was being read for school, took on different social purposes than it might have had it been read for pleasure. Moreover, the book did not stand alone as a text in this class, but became a part of a larger class text centered on a particular concept ("Coming of Age"). Thus, an attempt was made on the part of the teachers to create a socially situated intertext—comprised of classroom discussion, students' writings, and other texts about the coming of age—to which students would link *The Catcher in the Rye*. The text did not serve as a source of literary information, but rather as a tool for thinking about and examining the process of "coming of age."

In addition to whole-group discussions of text, *peer-led* discussions of literature have been used in participatory approaches as a way of decentering the teacher's authority and encouraging students to explore their own questions about the literature. These peer-led discussions yield yet another type of oral text, with differences that have important implications for classroom learning. Almasi (1994), for example, found that students who participated in peer-led discussions of texts produced significantly more elaborate and complex discussions than those who participated in teacher-led discussions. Moreover, the children who participated in the peer-led discussions were better able to recognize and resolve sociocognitive conflicts that arose during their discussions.

However, a number of teachers who have adopted literature-based, participatory approaches have found that they and their students struggle to negotiate a balance between a focus on skills and strategies and a focus on personal response to the literature. Enciso (1997), for example, highlighted her own struggle to understand connections made by two African American boys while reading *The Gold Cadillac* (Taylor, 1987). Although her first impression was that the boys had "misread" the text, she learned through her analysis of the episode that the boys' readings had to be understood in light of their particular social and cultural experiences. Thus, classroom teachers eager to incorporate students' "personal" texts are presented with the challenge of understanding and linking personal texts to published texts.

Other studies have identified issues of marginalization and silencing of others' voices in peer-led groups. Alvermann (1996) and Evans (1996) found that peer-led literature groups created to decenter teacher authority and encourage student participation often created the unintended consequence of allowing some students to dominate whereas other students were silenced. Consequently, the texts of peer-led groups may serve to enrich some students' learning while inhibiting the learning of other students.

Reading/Writing Workshops.   In reading/writing workshops, the most privileged texts are those that students choose or generate, although published texts chosen by the teacher are often used as models for writing themes and conventions (cf. Atwell, 1987; Calkins, 1994; Graves, 1983). Studies have demonstrated that encouraging students to generate and respond to one another's texts contributes to enhanced content learning and positive social growth by helping students learn social skills necessary for communication, cooperation, and collaboration (DiPardo & Freedman, 1988; Forman & Cazden, 1985). Thus, these approaches are said to provide opportunities for students to build the knowledge, experiences, and skills they bring to the classroom while also developing new knowledge, experiences, and skills—and thus, new texts. For example, McCarthey (1994) illustrated how students incorporated both "authoritative" and "internally persuasive" voices (cf. Bakhtin, 1981) into their written texts as a result of the oral texts ("talk") that they constructed in conferences with the teacher and other students.

Lensmire (1994), however, raised concerns about some aspects of workshop approaches. From his work with third-grade students, he concluded that texts—both published and student-generated—should not be used only as tools for modeling the writing process, but should also be examined by students for the assumptions and stereotypes that they offer to readers. He pointed out that because the texts students generated remained rooted in their particular conceptions of the world, students were not challenged to think differently about their texts or their worlds. As a result, some students—who came from nonmainstream social and cultural worlds—were implicitly, and sometimes explicitly, told by other children that their texts and worlds were inferior. Lensmire, then, envisioned that texts in a modified writer's workshop could be used as tools for challenging oppression and marginalization, but that students would need to be guided in the deconstruction of texts and in the construction of countertexts (Aronowitz & Giroux, 1991).

Other studies also examined how the texts generated or selected in expressivist approaches might silence or regulate diverse voices and texts in classrooms (Finders, 1996; McCarthey, 1996; Moje et al., in press; Willis, 1995). McCarthey (1996), for example, found that the teachers in expressivist, participatory classrooms often relied exclusively on mainstream literature and overlooked how students' cultural experiences might influence their engagement with and interpretations of the literature being used. Willis (1995) questioned how aspects of expressivist pedagogy such as the "author's chair" or "group shares" might silence or regulate diverse voices and perspectives in a reading/writing workshop, causing children to keep their personal texts separate from the classroom. In a study of the different texts that seventh-grade students produced in two writer's workshop classrooms in a diverse urban setting, Moje et al. (in press) found that students did indeed initially keep their personal and social texts separate from the texts they prepared to meet the demands of the official writer's workshop curriculum. Finders (1996) found similar results in her study of an ethnically homogeneous, but socioeconomically diverse, midwestern classroom. By engaging in intensive observation of and interaction with two groups of young women, Finders learned that many of the texts they read and wrote in their reading/writing workshop classroom were different from the texts they read and wrote in their out-of-school family and social interactions. Thus, although student-generated texts are given primacy in participatory approaches such as the writing workshop, what is considered appropriate or acceptable text by teachers and students may shape the kinds of texts students generate in both their written and oral work. Moje et al. (in press) and Fassio (1998), however, found that when the typical guidelines of expressivist pedagogy (such as group sharing and publication) were relaxed or modified, students in diverse classrooms began to construct countertexts drawn from their actual life experiences.

Project-Based Pedagogies.   Project-based pedagogies incorporate published and student-generated oral, written, electronic and pictorial texts into classroom practices as a way of engaging students in collaborative investigations of real-world problems (Blumenfeld et al., 1991; Marx et al., 1997). Typically, project-based pedagogies result in shared, student-created texts—such as exhibits, books, research reports, models, videotapes, or computer programs—that represent students' learning. In Maryland, for example, researchers, classroom teachers, and reading specialists have collaborated to develop Concept-Oriented Reading Instruction (CORI), designed to promote elementary students' engagement in literacy and science (Guthrie et al., 1996). CORI involves four phases, in which a variety of published and student-generated print, pictorial, and oral texts are integrated in a project-based curriculum. During each phase, teachers explicitly teach cognitive and metacognitive strategies to help students accomplish specific goals. Guthrie et al. (1996) found that the texts generated in CORI served as tools to increase students' literacy engagement and performance on a number of assessment measures, including writing, conceptual transfer, comprehension of informational text, and narrative interpretation.

Goldman (1997) described several classroom-based studies that relied on multiple texts— such as print texts, CDS, and the Internet—for students' research projects in different content areas. In the *Whole Day, Whole Year* (Goldman, 1997) project, for example, middle school students searched for relevant information in these texts, taking notes in their field journals. In the final phase of student-generated projects, students evaluated the information they had collected and integrated what they deemed trustworthy and relevant into written products. Especially important in this phase were the oral texts generated by students and teachers as they shared, evaluated, integrated, and composed.

Garner and Gillingham's (1996) study of the use of the Internet in six elementary and high school classrooms also reveals multiple uses of texts, broadly defined. In each of these classrooms, the Internet was the site for different kinds of student discourse, which became an essential part of daily classroom life. Similarly, at the Center for Learning Technologies in Urban Schools (LeTUS), researchers and teachers are working together to examine how learning and collaborative technologies can be used as catalysts for systemic change in U.S. urban schools (cf. Marx et al., 1997). Viewing texts as something more than published print, LeTUS bases the students' curriculum in the texts of their experience by asking students to identify community issues and problems, or driving questions, that they will study and work on through their research. Like Garner and Gillingham (1996), Goldman (1997), and the New London Group (1996), the LeTUS sees an important challenge ahead for students and teachers to broaden the role of text in classroom learning into one in which students are asked to negotiate a variety of text types, including printed, electronic, and multimedia texts; to collaborate with fellow students; to extract and synthesize information—or make meaning—across multiple resources; and to contribute to community development and change.

Moll et al. (1993) reported on a socioculturally focused, community-based project approach in which third-grade bilingual students conducted original research of their own community. Using two languages, the children wrote, piloted, and revised a questionnaire about community resources; tabulated the data they collected; revised and readministered the questionnaire; and reported their findings to the community. The children consulted multiple printed texts; generated their own oral, written, and graphic texts (interviews, questionnaires, and reports); worked with other children, their families, and community members while using these texts; and summarized, synthesized, and communicated their findings. Moll and Gonzales (1994) argued that the children's texts have an especially important role in classroom learning because they emphasize reading and writing in different languages. Similar projects include a participatory, community-based, bilingual social studies curriculum constructed for Navajo students (McCarty, Wallace, Lynch, & Benally, 1991); Mercado's (1992) work with Puerto Rican and African American students in New York; social-action projects generated by urban-school students in Salt Lake City, Utah (Moje & Fassio, 1997); and Warren et al.'s (1989) work with Haitian students in Boston.

In summary, participatory approaches have been studied and critiqued from different theoretical perspectives, thus focusing on different learning goals and issues. Some critiques have focused on problems of design and implementation—for example, tasks that are not challenging, inadequate strategy instruction or guidance for students, and inadequate support for teachers (e.g., Blumenfeld et al., 1991; Elmore, Peterson, & McCarthey, 1996), or the difficulties of teaching complex cognitive strategies using multiple texts (e.g., Goldman, 1997). Sociolinguistic and sociocultural perspectives that have critiqued peer-led discussions and reading/writing workshops have tended to focus on issues of multiple interpretations generated by students, the sometimes conflicting roles of teachers and students, choice of texts, the difficulties of challenging students to read and write critically for social change, the emphasis of process over product to the disadvantage of nonmainstream students, and the ability of all students to participate fully (e.g., Delpit, 1988; Dressman, 1993). Atwell (1997), who worked from expressivist literary perspectives, was concerned that by allowing students total choice, she was not exposing them to texts beyond their experiences.

Unlike transmission approaches, participatory approaches are all grounded in students' texts and experiences, whether individual, social, or cultural. Nevertheless, because they focus on the role of texts in classrooms and on connecting community texts to academic learning, the approaches at times overlook the texts that children and adolescents use to navigate the many different spaces—school, family, community, and youth social groups—in which they live and work every day. These texts often are unacknowledged and sometimes unsanctioned in each of their different communities. In the next section, we examine these different texts and their implications for student learning.

UNACKNOWLEDGED AND UNSANCTIONED TEXTS

Missing from many of the studies we have reviewed are the social—and often unsanctioned—writings that students generate. Although these texts often go unacknowledged and do not serve as texts for reading or content learning in the classroom, students nevertheless learn a great deal about themselves, about schooling, and about society from the texts they create and exchange. At times, these missing texts are a result of a disjuncture between home/community and school. For example, as Heath (1983) demonstrated, the home and community texts of various cultural groups she studied did not always match the texts that were valued in school. A number of other literacy studies have followed Heath's lead in examining the multiple texts that students generate in and out of school (cf. Camitta, 1990; Finders, 1996; Hartman, 1997; Heath & McLaughlin, 1993; Moje & Thompson, 1996; Moll et al., 1993; Myers, 1992) and have demonstrated that what students learn from the various texts they use outside of school often can be more powerful than what they learn in school. In particular, a number of these studies have examined the texts that children and adolescents view as important in their social interactions with other youth, rather than focusing only on the texts of various school, family, or community groups (cf. Camitta, 1990; Finders, 1996; Hartman, 1997; Moje, in press; Moje & Thompson, 1996; Myers, 1992).

Myers (1992) pointed out that "students must be seen as active participants in social activity even if they appear to be passive responders to external stimuli" (p. 302). One of the ways students actively construct their social and classroom contexts is to create their own texts, texts that serve multiple purposes in their in- and out-of-school learning. Camitta (1990), for example, drew on poststructural and cultural studies perspectives to study what she called the "vernacular writing" of high-school students to find that they used writing both in and out of the classroom to make a social space for themselves—*to write themselves into the world*. These texts were not only texts that were valued at home or in the community, but also were texts valued by other adolescents.

Similarly, Finders (1996) examined the out-of-classroom reading and writing practices of two groups of adolescent girls and learned that the girls used the texts that they read and generated not only to construct social spaces, but to define them and limit others' participation in them. A particularly interesting finding of her research revolved around the girls' uses of text in the classroom: Several of them reported reading very different kinds of texts in private spaces, but carrying and "reading" certain texts in school as a way of identifying themselves with particular groups for the benefit of both their peers and teachers. Hartman's (1997) study of the textual practices of two African American adolescents outside of school illustrated their multiple uses and generation of very diverse texts such as sermons in church and works of art in museums—texts that are not valued in their high school classrooms, but are also not necessarily valued in their larger communities. Moje (in press) illustrated that the gang-connected adolescents in the two classrooms she studied used graffiti and tagging texts, as well as conventional written texts about gang practices, to claim space and position in their social worlds. These texts were not validated in their schools, homes, churches, or communities, but were nevertheless quite powerful for the adolescents in their social interactions with other youth. Each of these studies raises questions about how to acknowledge the sophistication and power of these textual practices for young people without simply appropriating them into the official curriculum as "sanctioned" texts and requires that we begin to study more closely the texts that *we do not see* (cf. Mahiri, 1994).

CONCLUSIONS

As researchers and theorists, we need to be more explicit about what is counted as text and as learning as we make pedagogical recommendations. A number of the studies we reviewed did not make their perspectives on text explicit, but implicitly acknowledged only published, print texts as the texts to be valued and studied in classroom learning. We contend that to examine thoroughly the role of text in classroom learning, we must use multiple perspectives to look at what texts are, what learning is, and how texts could be used to learn. In effect, success and failure in our schools are defined by what counts as text and as learning and by how texts are actually used in classrooms to achieve particular learning goals. Success and failure, then, are relative to the perspective on texts and learning privileged in particular studies, classrooms, and assessment practices (cf. McDermott & Varenne, 1995; Rose, 1989). When notions of text and learning are broadened—in projects such as CORI (Guthrie et al., 1996), the Whole Day, Whole Year project (Goldman, 1997), or Heath's (1983) and Moll's work with teachers to learn about students' ways of knowing and "funds of knowledge" (Moll & Greenberg, 1990; Moll & Gonzales, 1994)—we begin to see how successful children and adolescents are in settings in which they are encouraged to use and learn from many different texts and where learning is assessed in many different ways. These studies also broaden definitions of "classroom" to include students' uses of and learning from multiple texts in multiple settings.

As reading/literacy researchers, we need to draw on more than one or two perspectives to inform our understanding of the role of text in classroom learning. In his forward to the book *Reconceptualizing the Literacies in Adolescents' Lives*, Vacca (1998) wrote, "Although we know more today about text and instructional variables from a psychological perspective, we know very little about what counts as literacy from adolescent perspectives or the literacies that adolescents engage in outside of an academic context" (p. xvi). We concur with Vacca's assessment of adolescent literacy, and of the reading/literacy field in general: If we count only print texts as text, and if we view learning as extracting important information or as individual responses or interpretations of text, then we miss many possibilities for engaging all students in learning in multiple ways from multiple texts. We also risk disenfranchising large groups of students for whom print texts are not paramount because they hold different social or cultural values. Operating from one perspective means that our pedagogical recommendations will remain rooted in finding ways to help students become successful according to certain predefined conceptions of success. This view privileges the learning and textual practices of some students and devalues the practices of others, thereby relegating some students to the status of "unsuccessful," "problem," or "at risk of failure." Using multiple approaches to text and learning, we may be able to expand our understanding of the role of text in classroom learning and work with more students to expand their textual, social, and cultural worlds.

REFERENCES

Ackerman, J. M., & Oates, S. (1996). Image, text, and power in architectural design and workplace writing. In A. H. Duin & C. J. Hansen (Eds.), *Nonacademic writing: Social theory and technology* (pp. 81–121) Mahwah, NJ: Lawrence Erlbaum Associates.

Almasi, J. (1994). The effects of peer-led and teacher-led discussions of literature on fourth graders' sociocognitive conflicts. In C. K. Kinzer & D. J. Leu (Eds.), *Multidimensional aspects of literacy research, theory, and practice: Forty-third yearbook of the National Reading Conference* (pp. 40–59). Chicago: National Reading Conference.

Alvermann, D. E. (1996). Peer-led discussions: Whose interests are served? *Journal of Adolescent and Adult Literacy, 39*, 282–289.

Alvermann, D. E., & Hayes, D. A. (1989). Classroom discussion of content area reading assignments: An intervention study. *Reading Research Quarterly, 24*, 305–335.

Alvermann, D. E., & Moore, D. W. (1991). Secondary school reading. In R. Barr, M. L. Kamil, P. B. Mosenthal, & P. D. Pearson (Eds.), *Handbook of reading research* (Vol. II, pp. 951– 983). New York: Longman.

Alvermann, D. E., Young, J. P., Weaver, D, Hinchman, K. A., Moore, D. W., Phelps, S. F., Thrash, E.C., & Zalewski, P. (1996). Middle and high school students' perceptions of how they experience text-based discussions: A multi-case study. *Reading Research Quarterly, 31*, 244–267.

Apple, M. W. (1986). *Teachers and texts: The political economy of class and gender relations in education*. Boston: Routledge & Kegan Paul.

Apple, M. W. (1989). Regulating the text: The socio-historical roots of state control. *Educational Policy, 3*, 107–123.

Applebee, A. (1984). *Writing in the secondary school*. Urbana, IL: National Council of Teachers of English.

Armbruster, B. B. (1984). The problem of inconsiderate text. In G. Duffy, L. Roehler, & J. Mason (Eds.), *Comprehension instruction: Perspectives and suggestions* (pp. 202–217). New York: Longman.

Armbruster, B. B., Anderson, T. H., Armstrong, J. O., Wise, M. A., Janisch, C., & Meyer, L.A. (1991). Reading and questioning in content-area lessons. *Journal of Reading Behavior, 23*, 35–60.

Aronowitz, S., & Giroux, H. A. (1991). *Postmodern education: Politics, culture, and criticism*. Minneapolis: University of Minnesota Press.

Atwell, N. (1987). *In the middle*. Portsmouth, NH: Heinemann.

Atwell, N. (1997, June). Cultivating our garden. *Council Chronicle, 6*(5), 16.

Bakhtin, M. (1981). *The dialogic imagination*. Austin: University of Texas Press.

Barthes, R. (1996). The photographic message. In P. Cobley (Ed.), *The communication theory reader* (pp. 134–147). London: Routledge. (Original work published 1977)

Beck, I. L., McKeown, M. G., & Gromoll, E. W. (1989). Learning from social studies texts. *Cognition and Instruction, 6*, 99–158.

Bellack, A. A., Kliebard, H. M., Hyman, R. T., & Smith, F. L., Jr. (1966). *The language in the classroom*. New York: Teachers College Press.

Bloome, D., & Egan-Robertson, A. (1993). The social construction of intertextuality in classroom reading and writing lessons. *Reading Research Quarterly, 28*, 304–333.

Bloome, D., & Green, J. (1984). Directions in the sociolinguistic study of reading. In P. D. Pearson, R. Barr, M. L. Kamil, & P. B. Mosenthal, (Eds.), *Handbook of reading research* (pp. 395–421). New York: Longman.

Blumenfeld, P. C., Soloway, E., Marx, R. W., Krajcik, J. S., Guzdial, M., & Palincsar, A. (1991). Motivating project-based learning: Sustaining the doing, supporting the learning. *Educational Psychologist, 26*, 369–398.

Calkins, L. M. (1994). *The art of teaching writing.* Portsmouth, NH: Heinemann.

Camitta, M. (1990). Adolescent vernacular writing: Literacy reconsidered. In A. A. Lunsford, H. Moglen, & J. Slevin (Eds.), *The right to literacy* (pp. 262–268). New York: Modern Language Association.

Campbell, J. R., Voelkl, K., & Donahue, P. L. (1997). *Report in brief, NAEP 1996 trends in academic progress.* Washington, DC: National Center for Education Statistics.

Carlsen, W. S. (1991). Questioning in classrooms: A sociolinguistic perspective. *Review of Educational Research, 61*, 157–178.

Cazden, C. B. (1985). The social context of learning to read. In H. Singer & R. B. Ruddell (Eds.), *Theoretical models and processes of reading* (3rd ed., pp. 595–610). Newark, DE: International Reading Association.

Cazden, C. (1986). *Classroom discourse.* In M. C. Wittrock (Ed.), *Handbook on Teaching* (3rd ed., pp. 432–460). New York: Macmillan.

Cohen, D. K., & Ball, D. L. (1990). Relations between policy and practice: A commentary. *Educational Evaluation and Policy Analysis, 12*, 249–256.

Cole, M. (1985). The zone of proximal development: Where culture and cognition create each other. In J. V. Wertsch (Ed.), *Culture, communication, and cognition: Vygotskian perspectives* (pp. 146–161). Cambridge: Cambridge University Press.

Cuban, L. (1984). *How teachers taught: Constancy and change in American classrooms 1880–1980* (2nd ed.). New York: Longman.

Cuban, L. (1986). Persistent instruction: Another look at constancy in the classroom. *Phi Delta Kappan, 68*, 7–11.

Cummins, J. (1986). Empowering minority students: A framework for intervention. *Harvard Educational Review, 56*, 18–36.

Davey, B. (1988). How do classroom teachers use their textbooks? *Journal of Reading, 31*, 340–345.

Delpit, L. D. (1988). The silenced dialogue: Pedagogy and power in educating other people's children. *Harvard Educational Review, 58*, 280–298.

Derrida, J. (1976). *Of grammatology.* (G. C. Spivak, Trans.). Baltimore, MD: Johns Hopkins University Press.

Derrida, J. (1982). *Margins of philosophy* (A. Bass, Trans.). Brighton: Harvester Press.

DiGisi, L. L., & Willett, J. B. (1995). What high school biology teachers say about their textbook use: A descriptive study. *Journal of Research in Science Teaching, 32*, 123–142.

Dillon, D. R., O'Brien, D. G., Moje, E. B., & Stewart, R. A. (1994). Literacy learning in science classrooms: A cross-case analysis of three qualitative studies. *Journal of Research in Science Teaching, 31*, 345–362.

Dillon, J. T. (1984). Research on questioning and discussion. *Educational Leadership, 42*, 50–56.

DiPardo, A. & Freedman, S. W. (1988). Peer response groups in the writing classroom: Theoretic foundations and new directions. *Review of Educational Research, 58*, 119–150.

Dole, J. A., & Niederhauser, D. S. (1989, December). *The effects of considerate and refutation text on learning conceptually easy and difficult science topics.* Paper presented at the meeting of the National Reading Conference, Austin, TX.

Dressman, M. (1993). Lionizing lone wolves: The cultural romantics of literacy workshops. *Curriculum Inquiry, 23*, 245–263.

Durkin, D. (1978–1979). What classroom observations reveal about reading comprehension instruction. *Reading Research Quarterly, 15*, 481–533.

Eco, U. (1992). *Interpretation and overinterpretation* (S. Collini, Ed.). Cambridge, UK: Cambridge University Press.

Eco, U. (1983). *Travels in hyperreality* (W. Weaver, Trans.). San Diego, CA: Harcourt Brace Jovanovich.

Eisner, E. W. (1994). *Cognition and curriculum reconsidered* (2nd ed.). New York: Teachers College Press.

Elmore, R. F., Peterson, P. L., & McCarthey, S. J. (1996). *Restructuring in the classroom: Teaching, learning, and school organization.* San Francisco, CA: Jossey-Bass.

Enciso, P. (1997, September). *Learning to be/read together: A sociocultural analysis of children's reading, art, and relationships.* Paper presented at the 1997 fall forum of the National Academy of Education, Boulder, CO.

Evans, K. (1996). A closer look at literature discussion groups: The influence of gender on student response and discourse. *New Advocate, 9*, 183–196.

Fassio, K. (1998, November). *The Mexican alliance in 2-b (on March 23, 1998): Children's political negotiations in a 2nd-grade classroom.* Paper presented at the annual meeting of the American Educational Studies Association, Philadelphia, PA.

Finders, M. (1996). "Just girls": Literacy and allegiance in junior high school. *Written Communication, 13*, 93–129.

Forman, E. A., & Cazden, C. B. (1985). Exploring Vygotskian perspectives in education: The cognitive value of peer interaction. In J. V. Wertsch (Ed.), *Culture, communication and cognition: Vygotskian perspectives* (pp. 323–347). New York: Cambridge University Press.

Fractor, J. S., Woodruff, M.. C., Martinez, M. G., & Teale, W. H. (1993). Let's not miss opportunities to promote voluntary reading: Classroom libraries in the elementary school. *The Reading Teacher, 46*, 476–484.

Garner, R., & Gillingham, M. G. (1996). *Internet communication in six classrooms: Conversations across time, space, and culture.* Mahwah, NJ: Lawrence Erlbaum Associates.

Golden, J. M. (1988). Structuring and restructuring text. In J. Green & J. Harker (Eds.), *Multiple perspective analyses of classroom discourse* (pp. 71–106). Norwood, NJ: Ablex.

Goldman, S. R. (1997). Learning from text: Reflections on the past and suggestions for the future. *Discourse Processes, 23*, 357–398.

Goodlad, J. I. (1984). *A place called school.* New York: McGraw-Hill.

Goodlad, J. I. (1994). *What schools are for.* Bloomington, IN: Phi Delta Kappa Educational Foundation.

Goodman, K. (1986). *What's whole in whole language?* Portsmouth, NH: Heinemann.

Goodman, K. (1989). Access to literacy: Basals and other barriers. *Theory into Practice, 28*, 410–421.

Goodman, K., Shannon, P., Freeman, Y., & Murphy, S. (1988). *Report card on basal readers.* New York: Richard C. Owen.

Gottfried, S. S., & Kyle, W. C., Jr. (1992). Textbook use and the biology education desired state. *Journal of Research in Science Teaching, 29*, 35–49.

Graves, D. (1983). *When children write.* Portsmouth, NH: Heinemann.

Guthrie, J. T., van Meter, P., McCann, A. D., Wigfield, A., Bennett, L., Poundstone, C. C., Rice, M. E., Faibisch, F. M., Hunt, B., & Mitchell, A. M. (1996). Growth of literacy engagement: Changes in motivations and strategies during concept-oriented reading instruction. *Reading Research Quarterly, 31*, 306–343.

Hartman, D. (1997, September). *Doing things with text: Mapping the textual practices of two African-American male high school students.* Paper presented at the fall forum of the National Academy of Education, Boulder, CO.

Heath, S. B. (1983). *Ways with words.* New York: Cambridge University Press.

Heath, S. B. (1994). The children of Trackton's children: Spoken and written language in social change. In R. B. Ruddell, M. R. Ruddell, & H. Singer (Eds.), *Theoretical models and processes of reading* (4th ed., pp. 208–230). Newark, DE: International Reading Association.

Heath, S. B., & McLaughlin, M. W. (Eds.). (1993). *Identity and inner city youth: Beyond ethnicity and gender.* New York: Teachers College Press.

Hinchman, K. A. (1987). The textbook and three content-area teachers. *Reading Research and Instruction, 26*, 247–263.

Hinchman, K. A., & Zalewski, P. (1996). Reading for success in a tenth-grade global-studies class: A qualitative study. *Journal of Literacy Research, 28*, 91–106.

Hoffman, J. V., McCarthey, S. J., Abbott, J., Christian, C., Corman, L., Curry, C., Dressman, M., Elliott, B., Matherne, D., & Stahle, D. (1994). So what's new in the new basals? A focus on first grade. *Journal of Reading Behavior, 26*, 47–74.

Jetton, T. L. (1994). *Teachers' and students' understanding of scientific exposition: How importance and interest influence what is assessed and what is discussed.* Unpublished doctoral dissertation, Texas A & M University, College Station.

Jetton, T. L., & Alexander, P. A. (1997). Instructional importance: What teachers value and what students learn. *Reading Research Quarterly, 32*, 290–308.

Kamberelis, G., & de la Luna, L. C. (1996). Constructing multiculturally relevant pedagogy: Signifying on the basal. In D. Leu, C. Kinzer, & K. A. Hinchman (Eds.), *Literacies for the 21st century: Research and practice: Forty-fifth yearbook of the National Reading Conference* (pp. 329–344). Chicago: National Reading Conference.

Langer, J., A., Applebee, A. N., Mullis, I. V. S., & Foertsch, M. A. (1990). *Learning to read in our nation's schools: Instruction and achievement in 1988 at grades 4, 8, and 12.* Washington, DC: National Assessment of Educational Progress.

Lantz, O., & Kass, H. (1987). Chemistry teachers' functional paradigms. *Science Education, 71*, 117–134.

Lemke, J. L. (1990). *Talking science: Language, learning, and values.* Norwood, NJ: Ablex.

Lensmire, T. (1994). *When children write.* New York: Teachers College Press.

Luke, A. (1993). Stories of social regulation: The micropolitics of classroom narrative. In B. Green (Ed.), *The insistence of the letter: Literacy studies and curriculum theorizing* (pp. 137–153). London: Falmer.

Luke, A., de Castell, S. C., & Luke, A. (1989). Beyond criticism: The authority of the school textbook. In S. C. de Castell, A. Luke, & C. Luke (Eds.), *Language, authority, and criticism* (pp. 245–260). London: Falmer.

Mahiri, J. (1994). Reading rites and sports: Motivation for adaptive literacy of young African-American males. In B. J. Moss (Ed.), *Literacy across communities* (pp. 121–146). Cresskill, NJ: Hampton Press.

Many, J. E. (1991). The effects of stance and age level on children's literary responses. *Journal of Reading Behavior, 23*, 61–85.

Marx, R.W., Blumenfeld, P. C., Krajcik, J. S., & Soloway, E. (1997). Enacting project-based science. *Elementary School Journal, 97*, 341–358.

McCarthey, S. (1994). Authors, text, and talk: The internalization of dialogue from social interaction during writing. *Reading Research Quarterly, 29*, 200–231.

McCarthey, S. (1996, December). *Learning the qualities of good writing: Literacy practices in elementary schools.* Paper presented at the annual meeting of the National Reading Conference, Charleston, SC.

McCarty, T. L., Wallace, S., Lynch, R. H., & Benally, A. (1991). Classroom inquiry and Navajo learning styles: A call for reassessment. *Anthropology and Education Quarterly, 22*, 42–59.

McDermott, R. P., & Varenne, H. (1995). Culture as disability. *Anthropology and Education Quarterly, 26*, 324–348.

McKeown, M. G., & Beck, I. L. (1990). The assessment and characterization of young learners' knowledge of a topic of history. *Reading Research Quarterly, 27*, 688–726.

McKeown, M. G., Beck, I. L., Sinatra, G. M., & Loxterman, J. A. (1992). The contribution of prior knowledge and coherent text to comprehension. *Reading Research Quarterly, 27*, 79–93.

McMahon, S., & Raphael, T. E. (1997). *The book club connection: Literacy learning and classroom talk.* New York: Teachers College Press.

McNeil, L. (1986). *Contradictions of control: School structure and social knowledge.* New York: Routledge.

Mercado, C. (1992). Researching research: A classroom-based student–teacher–researchers collaborative project. In A. Ambert & M. Alvarez (Eds.), *Puerto Rican children on the mainland: Interdisciplinary perspectives* (pp. 167–192). New York: Garland.

Michaels, S. (1981). "Sharing time": Children's narrative styles and differential access to literacy. *Language in Society, 10*, 423–442.

Moje, E. B., (1996). "I teach students, not subjects": Teacher-student relationships as contexts for secondary literacy. *Reading Research Quarterly, 31*, 172–195.

Moje, E. B. (1997). Exploring discourse, knowledge, and subjectivity in chemistry class. *Journal of Classroom Interaction, 32*, 35–44.

Moje, E. B. (in press). *To be part of the story: The literacy practices of gangsta adolescents.* New York: Teachers College Press.

Moje, E. B., & Fassio, K. (1997, December). *Revisioning the writer's workshop.* Paper presented at the annual meeting of the National Reading Conference, Scottsdale, AZ.

Moje, E. B., & Thompson, A. (1996, September). *Sociocultural practice and learning to write in school: Exploring the communicative and transformative potential of gang literacies.* Paper presented at the second Conference for Sociocultural Research, Vygotsky/Piaget Centennial, Geneva, Switzerland.

Moje, E. B., & Wade, S. E. (1997). What case discussions reveal about teacher thinking. *Teaching and Teacher Education, 13*, 691–712.

Moje, E. B., Willes, D. J., & Fassio, K. (in press). Constructing and negotiating literacy in a seventh-grade writer's workshop. In E. B. Moje & D. G. O'Brien (Eds.), *Constructions of literacy: Studies of teaching and learning in secondary classrooms and schools.* Mahwah, NJ: Lawrence Erlbaum Associates.

Moll, L. C. (1994). Literacy research in community and classrooms: A sociocultural approach. In R. B. Ruddell, M. R. Ruddell, & H. Singer (Eds.), *Theoretical models and processes of reading* (pp. 179–207). Newark, DE: International Reading Association.

Moll, L. C., & Gonzalez, N. (1994). Lessons from research with language minority children. *Journal of Reading Behavior, 26*, 439–456.

Moll, L. C., & Greenberg, J. (1990). Creating zones of possibilities: Combining social contexts for instruction. In L. C. Moll (Ed.), *Vygotsky and education* (pp. 319–348). Cambridge, England: Cambridge University Press.

Moll, L. C., Tapia, J., & Whitmore, K. (1993). Living knowledge: The social distribution of cultural resources for thinking. In G. Solomon (Ed.), *Distributed cognitions: Psychological and educational considerations* (pp. 139–163). Cambridge, England: Cambridge University Press.

Moore, D. W. (1996). Contexts for literacy in secondary schools. In D. J. Leu, C. K. Kinzer, & K. A. Hinchman (Eds.), *Literacies for the 21st century: Research and practice: Forty-fifth yearbook of the National Reading Conference* (pp. 15–46). Chicago: National Reading Conference.

Mullis, I. V. S., Campbell, J. R., & Farstrup, A. E. (1993). *NAEP 1992 Reading Report Card for the nation and the states.* Washington, DC: Office of Educational Research and Improvement, U.S. Department of Education.

Myers, J. (1992). The social contexts of school and personal literacy. *Reading Research Quarterly, 27*, 296–333.

New London Group. (1996). A pedagogy of multiliteracies: Designing social futures. *Harvard Educational Review, 66*, 60–92.

O'Brien, D. G., Stewart, R. A., & Moje, E. B. (1995). Why content literacy is difficult to infuse into the secondary curriculum: Strategies, goals, and classroom realities. *Reading Research Quarterly, 30*, 442–463.

Rex, L., Green, J., Dixon, C., & the Santa Barbara Classroom Discourse Group. (1998). Critical issues: What counts when context counts?: The uncommon "common" language of literacy research. *JLR: Journal of Literacy Research, 30*, 405–433.

Rogers, T. (1991). Students as literary critics: The interpretive experiences, beliefs, and processes of ninth-grade students. *Journal of Reading Behavior, 23*, 391–424.

Rogoff, B. (1990). *Apprenticeship in thinking.* Cambridge, England: Cambridge University Press.

Rose, M. (1989). *Lives on the boundary.* New York: Penguin.

Salinger, J. D. (1951). *The catcher in the rye.* New York: Modern Language Association.

Santa Barbara Discourse Group. (1994). Constructing literacy in classrooms: Literate action as social accomplishment. In R. B. Ruddell, M. R. Ruddell, & H. Singer (Eds.), *Theoretical models and processes of reading* (pp. 124–154). Newark, DE: International Reading Association.

Schumm, J. S., Vaughn, S., & Saumell, L. (1992). What teachers do when the textbook is tough: Students speak out. *Journal of Reading Behavior, 24,* 481–503.

Shannon, P. (1990). *The struggle to continue: Progressive reading instruction in the United States.* Portsmouth, NH: Heinemann.

Shymansky, J. A., Yore, L. D., & Good, R. (1991). Elementary school teachers' beliefs about and perceptions of elementary school sciences, science reading, science textbooks, and supportive instructional factors. *Journal of Research in Science Teaching, 28,* 431–454.

Siegel, M. (1995). More than words: The generative power of transmediation for learning. *Canadian Journal of Education, 20,* 455–475.

Sinclair, J. M., & Coulthard, R. M. (1975). *Towards an analysis of discourse: The English used by teachers and pupils.* London: Oxford University Press.

Sizer, T. R. (1985). *Horace's compromise: The dilemma of the American high school.* Boston: Houghton Mifflin.

Smith, F. R., & Feathers, K. M. (1983). The role of reading in content classrooms: Assumption vs. reality. *Journal of Reading, 27,* 262–267.

Stewart, R. A. (1990). A microethnography of a secondary science classroom: A focus on textbooks and reading (Doctoral dissertation, Purdue University, 1990). *Dissertation Abstracts International, 50,* 3540A.

Stodolsky, S. S. (1988). *The subject matters: Classroom activity in math and social studies.* Chicago: University of Chicago Press.

Stodolsky, S. S., & Grossman, P. (1995). The impact of subject matter on curricular activity: An analysis of five academic subjects. *American Educational Research Journal, 32,* 227–249.

Stodolsky, S. S., Salk, S., & Glaessner, B. (1991). Student views about learning math and social studies. *American Educational Research Journal, 28,* 89–116.

Street, B. V. (1995). *Social literacies: Critical approaches to literacy in development, ethnography, and education.* London: Longman.

Taylor, M. (1987). *The gold Cadillac: A fancy new car and an unforgettable drive.* New York: Puffin.

Tyson-Bernstein, H. (1988). *A conspiracy of good intentions: America's textbook fiasco.* Washington, DC: Council for Basic Education.

Vacca, R. T. (1998). Foreword. In D. E. Alvermann, K A., Hinchman, D. W. Moore, S. F. Phelps, & D. R. Waff (Eds.), *Reconceptualizing the literacies in adolescents' lives* (pp. xv– xvi). Mahwah, NJ: Lawrence Erlbaum Associates.

Vélez-Ibáñez, C. G. (1988). Networks of exchange among Mexicans in the U. S. and Mexico: Local level mediating responses to national and international transformations. *Urban Anthropology, 17*(1), 27–51.

Vygotsky, L. S. (1978). *Mind in society.* Cambridge, MA: MIT Press.

Vygotsky, L. S. (1986). *Thought and language* (A. Kozulin, Trans. & Ed.). Cambridge, MA: Harvard University Press. (Original work published 1934)

Warren, B., Rosebery, A., & Conant, F. (1989). *Cheche Konnen: Science and literacy in language minority classrooms* (Report No. 7305). Cambridge, MA: Bolt, Beranek, & Newman.

Wertsch, J. V. (1991). A sociocultural approach to understanding socially shared cognition. In L. B. Resnick, J. M. Levine, & S. D. Teasley (Eds.), *Perspectives on socially shared cognition* (pp. 85–100). Washington, DC: American Psychological Association.

Wildy, H., & Wallace, J. (1995). Understanding teaching or teaching for understanding: Alternative frameworks for science classrooms. *Journal of Research in Science Teaching, 32,* 143–156.

Willis, A. I. (1995). Reading the world of school literacy: Contextualizing the experience of a young African American male. *Harvard Educational Review, 65,* 30–49.

Yore, L. D. (1991). Secondary science teachers' attitudes toward and beliefs about science reading and science textbooks. *Journal of Research in Science Teaching, 28,* 55–72.

CHAPTER 34

Reading in the Content Areas: Social Constructivist Dimensions

Thomas W. Bean
University of Nevada

Since Volume II of the *Handbook*, with its related chapter on secondary reading (Alvermann & Moore, 1991), there has been a considerable shift in research emphasis and methodology in content area reading studies. Research reviewed for the 1991 volume reflected a quest for teaching and learning strategy validation, typically through experimental and quasi-experimental studies. That line of research has now given way to qualitative studies in content area classrooms aimed at understanding sociocultural underpinnings in teaching and learning (e.g., Bean, 1997; Hinchman & Zalewski, 1996; Moje, 1996; Sturtevant, 1996a). Thus, one of the goals of this review is to provide a picture of the past and present landscapes encompassing research in reading in the content areas with implications for theory, practice, policy, and future research.

I begin the chapter by first defining content area reading. Historical work is alluded to, and the earlier review of secondary reading research in Volume II of the *Handbook* (Alvermann & Moore, 1991) serves as a valuable departure point for the present review. Second, I explore four topics from a social constructivist perspective: (a) teacher beliefs and practices; (b) attitudes and interests in content reading; (c) the role of literature in content area classrooms; and (d) implications for research and future directions.

DEFINITION OF CONTENT AREA READING

In a historical exploration of content area reading instruction, Moore, Readence, and Rickelman (1983) noted:

> The specialty of content area reading instruction came about in recognition of the fact that readers require various strategies when they study particular subject areas and read many kinds of materials for different purposes. Content area reading instruction is designed to deliver those strategies. To date, the primary mission of this instruction is to develop students' reading-to-learn strategies. (p. 419)

The focus on teaching strategies in the content areas, although remaining a cornerstone of methods courses, has expanded to include other forms of communication, particularly writing and discussion. For example, our content methods text (Readence, Bean, & Baldwin, 1998, p. 4) used the more inclusive term *content area literacy* and the definition: "The level of reading and writing skill necessary to read, comprehend, and react to appropriate instructional materials in a given subject area." Similarly, Vacca and Vacca's (1996) methods text defined content literacy as "the ability to use reading and writing to learn subject matter in a given discipline" (p. 8).

The road to an expanded view of content area literacy, now anchored in text and reader-based research in the cognitive sciences (as well as more recent work in classroom-based ethnography) has been arduous. At times, content area literacy research has taken a back seat to the greater funding opportunities available for research in early literacy (Vacca, 1998). Yet, it is precisely at the point where young readers encounter content area texts that they often flounder (Readence et al., 1998). Even very early accounts of content area reading provide a picture of social stratification based on access and ability to handle the demands of technical writing. The next section considers some of the issues related to who had access to content area information in the past and how this information was managed.

HISTORICAL BACKGROUND

Reading and writing for informational purposes has its roots in ancient society. In Mesopotamia, scribes noted astronomical data to keep the calendar; they charted financial transactions, medical diagnoses, and chronicles of war (Manguel, 1996). Indeed, school tablets or early textbooks were common in the wealthier Mesopotamian households. Writing and reading were aristocratic activities in ancient society (Manguel, 1996). In Manguel's historical account of early informational texts, some of the problems that plague our information rich society were already causing problems in 323 b.c. in Egyptian society. The lofty goal of Alexandria's library was to "encapsulate the totality of human knowledge" (p. 189). However, without a system of organization, the vast records of the scribes on pig keeping, selling beer, and trading in roasted lentils overburdened the storage capacity of Alexandria. By 1250, Richard de Fournival created a library catalog system for content area reading topics including geometry, astronomy, physics, medicine, law, and so on. Thus, even in early society, crucial knowledge was contained in written documents to be read only by those with the power, knowledge, and skills to do so. Medieval libraries guarded access to books by keeping them chained to the shelves (Boorstin, 1983).

With the advent of Gutenberg's printing press in 1454 and the ability to mass produce books, access to content literacy expanded. Multiple copies of secular works by Aristotle and other great thinkers increased the public's motivation and interest in reading. Coupled with English dictionaries in the 1600s literacy was no longer the exclusive domain of a privileged few (Boorstin, 1983).

Following these early beginnings of informational text, content reading became linked with memorizing and reciting texts in the early 1900s (Moore et al., 1983). A few researchers such as Edmund Burke Huey and E. L. Thorndike tackled the difficult task of studying reading for meaning, but their landmark work languished in subsequent years with the rise of behaviorism. Harold Herber's revolutionary textbook *Teaching Reading in the Content Areas* (1970) and a series of research monographs highlighting empirical and quasi-empirical investigations in content area classrooms by promising doctoral students at Syracuse University changed the landscape.

Alvermann and Moore's (1991) earlier review of research related to secondary reading provides a sense of the cognitivist ethos of research in the 1980s and serves as a good departure point for the present review.

EARLIER RESEARCH IN SECONDARY READING

Alvermann and Moore (1991) tabulated and calculated the effectiveness of various teaching and learning strategies. They concluded that many of our teaching and learning strategies (e.g., graphic organizers) are moderately effective when the experimental and actual classroom conditions match. They found that 61% of the effective strategy interventions had the classroom teacher at the forefront, and only 48% of the effective interventions were conducted by experimenters. In addition, 76% of the studies used contrived rather than real content area text selections. Alvermann and Moore stressed four major problems with this research: (a) limited ecological validity, (b) limited teacher input, (c) limited texts, and (d) limited instruction in actual strategy use. They raised serious concerns about the decontextualized nature of the studies reviewed and argued for future research aimed at providing greater naturalistic detail about content area classrooms.

The five themes Alvermann and Moore identified included:

1. Single text use predominated in content classrooms.
2. Learning facts was a dominant goal.
3. Little preteaching of concepts and vocabulary occurred.
4. Teacher control and order were of paramount interest.
5. Accountability testing and time constraints limited teachers' efforts to implement content area reading strategies.

Has the landscape changed since the 1991 review, and if so, how?

THE INFLUENCE OF SOCIAL CONSTRUCTIVISM

The shift away from strategy validation studies steeped in the cognitivist tradition has been influenced, in large measure, by social constructivism. Social constructivist theory places the experiences and views of participants in a social context at the forefront (Au, 1998). Questions exploring how and why teachers and students use literacy in and out of classrooms have become paramount (Hinchman & Moje, 1998). Meaning is socially constructed by teachers and students as they interact with texts, media, and each other (Au, 1998). Some literacy practices are valued and others marginalized.

In a social constructivist view, classrooms are seen as complex, hegemonic contexts where participants negotiate multiple discourses with varying degrees of success (Hinchman & Moje, 1998). It is from this social constructivist stance that I selected and considered studies in content area literacy.

TEACHER BELIEFS AND PRACTICES

Preservice Teachers

A fairly extensive body of work informs our current understanding of content area teachers' beliefs and practices at both preservice and inservice levels (Bean, 1997; Dillon, O'Brien, Moje, & Stewart, 1994; Fox, 1994; Hinchman & Zalewski, 1996; Jetton & Alexander, 1997; Lloyd, 1996; Moje, 1996; Sturtevant, 1996a; Wilson, Konopak, & Readence, 1993). At the preservice level, there is substantial variability in beliefs and practices within the same content area. This variability is shaped partially by the sociocultural dimensions of individual biography, discipline subculture, and field-based experiences. Cooperating teachers exert substantial influence over preservice teachers' use of content strategies. In this social context where the cooperating teacher holds power, preservice teachers often opt for traditional transmission strategies that optimize control, rather than using content strategies that give students more agency in small-group structures. Studies of preservice content teachers in the fields of English, social studies, biology, and mathematics reveal the tension between stated beliefs and practices that emerge in the school context. Preservice teachers struggle with their desire to embrace an interactive model and their larger desire to please an expert cooperating teacher who may well be successful with a more traditional transmission model. For example, Fox (1994) conducted a qualitative case study of preservice English teachers engaged in teaching a literature course after learning about a reader-centered literature response curriculum in their university English methods class. Larry, one of the case study participants, continued his strong belief in a transmission model of teaching literature even after his methods class demonstration activities designed to counter this view. Unlike Larry, Mario knew from personal experience that a distant transmission model was not appropriate for powerful literature like Rudolfo Anaya's (1972) *Bless Me Ultima*. Fox (1994) found that preservice teachers needed opportunities to reflect on the internal conflicts they had about how to balance transmission and transactional models of teaching literature.

In a study of three preservice teachers from social studies, biology, and English, Bean and Zulich (1992) explored the beliefs and practices of nontraditional preservice teachers through the window of student–professor dialogue journals in a required content literacy course. Students expressed real interest in content area reading strategies introduced in the course, and they found graphic organizers in social studies and biology, and word concept maps in English, to be strategies they planned to use in their 2-day practicum. Unfortunately, their field placements with restrictive cooperating teachers limited their attempts to experiment with interactive strategies.

Bean (1997) charted preservice content area teachers' selection and use of specific vocabulary and comprehension strategies for a microteaching session in a field-based practicum attached to a required content area literacy course. Twenty-seven participants from science, social studies, mathematics, English, art, and music initially selected 14 strategies for microteaching. These included graphic organizers, anticipation-reaction guides, writing roulette, the verbal-visual strategy, word concept maps, study guides, prereading questions, analogical study guides, text previews, KWL, fictionary, jigsaw, parallel notes, and bingo games. However, in a subsequent semester, where students were interviewed in a 5-day practicum or student teaching, their selection and use of strategies narrowed dramatically. Only 2 out of 10 preservice teachers interviewed in this second phase of the study continued to use the strategy originally selected for microteaching. Eight of 10 preservice teachers were using one of the content literacy strategies introduced in the course. The most dominant influence in strategy selection and use was the cooperating teacher.

In a case study that sheds further light on the dichotomies that develop between preservice teachers' stated beliefs and the realities of secondary classrooms, Wilson et al. (1993) followed a student through the content literacy class to student teaching. Wilson et al. found that David, a 21-year-old preservice teacher, espoused beliefs about secondary reading that were largely interactive and reader-based in his first semester of content literacy and its related practicum in social studies. He felt positive about using graphic organizers and webs to guide students' text reading. However, during the subsequent semester of student teaching, he became very text based in his teaching, abandoning any use of content literacy prereading and postreading strategies. He typically lectured, wrote key points on the board, and adopted a transmission model of teaching, in direct opposition to his stated beliefs. In an interview, David stated that too much time is consumed by content reading strategies. In essence, he mirrored his cooperating teacher's approach to maintaining order, control, and easy accountability through low-level assessments and worksheets.

Even in less text-bound, more hands-on problem-based fields like mathematics, these same preservice teacher patterns persist. Sturtevant (1996b) examined five math student teachers from a military group transitioning into teaching as a new career. They took a content area literacy class prior to student teaching and identified a number of strategies that they planned to use in student teaching. Their actual instructional decisions, once in the school site, clashed with their original desire to use interactive content reading approaches. Interviews showed that the cooperating teacher's traditional style outweighed the preservice teachers' enthusiasm for content literacy strategies.

In recent years, alternative practicum models have been attempted in an effort to change the apprenticeship model that seems to diminish preservice teachers' efforts to try out promising content area literacy strategies (Banaszak, Wilson, & McClelland, 1995). These researchers described a Clinical Master Teacher Program model where the dual roles of campus student teaching supervisor and cooperating teacher are fulfilled by a master teacher. Careful selection of master teachers involves identifying individuals who possess a master's degree, 5 years of teaching experience, supervisory experience, and participation in a summer workshop. It remains to be seen what impact this model and others including compressed field-based certification programs will have on altering the traditional apprenticeship model.

A number of studies, increasingly in a qualitative vein, chart inservice teachers' beliefs and practices in content literacy (Fox, 1994; Hinchman & Zalewski, 1996; Konopak, Wilson, & Readence, 1994; Lloyd, 1996; Moje, 1996; Sturtevant, 1996a). At the inservice level, the following themes are evident (some of which intersect with the aforementioned preservice themes):

1. Teacher-centered approaches to content area instruction predominate, making more student-centered, small-group learning appear unusual.
2. Content teachers often espouse a desire to foster students' high-level interpretive thinking yet emphasize lower level questions and tasks in actual classroom practice.
3. Students are very adept at playing the game and sensing the signs and symbols that signal membership in each unique content area classroom.
4. Content teachers are highly idiosyncratic in classroom organization, use of content strategies, and delivery, partly due to content and pedagogical content knowledge.
5. Pacing and control issues also occupy inservice content teachers concerns, much like their preservice colleagues.

Inservice Teachers

Experienced content area teachers, although free of many of the constraints preservice teachers labor under (e.g., meeting the expectations of university and school-based supervisors), must cope with school and community expectations that may conflict with their beliefs. For example, in a study of 35 secondary social studies teachers, followed by an intensive case study of one teacher, the dichotomous nature of beliefs and practices emerged (Konopak et al., 1994). These teachers were primarily reader based in their stated beliefs about comprehension instruction. In a follow-up case study of George, a world geography teacher with 19 years of experience, he opted for literal-level questions and conducted discussions that were very teacher centered. Control won out in his teaching, despite espoused beliefs in reader-based instruction (Konopak et al., 1994).

Sturtevant (1996a) explored the role of content literacy in two high school history classes from the teachers' perspectives. Both teachers had 20 years of experience.

Using a qualitative case study approach including teacher autobiographies, observational field notes, and interviews, Sturtevant painted a contrasting picture of Dan and Joe. Dan believed strongly in a slow, methodical coverage of history content designed to help students grasp concepts in depth. His classroom style was very teacher directed with two to three guide questions and subsequent student recitation. As the semester progressed, he opted for an accelerated presentation of content. After digressing to discuss a local problem with students, he fell further behind his intended pacing and began speeding up the next day.

In contrast, Joe used listening guides to present content and tapped students' opinions as much as possible. Both teachers said interpretation of content was important but they devoted little time to this dimension.

In their autobiographical interviews, both teachers pinpointed key sociocultural influences in their beliefs about teaching. Dan viewed his former elementary teachers, his wife (a history teacher), his cooperating teacher during student teaching, and his students who struggled with concepts as influential. Joe recalled his junior high social studies teacher, his wife (an elementary teacher), a friend who taught English, and his students who struggled with the class as influential.

Sturtevant (1996a) argued that our reform efforts designed to infuse content literacy strategies in classrooms need to carefully consider the school-based dilemmas teachers wrestle with, as well as deeply ingrained belief systems teachers hold.

Other efforts to understand the social context of content classrooms were conducted by Dillon et al. (1994). They conducted an ethnographic study of three teachers in biology, chemistry, and earth science. The first teacher used a mastery learning model in biology that centered on study guides he wrote highlighting technical vocabulary, questions, and guidance about what parts of the textbook chapter students needed to read. He believed strongly that all students could learn biology, even if this was not a high-interest area for them. He placed students in small cooperative learning groups to discuss their responses to the study guides.

The second teacher, in chemistry, believed that science was best defined as an organizational system with inherent structure. She felt students would learn how to learn by acquiring organizational metacognitive strategies like SQ3R. In contrast to the biology teacher, she was very teacher directed in guiding text discussions where students took split-page notes on her lectures and wrote summaries of text information.

Similarly, the third teacher, in earth science, was very success oriented in his beliefs about student learning. He felt that connecting science to students' lives, creating a relaxed classroom atmosphere, and using humor were keys to student success. Therefore, he used the text only as a reference to create outlines of key points on the board with related teacher-directed lectures.

All three of these teachers held philosophies that valued student learning. Yet, they carried out their philosophies using instructional decisions about guiding content reading, writing, and talk in very idiosyncratic ways. Strategy selection flowed logically from their espoused philosophies, and the degree of student autonomy varied from small cooperative group learning using teacher-made study guides to a teacher-centered lecture-outline format. Dillon et al. (1994) concluded that philosophies about a content field and teaching are intertwined with instructional decisions in complex and varied ways.

In a study designed to explore how teachers in physical science signal important text information and how students react to this information, Jetton and Alexander (1997) looked at three teachers displaying varying levels of content knowledge in astrophysics. Using a textbook article about Stephen Hawking's work on black holes (Hurd, Silver, Bacher, & McLaughlin, 1988), these researchers found teachers' content pedagogical knowledge weighed heavily in students' understanding.

The first teacher possessed limited knowledge of astrophysics and felt compelled to cling to the text as her source of information. Using a very text-based style of presentation and lecturing, students gained little from this material. The second teacher, sidetracked by seductive details of Hawking's life in the article, did little to convey scientific information about black holes. Finally, the third teacher had a strong grounding in astrophysics and focused her class on the scientific concepts in the article.

Jetton and Alexander (1997) concluded that, in addition to beliefs and strategies, content knowledge and content pedagogical knowledge are crucial elements in instruction and learning. Although science teachers often embrace strategies like concept mapping, without adequate content knowledge, such strategies may have little impact.

In a critique of research efforts aimed at validating content literacy strategies and infusing them in secondary classrooms, O'Brien, Stewart, and Moje (1995) developed a strong case for naturalistic studies approaching classrooms as sociocultural communities. They took the position that strategy instruction, combined with small-group learning, flies in the face of control and management issues in classrooms. Content area literacy classes emphasize student centeredness, reader response literature circles, and collaboration in constructing meaning. But textbooks and tests serve to center authority on the teacher. "A primary goal of the secondary curriculum is to construct an efficient framework to control the transmission of formalized value-free knowledge, toward predictable outcomes measured with tests" (O'Brien et al., 1995, p. 447).

As a means of better understanding and overcoming some of the roadblocks to infusing content area literacy in secondary classrooms, O'Brien et al. called for studies approaching teaching and learning as social constructivist enterprises. Studies from this naturalistic stance seek an insider's perspective and view teachers' personal philosophies as important precursors to using or avoiding content area literacy approaches. Exploring teacher beliefs reflectively through autobiographies, dialogue journals, discussion of teaching cases, and field experiences coupled with debriefing and critiques could go a long way toward changing the technocratic and idiosyncratic nature of our classroom practice.

In a critical review of literacy research in secondary classrooms, Moore (1996) suggested that the current emphasis on social forces in classrooms shows the powerful influence of social contexts on students' content learning. Classroom situational contexts are coproduced by teachers and students actively interpreting the patterns and signals that arise in the course of daily instruction. He further argued that case studies help reduce our positivistic tendency to overgeneralize and overlook the individuality of teachers and students.

Individual agency, revealed in the more recent qualitative studies (Dillon et al., 1994; Hinchman & Zalewski, 1996; Lloyd, 1996; Moje, 1996; Sturtevant, 1996a), helps reduce overly deterministic views that broad societal forces shape situational contexts. Rather, teachers and students in the wide-ranging classrooms already charted in the present review forge unique situational contexts. Thus, the possibility for change is always there. Indeed, an evaluation study of a long-term intervention program for high school students from underrepresented groups struggling socioeconomically further supports the view that individual and collective agency can alter the status quo (see Bean & Valerio, 1997 for a complete account of Project AVID). Intervention projects that assist students in study strategies, as well as ways to communicate effectively with high school teachers, show great promise in providing students from underrepresented groups with the cultural capital necessary for success (Bean & Valerio, 1997).

The sociocultural theory of individual agency is perhaps best illustrated in a qualitative study contrasting a teacher's criteria for success in a 10th-grade global studies class with her students' views of success (Hinchman & Zalewski, 1996). The teacher defined success as conceptual understanding and used guide material coupled with lectures and discussion to foster student understanding. Students defined success as getting the grade, resulting in varying levels of effort from average to excellent. Students adopted a utilitarian stance, reading mainly to find answers. They used traditional study approaches, including skimming chapter material and rereading as needed. The teacher and students' conflicting notions of success reduced any sense of community in this classroom. Indeed, the teacher felt pressed to cover as much global studies content as possible. This undoubtedly sent a conflicting message to students that content coverage was more important than depth of understanding.

In a 2-year ethnography of a high school chemistry class, students learned both science concepts and study strategies that they could conceivably use in other classes, but they elected not to (Moje, 1996). Landy, an experienced chemistry teacher, believed strongly in science as organization, and she selected strategies mirroring this view. Using SQ3R, split-page notetaking, concept mapping, and graphic organizers, Landy cared about students' grasp of chemistry concepts. In turn, students viewed the use of these strategies as signs that they were members of this classroom culture. Students reported that they did not transfer the use of these strategies to other courses. The strategies were viewed as unique to Landy's style of teaching. Moje (1996) noted that students held socially constructed theories about the nature of knowledge and purposes of literacy in the chemistry classroom and other classes they were taking. They could differentiate those beliefs and practices teachers held and adjust their approach accordingly, even when the two viewpoints were in conflict with each other.

Another science classroom study looked at beliefs and practices of two high school biology teachers and the beliefs held by their students (Lloyd, 1996). Larry and Ed, the two teachers, held contrasting beliefs about learning that were evident in their science teaching. Larry held to a behaviorist stance emphasizing learning through repetition. He instructed his students to compile notebooks of their reading and lecture notetaking. In his view, the notebooks reinforced repetition of important information in biology. In contrast, Ed believed that students' prior knowledge was the key bridge to new concept learning. Notebooks in Ed's class became vehicles for analyzing and synthesizing ideas.

Students in Larry's class viewed his methods as largely ineffective. They were particularly unhappy about the absence of small-group interaction and opportunities for discussion of text material. Ed's students had ample opportunities for small-group interaction and cooperative lab activities to learn biology concepts.

These studies show the impact of teachers' and students' socially constructed beliefs about the nature of teaching and learning across a range of core content areas. When teachers' and students' views of learning conflict, important concepts may be glossed over. More importantly, students' sense of agency as learners is diminished.

In addition to research in content teacher beliefs and practices, a growing body of work chronicles the affective area of how students view literacy and voluntary reading at the secondary level.

ATTITUDES AND INTERESTS
IN CONTENT AREA LITERACY

McKenna, Kear, and Ellsworth (1995) surveyed students' attitudes toward recreational and academic reading through Grade 6. A total of 18,185 students responded to the survey, and the results chart a steady decline in attitudes toward recreational and academic reading as students advance in grade level. This finding was especially strong for less able readers. By sixth grade, students were largely indifferent to reading. The relation between attitude and reading frequency is critical, as reading frequency helps comprehension (McKenna et al., 1995). Thus, a decline in reading attitudes at middle and secondary levels has a marked impact on content learning and the potential effect of causing students to avoid difficult reading tasks.

Undergraduate college students also report little reading for pleasure, despite the ability to do so (Duchein & Mealey, 1993). In their study of 90 college students, these researchers found students had vivid memories of those few teachers who read aloud in class at the secondary level.

Similar declines in attitude toward reading have been found for adult preservice and inservice content area teachers by Bean and Readence (1995). Using autobiographical literacy histories, they explored 53 preservice and inservice teachers' attitudes toward reading from their earliest memories of home and school, through high school and their present college experiences. A precipitous decline in attitude toward reading occurred by the middle stage of their school experiences. Negative influences included dull textbooks, reading as a form of forced labor, and problems related to low-level tracking of some students. Positive influences involved time for book sharing and discussion. Journal writing about books, book clubs, and field trips linked to book reading were also viewed positively. Content teachers who introduced study strategies and socioculturally interesting material were recalled fondly. Thus, content teachers exert a tremendous influence on reading attitudes. This is especially true at middle and secondary levels where the nature of reading often centers exclusively on locating, analyzing, and synthesizing technical information to the exclusion of captivating fiction.

THE ROLE OF LITERATURE IN CONTENT AREA CLASSROOMS

The degree to which adolescents are motivated to engage in learning science, mathematics, history, and other content is heavily influenced by the nature of the material they encounter and opportunities for discussion (Bean, 1998).

An engaged reader is intrinsically motivated to use content area learning strategies to create connections between prior knowledge and new information (Guthrie, Alao, & Rinehart, 1997). The increasing use of thematic units incorporating literature within the content areas of science, mathematics, and social studies offers a model that is likely to increase students' engagement in reading. For example, the inclusion of well-crafted young adult novels linked to content area concepts illuminates otherwise turgid text. An award-winning book like David Klass' (1994) *California Blue*, where the main character finds an endangered butterfly in a northern California logging area, raises a number of issues for discussion in a social studies class about citizenship (Bean, Kile, & Readence, 1996).

Multicultural young adult literature explores issues of ethnic identity development, human relations, and rites of passage. A novel like *Heartbeat, Drumbeat* (Hernandez, 1992), where the main character explores her Navajo and Hispanic ethnicity, generates a rich array of topics that ninth-grade English students can explore (Bean, Valerio, Money-Senior, & White, 1997). In this research, reader response patterns in students' writing were investigated across a variety of topics. Students wrote about gender issues, researched and critiqued the authenticity of Navajo burial ceremonies in the novel, and carried on dialogue journal conversations with their peers in a classroom filled with computers and a small group of students in a Hawaii high school. Most importantly, the infusion of multicultural young adult novels expands the traditional literary canon and engages students in works relating to their cultures and lives (Godina, 1996).

The use of multicultural young-adult literature also engaged preservice teachers in a critical examination of their long-held beliefs about groups outside the European-American culture. For example, Chevalier and Houser (1997) conducted a one-semester action research project aimed at exploring preservice teachers' literature circle discussion of books by Walter Dean Myers and others in social studies and literacy methods classes. They found that preservice teachers initially believed in the value of assimilation of all cultures into the mainstream. Following novel reading and discussion, they began to experience a heightened level of awareness of other cultures. As a result, some of these preservice teachers developed plans to use multicultural young adult literature whereas others held to a resistance position. Similar to the earlier work reviewed on preservice teachers' beliefs and practices, the individuals approached these readings with biographical and institutional experiences that influenced how they thought about this literature.

Sociocultural theories (Bloome, 1991) lead to research questions exploring hidden curricular choices in what literature is taught and how this literature is discussed. For example, does the teacher control discussion, or are students able to engage in reader-response patterns where they can critique a work from their point of view? In essence, reader-response research now embraces a view of literacy as cultural practice with related questions about who gets to participate, and who decides what is read and how it is discussed (Bloome, 1991). Bloome (1991, p. 52) argued that "The questions being asked and the supporting arguments given can be viewed as a debate over what counts as the literary cultural capital of the society and what value or priority is given to the literary domain compared with other domains (e.g., skill development)."

Recent studies in reader response in content classrooms suggest that, although students' voices have been largely ignored in past work, there is a growing interest in exploring their unique views of classroom discussion. For instance, in a recent multicase study in five school sites, students viewed opportunities for discussion of literary and expository texts as almost nonexistent (Alvermann, et al., 1996). Interviews showed that these middle school and secondary students in English and social studies held views of good discussions emphasizing a preference for small groups of friends, each sharing equally by participating actively in discussion. Furthermore, they saw teacher guidelines for discussion as only moderately important and felt that their own approaches would result in effective, task-oriented talk. This study suggests that content teachers need to be willing to adopt a model of shared decisionmaking that respects students' ideas and approaches to text discussion. In addition, the absence of research on student discussion in mathematics, science, and other content classrooms suggests a need to explore cross-disciplinary differences in future studies (Alvermann et al., 1996).

Newell (1996, p. 149) asserted: "A fundamental assumption operating in many literature classrooms is that the author's meaning remains hidden until unveiled by the teacher's own interpretive agenda." In an effort to understand the contrast between reader-based and teacher-centered modes of literary discussion, Newell conducted a descriptive study of two classes of middle-track 10th-graders' discussion and writing about a short story. The teacher-centered classroom involved students in responding to teacher prompt questions for discussion and a five paragraph essay. Students in the reader-based classroom engaged in small-group discussion aimed at judging the main character's values and reporting this to the whole class. They also completed a free writing. Students in the reader-based classroom displayed more personal associations in their character discussion and demonstrated more interpretive engagement in their discussion and writing.

Reader-response studies in content classes show the potential of shared decision making. Students are more likely to socially construct personally meaningful interpretations of literature in settings that encourage and respect multiple perspectives. This is not to say that peer status rankings will not interfere with whose voice gets heard and who is silenced (cf. Dillon & Moje, 1998). Nevertheless, moving away from the teacher as the central source of knowledge has the potential to liberate students' knowledge construction.

In the final section, I want to summarize the current state of the art in content area literacy research and suggest some future directions that I think are critical if content area literacy is to move beyond our present knowledge base.

IMPLICATIONS FOR RESEARCH
AND FUTURE DIRECTIONS

At the outset of this chapter, I alluded to the issues uncovered in Alvermann and Moore's (1991) review of research in secondary reading. Their synthesis and critique of studies centered on the 1980s strategy validation research of that period. Four problems in research of that era surfaced in their review: (a) limited ecological validity, (b) limited teacher input, (c) limited texts, and (d) limited instruction in actual strategy use. These problems prompted me to raise the question, "Has the landscape changed since their 1991 review and, if so, how?"

I believe the landscape has changed and that contemporary researchers in content area literacy have expanded our understanding of classroom contexts dramatically. This fairly extensive line of work also points toward gaps in our knowledge, particularly as technical reading demands accelerate in many fields. Careers that, in the past, were primarily devoted to physical labor with minimal reading demands, increasingly involve the use of computers and at least some sociotechnical literacy (Bruce, 1997).

It seems clear that research in the 1990s has overcome the decontextualized nature of our earlier work by placing classroom social contexts at the forefront. Much of the more recent research in content area literacy is grounded in social constructivist theory (Au, 1998).

Studies (Bean, 1997; Bean & Zulich, 1992; Fox, 1994; Sturtevant, 1996b; Wilson et al., 1993) in preservice teachers beliefs and practices in content area literacy show the powerful sway of school contexts on what fledgling teachers say they believe and their tendency to acquiesce to the demands of the cooperating teacher. Although preservice content teachers vary somewhat in their beliefs and practices, they lean toward transmission styles of teaching that reinforce teacher control at the expense of content area strategies. Content area strategies rely on small-group work and reward student independence and agency. The continuing dominant use of single textbooks serves to further center instruction on the teacher. Thus, in many ways, we have not shifted away from the textbook as a source of authority, a recurring theme in Alvermann and Moore's (1991) review.

Inservice content teachers vary in their beliefs and practices but also veer toward teacher-centered approaches, particularly when they are pressed for time to cover content faster (Dillon et al., 1994; Lloyd, 1996). Content teachers often express a desire to develop students' critical thinking in their disciplines yet emphasize lower level questions and tasks in actual classroom practice (Sturtevant, 1996a). Students become skilled at discerning what is required "to do school" and quickly assess the signs and symbols signaling membership in content classrooms (Hinchman & Zalewski, 1996; Moje, 1996). Content teachers' pedagogical content knowledge drives how they approach a topic (Jetton & Alexander, 1997). When the knowledge base is low for a particular topic, and shared decision making with students is not part of their repertoire, a marked tendency to become very text based and teacher centered is the norm.

We have taken to heart Alvermann and Moore's (1991) call for more contextualized research in content literacy and learned a great deal from these studies. In many ways it seems that we now need to move on. We need studies that stay attuned to issues of social context while providing exemplars of the unusual. By that, I mean classrooms where small-group discussion is the norm, where the use of multiple texts is common, where students download informational text from the Internet and communicate with other classrooms and communities via electronic mail and video conferencing. These promising modes of learning are not well represented in our current research in content area literacy, and there is a danger that we will repeat what we already know from our rich array of studies in teachers beliefs and practices.

Strategy use is now seen as an integral part of the content teacher's personal and institutional biography, often tied closely to how a discipline organizes knowledge (Moje, 1996). For example, concept maps often appeal to science teachers, whereas social studies teachers may find anticipation-reaction guides stimulate discussion (Bean, 1997). These strategies are no longer the focal point of research in content area classrooms. Our research attention now centers on the social interaction patterns of teachers and students.

As our understanding of classroom social context has grown, we have documented a status quo world in schools, whereas students' attitudes toward recreational reading show precipitous declines as they advance into middle and secondary grades (Bean & Readence, 1995; Duchein & Mealey, 1993; McKenna, et al., 1995). Contemporary models of reading attitude show the powerful relation between attitude and reading frequency and its impact on reading comprehension (McKenna et al., 1995). Thus, I believe we need to explore the role of literature in a variety of content classrooms. Captivating young adult literature like David Klass's (1994) award-winning novel *California Blue* can serve to illuminate otherwise abstract concepts such as "citizenship" presented in textbooks (Bean et al., 1996). We need to study students' reactions to these works, their discussion patterns, and the impact of this work on content teachers' classrooms. Models of reader response and shared decision making need greater research attention, particularly in core content fields.

Another untapped area of research involves efforts to use young adult literature in content classrooms outside English (Bean, 1998). Given the large collection of outstanding books for young adults spanning science, social studies, physical education, and other fields, it is surprising that more work has not been undertaken in this area. For example, research questions might include:

1. What problems do content area teachers experience as they attempt to select young adult novels to use with particular topics?
2. How do content area teachers incorporate literature in their classrooms?
3. How do students react to the use of young adult literature in classrooms outside English?

In short, this dimension of literature and reader response is one that has yet to attract much research energy. Even adding a single novel like *California Blue* (Klass, 1994) that delves into science-related topics in ecology and environmental protection would be atypical in most science classrooms. It is precisely this sort of change in the use of single content area texts that is most likely to help students learn how to interpret, critique, and synthesize diverse points of view on a topic.

Subject areas often ignored in our literacy research offer contexts for exploring the infusion of literature. For example, music and physical education rarely receive much research attention in our literacy journals. Agriculture, art, vocational education, career education, guidance, and a host of other areas typically dealt with in high school are absent from our research lens. Novels like Gary Paulsen's (1994) *The Car* might captivate students' interest in vocational-technical classes (Bean, 1998). At this point, we simply have too little research in noncore content areas to speculate about the role of literature on students' attitudes and concept learning.

The use of multicultural young adult literature in content classrooms is beginning to expand the traditional literary canon to include underrepresented groups (Godina, 1996). Research gauging the impact of this work on content learning and ethnic identity awareness is still in the early stages. The potential for altering students' views of school as a place where only certain literary works are acceptable to read and discuss is very great, but we need in-depth studies of how this literature impacts content classrooms.

Another dimension of content literacy that needs greater attention is the impact of multiple texts on students' learning, interest, critical thinking, writing, and attitudes toward reading. Multiple texts have the potential to increase students' reasoning precisely because they present various viewpoints about a topic (Hartman & Allison, 1996; Palmer & Stewart, 1997; Perfetti, Britt, & Georgi, 1995; Stahl, Hynd, Britton, McNish, & Bosquet, 1996). For example, history is the story of events depicted in historical documents. In order to judge the truth value of historical documents, students need substantial practice in the process of weighing evidence across multiple texts (Perfetti et al., 1995). Using multiple texts has the advantage of capturing students' interest because each text is a novel representation of an event. As we begin to see more use of compact disk text storage and retrieval in classrooms, these hypertext representations offer a manageable means to engage students in sophisticated document comparison (Perfetti et al, 1995).

We need to conceptualize "texts" in a broad fashion to include the use of census data (Sweeney, Monteverde, & Garrett, 1993), multimedia (Hermanson & Kerfoot, 1994) in music and other fields, and Internet technology that is becoming more accessible in many schools (Bruce, 1997). We need careful descriptive studies of classrooms in history and other content fields where teachers are experimenting with multiple texts defined broadly to include print in all its recent forms. Studies exploring unusual classrooms where teachers and students are pushing into the future using technology to expand students' voices and connections with other students seem especially promising across content fields.

Research in content literacy has emerged from the cognitivist emphasis of the 1980s to embrace qualitative paradigms in the 1990s. Research reviews like Alvermann and Moore's (1991) compilation, and this one, serve to gauge where we have been and to speculate on where we might go next. Much like the voyages of the Polynesian double-hulled canoe, Hōkūle'a, we are engaged in what Will Kyselka (1987), in a wonderful book entitled, *An Ocean in Mind*, called "wayfinding" (p. x). Early theories of Polynesian voyaging held to a drift theory that viewed their voyages and landfalls as largely accidental. The numerous voyages of the Hōkūle'a, using ancient experiential forms of navigation, cast doubt on simplistic drift theories (Kyselka, 1987). Stars, cloud patterns, birds, and so on provided observational data modern-day Hawaiian navigator Nainoa Thompson and others used to guide Hōkūle'a to intended landfalls.

Kyselka (1987, p. 179) painted a powerful contrasting picture of traditional celestial navigation and wayfinding: "How different the ways of navigation. Instrument navigation is discontinuous, and we don't know where we are until we have a fix. The wayfinder on the canoe so close to us stays continuously oriented: external verification is neither a possibility nor is it wanted." Like astute Polynesian navigators, it seems we are now staying much closer to participants' experiences in content classrooms in our research than we did in the 1980s.

In the 1980s, we sought to validate content area literacy strategies in studies that often minimized the larger context of the classroom, teachers biography, and students' voices. Our quasi-experimental methodology, much like instrument navigation, charted students' performance in relation to the impact of various teaching strategies. In the 1990s our research embraced qualitative methodology, using interpretive participant-observation much like a navigational wayfinder paying close attention to patterns at sea.

Moving into and beyond the year 2000, I suspect that technology and alternative forms of data representation will play a profound role in how we study and share our discourse of discovery with colleagues (Eisner, 1997; Maring, Wiseman, & Myers, 1997). Electronic journals like the International Reading Association's *Reading Online* (http://www.readingonline.org) offer a forum to display classroom audio and video clips accompanying research studies. This feature, coupled with chat opportunities about a study, is altering the sharing and critique of research in content literacy. Technology-rich classrooms offer a vehicle for enriching language through web-site communities and multiple perspectives on content topics that we are just beginning to explore (Maring et al., 1997).

In a wide-ranging examination of alternative forms of data representation, Eisner (1997, p. 8) speculated that "as the use of alternative forms of data representation increases, we can expect new ways of seeing things, new settings for their display, and new problems to tackle." Sociocultural issues of access to literacy and knowledge, whose knowledge counts as legitimate in content classrooms, and teacher and student interaction patterns will remain important concerns in our research in content classrooms.

Where will our search take us next in content area literacy? The answer to that question will have to await our next decade of exploration combining the best of our recent forms of inquiry with new forms yet to be discovered.

ACKNOWLEDGMENT

The author thanks Paul Cantú Valerio, University of Nevada, Las Vegas doctoral student in literacy, for his valuable assistance in gathering library sources for this chapter.

REFERENCES

Alvermann, D. E., & Moore, D. W. (1991). Secondary school reading. In R. Barr, M. L. Kamil, P. B. Mosenthal, & P. D. Pearson (Eds.), *Handbook of reading research* (Vol. II, pp. 951–983) New York: Longman.

Alvermann, D. E., Young, J. P., Weaver, D., Hinchman, K. A., Moore, D. W., Phelps, S. F., Thrash, E. C., & Zalewski, P. (1996). Middle and high school students' perceptions of how they experience text-based discussions: A multicase study. *Reading Research Quarterly, 31*, 244–267.

Anaya, R. (1972). *Bless Me Ultima*. Berkeley, CA: Tonatiuh Quinto Sol International.

Au, K. H. (1998). Social constructivism and the school literacy learning of students of diverse backgrounds. *Journal of Literacy Research, 30*, 297–319.

Banaszak, R. A., Wilson, E. K., & McClelland, S. M. (1995). Redefining the student teaching triad. *Teacher Education and Practice, 11*, 50–59.

Bean, T. W. (1997). Preservice teachers' selection and use of content area literacy strategies. *Journal of Educational Research, 90*, 154–163.

Bean, T. W. (1998). Teacher literacy histories and adolescent voices: Changing content area classrooms. In D. Alvermann, D. Moore, S. Phelps, & D. Waff (Eds.), *Toward reconceptualizing adolescent literacy* (pp. 149–170). Mahwah, NJ: Lawrence Erlbaum Associates.

Bean, T. W., Kile, R. S., & Readence, J. E. (1996). Using trade books to encourage critical thinking about citizenship in high school social studies. *Social Education, 60*, 227–230.

Bean, T. W., & Readence, J. E. (1995). A comparative study of content area literacy students' attitudes toward reading through autobiography analysis. In K. A. Hinchman, D. J. Leu, & C. K. Kinzer (Eds.), *Perspectives on literacy research and practice: Forty-fourth yearbook of the National Reading Conference* (pp. 325–333). Chicago: National Reading Conference.

Bean, T. W., & Valerio, P. C. (1997). Constructing school success in literacy: The pathway to college entrance for minority students [Review of the book *Constructing school success: The consequences of untracking low-achieving students*]. *Reading Research Quarterly, 32*, 320–327.

Bean, T. W., Valerio, P. C., Money-Senior, H., & White, F. (1997, December). *Secondary English students' engagement in reading and interpreting a multicultural young adult novel*. Paper presented at the annual meeting of the National Reading Conference, Scottsdale, AZ.

Bean, T. W., & Zulich, J. (1992). A case study of three preservice teachers' beliefs about content area reading through the window of student-professor dialogue journals. In C. K. Kinzer & D. J. Leu (Eds.), *Literacy research, theory, and practice: Views from many perspectives: Forty-first yearbook of the National Reading Conference* (pp. 463–474). Chicago: National Reading Conference.

Bloome, D. (1991). Anthropology and research on teaching the English language arts. In J. Flood, J. M. Jensen, D. Lapp, & J. R. Squire (Eds.), *Handbook of research on teaching the English language arts* (pp. 46–55). New York: Macmillan.

Boorstin, D. J. (1983). *The discoverers*. New York: Random House.

Bruce, B. C. (1997). Literacy technologies: What stance should we take? *Journal of Literacy Research, 29*, 289–309.

Chevalier, M., & Houser, N. D. (1997). Preservice teachers' multicultural self-development through adolescent fiction. *Journal of Adolescent and Adult Literacy, 40,* 426–436.

Dillon, D. R., & Moje, E. B. (1998). Listening to the talk of adolescent girls: Lessons about literacy, school, and life. In D. E. Alvermann, K. A. Hinchman, D. W. Moore, S. F. Phelps, & D. R. Waff (Eds.), *Reconceptualizing the literacies in adolescents' lives* (pp. 193–223). Mahwah, NJ: Lawrence Erlbaum Associates.

Dillon, D. R., O'Brien, D. G., Moje, E. B., & Stewart, R. A. (1994). Literacy learning in secondary school science classrooms: A cross-case analysis of three qualitative studies. *Journal of Research in Science Teaching, 31,* 345–362.

Duchein, M. A., & Mealey, D. L. (1993). Remembrance of books past … long past: Glimpses into aliteracy. *Reading Research and Instruction, 31,* 84–97.

Eisner, E. W. (1997). The promise and perils of alternative forms of data representation. *Educational Researcher, 26,* 4–10.

Fox, D. L. (1994). What is literature? Two preservice teachers' conceptions of literature and of the teaching of literature. In C. K. Kinzer & D. J. Leu (Eds.), *Multidimensional aspects of literacy: Research, theory, and practice: Forty-third yearbook of the National Reading Conference* (pp. 394–405). Chicago: National Reading Conference.

Godina, H. (1996). The canonical debate-implementing multicultural literature and perspectives. *Journal of Adolescent & Adult Literacy, 39,* 544–549.

Guthrie, J. T., Alao, S., & Rinehart, J. M. (1997). Engagement in reading for young adolescents. *Journal of Adolescent & Adult Literacy, 40,* 438–446.

Hartman, D. K., & Allison, J. (1996). Promoting inquiry-oriented discussions using multiple texts. In L. B. Gambrell & J. F. Almasi (Eds.), *Lively discussions! Fostering engaged reading* (pp. 106–133). Newark, DE: International Reading Association.

Herber, H. L. (1970). *Teaching reading in content areas.* Englewood Cliffs, NJ: Prentice Hall.

Hermanson, C., & Kerfoot, J. (1994). Technology assisted teaching: Is it getting results? *American Music Teacher, 43,* 20–23.

Hernandez, I. B. (1992). *Heartbeat, drumbeat.* Houston, TX: Arte Publico Press.

Hinchman, K. A., & Moje, E. B. (1998). Locating the social and political in secondary school literacy. *Reading Research Quarterly, 33,* 117–128.

Hinchman, K. A., & Zalewski, P. (1996). Reading for success in a tenth-grade global-studies class: A qualitative study. *Journal of Literacy Research, 28,* 91–106.

Hurd, D., Silver, M., Bacher, B. A., & McLaughlin, C. W. (1988). *Stephen Hawking: Changing our view of the universe.* Prentice Hall Physical Science. Englewood Cliffs, NJ: Prentice Hall.

Jetton, T. L., & Alexander, P. A. (1997). Instructional importance: What teachers value and what students learn. *Reading Research Quarterly, 32,* 290–308.

Klass, D. (1994). *California blue.* New York: Scholastic.

Konopak, B. C., Wilson, E. K., & Readence, J. E. (1994). Examining teachers' beliefs, decisions, and practices about content area reading in secondary social studies. In C. K. Kinzer & D. J. Leu (Eds.), *Multidimensional aspects of literacy research, theory, and practice: Forty-third yearbook of the National Reading Conference* (pp. 127–136). Chicago: National Reading Conference.

Kyselka, W. (1987). *An ocean in mind.* Honolulu: University of Hawaii Press.

Lloyd, C. (1996). Scientific literacy in two high school biology classrooms: Considering literacy as social process. *Journal of Classroom Interaction, 31,* 25–30.

Manguel, A. (1996). *A history of reading.* New York: Viking.

Maring, G. H., Wiseman, B. J., & Myers, K. S. (1997). Using the world wide web to build learning communities: Writing for genuine purposes. *Journal of Adolescent & Adult Literacy, 41,* 196–207.

McKenna, M. C., Kear, D. J., & Ellsworth, R. A. (1995). Children's attitudes toward reading: A national survey. *Reading Research Quarterly, 30,* 934–956.

Moje, E. B. (1996). "I teach students, not subjects": Teacher-student relationships as contexts for secondary literacy. *Reading Research Quarterly, 31,* 172–195.

Moore, D. W. (1996). Contexts for literacy in secondary schools. In D. J. Leu, C. K. Kinzer, & K. A. Hinchman (Eds.), *Literacies for the 21st century: Research and practice: Forty-fifth yearbook of the National Reading Conference* (pp. 15–46). Chicago: National Reading Conference.

Moore, D. W., Readence, J. E., & Rickelman, R. J. (1983). An historical exploration of content area reading instruction. *Reading Research Quarterly, 18,* 419–438.

Newell, G. E. (1996). Reader-based and teacher-centered instructional tasks: Writing and learning about a short story in middle-track classrooms. *Journal of Literacy Research, 28,* 147–172.

O'Brien, D. G., Stewart, R. A., & Moje, E. B. (1995). Why content literacy is difficult to infuse into the secondary school: Complexities of curriculum, pedagogy, and school culture. *Reading Research Quarterly, 30,* 442–463.

Palmer, R. G., & Stewart, R. A. (1997). Nonfiction trade books in content area instruction: Realities and potential. *Journal of Adolescent and Adult Literacy, 40,* 630–641.

Paulsen, G. (1994). *The car.* San Diego, CA: Harcourt Brace.

Perfetti, C. A., Britt, M. A., & Georgi, M. C. (1995). *Text-based learning and reasoning studies in history.* Hillsdale, NJ: Lawrence Erlbaum Associates.

Readence, J. E., Bean, T. W., & Baldwin, R. S. (1998). *Content area literacy: An integrated approach* (6th ed.). Dubuque, IA: Kendall/Hunt.

Stahl, S. A., Hynd, C. R., Britton, B. K., McNish, M. M., & Bosquet, D. (1996). What happens when students read multiple source documents in history? *Reading Research Quarterly, 31*, 430–456.

Sturtevant, E. G. (1996a). Lifetime influences on the literacy-related instructional beliefs of two experienced high school history teachers: Two comparative case studies. *Journal of Literacy Research, 28*, 227–258.

Sturtevant, E. G. (1996b). Beyond the content literacy course: Influences on beginning mathematics teachers' uses of literacy in student teaching. In D. J. Leu, C. K. Kinzer, & K. A. Hinchman (Eds.), *Literacies for the 21st century: Research and practice: Forty-fifth yearbook of the National Reading Conference* (pp. 146–158). Chicago: National Reading Conference.

Sweeney, J. C., Monteverde, F. E., & Garrett, A. W. (1993). Social history, the census, and the blues: A high school application. *Social Studies, 84*, 107–112.

Vacca, R. T. (1998). Foreword. In D. Alvermann, D. Moore, S. Phelps, & D. Waff (Eds.), *Toward reconceptualizing adolescent literacy* (pp. xv–xvi). Mahwah, NJ: Lawrence Erlbaum Associates.

Vacca, R. T., & Vacca, J. L. (1996). *Content area reading* (5th ed.). New York: HarperCollins.

Wilson, E. K., Konopak, B. C., & Readence, J. E. (1993). A case study of a preservice secondary social studies teacher's beliefs and practices about content-area reading. In D. J. Leu & C. K. Kinzer (Eds.), *Examining central issues in literacy research, theory, and practice: Forty-second yearbook of the National Reading Conference* (pp. 335–343). Chicago: National Reading Conference.

CHAPTER 35

College Studying

Sherrie L. Nist[*]
Michele L. Simpson
University of Georgia

COLLEGE STUDYING

It is well accepted both in theory and in practice that academically successful college students know how to study. Yet research suggests that many students enter postsecondary institutions unprepared to meet the studying demands placed on them (e.g., Pressley, Yokoi, van Meter, Van Etten, & Freebern, 1997). This lack of preparation can be traced, in part, to the fact that studying is part of the "hidden curriculum" at the secondary level (Mayer, 1996). That is, study strategies are "hidden" because teachers at all levels assume that students already have a repertoire of studying behaviors when they enter their classrooms. As a result of this lack of preparation, a majority of colleges and universities offer some vehicle for students to become efficient and active learners (Maxwell, 1997). Some institutions have entire programs to provide students with a variety of academic assistance options; others offer "Learning to Learn" courses and Freshman Experience programs that focus on teaching students to be active learners.

But what does it mean to say that students know how to study or that they are active learners? And what is it that the research community knows about studying in college? Finally, in what directions does the field need to move given what we currently know about studying? It is on these questions that this chapter focuses.

Before we begin our discussion, however, we need to express the frustration we often felt in communicating the complexity of studying as we worked through numerous drafts of this chapter. Because of this complexity, we believed that it was imperative to at least acknowledge the importance of factors other than learning strategies. Thus, we begin our discussion of college studying with a brief historical perspective. Then we set the theoretical stage by examining models and taxonomies that have guided researchers as they have investigated studying. Using one model, we then review the research factors related to studying at the college level: course characteristics, learner characteristics, and learning strategies. Finally, we conclude the chapter with implications for practice and policy as well as suggesting recommendations for future research.

---

[*]Authors are listed alphabetically; both contributed equally to this chapter.

SEARCH PROCEDURES

We focused our literature review based on the idea that studying is an interactive process as portrayed in Thomas and Rohwer's (1986) component and process model. Starting with the components of this model as descriptors, we conducted a computer search of ERIC and examined the *Citation Index to Journals in Education, Resources in Education,* and did a cursory search of *Dissertation Abstracts.*

In addition, we searched scholarly books, yearbooks from the National Reading Conference for the past 15 years, and current issues of all pertinent journals. The reference lists from the book chapters and yearbooks were particularly helpful in leading us to other specific research studies. Similarly, the bibliographies of recent reviews of pertinent topics from the *Review of Educational Research* also assisted us in identifying relevant investigations and assured us that we had included the most up-to-date information in our search.

HISTORICAL BACKGROUND

College students have been identified as needing academic assistance or "remedial" help almost since the inception of institutions of higher education. In fact, as early as 1927, Book and others were bemoaning the fact that "they [students] have great difficulty in orientating themselves to the life and work of a college or university" (p. 529) and he suggested that students become part of "How to Study" groups. Book's recommendation caused quite a stir, and, as a result, many other colleges and universities—the University of Minnesota, New York University, Harvard, and Dartmouth, to name a few—designed courses or entire programs to improve college students' study skills. Some of these institutions continued to lead the way in college reading and studying programs for years to come.

The growth of programs to promote academic assistance and studying at the college level has been strongly tied in our society to particular landmark events, mostly through some type of federal legislation. These events, for a variety of reasons, have spurred greater enrollment in postsecondary institutions, thus causing a trickle-down effect for programs for the underprepared. For example, in 1944 the G.I. Bill of Rights caused tremendous change on college campuses. Likewise, the passage of the National Defense Act of 1958, which was precipitated by the launch of Sputnik 1 year earlier, provided loans and grants to nonveteran students, causing again a major increase in the numbers of students on college campuses. A third key event was the civil rights movement and the passage of the Higher Education Act of 1965. The focus now switched from primarily veterans to the recruitment and admission of minority students who had been historically underrepresented in higher education (Boylan, 1994).

Two major early movements—behaviorism in the 1940s and 1950s and humanism in the 1960s—influenced the types of programs and instruction available for college students and, to a lesser degree, in the types of studies that were conducted. Much of the research at this time examined the effectiveness of particular programs or materials in promoting students' reading rate, comprehension, and study skills. Researchers such as Kingston, Spache, Raygor, and McConihe, led the way with college reading studies that were presented at the Southwest Reading Conference, a precursor to the National Reading Conference (Baldwin et al., 1992).

In the 1960s, humanism also became evident in practice and pedagogy. Although it became more important at this time for students to feel good about themselves as readers and learners, this belief was evidenced more in practice than in research (Enright & Kerstiens, 1980) Research, however, continued to have a behavioristic influence (e.g., Bliesmer, 1968).

Two overriding conclusions can be drawn from this brief historical perspective. First, whether the need for assistance was because students lacked basic skills or because the transfer from high school to college was academically traumatic for students, the solutions to solve these problems were similar. Second, much of the early research in college reading and studying simply described effective reading or study skills courses or programs. However, as theoretical models were developed in the late 1970s and beyond, researchers began to base their investigations on stronger theoretical grounds.

THEORETICAL MODELS

Since the early 1980s, researchers committed to helping students become successful, active learners have based their studies on a variety of interactive, theoretical models. Albeit diverse, these models share a common assumption that there are a number of variables that impact students' learning from text. Jenkins's (1978) tetrahedral model of learning, for example, proposed that active learners consider the nature of the material to be learned and examine the criterial task, determining the products (i.e., recognition or recall) and levels of thinking embodied in that task. Moreover, active learners are also aware of their own characteristics, especially their own strengths and weaknesses in terms of the specified tasks and texts. Using that information about themselves as learners and the specified tasks and texts, active learners then determine the appropriate strategies to employ.

Gradually, researchers refined the tetrahedral model and created their own models, which included a variety of additional variables. Of these models, Thomas and Rohwer's (1986) component and process model perhaps best captures the factors impacting college students' studying. Their model proposes that the experiences, ability, and volition-related characteristics of students and the characteristics of a course (i.e., materials, tasks factors, course conditions) are filtered by students' perceptions or beliefs. These components interact to impact students' study activities and hence their performance. What particularly distinguishes this model is the research that Thomas and Rohwer (1987) conducted in classroom settings. They used their model to investigate study practices in social studies courses across the grade range of junior high school to college, finding that students' study activities are influenced by a relatively large number of course features or characteristics.

From the Thomas and Rohwer model and other theoretical models, several important generalizations about studying can be drawn. First, the models imply that there are no generic best strategies or methods of studying. Rather, strategies are considered appropriate when they match the demands of the texts and tasks and the beliefs and background knowledge of the learner. Moreover, studying involves more than a knowledge of the possible strategies. To be active learners, students must understand the *what, when, how,* and *why* of strategies if they are to apply them to their own tasks and texts (Paris, Lipson, & Wixson, 1983; Pressley, 1995). Third, these models suggest that there is a core of essential cognitive and metacognitive processes that cut across domains. These processes include selecting, transforming, organizing, elaborating, monitoring, planning, and evaluating (Mayer, 1996; Weinstein & Mayer, 1986). Finally, and most importantly, these models imply that active learning takes a long time to foster and develop (Butler & Winne, 1995; Pressley, 1995).

As we have suggested, studying and active learning involve considerably more than students employing strategies. In the sections that follow, we briefly address these other factors—course characteristics, learner characteristics, and belief systems—before discussing learning strategies.

FACTORS RELATED TO EFFECTIVE STUDYING
AND ACTIVE LEARNING

Course Characteristics

The first factor that influences studying at the college level is a student's ability to understand the situation and/or context (Alexander, 1995; Garner, 1990). Thomas and Rohwer described context as the characteristics of a course, or the external factors that influence reading and studying (Thomas, Bol, & Warkentin, 1991; Thomas & Rohwer, 1986). These external factors include the texts that are assigned and the academic tasks that are either tacitly or explicitly communicated by the professor. College students who know how to interact with texts and how to determine tasks independently can use this information to assist them in strategy selection. Given the fact that approximately 85% of all college learning involves reading, and that texts are central to learning at all levels of education (Voss & Silfies, 1996; Woodward, 1993), first we discuss the role of text. Then the role of academic task, which is beginning to make its way into the literature, is described.

Text.   Early research examining text was mainly concerned with text structure (see Vol. I of the *Handbook on Reading Research*, Meyer & Rice, 1984). Then, in the mid to late 1980s, research on text characteristics focused on how text aids and organization influenced text comprehension. Many of these foci were reviewed in Volume II of the *Handbook of Reading Research*. The research at this time, which was primarily quantitative in nature, had a rather profound influence on publishers of college textbooks, although some research suggested that text aids promoted passive processing (Schallert, Alexander, & Goetz, 1985). Publishers began inserting numerous aids, many of which had been scientifically researched, to help students better understand and organize text information. Text inserts providing additional background information, the inclusion of many visual aids, and inserted questions all made college texts more readable and considerate.

Currently, text research, especially as it is related to college studying, seems to be heading in two directions. First, there has been an emphasis more recently on how students approach text in a variety of domains, particularly in history and science (Carson, Chase, & Gibson, 1993; Donald, 1994; Simpson & Nist, 1997; Voss & Silfies, 1996; Wineburg, 1991), as well as students' beliefs about these texts. That is, rather than simply focusing on the differences between narrative and expository texts, researchers are examining differences between expository texts from a variety of disciplines using more qualitative methodology. In history, for example, Wineburg's (1991) descriptive research concerning students' beliefs about history text suggests that subtexts, or underlying texts, supplement the more explicit meaning of the text. In two other investigations, also in the domain of history, Simpson, Nist, and Sharman (1997) and Simpson and Nist (1997) found that college students' beliefs about history and history text influenced the strategies they selected and the way they interpreted task. Studies such as these represent a step forward and have important implications for college readers because they indicate that text, like strategies, does not operate independently of other factors (Alexander, 1992; Simpson & Nist, 1997). That is, researchers are considering other factors—metacognition (Kuhn, 1991), task (Simpson & Nist, 1997), study strategies (Schommer, 1990)—as they relate to beliefs about text in a variety of domains.

A second direction that currently is drawing interest from researchers is how students interact with lecture notes as texts, particularly how they attempt to organize and study these texts as part of test preparation (Kiewra, 1989; Kiewra, Benton, Kim, & Risch, 1995; King, 1991, 1992; van Meter, Yokoi, & Pressley, 1994). King (1992), for example, found that students who were trained to generate and answer their own questions over lecture content did significantly better on a delayed retention measure than those who wrote summaries or reviewed their notes. The results from these recent studies strongly support the notion that college students should use generative strategies (Wittrock, 1990) to interact with lecture notes, just as they should use generative strategies to interact with textbooks. In addition, these investigations are helping to create a theory of notetaking beyond the encoding-storage perspective that has dominated the notetaking literature.

Academic Tasks.   The second course-specific characteristic is academic task. Academic tasks are the products students are asked to formulate, (e.g., tests or papers) and the operations or thinking processes they should use to formulate these products (Doyle, 1983). In order to be successful in their studying, students must understand the characteristics and nuances of academic tasks and then adjust their strategies accordingly. Because many college students do not adjust their strategies to match the varying task demands, texts, or domains, they suffer from what has been termed *transfer-appropriate processing deficiencies* (Pressley et al., 1997).

As noted by Anderson and Armbruster (1984), tasks have been studied in a variety of ways in laboratory settings. In particular, previous researchers have investigated the impact of students having complete, partial, or no task knowledge on their recall or recognition test performance (e.g., Rickards & Friedman, 1978). Although these studies have contributed to our understanding of the importance of specific and accurate task knowledge, the more recent research studies have moved to actual classroom settings where academic tasks are no longer defined and manipulated by the researcher (Chase, Gibson, & Carson, 1994; Chiseri-Strater, 1991; Donald, 1994; Hofer, 1998).

Current research on academic tasks has focused on two areas. First, some researchers have investigated how tasks vary across domains (Burrell, Tao, Simpson, & Mendez-Burreuta, 1996; Chase et al., 1994; Donald, 1994; Schellings, Van Hout-Wolters, & Vermunt, 1996a, 1996b; Simpson & Nist, 1997). In general, the findings from these studies have suggested that academic tasks are not only specific to a domain, but also specific to a professor and a setting. Moreover, the findings indicate that students and professors frequently have different perceptions of what is considered the essential thinking processes in a particular domain. Donald (1994), for example, found that in the sciences, the match in task perceptions between professors and students was the closest in engineering courses and the furthest away from congruency in physics courses.

Other studies have investigated academic tasks using case study methodology in order to describe the patterns that seem to exist between students' interpretation of academic tasks, their choice of strategies, and their subsequent academic performance. For example, Simpson and Nist (1997) concluded that students who earned high grades in a history course were those who either initially understood the professor's tasks, or were flexible enough to modify their task perceptions and strategies.

Characteristics of the Learner

In their model, Thomas and Rohwer also considered the characteristics that college students bring to each learning environment. Among the learner characteristics that are important to active learning are prior knowledge, students' metacognitive abilities, their motivational levels, and interest in what they are reading or studying.

Prior Knowledge.   In a special issue of *Educational Psychologist* (Vol. 31, 1996), Alexander divided the research that has examined the role of knowledge on comprehension and learning into two periods: First Generation of knowledge, which laid the groundwork, and Second Generation of knowledge, which examines knowledge as it relates to social and cultural contexts. Most closely related to the focus of this chapter is the role that domain knowledge has on college students' abilities to understand and learn through text or lecture as well as the interaction between domain and strategy knowledge. *Domain knowledge* is defined as the knowledge learners have about a specific field of study (Alexander & Judy, 1988). As such, domain knowledge involves declarative, procedural, and conditional knowledge (Paris et al., 1983). Alexander (1992) aptly pointed out that researchers have not been quick to understand the relationship between domain knowledge and strategy research as a way of building a more complete model of learning and suggested that both are crucial if we want to understand more about how knowledge is acquired and used.

Current researchers seem to be taking Alexander's ideas to heart, focusing on the more complex questions about domain knowledge, strategy selection, and other factors that may influence performance. What seems to be emerging in the recent literature is the degree to which both domain knowledge and topic knowledge influence not only strategy choice, but also the performance level of students (Alexander, Kulikowich, & Schulze, 1994). Stanovich's (1986) idea that "the rich get richer" seems to be thriving in the domain knowledge arena.

We also currently see a line of research that examines the degree to which interest interacts with domain knowledge (Garner, Alexander, Gillingham, Kulikowich, & Brown, 1991). Moreover, other research suggests that some knowledge that college students bring to learning situations is highly resistant to change, even when they have read information to the contrary (e.g., Alvermann & Hynd, 1989; Marshall, 1989), and that prior knowledge can inhibit comprehension (Pace, Marshall, Horowitz, Lipson, & Lucido, 1989). Such resistance indicates that an affective as well as a cognitive component is at work as students attempt to make sense of information (Dole & Sinatra, 1994). The results of this and similar research, once again, indicate the interaction of numerous variables in the learning and studying processes.

Metacognitive Ability.   Paris, Wasik, and van der Westhuizen (1988) pointed out that many of the early metacognitive papers were not empirical in nature, but instead "simply extolled the virtues of metacognition for understanding reading" (p. 162). Subsequent studies, most of which have been intervention or correlational in nature, have confirmed the idea that in order to be successful college students need well-developed metacognitive skills.

In the first volume of the *Handbook*, Baker and Brown (1984) concluded that mature readers may have limited metacognitive skills, and that college students often also failed to monitor their comprehension. These two conclusions still hold true today. College students, who may or may not be mature readers, not only have persistent problems in monitoring text reading (Bielaczyc, Pirolli, & Brown, 1991; Maki & Berry, 1984; Pressley, 1995), but they also have monitoring problems when it comes to test preparation and subsequent prediction concerning how well they have performed on tests for which they have studied (e.g., Nist, Simpson, Olejnik, & Mealey, 1991; Pressley, Snyder, Levin, Murray, & Ghatala, 1987). Intervention research has also confirmed the idea that students can be trained to monitor their learning, thus becoming more metacognitively aware (Dunlosky & Nelson, 1994; Nelson & Narens, 1990; Pressley et al.,1987; Shenkman and Cukras, 1986; Thiede & Dunlosky, 1994). It appears, then, that there is a large payoff when college students are taught metacognitive skills.

The current trend in metacognitive research seems to be heading in two directions. First, metacognition is being studied more in how it relates to self-regulated learning (SRL), rather than in isolation. Drawing on theoretical models of SRL (Butler & Winne, 1995; Metcalfe & Shimamura, 1994), Winne (1996) suggested that cognitive and metacognitive tasks are highly interrelated, yet admitted that there is a "relatively small population of (empirical) studies that directly examine how metacognition is used within SRL."

The second area in which there has been a considerable amount of interest has been how to measure metacognition (Dennison, 1997). Several instruments have subscales that tap not only cognitive but metacognitive abilities as well. The best known of these instruments are perhaps the Learning and Study Strategies Inventory (LASSI) (Weinstein, Palmer, & Schulte, 1987) and the Motivated Strategies for Learning Questionnaire (MSLQ) (Pintrich, Smith, Garcia, & MeKeachie, 1991). Although these instruments seem to have some reliability and validity problems, when used under appropriate conditions, they can provide valuable information.

Motivation.   Much of the research on college students' motivation has been done in isolation of strategic learning, thus portraying what Pintrich and Garcia (1994) called a "motivationally inert" learner (p. 123). That is, there is a considerable amount of research on motivation as well as strategic learning or studying, but researchers are just beginning to examine how these constructs interact. Researchers term the blending of motivation with cognition "hot" cognition (e.g., Winne, 1996).

The role that motivation plays in strategic learning and self-regulation is portrayed nicely in the Reciprocal Empowerment Model (McCombs, 1994). In this model, skill, will, and social support are deemed essential if maximum motivation is to occur, but the will component is the center if a student is to become truly self-regulated. Likewise, Mills (1991) claimed that students must be able to gain control over their own thinking processes rather than to be controlled by external standards. It is only then that they will be open to learning new strategies. Moreover, if students believe that strategies are useful in meeting their goals, they will have higher levels of motivation and put forth greater effort (Schunk & Swartz, 1991). In a somewhat different perspective, Paris and Turner (1994) presented what they referred to as *situated motivation*, the idea that students' motivation is dynamic, thus changing as the situation changes.

Much of the research that examines the interaction between college students' strategy use and motivation is correlational in nature. For example, when correlating different subscales from the MSLQ, Pintrich and his colleagues (Pintrich & Garcia, 1991; Pintrich & Schrauben, 1992) found that those who are intrinsically motivated, value task, and are highly self-efficacious are more likely to be strategic and metacognitively aware. Moreover, students who use motivational strategies, such as self-handicapping and defensive pessimism (Garcia, 1993) when they are in "risky" situations, improve their cognitive engagement (Garcia, 1993).

Interest.   Hidi's (1990) synthesis on the role that interest plays in learning has contributed much to what we know about both individual and situational interest. Hidi drew two major conclusions in this synthesis. First, she concluded that interest is key in determining how students process information. Second, Hidi also concluded that interesting information seems to be processed differently than that which is uninteresting.

Other research with college students has found that interest played a role in how they responded to text, but that domain knowledge (Garner et al., 1991) and the nature of the text (Schallert, Meyer, & Fowler, 1995) also made a difference. Garner et al. found that interestingness had a particular effect on recall if the participants had little domain knowledge about the topic. Similarly, Schallert et al. found that when students responded to text, both related to and not related to their own majors, they had significantly more interest and involvement in readings for which they had the most domain knowledge. However, the considerateness of the text also played a role.

In a review exploring the intersection of the importance of text information and interest, Alexander and Jetton (1996) concluded that: (a) discrepancies in findings may be more due to how researchers have defined these constructs rather than reflecting any real discrepancies; (b) developmental studies that examined both importance and interest were nonexistent; (c) researchers need to investigate the role of importance and interest using nonlinear texts as well as authentic classroom situations; and (d) research should expand into other domains and topics.

Students' Beliefs as Filters

What college students believe about learning has an influence on how they interpret the task, how they interact with text, and, ultimately, the strategies they select. Because student beliefs are so important, Thomas and Rohwer (1987) suggested that beliefs serve as the "filter" through which students decipher and interpret the other components of their model. College students' beliefs about knowledge, or epistemologies, and how those beliefs influence learning are currently receiving considerable attention from researchers.

Perry (1968, 1970) was the first to discuss epistemologies in an academic setting, and much of the subsequent work is rooted in his findings. The most current line of research defines epistemological beliefs that may influence students' performance on academic tasks. Schommer (1990, 1993, 1994) and her colleagues (Schommer & Hutter, 1995; Schommer & Walker, 1995) characterized epistemologies as individuals' beliefs about the nature of knowledge and learning. These beliefs include a student's belief about the certainty of knowledge, the organization of knowledge, and the control of knowledge acquisition (Schoenfeld, 1988; Schommer, 1994; Schommer, Calvert, Gariglietti, & Bajaj, 1997; Schommer & Hutter, 1995).

A slightly different approach, the reflective judgment model (King & Kitchener, 1981; Kitchener, King, Wood, & Davidson, 1989), posits that epistemological beliefs are developmental and assumes that individuals progress through seven stages, without skipping any. Although these approaches to thinking about epistemologies differ in some respects, all models assume that individuals move from naive to mature beliefs with experience.

Some of the most recent epistemological research focuses on how beliefs influence factors such as motivation, strategy use, and performance. In a series of correlational studies, Schommer (1990, 1993) found significant relationships between certain scales on the epistemological questionnaire she developed and student performance. In her later studies (Schommer, 1993), she concluded that beliefs about knowledge may also influence students' self-report of strategy use.

Other researchers are looking at the role that students' beliefs play in task interpretation and strategy selection. For example, Ryan (1984) found that epistemological beliefs (whether students were dualists or relativists as defined by Perry's theory) influenced how students monitored their reading and learning. Moreover, Simpson and Nist (1997) and Simpson et al. (1997) concluded that students' beliefs about knowledge in general, and more specifically their beliefs about what history is, strongly influenced the strategies they selected and their interpretation of the task in a college history class.

One final area currently of interest related to epistemological beliefs is the controversy over whether beliefs are domain specific or whether college students have the same underlying beliefs across all domains (Hofer & Pintrich, 1997). Most of the research indicates that epistemological beliefs are developmental in nature, suggesting that at a particular point in time, a student's beliefs would be at the same stage across all domains (e.g., Schommer & Walker, 1995). Yet, as noted by Hofer and Pintrich, the issue of domain specificity as related to epistemological beliefs has received little attention.

Learning Strategies

Learning strategies are the "behaviors of a learner that are intended to influence how the learner processes information" (Mayer, 1988, p. 11). Although learning strategies have been part of an assumed or hidden curriculum, researchers have acknowledged their importance and have churned out a plethora of studies investigating their efficacy. Most of the studies during the 1960s, 1970s, and early 1980s were experimental or correlational and attempted to isolate a superior study strategy system or to determine which strategy was more effective in a particular situation.

These earlier studies offered an equivocal array of findings for practitioners and researchers. For example, the conclusions from the numerous studies on notetaking and outlining indicated that these strategies were no more effective than passive techniques such as rereading and memorizing (Brown, 1982). Accordingly, the reviews of the extant literature on learning strategy instruction and strategy programs were cautious, at best, and not particularly positive. In Volume I of the *Handbook of Reading Research*, Anderson and Armbruster (1984) concluded that "empirical research fails to confirm the purported benefits of the popular strategies" and "the effort to find the one superior method has not been successful" (p. 665). In addition, Anderson and Armbruster suggested that most learning strategies were being taught because of tradition or instructors' personal beliefs about their effectiveness rather than because the empirical research confirmed their advantages and benefits.

The strategy research studies conducted during the mid 1980s and 1990s changed focus in several significant ways. Rather than attempting to identify a superior strategy, most of these studies investigated whether the performance of college students could be altered if they received an instructional intervention. These later studies were particularly noteworthy in that the interventions were usually quite intensive, employing what Brown, Campione, and Day (1981) characterized as informed training. Such training encouraged students to use a strategy and provided them conditional and procedural knowledge.

However, during this period the most significant change in the research on studying occurred with the emergence of the "cognitive constructivist vision of learning" (Mayer, 1996, p. 364). These studies typically occurred in more authentic contexts and viewed the learner as an active participant and "sense maker." These researchers, albeit diverse in their approaches, agreed that learning strategies embodied the essential cognitive and metacognitive processes necessary for college students to make meaning or sense of the world of academia (e.g., Mayer, 1996; McKeachie, Pintrich, Smith, & Lin, 1986; Thomas & Rohwer, 1986; Weinstein, 1994).

Although these methodological and philosophical changes had an impact on investigations focusing on studying at the college level, the reality was that there were still a considerable number of atheoretical studies being conducted that repeated the questions and mirrored the methodologies of the past. Hence, it is not surprising that reviews of the more recent literature on studying have yielded conclusions and cautious recommendations similar to those of Anderson and Armbruster in 1984. For example, McWhorter's meta-analysis (1993) of 54 studies found only a moderate effect size for learning strategy interventions on students' test performance. Hattie, Biggs, and Purdie (1996) reviewed 51 studies in which the interventions were aimed at enhancing student learning with one or more study skills or learning strategies. The 18 studies that focused on college students' performance on subject area tests, grade point averages, and tests of general ability found only a small effect of 0.27. Finally, Hadwin and Winne (1996) reviewed 566 strategy intervention studies conducted at the college level. After eliminating 96.7% of the studies, they concluded from their review of the remaining 21 studies that there was a scant research base for the strategies typically recommended by practitioners and commercial materials. However, we should point out that the major limitation of this meta-analysis was the small number of studies included.

Although the results of these meta-analyses are certainly equivocal, we believe that important generalizations about studying and active learning have emerged from the large body of research studies. Three generalizations seem particularly relevant.

Quality Strategy Instruction Can Promote Active Learning

As noted by Paris, Wasik, and Turner (1991) and Alvermann and Moore (1991) in Volume II of the *Handbook*, it is imperative that students receive quality learning strategy instruction if the goal is to insure that they can apply the strategies to their tasks and texts. One important legacy from the research studies of the eighties is that we have a clearer sense of the characteristics of quality strategy instruction or training.

First, we know that in order to develop active learners who have a repertoire of strategies, a substantial amount of time must be committed to instruction (Garner, 1990; Paris, 1988; Pressley, 1995). Such instruction should not only be intensive, but should also be of significant duration. In a study that validated the importance of sustained time, Nist and Simpson (1990) found that students' metacognition gradually improved over time, but distinct and significant improvement did not emerge until 4 weeks after the initial instruction. Had the instruction and data collection ended with the first test after only 1 week of intensive instruction, improvement would not have been detected.

Second, strategy instruction should include not only the declarative knowledge about a strategy, but also the procedural and conditional knowledge (Butler & Winne, 1995; Garner, 1990; Paris, 1988; Pressley, 1995). For students to gain conditional knowledge, it is critical that they practice strategies with authentic texts and authentic tasks and that they learn how to analyze the texts and tasks in order to determine which strategies are the most appropriate (Butler & Winne, 1995; Simpson, Hynd, Nist, & Burrell, 1997). Moreover, the texts and tasks should be challenging and complex enough so that students will not opt for a more "primitive" routine (e.g., rereading) that is familiar to them and deemed more cost effective (Garner, 1990; Paris & Byrnes, 1989; Pressley, 1995).

Third, and perhaps most important, is that instruction should occur within a specific context and specific domain (Alexander, 1996; Garner, 1990; Mayer, 1996; Perkins & Salomon, 1989; Pressley, 1995). As Garner (1990) pointed out, "One thing that we already know about strategy use is that it is embedded. It does not occur in a vacuum. When context varies, the nature of strategic activity often varies as well" (p. 523). Such contextualized instruction, however, is very rare at the college level (Hadwin & Winne, 1996; Simpson et al., 1997).

Finally, effective strategy instruction should be explicit and direct (Garner, 1990; Pressley, 1995; Winograd & Hare, 1988). In addition, students should receive specific instructor feedback on their practice attempts because such process checks are critical to the development of active learners (Butler & Winne, 1995). We have observed that very few researchers have actually collected and analyzed students' strategies to determine whether they have correctly interpreted and applied the strategy, and few, if any, have shared that information with the students during the training period (Simpson et al., 1997).

Research-Validated Strategies Are Few in Number

The second generalization focuses on research validated strategies. Most researchers and practitioners would agree that it is best to teach students a limited number of validated strategies (Levin, 1986; McKeachie et al., 1986; Pressley, 1995). Interestingly, that recommendation is quite easy to adopt given that there is a limited number of research validated strategies appropriate for college students. The four strategies we examine here have been validated in several research studies and have been conducted, in most situations, by a variety of researchers rather than just one. In addition, these studies have included explicit instruction, using high school or college students as their participants. However, one caveat should be noted: Their selection in no way implies that they are useful for all students, domains, or tasks. Research that has investigated these variables in a consistent manner simply does not exist.

Question Generation and Answer Explanation.   When students generate questions about what they have read, they are actively processing text information and monitoring their understanding of that information. As a result, their text comprehension improves (Graesser & McMahen, 1993; King, 1990, 1995; Palinscar & Brown, 1984; Rosenshine, Meister, & Chapman, 1994; Spires & Donley, 1998).

In order to train students in how to create task-appropriate questions which elicit higher levels of thinking, several methods have been used. For example, King (1989, 1992) used generic questions stems that asked students to analyze, predict, compare and contrast, apply, and evaluate (e.g., "What is an example of ...?"). Other research studies capitalized on the power of reciprocal teaching, in which students worked cooperatively in pairs or small groups, asking each other questions and answering them in a reciprocal manner (e.g., King, 1990; King & Rosenshine, 1993; Palinscar & Brown, 1984). The findings from these studies and others have suggested that the question answering is equal in importance to the question asking because students are encouraged to clarify concepts, create alternative examples, or relate ideas to their partners' prior knowledge in order to answer the question from their partner (King, 1995).

Text Summarization.   Writer-based summaries are external products that students create for themselves in order to reduce and organize information for their subsequent study and review. According to Wittrock's (1990) model of generative comprehension, for a summary to be effective, students must use their own words to form connections across the concepts and relate the concepts to their own prior knowledge and experiences. Such a definition of summarization implies that it is not a strategy quickly mastered (Brown & Day, 1983; Pressley et al., 1997). Because of the inherent difficulties in producing generative summaries, many of the early research studies, which did not provide explicit instruction of some duration, found that summaries had no impact on students' performance (e.g., Howe & Singer, 1975). However, the majority of the more recent studies have found that writer-based summaries not only improve students' comprehension, but also help them monitor their understanding (Brown & Day, 1983; Hare & Borchardt, 1984; King, 1992; O'Donnell & Dansereau, 1992; Wittrock, 1990).

Summarization as a study strategy has taken a variety of forms. Many of the studies in the mid 1980s taught students rules for summarizing, hoping to make explicit the steps that expert readers use when they read and study text (Day, 1980; Hare & Borchardt, 1984). Other investigations (e.g., Palinscar & Brown, 1984; O'Donnell & Dansereau, 1993) examined the combined impact of dyad learning and summarization on students' performance. Nist and Simpson (1988) incorporated many of Wittrock's principles of summarization into a text-marking strategy called annotation, training students to write brief summaries in the margins of their texts. These researchers and others have found that students' test performance and summary writing abilities improved when they were taught to summarize and annotate (Harris, 1991; Hynd, Simpson, & Chase, 1990; Strode, 1991).

Student-Generated Elaborations.   When students generate elaborations, they create examples or analogies, draw inferences, and explain the relationships between two or more concepts (Gagne, Weidemann, Bell, & Anders, 1984). Since Anderson and Armbruster's (1984) review of studying, there have been several studies investigating the impact of elaboration (Pressley, McDaniel, Turnure, Wood, & Ahmad, 1987; Simpson, Olejnik, Tam, & Supattathum, 1994; Woloshyn, Willoughby, Wood, & Pressley, 1990). These more recent studies have demonstrated rather consistently that students can be trained to create elaborations and that self-generated elaborations can significantly effect students' performance on both recall and recognition measures.

Pressley and his colleagues have conducted numerous studies on elaborative interrogation (e.g., Kaspar & Wood, 1993; Pressley, McDaniel, Turnure, Wood, & Ahmad, 1987; Pressley, Symons, McDaniel, Snyder, & Turnure, 1988; Woloshyn et al., 1990). Elaborative interrogation involves students in making connections between ideas they have read and their prior knowledge by generating "why" questions and then answering those questions. The findings from the elaborative interrogation studies have suggested that the quality of the generated elaborations does not impact students' understanding when the targeted topic domain is one for which they have some prior knowledge.

In a different type of elaboration study, Simpson et al. (1994) trained students to generate their own elaborations and then to recite them orally. Like the findings from the elaborative interrogation studies, the students who produced oral elaborations performed significantly better than their counterparts on immediate recall and recognition measures. However, Simpson et al. also investigated the long-term impact of the strategy, discovering that oral elaborations had a significant effect on students' performance on a delayed recall measure that occurred 2 weeks after the immediate testing.

Organizing Strategies.   Perhaps most researched of all validated strategies are those that help students organize information. Several researchers have sought to validate the effectiveness of strategies that assist students in visually organizing and representing important relationships among ideas present in written or oral text (Bernard & Naidu, 1992; Briscoe & LeMaster, 1991; Kiewra, 1994; Lambiote, Peale, & Dansereau, 1992; McCagg & Dansereau, 1991). Most of these organizing strategies involve students in identifying main ideas and subordinate ideas, making connections among those ideas, and then choosing a way in which to visually represent those relationships in an abbreviated spatial format. Although there are variations in these organizing strategies, the two basic types are concept maps and network representations, both of which are closely associated with the network and propositional models of memory.

Concept maps generally depict a hierarchical or linear relationship, and can be created in such a way as to represent complex interrelationships among ideas. When researchers have provided training in how to map, they have found that students who studied these maps performed better on dependent measures than their counterparts (Bernard & Naidu, 1992; Lipson, 1995). Mapping appears to be especially effective in situations where students must read and study complex expository text and then demonstrate their understanding on measures requiring higher levels of thinking such as synthesis and application (Bernard & Naidu, 1992; Briscoe & LeMaster, 1991). As such, much of the research on mapping has been conducted in the sciences. In addition, the studies seem to suggest that mapping best benefits students who are persistent in using the strategy and who have high content knowledge in a particular domain (Hadwin & Winne, 1996).

According to the researchers at Texas Christian University, network representations differ from concept maps in that students link key ideas with a canonical set of labels or links (Lambiote, Dansereau, Cross, & Reynolds, 1989). Perhaps the earliest study on a network representation was done by Diekhoff, Brown, and Dansereau (1982), who found that college students using the NAIT strategy (Node Acquisition and Integration Technique) performed significantly better on the recall measures than their counterparts who self-selected their own strategies.

NAIT gradually evolved into a strategy that was renamed the knowledge map or k-map. The effectiveness of the k-map has been investigated with both oral and written text (Lambiote et al., 1992; McCagg & Dansereau, 1991). In both studies, the researchers found that students using k-maps performed better than their counterparts using alternative methods. It should be noted, however, that the type of thinking demanded on the dependent measure and the domain (e.g., physiology vs. statistics) used as the study material has influenced the success of k-maps. In general, the findings from these organizing strategies have not been as compelling as with the findings from other strategies such as self-questioning and elaborating.

Students' Cognitive and Metacognitive Processing Is Important

The third generalization that emerged from the extant literature reaffirms the importance of students' cognitive and metacognitive processing. In a quest to determine a superior strategy or to train students to use a specific strategy, previous researchers targeted their efforts totally on the strategy itself, thus overlooking processes underlining that strategy. Recent researchers (e.g., Mayer, 1996; Pintrich, Smith, Garcia, & McKeachie, 1993), however, have focused their investigations more on processes, believing that what makes a difference in students' learning is the cognitive and metacognitive processes that students enact as they read and study. Although there are some slight differences in the terminology, the processes typically include selecting and transforming ideas, organizing, elaborating, monitoring, planning, and evaluating (Hadwin & Winne, 1996; Mayer, 1996; Pintrich et al., 1993; Weinstein, 1994).

The cognitive and metacognitive processes essential to active learning have been studied in a variety of ways. Mayer (1996), for example, has theorized that the selection–organization–integration model represents the cognitive processes involved in students' meaningful learning from expository text and has identified several strategies for enhancing each process. Other researchers have trained students to employ certain processes such as elaborating, planning, monitoring, and evaluating (Pressley, McDaniel, et al., 1987; Nist & Simpson, 1990).

A majority of these studies have used quantitative methodologies, and, in particular, correlational designs that have attempted to determine what relationships exist between students' self-reported cognitive and metacognitive processes and their performance in a particular domain or their overall grade point averages. For example, Pintrich and Garcia (1991) concluded that students who were engaged in deeper levels of processing, such as elaboration and organization, were more likely to do better in terms of grades on assignments or exams, as well as overall course grades.

The renewed emphasis on process rather than strategies has significant implications for program evaluation efforts and for studies on strategy transfer. That is, students could be employing certain cognitive or metacognitive processes as they read and study, but not using the specific strategy that embodies these processes. When practitioners and researchers ask students in interviews or in questionnaires to list or check the strategies they are presently using, they may be overlooking the most important data. The irony of this oversight is that we want students to focus on the processes they are using when they study, not just the strategies. If students can learn to think about the cognitive and metacognitive processes demanded in a task, they then can define their goals and study appropriately (Hadwin & Winne, 1996; Pressley, 1995).

IMPLICATIONS OF THE CURRENT RESEARCH

In this section we examine the implications of the extant research and theory. We describe four components of effective college studying programs and courses, comparing and contrasting, when appropriate, the "ideal" to the status quo. Then we examine the implications of current research for public policy. Finally, we offer suggestions for future research endeavors.

Courses and Programs

Based on our review of the literature, we recommend the following for programs and courses.

Programs Should Reflect Students' Academic Tasks.   Although it may seem obvious, our first recommendation is that programs and courses should reflect the academic tasks and texts that professors assign. Our 20 years of experience in the field have taught us that many college studying programs still use a generic model that relies on commercial materials to dictate what students will be taught. A more powerful approach is for instructors to begin curriculum development with an explicit understanding of the tasks and texts expected of students *at their institutions*. For example, are students in humanities courses asked to read a variety of primary and secondary sources and take essay exams over these texts? If so, then the objectives of the studying course should reflect these tasks.

When instructors emphasize the teaching of processes and strategies within a specific domain, the approach is usually classified as the embedded approach. Perkins and Salomon (1989) described the embedded approach as one that "calls for the intimate intermingling of generality and context-specificity in instruction" (p. 24). Although there are a variety of embedded approaches that acknowledge college students' tasks and texts, the two most prevalent are "Learning to Learn" courses and paired courses. "Learning to Learn" courses are designed to teach students a variety of study strategies, which they then apply to their own tasks and texts. These courses have been implemented by a variety of larger universities such as the University of Michigan, the University of Texas, and the University of Georgia. In paired courses, also known as supplemental instruction (Martin & Arendale, 1994), an instructor "pairs" strategy instruction to a particular high-risk college course. The instructor attends the targeted course, reads the assigned material, takes lecture notes, and then organizes sessions outside the class period on how to study, making sure that the strategies pertain to the professor's tasks and texts.

Programs Should Encourage Students to Decipher Academic Tasks and Become Aware of Personal Epistemologies.   In order to succeed, students must understand their professors' objectives and goals, build an awareness of how professors think about their domain, and learn how to organize that information. The paired course approach is an ideal situation for teaching students how to interpret academic tasks because the study strategy instructor and the students are both placed in a specific context. However, the embedded model presents only one learning context to students. Hence, instructors wanting to build task awareness might consider using scenarios or case studies to sensitize students to the nuances of tasks and the many ways in which professors directly and indirectly communicate tasks.

In addition to teaching students to decipher academic tasks, it is important for students to become aware of their personal beliefs/epistemologies about learning and to realize that their professors may have differing belief systems. General or domain specific beliefs about learning are important because they impact students' choices on how they read, process, and choose to study (Gibbs, 1990; Schommer, 1993).

Programs Should Emphasize a Variety of Validated Strategies and Processes. Because the extant literature suggests that there is no superior study strategy or study system, it seems reasonable that students should be taught a repertoire of strategies, some of which are general cognitive and metacognitive strategies and some of which are domain specific (i.e., problem-solving steps for mathematics). More important than the decision of which research validated strategies to teach is the commitment to making sure that students know how to select, transform, organize, elaborate, plan, monitor, and evaluate all critical thinking processes. In addition to these cognitive processes, instructors should address the pivotal role that motivation plays in active learning.

Programs Should Encourage Strategy Transfer and Modification. The extant literature suggests that students do not automatically or immediately transfer strategies in a flexible manner (Garner, 1990; Pressley, 1995). For transfer to occur, students must understand strategies and be able to discuss "knowingly" the domains and tasks for which they are appropriate (Butler & Winne, 1995; Campione, Shapiro, & Brown, 1995). In addition, students must understand the advantages of a particular strategy, especially if they are expected to abandon their usual approaches, which may be more comfortable and accessible (Pressley, 1995; Winne, 1995). Finally, students must learn how they can modify a strategy to fit situations slightly different from those in which they originally learned the strategy (Pressley, Harris, & Marks, 1992).

To encourage strategy transfer, instructors should provide students with explicit instruction and practice opportunities with a diverse set of tasks across domains. As students analyze these academic tasks and try out the strategies, instructors should gently nudge them toward the belief that learning is not always quick and easy. Finally, in order to promote flexible strategy employment, instructors should arrange opportunities for students to reflect and evaluate (Campione et al., 1995).

Policy

Unlike emerging literacy and the paradigm wars concerning reading methodologies, very few literacy professionals currently seem concerned about active learning and whether students are being taught how to study. As mentioned earlier, the lack of concern is probably due, in part, to the fact that studying is a part of the hidden curriculum in our public schools (Mayer, 1996). As a result, many college students are totally unprepared for the academic demands and tasks they encounter in their courses (Simpson & Nist, 1997; Weinstein, 1994). Realizing that they lack the strategies necessary for the more demanding tasks in college, many students, sometimes the very brightest high school graduates, seek out courses on how to study. Ironically, these are the courses being reduced or cut altogether because college administrators erroneously believe such courses to be "remedial" and unnecessary.

Although there are no easy solutions to these problems, we suggest that researchers and instructors specializing in the area of study strategies forge cooperative relationships with individuals in decision-making positions such as legislators, members of boards of education, and administrators. These individuals must first realize that reading to learn and studying are essential processes that must be incorporated into the K–12 curriculum so that students are continually using active reading and learning strategies, whether it be for 4th-grade social studies or 11th-grade chemistry.

Research

We divide our research agenda into two parts. First, we discuss the more methodological issues related to designing investigations related to studying. Second, we outline specific gaps that we perceive, suggesting future directions that the research on studying might take.

Methodological Issues.   We see three overriding methodological issues that need to be addressed. First, a major problem with the extant studies, particularly those that are correlational in nature, concerns the instruments used to measure both cognitive and affective factors related to studying. The most commonly used instruments have both reliability and validity problems that, at the very least, call into question research results. It is not that we believe that these instruments are poorly constructed. Rather, they simply are not appropriate in all research settings. Therefore, we suggest that future studies pilot instruments on students similar to those they will use in their actual studies. Furthermore, researchers should consider collecting information using a variety of instruments and data collection methods. For example, reliable and valid standardized instruments could be coupled with data from interviews and observations as a way of triangulating information.

Second, we need additional studies that use alternative methodologies. We believe that qualitative methodology lends itself well to investigating college studying because such methods allow for greater insights into the complexity of studying at the student level. Moreover, researchers interested in quantitative methodology should move beyond simple correlational and regression studies, working toward building models of studying through structural equation modeling. Furthermore, although some comparison studies still provide valuable information, the last thing the field needs is more studies comparing one strategy with another or a specific strategy with no treatment at all.

Finally, both qualitative and quantitative researchers need to conduct more long-term investigations to determine how students' studying behaviors evolve over time. It is only through long-term studies that researchers can understand strategy transfer and make better sense of the factors that play a role in students' studying behaviors.

Future Directions.   First and foremost, we need to focus future research studies on the interactive nature of studying. In the past, the majority of studies that have examined interactions have concentrated on how strategy use interacts with one other variable such as domain knowledge or text type. As outlined in the Rohwer and Thomas model, we need to know more about how factors such as text, academic task, and students' beliefs impact and interact with strategy use.

Second, we need further research on the processes that underlie studying rather than on specific strategies. Some researchers have done an admirable job of beginning to identify the processes (Mayer, 1988, 1996; Weinstein & Mayer, 1986), but, clearly, we do not understand how these processes interact.

Third, we need additional studies that focus on course characteristics, concentrating on the role that both academic tasks and texts play in student learning. That is, it is important to determine how academic tasks are communicated in college classrooms and how students go about interpreting those tasks within varying contexts. What kinds of compensatory strategies do students use when tasks are conveyed only implicitly, or not at all? In terms of text, one of the major gaps in the research is how students deal with the problem of multiple texts.

Fourth, studies that examine the role of student beliefs as they relate to strategy selection, motivation, task interpretation, and academic performance are lacking. Our experiences suggest that most students have little idea about their own beliefs about learning and knowing, let alone how these beliefs influence their academic performance. Moreover, research findings indicate that professor beliefs and student beliefs are generally disparate (Wineburg, 1991). We need additional studies examining these issues within classroom settings across a variety of domains.

Finally, program evaluation studies on "Learning to Learn" or study strategy courses are virtually nonexistent, except for a few presented at conferences or published in tertiary journals. We believe that this lack of evaluation has occurred for several reasons. First, good evaluation studies are challenging to design. Second, evaluation studies are difficult to get published, particularly in the better research journals. We applaud the efforts of researchers such as Dubois, Staley, and Dennison (1998) and Weinstein et al. (1997), who have designed and reported long-term evaluation studies, but such investigations are rare, or perhaps just rarely reported. Third, good evaluation studies involve the researchers in a long-term commitment because data on students' academic achievement must be collected for at least 2 years after they have completed such a program or course. Finally, program and course evaluations can be politically charged. Because pressure can be exerted administratively to indicate that such programs and courses are worthy, many program evaluation studies are often designed using instruments and variables guaranteed to show growth. Given these reasons why evaluation studies are scant in the literature, well-planned studies are important if how to study or "Learning to Learn" programs at the college level are to survive.

REFERENCES

Alexander, P. A. (1992). Domain knowledge: Evolving themes and emerging concerns. *Educational Psychologist, 27*, 33–51.

Alexander, P. A. (1995). Superimposing a situation-specific and domain-specific perspective on an account of self-regulated learning. *Educational Psychologist, 30*, 189–193.

Alexander, P. A. (1996). The past, present, and future of knowledge research: A reexamination of the role of knowledge in learning and instruction. *Educational Psychologist, 31*, 89–92.

Alexander, P. A., & Jetton, T. L. (1996). The role of importance and interest in the processing of text. *Educational Psychology Review, 8*, 89–122.

Alexander, P. A., & Judy, J. E. (1988). The interaction of domain-specific knowledge in academic performance. *Review of Educational Research, 58*, 375–404.

Alexander, P. A., Kulikowich, J. M., & Schulze, S. K. (1994). The influence of topic knowledge, domain knowledge, and interest on the comprehension of scientific exposition. *Learning and Individual Differences, 6*, 379–397.

Alvermann, D. E., & Hynd, C. R. (1989). Study strategies for correcting misconceptions in physics: An intervention. In S. McCormick & J. Zutell (Eds.), *Cognitive and social perspectives for literacy research and instruction: Thirty-eighth yearbook of the National Reading Conference* (pp. 353–361). Chicago: National Reading Conference.

Alvermann, D. E., & Moore, D. W. (1991). Secondary school reading. In R. Barr, M. L. Kamil, P. B. Mosenthal, & P. D. Pearson (Eds.), *Handbook of reading research* (Vol II, pp. 951–983). New York: Longman.

Anderson, T. H., & Armbruster, B. B. (1984). Studying. In P. D. Pearson, R. Barr, M. Kamil, & P. Mosenthal (Eds.), *Handbook of reading research* (Vol. I, pp. 657–679). New York: Longman.

Baker, L., & Brown, A. L. (1984). Metacognitive skills and reading. In P. D. Pearson, R. Barr, M. Kamil, & P. Mosenthal (Eds.), *Handbook of reading research* (Vol. I, pp. 353–394). New York: Longman.

Baldwin, R. S., Readence, J. E., Schumm, J. S., Konopak, J. P., Konopak, B. C., & Klingner, J. K. (1992). Forty years of NRC publications: 1952–1991. *Journal of Reading Behavior, 24*, 505–532.

Bernard, R. M., & Naidu, S. (1992). Post-questioning, concept mapping, and feedback: A distance education field experiment. *British Journal of Educational Technology, 23*, 48–60.

Bielaczyc, K., Pirolli, P., & Brown, A. L. (1991, April). *The effects of training in explanation strategies on the acquisition of programming skills.* Paper presented at the annual meeting of the American Educational Research Association, Chicago.

Bliesmer, E. P. (1968). 1968 review of research on college-adult reading. *Psychology of Reading Education, 8*, 79–99.

Book, W. F. (1927). Results obtained in a special "How to Study" course given to college students. *School and Society, 26*, 529–534.

Boylan, H. R. (1994). Educating all the nation's people: The historical roots of developmental education. In M. A. Maxwell (Ed.), *From access to success* (pp.3–7). Clearwater, FL: H & H.

Briscoe, C., & LeMaster, S. U. (1991). Meaningful learning in college biology through concept mapping. *American Biology Teacher, 53*, 214–219.

Brown, A. L. (1982). Learning to learn from reading. In J. A. Langer & M. T. Smith-Burke (Eds.), *Reader meets author/Bridging the gap* (pp. 26–54). Newark, DE: International Reading Association.

Brown, A. L., Campione, J. C., & Day, J. D. (1981). Learning to learn: On training students to learn from text. *Educational Researcher, 10*, 14–21.

Brown, A. L., & Day, J. D. (1983). Macrorules for summarizing texts: The development of expertise. *Journal of Verbal Learning and Verbal Behavior, 22*, 1–4.

Burrell, K. I., Tao, L., Simpson, M. L., & Mendez-Burreuta, H. (1996). How do we know what we are preparing students for? A reality check of one university's academic literacy demands. *Research and Teaching in Developmental Education, 13*, 55–70.

Butler, D. L., & Winne, P. H. (1995). Feedback and self-regulated learning: A theoretical synthesis. *Review of Educational Research, 65*, 245–281.

Campione, J. C., Shapiro, A. M., & Brown, A. L., (1995). Forms of transfer in a community of learners: Flexible learning and understanding. In A. McKeough, J. Lupart, & A. Marini (Eds.), *Teaching for transfer: Fostering generalization in learning* (pp. 35–68), Mahwah, NJ: Lawrence Erlbaum Associates.

Carson, J. G., Chase, N. D., & Gibson, S. U. (1993). *A model for faculty collaboration: Focus on academic literacy.* Atlanta: Center for Adult Literacy, Georgia State University.

Chase, N. D., Gibson, S. U., & Carson, J. G. (1994). An examination of reading demands across four college courses. *Journal of Developmental Education, 18*, 10–16.

Chiseri-Strater, E. (1991). *Academic literacies: The public and private discourse of university students.* Portsmouth, NH: Boynton/Cook.

Day, J. D. (1980). *Training summarization skills: A comparison of teaching methods.* Unpublished doctoral dissertation, University of Illinois, Champagne-Urbana.

Dennison, R. S. (1997, March). *Relationships among measures of metacognitive monitoring.* Paper presented at the annual meeting of the American Educational Research Association, Chicago.

Diekhoff, G. M., Brown, P. J., & Dansereau, D. F. (1982). A prose learning strategy training program based on network and depth-of-processing models. *Journal of Experimental Education, 50*, 180–184.

Dole, J. A., & Sinatra, G. M. (1994). Social psychology research on beliefs and attitudes: Implications for research on learning from text. In R. Garner & P. A. Alexander (Eds.), *Beliefs about text and instruction with text* (pp. 245–264). Hillsdale, NJ: Lawrence Erlbaum Associates.

Donald, J. G. (1994). Science students' learning: Ethnographic studies in three disciplines. In P. R. Pintrich, D. R. Brown, & C. E. Weinstein (Eds.), *Student motivation, cognition, and learning* (pp. 79–112). Hillsdale, NJ: Lawrence Erlbaum Associates.

Doyle, W. (1983). Academic work. *Review of Educational Research, 53*, 159–199.

DuBois, N. F., Staley, R., & Dennison, R. S. (1998, April). *Longitudinal analysis of a college study skills course: Motivation, study tactics, and GPA relationships.* Paper presented at the annual meeting of the American Educational Research Association, San Diego, CA.

Dunlosky, J., & Nelson, T. O. (1994). Does the sensitivity of judgments of learning (JOLs) to the effects of various study activities depend on when the JOLs occur? *Journal of Memory and Language, 33*, 545–565.

Enright, G. & Kerstiens, G. (1980). The learning center: Toward an expanded role. In O. T. Lenning & R. L. Nayman (Eds.), *New directions in learning assistance* (pp. 1–24). San Francisco, CA: Jossey-Bass.

Gagne, E. D., Weidemann, C., Bell, M. S., & Anders, T. D. (1984). Training thirteen-year-olds to elaborate while studying. *Human Learning, 3*, 281–294.

Garcia, T. (1993). *Skill and will for learning: Self-schemas, motivational strategies, and self-regulated learning.* Unpublished doctoral dissertation, University of Michigan, Ann Arbor.

Garner, R. (1990). When children and students do not use learning strategies: Toward a theory of settings. *Review of Educational Research, 60*, 517–529.

Garner, R., Alexander, P. A., Gillingham, M. G., Kulikowich, J. M., & Brown, R. (1991). Interest and learning from text. *American Educational Research Journal, 28*, 643–659.

Gibbs, G. (1990). *Improving student learning project briefing paper.* Oxford, UK: Oxford Centre for Staff Development, Oxford Polytechnic.

Graesser, A. C., & McMahen, C. L. (1993). Anomalous information triggers questions when adults solve quantitative problems and comprehend stories. *Journal of Educational Psychology, 85*, 136–141.

Hadwin, A. F., & Winne, P. H. (1996). Study strategies have meager support. *Journal of Higher Education, 67*, 692–715.

Hare, V., & Borchardt, K. M. (1984). Direct instruction of summarization skills. *Reading Research Quarterly, 21*, 62–78.

Harris, J. (1991, November). *Text annotation and underlining as metacognitive strategies to improve comprehension and retention of expository text.* Paper presented at the meeting of the National Reading Conference, Miami, FL.

Hattie, J., Biggs, H. J., & Purdie, N. (1996). Effects of learning skills interventions on student learning: A meta-analysis. *Review of Educational Research, 66*, 99–136.

Hidi, S. (1990). Interest and its contribution as a mental resource for learning. *Review of Educational Research, 60*, 549–571.

Hofer, B. K. (1998, April). *Personal epistemology in context: Student interpretations of instructional practice*. Paper presented at the annual meeting of the American Educational Research Association, San Diego.

Hofer, B. K., & Pintrich, P. (1997). The development of epistemological theories: Beliefs about knowledge and knowing and their relation to learning. *Review of Educational Research, 67*, 88–140.

Howe, M. J. A., & Singer, L. (1975). Presentation variables and students' activities in meaningful learning. *British Journal of Educational Psychology, 45*, 52–61.

Hynd, C. R., Simpson, M. L., & Chase, N. D. (1990). Studying narrative text: The effects of annotation vs. journal writing on test performance. *Reading Research and Instruction, 29*, 44–54.

Jenkins, J. J. (1978). Four points to remember: A tetrahedral model of memory experiments. In L. S. Cermak & F. I. M. Craik (Eds.), *Levels of processing and human memory* (pp. 425–445). Hillsdale, NJ: Lawrence Erlbaum Associates.

Kaspar, V., & Wood, E. (1993, April). *Academic achievement as a predictor of adolescent success in elaboration strategies*. Paper presented at the annual meeting of the American Educational Research Association, Atlanta, GA.

Kiewra, K. A. (1989). A review of note-taking: The encoding-storage paradigm and beyond. *Educational Psychology Review, 1*, 147–172.

Kiewra, K. A. (1994). The matrix representation system: Orientation, research, theory, and application. In J. Smart (Ed.), *Higher education: Handbook of theory and research* (pp. 331–373). New York: Agathon.

Kiewra, K. A., Benton, S. L., Kim, S. L., & Risch, N. (1995). Effects of note-taking format and study technique on recall and relational performance. *Contemporary Educational Psychology, 20*, 1995.

King, A. (1989). Effects of self-questioning training on college students' comprehension of lectures. *Contemporary Educational Psychology, 14*, 1–16.

King, A. (1990). Enhancing peer interaction and learning in the classroom through reciprocal questioning. *American Educational Research Journal, 27*, 664–687.

King, A. (1991). Improving lecture comprehension: Effects of a metacognitive strategy. *Applied Cognitive Psychology, 5*, 331–346.

King, A. (1992). Comparison of self-questioning, summarizing, and note taking review as strategies for learning from lectures. *American Educational Research Journal, 29*, 303–323.

King, A. (1995). Cognitive strategies for learning from direct teaching. In E. Wood, V. Woloshyn, & T. Willoughby (Eds.), *Cognitive strategy instruction for middle and high schools* (pp. 18–65). Cambridge, MA: Brookline Books.

King, A., & Rosenshine, B. (1993). Effects of guided cooperative questioning on children's knowledge construction. *Journal of Experimental Education, 61*, 127–148.

King, K. S., & Kitchener, P. M. (1994). *Developing reflective judgement*. San Francisco: Jossey-Bass.

Kitchener, P. M., King, K. S., Wood, P. K, & Davidson, M. L. (1989). Sequentially and consistency in the development of reflective judgement: A six-year longitudinal study. *Journal of Applied Psychology, 10*, 73–95.

Kuhn, D. (1991). *The skills of argument*. Cambridge, England: Cambridge University Press.

Lambiote, J. G., Dansereau, D. F., Cross, D. R., & Reynolds, S. B. (1989). Multirelational maps. *Educational Psychology Review, 1*, 331–367.

Lambiote, J. G., Peale, J., & Dansereau, D. F. (1992, April). *Knowledge maps as review devices: Like 'em or not*. Paper presented at the annual meeting of the American Educational Research Association, San Francisco.

Levin, J. R. (1986). Four cognitive principles of learning strategy instruction. *Educational Psychologist, 21*, 3–17.

Lipson, M. (1995). The effect of semantic mapping instruction on prose comprehension of below-level college readers. *Reading Research and Instruction, 34*, 367–378.

Maki, R. H., & Berry, S. L. (1984). Metacomprehension of text material. *Journal of Experimental Psychology: Learning, Memory, and Cognition, 10*, 663–697.

Marshall, N. (1989). Overcoming problems with incorrect prior knowledge: An instructional study. In S. McCormick & J. Zutell (Eds.), *Cognitive and social perspectives for literacy research and instruction: Thirty-ninth yearbook of the National Reading Conference* (pp. 323–330). Chicago: National Reading Conference.

Martin, D. C., & Arendale, D. (1994, February). *Review of research concerning the effectiveness of SI from the University of Missouri-Kansas City and other institutions across the United States*. Paper presented at the annual conference of the Freshmen Year Experience, Columbia, SC. (ERIC Document Reproduction Service No. ED 370 502).

Maxwell, M. (1997). *Improving student learning skills*. Clearwater, FL: H & H Publishing.

Mayer, R. E. (1988). Learning strategies: An overview. In C. E. Weinstein, E. T. Goetz, & P. A. Alexander (Eds.), *Learning and study strategies: Issues in assessment, instruction, and evaluation* (pp. 11–22). San Diego, CA: Academic Press.

Mayer, R. E. (1996). Learning strategies for making sense out of expository text: The SOI model for guiding three cognitive processes in knowledge construction. *Educational Psychology Review, 8*, 357–371.

McCagg, E. C., & Dansereau, D. F. (1991). A convergent paradigm for examining knowledge mapping as a learning strategy. *Journal of Educational Research, 84*, 317–324.

McCombs, B. L. (1994). Strategies for assessing and enhancing motivation: Keys to promoting self-regulated learning and performance. In H. F. O'Neil, Jr. & M. Drillings (Eds.), *Motivation: Theory and research* (pp. 49–69). Hillsdale, NJ: Lawrence Erlbaum Associates.

McKeachie, W. J, Pintrich, P. R., Smith, D.A., & Lin, Y. G. (1986). *Teaching and learning in the college classroom: A review of the research literature.* Ann Arbor, MI: National Center for Research to Improve Postsecondary Teaching and Learning.

McWhorter, J. Y. (1993). *The effects of postsecondary learning strategy use on performance.* Unpublished doctoral dissertation, University of Georgia, Athens.

Metcalf, J., & Shimamura, A. (1994). *Metacognition: Knowing about knowing.* Cambridge, MA: Bradford Books.

Meyer, B. J. F., & Rice, G. E. (1984). The structure of text. In P. D. Pearson (Ed.), *Handbook of reading research* (pp. 319–352). New York: Longman.

Mills, R. C. (1991). A new understanding of self: The role of affect, state of mind, self understanding, and intrinsic motivation. In B. L. McCombs (Ed.), Unraveling motivation: New perspectives from research and practice [Special issue]. *Journal of Experimental Education,* fall.

Nelson, T. O., & Narens, L. (1990). Metamemory: A theoretical framework and new findings. In G. H. Bower (Ed.), *The psychology of learning and motivation* (pp. 125–173). New York: Academic Press.

Nist, S. L., & Simpson, M. L. (1988). The effectiveness and efficiency of training college students to annotate and underline texts. In J. E. Readence & R. S. Baldwin (Eds.), *Dialogues in literacy research: Thirty-seventh yearbook of the National Reading Conference* (pp. 251–257). Chicago: National Reading Conference.

Nist, S. L., & Simpson, M. L. (1990). The effect of PLAE upon students' test performance and metacognitive awareness. In J. Zutell & S. McCormick (Eds.), *Literacy theory and research: Analyses from multiple paradigms: Thirty-ninth yearbook of the National Reading Conference* (pp. 321–328). Chicago: National Reading Conference.

Nist, S. L., Simpson, M. L., Olejnik, S., & Mealey, D. L. (1991). The relation between self-selected study processes and performance. *American Educational Research Journal, 28,* 849–874.

O'Donnell, A. M., & Dansereau, D. F. (1992). Scripted cooperation in student dyads: A method for analyzing and enhancing academic learning and performance. In R. Hertz-Lazarowitz & N. Miller (Eds.), *Interaction in cooperative groups: The theoretical anatomy of group learning* (pp. 120–141). New York: Cambridge University Press.

O'Donnell, A. M., & Dansereau, D. F. (1993). Learning from lectures: Effects of cooperative review. *Journal of Experimental Education, 6,* 116–125.

Pace, A. J., Marshall, N., Horowitz, R., Lipson, M. Y., & Lucido, P. (1989). When prior knowledge doesn't facilitate text comprehension: An examination of some of the issues. In S. McCormick & J. Zutell (Eds.), *Cognitive and social perspectives for literacy research and instruction: Thirty-eighth yearbook of the National Reading Conference* (pp. 213–224). Chicago: National Reading Conference.

Palincsar, A. S., & Brown, A. L. (1984). Reciprocal teaching of comprehension-fostering and monitoring activities. *Cognition and Instruction, 1,* 117–175.

Paris, S. G. (1988). Models and metaphors of learning strategies. In C. E. Weinstein, E. T. Goetz, & P. A. Alexander (Eds.), *Learning and study strategies: Issues in assessment, instruction, and evaluation* (pp. 299–321). San Diego, CA: Academic Press.

Paris, S. G., & Byrnes, J. P. (1989). The constructivist approach to self-regulation and learning in the classroom. In B. J. Zimmerman & D. H. Schunk (Eds.), *Self-regulated learning and academic achievement: Theory, research, and practice* (pp. 169–200). New York: Springer-Verlag.

Paris, S. G., & Turner, G. C. (1994). Situated motivation. In P. R. Pintrich, D. R. Brown, & C. E. Weinstein, (Eds.), *Student motivation, cognition, and learning* (pp. 213–238). Hillsdale, NJ: Lawrence Erlbaum Associates.

Paris, S. G., Lipson, M. Y., & Wixson, K. (1983). Becoming a strategic reader. *Contemporary Educational Psychology, 8,* 293–316.

Paris, S. G., Wasik, B. A., & Turner, J. C. (1991). The development of strategic readers. In R. Barr, M. L. Kamil, P. B. Mosenthal, & P. D. Pearson (Eds.), *Handbook of reading research* (Vol. II, pp. 609–640). New York: Longman.

Paris, S. G, Wasik, B. A., & van der Westhuizen, G. (1988). Meta-metacognition: A review of research on metacognition and reading. In J. R. Readence & R. S. Baldwin (Eds.), *Dialogues in literacy research: Thirty-seventh yearbook of the National Reading Conference* (pp. 143–166). Chicago: National Reading Conference.

Perkins, D. N., & Salomon, G. (1989). Are cognitive skills context-bound? *Educational Researchers, 18,* 16–25.

Perry, W. G. (1968). *Patterns of development in thought and values of students in a liberal arts college: A validation of a scheme.* Cambridge, MA: Harvard University. (ERIC Document Reproduction Service No. ED 024315)

Perry, W. G. (1970). *Forms of intellectual and ethical development in the college years: A scheme.* New York: Holt, Rinehart, & Winston.

Pintrich, P. R., & Garcia, T. (1991). Student goal orientation and self-regulation in the college classroom. In M. L. Maehr & P. R. Pintrich (Eds.), *Advances in motivation and achievement: Goals and self-regulatory processes* (Vol. 7, pp. 371–402). Greenwich, CT: JAI Press.

Pintrich, P. R., & Garcia, T. (1994). Self-regulated learning in college students: Knowledge, strategies and motivation. In P. R. Pintrich, D. R. Brown, & C. E. Weinstein (Eds.), *Student motivation, cognition, and learning* (pp. 113–133). Hillsdale, NJ: Lawrence Erlbaum Associates.

Pintrich, P. R., & Schrauben, B. (1992). Students' motivational beliefs and their cognitive engagement in classroom tasks. In D. H. Schunk & J. Meece (Eds.), *Student perceptions in the classroom: Causes and consequences* (pp. 149–183). Hillsdale, NJ: Lawrence Erlbaum Associates.

Pintrich, P. R., Smith, D. A., Garcia, T., & McKeachie, W. J. (1991). *A manual for the use of the Motivated Strategies for Learning Questionnaire (MSLQ).* Ann Arbor, MI: University of Michigan National Center for Research to Improve Postsecondary Teaching and Learning.

Pintrich, P. R., Smith, D. A., Garcia, T., & McKeachie, W. J. (1993). Reliability and predictive validity of the Motivation Strategies for Learning Questionnaire (MSLQ). *Educational and Psychological Measurement, 53,* 801–813.

Pressley, M. (1995). More about the development of self-regulation: Complex, long-term, and thoroughly social. *Educational Psychologist, 30,* 207–212.

Pressley, M., Harris, K. R., & Marks, M. B. (1992). But good strategy instructors are constructivists! *Educational Psychologist, 4,* 1–32.

Pressley, M., McDaniel, M. A., Turnure, J. E., Wood, E., & Ahmad, M. (1987). Generation and precision of elaboration: Effects on intentional and incidental learning. *Journal of Experimental Psychology: Learning, Memory, and Cognition, 13,* 291–300.

Pressley, M., Snyder, B. L., Levin, J. R., Murray, H. G., & Ghatala, E. S. (1987). Perceived readiness for examination performance (PREP) produced by initial reading of text and text containing adjunct questions. *Reading Research Quarterly, 22,* 219–236.

Pressley, M., Symons, S., McDaniel, M. A., Snyder, B. L., & Turnure, J. E. (1988). Elaborative interrogation facilitates acquisition of confusing facts. *Journal of Educational Psychology, 80,* 268–278.

Pressley, M., Yokoi, L., van Meter, P., Van Etten, S., & Freebern, G. (1997). Some of the reasons preparing for exams is so hard: What can be done to make it easier? *Educational Psychology Review, 9,* 1–38.

Rickards, J. P., & Friedman, F. (1978). The encoding versus external storage hypothesis in notetaking. *Contemporary Educational Psychology, 3,* 136–143.

Rosenshine, B., Meister, C., & Chapman, S. (1994). Reciprocal teaching: A review of the research. *Review of Educational Research, 64,* 479–530.

Ryan, M. P. (1984). Monitoring text comprehension: Individual differences in epistemological standards. *Journal of Educational Psychology, 76,* 248–258.

Schallert, D. L., Alexander, P. A., & Goetz, E. T. (1985). What do instructors and authors do to influence the textbook-student relationship? In J. A. Niles & R. V. Lalik (Eds.), *Issues in literacy: A research perspective: Thirty-fourth yearbook of the National Reading Conference* (pp. 110–115). New York: National Reading Conference.

Schallert, D. L., Meyer, D. K., & Fowler, L. A. (1995). The nature of engagement when reading in and out of one's discipline. In K. A. Hinchman, D. J. Leu, & C. K. Kinzer (Eds.), *Perspectives on literacy research and practice: Forty-fourth yearbook of the National Reading Conference* (pp. 119–125). Chicago: National Reading Conference.

Schellings, G. L. M., Van Hout-Wolters, B. H. A. M., & Vermunt, J. D. (1996a). Individual differences in adapting to three different tasks of selecting information from texts. *Contemporary Educational Psychology, 21,* 423–446.

Schellings, G. L. M., Van Hout-Wolters, B. H. A. M., & Vermunt, J. D. (1996b). Selection of main points in instructional texts: Influences of task demands. *Journal of Literacy Research, 28,* 355–378.

Schoenfeld, A. H. (1988). When good teaching leads to bad results: The disasters of "well-taught" mathematics courses. *Educational Psychologist, 23,* 498–504.

Schommer, M. (1990). Effects of beliefs about the nature of knowledge on comprehension. *Journal of Educational Psychology, 85,* 498–504.

Schommer, M. (1993). Comparisons of beliefs about the nature of knowledge and learning among post-secondary students. *Research in Higher Education, 43,* 355–370.

Schommer, M. (1994). An emerging conceptualization of epistemological beliefs and their role in learning. In R. Garner & P. A. Alexander (Eds.), *Beliefs about text and instruction with text* (pp. 25–40). Hillsdale, NJ: Lawrence Erlbaum Associates.

Schommer, M., Calvert, C., Gariglietti, G., & Bajaj, A. (1997). The development of epistemological beliefs among secondary students: A longitudinal study. *Journal of Educational Psychology, 89,* 37–40.

Schommer, M., & Hutter, R. (1995, April). *Epistemological beliefs and thinking about everyday controversial issues.* Paper presented at the annual meeting of the American Educational Research Association, San Francisco.

Schommer, M., & Walker, K. (1995). Are epistemological beliefs similar across domains? *Journal of Educational Psychology, 87,* 424–432.

Schunk, D. H., & Swartz, C. W. (1991, April). *Process goals and feedback: Effects on children's self-efficacy and skills.* Paper presented at the annual meeting of the American Educational Research Association, Chicago.

Shenkman, H., & Cukras, G. (1986). Effects of a metacognitive study training program on underprepared college students. In J. A. Niles & R. V. Lalik (Eds.), *Solving problems in literacy: Learners, teachers, and researchers: Thirty-fifth yearbook of the National Reading Conference* (pp. 222–226). Chicago: National Reading Conference.

Simpson, M. L., Hynd, C. R., Nist, S. L., & Burrell, K. I. (1997). College academic assistance programs and practices. *Educational Psychology Review, 9*, 39–87.

Simpson, M. L., & Nist, S. L. (1997). Perspectives on learning history: A case study. *Journal of Literacy Research, 29*, 363–395.

Simpson, M. L., Nist, S. L., & Sharman, S. J. (1997, December). *"I think the big trick of history is": A case study of self-regulated learning.* Paper presented at the annual meeting of the National Reading Conference, Scottsdale, AZ.

Simpson, M. L., Olejnik, S., Tam, A. Y., & Supattathum S. (1994). Elaborative verbal rehearsals and college students' cognitive performance. *Journal of Educational Psychology, 86*, 267–278.

Spires, H. A., & Donley, J. (1998). Prior knowledge activation: Inducing engagement with informational texts. *Journal of Educational Psychology, 90*, 249–260.

Stanovich, K. (1986). Matthew effects in reading: Some consequences of individual differences in the acquisition of literacy. *Reading Research Quarterly, 21*, 360–407

Strode, S. L. (1991). Teaching annotation writing to college students. *Forum for Reaching, 23*, 33–44.

Thiede, K. W., & Dunlosky, J. (1994). Delaying students' metacognitive monitoring improves their accuracy in predicting their recognition performance. *Journal of Educational Psychology, 86*, 290–302.

Thomas, J. W., Bol, L., & Warkentin, R. W. (1991). Antecedents of college students' study deficiencies: The relationship between course features and students' study activities. *Higher Education, 22*, 275–296.

Thomas, J. W., & Rohwer, W. D. (1986). Academic studying: The role of learning strategies. *Educational Psychologist, 21*, 19–41.

Thomas, J. W., & Rohwer, W. D. (1987). Grade-level and course-specific differences in academic studying: Summary. *Contemporary Educational Psychology, 12*, 381–385.

van Meter, P., Yokoi, L., & Pressley, M. (1994). College students' theory of note-taking derived from their perceptions of note-taking. *Journal of Educational Psychology, 86*, 323–338.

Voss, J. F., & Silfies, L. N. (1996). Learning from history text: The interaction of knowledge and comprehension skill with text structure. *Cognition and Instruction, 14*, 45–68.

Weinstein, C. E. (1994). Strategic learning/strategic teaching: Flip sides of a coin. In P. R. Pintrich, D. R. Brown, & C. E. Weinstein (Eds.), *Student motivation, cognition, and learning* (pp. 257–273). Hillsdale, NJ: Lawrence Erlbaum Associates.

Weinstein, C. E., Dierking, D., Husman, J., Roska. L. & Powdril, L. (1998). The impact of a course in strategic learning on the long-term retention of college students [Monograph]. *Developmental Education: Preparing successful college students, 24*, 85–96.

Weinstein, C. E., & Mayer, R. F. (1986). The teaching of learning strategies. In M. C. Wittrock (Ed.), *Handbook of research on teaching* (pp. 315–327). New York: Macmillan.

Weinstein, C. E., Palmer, D. R., & Schulte, A. C. (1987). *Learning and Study Strategies Inventory.* Clearwater, FL: H & H Publishing.

Wineburg, S. (1991). On the reading of historical texts: Notes on the breach between school and academy. *American Educational Research Journal, 28*, 495–519.

Winne, P. H. (1995). Inherent details in self-regulated learning. *Educational Psychologist, 30*, 173–187.

Winne, P. H. (1996). A metacognitive view of individual differences in self-regulated learning. *Learning and Individual Differences, 8*, 327–353.

Winograd, P., & Hare, V. C. (1988). Direct instruction of reading comprehension strategies: The nature of teacher explanation. In C. E. Weinstein, E. T. Goetz, & P. A. Alexander (Eds.), *Learning and study strategies* (pp. 121–140). San Diego, CA: Academic Press.

Wittrock, M. C. (1990). Generative processes of comprehension. *Educational Psychologist, 24*, 345–376.

Woloshyn, V. E., Willoughby, T., Wood, E., & Pressley, M. (1990). Elaborative interrogation facilitates adult learning of factual paragraphs. *Journal of Educational Psychology, 82*, 513–524.

Woodward, A. (1993). Introduction: Learning from textbooks. In B. K. Britton, A. Woodward, & M. Binkley (Eds.), *Learning from textbooks* (pp. vii–x). Hillsdale, NJ: Lawrence Erlbaum Associates.

CHAPTER 36

Re-Mediating Reading Difficulties: Appraising the Past, Reconciling the Present, Constructing the Future

Laura Klenk
Michael W. Kibby
University at Buffalo

A small but significant portion of otherwise normal American children encounter major difficulties in learning to read when provided regular classroom reading instruction. These children (heretofore called "remedial readers") and the special intervention programs designed to help them become better readers (heretofore called "remedial reading") are the dual foci of this chapter. We offer a caveat, however: The fact that there exists a sizable number of children who have reading difficulties need not be interpreted as a negative reflection on the overall status of reading ability of American students. It is an irrefutable fact that children in Grades K–8 today read as well or better than children at any other time in the history of the United States (Berliner & Biddle, 1995; Farr, Fay, Myers, & Ginsberg, 1987; Kibby, 1993, 1995a, b). Even in the last 30 years—and in spite of the surfeit of negativity in the media—reading achievement has improved significantly for 9- and 13-year olds (Campbell, Voekl, & Donahue, 1997). Further, although some studies find that the achievement of high school students since 1963 has not increased—indeed, has decreased slightly (Gates & MacGinitie, 1978; MacGinitie & MacGinitie, 1989)—the general conclusion from the NAEP data (Campbell et al., 1997) and an analysis of changes in median scores on the nation's major reading achievement tests (Linn, Graue, & Sanders, 1990) is that, even at the high school level, reading ability has increased during this era.

Added to the fact that children read as well or better today than at any other time in the history of the United States is the fact that American children today score more than a full standard deviation above the scores of children in 1932 on individually administered IQ tests (Flynn, 1984a, 1984b, 1987). By analysis of restandardization data, Flynn found that the scores on 1930s/1940s IQ tests (Stanford-Binet and WISC) by

1970s/1980s students were 15–22 points higher than the actual scores on these tests by 1930s/1940s students. Further, in the International Education Association (Elley, 1992) comparison of reading tests scores of 9-year-old students from 27 countries, Americans had the second highest scores, exceeded by only Finland; in the comparison of 15-year-olds from 31 countries, American students tied for fifth place with 6 other countries, exceeded by Finland, France, Sweden, and New Zealand. In terms of reading and knowledge acquisition, American schools are doing something right (although it is rare that one ever hears of such in the media). In spite of these and many other successes, there remains a segment of the population of school children who struggle to learn to read in their first years of school; in addition, there are those who, after years of classroom reading instruction, have not learned to read at a level that is thought appropriate for their other abilities, age, or grade. We now turn our attention toward these students and the remedial programs to which they are often assigned.

The field of remedial reading is rooted in noble social intentions, yet mired in theoretical and practical contentions. Despite advances in our understanding of the developmental process of literacy acquisition, we are besieged in the professional and lay community with arguments over what counts as legitimate research and appropriate remedial instruction. Some of these arguments are steeped in political rhetoric rather than scholarly or pedagogical logic. Repeated calls for an end to the "reading wars" not withstanding (Kameenui, 1993; Matson, 1996; Spiegel, 1992; Stanovich, 1990), we continue to labor under widespread mistrust and popular misconceptions that are fueled, in part, by partisan rhetoric and our own history of limited success in remediating reading difficulties. In fact, the field of remedial reading long has been fertile ground for questionable "remedies" that have coexisted alongside an honorable tradition of research and practice. In this chapter we celebrate past achievements and recognize past failures, we confront current controversies, and, hopefully, we encourage momentum for a dynamic future. We begin with an historical review of research and practice in remedial reading, followed by a discussion of current trends and controversies.

APPRAISING THE PAST: A HISTORICAL PERSPECTIVE ON REMEDIAL READING

Today, it is generally accepted that most children who struggle to read do not require instruction that is substantially different from their more successful peers; rather, they require a greater intensity of "high-quality instruction" (Snow, Burns, & Griffin, 1998). But the trail of theory and practice in reading intervention programs has, at times, sharply diverged from theory and practice in general developmental reading. In this review, we characterize these points of divergence as "non-print based," describing "remedies" for reading difficulties from such diverse professions as optometry, neurology, pharmacology, and occupational therapy. "Print-based" responses are usually, but not always, those that have more closely paralleled the mainstream, whether from behaviorist, cognitive, or social-constructivist perspectives of learning.

Hypotheses About the Causes of Reading Disability

Perhaps the most unfortunate component of the conceptualization of children who have difficulty learning to read—seemingly from the very first notice of reading difficulties (Morgan, 1896)—was the assumption that something must be wrong with children if they do not learn to read—something other than not learning to read, that is. Morgan, a British ophthalmologist, used the term *congenital word blindness* to describe a 14-year-old boy with apparently average intellect who had failed to learn to read.

Fisher (1905) and Hinshelwood (1917) also used this term. The use of intelligence tests in public education may have had a major role in drawing attention to reading problems and to searching out their cause. In the late 1920s, after the publication of group intelligent tests and the individually administered Stanford-Binet Intelligence Test, it became increasingly obvious that most children who were failing in reading had intellectual abilities that far surpassed their reading abilities, many having above-average IQ scores. A major research focus of the second quarter of the century was attempting to delineate the cause (or causes) of reading difficulties. This is known as the *medical model* of reading diagnosis. Among the major variables studied were visual acuity, auditory acuity, general physical status, neurological factors, emotional/psychiatric factors, and intelligence. Particularly noteworthy from this era are the comprehensive studies of groups of disabled readers by Marion Monroe (1932) and Helen M. Robinson at the University of Chicago (1946). Robinson's study included a review of extant research on each of the hypothesized causes of reading difficulty and an exhaustive evaluation of 30 children with severe reading problems by a team of physicians (e.g., pediatricians, otologists, ophthalmologists, psychiatrists, neurologists), clinical/school psychologists, social workers, and teachers. These and other smaller scale studies gave little support for attributing reading difficulties to any single cause, even for a given child. By the middle of the 20th century, it was obvious from 30 years of accumulated research that the medical model of reading diagnosis—to search for the cause of the reading difficulty—was no longer a valid line of research. It was at this time that reading diagnosis took a major turn (Pelosi, 1977), and moved from the medical model to the intensive instructional intervention model of "a process of gaining a thorough knowledge of a person's reading performance, strategies, skills, and instructional needs through accurate observations for the purpose of modifying instruction" (Kibby, 1995c, p. 2).

Not all research on the causes of reading difficulty disappeared in the 1940s and 1950s, however, most especially in special education. Research on the neurological or perceptual bases of reading disability was prevalent during this era. Orton continued his research on the role of hemispheric dominance in reading difficulties, and his theories were transformed by Gillingham and Stillman (1960) into the Orton–Gillingham method of teaching phonics (a method still widely in use). At the same time, Heinz Werner and Alfred Strauss, both having fled Nazi Germany in the late 1930s, were working at the Wayne County Training School in Detroit, MI, with children known to have brain injury or brain disease. It was during this time that children who did not actually have a history of brain trauma or brain disease, but who shared some of the symptoms of brain-damaged children (called "soft signs"), came to be referred to as *minimally brain dysfunctioned* or *minimally brain damaged* (MBD). Soft signs included difficulties in perception, distractibility, and emotional lability, in addition to difficulties in reading and spelling.

At the same time the concept of MBD was taking hold, three men with new PhD degrees in psychology or special education went to Detroit to study with Werner and Strauss: William M. Cruickshank, Newell C. Kephart, and Samuel A. Kirk. Each became a founding father of learning disabilities (Hallahan & Cruickshank, 1973; Kavale & Forness, 1985; Weiderholt, 1974). In this era, the major domains of special education (besides physical handicaps) were mental retardation and emotional disturbance; thus, parents of children diagnosed as MBD not only had to reconcile themselves to the harshness of this label, but also found their child's difficulties often confused with mental retardation and emotional disturbance. In 1963, at a meeting of parents of MBD children in Chicago, Sam Kirk coined the term *learning disabled* to describe children of normal (or higher) intellectual abilities who failed to learn to read in spite of seemingly adequate classroom developmental reading programs and individual remedial reading instruction.

Effects of Labeling and Blaming

By the late 1960s, the term MBD had mostly disappeared and terms such as *learning disability* or *learning adjustment* were gaining wider use. The neurological attributions (stemming back to the work of Werner and Strauss) remained, however, even if no tests existed to measure or validate these neurological problems (Cruickshank, 1979). Regardless of the terms used, educators and psychologists have exerted a subtle, unique, and probably unintended effect of blaming the child for reading or learning problems through the process of labeling (e.g., attention-deficit syndrome, perceptually handicapped) and classification for special education programs (e.g., learning disabled). Indeed, P.L. 90-142, the 1975 federal legislation originally mandating instruction for children with handicapping conditions in the least restrictive environment, defined learning disability as:

> a disorder in one or more of the basic psychological processes involved in understanding or in using language, spoken or written, which disorder may manifest itself in imperfect ability to listen, think, speak, read, write, spell, or to do mathematical calculations.

Note that the child does not simply have difficulty reading but is afflicted with a "basic psychological" processing "disorder," which in turn causes the reading problem. Such reasoning follows logically from the medical model.

In medical diagnoses, physicians do search for causes, but reading clinicians do not search for causes in their reading diagnoses (Gil, Hoffmyer, VanRokel, & Weinshank, 1979; Gil, Vinsonhaler, & Sherman, 1979; Gil, Vinsonhaler, & Wagner, 1979; Gil, Wagner, & Vinsonhaler, 1979; Vinsonhaler, 1979). In these studies, both physicians and reading clinicians were observed as they conducted diagnoses. Although both groups conceptualized diagnosis as a problem-solving process, the researchers found that the diagnostic process in medicine differs significantly from that in reading. First, medical diagnoses generally concentrate only on the problems presented by the patient, but reading diagnoses account for both a reader's strengths and problems. Second, in medical diagnoses, causal statements about problems are the rule; in reading diagnoses, statements about the cause of a reading problem are rare. Third, deductive thinking predominates in medical diagnoses, whereas inductive thinking predominates in reading diagnoses.

When applied to reading diagnosis, the logic of the medical model becomes twisted. Instead of saying, "Here is a child and that child has difficulty reading," we now say, "Here is a learning disabled child." We have moved from stating one aspect of a child with no attributions at all, to labeling and identifying the whole of the child by just one attribute: that is, the unspecified— indeed, unknown—internal attributes of the child that are to be blamed for his or her learning difficulties.

The influence of this line of thinking on special educators remains today and is manifested in the vast gulf between reading educators and some special educators in conceptualizing reading difficulties. Today's well-informed reading educators view reading difficulty as having no precise etiology and consider that the only avenue to a possible correction of this reading difficulty is a print-based reading instruction program. Learning disability, however, is viewed by special educators as a perceptual or neurological disability that requires extraordinary forms of instruction, including development of perceptual abilities. Applied to reading difficulties, this perspective was the foundation for many non-print-based remedial reading methods.

NON-PRINT-BASED METHODS

Perceptual Training and Perceptual-Based Programs

There is little question that learning to read words is largely a cognitive-perceptual task, a process of learning to recognize words by their visually distinctive or distinguishing characteristics (Ehri, 1994; Gibson, 1965; Gibson & Levin, 1975). There is also little question that difficulty in learning to read is rarely the result of visual-spatial perceptual or perceptual-motor deficits (Vellutino, 1979). In spite of the fact that issues related to perceptual handicaps should have been dismissed from consideration by classroom and reading teachers more than a quarter of a century ago, these persist.

In a survey of classroom and specialist teachers' beliefs about perception and reading, Allington (1987) found that 40% of the classroom and specialist teachers believed that "visual perceptual handicaps are the most prevalent cause of reading disability"; 52% believed that reversing such words as *was* or *on* are indicators of "disturbed visual perceptual processes"; and 49% believed children with learning or reading disabilities who "have a strength in the visual modality learn most effectively when reading instruction focuses on the visual aspects of words." A greater proportion of classroom teachers held these beliefs than specialist teachers, but far too many specialists still persist in believing that perceptual abilities are the root of reading problems. In addition, perception continues to play a role in school psychological evaluations, a common outcome of which is to place children into one of two programs: those that provide no print-based instruction but, instead, focus on developing visual-perceptual or visual-motor skills; or modality matching programs that emphasize only one mode of instruction (such as phonics for children who are thought to have limited visual-perceptual skills or whole-word methods for children who are thought to have limited auditory skills).

The validity of perceptual training programs as a method of improving reading has long been debunked (Balow, 1971/1996; Coles, 1978; Kavale, 1982, 1984; Perfetti, 1985; Vellutino, 1977, 1979, 1987; Vellutino & Scanlon, 1987). The conclusion from decades of research on this topic is abundantly clear: Perceptual training programs, although perhaps increasing perceptual ability, have no substantive affect on reading ability. Similarly, modality matching has not been supported by research. On tests of visual and auditory perception, Robinson (1972) found that only 11% of nearly 550 first graders demonstrated mixed modalities (high visual/low auditory [HV/LA] or low visual/high auditory [LV/HA]). Further, when taught by a phonic program, both groups learned equally well; and when taught by a whole-word program, both groups learned equally well. Robinson's data lent no support to the hypothesis that children who have higher performance in one modality (visual or auditory) than the other learn best when taught by a teaching method thought to match the preferred modality. Indeed, both the HV/LA and LV/HA groups in Robinson's study were reading at an average level at the end of Grade 1 and at the end of Grade 3. The children with far-below-average reading scores in both grades were the children who had low scores on both the visual and auditory perceptual tests.

Visual perceptual training with nonprint stimuli and modality matching have utterly failed in study after study; there is no room in remedial reading for these totally debunked notions of perceptual deficit, perceptual training, or modality matching. Reading instruction for children who have difficulty reading must be print based (Gibson, 1965; Gibson & Levin, 1975)—there is no other way.

Effects of Ritalin on Reading Achievement

A more recent nonprint intervention that has gained wide acceptance amongst teachers, parents, psychologists, and physicians is the use of pharmacological remedies—particularly methylphenidate, a stimulant commonly known as *Ritalin*. Based on information from the Drug Enforcement Administration, several state departments of health, and national prescription audits, Safer, Zito, and Fine (1996) estimated that 1.4 million children from 5 to 18 years old currently receive pharmacological treatment for problems of behavior, attention, and learning. Methylphenidate (Ritalin) is the drug most often prescribed for this purpose (Stoner, Carey, Ikeda, & Shinn, 1994).

Although the literature includes numerous studies on the effects of methylphenidate on reading achievement, most of these are limited due to: (a) small numbers of participants; (b) inadequate (if any) descriptions of the reading instruction received by participants; (c) reliance on teacher and/or parent reports rather than direct evidence of achievement; (d) reliance on indicators of the quantity of work completed (i.e., the number of worksheets or problems completed), rather than on the quality of the work; (e) too brief interventions (less than 1 month); (f) lack of attention to dosage levels administered to participants; and (g) high levels of comorbidity with attention and conduct disorders.

At this time, no reliable evidence can be found to indicate that Ritalin is effective in ameliorating reading difficulties apart from concurrent, effective reading instruction. At best, Ritalin may allow some children to become more sensitive to behavioral management, thus leading to higher levels of participation in academic tasks, including reading (Ajibola & Clement, 1995; Forness, Swanson, Cantwell, Youpa, & Hanna, 1992; Stoner et al., 1994). Concerns persist regarding overreliance on Ritalin as an educational intervention due to the potential for numerous side effects (Safer et al., 1996). However, as long as reading difficulties are perceived to be inherent within the child, non-print-based interventions (including Ritalin) will likely remain popular options for many educators and parents.

Print-Based Instruction: A Review of Fluency Research

A hallmark of children who have difficulty in reading is a lack of fluency. Fluency is reading smoothly, without hesitation, and with comprehension (Harris & Hodges, 1995). In fluent oral reading, word recognition is also mostly accurate. LaBerge and Samuels' (1974) term *automaticity* is the same as fluency. The improvement of reading fluency is considered a major goal, if not the major goal, of programs of intensive intervention in reading. Allington (1983) was an early advocate of fluency instruction as part of both developmental and intensive intervention reading programs, and Samuels (1979) is often credited as the first person to conduct research on the validity of repeated readings to facilitate reading fluency. Clay (1979, 1993b) built repeated readings into her Reading Recovery methods as a means of developing reading fluency, and these remain a key component of Reading Recovery.

Today, methods of developing fluency, especially in primary grades and in intensive reading intervention programs, usually conjoin two major components: teacher modeling of the text that the student will be reading, and repeated readings. Teacher modeling is when the teacher reads a text aloud to a student(s) as that student follows along in the reading, and then the student reads the text several times. Modeling may or may not be done with finger-pointing of each word or group of words as they are read. Repeated readings is when a student reads the same text repeatedly, time after time, until the rate of reading, comprehension, or errors while reading (or all three) reach a specific criterion. This repeated reading is almost always aided: that is, the teacher assists the child during the reading when needed (see Clay, 1993b). Teacher modeling and repeated readings are sometimes conjoined with direct teaching of difficult words (sight vocabulary) in the text to be read (Arya, Kutno, & Kibby, 1995).

The theory underlying fluency is that while reading, a reader has only so much attention to focus on meaning. If part of that attention is diverted from comprehension and understanding, the result is limited reading fluency and comprehension (LaBerge & Samuels, 1974). Beginning readers and children with reading difficulties who have not experienced processing words and meaning automatically and fluently will find it more difficult to: (a) monitor their reading; (b) comprehend the text; and (c) perhaps most important, know how it sounds and feels to read text fluently. Teacher modeling and guided repeated readings are designed to help such students to gain each of these abilities.

Working with second graders, Dowhower (1987) found that oral reading rate, accuracy, and comprehension improved significantly with repeated reading practice. Similar positive results have been found for first graders (Simons, 1992; Turpie & Paratore, 1994; Young, Bowers, & MacKinnon, 1996;); for second and third graders (Richek & McTague, 1988; Stahl, 1994); and for children who have reading difficulties (Homan et al., 1993; Koskinen & Blum, 1986; Rashotte & Torgesen, 1985; Rasinski, 1990; Weinstein & Cooke, 1992; Young et al., 1996). Although there is only a modest research base on teacher modeling, studies by Maxson (1996), Rasinski (1990), and Young et al. (1996) found that it facilitates oral reading accuracy, fluency, and comprehension.

Summary

What has become clear as we near the end of a century is that, given adequate social and cognitive assistance, children learn to read through engagement in a variety of age-appropriate and developmentally appropriate print-related activities. These activities may focus the learner's attention on one or more specific facets of reading including: print concepts such as alphabet recognition (Walsh, Price, & Gillingham, 1988); metalinguistic awareness (Clay, 1979); phonemic awareness (Adams, 1990; Adams, Treiman, & Pressley, 1998); assisted reading for fluency or comprehension (Fountas & Pinnell, 1996; Palincsar & Brown, 1984); assisted writing (Englert, Raphael, Fear, & Anderson, 1988; Graham & Harris, 1989); and explicit "word study" consisting of phonics, sight vocabulary, and spelling instruction (Bear, Invernezzi, Templeton, & Johnston, 1996). Although vociferous arguments persist as to the balance and particular focus of these activities, there is little, if any, justification for remedial reading methods that assume an unknown cause or that proceed from non-print-based methods.

RECONCILING THE PRESENT: CURRENT ISSUES AND TRENDS IN REMEDIAL READING

Several trends and issues have dominated remedial reading during the past decade. First is the current emphasis on the prevention of reading difficulties through early intervention, in contrast to the more typical practice of providing remedial services to children after they have demonstrated considerable difficulty and even failure (Snow et al., 1998). To this end, elementary teachers—particularly in the primary grades—are being held to greater accountability for the results of reading instruction provided within general classrooms. Another trend is the call by many scholars and practitioners for "balanced instruction," a term that defies common understanding (Freppon & Dahl, 1998) Although, in a popular sense, it has come to mean that both "wholistic" and "skill-based" instruction have value for struggling readers. A third trend is noted in a more expansive view of remedial reading in which writing and thinking skills are recognized as crucial elements of remedial instruction. For example, writing (including the use of "invented" or "functional" spellings by young children) has become an important component of many early intervention programs (Hiebert & Taylor, 1994).

Other significant trends in remedial reading can be traced to the influence of Marie Clay's (1979) early intervention known as Reading Recovery. Conceptually, Clay's work has popularized the notion of accelerating reading development in young children in order to prevent failure. In addition, success in Reading Recovery is defined as reading at grade level. For a field in which discussions of success—let alone a consensus on the definition of success—have been conspicuously absent, this conception is bold. On a practical level, Reading Recovery has legitimized the tutorial model of remedial instruction in contrast to the drill-and-skill models of the past. Finally, Reading Recovery has revived interest in the legitimacy of the one-to-one model of remedial instruction taught by highly trained experienced teachers. This revival comes at a time when fiscal constraints have led to increasing use of small-group and whole-class models of remedial instruction and an increasing reliance on nonprofessionals to staff remedial programs.

Recent research on the role of phonemic awareness in early reading has received intense publicity, if not public scrutiny. In particular, numerous studies sponsored by the National Institute of Child Health and Human Development (NICHD) have been cited frequently in the popular press and by policymakers as providing definitive support for explicit instruction in phonics and the alphabetic principle. Lovett et al. (1994) and Foorman, Francis, Fletcher, Schatschneider, and Mehta (1998), among others, report consistent results for the positive effects of phonemic awareness and phonics training on measures of isolated word recognition, pseudo-word decoding, and word- or sentence-level comprehension. Critics of this research claim that the results are exaggerated and misleading, and that they are frequently misinterpreted to promote a specific instructional and/or political agenda. Allington and Woodside-Jiron (1997) pointed out that measures of fluency, reading rate, and comprehension of extended text are missing in this work. Moreover, the NICHD studies lack specificity regarding the general classroom instruction provided to the children in these interventions, attributing gains solely to the experimental conditions. The extent to which these studies will be used to shape legislative initiatives for early literacy is a cause of concern for many reading researchers.

Other perennial controversies swirling around the field are centered on questions such as: Who should provide remedial services? Where should these services be situated? What are the most appropriate and efficacious remedial methods for children with reading difficulties? Particularly onerous is the present tension over what counts as legitimate research (and, therefore, practice) in remedial reading. Some of these tensions are played out as turf wars across professional organizations in reading and special education, and others are reflected in a decade of federal funding and initiatives for improving remedial reading.

Title I Remedial Reading

Funds for compensatory education in reading were first allocated by the federal government in 1966 through Title I of the Elementary and Secondary Education Act (ESEA), for the explicit purpose of improving the instructional opportunities and outcomes in schools serving populations with high concentrations of poverty. Approximately half of all Title I funds are distributed as basic, concentration, and targeted grants to local education agencies (LEAs). The budget for grants to LEAs has grown from less than $1 billion in 1966 to $7.3 billion in 1998; however, when adjusted to 1988 dollars, the current figure for 1998 is $5.48 billion (Office of Compensatory Education Programs, December 1997). In 1996, nearly 13.5% (3,618,859) of elementary school children and 5.6% (774,564) of secondary students in the United States received remedial reading services (Digest of Education Statistics, 1996). In addition, it is estimated that 80% (1,864,650) of K–12 students receiving services for specific learning disabilities have reading problems for which they receive services through special education (U.S. Department of Education, 1996), or from a combination of Title I and special education programs. These figures do not reflect children who receive remedial reading instruction in schools that do not qualify for Title I funding.

Effectiveness of Remedial Services

Because Title I (known from 1981 to 1994 as Chapter 1) is a funding mechanism rather than a remedial program per se, evaluation of Title I programs has proven difficult. Funds are distributed to states, then redistributed to LEAs where they are applied with wide variation. Due to the lack of adequate control groups and dissimilar (and questionable) procedures employed in local and state program evaluations, large-scale evaluations are limited (Borman & D'Agostino, 1996). However, reports throughout the past 20 years have concluded that, although students served in Title I programs may demonstrate higher achievement than nonparticipating peers, these students fail to achieve or maintain levels of success comparable to their mainstream peers (Kennedy, Birman, & Demaline, 1986; Puma et al., 1997). A meta-analysis of 17 evaluation studies by Borman & D'Agostino (1996) confirmed this finding, citing a modest trend for improved effectiveness over time, due, in part, to increased funding, greater awareness of students' needs, and increasing flexibility in the use of Title I funds.

Several explanations for the limited success of Title I programs have been offered (McGill-Franzen, 1994). First, typical instruction in these programs has been characterized as both *limited* in emphasis and *limiting* to recipients. With a predominant focus on repetitive practice of low-level, rigidly sequenced skills, typical remedial instruction is neither challenging, authentic, nor contextualized to students' lives beyond the remedial classroom (Allington, 1991; Knapp, 1995; Means & Knapp, 1991; Millsap, Moss, & Gamse, 1993). Students in such programs are considered to be further disadvantaged by the lack of access to instruction in higher order cognitive skills. Simultaneously, the lack of challenge and/or success leads to diminished motivation.

Observational studies point to a second explanation for the limited success of remedial programs: incongruence between the theoretical, philosophical, and instructional basis of general and remedial classrooms (Allington, 1994; Glynn, Bethune, Crooks, Ballard, & Smith, 1992). This lack of congruence, it is argued, leads to confusion and further difficulties for students who are already struggling to learn to read. Adding support to these observations, Tancock's (1995) interviews of 27 classroom teachers and 3 reading specialists revealed that the two groups of teachers differed on instructional matters and in their philosophies of remediation, as well as in their overall perceptions of remedial programs. These teachers lacked common planning times and other opportunities for communication that might have lead to greater congruence among programs. D'Agostino (1996) observed reading instruction in 52 self-contained Title I classes serving children in Grade 3. These students did not receive reading instruction in any other setting. Observers in this study documented instances in which children were engaged in "authentic instruction," as evidenced by: (a) engagement in higher order thinking skills, such as making inferences or predictions, developing opinions, and building concepts; (b) coherence of instruction, characterized by the depth of concept coverage, and the extent to which topics were interrelated through sequencing and structuring; (c) direct connections to students' prior and current life experiences; (d) amount of substantive dialogue and conversation; and (e) level of social support provided by the teacher and student engagement. D'Agostino reported that two of the most crucial principles of authentic instruction—higher order skills and connections to personal experience—were rarely observed in these classrooms.

Bean, Cooley, Eichelberger, Lazar, and Zigmond (1991) summarized the major concerns regarding pull-out programs. In addition to the lack of congruence between remedial and general education teachers, these authors pointed to lost instructional time in the transition between the classroom and the remedial setting and the negative consequences of labeling students as learning or reading disabled. These consequences involve lowered expectations on the part of remedial and special education teachers, which too often lead to the impoverished instruction noted earlier. In perhaps the strongest critique of remedial reading programs to date, Allington (1994) asserted that the now fully institutionalized, entrenched "second tier" system of compensatory and special education has failed in its promise to lift at-risk students out of school failure. Allington called for dramatic improvements in the "first tier" (general education) programs to circumvent many of the difficulties encountered by children in their early experiences with literacy instruction.

One antidote to pull-out programs has been inclusion, or "pull-in" programs, in which children with reading difficulties remain in their general education classrooms for whole-class instruction. Schumm, Moody, and Vaughn (1996) observed reading instruction in 29 third-grade classrooms in which struggling readers (including those identified as learning disabled) made little or no progress in reading. Similar results were reported for LD students in general education classrooms in which whole-class instruction, with no modifications for individual differences, was the norm (Klingner, Vaughn, Schumm, Hughes, & Elbaum, 1997; Schumm, Vaughn, Haager, & Klingner, 1994; Zigmond et al., 1995). In contrast, Cunningham, Hall, and Defee (1998) reported high rates of success for low-achieving first- and second-grade students given whole class instruction that is structured around four intensive, theme-related "blocks" or instructional activities, including guided reading, word study, writing, and self-selected reading. Additional support is given to struggling readers in these classrooms through flexible, heterogeneous, small-group activities similar to the four blocks.

The failure of struggling readers in some general education classes is attributed to the lack of specific, systematic skills instructions, and a lack of teacher guidance in basal reader manuals for individualizing instruction (Schumm et al., 1994; Vaughn, Moody, & Schumm, 1998). However, based on the Cunningham et al. (1998) report, whole-class or "pull-in" reading instruction can be effective in preventing and ameliorating reading difficulties, given appropriate support and sufficient opportunities for engagement in a variety of print-based activities.

Federally Funded Initiatives

Several major legislative initiatives been enacted since the late 1980s with the purpose of improving Title I services. The Hawkins-Stafford Amendments of 1988 revised the purpose of Chapter 1 by requiring instruction in basic and advanced skills in all funded programs. More recent federal initiatives, including the 1994 reauthorization of the ESEA as the Improving America's Schools Act (IASA), have continued to stress this requirement: "The new Title I has one overriding goal: to improve the teaching and learning of children in high-poverty schools to enable them to meet challenging academic content and performance standards" (Fowler, 1995). The authors of the IASA also addressed the issues raised by critics of pull-out remedial programs. A major emphasis of this initiative was to "promote instruction through an enhanced and accelerated curriculum—delivered through such mechanisms as extended-day and extended-year programs rather than 'pull-out' remedial efforts that compete with, rather than complement, the regular curriculum" (Fowler, 1995, p. 9).

Federal initiatives since 1988 have encouraged greater flexibility in the application of federal funds for remedial services. No longer limited to the "pull-out" model of remediation, school-wide projects, aimed at improving the curriculum of general education classes, have become popular. These projects are designed to meet local needs and range from staff development projects, to implementation of early intervention programs, to lowering class size by assigning remedial reading teachers and some administrators, to general elementary classrooms. Because evaluations are conducted locally and with as many variations as are found in the projects themselves, it is difficult to conduct meta-analyses of quantitative evaluations. One major survey of school-wide programs indicates enthusiasm on the part of administrators, parents, classroom teachers, and Title I teachers for such programs (Schenck & Beckstrom, 1993). Evaluation reports by numerous individual districts have been published as unreviewed ERIC documents. Virtually all of these reports indicate improvement in some areas of reading achievement following implementation of school-wide projects.

The most current federal initiatives for reading are the 1997 America Reads Challenge and the Reading Excellence Act (H. R. 2614, 1997). A prominent provision of this initiative provides funds for the training of 1 million volunteer reading tutors by the year 2000 through VISTA, AmeriCorps, and work-study programs. Volunteers are currently tutoring children in preschool programs such as Head Start and Even Start, as well as working with children in the primary grades in a variety of in-school and after-school programs.

In sum, the three primary goals for federally funded programs during the past decade include improving the quality and level of instruction in pull-out remedial classrooms; school-wide improvements in reading instruction in general education classes; and early intervention efforts to prevent reading difficulties and reduce the need for remedial services in the elementary and secondary schools. One of the practical dilemmas facing educators charged with meeting these goals concerns who is qualified to teach remedial reading.

Who Should Teach Remedial Reading?

Depending on local circumstances, children may receive remedial reading instruction from certified reading teachers or learning disabilities teachers, from paraprofessionals (classroom aides), or from volunteer tutors. Contentions surrounding this question arise primarily from two sources: first, the need to stretch limited resources; and second, from professional feuds over the nature of reading difficulties and paradigms of instruction.

Paraprofessionals.   School districts faced with increasing enrollment, class sizes, and numbers of at-risk learners often stretch Title I funds by hiring paraprofessionals rather than certified reading teachers. In 1994, an issue paper released by the International Reading Association (IRA) aired concerns regarding the employment of paraprofessionals in remedial reading. According to the IRA report, which summarized findings from several major evaluations of Title I, the number of full-time certified reading teachers rose 4.3% from 1985 to 1992, while the number of full-time aides rose 10.1%—more than double the percent of increase for teachers during the same period. In 1992 there were 72,000 full-time Title I teachers and 65,000 full-time aides. The employment of teacher aides can have positive consequences in schools, particularly in providing linguistic and cultural diversity; further, career opportunity programs offer potential for diversifying the urban teaching pool by recruiting paraprofessionals from minority communities (Haselkorn & Fideler, 1995).

The primary concern raised by the IRA regarding aides is that they provide instruction to at-risk children despite being poorly trained (if at all) and unsupervised.

Forty-four percent of Title I aides reportedly deliver instruction, independent of a teacher, to an average of 25 or more children per day. This practice is most common in high-poverty schools. Particularly disconcerting is the assertion that the majority of interactions between students and aides are characterized as low-level forms of assistance that foster dependency on the aide rather than leading to independent learning. At a time when the mandates for Title I reform emphasize instruction for higher level cognitive skills, the use of untrained paraprofessionals is particularly ironic.

Although the "IRA would discourage the widespread, routine hiring of aides with Chapter 1 funds," (IRA, 1994, p. 3), the continued use of aides was recognized as inevitable, given financial constraints on many school districts. Therefore the report set forth recommendations for establishing federal funding and guidelines for state certification programs for Title I aides. In addition, classroom and Title I teachers must be better prepared for supervising and mentoring the paraprofessionals who assist them. One model cited in this report is the training program for Head Start aides, known as the Child Development Associate Credential and administered by a professional organization of early childhood educators (National Association for the Education of Young Children).

Volunteer Tutors

Despite steady increases in the number of Title I teachers and paraprofessionals, many at-risk children in impoverished schools still do not have access to individual reading instruction. Volunteer reading tutors comprise an alternative to formal programs for these children. Even before the Clinton administration proposed the America Reads Challenge in 1997, nearly 1 million volunteers were already assisting in various capacities in American public schools through federally funded programs such as Foster Grandparents, VISTA and AmeriCorps volunteers, along with parents and other community volunteers (Michael, 1990).

Volunteer programs vary on numerous dimensions. Volunteers may be paid or unpaid; some receive little or no training and supervision, whereas others go through extensive and ongoing training and supervision. In the Reading Recovery/America-Corps partnership, for example, paid volunteers receive 150 hours of training, in addition to online supervision (DeFord, Pinnell, & Lyons, 1997). The level of volunteer engagement with children ranges from simply providing incentives for reading books, to listening to children read, to providing direct instruction in skills and strategies. Tutoring sessions may last from 30 min to 2 hr, and volunteers may meet their tutees 1 day per week or up to 4 days per week. Programs may run for the duration of a school year or for a fraction of a semester.

Evaluations of volunteer programs are sparse, and rigorous evaluation designs are even more rare. In a recent review of 17 adult volunteer programs, Wasik (1998) reported that only 3 of these programs employed equivalent treatment and control groups. Of programs that reported results, measures varied from standardized achievement tests (Metropolitan Achievement Test, The Iowa Test of Basic Skills, Woodcock), to word recognition and oral reading passages from basal readers. In a candid evaluation of their volunteer tutoring program, Vadasy, Jenkins, Antil, Wayne, and O'Conner (1997) reported difficulties such as scheduling appropriate space for an after-school program, unreliable volunteers (in this case, paid high school volunteers and community volunteers), and difficulty maintaining fidelity to components of the instructional program. Despite these conflicts, first-grade children in this study demonstrated significant improvements on several measures.

Evidence from other programs indicates that volunteer programs can effect positive change in struggling readers, although results are not consistent across participants. Juel (1996), whose study of college athletes as tutors is among the most innovative, well-designed, and evaluated programs, reported that the children who were tutored in this program demonstrated improvements over their nontutored peers. However, these children scored below their age and grade norms, with wide variations in progress as noted in the high *SD* reported in this study.

In addition to programs using adult tutors, several cross-age tutoring programs have been reported (Labbo & Teale, 1990; Taylor, Hanson, Justice-Swanson, & Watts, 1997). In the Taylor et al. program, a small-group Title I intervention for students in second grade was supplemented with cross-age tutoring by trained fourth-grade students who, like the student athletes in Juel's program, were also struggling readers. In each of these studies, the tutors, as well as their younger tutees, made demonstrable progress in reading, as has been found in earlier studies of cross-age tutoring (Cohen, Kulik, & Kulik, 1982).

Insights on Nonprofessional Reading Tutors.   Data on the effectiveness of volunteer tutors and paraprofessionals are mixed, and several recommendations are offered. First, effective programs require adequate training for tutors, whether these are college students, community volunteers, or other children. Second, supervision of tutors is essential. The qualitative observations of tutors in Juel's study indicated that a tutor's level of sophistication in scaffolding assistance for tutees can either enhance or compromise the efficacy of the tutoring. Third, tutoring sessions must be carefully planned—although not necessarily scripted—for maximum benefit. Vadasy et al. (1997) planned a tutoring program that included activities similar to those followed in Reading Recovery. In addition, they incorporated a component of phonemic awareness activities. Most of their tutors were unable to demonstrate fidelity to the highly scripted lessons that were planned for them, despite initial and ongoing training and supervision.

The services of volunteer tutors are an increasingly popular option for financially strapped school districts with many needy children; however, the short- and long-term efficacy of volunteer tutors remains ambiguous. It is imperative that resources be allocated to design and implement sophisticated evaluations of tutoring efforts.

Learning Disabilities Teachers.   Nearly 80% of students identified as learning disabled—and thus eligible for special education services—have reading difficulties (National Center for Educational Statistics, 1994). By legislative fiat, most learning disabled students with reading difficulties receive instruction from special education teachers rather than from reading specialists. Since 1995, the leadership of the International Reading Association has actively challenged the exclusion of reading specialists from providing instructional services to children identified as learning disabled. In a 1995 position paper entitled "Learning Disabilities: A Barrier to Literacy Instruction," the IRA expressed concerns regarding both the overidentification (and misidentification) of children with learning disabilities and the inadequate preparation of learning disabilities (LD) teachers to provide remedial reading instruction.

A recent study of reading instruction in 14 LD classrooms substantiates concerns aired in the IRA position paper (Vaughn et al., 1998). Children in these classrooms received whole-class instruction. Individual modifications or individualized support were rarely observed. Based on standardized achievement test scores, the children in these classrooms made "little to no growth in reading" (Vaughn et al., 1998, p. 220). Similarly, Morris, Ervin and Conrad (1996) traced the failure of a sixth-grade LD student to achieve independent reading, despite his retention in kindergarten and 4 years of instruction in a self-contained LD class. These authors attributed the failure of instruction in these instances to several factors. First, the LD teachers were following a "whole-language" trend, including whole-class instruction. Second, Vaughn et al.

(1998) observed that reading groups in the LD classrooms ranged from 5 to 19 students, making individualized instruction difficult at best. These authors also speculated that, because the LD teachers had no special preparation in reading (they received the same required preservice reading course as general education teachers), they tended to implement instruction similar to what might be recommended for a general classroom.

The IRA position paper fueled tensions between the leadership of professional organizations in reading and learning disabilities, as both sides lobbied for federal support of their respective programs. The Council for Exceptional Children–Division of Learning Disabilities (CEC-DLD) responded to criticism of LD teachers by questioning the preparation of reading teachers to provide instruction to children with learning disabilities (Council for Exceptional Children, 1997). Despite the sometimes hostile public rhetoric accompanying this fray, members of both factions have come to agreement on several points, including the need to streamline and shorten the lengthy process of referral to special education services, and the desirability of preventive versus remedial interventions for children with reading difficulties (Council for Exceptional Children, 1997; Pikulski, 1998).

Even as Congress deliberates the matter of allowing reading specialists to provide services to children with learning disabilities, at least one state (New York) has passed legislation to this effect. Given that children identified as learning disabled are generally indistinguishable from generic poor readers (Spear-Swerling & Sternberg, 1996), there is no logical reason for withholding from these youngsters the services of highly trained reading teachers. In the next section, we describe the professional standards of and expectations for reading specialists, along with recommendations for future research.

CONSTRUCTING THE FUTURE OF REMEDIAL READING: BELIEFS, REALITY, AND NEEDED FUTURE RESEARCH

In the domain of reading, most particularly in regards to reading difficulties, there are many widely held beliefs. As the discussion in the appendix shows, some of these beliefs are logically or empirically indefensible; others are perhaps logical, but not supported by extant research. It is hoped that this listing and description and the calls for research will promote research to investigate the validity of these beliefs.

Requiem for Remedial Reading

Along with the theoretical and practical contentions that dog the field, remedial reading is mired in arcane terminology representing an outdated conceptualization of reading problems. The requiem we compose here is not a signal for the demise of intensive instructional interventions for children who struggle to acquire print literacy; rather, the intent is to note publicly a turning point, a new era in the field.

The word *remedial* as used in both "remedial reading" and "remedial reader" is most problematic. It derives from *remedy*, meaning "to cure" or to "restore to natural or proper condition" (*Random House Dictionary of the English Language*, Second Unabridged Edition, 1987). For two reasons, the remedying aspect of remedial does not fit the typical case of a child with a reading problem. First, it is the rare child who makes appropriate progress in the initial stages of reading, then falters. Children who need what was previously called "remedial reading" are children whose learning lagged from the first day of developmental reading instruction—and became further and further behind as readily learning peers made ever-increasing progress in reading. These children had never been at a "proper" level of reading to which remedial reading would "restore" them. Indeed, the term *Matthew effect* has been used to describe this ever-widening gulf between children who make continuous progress in reading lessons, and those children who never seem to get out of the starting blocks, falling further and further behind their faster learning peers (Stanovich, 1986).

The second reason the term *remedial* fails (although most in reading would prefer to overlook this point) is that most children provided remedial reading never come fully up to grade level, that is, their reading problems are not "cured." This includes not only children in economically depressed areas but also children attending schools in affluent suburbs.

The term *remedial reading* must be cast off. This argument was previously made by Johnston and Allington (1991). We propose a deliberate shift from the metaphor of the *remedy* to that of *mediation* as in the *remediational* (or *remedial*) context. This shift is based on the sociohistorical theories of Vygotsky (1962, 1978) and neo-Vygotskian scholars such as Cole (1990) and Tharp and Gallimore (1988). A basic tenet of sociohistorical theory is that psychological processes are "culturally mediated, historically developing, and arise from practical activity" (Cole, 1990, p. 91). The notion of historical development is most pertinent to the present discussion. Gallimore and Tharp (1990) described learning and development as movement, with various levels of assistance, or mediation, through recursive stages of the zone of proximal development. "Assisted performance" marks the first level, in which the learner is engaged in activity with the assistance of a teacher. At the second level, the learner demonstrates self-assisted performance in the form of self-directed speech. The third level is characterized by independent performance, as learning has become internalized and automatic. Recursiveness kicks in at the fourth level, when the learner confronts a new task. Throughout this process, learners are assumed to be actively involved in problem-solving with print. This perspective stands in contrast to those in which struggling readers are viewed as passive, helpless victims of circumstance or heredity.

As St. Augustine noted 1,700 years ago (Saint Augustine, 1942), learning to read is not accomplished as naturally as learning to speak but, as is the case in most learning, if children learn to read, they must learn far more than what their teachers explicitly teach them or make them practice. That is, learning to read is not learning solely a set of skills the teacher demonstrates and makes students practice; rather, children who have learned to read have taken bits and pieces of what they have been taught and practiced, constructed their own generalizations and understanding of the reading process, and organized and integrated the strategies and skills of reading. Every child must engage in this constructive process to become a mature, fluent, analytic, critical reader. This description of the constructivist view of learning to read casts the teacher into a role far greater than that of a presenter of skills and concrete information, but rather describes the teacher as someone who carries out a variety of roles that mediate learning. These roles include modeling, encouraging, reminding, hinting, questioning, challenging, correcting, directly teaching, reteaching, reviewing, and, when necessary, just letting the learner be. The teacher's role in teaching children to read is best described as mediator. To learn, children also must act as mediators—attending to and analyzing finer and finer aspects of print and text and constructing their own interpretation and organization of orthography, text, and meaning-gaining strategies. Thus, if we consider normal, developmental reading instruction to be a mediational process for both teachers and students, then when children fail to learn to read during this mediation, both teacher and children must encounter this learning task once again—hence, re-mediation.

As we mark the beginning of a new century, the knowledge base in re-medial reading is robust, having the breadth and depth of multiple research and instructional perspectives. Public interest in—and criticism of—reading programs is strong, albeit often based on narrow perspectives, misperceptions, and myths. Enduring tensions will continue within the field; however, the momentum created by the current wave of public interest affords opportunities for reading professionals to correct public misperceptions about the nature of reading acquisition and reading difficulties, and to create public support for programs of research and practice that reflect the breadth and depth of this dynamic field.

APPENDIX: BELIEFS, REALITY, AND NEEDED FUTURE RESEARCH

Belief: Reading Failure Results From Poor Schools and Poor Teaching

Unquestionably, many reading problems result from poor schools and teaching, but it is also the case that in the same first- or second-grade classroom where one child or a small group of children failed to learn to read, the vast majority usually did learn to read. There is too little research that examines reading development over a period of time (e.g., 4 or 5 years), teacher by teacher. The First-Grade Studies (Bond & Dykstra, 1967) found greater achievement variation within a large number of classrooms taught by a given reading method than between the average scores of classrooms taught by different instructional methods. The authors of that study concluded that this "greater variation within than between groups" outcome resulted from teacher differences; however, none of the projects in the First-Grade Studies actually accounted for teaching or teachers. It is important to know if, in controlled studies, some primary-grade teachers consistently end the school year with larger numbers of children with reading difficulties and if another group of teachers consistently end the school year with few or no children with reading difficulties. It is commonly believed that such teaching variation exists, but research documentation of this belief is scant.

Belief: Curricular Congruence Is Important

Curricular congruence is when there is a strong similarity in the rationale, methods, and materials of the reading instruction that a student receives in the classroom and in remedial reading. Curricular congruence is not viewed here as "narrow-based" instruction (e.g., all phonics in a skills-based program, all context in a literature-based program) but, by definition, it demands goals, methods, and materials adhered to by both the classroom and reading teacher. Although, at first blush, this notion of curricular congruence has intuitive appeal, the reading research community has failed to establish its validity. Curricular congruence may be open to at least three specific criticisms. First, the specificity required if classroom and remedial teachers convene to design a reading program will delimit options in reading instruction. From the constructivist position, teaching reading is not laying out a bounded set of goals and activities that the child follows in a more-or-less straight line, but rather is a process of exposing the child to a multitude of varying literacy experiences frequently revised in light of the child's progress and learning. The teacher's role here is to expose children to a multitude of skills and strategies that they may use to learn to read, to assist children in their initial applications of those skills and strategies, and to guide children in revising their notions of the reading process. Curricular congruence could have the effect of limiting the options available to children in trying to learn what they need to learn in order to be able to learn to read.

Further, although remedial reading has not wiped out the nation's reading difficulties, many children have made large gains in reading proficiency and motivation via remedial reading instruction. Perhaps it is just the remedial reading instruction that causes this growth in reading, but just as valid an explanation is the hypothesis that the joint action (interaction) of the classroom program and the remedial program caused the growth. We do not know, and this state of ignorance only exacerbates the need for further researching the validity of curricular congruence.

Yet another reason to call for research on the validity of curricular congruence is that most reading specialists have found themselves in the position of providing remedial reading to children whose previous reading instruction was not only narrow in focus, but also poorly conducted. In this case, perhaps a form of curricular congruence is truly called for—the classroom teacher should teach the way the reading specialist is teaching.

Research on curricular congruence is in short supply, but a recent dissertation by Wilson-Bridgeman (1998) failed to find that curricular congruence was associated with gains in reading ability. Research on the content and construct validity of curricular congruence is sorely needed.

Belief: Skilled Reading Teachers Have Special Knowledge and Abilities for Teaching Reading

[handwritten margin note: Evidence of philosophy of teaching → demon in classroom]

Much time, effort, and expense is given by many to graduate reading programs for previously certified classroom teachers. These programs require as many as six to eight reading courses or practicums. Such expense and effort would not be expended if we did not believe that, at the completion of these programs, reading teachers would have gained knowledge, insights, abilities, and techniques beyond those of most classroom teachers. Following are seven commonly accepted beliefs about what it is that reading teachers know and can do. In spite of the fact that references can be found for most of these beliefs, there is little or no data to support any.

First, expert reading teachers have knowledge and models of good readers at the various stages of reading development (Chall, 1983). They know what a good reader at a given stage is able to do and not do, and they are able to contrast this model to children they are teaching who have reading difficulties to build reasonable goals for that child (Kibby & Barr, in press). They also have internalized and used models of effective teaching (Allington & Cunningham, 1996, p. 163). Perhaps most importantly, an expert reading teacher is an excellent "systematic observer" who "drops all presuppositions about a child … and listens very carefully and records very precisely what the child can in fact do" (Clay, 1993a, p. 3). Eisner (1991) would say that these excellent reading teachers had developed "the enlightened eye." They also have developed a decision-making model of the diagnostic assessment that provides an overall perspective, or gestalt, of the components and strategies important to successful reading and a sequence for routinely evaluating those components and strategies in a rational and efficient manner (Gil et al., 1979; Kibby, 1995c; Kibby & Barr, in press; O'Flahavan et al., 1992; Polin, 1981; Snow et al., 1998, p. 287).

Second, for any given intensive intervention reading lesson, good reading teachers can substantiate, document, or explain why they are providing the instruction they are—that is, they can explain what the child is able to do and how they know; they can explain what are children's successive needs to learn; they can explain the nature of the instruction the children require to learn what they next need to learn and how they know; and they can explain the form of supporting guidance and review that children will need in applying or practicing this new knowledge and how they know (Clay, 1993b; Pinnell, Fried, & Estice, 1990).

Third, good reading teachers view all their planned instruction as "responsive instruction" (Shanahan & Barr, 1995, p. 963) or "diagnostic teaching" (Kibby, 1995c, p. 49). One outcome of this rationale is that they presume that every lesson that they design requires adjustment as they implement it (Allington & Cunningham, 1996, p. 164;

Clay, 1993b; Pinnell et al., 1990). This adjustment of in-process instruction is continuous and requires critical analyses of children's responses to the text being read (prior to, while, and after reading), knowledge of the demands of the text, and ability to implement a wide range of instructional techniques. Another outcome of viewing all instruction as diagnostic teaching is that every individual lesson is a diagnosis, and any one lesson must be based upon the results of the previous diagnostic lesson (Clay, 1993b; Morris, Ervin, & Conrad, 1996).

Fourth, it surely is the case when children read a text with a reading teacher's instruction that comprehension of the text's content is paramount. In reading instruction, however, the goal of instruction is not the information gained per se, but to teach the reading strategies and skills required for children to gain this information from independent reading.

Fifth, good reading teachers know that solid reading instruction requires a balance of easy (independent, nondirected, or unguided) reading and more difficult (instructional, directed, or guided) reading. They know that learning to read is moving from not knowing, to knowing how, to doing, to doing with ease, accuracy, and speed. Whether a child is still attempting to master the essentials of word recognition or striving to develop the comprehension strategies of analysis and synthesis, fluency is required. Therefore, not all of every instructional session can be devoted entirely to teaching children new strategies, skills, or information, but some of every lesson must be devoted to help children do what has already been learned, but more rapidly, with less attention, and with fewer errors (i.e., with greater fluency) (Clay, 1993b; Snow et al., 1998).

Sixth, Barr (1973–1974) found in first-grade classrooms that the amount learned was highly dependent on instructional pace, that is, the rate at which teachers accomplished the basal reader's lessons. Expert reading teachers know that children with reading difficulties not only need greater amounts of high-quality reading instruction but also that the pace of instruction in the intervention program must be intense.

Finally, good reading teachers realize that the purpose of any lesson is children's learning, not the mere accomplishment of the lesson. This child focus means that the teacher's perception is affixed to what is and is not being learned, not to the instructional activity itself.

Belief: Almost Every Child Should Be Reading on Grade Level

The basic premise of all intervention, remedial, or learning disability programs is to "get the child up to grade level." Some may say that this is not logical; it would be the same as saying that every child will be approximately average in height, or taller (Cannell, 1987). Speaking strictly statistically, this is correct; the Lake Woebegone Effect of everybody scoring at or above *average* on a normed test is impossible. The statistical word *average* is the problem, and should be replaced with the more general term *on grade level*. The term *grade level* here is not a grade equivalent score on a standardized test but is the ability to read texts generally considered appropriate for children's age or grade. Given this interpretation of average, then the notion of *almost every child reading on grade level* may not be dismissed on purely logical grounds.

Allington (1995) listed six pieces of conventional wisdom he believed are erroneous; the first of these deceptive ad hominems is "not all children can become literate with their peers." He suggests that the basis of this deceptive conventional wisdom is the "enormous range of differences in children when they begin school" (p. 6). One of those variables that has been thought to limit progression in reading is intelligence, but in the primary grades, IQ scores correlate with reading achievement at only the .2 to .45 level. There is nothing so complicated about learning to read that would keep any child who is not mentally retarded from being able to learn to read near, on, or above grade level, provided that this child is given enough instruction and instruction of sufficient quality. And because, within a normally distributed population, about 95% of the population will, theoretically, have IQ scores of 80 and above, then in accordance with the thinking of Bloom (1968), Carroll (1964, 1989), and Allington (1995), almost every child in elementary school should be reading on grade level at grade level.

Those who claim that every elementary school child should be reading at grade level (this includes the authors) find little to support this belief beyond faith. The dualfold data nullifying this belief include:

1. Not every child does learn to read, some in spite of high IQs, homes that value and encourage language and reading, excellent developmental reading instruction, and excellent remedial reading instruction.
2. Those who hold this belief (including the authors) have been unable to proffer methods that guarantee success for all. Even in Reading Recovery, children who do not make success after 60 lessons are dropped from the program and returned to the regular classroom or referred to a special education program.

There certainly have been numerous major attempts to eliminate reading difficulties within our society (e.g., Title I, Special Education, Remedial Reading, Reading Recovery, Success for All), but there are still significant numbers of children who have difficulty reading. Studies are needed in which a school or a school district commits itself to not allowing a single child in an entire cohort of 4-year-olds (or younger) to fall significantly behind in learning to read through grade five or six. Funding for this project would permit whatever form of instruction, including a great deal of one-to-one teaching if such were deemed necessary. It is important to know if it is only limited funding and staffing that stands in the way of success for all, or if it is a lack of reading theory and instructional methods.

REFERENCES

Adams, M. J. (1990). *Beginning to read: Thinking and learning about print.* Cambridge, MA: MIT Press.

Adams, M. J., Treiman, R., & Pressley, M. (1998). Reading, writing, and literacy. In I.E. Siegel & K. A. Renninger, (Eds.). *Handbook of child psychology, Vol. 4: Child psychology in practice* (5th ed., pp. 275–355). New York: Wiley.

Ajibola, O., & Clement, P. W. (1995). Differential effects of methylphenidate and self-reinforcement on attention-deficit hyperactivity disorder. *Behavior Modification, 19*(2), 211–233.

Allington, R. L. (1983). Fluency: The neglected reading goal. *Reading Teacher, 36*(6), 556–561.

Allington, R. L. (1987). The persistence of teachers beliefs in facets of the visual perceptual hypothesis. *Elementary School Journal, 87*(4), 351–359.

Allington, R. L. (1991). The legacy of "slow it down and make it more concrete." In J. Zutell & S. McCormick (Eds.) *Learner factors/teacher factors: Issues in literacy research and instruction* (pp. 19–30). Chicago: National Reading Conference.

Allington, R. L. (1994). What's special about special programs for children who find learning to read difficult? *Journal of Reading Behavior, 26*(1), 95–115.

Allington, R. L. (1995). Literacy lessons in the elementary schools: Yesterday, today, and tomorrow. In R. L. Allington & S. A. Walmsley (Eds.), *No quick fix: Rethinking literacy programs in America's elementary schools* (pp. 1–15). New York: Teachers College Press.

Allington, R. L., & Cunningham, P. M. (1996). *Schools that work: Where all children read and write.* New York: HarperCollins.

Allington, R. L., & Woodside-Jiron, H. (1997). *Adequacy of a program of research and of a "research synthesis" in shaping educational policy* (Rep. Ser. 1.15). National Research Center on English Learning and Achievement. Albany, NY: State University of New York at Albany.

Arya, P., Kutno, S., & Kibby, M. W. (1995, December). *Creating fluent readers: A comparison of two teaching strategies for dysfluent readers.* Paper presented at the 48th annual meeting of the National Reading Conference, New Orleans.

Balow, B. (1996). Perceptual-motor activities in the treatment of severe reading disability. *Reading Teacher*, *50*(2), 88–97. (Original work published 1971)

Barr, R. (1973–1974). Instructional pace differences and their effect on reading acquisition. *Reading Research Quarterly*, *9*(4), 526–554.

Bean, R. M., Cooley, W. W, Eichelberger, R. T., Lazar, M. K., & Zigmond, N. (1991). In class or pullout: Effects of setting on the remedial reading program. *Journal of Reading Behavior*, *23*(4), 445–464.

Bear, D. R., Invernezzi, M., Templeton, S., & Johnston, F. (1996). *Words their way: Word study for phonics, vocabulary, and spelling instruction*. Englewood Cliffs, NJ: Merrill.

Berliner, D. C., & Biddle, B. J. (1995). *The manufactured crisis: Myths, fraud, and the attack on America's public schools*. Reading, MA: Addison-Wesley.

Bloom, B. S. (1968). Learning for mastery. *Evaluation Comment*, *1*(2). University of California, Los Angeles, Center for the Study of Evaluation and Instructional Programs.

Bond, G. L., & Dykstra, R. (1967). The cooperative research program in first-grade reading instruction. *Reading Research Quarterly*, *2*(4), 5–142.

Borman, G. D., & D'Agostino, J. V. (1996). Title I and student achievement: A meta-analysis of federal evaluation results. *Educational Evaluation & Policy Analysis*, *18*(4), 309–326.

Campbell, J. R., Voekl, K. E., & Donahue, P. L. (1997, September). *NAEP 1996 trends in academic progress*. Princeton, NJ: Educational Testing Service.

Cannell, J. J. (1987). *Nationally normed elementary achievement testing in America's public schools; How all 50 states are above the national average* (2nd ed.). Daniels, WV: Friends for Education.

Carroll, J. B. (1964). A model of school learning. *Teachers College Record*, *64*, 222–228.

Carroll, J. B. (1989). The Carroll Model: A 25-year retrospective and prospective view. *Educational Researcher*, *18*, 26–31.

Chall, J. S. (1983). *Stages of reading development*. New York: McGraw-Hill.

Clay, M. M. (1979). *The early detection of reading difficulties*. Auckland, NZ: Heinemann.

Clay, M. M. (1993a). *An observation schedule of early literacy achievement*. Portsmouth, NH: Heinemann.

Clay, M. M. (1993b). *Reading recovery: A guidebook for teachers in training*. Portsmouth, NH: Heinemann.

Cohen, P. A., Kulik, J. A., & Kulik, C. C. (1982). Education outcomes of tutoring: A meta-analysis of findings. *American Educational Research Journal*, *19*(2), 237–248.

Cole, M. (1990). Cognitive development and formal schooling: The evidence from cross-cultural research. In L. C. Moll (Ed.), *Vygotsky and education: Instructional implications and applications of sociohistorical psychology* (pp. 89–110). Cambridge: Cambridge University Press.

Coles, G. S. (1978). The learning-disabilities test battery: Empirical and social issues. *Harvard Educational Review*, *48*, 313–340.

Council for Exceptional Children. (1997). Reading difficulties vs. learning disabilities. *CEC Today*, *4*(5). Reston, VA: Council for Exceptional Children. [Online]. http://www.cec.sped.org/bk/cectoday/today.htm

Cruickshank, W. C. (1979). Learning disabilities: A definitional statement. In E. Polak (Ed.), *Issues and initiatives in learning disabilities* (pp. 80–110). Syracuse, NY: Syracuse University Press.

Cunningham, P. M., Hall, D. P., & Defee, M. (1998). Nonability grouped, multilevel instruction: Eight years later. *Reading Teacher*, *51*(8), 652–664.

D'Agostino, J. V. (1996). Authentic instruction and academic achievement in compensatory education classrooms. *Studies in Educational Evaluation*, *22*(2), 139–155.

Deford, D. E., Pinnell, G. S., & Lyons, C. (1997, December). *AmeriCorps for literacy and math*. Paper presented at the annual meeting of the National Reading Conference. Scottsdale, AZ.

Dowhower, S. L. (1987). Repeated reading revisited: Research into practice. *Reading Research Quarterly*, *22*(4), 389–406.

Ehri, L. (1994). Development of the ability to read words: Update. In R. Ruddell, M. Ruddell, & H. Singer (Eds.), *Theoretical models and processes of reading* (4th ed., pp. 323–358). Newark, DE: International Reading Association.

Eisner, E. W. (1991). *The enlightened eye: Qualitative inquiry and the enhancement of educational practice*. New York: Macmillan.

Elley, W. B. (1992). *How in the world do students read? IEA study of reading literacy*. Hamburg, Germany: International Association for the Evaluation of Educational Attainment.

Englert, C. S., Raphael, T. E., Fear, K. L., & Anderson, L. M. (1988). Students' metacognitive knowledge about how to write informational texts. *Learning Disability Quarterly*, *11*(1), 18–46.

Farr, R., Fay, L., Myers, J., & Ginsberg, M. (1987). *Then and now: Reading achievement in Indiana 1944–45, 1976, and 1986*. Bloomington, IN: Center for Reading and Language Studies, School of Education, Indiana University.

Fisher, J. H. (1905). A case of congenital word-blindness. *Review*, *19*, 315–318.

Flynn, J. R. (1984a). The mean IQ of Americans: Massive gains 1932–1938. *Psychological Bulletin*, *95*(1), 29–51.

Flynn, J. R. (1984b). IQ gains and the Binet Decrements. *Journal of Educational Measurement*, *21*(3, fall), 283–290.

Flynn, J. R. (1987). Massive IQ gains in 14 nations: What IQ tests really measure. *Psychological Bulletin*, *101*(2), 171–191.

Foorman, B. R., Francis, D. J., Fletcher, J. M., Schatschneider, C., & Mehta, P. (1998). The role of instruction in learning to read: Preventing reading failure in at-risk children. *Journal of Educational Psychology, 90*(1), 37–55.

Forness, S. R., Swanson, J. M., Cantwell, D. P., Youpa, D., & Hanna, G. L. (1992). Stimulant medication and reading performance: Follow-up on sustained dose in ADHD boys with and without conduct disorders. *Journal of Learning Disabilities, 25*(2), 115–123.

Fountas, I. C., & Pinnell, G. S. (1996). *Guided reading: Good first teaching for all children*. Portsmouth, NH: Heinemann.

Fowler, T. (1995). *Improving America's Schools Act of 1994: Reauthorization of the ESEA*. Washington, DC: U.S. Department of Education.

Freppon, P. A., & Dahl, K. L. (1998). Balanced instruction: Insights and considerations. *Reading Research Quarterly, 33*(2), 240–251.

Gallimore, R., & Tharp, R. G. (1990). Teaching mind in society. In L. C. Moll (Ed.). *Vygotsky and education: Instructional implications and applications of sociohistorical psychology* (pp.175–205). Cambridge: Cambridge University Press.

Gates, A. R. & MacGinitie, W. H. (1978). *Technical Report: Gates-MacGinitie Reading Tests* (2nd ed.). Chicago: Riverside.

Gibson, E. J. (1965). Learning to read. *Science, 148*, 1066–1072.

Gibson, E. J., & Levin, H. (1975). *The psychology of reading*. Cambridge, MA: MIT Press.

Gil, D., Hoffmyer, E., VanRoekel, J., & Weinshank, A. (1979). *Clinical problem solving in reading: Theory and research* (Research Ser. No. 45). East Lansing, MI: Institute for Research on Teaching, Michigan State University.

Gil, D., Vinsonhaler, J. F., & Sherman, G. (1979). *Defining reading diagnosis: Why, what, and how?* (Research Ser. No. 46). East Lansing, MI: Institute for Research on Teaching, Michigan State University.

Gil, D., Vinsonhaler, J. F., & Wagner, C. C. (1979). *Studies of clinical problem solving behavior in reading diagnosis* (Research Ser. No. 42). East Lansing, MI: Institute for Research on Teaching, Michigan State University.

Gil, D., Wagner, C. C., & Vinsonhaler, J. F. (1979). *Simulating the problem solving of reading clinicians* (Research Ser. No. 30). East Lansing, MI: Institute for Research on Teaching, Michigan State University.

Gillingham, A., & Stillman, B. W. (1960). *Remedial training for children with specific disability in reading, spelling, and penmanship*. Cambridge, MA: Educators Publishing Service.

Glynn, T., Bethune, N., Crooks, T., Ballard, K., & Smith, J. (1992). Reading Recovery in context: Implementation and outcome. *Educational Psychology, 12*(3-4), 249–261.

Graham, S., & Harris, K. R. (1989). Improving learning disabled students' skills at composing essays: Self-instructional strategy training. *Exceptional Children, 56*(3), 201–216.

Hallahan, D. P., & Cruickshank, W. M. (1973). *Psychoeducational foundations of learning disabilities*. New York: Prentice-Hall.

Harris, T. L., & Hodges, R. E. (1995). *The literacy dictionary: The vocabulary of reading and writing*. Newark, DE: International Reading Association.

Haselkorn, D., & Fideler, E. (1996). *Breaking the class ceiling: Paraeducator pathways to teaching*. Belmont, MA: Recruiting New Teachers.

Hiebert, E. H., & Taylor, B. M. (1994). *Getting reading right from the start: Effective early literacy interventions*. Boston: Allyn & Bacon.

Hinshelwood, J. (1917). *Congenital word-blindness*. London: H. K. Lewis.

Homan, S. P., Klesius, J. P., & Hite, C. (1993). Effects of repeated readings and nonrepetitive strategies on students' fluency and comprehension. *Journal of Educational Research, 87*(2), 94–99.

International Reading Association. (1994). *Position paper: Who is teaching our children? A look at the use of aides in Chapter 1*. Newark, DE: International Reading Association.

International Reading Association. (1995). *Position paper: Learning disabilities: A barrier to literacy instruction*. Newark, DE: International Reading Association.

Johnston, P. & Allington, R. (1991). Remediation. In R. Barr, M. L. Kamil, P. B. Mosenthal, & P. D. Pearson (Eds.), *Handbook of reading research* (Vol. II, pp. 984–1012). New York: Longman.

Juel, C. (1996). What makes literacy tutoring effective? *Reading Research Quarterly, 31*(3), 268–289.

Kameenui, E. J. (1993). Diverse learners and the tyranny of time: Don't fix blame; fix the leaky roof. *Reading Teacher, 46*(5), 376–383.

Kavale, K. A. (1982). Meta-analysis of the relationship between visual perceptual skills and reading achievement. *Journal of Learning Disabilities, 15*, 42–51.

Kavale, K. A. (1984). A meta-analytic evaluation of the Frostig training program. *Exceptional Children, 31*, 131–141.

Kavale, K. A., & Forness, S. R. (1985). Learning disabilities and the history of science: Paradigm or paradox. *Remedial and Special Education, 6*, 12–23.

Kennedy, M. M., Birman, B. F., & Demaline, R. (1986). *The effectiveness of Chapter 1 services: Second interim report from the National Assessment of Chapter 1*. Washington, DC: Office of Educational Research and Improvement, U.S. Department of Education.

Kibby, M. W. (1995a). *Student literacy: Myths and realities*. Bloomington, IN: Phi Delta Kappa.

Kibby, M. W. (1995b). What reading teachers should know about reading achievement in America. *Journal of Reading, 37*(1), 28–40.

Kibby, M. W. (1995c). *Practical steps for informing literacy instruction: A diagnostic decision-making model.* Newark, DE: International Reading Association.

Kibby, M. W., & Barr, R. (in press). The education of reading clinicians. *Reconsidering the role of the reading clinic in a new age of literacy* Advances in Reading/Language Research (Vol. 6). Greenwich, CT: JAI Press.

Klingner, J. K., Vaughn, S., Schumm, J. S., Hughes, M., & Elbaum, B. (1997). Outcomes for students with and without learning disabilities in inclusive classrooms. *Learning Disabilities Research & Practice, 13*(3), 153–161.

Knapp, M. S. (1995). *Teaching for meaning in high-poverty classrooms.* New York: Teachers College Press.

Koskinen, P. S., & Blum, I. H. (1986). Paired repeated reading: A classroom strategy for developing fluent reading. *Reading Teacher, 40*(1), 70–75.

Labbo, L. D., & Teale, W. H. (1990). Cross-age reading: A strategy for helping poor readers. *Reading Teacher, 43*(6), 362–369.

LaBerge, D., & Samuels, S. J. (1974). Toward a theory of automatic information processing in reading. *Cognitive Psychology, 6*, 293–323.

Linn, R. L., Graue, M. E., & Sanders, N. M. (1990). Comparing state and district tests results to national norms: The validity of claims that "everyone is above average." *Educational Measurement: Issues and Practice, 10*(fall), 5–14.

Lovett, M., Borden, L., DeLuca, T., Lacerenza, L., Benson, N., & Brackstone, D. (1994). Treating core deficits of developmental dyslexia: Evidence of transfer of learning after phonologically—and strategy-based reading training programs. *Developmental Psychology, 30*, 805–822.

MacGinitie, W. H. & MacGinitie, R. K. (1989). *Technical Report: Gates-MacGinitie Reading Tests* (3rd ed.). Chicago: Riverside.

Matson, B. (1996). Whole language or phonics? Teachers and researchers find the middle ground most fertile. *Harvard Education Letter, 12*(2), 1–5.

Maxson, S. P. (1996, February). *The influence of teachers' beliefs on literacy development for at-risk first grade students.* Paper presented at the Annual Meeting of the American Association for Teacher Educators, Chicago.

McGill-Franzen, A. (1994). Compensatory and special education: Is there accountability for learning and belief in children's potential? In E. H. Hiebert & B. M. Taylor, (Eds.), *Getting reading right from the start: Effective early literacy instruction* (pp. 3–35). Needham Heights, MA: Allyn & Bacon.

Means, B., & Knapp, M. S. (1991). *Teaching advanced skills to educationally disadvantaged students.* Washington, DC: Policy Studies Associates, and Menlo Park, CA: SRI International.

Michael, B. (1990). *Volunteers in public schools.* Washington, DC: National Academy Press.

Millsap, M. A., Moss, M., & Gamse, B. (1993). *Chapter 1 implementation study: Chapter 1 in public schools.* Washington, DC: U.S. Department of Education, Office of Policy and Planning.

Monroe, M. (1932). *Children who cannot read.* Chicago: University of Chicago Press.

Morgan, W. P. (1896). A case of congenital word-blindness. *British Medical Journal, 2*, 1543–1544.

Morris, D., Ervin, C., & Conrad, K. (1996). A case study of a middle school reading disability. *Reading Teacher, 49*(5), 368–377.

National Center for Education Statistics. (1994). *U.S. Department of Education statistics.* Washington, DC: United States Department of Education.

O'Flahavan, J., Gambrell, L., Guthrie, J., Stahl, J., Baumann, J. F., & Alvermann, D. E. (1992). Poll results guide activities for research center. *Reading Today, 10*, 12.

Office of Compensatory Education Programs. (1997, December). *Title I (pamphlet).* Washington, DC: U.S. Department of Education.

Palincsar, A. S., & Brown, A. L. (1984). Reciprocal teaching of comprehension-fostering and monitoring activities. *Cognition and Instruction, 1*(2), 117–175.

Pelosi, P. L. (1977). *The origin and development of reading diagnosis in the United States: 1896–1946.* Unpublished doctoral dissertation, University at Buffalo.

Perfetti, C. A. (1986). Continuities in reading acquisition, reading skill, and reading disability. *Remedial & Special Education, 7*(1), 11–21.

Pikulski, J. J. (1998, February/March). IRA and leaning disabilities: Another update. *Reading Today,* p. 39.

Pinnell, G. S., Fried, M. D., & Estice, R. M. (1990). Reading recovery: Learning how to make a difference. *Reading Teacher, 43*, 282–295.

Polin, R. M. (1981). *A study of preceptor training of classroom teachers in reading diagnosis.* (Research Ser. No. 110). East Lansing, MI: Institute for Research on Teaching, Michigan State University.

Puma, M. J., Karweit, N., Price, C., Ricciuti, A., Thompson, W., & Vaden-Kiernan, M. (1997). *Prospects: Student outcomes—Final report.* U.S. Department of Education, Planning and Evaluation Service. Cambridge, MA: Abt Associates, Inc.

Random House. (1987). *Random House dictionary of the English language,* Second Unabridged Edition. New York: Author.

Rashotte, C. A., & Torgesen, J. K. (1985). Repeated reading and reading fluency in learning disabled children. *Reading Research Quarterly, 20*(2), 180–188.

Rasinski, T. V. (1990). Effects of repeated reading and listening while reading on reading fluency. *Journal of Educational Research, 83*(3), 147–150.

Richek, M. A., & McTague, B. K. (1988). The "Curious George" strategy for students with reading problems. *Reading Teacher, 42*(3), 220–226.

Robinson, H. M. (1946). *Why pupils fail in reading?* Chicago: University of Chicago Press.

Robinson, H. M. (1972). Visual and auditory modalities related to methods for beginning reading. *Reading Research Quarterly, 8,* 7–39.

Safer, D. J., Zito, J. M., & Fine, E. M. (1996). Increased methylphenidate usage for Attention Deficit Disorder in the 1990s. *Pediatrics, 98*(6), 1084–1088.

Saint Augustine. (1942). *The confessions of Saint Augustine, Books I–X.* Translated by F. J. Sheed. New York: Sheed & Ward.

Samuels, S. J. (1979). The method of repeated readings. *Reading Teacher, 32*(4), 403–408.

Schenck, E. A., & Beckstrom, S. (1993). *Chapter 1 schoolwide project study—Final Report.* Portsmouth, NH: RMC Research Corp.

Schumm, J. S., Moody, S. W., & Vaughn, S. (1996). *Grouping for reading instruction: General education teacher's perceptions and practices.* Unpublished manuscript.

Schumm, J. S., Vaughn, S., Haager, D., & Klingner, J. (1994). Literacy instruction for mainstreamed students: What suggestions are provided in basal reading series? *Remedial and Special Education, 15*(1), 14–20.

Shanahan, T., & Barr, R. (1995). Reading Recovery: An independent evaluation of the effects of an early intervention for at-risk learners. *Reading Research Quarterly, 30*(4), 958–996.

Simons, H. D. (1992, December). *The effect of repeated reading of predictable texts on word recognition and decoding: A descriptive study of six first grade children.* Paper presented at the 42nd annual meeting of the National Reading Conference, San Antonio, TX.

Snow, C. E., Burns, M. S., & Griffin. P. (1998). *Preventing reading difficulties in young children.* Washington, DC: National Academy Press.

Spear-Swerling, L., & Sternberg, R. J. (1996). *Off track: When poor readers become "learning disabled."* Boulder, CO: Westview Press.

Spiegel, D. L. (1992). Blending whole language and systematic direct instruction. *Reading Teacher, 46*(1), 38–44.

Stahl, S. A. (1994, November). *Fluency-oriented reading instruction.* Paper presented at the 44th annual meeting of the National Reading Conference, San Diego, CA.

Stanovich, K. E. (1986). Matthew effects in reading: Some consequences of individual differences in the acquisition of literacy. *Reading Research Quarterly, 21,* 360–407.

Stanovich, K. E. (1990). A call for an end to the paradigm wars in reading research. *Journal of Reading Behavior, 22*(3), 221–31.

Stoner, G., Carey, S.P., Ikeda, M. J., & Shinn, M. (1994). The utility of curriculum based measurement for evaluating the effects of methylphenidate on academic performance. *Journal of Applied Behavior Analysis, 27*(1), 101–113.

Sulzby, E. (1985). Children's emergent reading of favorite storybooks: A developmental study. *Reading Research Quarterly, 20*(3), 458–481.

Tancock, S. M. (1995). Classroom teachers and reading specialists examine their Chapter 1 reading programs. *Journal of Reading Behavior, 27*(3), 315–335.

Taylor, B. M., Hanson, B. E., Justice-Swanson, K., & Watts, S, M. (1997). Helping struggling readers: Linking small-group intervention with cross-age tutoring. *Reading Teacher, 51*(3), 196–209.

Tharp, R. G., & Gallimore, R. (1988). *Rousing minds to life.* Cambridge: Cambridge University Press.

Turpie, J. J., & Paratore, J. R. (1994, November). *Using repeated reading to promote reading success in a heterogeneously grouped first grade.* Paper presented at the 44th annual meeting of the National Reading Conference, San Diego, CA.

U.S. Department of Education. (1996). *Digest of education statistics.* Table 369. Public and private school students receiving federally funded Chapter 1 services, by selected school characteristics: School year 1993–1994. [Online]. http//nces.ed.gov/pubs/d96/D96/T369.html

U.S. Department of Education. (1997). *Digest of education statistics.* Washington, DC: National Center for Education Statistics. [Online]. http://nces.ed.gov/pubsearch/pubsinfo.asp?pubid=98015

Vadasy, P. F., Jenkins, J. R., Antil, L. R., Wayne, S. K., & O'Conner, R. E. (1997). The effectiveness of one-to-one tutoring by community tutors for at-risk beginning readers. *Learning Disability Quarterly, 20,* 126–139.

Vaughn, S., Moody, S. W., & Schumm, J. S. (1998). Broken promises: Reading instruction in the resource room. *Exceptional Children, 64*(2), 211–225.

Vellutino, F. R. (1977). Alternative conceptualizations of dyslexia: Evidence in support of a verbal deficit hypothesis. *Harvard Educational Review, 47,* 334–354.

Vellutino, F. R. (1979). *Dyslexia: Theory and research.* Cambridge, MA: MIT Press.

Vellutino, F. R. (1987). Dyslexia. *Scientific American, 256*(3), 34–41.

Vellutino, F. R., & Scanlon, D. M. (1987). Linguistic coding and reading ability. In S. Rosenberg (Ed.), *Advances in applied psycholinguistics, Vol. 2, Reading, writing, and language learning* (pp. 1–69). New York: Cambridge University Press.

Vinsonhaler, J. F. (1979). *The consistency of reading diagnosis* (Research Ser. No. 28). East Lansing, MI: Institute for Research on Teaching, Michigan State University.

Vygotsky, L. S. (1962). *Thought and language.* Cambridge, MA: Harvard University Press.

Vygotsky, L. (1978). *Mind in society: The development of higher psychological processes* (M. Cole, V. John-Steiner, & E. Souberman, Eds.). Cambridge, MA: Harvard University Press.

Walsh, D. J., Price, G. G., & Gillingham, M. G. (1988). The critical but transitory importance of letter naming. *Reading Research Quarterly, 23*(1), 108–122.

Wasik, B. A. (1998). Volunteer tutoring programs in reading: A review. *Reading Research Quarterly, 33*(3), 268–289.

Weiderholt, J. L. (1974). Historical perspectives on the education of the learning disabled. In L. Mann & D. Sabatino (Eds.), *The second review of special education* (pp. 103–152). Philadelphia: Journal of Special Education Press.

Weinstein, G., & Cooke, N. L. (1992). The effects of two repeated reading interventions on generalization of fluency. *Learning Disability Quarterly, 15*(1), 21–28.

Wilson-Bridgeman, J. (1998). *Curricular and communicative congruence: A key to success for students at risk of reading failure.* Unpublished doctoral dissertation, University at Buffalo.

Young, A. R, Bowers, P. G., & MacKinnon, G. E. (1996). Effects of prosodic modeling and repeated reading on poor readers' fluency and comprehension. *Applied Psycholinguistics, 17*(1), 59–84.

Zigmond, N., Jenkins, J., Fuchs, L. S., Deno, S., Fuchs, D., Baker, J. N., Jenkins, L., & Couthino, M. (1995). Special education in restructured schools: Findings from three multi-year studies. *Phi Delta Kappan, 76*(7), 531–540.

CHAPTER 37

Teacher Research in the Contact Zone

Susan L. Lytle
University of Pennsylvania

For over a decade there has been enormous growth in the number of teachers conducting inquiry into literacy teaching and learning in their own schools and classrooms. A considerable portion of this work has been published and disseminated nationally as research monographs, edited volumes, and journal articles. Much of it, however, has been published in newsletters or network collections and has remained intentionally local, not readily available beyond the particular setting to which it is connected. What counts as the literature of teacher research[1] is thus at issue because the texts available for a review in a handbook such as this one, although numerous, likely constitute a small proportion of what is actually being written in the field.

The problem of reviewing the literature of teacher research is further complicated in that over this same period of time, there has emerged an extensive literature *about* teacher research written almost solely by university-based researchers. Relatively little of the scholarship about teacher research draws explicitly on the published texts of teacher researchers. Instead, this work describes, theorizes, and critiques teacher research from various authors' stances as participants in and/or analysts of the movement. Additionally there have been, to date, no comprehensive reviews of teacher research in any area that treat it as a literature or body of knowledge. Only recently has the topic of teacher inquiry been regarded as sufficiently prominent to merit inclusion in a major handbook (Baumann, Bisblinghoff, & Allen, 1997; Burton, 1991; Henson, 1996; Zeichner & Noffke, in press), and other chapters in these handbooks contain few,

---

[1] I use the term *teacher research* throughout this chapter to encompass broadly the forms of inquiry that others in the field of literacy may refer to as action research, practitioner inquiry, or teacher inquiry. The chapter is constructed by juxtaposing the literature of K–12 teacher research in literacy as the primary source with conceptual work on teacher research done for the most part by university-based researchers. Sources for teacher research in literacy for this chapter were selected from an extensive literature search for work published in the last 10 years—including monographs, edited volumes, book chapters, and journal articles. In no way intended to diminish the value and relevance of local publications, for the purpose of this chapter citations were limited to sources accessible nationally, with the exception of teacher research published online. Teacher writing was considered teacher research if the writer so specified. Although I reference practitioner inquiry in the field of adult literacy, I do not focus on this work, nor do I attempt to deal explicitly with the many issues surrounding the use of teacher research in preservice teacher education. This chapter does not take up methodological issues in teacher inquiry which are dealt with in the chapter by J. Baumann.

if any, citations to the work of teacher researchers. There is considerable question, then, about what counts as the literature of teacher research and to whom.

The "what counts and to whom" question, however, is not simply one of the difficulties in locating literatures or in selecting from the wide range of texts that call themselves "teacher research," but is rather a problem endemic to the very nature of the work. In this chapter, I place this question at the center of my inquiry in order to emphasize the tensions that characterize what is at issue in the field. By taking seriously this question, the chapter illuminates the ways in which the intellectual and material worlds of research and practice, schools and universities, local and public ways of acting and knowing are being continuously negotiated, and thus how the arena of teacher research has become contested territory. I argue that understanding the work's history, current status, and potential contributions to the field of literacy education hinges on understanding the nature of this contestation.

The argument of this chapter is animated by Mary Louise Pratt's (1991) notion of a contact zone as a "social space where cultures meet, clash and grapple with each other, often in contexts of highly asymmetrical relations of power" (p. 34). In order to reveal what is at issue in the contact zone of teacher research, the chapter is organized into four areas of contestation. These areas are intentionally designed using metaphors of place and space in order to avoid the construction of a definitive typology and instead to suggest a generative framework for provoking further conversation and interpretation. These areas include the *legacy* of teacher research, that is, where it comes from and what it is connected to; the *location* of the researcher, that is, who is doing the work; the *orientation* of the work, that is, what it is about, what it is for, and why; and, finally, how the work is structured by *community*. The concluding section explores the concept of *neighborhood* as a way to envision alternative social spaces for the future of teacher research.

LEGACY

Teacher research in the field of literacy came into prominence as an alternative research tradition in the mid 1980s and has since become one of the signature strands of the contemporary North American teacher research movement (Anderson, Herr, & Nihlen, 1994; Cochran-Smith & Lytle, 1993, 1999; Zeichner & Noffke, in press).[2] Several complementary and converging lines of thought about the relationships of language and learning created the immediate context for this to occur.

The first, marked by the publication of Dixie Goswami and Peter Stillman's "Reclaiming the Classroom: Teacher Research as an Agency for Change" (1987), an edited collection of conceptual essays and pieces of teacher research, emphasized inquiry as both a basis for pedagogy and as an agency for change.[3] Tracing its central metaphors to the influence of British educator Lawrence Stenhouse (1983; also Rudduck &

---

[2]This chapter does not trace the history nor explore the range of traditions of teacher research/action research/practitioner inquiry as they have evolved in the United States or abroad. See Zeichner and Noffke (in press) for references to historical analyses. See Hollingsworth (1997) for sources from an international perspective. Teacher research in the United States dates back at least to the 1950s but literacy-related teacher research did not become prominent in the field until the mid to late 1980s.

[3]Goswami and Stillman's volume emanated from courses and programs at the Bread Loaf School of English. It highlighted the significance of teachers' and students' questions as well as the critical role of teacher observation and documentation in developmental approaches to children's learning (see, e.g., the work of Emig, Martin, Britton, Dixon, Cazden, Royster, Lunsford, Graves, Heath, Berthoff, Burgess, Armstrong, Medway, Moffett, etc). Over time, Goswami and others (e.g., Atwell, 1987/1998; Branscombe et al., 1992; Christian, 1997) have continued to explore this vision. For a recent publication of Bread Loaf teacher researchers' work, see the summer 1998 *Bread Loaf Rural Teacher Network Magazine* published by Bread Loaf School of English, Middlebury College. It is important to note that in the mid 1980s other very similar approaches to teacher research in literacy were being developed by Robinson (1990) and Stock (1995) in Michigan and, with a somewhat different valence, by Myers (1985) in California.

Hopkins, 1985), Ann Berthoff (1987), and James Britton (1987), the volume drew extensively on the literature and dialogue since the 1970s among English educators and writing teachers in the United States and United Kingdom about students as language learners and about inquiry as a basis for teaching, classroom discourse, reading, and writing. What many regard as the seminal book in a second strand, "Working Together: A Guide for Teacher Researchers," was written by classroom teachers and National Writing Project teacher-consultants Marion Mohr and Marian Maclean and drew primarily on their experience as teachers facilitating other teachers' learning. Instrumental in the proliferation of teacher groups in subsequent years, this book guided many teachers in methods for conducting teacher research and in strategies for forming and sustaining communities built around sharing individual teachers' classroom research. Nancie Atwell's influential volume "In the Middle" provided a kind of connecting link between the two strands by offering a detailed account of how she embedded research in practice, thus making immediately accessible images of classroom teaching congruent with ongoing documentation.

All three of these volumes were published in 1987 and were written primarily for audiences of teachers. A fourth volume in that same year (Bissex & Bullock, 1987) elaborated the idea of case study research in writing and offered examples of year-long classroom-based studies by teachers in K–12 classrooms as well as case studies of writers conducted as part of graduate study. Taken together, this work planted seeds for a "quiet revolution" (Bullock, 1987), for an indigenous or homegrown form of teacher-initiated study of literacy practice to take root. As an extension of the process writing and language-across-the-curriculum movements of the 1970s, this work built on a set of fundamental assumptions about the nature of language and literacy learning and applied them to the act of teaching in order to argue that there are critical connections between the ways that students and teachers learn and co-construct knowledge.

The primary organizations responsible for forwarding these ideas—the Bread Loaf School of English and the National Writing Project—each had more than a decade of experience in connecting teachers, school districts, and higher education in partnerships that by design attempted to interrupt the dominant theory-to-practice model of knowledge utilization. The concept of "teacher as researcher" thus added depth and purpose to established teacher networks already having national reach, as well as supported teachers and teacher educators poised to invent new linkages and relationships. Importantly, the version of teacher research that emerged in literacy not only had pedagogical appeal, but was intentionally quite general, conceptually coherent but only loosely aligned with particular ideologies or research methods. This spirit was evident in Goswami and Stillman's Preface, where as editors they proposed that "following another's blueprint is inimical to the spirit of classroom research." Thus the framework that jump-started teacher research in literacy was deeply practice and classroom focused and supportive of invention and initiative, but also sought the institutionalization of teacher research by making inquiry part of the professional lives of teachers (Myers, 1987). Not insignificantly, teacher researchers in literacy understood writing as central to learning for both their students and themselves and as a consequence were poised to take leadership in developing opportunities for teachers to write proposals for grants, present at local and national conferences, and contribute to a range of publications. Over time, support for and sponsorship of teacher research has been taken on by virtually all of the major professional organizations associated with reading and language research (see Table 37.2 in the section on Community).

A range of other approaches to teacher research—affiliated with different traditions and practices here as well as in other countries such as England and Australia—were being developed, theorized, adapted, and critiqued by university-based researchers over the same period of time. This work conceptualizes teacher research in a range of ways from an activity or process to a method, project, program, or type of text to an emerging genre of research. Core concepts such as "research," "inquiry," "action," "collaborative," and "critical" are used in combination with one another and with the term *teacher* or *practitioner* to signal a range of meanings for "insider" investigations into life in classrooms, schools or other educational settings (Anderson et al., 1994; Carr & Kemmis, 1986; Cochran-Smith & Lytle, 1993; Elliott, 1991; Kincheloe, 1991; Zeichner & Noffke, in press).

It may be helpful to spin out a few ways in which the language here is problematic. Typically, the term teacher *research* describes investigations of practice that are intentionally in the tradition of qualitative, interpretive and ethnographic methods and methodologies as distinguished from the tradition, for example, of "reflective practice" attributed to Schon (1983). *Action research,* on the other hand, has frequently differentiated itself through its definition as joint investigation, curriculum construction, or project with an activist and democratic orientation (Beyer, 1988; Elliott, 1991; Noffke & Stevenson, 1995). Further complicating the discourse, an investigation designated as *action* research may carry the political and social connotations suggested by affixing the terms *critical* or, in some cases, *collaborative,* or it may not (Carr & Kemmis, 1986; Krater, Zeni & Cason, 1994; Goldblatt, 1995; Hollingsworth, 1997; Noffke & Stevenson, 1995; Sagor, 1992).

Some literacy-related teacher research literature has favored the term *practitioner* research over teacher research, in part to signal collaboration with other stakeholders in the educational arena such as administrators, counselors, tutors, social workers, parents, and community members (Anderson et al., 1994). Frequently the term *inquiry* has begun to be substituted for research. For some teachers, calling the work *inquiry* is an effort to make more visible and explicit the connection between the stance of the teacher who is conducting the inquiry and the inquiry stance of the learners involved, and thus to resonate with popular notions of classrooms as learning communities and with constructivist, whole-language, and learner-centered pedagogies (Baroz, 1998; Locklear, 1994; Murphy, 1994; J. Schwartz, 1990; Thomas & Oldfather, 1996). For others, using *inquiry* represents a self-conscious attempt to distinguish or disassociate their work from academic or university-based research, which calls up prior images of research they regard as irrelevant, inaccessible, and/or impositional.

Proliferating terms and traditions have been an inevitable consequence of the wide range of participants in the teacher research movement (Cochran-Smith & Lytle, 1999). Universities, school districts, state education departments, and national reform networks have begun to attach some form of teacher inquiry to all manner of teacher education and professional development, school reform, and curricular improvement (see, e.g., Allen, Cary, & Delgado, 1995; Hollingsworth & Sockett, 1994b; Little, 1993; Richardson, 1994a). Teacher research also plays a role in discipline-based research on practice (in the writing field, see, e.g., Daiker & Morenberg, 1990; North, 1987; Ray, 1993), as well as the newer national reform networks (e.g., most recently, the Annenberg Institute). For more than 10 years, teacher research has been forwarded by all of the major national literacy-related research centers, each of which has framed and reframed what teacher inquiry is, what it is for, and how it ought to look, according to its own mission and mix of disciplinary and interdisciplinary perspectives (see Table 37.2 in the section on Community). Most of this work has required, not incidentally, establishing and negotiating new relationships between and among school-based teacher researchers and collaborative partners from the university or school districts. Concurrent with this spread and growth has been an intensified debate about whether teacher research is a new *paradigm,* a new *genre* of research that is part of a wider social and political movement, or even qualifies, epistemologically and methodologically, as *research* at all (Anderson et al., 1994; Cochran-Smith & Lytle, 1993; Fenstermacher, 1994; Huberman, 1996; Ray, 1993).

As a consequence of their particular legacies, the texts of teacher research in literacy thus vary considerably in the ways in which teacher researchers connect their work—explicitly or by implication—with established or alternative research traditions or particular bodies of knowledge. Although the epistemological and methodological frames teachers bring to research that in turn inform their analyses and interpretations are being debated in the literature *about* teacher research, most teacher researchers have not taken this on directly. In contrast to research in the academy that emphasizes the deliberate selection of key concepts and the location of work in relation to established traditions, a large proportion of teacher research in literacy has spread as a more organic, grass-roots phenomenon that rarely identifies its roots and relatives.[4] In a sense, the literature of teacher research in literacy does not constitute a "tradition" as the academy understands that idea; it does not appear to be evolving necessarily from any agreed-on set of questions, beliefs or assumptions about literacy, teaching, learning, or inquiry itself. Only relatively rarely (and mostly in teacher research dissertations or writing based on them) do teacher researchers choose to frame their texts with extensive reference to academic literatures or methodological traditions (see, e.g., Barbieri, 1995; Duthie, 1996; Fecho, 1998; Goldblatt, 1995; Wilhelm, 1996).

In the literature of teacher research in literacy, the most salient "legacies" indicated in the work are often researchers' own social, cultural, political, and educational frameworks, their experiences in and out of the profession, and their indigenous questions (see, e.g., Hankins, 1998; Trotman, 1998; Yagelski, 1990). These sources may be investigated through the construction, for example, of literacy autobiographies as initial sections that explore the origins of the research questions in order to link (and critique) cultural, family, community, and educational frameworks and experiences (see, e.g., Bullough & Gitlen, 1995; Meyer, 1996; Mies, 1982 as cited in Kincheloe, 1991; Smythe, 1992).[5] Some pieces examine what it means to "read" as teachers, to engage current research critically and dialectically in light of what they know and are learning from their own classrooms (see, e.g., Allen et al., 1995; Fecho, 1993; Gallas, 1994). Whether and how teacher researchers make or make explicit these kinds of connections—to particular iterations of teacher research, to established bodies of knowledge on similar topics, to methodological traditions, and/or to their own life experiences, including the conceptual frameworks or theories of practice they bring to teaching—has implications for how their texts are understood and valued by different audiences.

LOCATION

What it means for classroom teachers to do research has been a subject of debate since the movement began. Some formulations emphasize the unique position of the teacher in the research, arguing that this work is intentionally and necessarily local, rooted in the practices and issues of the everyday life world (Bissex & Bullock, 1987; Britton, 1987; Goswami & Stillman, 1987; Hubbard & Power, 1993; Lytle & Cochran-Smith, 1992; Meier, 1997; Wells, 1994; Wells & Chang-Wells, 1992). In contrast to other researchers who enter schools for a bounded period of time as participant observers, in this view teacher researchers are understood to inhabit the research site as *observant participants* (Erickson, 1986; Florio-Ruane & Walsh, 1980) with immediate and deliber-

---

[4]Notable exceptions include the collaborative school-university work of the Santa Barbara Discourse Group (see Green & Dixon, 1993) and the Brookline Teacher Research Group (see Gallas et al., 1996) from sociolinguistic and sociocultural perspectives on classroom language and the Philadelphia Teachers Learning Cooperative (1984) from a phenomenological approach.

[5]Some exceptions include the few studies in literacy that also provide extensive analyses of teacher researchers' own research histories, including their education in various literatures and methodologies (see, e.g., Fleischer, 1994, 1995; Vinz, 1996; Hankins, 1998; Wilhelm, 1996).

ate commitments to the task at hand. As insiders studying their own setting, it is argued that teacher researchers bring a unique perspective that can make visible the co-construction of knowledge and the curriculum; drawing on their phenomenal experience, teacher researchers are in a position to interrogate (and alter) classroom and school culture from within (Cochran-Smith & Lytle, 1993; Knoblauch & Brannon, 1993; Vinz, 1996). Some argue that teachers have different perceptions, a "teacherly" way of viewing the world (Jackson, 1986, as quoted in Ray, 1993)—abilities Ray (1993) identifies as "noticing details, processing a considerable amount of information at a glance, perceiving irregularities and trouble spots immediately, thinking in a 'future-oriented' way so as to see possibilities that others miss, and responding appropriately to a variety of behaviors" (p. 59).

At the same time, a range of epistemological and methodological critiques has been offered of the notion of a "privileged" kind of emic stance and the attribution of a special kind of knowledge (Fenstermacher, 1994; Huberman, 1996; Cochran-Smith & Lytle, 1998). Although it is acknowledged that practitioners are centrally positioned to test theory because they have access to their own intentions and motives, long-term experience of the setting, and well-established relationships, the argument is nevertheless made that self-knowledge is not necessarily valid; because insiders process knowledge implicitly on the basis of practice-based concerns, the argument is made that they cannot necessarily understand what is going on in a wider context (Hammersley, 1993). Fenstermacher (1994) and Huberman (1996) question the epistemic merit of teacher research as well as its claims for a distinctive methodology, an argument that has been interpreted as applying essentially conventional standards to constructing and assessing teacher research (Cochran-Smith & Lytle, 1998). On the other end of the continuum, Manning and Harste (1994) argue that much "research ON education" is part of a "discourse of emasculation," used to control teachers' practice and undermine their professional judgments; it is teacher research "done by teachers and kids in their classrooms" that they regard as "real educational research" (p. 2).

Other conceptual and empirical literatures (written by variously situated teacher researchers and university-based scholars) position teacher researchers as both insiders *and* outsiders who need to renegotiate traditional relationships between schools and universities and rethink assumptions about the relationships of research and practice (Cochran-Smith & Lytle, 1993; Freedman, Simons, Kalnin, & Casareno, 1999; Hollingsworth, 1994; Noffke & Stevenson, 1995). By resisting both the unproblematized celebration of teachers' voices and the critiques that would circumscribe teacher research by relying primarily on normative frameworks, these accounts raise deeper issues about what is at stake for teachers doing research, that is, what it means to be implicated in every part of this work as practicing teachers and simultaneously as researchers/writers.

There is little disagreement that teacher researchers have complicated relationships to their teaching and research; it is the nature of that complication and its significance to teachers and others that is at issue. In much of the literature of teacher research in literacy, teachers' questions surface first from their practice. Typically they are not expressly (at least initially) tied to issues that others might view as significant for building knowledge in the field, but rather emerge from some discrepancy, nudge, problem, curiosity, desire, surprise, contradiction, and/or "felt need" that is directly tied to their particular setting (see, e.g., Ballenger, 1998; Root, 1996; Schiller, 1996; Waff, 1995b). These questions have "stories" in that they may be traced to the teacher's prior or current educational experiences and pedagogical stance, but they are rarely stable, evolving in relationship to the day-to-day exigencies and insights of ongoing work with learners and with their colleagues (Buchanan, 1994; Cone, 1994/1997; E. Schwartz , 1992; Sims, 1993). Investigating their questions requires that teacher researchers both immerse themselves in lived experience and at once step back from it.

Teachers thus have the opposite dilemma of university-based researchers who come into classrooms, in that as part of the research process teacher researchers need to seek a more distanced perspective on what is closest and perhaps taken for granted in their own practice.

Taking the dual stance of teacher and researcher has indeterminate and sometimes problematic implications for the role of teacher researcher as teacher, raising issues about what it really means to attempt to embed research in practice. The literature of teacher research in literacy suggests that decisions about whether to stand back or intervene in classroom behavior, whether to record or attempt to alter an interaction, to interrupt a silence or let a situation play itself out, become at best knottier (Gaughan, 1996; Hartman, 1994). Teaching issues and research issues thus become complexly entangled with each other (Atwell, 1987/1998; Johnston, 1992; Mohr, 1994). Furthermore, although there are many richly documented accounts in the literature of teachers speaking to the positive effects of researching their classrooms on their teaching, there is also a concern about whether the roles are conflicting or compatible (see, e.g., Baumann, 1996; Curtis, 1993; Dudley-Marling, 1995). Much of the published work points to teacher research as complicating, intentionally, the teachers' relationships to students, as teachers style their research as *with* or *for* students rather than about them, and as they engage students as co-researchers and therefore need to negotiate the roles of the students in the research process (Branscombe, Goswami, & Schwartz, 1992; Kutz, 1992). As a consequence, issues some identify as those associated with "studying down" may color and complicate already complex power dynamics between students and teachers (Ray, 1993).

In arenas beyond the classroom, there is much at stake for teachers when they present their work to others, whether in their own schools or in other educational settings. Teachers' accounts of their classroom-based research make public aspects of their pedagogy—everything from choices made in leading discussions of literary texts to ways of structuring literacy tasks for students to formative or summative assessments of writing and learning (Parker, 1997; Reilly, 1995; Swain, 1994; Udall, 1998). Thus teacher researchers open their teaching *practice* up to comment and validation but also to examination, critique, and evaluation. When teachers explain the sources of their questions, for example, these stories provide insight into who they are in their classrooms. There is thus a possibility that something will be revealed that is not intended, for example, that the practices made "public" through the research appear incompatible with the teacher's stated beliefs. Always deeply implicated in the culture of the school, teacher researchers often need to negotiate and renegotiate relationships with their colleagues, administrators, parents, and other staff around the connections between their immediate responsibilities for groups of students' learning and their assumption of an inquiry stance on their practice (Chin, 1996; Headman, 1993; Jumpp & Strieb, 1993; Resnick, 1996).

The teacher research literatures make evident the vulnerability of the teacher researcher (Hammack, 1997; Lytle, 1993; Nagle, 1997; Ray, 1993, 1996; J. Schwartz, 1990; Zeni, 1996). Researching one's own practice involves not only revealing the contours of one's teaching life over time but also portraying the experiences of students and the variable landscapes of a teaching context. Teacher research is not all about good news, not simply about "revealed excellence" (see, e.g., Baum-Brunner, 1993; Deshon, 1997; Keep-Barnes, 1994; Kucera, 1995). At best, presenting to wider audiences increases teachers' mutual dependence and trust. But the processes of "seeing collectively" may also reveal messy ethical issues in co-investigating school practices with students, or inadvertently may display students' struggles in ways that reinforce stereotypes (Ray, 1993). This has implications for what and how teachers choose to investigate in light of their ongoing relationships with their students, colleagues, schools, and communities (Newkirk, 1992).

Some teacher research highlights these institutional politics and the potential for conflict around the responses of administrators, parents, and colleagues to the critical stance of some practitioner research (e.g., Chase & Doan, 1996; Ellwood, 1992; Lytle & Fecho, 1992; Schaafsma, 1993; Trotman, 1998). As Ray (1993) pointed out, there are clearly issues here about what has been referred to as the good teacher versus the good researcher. Also dealt with in the literature about teacher research, these issues sometimes have a different valence. Contending that practitioner research "must challenge the sociopolitical status quo" of the setting, for example, Anderson et al. (1994) urged that teachers should not fall into reporting what they call "sanitized" forms of practitioner research. Others argue for methodological rigor without accounting for inevitable constraints in teachers' work lives or for the possibility of repercussions in their workplaces (see, e.g., Huberman, 1996).

The subset of teacher research in literacy done by pairs of school–university collaborators makes visible a kind of "dynamic tension" that requires redefinition of roles (Ray, 1993). Differences are noted in whose questions drive the investigation and how they are identified, what counts as inquiry, what analytic frameworks are used for interpreting the data and where they come from, as well as who or what is expected to change as a consequence of the work together. Some studies, for example, are driven by a teacher's question (Butler, 1992; Ellison, 1997; Keenan, Willett, & Solsken, 1993), some by a university-based researcher's question about the teacher's classroom (Fairbanks, 1995; Henkin, 1995; Snyder, 1992), and some by questions from each participant (Carroll, 1994; Pappas, Oyler, Barry & Rassel, 1993; Taylor & McIntyre, 1992), whereas the majority report studies based on questions developed collaboratively by the participants (Bianchi & Cullere, 1996; Busching & Slesinger, 1995; Chinn & Iding, 1997; Commeyras & Sumner, 1995; Edelsky & Boyd, 1993; Fecho & Lytle, 1993). These collaborative arrangements have been described as social interventions in the lives of participants (Wagner, 1997) that entail issues of power, access, ownership, credit/reward, voice, audience, and purpose (Allen, Buchanan, Edelsky & Norton, 1992; Ellwood, 1992).

Edelsky and Boyd (1993), a university-based researcher and a school-based teacher researcher, pointed to an array of factors and potential struggles that influence the work, including research approaches, abilities, and stances, as well as the nature of mentoring relationships, collegial arrangements (e.g., a dissertation done in a colleague's classroom; see Buchanan & Schultz, 1993; Cohen, 1993), and various other permutations that color how the concepts of research "with" and writing "with" are instantiated. Arguing for ethical guidelines for both collaborative and noncollaborative research, teams of school and university-based researchers have noted that what is at issue in collaborative research for teachers includes ambiguity about being the researcher and the researched, status inequalities, differences in working conditions, and disparities in credit for writing and publication (Alvermann, Olson, & Umpleby, 1993; Fecho & Lytle, 1993; Hudelson & Lindfors, 1993; Mackinson & Peyton, 1993; Mangiola & Pease-Alvarez, 1993). It is not irrelevant that the most widely used computer program for bibliographies has no function for research "with."[6]

The complex relationships of teachers to teacher research, schools, districts, and universities constitute sites of conflict considerably more nuanced than the simple opposition of "us" and "them." What is particularly generative about *location* may be the seemingly contradictory set of relationships between and among participants in what we often take for granted are the separate worlds of the school and university. In teacher research, school-based and university-based researchers are not so easily distinguished from one another: they are at once in union, in opposition, and in response or challenge to each other; none live in a vacuum, speaking just their own language.

---

[6]The software referred to here is Endnote.

This arena of teacher research thus resembles what Gloria Anzaldua (1987) described as a borderland, a vague or undetermined situation or place where two or more cultures edge each other, where differently situated people occupy the same territory and where very similar people find themselves "across the borders" from one another, in different territories. From this perspective, the role of the teacher as a researcher lends itself to a further reinterpretation aligned with Anzaldua's concept of *mestiza* consciousness: in her view, rather than resisting the construction of duality by seeing oneself as having separate identities, clashing with each other, one can instead decide to see this *mestiza* consciousness as something powerful to cultivate. The positioning or *location* of teachers as researchers interrupts the easy distinctions often made between "insider" and "outsider" and destabilizes the boundaries of research and practice—creating a space where a radical realignment and redefinition may be possible.

ORIENTATION

A content analysis of teacher research in literacy would be an expected dimension of an inquiry such as this one. However, analyzing the content of teacher research in literacy primarily to demonstrate patterns of what it is about is problematic for three reasons. First, the genres of teacher research in literacy vary widely, thereby provoking questions about the significance of relationships between the form and the particular questions or topics that are taken up. Second, the ways purpose is married with content raise questions as to why texts address particular themes, that is, why it is about what it is about and how knowing that (or not) alters how we think about the specific content. Third, the range of readers or audiences for the pieces varies so widely that understanding the content often depends on understanding the teacher researcher's intended relation to a known and/or distal readership. In order to elaborate fully the significant dimensions related to content, a richer notion is required, one that takes into account the intricacies of genre, topic, purpose and audience—what is here called an *orientation*.

This said, it is not unuseful to organize the literature thematically, because the range and variation of content foci provide an overview of the areas literacy teacher-researchers regard as important enough to merit systematic investigation. Table 37.1 displays teacher research studies organized broadly by thematic frames, separating work done by individuals or pairs of teacher researchers from publications describing the work of teacher groups or communities.

When looking across the literature for themes and patterns, it is clear that the majority of the pieces focus on issues directly related to classroom pedagogy. These include teachers' analyses of individual students and classroom interactions, instructional strategies related primarily to aspects of learner- or response-centered teaching, and analyses of students' expressive and creative abilities and the purposes, attitudes, interests, linguistic and cultural resources students bring to learning. Teacher research on pedagogy often makes problematic the nature and purposes for reading, writing, and talking in school as well as criteria for developing curricula for use in different contexts. Some of this work investigates pedagogical concerns by highlighting the social and organizational structures and oral and written discourse of classrooms as learning environments co-constructed by teachers and students through language and interaction. Other texts link issues of teaching and learning and the patterns of classroom literacy practices explicitly to issues of race, gender, and ethnicity, as well as what it means to make problematic teachers' and students' assumptions about culture and community in various urban, suburban and rural contexts.

The corpus of teacher research in literacy also encompasses work that contributes to a transformed and expanded notion of practice (Cochran-Smith & Lytle, 1999). Some of this work explores the cultures of teaching and learning in and out of schools, partic-

TABLE 37.1

Teacher Research in Literacy—Four Thematic Frames for Researching Practice[a]

	Individuals and Pairs[a]			Groups
I. Pedagogy **A. Classroom instruction, curriculum, and assessment**	Baum-Brunner (1993) Buchanan (1993) Christian (1997) Cone (1994/1997) Duthie (1996) Feldgus (1993) Five (1986, 1989) Gallas (1991/1997) Hoffman (1996)	Johnson (1995/1997) Johnston (1992) Lewis (1993) Madigan & Koivu-Rybicki (1997) Meier (1997) Ray (1987) Reilly (1995) Schwartz, E. (1992)	Sims (1993) Stock (1995) Strieb (1993) Swaim (1998) Udall (1998) Whitin (1996) Wilhelm (1996) Wyshynki & Paulsen (1995) Yagelski (1990)	Livdahl et al. (1995) McMahon & Raphael (Eds.) (1996) Newman (Ed.) (1990, 1998) Phillips et al. (1993) Strickland, Dillon, Funkhouse, Glick, & Rogers (1989) Taylor (1990) Wells (1993)
B. Classroom environment and organization	Ackerman (1997) Allen, J. (1997) Allen, S. (1992) Atwell (1987, 1987/1998) Avery (1993) Banford (1996) Barbieri (1987)	Baroz (1998) Chase & Doan (1996) Cone (1990, 1992, 1993) Deshon (1997) Fraser & Skolnick (1994) Gallas (1992, 1994) Juska (1995)	Lott (1994) Paley (1995) Seabrook (1991/1997) Whitmore & Crowell (1994)	Meyer (1996) Tuyay, Floriani, Yeager, Dixon, & Green (1995)
II. Culture and community	Ballenger (1992/1997, 1996a, 1996b, 1998) Barbieri (1995) Brown (1993) Cziko (1996) Fecho (1994, 1996, 1998)	Gallas (1998) Gaughan (1996) Hunt (1995) Macphee (1997) Moore (1998) Murphy (1994) Newland (1990)	Schaafsma (1993) Schiller (1996) Schwartz, J. (1990) Skelton (1998) Stumbo (1992) Temple (1998) Waff (1995a, 1995b, 1996)	Dyson with the San Francisco East Bay Teacher Study Group (1997) Freedman, Simons, Kalnin, Casareno & M-Class Teacher Researchers (1999) Krater et al. (1994)

(Continues)

TABLE 37.1 (Continued)

	Individuals and Pairs	Groups
III. Cultures of teaching in/out of schools	Austin (1994) Buchanan (1994) Chin (1996) Colgan-Davis (1993) Christian (1998) Fecho (1993) Fleischer (1995) Harris (1993) Headman (1993) Jumpp (1996) Jumpp & Strieb (1993) Kaltenbach (1993) Kanevsky (1993) Kieffer (1996) Mohr (1987) Parker (1997) Pincus (1993) Resnick (1996) Swain (1994) Wunner (1993)	Allen, Cary, & Delgado (1995) Duckworth et al. (1997) Florio-Ruane (1990) Gallas et al. (1996) Gonzalez et al. (1993) Hollingsworth (1994) Meyer et al. 1998
IV. Access, equity, and democratic education	Allen, A. (1997) Branscombe & Thomas (1992) Goldblatt (1995) Sylvester (1994/1997) Vasquez (2000)	Allen, J. (Ed.) (1999) Beyer & Liston (Eds.) (1996) Gitlin et al. (1992) Lytle et al. (1994) Taylor et al. (1997)

[a]The citations here do not include teacher–researcher collaborative pairs.

ularly the changing nature of schools as workplaces and sites of the intersection of school practices with families, community organizations, and school–university partnerships. The work reflects teachers' efforts to assume leadership roles, to connect parents and schools, and to build communities with other teachers and their students across classroom and school boundaries. Research considering issues of professional socialization including teacher-to-teacher collaboration and inquiry as a mode of collegial learning is also evident. A smaller number of studies address issues of access, equity, and democratic education by explicitly framing their work within broad societal issues, including social, economic, political, and moral concerns, and often with a focus on democracy and social justice.

Looking at the content of this literature reveals areas that teachers have identified as important to investigate in their practice, broadly construed. The texts themselves, however, reveal considerable diversity in type or genre and thus invite questions about how researching teachers understand relationships between the form and content, particularly when there is little in the texts themselves to illuminate the rationale for these choices.[7] More specifically, publications by teacher researchers represent a range of texts both conceptual and empirical, including reflective essays, studies or inquiries, oral inquiries, monographs, and dissertations. Some of these now appear as well in online journals or web sites. Teacher research publications are variously referred to as stories, anecdotes, vignettes, reports, case studies, journals, narratives, autobiographies, personal accounts, qualitative, interpretive, ethnographic or autoethnographic reports (Calkins, 1985; Grimmett & MacKinnon, 1992; Knoblauch & Brannon, 1993; Lytle & Cochran-Smith, 1990; Stock, 1995). Over more than a decade, literacy teachers have also invented new genres or forms for depicting their research, with some bringing together multiple voices (such as multigenre pieces, multivoiced collages, reader's theater, and other performative modes) and others adapting fictional or poetic modes including satire and parody. Although these texts differ considerably in their interpretations of what it means to gather and make sense of data in schools and classrooms and to communicate results of research to others, there is no necessary hierarchy, for example, a scheme for valuing or evaluating how the content is formed or transformed to construct a reflective essay, in contrast to an ethnographic study or reader's theater piece. This variation, however, does raise questions about the relationships between content and purpose, that is, why the work is about what it is about and why it is represented or written in a particular way.

The notion of purpose for teacher research is a particularly contested territory. That the site of inquiry is infused with immediate and consequential actions and meanings is one of the defining features of this research. Taking the literature of teacher research in literacy as a set, the primary purpose most teachers articulate for their research is to *teach better*, to act or understand something differently so that their students' learning is enhanced. Conspicuous across texts are teachers' concerns about the immediate consequences of actions for particular learners, families, schools, and communities (Meier, 1997; Parker, 1997; Swain, 1994; Taylor, Coughlin, & Marasco, 1997). The purpose is not to "do research," but to observe, document, and analyze the daily work of literacy teaching and learning as it occurs in and out of classroom and school contexts. Thus the choices teachers make about genre are almost always deeply informed by the particular purpose and often local "audience" for whom they are writing, presenting, or performing.

Looking across the literature of teacher research in literacy, there appears to be consistency at the most general level about teacher research as a vehicle for making change. However, there is little in the teacher research literature itself that conceptual-

---

[7]Ray (1993) linked issues around genre to methodological eclecticism, resulting in difficulties in putting the written products in standard research genres and creating "a kind of hybrid text—part narrative, part case study, part experiment, part ethnography, part discourse analysis" (p. 93).

izes, elaborates, or interrogates the nature of change. The change agenda may be assumed or implicit, emanating from the particular nudge or discrepancy that frames the work rather than from a detailed research problem or contextualized question. Thus the rationale for change—a more formal statement of the problem in the classroom or in the world that the research responds to—may not be explicitly narrated or argued.

The literature *about* teacher research, on the other hand, reveals considerable attention to various notions of purpose and change and what it means that change is named, defined and valued differently in various educational contexts. In this literature, the concepts of change evolve from particular theoretical orientations to teacher research and are reflected in conversations in the academy linking teacher research with the discourses of reform, critical social theory, professional development, and teacher education (Cochran-Smith, 1994; Hargreaves, 1994, 1996; Hollingsworth & Sockett, 1994; Lieberman & Miller, 1994; Little & McLaughlin, 1993; Pappas & Zecker, in press-a, in press-b; Richardson, 1994b; Stevenson, 1995). And although university-based researchers consistently affirm the significance of the work for the local context, much of the debate has concerned itself with the value of teacher research in the so-called "wider" or "public" sphere. Often the unit of analysis is foregrounded, so that the concepts structuring the debate emphasize who or what is the object of change. Reviewing the literature for this chapter reveals that the key distinctions about purpose in teacher research often fall out along the lines of the locus of change, that is, change that is directed at individual, institutional, and/or societal change. They are elaborated here in order to sketch the territories within which significant questions of use and value get inscribed and debated.

In the literature *about* teacher research, studies that show the improvement of a teacher's classroom practice are thought to reflect an *individual* kind of change. From this perspective, teachers do research to observe and document learners' lives in and sometimes outside of classrooms to understand, and perhaps improve, how they and their students construct understandings of educational processes. The agenda of individually oriented change is understood to bring about a more complex or textured view of daily practice, including its tensions, ambiguities, and multiple interpretations. Work characterized as directed toward individual change may attempt to reveal how teachers and their students negotiate what counts as knowledge in—and out—of the classroom, who can have it, and how their own interpretations of classroom, school, family, and community life are shaped. Teacher research in this category may be understood to be aiming for a clarification of theoretical or interpretive frameworks and for interrogating assumptions, with an eye to changing perspectives and actions.

Studies understood as trying to make impact more broadly than the classroom are considered as those attempting to make some kind of *institutional* change. Teacher research understood to be in this category typically has issues of reform and the restructuring or transformation of schools, programs, district practices, or policies at its center. The intent of this work is understood as an attempt to influence administrative, curricular, or programmatic structures or to make these structures more visible by questioning specific practices. This kind of teacher research includes efforts to change the cultures of teaching and learning in schools and school systems, to make teachers' work more integrated or interdependent, and sometimes to document the work of collaborative communities within or across school sites.

Studies that frame the problem within broad social and political issues are considered aimed at some form of *societal* change. This work articulates the intent to work for and understand, for example, democratic education, antiracist teaching, or pedagogy for social justice—often by interrogating common understandings and challenging school practices that reproduce social inequalities. And although not the sole or even primary focus of the research, some work within this category is understood to seek to challenge traditional paradigms of educational research and practice, and thus intentionally to provoke questions about the role of practitioners in *changing research*, that is, the ways research is conducted, valued, and promoted, by and for whom. Research from this perspective raises questions about who sets the agenda for educational inquiry and whose interests are served.

At issue in the literature about teacher research is the extent to which teacher research is concerned with practitioners improving their own practice and enhancing their self-knowledge and the extent to which these individual transformations are part of efforts to improve the situations in which practices occur as well as efforts to change social and institutional structures (Anderson et al., 1994; Noffke, 1997; Noffke & Stevenson, 1995; Zeichner & Noffke, in press). Approaches characterized as individualistic and self-improvement oriented are weighed against changing organizational structures, introducing new programs, or seeking to rectify school services that function to maintain inequitable arrangements among students. What is being questioned, in part, are the relationships between changing individuals and changing societal structures, or what differently positioned participants in the debate understand as the social value of individual change, the classroom as a site of cultural and political work, and the role of individual acts in making more fundamental change.

Within this conversation is a concern with whether teacher research is fulfilling its potential to contribute to a more socially just world (Zeichner, 1994). Some point out that much of reflective practice has been co-opted, cast as a technology, and rather than challenging standard practices, supports them (Smythe, 1992); similar caveats have been made about teacher research becoming anything and everything, and thus nothing of consequence (Cochran-Smith & Lytle, 1999; Lytle, 1993). There is considerable discussion about whether classrooms can and do function as arenas for social, cultural, and political struggle and as sites for identifying alternatives to current practices (Noffke, 1997; Zeichner, 1994). A point of critique is what some construe as the limited amount of practitioner work addressing social justice or social equity issues in teaching and schooling (Noffke & Stevenson, 1995). Furthermore, those who are conceptualizing change as a consequence or outcome of teacher research point out that insofar as teachers can identify ways to alter their practice through the research process, they can also reproduce what already exists, solidify inequities, and make changes with little consequence for improving the quality of teaching and learning (Ellwood, 1992; Gore & Zeichner, 1995; Wells, 1993; Zeichner, 1992).

Questions of the use and value of teacher research are thus typically construed in the literature *about* teacher research within a framework of "the greater good," whereas teacher research itself often frames these questions within the immediate context and with reference to local purposes and meanings. And although the themes apparent in the teacher research literature on literacy may appear to map onto the framework of individual, institutional, and societal change, such distinctions are less compelling from the more nuanced and complicated view of *orientation*, which highlights the critical intersections of what teacher research is about, what it is for, and why. A teacher's research on pedagogy, for example, may be at once concerned with or at least potentially relevant to all three "takes" or loci of change. Nor is it obvious what kinds of texts appeal to whom and thus what work has the potential for contributing to what kinds of change.

The paucity of discussion in the literature *of* teacher research that interrogates the use and value of different kinds of change juxtaposed with the persistent emphasis in the literature *about* teacher research suggests the need for opening up conversations within and across communities and across the two literatures about what this work is for and about and how it is represented. Zeichner and Noffke (in press) make a related point in their call for ways to bridge the "current divide between academic discussions of critical and emancipatory goals for practitioner research and practitioners' discussions of the classroom as a site for political struggle" (p. 88). There are provocative questions about the relationship between the so-called public arena of discussion about change within the academy and the particular contexts of teacher research wherein questions of use and value are necessarily defined and negotiated initially if not ultimately in local terms and for local purposes.

COMMUNITY

As a critical part of the reform agenda begun in the mid 1980s, the move to create professional community has been recognized by many schools, districts, and universities as a central component in making change. And although historically there have been teacher groups outside of these formal organizational structures, such as the Philadelphia Teachers Cooperative (1984) and the Harvard Educator's Forum (Evans, 1989) and likewise individual teachers who inquired into and wrote about their practice (e.g., Ashton-Warner, 1963; Harris, 1993; Strieb, 1985; Wigginton, 1985), there is evidence that the growth of these many differently configured professional communities in and out of schools, districts, and universities has contributed to and in some cases resulted from the growth of the teacher research movement (Cochran-Smith & Lytle, 1999).

Over more than 15 years there has evolved a complicated set of social and organizational structures that shape and are sometimes shaped by the work of teacher researchers. From its inception, the teacher research movement in literacy has been, not surprisingly, a profoundly social and collaborative enterprise in which research has been conducted primarily in voluntary communities of teachers within and across schools and school districts and constructed through sets of literacy practices that vary according to the context of the group (see, e.g., Allen et al., 1995; Freedman et al., 1999; Gitlen et al., 1992; Lytle, 1998; Lytle et al., 1994; Meyer et al., 1998; Michaels, 1998; Pappas & Zecker, in press-b; Phillips et al., 1993). These groups have not typically been free-floating, but rather attached in complex ways to some other structure—a university, school, school-within-a-school, project, or network. To these inquiry communities teachers bring their "legacy"—including what they know or expect about the purpose and nature of the group's activity based on their own educational background and theories of practice. They also bring their "location," their positions relative to other systems or organizations, and thus the particularities of school context and collegial relationships, stance on practice, relationships with students, questions and etiologies of questions as well as their perceptions of the complex relationships of teaching and research.

The unique literacy practices of each teacher research group are in part co-constructed from these individual profiles and proclivities and often function as heuristic sites for envisioning an altered classroom community where students become more active constructors of knowledge (Allen, Cary & Delgado, 1995; Waff, 1996). In teacher inquiry or action research communities, discussion and debate around "orientation" are often the ways these dimensions get played out in the particular, that is, through how their written texts reflect participants' views of content and purpose for looking at some classroom, school, or system, as well as decisions about how the investigation will be written up/about and published for particular audiences. The intensity of the group dynamic—in contrast with how teachers describe their profound experiences with isolation over time—reflects the local connotation and collision of legacy, location and orientation.[8]

---

[8]Table 37.1 separates teacher research conducted by individuals and pairs of teachers from research conducted and published by teacher research communities to highlight the new genres of publication by groups. Research done by individuals (and pairs of teachers/university-based researchers) often grows out of the work of a community that functions as the social and organizational support for the work accomplished, although this is often not explained in the text.

Table 37.2 displays the sponsorship of teacher research related to literacy over the last 10 years as a multilevel set of loosely interrelated systems providing material and human resources to support various iterations of teacher research.[9] Although not exhaustive, it provides an overview of a range of social and organizational structures that have played a visible and critical role in this evolving field.[10]

In the teacher research literature itself, unless part of a collection or monograph in which the university or district sponsors (or more rarely, a teacher facilitator or participant) explain the social and organizational context from their perspective, there is typically very little written in the individual pieces about the complex layers of sponsorship, especially issues related to the macro context of the work. Furthermore, the meanings or implications of being funded by particular organizations such as foundations, government agencies, school districts, businesses, individuals, or professional networks, the choices to publish with particular presses or in particular journals, and the significance of being affiliated with various groups and universities are rarely discussed.

Issues of the depth and valence of support—types of resources, amount and duration, degrees of internal and external structure and control—merit further analysis. In the contact zone of teacher research, the relationships of funders and funded, sponsors and sponsored, university and school cultures compose the subtext of much of the teacher research literature, and suggest a number of critical issues that are at stake in the continued health and growth of the teacher research movement.

How are the relationships between organizations and teachers in communities shaped by negotiations conducted between sponsoring organizations and universities, which in turn make decisions about the allocations of resources and participants' roles? What do foundations or universities or school districts or counties want from the work of teacher researchers and how are those desired outcomes communicated, defined, and assessed? To what extent are teachers who participate in communities allied with universities, for example, positioned to make choices about the conceptual framework—the legacy and orientation—that govern the work, or its linkage to particular reform agendas, university research priorities, or foundation criteria? How are the collaborators' different agendas made visible, or not? What does it mean to fulfill an "outsider's" vision of the work in contrast to investigating and inventing one from within? In whose interests is the research in and on the community designed and carried out, and who stands to benefit from its completion and dissemination?

---

[9]Missing from the table, however, are the countless school-based and district-based inquiry groups that have been a salient dimension of reform initiatives, many with strong literacy-related components (e.g., Erickson & Christman, 1996; Zeichner, 1997), as well as an indeterminate number of teacher groups without outside funding or with less formal social and organizational structures (e.g., Colgan-Davis, 1993). Also not accounted for are the particular emphases of different sponsors, that is, teacher research as professional development, as school or organizational development, as knowledge generation, and so on.

[10]On the national level, supportive structures have included grants for individual and group projects, seminars, institutes and conferences, publication, and network leadership. Both the National Writing Project (through the more than 150 sites and subnetworks involving urban and rural teachers across the country) and the Bread Loaf School of English through the Rural Teacher Network in eight states have continued to take leadership through grant-funded special projects and online communities. Foundations have also become organizational sponsors; to strengthen the community of practitioner researchers and build teachers' research capacity, for example, through its Practitioner-Initiated Communication and Mentoring Grants Program, the Spencer Foundation has supported individuals and group programs of teacher research, including research mentoring and conferences, publications, and electronic networks. Teachers and teacher educators have worked successfully through professional organizations to open new avenues for funding, dissemination and recognition of the work of teacher researchers. A number of states, school districts, and public education funds have provided a range of supports for inquiry-based professional development. Notable efforts to publish teacher research locally over many years include the Madison Metropolitan School District, Madison, WI; the Alaska Teacher Researcher Network; the CRESS Center at UCDavis; the N. Virginia Writing Project; and the UCLA Writing Project. Countless numbers of colleges and universities have supported research communities of both preservice and inservice teachers through degree programs, collaborative partnerships with districts, and continuing education and research centers.

TABLE 37.2
Sponsorship of Literacy-Related Teacher Research: Social and Organizational Structures

Types of Structure	Examples of Organizations
Federal government	National Institute for Literacy (NIFL) Office of Educational Research and Improvement—U.S. Department of Education
National professional organizations	American Educational Research Association (AERA) (Teacher as Researcher SIG and Division K) International Reading Association (IRA) National Council of Teachers of English (NCTE) National Reading Conference (NRC) Teachers of English to Speakers of Other Languages (TESOL)
National networks	Bread Loaf Rural Teachers Network Foxfire National Writing Project
National centers	Annenberg Institute for School Reform (Providence, RI) Center for the Study of Writing and Literacy (UCBerkeley) Center on English Learning and Achievement (SUNY Albany) National Center for Research on Cultural Diversity and Second Language Learning (UCSanta Cruz) National Center for the Study of Adult Learning and Literacy (Harvard) National Center for Restructuring Education, Schools, and Teaching (Teachers College, Columbia) National Center on Adult Literacy (UPenn) National Reading Research Center (UGa) National Research Center on Literature Teaching and Learning (SUNY Albany)
National foundations	DeWitt-Wallace Readers Digest Foundation Spencer Foundation UPS Foundation
University centers/ networks	Center X (UCLA) Center for Educational Improvement Through Collaboration (UMichigan) Center for Literacy Studies (CUNY) Cooperative Research and Extension Services for Schools (UCDavis) Educators' Forum (Harvard) Jacob Hiatt Center for Urban Education (ClarkU) League of Professional Schools (UGa) Partnership Teacher Network (Univ. S. Maine)

(Continues)

TABLE 37.2 (Continued)

Types of Structure	Examples of Organizations
Journals	*English Education, English Journal, Language Arts, Research in the Teaching of English* (NCTE) *Harvard Educational Review* *New Advocate* *Teacher Research: A Journal of Classroom Inquiry* *Quarterly of the National Writing Project and the Center for the Study of Writing and Literacy* *Teaching and Change* (National Education Association and Corwin/Sage)
Publishers	Christopher Gordon Falmer Press Heinemann Boynton-Cook Lawrence Erlbaum Associates Stenhouse Publishers Teachers College Press

Note. Table includes organizations known to have supported literacy-related teacher research at some time over the past 10 years; there are many other organizations supporting teacher research with other or more general foci.

Within the community itself, how are relationships negotiated and represented? What are the implications when some participants in the community are funded as facilitators and others receive stipends for participation? What are the roles of university and teacher participants in decisions related to writing and publishing, and what happens, for example, when a group member pursues a project "out of line" with the ethos or politics of the group's work? When some participants elect not to write? Whose stories get told and whose published, and how are decisions made about positioning jointly authored work in the world, that is, which publisher, who writes the forward, and what are the status and political implications of these choices for differently situated coauthors?

Questions such as these move to the wider terrain of how the long-established research cultures of universities are shaping the newly emerging research cultures of teachers and vice versa, how the long-established but changing cultures of schools and school systems are shaping and/or being shaped by communities of teachers (Anderson & Herr, 1999; Lytle & Cochran-Smith, 1995). It is becoming increasingly important to understand how and to what extent these dimensions enhance teachers' agency and participation, through their research, in the wider discourse of policy and change. The profoundly social nature of teacher research in literacy suggests that we need to pay more attention to the structures that play a pivotal role in determining how and whether the work supports or interrupts the status quo.

DIRECTIONS FORWARD

The metaphor of the contact zone suggests a "read" of teacher research as a site of struggle that probes and at least partially illuminates the deeply relational context for this work. It invites movement from unproblematized notions of insider and outsider to consider more complexly what is possible in a third space—where the various constituencies recognize complementarity as well as difference and open up the productive possibilities of what Pratt (1991) referred to as oppositional discourse, resistance and critique. The goal here is neither contentiousness nor consensus, but rather acknowledging, understanding, and drawing on the richness of roles and identities and searching for new language with which to talk and think and new social practices with which to structure and support the work.

The distinctive contribution of teacher research in literacy as at once a grass-roots movement, and not, suggests the need to interrogate the ways we envision the "local" and the terms we set against it. Usage of concepts such as "the wider academic community" and the "public sphere" implicitly depends on a margin and center framework that designates teachers' knowledge and action as local and the actions and ways of knowing in the academy as something broader, bigger, and by implication more significant. Contrasting the local with the public reifies these terms. An alternative would be to explore the possibilities of reimagining or redefining the local as what Moshenberg (1996) called a "neighborhood"—a conceptual space or vicinity in which the salient concern is not an essentialized identity but rather one's location relative to others. What's important becomes not "who am I?" (or, "who are you?") but where, how, what, why and when [are we] (Trinh, 1992). From this perspective, what is more or less local, then, is relative to where one is. In this view, not only is the classroom or school local to teachers, for example, but the university is local to academics, and the American Educational Research Association (AERA) is local to both academics and teacher researchers who have elected to become part of that conversation. The local then is not a narrow given or solely the domain of the particular, but rather constructed and reconstructed to further a range of possibilities for the imaginative organization of new kinds of communities.

A reenvisioned local invites other ways of thinking about the many texts *of* and *about* teacher research, and especially the so-called fugitive literatures (Zeichner, 1994), the publications of teacher groups that are not disseminated nationally. We need to inquire to whom these literatures are "fugitive"—a term associated with the runaway or absconder, or alternately, a mischiefmaker or ruffian—and to ask who writes and reads this work and for what purposes. Who is the literature about teacher research intended for? What happens when a "local group" reads and interprets the layered "public" conversation of the academy about the processes and meanings of teacher research? What happens when academics read into the locally disseminated literatures? How does one teacher research group read—or review—the writing of another? What does it mean that many who write about this work do not read its texts or find them useful? What does it mean to "take this work seriously" and who are the "takers"?

An extension of these issues related to the diverse literatures of teacher research is what might be called "the missing conversations"—connections among the texts of teacher research and their linkages with other literatures. Envisioning the neighborhoods of teacher research raises questions about what it means that the literature of teacher research in literacy exists almost entirely as a collection of separate studies, essays, monographs, and so on without internal reference or citation to others whose research may inform the work at hand. In the literature about teacher research there are very different perspectives on how and whether the university's theoretical and analytic frameworks are needed or appropriate for this work (Calkins, 1985; Hubbard & Power, 1993). Although many agree that the task is not to make teacher research look more like university research, the question still remains as to how that issue is being taken up and interrogated and by whom. What would it mean to create more opportunities for the "constructive disruption of university culture" (Lytle & Cochran-Smith, 1995) and who needs to be part of these conversations? When is the circle better narrowed than made wider? As teacher researcher Threatt (Threatt et al., 1994) pointed out, there are important questions about who is having what discussion and who is being rewarded for making sense of who's work. What conversation is going on among teachers that is not visible in the published texts—and why does that matter? How and with what consequences have the conversations about university-based research that take place in university courses, professional development seminars, and the many gatherings of teacher networks been altered by the appearance of this "other" writing? Are the systems of citation and documentation endemic to the academy relevant and useful to the work of teacher researchers? How would a system of *lateral* citation, defined as a "less hierarchical and less traditional method of citation ... emphasizing collaboration and connection over argument and defense" (Franke, 1995, p. 376), reflect more accurately the real world relationships that inform the work? Engaging the concept of neighborhood has the potential to alter dramatically the bounded debate about "what counts as teacher research and to whom" and to embrace instead significant questions of use and value that are called up when such differently situated participants work together and separately for change.

ACKNOWLEDGMENTS

Preparation of this chapter was supported in part by the Spencer Foundation. I am grateful for the important insights and critical assistance of Elizabeth Cantafio and Mollie Blackburn and to the many colleagues who read and reacted to this chapter, especially Bob Fecho and Kathy Schultz.

REFERENCES

Ackerman, M. (1997). Can I speak Gussak? Using literature with a special education class. In M. Barbieri & C. Tateishi (Eds.), *Meeting the challenges: Stories from today's classrooms* (pp. 1–11). Portsmouth, NH: Heinemann.

Allen, A. M. A. (1997). Creating space for discussions about social justice and equity in an elementary classroom. *Language Arts, 74*(7), 518–524.

Allen, J. (1997). Exploring literature through student-led discussions. *Teacher Research, 4*(2), 124–139.

Allen, J. (Ed.). (1999). *Class actions: Literacy education for democracy.* New York: Teachers College Press.

Allen, J., Buchanan, J., Edelsky, C., & Norton, G. (1992). Teachers as "they" at NRC: An invitation to enter the dialogue on the ethics of collaborative and non-collaborative classroom research. In C. K. Kinzer & D. J. Leu (Eds.), *Literacy research, theory, and practice: Views from many perspectives: The Forty-first yearbook of the National Reading Conference* (pp. 357 –365). Chicago: National Reading Conference.

Allen, J., Cary, M., & Delgado, L. (Eds.). (1995). *Exploring blue highways: Literacy reform, school change, and the creation of learning communities.* New York: Teachers College Press.

Allen, S. (1992). Student-sustained discussion: When students talk and the teacher listens. In N. A. Branscombe, D. Goswami, & J. Schwartz (Eds.), *Students teach, teachers learn* (pp. 81–95). Portsmouth, NH: Boynton/Cook.

Alvermann, D. E., Olson, J., & Umpleby, R. (1993). Learning to do research together. In S. J. Hudelson & J. W. Lindfors (Eds.), *Delicate balances: Collaborative research in language education* (pp. 112–124). Urbana, IL: National Council for Teachers of English.

Anderson, G. L., & Herr, K. (1999). The new paradigm wars: Is there room for rigorous practitioner knowledge in schools and universities? *Educational Researcher, 28*(5), 12–21, 40.

Anderson, G. L., Herr, K., & Nihlen, A. S. (1994). *Studying your own school: An educator's guide to qualitative practitioner research.* Thousand Oaks, CA: Corwin Press.

Anzaldua, G. (1987). *Borderlands/La Frontera: The new mestiza.* San Francisco: spinsters/aunt lute.

Ashton-Warner, S. (1963). *Teacher.* New York: Simon & Schuster.

Atwell, N. (1987). Everyone sits at a big desk: Discovering topics for writing. In D. Goswami & P. R. Stillman (Eds.), *Reclaiming the classroom: Teacher research as an agency for change* (pp. 178–187). Upper Montclair, NJ: Boynton/Cook.

Atwell, N. (1998). *In the middle* (2nd ed.). Portsmouth, NH: Heinemann. (Original work published 1987)

Austin, T. (1994). *Changing view: Student-led parent conferences.* Portsmouth, NH: Heinemann.

Avery, C. (1993). *... And with a light touch: Learning about reading, writing, and teaching with first graders.* Portsmouth, NH: Heinemann.

Ballenger, C. (1996a). Learning the ABCs in a Haitian preschool: A teacher's story. *Language Arts, 73*(5), 317–323.

Ballenger, C. (1996b). Oral preparation for literature: Text and interpretation in a Haitian preschool. *Teacher Research, 4*(1), 85–103.

Ballenger, C. (1997). Because you like us: The language of control. In I. Hall, C. H. Campbell, & E. J. Miech (Eds.), *Class acts: Teachers reflect on their own classroom practice* (pp. 33–43). Cambridge: Harvard Educational Review. (Original work published 1994)

Ballenger, C. (1998). *Language and literacy in a Haitian Preschool: A perspective from teacher research.* New York: Teachers College Press.

Banford, H. (1996). The blooming of Maricar: Writing workshop and the phantom student. *In Cityscapes: Eight views from the urban classroom* (pp. 3–24). Berkeley, CA: National Writing Project.

Barbieri, M. (1987). Writing beyond the curriculum: Why seventh grade boys write? *Language Arts, 64*(5), 497–504.

Barbieri, M. (1995). *Sounds from the heart.* Portsmouth, NH: Heinemann.

Baroz, R. (1998, Summer). Something invisible became visible. *Bread Loaf Rural Teacher Network Magazine,* 34–37.

Baum-Brunner, S. (1993). Classroom and school studies: Stepping in and stepping out: The making of hindsight. In M. Cochran-Smith & S. L. Lytle, *Inside/outside: Teacher research and knowledge* (pp. 203–212). New York: Teachers College Press.

Baumann, J. F. (1996). Conflict or compatibility in classroom inquiry? One teacher's struggle to balance teaching and research. *Educational Researcher, 25*(7), 29–36.

Baumann, J. F., Bisblinghoff, B. S., & Allen, J. (1997). Methodology in teacher research: Three cases. In J. Flood, S. B. Heath, & D. Lapp (Eds.), *Handbook of research on teaching literacy through the communicative and visual arts* (pp. 121–143). New York: Simon & Schuster Macmillan.

Belanger, J. (1992). Teacher research as a lifelong experiment. *English Journal, 81*(8), 16–23.

Berthoff, A. E. (1987). The teacher as REsearcher. In D. Goswami & P. Stillman (Eds.), *Reclaiming the classroom: Teacher research as an agency for change* (pp. 28–38). Upper Montclair, NJ: Boynton/Cook.

Beyer, L. (1988). *Knowing and acting: Inquiry and educational studies.* New York: Falmer Press.

Beyer, L. E., & Liston, D. P. (Eds.). (1996). *Creating democratic classrooms: The struggles to integrate theory and practice.* New York: Teachers College Press.

Bianchi, L. L., & Cullere, B. A. (1996). Research as duet: Teachers with complementary literacies study orality's links to literacy. *Language Arts, 73*(4), 241–247.

Bissex, G. L., & Bullock, R. H. (Eds.). (1987). *Seeing for ourselves.* Portsmouth, NH: Heinemann.

Branscombe, N. A., Goswami, D., & Schwartz, J. (Eds.). (1992). *Students teaching, teachers learning.* Portsmouth, NH: Boynton/Cook.

Branscombe, A., & Thomas, C. (1992). Student and teacher co-researchers: Ten years later. In N. A. Branscombe, D. Goswami, & J. Schwartz (Eds.), *Students teaching, teachers learning* (pp. 5–18). Portsmouth, NH: Boynton/Cook.

Britton, J. (1987). A quiet form of research. In D. Goswami & P. Stillman (Eds.), *Reclaiming the classroom: Teacher research as an agency for change* (pp. 13–19). Upper Montclair, NJ: Boynton/Cook.

Brown, S. P. (1993). Essays: Lighting fires. In M. Cochran-Smith & S. L. Lytle, *Inside/outside: Teacher research and knowledge* (pp. 241–249). New York: Teachers College Press.

Buchanan, J. (1993). Listening to the voices. In M. Cochran-Smith & S. L. Lytle, *Inside/outside: Teacher research and knowledge* (pp. 212–220). New York: Teachers College Press.

Buchanan, J. (1994). Teacher as learner: Working in a community of teachers. In T. Shanahan (Ed.), *Teachers thinking, teachers knowing: Reflections on literacy and language education* (pp. 39–52). Urbana, IL: National Council of Teachers of English.

Buchanan, J., & Schultz, K. (1993). Looking together: Collaboration as an inquiry process. In S. J. Hudelson & J. W. Lindfors (Eds.), *Delicate balances: Collaborative research in language education* (pp. 37–52). Urbana, IL: National Council for Teachers of English.

Bullock, R. H. (1987). A quiet revolution: The power of teacher research. In G. L. Bissex & R. H. Bullock (Eds.), *Seeing for ourselves* (pp. 21–27). Portsmouth, NH: Heinemann.

Bullough, R. V., Jr., & Gitlin, A. (1995). *Becoming a student of teaching: Methodologies for exploring self and school context.* New York: Garland.

Burton, F. R. (1991). Teacher-researcher projects: An elementary school teacher's perspective. In J. Flood, J. M. Jensen, D. Lapp, & J. R. Squire (Eds.), *Handbook of research on teaching the English language arts* (pp. 226–230). New York: Macmillan.

Busching, B. A., & Slesinger, B. A. (1995). Authentic questions: What do they look like? Where do they lead? *Language Arts, 72*(5), 341–351.

Butler, S. (1992). DISKovery: Writing with a computer in grade one: A study in collaboration. *Language Arts, 69*(8), 633–640.

Calkins, L. M. (1985). Forming research communities among naturalistic researchers. In B. W. McClelland & T. R. Donovan (Eds.), *Perspectives on research and scholarship in composition* (pp. 125–144). Urbana, IL: National Council of Teachers of English.

Carr, W., & Kemmis, S. (1986). *Becoming critical: Education, knowledge and action research.* London: Falmer Press.

Carroll, P. S. (1994). Metamorphosis: One teacher's change/One class' reaction. *English Journal, 83*(6), 22–28.

Chase, P., & Doan, J. (1996). *Choosing to learn: Ownership and responsibility in a primary multiage classroom.* Portsmouth, NH: Heinemann.

Chin, C. (1996). "Are you the teacher who gives parents homework?" In *Cityscapes: Eight views from the urban classroom* (pp. 145–163). Berkeley, CA: National Writing Project.

Chinn, P. & Iding, M. K. (1997). High school chemistry students' self-concepts as writers and scientists. *Teaching and Change, 4*(3), 227–244.

Christian, S. (1997). *Exchanging lives: Middle school writers online.* Urbana, IL: National Council of Teachers of English.

Christian, S. (1998, Summer). Becoming a network of teachers. *Bread Loaf Rural Teacher Network Magazine,* 3–5.

Cochran-Smith, M. (1994). The power of teacher research in education. In S. Hollingsworth & H. Sockett (Eds.), *Teacher research and educational reform* (pp. 142–165). Chicago: University of Chicago Press.

Cochran-Smith, M., & Lytle, S. L. (1993). *Inside/outside: Teacher research and knowledge.* New York: Teachers College Press.

Cochran-Smith, M., & Lytle, S. L. (1998). Teacher research: The question that persists. *International Journal of Leadership in Education, 1*(1), 19–36.

Cochran-Smith, M., & Lytle, S. L. (1999). The teacher research movement: A decade later. *Educational Researcher, 28*(7), 15–25.

Cohen, J. (1993). *Restructuring instruction in an urban high school: An inquiry into texts, identities, and power.* Unpublished doctoral dissertation, University of Pennsylvania, Graduate School of Education.

Colgan-Davis, P. (1993). Oral inquiries: Learning about learning diversity. In M. Cochran-Smith & S. L. Lytle, *Inside/outside: Teacher research and knowledge* (pp. 163–169). New York: Teachers College Press.

Commeyras, M., & Sumner, G. (1995). *Questions children want to discuss about literature: What teachers and students learned in a second-grade classroom* (Instructional Resource 47). Athens, GA: National Reading Research Center.

Cone, J. K. (1990). Literature, geography, and the untracked English class. *English Journal, 79*(8), 60–67.

Cone, J. K. (1992). Untracking Advanced Placement English: Creating opportunity is not enough. *Phi Delta Kappan, 73*(9), 712–717.

Cone, J. K. (1993). Using classroom talk to create community and learning. *English Journal, 82*(6), 30–38.

Cone, J. K. (1997). Appearing acts: Creating readers in a high school English class. In I. Hall, C. H. Campbell, & E. J. Miech (Eds.), *Class acts: Teachers reflect on their own classroom practice* (pp. 67–91). Cambridge, MA: Harvard Educational Review. (Original work published 1994)

Curtis, J. P. (1993). Balance the basics: Teaching and learning. *Teacher Research, 1*(1), 58–63.

Cziko, C. (1996). Dialogue journals: Passing notes the academic way. In *Cityscapes: Eight views from the urban classroom* (pp. 99–110). Berkeley, CA: National Writing Project.

Daiker, D. A., & Morenberg, M. (Eds.). (1990). *The writing teacher as researcher.* Portsmouth, NH: Boynton/Cook.

Deshon, J. A. P. (1997). Innocent and not-so-innocent contributions to inequality: Choice, power, and insensitivity in a first grade writing workshop. *Language Arts, 74*(1), 12–16.

Duckworth, E., & the Experienced Teachers Group. (1997). *Teacher to teacher: Learning from each other.* New York: Teachers College Press.

Dudley-Marling, C. (1995). Uncertainty and the whole language teacher. *Language Arts, 72*(4), 252–257.

Duthie, C. (1996). *True stories: Nonfiction literacy in the primary classroom.* York, ME: Stenhouse.

Dyson, A. H. (1997). *What difference does difference make?: Teacher reflections on diversity, literacy, and urban primary school.* Urbana, IL: National Council of Teachers of English.

Edelsky, C., & Boyd, C. (1993). Collaborative research: More questions than answers. In S. J. Hudelson & J. W. Lindfors (Eds.), *Delicate balances: Collaborative research in language education* (pp. 4–20). Urbana, IL: National Council of Teachers of English.

Elliott, J. (1992). *Action research for educational change.* Philadelphia: Open University Press. (Original work published 1991)

Ellison, V. L. (1997). Having students select spelling words. *Teaching and Change, 4*(1), 77–89.

Ellwood, C. (1992, April). *Teacher research for whom?* Paper presented at the American Educational Research Association, San Francisco.

Erickson, F. (1986). Qualitative methods in research on teaching. In M. C. Wittrock (Ed.), *Handbook of research on teaching* (3rd ed., pp. 119–161). New York: Macmillan.

Erickson, F., & Christman, J. B. (1996). Taking stock/Making change: Stories of collaboration in local school reform. *Theory Into Practice, 35*(3), 149–157.

Evans, C. (1989, April). *The educators' forum: Teacher-initiated research in progress.* Paper presented at the American Educational Research Association, San Francisco.

Fairbanks, C. M. (1995). Reading students: Texts in contexts. *English Education, 27*(1), 40–52.

Fecho, B. (1993). Reading as a teacher. In M. Cochran-Smith & S. L. Lytle, *Inside/outside: Teacher research and knowledge* (pp. 265–272). New York: Teachers College Press.

Fecho, B. (1994). Language inquiry and critical pedagogy. In M. Fine (Ed.), *Chartering urban school reform* (pp. 180–191). New York: Teachers College Press.

Fecho, B. (1996). Learning from Laura. In *Cityscapes: Eight views from the urban classroom* (pp. 57–71). Berkeley, CA: National Writing Project.

Fecho, B. (1998). Crossing boundaries of race in a critical literacy classroom. In D. E. Alvermann, K. A. Hinchman, D. W. Moore, S. F. Phelps, & D. R. Waff (Eds.), *Reconceptualizing the literacies in adolescents' lives* (pp. 75–101). Mahwah, NJ: Lawrence Erlbaum Associates.

Fecho, B., & Lytle, S. (1993). Working it out: Collaboration as subject and method. In S. J. Hudelson & J. W. Lindfors (Eds.), *Delicate balances: Collaborative research in language education* (pp. 125–141). Urbana, IL: National Council of Teachers of English.

Feiman-Nemser, & Floden, R. E. (1986). The cultures of teaching. In M. C. Wittrock (Ed.), *Handbook of research on teaching* (3rd ed., pp. 505–526). New York: Macmillan.

Feldgus, E. G. (1993). Classroom and school studies: Walking to the words. In M. Cochran-Smith & S. L. Lytle, *Inside/outside: Teacher research and knowledge* (pp. 170–178). New York: Teachers College Press.

Fenstermacher, G. (1994). The knower and the known: The nature of knowledge in research on teaching. In L. Darling Hammond (Ed.), *Review of research in education* (Vol. 20, pp. 3–56). Washington, DC: American Educational Research Association.

Five, C. (1986). Fifth graders respond to a changed reading program. *Harvard Educational Review, 56*(4), 395–405.

Five, C. (1989). A garden of poets. In N. Atwell (Ed.), *Workshop 1 by and for teachers: Writing and literature* (pp. 61–71). Portsmouth, NH: Heinemann.

Fleischer, C. (1994). Researching teacher research: A practitioner's retrospective. *English Education, 26*(2), 86–124.

Fleischer, C. (1995). *Composing teacher-research: A prosaic history.* Albany: State University of New York Press.

Florio-Ruane, S. (1990). The written literacy forum: Analysis of teacher/researcher collaboration. *Journal of Curriculum Studies, 22*(4), 313–323.

Florio-Ruane, S., & Walsh, M. (1980). The teacher as colleague in classroom research. In H. Trueba, G. Guthrie, & K. Au (Eds.), *Culture in the bilingual classroom: Studies in classroom ethnography* (pp. 87–101). Rowley, MA: Newbury House.

Franke, D. (1995). Writing into unmapped territory: The practice of lateral citation. In L. W. Phelps & J. Emig (Eds.), *Feminine principles and women's experiences in American composition and rhetoric* (pp. 375–384). Pittsburgh: University of Pittsburgh Press.

Fraser, J., & Skolnick, D. (1994). *On their way: Celebrating second graders as they read and write.* Portsmouth, NH: Heinemann.

Freedman, S. W., Simons, E. R., Kalnin, J. S., Casareno, A., & the M-CLASS Teacher Researchers. (1999). *Inside city schools: Investigating literacy in multicultural classrooms.* New York: Teachers College Press.

Gallas, K. (1992). When the children take the chair: A study of sharing time in a primary classroom. *Language Arts, 69*(3), 172–182.

Gallas, K. (1994). *The language of learning: How children talk, write, dance, draw, and sing their understanding of the world.* New York: Teachers College Press.

Gallas, K. (1997). Arts as epistemology: Enabling children to know what they know. In I. Hall, C. H. Campbell, & E. J. Miech (Eds.), *Class acts: Teachers reflect on their own classroom practice* (pp. 93–105). Cambridge: Harvard Educational Review. (Original work published 1991)

Gallas, K. (1998). *"Sometimes I can be anything": Power gender and identity in primary classroom.* New York: Teachers College Press.

Gallas, K., Anton-Oldenberg, M., Ballenger, C., Beseler, C., Griffin, S., Pappenheimer, R., & Swaim, J. (1996). Focus on research: Talking the talk and walking the walk: Researching oral language in the classroom. *Language Arts, 73*(8), 608–617.

Gaughan, J. (1996). Taking a walk in the contact zone. *Teacher Research, 4*(1), 1–12.

Gitlin, A., Bringhurst, K., Burns, M., Cooley, V., Myers, B., Price, K., Russell, R., & Tiess, P. (1992). *Teachers' voices for school change.* New York: Teachers College Press.

Goldblatt, E. C. (1995). *'Round my way.* Pittsburgh: University of Pittsburgh Press.

Gonzalez, N., Moll, L. C., Floyd-Tenery, M., Rivera, A., Rendon, P., Gonzales, R., & Amanti, C. (1993). *Teacher research on funds of knowledge: Learning from households.* Santa Cruz, CA: National Center for Research on Cultural Diversity and Second Language Learning.

Gore, J., & Zeichner, K. (1995). Connecting action research to genuine teacher development. In J. Smythe (Ed.), *Critical discourses on teacher development* (pp. 203–214). London: Casell.

Goswami, D., & Stillman, P. (Eds.). (1987). *Reclaiming the classroom: Teacher research as an agency for change.* Upper Montclair, NJ: Boynton/Cook.

Green, J., & Dixon, C. (1993). Talking knowledge into being: Discursive and social practices in classrooms. *Linguistics and Education, 5*(3&4), 231–239.

Grimmett, P., & MacKinnon, A. (1992). Craft knowledge and the education of teachers. In G. Grant (Ed.), *Review of research in education* (Vol. 18, pp. 385–346). Washington, DC: American Educational Research Association.

Hammack, F. M. (1997). Ethical issues in teacher research. *Teachers College Record, 99*(2), 247–265.

Hammersley, M. (Ed.). (1993). *Controversies in classroom research* (2nd ed.). Buckingham: Open University Press.

Hankins, K. H. (1998). Cacophony to symphony: Memoirs in teacher research. *Harvard Educational Review, 68*(1), 80–95.

Hargreaves, A. (1994). *Changing teachers, changing times.* New York: Teachers College Press.

Hargreaves, A. (1996). Transforming knowledge: Blurring the boundaries between research, policy, and practice. *Educational evaluation and policy analysis, 18*(2), 161–178.

Harris, M. (1993). Journals: Looking back: 20 Years of a teacher's journal. In M. Cochran-Smith & S. L. Lytle, *Inside/outside: Teacher research and knowledge* (pp. 130–140). New York: Teachers College Press.

Hartmann, W. (1994). A teacher-researcher's reflection. *English Journal, 83*(6), 55–58.

Headman, R. (1993). Classroom and school studies: Parents and teachers as coinvestigators. In M. Cochran-Smith & S. L. Lytle, *Inside/outside: Teacher research and knowledge* (pp. 220–230). New York: Teachers College Press.

Henkin, R. (1995). Insiders and outsiders in first-grade writing workshops: Gender and equity issues. *Language Arts, 72*(6), 429–434.

Henson, K. T. (1996). Teachers as researchers. In J. Sikula (Ed.), *Handbook of research on teacher education* (pp. 53–64). New York: Macmillan.

Hoffman, M. (1996). *Chasing hellhounds: A teacher learns from his students.* Minneapolis, MN: Milkweed Editions.

Hollingsworth, S. (1994). *Teacher research & urban literacy education.* New York: Teachers College Press.

Hollingsworth, S. (Ed.). (1997). *International action research: A casebook for educational reform.* London: Falmer Press.

Hollingsworth, S., & Sockett, H. (1994a). Positioning teacher research in educational reform: An introduction. In S. Hollingsworth & H. Sockett (Eds.), *Teacher research and educational reform: Ninety-third yearbook of the National Society for the Study of Education* (pp. 1–20). Chicago: University of Chicago Press.

Hollingsworth, S., & Sockett, H. (Eds.). (1994b). *Teacher research and educational reform: Ninety-third yearbook of the National Society for the Study of Education.* Chicago: University of Chicago Press.

Hubbard, R. S., & Power, B. M. (1993). *The art of classroom inquiry.* Portsmouth, NH: Heinemann.

Huberman, M. (1996). Focus on research: Moving mainstream: Taking a closer look at teacher research. *Language Arts, 73*(2), 124–140.

Hudelson, S. J., & Lindfors, J. W. (Eds.). (1993). *Delicate balances: Collaborative research in language education.* Urbana, IL: National Council for Teachers of English.

Hunt, S. (1995). Choice in the writing class: How do students decide what to write and how to write it? *Quarterly of the National Writing Project and the Center for the Study of Writing, 17*(2), 7–11, 33.

Johnson, J. A. (1997). Life after death: Critical pedagogy in an urban classroom. In I. Hall, C. H. Campbell, & E. J. Miech (Eds.), *Class acts: Teachers reflect on their own classroom practice* (pp. 107–125). Cambridge, MA: Harvard Educational Review. (Original work published 1995)

Johnston, P. (1992). Coming full circle: As teachers become researchers so goes the curriculum. In N. A. Branscombe, D. Goswami, & J. Schwartz (Eds.), *Students teach, teachers learn* (pp. 66–80). Portsmouth, NH: Boynton/Cook.

Jumpp, D. (1996). Extending the literate community: Literacy over a life span. In *Cityscapes: Eight views from the urban classroom* (pp. 133–143). Berkeley, CA: National Writing Project.

Jumpp, D., & Strieb, L. Y. (1993). Journals: Journals for collaboration, curriculum, and assessment. In M. Cochran-Smith & S. L. Lytle, *Inside/outside: Teacher research and knowledge* (pp. 140–149). New York: Teachers College Press.

Juska, J. (1995). The wall. *Quarterly of the National Writing Project and the Center for the Study of Writing, 17*(1), 42–48.

Kaltenbach, S. (1993). What do you think? A parent-child classroom study. *Teacher Research, 1*(1), 49–57.

Kanevsky, R. D. (1993). Oral Inquiries: Descriptive review of a child: A way of knowing about teaching and learning. In M. Cochran-Smith & S. L. Lytle (Eds.), *Inside/outside: Teacher research and knowledge* (pp. 150–163). New York: Teachers College Press.

Keenan, J. A. W., Willett, J., & Solsken, J. (1993). Focus on research: Constructing an urban village: School/home collaboration in a multicultural classroom. *Language Arts, 70*(3), 204–214.

Keep-Barnes, A. (1994). Real teachers don't always succeed. *Teacher Research, 2*(2), 1–7.

Kieffer, C. C. (1996). *A class study of informal drama in the fourth grade* (Instructional Resource 16). Athens, GA: National Reading Research Center.

Kincheloe, J. L. (1991). *Teachers as researchers: Qualitative inquiry as a path to empowerment.* London: Falmer Press.

Knoblauch, C. H., & Brannon, L. (1993). *Critical teaching & the idea of literacy.* Portsmouth, NH: Boynton/Cook.

Krater, J., Zeni, J., & Cason, N. D. (1994). *Mirror images: Teaching writing in black and white.* Portsmouth, NH: Heinemann.

Kucera, C. A. (1995). Detours and destinations: One teacher's journey into an environmental writing workshop. *Language Arts, 72*(3), 179–187.

Kutz, E. (1992). Teacher research: Myths and realities. *Language Arts, 69*(3), 193–197.

Lewis, C. (1993). "Give people a chance": Acknowledging social differences in reading. *Language Arts, 70*(6), 454–461.

Lieberman, A., & Miller, L. (1994). Problems and possibilities of institutionalizing teacher research. In S. Hollingsworth & H. Sockett (Eds.), *Teacher research and educational reform: Ninety-third yearbook of the National Society for the Study of Education* (pp. 204–220). Chicago: University of Chicago Press.

Little, J. W. (1993). Teachers' professional development in a climate of educational reform. *Education evaluation and policy analysis, 15*(2), 129–151.

Little, J. W., & McLaughlin, M. W. (1993). *Teachers' work: Individuals, colleagues, and contexts.* New York: Teachers College Press.

Livdahl, B. S., Smart, K., Wallman, J., Herbert, T. K., Geiger, D. K., & Anderson, J. L. (1995). *Stories from response-centered classrooms.* New York: Teachers College Press.

Locklear, G. (1994). Thinking for themselves: Students examine the writing group process. *Teaching and Change, 2*(1), 61–72.

Lott, J. G. (1994). *A teacher's stories: Reflections on high school writers.* Portsmouth, NH: Heinemann.

Lytle, S. L. (1993). Risky business. *Quarterly of the National Writing Project and the Center for the Study of Writing and Literacy, 15*(1), 20–23.

Lytle, S. L. (1998, April). *Inquiry as a stance on teaching: The inservice case.* Paper presented at the American Educational Research Association, San Diego.

Lytle, S. L., Christman, J., Cohen, J., Countryman, J., Fecho, B., Portnoy, D., & Sion, F. (1994). Learning in the afternoon: When teacher inquiry meets school reform. In M. Fine (Ed.), *Chartering urban school reform* (pp. 157–179). New York: Teachers College Press.

Lytle, S. L., & Cochran-Smith, M. (1990). Learning from teacher research: A working typology. *Teachers College Record, 92*(1), 83–103.

Lytle, S. L., & Cochran-Smith, M. (1992). Teacher research as a way of knowing. *Harvard Educational Review, 62*(4), 447–474.

Lytle, S. L., & Cochran-Smith, M. (1995, March). *Teacher research and the constructive disruption of university culture.* Paper presented at the Ethnography Forum, Philadelphia.

Lytle, S. L., & Fecho, R. (1991). Meeting strangers in familiar places: Teacher collaboration by cross-visitation. *English Education, 23*(1), 5–28.

Mackinson, J., & Peyton, J. K. (1993). Interactive writing on a computer network: A teacher/researcher collaboration. In S. J. Hudelson & J. W. Lindfors (Eds.), *Delicate balances: Collaborative research in language education* (pp. 21–36). Urbana, IL: National Council of Teachers of English.

Macphee, J. S. (1997). "That's not fair!": A white teacher reports on white first graders' responses to multicultural literature. *Language Arts, 74*(1), 33–40.

Madigan, D., & Koivu-Rybicki, V. T. (1997). *The writing lives of children.* York, ME: Stenhouse.

Mangiola, L., & Pease-Alvarez, L. (1993). Learning and teaching together. In S. J. Hudelson & J. W. Lindfors (Eds.), *Delicate balances: Collaborative research in language education* (pp. 53–66). Urbana, IL: National Council for Teachers for English.

Manning, A., & Harste, J. (1994). Teacher research: Demonstrations of possibilities. *Reading, 28*(1), 2–4.

McMahon, S. I., & Raphael, T. E. (Eds.). (1996). *The Book Club connection: Literacy learning and classroom talk.* New York: Teachers College Press.

Meier, D. (1997). *Learning in small moments: Life in an urban classroom.* New York: Teachers College Press.

Meyer, R. J. (1996). *Stories from the heart: Teachers and students researching their lives.* Mahwah, NJ: Lawrence Erlbaum Associates.

Meyer, R. J., Brown, L., DeNiro, E., Larson, K., McKenzie, M., Ridder, K., & Zetterman, K. (1998). *Composing a teacher study group: Learning about inquiry in primary classrooms.* Mahwah, NJ: Lawrence Erlbaum Associates.

Michaels, S. (1998, Spring). Stories in contact: Teacher research in the academy. *Association of Departments of English (ADE) Bulletin, 22,* 59–64.

Mohr, M. (1987). Teacher-researchers and the study of the writing process. In D. Goswami & P. R. Stillman (Eds.), *Reclaiming the classroom: Teacher research as an agency for change* (pp. 94–107). Upper Montclair, NJ: Boynton/Cook.

Mohr, M. M. (1994). Teacher-researchers at work. *English Journal, 83*(6), 19–21.

Moore, R. (1998, Summer). Teaching standard English to African American students. *Bread Loaf Rural Teacher Network Magazine,* 12–15.

Moshenberg, D. (1996). Standing in the neighborhood. In J. Slevin & A. Young (Eds.), *Critical theory and the teaching of literature* (pp. 75–92). Urbana, IL: National Council of Teachers of English.

Murphy, P. (1994). Antonio: My student, my teacher. My inquiry begins. *Teacher Research, 1*(2), 75–88.

Myers, M. (1985). *The teacher-researcher: How to study writing in the classroom.* Urbana, IL: National Council of Teachers of English.

Myers, M. (1987). Institutionalizing inquiry. *National Writing Project Quarterly, 9,* 1–4.

Nagle, J. P. (1997). Looking inward: Reflections on gender identity. *Teacher Research, 5*(1), 75–82.

Newkirk, T. (1992). Silences in our teaching stories: What do we leave out and why? In T. Newkirk (Ed.), *Workshop 4 by and for teachers: The teacher as researcher* (pp. 21–30). Portsmouth, NH: Heinemann.

Newland, A. (1990). Teacher inquiry in the classroom: Broadening perspectives. *Language Arts, 67*(1), 70–75.

Newman, J. (Ed.). (1990). *Finding our own way: Teachers exploring their assumptions.* Portsmouth, NH: Heinemann.

Newman, J. M. (1998). *Tensions of teaching: Beyond tips to critical reflection.* New York: Teachers College Press.

Noffke, S. (1995). Action research and democratic schooling: Problems and potentials. In S. E. Noffke & R. B. Stevenson (Eds.), *Educational action research: Becoming practically critical* (pp. 1–10). New York: Teachers College Press.

Noffke, S. (1997). Professional, personal, and political dimensions of action research. In M. W. Apple (Ed.), *Review of research in education* (Vol. 22, pp. 305–343). Washington, DC: American Education Research Association.

Noffke, S., & Brennan, M. (1997). Reconstructing the politics of action in action research. In S. Hollingsworth (Ed.), *International action research* (pp. 49–60). London: Falmer Press.

Noffke, S. E. & Stevenson, R. B. (Eds.). (1995). *Educational action research: Becoming practically critical.* New York: Teachers College Press.

North, S. (1987). *The making of knowledge in composition.* Portsmouth, NH: Heinemann.

Paley, V. G. (1995). *Kwanzaa and me.* Cambridge, MA: Harvard University Press.

Pappas, C., & Zecker, L. (Eds.). (in press a). *Teacher inquiries in literacy teaching-learning: Learning to collaborate in elementary classrooms.* Mahwah, NJ: Lawrence Erlbaum Associates.

Pappas, C., & Zecker, L. (Eds.). (in press b). *Working with teacher researchers in urban classrooms: Transforming literacy curriculum genres.* Mahwah, NJ: Lawrence Erlbaum Associates.

Pappas, C. C., Oyler, C., Barry, A., & Rassel, M. (1993). Focus on research: Collaborating with teachers developing integrated language arts programs in urban schools. *Language Arts, 70*(4), 297–303.

Parker, D. (1997). *Jamie: A literacy story.* York, ME: Stenhouse.

Philadelphia Teachers Learning Cooperative. (1984). On becoming teacher experts: Buying time. *Language Arts, 61,* 731–736.

Phillips, A., Ballenger, C., Black, S., Gallas, K., Griffin, S., Morton, C., Swaim, J., Williams, K. S., & Gee, J. P. (1993). *Childrens' voices, teachers' stories: Papers from the Brookline Teacher Researcher Seminar* (Tech. Rep. No. 11). Newton, MA: Literacies Institute.

Pincus, M. R. (1993). Essays: Following the paper trail. In M. Cochran-Smith & S. L. Lytle, *Inside/outside: Teacher research and knowledge* (pp. 249–255). New York: Teachers College Press.

Pratt, M. L. (1991). Arts of the contact zone. In *Profession 91* (pp. 33–40). New York: Modern Language Association.

Ray, L. (1987). Reflections on classroom research. In D. Goswami & P. R. Stillman (Eds.), *Reclaiming the classroom: Teacher research as an agency for change* (pp. 219–242). Upper Montclair, NJ: Boynton/Cook.

Ray, R. (1996). Afterword: Ethics and representation in research. In P. Mortensen & G. Kirsch (Eds.), *Ethics and representation in qualitative studies of literacy* (pp. 287–300). Urbana, IL: National Council of Teachers of English.

Ray, R. E. (1993). *The practice of theory.* Urbana, IL: National Council of Teachers of English.

Reilly, K. C. (1995). Making new audiences: Moving through classroom walls. *Teacher Research, 2*(2), 49–60.

Resnick, M. (1996). Making connections between families and school. In *Cityscapes: Eight views from the urban classroom* (pp. 115–132). Berkeley, CA: National Writing Project.

Richardson, V. (Ed.). (1994a). *Teacher change and the staff development process.* New York: Teachers College Press.

Richardson, V. (1994b). Teacher inquiry as professional staff development. In S. Hollingsworth & H. Sockett (Eds.), *Teacher research and educational reform* (pp. 186–203). Chicago: University of Chicago Press.

Robinson, J. (1990). *Conversation on the written word.* Upper Montclair, NJ: Boynton/Cook.

Root, C. H. (1996). Having art students use a journal. *Teaching and Change, 3*(4), 331–355.

Rudduck, J., & Hopkins, D. (Eds.). (1985). *Research as a basis for teaching: Readings from the work of Lawrence Stenhouse.* London: Heinemann.

Sagor, R. (1992). *How to conduct collaborative action research.* Alexandria, VA: Association for Supervision and Curriculum Development.

Schaafsma, D. (1993). *Eating on the street: Teaching literacy in a multicultural society.* Pittsburgh: University of Pittsburgh Press.

Schiller, L. (1996). Coming to America: Community from diversity. *Language Arts, 73*(1), 46–51.

Schon, D. (1983). *The reflective practitioner.* San Francisco: Jossey-Bass.

Schwartz, E. (1992). The round table: Emergent curriculum in a primary class. In N. A. Branscombe, D. Goswami, & J. Schwartz (Eds.), *Students teaching, teachers learning* (pp. 22–45). Portsmouth, NH: Boynton/Cook.

Schwartz, J. (1990). On the move in Pittsburgh: When students and teacher share research. In D. A. Daiker & M. Morenberg (Eds.), *Writing teachers as researchers* (pp. 153–166). Portsmouth, NH: Boynton/Cook.

Seabrook, G. (1997). A teacher learns in the context of a social studies workshop. In I. Hall, C. H. Campbell, & E. J. Miech (Eds.), *Class acts: Teachers reflect on their own classroom practice* (pp. 165–177). Cambridge, MA: Harvard Educational Review. (Original work published 1991)

Sims, M. (1993). Essays: How my question keeps evolving. In M. Cochran-Smith & S. L. Lytle, *Inside/outside: Teacher research and knowledge* (pp. 283–289). New York: Teachers College Press.

Skelton, S. (1998, Summer). Watching and listening in and outside the classroom. *Bread Loaf Rural Teacher Network Magazine,* 18–23.

Smythe, J. (1992). Teachers' work and the politics of reflection. *American Educational Research Journal, 29*(2), 267–300.

Snyder, I. (1992). "It's not as simple as you think!" Collaboration between a researcher and a teacher. *English Education, 24*(4), 195–211.

Stenhouse, L. (1983). *Authority, education and emancipation.* London: Heinemann.

Stevenson, R. (1995). Action research and supportive school contexts: Exploring the possibilities for transformation. In S. Noffke & R. Stevenson (Eds.), *Education action research* (pp. 197–209). New York: Teachers College Press.

Stock, P. L. (1995). *The dialogic curriculum: Teaching and learning in a multicultural society*. Portsmouth, NH: Boynton/Cook Heinemann.

Strickland, D. S., Dillon, R. M., Funkhouse, L., Glick, M., & Rogers, C. (1989). Research currents: Classroom dialogue during literature response groups. *Language Arts, 66*(2), 192–200.

Strieb, L. (1985). *A (Philadelphia) teacher's journal: North Dakota Study Group Center for Teaching and Learning.* Grand Forks, ND: North Dakota Study Group Center for Teaching and Learning.

Strieb, L. Y. (1993). Journals: Visiting and revisiting the trees. In M. Cochran-Smith & S. L. Lytle, *Inside/outside: Teacher research and knowledge* (pp. 121–130). New York: Teachers College Press.

Stumbo, C. (1992). Giving their words back to them: Cultural journalism in Eastern Kentucky. In N. A. Branscombe, D. Goswami, & J. Schwartz (Eds.), *Students teaching, teachers learning* (pp. 124–150). Portsmouth, NH: Boynton/Cook.

Swaim, J. (1998). In search of an honest response. *Language Arts, 75*(2), 118–125.

Swain, S. S. (1994). *I can write what's on my mind.* Portsmouth, NH: Heinemann.

Sylvester, P. (1997). Elementary school curricula and urban transformation. In I. Hall, C. H. Campbell, & E. J. Miech (Eds.), *Class acts: Teachers reflect on their own classroom practice* (pp. 179–201). Cambridge, MA: Harvard Educational Review. (Original work published 1994)

Taylor, D. (1990). Teaching without testing: Assessing the complexity of children's literacy learning. *English Education, 22*(1), 4–74.

Taylor, D., Coughlin, D., & Marasco, J. (1997). *Teaching and advocacy.* York, ME: Stenhouse.

Taylor, J. B., & McIntyre, G. G. (1992). Negotiating the curriculum: Children, teaching intern, and university professor together. In N. A. Branscombe, D. Goswami, & J. Schwartz (Eds.), *Students teaching, teachers learning* (pp. 245–273). Portsmouth, NH: Boynton/Cook.

Temple, E. (1998, Summer). Observing student language in the classroom. *Bread Loaf Rural Teacher Network Magazine,* 6–11.

Thomas, S., & Oldfather, P. (1996). *Enhancing student and teacher engagement in literacy learning: A shared inquiry approach* (Instructional Resource 17). Athens, GA: National Reading Research Center.

Threatt, S., Buchanan, J., Morgan, B., Yermanock Strieb, L., Sugarman, J., Swenson, J., Teel, K., & Tomlinson, J. (1994). Teacher's voices in the conversation about teacher research. In S. Hollingsworth & H. Sockett (Eds.), *Teacher research and educational reform: Ninety-third yearbook of the National Society for the Study of Education* (pp. 222–244). Chicago: University of Chicago Press.

Trinh, M. T. (1992). *Framer framed.* New York: Routledge.

Trotman, M. V. (1998). "Would Queenie be in our class?": Questioning social inequity in advanced classes. *New Advocate, 11*(1), 55–65.

Tuyay, S., Floriani, A., Yeager, B., Dixon, C., & Green, J. (1995). Constructed in integrated, inquiry-oriented approach in classrooms: A cross case analysis of social, literate and academic practices. *Journal of Classroom Interaction, 30*(2), 1–15.

Udall, R. (1998, Summer). "Have you graded our essays yet?". *Bread Loaf Rural Teacher Network Magazine,* 18–23.

Vasquez, V. (2000). Seeking out possibilities in the lives of learners: Classroom inquiry into the incidental unfolding of social justice issues with young children from a critical literacy perspective. In B. Comber & S. Cakmac (Eds.), S. Boran & B. Comber (Eds.), *Inquiry into What? Empowering today's young people, tomorrow's citizens using whole language.* Urbana, IL: National Council of Teachers of English and Whole Language Umbrella.

Vinz, R. (1996). *Composing a teaching life.* Portsmouth, NH: Boynton/Cook.

Waff, D. (1995). Girl talk: Creating community through social exchange. In M. Fine (Ed.), *Chartering urban school reform* (pp. 192–203). New York: Teachers College Press.

Waff, D. (1995). Romance in the classroom: Inviting discourse on gender and power. *Quarterly of the National Writing Project and the Center for the Study of Writing, 17*(2), 15–18.

Waff, D. (1996). Talking across boundaries: The collaborative construction of community. *In Literacy Networks, 2.* Mount Pleasant, MI: Central Michigan University.

Wagner, J. (1997). The unavoidable intervention of education research: A framework for reconsidering researcher-practitioner cooperation. *Educational Researcher, 26*(7), 13–22.

Wells, G. (1993). *Changing schools from within: Creating communities of inquiry.* Portsmouth, NH: Heinemann.

Wells, G. (1994). *Changing schools from within: Creating communities of Inquiry.* Toronto: Disc Press.

Wells, G., & Chang-Wells, G. L. (1992). *Constructing knowledge together: Classrooms as centers of inquiry and literacy.* Portsmouth, NH: Heinemann.

Whitin, P. (1996). *Sketching stories, stretching minds: Responding visually to literature.* Portsmouth, NH: Heinemann.

Whitmore, K. F., & Crowell, C. G. (1994). *Inventing a classroom.* York, ME: Stenhouse.

Wigginton, E. (1985). *Sometimes a shining moment: The Foxfire experience.* Garden City, NY: Archer Press/Doubleday.

Wilhelm, J. D. (1996). To make reading visible: The process of one teacher researcher. *Teacher Research, 4*(1), 52–62.

Wunner, K. E. (1993). Classroom and school studies: Great expectations. In M. Cochran-Smith & S. L. Lytle (Eds.), *Inside/outside: Teacher research and knowledge* (pp. 230–240). New York: Teachers College Press.

Wyshynski, R., & Paulsen, D. (1995). Maybe I will do something: Lessons from coyote. *Language Arts, 72*(4), 258–264.

Yagelski, R. P. (1990). Searching for "Sloppy Trees": How research shapes teaching. In D. A. Daiker & M. Morenberg (Eds.), *Writing teachers as researchers* (pp. 142–152). Portsmouth, NH: Boynton/Cook.

Zeichner, K. (1992, April). *Teacher research: Toward what end.* Paper presented at the American Educational Research Association, San Francisco.

Zeichner, K. (1994). Personal renewal and social reconstruction through teacher research. In S. Hollingsworth & H. Sockett (Eds.), *Teacher research and educational reform: Ninety-third yearbook of the National Society for the Study of Education* (pp. 66–84). Chicago: University of Chicago Press.

Zeichner, K. (1997, March). *Action research as a professional development in one urban school district.* Paper presented at the American Educational Research Association.

Zeichner, K., & Noffke, S. (in press). Practitioner research. In V. Richardson (Ed.), *Handbook of research on teaching* (4th ed.). New York: Macmillan.

Zeni, J. (1996). A picturesque tale from the land of kidwatching: Teacher research and ethical dilemmas. *Quarterly of the National Writing Project and the Center for the Study of Writing, 18*(1), 30–35.

CHAPTER 38

Teaching Teachers to Teach Reading: Paradigm Shifts, Persistent Problems, and Challenges

Patricia L. Anders
University of Arizona-Tucson

James V. Hoffman
University of Texas-Austin

Gerald G. Duffy
Duffy 4 Education Consultants

How should teachers be taught to teach reading? This question has received little attention from the reading research community. Reading researchers have attended to the reading process, drawing inferences and conducting studies to test their theories. Relatively few researchers have asked questions about the processes that teachers go through as they learn and continue to learn to teach reading. We sense, however, that reading researchers are beginning to turn their attention to this crucial question. Many reading researchers are involved in teacher education programs and are frustrated by the lack of empirical evidence to guide decisions about programs, curriculum, and instruction. Further, across the United States, schools of education and teacher education programs are the focus of policymakers and legislators, and educators need to respond to their pressures and queries with empirical knowledge. Moreover, researchers in teacher education have argued persuasively, and reading educators are beginning to listen, that teaching is more than using "best practices," good classroom management, or certain material.

Indeed, published research in reading teacher education has increased since the publication of the second *Handbook of Reading Research* (Barr, Kamil, Mosenthal, & Pearson, 1991), which, like the first volume of the *Handbook* (Pearson, Barr, Kamil, & Mosenthal, 1984), had no chapter dedicated exclusively to teacher education research.

To gauge interest in teacher education research, two *Yearbooks of the National Reading Conference* (Kinzer, Hinchman, & Leu, 1997; Zutell & McCormick, 1990) were sampled for articles about teacher education. In the Zutell and McCormick yearbook, 9 articles (2%) addressed teacher education, whereas in the Kinzer, Hinchman, and Leu yearbook, 17 articles (37%) dealt with teacher education. This is a dramatic increase and suggests powerfully that interest in teacher education research has become an important topic among reading researchers.

We have organized this chapter to present a historical perspective and to provide a report of what little we think we know and what we need to know about how teachers should be taught to teach reading. To do this, we first present a "review of the reviews." This section reveals the focus of reading teacher education research over the decades and provides a picture of the way that teacher education has been conceptualized by reading researchers. Second, we summarize literature that relates to preservice education. Our analysis of this literature is presented in thesis statements representing our interpretation of the research. In a similar manner, we present the inservice education literature. We then discuss examples of problems that we face as teacher educators, about which we can find little empirical information. The chapter concludes with reflections about future directions of reading teacher education research.

A REVIEW OF THE REVIEWS

The history of reviews about reading teacher education is short and corresponds conceptually to three trends in teacher education (Russell & Korthagen, 1995, pp. 187–188). First, from roughly 1900 until the 1960s, the apprenticeship model was central. Second, from the 1960s to the early 1980s, the trend was to help teachers improve their knowledge base and to improve their application of knowledge about both content and methods. And third, from the mid 1980s through the 1990s, these older models were challenged. Issues were raised regarding the connection between formal, theoretical, and abstract knowledge, and informal, personal, and practical knowledge of the reflective practitioner (Fenstermacher, 1994; Schön, 1983).

The reviews before the 1960s emphasized what teachers should learn in course work and from their mentors as apprentices. Reading researchers presented the content knowledge that teachers needed in two reviews (Gray, 1961; Russell & Fea, 1963). Emphasis on content knowledge was a theme occurring throughout the history of reading teacher education. Austin (1968) and Chall (1975) reviewed research on preparing classroom teachers to teach reading. Austin suggested an increase in practical experiences, and Chall concluded that elementary school teachers educated "during the 1960s and 1970s were not receiving adequate instruction" (p. 47). Artley (1978) agreed and, after reviewing the key survey studies of teacher preparation (e.g., Austin & Morrison, 1961), he recommended a teacher education program requiring future teachers to take an increased number of credit hours in reading and more preservice experiences teaching reading. Chall's and Artley's recommendations are consistent with the "apprenticeship" model of teacher education, which was dominant before the 1980s.

The reviews of research about teaching reading during the 1980s (Barr, 1984; Calfee & Drum, 1986; Otto, Wolf, & Eldridge, 1984; Raphael, 1987; Rosenshine & Stevens, 1984; Tierney & Cunningham, 1984) reflected the idea that if research-based effective practices were used properly by teachers, their students' learning would improve. Calfee and Drum's (1986) review illustrated this perspective. Their chapter reviewed what reading teachers needed to know, and it described learners' progress when they were taught. It did not, however, describe how teachers accomplished the teaching of reading. The authors noted the lack of attention to the teacher and instruction by writing: "the present study would have been more informative if grounded in a theoretical framework of the curriculum and the pedagogy of the task" (p. 819).

Rosenshine and Stevens (1984) reviewed research about classroom instruction in reading. Their purpose was to report on instructional procedures, the content covered, academic engaged time and allocated time, and the error rate. The first major section, "general instructional procedures," reviewed research related to student learning when teachers offered teacher-directed, academically oriented instruction to individuals, to small groups, and to the whole class. Their chapter concluded by recognizing the impact that teachers can have on students' achievement and by suggesting that teacher training manuals should be revised. They did not call for the study of *how* teachers learn to implement new methods, which typifies the low status of reading teacher education of the 1980s.

"But what can I teach on Monday?" was the question posed by Raphael (1987) in the title of her review. One of several organizing questions in her study was, "What do teachers need to know about learning, reading, and instruction to improve what may already be a reasonable reading program?" The content knowledge promoted by Raphael represented the assumptions guiding the "process-product" research paradigm. She suggested strategies and methods a teacher should use to cause increased student learning. She did not discuss the acquisition of this knowledge, nor did she discuss the ways that teachers might use it in practice.

The question Barr (1984) addressed was, "How should children be taught to read?" She echoed the process-product paradigm by organizing her review around methods used to teach reading. Except for two studies, teachers were not participants in the studies. The first was a report of the Institute for Research on Teaching (IRT) on reading conceptions. She pointed out that the mental life and decision making of teachers were studied for their instructional consequences. The second study caused Barr to suggest that "it may be important to characterize the behavior or teachers ... (A) general description of teaching may not adequately represent that received by different groups in a class" (p. 573).

Like Barr (1984), Otto et al. (1984) called for more in-depth studies of teachers' behavior as indicators of their beliefs and perceptions. Their review reported on the management of reading instruction and on teachers' planning and decision making. They called for the study of teachers' personal perceptions and beliefs, predicting that perceptions and beliefs may be as influential in *how* one teaches as other considerations such as materials or methods.

Tierney and Cunningham (1984) provided a review of the methods teachers might use to teach reading comprehension. They concluded their chapter with a plea to "reading-comprehension instructional researchers to have a vision of how the research being reported fits into a larger picture of a 'best' program" (p. 640). They suggested that two of the four components of such a vision were to have "a vision of teachers" and "a vision of teacher support and change" (p. 641).

These reviews portray reading teacher education of the 1980s as translation of theory to practice. Shulman's (1986) description of the state of teacher education corresponded with the state of reading teacher education: "Teacher education programs ... seem to be based on the view that teacher candidates will teach effectively once they have acquired subject matter knowledge, become acquainted with models of innovative curriculum, and have practiced using them" (p. 8).

These reviews suggested, however, that "change was in the wind." Three of the studies implied that new questions about teachers' decision making, beliefs, and ways of learning and teaching needed to be studied (Barr, 1984; Otto et al., 1984; Tierney & Cunningham, 1984). These questions were also being asked by teacher education researchers. Russell and Korthagen (1995, pp. 187–188) argued for a new approach to teacher education by analyzing the failure of the old process-product paradigm. This approach was characterized by emphasizing reflective teaching, and by introducing new methods such as action research by (student) teachers and reflective journal writing.

Despite changes in teacher education and in the writings of some reading researchers, the shift from process-product studies toward studies of teachers and their beliefs, understandings, and practices were *not* evidenced in the reading research reviews of the 1990s. Volume II of the *Handbook of Reading Research* (Barr et al., 1991) included nine chapters organized in a section called "Literacy and Schooling." Three of these chapters discussed the implications of the reviewed research for teacher education (Hoffman, 1991; Pearson & Fielding, 1991; Roehler & Duffy, 1991). Pearson and Fielding proposed "principles of comprehension instruction." One trend they discovered was the "subtle but important" (p. 849) differences between the teacher's role in explicit instruction and in scaffolded instruction. They pointed out that scaffolded instruction requires the teacher to analyze the learner's developing understanding "online," so to speak, to decide the direction(s) the lesson should go (this is different from explicit instruction that relies on the teacher's predetermined plan for teaching). Further, Pearson and Fielding drew attention to another trend that considered the teacher a "facilitator of learning and as a co-equal with students in a literacy community" (p. 849).

Roehler and Duffy's (1991) chapter described "teachers' instructional actions." They asked how teacher educators might help teachers learn to make the instructional moves that seem to promote learning. Their chapter concluded by postulating that not enough is known and that the next wave of reading teacher education research needs to inform the field. Hoffman (1991) ended his chapter similarly, decrying the paucity of research related to teacher and school effects on learning. He wrote that a breakthrough will come as "more researchers, without enormous resources but with a scientific model, move into schools to observe and systematically study reading instruction and learning to read in classrooms" (p. 948). Other chapters in the *Handbook* suggested similar new directions for teacher education research (e.g., Paris, Wasik, & Turner, 1991).

The reviews published in *The Teacher Educator's Handbook* (Murray, 1996) about the teaching of reading (Ehri & Williams, 1996; Graves, Pauls, & Sallinger, 1996) represented the process-product paradigm rather than the "new directions" suggested by Paris, Wasik, and Turner (1991). Ehri and Williams pointed out that learning to teach reading is a process that develops over a teacher's career. They reported that preservice teacher education provides background knowledge about the "structure of written language, the nature of reading processes and reading disabilities, alternative methods of teaching reading, and how to assess students' reading capabilities" (p. 240). Little in this recommendation differed from the earliest goals of teacher education. Likewise, Graves et al. (1996) emphasized the content knowledge beginning teachers must have to launch their careers.

Barr (in press) confirmed our sense of the reading research community's position on teacher education when she wrote:

> We do not gain an understanding from these global descriptions of how teachers using the same approach differ, or learn about how teachers think: what guides their participation and how they evolve instructional patterns that differ in unique ways from other teachers espousing similar philosophical perspectives. Studies that focus on learner response provide the basis for understanding learners, but they are not useful in developing an understanding of how teachers think and act. The descriptions of how children make sense of their instruction would be of interest to new and experienced teachers, but the description might be more informative with a more elaborated representation of teaching. The assumption that researchers must choose between a focus on teaching and learning can be questioned; we learn most when both aspects of this interactive whole are represented. (p. 23)

Alvermann (1990) focused on both reading specialists and classroom teachers, and reviewed trends in certification and licensure. She framed teacher education by describing three dominant traditions: the traditional-craft, the competency-based, and the inquiry-oriented. She described common themes among inquiry-oriented researchers:

> Nearly all of the studies reported have incorporated teacher decision making and reflection, either as part of an intervention or as a means for studying teachers' thought processes. Most have been long-term studies, some extending for a year or more. Thematically, the studies have been concerned with how teachers acquire knowledge of complex reading instructional strategies and what beliefs, or implicit theories of teaching they use to guide their reading instruction. (p. 689)

Alvermann (1990) concluded her review by noting "a growing interest in the inquiry-oriented approach ... [it] promises new perspectives on how preservice and inservice teachers acquire knowledge and how their beliefs influence practice." Barr (in press) concurred and noted that an important question remains: "How do teachers learn and how can teacher educators foster this process?" (p. 49).

This "review of the reviews" reveals the focus of reading research over the decades: reading researchers have overwhelmingly devoted attention to the process of reading and to the learning of reading. Recent reviewers have suggested turning attention to *how* teachers learn and how that learning is enacted in their professional responsibilities. A nagging question for us is what teacher educators should do to promote that learning. We reviewed research to provide insights to these questions.

RESEARCH IN TEACHER EDUCATION

To summarize and interpret this literature, we looked first at research on preservice education. Our analysis of this literature resulted in thesis statements representing our interpretation of the research. Likewise, the inservice education literature suggested to us six generalizations, which represent the status of this research.

Research in Preservice Teacher Education

Austin and Morrison (1961) reported the results of their investigation into the preparation of elementary teachers to teach reading. The study employed a survey and a field study of teacher preparation institutions across the country. The authors criticized the lack of specific course offerings for prospective teachers, the lack of field/practicum experiences, and the qualifications of those teaching the teachers. Twenty-two recommendations were made, including the following: systematic screening of candidates; senior faculty playing a more active role instructing future teachers; and requiring the equivalent of three semester hours of credit in reading. Practice teaching was perceived to be at the heart of the teacher education experience. This study was replicated (Morrison & Austin, 1977) to determine if any changes were being made. Results suggested that 14 of the recommendations were in effect, and 2 recommendations were reported as somewhat implemented: More courses were being required, more courses were being taught in field-based settings, and more active use of simulations and practicums were reported. Little progress was found, however, in several areas (e.g., the recommendation to follow up on program graduates was lacking in most institutions). These two studies frame our understanding of the status of preservice teacher education. Although informative and valuable to those who have argued for fundamental changes in practice, they described reading teacher education superficially. The more interesting questions (e.g., What goes on in reading teacher preparation? Which students are being taught? How are they being taught? With what effects?) were unaddressed in survey studies.

To look closely at reading teacher education at the preservice level, we read and analyzed the studies between the original *Torch Lighters* study (Austin & Morrison, 1961; Morrison & Austin, 1977) and the present. We reviewed the preservice teacher education research published over this 30-year period to identify major findings, themes, and trends. The database for this review is represented in the Annual Summary of Investigations of Reading (1965–1996).

In the past 30 years, 19,457 studies have been conducted in reading, and 140 studies have focused in preservice reading education. During the decade of 1965–1975, 3,716 studies were conducted in reading and 19 of those focused on reading education. Likewise, during the decade of 1975–1985, 8,941 studies on reading were reported and 37 of those were in preservice reading education. Finally, in the years between 1985–1995, 6,800 studies were reported and 84 of those related to preservice reading teacher education. The 140 studies identified through this search varied in methodology, factors investigated, and significance of findings. They also varied in the quality and rigor of the research—a caution and sometimes a lament, expressed often by those who have compiled the annual summary. At best, a review of these studies offers a general sense of the nature of the inquiry into teacher education.

Based on this review, we have identified seven thesis statements regarding preservice teacher education in reading. These statements and supporting commentary reflect our interpretation of the status of research about teaching teachers to teach reading.

1. *Preservice teacher education has not been a high priority within the reading research community.* Representing less than 1% of the total studies conducted in reading over the past 30 years, we conclude that either preservice teacher education is lacking compelling questions, or it is such a difficult and undersupported area of study that researchers have shied away from systematic inquiry. We strongly suspect the latter to be the case. Few of the 140 studies suggest a program that builds on previous research or links to a theoretical basis. Further, few of the reported studies identify a major funding source or that the project is part of a supported research context (e.g., a research center). Most distressing is the finding that few of the studies have generated specific findings that have had a substantial impact on practice. We recognize there are exceptions to each of these claims, but in the context of less than 1% of the total, the exceptions are outliers in the field.

2. *There has been an increase in teacher education research in the most recent decade.* Consider that in the decade 1985 to 1995 more than four times the number of reading teacher education articles was published than in the decade between 1965 and 1975. This trend suggests an increased number of researchers who have been teaching, directing, or designing teacher education programs. For example, Gipe and her colleagues (Gipe, Duffy & Richards, 1989; Gipe & Richards, 1990) investigated the effects of journaling and two types of field experiences on students. Walker and Roskos (1994; Roskos & Walker, 1994) conducted numerous studies reflecting an inquiry stance. Risko (1992; Risko, McAllister, Peter, & Bigenho, 1994) studied the effects of video disk-based case methodology on preservice students' learning. Niles and Lalik (1987) studied their own program design with its emphasis on cooperative planning. These studies and others involve researchers studying practices in the context of their teaching environment (e.g., Whitmore & Goodman, 1996).

3. *In recent years, diverse research methodologies have been used.* We could locate few studies in the 1965–1985 period that drew on qualitative/interpretive research perspectives. There were numerous "questionnaire" studies, but these tended toward positivistic frames of reference. Between 1985 and 1995, we identified 20 studies (about 25%) that adopted an interpretive stance and used research methods ranging from

ethnographies, to sociolinguistic analyses of classroom interaction patterns, to case studies of students working through entire programs of study. Studies of students journaling in the context of course work and field work were conducted (e.g., Bean & Zulich, 1992; Moore, 1986); interviews with students were transcribed and analyzed (Kinzer, 1989); task/case analyses were developed (Comas & Farr, 1989; Roskos & Walker, 1993, 1994); simulations and microteaching were studied (e.g., Klesius, Zielonka, & LaFramboise, 1990; Phelps & Weidler, 1993); planning and reflection were investigated (Walker & Ramseth, 1993); individual case studies were developed (Mosenthal, 1994); and combinations of strategies were researched (O'Brien & Stewart, 1990). These qualitative-type studies represent a trend toward broadening the conception of "what counts" as research in the reading teacher education community.

4. *We have no coherent, comprehensive data base, or reference point, for preservice teacher education programs.* Attempts to describe the organization, content, and structure of preservice teacher education programs have been less than successful. The course hours required in reading have been a focal point for a number of survey type studies (e.g., Johnson, Phillips, & Sublett, 1974; Roeder, 1972; Roeder, Beal, & Eller, 1973; Smith, Fairbanks, & Saltz, 1984). In some cases, these surveys have focused on specific content issues such as the degree of attention given to second-language learners in courses (Gonzales, 1980), the preparation needed for early childhood education (Bailey, Durkin, Nurss, & Stammer, 1982), and clinical (i.e., disability) experiences and focus (Rogers, Merlin, Brittain, Palmatier, & Terrell, 1983). Outside the United States, similar studies have focused on teacher education programs in Canada (Start & Strange, 1980). Flippo and Hayes (1984) surveyed state departments of education to learn the reading course work required for elementary certification. They found a two-course requirement in 24 states, one course in 17 states, and 9 states leaving this decision to the local institutions.

5. *We have continued to struggle with conceptions of teacher knowledge, beliefs, attitudes and habits—how they are formed, how they are affected by programs, and how they impact development over time.* This is a ubiquitous trend but is difficult to unravel because the use of terms varies from study to study and from time period to time period. Throughout the 30 years of research, we found several studies looking at prospective teachers' own reading abilities/skills (e.g., Adams, 1967; Askov, Kamm, Klumb, & Barnette, 1980; Eckert & Wollenberg, 1984; Laine, 1984; Neal, Schaer, Ley, & Wright, 1990; Sullivan, 1976); their reading habits (Hawkins, 1967); their reading attitudes (Mikulecky & Ribovich, 1977; Smith, 1989); their own early literacy experiences at home (Lickteig, Johnson, & Johnson, 1994); and their experiences learning to read in school (e.g., Artley, 1975; Bush & Putnam, 1968; Moss, 1991; Warner, 1970). At their best, these studies have offered insights into the characteristics of those who hope to teach. At their worst, they have been used negatively to characterize those who aspire to teach as having poor reading habits and attitudes. In the decades of the 1960s and 1970s, we have found consideration of knowledge and beliefs focusing on issues such as: What is necessary to know as a teacher of reading? And how can this knowledge be measured?

Studies have examined prospective teachers' knowledge in terms of performance on tests such as the National Teachers Examination (NTE). Barter (1974), for example, found no relationship between reading abilities and performance on the NTE. More specific to reading, investigators explored the validity of such instruments as the Mastery Assessment of Basic Reading Concepts (Pavlik, 1975), the Inventory of Teacher Knowledge of Reading (Kingston, Brosier, & Hsu, 1975), and the Artley-Hardin Inventory (e.g., Koenke, 1976). In most cases, studies investigating these instruments demonstrated limited validity for representing reading teacher knowledge.

In the later 1970s and 1980s, reading teacher education research has followed general trends in cognitive psychology—moving away from knowledge as static to focus more on mental constructs, theoretical orientations, and beliefs about reading. Kinzer

(1989), for example, contrasted the mental models and frames used by preservice and experienced teachers based on structured interviews. Preservice teachers presented a limited frame of reference as contrasted with experienced teachers. Using the Theoretical Orientation to Reading Profile (Deford, 1985), Stice, Bertrand, Leuder, and Dunn (1989) investigated the relationship between theoretical orientation and selected psychological characteristics. They found differences (e.g., teachers with a phonics orientation tended to be "judgers," whereas teachers with a whole-language orientation tended to be "perceivers").

In recent years, researchers have examined how this knowledge and these belief systems are constructed, how they are accessed and represented, and how they are lived in the context of instruction. Shefelbine and Shiel (1990), for example, studied preservice teachers' model of reading diagnosis as related to instructional decision-making. Some components of the model were useful to students, but others were not—six types of misinterpretations were identified that led to inappropriate decisions. Herrmann (1990) studied teachers' knowledge structures and how they developed over a series of course experiences. Preservice teachers' knowledge structures tended to be less extensive but more coherent over time.

Progress in understanding knowledge representation and knowledge use has been slow, but no slower than in other areas of psychology. The driving questions are constantly being reshaped and new methodologies are explored. This is good news for the future of the inquiry, although criticisms may surround current efforts.

6. *We can make few claims from our current research base on what is effective in reading teacher education at the preservice level.* The "what works" question plagues our profession. Little empirical evidence is available to inform teacher educators about how certain educative experiences affect teachers' long-term development. Typically, research has been designed to map short-term program components to the acquisition of attitudes, knowledge, and skills.

A large portion of program "effectiveness" studies involve participants' retrospective introspections. Furr (1965) was one of the earliest investigators to survey and to interview graduates of a program regarding its perceived value. Smith, Otto, and Harty (1970) surveyed elementary teachers concerning their attitudes toward their preparation to teach reading. They found that primary teachers were more positive than intermediate grade teachers, and that the more experienced teachers were more positive than the more recent graduates. Britton (1973; 1975) surveyed graduates of a program that emphasized field and practicum experiences and found that the experiences were given high (or excellent) ratings by nearly all of the participants (see also, Cheek, 1982; Hyatt, Foster, Menter, & Riley, 1994; Wendelin & Murphy, 1986). Noe (1994), in one of the few reports of a program evaluation to follow up with students after their first year of teaching, investigated the influence of curriculum integration on beginning teachers' practices. Findings suggested that teachers were influenced, in both their teaching philosophies and practices, by their undergraduate preparation. Specifically, they reported that the program helped them to integrate reading and writing instruction.

A number of studies evaluated program impact on students in specific areas. Some studies have looked at program impact on student beliefs (Bacharach, 1993; Lefever-Davis & Helfeldt, 1994; Shaw, 1994; Wham, 1993). In most cases, these studies suggested that students' changes in theoretical orientation are related to specific program features, contexts, or components. Investigations of program impact and focused training on student learning have been conducted in such areas as teacher questioning (Johnson & Evans, 1992), diagnosis (e.g., Shefelbine & Shiel, 1990; Walker & Roskos, 1994; Wedman & Robinson, 1988), teaching strategic reasoning (e.g., Herrmann & Sarracino, 1992), evaluating text materials and commercial programs (e.g., Comas & Farr, 1989; Miller, 1978), phonics instruction (e.g., Strickler, 1976), and portfolio assessment (e.g., Ford, 1993; Fox, 1996; Seaboard, Mohr, Fowler,

& Lyons, 1993). In almost every case, these studies have shown a positive impact for instruction and training. A number of researchers evaluated program context and its effects, focusing on the contribution of field and practicum experiences as part of the program (e.g., Boehnlein & Gans, 1975; Britton, 1975; Gipe et al., 1989). In all cases, the studies have shown a positive impact for the field-based settings and practicum components.

The good news from these kinds of studies is that future teachers do learn what they are taught. The bad news is that questions of long-term effects and uses—and overall program impact on career development or on teaching effectiveness—have not been adequately addressed.

7. *Teacher education programs have become more complex, and the labels we use have become inadequate to describe practice.* This is apparent as we look at the language used to describe certain components of programs. For example, the focus on "courses" that fills much of the early literature gives way more recently to descriptions of "course sequences" or "program phases." This suggests that teacher educators are developing coherent programs that pave the way for teachers to more easily integrate content knowledge and practice. They require that teacher educators' courses be coordinated and that students be provided experiences that build on each other. These programs are more integrated and complex than the programs of previous generations.

This trend is also apparent in the conception of field-based instruction. What does field-based mean? Miller and Rand (1978) described a practicum experience totaling 22 hours. In the 1998 reading concentration program at the University of Texas, students spent a total of 1,000 hours in field and practicum settings. This difference suggests questions about when is a field-based program a field-based program, and what are expectations for the quality of the experience, the supervision involved, and the responsibilities of all concerned.

Conclusions.   Based on the research just reviewed, what do we have to say to those who would question us regarding effective teacher education practices and programs, the status of preservice reading teacher education, or the relative contribution of the investment in teacher education and the performance of students in schools? Our sense is that we have much to say, but few of our claims stand on a solid research base rather as practice informed by practice. This is a dangerous position for a field that is so vulnerable to public opinion and political whim.

What we need are the following:

- Case reports of excellence in programming. We could find none in our literature search that provides compelling evidence for their effectiveness. Where are the exemplary programs in reading teacher education? We have sufficient basic criteria to identify a core group that would demonstrate three important principles: It is possible to develop quality programs; quality programs make a difference in the lives of teachers and students; and excellent programs share commonalities with room for diversity and creativity.
- A national database on reading teacher education programs, clients, and practices. It is difficult to set goals, chart progress, and evaluate innovations without a sense of what exists. The American Association of Colleges of Teacher Education initiated the RATE (Research About Teacher Education) project in 1987. This project provides a national database on programs, program features, and participants and is being maintained. Researchers and policymakers in reading teacher education need this kind of information to do their work.

- More researchers studying their own practice. Excellent strides have been made in this area; however, these efforts need support and encouragement by teacher education administrators. Also, outlets for publication related to this work need to be more available.
- Increased opportunities for professional dialogue. Special conferences and forums for critical reflection and collaboration are needed for change to occur. Ultimately, it will be through dialogue, critical reflection, and collaboration that changes will be made.
- Longitudinal studies of program effectiveness. The 'what works?' question will continue to plague the field. We must demonstrate the cost effectiveness of programs to speak clearly and persuasively to policy makers. The work of Linda Darling-Hammond (1996, 1997) in teacher education has been exemplary in this area. We should be able to provide data and documentation showing to the public and to policy makers that an increased investment in teacher education will pay off directly in improved student learning. It is the only language the policy makers speak and we must become bilingual or we will continue to flounder and to talk only to one another.

Research in Inservice Teacher Education

We have read and analyzed the studies of inservice teacher education from the original *First R* (Austin & Morrison, 1963) study to the present and have identified major findings, themes, and trends. The data base for this review is essentially the same as that used in the review of preservice teacher education just reported. The total number of studies reported in reading education ($n = 19,457$) and the total number that focused on reading inservice for classroom teachers ($n = 140$) are represented in the following proportions by decade: 1965–1975, 3,716:19; 1975–1985, 8,941:37; and 1985–1995, 19,457:140.

In many cases, it was challenging to identify inservice teacher education studies. We did not rely solely on the researchers' use of the term *inservice* or *teacher education* to achieve identification. We were interested in research promoting changes in practice by affecting the teacher but, this may not have been the researcher's primary goal. For example, in experimental studies involving classroom research, teachers may have been trained in some particular method or technique. Is this teacher education? Or, is this simply an experimental condition without regard for long-term effects on teacher thinking or practices? We attempted to focus on those studies that have the goal of affecting teacher knowledge and practices with a long-term effect in mind. When there was uncertainty or ambiguity, however, we tended to include rather than to exclude a particular study. As with our review of the preservice literature, the studies vary enormously in terms of methodology, factors investigated, rigor, and significance of findings. On the basis of this review, we have identified six thesis statements.

1. *Inservice teacher education has not been a high priority within the reading research community, but interest may be increasing.* As in the preservice arena, studies focused on inservice teacher education represent less than 1% of the total. One constant in the findings across the three decades has been that teachers want more and better inservice support. Marcus (1968) found a mismatch between what supervisors offered in terms of support (i.e., help with supplementary materials and reading lists) as contrasted with what teachers wanted (i.e., help with the diagnosis of disabled readers and the identification of goals and objectives). Interest in issues of disability has been strong over the years (e.g., Goodacre & Clark, 1973; Logan & Erickson, 1979; Smith et

al., 1970). In the 1980s, interest increased for inservice in the teaching of reading comprehension (e.g., Anders & Gallego, 1989; Bailey & Guerra, 1984), and interest in reading disabilities continued. Preferences and interests in the late 1980s and the 1990s shifted toward integrated instruction and thematic teaching (e.g., Erickson, Johnson & Logan, 1992; Hosking, 1991).

2. *Inservice has been of use.* This is not intended as an "anything goes/everything works" kind of assertion. Studies have suggested that resources committed to changes in teacher thinking and practices do affect change. Positive effects have been shown across a variety of areas ranging from targeted interventions on teacher questioning (e.g., Conley, 1986), to skills instruction (e.g., DeCarlo & Cleland, 1970), to comprehension instruction (e.g., Conley, 1983), to impact on general approaches and philosophies such as "whole language" (e.g., Nelson, Pryor & Church, 1990; Otto & Iacono, 1991). The impact of inservice has been shown on the development of teacher knowledge (e.g., Sawyer & Taylor, 1968), attitudes (e.g., Stieglitz & Oehlkers, 1989), beliefs (e.g., Bean, Bishop, & Leuer, 1981; Scheffler, Richmond, & Kazelskis, 1993), practices (e.g., Trickey & Crispin, 1982), and teacher satisfaction (e.g., Dworkin, 1979). The impact has even been demonstrated in terms of positive effects on student growth in decoding (e.g., Strickler, 1976), comprehension (e.g., Kurth & Stromberg, 1983; Mosenthal, 1987; Miller & Ellsworth, 1985), cooperation (e.g., Talmadge, Pascarella & Ford, 1984), and attitudes (e.g., Streeter, 1986). The impact has been shown across classroom-based (e.g., Kieffer & Morrison, 1994), school-based, and district-based efforts (e.g., Boehnlein, 1984; Conley, 1983); short-term and long-term projects (e.g., Chadwick & Chadwick, 1976; Raphael, 1984); and across research methodologies ranging from case studies (e.g., Brown & Coy-Ogan, 1993) to full experimental designs (e.g., Sanger & Stick, 1984).

3. *The development of research in inservice teacher education has had important connections to the developments in research on teaching.* As noted earlier in this chapter, this relationship was first apparent in the late 1970s as the process-product paradigm for research in teaching gained momentum. In the middle to late 1980s, the research in teaching literature embraced teacher knowledge, thinking, and decision-making as the "missing paradigm" in the quest to understand teaching (Shulman, 1986). Two programs of research exemplified this shift. Duffy, Roehler, and their colleagues conducted a series of studies in which they examined the impact of interventions focused on the development of explicit teacher "explanations" (Book, Duffy, Roehler, Meloth, & Vavrus, 1985; Duffy, 1983; Duffy, Roehler, & Putnam, 1987; Duffy, Roehler, & Rackliffe, 1986; Roehler, Duffy & Meloth, 1984; Sivan & Roehler, 1986). In these studies, teachers grew in their abilities to translate skills into strategies in the context of reading instruction. The growth in this ability and the associated "explicitness" of teaching led to positive gains in student achievement. Pressley and his colleagues (El-Dinary, Pressley, & Schuder, 1992; Pressley, Bergman, & El-Dinary, 1992) conducted a series of studies into the effectiveness of transactional strategies instruction. Comprehension instruction was promoted and student learning was enhanced through the application of transactional teaching strategies. Both programs of research shared the complexity of the instructional intervention, the complexity of teaching, and the complexity of reading.

This complexity was further exhibited by programs of research in the early 1990s, when researchers began to look into the processes of teacher change as offering insight into effective teacher education practices. These investigations involved collaboration and interaction between teachers, teacher educators, and researchers. Hoffman, Roser and their colleagues (Hoffman, Roser, Battle, Farest, & Isaacs, 1990; Hoffman, Roser, & Farest, 1988) studied the changes in teacher insights and instructional strategies associated with the implementation of a literature-based program. Pace (1992) investigated the tensions associated with grass-roots change efforts as they moved from traditional textbook-based instruction to a more learner-centered curriculum. Scharer (1991, 1992) critiqued teachers in transition as they moved from traditional to literature-based teaching. Lloyd and Anders (1994) observed and analyzed a collaborative staff development effort in which teachers worked to improve comprehension instruction. These efforts involved substantial collaboration among all participants, and also documented impact on students' learning to read. These studies also assumed a broader perspective on classroom reading instruction than merely a focus on a particular strategy, process, or type of student. Our sense is that the field has abandoned the simplistic idea that the findings from teacher effectiveness research (e.g., "teaching behaviors" that correlate with student gains) and treat that as the basis for the curriculum in teacher education. Rather, we are seeing the processes of teacher learning as a model for constructing more effective program contexts. This change in perspective suggests that the complexities of teacher change are constituted by shifting definitions of reading, of increased awareness of the contexts in which teachers teach, and of sensitivity to the possibilities of collaboration among educators.

4. *There have been common features that could be used to characterize quality teacher education efforts at the inservice level.* We found few studies comparing method A of teacher education with method B of teacher education. Hence, we extracted common elements or features that appear salient. We offer the following list.

Intensive/extensive commitments. Most of the studies have suggested that intensive levels of support, with sustained and concentrated effort, are critical for success (e.g., Anders & Evans, 1994; Coladarci & Gage, 1984; Lamme & Hysmith, 1991; Miller & Ellsworth, 1985; Thistlewaite, Barclay, Castle & Lewis, 1991).

Monitoring/coaching/clinical support. This follow-up and support have ranged in scope and focus from follow-up contact to supporting connections to actual practice (e.g., Moore, 1991), to oversight of strict implementation of key features of an innovation (e.g., Reay, Von Harrison, & Gottfredson, 1984). The salient point is that teacher change needs support in the context of practice.

Reflection. The theme of reflection has appeared time and again in this literature. It appears that an important part of inservice teacher education is to provide opportunities and tools for teachers to reflect on their own practices systematically as they move toward change (e.g., Anders, 1991; Bos & Anders, 1994; Fleisher, 1992).

Deliberation, dialogue, and negotiation. Many studies have suggested that conversation and discussion make up a critical element in supporting the change process (e.g., Anders & Richardson, 1991; Combs, 1994; Hollingsworth, 1994; Kraus, 1992; Shepperson & Nistler, 1991, 1992).

Voluntary participation/choice. Most effective inservice teacher education programs have involved teachers who choose to participate. El-Dinary, Beard and Schuder (1993) demonstrated the differences in teacher patterns of adoption of "transactional" strategy instruction as a function of their "choice" to be involved.

Collaboration. Several reports of successful programs have suggested collaboration among different role groups (e.g., university-based researchers, school-based teacher educators, and teachers). Jennings, Hieshima, Pierce, Shapiro, and Ambardar (1994), for example, reported on a successful collaboration in the Chicago public schools to promote reading and writing activity (see also Nistler & Shepperson, 1993–1994; Paratore & Indrisano 1994; Short & Kauffman, 1992).

These features of teacher education inservice suggest that teacher change is more than "trying a good idea." These programs involved participants who are in the classroom and those who influence the classroom. They also provided time and space for change to be considered, accepted or rejected, and reflected upon.

5. *There have been strong forces working against initial change and the sustaining of change.* Change is difficult. Teacher education involves change and must attend to the

individual who is changing to the context in which they work. Many studies offered insights into potential barriers to change, including the following: resource commitments, role confusion, stability (turnover) of personnel, and institutional constraints (Thomas & Rinehart, 1994); constraints within the school district (e.g., evaluation, parental questioning, personal risk, program organization); those imposed outside the school district (e.g., achievement test, professional outsiders); and those imposed by time (preparation time, scheduling, feeling of being overwhelmed) (Bergeron, 1994). In addition, Placier and Hamilton (1994) described the nature of the school culture and personal conflict (e.g., based on philosophy) issues as impediments to change.

Even when change has occurred, it has not been necessarily sustainable (e.g., Morrison, Harris, & Auerbach, 1969) One of the more telling illustrations of this challenge was reported by Duffy, Roehler, and Putnam (1987). Through their work with a group of teachers, they were able to achieve positive changes in explicit teacher explanations, which had a positive affect on student learning. In follow-up conferences however, teachers reported that it was difficult to maintain their decision-making role due to constraints and pressures. We are only beginning to understand the context effects that affect and often constrain long-term teacher education efforts.

6. *There have been noteworthy examples of long-term staff development efforts that have suggested positive features and valuable processes and frameworks to follow.* Through our review of this literature we identified four plans for inservice reading teacher education that are distinct but not necessarily independent of one another.

Inquiry. Teacher research (action research) has proven to be a rich path for teacher inservice. Gove and Kennedy-Calloway (1992) reported on a project in which teachers engaged in the study of the instructional support offered to "at-risk" students. These researchers concluded that the participation in the research itself was directly related to shifts in knowledge, beliefs, and practices. Similarly, Gray-Schlegel and Matanzo (1993) found that a teacher research project initiated in a graduate course focusing on classroom practices served as a positive force for change. Likewise, Hancock, Turbill, and Cambourne (1994) collaborated with teacher researchers South Australia. The findings suggested that new knowledge gained through research led to more effective teaching and gave inservice teachers greater ownership and trust in the practices adopted.

Portfolios. This point of entry into teacher change has been useful across many contexts. Whether the usefulness has been rooted in portfolios as a specific process or in attention to assessment in general is difficult to unravel. At least for the present, portfolios are a productive focal point (Lyons, 1993). Kieffer and Faust (1994), for example, reported on the positive impact of an inservice project focused on the use of portfolios as opposed to traditional alternatives for assessment. Research with portfolios has been interesting in the way it has revealed the complex interaction between the "beliefs" of the participants (e.g., Lamme & Hysmith, 1991; Stewart & Paradis, 1993) and their success at implementation. When there is a mismatch, significant changes are less likely to occur.

Journaling. Encouraging reflective practice through journaling has been a positive point for inservice activity. Moore (1991), for example, found positive effects for journaling and the analysis of journal entries on a group of elementary teachers enrolled in a graduate course. Botel, Ripley, and Barnes (1993) demonstrated the powerful mediating effect for journaling in the implementation of a "new" conception of literacy (constructive, social, learner-centered).

Book clubs/literacy groups/study groups. Researchers have shown the positive effects for teachers working together in book clubs (reading and discussing literature). Flood, Lapp, Ranck-Buhr, and Moore (1995) found book-club reading and discussion among elementary teachers and their principal led to growth in understanding of multiculturalism, to increased insights into their pupils, and to changes in some teaching practices. Bealor (1992) demonstrated positive effects for a teacher book-club project focused on cultural issues and diversity. She found that the participating teachers gained insights regarding relationships between culture and teaching, and pupil interests. Study groups have shown similar benefits. Matlin and Short (1996) reported on groups organized to respond to a mandate for change from a basal series to a new literature program. The group voluntarily studied for three years, involving the principal as a colleague, and the group was responsible for setting the agendas.

Comments, Conclusions, and Questions.   As with the preservice literature, there is much to be excited about here in terms of progress, but the challenges are many. We note the following:

- There are major gaps in this literature. For example, little is reported that examines the experiences of first-year or novice teachers.
- There is a mismatch between the amount of effort invested in inservice education and the amount of research being reported. Where is the research of those consultants who do this work as a full-time job?
- The distinction between training and teacher education needs to be examined. We know how to "train" teachers (e.g., with specific behavioral outcomes targeted), but we need to know more about educating teachers (e.g., with the goal of conceptual change, enhanced decision-making capabilities, or strategic teaching).
- A "packaging mentality" is sweeping the country regarding teacher education and inservice. School districts are purchasing inservice packages for school districts. Why? And with what outcomes? We fear that such a movement might lead some to conduct research on inservice programs comparing "method A" to "method B" (e.g., Lyons, 1991). In the process of doing this kind of research, the teacher becomes subservient to the method. We have made this mistake too often, and we are in danger of going down this path again.

On the basis of these reviews, the answers to questions about teacher education are unclear, at best. We have learned that there are two traditions in teacher education (preservice and inservice) and that neither explains how teachers of reading are created, how they teach, nor how they change.

Unresolved Problems of Reading Teacher Education.

Despite evidence that the quantity of teacher education research has increased, the results leave reading educators with more questions than answers. The three authors of this chapter are illustrative. We are reading educators. Much of our professional time is spent planning and teaching reading methods courses and collaborating with teachers in schools. Nevertheless, research inadequately informs us about day-to-day problems—like the ones described next.

What should the goal be? Research on teaching tells us that the best teachers are thoughtfully adaptive (e.g., Duffy, 1994; Hoffman et al., 1998; Pressley et al., 1998; Shanahan & Neuman, 1997). Dilemmas characterize the nature of classroom teaching generally and the teaching of reading in particular; creative responsiveness, rather than technical compliance, characterizes the nature of effective teachers. In short, classrooms are complex places, and the best teachers are successful because they are thoughtful opportunists who create instructional practices to meet situational demands. It follows that teacher education ought to focus on developing adaptive teachers. Reading educators, in particular, should be trying to develop teachers who analyze reading instructional situations and then, in a thoughtful way, construct appropriate responses. In doing so, professional knowledge about reading is perceived not as an end in itself but as grist for thinking and problem solving. A constructivist model is often recommended (see Richardson, in press).

But reading educators also know that there are some teaching problems that are technical, that we do have answers for some problems, and that teachers need to have some of these answers. So, like most thoughtful reading educators, we are torn. We encourage our teachers to become problem solvers who can live the uncertain and ambiguous life of classroom teaching. We worry, though, about whether our students are getting "essentials" that might ease their beginning teaching.

What is the knowledge appropriate for beginning teachers? We reading educators are often fascinated with the subtle distinctions we discover about reading, and we love to talk about them. But do beginning teachers need to know these subtleties? Typically, the question is not whether we should teach a topic or not; the question is how far to go with it. Research does not tell us what or how much teachers need to know. Consequently, we decide by opinion or trial and error.

How do we teach problem solving anyway? We have little research to guide us, particularly as it relates to teachers and teaching. For instance, much of the research on effective teaching suggests that ability to identify and reframe problems is crucial (Schön, 1983). Consequently, when we present teaching as a problematic endeavor, we should be teaching our teachers how to identify and re-frame problems. A small body of literature, identified as inquiry-based instruction, is emerging but it is not yet sufficient for addressing this issue (see Short & Burke, 1989).

Similarly, it is assumed that problem solvers "think on their feet" or make "on-the-fly" decisions. At a still more subtle level, teachers must master the making of "imperfect decisions" in which one horn of a complex dilemma is dealt with immediately and another horn of the same dilemma is bypassed to be dealt with later (Buchmann, 1990). But research on teacher education offers us little guidance for teaching about these dilemmas.

What about teacher beliefs? Beliefs have been researched (e.g., Clark & Petersen, 1986; Pajares, 1992; Richardson, 1996; Richardson, Anders, Tidwell, & Lloyd, 1991), and Barr (in press) said that "exploration of belief is pivotal" and that changes cannot be incorporated into classroom practice "unless the teacher's conception of the work of the class supports such incorporation." Such views are sensible, but there are two problems. The first is that little agreement exists about the impact of beliefs, and the second is that we do not know enough about the construct to effect change (Duffy & Anderson, 1984; Hollingsworth, 1989). Consequently, reading methods professors are left with little guidance.

How do we decide on assignments/activities for our classes? Research on academic work tells us that school children make sense of school work by noting what tasks are assigned and what the teacher is particularly interested in grading (e.g., Doyle, 1983; Winne & Marx, 1982). It is sensible that the academic work principle operates in the same way with teachers as with children, but we do not know.

What should we do to develop mental strength? We hear that the best teachers display a certain spiritual strength, morality, or mental toughness that sustains them through the difficulties of teaching (e.g., Garrison, 1997; Purpel, 1989). We sense that the best teachers possess what Duffy (1998) calls a "moral compass," allowing them to navigate effectively through daily classroom dilemmas. It is an intangible attribute about which research is needed.

What is happening outside my course? An enduring problem of teacher education is whether the left hand knows what the right hand is doing. Teachers in preparation are influenced by other professors and course work, work in the field, and early on-the-job experiences. Each of these contexts is likely to be contradictory and to create conflicts for the neophyte teacher (Guilfoyle, 1996). Because we lack program-level research, teacher educators and teachers struggle to cope with these contradictions (Lampert, 1981).

How can we prepare teachers for the students they will face? In an increasingly diverse society, we need teachers who can recognize, accept, and build on differences (Dahl & Freppon, 1995). This problem has two sides: One side is that teachers of color need to be recruited and retained in the field; and second, teachers who are middle class and White need to learn that students who are different from themselves are a source of vitality, growth, and strength (see Moll, 1998). This requires that teachers recognize the potential that differing cultures have for creating the classroom culture (McDiarmid, 1992). Teacher educators, most of whom are culturally similar to the majority of teachers, need knowledge to address this issue (see Zeichner, 1995). An emerging literature in social literacies (Street, 1995) may inform this problem, but its consideration in teacher education is unrealized (Anders & Whitman, 1998).

REFLECTIONS

Is our ambivalence about the state of research on teacher education evident? We expect it is. On the one hand, reading teacher education is getting more research attention; on the other hand, this attention has not provided answers to our most pressing questions. At this point in history, with teacher education under intense fire, we need some answers (Fenstermacher, 1993). Teacher education has long been a favorite "whipping boy" of educational critics. The past year, however, has produced an unprecedented attack. Politicians and pundits charge that teachers are poorly prepared to teach reading (Darling-Hammond, 1996); schools of education are threatened (Ducharme & Ducharme, 1996); and legislatures are making preparation of reading teachers a priority of the reform agenda (Farkas & Johnson, 1997). Even highly respected agencies, such as the National Commission on Teaching and America's Future (Darling-Hammond, 1997), point out that the United States has no system for ensuring that teachers get access to knowledge; that preparation, licensing, and induction are often fragmented; and that professional development of teachers receives little emphasis. We have difficulty responding to these criticisms because we lack answers about how best to prepare reading teachers.

Unlike most critics, however, Darling-Hammond (1997) does more than point out flaws. She also has established the importance of teacher education by providing compelling data about the benefits of investing in teacher education. Basing her conclusions in a variety of studies from around the country, she has argued that teacher education is the key to instructional improvement, saying, "spending on teacher education swamped other variables as the most productive investment for schools" (p. 9). Knowing that investment in teacher education pays off is not enough. We need empirical evidence regarding how to invest resources.

We do not have that evidence. To gather that evidence and to respond to the questions posed in this chapter, teacher education research must be a priority. Like the state of research on teaching in the late 1960s—when a dormant agenda was transformed into a major force to improve classroom teaching—research on reading teacher education could likewise surge and become a major force in the education of reading teachers. Accomplishing such a surge would require hard choices (Goodman & Short, 1996). We must commit our energies to studying our programs, our courses, our teaching, and our expectations and requirements. In short, it means consenting to be the subject of study ourselves. It will take courage and creativity. Now is the time to start.

REFERENCES

Adams, E. K. (1967). Reading performance of elementary teachers in a developing institution. In G. B. Schick & M. M. May (Eds.) *Junior college and young adult reading programs: Expanding fields: Sixteenth yearbook of the National Reading Conference,* (pp. 47–57). Clemson, NC: National Reading Conference.

Alvermann, D. E. (1990). Reading teacher education. In R. W. Houston, M. Haberman, & J. Sikula (Eds.), *Handbook of research on teacher education* (pp. 687–704). New York: Macmillan.

Anders, P. L. (1991). The relationship between reading practices literature and teachers' talk about practices. In J. Zutell & S. McCormick (Eds.), *Learner factors/teacher factors: Issues in literacy research and instruction* (pp. 211–217). Chicago: National Reading Conference.

Anders, P. L., & Evans, K. S. (1994). Relationship between teachers' beliefs and their instructional practice in reading. In R. Garner & P. Alexander (Eds.), *Beliefs about text and instruction with text* (pp. 137–154). Hillsdale, NJ: Lawrence Erlbaum Associates.

Anders, P. L., & Gallego, M., A. (1989). Adoption of theoretically linked vocabulary-reading comprehension practices. In S. McCormick & J. Zutell (Eds.), *Cognitive and social perspectives for literacy research and instruction* (pp. 481–487). Chicago: National Reading Conference.

Anders, P. L., & Richardson, V. (1991). Research directions: Staff development that empowers teachers' reflection and enhances instruction. *Language Arts, 68,* 316–321.

Anders, P. L., & Whitman, R. (1998, December). *"Everything's changing all the time": Lived experiences, conceptual change (and ideology?) in content area literacy.* Presented at the National Reading Conference, Austin, TX.

Artley, A. S. (1975). Good teachers of reading—Who are they? *Reading Teacher, 29,* 26–31.

Artley, A. S. (1978). The education and certification of elementary and secondary teachers of reading. *Journal of Research and Development in Education, 11*(3), 34–43.

Askov, E. N., Kamm, K., Klumb, R., & Barnette, J. J. (1980). Study skills mastery: Comparisons between teachers and students on selected skills. In M. L. Kamil & A. J. Moe (Eds.), *Perspectives on reading research and instruction: Twenty-ninth yearbook of the National Reading Conference* (pp. 207–212). Washington DC: National Reading Conference.

Austin, M. C. (1968). Professional training of reading personnel. In H. M. Robinson (Ed.), *Innovation and change in reading instruction: Sixty-seventh yearbook of the National Society for the Study of Education,* (Part II, pp. 357–396). Chicago: University of Chicago Press.

Austin, M. C., & Morrison, C. (1961). *The torch lighters: Tomorrow's teachers of reading.* Cambridge, MA: Harvard University Press.

Austin, M. C., & Morrison, C. (1963). *The first R: The Harvard report on reading in elementary schools.* New York: Macmillan.

Bacharach, N. (1993). Facilitating emerging theories of reading in preservice students. *Journal of Reading Education, 19,* 8–16.

Bailey, M. H., Durkin, D., Nurss, J. R., & Stammer, J. D. (1982). Preparation of kindergarten teachers for reading instruction. *Reading Teacher, 36,* 307–311.

Bailey, M. H., & Guerra, C. L. (1984). Inservice education in reading: Three points of view. *Reading Teacher, 38,* 174–176.

Barter, A. (1974). An analysis of the relationship between student performance on the National Teachers Examination and that on the Cooperative English Test, Form 1B, Reading. *Educational and Psychological Measurement, 34,* 375–378.

Barr, R. (1984). Beginning reading instruction: From debate to reformation. In P. D. Pearson, R. Barr, M. L. Kamil, & P. Mosenthal (Eds.), *Handbook of reading research* (pp. 545–581). New York: Longman.

Barr, R. (in press). Research on the teaching of reading. In V. Richardson (Ed.), *Handbook of research on teaching* (4th ed.). Washington, DC: American Educational Research Association.

Barr, R, Kamil, M., Mosenthal, P., & Pearson, P. D. (1991). *Handbook of reading research* (Vol. II). White Plains, NY: Longman.

Bealor, S. (1992). Minority literature book groups for teachers. *Reading in Virginia, 17,* 17–21.

Bean, T. W., Bishop, A., & Leuer, M. (1981). The effect of a mini-conference on teacher beliefs about the reading process. *Reading Horizons, 22,* 85–90.

Bean, T. W., & Zulich, J. (1992). Teaching students to learn from text: Preservice content teachers' changing view of their role through the window of their student-professor dialogue journals. In J. Zutell & S. McCormick (Eds.), *Literacy theory and research: Analyses from multiple paradigm: Thirty-ninth yearbook of the National Reading Conference* (pp. 171–178). Chicago: National Reading Conference.

Bergeron, B. S. (1994). Practitioners and curricular control: Exploring constraints to literacy change. *Journal of Reading Education, 20,* 28–34.

Boehnlein, M. M. (1984). Can all teachers *really* teach reading? *Ohio Reading Teacher, 18*(4), 17–21.

Boehnlein, M. M., & Gans, T. G. (1975). Competency in teaching reading of field based and on-campus university students. *Journal of Reading, 20,* 28–34.

Book, C. L., Duffy, G. G., Roehler, L. R., Meloth, M. S., & Vavrus, L. G. (1985). A study of the relationship between teacher explanation and student metacognitive awareness during reading instruction. *Communication Education, 34,* 29–36.

Bos, C. S., & Anders, P. L. (1994). The study of student change. In V. Richardson (Ed.), *Teacher change and the staff development process: A case in reading instruction* (pp. 181–198). New York: Teachers College Press.

Botel, M., Ripley, P. M., & Barnes, L. A. (1993). A case study of an implementation of the "new literacy" paradigm. *Journal of Research in Reading, 16*, 112–127.

Britton, G. E. (1973). Preservice reading methods instruction: Large group/on-site/individualized. *Reading Improvement, 10*, 29–32.

Britton, G. E. (1975). Assessing preservice reading methods courses. *Reading Improvement, 10*, 29–32.

Brown, R., & Coy-Ogan, L. (1993). The evolution of transactional strategies instruction in one teacher's classroom. *Elementary School Journal, 94*, 221–233.

Buchmann, M. (1990). Beyond the lonely, choosing will: Professional development in teacher thinking. *Teachers College Record, 91*, 481–508.

Bush, C., & Putnam, L. (1968). Student teachers' experiences in reading instruction at Newark State College. *Journal of the Reading Specialist, 8*(1), 3–6, 18.

Calfee, R., & Drum, P. (1986). Research on teaching reading. In M. C. Wittrock (Ed.), *Handbook of research on teaching* (3rd ed., pp. 804–849). New York: Macmillan.

Chadwick, E. H., & Chadwick, S. C. (1976). In Vermont, an inservice program worth noting. *Reading Teacher, 30*, 193–196.

Chall, J. (1975). The reading problem: A diagnosis of the national reading problem; a national strategy for attacking the reading problem; legislative and administrative actions. In J. Carroll (Ed.), *Toward a literate society: The report of the Committee on Reading of the National Academy of Education* (pp. 3–45). New York: The National Academy.

Cheek, M. C. (1982). Preservice education in reading: What do the teachers say? *Reading Psychology, 3*, 25–35.

Clark, C., & Petersen, P. (1986). Teachers' thought processes. In M. Wittrock (Ed.), *Handbook of research on teaching* (3rd ed., pp. 255–296). New York: Macmillan.

Coladarci, T., & Gage, N. L. (1984). Effects of a minimal intervention on teacher behavior and student achievement. *American Educational Research Journal, 21*, 539–555.

Comas, J. C., & Farr, R. (1989). Training preservice teachers to analyze and evaluate textbooks. *Book Research Quarterly, 5*, 5–15.

Combs, M. (1994). Implementing a holistic reading series in first grade: Experiences with a conversation group. *Reading Horizons, 34*, 196–207.

Conley, M. W. (1983). Increasing students' reading achievement via inservice education. *Reading Teacher, 36*, 804–808.

Conley, M. W. (1986). The influence of training on three teachers' comprehension questions during content area lessons. *Elementary School Journal, 87*, 17–27.

Dahl, K. L., & Freppon, P. A. (1995). A comparison of inner-city children's interpretations of reading and writing instruction in the early grades in skills-based and whole language classrooms. *Reading Research Quarterly, 30*, 50–74.

Darling-Hammond, L. (1996). *What matters most: Teaching for America's future.* New York: National Commission on Teaching and America's Future.

Darling-Hammond, L. (1997). *Doing what matters most: Investing in quality teaching.* New York: National Commission on Teaching and America's Future.

DeCarlo, M. R., & Cleland, D. L. (1968). A reading in-service education program for teachers. *Reading Teacher, 22*, 163–169.

Deford, D. (1985). Validating the construct of theoretical orientation in reading instruction. *Reading Research Quarterly, 20*, 351–367.

Doyle, W. (1983). Academic work. *Review of Educational Research, 53*, 159–199.

Ducharme, E., & Ducharme, M. (1996). Development of the teacher education professoriate. In F. Murray (Ed.), *The teacher educator's handbook: Building a knowledge base for the preparation of teachers* (pp. 691–714). San Francisco: Jossey-Bass.

Duffy, G. G. (1983). From turn taking to sense making: Broadening the concept of reading teacher effectiveness. *Journal of Educational Research, 76*, 134–139.

Duffy, G. (1994). Teachers' progress toward becoming expert strategy teachers. *Elementary School Journal, 94*(2), 109–120.

Duffy, G. (1998). Teaching and the balancing of round stones. *Phi Delta Kappan, 79*(10), 777–780.

Duffy, G., & Anderson, L. (1984). Teachers' theoretical orientations and the real classroom. *Reading Psychology, 5*(2), 97–104.

Duffy, G. G., Roehler, L. R., & Putnam, J. (1987). Putting the teacher in control: Basal reading textbooks and instructional decision making. *Elementary School Journal, 87*, 357–366.

Duffy, G. G., Roehler, L. R., & Rackliffe, G. (1986). How teachers' instructional talk influences students' understanding of lesson content. *Elementary School Journal, 87*, 3–16.

Dworkin, N. E. (1979). Changing teachers' negative expectations. *Academic Therapy, 14*, 517–531.

Eckert, M. S., & Wollenberg, J. (1984). Competency model for preservice teachers in a basic skills course. *Reading Horizons, 24*, 238–242.

Ehri, L., & Williams, J. (1996). Learning to read and learning to teach reading. In F. B. Murray (Ed.), *The teacher educator's handbook* (pp. 231–241). San Francisco, CA: Jossey-Bass.

El-Dinary, P. B., Pressley, M., & Schuder, T. (1992). Teachers' learning transactional strategies instruction. In C. K. Kinzer & D. J. Leu (Eds.), *Literacy research, theory, and practice: Views from many perspectives* (pp. 453–462). Chicago: National Reading Conference.

El-Dinary, P. B., & Schuder, T. (1993). Seven teachers' acceptance of transactional strategies instruction during their first year using it. *Elementary School Journal, 94,* 207–219.

Erickson, L., Johnson, M., & Logan, J. (1992). A survey of Illinois K–8 teachers' reading and writing preservice and staff development perceptions. *Illinois Reading Council Journal, 20,* 31–39.

Farkas, S., & Johnson, J. (1997). *Different drummers: How teachers of teachers view public education.* New York: Public Agenda.

Fenstermacher, G. D (1993). *Where are we going? Who will lead us there?* Washington, DC: American Association of Colleges of Teacher Education.

Fenstermacher, G. D (1994). The knower and the known: The nature of knowledge in research on teaching. In L. Darling-Hammond (Ed.), *Review of educational research, 20,* 3–56. Washington, DC: American Educational Research Association.

Fleisher, B. M. (1992). Videotaping: A tool for self-evaluation. *Journal of College Reading and Learning, 24,* 40–47.

Flippo, R. F., & Hayes, D. A. (1984). Preparation in reading and educator certification: Requirements, needs, issues. In G. H. McNinch (Ed.), *Reading teacher education: Fourth yearbook of the American Reading Forum* (pp. 27–29). Athens, GA: American Reading Forum.

Flood, J., Lapp, D., Ranck-Buhr, W., & Moore, J. (1995). What happens when teachers get together to talk about books? Gaining a multicultural perspective from literature. *Reading Teacher, 48,* 720–723.

Ford, M. P. (1993). The process and promise of portfolio assessment in teacher education programs: Impact on students' knowledge beliefs, and practices. In T. V. Rasinski & N. D. Padak (Eds.), *Inquiries in literacy learning and instruction* (pp. 145–152). Pittsburg, KS: College Reading Association.

Fox, D. L. (1996). The struggle for voice in learning to teach: Lessons from one preservice teacher's portfolio. In K. Whitmore & Y. Goodman (Eds.), *Whole language voices in teacher education* (pp. 285–296). York, ME: Stenhouse.

Furr, O. R. (1965). The effectiveness of a college course in the teaching of reading. In J. A. Figurel (Ed.), *Reading and inquiry,* Proceedings of the International Reading Association (pp. 370–372). Newark, DE: International Reading Association.

Garrison, J. (1997). *Dewey and eros: Wisdom and desire in the art of teaching.* New York: Teachers College Press.

Gipe, J. P., Duffy, C. A., & Richards, J. C. (1989). A comparison of two types of early field experiences. *Reading Improvement, 26,* 254–265.

Gipe, J. P., & Richards, J. C. (1990). Promoting reflection about reading instruction through journaling. *Journal of Reading Education, 15,* 6–13.

Gonzales, P. C. (1980). Teacher preparation: Meeting the needs of the limited English speaking student. *Reading World, 19,* 375–382.

Goodacre, E. J., & Clark, M. M. (1973). Initial approaches to teaching reading in Scottish and English schools. *Reading, 5*(2), 15–21.

Goodman, Y. M., & Short, K. G. (1996). Heightening political awareness and action: Liberating our teaching. In K. Whitmore & Y. Goodman (Eds.), *Whole language voices in teacher education* (pp. 319–329). York, ME: Stenhouse.

Gove, M. K., & Kennedy-Calloway, C. (1992). Action research: Empowering students to work with at-risk students. *Journal of Reading, 35,* 526–534.

Graves, M. F., Pauls, L. W., & Sallinger, T. (1996). Reading curriculum and instruction. In F. B. Murray (Ed.), *The teacher educator's handbook* (pp. 217–230). San Francisco, CA: Jossey-Bass.

Gray, W. S. (1961). The role of teacher education. In N. B. Henry (Ed.), *Development in an through reading: Sixtieth Yearbook of the National Society for the Study of Education* (Part 1, pp. 144–164). Chicago: University of Chicago Press.

Gray-Schlegel, M. A., & Matanzo, J. B. (1993). Action research: Classroom teachers' perception of its impact on the teaching of reading. In T. B. Rasinski & N. D. Padak (Eds.), *Inquiries in literacy learning and instruction* (pp. 135–142). Pittsburg, KS: College Reading Association.

Guilfoyle, K. (1996). My journey through the land of transformation: Navigating uncharted territory. In K. Whitmore & Y. Goodman (Eds.), *Whole language voices in teacher education* (pp. 25–36). York: ME: Stenhouse.

Hancock, J., Turbill, J., & Cambourne, B. (1994). Assessment and evaluation of literacy learning. In S. W. Valencia, E. H. Hiebert, & P. P. Afflerback (Eds.), *Authentic reading assessment: Practices and possibilities* (pp. 46–62). Newark, DE: International Reading Association.

Hawkins, M. L. (1967). Are future teachers readers? *Reading Teacher, 21,* 138–140, 144.

Herrmann, B. A. (1990). A longitudinal study of preservice teachers' knowledge structures. In J. Zutell & S. McCormick (Eds.), *Literacy theory and research: Analyses from multiple paradigms: Thirty-ninth yearbook of the National Reading Conference* (pp. 145–152). Chicago: National Reading Conference.

Herrmann, B. A., & Sarracino, J. (1992). Effects of an alternative approach for teaching preservice teachers how to teach strategic reasoning: Two illustrative cases. In C. K. Kinzer & D. J. Leu (Eds.), *Literacy research, theory and practice: Views from many perspectives* (pp. 331–339). Chicago: National Reading Conference.

Hoffman, J. V. (1991). Teacher and school effects in learning to read. In R. Barr, M. Kamil, P. Mosenthal, & P. D. Pearson (Eds.), *Handbook of reading research* (Vol. II, pp. 911–950). White Plains, NY: Longman.

Hoffman, J. V., McCarthey, S., Elliott, B., Bayles, D., Price, D., Ferree, A., & Abbott, J. (1998). The literature-based basals in first-grade classrooms: Savior, satan or same-old, same-old. *Reading Research Quarterly, 33,* 168–197.

Hoffman, J. V., Roser, N.L., Battle, J., Farest, C., & Isaacs, M. E. (1990). Teachers' developing insights about the use of children's literature for language and literacy growth. In J. Zutell & S. McCormick (Eds.), *Literacy theory and research: Analyses from multiple paradigms* (pp. 89–98). Chicago: National Reading Conference.

Hoffman, J. V., Roser, N. L., & Farest, C. (1988). Literature-sharing strategies in classrooms serving students from economically disadvantaged and language different home environments. In J. E. Readence & R. S. Baldwin (Eds.), *Dialogues in literacy research* (pp. 331–337). Chicago: National Reading Conference.

Hollingsworth, S. (1989). Prior beliefs and cognitive change in learning to teach. *American Educational Research Journal, 26*(2), 160–189.

Hollingsworth, S. (1994). *Teacher research and urban literacy education: Lessons and conversations in a feminist key.* New York: Teachers College Press.

Hosking, N. J. (1991). A comparative study to determine appropriate implementation strategies for Saskatchewan's new elementary English language arts curriculum. *Reflections on Canadian Literacy, 9,* 82–89.

Hyatt, A., Foster, T., Menter, I., & Riley, S. (1994). Teaching students, learning reading. *Reading, 28,* 45–49.

Jennings, J. H., Hieshima, J. A., Pearce, D. L., Shapiro, S., & Ambardar, A. K. (1994). A staff development project to improve literacy instruction in an urban school. *Illinois Reading Council Journal, 22,* 47–59.

Johnson, C. S., & Evans, A. D. (1992). Improving teacher questioning: A study of a training program. In N. D. Padak, T. V. Rasinski, & J. Logan (Eds.), *Literacy research and practice: Foundations for the year 2000* (pp. 65–70). Provo, UT: College Reading Association.

Johnson, J. C., Phillips, G. O., & Sublett, H. L. (1974). An inventory of reading courses and practices in major black institutions. In P. L. Nacke (Ed.) *Interaction: Research and practice for college-adult reading: Twenty-third yearbook of the National Reading Conference* (pp. 293–295). Clemson, SC: National Reading Conference.

Kieffer, R. D., & Faust, M. A. (1994). Portfolio process and teacher change: Elementary, middle, and secondary teachers reflect on their initial experiences with portfolio evaluation. In C. K. Kinzer & D. J. Leu (Eds.), *Multidimensional aspects of literacy research, theory, and practice.* (pp. 82–88). Chicago: National Reading Conference.

Kieffer, R. D., & Morrison, L. S. (1994). Changing portfolio process: One journey toward authentic assessment. *Language Arts, 71,* 411–418.

Kingston, A. J., Brosier, G. F., & Hsu, Y. (1975). The inventory of teacher knowledge of reading—A validation. *Reading Teacher, 29,* 133–136.

Kinzer, C. K. (1989). Mental models and beliefs about classrooms and reading instruction: A comparison between preservice teachers, inservice teachers, and professors of education. In S. McCormick & J. Zutell (Eds.), *Cognitive and social perspectives for literacy research and instruction* (pp. 489–499). Chicago: National Reading Conference.

Kinzer, C. K., Hinchman, K. A., & Leu, D. J. (Eds.) (1997). *Inquiries in literacy theory and practice: Forty-sixth yearbook of the National Reading Conference.* Chicago: National Reading Conference.

Klesius, J., Zielonka, P., & LaFramboise, K. (1990). Training preservice teachers to effectively implement the directed reading activity: Positive and negative influences. *Journal of Reading Education, 15,* 40–50.

Koenke, K. (1976). Ascertaining knowledge of reading with the Artley-Hardin Inventory. In W. D. Miller & G. H. McNinch (Eds.), *Reflections and investigations on reading: Twenty-fifth yearbook of the National Reading Conference* (pp. 141–146). Clemson, SC: National Reading Conference.

Kraus, D. D. (1992). Changes in primary teachers' instructional practices after year 1 of a collaborative whole language project. In N. D. Padak, T. B. Rasinski, & J. Logan (Eds.), *Literacy research and practice: Foundations for the year 2000* (pp. 70–86). Provo, UT: College Reading Association.

Kurth, R. J., & Stromberg, L. J. (1983). Improving comprehension instruction in elementary classrooms. In G. H. McNinch (Ed.) *Reading research to reading practice,* Third yearbook of the American Reading Forum (pp. 127–131). Athens, GA: American Reading Forum.

Laine, C. (1984). Reading and writing skills of prospective teachers. In G. H. McNinch (Ed.), *Reading teacher education,* Fourth yearbook of the American Reading Forum (pp. 53–55). Athens, GA: American Reading Forum.

Lamme, L. L., & Hysmith, C. (1991). One school's adventure into portfolio assessment. *Language Arts, 68,* 629–640.

Lampert, M. (1981). How teachers manage to teach: Perspectives on the unsolvable dilemmas in teaching practice. *Dissertation Abstracts International, 42,* 3122A. (University Microfilms No. 81-26, 203)

Lefever-Davis, S., & Helfeldt, J. P. (1994). The efficacy of a site-based literacy methods course developed within the context of a school-university partnership. In E. G. Strurtevant & W. M. Linek (Eds.), *Pathways for literacy: Learners teach and teachers learn* (pp. 183–194). Pittsburg, KS: College Reading Association.

Lickteig, J., Johnson, B., & Johnson, D. (1994). Future teachers' reflections, perceptions, and anticipations about reading and writing. *Journal of Reading Education, 19,* 22–43.

Lloyd, C. V., & Anders, P. L. (1994). Research-based practices as the content of a staff development process. In V. Richardson (Ed.), *Teacher change and the staff development process: A case of reading instruction* (pp. 68–89). New York: Teachers College Press.

Logan, J., & Erickson, L. (1979). Elementary teachers' reading inservice preferences. *Reading Teacher, 33,* 330–334.

Lyons, C. A. (1991). A comparative study of the teaching effectiveness of teachers participating in a year-long or 2-week inservice program. In J. Zutell & S. McCormick (Eds.), *Learner factors/teacher factors: Issues in literacy research and instruction* (pp. 367–375). Chicago: National Reading Conference.

Lyons, N. (1993). Constructing narratives for understanding: Using portfolio interviews to structure teachers' professional development. In P. H. Dreyer (Ed.), *Learning from learners: Fifty-seventh yearbook of the Claremont Reading Conference* (pp. 1–17). Claremont, CA: Claremont Graduate School.

Marcus, M. (1968). The status of reading instruction—Greater New Orleans area. *Journal of the Reading Specialist, 7,* 153–163, 169.

Matlin, M. L., & Short, K. G. (1996). Study groups: Inviting teachers to learn together. In K. Whitmore & Y. Goodman (Eds.), *Whole language voices in teacher education* (pp. 85–92). York, ME: Stenhouse.

McDiarmid, G. (1992). What to do about differences? A study of multicultural education for teacher trainees in the Los Angeles Unified School District. *Journal of Teacher Education, 43*(2), 83–93.

Mikulecky, L. J., & Ribovich, J. K. (1977). Reading competence and attitudes of teachers in preparation. *Journal of Reading, 20,* 573–580.

Miller, J. W. (1978). Teachers' abilities to judge the difficulty of reading materials. *Reading Horizons, 19,* 151–158.

Miller, J. W., & Ellsworth, R. (1985). The evaluation of a two-year program to improve teacher effectiveness in reading instruction. *Elementary School Journal, 85,* 484–495.

Miller, J. W., & Rand, D. C. (1978). Practical teaching experiences in reading for preservice teachers. *Reading Improvement, 15,* 305–308.

Moll, L. C. (1998). Turning to the world: Bilingual schooling, literacy, and the cultural mediation of thinking. In T. Shanahan & F. V. Rodriguez-Brown (Eds.), *National reading conference yearbook* (pp. 59–75). Chicago: The National Reading Conference.

Moore, M. (1991). Reflective teaching and learning through the use of learning logs. *Journal of Reading Education, 17,* 35–49.

Moore, S. A. (1986). A comparison of reading education students, instructional beliefs and instructional practices. In J. A. Niles, & R. V. Lalik (Eds.) *Solving problems in literacy: Learners, teachers, and researchers: Twenty-fifth yearbook of The National Reading Conference* (pp. 143–146). Rochester, NY: National Reading Conference.

Morrison, C., & Austin, M. C. (1977). *The torch lighters revisited.* Newark, DE: International Reading Association.

Morrison, C., Harris, A. J., & Auerbach, I. T. (1969). Staff aftereffects of participation in reading research project: A follow-up study of the CRAFT project. *Reading Research Quarterly, 4,* 366–395.

Mosenthal, J. H. (1987). Learning from discussion: Requirements and constraints on classroom instruction in reading comprehension strategies. In J. E. Readence & R. Scott Baldwin (Eds.), *Research in literacy: Merging perspectives: Thirty-sixth yearbook of the National Reading Conference* (pp. 169–176). Rochester, NY: National Reading Conference.

Mosenthal, J. (1994). Constructing knowledge and expertise in literacy teaching: Portfolios in undergraduate teacher education. In C. K. Kinzer & D. J. Leu (Eds.), *Multidimensional aspects of literacy research, theory, and practice* (pp. 407–417). Chicago: National Reading Conference.

Moss, B. (1991). Preservice teachers' reminiscences of positive and negative reading experiences: A qualitative study. In N. D. Padak, T. V. Rasinski, & J. Logan (Eds.), *Literacy research and practice: Foundations for the year 2000* (pp. 29–35). Provo, UT: College Reading Association.

Murray, F. B. (Ed.). (1996). *The teacher educator's handbook.* San Francisco, CA: Jossey-Bass.

Neal, K. S., Schaer, B. B., Ley, T. C., & Wright, J. P. (1990). Predicting achievement in a teacher preparatory course of reading methods from the ACT and Teale-Lewis Reading Attitude scores. *Reading Psychology, 11,* 131–139.

Nelson, O., Pryor, E., & Church, B. (1990). Process of change in teachers' beliefs, attitudes, and concerns during a series of whole language reading and writing workshops. In N. D. Padak, T. V. Rasinski, & J. Logan (Eds.), *Challenges in reading* (pp. 53–62). Pittsburg, KS: College Reading Association.

Niles, J. A., & Lalik, R. V. (1987). Learning to teach comprehension: A collaborative approach. In J. E. Readence & R. S. Baldwin (Eds.), *Research in literacy: Merging perspectives: Thirty-sixth yearbook of the National Reading Conference* (pp. 153–160). Rochester, NY: National Reading Conference.

Nistler, R. J., & Shepperson, G. M. (1993-1994). Negotiating change: Teachers and university professors working together. *Journal of Reading Education, 19,* 29–45.

Noe, K. (1994). Effectiveness of an integrated methods curriculum: Will beginning teachers teach as we have taught them? *Journal of Reading Education, 19,* 45–49.

O'Brien, D. G, & Stewart, R. A. (1990). Preservice teachers' perspectives on why every teacher is not a teacher of reading: A qualitative analysis. *Journal of Reading Behavior, 22,* 101–129.

Otto, B., & Iacono, M. (1991). Implementing changes in reading instruction. *Illinois Reading Council Journal, 19,* 25–33.

Otto, W., Wolf, A., & Eldridge, R. G. (1984). Managing instruction. In P. D. Pearson, R. Barr, M. L. Kamil, & P. Mosenthal (Eds.), *Handbook of reading research* (Vol. I, pp. 799–828). New York: Longman.

Pace, G. (1992). Stories of teacher-initiated change from traditional to whole-language literacy instruction. *Elementary School Journal, 92*, 461–476.

Pajares, M. (1992). Teachers' beliefs and educational research: Cleaning up a messy construct. *Review of Educational Research, 62*(3), 307–332.

Paratore, J. R., & Indrisano, R. (1994). Changing classroom instruction in literacy. *Journal of Education, 176*(1), 49–66.

Paris, S. G., Wasik, B. A., & Turner, J. C. (1991). The development of strategic readers. In R. Barr, M. Kamil, P. Mosenthal, & P. D. Pearson (Eds.), *Handbook of reading research* (Vol. II, pp. 609–640). White Plains, NY: Longman.

Pavlik, R. A. (1975). An assessment of undergraduate preparation available at the University of Northern Colorado for the teaching of reading in the elementary school. *Colorado Journal of Educational Research, 14*, 22–28.

Pearson, P. D., Barr, R., Kamil, M. L., & Mosenthal, P. (1984). *Handbook of reading research* (Vol. I). New York: Longman.

Pearson, P. D., & Fielding, L. (1991). Comprehension instruction. In R. Barr, M. Kamil, P. Mosenthal, & P. D. Pearson (Eds.), *Handbook of reading research* (Vol. II, pp. 815–860). White Plains, NY: Longman.

Phelps, S., & Weidler, S. D. (1993). Preservice teachers' perceptions of effective teaching. *Journal of Educational Psychology, 84*, 231–246.

Placier, P., & Hamilton, M. L. (1994). Schools as contexts: A complex relationship. In V. Richardson (Ed.), *Teacher change and the staff development process: A case in reading instruction* (pp. 135–158). New York: Teachers College Press.

Pressley, M., Allington, R., Morrow, L., Baker, L., Nelson, E., Wharton-McDonald, R., Block, C., Tracey, D., Brooks, G., Cronin, J., & Woo, D. (1998). *The nature of effective first-grade literacy instruction.* Unpublished paper, National Research Center on English Learning and Achievement, State University of New York, Albany.

Pressley, M., Bergman, J. L., & El-Dinary, P. B. (1992). A researcher-educator collaborative interview study of transactional comprehension strategies instruction. *Journal of Educational Psychology, 84*, 231–246.

Purpel, D. (1989). *The moral and spiritual crisis in education.* New York: Bergin & Garvey.

Raphael, T. E. (1984). Teacher explanations and students' understanding of sources of information for answering questions. In J. A. Niles & L. A. Harris (Eds.), *Changing perspectives on research in reading/language processing and instruction: Thirty-third yearbook of the National Reading Conference* (pp. 214–222). Rochester, NY: National Reading Conference.

Raphael, T. E. (1987). Research on reading: But what can I teach on Monday? In V. Richardson-Koehler (Ed.), *Educators' handbook: A research perspective* (pp. 26–49). White Plains, NY: Longman.

Reay, D. G., Von Harrison, G., & Gottfredson, C. (1984). The effect on pupil reading achievement of teacher compliance with prescribed methodology. *Reading in Education, 32*, 17–23.

Richardson, V. (1996). The role of attitudes and beliefs in learning to teach. In J. Sikula (Ed.), *Handbook of research on teacher education* (2nd ed., pp. 102–119). New York: Macmillan.

Richardson, V. (in press). Teacher education and the construction of meaning. In G. Griffin (Ed.), *Teacher education for a new century: Emerging perspectives, promising practices, and future possibilities,* (NSSE Yearbook). Chicago: University of Chicago Press.

Richardson, V., Anders, P., Tidwell, D., & Lloyd, C. (1991). The relationship between teachers' beliefs and practices in reading comprehension. *American Educational Research Journal, 28*(3), 559–586.

Risko, V. J. (1992). Developing problem solving environment to prepare teachers for instruction of diverse learners. In B. L. Hayes & K. Camperell (Eds.), *Developing lifelong readers: Policies, procedures and programs* (pp. 1–13). Athens, GA: American Reading Forum.

Risko, V. J., McAllister, D., Peter, J., & Bigenho, F. (1994). Using technology in support of preservice teachers' generative learning. In E. G. Sturtevant & W. M. Linek (Eds.), *Pathways for literacy: Learners teach and teachers learn* (pp. 156–167). Pittsburg, KS: College Reading Association.

Roeder, H. H. (1972). Mississippi teachers better prepared to teach reading than California grads. *California Journal of Educational Research, 23*, 177–181.

Roeder, H. H., Beal, D. K., & Eller, W. (1973). What Johnny knows that teacher educators don't. *Journal of Research and Development in Education, 7*(1), 3–10, F 73.

Roehler, L. R., & Duffy, G. G. (1991). Teachers' instructional actions. In R. Barr, M. Kamil, P. Mosenthal, & P. D. Pearson (Eds.), *Handbook of reading research* (Vol. II, pp. 861–883). White Plains, NY: Longman.

Roehler, L. R., Duffy, G. G., & Meloth, M. S., (1984). The effects and some distinguishing characteristics of explicit teacher explanation during reading instruction. In J. A. Niles & L. A. Harris (Eds.), *Changing perspectives on research in reading/language processing and instruction: Thirty-third yearbook of the National Reading Conference* (pp. 223–229). Rochester, NY: National Reading Conference.

Rogers, S. F., Merlin, S. B., Brittain, M. M., Palmatier, R., & Terrell, P. (1983). A research view of clinic practicum in reading education. *Reading World, 23*, 134–146.

Rosenshine, B., & Stevens, R. (1984). Classroom instruction in reading. In P. D. Pearson, R. Barr, M. L. Kamil, & P. Mosenthal (Eds.), *Handbook of reading research* (Vol. I, pp. 745–798). New York: Longman.

Roskos, K., & Walker, B. J. (1993). Preservice teachers' epistemology in the teaching of problem readers. In D. J. Leu & C. K. Kinzer (Eds.), *Examining central issues in literacy research, theory, and practice* (pp. 325–334). Chicago: National Reading Conference.

Roskos, K., & Walker, B. (1994). An analysis of preservice teachers' pedagogical concepts in the teaching of problem readers. In C. K. Kinzer & D. J. Leu (Eds.), *Multidimensional aspects of literacy research theory and practice* (pp. 418–428). Chicago: National Reading Conference.

Russell, D. H., & Fea, H. R. (1963). Research on teaching reading. In N. L. Gage (Ed.), *Handbook of research on teaching* (pp. 865–928). Chicago: Rand McNally.

Russell, T., & Korthagen, F. (Eds.) (1995). *Teachers who teach teachers: Reflections on teacher education.* Washington, DC: Falmer Press.

Sanger, D. D., & Stick, S. L. (1984). A workshop to incorporate language development in teaching reading. *Reading Horizons, 24,* 266–274.

Sawyer, R., & Taylor, L. B. (1968). Evaluating teacher effectiveness in reading instruction. *Journal of Reading, 2,* 415–418, 483–488.

Scharer, P. L. (1991). Moving into literature-based reading instruction: Changes and challenges for teachers. In J. Zutell & S. McCormick, (Eds.), *Learner factors/teacher factors: Issues in literacy research and instruction* (pp. 409–421). Chicago: National Reading Conference.

Scharer, P. L. (1992). Teachers in transition: An exploration of changes in teachers and classrooms during implementation of literature-based reading instruction. *Reading Psychology, 14,* 1–13.

Scheffler, A. J., Richmond, M., & Kazelskis, R. (1993). Examining shifts in teachers' theoretical orientations to reading. *Reading Psychology, 14,* 1–13.

Schön, D. (1983). *The reflective practitioner.* New York: Basic Books.

Seaboard, M. B., Mohr, K., Fowler, T. J. & Lyons, C. (1993). Preservice teachers' learning processes: A descriptive analysis of the impact of varied experiences with portfolios. In C. K. Kinzer & D. Leu (Eds.), *Multidimensional aspects of literacy research, theory, and practice* (pp. 440–447). Chicago: National Reading Conference.

Shanahan, T., & Neuman, S. (1997). Conversations: Literacy research that makes a difference. *Reading Research Quarterly, 32,* 202–211.

Shaw, P. A. (1994). The effects of teacher training on preservice elementary education majors' conceptual framework of reading. *Reading Horizons, 34*(3), 216–233.

Shefelbine, J., & Shiel, G. (1990). Preservice teachers' schemata for a diagnostic framework in reading. *Reading Research and Instruction, 30,* 30–43.

Shepperson, G. M., & Nistler, R. J. (1991). Whole language collaboration project: Three case studies to represent change. In T. V. Rasinski, N. D. Padak, & J. Logan (Eds.), *Reading is knowledge: The yearbook of the College Reading Association* (Vol. XIII, pp. 129–137). Pittsburg, KS: College Reading Association.

Shepperson, G. M., & Nistler, R. J. (1992). Whole language collaboration project: Implementing change in one elementary school. *Reading Horizons, 33,* 55–56.

Short, K. G., & Burke, C. (1989). New potentials for teacher education: Teaching and learning as inquiry. *Elementary School Journal, 90*(2), 193–206.

Short, K. G., & Kauffman, G. (1992). Hearing students' voices: The role of reflection in learning. *Teachers Networking: The Whole Language Newsletter, 11*(3), 1–6.

Shulman, L. S. (1986). Those who understand: Knowledge growth in teaching. *Educational Researcher, 15*(2), 4–14.

Sivan, E., & Roehler, L. (1986). Motivational statements in explicit teacher explanations, and their relationship to students' metacognition in reading. In J. A. Niles & R. V. Lalik, (Eds.), *Solving problems in literacy: Learners, teachers, and researchers: Thirty-fifth yearbook of the National Reading Conference* (pp. 178–184). Rochester, NY: National Reading Conference.

Smith, C. M. (1989). Reading attitudes of preservice education majors. *Reading Horizons, 29,* 231–234.

Smith, P. K., Fairbanks, M. M., & Saltz, M. (1984). Status and content of reading foundation courses. *Reading Improvement, 21,* 232–239.

Smith, R. J., Otto, W., & Harty, K. (1970). Elementary teachers' preferences for preservice and in-service training in the teaching of reading. *Journal of Educational Research, 63,* 445–449.

Start, K. B., & Strange, L. (1980). Primary reading and mathematics method in eight state colleges of Victoria. *British Journal of Teacher Education, 6,* 131–138.

Stewart, R. A., & Paradis, E. E. (1993). Portfolios: Agents of change and empowerment in classrooms. In D. J. Leu & C. K. Kinzer (Eds.), *Examining central issues in literacy research, theory, and practice* (pp. 109–116). Chicago: National Reading Conference.

Stice, C. F., Bertrand, N. P., Leuder, D. C., & Dunn, M. B. (1989). Personality types and theoretical orientation to reading: An exploratory study. *Reading Research and Instruction, 29,* 39–51.

Stieglitz, E. L., & Oehlkers, W. J. (1989). Improving teacher discourse in a reading lesson. *Reading Teacher, 42,* 374–379.

Street, B. V. (1995). *Social literacies: Critical approaches to literacy in development, ethnography and education.* New York: Longman.

Streeter, B. B. (1986). The effects of training experienced teachers in enthusiasm on students' attitudes toward reading. *Reading Psychology, 7*(4), 249–259.

Strickler, D. (1976). A systematic approach to teaching decoding skills. In B. L. Courtney (Ed.), *Reading interaction: The teacher, the pupil, the materials* (pp. 49–57). Newark, DE: International Reading Association.

Sullivan, E. P. (1976). Functional literacy of teacher trainees. In W. D. Miller & G. H. McNinch (Eds.), *Reflections and investigations on reading: Twenty-fifth yearbook of the National Reading Conference* (pp. 147–151). Clemson, SC: National Reading Conference.

Talmadge, H., Pascarella E. T., & Ford, S. (1984). The influence of cooperative learning strategies on teacher practices, student perceptions of the learning environment, and academic achievement. *American Educational Research Journal, 21*, 163–179.

Thistlethwaite, L., Barclay, K. D., Castle, M., & Lewis, W. J. (1991). Multi-session reading inservice: A step in the right direction. *Reading Horizons, 31*, 299–311.

Thomas, K. F., & Rinehart, S. D. (1994). Instituting whole language: Teacher power and practice. *Reading Horizons, 35*(1), 71–88.

Tierney, R. J., & Cunningham, J. W. (1984). Research on teaching reading comprehension. In P. D. Pearson, R. Barr, M. L. Kamil, & P. Mosenthal (Eds.), *Handbook of reading research* (Vol. I, pp. 609–655). New York: Longman.

Trickey, G., & Crispin, L. (1982). A reading project in Barking. *Special Education, 9*(4), 6–9.

Walker, B. J., & Ramseth, C. (1993). Reflective practice confronts the complexities of teaching reading. In T. V. Rasinski & N. D. Padak (Eds.), *Inquiries in literacy learning and instruction* (pp. 171–177). Pittsburg, KS: College Reading Association.

Walker, B. J., & Roskos, K. (1994). Preservice teachers' epistemology of diagnostic reading instruction: Observations of shifts during coursework experience. In E. G. Sturtevant & W. M. Linek (Eds.), *Pathways for literacy: Learners teach and teachers learn* (pp. 59–71). Pittsburg, KS: College Reading Association.

Warner, D. (1970). Future teachers look at reading instruction. *Reading Horizons, 10*(2), 53–58.

Wedman, J. M., & Robinson, R. (1988). Effects of a decision making model on preservice teachers' decision making practices and materials use. *Reading Improvement, 23*, 21–26.

Wendelin, K. H., & Murphy, C. C. (1986). Preservice teachers' perceptions of their reading methods preparation. *Reading Improvement, 23*, 21–26.

Wham, M. A. (1993). The relationship between undergraduate course work and beliefs about reading instruction. *Journal of Research and Development in Education, 27*, 9–17.

Whitmore, K. F., & Goodman, Y. M. (1996). *Whole language voices in teacher education.* York, ME: Stenhouse.

Winne, P., & Marx, R. (1982). Students' and teachers' views of thinking processes for classroom learning. *Elementary School Journal, 82*, 493–518.

Zeichner, K. M. (1995). Reflections of a teacher educator working for social change. In T. Russell & F. Korthagen (Eds.), *Teachers who teach teachers: Reflections on teacher education* (pp. 11–24). Washington, DC: Falmer Press.

Zutell, J., & McCormick, S. (Eds.). (1990). *Literacy theory and research: Analyses from multiple paradigms: Thirty-ninth yearbook of the National Reading Conference.* Chicago: National Reading Conference.

CHAPTER 39

Literacy and Technology: Deictic Consequences for Literacy Education in an Information Age

Donald J. Leu, Jr.
Syracuse University

Change increasingly defines the nature of literacy in an information age. Literacy is rapidly and continuously changing as new technologies for information and communication repeatedly appear and new envisionments for exploiting these technologies are continuously crafted by users. Moreover, these new technologies for information and communication permit the immediate exchange of even newer technologies and envisionments for their use. This speeds up the already rapid pace of change in the forms and functions of literacy, increasing the complexity of the challenges we face as we consider how best to prepare students for their literacy futures. Today, continuous, rapid change regularly redefines the nature of literacy. This simple observation has profound implications for literacy education.

Although some might deny the value of these changes for education (Oppenheimer, 1997; Roszak, 1994; Stoll, 1995) or for literacy (Birkerts, 1994; Rochlin, 1997), it is no longer possible to ignore them in a world of networked information resources. Simply visit one of many classrooms now accessible through a recent technology for information and communication—the Internet. You might, for example, pay a visit to the K–2 classrooms of Tim Lauer and Beth Rohloff at Buckman Elementary School in Portland, OR (http://buckman.pps.k12.or.us/room100/room100.html), Gary Cressman's U.S. History classroom at Enumclaw Junior High in Enumclaw, WA (http://www.learningspace.org/socialstudies/ejhs/), Maggie Hos-McGrane's fifth-sixth-grade classroom at the International School of Amsterdam (http://www.xs4all.nl/~swanson/origins/intro.html), Sue Pandiani's third-grade classroom on Cape Cod (http://www.capecod.net/voyage/), the classrooms at Loogootee Elementary West in Indiana (http://www.siec.k12.in.us/west/), or one of thousands of other schools located at Web66: International School Web Site Registry (http://web66.coled.umn.edu/schools.html). Many of us will find that literacy, in these and many other classrooms, differs substantially from the literacy on which most of the research in our field is based. And, it is not just that literacy has changed; it is also that literacy *continuously* changes in these classrooms. Return several months after your first visit and note the new forms of literacy as new technologies for information and communication, and new visions for using these technologies, are enacted by both students and teachers. Clearly, the literacy of yesterday is not the literacy of today, and it will not be the literacy of tomorrow.

A THEORETICAL PERSPECTIVE

As we begin this review of research on the instructional applications of technology for literacy, recent theoretical work helps us to better understand the central relationship between literacy and technology. Our view of the relation between literacy and technology profoundly influences how we might view research on the inchoate patterns so characteristic of this area. One might, for example, take a transformative stance, observing that technology transforms the nature of literacy (Reinking, 1998). From this perspective, a review of research would seek to understand the new forms of literacy possible within new technologies. It would include studies of how multimedia, e-mail, and other technologies transform literacy and literacy learning in school classrooms and other contexts (e.g., Reinking, 1995; Reinking, McKenna, Labbo, & Kieffer, 1998; van Oostendorp & de Mul, 1996). Such an approach provides important insights into the many changes currently taking place in the nature of literacy and literacy learning.

Alternatively, one might take a transactional stance, observing that technology and literacy transact in multiple ways, mutually influencing one another (Bruce, 1997b; Garton & Wellman, 1995; Haas, 1996). According to this view, technology transforms literacy but literacy also transforms technology as users envision new ways of using emergent technologies for literate acts. We see an example of how earlier technologies were transformed by literacy envisionments in work by Labbo, Phillips, and Murray (1995–1996). They found teachers transforming existing technology to meet their literacy envisionments as an IBM Writing to Read lab was transformed into a more student-directed context for literacy and learning. We can also find examples on the Internet where teachers and children transform the Internet every day and share these transformations with other teachers. Often, this takes place through Internet projects that teachers envision and post at locations such as Global SchoolNet's Internet Projects Registry (http://www.gsn.org/pr/index.cfm). Stories of these Internet envisionments are beginning to appear at locations such as EDs Spotlight on Effective Practice (www.EDsOasis.org/Spotlight/Spotlight.html) or What's Working (http://www.techlearning.com/content/working/articles/articles.html) and are beginning to be studied more formally by some (Karchmer, 1998; Leu, Karchmer, & Hinchman, 1999). From a transactional perspective, a review of research would focus as much on the new envisionments for literacy, as on the literacy transformations produced by changing technologies. One might explore the important transformations in literacy resulting from word processing, multimedia, e-mail, Internet, and other technologies. But one might also explore how and why teachers and children generate new envisionments for literacy with the use of new technologies (e.g., Bijker, Hughes, & Pinch, 1987; Bromley, 1997; Cuban, 1986; Labbo & Kuhn, 1998; Labbo et al., 1995–1996; Lemke, 1994, 1998; Leu et al., 1998; Leu, Karchmer, & Leu, 1999).

Both of these views are useful and lead to important insights about literacy within new technologies. This chapter, however, argues that a comprehensive theory about the relationship between literacy and technology must also include a third view. It is not only that literacy has changed because of the introduction of new technologies and the envisionments for literacy that they initiate. In addition, it is essential to recognize that we have entered a period of rapid and continuous change in the forms and functions of literacy. Today, changing technologies for information and communication and changing envisionments for their use rapidly and continuously redefine the nature of literacy (Leu, 1997a; Leu & Kinzer, in press; Leu, in press).

Linguists and others have used the term *deixis* to capture the special qualities of words like *today*, *tomorrow*, and *here* whose meanings change quickly, depending on the time or space in which they are uttered (Fillmore, 1972; Murphy, 1986). For example, if I say "today" at this moment in time, it means today; if I say "today" tomorrow, it means tomorrow. And, by the time you read this, the meaning of my "today" is many days in the past. In a world of rapidly changing technologies and new envisionments for their use, literacy appears to be increasingly deictic; its meaning is regularly redefined, not by time or space, but by new technologies and the continuously changing envisionments they initiate for information and communication (Leu, 1997a). It is the rapid and continuously changing nature of literacy, literacy as technological deixis, that requires our attention as we consider research in this area and the implications for literacy learning.

In order to explore the essence of the transformative (Reinking et al., 1998), transactional (Bruce, 1997b), and deictic relationships between technology and literacy, I begin by briefly reviewing both the historical and the social context for the changing technologies and envisionments of literacy. This helps us to understand the unique situation in which we conduct research on the application of technology to literacy education. I then explore research on using the most recent technologies for information and communication, keeping in mind the special nature of literacy research in an era of rapid technological change and the changing envisionments for literacy that regularly occur. I conclude by exploring the consequences of viewing literacy as deixis for several areas: the nature of literacy, literacy research, literacy learning, teacher education, and public policy. In each area, the general principles at work in reshaping contemporary notions of literacy and literacy education are identified.

EXPLORING THE HISTORICAL CONTEXT

Historically, the nature of literacy has always changed through different historical and cultural contexts as the technologies of information and communication have changed and as individuals have seen new possibilities within these technologies for literate acts (Boyarin, 1993; Diringer, 1968; Illera, 1997; Manguel, 1996). Thus, in a broad, historical sense, literacy has always been deictic, its meaning dependent on the technologies and envisionments within many historical, religious, political, and cultural contexts.

The changing meanings for literacy have appeared as a variety of forces have influenced the development of new technologies and the literacy envisionments they prompt. In earliest societies, literacy was a way to record land, livestock, and crops, often for taxes or to record business transactions. In Mesopotamia, for example, Sumerians used cuneiform writing on clay tablets to keep these types of records (Boyarin, 1993; Diringer, 1968).

In many religions, literacy has been used to enforce a common dogma. This was accomplished in medieval Europe, for example, through hand-copied religious texts and a literate priesthood established to read and interpret religious texts to others (Manguel, 1996).

In post-Reformation Europe, literacy became a way to seek individual salvation, as Luther argued one need not rely solely on a priest to interpret religious texts. Instead, Luther and his Protestant followers believed individuals were responsible for their own salvation through independent reading and study of religious texts. Importantly, this changing envisionment for literacy occurred only after several new technologies, developed by Johann Gutenberg, made the Bible widely available (Mathews, 1966).

In a Jeffersonian democracy, literacy was viewed as central to the survival of government as informed citizens made reasoned decisions at the ballot box (Ellis, 1997; Sterne, 1993). The rise of this political form became possible, in part, because of important changes in printing and other technologies enabling greater distribution of news and information along with an important emphasis on universal public schooling and widespread literacy (Mathews, 1966; Smith, 1965).

In an industrial world, literacy was seen as a means to accurately transmit production information from top to bottom in a hierarchically organized company. Memos, typewriting technologies, and large numbers of typists and stenographers became important to communicate information down the organizational structure to optimize production and sales.

In the information age or post-information age (Negroponte, 1995) in which we live, literacy is essential to enable individuals, groups, and societies to access the best information in the shortest time to identify and solve the most important problems and then communicate this information to others. Accessing information, evaluating information, solving problems, and communicating solutions are essential to success in this new era (Bruce, 1997a; Mikulecky & Kirley, 1998).

Clearly, literacy has always been deictic, its meaning changing in each of these contexts, and many others, as new technologies appeared and people envisioned new ways of using these technologies for information and communication. What is unique about the current period is that the technologies and envisionments for literacy repeatedly change within such short periods of time, affecting so many individuals. Our era is defined largely by repeated, rapid, and revolutionary changes in the technologies of information and communication (Harrison & Stephen, 1996; Johnson, 1997; Negroponte, 1995). Within just 20 years, we have seen the widespread appearance of, among others, word processing technologies, electronic database technologies, multimedia/hypermedia technologies, e-mail technologies, and Internet technologies. Each has helped to redefine the nature of literacy and each has seen new envisionments for its use redefine the technology itself.

Moreover, the nature of literacy within each technology continuously changes as even newer technologies and newer envisionments regularly appear. Most of us, for example, have changed or upgraded word processing and e-mail software several times as new technologies regularly require us to develop new literacy skills appropriate for the communication software we use and the new possibilities we envision for its use. The same is also true for many other types of information and communication software including web-browser software, a technology that seems to change almost daily as upgraded browsers and new plug-ins appear with rapid regularity and as web pages are regularly redesigned to exploit newer technologies and envisionments for their effective use.

Although literacy and literacy learning have always been intimately related to technology, never before have so many new envisionments for literacy been developed within so many new technologies that regularly change within such short periods of time. Increasingly, it appears that literacy is defined largely by change itself, its meaning dependent on rapidly changing technologies for information and communication and the envisionments for literacy they repeatedly inspire.

THE SOCIAL CONTEXT FOR RAPIDLY CHANGING
TECHNOLOGIES AND LITERACIES

Why does rapid change characterize the technologies of information and communication and the envisionments for literacy we create in today's world? At least one answer to this question is related to the information economies and the global competition defining the age in which we find ourselves. A number of recent analyses (Reich, 1992; Rifkin, 1995) demonstrate that we have moved from a time when land, labor, or capital defined power and influence, to one where power and influence accrue to those most effective at using information for solving important problems. Moreover, it is increasingly clear that networked, digital technologies provide rapid access to vast amounts of information, increasing the importance of effective information use (Harrison & Stephen, 1996).

To succeed in an increasingly competitive global marketplace, many organizations have changed the way in which they work (Mikulecky & Kirley, 1998; Reich, 1992) as they transform themselves into "high-performance" workplaces. In most cases, this has required fundamental change in several areas. First, it requires change from a centrally planned organization to one that relies increasingly on collaborative teams at all levels in order to assume initiative for planning ways to work more efficiently. Second, problem-solving skills become critical to successful performance. As collaborative teams seek more effective ways of working, they identify problems important to their unit and seek appropriate solutions. To succeed in this task, it appears a third change is also taking place: Effective collaboration and communication skills become increasingly important. The changes from a centralized to a decentralized workplace require collaboration and communication skills so the best decisions get made at every level in an organization and so that changes at one level are clearly communicated to other levels. Finally, there is a fourth change taking place in many organizations: Effective information access and use become increasingly important to success. Individuals and organizations who can access information most rapidly and use it effectively to solve important problems become the ones who succeed in these challenging times. As a result, informational literacy within new technologies has become a crucial determinant of success in the age in which we live (Bruce, 1997a; Drucker, 1994; Mikulecky & Kirley, 1998).

The continuously changing technologies of information and communication are largely driven by these global forces in the nature of work. As individuals or organizations identify problems, gather information, and seek solutions, digital bits become faster and cheaper than atoms (Negroponte, 1995), and in a highly competitive context, speed, information, and cost become paramount. Most of the technologies of literacy are driven by these three considerations. Successful information and communication technologies allow faster access to more information at a cheaper cost than alternatives. Moreover, the globally competitive context in which we find ourselves ensures that new technologies for information and communication will continually be developed, resulting in continuously changing literacies and envisionments for literacy.

It is possible to view these changes strictly from an economic or political view, suggesting that new technologies and envisionments for literacy are derived solely for economic gain or political control (Selfe & Selfe, 1996; Virillo, 1986), often by those most economically advantaged with a hegemonic desire to maintain and expand political power. This would not be a new development, for, as many have observed, literacy typically serves those in power, not those out of power (Graff, 1981; Harris, 1989; Levi-Strauss, 1973; Shannon, 1996). At the same time, however, Giroux and Freire (1987) noted the emancipatory effects of acquiring literacy and the humanizing developments that result. Moreover, Stotsky (1996) demonstrated the important ways in which individuals exploit political structures, achieving personal ends that often run counter to prevailing political power structures through participatory writing. It is also but a short step to consider the historical example of *samizdat* in Russia, the Soviet Union, and Eastern Europe within the context of new electronic networks, such as the Internet, and expect these new electronic forms of literacy to provide potentially powerful opportunities for developing alternative views to prevailing political or economic forces.

Thus, it is possible to view these rapid and continuous changes in literacy as the result of the competition between nations for creating economically and politically powerful societies. Alternatively, one could view these changes as new potentials within which to create more "just" societies. In truth, it is probably a bit of both, because historical realities clearly demonstrate the former cannot long survive without the latter and the latter will not long exist without the former. In either case, however, information economies, global competition, and the changing nature of work are, perhaps, the most powerful forces driving the changing nature of literacy in school classrooms. They prompt very real consequences for literacy education as we seek to prepare our students for the futures they deserve.

These consequences are increasingly clear to governments as they consider how best to prepare students for the changing demands of new electronic literacies in a globally competitive world. Policy decisions and discussions in many countries seek to ensure that students leaving school are able to use new electronic literacies in order to identify central problems, find appropriate information quickly, and then use this information to solve problems and effectively communicate the solutions to others. Consider just three examples: the United States, the United Kingdom, and Finland.

In the United States, with a long history of local control over education and little federal influence, we now find federal agencies as diverse as the Federal Communications Commission (FCC), the Commerce Department, and the Justice Department initiating policy discussions and implementing decisions related to the new literacy needs of students and schools. The FCC, for example, has a major section of its web page devoted to educational policy initiatives, LearnNet (http://www.fcc.gov/learnnet/). Here you discover a federal program providing up to $2.25 billion annually in financial support to schools and libraries for Internet access, based on indicators of financial need. This revolutionary program (known formally as the Universal Service Support Mechanism for Schools and Libraries and informally as the "e-rate program") was established by Congress under the Telecommunications Act of 1996 and is administered by the Schools and Libraries Division of the Universal Service Administrative Company (http://www.sl.universalservice.org/), a not-for-profit organization established by the FCC for this purpose. Although telecommunications companies seek to reduce the revenue stream for this program—financed largely from a surcharge to their customers—it appears that popular support for this program is strong and will continue.

Public policy initiatives are also underway in Great Britain to prepare their children for a future in a world where effective use of information technology (IT) is the new touchstone for success. The Labour government, elected in 1990, is moving aggressively in this area. It has already implemented policies to provide free connections to the Internet and subsidized phone rates to all schools. Moreover, it has stated publicly the goals of connecting every school to the Internet by the year 2002, free of charge, and ensuring 500,000 teachers are trained in IT by that time. In addition, the government has established a "National Grid for Learning" (http://www.ngfl.gov.uk/ngfl/) to help identify and organize electronic information resources for use in the schools.

Public policy initiatives to prepare students for their literacy futures are also underway in Finland. In 1996, the Ministry of Education launched a 3-year program to teach students effective use of information technology in schools. This program includes developing new teaching methods for the use of IT, connecting all schools to the Internet before the year 2000, providing new computers to schools, and providing teachers with a 5-week course of study in the effective instructional use of new information technologies (R. Svedlin, personal communication, January 8, 1998). These policy initiatives are being carried out by the National Board of Education (http://www.edu.fi/english/).

Information economies, global competition, changes in workplace settings, and new national policy initiatives make solid research, especially in educational settings, critically important as we seek insights into preparing children for their literacy futures. We require useful data in order to prepare students for new technologies and new envisionments as we explore the boundaries of an information society, increasingly dependent on networked, digital technologies for information and communication.

USING NEW TECHNOLOGIES FOR LITERACY AND LEARNING: THE RESEARCH BASE

Recent reviews (e.g., Ayersman, 1996; Chen & Rada, 1996; Cochran-Smith, 1991; Mayer, 1997; Reinking, 1995; Reinking, Labbo, & McKenna, 1997; Scott, Cole, & Engel, 1992; U.S. Congress, 1995) and edited volumes (e.g., Flood, Heath, & Lapp, 1997; Reinking et al., 1998; Rouet, Levonen, Dillon, & Spiro, 1996; van Oostendorp & de Mul, 1996) provide a number of observations about the use of technologies to support literacy and learning. An important challenge arises, however, as one seeks to incorporate their conclusions into the use of even newer technologies for information and communication available today and the literacy envisionments they inspire. The challenge is closely related to the increasingly deictic nature of literacy within rapidly changing technologies of information and communication: As newer technologies of information and communication continually appear, they raise concerns about the generalizability of findings from earlier technologies.

Mayer (1997) reminded us that it is important to be cautious about generalizing findings from traditional texts to different forms of hypermedia because each technology contains different contexts and resources for constructing meanings and requires somewhat different strategies for doing so. It is equally important to recognize that we must also be cautious about generalizing patterns from older digital technologies to newer digital technologies. Thus, we should be cautious about generalizing from word processing technologies to e-mail technologies, and from hypermedia within CD-ROM or videodisc technologies to hypermedia within various Internet technologies. In addition, we should also be cautious about generalizing from one iteration within a particular technology to a newer iteration where the interface, speed, and resources may differ substantially. To what extent does research from older e-mail software generalize to newer, more powerful e-mail software? The answer to this question is not clear. What is clear is that the two contexts will be substantially different, requiring new strategies to effectively exploit new resources, permitting different opportunities for communication.

To further problematize the issue of generalizability, one must keep in mind that individuals often create different envisionments for literacy within each technology. I may envision the use of current e-mail technologies for helping students acquire information from knowledgeable, unfamiliar others. You may envision the use of current e-mail technologies to help students share literary responses with friends and colleagues. To what extent does research from my envisionment for using e-mail generalize to your envisionment when the pragmatic aspects of these communication tasks differ so substantially? Clearly the challenges are enormous as we consider the utility of literacy research from one technology to another, from one iteration of a technology to another, and from one envisionment of literacy to another. Issues of ecological validity caused by rapidly changing technologies for information and communication and the increasingly deictic nature of literacy are critically important as we explore the literacy potentials of digital environments.

Although the focus of this review is on the use of newer technologies, including hypermedia/multimedia and Internet technologies, one must be extraordinarily cautious about generalizing from work in one specific context in which digital technologies are used to any other context that might appear in the future. The differences, to draw on historical examples, may be as different as reading a cuneiform tablet in order to determine taxes versus viewing a television news program in order to make a reasoned decision at the ballot box. It is just that historical time has become compressed in an age when the technologies of literacy change so rapidly.

Unfortunately, in addition to questions of ecological validity, there is a second general problem that one must recognize when reviewing work in this area: Only a small number of investigations have been published in traditional forums for reading and writing research. Kamil and Lane (1998) reported that during the period 1990–1995, only 12 out of 437 research articles appearing in the four major journals of reading and writing research studied technology issues of literacy. Although a number of investigations of new technologies for literacy and learning have appeared outside of the traditional literacy journals (Kamil, 1997), these are less likely to evaluate questions directly related to issues of literacy in classroom learning contexts. Often, this work evaluates adult performance, takes epistemological approaches less familiar to many in the literacy research community, focuses more on learning outcomes rather than literacy outcomes, or evaluates learning outside of classroom contexts.

Previous reviews have tended to evaluate work from one of two research communities: the literacy research community (e.g., Cochran-Smith, 1991; Reinking, 1995; Reinking et al., 1997) or the information technology (IT) community (e.g., Ayersman, 1996; Chen & Rada, 1996; Mayer, 1997; U.S. Congress, 1995). This review attempts to integrate these two bodies of research, an approach we must increasingly attempt if we hope to maximize our understanding of literacy and learning within new technologies. It focuses on recent technologies and especially on the challenges we face in conducting and interpreting work in this area for classroom use. Although we face extraordinary challenges in interpreting the results of research on literacy within continually changing technologies, it is important to identify extant patterns at the same time that we are extremely cautious about their significance for new technologies, new iterations, and new envisionments that will regularly redefine the nature of literacy.

Interest and Other Motivational Factors

One of the more common patterns in research, within the greater interactivity and wider bandwidth media possible with newer technologies, is a generally high level of engagement, interest, or attitude (U.S. Congress, 1995) among both teachers and students when newer technologies are used. This appears to be the case among both preservice and inservice teachers who received instruction in the use of hypermedia for teaching and learning (Reed, Ayersman, & Liu, 1995a, 1995b). Teachers seemed to be most attracted by the learner-controlled nature of hypermedia learning environments and the potential of this feature for educational settings. This may suggest that hypermedia learning contexts will meet with less resistance in the classroom than previous technologies because they appear to be more consistent with concerns that teachers have for instructional relevance. On the other hand, this finding may be due to these teachers' beliefs about learning. This feature is more consistent with constructivist, student-directed beliefs about learning, and this study did not evaluate participating teachers' beliefs.

Newer technologies, permitting greater control by both teachers and students as they navigate rich information resources and construct meanings appropriate to their teaching and learning needs, may permit us to overcome a fundamental paradox clear to many who have studied the use of previous technologies in classrooms: Although these technologies became more widely available, they were not always appropriated by teachers and systematically integrated into the curriculum (Anderson, 1993; Becker, 1993; Miller & Olson, 1994; Papert, 1993; Reinking & Bridwell-Bowles; 1991; U.S. Congress, 1995). Although not all teachers take a more student-centered, constructivist stance, more open information and communication environments such as the Internet permit both teacher-directed and student-directed learning activities, thus inviting teachers from a wider spectrum of beliefs into this new learning context (Leu & Kinzer, 1998). The same is not true for earlier skill-oriented software, which is only consistent with more teacher-directed beliefs.

Limited evidence also suggests that hypermedia's defining characteristic, the ability to respond to the needs of an individual learner for information, results in an increased sense of control over the learning environment and higher levels of intrinsic motivation (Becker & Dwyer, 1994). These aspects have related patterns in the research on locus of control within traditional reading contexts, where internal locus of control is associated with higher reading achievement in reading comprehension (Hiebert, Winograd, & Danner, 1984; Wagner, Sprat, Gal, & Paris, 1989). Thus, it may suggest the interactive features of hypermedia and the users' ability to control the direction they take within these rich information contexts may explain some of the learning gains in comprehension as users develop more intrinsic motivation and a greater sense of control over their own comprehension.

Some work, albeit with earlier technologies, has begun to explore the nature of locus of control within electronic learning environments (Gray, 1989; Gray, Barber, & Shasha, 1991). Gray et al. found internal locus of control subjects performed better at information retrieval and retention than external locus of control subjects in an early hypertext system. It would seem logical to expect much more work in this area, especially in relation to newer hypermedia technologies, such as the Internet, exploring their potential to change locus of control from external to internal attributions. Because locus of control has been a useful construct and since the Internet is user driven, one would expect Internet use might enhance locus of control and this might lead to greater comprehension over time. Although the evidence in this area is merely suggestive, the potential for this explanatory mechanism seems especially important to explore with additional work.

Locus of control and the potential of hypermedia to increase intrinsic motivation may also be important to explore in authoring studies using hypermedia authoring tools or newer forms of communication software. Finkelman and McMunn (1995), for example, found that sixth-grade language arts students reported an especially satisfying aspect of using hypermedia authoring tools was the greater control over the nature of their presentations. A similar pattern appears in the extensive data presented by Tierney and his colleagues (Tierney et al., 1997).

In classroom studies such as these, however, it is difficult to separate out effects due to the technology from the instructional strategies used with the technology. As Brush (1996) discovered, students who used hypermedia from an Integrated Learning System, while working within collaborative learning groups, reported significantly more positive attitudes about both math and computer math lessons than did students who worked alone using the same computer software. This suggests that the positive effects on attitude demonstrated in the authoring studies by Finkelman and McMunn (1995) and Tierney and his colleagues (Tierney et al., 1997) may be an artifact of the instructional condition more than the consequence of the hypermedia authoring opportunities. Each contained elements of collaborative instructional strategies.

In addition to the potential confounding of instructional condition, work on interest and other motivational aspects within recent technologies suffers from a tendency to use limited measures of interest, sometimes with only a few items presented in a simple Likert scale. Moreover, these data are often collected either before or after interactions with hypermedia software, never during the actual use of the software environment: data that would be especially important for evaluating the effects of multiple media forms and various design features typical of hypermedia and Internet technologies.

Finally, this work does not appear to evaluate distinctions between what Hidi (1990) referred to as situational interest and individual interest. Situational interest is transitory and specific to a learning situation. Often it is measured after a learning experience. Individual interest is a result of long-term experiences with a topic or a domain and is much more permanent. Often it is measured before a learning experience. This distinction may be important to explore within the new technologies of literacy because Garner and Gillingham (1992) observed that individual interest may actually impede learning. This may be especially true when students have extensive experiences with electronic games (Schick & Miller, 1992). Students who enter into hypermedia learning environments expecting to encounter a game may be less interested in exploring this context to acquire important knowledge and thus less likely to learn important information.

As important as it is to evaluate the consequences of new digital literacies for interest and other motivational factors, clearly this work is in its early stages (Leu & Reinking, 1996). Richer theoretical constructs, more complex and sophisticated measures, more online assessment of motivational aspects, and more systematic attempts to distinguish between situational and individual interest will help us to develop richer, more comprehensive insights into the changing technologies for information and communication.

Evaluating Individual Differences and Cognitive Learning Styles

There are both intuitive and theoretical reasons for expecting newer technologies for information and communication to be especially sensitive to individual differences. Intuitively, one would expect individual differences to be accommodated better within the newer technologies for information and communication. Hypermedia, Internet, and other recent technologies combine multiple media forms within a dynamic and interactive information structure under the control of the user. One would expect these contexts to allow individuals to explore information resources most consistent with individual learning needs or styles, each using the particular information or media forms they require to optimize understanding.

Recent work is consistent with this intuitive expectation, showing how students may travel different routes through a rich, digital information structure, using different media resources, allowing each to perform at similarly high levels (Hillinger & Leu, 1994; Horney & Anderson-Inman, 1994; Liu & Reed, 1994; Toro, 1995). Hillinger and Leu (1994), for example, found a hypermedia program led to similar high performance among both high and low prior knowledge adults on a variety of comprehension and performance tasks related to the repair and maintenance of a turboprop engine. Low prior knowledge participants achieved the same high level of learning with the hypermedia program as did high prior knowledge participants, suggesting that hypermedia may have the potential for overcoming limitations in prior knowledge for comprehension and learning, at least among adults.

Theoretically, several perspectives have been used to direct work on individual learning style differences in the use of hypertext and hypermedia: locus of control (discussed earlier), the dual coding theory of Paivio (1979, 1986), and theoretical perspectives related to field independent and field dependent learners. Studies have explored each of these theoretical perspectives.

Multimodal learning theories, such as the dual coding theory of Paivio, typically suggest that information presented within multiple modalities maximizes learning for a wider variety of students, some of whom optimize information presented within a verbal context and others who optimize information presented within an imaginal (visual) context. Some results appear to be consistent with this theoretical orientation. Daiute and Morse (1994) reviewed much of the multiple modality research, concluding that appropriately combined images and sound may enhance both the comprehension and the production of text. Reinking and Chanlin (1994), however, reviewed many of the more problematic aspects of research exploring multimedia capabilities of electronic texts, especially early work in this area. Although the potential continues to remain promising—especially with the greater variety and wider bandwidth media available in newer technologies—we are still waiting for more thoughtfully designed studies to systematically explore the utility of multimodal learning theories in this area.

A few studies have explored field independence and field dependence within hypermedia technologies. Field-independent learners tend to be skilled at identifying useful information quickly from a complex context, whereas field-dependent learners perform less efficiently. Given the increasingly complex visual displays appearing within Internet and other newer technologies (Caroff, Fringer, & Kletzien, 1997; Tufte, 1997), one would expect field independence and field dependence theories to be useful to explore individual differences. Marrison and Frick (1994) evaluated this distinction among undergraduate economics students. Field-independent students found a hypermedia learning context easier to use and more exciting than field-dependent students. Leader and Klein (1994) reported a study in which field-independent students achieved at a level significantly higher than field-dependent students with certain search tools in a hypermedia program. Weller, Repman, and Rooze (1994) and Weller, Repman, Lan, and Rooze (1995) reported two studies in which field-independent, eighth-grade students learned computer ethics better than field-dependent students in a hypermedia program.

A number of feminist scholars (Belenky, Clinchy, Goldberger, & Tarule, 1986; Gilligan, 1982) proposed that gender often determines learning style. As a result, an increasingly important area of exploration concerns gender differences in the use of newer technologies for information and communication (Grint & Gill, 1995; Lay, 1996; Selfe, 1990; Turkle & Papert, 1990). Work on the computer culture in general, and especially with older technologies among college students, suggested it was a greater challenge for women to become engaged with information and communication technologies than for men. A number of reasons were found for this pattern: a sense of isolation within the technology (Durndell, 1990), a lack of confidence in math skills Clarke (1990), and a dislike of competition and aggression (Clarke, 1990). Some suggest, however, that collaboration, conferencing, and networking experiences—all central characteristics of newer networked technologies such as the Internet—may be especially inviting to women and young girls (Eldred & Hawisher, 1995; Lay, 1996). This work only hints at possible opportunities to limit gender bias within the newer technologies. If we hope to provide optimal learning experiences for all children, exploring questions related to this issue will be an important challenge as networked communication technologies enter the classroom.

Generally, the work on individual differences and learning styles within the newer technologies for information and communication has not yet produced a consistent body of results clearly demonstrating the primacy of a particular theoretical perspective or the clear-cut efficacy of hypermedia and newer technologies for accommodating varied individual differences or learning styles. In a meta-analysis of hypertext studies from 1988 to 1993, Chen and Rada (1996) found a generally small overall effect size for several cognitive styles on measures of either effectiveness or efficiency. Individual differences in spatial ability, though, consistently produced a large effect size on efficiency measures. It should be noted, however, that the studies in this review contained far fewer multimedia resources than are currently available in the newest technologies for information and communication. Thus, it is possible newer technologies, with more media resources, more sophisticated interface designs, and more opportunities for networking, may produce more substantial effects.

As this work moves forward, we need to pay attention to several methodological issues. First, much of the current work on individual differences only explores issues with adult participants. Research needs to include children in classroom contexts to better understand the variety of individual differences in relation to the newer technologies. This is especially important because these technologies provide greater opportunity for individual control and direction of information resources. Second, work on individual difference within the technologies of literacy often fails to ensure all students are equally familiar and skilled in navigating these environments. Thus, differences may be due to a potential confounding with navigational knowledge. In future studies, great care needs to be taken to ensure that participants possess sufficient metacognitive knowledge about navigational strategies to exploit insightfully the additional media resources and more complex interfaces. Although many studies of hypertext and hypermedia tend to assume strategic knowledge among participants about how best to navigate within a particular interface, this problem is especially important for studies that evaluate individual differences. Schroeder (1994), for example, found that students using a hypertext information environment performed at initially lower levels of achievement until they became more familiar and comfortable with the user interface. The failure to adequately demonstrate that participants can navigate effectively may be an explanation for studies that find little or no difference between learning-style groups in this literature.

Literacy and Learning Tasks

Not all tasks within the new technologies of information and communication are alike (Jonassen, 1993). Some require one to simply find a specific piece of information. Others are far more complex, requiring participants to gather and organize multiple information resources, evaluating their appropriateness as they work toward a vaguely defined goal that may change along the way. Within the information technology community, tasks have been analyzed in many ways, but they often cluster around polar constructs such as closed and open tasks (Chen & Rada, 1996; Marchionini, 1989), or search and browsing tasks (Carmel, Crawford, & Chen, 1992; Rada & Murphy, 1992). Closed or search tasks tend to focus on specific goals, often specific, factual information, within complex information environments. An example would be searching for the answer to a given question such as, "When is the scheduled departure for the next Space Shuttle?" Open or browsing tasks tend to have open goals, often requiring users to find, evaluate, and integrate information from several sources. An example would be to compare how several authors of children literature approach their work and write a book.

In a review of earlier technologies, Chen and Rada (1996) found hypertext yielded significantly greater effect sizes for open tasks than closed tasks on measures of effectiveness. This suggests that the more complex and rich information resources characteristic of hypertext systems may be especially suited for effective completion of cognitively complex tasks.

Hillinger and Leu (1994), however, reported a somewhat different pattern of results within hypermedia when individual differences in prior knowledge were evaluated. The hypermedia program developed for the study explained how a turboprop engine generated propulsion and showed how to take apart and put together the main components of this engine. The hypermedia program contained video, text, animation, digitized speech, and tools allowing the user to take apart the engine on the screen. Although all participants performed better on closed tasks than open tasks, this was largely due to low prior knowledge participants who performed significantly better on closed tasks than they did on open tasks. High prior knowledge participants performed at comparable levels for both closed and open tasks. These differences suggest prior knowledge may interact with the nature of a comprehension task. It may also suggest that hypermedia technologies yield a different pattern of results from hypertext. In either case, it argues for additional work within the newer information technologies, exploring both individual differences and the effects of different types of tasks on learning outcomes.

Specific Applications of Newer Technologies for Literacy and Learning

Research in each of the preceding sections indirectly informs research on the use of new technologies in classrooms for literacy and learning. It is helpful as we seek to inform policymakers, teacher educators, and others about the optimal use of new technologies for teaching and learning. In addition, however, a number of other studies have looked at more specific applications of newer technologies for classroom literacy and learning.

One area drawing recent attention has been the use of talking books among younger readers. Talking books are hypermedia texts with digitized pronunciations of words and larger textual units. Sometimes they also include animated illustrations and other features. Although talking storybooks are designed to improve comprehension and reduce the decoding difficulties experienced by beginning readers, most of this work has taken place among students 8 years of age or older, often with students experiencing difficulties learning to read (e.g., Farmer, Klein, & Bryson, 1992; Greenlee-Moore & Smith, 1996; Lundberg & Olofsson, 1993; Miller, Blackstock, & Miller, 1994; Olofsson, 1992; Olson, Foltz, & Wise, 1986; Scoresby, 1996; Wise & Olson, 1994; Wise et al, 1989). Less work has taken place to explore the potential of talking books for those at the very beginning stages of reading instruction, although some work has been done with this population (Hastings, 1997; Lewin, 1997; McKenna, 1998; Reitsma, 1988). Although much more work remains to more fully understand the supportive opportunities for multimedia software among younger readers, the results have been sufficiently promising to encourage additional work. Generally, this works shows that comprehension increases when children can access digitized speech support. There is some indication (Miller et al., 1994; Reitsma, 1988; Olson et al., 1986; Olson & Wise, 1992; Wise & Olson, 1994) that decoding ability may also increase, although the exact manner in which these two patterns are related within talking book software for different populations remains an open question. Future work needs to explore the relationship between these two patterns for different populations, as well as explore optimal interface designs and strategies to connect reading and writing within these contexts. The latter is especially important given recent work by Labbo (1996) showing the importance of early writing experiences within multimedia software.

Other work within hypermedia software has focused more on comprehension and learning using "responsive text" (Hillinger, 1992; Hillinger & Leu, 1994; Leu & Hillinger, 1994) and "supportive text" (Anderson-Inman & Horney, 1998; Anderson-Inman, Horney, Chen, & Lewin, 1994). Generally, this work shows a positive effect on learning, although much more research on optimizing the interface of supportive structures appears to be necessary. Not all supposedly supportive aids always lead to increases in learning or comprehension. Scoresby (1996), for example, found that interactive animation within the pictures of a story actually impedes comprehension.

The work by the literacy community on early reading, comprehension, or learning tends to suffer from an emphasis on comprehension or learning as an outcome measure. In a world where time is increasingly important and where busy classrooms and limited computer time are all too common, we also need to evaluate the amount of time it takes to achieve important outcome measures. Here, the literacy community might learn from the information technology (IT) community. Time is almost always included as a dependent measure in work from the IT community; it is seldom included in work from the literacy community. In a recent study using a virtual world to help students learn a challenging scientific concept, for example, Hillinger and Leu (1997) found this hypermedia context achieved the same level of learning as a classroom approach using "hands-on" experiments but required one-third less time. We should begin to think about efficiency with these new technologies as much as we think about achievement levels.

Another area of recent research is on the use of networked information environments such as Integrated Learning Systems (ILS) and the Internet. With a longer history of classroom use, ILS research is much more extensive than the use of the Internet in classrooms. ILS research does not provide conclusive evidence for its positive outcomes, despite studies showing positive satisfaction by students, teachers, and administrators (Sherry, 1990; Trotter, 1990). A meta-analysis of almost 100 ILS studies showed many methodological flaws and little conclusive evidence of ILS impact on achievement (Becker, 1992).

The Internet has attracted much recent attention and a number of books and articles describing its use in classroom contexts (Garner & Gillingham, 1996, Leu & Leu, 1998; Peha, 1995). To date, however, we have little empirical evidence evaluating its effectiveness supporting literacy and learning in classrooms. The largest, most systematic work is a study, jointly funded by Scholastic Network, the Council of Great City Schools, and the Center for Applied Special Technology (CAST). Participants included 500 students in Grades 4 and 6 in seven urban school districts around the United States (CAST, 1996; Follansbee, Hughes, Pisha, & Stahl, 1997). Each classroom completed an integrated learning unit on civil rights using a common curricular framework and common activities. Each class was encouraged to use traditional library resources as well as technology resources, including computers and multimedia software. The experimental classes also used the Internet for online resources, activities, and communication. Each student completed a project as a result of their participation in the unit. Evaluation of the final project showed greater achievement on a number of measures for classrooms using Internet resources.

This study provides important support for suggestions about the potential of Internet resources for classroom learning, but it is also clear that we require a larger, consistent body of work in this area before conclusive claims may be made. In addition, we require important new work evaluating how teachers optimize learning within the Internet, how new envisionments for literacy are initiated by this resource in the classroom, how the Internet may restructure traditional student–teacher relationships, and a host of issues related to the use of Internet technologies in classroom settings. It is likely that this will be the most important area of research in the near future as this powerful resource enters classrooms around the world.

A central issue in the classroom use of Internet and other new technologies for literacy and learning is their integration into the classroom. The data on classroom integration with earlier technologies is instructive, revealing the important challenge we face. U.S. schools had 5.8 million computers in use for instruction during the spring of 1995, approximately 1 for every 9 students or 2–3 per classroom (U.S. Congress, 1995). Despite this, however, teachers reported minimal use of computers for instructional purposes. Reports from secondary schools indicated only 9% of students used computers for English class, 6% to 7% for math class, and only 3% for social studies class (U.S. Congress, 1995). In elementary schools, computers were seldom integrated into central areas of the curriculum; often they were used after assigned work had been completed, for games and game-like experiences (Becker, 1993; U.S. Congress, 1995).

As technological change occurs more and more rapidly, redefining potentials for literacy and learning, how do we ensure that teachers fully exploit these potentials during classroom instruction? Part of the challenge will require far more teacher education and staff development to continually support teachers as new technologies regularly appear and as resources become available for its purchase. Current levels of support appear inadequate if we expect the continuous progression of new technologies to become integrated into central locations of the curriculum (U.S. Congress, 1995). U.S. schools only spend about 20% of the amount recommended by the U.S. Department of Education for staff development with technology (CEO Forum, 1999).

There is also increasing evidence that any new technology is not value free; its integration or resistance will be determined largely by the values and practices of the teacher and the organization into which it is placed (Becker, 1993; Cuban, 1986; Hodas, 1993; Miller & Olson, 1994). Thus, rapid revolutionary change is unlikely as new technologies enter school classrooms. Instead, it is more likely teachers will adopt those technologies that already fit existing practices or can be adapted easily. Some of the newer technologies for literacy and learning may make it more likely for teachers to integrate these into classroom instruction. The greater resources, interaction, and connectivity of the Internet, for example, make possible teaching and learning practices from a wider range of beliefs, accommodating teachers who take a specific skill perspective to literacy issues, those who take more of a holistic language perspective, and those who fall somewhere in between (Leu & Kinzer, 1998). Clearly, however, much support will continually be required for teachers as technologies for information and communication continue to change (Schrum, 1995).

An important new solution to the challenge of classroom integration of new technologies, at least at the university level, may be literacy education that takes place within the technologies themselves. This is the approach taken recently in work completed at Vanderbilt University by Risko, Kinzer, and their colleagues (Kinzer & Risko, 1998; Risko, 1995; Risko, Peter, & McAllister, 1996; Risko, Yount, & McAllister, 1992) using multimedia, cased-based instruction. This approach, perhaps regularly extended to new technologies as they appear, may naturally enable new envisionments for their use and provide an important solution to the challenge of classroom integration.

Even if adequate support appears and teachers are prepared for using new technologies in their classrooms, important equity issues, unless they are resolved, will impede our ability to prepare all children for their literacy futures. Although simple data on the number of computers raise concerns about equity between urban and suburban, rich and poor, small schools and large schools, the issue is much more complicated than these simple contrasts might suggest (Sutton, 1991; U.S. Congress, 1995). Increasingly, important equity issues revolve around the age of technology, how it is used, where it is located, and who uses it (Sayers, 1995; Sutton, 1991; U.S. Congress, 1995). Bold, new initiatives such as the recent Universal Service Support Mechanism for Schools and Libraries will need to be continually developed to ensure equity of access for all children as new technologies regularly appear, creating new and potentially harmful disparities in equity of access to future technologies and future literacies. Just as important will be local and even classroom solutions to access to technologies. Given the complexity of equity issues, individual decisions by districts, schools, and teachers may be just as important as state and national policy initiatives.

Although many political obstacles may currently exist to Internet equity, this goal is important for all of us. As we provide access to the Internet for all children, we increase the potential of their contribution to our global community. Providing access to the Internet increases opportunities for each one of us as new discoveries are made and new advancements take place to improve the quality of everyone's life. Although perfect solutions to equity issues are seldom possible, nations, states, cities, and school districts must make every effort to help each child realize their literacy futures possible in a world with new and powerful sources of information and communication.

Lessons from the Research Literature

Standing back for a moment and looking at the broad sweep of research, one notices several important lessons. Most obvious, perhaps, is the need to think systematically about work taking place from many different areas, with many different traditions. The clearest example of this problem is the work taking place within the IT and literacy communities. These studies almost never draw on the work taking place within the other community. We need to begin to explore one another's work, drawing important insights from the special perspective each brings to questions of literacy and learning within rapidly evolving technologies of information and communication. Most of the IT research, for example, explores the most recent technologies but often with adult users. Most of the research from the literacy community explores older technologies but often in wonderfully rich classroom contexts with children. At the very least, the IT community can provide useful insights into the latest technologies, whereas the literacy community can provide useful insights into the use of these technologies within classrooms. Collaborative work might find even more useful synergies.

Another lesson to draw from this review is this: We have often focused more on the technology itself rather than how any technology is used in the classroom. Brush (1996), for example, reminded us that important differences in outcomes arise for any technology, depending on how it is used in the classroom. This is one of the few studies to vary instructional condition within the use of hypermedia, demonstrating clear differences due to instructional condition. More work such as this needs to be attempted in an effort to discover the instructional conditions that maximally exploit the learning potentials within various forms of digital literacies. As Owston (1997) pointed out, the potential of new technologies for learning, such as the World Wide Web, is likely to be found in the way in which these new technologies are exploited, not in the technologies themselves.

To guide us in this work, we also require new theoretical perspectives and new research strategies to explore the continually changing technologies of literacy and learning. Some new theoretical work is beginning to appear, such as the work on anchored instruction and situated learning (Cognition and Technology Group at Vanderbilt, 1990) and work on cognitive flexibility theory (Spiro & Jeng, 1990). We need additional theoretical perspectives for literacy developed within new digital technologies as these are used in classroom contexts to support literacy and learning.

New research strategies are also beginning to appear. One of the promising approaches is work using a formative experimental model initially proposed by Newman (1990) and currently being explored by Reinking and colleagues (Reinking & Pickle, 1993; Reinking & Watkins, 1997). Additionally, case studies are increasingly being used to explore the unique situational contexts of new technologies within individual classrooms (Garner & Gillingham, 1996). It is important that additional research models also emerge out of the new contexts and new envisionments possible within new technologies.

Another lesson also exists in these studies: Often outcomes from traditional teaching and learning contexts are evaluated, rather than evaluating new outcomes that are becoming increasingly important in a global information environment where problem solving, information evaluation, speed, and communication are essential to success. Earlier I suggested that we begin to consider the speed it takes to acquire information as an important measure of success within various technologies. We also need to begin to explore how effective various technologies are for supporting collaboration, problem solving, information evaluation, and communication. All will be increasingly important literacy tasks in the years ahead.

Although some work is taking place on electronic communication within networked environments, bringing new insights and new definitions to literacy (Eldred

& Hawisher, 1995; Tao, Montgomery, & Pickle, 1997), much more needs to take place, especially with children and in classroom contexts. It is likely that work on pragmatic aspects of effective communication within e-mail and new video conferencing technologies will be especially important in preparing children for the communication requirements in their futures.

There is another important point to keep in mind as we explore research in these contexts. Roszak (1994) argued that we need to understand the important distinction between information and knowledge. Most of the research in this area has explored new ways of presenting and acquiring information. Little has explored new ways of acquiring knowledge, or using the information one acquires in productive ways. Much more attention should be paid to this distinction. Future work needs to include evaluations of how to optimize the underlying nature of knowledge, not merely how to optimize the acquisition of information.

Finally, we need to understand better how new envisionments for literacy develop and are disseminated as new technologies for information and communication continually appear. It is clear that new envisionments appear with each new technology (Bruce, 1997b; Lemke, 1998), and it is clear that young children build these envisionments as they are engaged with digital literacy tasks with new technologies (Labbo, 1996; Labbo & Kuhn, 1998). Many new envisionments take place every day on the Internet as teachers construct new collaborative projects for classrooms and invite others to join (Garner & Gillingham, 1996; Leu & Leu, 1998). We know little about how this process develops and about the literacy and learning that develop from these encounters. This information will be essential to assist new teachers entering these powerful contexts for collaboration, communication, and learning.

LITERACY AS DEIXIS: REDEFINING LITERACY, LITERACY RESEARCH, CLASSROOM LEARNING, TEACHER EDUCATION, AND PUBLIC POLICY

Reviews of various technologies and their application to instruction serve to capture the state of our knowledge at a particular moment in time. They fail, however, to capture the larger view of changing technologies, changing literacies, and changing envisionments. As a result, they quickly lose their power to inform either instruction or research.

In this chapter, I have argued that literacy is rapidly changing because information and communication technologies change quickly, as do the literacy envisionments that they inspire. Moreover, new technologies for information and communication, themselves, increasingly permit the immediate exchange of new technologies and envisionments for literacy. This speeds up the already rapid pace of change in the forms and functions of literacy as society regularly discovers new ways to exploit these technological means to accomplish new social ends. Changing technologies and concomitantly changing literacies and envisionments for literacy regularly redefine our instructional worlds.

Fifteen years ago, students did not need to know word processing technologies. Ten years ago, students did not need to know how to navigate through the rich information environments possible in multimedia, CD-ROM technologies. Five years ago, students did not need to know how to search for information on the Internet, set a bookmark, use a web browser, create an HTML document, participate in a mailing list, engage in a collaborative Internet project with another classroom, or communicate via e-mail. Today, however, each of these technologies and each of these envisionments is appearing within classrooms forcing teachers, students, and researchers to continually adapt to new definitions of literacy.

As we consider the lessons we might draw from this observation, we must step back to consider the broader issues that come into focus when one views literacy as technological deixis. To simply review the research on the instructional applications of technology in our field would only serve to look back at *what was*. Its would provide only limited guidance about *what might be* in our literacy futures.

Given the increasingly deictic nature of literacy, it would not be too extreme to draw an important conclusion: For the first time in our history, we are unable to accurately anticipate the literacy requirements expected at the time of graduation for children who will enter school this year. If, only 5 years ago, we were unable to anticipate the important role Internet technologies would play in our literacy lives today, how can we anticipate the nature of literacy in 13 years for children who are in kindergarten classrooms today? This observation has important consequences for thinking about the instructional applications of technology, because most of our research, instruction, and policies still assumes the literacy of tomorrow will be the same as the literacy of today. How do we plan for changes in technology and literacy that we cannot yet imagine? Although we cannot accurately define the nature of literacy in the future, we must begin to define the general principles at work in several areas, continuously reshaping contemporary notions of what it means to become literate.

The Nature of Literacy

First, let us consider the general nature of literacy in this new context. It is likely that reading and writing ability will become even more important in the future than they are today. This is due to the increasing need for acquiring and communicating information rapidly in a world of global competition and information economies. In this context, success will often be defined by one's ability to quickly locate useful information to solve important problems and then communicate the solution to others. Proficient readers can acquire many types of information more rapidly by reading than they can by listening to speech or viewing a video. In an age when speed of information access is central to success, reading proficiency will be even more critical to our children's futures.

Writing will also become more important in our literacy futures. We can acquire information faster by reading a written text than by listening. In addition, the greater planning time possible with written communication enables skilled authors to make meaning more explicit and precise; greater planning time also allows skilled authors to make meaning more deliberately ambiguous when that purpose might suit their needs. Finally, written messages may be stored in a manner that permits faster retrieval when they are needed. Pragmatically, audiences will increasing find value in written texts over oral texts when time is essential to communicate information precisely. For all of these reasons, reading and writing will become even more important in an information age as we access information rapidly and as we communicate new solutions to important problems.

As reading and writing become more important, a deictic perspective on literacy predicts that each will also change in important ways. First, strategic knowledge will become even more important to successful literacy activities than it is today. Navigating the increasingly complex information available within global information networks that continually change will require greater strategic knowledge than is required within more limited and static, traditional texts. It is likely, too, that new forms of strategic knowledge will be required (Gilster, 1997). Becoming literate will require our students to acquire new and increasingly sophisticated strategies for acquiring information within these complex and continually changing information contexts.

Second, literacy within global information networks will require new forms of critical thinking and reasoning from all of us. Anyone may publish anything on open networks like the Internet. Traditional forces guaranteeing some degree of control over the accuracy of information in traditionally published works do not exist. As a result, we encounter web pages created by people who have political, religious, or ideological stances that profoundly distort the nature of the information that they present to others. In this type of information environment, we must assist students to become more critical consumers of the information they encounter. Such skills have not always been important in classrooms where textbooks and other traditional information resources are often assumed to be correct.

Third, we need to help children become more aware of the variety of meanings inherent in the multiple media forms in which messages will increasingly appear (Flood & Lapp, 1995; Labbo, 1996; Labbo & Kuhn, 1998; Meyers, Hammett, and McKillop, 1998). Information resources now have the ability to combine many different media forms, making it possible to impart many new meanings, often in very subtle ways. This may either problematize or assist the construction of meaning. Within the area of communication and composition, new media are increasingly available in digital authoring tools. These also make for more complex communication skills. Clearly, the new meanings possible by combining multiple media sources create important challenges for us as we prepare students for their futures with new media and new literacies.

Fourth, literacy will increasingly become a continuous learning task for each of us. Since new technologies and new envisionments for literacy will regularly appear, we will need to continually learn new ways to acquire information and communicate with one another. Increasingly, *becoming literate* will become a more precise term than *being literate*, reflecting the continual need to update our abilities to communicate within new technologies that regularly appear.

Finally, changes in reading and writing will bring to the forefront the issue of language and cultural dominance. In the past, languages and cultures have been dominated by nations possessing superior military and economic power. In our digital futures, languages and cultures will be dominated by nations possessing superior information resources on global information networks such as the Internet. Currently, the vast majority of Internet sites and Internet traffic takes place to and from locations in the United States. One worries about the consequences of this for the rich heritage of diverse languages and cultures that characterize our world, permitting varied and unique interpretations of the reality we all inhabit. Will the Internet mean that English will become the only language of international communication? Will the Internet provide a vehicle for the dominance of U.S. culture? One hopes not, but the signs are already becoming clear that we may quickly lose our linguistic and cultural diversity if we all inhabit the same information and communication space on the Internet (Leu, 1997b).

Literacy Research

A deictic perspective about literacy within rapidly changing technologies and envisionments for their use generates two important paradoxes for the literacy community to carefully consider. These will require us to rethink several aspects of traditional approaches to research in literacy contexts.

The first paradox is that technology often changes faster than we can effectively evaluate its utility for literacy and learning (Kamil & Lane, 1998). Because literacy is so intimately related to the technologies of information and communication as well as the envisionments they inspire, rapidly changing technologies make it difficult, if not impossible, to develop a consistent body of research within traditional forums before the technology on which it is based is replaced by an even newer technology. Unless this situation changes, and strategies for publishing research in traditional forums speed up their processes or new forums appear, it is likely that traditional research will play an increasingly less important role in defining our understanding of new technologies and new literacies. Our understanding may be informed more often by individuals who use various technologies on a daily basis and less often by traditional forms of research. Perhaps, as Broudy (1986) suggested, we will have to depend increasingly on the credibility of advocates to different claims rather than on the truth of their claims.

There is also a second paradox for research resulting from a deictic perspective about literacy and technology: It may become unimportant to demonstrate the advantages of new technologies for educational contexts if it is already clear those technologies will define the literacies of our students' futures. Technologies and the literacies they prompt are changing so quickly that their importance to our children's future is often clear before a consistent body of research evidence appears objectively demonstrating their efficacy. Several authors (Oppenheimer, 1997; Rochlin, 1997; Roszak, 1994; Stoll, 1995) recently criticized the educational community for committing enormous amounts of money to technology without providing a compelling body of research evidence demonstrating the learning gains that will result. On the other hand, who needs hard data on the beneficial outcomes of new technologies for literacy or learning when it becomes clear that these technologies, or their related successors, will be the technologies of our children's futures? Although some would argue we must wait until compelling data are available; I would argue that to wait for these data will make them useless because new technologies will have appeared by then. If it is already clear that workplaces and higher education have become dependent on networked information environments such as the Internet, who has the luxury of time to wait for a consistent body of research to appear, demonstrating its effectiveness? Research might be better spent exploring issues of how to support teachers' efforts to unlock the potentials of new technologies, not demonstrating the learning gains from technologies we already know will be important to our children's success at life's opportunities.

If technologies continually change in the years ahead, it may become increasingly important to study teachers' envisionments of these technologies for literacy and learning. Teachers' envisionments, in a time of rapid technological change, may be one of the more stable components of literacy education in the future. Clearly, new envisionments for literacy and learning are taking place now, within current Internet technologies. We see these as teachers and educators develop a wide variety of keypal and Internet projects, many of which occur between students in different countries and cultures (El-Hindi, 1998; Iannone, 1998; Leu, Karchmer, & Leu, 1999; Leu & Leu, 1998). Unfortunately, there has been no work into how and why teachers envision and gravitate toward these new envisionments with this new technology. How do they emerge? What defines effective envisionments? How do teachers modify their envisionments over time? Why does this take place? All of these are important questions we must begin to address.

Classroom Learning Contexts

The rapidly changing nature of literacy predicted by a deictic perspective also has important consequences for designing classroom learning contexts. Because the technologies for information and communication are increasingly powerful, complex, and continually changing, no one person can hope to know everything about the technologies of literacy. As a result, literacy learning will be increasingly dependent on social learning strategies, even more than traditional contexts for literacy learning. I may know how to digitize video scenes from a classroom lesson, but you may know how best to design a web page for a class in literacy education. By exchanging information, we both discover new potentials for literacy and learning.

If literacy learning will become increasingly dependent on social learning strategies, socially skilled learners will be advantaged; "monastic learners," children who rely solely on independent learning strategies, will be disadvantaged. This may be an important change in many classrooms, because individual learning has often been the norm, privileging children who learn well independently. Increasingly, we must attend to this individual difference in classrooms, supporting children who are unfamiliar or ineffective with social learning strategies.

Workshop experiences and cooperative learning activities may be especially useful with complex and continually changing technologies of literacy because they allow groups of students to share experiences and learn from one another. It may be the case that classroom use of new literacy technologies will increasingly be organized around these strategies for instruction.

Teacher Education

A deictic perspective of literacy and technology also generates important consequences for teachers. Traditionally, we have selected teachers who were already literate and could pass their literacy along to our children. Now, however, the very nature of literacy is regularly changing because of new information and communication technologies. Many teachers literate in older technologies quickly become illiterate as newer technologies of information and communication replace previous technologies. If educators fail to continually become literate with rapidly changing technologies, how will they help their students become literate? We must begin to develop strategies to help each of us keep up with the continually changing definitions of literacy that will exist in our world. School systems have never faced the amount of professional support and continual reeducation these new technologies will require. Determining the most effective ways to support teachers in new electronic worlds will be an important challenge for policymakers and educational leaders.

Public Policy

A deictic perspective on technology suggests there are at least three important public policy issues that will become important in a world where technologies and envisionments for literacy continuously change. We have already discussed the first: equity issues in a world of continually changing technologies and envisionments for literacy. Somehow, we must develop equal access to these continuously changing technologies for all students. We must be prepared to continually provide support for schools and children to ensure equity in these new worlds for each and every child.

The second issue is related to the recent emphasis on setting national, state, and local standards for education in various subject areas. Current approaches to identifying specific literacy standards or benchmarks become somewhat meaningless if new technologies regularly redefine the very nature of literacy. Although these may be appropriate for some areas, a deictic perspective on literacy suggests they may be somewhat misguided, because standards and benchmarks assume the nature of literacy will remain constant. If we are unable to accurately anticipate the type of literacy expected at the time of graduation for children who enter school this year, how can we develop assessment tools to guide us on the journey? Clearly, if literacy is regularly redefined by new technologies and new envisionments, assessment must also be regularly redefined in the electronic futures our schools will inhabit. The challenge, however, is to develop assessment systems that keep up with the continually changing nature of literacy. A deictic perspective would suggest that the ability to learn continuously changing technologies and new envisionments for literacy may be a better target than literacy itself.

Finally, the financing of new technologies presents major new hurdles to any society. A deictic perspective would suggest that continually changing technologies of information and communication will require regular capital investments by schools if they wish to help their students keep up with the changing nature of literacy. We have never before been faced with the expenses of our literacy futures. Somehow, this challenge must be met if we hope to adequately prepare children for their literacy futures.

SUMMARY AND CONCLUSIONS

In this chapter, I have suggested that rapid changes in information and communication technologies have resulted in literacy becoming technological deixis, its meaning continuously changing as new technologies appear and as new envisionments for their use are crafted. Although literacy has always been deictic in an historical sense, the current period is unique because of the rapid changes in the technologies of information and communication as well as the envisionments they inspire. As a result, literacy is regularly being redefined within shorted time periods. This takes place as rapidly changing technologies for information and communication transform literacy and as users envision new ways of using these technologies for literate acts, transforming, in turn, the nature of these technologies.

What is especially interesting about these changes is that they appear to be driven less by traditional research on the effectiveness of any technology to support literacy or learning, perhaps because changes in the new technologies of information and communication occur more rapidly than we can develop a traditional research base on which to draw conclusions. Instead, larger social and economic factors appear to exert a powerful force on the use of information and communication technologies in classrooms as we seek to prepare students for the literacies of their futures.

In reviewing the recent literature on newer technologies, I have suggested that a deictic perspective makes it just as important to look forward into the consequences for our futures as it is to look backward to the research base. Because we cannot accurately define the nature of literacy in the future, I have suggested it is critical to define the general principles at work in reshaping contemporary notions of literacy. A central challenge is how to plan for education when the very heart of the system, literacy, will be changing regularly as new information and communication technologies continually appear and as teachers and students envision new ways to exploit these resources. To assist in this task, I identified a number of principles that might be drawn from a deictic perspective in several areas: the nature of literacy, literacy research, classroom learning contexts, teacher education, and public policy. These principles may be useful to help frame the exploration of issues in our literacy futures.

ACKNOWLEDGMENTS

I thank Allyson J. Crawley for her research assistance in the preparation of this chapter. I also thank the following colleagues for the many important insights they graciously shared in response to an earlier draft: Maya Eagleton, Dana Grisham, Lee Gunderson, Michael Hillinger, Rachel Karchmer, Jamie Kirkley, Linda Labbo, Larry Mickulecky, David Reinking, Bob Rickleman, Victoria Risko, and William Valmont. Each has helped me to see these issues in new ways. None, however, should be held responsible for any of my errors.

REFERENCES

Anderson, R. E. (1993). The technology infrastructure of U.S. schools. *Communications of the ACM, 36*(5), 72.

Anderson-Inman, L., & Horney, M. A. (1998). Transforming text for at-risk readers. In D. Reinking, M. McKenna, L. D. Labbo, & R. Kieffer, (Eds.), *Handbook of literacy and technology: Transformations in a post-typographic world* (pp. 15–44). Mahwah, NJ: Lawrence Erlbaum Associates.

Anderson-Inman, L., Horney, M. A., Chen, D. T., & Lewin, L. (1994). Hypertext literacy: Observations from the ElectroText project. *Language Arts, 71*, 279–287.

Ayersman, D. J. (1996). Reviewing the research on hypermedia-based learning. *Journal of Research on Computing in Education, 28*, 500–525.

Becker, H. J. (1992). Computer-based integrated learning systems in the elementary and middle grades: A critical review and synthesis of evaluation reports. *Journal of Educational Computing Research, 8*, 1–41.

Becker, H. J. (1993). Computer experience, patterns of computer use, and effectiveness—An inevitable sequence or divergent national cultures? *Studies in Educational Evaluation, (19)*, 127–148.

Becker, D. A., & Dwyer, M. M. (1994). Using hypermedia to provide learner control. *Journal of Educational Multimedia and Hypermedia, 3*, 155–172.

Belenky, M., Clinchy, B. M., Goldberger, N. R., & Tarule, J. M. (1986). *Women's ways of knowing: The development of self, voice, and mind.* New York: Basic Books.

Bijker, W. E., Hughes, T. P., & Pinch, T. (1987). *The social construction of technological systems.* Cambridge, MA: MIT Press,

Birkerts, S. (1994). *The Gutenberg elegies.* New York: Ballentine Books.

Boyarin, J. (Ed.) (1993). *The ethnography of reading.* Berkeley: University of California Press.

Bromley, H. (1997). The social chicken and the technological egg. *Educational Theory, 47*, 51–65.

Broudy, H. S. (1986). Technology and citizenship. In J. Culbertson & L. L. Cunningham (Eds.), *Microcomputers in education: Eighty-fifth yearbook of the National Society for the Study of Education* (pp. 234–253). Chicago: University of Chicago Press.

Bruce, B. C. (1997a). Current issues and future directions. In J. Flood, S. B. Heath, & D. Lapp (Ed.), *Handbook of research on teaching literacy through the communicative and visual arts* (pp. 875–884). New York: Simon & Schuster Macmillan.

Bruce, B. C. (1997b). Literacy technologies: What stance should we take? *Journal of Literacy Research, 29*, 289–309.

Brush, T. A. (1996, February). *The effects on student achievement and attitudes when utilizing cooperative learning of ILS-delivered instruction.* Paper presented at the annual meeting of the Eastern Educational Research Association, Cambridge, MA.

Carmel, E., Crawford, S., & Chen, H. (1992). Browsing in hypertext: A cognitive study. *IEEE Transactions on Systems, Man, and Cybernetics, 22*, 865–884.

Caroff, S., Fringer, V., & Kletzien, S. (1997, December). *Writing for publication in electronic media: Redefining authorship.* Paper presented at the annual meeting of the National Reading Conference, Scottsdale, AZ.

CEO Forum. (1999). *Professional development: A link to better learning.* [Online] Retrieved on March 1, 1999 from URL http://www.ceoforum.org/report99/99report.pdf.

Center for Applied Special Technology. (1996). *The role of online communications in schools: A national study.* [Online]. Retrieved on January 1, 1997, from URL http://www.cast.org/stsstudy.html

Chen, C., & Rada, R. (1996). Interacting with hypertext: A meta analysis of experimental studies. *Human-Computer Interaction, 11*, 125–156.

Clarke, V. (1990). Sex differences in computing participation: Concerns, extent, reasons, and strategies. *Australian Journal of Education, 34*, 52–66.

Cochran-Smith, M. (1991). Word processing and writing in elementary classrooms: A critical review of related literature. *Review of Educational Research, 61*, 107–155.

Cognition and Technology Group at Vanderbilt. (1990). Anchored instruction and its relationship to situated cognition. *Educational Researcher, 19*(3), 2–10.

Cuban, L. (1986). *Teachers and machines: The classroom use of technology since 1920.* New York: Teachers College Press.

Daiute, C., & Morse, F. (1994). Access to knowledge and expression: Multimedia writing tools for students with diverse needs and strengths. *Journal of Special Education Technology, 12*, 221–256.

Diringer, D. (1968). *The alphabet: A key to the history of mankind.* New York: Funk and Wagnalls.

Drucker, P. F. (1994, November). The age of social transformation. *Atlantic Monthly*, pp. 53–80.

Durndell, A. (1990). Why do female students tend to avoid computer studies? *Research in Science and Technological Education, 8*(2), 163–170.

Eldred, J. C., & Hawisher, G. E. (1995). Researching electronic networks. *Written Communication, 12*(3), 330–359.

El-Hindi, A. E. (1998). Beyond classroom boundaries: Constructivist teaching with the Internet. *Reading Teacher, 51*, 694–700.

Ellis, J. E.. (1997). *American Sphinx: The character of Thomas Jefferson.* New York: Knopf.

Farmer, M., Klein, R., & Bryson S. (1992). Computer-assisted reading: Effects of whole word feedback on fluency and comprehension in readers with severe disabilities. *Remedial and Special Education, 13*, 50–60.

Fillmore, C. J. (1972). How to know whether you're coming or going. In K. Huldgaard-Jensen (Ed.), *Linguistik 1971* (pp. 369–379). Amsterdam: Athemaiim.

Finkelman, K., & McMunn, C. (1995). *Microworlds as a publishing tool for cooperative groups: An affective study* (Report No. 143). Charlottesville, VA: Curry School of Education, University of Virginia. (ERIC Document Reproduction Service No. ED 384 344)

Flood, J., Heath, S. B., & Lapp, D. (Eds.). (1997). *Handbook of Research on teaching literacy through the communicative and visual arts.* New York: Simon & Schuster Macmillan.

Flood, J. & Lapp, D. (1995). Broadening the lens: Toward an expanded conceptualization of literacy. In K. A. Hinchman, D. J. Leu, & C. K. Kinzer (Eds.), *Perspectives on literacy research and practice* (pp. 1–16). Chicago: National Reading Conference.

Follansbee, S., Hughes, B., Pisha, B., & Stahl, S. (1997). Can online communications improve student performance? Results of a controlled study. *Journal of School Research and Information, 15,* 15–26.

Garton, L., & Wellman, B. (1995). Social impacts of electronic mail in organizations: A review of the research literature. *Communication Yearbook, 18,* 434–453.

Garner, R., & Gillingham, M. G. (1992). Topic knowledge, cognitive interest, and text recall: A microanalysis. *Journal of Experimental Education, 59,* 310–319.

Garner, R., & Gillingham, M. G. (1996). *Internet communication in six classrooms: Conversations across time, space, and culture.* Mahwah, NJ: Lawrence Erlbaum Associates.

Gilligan, C. (1982). *In a different voice: Psychological theory and women's development.* Cambridge, MA: Harvard University Press.

Gilster, P. (1997). *Digital literacy.* New York: John Wiley & Sons.

Giroux, H. A., & Freire, P. (1987). Series introduction. In D. Livingston (Ed.), *Critical pedagogy and cultural power* (pp. xi–xvi). South Hadley, MA: Bergin & Garvey.

Graff, H. J. (Ed.). (1981). *Literacy and social development in the West: A reader.* Cambridge, UK: Cambridge University Press.

Gray, S. H. (1989). The effect of locus of control and sequence control on computerized information retrieval and retention. *Journal of Educational Computing Research, 5,* 459–471.

Gray, S., Barber, C., & Shasha, D. (1991). Information search with dynamic text vs. paper text: An empirical comparison. *International Journal of Man-Machine Studies, 35,* 575–596.

Greenlee-Moore, M., & Smith, L. (1996). Interactive computer software: The effects on young children's reading achievement. *Reading Psychology: An International Quarterly, 17,* 43–64.

Grint, K., & Gill, R. (Eds.). (1995). *The gender–technology relation.* London: Taylor & Francis.

Haas, C. (1996). *Writing technology: Studies in the materiality of literacy.* Mahwah, NJ: Lawrence Erlbaum Associates.

Harris, W. V. (1989). *Ancient literacy.* Cambridge, MA: Harvard University Press.

Harrison, T. M., & Stephen, T. (Eds.). (1996). *Computer networking and scholarly communication in the twenty-first-century university.* Albany, NY: State University of New York Press.

Hastings, E. (1997). *Effects of CD-ROM talking storybooks on word recognition and motivation in young students with reading disabilities: An exploratory study.* Unpublished manuscript, Syracuse University.

Hidi, S. (1990). Interest and its contribution as a mental resource for learning. *Review of Education Research, 60,* 549–571.

Hiebert, E. H., Winograd, P.N., & Danner, F. W. (1984). Children's attributions for failure and success in different aspects of reading. *Journal of Educational Psychology, 76,* 1139–1148.

Hillinger, M. L. (1992). Computer speech and responsive text. *Reading and Writing: An Interdisciplinary Journal, 4,* 219–229.

Hillinger, M., & Leu, D. J. (1994). Guiding instruction in hypermedia. *Proceedings of the Human Factors and Ergonomics Society's 38th Annual Meeting,* 266–270.

Hillinger, M. L., & Leu, D. J. (1997). *Using multimedia to promote conceptual change.* (SBIR Phase I Final Report. National Science Foundation: Grant No. 9660334). Sharon, VT: LexIcon Systems.

Hodas, S. (1993). *Technology refusal and the organizational culture of schools.* (ERIC Document Reproduction Service No. ED 366 328)

Horney, M. A., & Anderson-Inman, L. (1994). The electrotext project: Hypertext reading patterns of middle school students. *Journal of Educational Multimedia and Hypermedia, 3,* 71–91.

Iannone, P. V. (1998). Just beyond the horizon: Writing-centered literacy activities for traditional and electronic contexts. *Reading Teacher, 51,* 438–443.

Illera, J. L. R. (1997). De la lectura en papel a la lectura multimedia. In Fundalectura (Ed.), *Lectura y nuevas tecnologías: 3er congreso nacional de lectura* (pp. 69–88). Bogotá, Colombia: Fundación para el Fomento de la Lectura.

Johnson, S. (1997). *Interface culture : How new technology transforms the way we create and communicate.* San Francisco: HarperCollins.

Jonassen, D. H. (1993). Acquiring structural knowledge from semantically structured hypertext. *Journal of Computer-Based Instruction, 20,* 1–8.

Kamil, M. (1997, December). *Qualitative trends in publication of research on technology and reading, writing, and literacy.* Paper presented at the meeting of the National Research Conference, Scottsdale, AZ.

Kamil, M. L., & Lane, D. M. (1998). Researching the relationship between technology and literacy: An agenda for the 21st century. In D. Reinking, M. McKenna, L. D. Labbo, & R. Kieffer (Eds.), *Handbook of lit-*

eracy and technology: Transformations in a post-typographic world (pp. 323–342). Mahwah, NJ: Lawrence Erlbaum Associates.

Karchmer, R. A. (1998). *Understanding teachers' perspectives of Internet use in the classroom: Implications for teacher education and staff development programs*. Unpublished manuscript, Syracuse University.

Kinzer, C. K., & Leu, D. J. (1997). The challenge of change: Exploring literacy and learning in electronic environments. *Language Arts, 74,* 126–136.

Kinzer, C. K., & Risko, V. J. (1998). Multimedia and enhanced learning: Transforming preservice education. In D. Reinking, M. McKenna, L. D. Labbo, & R. Kieffer (Eds.), *Handbook of literacy and technology: Transformations in a post-typographic world* (pp. 185–202). Mahwah, NJ: Lawrence Erlbaum Associates.

Labbo, L. (1996). A semiotic analysis of young children's symbol making in a classroom computer center. *Reading Research Quarterly, 51,* 356–385.

Labbo, L. & Kuhn, M. (1998). Electronic symbol making: Young children's computer-related emerging concepts about literacy. In D. Reinking, M. McKenna, L. D. Labbo, & R. Kieffer (Eds.), *Handbook of literacy and technology: Transformations in a post-typographic world* (pp. 79–92). Mahwah, NJ: Lawrence Erlbaum Associates.

Labbo, L. D., Phillips, M., & Murray, B. (1995–1996). Writing to read: From inheritance ti innovation and invitation. *Reading Teacher, 49,* 314–321.

Lay, M. M. (1996). The computer culture, gender, and nonacademic writing: An interdisciplinary critique. In A. H. Duin & C. J. Hansen (Eds.), *Nonacademic writing: Social theory and technology* (pp. 57–80). Mahwah, NJ: Lawrence Erlbaum Associates.

Leader, L. F., & Klein, J. D. (1994, February). *The effects of search tool and cognitive style on performance in hypermedia database searches*. Paper presented at the national convention of the Association for Educational Communications and Technology, Nashville, TN. (ERIC Document Reproduction Service No. ED 373 729)

Lemke, J. L. (1994). *Multiplying meaning: Literacy in a multimedia world*. Paper presented at the 1993 annual meeting of the National Reading Conference, Charleston, SC (December 1993). (ERIC Document Reproduction Service No. ED 365 940)

Lemke, J. L. (1998). Metamedia literacy: Transforming meanings and media. In D. Reinking, M. McKenna, L. D. Labbo, & R. Kieffer (Eds.), *Handbook of literacy and technology: Transformations in a post-typographic world* (pp. 283–302). Mahwah, NJ: Lawrence Erlbaum Associates.

Leu, D. J., Jr. (1997a). Caity's question: Literacy as deixis on the Internet. *Reading Teacher, 51,* 62–67.

Leu, D. J., Jr. (1997b). Internet en el aula: Nuevas oportunidades para la educación, el aprendizaje y la enseñanza. In Fundalectura (Ed.) *Lectura y nuevas tecnologías: 3er congreso nacional de lectura* (pp. 47–68). Bogotá, Colombia: Fundación para el Fomento de la Lectura.

Leu, D. J., Jr. (in press). The new Literacies: Research on reading instruction with the Internet and other digital technologies. In J. Samuels & A. E. Farstrup (Eds.), *What research has to say about reading instruction*. Newark, DE: International Reading Association.

Leu, D. J., & Hillinger, M. (1994, December). *Reading comprehension in hypermedia: Supporting changes to children's conceptions of a scientific principle*. Paper presented at the annual meeting of the National Reading Conference, San Diego.

Leu, D. J., Hillinger, M., Loseby, P. H., Balcom, M., Dinkin, J., Eckels, M., Johnson, J., Mathews, K., & Raegler, R. (1998). Grounding the design of new technologies for literacy and learning in teachers' instructional needs. In D. Reinking, M. McKenna, L. D. Labbo, & R. Kieffer (Eds.), *Handbook of literacy and technology: Transformations in a post-typographic world* (pp. 203–220). Mahwah, NJ: Lawrence Erlbaum Associates.

Leu, D. J., Jr., Karchmer, R., & Leu, D. D. (1999). The Miss Rumphius effect: Envisionments that transform literacy and learning on the Internet. *Reading Teacher, 52,* 636–642.

Leu, D. J., Jr., Karchmer, R., & Hinchman, K. A. (1999, April). *Using the Internet to study Internet use in classrooms: Expanding individual e-mail data with collaboratively constructed listserv data*. Paper presented at the annual meeting of the American Educational Research Association, Montreal, Canada.

Leu, D. J., Jr., & Kinzer, C. K. (1998). *Effective literacy instruction* (4th ed.). Englewood Cliffs, NJ: Merrill.

Leu, D. J., Jr., & Kinzer, C. K. (in press). The convergence of literacy instruction and communication. *Reading Research Quarterly*.

Leu, D. J., Jr., & Leu, D. D. (1998). *Teaching with the Internet: Lessons from the classroom* (2nd ed.). Norwood, MA: Christopher-Gordon.

Leu, D. J., Jr., & Reinking, D. (1996). Bringing insights from reading research to research on electronic learning environments. In H. van Oostendorp (Ed.), *Cognitive aspects of electronic text processing* (pp. 43–75). Norwood, NJ: Ablex.

Levi-Strauss, C. (1973). *Tristes tropiques* (J. Weightman & D. Weightman, Trans.). London: Jonathan Cape.

Lewin, C. (1997). Evaluating talking books: Ascertaining the effectiveness of multiple feedback modes and tutoring techniques. In C. K. Kinzer, K. A. Hinchman, & D. J. Leu (Eds.), *Inquiries in literacy theory and practice* (pp. 360–371). Chicago: National Reading Conference.

Liu, M., & Reed, W. M. (1994). The relationship between the learning strategies and learning styles in a hypermedia environment. *Computers in Human Behavior, 10,* 419–434.

Lundberg, I., & Olofsson, A. (1993). Can computer speech support reading comprehension? *Computers in Human Behavior, 9,* 283–293.

Manguel, A. (1996). *A history of reading.* New York: Viking.

Marchionini, G. (1989). Information-seeking strategies of novices using a full-text electronic encyclopedia. *Journal of the American Society for Information Science, 40,* 54–66.

Marrison, D. L., & Frick, M. J. (1994). The effect of agricultural students' learning styles on academic achievement and their perceptions of two methods of instruction. *Journal of Agricultural Education, 35,* 26–30.

Mathews, M. (1966). *Teaching to read: Historically considered.* Chicago: University of Chicago Press.

Mayer, R. E. (1997). Multimedia learning: Are we asking the right questions? *Educational Psychologist, 32,* 1–19.

McKenna, M. (1998). Electronic texts and the transformation of beginning reading. In D. Reinking, M. McKenna, L. D. Labbo, & R. Kieffer (Eds.), *Handbook of literacy and technology: Transformations in a post-typographic world* (pp. 45–60). Mahwah, NJ: Lawrence Erlbaum Associates.

Meyers, J., Hammett, R., & McKillop, A. M. (1998). Opportunities for critical literacy/pedagogy in student authored hypermedia. In D. Reinking, M. McKenna, L. D. Labbo, & R. Kieffer (Eds.), *Handbook of literacy and technology: Transformations in a post-typographic world* (pp. 63–78). Mahwah, NJ: Lawrence Erlbaum Associates.

Mikulecky, L., & Kirley, J. R. (1998). Changing workplaces, changing classes: The new role of technology in workplace literacy. In D. Reinking, M. McKenna, L. D. Labbo, & R. Kieffer (Eds.), *Handbook of literacy and technology: Transformations in a post-typographic world* (pp. 303–320). Mahwah, NJ: Lawrence Erlbaum Associates.

Miller, L., Blackstock, J., & Miller, R. (1994). An exploratory study into the use of CD-ROM storybooks. *Computers in Education, 22,* 187–204.

Miller, L., & Olson, J. (1994). Putting the computer in its place: A study of teaching with technology. *Journal of Curriculum Studies, 26,* 121–141.

Murphy, S. M. (1986). Children's comprehension of deictic categories in oral and written language. *Reading Research Quarterly, 21,* 118–131.

Negroponte, N. (1995). *Being digital.* New York: Knopf.

Newman, D. (1990). Opportunities for research on the organizational impact of school computers. *Educational Researcher, 19*(3). 8–13.

Olofsson, A. (1992). Synthetic speech and computer aided reading for reading disabled children. *Reading and Writing: An Interdisciplinary Journal, 4,* 165–178.

Olson, R., Foltz, G., & Wise, B. (1986). Reading instruction and remediation with the aid of computer speech. *Behavior Research Methods, Instruments, and Computers, 18,* 93–99.

Olson, R., & Wise, B. (1992). Reading on the computer with orthographic and speech feedback: An overview of the Colorado remediation project. *Reading and Writing: An Interdisciplinary Journal, 4,* 107–144.

Oppenheimer, T. (1997, July). The computer delusion. *The Atlantic Monthly, 280* [Online]. Retrieved on January 1, 1998 from URL http://www.theatlantic.com/issues/97jul/computer.htm

Owston, R. D. (1997). The World Wide Web: A technology to enhance teaching and learning? *Educational Researcher, 26*(2), 27–33.

Paivio, A. (1979). *Imagery and verbal processes.* Hillsdale, NJ: Lawrence Erlbaum Associates.

Paivio, A. (1986). *Mental representations: A dual coding approach.* New York: Oxford University Press.

Papert, S. (1993). *The children's machine: Rethinking school in the age of the computer.* New York: Basic Books.

Peha, J. M. (1995). How K–12 teachers are using computer networks. *Educational Leadership,* (3), 18–33.

Rada, R., & Murphy, C. (1992). Searching versus browsing in hypertext. *Hypermedia, 4,* 1–30.

Reed, W. M., Ayersman, D. J., & Liu, M. (1995a). The effect of hypermedia instruction on stages of concern of students with varying authoring language and prior hypermedia experience. *Journal of Research on Computing in Education, 27,* 297–317.

Reed, W. M., Ayersman, D. J., & Liu, M. (1995b). The effects of three different hypermedia courses on students' attitudes. *Computers in Human Behavior, 11,* 495–509.

Reich, R, (1992). *The work of nations.* New York: Vintage Books.

Reinking, D. (1995). Reading and writing with computers: Literacy research in a post-typographic world. In K. A. Hinchman, D. J. Leu, & C. K. Kinzer (Eds.), *Perspectives on literacy research and practice.* Chicago: National Reading Conference.

Reinking, D. (1998). Synthesizing technological transformations of literacy in a post-typographic world. In D. Reinking, M. McKenna, L. D. Labbo, & R. Kieffer (Eds.), *Handbook of literacy and technology: Transformations in a post-typographic world* (pp. xi–xxx). Mahwah, NJ: Lawrence Erlbaum Associates.

Reinking, D., & Bridwell-Bowles, L. (1991). Computers in reading and writing. In R. Barr, M. L., Kamil, P. B. Mosenthal, & P. D. Pearson (Eds.), *Handbook of reading research* (Vol. 2, pp. 310–340). New York: Longman.

Reinking, D., & Chanlin, L. J. (1994). Graphic aids in electronic texts. *Reading Research and Instruction, 33,* 207–232.

Reinking, D., Labbo, L., & McKenna, M. (1997). Navigating the changing landscape of literacy: Current theory and research in computer-based reading and writing. In J. Flood, S. B. Heath, & D. Lapp (Eds.), *Handbook of research on teaching literacy through the communicative and visual arts* (pp. 77–92). New York: Simon & Schuster Macmillan.

Reinking, D., McKenna, M. Labbo, L., & Kieffer, R. (Eds.). (1998). *Handbook of literacy and technology: Transformations in a post-typographic world.* Mahwah, NJ: Lawrence Erlbaum Associates.

Reinking, D., & Pickle, J. M. (1993). Using a formative experiment to study how computers affect reading and writing in classrooms. In D. J. Leu & C. K. Kinzer (Eds.), *Examining central issues in literacy research, theory, and practice* (pp. 263–270.) Chicago: National Reading Conference.

Reinking, D., & Watkins, J. (1997). *A formative experiment investigating the use of multimedia book reviews to increase elementary students' independent reading* (Research report). University of Georgia, University of Maryland: National Reading Research Center.

Reitsma, P. (1998). Reading practice for beginners: Effects of guided reading, reading-while-listening, and independent reading with computer-based speech feedback. *Reading Research Quarterly, 23,* 219–235.

Rifkin, J. (1995). *The end of work: The decline of the global labor force and the dawn of the post-market era.* New York: G. P. Putnam's Sons.

Risko, V. J. (1995). Using videodisc-based cases to promote preservice teachers' problem solving and mental model building. In W. M. Linek & E. G. Sturtevant (Eds.), *Generations of literacy* (pp. 173–187). Pittsburg, KS: College Reading Association.

Risko, V. J., Peter, J., & McAllister, D. (1996). Conceptual changes: Preservice teachers' pathways to providing literacy transaction. In E. Sturtevant & W. Linek (Eds.), *Growing literacy* (pp. 103–119). Commerce, TX: College Reading Association.

Risko, V. J., Yount, D., & McAllister, D. (1992). Preparing preservice teachers for remedial instruction: Teaching problem solving and use of content and pedagogical knowledge. In N. Padak, T. V. Rasinski, & J. Logan (Eds.), *Inquiries in literacy learning and instruction* (pp. 178–189). Pittsburg, KS: College Reading Association.

Rochlin, G. I. (1997). *Trapped in the Net: The unanticipated consequences of computerization.* Princeton, NJ: Princeton University Press.

Roszak, T. (1994). *The cult of information: A neo-luddite treatise on high tech, artificial intelligence, and the true art of thinking.* Berkeley, CA: University of California Press.

Rouet, J., Levonen, J., Dillon, A., & Spiro, R. (Eds.). (1996). *Hypertext and cognition.* Mahwah, NJ: Lawrence Erlbaum Associates.

Sayers, D. (1995). Educational equity issues in an information age. *Teachers College Record, 96,* 769–773.

Schick, J. E., & Miller, R. M. (1992, April). *Learner control in a hypertext environment with linguistic-minority students.* Paper presented at the annual meeting of the American Educational Research Association, Atlanta, GA.

Schroeder, E. E. (1994, February). *Navigating through hypertext: Navigational technique, individual differences, and learning.* Paper presented at the national convention of the Association for Educational Communications and Technology, Nashville, TN. (ERIC Document Reproduction Service No. ED 373 760)

Schrum, L. (1995). Educators and the Internet: A case study of professional development. *Computers and Education, 24,* 221–228.

Scoresby, K. (1996). *The effects of electronic storybook animation on third graders' story recall.* Unpublished doctoral dissertation, Brigham Young University.

Scott, T., Cole, M., & Engel, M. (1992). Computers and education: A cultural constructivist perspective. In G. Grant (Ed.), *Review of research in education* (Vol. 18, pp. 191–251). Washington, DC: American Educational Research Association.

Selfe, C. L. (1990). Technology in the English classroom: Computers through the lens of feminist theory. In C. Handa (Ed.), *Computers and community: Teaching composition in the 21st century* (pp. 118–139). Portsmouth, NH: Boynton/Cook, Heinemann.

Selfe, C. L., & Selfe, R. J., Jr. (1996). Writing as democratic social action in a technological world: Politicizing and inhabiting virtual landscapes. In A. H. Duin & C. J. Hansen (Eds.), *Nonacademic writing: Social theory and technology* (pp. 325–358). Mahwah, NJ: Lawrence Erlbaum Associates.

Shannon, P. (1996). Poverty, literacy, and politics: Living in the USA. *Journal of Literacy Research, 28,* 430–439.

Sherry, M. (1990). Implementing an integrated learning system: Critical issues. *Phi Delta Kappan, 72,* 118–120.

Smith, N. B. (1965). *American reading instruction.* Newark, DE: International Reading Association.

Spiro, R. J., & Jeng, J. (1990). Cognitive flexibility and hypertext: Theory and technology for the non-linear and multidimensional traversal of complex subject matter. In D. Nix & R. Spiro (Eds.), *Cognition, education and multimedia: Exploring ideas in high technology* (pp. 163–205). Hillsdale, NJ: Lawrence Erlbaum Associates.

Sterne, R. W. (1993). *Thomas Jefferson : A life.* New York : Holt.

Stoll, C. (1995). *Silicon snake oil: Second thoughts on the information highway.* New York: Doubleday.

Stotsky, S. (1996). Participatory writing: Literacy for civic purposes. In A. H. Duin & C. J. Hansen (Eds.), *Nonacademic writing: Social theory and technology* (pp. 227–256). Mahwah, NJ: Lawrence Erlbaum Associates.

Sutton, R. E. (1991). Equity and computers in the schools: A decade of research. *Review of Educational Research, 61,* 475–503.

Tao, L., Montgomery, T., & Pickle, M. (1997). Content analysis in e-mail research: A methodological review. In C. K. Kinzer, K. A. Hinchman, & D. J. Leu (Eds.), *Inquiries in literacy theory and practice* (pp. 474–482). Chicago: National Reading Conference.

Tierney, R. J., Kieffer, R., Whalin, K., Desai, L. Moss, A. G., Harris, J. E., & Hopper, J. (1997). Assessing the impact of hypertext on learners' architecture of literacy learning spaces in different disciplines: Follow-up studies. *Reading Online*. Available: http://www.readingonline.org/research/impact/index.html [1997, December 28].

Toro, M. A. (1995). The effects of Hypercard authoring on computer-related attitudes and Spanish language acquisition. *Computers in Human Behavior, 11,* 633–647.

Trotter, A. (1990). Computer learning. *American School Board Journal, 177,* 12–18.

Tufte, E. R. (1997). *Visual explanations: Images, quantities, evidence and narrative.* Chesire, CT: Graphics Press.

Turkle, S., & Papert, S. (1990). Epistomological pluralism: Styles and voices within the computer culture. *Signs, 16,* 128–157.

U.S. Congress, Office of Congressional Assessment. (1995). *Teachers and technology: Making the connection.* Washington, DC: U.S. Government Printing Office.

van Oostendorp, H. & de Mul, S. (Eds.). (1996). *Cognitive aspects of electronic text processing.* Norwood, NJ: Ablex.

Virillo, P. (1986). *Speed and politics: An essay on domology* (M. Polizzotti, Trans.). New York: Semiotext(e).

Wagner, D. A., Spratt, J. E., Gal, I., & Paris, S. G. (1989). Reading and believing: Beliefs, attributions, and reading achievement in Moroccan school children. *Journal of Educational Psychology, 81,* 283–293.

Weller, H. G., Repman, J., & Rooze, G. E. (1994). The relationship of learning, behavior, and cognitive style in hypermedia-based instruction: Implications for the design of HBI. *Computers in the Schools, 10,* 401–420.

Weller, H. G., Repman, J., Lan, W., & Rooze, G. E. (1995). Improving the effectiveness of learning through hypermedia-based instruction: The importance of learner characteristics. *Computers in Human Behavior, 11,* 451–465.

Wise, B., & Olson, R. (1994). Computer-based phonological awareness and reading instruction. *Annals of Dyslexia, 45,* 99–122.

Wise, B., Olson, R., Anstett, M., Andrews, L., Terjak, M., Schneider, V., Kostuch, J., & Kriho, L. (1989). Implementing a long-term computerized remedial reading program with synthetic speech feedback: Hardware, software, and real-world issues. *Behavior Research Methods, Instruments, and Computers, 21,* 172–180.

CHAPTER 40

The Effects of Other Technologies on Literacy and Literacy Learning

Michael L. Kamil
Sam M. Intrator[*]
Helen S. Kim
Stanford University

Reviewing the research on literacy and "technology" is something of a conundrum, for literacy and literacy instruction are, themselves, technologies. Moreover, in current usage, technology typically refers to computer technology, disregarding other technologies. The use of computer technology in reading has a relatively short history, extending primarily to the work of Atkinson and Hansen (1966–1967).

There was no review of reading (or writing) and other technologies in the first volume of the *Handbook of Reading Research*. Reinking and Bridwell-Bowles (1991) reviewed research on both reading and writing in the second volume.

The *NRC Yearbooks* have contained three reviews of technology and reading (Kamil, 1982; Reinking, 1995; Spache, 1967). It is instructive to note that the emphasis on technology and reading differed among these three reviews. Spache focused on the use of reading machines to train students to read better and faster. His review was early enough that computer technology did not play as prominent a role except in the analysis of text. In 1982, the computer "revolution" was in full swing and the focus was on the capabilities of computers and software. Much of Kamil's emphasis was on the use of the computer as a tool in research and on the use of technology to teach reading. Reinking's review focused on the notion of text and how it has been, or will be, altered by computer technology. The concern was more with the shape of literacy in the future than it was for any concerns of the present. This review represented a clear disconnect from earlier perspectives, as Reinking suggested that new conceptions of literacy were needed. There was little emphasis on CAI or instructional processes.

---

[*]Sam M. Inrator is now at Smith College.

A fourth review, Flood and Lapp (1995), dealt peripherally with issues of visual literacy. By its very nature, this topic overlaps substantially with technological developments, but the review did not isolate those effects. Neuman (1991) reviewed most of the research on television and literacy. She concluded that it would be best to incorporate television in literacy rather than trying to banish it or eliminate it from children's lives. However, as Kamil and Intrator (1998) pointed out, there is simply not a large body of research on these issues, and more systematic and programmatic research is needed to validate these speculations.

There have been several reviews limited to writing and computer technologies. Cochran-Smith (1991) looked at classroom effects of word processing on writing, and Bangert-Drowns (1993) conducted a meta-analysis of word processing in writing instruction. Hawisher, LeBlanc, Moran, and Selfe (1996) dated the history of teaching writing with computers to the early 1970s. By all accounts, at least the computer technologies have a history of some four decades or less.

A recent volume (Reinking, McKenna, Labbo, & Kieffer, 1998) is devoted entirely to topics in literacy and computer technology. However, only a few chapters deal exclusively with research or research topics.

Kamil and Lane (1998) examined research over the years 1990–1995. They found that there were only 12 research articles about technology and reading or writing in the four reading and writing journals (*Written Communication, Research in the Teaching of English, Reading Research Quarterly,* and *Journal of Reading Behavior,* since changed to *Journal of Literacy Research*) with the highest citation rates for literacy research (Shanahan & Kamil, 1994). There was a total of 437 articles published in those journals over the same time period.

Out of a total of 256 articles in the two reading journals, only 3, a little more than 1%, dealt with technology issues directly. (One of these was about television, another about audio, and one was about computers.) The situation was somewhat better for the two writing journals. There were 9 articles dealing with writing and technology, out of a total of 181 articles, or approximately 5%. Combined, the total number of technology articles published in these four journals was 12 out of a total of 437 articles, or 2.7%. An important datum is that the bulk of the technology articles in the 5-year period was published in 1991 and 1992. These two years account for all but 2 of the technology articles across all of the four journals in the years between 1990 and 1995.

Kamil and Intrator (in press) conducted a more complete review of the research in literacy and technology and found that between 1986 and 1996 there were only 350 research journal articles about reading and writing published. The proportion was relatively constant over that time period, ranging from 2% to 5% of the total of all research articles on reading and writing.

PROBLEM SELECTION

Despite the paucity of research and the particular lack of research in mainstream reading and writing journals, there are definite trends and findings that can be represented in the limited dataset. In order to deal with the research in a systematic manner, we relied on the findings of Intrator and Kamil (1998) and Kamil and Intrator (1998) to categorize the problems that have been studied. They used a combination of quantitative and qualitative criteria to analyze the research. They found areas that had been the focus of intensive study, areas that seemed to be sparsely researched (but promising), and areas that were largely unresearched. For each of the areas, we attempt to summarize major findings and point to productive directions. Given the relatively small numbers of studies in many of these areas, the reviews are interpretive rather than quantitative. We do, however, refer to quantitative reviews where they have been conducted.

COMPUTER AND COMPOSITION

Of all the uses of technology in literacy and literacy instruction, word processing seems tailor-made. Philosophically and practically, word processing fits with current educational thought and pedagogy. There is probably no other single technological application that seems to be as well designed for the educational purposes to which it is put. Simply, there is no other alternative that will allow students and teachers to operate in composing, editing, revising, and publishing with so little compromise. Process writing predates the advent of word processors, but the two concepts seem to be so matched that they seem to have sprung from the same intellectual root. Computer technology is the quintessential tool for process writing.

Word processing studies fall into two of the categories that Intrator and Kamil (1998) used to classify research studies studying computer technology: those in which technology is a simple replacement, and those in which technology augments an older skill or practice. (There was also a third category which was an entirely new process. They found none of the word processing studies belonged in this category.) In some of the studies, word processing is simply being used to replace, rather than augment, the process of writing. Many studies (e.g., Rice, 1994; Snyder, 1993) simply compared word processing with using pen and paper. Indeed, this is similar to the basis for the meta-analysis that Bangert-Drowns (1993) conducted. He reviewed 32 studies where two groups of students received identical writing instruction but only one group was allowed to use word processing. The strong conclusion was that the quality of writing was higher for word processing groups, although the effect size was relatively small. Using word processing did not have an effect on attitudes toward writing, although students did produce longer documents. Although the evidence on revisions was difficult to interpret, there is other evidence to suggest that revisions may not automatically result from word processing (Daiute, 1986; Daiute & Kruideneir, 1985). In her work, Daiute added revision prompts and found that students did produce more revisions under such circumstances. This clearly forms the basis for recommendations (including that of Bangert-Drowns) that adapting word processing programs to instruction may make them even more effective.

Cochran-Smith (1991) suggested that there was more known about the cognitive aspects of word processing than the social. In particular, she recommended that we needed to know much more about the implementations of technologies like word processing and how they interact with the social environment of classrooms. Since 1991, we have found little in the literature to put this issue to rest. The updated version of this concern is that, with networked and collaborative writing becoming more commonplace (e.g., Beach & Lundell, 1998), we need to extend our efforts to determine how the social aspects of collaborative networks affect writing and writing instruction. (We address this again later in this chapter.)

We believe that writing with computers will continue to have a strong presence in the body of research literature on literacy and technology. It is also clear that word processing is one of the uses of computer technology that gets a strong recommendation for implementation from the currently available research.

HYPERMEDIA, HYPERTEXT, AND LITERACY

One of the interesting trends that Kamil and Intrator (1998) found was that there was only a small body of research on hypertext and hypermedia. Although there is a reasonable body of theory about hypertext, and promises of its importance to literacy (e.g., Rouet, Levonen, Dillon, & Spiro, 1996; Purves, 1998), we have few empirical studies of the cognitive consequences of reading this type of nontraditional text.

There seem to be at least three separate situations in which hypertext is used. There is a literary version of hypertext in which a reader is encouraged to create a unique story. A second use of hypertext is to add information to allow readers to explore text material in greater detail. A third use is to create study environments. Our review of the research shows so little work on each of these areas that it is difficult to reach a strong conclusion. This is in spite of the review of research by Chen and Rada (1996). They reviewed 23 studies for a meta-analysis in which an assortment of variables was examined. We believe that there were too few studies in each group to make strong conclusions. Further, Chen and Rada used very little in the way of theory to guide their classification of hypertext. Finally, not all of the studies were about reading, even if they involved hypertext. That is, in some of the studies, the issues at hand only involved hypertext in an incidental manner.

There is, however, promising research in this area, and we would hope that there will be even more work. Of particular interest is Gillingham's (1993) study, which showed that hypertext slowed the search for the answer to a known question. Although this is not a typical use for hypertext, it does raise several considerations about computerized text in general and hypertext in particular. For example, how does having the capability to electronically search for material in a text affect comprehension and studying? For some purposes, the electronic search is clearly faster, provided the query can be appropriately structured.

Horney and Anderson-Inman (1994) categorized the hypertext reading of middle school students as exhibiting six possible strategies: skimming, checking, reading, responding, studying, and reviewing. However, we still do not have general agreement in the field about how to line up these sorts of data with instruction in reading.

One of the issues here is, as Kamil and Lane (1998) pointed out, that there is a conceptual problem that remains unaddressed. When a reader encounters a hyperlink in text, there is often no way to predict whether the information to be acquired by following that link is going to be useful. Anderson-Inman and her colleagues developed a system of "supported text" in which the reader can choose the information to be obtained by using a "link" (see, e.g., Anderson-Inman, 1991; Anderson-Inman & Horney, 1998).

One more issue seems to be impeding the research on hypertext. We have no coherent account of the nature of hyperlinks, independent of the utilization of them. Kamil (1998) proposed a taxonomy of hyperlinks that classifies links on the basis of their uses and consequences for the reader. However, we still do not have comprehensive, usable, and testable theoretical accounts of hypertext against which to do empirical studies. Purves (1998) raised many important issues, but brought little empirical data to bear on those issues.

With the increasing use of the Internet and its highly intricate set of hyperlinks, we need to address this issue with some urgency. As schools become wired and the Internet becomes an instructional tool (see Leu, this volume), we must dedicate ourselves to determining how best to teach students to read the sorts of materials they may encounter.

MULTIMEDIA EFFECTS ON LITERACY

A recent line of research has explored the effects on literacy of using multimedia presentations that actively integrate text and visuals. Dynamically combining text and narratives with illustrations and sound, multimedia applications such as interactive CD-ROMS, videos, the Internet, and hypertext are offering new modalities for using and acquiring literacy. Reinking (1995, 1998) offered some insight into the societal implications of these new technologies that integrate text and visuals on literacy acquisition, and the challenges they pose to traditional conceptualizations of literacy. Flood and Lapp (1995) further explored the impact of visual media on learning, and assessed the implications of expanding traditional notions of literacy on instructional design and student learning.

A debate on whether or not learning is ultimately dependent on the medium used to deliver instruction has been rather lively (Clark, 1983, 1994; Kozma, 1991, 1994; Jonassen, Campbell, & Davidson, 1994). This debate among instructional designers is reflective of contrasting views across the entire spectrum of technology users in learning environments. There seems to be little hope for resolving the theoretical issues in favor of one side of the instructional design debate.

Correspondingly, the issue of how best to facilitate comprehension using different modes of representation has recently been the subject of much empirical inquiry (e.g., Mayer, 1997; Mayer & Moreno, 1998; Sharp et al., 1995). This work draws heavily on visual representations, displays of information, and mental model building. Recent research in multimedia and literacy acquisition has examined the affordances of technology to create dynamic, interactive, and visually salient learning environments. Multimedia applications that integrate text/narratives with visual representations can confer unique learning advantages because they do not require knowledge of how to read or speak English. As discussed in a separate section, multimedia has also offered many instructional alternatives and unique learning opportunities for learners whose educational needs might not be sufficiently met through more traditional modes of instruction.

Paivio's (1986) dual coding theory posits the existence of separate codes for processing visual and verbal material. One possible implication of this model is that when information is processed both visually and verbally, the information may be more memorable as there are two memory traces instead of one. Multimedia applications are replete with opportunities to test a possible facilitating effect of contiguous visual and verbal input. In this direction, Mayer and Moreno (1998) found preliminary support for augmented learning outcomes and a split attention effect, with subjects in treatment conditions of simultaneous visual and audio support outperforming subjects in simultaneous visual pictures and visual text conditions on learning measures such as recall and problem solving transfer. In assessing the effects of multimedia presentations, some recent studies have also emphasized the role that integrated support may have in facilitating the formation of mental models for comprehending information (e.g., Plass, Chun, Mayer, & Leutner, 1998; Mayer, 1997; Sharp et al., 1995).

Rather than focusing solely on instructional effects, recent studies have also probed deeper into understanding the specific cognitive processes involved in how learners synthesize multimedia information, and analyzing the effects of learner and task characteristics. For example, in a review of six studies involving multimedia instruction and coordinated presentations, Mayer (1997) found differential strengths of instructional effects between low prior knowledge and high spatial ability students, as well as learning styles. He found that learners with little prior knowledge did better with multimedia learning. Learners who could be classified as visual or auditory also showed better learning in that modality. In a study of two above average fourth-grade classes, Greenlee-Moore and Smith (1996) found augmented comprehension from the reading of narrative texts on interactive CD-ROM software versus printed paper, but only for longer and more difficult passages. There is a paucity of research on the differential learning effects of multimedia instruction. The studies just described serve to underscore the need for further investigation of the circumstances of how, when, and for whom learning with multimedia occurs.

As computer technology and multimedia videos continue to be integrated into educational instruction, the body of research is starting to reflect more specific lines of inquiry into the particular characteristics of multimedia applications that are most efficacious. For example, the role of dynamic visuals (in contrast to static images), such as animations and computer simulations, has been suggested as a superior medium for mental model building and story comprehension (Sharp et al., 1995). Sharp et al. found that children in the treatment condition that included dynamic visual support had the highest ability to recall the ending of the stories and connect it with previous story elements in comparison to the static images and text only groups. One reason the researchers theorized that dynamic images were found to be superior is the augmented support for encoding visual and spatial information from the story. Dynamic videos may also enable children to see changes in spatial relationships, which can be difficult for younger children to imagine on their own. There is also an expectation that multimedia presentations of literacy material will motivate students more effectively than traditional presentations. We consider these issues in a separate section.

Collectively, these trends in research underscore a cognitively based approach to understanding the effects of multimedia on literacy acquisition. In the literature, the study of visual representations has moved from merely assessing instruction effects of using a specific medium, to searching for a deeper understanding of the underlying cognitive mechanisms involved, and the circumstances of how and when individual learning occurs (Mayer, 1997). Concomitant with advances in visual learning theory and multimedia instruction, the need to devise new assessments of learning outcomes and measures comprises another important research direction that has not been sufficiently explored in the current literature. One emerging conclusion is that multimedia applications facilitate the construction of mental models and augment learning outcomes. Much more empirical inquiry is needed to uncover the underlying cognitive processes.

Another unexplored, but important, research topic for literacy and technology is the role of cognitive strategies involved in the comprehension of graphics and text. The study of whether (and how) referential connections between visuals and text can be explicitly taught is particularly important. Finally, careful study of multimedia literacy learning, including determining whether developmental trends and differences exist, is critical for design and implementation of programs.

SPECIAL POPULATIONS

Another body of work in technology and literacy reflects the interventional use of technology to benefit individuals who may not learn as easily or effectively from traditional modes of instruction. These individuals may include the persons diagnosed with learning disabilities, persons facing physical challenges, and preliterate children. Relevant here is the use of technology with intentions to remediate specific difficulties in literacy acquisition or to facilitate more rapid literacy acquisition. As Ferrier and Shane (1987) attested, the computer can represent a diverse array of assistive tools because of its many functions and forms of output, including the visual representations, print, and voice/communication capabilities. In fact, the use of technology to assist persons with special learning needs has a rich history in the literature. Woodward and Rieth (1997) undertook a comprehensive review of the extant literature on technology research in special education since 1980, including a review of several divergent strands of research in the field. Recently, the literature on technology and literacy has begun to reflect several advances in the use of multimedia applications to address individual needs and learning styles. Many of the reported benefits have not been limited to literacy gains but encompass positive attitudinal and motivational aspects as well.

Several advances have been made with the use of technology to help students diagnosed with learning disabilities. One area of literacy that is currently under investigation regards the role of enhanced word processing programs in helping to facilitate the writing process for students with learning disabilities. Conferring advantages beyond mere wordprocessing, advances in technology have included developments such as speech synthesis and word prediction. Speech synthesis, which allows the user to hear the computer pronounce the words typed into the program, has rendered some promising results in allowing college students to detect a higher percentage of errors in their writing (Raskind & Higgins, 1995). Word prediction is another intervention that helps students by using the computer to predict and offer choices of words as users begin to type the letters. More recently, MacArthur (1998) explored the use of a word processing program with speech synthesis and word prediction with young students with learning disabilities and difficulties with writing. Although a small sample size precludes the ability to draw strong inferences, the study found that users of the special programs demonstrated increased spelling accuracy and legibility. However, major gaps in the research literature continue to exist regarding the efficacy of these programs in improving the length or quality of writing, as well as a deeper understanding of the learning styles and specific challenges that are best addressed through these programs.

Another current trend found in the research involves the adaptive use of technology to help facilitate literacy acquisition with learners facing physical challenges. More conventional applications of technology to facilitate literacy acquisition for learners facing visual impediments have included using computers to increase the size of text, audio descriptions, Braille displays, and screen magnifiers. As multimedia increasingly offers new modes of representation and the versatility to create unique learning environments, studies continue to assess the best ways to utilize these benefits. Steelman, Pierce, and Koppenhaver (1993) highlighted several advantages of using computer technology to develop literacy in children with severe speech and physical impairments, including the flexibility to tailor programs to different learning styles, as well as allowing physical access to literacy materials. Nelson and Camarata (1996) underscored the potential benefits of using multimedia supports to help integrate sign, speech, and text for children facing severe to profound hearing impairments.

With respect to future directions in the assistive use of technology and literacy, a growing body of literature reflects the extension and application of multimedia learning to benefit second-language learners, at-risk children, and very young, preliterate children. Much of the current research with multimedia support for second-language learners involves an emphasis on considering learning styles and individual needs. Preliminary findings in this domain appear to be quite promising. Plass, Chun, Mayer, and Leutner (1998) found augmented story comprehension and recall of word translations with the support of verbal and visual learning preferences to teach English to second language learners. Using a hypermedia-assisted second-language learning program, Liu and Reed (1995) also found positive gains in vocabulary and improvements in the correct use of words in context by a group of international students learning English.

As mentioned earlier, the prospect of introducing multimedia literacy programs at increasingly earlier ages and to preliterate children has garnered much interest. Labbo, Reinking, and McKenna (1995) undertook an ethnographic case study to evaluate the potential of the computer as an informal tool for literacy development in kindergarten children and emphasized the importance of considering the facilitative role of the teacher in the process. Although there is still little research in this area, Boone, Higgins, Notari, and Stump (1996) found some positive implications for the further development of multimedia programs to teach prereading lessons to kindergarten students of differential abilities. As these preliminary findings suggest, with the new instructive possibilities rendered by advances in integrative multimedia, the time is especially auspicious for the study of how these technologies can be applied and tailored to accommodate special needs and learning styles.

The study of technology and literacy for special populations has had a long history. It continues to show ever greater promise at bringing the promises of assistive technology to bear on what have been very difficult problems.

MOTIVATION

In the research on the impact of computer use on the classroom structure, the most consistently found effect is an increase in motivation and closely related constructs such as interest and enjoyment of schoolwork, task involvement, persistence, time on task, and retention in school (Hague & Mason, 1986; Kulik & Kulik, 1991; Kulik, Kulik, & Peter 1980; Schofield, 1997). Lepper and his research group have conducted the most complete series of investigations into the impact of computers on motivation. They concluded that computer-based educational activities can increase factors associated with the intrinsic motivation of students to the extent that they increase the opportunities to customize one's work and increase the control, curiosity, and challenge of the task (Lepper & Chabay, 1987; Lepper & Malone, 1985). Specifically related to literacy development, computer use by children can increase their involvement in and enjoyment of writing and reading, thereby, improving the quality of what they produce (Daiute, 1983; Montague, 1990; Papert, 1980; Sheingold, Kane, & Endreweit, 1983). The studies exploring the motivational attributes of technology and literacy fall into two distinct categories: the motivational effects on literacy tasks in technology environments, and the motivational effects of technology on the literacy learning of special populations of learners.

Motivational Effects of Technology Environments

One species of studies highlighting the motivational attributes of literacy and technology involved the comparison of tasks like essay writing with a pen and paper versus essay writing with a computer. These studies reported that students exhibited a higher level of motivational engagement when using technological tools (e.g., Daiute, 1983). Studies that compared word processing revision versus hand-written revision commonly found that students were more highly motivated to revise, which led to more time spent on the revision process. In a series of word processing studies, Daiute (1983) discovered that children found word processing more fun than hand revision because it dispensed with recopying their writings. Children also persisted on tasks longer when using word processing. Hague and Mason (1986) investigated whether the use of computer readability measures as a feedback mechanism to student writers would foster more effective revision processes. They found an increase in grade level from the original drafts to revised versions. They attributed this to a motivational effect. Baer's (1988) descriptive case study portrayed a seventh-grade classroom where computer composition heightened the enjoyment of writing assignments. McMillan and Honey (1993) conducted a year-long study with a class of 25 eighth graders who were given the use of laptop computers. Students used laptops as portable diaries to keep journals, write stories, and complete assignments. A holistic measure of writing scores for a randomly selected group of students indicated marked improvement in their ability to communicate persuasively, organize their ideas effectively, and use a broad vocabulary effectively. The researchers attributed this increase to the heightened motivation attached to using laptop computers.

Other research explored how technology could be used to enhance student interest when learning "dry" material. For example, Becker and Dwyer (1994) found that students who used hypertext to learn technical information experienced an increased sense of control and an increased level of intrinsic motivation to learn among hypertext users. More extensive research in the motivational aspects of reading and studying in these types of environments is clearly desirable.

Motivating Special Populations

Studies that have explored the motivational effects of technology environments on special populations of literacy learners have also encompassed the second category of studies. Scott, Kahlich, and Barker (1994) found that rich context of a technology environment can provide the incentive required to invite at-risk students into literacy experiences. The study noted that technology encourages at-risk students to persist at reading and writing by evoking self-interest and self-motivation. Miller (1993) found that students who seem passive and lethargic in conventional classroom settings may virtually come alive in the ENFI (Electronic Network For Information) environment. Smith (1992) studied a project designed to increase the historically low reading performance of Native American students. The project created a hypertext computer reading program to sensitively address Navajo learning styles and cultural content. Other studies explored how programs like MOST (Multimedia Environments that Organize and Support Text) from Vanderbilt's Learning Technology Center attempt to accelerate children's learn by organizing instruction around visually rich, meaningful "macrocontexts" that enhance student motivation. These literacy initiatives and research programs advance a theoretical case that context-specific learning activities will enhance learner motivation.

Several studies have highlighted how heightened motivation in a technological environment can increase the sense of efficacy of students diagnosed with learning disabilities. Cutler and Truss (1989) investigated a program designed to help junior high school remedial reading students increase their reading motivation by immediately providing definitions for unknown words. The study concluded that the program helps to increase students' reading rates and actively engages students in reading novels. Another study (Elkins, 1986) found that learners with writing and spelling difficulties who used word processing and spell-checking programs were motivated to become more independent writers.

Although the evidence suggests that technology environments can be more motivating than conventional environments, we still know very little about what specific factors contribute to levels of heightened motivation in the technology environment. Further, it was suggested that the motivational value of many computer learning activities may actually harm student learning (Balajthy, 1989; Postman, 1995). Others attributed the "motivational bounce" that comes with technology use to the novelty value (Schofield, 1997) of the experience. This line of consideration suggests that as computers continue to become more commonly used by learners, the "motivational bounce" derived from the nonroutine experience will dissipate. Lastly, further research that distinguishes between the approaches that attempt to motivate through fun, glitzy, arcade-like edutainment and those initiatives that attempt to increase motivation by focusing on authentic, educative work seems to be necessary in the future.

COMPUTERS AND COLLABORATION

As the role of technology in literacy instruction becomes more prominent, the social milieu of the classroom and the interactional processes between learners and teacher will undergo change. Intrator and Kamil (1998) noted that research that has explored the role and impact of technology on literacy communities and on social interaction in the classroom has increased in the last 3 years. These studies have emerged from the social constructivist tradition and focus on the interactive complexities of teaching and learning in technologically rich environments. The studies exploring the dimensions of social interactions in literacy learning fall into three categories: the effects of collaborative literacy practices in the classroom; the effects of collaborative writing in the professional environment; and the effects of technology on the interactional patterns and relationships between teachers and students.

Collaborative Literacy Practice in the Learning Environment

Eldred and Hawisher (1995) reviewed research that focused on some social aspects of composition, particularly with regard to communication among collaborative writers. They raised questions about the role of gender in light of reduced social cues in computer-mediated communication. They note that these roles may not reflect traditional models of gender interactions. More than anything else, however, they called for more extended research focusing on these issues.

A long-standing concern involving the use of the computer as a tool for learning involved the fear that learners would work in solitude and be cut off from human interaction (Schofield, 1997). Ironically, research suggests that the use of computers fosters higher levels of interaction and collaboration, particularly in the domain of writing (Bump, 1990; Dickinson, 1986; Hawkins Sheingold, Gearhart, & Berger, 1982; Mehan, Moll, & Riel, 1985).

Dickinson's (1986) study of the writing program of a first–second-grade classroom showed that collaborative work at the computer created a new social organization that affected interactional patterns. He found that during normal individual writing assignments, students rarely spoke to each other; however, during collaborative computer writing, students spoke to each other about plans, revision, and issues of meaning and style.

Other studies have found that the variety and complexity of language use increased during collaborative writing projects on the computer. Kent and Rakestraw (1994) studied two first-grade boys interacting during writing with the computer. They concluded that the computer was a valuable tool for facilitating complex language use. Gonzalez-Edfelt's (1990) study of limited English speakers discovered that the quantity and quality of oral discourse were raised during collaborative computer activities.

Still other studies have shown that collaborative work with computers can improve the error monitoring of handicapped students (Hine, Goldman, & Cosden, 1990). The potential for collaborative writing projects to include an authentic audience for the task also increased the quality of student work.

Two promising lines of research have looked beyond global characterizations of the amount of interaction and systematically identified interaction components. Allen and Thompson (1995) found that when fifth graders knew they would be sending their writing to outside readers who gave prompt responses, there was a positive effect on the quality of writing.

Forman (1990) investigated the interactional dynamics of the computer-supported group work of student project teams. Powerful individuals—experts and advocates—determined how the groups used technology to support their group writing. This demonstrates the need for care in constituting collaborative groups.

Studies in the college classroom have found that technology use also alters the patterns of social interaction. Gruber's (1995) study of asynchronous communication in the classroom context found that patterns of social interaction were significantly altered by the use of networked computers. Bump's (1990) study of freshman and senior English literature students and graduate humanities students tested a synchronous local area computer network and found that the advantages of computer-assisted classroom discussion far outweighed disadvantages. Advantages included greater student participation and a sense of liberation among minority students. Romano's (1993) observational study similarly found that computer-networked composition provided conditions that allowed egalitarian narrative to flourish. Warschauer's (1995–1996) study of computer-mediated communication found more equal participation among students by comparing face-to-face and electronic discussion. Findings revealed a tendency toward more equal participation in the computer mode. They also used more lexically and syntactically formal language in electronic than in face-to-face discussion.

A series of studies that explored collaborative literacy practices in the classroom emerged from Gallaudet University's Electronic Networks for Interaction (ENFI) project, which began in 1985. ENFI was designed to allow computers to simulate spoken conversation and allow deaf people to directly experience and participate in a live group discussion of English (Batson, 1993b). Most of the studies point to positive developments in the patterns of social interaction around writing. However, several studies have highlighted ways that collaborative work in technology environments occasionally results in interactions that do not approximate what is normally considered literate discourse. Kremers (1990) observed that students often engage in off-topic and confused discussion. In a reflective research piece about his own classroom, Miller (1993) warned that the medium can occasionally encourages inappropriate "flaming" that results in "cheap shots" and criticism. Miller and Olson (1995) found that some teachers often allowed students to work on programs with little supervision, and overlooked miseducative "mouse wars" between paired students. Kumpulainen (1996) explored the quality of primary-student language during the process of collaborative writing with the word processor. She discovered that children's verbal interactions were highly task related, procedural, and bound by context. Very little exploratory talk was found.

The variable nature of these findings suggests the need for extensive work to understand how instructional practices should be designed to maximize collaborative learning in technology environments.

Collaborative Literacy Practice in the Professional Environment

The second set of studies explored how collaborative literacy practices affect professional environments. Plowman (1993) attempted to understand the process of collaborative writing by investigating the transcripts from a group of five authors working closely with a text. Plowman argued that the different modes of talk (procedural, executive, or substantive) would be exceedingly difficult to reproduce if face-to-face social interaction were replaced by electronic mediums. Writing about management training, McConnell (1997) pointed out that gender issues in interaction patterns in online group work become an issue and that participants must be careful about overloading the group with information.

Researchers writing for business publications have examined the effects of computer use on collaborative processes in workplace settings. Although many of these studies were done with MBA (master's degree in business administration) students, the implications generated were intended for those concerned with communication in the workplace. Some studies focused on how collaborative processes mediated by technology could increase quality of presentation. Sormunen and Ray (1996) ran an experiment that compared the use of face-to-face collaboration with collaborations using group systems software. Posttest performance was significantly higher for both groups, but software users had significantly higher performance on the content and organization components of writing. Forman (1990) studied the performance of novice strategic report writers and novice users of technology that supported group writing. She highlighted how unfamiliarity with technologically supported collaborative writing processes could amplify uncertainty around new tasks in the business environment. Mabrito (1992) explored how business documents collaboratively planned over electronic mail enhanced the collaborative process.

Teacher–Learner Interactions

Many researchers have predicted that, despite the promising rhetoric about technology's potential for driving innovative practice in the classroom, dominant cultural beliefs about teaching, learning, and proper knowledge will inhibit computer use and deter shifts in both practice and in teacher-student relationships (Cuban, 1986, 1993; Oppenheimer, 1997). This category of studies has explored changing dynamics of interaction between teachers and learners when technology is a central tool in the practice. These studies have examined effects involving a shift in the teacher's role from the conductor of whole-class instruction to interacting with individual students or with small groups (Hativa, Shapira, & Navon, 1990; Schofield, 1997).

Burnett's (1986) exploration of the writing process of elementary school students found that teacher–student writing conferences involved more sophisticated interactions when a word processor was used, and this difference may have explained the enhanced writing of the word-processed compositions. Phenix and Hannan (1984) reported that when word processors were used the frequency of teacher–student conferences increased. Other studies have reported that the teacher's role and pattern of interaction with students underwent little change with the infusion of computers into their literacy practices. Michaels (1986) observed that in the two primary classrooms she researched, the organization and pacing of instruction changed very little once word processing methods, programs, and instruction were introduced.

In the college environment, Batson (1993b) described changes in the interactional pattern between student and teacher as the *horizontality* of the ENFI classroom and suggested that online interactivity literally and figuratively levels the traditional hierarchical teacher-student relationship. He found that the tension between verticality and hierarchiality was more acute in the writing classroom where developing a sense of audience for one's writing was critical (Batson, 1993a). D'Agostino and Varone (1991) described a classroom research project that explored verbal response to on-screen student texts and considered how teachers could work more effectively with basic writers in a computer classroom where writing practice and oral feedback were emphasized. Hartman (1991) examined the effects of computer network technologies on teacher–student and student–student interactions. The study found that teachers in networked sections interacted more with their students than did teachers in regular sections and that these teachers communicated more electronically with less able students than with more able students. Palmquist's (1993) study of two sections of an introductory composition course found that students used the network to collaborate with professors in different ways, including submitting unsolicited rough drafts to the instructor and discussing course-related concerns.

SOME RECURRENT PROBLEMS

We have yet to come to grips with a few older problems that seem to have been neglected, but that still have important consequences. One of these is reading at computer screens compared to reading hard copy. There is a pervasive feeling that reading at a computer screen is less comfortable than reading from a page. This particular problem has a long history, although it seems to have been neglected recently. In short, the older conclusion is that reading at a computer screen is slower and less efficient (in terms of comprehension or proofreading) than reading from hard copy (Gould & Grischkowsky, 1984; Haas & Hayes, 1985). Although there is some counterevidence (e.g., Gambrell, Bradley, & McLaughlin, 1987; Reinking, 1988), current interpretations suggest that reading at a computer screen is less efficient than from hard copy (Kamil & Lane, 1998; Neilsen, 1998). Some evidence suggests that higher resolution screens may, in fact, alleviate these problems (Gould & Grischkowsky, 1984; Haas & Hayes, 1985;

Neilsen, 1998). This is a critical research issue given the new versions of electronic books being brought to market, as well as proposals to replace textbooks with laptop computers.

A second unresolved problem is what we can use the computer to teach in reading and writing. Current research largely ignores the traditional questions about the effects on achievement of teaching reading by computer. In the past, it has clearly been shown that there were effects, often fairly substantial (Niemiec, 1987; Niemiec & Walberg, 1985). Although the trend in using computers has been to emphasize less comprehensive programs, there does seem to be evidence that teaching by computer raises achievement.

Coupled with the issue of how effective computers can be in teaching reading is the more general question of the cost-effectiveness of computers for teaching reading. This was an intense area of concern in the late 1980s (Levin, Glass, & Meister, 1987; Levin & Meister, 1986; Niemiec & Walberg, 1986). Now that computers have become far more powerful and far cheaper, the cost-effectiveness should be even greater. This has not been a concern of current research or implementation, even though there are often promises of improved achievement as a result of computer usage (see, e.g., Forcier, 1995; Mendels, 1998).

For special populations, the notion of cost-effectiveness may be very different. Some nontechnological instructional environments may be very costly because a low student-to-teacher ratio is required. For these environments, computer technology can be cost-effective. In other applications, only computers can fulfill certain assistive functions. In these cases, cost-effectiveness considerations may not be meaningful. There is simply no other way to achieve the desired ends.

CONCLUSIONS: THE FUTURE

We view the research on other technologies and literacy as a tapestry under construction. The warp and woof of the fabric have not yet entirely come together. Rather, we have bits and pieces of an overall design. It is important that the lacunae be filled in if we are ever to make substantial progress in the application of other technologies to literacy.

We have shown that, despite the paucity of research, there are clear areas in which one can currently make confident conclusions. We have elaborated on six of these: writing and composition, hypermedia, multimedia, work with special populations, motivation, and collaboration. We feel that there is even greater potential in the application of other technologies to literacy.

What is the future likely to bring? First, there will be increasing pressure to produce implementations for literacy. There seems to be a groundswell of public opinion supporting the use of computers in education. Despite the contrary opinions about the efficacy of computers (e.g., Cuban, 1986; Oppenheimer, 1997; Wenglinsky, 1998), there are already many uses for computers in literacy and literacy instruction. What we need is programmatic research—research that will allow the discovery of transferable *principles*, not context-specific information. We may not see dramatic changes in the rate of adoption and integration in the reading curriculum until such research demonstrates the efficacy of computer technology for reading instruction.

Although some may argue (e.g., Leu, this volume) that the technology changes too rapidly to conduct research, we see no reason to assume that research must be so closely identified with technological change. We suggest that the underlying principles of obtaining meaning from text will not and simply cannot change as rapidly as either hardware or software. It is relatively unimportant whether text is presented on a screen driven by a 100- or a 300-MHZ processor, or whether students use an ergonomic or conventional keyboard, for example. What is far more important is how the text is laid out on a screen or how the ancillary aids to understanding are brought to the reader. Also critical is the need for more research on the interaction between and among students, teachers, and computers. These are elements that do not change with anything like the rapidity of hardware product cycles.

Because of the low installed base of users for many literacy applications, we may have to learn to answer questions through the use of formative experiments (see, e.g., Reinking & Watkins, 1996). This approach seeks to ask questions about how many resources are required to produce a given result, rather than questions about whether an intervention works. This approach is most suitable to answer the sorts of questions we have in a rapidly changing technology environment.

We found little research on what we consider to be some important, cutting-edge topics: the use of voice recognition technology instead of manual keyboarding; voice recognition as part of reading instructional software; the use of smaller, alternative computing devices; or the use of portable electronic books (see, e.g., Neilsen, 1998). Voice recognition is a vital necessity if software is to be useful in teaching oral reading. We believe these are important developments near the horizon of technology implementation. Concerted, programmatic research and conceptualization are required if pedagogical needs are to drive the market rather than technological capabilities.

A particularly crucial (and largely unresearched) area is that of curricular integration. That is, we need to determine optimal combinations of other technology and conventional literacy instruction. We need research in ways to make implementation of technology appropriate, useful, and beneficial for students and teachers. Above all, we need ways to demonstrate that value can be added to the curriculum if other technologies are brought to bear on literacy.

All of these may require new research areas in alternative forms of assessment to examine, for example, the effects of multimedia technology on literacy. The combination of text and graphics represents special challenges for which we have little or no guidance from the research literature. The popularity of multimedia applications makes this line of research crucial

We also believe that the adaptive nature of software has been largely untapped. This is partially due to the state of the general technology of instruction. As we come to specify teaching and instruction in sufficient detail, we will develop "smarter" software that will adapt to the student. This may be even more critical for special populations.

Finally, we believe that we need to know more about the interactions of users with other technologies. That is, we need to know what the effect of simply *using* other technologies has on literacy. Questions of engagement, self-efficacy, and cognitive strategies seem to be most urgent.

We have a long way to go before the tapestry is filled in and the promise of the original application of computer technology to reading (Atkinson & Hansen, 1966–1967) is brought to complete fruition. We also believe that this will happen as other technologies become more adaptable. It is also important that these issues become part of the mainstream, lest they be determined by noneducational influences.

REFERENCES

Allen, G., & Thompson, A. (1995). Analysis of the effect of networking on computer-situated collaboration writing in a fifth-grade classroom. *Journal of Educational Computing Research, 12,* 65–76.

Anderson-Inman, L. (1991). Enabling students with learning disabilities: Insights from research. *Computing Teacher, 8,* 26–29.

Anderson-Inman, L., & Horney, M. (1998). Transforming text for at-risk readers. In D. Reinking, M. McKenna, L. Labbo, & R. Kieffer (Eds.), *Handbook of literacy and technology: transformations in a post-typographic world* (pp. 323–341). Mahwah, NJ: Lawrence Erlbaum Associates.

Atkinson, R., & Hansen, D. (1966–1967). Computer-assisted instruction in initial reading: The Stanford project. *Reading Research Quarterly, 2,* 5–26.

Baer, V. E. H. (1988). Computers as composition tools: A case study of student attitudes. *Journal of Computer-Based Instruction, 15,* 144–148.

Balajthy, E. (1989). *Computers and reading: Lessons from the past and the technologies of the future.* Englewood Cliffs, NJ: Prentice Hall.

Bangert-Drowns, R. (1993). The word processor as an instructional tool: A meta-analysis of word processing in writing instruction. *Review of Educational Research, 63,* 69–93.

Batson, T. (1993a). ENFI research. *Computers and Composition, 10,* 93–101.

Batson, T. (1993b). The origins of ENFI. In J. K. Peyton, B. C. Bruce, & T. Batson (Eds.), *Network-based classrooms: Promises and realities* (pp. 87–105). Cambridge: Cambridge University Press.

Beach, R., & Lundell, D. (1998). Early adolescents' use of computer-mediated communication in writing and reading. In D. Reinking, M. McKenna, L. Labbo, & R. Kieffer (Eds.), *Handbook of literacy and technology: Transformations in a post-typographic world* (pp. 323–341). Mahwah, NJ: Lawrence Erlbaum Associates.

Becker, D., & Dwyer, M. M. (1994). Using hypermedia to provide learner control. *Journal of Educational Multimedia and Hypermedia, 3,* 155–172.

Boone, R., Higgins, K., Notari, A., & Stump, C. S. (1996). Hypermedia pre-reading lessons: Learner-centered software for kindergarten. *Journal of Computing in Childhood Education, 7,* 39–70.

Bump, J. (1990). Radical changes in class discussion using networked computers. *Computers and the Humanities, 24,* 49–65.

Burnett, J. (1986). *Word processing as a writing tool of an elementary school student.* Unpublished doctoral dissertation, University of Maryland, College Park.

Chen, C., & Rada, R. (1996). Interacting with hypertext: A meta-analysis of experimental studies. *Human Computer Interaction, 11,* 125–156.

Clark, R. E. (1983). Reconsidering research on learning from media. *Review of Educational Research, 53,* 445–459.

Clark, R. E. (1994). Media will never influence learning. *Educational Technology Research and Development, 42,* 21–29.

Cochran-Smith, M. (1991). Word processing and writing in elementary classrooms: A critical review of related literature. *Review of Educational Research, 61,* 107–155

Cuban, L. (1986). *Teachers and machines: The classroom use of technology since 1920.* New York: Teachers College Press.

Cuban, L. (1993). Computers meet classroom: Classroom wins. *Teachers College Record, 95,* 185–210.

Cutler, R. B., & Truss, C. V. (1989). Computer aided instruction as a reading motivator. *Reading Improvement, 26,* 103–109.

D'Agostino, K., & Varone, S. D. (1991). Interacting with basic writers in the computer classroom. *Computers and Composition, 8,* 39–49.

Daiute, C. (1983). *Writing and computers.* Reading, MA: Addison Wesley.

Daiute, C. (1986). Physical and cognitive factors in revising: Insights from studies with computers. *Research in the Teaching of English, 20,* 141–159.

Daiute, C., & Kruideneir, J. (1985). A self-questioning strategy to increase young writers' revising processes. *Applied Psycholinguistics, 6,* 307–318.

Dickinson, D. K. (1986). Cooperation, collaboration, and a computer: Integrating a computer into a first-second grade writing program. *Research in the Teaching of English, 20,* 357–378.

Eldred, J. C., & Hawisher, G. E. (1995). Researching electronic networks. *Written Communication, 12* 330–359.

Elkins, J. (1986). Self-help for older writers with spelling and composing difficulties: Using the word processor and spelling checker. *Exceptional Child, 33,* 73–76.

Ferrier, L. J., & Shane, H. C. (1987). Computer-based communication aids for the nonspeaking child with cerebral palsy. *Seminars in Speech & Language, 8,* 107–122.

Flood, J., & Lapp, D. (1995). Broadening the lens: Toward an expanded conceptualization of literacy. In K. A. Hinchman, D. J. Leu, & C. K. Kinzer (Eds.), *Perspectives on literacy research and practice: Forty-fourth yearbook of the National Reading Conference* (pp. 1–16). Chicago: National Reading Conference.

Forcier, R. C. (1995). *The computer as a productivity tool in education.* Paramus, NJ: Prentice Hall.

Forman, J. (1990). Leadership dynamics of computer-supported writing. *Computers and Composition, 7,* 35–46.

Gambrell, L., Bradley, V., & McLaughlin, E. (1987). Young children's comprehension and recall of computer screen displayed text. *Journal of Research in Reading, 10,* 156–163.

Gillingham, M. (1993). Effects of question complexity and reader strategies on adults' hypertext comprehension. *Journal of Research on Computing in Education, 26,* 1–15.

Gonzalez-Edfelt, N. (1990). Oral interaction and collaboration at the computer. *Computers in the Schools, 7,* 53–90.

Gould, J., & Grischkowsky, N. (1984). Doing the same work with hardcopy and with CRT terminals. *Human Factors, 26,* 323–337.

Greenlee-Moore, M. E., & Smith, L. L. (1996). Interactive computer software: The effects on young children's reading achievement. *Reading Psychology, 12,* 43–64.

Gruber, S. (1995). Re: Ways we contribute: Students, instructors and pedagogies in the computer-mediated writing classroom. *Computers and Composition, 12*, 61–78.

Haas, C., & Hayes, J. (1985). *Reading on the computer: A comparison of standard and advanced computer display and hardcopy* (CDC Tech. Rep. No. 7.) Pittsburgh, PA: Carnegie-Mellon University, Communications Design Center.

Hague, S. A., & Mason, G. (1986). Using the computers readability measure to teach students to revise their writing. *Journal of Reading, 30*, 14–17.

Hartman, K. (1991). Patterns of social interaction and learning to write: Some effects of network technologies. *Written Communication, 8*, 79–113.

Hativa, N., Shapira, R., & Navon, D. (1990). Computer-managed practice: Effects on instructional methods and teacher adoption. *Teacher and Teacher Education, 6*, 55–68.

Hawisher, G., LeBlanc, P., Moran, C., & Selfe, C. (1996). *Computers and the teaching of writing in American higher education, 1979–1994: A history.* Norwood, NJ: Ablex.

Hawkins, J., Sheingold, K., Gearhart, M., &, & Berger, C. (1982). Microcomputers in schools: Impact on the social life of elementary classrooms. *Journal of Applied Developmental Psychology, 3*, 361–373.

Hine, M., Goldman, S. R., & Cosden, M., A. (1990). Error monitoring by learning handicapped students engaged in collaborative microcomputer-based writing. *Journal of Special Education, 23*, 407–422.

Horney, M. A., & Anderson-Inman, L. (1994). The electrotext project: hypertext reading patterns of middle school students. *Journal of Educational Multimedia and Hypermedia, 3*, 71–91.

Intrator, S., & Kamil, M. L. (1998, April). *Qualitative trends in publication of research on technology and reading, writing, and literacy.* Paper presented at the annual meeting of the American Educational Research Association, San Diego, CA.

Jonassen, D., Campbell, J., & Davidson, M. (1994). Learning *with* media: Restructuring the debate. *Educational Technology Research and Development, 42*, 31–39.

Kamil, M. L. (1982). Technology and reading: A review of research and instruction. In J. Niles & L. Harris (Eds.), *New inquiries in reading research and instruction: Thirty-first yearbook of the National Reading Conference* (pp. 251–260). Rochester, NY: National Reading Conference.

Kamil, M. L. (1998, December). *A taxonomy of hypertext links.* Paper presented at the annual meeting of the National Reading Conference, Austin, TX.

Kamil, M. L., & Intrator, S. (1998). Quantitative trends in publication of research on technology and reading, writing, and literacy. In T. Shanahan & F. Rodriguez-Brown (Eds.), *National Reading Conference Yearbook 47* (pp. 385–396). Chicago: National Reading Conference.

Kamil, M. L., & Lane, D. (1998). Researching the relationship between technology and literacy: An agenda for the 21st century. In D. Reinking, M. McKenna, L. Labbo, & R. Kieffer (Eds.), *Handbook of literacy and technology: Transformations in a post-typographic world* (pp. 323–341). Mahwah, NJ: Lawrence Erlbaum Associates.

Kent, J. F., & Rakestraw, J. (1994). The role of computers in functional language: A tale of two writers. *Journal of Computing in Childhood Education, 5*, 329–337.

Kozma, R. B. (1991). Learning with media. *Review of Educational Research, 61*, 179–211.

Kozma, R. B. (1994). *Will* media influence learning? Reframing the debate. *Educational Technology Research and Development, 42*, 7–19.

Kremers, M. (1990). Sharing authority on a synchronous network: The case for riding the beast. *Computers and Composition, 7*, 69–77.

Kulik, C. C., & Kulik, J. A. (1991). Effectiveness of computer-based instruction: An updated analysis. *Computers in Human Behavior, 7*, 75–94.

Kulik, J. A., Kulik, C. C., & C., Peter A. (1980). Effectiveness of computer-based college teaching: A meta-analysis of findings. *Review of Educational Research, 50*, 525–544.

Kumpulainen, K. (1996). The nature of peer interaction in the social context created by the use of word processors. *Learning and Instruction, 6*, 243–261.

Labbo, L. D., Reinking, D., & McKenna, M. (1995). Incorporating the computer into kindergarten: A case study. In K. A. Hinchman, D. J. Leu, & C. K. Kinzer (Eds.), *Perspectives on literacy research and practice: Forty-fourth yearbook of the National Reading Conference* (pp. 459–465). Chicago: National Reading Conference.

Lepper, M., & Chabay, R. (1985). Intrinsic motivation and instruction: Conflicting views on the role of motivational processes in computer-based education. *Educational Psychologist, 20*, 217–230.

Lepper, M., & Malone, T. W. (1987). Intrinsic motivation and instructional effectiveness in computer-based education. In R. E. Snow & M. J. Farr (Eds.), *Aptitude, learning and instruction* (pp. 255–296). Hillsdale, NJ: Lawrence Erlbaum Associates.

Levin, H. M., Glass, G., & Meister, G. (1987). Cost-effectiveness of computer-assisted instruction. *Evaluation Review, 11*, 50–72.

Levin, H. M., & Meister, G. (1986). Is CAI cost-effective? *Phi Delta Kappan, 67* 745–749.

Liu, M., & Reed, W. M. (1995). The effect of hypermedia assisted instruction on second language learning. *Journal of Educational Computing Research, 12*, 159–175.

Mabrito, M. (1992). Computer-mediated communication and high-apprehensive writers: Rethinking the collaborative process. *Bulletin of the Association for Business Communication, 55*, 26–29.

MacArthur, C. A. (1998). Word processing with speech synthesis and word prediction: Effects on the dialogue journal writing of students with learning disabilities. *Learning Disability Quarterly, 21*, 151–166.

Mayer, R. (1997). Multimedia learning: Are we asking the right questions? *Educational Psychologist, 32*, 1–19.

Mayer, R. E., & Moreno, R. (1998). A split-attention effect in multimedia learning: Evidence for dual processing systems in working memory. *Journal of Educational Psychology, 90*, 312–320.

McConnell, D. (1997). Computer support for management learning. In J. Burgoyne & M. Reynolds (Ed.), *Management learning: Integrating perspectives in theory and practice* (pp. 283–294). London: Sage.

McMillan, K., & Honey, M. (1993). *Year one of project pulse: Pupils using laptops in science and English* (Tech. Rep. 26). New York: Center for Technology in Education.

Mehan, H., Moll, L., & Riel, M.M. (1985). *Computers in classrooms: A quasi-experiment in guided change* (Final report NIE 6-83-0027). San Diego: University of California.

Mendels, P. (1998, April 27). U.S. official calls for studies of technology in classrooms. *The New York Times on the Web* [Online]. Available: http://home.earthlink.net/~aske/education/technology1.htm

Michaels, S. (1986, April). *Computer as dependent variable*. Paper presented at the annual meetings of the American Educational Research Association, San Francisco, CA.

Miller, J. D. (1993). Script writing on computer network: Quenching the flames or feeding the fire. In J. Kreeft Peyton, B. C. Bruce, & T. Batson (Eds.), *Network-based classrooms: Promises and realities* (pp. 124–137). Cambridge: Cambridge University Press.

Miller, L., & Olson, J. (1995). How computers live in schools. *Educational Leadership, 53*, 74–77.

Montague, M. (1990). *Computers cognition, and writing instruction*. Albany, NY: State University of New York Press.

Neilsen, J. (1998). Electronic books—A bad idea. *The Alertbox: Current Issues in Web Usability* [Online]. Available: http://www.useit.com/alertbox/980726.html

Nelson, K. E., & Camarata, S. M. (1996). Improving English literacy and speech-acquisition learning conditions for children with severe to profound hearing impairments. *Volta Review, 98*, 17–41.

Neuman, S. (1991). *Literacy in the television age*. Norwood, NJ: Ablex.

Niemiec, R. P. (1987). Comparative effects of computer-assisted instruction: A synthesis of reviews. *Journal of Educational Computing Research, 3*, 19–37.

Niemiec, R. P., & Walberg, H. J. (1985). Computers and achievement in the elementary schools. *Journal of Educational Computing Research, 1*, 435–440.

Niemiec, R. P., & Walberg, H. J. (1986). CAI can be doubly effective. *Phi Delta Kappan, 67*, 750–751.

Oppenheimer, T. (1997, July). The computer delusion. *Atlantic Monthly*, pp. 45–62.

Paivio, A. (1986). *Mental representations: A dual coding approach*. Oxford: Oxford University Press.

Palmquist, M. (1993). Network-supported interaction in two writing classes. *Computers and Composition, 10*, 25–53.

Papert, S. (1980). *Mindstorms*. Cambridge, MA: MIT Press.

Phenix, J., & Hannan, E. (1984). Word processing in the grade one classroom. *Language Arts, 61*, 804–812.

Plass, J. L., Chun, D. M., Mayer, R. E., & Leutner, D. (1998). Supporting visual and verbal learning preferences in a second-language multimedia learning environment. *Journal of Educational Psychology, 90*, 25–36.

Plowman, L. (1993). Tracing the evolution of co-authored text. *Language and Communication, 13*, 149–161.

Postman, N. (1995). *The end of education*. New York: Alfred Knopf.

Purves, A. C. (1998). *The web of text and the web of god: An essay on the third information transformation*. New York: Guilford Press

Raskind, M. H., & Higgins, E. L. (1995). Special issue: Technology for persons with learning disabilities. *Learning Disability Quarterly, 18*, 141–158.

Reinking, D. (1988). Computer-mediated text and comprehension differences: The role of reading time, reader preference, and estimation of learning. *Reading Research Quarterly, 23*, 484–498.

Reinking, D. (1995). Reading and writing with computers: Literacy research in a post-typographic world. In K. Hinchman, D. Leu, & C. Kinzer (Eds.), *Perspectives on literacy research and practice* (pp. 17–33). Chicago: National Reading Conference.

Reinking, D. (1998). Introduction: Synthesizing technological transformations of literacy in a post-typographic world. In D. Reinking, M. McKenna, L. Labbo, & R. Kieffer (Eds.), *Handbook of Literacy and Technology* (pp. xi–xxx). Mahwah, NJ: Lawrence Erlbaum Associates.

Reinking, D., & Bridwell-Bowles, L. (1991). Computers in reading and writing. In R. Barr, M. L. Kamil, P. Mosenthal, & P. D. Pearson (Eds.), *Handbook of Reading Research* (Vol. II, pp. 310–340). New York: Longman.

Reinking, D., McKenna, M., Labbo, L., and Kieffer, R. (Eds.). (1998). *Handbook of literacy and technology: Transformations in a post-typographic world*. Mahwah, NJ: Lawrence Erlbaum Associates.

Reinking, D., & Watkins, J. (1996). *A formative experiment investigating the use of multimedia book reviews to increase elementary students' independent reading* (Reading Research Rep. No. 55). National Reading Research Center, University of Georgia, Athens.

Rice, G. (1994). Examining constructs in reading comprehension using two presentation modes: Paper vs. computer. *Journal of Educational Computer Research, 11*, 153–178

Romano, S. (1993). The egalitarianism narrative: Whose story? Which yardstick? *Computers and Composition, 10*, 5–28.

Rouet, J., Levonen, J., Dillon, A., & Spiro, R. (Eds.). (1996). *Hypertext and cognition.* Hillsdale, NJ: Lawrence Erlbaum Associates.

Schofield, J. W. (1997). Computers and classroom social processes—A review of the literature. *Social Science Computer Review, 15*, 27–39.

Scott, D., Kahlich, P., & Barker, J. (1994). Motivating at-risk students using a literature based writing unit with computers. *Journal of Computing in Childhood Education, 5*, 311–317.

Shanahan, T., & Kamil, M. (1994). *Academic libraries and research in the teaching of English.* Champaign, IL: National Conference on Research in English and Center for the Study of Reading.

Sharp, D. L. M., Bransford, J. D., Goldman, S. R., Risko, V., Kinzer, C., & Vye, N. (1995). Dynamic visual support for story comprehension and mental model building by young, at-risk children. *Educational Technology Research & Development, 43*, 25–42.

Sheingold, K., Kane, J. H., & Endreweit, M.E. (1983). Microcomputer use in schools: Developing a research agenda. *Harvard Educational Review, 4*, 412–432.

Smith, K. (1992). Using multimedia with Navajo children: An effort to alleviate problems of cultural learning style, background of experience, and motivation. *Reading & Writing Quarterly: Overcoming Learning Difficulties, 8*, 287–294.

Snyder, I. (1993). The impact of computers on students' writing: A comparative study of the effects of pens and word processors on writing context, process and product. *Australian Journal of Education, 37*, 5–25.

Sormunen, C., & Ray, C. (1996). Teaching collaborative writing with group support systems software—An experiment. *Delta Pi Epsilon Journal, 38*, 125–138.

Spache, G. (1967). Reading technology. In G. Schick & M. May (Eds.), *Junior college and adult reading programs—Expanding fields: Sixteenth yearbook of the National Reading Conference* (pp. 178–184). Milwaukee, WI: National Reading Conference.

Steelman, J. D., Pierce, P. L., & Koppenhaver, D. A. (1993). The role of computers in promoting literacy in children with severe speech and physical impairments (SSPI). *Topics in Language Disorders, 13*, 76–88.

Warschauer, M. (1995–1996). Comparing face-to-face and electronic discussion in the second language classroom. *CALICO Journal, 13*, 7–25.

Wenglinsky, H. (1998). *Does it compute? The relationship between educational technology and student achievement in mathematics.* Policy Information Reports. Princeton, NJ: ETS Policy Information Center.

Woodward, J., & Rieth, H. (1997). A historical review of technology research in special education. *Review of Educational Research, 67*, 503–536.

PART V

Literacy Policies

CHAPTER 41

Second-Language Reading as a Case Study of Reading Scholarship in the 20th Century

Elizabeth B. Bernhardt
Stanford University

This chapter discusses the conflation of factors surrounding the concept of *second- language reading*. Indeed, the term *second-language reading* signifies different phenomena depending on the context in which the term is used. If one chooses to emphasize *reading*, then the term may refer to the interesting role that second languages have played as contributors to early *theories of reading*. At the same time, at the level of practice, the single purpose frequently cited for learning a second language is for *reading* it. Or, at the research level, the term may signify the process of *reading* in a language other than the mother tongue. If one chooses to emphasize the first part of the term, *second language*, other images are evoked. At the level of policy, the term may signify much of what became critical problems for public school educators, mainly reading educators, centered on the notion of immigrant children learning to read in English, their *second language*. Or, at the level of practice, the term may refer to the principle *vehicle* for learning a second language—*reading material*. At the level of research, the term may evoke notions of cross-lingual comparisons. Yet another dimension to the term is that of *language*. In the notoriously monolingual Anglophone world *language* is frequently synonymous with *English* and, therefore, *second language* refers to all languages other than English. This monolingualism, that is, English-language monolingualism, is such a dominant dimension in the Anglophone world that it is often difficult to get even the most astute scholars to think about the world in ways other than with an Anglophone view. Scholarship on language planning, referring to concepts such as linguistic imperialism (Phillipson, 1992; Tollefson, 1991), and on multiculturalism (McKay & Weinstein-Shr, 1993), documents this construction. Whatever the emphasis or whichever component is chosen for foregrounding, it is clear that all of these significations conflate to form a diverse, complicated, and frustrating landscape to traverse, let alone explain or predict.

"Reading" as a field of scholarly inquiry contains interesting reflections of the multiple meanings of *second-language reading* as a part of the Anglophone world. "Reading scholarship" by and large exists in the English-speaking world of North America, England, Israel, Australia and New Zealand. The only real exception to this overgeneralization is reading scholarship in the Netherlands. The French and the Russians, who have had such an influence on literary reading and on late-20th-century text interpretation (e.g., Bahktin, 1981; Foucault, 1972) and the Spanish and the Germans, too, have no concept of reading (as in "learning to read") other than in the sense of reading difficulty and disability (Biglmaier, 1991). This chapter considers the extent to which these factors, Anglophilia in particular, have contributed to the construction of the field of reading and to reading research in the 20th century.

THE HISTORICAL ROLE OF SECOND-LANGUAGE READING IN READING RESEARCH, PRACTICE, AND POLICY

Second Language and Early Reading Research

Reading research, in its earliest inception, actually acknowledged reading in languages other than "the vernacular" as an important dimension of investigations into the reading process. Javal (1878) and Cattell (1886) each used foreign words in their studies on perception in the reading process. They found that the reading of a foreign language text was more cognitively fatiguing than the reading of a native language text. In the same time period, Huey (1909) cited the work of Erdmann and Dodge (1898), working in Germany, which uncovered similar evidence. By the close of the 19th century, it was generally accepted knowledge that foreign language reading is a case of effortful reading even among highly literate adult subjects.

Huey (1909) used foreign language reading as examples and counterexamples to illustrate the psychology of reading. In a general explanation of the reading process, one eerily predictive of several late-20th-century findings, he stated:

> Our words are thoroughly organized according to these general associative habits of our language, and when any given series has occurred in our reading, the sort of words and the sentence forms that belong in sequence with these are subexcited in advance of their appearance on the page, and need but slight cues from the page to cause them to spring into perpetual consciousness. (p. 142)

> That the general meaning dawns upon the reader precedent to the full sentence-utterance is evidenced by the many cases in which variant words of equivalent meaning are read, and also by the comparative ease with which a reader may paraphrase the thought of what he reads. This is especially noticeable in the case of a person reading a foreign language which he does not pronounce easily but which he comprehends rather rapidly. Here the visual word and the phrase precepts touch off total meanings which clothe themselves, as the meanings become articulate, in English sentences, and we have as a result the mongrel reading which passes for French or German in so many modern language classes. (p. 148)

In the final section of *The Psychology and Pedagogy of Reading*, Huey turns to issues of curricular time, arguing that reading research will contribute to efficiency. In this arena, too, he uses the example of foreign language learning, writing that "the learning of foreign languages, ancient or modern, will in many quarters undergo considerable revision in the direction of economy, when the facts are clearly grasped as to what constitutes the essence of natural reading" (p. 428). This is an interesting concern on the part of Huey given that, as this chapter argues, that concern virtually disappeared from reading research in the century that followed.

It did not disappear, however, without capturing the attention of two additional reading researchers, Judd and Buswell, who might be considered precursors of the modernist-psychological view of reading. In the justification for their watershed work on investigating silent reading as a viable means of reading instruction, Judd and Buswell (1922) noted: "It was the purpose of this investigation to deal with the foreign languages as examples of reading for the purpose of throwing light on the general psychological and educational character of the reading process." They continued, "let it be said explicitly that this is an inquiry into reading. … it deals with these languages as specimens" (p. 91).

Judd and Buswell were intent on understanding the subprocesses involved in reading silently for comprehension and for examining "reading attitude," meaning different dispositions toward text with regard to reading purpose and text type. They contrast the "mechanical approach" (p. 4) of the "grammatical attitude" (p. 5) with an active approach. They summarized their work with:

> A printed page turns out to be, as shown by this study, a source of a mass of impressions which the active mind begins to organize and arrange with reference to some pattern which it is trained to work out. … Given a printed book, a pair of eyes, an active brain, and it is assumed that whatever associations are being set up must be of the same general type as those set up when a book printed in the vernacular is similarly held before eyes and active brain. The fact is that a great variety of results can issue from the coming together of books, eyes, and brains. (pp. 4–5)

In fact, the main conclusion to the second-language dimension of the study was indeed that

> most of the pupils who have had a corresponding amount [three years] of French show characteristic symptoms of reading, although their reading is of a labored type. … mature foreign-language records show that a foreign language can be read in a manner directly comparable to the reading of the vernacular … the manner of reading is fundamentally the same. (p. 91)

In the study, Judd and Buswell contended there were significant differences between the reading of French and Latin; French showed characteristic symptoms of reading, and Latin did not. They noted, for example, "that in no case does a third-year student of the best grade in seven high schools in and around Chicago read Latin" (p. 91). Perhaps further archival research would reveal additional agendas behind their work. In the policy implications section of their report on the Chicago public schools, Judd and Buswell noted that the continuation of Latin in the schools is "preposterous" (p. 156) and seemed to conceive of the learning of French as school time relatively well spent.

One wonders, of course, that if the Judd–Buswell investigation was purely about reading, what actually motivated the vociferous attack on the learning of Latin? Judd and Buswell were highly visible advocates of a scientific approach to solving educational problems. Perhaps they simply wanted to begin pushing the educators making curriculum recommendations to base them on laboratory studies. Judd and Buswell were reflections of their own time, and their writings are clear artifacts of particular views of public schooling.

Second Language and the Early Phase of American Public Education

Languages other than English in the American school curriculum have a history as old as the curriculum itself. Major figures in American intellectual history such as Franklin, Jefferson, and Webster all weighed in on the issue as a part of the Puritan legacy. The Puritans, "although proud of unrestricted immigration, … wanted to ensure that such diversity would not destroy what … was freedom's prototype. To overcome the heterogeneity that they feared threatened the unity and example of their country, they relied on education" (Carlson, 1975, p. 4). Puritan education focused on Protestant-based values and systems and dismissed as damnable (literally) and anti-Christian any alternative views. The Puritans were so focused on complete acceptance of their lifestyle that they held no compunction about massacring native peoples or of stockading even clergy whom they suspected of some degree of disloyalty. Acceptance and "the imperious quest for conformity" (Carlson, 1975, p. 11), characterized the 17th-century legacy handed to the Founders.

The Puritan legacy of "educating for homogeneity" (Carlson, 1975, p. 14)—based as it was on a religious agenda—found its way into the 18th century as part of a secular political agenda embodied most clearly, but not exclusively, by Franklin (Carlson, 1975). In the guise of providing intellectual leadership, Franklin, for example, opened charity schools for German immigrants. The express purpose, however, was to eliminate the German language and German mentality from the colonies. Franklin considered the English system far superior. Franklin's writings also contain generally disparaging comments about students wasting time learning modern languages "often without Success" (Labaree, 1961, p. 108).

It is, of course, true that other Founders such as Jefferson and Webster were not completely hostile to the notion of the learning of languages. Jefferson called for modern languages in his 1817 curriculum (Jefferson, 1955). Webster also included the study of modern languages other than English in his interest in vocational study (Rudolph, 1965). Yet dominant was the spirit of a standardized American language that would not only unify the country politically, but potentially out-English the English. Both Adams (1852) and Webster (1789) underlined the critical link between national unity and linguistic unity (Rudolph, 1965). Bernhardt (1998) commented that "early America can be characterized by the dialectic between a utilitarian view of language study and the messianic establishment of American English as a manifest destiny" (p. 43).

This backdrop of the 18th and 19th centuries is particularly key in conceptualizing the relationship of second languages to American schooling and most specifically in confronting the role of second languages in reading research. Yet, it is, of course, the first 20 years of the 20th century—the American century—that make the case for the argument. These years, marked by major southern and eastern European immigrations, the American Industrial Revolution, and the First World War, critically influenced the beginnings of the public school bureaucracy.

The major political movement of the time was known as "Americanization." It became particularly strong after the First World War, in which American sentiments for fighting for the world were high and so were feelings of suspicion toward foreigners. In 1918, the U.S. Commissioner of Education referred to Americanization "as a war measure" (Report of the Commissioner of Education, 1918, p. 132).

The federal office charged with implementing Americanization programs was the Department of the Interior, due to its control over immigration matters. In a critical speech in New York City in 1919, Franklin Lane, Secretary of the Interior, laid out the philosophical groundwork of Americanization:

> There is no one thing so supremely essential in a government such as ours, where decisions of such importance must be made by public opinion, as that every man and woman and child shall know one tongue—that each may speak to every other and that all shall be informed. There can be neither national unity in ideals or in purpose unless there is some common method of communication through which may be conveyed the thought of the Nation. All Americans must be taught to read and write and *think* [emphasis from Lane] in one language; this is a primary condition to that growth which all nations expect of us, and which we demand of ourselves. (p. 11)

In order to meet this patriot demand, the Americanization Bill was forwarded to Congress in 1919. This bill called for a program in the education of "illiterates" and for persons "unable to understand, speak, read, or write in English" and in the "training and preparation of teachers, supervisors, and directors, for such educational work" (Department of the Interior, 1919, p. 3). The bill allocated $12,500,000 over 7 years for teacher salaries and an additional $750,000 over 7 years for teacher and supervisor preparation programs.

Documents such as Suggestions for Americanization Work Among Foreign-Born Women (U.S. Naturalization Bureau, 1921), books such as *Democracy and Assimilation: The Blending of Immigrant Heritages in America* (Drachsler, 1920) and *Adult Immigration Education: Its Scope, Content, and Methods* (Sharlip & Owens, 1925), and studies such as Schooling of the Immigrant (Thompson, 1920), sponsored by the Carnegie Foundation, laid out the groundwork for effective Americanization programs in educational settings. The first principle in using "the school as the chief instrument of Americanization" (Thompson, 1920, p. 1) found in any of these documents is to insure the use of English as the sole language of the classroom.

The descriptions of the receiving end of Americanization programs are generally dismal. Cavello (1958) wrote that "we soon got the idea that Italian meant something inferior, and a barrier was erected between children of Italian origin and their parents" (p. 43). Cavello's volume, a biography of an immigrant who became an educator, is a sad yet inspirational tale of the feelings surrounding the process of being "Americanized" in school. Jane Addams, in fact, concurred with Cavello's description. Addams (1930), noting the primary role of the American school in the Americanization process, indicated that

> There is a certain indictment which may be justly brought, in that the public school too often separates the child from his parents and widens that old gulf between fathers and sons which is never so cruel and so wide as it is between the immigrants who come to this country and their children who have gone to public school and feel that they have learned it all. (Lagemann, 1985, pp. 136–137)

Addams continued by arguing that while the numbers of incarcerations of immigrants were actually lower than of native-born Americans, arrests of immigrant children were twice as high as compared with the children of native-born Americans. She attributed these statistics to a failure of the schools—that the American public school was deliberately forcing a disconnection with parental values and, hence, sending children without proper guidance "into the perilous business of living" (p. 138).

Immigrant organizations themselves were caught in the dilemma of participating in Americanization and in maintaining their own identities. An excellent example is that of Jewish immigration in New York City. In the summer of 1890 the Baron de Hirsch Foundation endowed classes in English for children and adults. Although hundreds of children and adults were supported by these schools, there was significant resistance to them because many children were schooled in Jewish schools known as "cheder." Joseph (1935) indicates that "the greatest difficulty experienced by visitors [leaders of the Jewish community—E. B.] was to persuade parents to remove their children from the 'cheder', and to impress upon them that the Baron de Hirsch schools were not a scheme for weaning the children from orthodoxy" (p. 254). Also established at the time was a library (which eventually became the Seward Park Division of the New York Public Library) containing books in Hebrew and Russian (Joseph, 1935).

It would be inappropriate to interpret this portion of the essay as a political diatribe against the learning of English and in blind support of multilingualism. Immigrants arrived in America precisely to escape many of the horrors they lived with in their native countries. The price that they paid explicitly for the privilege of living in America was to be Americanized—a process that entailed the leaving behind of a culture and language. The point for this essay is to uncover the political circumstances under which second-language speakers entered American schooling and to understand that the tensions surrounding the role of second language are more than 200 years old.

CURRENT TRENDS AND ISSUES IN SECOND-LANGUAGE READING RESEARCH

Second-language reading has often been accused of being a slavish imitation of first-language reading research. In fact, in the *Second Handbook*, Weber (1991) characterized second language reading at several points in her essay as derivative: "research efforts in bilingual reading have to some extent reflected research trends in first-language reading, particularly in the turn to qualitative methods" (p. 104); "The direction of research on second-language reading in academic and laboratory settings follows recent trends in first-language reading, especially comprehension" (p. 108); "research on reading and learning to read more than one language can be seen largely as an extension of inquiry undertaken in first-language reading" (p. 114). All of these statements imply that the research area "as limited as it is" (p. 115) has failed to do little more than replicate both the tasks and the findings of first-language research based in English.

The Weber essay provides exceptional support for the Anglophilial thesis of the current essay. The word "English" is mentioned no less often than 136 times in her essay called "Linguistic Diversity and Reading in American Society"; Spanish is mentioned 31 times; French, 17; Chinese, 11; and German, Haitian Creole, Cantonese, Latin, Japanese, and Arabic in single digits. The essay, in fact, begins with "English is the paramount language of the United States" (p. 97) and ends with "The predominance of English in U.S. society is apparent from the research on reading in more than one language" (p. 114). The dictionary definition of *paramount* as "superior to all others" reflects the linguistic hegemony that characterizes the Weber essay as does the use of the word *predominant*, defined as "having superior strength, influence, or authority."

Research Syntheses, 1990–Present

Indeed, although the negative spin on the area of research in second-language reading is unfortunate, it is probably deserved: the most substantial and comprehensive review of second-language reading research (Bernhardt, 1991) indicates that topics explored in the late 1970s and the 1980s (schema theory and its attendant background knowledge issues, text structure, word recognition, etc.) are all found in the second-language reading database with relatively little that could be identified as "unique." Many studies not only committed the sins of their fathers in first language reading research, but also used exactly the same texts—only in a translated version. This has led Bernhardt to comment that a lot is known about reading texts in a second language that would never actually be read in an authentic literacy setting.

Weber separates second-language reading research into two areas: word recognition, which she decries as lacking in second-language reading research, and comprehension studies. This is a curious duality. Bernhardt (1991) described the empirical base of second-language studies (principally referring to studies that examined adolescent and adult readers—i.e., readers who generally possessed a *first* literacy) as consisting of nine categories. She acknowledged that these nine categories were constructed from theoretical models of reading such as Goodman (1968), LaBerge and Samuels (1974), and Spiro, Bruce, and Brewer (1980), as prototypic representatives of the schema-theory movement. These models, along with Coady (1979), who made the first formal statement of variables entailed in the second-language reading process, isolated *word recognition; background knowledge factors; text structure analyses; oral–aural factors; syntactic features; cross-lingual processing strategies; testing;* and *instruction.* A less extensive review published at approximately the same time provided validation for these groupings of second-language studies (Grabe, 1991). Grabe separated the field into five, rather than nine, categories: *schema theory, automaticity, vocabulary, comprehension strategies,* and *reading/writing.* Several years later, Fitzgerald (1995a, 1995b) focused her research synthesis exclusively on English in the United States, thereby eliminating a handful of studies included in Bernhardt (1991) and Grabe (1991). Her synthesis, nevertheless, delimited seven categories consistent with previous reviews. Finally, a synthesis focused explicitly on the concept of "professional reader" included five categories also consistent with previous reviews (Ulijn & Salager-Meyer, 1998).

In her synthesis, Bernhardt relied on the authors' determination of independent sets and dependent variables. As Weber pointed out, there are not many word recognition studies, yet considerably more than she cites. Bernhardt argued that the studies themselves are fairly consistent, indicating that speed of processing is indeed related to fluency and that phonological factors are key to word recognition even in languages that are nonalphabetic and considered to be more conceptual in nature (Brown & Haynes, 1985; Favreau, Komoda, & Segalowitz, 1980; Favreau & Segalowitz, 1982; Hatch, Polin, & Part, 1974; Hayes, 1988; Haynes, 1981; Koda, 1987; Meara, 1984; Walker, 1983). The *background knowledge* studies, too, reflect general findings from the first-language reading data set: The knowledge a reader brings influences comprehension, and manipulations of content can lead to differences in comprehension (Adams, 1982; Alderson & Urquhart, 1988; Campbell, 1981; Carrell, 1983, 1987; Carrell & Wallace, 1983; Connor, 1984; Hudson, 1982; Johnson, 1981, 1982; Lee, 1986; Mohammed & Swales, 1984; Nunan, 1985; Olah, 1984; Omaggio, 1979; Parry, 1987; Perkins & Angelis, 1985; Steffensen, Joag-Dev, & Anderson, 1979; Zuck & Zuck, 1984). A number of studies examined *text structure.* These studies found second-language readers sensitive to structural differences in texts (Carrell, 1984a; Cohen, Glasman, Rosenbaum-Cohen, Ferrar, & Fine, 1979; Davis, 1984; Davis, Lange, & Samuels, 1988; Flick & Anderson, 1980; Perkins, 1987; Stanley, 1984; Steffensen, 1988; Urquhart, 1984). *Aural/oral factors,* a fourth area, is diverse in its findings because this area includes any studies referring to oral reading (i.e., generally using miscue analysis) (Bernhardt, 1983; Connor, 1981; Devine, 1981, 1984; Ewoldt, 1981; Grosse & Hameyer, 1979; Hodes, 1981; Muchisky, 1983; Nehr, 1984; Neville & Pugh, 1975; Reeds, Winitz, & Garcia, 1977; Romatowski, 1981; Tatlonghari, 1984). *Syntactic factors* in second-language reading parallel a number of first language findings; syntactic complexity does not necessarily predict text difficulty for second-language readers (Barnett, 1986; Bean, Potter, & Clark, 1980; Bhatia, 1984; Guarino & Perkins, 1986; Jarvis & Jensen, 1982; Olshtain, 1982; Robbins, 1983; Strother & Ulijn, 1987). *Metacognition* and *affect* were investigated over the years in only a few studies. The studies isolated a set of strategies that are found among all readers—good readers keep the meaning of a text in mind as they read; they read in word groups; their motivation influences the types of strategies they use (Fransson, 1984; Hosenfeld, 1977; Neville, 1979; Shohamy, 1982). In summary, based on these studies, Weber is to a large extent justified in her commentary that there is considerable overlap between the first- and second-language reading databases.

Bernhardt (1991) attempted to synthesize these factors in order to get to a holistic picture of variables as they interact in the second language reading process. The synthesis was set against the backdrop of her literature review and included new data that used recall in the first language as a integrative measure of reading comprehension in a second language. That synthesis produced a developmental plot characterized as sets of curves: rapidly declining error rates in word recognition and phono-graphemic confusions over time; increasing syntactic errors that then decrease over time; and the use of background knowledge and intratextual perceptions and impressions that seemed to be unrelated to length of learning time.

Two features of the synthesis are not immediately intuitively obvious. First, the fact that syntactic errors actually increase with learning time is evidence that as learners become more sophisticated in their use of language they make more sophisticated errors. This finding is consistent with all of the language development literature—both first and second. "U-shaped" developmental patterns—correct behaviors followed by overgeneralized incorrect patterns, followed by distinguished correct patterns—are not uncommon. The second element that requires commentary involves metacognition. The synthesis revealed that knowledge and affect are linked to individual readers. Bringing knowledge to bear on some dimension of text context or choosing to respond to that text in a personal or aesthetic manner does not seem to be related to any particular learning phenomenon or to any proficiency level.

This particular statement (Fig. 41.1) of the theoretical distribution of factors involved in second-language reading was never tested. It suffers from having been generated on cognate languages (namely, French, German, and Spanish) whose structures and vocabularies are more like English than not. It was also developed using one assessment technique—recall in the first language. But, most importantly, it did *not* acknowledge what was to be discovered as the most critical variable in the second-language process—the first language (see following section). It nevertheless remains as the only fully articulated model of the second-language reading process currently published.

In the late 1990s, a number of areas remained consistent instances of research interest: *affective factors, text structure, syntactic features,* and *word knowledge* and *instruction.* A further area, relationships between *other language modalities* and reading, also emerged. Affective factors, for example, metamorphosed into an interest in literature and interpretation (Chi, 1995; Kramsch & Nolden, 1994; Davis, 1992; Davis, Caron-Gorell, Kline, & Hsieh, 1992; Tian, 1991). Chi, Kramsch and Nolden, Tian, and Davis all examined the manner in which readers' first-language general knowledge, literacy knowledge, and literature knowledge come into play in their learning of inter-

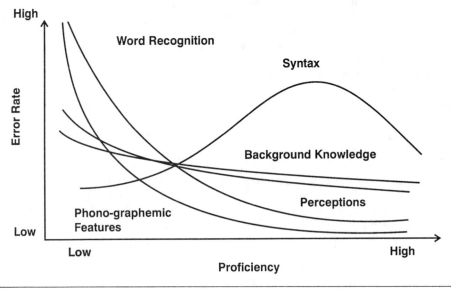

FIG. 41.1. Theoretical distribution of factors in second-language reading. Redrawn from Bernhardt (1991).

pretive skills in a second language. In an important attitude survey, Davis et al. examined the stance that foreign-language learners take toward the use of literature in its role as instructional text. They found that majors and minors in languages held very positive attitudes about the use of literature; interestingly, though, they found no relationship between foreign travel experience and attitudes toward literature and a negative relationship between knowledge of the other culture and an appreciation of its literature. Given that literary texts are the principle form of instructional text for almost all of foreign language instruction, it is critical that there be better understandings of the interactions of students and text within this context. The *structure of texts*, too, remained an active part of the database. Yano, Long, and Ross (1994) modified texts in three different ways and then posed multiple-choice questions. Because there were statistical interactions between the modifications and test items, the researchers concluded that "different kinds of text modification facilitate different levels of comprehension" (p. 190). They found that elaborated texts—text with more language rather than less—were more successful as learning tools for second language readers. Riley (1993) examined story structure. She found that naturally occurring structures in stories—rather than texts that were restructured in some fashion—led to higher performance. She also found, however, a language proficiency effect. Tang (1992) found that presenting students with graphic organizers was a method to facilitate reading comprehension.

Investigations of *morphosyntactic features* also remained. Three studies examined the effects of particular language features on second-language comprehension. Both Berkemeyer (1994) and Kitajima (1997) examined referential ties. Examining English readers of German as a second language, Berkemeyer found that the greater the ability of readers to identify anaphoric relations in German correctly, the higher was their general comprehension ability. Kitajima investigated learners of Japanese and, in corollary results, found that learners trained in understanding the coreferential system of Japanese attained higher comprehension scores. Takahashi and Roitblatt (1994) examined the understanding of Japanese learners of English reading indirect speech acts. By calculating reading speed, they found that learners do indeed seem to process both literal and nonliteral meanings during reading.

Vocabulary actually became a more significant area of study throughout the late 1990s. Kim (1995) identified vocabulary as a key problem for second-language readers. Learners' dictionary use led to positive gains in vocabulary acquisition (also Knight, 1994), yet students were also frequently misled by dictionary entries. In addition, it appears that dictionary use significantly decreased reading speed (Luppescu & Day, 1993). Leffa (1992) found that electronic glossing (in contrast to a conventional dictionary) led to higher reading comprehension scores in reading English as a foreign language, although Davis (1989) did not. Laufer and Hadar (1997) also looked at dictionary use; they found no consistency in effect for bilingual, bilingualized or monolingual dictionaries on the performances of second language learners. Parry (1991) found students struggling to acquire vocabulary through academic reading. Using case studies of a number of learners, Parry found no consistently productive strategy to acquire new words. Zimmerman (1997) found that direct vocabulary instruction in conjunction with significant amounts of reading was more productive than simply relying on extensive reading. Chun and Plass (1996) found that multimedia presentations including advance organizers and vocabulary support enhanced the recall of propositions from a text. Hulstijn (1993) examined the conditions under which learners choose to look up words. He found that readers generally chose to look up words based on their perceived relevance to the text, and that this general—by no means universal—behavior was not particularly related to the word knowledge that a reader already had. De Bot, Paribakht, and Wesche (1997) examined the use of lexical processing strategies.

Finally, a concern with *instruction* remained. Two substantial reviews conducted in the mid 1990s reflect the conflation of issues in second language reading. Fitzgerald (1995a, 1995b) reviewed the practice/methodology literature, yet included studies involving only English as a second language. Investigations that examined literacy instruction in language other than English were not perceived to be germane to the issue of developing second-language literacy. Fitzgerald concluded, in parallel to Weber (1991), that there is little that is actually unique in the practice literature on second-language reading development. Another review of the practice literature, Bernhardt (1994), examined how the issue of second-language reading is considered in textbooks used in language arts and reading methods courses as well as in practice-oriented reading and language arts journals. Examining 75 textbooks published between 1980 and 1992 and issues of *The Reading Teacher, Journal of Reading,* and *Language Arts* indicated a minimal treatment of the topic.

At the level of individual investigations, the 1990s provided a number of substantive studies that examined efficacious *instructional approaches* (Blum, Koskinen, Tennant, Parker, Straub, & Curry, 1995; Elley, 1991; Hudson, 1991; Lai, 1993; Mason & Krashen, 1997). These studies examined learners of different ages exposed to a variety of approaches to extensive, content-based (rather than grammar-focused) reading. These studies found that providing students extended reading experiences over time with authentic, not grammatically sequenced or altered, texts promoted the greatest gains in comprehension over time. A second approach to facilitating second-language reading comprehension focused on the use of strategies. Rusciolelli (1995) indicated that students self-reported the positive impact of skimming and word guessing practice on their reading comprehension; Stavans and Oded (1993) found, similarly, that students all seem to use a certain set of strategies, but some of them use them more effectively than others. Their study, which concluded that teachers need to rely on individual student's strategy use rather than the converse, is compatible with Auerbach and Paxton (1997). Subjects in the latter study were given the opportunity to reflect and articulate their individual use of strategies that had a facilitative impact on their comprehension processes. Filling a gap in the instruction literature are Johnson (1992) and Graden (1996). Each of these studies was conducted within the teacher beliefs paradigm. Each caution that teachers do not necessarily match what they believe to what they do instructionally and that they do not necessarily have research-based information about the second-language reading process at hand.

Relationships with *other language modalities*, that is, reading/writing relationships (Carrell & Connor, 1991; Hedgcock & Atkinson, 1993), were new areas of investigation in the 1990s. Hedgcock and Atkinson found little relationship between the quantity and ability to *read* and writing proficiency in a second language. Carrell and Connor found that reading and writing are genre related and provided some developmental evidence for genre across reading, but not across writing. The corollary, listening/reading relationships (Lund, 1991), also remained areas of interest. Lund documented differences between comprehension performances based on modality, with readers recalling more detail, listeners able to comprehend more globally.

Significant Challenges to the Present Database

Two additional important and influential areas that received significant attention in the 1990s, *testing* and *cross-lingual processing*, deserve special consideration. They are key toward establishing (re)interpretations of the data base and for directing developments in it.

In her 1991 synthesis, Bernhardt indicated that 50% of the studies in the second-language reading database relied on measures that are not considered to be appropriate measures—cloze, because of its inability to assess passage integration; recall in the second language, for its deliberate conflating of second-language writing abilities with comprehension abilities; and oral reading, for its inability to distinguish between miscues and mispronunciations.

A handful of the *testing* studies that emerged in the 1990s actually address the issue of "appropriate measure." Found in the foreign language literature are Wolf (1993) and Riley and Lee (1996), each of which explored different methods of assessment—studies that are corollary to Shohamy (1984). Each found that task and the language of response (native or nonnative) exert profound impacts on students' revealed performance. The majority of studies that use English-as-a-second-language populations focus on large-scale multiple choice testing. This focus is largely driven by the international TOEFL industry. Some focus specifically on the TOEFL test (Freedle & Kostin, 1993; Pierce, 1992). Others examine statistical and other analysis techniques attached to multiple choice tests of various forms (Allan, 1992; Choi & Bachman, 1992; Lumley, 1993; Perkins, Gupta, & Tammana, 1995; Young, Shermis, Brutten, & Perkins, 1996). Two studies are of particular note in this regard: Anderson, Bachman, Perkins, and Cohen (1991), and Gordon and Hanauer (1995). Each used external evidence—principally think-aloud data—for interpreting the results of learner performance on multiple-choice tests. Each found an interaction of knowledge source and individual test item performance. Ironically, Anderson et al. (1991) suggested the following as a remedy:

> Of concern to the second language classroom teacher is how readers should be taught to take standardized tests so that their scores will more appropriately reflect their students [sic] language abilities. (p. 61)

Gordon and Hanauer (1995) concluded differently:

> As we have seen in this study, responses to items were based on a number of knowledge sources including information in the test itself. Furthermore, the responses were at times correct for reasons that did not reflect reading ability. As a result, inferences made about a person's reading ability based upon the responses which are given on reading tasks may not be valid. Consequently, because much research on the reading process is based upon results of reading comprehension tests, invalid inferences might be made about the comprehension processes if the processing involved in performing those tasks was not analyzed well. (p. 320)

A final thrust of assessment research continues to be the examination of cloze testing—a topic that has virtually disappeared from the first-language scene. Jonz (1991) continued the debate of whether cloze measures only local-level syntactic sensitivity or whether it is indeed sensitive to intersentential processing. Jonz (1991) found the cloze procedure sensitive at an array of discourse levels. Given that the study used scrambled passages, it is still unclear whether the findings hold across authentic reading experiences.

The validity of measures question is a concern in all of educational research. Why it is of particular concern in the second-language domain is the foreknowledge that there exist two languages and two literacies within each subject. When studies use only one dependent variable, it is often unclear what precisely is being measured. This is the critical issue with using the second language as a response measure in a comprehension task. Given that there are always substantial distances between comprehension and productive abilities in a second language, distances that by and large do not exist in first languages, this is an absolutely crucial distinction that must be maintained in research.

The second critical area, and in fact the area that bridges to the future, is the area that focuses on the relationship between first and second languages, *cross-lingual processing strategies.* In the earlier state of the research area, studies that examined an array of readers at different proficiency levels reading in a particular language indicated developmental patterns (Barrera, Valdes, & Cardenes, 1986; Bernhardt, 1986; Block, 1986; Cziko, 1978, 1980; Devine, 1981; Kendall, Lajeunesse, Chmilar, Shapson, & Shapson, 1987; McLeod & McLaughlin, 1986; Rigg, 1978; Padron & Waxman, 1988). In other words, as readers increase in language proficiency, they acquire greater reading fluency and display sophisticated "symptoms of reading," to use Judd and Buswell's term. Such studies lend credence to statements about reading universals.

The more critical set of studies, however, surrounds the relationship of one language to the other—the absolute essence of the second-language experience. In the earlier iterations of the field of second-language reading, that set of studies argued for a transfer of reading behaviors from one language to another (Clark, 1979, 1980; Elley, 1984; Groebel, 1980; Roller, 1988; Sarig, 1987; Wagner, Spratt, & Ezzaki, 1989). Another set infers interference from one language to another (de Suarez, 1985; Irujo, 1986). A third argues that the first-language literacy behaviors are the principal control mechanism over second-language literacy (Dank & McEachern, 1979; Douglas, 1981; MacLean & d'Anglejan, 1986). Bernhardt (1991) commented:

> Transfer and interference data parallel a long-running debate in second language acquisition research in general. The extent to which first language strategies facilitate acquisition and the extent to which they impede acquisition—in this case, of second language reading skills—remains unclear. (p. 52)

Distinguishing a *second* language *process* from a *first* language *process* is a powerful question. At some level, it is a Whorfian question—is there thought without language and language without thought? If there are phenomena known as literacy phenomena, how does one distinguish them? That is, does one tease them apart in the two, that is, first and second language, contexts? This has been a significant question in the history of all second language issues. To be succinct, when a measure is taken is it a measure of second language, of first language, or a hybrid of the two?

The 1990s have seen a revisiting of the relationship between the processing of first-language (L1) texts and second-language (L2) texts. The term *revisiting* is used deliberately: In some sense the question of the L1/L2 relationship is precisely what Cattell and Buswell were after in the early part of the century. Research in the latter part of the century has returned to the issue after a series of studies that examined text processing in languages *other than* English. A significant question still remains about the role of the first language in text processing. Work in the 1990s has examined the role that cultural difference plays in strategy use (Abu-Rabia, 1996, 1998; Block, 1992; Parry, 1996); the extent to which second language readers rely on translation as a strategy (Kern, 1994); relationships between working memory and comprehension abilities (Barry & Lazarte, 1998; Harrington & Sawyer, 1992); and relationships between first-language and second-language syntactic and word recognition processing strategies (Chikamatsu, 1996; Everson, 1998; Everson & Ke, 1997; Horiba, 1996; Koda, 1993; Royer & Carlo, 1991; Tang, 1997).

These studies, in parallel to those conduced earlier, indicate that there is a definite reliance on the first language (that both facilitates and interferes with) within second-language processing. In 1984 the question was fully articulated by Alderson (1984), and the 1990s witnessed a set of revelatory studies that displayed remarkable consistency across varied subject groups or language family. Hacquebord (1989), Bossers (1991), Carrell (1991), Brisbois (1995), and Bernhardt and Kamil (1995) all used regression techniques to get at the contribution of a first language literacy to a second. Two Turkish/Dutch studies, one French/English, and two Spanish/English studies estimated the contribution of first-language literacy to be between 14% and 21%. This estimate is remarkably consistent considering that both children and adults were in-volved in the studies; that there is evidence from a noncognate language; and that a va-riety of measures—from traditional multiple choice through free recall in the first language—were employed. The other reasonably consistent finding across the studies is the influence of basic second-language ability (crassly stated as "grammar") in sec-ond-language reading. Estimates hovered around 30%. Bernhardt and Kamil (1995) concluded, then, that *second-language reading is a function of L1 reading ability and sec-ond-language grammatical ability.*

How are these findings to be reconciled with findings from the 1990s as well as with previous theoretical statements? Clearly, the theoretical distribution of factors dis-cussed earlier (Fig. 41.1) should not be perceived in a generic fashion. That distribution is related to the level of first-language literacy and to actual language knowledge. At the same time, however, the relationship of factor to factor is probably also a function of the linguistic overlap between two languages (Spanish–German, for example, shar-ing an overlapping orthographic system; Spanish–Thai, having virtually nothing in common linguistically).

These recognitions mandate the formulation of a different view based on the inter-relationships of languages, on the impact of linguistic and literacy knowledge, and on principles of learning. Fig. 41.1, for example, portrayed the snapshot of a reader at a particular point in time, yet we know that readers do get to be better comprehenders over time. An alternative conceptualization must capture these features. The alterna-tive is displayed in Fig. 41.2.

Figure 41.2 displays two axes: The x axis refers to time in learning, time in instruc-tion, or to the concept of development; the y axis denotes the ability to understand con-

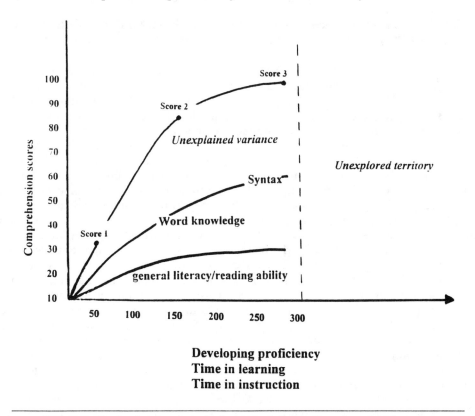

FIG. 41.2. Revised statement of a theoretical distribution of reading factors.

nected text or comprehension. Score 1, 2, and 3 refer to three points in time, either attained by one person or by three different persons at progressive developmental or learning stages. What the research referred to earlier indicates is the constitution of these scores: general literacy ability (about 20% of any given score), grammar (about an additional 30% of any given score, 27% of which is word knowledge and 3% syntax), and 50% of any given score at any particular point in time unexplained.

This formulation has several significant advantages. First, this model acknowledges the significant contribution of first-language reading ability to second-language comprehension. Second, this model enables the conceptualization of comprehension scores as consisting of different elements and thereby facilitates new ways of thinking about the components of scores. Third, it concedes that in the reading of cognate languages there is no such thing as "no knowledge." Fourth, it promotes the consideration of unexplained variance in individual performance *and* after considerable time in instruction.

Despite the advantages of the model in Fig. 41.2 over the model in Fig. 41.1, a significant disadvantage remains—the representation of syntactic development. In part, Fig. 41.1 is an artifact of qualitative data analysis whereas Fig. 41.2 is influenced by quantitative analysis. Syntax is an extremely important component in the conceptualization of the second-language reading process illustrated in Fig. 41.1. In fact, it is the component that is most consistent with the bulk of second-language acquisition research. Yet, the operation of syntax cannot be reconciled in Fig. 41.2, which is by and large consistent with the bulk of literacy research. Within the chapter's theme of "case study," the building of second-language reading models is an excellent illustration of the tensions in the term *second-language reading* discussed in the initial pages.

IMPLICATIONS OF SECOND-LANGUAGE READING RESEARCH FOR FUTURE THEORY, PRACTICE, POLICY, AND RESEARCH

The theme of case study is used in this essay in order to underline that the field of second-language reading is simultaneously a subfield and a microcosm of literacy issues as they unfold into the next century. The issues that literacy in general faces are at play in the second-language arena—so much so that often the issues are easier to perceive and comprehend from the second-language perspective than from a first.

The simulation of early reading acquisition can be done convincingly within second-language contexts. On the one hand, it is possible to perceive a beginner reader's process through adult reading and therefore to achieve a picture of actual difficulty and effort, as well as having a highly articulate subject describe and have words for processes that children simply cannot yet describe. Cultural subtleties related to literacy are also much more visible through cultures that are distinctly different rather than through the lens of subcultures of the larger whole. To discuss literacy differences in rural versus urban America (clearly distinct cultural contexts in some sense) is possible, yet not always productive: Issues of socioeconomic status, level of education, and the influence of mass media inevitably intervene and bring the discussion to a standstill. Discussing literacy differences between a Western/technological/North American Anglophone view and a Southeast Asian/rural/Hmong-speaking view leads to clearly capturable and productive distinctions. And processing issues, too, are far more discernible within second-language contexts, particularly when languages are not overlapping. How does a strict view of "whole language" hold up within learning Mandarin, for example, in which learners clearly need to search for consistencies within the visual and phonological field? In like manner, how far will a phonics-based or any other strictly analytic approach take a learner who is learning Chinese? Not far, as we know from the millions of learners who have tried and failed because they could not gain access to the language because of the symbolic system.

At the level of literacy policy, too, second-language issues can be revelatory. Literacy, particularly as established by the American literacy industrial complex, is seated in a Western value system based in large part on notions of relatively unrestricted access to knowledge and of empowerment. Not all cultures accept these values; accepting these values inevitably means changes in cultural beliefs and practices. Writing down a language for those who are not literate (Hmong is the recent late-20th-century example) means expecting and inviting (and in some cases insisting) that speakers of Hmong become Western. The history of Western literacy has often been tied up with such conflicts, and yet, in the literacy establishment's zeal to provide literacy, it has inevitably destroyed some cultural features, leading toward homogenized literate culture.

Second-language perspectives also liberate reading theory from the constraints of a single linguistic system, namely, English, as the single platform from which to build both cognitive and social models of reading. Given that the vast majority of the world receives its technical information through the mode of second-language literacy, it is arguable that no more critical issue exists than understanding the processing involved in using second-language texts. As noted earlier, current models of second-language reading acknowledge the impact of first-language literacy knowledge on the learning and the use of the second as well as the importance of grammatical knowledge of the second language. These findings fall short of providing satisfying explanations of the second-language process or of second-language reading instruction. They underline, for example, the vastness of the territory yet to be investigated. The role of affect and interest in second-language text processing is yet to be understood. The role of alternative conceptions of literacy (i.e., non-Western) and the impact such conceptions have on cognitive processes are critical toward understanding how persons read and learn to read when one oral language already exists in cognition.

Finally, how instruction is to accommodate (rather than ignore) the array of first languages that come into play among learners of second-language literacy remains perhaps the most pressing practical issue that faces the field. The century began with restricting access to freedom in the United States by means of English-language literacy tests. The century ends with a covert version of the access question. Ninety-five percent of what appears on the Internet (personal communication, Michael Kamil, April 18, 1997), as well as the vast majority of published technical information available globally, is written in English. Whether the information is about building a better mousetrap, how to prevent communicable diseases, or how to construct a nuclear weapon, the information is written and must be read in English, a *second language* for the majority of the world's population. Having appropriate and, more importantly, *accurate* access to this information—access that one receives through substantive instruction—is indeed one of the great challenges that faces the literacy community. Huey told us at the beginning of the century that reading research would lead to efficient instruction in all languages. After a 70-year hiatus, the time has returned to revisit and understand the variables involved in and that contribute toward comprehension in a second language.

REFERENCES

Abu-Rabia, S. (1996). The influence of culture and attitudes on reading comprehension in SL: The case of Jews learning English and Arabs learning Hebrew. *Reading Psychology, 17*(3), 253–271.

Abu-Rabia, S. (1998). The learning of Hebrew by Israeli Arab students in Israel. *Journal of Social Psychology, 138*(3), 331–341.

Addams, J. (1930). *The second twenty years at Hull House, September 1909 to September, 1929, with a record of a growing world consciousness.* New York: Macmillan.

Adams, S. J. (1982). Scripts and the recognition of unfamiliar vocabulary: Enhancing second language reading skills. *Modern Language Journal, 66,* 155159.

Adams, J. (1852). *The works of John Adams* (Vol. 7). Boston: Little.

Alderson, J. C. (1984). Reading in a foreign language: A reading problem or a language problem? In J. C. Alderson & A. H. Urquhart (Eds.), *Reading in a foreign language* (pp. 1–24). London: Longman.

Alderson, J. C., & Urquhart, A. H. (1988). This test is unfair: I'm not an economist. In P. C. Carrell, J. Devine, & D. E. Eskey (Eds.), *Interactive approaches to second language reading* (pp. 168–182). Cambridge: Cambridge University Press.

Allan, A. (1992). Development and validation of a scale to measure test-wiseness in EFL/ESL reading test takers. *Language Testing, 9*,101–122.

Anderson, N., Bachman, L., Perkins, K. & Cohen, A. (1991). An exploratory study into the construct validity of a reading comprehension test: Triangulation of data sources. *Language Testing, 8*(1), 41–66.

Auerbach, E. , & Paxton, D. (1997). "It's not the English thing": Bringing reading research into the ESL classroom. *TESOL Quarterly, 31*(2), 237–261.

Bahktin, M. (1981). *The dialogical imagination.* Austin: University of Texas Press.

Barnett, M. (1986). Syntactic and lexical/semantic skill in foreign language reading: Importance and interaction. *Modern Language Journal, 70*, 343349.

Barrera, B. R., Valdes, G., & Cardenes, M. (1986). Analyzing the recall of students across different language-reading categories: A study of third-graders' Spanish-L1, English-L2, and English-L1 comprehension. In J. A. Niles & R. V. Lalik (Eds.), *Thirty-fifth yearbook of the National Reading Conference* (pp. 375381). Rochester, NY: National Reading Conference.

Barry, S., & Lazarte, A. A. (1998). Evidence for mental models: How do prior knowledge, syntactic complexity, and reading topic affect inference generation in a recall task for nonnative readers of Spanish? *Modern Language Journal, 82*(2), 176–193.

Bean, T. W., Potter, T. C., & Clark, C. (1980). Selected semantic features of ESL materials and their effect on bilingual students' comprehension. In M. Kamil & A. Moe, (Eds.), *Perspectives on reading research and instruction: Twenty-ninth yearbook of the National Reading Conference* (pp. 1–5). Washington, DC: National Reading Conference.

Berkemeyer, V. (1994). Anaphoric resolution and text comprehension for readers of German. *Die Unterrichtspraxis, 27*(2), 15–22.

Bernhardt, E. B. (1983). Three approaches to reading comprehension in intermediate German. *Modern Language Journal, 67*, 111–115.

Bernhardt, E. B. (1986a). Cognitive processes in L2: An examination of reading behaviors. In J. Lantolf & A. Labarca (Eds.), *Research in second language acquisition in the classroom setting* (pp. 35–51). Norwood, NJ: Ablex.

Bernhardt, E. B. (1994). A content analysis of reading methods texts: What are we told about the nonnative speaker of English? *Journal of Reading Behavior, 26*, 159–189.

Bernhardt, E. B. (1991). *Reading development in a second language: Theoretical, empirical, and classroom perspectives.* Norwood, NJ: Ablex.

Bernhardt, E. B. (1998). Socio-historical perspectives on language teaching in modern America. In H. Byrnes (Ed.), *Perspectives on research and scholarship in second language learning* (pp. 39–57). New York: Modern Language Association.

Bernhardt, E. B., & Kamil, M. L. (1995). Interpreting relationships between L1 and L2 reading: Consolidating the linguistic threshold and the linguistic interdependence hypotheses. *Applied Linguistics, 16*, 15–34.

Bhatia, V. K. (1984). Syntactic discontinuity in legislative writing for academic legal purposes. In A. K. Pugh & J. M. Ulijn (Eds.), *Reading for professional purposes: Studies and practices in native and foreign languages* (pp. 90–96). London: Heinemann.

Biglmaier, F. (1991). Recent political changes in Germany and their impact on teaching reading. *Reading Teacher, 44*(9), 634–637.

Block, E. (1992). See how they read: Comprehension monitoring of L1 and L2 readers. *TESOL Quarterly, 26*(2), 319–343.

Blum, I., Koskinen, P., & Tennant, N., Parker, E., Straub, J., & Curry, C. (1995). Using audiotaped books to extend classroom literacy instruction into the homes of second-language learners. *Journal of Reading Behavior, 27*(4), 535–563.

Bossers, B. (1991). On thresholds, ceiling, and short circuits: The relation between L1 reading, L2 reading, and L1 knowledge. *AILA Review, 8*, 45–60.

Brisbois, J. (1995). Connections between first- and second-language reading. *Journal of Reading Behavior, 24*(4), 565–584.

Brown, T. L., & Haynes, M. (1985). Literacy background and reading development in a second language. In T. H. Carr (Ed.), *The development of reading skills* (pp. 19–34). San Francisco: Jossey-Bass.

Campbell, A. J. (1981). Language background and comprehension. *Reading Teacher, 35*, 10–14.

Carlson, R. A. (1975). *The quest for conformity: Americanization through education.* New York: John Wiley & Sons.

Carrell, P. L. (1983). Three components of background knowledge in reading comprehension. *Language Learning, 33*, 183–207.

Carrell, P. L. (1984a). Evidence of a formal schema in second language comprehension. *Language Learning, 34*, 87–112.

Carrell, P. L. (1987). Content and formal schemata in ESL reading. *TESOL Quarterly, 2*(3), 461–481.

Carrell, P. (1991). Second language reading: Reading ability or language proficiency? *Applied Linguistics, 12,* 159–179.

Carrell, P., & Connor, U. (1991). Reading and writing persuasive texts. *Modern Language Journal, 75*(3), 314–324.

Carrell, P., & Wallace, B. (1983). Background knowledge: Context and familiarity in reading comprehension. In M. A. Clarke & J. Handscombe (Eds.), *On TESOL '82* (pp. 245–308). Washington, DC: TESOL.

Cattell, J. M. (1886). The inertia of the eye and the brain. *Brain, 8,* 295–312.

Cavello, L. (1958). *The heart is the teacher.* New York: McGraw-Hill.

Chi, F.-M. (1995). EFL readers and a focus on intertextuality. *Journal of Reading, 38*(8), 638–644.

Chikamatsu, N. (1996). The effects of L1 orthography on L2 word recognition: A study of American and Chinese learners of Japanese. *Studies in Second Language Acquisition, 18*(4), 403–432.

Choi, I.-C., & Bachman, L. (1992). An investigation into the adequacy of three IRT models for data from two EFL reading tests. *Language Testing, 9,* 51–78.

Chun, D., & Plass, J. (1996). Facilitating reading comprehension with multimedia. *System, 24*(4), 503–519.

Clarke, M. A. (1979). Reading in Spanish and English: Evidence from adult ESL students. *Language Learning, 29,* 121–150.

Clarke, M. A. (1980). The short circuit hypothesis of ESL reading: Or when language competence interferes with reading performance. *Modern Language Journal, 64,* 203–209.

Coady, J. (1979). A psycholinguistic model of the ESL reader. In R. Mackay, B. Barkman, & R. R. Jordan (Eds.), *Reading in a second language* (pp. 5–12). Rowley, MA; Newbury House.

Cohen, A., Glasman, H., Rosenbaum-Cohen, P., Ferrar, J., & Fine, J. (1979). Reading English for specialized purposes: Discourse analysis and the use of student informants. *TESOL Quarterly, 3,* 551–564.

Connor, U. (1981). The application of reading miscue analysis to diagnosis of English as a second language learners' reading skills. In C. W. Twyford, W. Diehl, & K. Feathers (Eds.), *Reading English as a second language: Moving from theory* (pp. 47–55). Bloomington, IN: Indiana University School of Education.

Connor, U. (1984). Recall of text: Differences between first and second language readers. *TESOL Quarterly, 18,* 239–255.

Cziko, G. A. (1978). Differences in first- and second-language reading: The use of syntactic, semantic, and discourse constraints. *Canadian Modern Language Review/La revue canadienne des langues vivantes, 34,* 473–489.

Dank, M., & McEachern, W. (1979). A psycholinguistic description comparing the native language oral reading behavior of French immersion students with traditional English language students. *Canadian Modern Language Review/La revue canadienne des langues vivantes, 35,* 366–371.

Davies, A. (1984). Simple, simplified and simplification: What is authentic? In J. C. Alderson & A. H. Urquhart (Eds.), *Reading in a foreign language,* (pp. 181–195). London: Longman.

Davis, J. (1989). Facilitating effects of marginal glosses on foreign language reading. *Foreign Language Annals, 21*(6), 547–550.

Davis, J. (1992). Reading literature in the foreign language: the comprehension/response connection. *French Review, 65*(3), 359–370.

Davis, J., Caron-Gorell, L., Kline, R., & Hsieh, G. (1992). Readers and foreign languages: A survey of undergraduate attitudes toward the study of literature. *Modern Language Journal, 73*(3), 320–332.

Davis, J. N., Lange, D. L., & Samuels, S. J. (1988). Effects of text structure instruction on foreign language readers' recall of a scientific journal article. *Journal of Reading Behavior, 22*(3), 203–214.

De Bot, K., Paribakht, T., & Wesche, M. (1997). Toward a lexical processing model for the study of second language vocabulary acquisition: Evidence from ESL reading. *Studies in Second Language Acquisition, 19,* 309–329.

de Suarez, J. (1985). Using translation communicatively in ESP courses for science studies. In J. M. Ulijn & A. K. Pugh (Eds.), *Reading for professional purposes: Methods and materials in teaching languages* (pp. 56–68). Leuven, Belgium: Acco.

Devine, J. (1981). Developmental patterns in native and non-native reading acquisition. In S. Hudelson (Ed.), *Learning to read in different languages* (pp. 10–114). Washington, DC: Center for Applied Linguistics.

Devine, J. (1984). ESL reader's internalized models of the reading process. In J. Handscombe, R. Orem, & B. Taylor (Eds.), On TESOL '83 (pp. 95–108). Washington, DC: TESOL.

Douglas, D. (1981). An exploratory study of bilingual reading proficiency. In S. Hudelson (Ed.), *Learning to read in different languages* (pp. 93–102). Washington, DC: Center for Applied Linguistics.

Drachsler, J. (1920). *Democracy and assimilation, the blending of immigrant heritages in America.* New York: Macmillan.

Elley, W. (1991). Acquiring literacy in a second language: The effects of book-based programs. *Language Learning, 41*(3), 375–411.

Elley, W. B. (1984). Exploring the reading difficulties of second language readers and second-languages in Fiji. In J. C. Alderson & A. H. Urquhart (Eds.), *Reading in a foreign language* (pp. 281–297). London: Longman.

Erdmann, B., & Dodge, R. (1898). *Psychologische Untersuchungen ueber das Lesen, auf Experimenteller Grundlage.* Halle: Niemeyer.

Everson, M. E. (1998). Word recognition among learners of Chinese as a foreign language: Investigating the relationship between naming and knowing. *Modern Language Journal, 82*(2), 194–204.

Everson, M., & Ke, C. (1997). An inquiry into the reading strategies of intermediate and advanced learners of Chinese as a foreign language. *Journal of the Chinese Language Teachers Association, 32*(1), 1–20.

Ewoldt, C. (1981). Factors which enable deaf readers to get meaning from print. In S. Hudelson (Ed.), *Learning to read in different languages* (pp. 45–53). Washington, DC: Center for Applied Linguistics.

Favreau, M., Komoda, M. K., & Segalowitz, N. S. (1980). Second language reading: Implications of the word superiority effect in skilled bilinguals. *Canadian Journal of Psychology/Revue canadienne de psychologie, 34,* 370–380.

Favreau, M., & Segalowitz, N. S. (1982). Second language reading in fluent bilinguals. *Applied Psycholinguistics, 3,* 329–341.

Fitzgerald, J. (1995a). English-as-a-second-language learners' cognitive reading processes: A review of research in the United States. *Review of Educational Research, 65*(2), 145–190.

Fitzgerald, J. (1995b). English-as a second language reading instruction in the United States: A research review. *Journal of Reading Behavior, 27*(2), 115–152.

Flick, W. C., & Anderson, J. L. (1980). Rhetorical difficulty in scientific English: A study in reading comprehension. *TESOL Quarterly, 14,* 345–351.

Foucault, M. (1972). *The archaeology of knowledge.* London: Tavistock.

Fransson, A. (1984). Cramming or understanding? Effects of intrinsic and extrinsic motivation on approach to learning and test performance. In J. C. Alderson & A. H. Urquhart (Eds.), *Reading in a foreign language* (pp. 86–115). London: Longman.

Freedle, R., & Kostin, I. (1993). The prediction of TOEFL reading item difficulty: Implications for construct validity. *Language Testing, 10,* 133–170.

Goodman, K. (Ed.). (1968). *The psycholinguistic nature of the reading process.* Detroit, MI: Wayne State University Press.

Gordon, C., & Hanauer, D. (1995). The interaction between task and meaning construction in EFL reading comprehension tests. *TESOL Quarterly, 29*(2), 299–324.

Grabe, W. (1991). Current developments in second language reading research. *TESOL Quarterly, 25*(3), 375–406.

Graden, E. (1996). How language teachers' beliefs about reading instruction are mediated by their beliefs about students. *Foreign Language Annals, 29*(3), 387–395.

Groebel, L. (1980). A comparison of students' reading comprehension in the native language with their reading comprehension in the target language. *English Language Teaching Journal, 35,* 54–59.

Grosse, C., & Hameyer, K. (1979). Dialect and reading interferences in second language perception and production. *Die Unterrichtspraxis, 12,* 52–60.

Guarino, R., & Perkins, K. (1986). Awareness of form class as a factor in ESL reading comprehension. *Language Learning, 36,* 77–82.

Hacquebord, H. (1989). *Reading comprehension of Turkish and Dutch students attending secondary schools.* Groningen: RUG.

Harrington, M., & Sawyer, M. (1992). L2 working memory capacity and L2 reading skill. *Studies in Second Language Acquisition, 14,* 25–38.

Hatch, E., Polin, P., & Part, S. (1974). Acoustic scanning and syntactic processing: Three reading experiments: First and second language learners. *Journal of Reading Behavior, 6,* 275–285.

Hayes, E. B. (1988). Encoding strategies used by native and non-native readers of Chinese Mandarin. *Modern Language Journal, 72*(2), 188–195.

Haynes, M. (1981). Patterns and perils of guessing in second language reading. In J. Handscombe, R. Oren, & B. Taylor (Eds.), *On TESOL '83* (pp. 163–176). Washington, DC: TESOL.

Hedgcock, J., & Atkinson, D. (1993). Differing reading–writing relationships in L1 and L2 literacy development? *TESOL Quarterly, 27*(2), 329–333.

Hodes, P. (1981). Reading: A universal process. In S. Hudelson (Ed.), *Learning to read in different languages* (pp. 27–31). Washington, DC: Center for Applied Linguistics.

Horiba, Y. (1996). Comprehension processes in L2 reading: Language competence, textual coherence, and inferences. *Studies in Second Language Acquisition, 18,* 433–473.

Hosenfeld, C. (1977). A preliminary investigation of the reading strategies of successful and nonsuccessful second language readers. *System, 5,* 110–123.

Hudson, T. (1982). The effects of induced schemata on the "short circuit" in L2 reading: Non-decoding factors in L2 reading performance. *Language Learning, 32,* 1–32.

Hudson, T. (1991). A content comprehension approach to reading English for science and technology. *TESOL Quarterly, 25*(1), 77–104.

Huey, E. B. (1909). *The psychology and pedagogy of reading.* New York: Macmillan.

Hulstijn, J. (1993). When do foreign-language readers look up the meaning of unfamiliar words? The influence of task and learner variables. *Modern Language Journal, 77*(2), 139–147.

Irujo, S. (1986). Don't put your leg in your mouth: Transfer in the acquisition of idioms in a second language. *TESOL Quarterly, 20,* 287–304.

Jarvis, D. K., & Jensen, D. C. (1982). The effect of parallel translations on second language reading and syntax acquisition. *Modern Language Journal, 66,* 18–23.

Javal, E. (1878). Essai sur la physiologie de la lecture. *Annaels d'oculistique, 82,* 242–253.

Jefferson, T. (1955). *Notes on the state of Virginia.* Chapel Hill: University of North Carolina Press.

Johnson, K. E. (1992). The relationship between teachers' beliefs and practices during literacy instruction for nonnative speakers of English. *Journal of Reading Behavior, 24*(1), 83–108.

Johnson, P. (1981). Effects on reading comprehension of language complexity and cultural background of a text. *TESOL Quarterly, 15*, 169–181.

Johnson, P. (1982). Effects on comprehension of building background knowledge. *TESOL Quarterly, 16*, 503–516.

Jonz, J. (1991). Cloze item types and second language comprehension. *Language Testing, 8*(1), 1–22.

Joseph, S. (1935). *History of the Baron de Hirsch Fund: The Americanization of the Jewish immigrant.* New York: Jewish Publication Society.

Judd, C. H., & Buswell, G. T. (1922). *Silent reading: A study of the various types.* Chicago: University of Chicago.

Kendall, J. R., Lajeunesse, G., Chmilar, P., Shapson, L. R., & Shapson, S. M. (1987). English reading skills of French immersion students in kindergarten and grades 1 and 2. *Reading Research Quarterly, 22*(2). 135–159.

Kern, R. G. (1994). The role of mental translation in second language reading. *Studies in Second Language Acquisition, 16*, 441–461.

Kim, S.-A. (1995). Types and sources of problems in L2 reading: A qualitative analysis of the recall protocols of Korean high school EFL students. *Foreign Language Annals, 28*(1), 49–70.

Kitajima, R. (1997). Referential strategy training for second language reading comprehension of Japanese texts. *Foreign Language Annals, 30*(1), 84–97.

Knight, S. (1994). Dictionary: The tool of last resort in foreign language reading? A new perspective. *Modern Language Journal, 78*(3), 285–299.

Koda, K. (1987). Cognitive strategy transfer in second language reading. In J. Devine, P. L. Carrell, & D. E. Eskey (Eds.), *Research in reading in English as a second language* (pp. 125–144). Washington, DC: TESOL.

Koda, K. (1993). Transferred L1 strategies and L2 syntactic structures in L2 sentence comprehension. *Modern Language Journal, 77*(iv), 490–499.

Kramsch, C., & Nolden, T. (1994). Redefining literacy in a foreign language. *Die Unterrichtspraxis, 27*(1), 28–35.

Labaree, L. (1961). (Ed.). *The papers of Benjamin Franklin* (Vol. 4). New Haven, CT: Yale University Press.

LaBerge, D., & Samuels, S. J. (1974). Toward a theory of automatic information processing in reading. *Cognitive Psychology, 6*, 293–323.

Lagemann, E. C. (Ed.). (1985). *Jane Addams on education.* New York: Teachers College Press.

Lai, F.-K. (1993). The effect of a summer reading course on reading and writing skills. *System, 27*(1), 87–100.

Lane, F. K. (1919). *Americanization speech at Hotel Astor, New York.* Washington, DC: Government Printing Office.

Laufer, B., & Hadar, L. (1997). Assessing the effectiveness of monolingual, bilingual, and "bilingualized" dictionaries in the comprehension and production of new words. *Modern Language Journal, 81*(2), 189–196.

Lee, J. F. (1986). Background knowledge and L2 reading. *Modern Language Journal, 70*, 350–354.

Leffa, V. (1992). Making foreign language texts comprehensible for beginners: An experiment with an electronic glossary. *System, 20*(1), 63–73.

Lumley, T. (1993). The notion of subskills in reading comprehension tests: An EAP example. *Language Testing, 10*, 211–234.

Lund, R. (1991). A comparison of second language listening and reading comprehension. *Modern Language Journal, 75*(2), 196–204.

Luppescu, S., & Day, R. (1993). Reading, dictionaries, and vocabulary learning. *Language Learning, 42*(2), 263–287.

MacLean, M., & d'Anglejan, A. (1986). Rational cloze and retrospection: Insights into first and second language reading comprehension. *Canadian Modern Language Review/La revue canadienne des langues vivantes, 42*, 814–826.

Mason, B., & Krashen, S. (1997). Extensive reading in English as a foreign language. *System, 25*(1), 91–102.

McKay, S., & Weinstein-Shr, G. (1993). English literacy in the U.S.: National policies, personal consequences. *TESOL Quarterly, 27*(3), 399–419.

McLeod, B., & McLaughlin, B. (1986). Restructuring or automaticity? Reading in a second language. *Language Learning, 36*, 109–123.

Meara, P. (1984). Word recognition in foreign languages. In A. K. Pugh & J. M. Ulijn (Eds.), *Reading for professional purposes: Studies and practices in native and foreign languages* (pp. 97–105). London: Heinemann.

Mohammed, M. A. H., & Swales, J. M. (1984). Factors affecting the successful reading of technical instructions. *Reading in a Foreign Language, 2*, 206–217.

Muchisky, D. M. (1983). Relationships between speech and reading among second language learners. *Language Learning, 33*, 77–102.

Nehr, M. (1984). Audio-lingual behaviour in learning to read foreign languages. In A. K. Pugh & J. M. Ulijn (Eds.), *Reading for professional purposes: Studies and practices in native and foreign languages* (pp. 82–89). London: Heinemann.

Neville, M. H. (1979). An Englishwoman reads Spanish: Self-observation and speculation. *English Language Teaching Journal, 33*, 274–281.

Neville, M. H., & Pugh, A. K. (1975). An exploratory study of the application of time-compressed and time-expanded speech in the development of the English reading proficiency of foreign students. *English Language Teaching Journal, 29*, 320–329.

Nunan, D. (1985). Content familiarity and the perception of textual relationships in second language reading. *RELC Journal, 16*, 43–51.

Olah, E. (1984). How special is special English? In A. K. Pugh & J. M. Ulijn (Eds.), *Reading for professional purposes: Studies and practices in native and foreign languages* (pp. 223–226). London: Heinemann.

Olshtain, E. (1982). English nominal compounds and the ESL/EFL reader. In M. Hines & W. Rutherford (Eds.), *On TESOL 81* (pp. 153–167). Washington, DC: TESOL.

Omaggio, A. C. (1979). Pictures and second language comprehension: Do they help? *Foreign Language Annals, 12*, 107–116.

Padron, Y. N., & Waxman, H. C. (1988). The effect of ESL students' perceptions of their cognitive strategies on reading achievement. *TESOL Quarterly, 22*(1), 146–150.

Parry, K. J. (1987). Reading in a second culture. In J. Devine, P. L. Carrell, & D. E. Eskey (Eds.), *Research in reading in English as a second language* (pp. 59–70). Washington, DC: TESOL.

Parry, K. (1991). Building a vocabulary through academic reading. *TESOL Quarterly, 25*(4), 629–653.

Parry, K. (1996). Culture, literacy, and L2 reading. *TESOL Quarterly, 30*(4), 665–692.

Perkins, K. (1987). The relationship between nonverbal schematic concept formation and story comprehension. In J. Devine, P. L. Carrell, & D. E. Eskey (Eds.), *Research in reading in English as a second language* (pp. 151–171). Washington, DC: TESOL.

Perkins, K., & Angelis, P. J. (1985). Schematic concept formation: Concurrent validity for attained English as a second language reading comprehension? *Language Learning, 35*, 269–283.

Perkins, K., Gupta, L., & Tammana, R. (1995). Predicting item difficulty in a reading comprehension test with an artificial neural network. *Language Testing, 12*, 34–53.

Phillipson, R. (1992). *Linguistic imperialism*. Oxford: Oxford University Press.

Pierce, B. (1992). Demystifying the TOEFL reading test. *TESOL Quarterly, 26*(4), 665–691.

Reeds, J. A., Winitz, H., & Garcia, P. A. (1977). A test of reading following comprehension training. *IRAL, 15*, 307–319.

Report of the Commissioner of Education. (1918). Washington: Government Printing Office.

Rigg, P. (1978). The miscue-ESL project. In H. D. Brown, C. Yorio, & R. Crymes (Eds.), *On TESOL 77* (pp. 109–117). Washington, DC: TESOL.

Riley, G. (1993). A story structure approach to narrative text comprehension. *Modern Language Journal, 77*(4), 417–430.

Riley, G., & Lee, J. F. (1996). A comparison of recall and summary protocols as measures of second language reading comprehension. *Language Testing, 12*, 173–187.

Robbins, B. (1983). Language proficiency level and the comprehension of anaphoric subject pronouns by bilingual and monolingual children. In P. Larson, E. L. Judd, & D. S. Messerschmitt (Eds.), *On TESOL 84* (pp. 45–54). Washington, DC: TESOL.

Roller, C. M. (1988). Transfer of cognitive academic competence and L2 reading in a rural Zimbabwean primary school. *TESOL Quarterly, 22*(2), 303–328.

Romatowski, J. (1981). A study of oral reading in Polish and English: A psycholinguistic perspective. In S. Hudelson (Ed.), *Learning to read in different languages* (pp. 21–31). Washington, DC: Center for Applied Linguistics.

Royer, J., & Carlo, M. (1991). Transfer of comprehension skills from native to second language. *Journal of Reading, 34*(6), 450–455.

Rudolph, R. (Ed.). (1965). *Essays on education in the early republic*. Cambridge, MA: Belknap Press.

Rusciolelli, J. (1995). Student responses to reading strategies instruction. *Foreign Language Annals, 28*(2), 262–273.

Sarig, G. (1987). High-level reading in the first and in the foreign language: Some comparative process data. In J. Devine, P. L. Carrell, & D. E. Eskey (Eds.), *Research in reading in English as a second language* (pp. 105–120). Washington, DC: TESOL.

Sharlip, W., & Owens, A. (1925). *Adult immigration education: Its scope, content, and methods*. New York: Macmillan.

Shohamy, E. (1982). Affective considerations in language testing. *Modern Language Journal, 66*, 13–17.

Shohamy, E. (1984). Does the testing method make a difference? The case of reading comprehension. *Language Testing, 1*, 147–170.

Spiro, R. J., Bruce, B. C. and Brewer, W. F. (Eds.). (1980). *Theoretical issues in reading comprehension*. Hillsdale, NJ: Lawrence Erlbaum Associates.

Stanley, R. M. (1984). The recognition of macrostructure: A pilot study. *Reading in a Foreign Language, 2*, 156–168.

Stavans, A., & Oded, B. (1993). Assessing EFL reading comprehension: The case of Ethiopian learners. *System, 21*(4), 481–494.

Steffensen, M. S. (1988). Changes in cohesion in the recall of native and foreign texts. In P. L. Carrell, J. Devine, & D. E. Eskey (Eds.), *Interactive approaches to second language reading* (pp. 140–151). Cambridge: Cambridge University Press.

Steffensen, M. S., Joag-Dev, C., & Anderson, R. C. (1979). A cross-cultural perspective on reading comprehension. *Reading Research Quarterly, 15*, 10–29.

Strother, J. B., & Ulijn, J. M. (1987). Does syntactic rewriting affect English for science and technology text comprehension? In J. Devine, P. L. Carrell, & D. E. Eskey (Eds.), *Research in reading in English as a second language* (pp. 89–100). Washington, DC: TESOL.

Takahashi, S., & Roitblatt, H. (1994). Comprehension processes of second language indirect requests. *Applied Psycholinguistics, 15,* 475–506.

Tang, G. (1992). The effect of graphic representation of knowledge structures on ESL reading comprehension. *Studies in Second Language Acquisition, 14,* 177–195.

Tang, H. (1997). The relationship between reading comprehension processes in L1 and L2. *Reading Psychology, 18*(3), 249–301.

Tatlonghari, M. (1984). Miscue analysis in an ESL context. *RELC Journal, 15,* 75–84.

Thompson, F. V. (1920). *Schooling of the immigrant.* New York: Harper & Brothers.

Tian, G. S. (1991). Higher order reading comprehension skills in literature learning and teaching at the lower secondary school level in Singapore. *RELC Journal, 22*(2), 29–43.

Tollefson, J. (1991). *Planning language, planning inequality: Language policy in the community.* London: Longman.

Ulijn, J. & Salager-Meyer, S. (1998). The professional reader and the text: Insights from L2 research. *Journal of Research in Reading, 21*(2), 79–95.

U.S. Naturalization Bureau. (1921). *Suggestions for Americanization work among foreign-born women.* Washington, DC: Government Printing Office.

Urquhart, A. H. (1984). The effect of rhetorical ordering on readability. In J. C. Alderson & A. H. Urquhart (Eds.), *Reading in a foreign language* (pp. 160–175). London: Longman.

Wagner, D. A., Spratt, J. E., & Ezzaki, A. (1989). Does learning to read in a second language always put the child at a disadvantage? Some counter evidence from Morocco. *Applied Psycholinguistics, 10,* 31–48.

Walker, L. J. (1983). Word identification strategies in reading in a foreign language. *Foreign Language Annals, 16,* 293–299.

Weber, R. (1991). Linguistic diversity and reading in American society. In R. Barr (Ed.), *Handbook of reading research* (Vol. II, pp. 97–119). New York: Longman.

Webster, N. (1789). *Dissertations on the English language.* Boston: I. Thomas.

Wolf, D. F. (1993). A comparison of assessment tasks used to measure FL reading comprehension. *Modern Language Journal, 77*(iv), 473–489.

Yano, Y., Long, M., & Ross, S. (1994). The effects of simplified and elaborated texts on foreign language reading comprehension. *Language Learning, 44*(2), 189–219.

Young, R., Shermis, M., Brutten, S., & Perkins, K. (1996). From conventional to computer-adaptive testing of ESL reading comprehension. *System, 24*(1), 23–40.

Zimmerman, C. (1997). Do reading and interactive vocabulary instruction make a difference? An empirical study. *TESOL Quarterly, 31*(1), 121–140.

Zuck, L. V., & Zuck, I. G. (1984). The main idea: Specialist and nonspecialist judgments. In A. K. Pugh & I. M. Ulijn (Eds.), *Reading for professional purposes: Studies and practices in native and foreign languages* (pp. 130–135). London: Heinemann.

CHAPTER 42

Bilingual Children's Reading

Georgia Earnest García
University of Illinois at Urbana-Champaign

Many children throughout the world acquire a second language. A 1991 United Nations survey of 104 countries indicated that 46 countries provide elementary school children with instruction in at least two official languages (Cavicchiori & Erickson, 1991). Current U.S. demographics show that 9.9 million children, or 22% of the school-age population, live in homes where a language other than English is spoken (Anstrom, 1996; Crawford, 1997). According to the 1990 U.S. census, over 6.3 million children between the ages of 5 and 17 years actually spoke a language other than English at home. Two-thirds of these children were Spanish speakers.

This chapter focuses on the reading of children (preschool to Grade 12) who speak two languages or who are in the process of acquiring two languages. A range of terms have been used to describe these children—among others, *bilingual students*, *English language learners*, *learners of English-as-a-second-language* (ESL), *second-language learners*, and *students who are limited-English-proficient*. As Dworin (in press) explained, *biliteracy* refers to children's literate development in "two languages, to whatever degree, developed either simultaneously or successively." True bilinguals who are completely fluent in both languages are exceedingly rare.

A problem in locating research on bilingual reading is that the topic historically has been ignored in the second-language field, and only recently addressed in the reading field. In 1989, Carrell observed that researchers in the field of second-language acquisition historically had focused on oral language development, neglecting the study of second-language students' literate development. Weber's 1991 chapter in the second volume of the *Handbook on Reading Research* was the first chapter on linguistic diversity to appear in the *Handbook*. Her chapter focused on the second-language reading of adults and children in bilingual, ESL, and foreign language contexts in the United States. As she noted, the research on second-language children's reading was limited in scope and quantity, with much of it evaluating the reading progress of children in U.S. bilingual education programs. Fitzgerald published a review of ESL learners' cognitive reading processes (1995a) and a review of ESL reading instruction (1995b). In both reviews, she collapsed the adult and children's findings and limited her focus to the ESL reading of limited-English-proficient students in the United States.

To give a more complete interpretive account of bilingual children's reading I have included research from other countries and the United States. In addition, I have drawn from literature in bilingual education, education, ESL, linguistics, psychology, reading, and second-language acquisition. Due to space limitations, my major focus is on research published between 1989 and 1997. Studies on bilingual writing or oral language are included if they report information related to bilingual reading. I have excluded research on deaf children or children who are learning a foreign language.

I have organized the chapter so that I begin with a brief review of theoretical assumptions and sociocultural factors related to bilingual children's reading and a short overview of U.S. bilingual educational policy and evaluation findings. Next comes the heart of the chapter: a discussion of young (Preschool to Grade 2) bilingual children's reading acquisition and instruction, followed by a discussion of older bilingual children's (Grades 3–12) reading development and instruction. Under the heading of related issues, I review research on teacher attitudes and knowledge, reading and instructional materials, assessment, and student motivation. I end the chapter by summarizing the research on young and older bilingual children's reading development and instruction and by delineating various educational and research implications.

THEORETICAL ASSUMPTIONS
AND SOCIOCULTURAL FACTORS

Weber (1991) reviewed the major assumptions that underlie bilingual education. Most of these still hold, although not all researchers agree on the level of second-language oral proficiency that bilingual children must have before they optimally can learn to read and write in a second language (see August & Hakuta, 1997; García, Pearson, & Jiménez, 1994; Snow, Burns, & Griffin, 1998). Cummins's interdependence and threshold hypotheses (1981, 1989), in which he proposed that the successful transfer of knowledge and expertise across languages was dependent on the development of cognitive proficiency in one language—usually the dominant language—still is widely cited as a major reason for providing U.S. bilingual children with native-language literacy instruction. Findings from Collier and Thomas's (1989) longitudinal study of the U.S. academic performance of immigrant children from advantaged families have substantiated Cummins's hypothesis. They reported that non-English-speaking immigrant children did best in American schools when they arrived in the United States at ages 8 and 9, with already developed literacy skills in their native languages, as compared to younger children who arrived at ages 5 and 6 without native-language literacy skills. In fact, their findings revealed that it took more than 5–7 years of instruction in the United States for the 8- and 9-year-olds to perform at grade level in English, and 7–10 years of instruction for the 5- and 6-year olds.

Hornberger's (1992) comparative analysis of biliteracy in Puerto Rican and Cambodian communities in Philadelphia illustrated the range of factors that can impact students' biliterate development. She argued that for students to become biliterate, they have to be supported along three continua: the macro–micro continuum (political and economic factors that support or detract from the development and acceptance of biliteracy), the monolingual–bilingual continuum (the use of both languages in school and societal contexts), and the oral–literate continuum (the use and support of oral and written language by the school and community). Hornberger explained that, despite an English-only legislative bias, the Puerto Rican community generated the institutional support necessary to provide its children with Spanish literacy instruction through the sixth grade. On the other hand, because the children's Spanish language development was not tied to their ethnic identity, and because they did not continue to receive instruction in Spanish after sixth grade, their attitude toward Spanish and their long-range use of it were adversely affected.

In contrast, the Cambodian community provided institutional support for the maintenance of religious and traditional customs. There was no community or school support for the Khmer language or literacy. The children only received ESL instruction, eventually losing their ability to communicate appropriately in Khmer. When school personnel used the children as translators to tell their parents about their school progress and performance, social disruption occurred due to the children's inappropriate language use and shift in roles between parents and children.

Recognition that English fluency and literacy do not necessarily result in second-language students' academic success in the United States is a topic that has garnered attention. Cummins (1989) argued that language minority students' school success depends on whether the schools accept or redefine the power relations reflected in broader society. Necessary prerequisites include the incorporation of students' languages and cultures into the school culture, the implementation of pedagogical empowerment strategies, and parental and community involvement in the students' school experiences. Cummins (1996) also warned that the quality of teacher–student interactions and peer interactions could be much more important to student success than specific teaching methods.

U.S. BILINGUAL EDUCATIONAL POLICY AND EVALUATION

The passage of the first U.S. bilingual education act in 1968 marked the federal government's acknowledgment that children who were not proficient in English could benefit from instruction that addressed their second-language status (see Crawford, 1991). The *Lau v. Nichols* (1974) court case, brought against the San Francisco Unified School District because the district did not address Chinese-speaking children's limited English status, resulted in the Office of Civil Rights requirement that all school districts had to meet the needs of their second-language students. During the 1970s, the Office of Civil Rights recommended that districts meet the educational and ESL needs of limited-English-proficient students through bilingual/bicultural educational programs.

Politics rather than program evaluation findings or research has stimulated many of the federal policy changes. Fitzgerald (1993) recounted how the federal attitude toward bilingual education changed between the 1970s and 1990s. In 1974, the wording in the Bilingual Education Act, Title VII of the Elementary and Secondary Education Act, stated that programs receiving federal support had to include instruction that included students' native languages and cultures. However, in 1978, this wording was amended to state that the native language was to be used for the explicit purpose of transitioning students into English. By 1984, 25% of the funding under the Bilingual Education Act was available for Special Alternative Instructional Programs, which did not provide any native language instruction (Crawford, 1997). By 1988, programs that provided English-only instruction were accepted and funded along with bilingual education programs (Fitzgerald, 1993).

A criticism of past bilingual program evaluations was that they did not take into account variations in instructional approaches or the amount of time spent teaching in the children's native language and English (García et al., 1994). In an attempt to control for this type of variation, Rámirez, Yuen, and Ramey (1991) conducted a longitudinal evaluation that carefully examined the language use and instruction that occurred in three types of programs serving predominantly low-income Spanish speakers: early-exit transitional bilingual education—a 3- to 4-year program in which children typically receive Spanish and ESL instruction until they are deemed capable of performing in English; structured immersion—a 3- to 4-year program in which children are taught solely in English by a teacher who knows Spanish; and late-exit transitional bilingual education—a 5- to 6-year program, similar to the early-exit program, except that children are moved into English instruction at a slower pace and often continue to receive instruction in Spanish throughout the program. The authors found that children in the early-exit programs received considerably more instruction in English during Grades K–1 (about 66%) than they had expected. In addition, teachers in all three types of programs employed a passive instructional style that resulted in limited opportunities for student development of complex language and higher order thinking skills.

Most importantly, Rámirez et al. (1991) reported that by the end of third grade, there was no significant difference in the standardized English language and reading test performance of Spanish-speaking students enrolled in the structured immersion and early-exit programs, even though students in the early-exit programs had received much less English instruction. They concluded that instruction in Spanish had not impeded the students' English language and reading performance. When they examined the performance of students in the late-exit programs, they discovered that those students who had the most opportunity to develop their Spanish between kindergarten and sixth grade actually increased their standardized English language and reading test performance at a significantly greater rate than students in the other late-exit classrooms or the normed sample from the standardized test. Rámirez et al. were surprised by this finding because it generally is difficult for low-income children in poor schooling situations to gain on their middle-class peers. They estimated that if the projected growth rate were sustained, students who had received instruction in Spanish 40% of the time would eventually catch up with their English-speaking peers and perform at grade level in English.

EARLY READING ACQUISITION
(PRESCHOOL TO GRADE 2)

Few researchers have studied young children's biliterate development. Titone (1985) argued that young bilingual children should be given the opportunity to become biliterate, given the advantage they often display on metalinguistic tasks compared to monolingual children. He also reminded us that by the age of 3 most bilingual children, raised in dual language settings, have learned to differentiate the languages they hear around them (Arneberg & Arneberg, 1992; McLaughlin, 1984). Therefore, they should not be confused by the presence of different written languages.

Metalinguistic Awareness

In a review of the metalinguistic literature, García, Jiménez, and Pearson (1998) pointed out that bilingual children up to the age of 6 tend to outperform monolingual children on isolated tasks of metalinguistic awareness related to reading. For example, in a comparative study of Yugoslavian preschool and kindergarten children, Göncz and Kodzopeljic (1991) found that bilingual children were significantly better than monolingual children at explaining how words such as "mosquito" and "ox" differed in their length and referents. Bruck and Genesee (1995) reported that bilingual English-speaking kindergarten children enrolled in French immersion schools in Canada significantly outperformed their monolingual English-speaking peers on tests of onset-rime awareness. Galambos and Goldin-Meadow (1990) found that young Spanish–English bilinguals in El Salvador outperformed their monolingual Spanish counterparts on sentence grammaticality tests in Spanish. When the bilingual children's performance on sentence grammaticality tests in English was compared to that of U.S. English monolinguals, there was no significant difference in the two groups' performance even though the bilingual children's English language proficiency was significantly lower.

Bialystok (1997) reported that 4- and 5-year-old bilingual preschoolers (French–English and Mandarin–English speakers) in Canada outperformed monolingual English-speaking preschoolers on a metalinguistic task specifically related to beginning reading: a moving word task, in which a word placed under its corresponding picture was accidentally moved to a different picture. She interpreted the superior performance of the bilingual children, and the fact that they performed the task equally well in both languages, to mean that they not only had a heightened knowledge of symbolic representation as encoded in text, but that they also could transfer this knowledge from one language to the other. On the other hand, only the 5-year-old Mandarin–English speakers outperformed the other children on a word-size task, which involved matching the length of words with their phonological representations when conflicting pictures based on the word meanings (e.g., dandelion–bus) were included. Bialystok hypothesized that the lower performance of the 4-year old Mandarin–English speakers on the word-size task might have been due to the initial confusion that young bilingual children face when they first are exposed to two radically different writing systems. In contrast, the superior performance of the 5-year-old Mandarin–English speakers seemed to indicate that once bilingual children figure out the differences, they develop more advanced awareness of specific representational properties than monolingual children.

In explaining the metalinguistic advantage held by young bilingual children, Bruck and Genesee (1995) pointed out that bilingualism seems to provide a type of "contrastive linguistics instruction which leads bilingual children to compare and analyze the structural aspects of language in more advanced ways than monolinguals" (p. 308). Why bilingual children's metalinguistic advantage generally seems to disappear after the age of 6 is not known, although García et al. (1998) speculated that it could be due to the predominant tendency to school bilingual children only in one language, effectively limiting their continued bilingual development.

Cross-Linguistic Transfer of Reading Skills

Very few researchers have investigated the specific types of reading skills and knowledge that young bilingual children transfer from one language to another (Durgunoğlu, Nagy, & Hancin-Bhatt, 1993; Verhoeven, 1994). This type of research predominantly has been informed by an information-processing paradigm, and has employed isolated tasks related to reading as well as multivariate analyses and regression techniques. For example, Durgunoğlu et al. administered a letter naming test, an English word recognition test, a Spanish word recognition test, Spanish phonological tasks, and English and Spanish oral proficiency tests to U.S. Spanish-speaking first graders who were beginning readers. To test for transfer of phonological awareness, they taught the children to read English-like pseudo words and later asked them to identify English words that included the onsets and rimes of the pseudo words previously taught.

Durgunoğlu et al. (1993) reported that the children's Spanish phonological awareness and Spanish word recognition significantly predicted their English word recognition and pseudo word recognition, indicating cross-linguistic transfer. Children who had phonological awareness and Spanish word recognition skills performed better on the transfer tasks compared to those children who could read some Spanish words but who demonstrated low Spanish phonological awareness. Durgunoğlu et al. concluded that the former children were able to transfer metalinguistic abilities related to phonological awareness in Spanish to English word recognition, without formal instruction in English phonological awareness, because similar types of word recognition processing underlie the two languages.

In an attempt to test Cummins's interdependence hypothesis, Verhoeven (1994) compared the oral language and reading comprehension of first- and second-grade

Turkish students in the Netherlands. Three-quarters of the students had been taught to read in Dutch (a submersion approach with 3 hours of weekly Turkish instruction), whereas the other quarter had been taught to read in Turkish before being transitioned into Dutch reading (a transitional approach). Verhoeven (1994) found that the submersion students' performance on Dutch word reading efficiency and reading comprehension measures were good predictors of their Turkish performance; likewise, the transitional students' performance on Turkish word reading efficiency and reading comprehension measures were good predictors of their Dutch performance. He concluded that both groups of children applied reading skills learned in one language to their other language, providing support for a bidirectional interpretation of Cummins's interdependence hypothesis.

Geva, Wade-Woolley, and Shany (1993) conducted one of the few studies to examine bilingual children's concurrent reading and spelling development in two languages. They reported that first-grade, English-speaking children in Canada who were acquiring Hebrew as a second language did not become confused when they were provided with concurrent literacy instruction in Hebrew and English. On the other hand, when they compared the children's first- and second-grade reading and spelling performance, they found that the children performed significantly better on Hebrew decoding tasks than on Hebrew spelling or English decoding tasks, reflecting the more consistent and regular grapheme–phoneme correspondence of Hebrew as compared to English. They also scored higher on the English spelling tasks than on the English decoding tasks. Geva et al. observed that learning to spell in Hebrew probably was more difficult than decoding because of orthographic complexities in Hebrew that are not phonologically based. Based on their findings, they proposed that the decoding and spelling development of bilingual children might vary according to the language structures being learned.

The extent to which bilingual children need to be taught phonological or orthographic elements characteristic of their second language, but not that salient to their native language, is a topic that needs further investigation. Both Durgunoğlu et al. (1993) and Verhoeven (1994) interpreted young bilingual children's cross-linguistic transfer of skills to be indicative of their metalinguistic competence rather than their ability to use language specific skills. Fashola, Drum, Mayer, and Kang (1996) predicted that bilingual children learning to spell in their second language would temporarily rely on first-language phonological and orthographic processes to spell second-language words with unfamiliar phonemes or graphemes. They compared the English spelling of second-, third-, fifth-, and sixth-grade Spanish-speaking children who were learning to spell in English with that of English-speaking children. Although there were no significant differences in the two groups' random spelling errors, the Spanish-speaking children made significantly more predictable errors, based on their Spanish phonemic and orthographic knowledge, than the English-speaking children, supporting the Fashola et al. prediction.

The Relationship Between Oral Language Proficiency and Reading

Almost all of the recent quantitative research, which has tested the relationship between young bilingual children's oral proficiency in their two languages and their performance on related reading tasks, has indicated that variables other than oral language proficiency were more powerful predictors of the children's reading task performance in either language (Durgunoğlu et al., 1993; Geva et al., 1993; Verhoeven, 1994). A partial explanation for this finding is that not all young children (monolingual and bilingual) who are orally proficient in a language can read in that language. On the other hand, the Geva et al. study on the concurrent literacy development of English-speaking children who were learning Hebrew as a second language revealed that the children's limited proficiency in Hebrew did not adversely affect their Hebrew spelling or decoding, which had been explicitly taught. The children were able to spell and decode at levels beyond their beginning second-language status as indicated on oral proficiency measures. The respective findings of Durgunoğlu et al. (1993) and Verhoeven (1994) implied that a key predictor of bilingual children's reading in the second language was their ability to transfer knowledge about reading from one language to another. In fact, Durgunoğlu, et al. reported that tests of first-language word recognition were better predictors of her bilingual subjects' second-language performance on reading tasks than their second-language oral proficiency. Geva (personal communication, 1998) speculated that the oral proficiency measures used with young children did not capture the types of oral language knowledge and skills that predicted their reading.

Although the Geva et al. (1993) findings and those of Verhoeven (1994) support the earlier claims of Barrera (1984) and Hudelson (1984) that bilingual children can learn to read and write in a second language as they develop their second-language oral competency, they do not mean that oral language development does not influence bilingual children's reading development. Other researchers, such as Seda and Abramson (1990) and Schmidt (1993), who have used qualitative methods to document the literacy progress of U.S. second-language learners enrolled in multilingual or all-English classroom settings, have shown that children who are not fluent in English do not develop aspects of their English literacy as quickly as their monolingual peers. In addition, Geva et al. warned that it was very likely that bilingual children's reading comprehension of second-language texts would be adversely affected by their limited second-language status.

EARLY READING INSTRUCTION
(PRESCHOOL TO GRADE 2)

Family Literacy Issues

Several researchers have noted the cultural conflicts that often occur between U.S. teachers and second-language parents when shared expectations regarding the school and parents' responsibilities are not clear (Delgado-Gaitán, 1990; Godina, 1997; Valdés, 1996). Valdés's ethnographic account of 10 immigrant Mexican families showed that the parents did not understand why U.S. teachers wanted their children to know the alphabet. To them, the alphabet was meaningless because in Mexican reading instruction, it was far more important for children to know the sounds of key syllables. Godina's (1997) ethnographic account of literacy practices in a rural, Mexican-American migrant community and Teale's (1986) study of emergent literacy in low-income homes, including Latina/o homes, revealed that parent–child book reading was not a common activity. Because writing accounted for over half of the literacy events that Teale documented, he recommended that additional research examine the role of writing in young children's literacy development.

Intergenerational literacy programs, usually based on a middle-class model of emergent literacy (Auerbach, 1989), have been developed in Spanish (Rodriguez-Brown & Mulhern, 1993; Shanahan, Mulhern, & Rodriguez-Brown, 1995) and English (Thornburg, 1993). The developers of Project FLAME (Shanahan et al., 1995) tried to offset a mainstream bias by focusing on what Latina/o parents deem important. Their program provides parents with Spanish literacy and ESL instruction, reading materials, book reading, and early literacy training. Despite the emphasis on parents, Shanahan et al. reported that the children's knowledge of basic concepts, letter names, and print awareness in Spanish had improved significantly. Thornburg did not report an increase in the children's English literacy performance, but did report an increase in their English oral fluency.

Reading Instruction in the First Language

Concerns have been voiced about the type of Spanish reading instruction bilingual children receive. Spanish adaptations of Reading Recovery (Escamilla, Andrade, Basurto, & Ruiz, 1990, 1991) and Success for All, termed Bilingual Cooperative Integrated Reading and Composition (Calderón, Tinajero, & Hertz-Lazarowitz, 1992), have been tried with U.S. Spanish-speaking children, but the results still have not been widely evaluated or published. In an experiment with Spanish-speaking kindergartners, Goldenberg (1994) reported that children who were taught to read through an academic code approach (which emphasized vowels, consonants, syllables, and words) outperformed children who received a reading-readiness or a storybook approach (where children took home books they had heard read at school). When Goldenberg added a code emphasis to the storybook reading approach, then there was no difference in performance between the two groups, leading him to question why early childhood educators were opposed to providing kindergartners with academic reading instruction. In subsequent observational research, Goldenberg criticized the slow pace of first- and second-grade reading instruction that was "weighted toward a phonics-based, bottom-up approach" (p. 187). He credited improvements in first- and second-graders' standardized reading test scores to the inclusion of an academic focus in kindergarten, a more balanced code-literature reading approach in first grade, and systematic efforts that involved the children's families in their early literacy development.

Pérez (1994) used ethnographic methods to investigate the reading development of 20 low-income Hispanic children in four bilingual "whole-language" classrooms (kindergarten, first, second, and fourth grade). By the end of the school year, four children still had difficulty decoding. Although the teachers were relatively inexperienced whole-language teachers, Pérez criticized three of them for not providing the students with efficient decoding strategies or helping them with print-specific skills.

In an interesting twist, Chang and Watson (1988) evaluated the use of predictable texts for the teaching of reading in Chinese to bilingual Chinese kindergartners enrolled in a weekend Chinese school in the United States. Their findings suggested that the kindergartners transferred what they knew about reading in English (their second language) to their reading in Chinese (their native/first language). In addition, after 15 weeks of weekly reading of predictable texts, the students recognized Chinese characters and were able to combine them to create new characters.

Reading Instruction in a Second Language

The extent to which second-language preschool children enrolled in ESL or all-English settings benefit from oral book reading in English has been questioned. In an ethnographic account of a multilingual preschool classroom—involving Chinese, Pakistani, Russian, and African children—García and Godina (1994) observed that the ESL learners had a difficult time paying attention to oral book reading in English. On the other hand, they were attentive during native-language book reading, responsive to English print in the classroom, and actively participated in literacy centers that allowed them to use their native languages and English (such as a post office, airport, restaurant). Thornburg (1993) reported that teachers involved in an intergenerational literacy program could not get ESL children to respond to English storybook reading when they used a cognitive approach that emphasized story grammar and prediction questions. When the teachers asked the children to relate their personal lives to what was being read, then their participation increased.

Other researchers have reported that storybook reading in English can work with ESL learners when native language support and sheltered English techniques, such as multiple modalities (seeing, hearing, touching) and structured repetition, are provided. For example, Battle (1993) described how a bilingual teacher used native-language support to structure daily storybook read alouds in English for her Mexican-American kindergartners. The teacher presented summaries of the books in Spanish, translated parts of the books during the read-aloud according to the children's responses, and allowed the children to participate in either language during group discussions. Blum et al. (1995) used single-subject reversal design with multiple baselines to study whether repeated home readings with audio tapes would improve five ESL first graders' reading fluency, monitoring, and motivation as compared to the home readings of books without the audio tapes. The authors concluded that the children improved their reading fluency when they used the audio tapes, but only made limited progress without the audio tapes.

READING DEVELOPMENT IN OLDER CHILDREN (GRADES 3–12)

Historically, two approaches have characterized the type of reading research conducted with older bilingual children. The first approach tends to compare the performance of bilingual readers with that of monolingual readers. The research design and interpretation generally are informed by monolingual research, and the bilingual students' reading performance in the second-language is the basis for comparison. In the second approach, a bilingual perspective is employed. Researchers investigate and identify "findings unique to bilinguals at the same time that [they] carefully evaluate the application of monolingual findings to bilingual populations" (García, 1998, p. 253). Much of this research has examined the variation that occurs within bilingual reading and has focused on bilingual students' reading in two languages.

Differences in Cultural Schemata and Vocabulary Knowledge

Differences in bilingual and monolingual children's cultural schemata for reading have been documented, with bilingual children generally knowing less about topics included in second-language texts (Droop & Verhoeven, 1997; García, 1991; Jiménez, García, & Pearson, 1995, 1996). García reported that even when U.S. Spanish-speaking, Latina/o and monolingual Anglo (non-Latina/o White) fifth and sixth graders had been in the same English-speaking classrooms for 2 years, they significantly differed in their background knowledge for standardized reading test passages in English, with the Latina/o students knowing less about specific topics. When differences in prior knowledge were controlled, then there was no significant difference in the two groups of students' reading test performance, although the Latina/o students still scored significantly more poorly on questions that required them to use background knowledge. García wondered if the low- and average-performing Latina/o students' literal interpretation of the text was due to the type of instruction they had received. Delgado-Gaitán's finding (1989) that teachers of bilingual students do not always encourage them to use their personal knowledge to construct meaning from text suggested that there could be an instructional relationship.

Droop and Verhoeven (1998) reported that the linguistic complexity of a text could impede bilingual students' performance on culturally relevant text. They found that Turkish and Moroccan third-grade children who were learning Dutch as a second language in the Netherlands performed significantly worse than Dutch children on texts from the Netherlands reading curriculum that emphasized Dutch culture. When the texts reflected the Turkish and Moroccan children's culture and were linguistically simple, then these children performed significantly better than the Dutch children. When the texts were linguistically complex, then the differences were negated due to the Turkish and Moroccan children's lower proficiency in Dutch.

García's (1991) comparison of the Latina/o and Anglo students' reading test performance in English also revealed that the Latina/o students knew significantly less of the English vocabulary in the test passages than the Anglo students. Interview data with a subsample of the students indicated that unfamiliar English vocabulary was the major linguistic factor that adversely affected the Latina/o students' reading test performance.

Differences in Metacognitive and Cognitive Reading Strategies

At least two sets of researchers have developed theoretical taxonomies to explain the types of strategies that monolingual and bilingual readers employ while reading (see Chamot & O'Malley, 1994; Jiménez et al., 1996). Chamot and O'Malley identified three types of interrelated strategies that they thought characterized the reading of monolingual and bilingual readers. In their framework, *metacognitive reading strategies* refer to students' conscious thinking about and reflections on reading (e.g., comprehension planning and monitoring). *Cognitive reading strategies* refer to how students accomplish reading (e.g., use of prior knowledge and inferencing), and *social and affective strategies* refer to how students interact with others during the act of reading (e.g., asking clarification questions). The Jiménez et al. framework included many of the same metacognitive and cognitive strategies as Chamot and O'Malley, but they categorized them as text-initiated strategies, interactive strategies, and reader-initiated strategies. Although Chamot and O'Malley listed linguistic transfer—bilingual students' recognition and use of similarities in their native language and second language—as a general cognitive reading strategy, Jiménez et al. specified the types of transfer strategies that bilingual students were observed using. I have chosen to discuss transfer strategies under the heading of cross-linguistic transfer.

Most of the research on bilingual students' use of strategies has focused on their employment of metacognitive and cognitive reading strategies. Very little research has examined their use of social and affective strategies. Previous research by Padrón, Knight, and Waxman (1986) with third- and fifth-grade bilingual Latina/o and monolingual Anglo students indicated that bilingual readers used fewer and less sophisticated metacognitive and cognitive strategies than monolingual readers. However, the Jiménez et al. (1995, 1996) think-aloud study of bilingual, Latina/o, middle school students' reading revealed similarities and differences in strategy use between 3 monolingual Anglo readers and 11 bilingual readers, depending on the bilingual students' reading level. The 3 less successful bilingual readers demonstrated the fewest and least sophisticated strategies, whereas, the 8 bilingual successful readers did not differ substantially from the monolingual successful readers in their comprehension monitoring, meaning construction, use of prior knowledge, or inferencing. On the other hand, similar to García's findings (1991), both the successful and less successful bilingual readers encountered more unknown English vocabulary and had less knowledge about the topics being read than the successful monolingual readers.

Cross-Linguistic Transfer of Knowledge and Strategies

A number of researchers have attempted to determine the extent to which bilingual students use the same metacognitive and cognitive strategies while reading in their two languages. Findings from self-report surveys indicated that intermediate (Calero-Breckheimer & Goetz, 1993) and high school (Pritchard, 1990) bilingual Latina/o students reported using the same strategies while reading in English and Spanish, implying cross-linguistic transfer. Researchers who employed qualitative methodologies, using think-alouds, interviews, and retellings, documented similarities in Spanish–English bilingual students' (fourth to seventh grade) reading profiles across languages (García, 1998; Jiménez et al., 1995; Langer, Bartolomé, Vásquez, & Lucas, 1990). However, García observed that it was very difficult to determine whether fourth-grade bilingual readers used exactly the same strategies across languages because their use of strategies varied according to the text genre, text difficulty, their language dominance, and reading ability. In fact, text genre rather than language seemed to characterize their use of strategies; that is, the students demonstrated similar strategies while reading expository text compared to narrative text, regardless of the language.

Spanish–English bilingual children's use of transfer strategies unique to their bilingual status also has been investigated. A cross-linguistic strategy that could help Latina/o children figure out unknown vocabulary in English is their recognition and use of Spanish–English cognates (words in Spanish/English with common ancestral roots that are similar in form and meaning). In a study with fourth-, fifth-, and sixth-grade Latina/o students, Nagy, García, Durgunoğlu, and Hancin-Bhatt (1993) found that when the students' English vocabulary knowledge was controlled, their Spanish vocabulary knowledge and post hoc ability to recognize cognates significantly predicted their English reading comprehension, indicating that they were making use of cognate relationships in their English reading. On the other hand, the fourth graders performed significantly more poorly than the fifth and sixth graders on the cognate recognition assessment, leading Nagy et al. to question whether the fourth graders' lower cognate recognition was due to developmental differences.

In a content analysis of the cognate recognition data, García and Nagy (1993) discovered that a majority of the students at all grade levels had identified less than half of the cognates that they previously had reported knowing separately in both Spanish and English. They also tended to identify words that were very close in orthographic correspondence. García and Nagy concluded that the students had an emerging concept of cognates and had underutilized cognate strategies in their reading.

Jiménez et al. (1995, 1996) and García (1998) argued that Spanish–English bilingual students' use of cross-linguistic strategies played a greater role in their reading comprehension than previously had been assumed. Jiménez et al. observed that what really differentiated the middle school bilingual successful readers from the less successful bilingual readers was their unitary view of reading across the two languages, use of knowledge across the two languages, occasional use of cognate strategies to figure out unknown vocabulary, code-switching (switching between languages at sentence boundaries to figure out what is being read), and translating (using one language to explain what was read in the other). Similar to the Nagy et al. (1993) findings, García found that her fourth-grade bilingual students made very little use of cognate strategies. On the other hand, they used code-switching, code-mixing (trying out a word from the other language within a sentence), and translating with much greater frequency than the middle school students in the Jiménez et al. (1996) study, who had much less experience in bilingual education. Paraphrased translating, where students put the translation into their own words, was more effective than direct or word-to-word translating. García argued that the students' code-mixing, code-switching, and paraphrased translating should not be viewed as compensatory strategies, but as resources that reflected their bilingual identity.

Interdependence Between Oral Language Proficiency and Reading

Several researchers (Langer et al., 1990; Peregoy & Boyle, 1991) have investigated the relationship between older bilingual children's second-language oral proficiency and their second-language reading performance in an attempt to determine whether bilingual students' reading ability in their second language is more dependent on their second-language oral proficiency or their first-language reading performance. In a think-aloud study that focused on the bilingual reading of 12 fifth-grade Mexican-American students, Langer et al. reported that beyond a need for basic English, what characterized the better English readers was their use of meaning-making strategies in Spanish and English reading, and not their English or Spanish oral proficiency. On the other hand, in a quantitative study, Peregoy and Boyle reported a strong and significant relationship between the English reading performance and English oral language proficiency of third-grade bilingual Latina/o students. The contradictory findings appear to be due to the variation in the students' ages, reading levels, types of assessments used, and the type of instruction the children received (see García et al., 1994). For example, the children in Peregoy and Boyle's study had received English instruction since kindergarten, but some of them were in bilingual educational programs; others were in all-English classrooms. Peregoy and Boyle acknowledged that there was wide variation in the low readers' performance, with some of the children demonstrating fairly high English proficiency but an inability to read in English.

Miramontes's (1990) comparative analysis of the oral miscue and retelling performance of three types of Mexican-American students demonstrated the importance of acknowledging differences in students' instructional backgrounds and language and reading proficiencies. A factor analysis indicated that there were significant differences in the reading strategy profiles of "good English readers" (students who had always received instruction in English) and "good ESL readers" (students who had received ESL and Spanish literacy instruction since kindergarten). The good ESL readers were better at grammatical relationships than the good English readers or the "mixed dominant students" (students who were Spanish speakers but whose instruction always had been in English), implying that they had a heightened awareness of grammar/correct forms in English. Miramontes also reported that although the mixed dominant students' comprehension strategies were similar to those of the good ESL readers, and their story recalls were better than those of the good English readers, their reading fluency scores were significantly lower than both groups. She speculated that the teachers were not aware of the mixed dominant students' sophisticated reading strategies because they were fooled by their low reading fluency.

READING INSTRUCTION OF OLDER STUDENTS (GRADES 3–12)

Because many U.S. bilingual children are enrolled in underfunded urban districts (Rámirez, et al., 1991), they frequently do not receive high-quality reading instruction. Padrón (1994) used the Classroom Observation Schedule to compare the type of reading instruction that an urban district provided to fourth and fifth graders in eight predominantly Hispanic schools (50% of the students were limited-English-proficient) with that of students from diverse populations in seven other schools. She found that the reading instruction in both types of schools was very passive, with most of the students receiving instruction in whole-class settings. Neither group of students spent much time actually reading; instead, most of their time was spent listening or watching their teachers.

Literature-Based and Whole-Language Approaches

The use of book clubs, whole-language approaches, and storybook reading with second-language learners of English has been examined in a variety of settings: all-English, ESL, and ESL transitional (Brock & Raphael, 1994; Elley, 1991, 1994; Reyes, 1991). Whether these approaches help the children to improve aspects of their English reading performance seems to depend on the extent to which they explicitly address their second-language needs. Reyes used a case study approach to analyze the literacy performance of 10 sixth-grade Hispanic bilingual students, whose teacher ascribed to a whole-language approach. According to Reyes, the students did not receive explicit instruction on selecting, analyzing, and discussing books, and, as a result, their English reading comprehension suffered. In addition, the mini-lessons that the teacher gave on English writing did not appear to be effective. The only time that the students made corrections in their literature log or dialogue journal writing was when the teacher explicitly corrected their writing in the log or journal.

Elley's (1991) findings showed that when literature-based activities were combined with quality ESL instruction they were effective with second-language learners who already were literate in their first language. He reviewed findings from two experiments conducted in the South Pacific (Niue, Figi) and Southeast Asia (Singapore) with 8- to 10-year-old, second-language learners of English, who already were literate in their first language but who were in their first year of English transition. In each of the experiments, the students who participated in a high-interest storybook approach, with a book flood, independent book choice, and silent reading, along with English instruction based on Krashen's (1985) comprehensible input theory, had significantly higher reading comprehension scores than students who participated in a controlled reading and audio-lingual approach or a structured reading and systematic oral instructional approach.

Metacognitive and Cognitive Strategy Instruction

Other researchers have tested the efficacy of monolingual interventions designed to improve students' metacognitive and cognitive reading strategies. Padrón (1992) found that third-, fourth-, and fifth-grade bilingual Latina/o students significantly improved their reported use of selected reading strategies in English after participating in a month of cognitive strategy instruction (30 minutes twice a week) that either emphasized reciprocal teaching or question–answer–response instruction. Muñiz-Swicegood (1994) reported that third-grade Latina/o students benefited from 6 weeks of Spanish metacognitive strategy instruction (90 minutes per day) that emphasized self-generating questions. In addition, the students significantly improved their standardized reading test performance in Spanish and English, implying that they transferred strategies learned in Spanish to their English reading.

Based on their taxonomy of metacognitive and cognitive strategies, Chamot and O'Malley (1996) developed the Cognitive Academic Language Learning Approach (CALLA) to aid ESL students in their English language development and comprehension of content area domains, such as mathematics, science, social studies, and literature. CALLA essentially provides students with content area ESL instruction that includes explicit strategy instruction to facilitate their comprehension of a specific content area. The rationale for CALLA is that (a) language is involved in all learning, and, therefore, teaching students vocabulary and linguistic structures relevant to a content area domain provides them with an authentic context for learning and an opportunity to develop their academic English; and (b) to actually become strategic learners, students must be involved in a setting where they have an authentic purpose for using the metacognitive and cognitive strategies being taught. Although CALLA appears promising, Chamot and O'Malley acknowledged that the newness of the approach has meant that there is very limited information available on its effectiveness in terms of student achievement and ESL development.

Jiménez (1997) used findings from his research with successful bilingual readers (Jiménez et al., 1996) to conduct a formative experiment with five low-literacy, seventh-grade, Latina/o students. In his cognitive strategy lessons, he emphasized reading fluency and word recognition skills; taught strategies for resolving unknown vocabulary, asking questions, and making inferences; and encouraged searching for cognates, translating, transferring knowledge, and reflecting on text in both languages. Jiménez reported that the use of culturally familiar text resulted in the students producing extended discourse about the text, which aided their inferencing. After 2 weeks of instruction, all of the students had increased their reading engagement.

Vocabulary Instruction

Although unknown vocabulary in the second language is a major problem for bilingual readers (García, 1991), few researchers have developed programs to improve students' second-language reading vocabulary. García (1996) reported that after receiving individualized scaffolded instruction on cognate recognition and use while reading, 10 out of 13 fourth-grade, Mexican-American students were able to access cognates to figure out unknown English vocabulary while reading. Neuman and Koskinen (1992) concluded that viewing captioned television provided seventh- and eighth-grade bilingual students (predominantly Cambodian) with the type of comprehensible input (Krashen, 1985) they needed to significantly improve their acquisition of English reading vocabulary. On the other hand, when Neuman and Koskinen examined the students' oral English proficiency scores, they discovered that those students who were most proficient in English had the highest vocabulary scores. They cautioned that there might be a threshold level of second-language competency that students need before they can benefit from captioned television without explicit teacher help.

Culturally Responsive Pedagogy

Moll and González (González et al., 1995; Moll, 1990; Moll & González, 1994) questioned the educational emphasis placed on traditional literacy activities that are commonplace in many Anglo, middle-class homes. Instead, they have shown how teachers can tap into and build on the "cultural funds of knowledge" of working-class, Latina/o (predominantly Mexican) families. Their approach first gets teachers to serve as ethnographers, investigating the funds of knowledge in children's families and community; then they work with teachers to connect their literacy instruction to the cultural resources they have documented outside of the classroom. As Moll and González explained, a major implication of the teachers' research has been "debunking ideas of working-class, language minority households as lacking worthwhile knowledge and experiences" (p. 444). Writings by the teachers have demonstrated a positive shift in their attitudes and knowledge about Latina/o students, families, and community (González et al., 1995).

RELATED ISSUES

Given the serious shortage of bilingual teachers in the United States (see August & Hakuta, 1997), it should not be too surprising to learn that many teachers who work with bilingual students lack relevant training. In a multischool instructional study that involved seven schools in California and Texas, Gersten (1996) reported that only 6 of the 19 third- to sixth-grade teachers, who worked with students transitioning into all-English instruction, had completed course work in ESL or sheltered English. Most of them knew that they should modulate the language-based curriculum that they implemented, but not all of them had effective strategies for doing so. Rueda and García's (1996) study on the attitudes and approaches of third- and fourth-grade teachers who worked with bilingual students revealed that certified bilingual teachers and temporary, emergency-credentialed bilingual teachers tended to view bilingualism and biculturalism more positively than special education teachers. However, none of the teachers fell at the constructivist end of the literacy or assessment continuum. Due to the pressure on them to teach English, all of them, even the bilingual credentialed teachers, said that they were reluctant to use native-language instruction.

The general consensus of researchers who have analyzed the second-language content of teaching resource materials is that teachers are not given the information they need to work effectively with bilingual or ESL students in all-English classrooms (Bernhardt, 1994; García, Montes, Janisch, Bouchereau, & Consalvi, 1993; Schumm, Vaughn, Klingner, & Haager, 1992). According to Bernhardt, textbook authors generally categorized second-language children with dialect speakers or with handicapped children. Few of them discussed the role of native-language literacy. García et al. reported that less than 6% of the reading and language arts journals dealt with second-language topics. Examination of the basal reading materials revealed that most of them dealt with English oral language development rather than literacy development.

Although several basal reading series now are published in Spanish, trade books in Spanish and reading materials in other native languages are in short supply. Pucci's (1994) case study of public and school libraries in the Los Angeles, California, area revealed a serious shortage of books in Spanish, as well as negative library practices that did not encourage the reading of Spanish books. Several researchers have voiced concerns about the shortage of multicultural children's literature—in English, Spanish, and other languages—that allows children to learn about their histories, see themselves reflected in the pages, and experience what it is like to read culturally familiar material for which they have the appropriate schemata (Aloki, 1993; Barrera, Liguori, & Salas, 1993; Nieto, 1993).

Fernández, Pearson, Umbel, and Oller's (1992) findings, along with those of García (1991), illustrate the difficulties involved in accurately assessing bilingual students' literacy development. Fernández et al. found that the word order difficulty on the Peabody Picture Vocabulary Test–Revised, Form L (1981), and its Spanish version, Test de Vocabulario en Imagenes Peabody, Adaptacion Hispanoamericana (1986), differed substantially for Cuban preschoolers in Miami, compared to the norming samples for monolingual preschoolers in English and Spanish. Fernández et al. also warned that single-language vocabulary tests would underestimate bilingual children's conceptual knowledge because they do not capture what children know in the other language.

García (1991) cautioned against overrelying on bilingual students' reading test scores in English to evaluate their English reading performance. She identified a number of testing factors—unfamiliar passage vocabulary, paraphrased vocabulary in test items, unfamiliar passage topics, scriptally implicit questions, limited time to complete the test—that adversely affected the standardized English reading test performance of Latina/o fifth and sixth graders compared to that of Anglo students.

Interviews with the Latina/o students, often in Spanish, revealed more information about their English reading comprehension than their actual test performance. The extent to which similar factors will adversely affect the performance assessment of bilingual students' reading in English has been discussed but not investigated (see García & Pearson, 1994).

Few researchers have studied the influence of affective factors on bilingual students' reading. When this type of research has occurred, it tends to look at students' English reading achievement in terms of their U.S. acculturation (García-Vázquez, 1995). Rarely is information presented on how the students view their home cultural and language backgrounds or how their home culture and language were used in school, so it is not possible to know if the students who attained high levels of English reading achievement also viewed their home languages and cultures positively.

SUMMARY AND IMPLICATIONS

Although more researchers have directed their attention to bilingual children's reading since Weber's (1991) review, the level and quality of the research still have not kept pace with the numbers of bilingual children living in the United States and throughout the world. In many cases, only a few researchers have investigated a key issue. The inclusion of international findings has helped to expand what is known about bilingual children's reading, especially that of young bilingual children. On the other hand, it is important to remember that the applicability of findings to other bilingual groups may vary according to the language and instructional contexts, and social, economic, and political status of the group (Collier & Thomas, 1989; Cummins, 1989, 1996; Hornberger, 1992; Rámirez et al., 1991). Although researchers from other countries focused on children who were not Spanish speakers, most of the U.S. researchers focused on this group of children.

Researchers who contributed to our knowledge of young bilingual children's reading focused on three interrelated topics: metalinguistic awareness, cross-linguistic transfer, and the relationship between oral language proficiency and reading. In addition, two of the international researchers provided some evidence in support of young children's biliteracy development. However, the metalinguistic topic is the only one for which there is considerable research. Previous researchers (among others, Ben-Zeev, 1977; Feldman & Shen, 1971; Ianco-Worrall, 1972) corroborated the finding that bilingual children younger than 6 years outperform their monolingual counterparts on isolated metalinguistic tasks related to reading. Why this advantage appears to disappear after the age of 6 needs to be researched. Miramontes (1990) was the only researcher who documented a metalinguistic advantage in older U.S. bilingual readers. Interestingly, these students had received Spanish and ESL instruction since kindergarten, supporting the García et al. (1998) contention that continued exposure to two languages throughout the schooling years might result in enhanced metalinguistic awareness.

Although the ability of young bilingual children to transfer knowledge and strategies from one language to the other is a key assumption underlying bilingual education, only two sets of researchers actually specified the types of knowledge and strategies that young bilingual children (Spanish–English bilinguals) seemed to transfer across languages. Four sets of researchers concluded that young bilingual children from diverse language backgrounds (Spanish–English, French–English, Mandarin–English, Turkish–Dutch, Hebrew–English) were able to transfer metalinguistic awareness related to reading. On the other hand, several of them thought that young bilingual children might need explicit instruction on structural features of the second language that were not characteristic of the first language. Whether this type of in-

struction actually is needed, what should be emphasized, and whether it can accelerate bilingual students' second-language reading development needs to be
investigated. In addition, more attention needs to be devoted to identifying specific
skills or strategies that transfer in young bilingual children's reading. This type of research needs to occur both in experimental settings (to see what is possible) and in natural, uncontrived settings (to see what actually happens).

None of the oral proficiency measures used by the researchers predicted the young
children's reading task performance. As mentioned earlier, this does not mean that
oral proficiency does not play a role in bilingual children's reading. It could be that the
measures do not accurately reflect aspects of oral knowledge that are important for
reading. On the other hand, several of the researchers reported that measures related
to first-language reading were better predictors of the children's second-language
reading development than oral proficiency measures. Additional research needs to
untangle the role of oral language and first-language reading development in young
bilingual children's second-language reading.

Unfortunately, the instructional research on young bilingual children's reading
does not help us to understand any of the issues just defined. Although
intergenerational literacy programs have been developed in Spanish and English, very
few researchers have examined how culturally relevant literacy activities in children's
homes affect their emergent literacy development. Two researchers argued that beginning reading instruction in Spanish was more effective when explicit attention to decoding and print-specific skills was combined with literature-based activities. Others
reported that young second-language learners of English had a difficult time participating in storybook reading in English when a cognitive approach was used or when
native-language support, multiple modalities, or structured repetition was not used.
The Rámirez et al. (1991) evaluation of the reading instruction provided to Spanish-speaking students in structured immersion, early-exit, and late-exit transitional bilingual education classrooms revealed that all of the students, regardless of the
language of instruction, received passive, teacher-directed instruction that did not
promote their development of complex language and higher order thinking skills.
Clearly, more researchers need to see what is possible when young bilingual children
receive quality reading instruction in their first and/or second languages. How different types of reading instruction affect their bilingual reading development also needs
to be explored. This type of research needs to focus on Spanish speakers as well as children from other diverse language backgrounds who usually are placed in an ESL or
all-English setting.

Even though more attention has focused on the reading development of older bilingual children compared to younger children, the research base still is limited, with
only a few researchers investigating each of the topics. Two types of research approaches have contributed to our understanding of older bilingual students' reading.
In the first approach, researchers compared the second-language reading performance
of bilingual students with that of monolingual students, who were reading in their native language. Findings from this type of research suggested that bilingual students'
second-language reading comprehension was adversely affected by their second-language status. They knew less about the topics included on reading tests and
reading curriculum passages, had difficulty with questions that required them to use
their background knowledge, had problems with unfamiliar vocabulary, and were adversely affected by linguistically complex text. The extent to which their problems
with background knowledge were due to instruction was raised but not answered.
Textual factors, such as textual cohesion or rhetorical structure, were not investigated.
Additional research needs to explore the obstacles that bilingual readers face while
reading in the second language as well as document how they react to and resolve such
obstacles.

Researchers who employed the second approach, which I termed a bilingual perspective, sometimes compared the second-language reading performance of U.S. Latina/o bilingual students to that of monolingual English-speaking students. However, they also examined the variation in performance that occurred among bilingual readers and often investigated their reading in two languages. Findings from this type of research suggested that comparative studies of monolingual and bilingual reading need to differentiate between successful and less successful bilingual readers. The Jiménez et al. (1996) qualitative study of successful and less successful middle school bilingual readers indicated that the less successful bilingual readers used fewer and less sophisticated metacognitive and cognitive strategies than the successful monolingual readers. In contrast, the successful bilingual and monolingual readers used similar metacognitive and cognitive strategies. The extent to which other successful and unsuccessful bilingual readers are characterized by similar reading profiles needs to be examined on a much larger basis.

Cross-linguistic transfer in older bilingual students' reading was investigated by several researchers. Findings based on self-report surveys indicated that bilingual readers reported using the same strategies while reading in their two languages. Qualitative studies also revealed that bilingual students generally had similar reading profiles across the two languages. However, as García (1998) noted, it was difficult to evaluate the cross-linguistic transfer of specific metacognitive and cognitive strategies because students' use of the strategies varied according to textual and reader features. The Jiménez et al. (1995, 1996) study of successful and less successful bilingual readers indicated that bilingual students' use of cross-linguistic transfer strategies was not automatic. Further research needs to examine to what extent, and under what conditions, bilingual readers utilize cross-linguistic transfer strategies.

Findings regarding the relationship between older bilingual students' oral language proficiency and their reading in a second language seemed to depend on whether the study was qualitative or quantitative, the ages and reading levels of the students, their instructional backgrounds, and how oral language proficiency was measured. It could be that the oral language proficiency measures that are used with older bilingual students measure aspects of second-language proficiency (e.g., knowledge of vocabulary and linguistic complexity) that are more related to the second-language reading of older bilingual students than what is measured on the oral proficiency measures used with younger students. Nonetheless, additional research needs to examine the extent to which a range of factors, including first-language reading development, the use of cross-linguistic strategies, instructional experiences, and second-language oral proficiency, predict older bilingual children's second-language reading performance.

The instructional research on older bilingual children's reading is meager. Limited evidence suggested that immersing second-language children in second-language, literature-based activities, such as storybook reading or process writing, without taking into account their second-language status was not very effective. On the other hand, the few researchers who implemented and tested metacognitive and cognitive strategy instruction in the first- or second-language appeared to obtain positive results. Using captioned television to develop reading vocabulary and teaching bilingual students how to use cognates and employ strategies similar to those of successful bilingual readers seemed to be promising but need to be investigated on a much larger scale.

Key topics, such as the extent to which bilingual children are taught how to use strategies and knowledge acquired in their first language in second-language reading or how students are transitioned into English reading and writing, received little attention. Although Rámirez et al. (1991) reported that continued exposure to Spanish language instruction through Grade 6 appeared to enhance low-income, U.S. Latina/o students'

English reading performance, how or why this instruction helped these students to develop their English reading has not been documented.

In closing, it is clear that considerably more research needs to focus on investigating the reading development and instruction of bilingual children. Longitudinal studies need to be conducted that examine bilingual children's reading process development in their two languages, taking into account the different types of instruction they receive, the settings in which they are taught, and the influence of social and contextual factors, such as the support and use of children's home languages and cultures. The metalinguistic findings for young bilingual children and the findings of Rámirez et al. (1991) and Collier and Thomas (1989) suggest that such research needs to begin and extend beyond the grades in which most bilingual children typically receive second-language services. Finally, improved research on bilingual children's reading and instruction will require funds and commitment, two items that have been sorely missing in the United States and other countries where bilingual students often are a language minority.

ACKNOWLEDGMENTS

I thank Rose-Marie Weber, Rosalinda Barrera, Robert T. Jiménez, and Michael Kamil for feedback on an early draft. I also thank Joan Primeaux and Jia-Ling Yau for their research assistance.

REFERENCES

Aloki, E. M. (1993). Turning the page: Asian Pacific American children's literature. In V. J. Harris (Ed.), *Teaching multicultural literature in grades K–8* (pp. 109–135). Norwood, MA: Christopher-Gordon.

Anstrom, K. (1996). Defining the limited-English-proficient student population. *Directions in Language and Education, 1*(9) (Summer). Washington, DC: National Clearinghouse for Bilingual Education.

Arneberg, L. N., & Arneberg, P. W. (1992). Language awareness and language separation in the young bilingual child. In R. J. Harris (Ed.), *Cognitive processing in bilinguals* (pp. 475–500). Amsterdam, The Netherlands: Elsevier.

Auerbach, E. R. (1989). Toward a social-contextual approach to family literacy. *Harvard Educational Review, 59,* 165–181.

August, D., & Hakuta, K. (Eds.). (1997). *Improving schooling for language-minority children: A research agenda.* Washington, DC: National Academy Press.

Barrera, R. (1984). Bilingual reading in the primary grades: Some questions about questionable views and practices. In T. H. Escobedo (Ed.), *Early childhood bilingual education: A Hispanic perspective* (pp. 164–184). New York: Teachers College Press.

Barrera, R., Liguori, O., & Salas, L. (1993). Ideas a literature can grow on. In V. J. Harris (Ed.), *Teaching multicultural literature in grades K–8* (pp. 203–241). Norwood, MA: Christopher-Gordon.

Battle, J. (1993). Mexican-American bilingual kindergarten collaborations in meaning making. In D. J. Leu & C. K. Kinzer (Eds.), *Examining central issues in literacy research, theory, and practice: Forty-second yearbook of the National Reading Conference* (pp. 163–169). Chicago: National Reading Conference.

Ben-Zeev, S. (1977). The influence of bilingualism on cognitive strategy and cognitive development. *Child Development, 48,* 1009–1018.

Bernhardt, E. B. (1994). A content analysis of reading method texts: What are we told about the non-native speaker of English? *Journal of Reading Behavior, 26*(2), 159–189.

Bialystok, E. (1997). Effects of bilingualism and biliteracy on children's emerging concepts of print. *Developmental Psychology, 33*(3), 429–440.

Blum, I. H., Koskinen, P. S., Tennant, N., Parker, E. M., Straub, M., & Curry, C. (1995). Using audiotaped books to extend classroom literacy instruction into the homes of second-language learners. *Journal of Reading Behavior, 27*(4), 535–563.

Brock, C. H., & Raphael, T. E. (1994). Mei: Constructing meaning during a sixth-grade social studies unit. In C. K. Kinzer & D. J. Leu (Eds.), *Multidimensional aspects of literacy research, theory, and practice: Forty-third yearbook of the National Reading Conference* (pp. 89–100). Chicago: National Reading Conference.

Bruck, M., & Genesee, F. (1995). Phonological awareness in young second language learners. *Child Language, 22,* 307–324.

Calderón, M. E., Tinajero, J. V., & Hertz-Lazarowitz, R. (1992). Adapting Cooperative Integrated Reading and Composition (CIRC) to meet the needs of bilingual students. *Journal of Educational Issues of Language Minority Students, 10,* 79–106.

Calero-Breckheimer, A., & Goetz, E. T. (1993). Reading strategies of biliterate children for English and Spanish texts. *Reading Psychology, 14*(3), 177–204.

Carrell, P. (1989). SLA and classroom instruction: Reading. *Annual Review of Applied Linguistics, 9*, 223–242.

Cavicchiori, V., & Erickson, A. (1991). *Statistical issues. Special survey on primary education* (STE-4). Paris, France: United Nations Educational, Scientific, and Cultural Organization. (Microfiche 4110-D35.5)

Chang, Y., & Watson, D. J. (1988). Adaptation of prediction strategies and materials in a Chinese/English bilingual classroom. *Reading Teacher, 42*, 36–44.

Chamot, A. U., & O'Malley, J. M. (1996). The cognitive academic language learning approach: A model for linguistically diverse classrooms. *Elementary School Journal, 96*(3), 259–273.

Collier, V. P., & Thomas, W. P. (1989). How quickly can immigrants become proficient in school English? *Journal of Educational Issues of Language Minority Students, 16*(1–2), 187–212.

Crawford, J. (1991). *Bilingual education: History, politics, theory and practice* (2nd ed.) Los Angeles, CA: Bilingual Educational Services.

Crawford, J. (1997). *Best evidence: Research foundations of the Bilingual Education Act.* Washington, DC: National Clearinghouse for Bilingual Education.

Cummins, J. (1981). The role of primary language development in promoting educational success for language minority students. In California State Department of Education (Ed.), *Schooling and language minority students: A theoretical framework* (pp. 3–49). Los Angeles: Evaluation, Dissemination and Assessment Center, California State University.

Cummins, J. (1989). *Empowering minority students.* Sacramento, CA: California Association for Bilingual Education.

Cummins, J. (1996). *Negotiating identities: Education for empowerment in a diverse society.* Ontario, CA: California Association for Bilingual Education.

Delgado-Gaitán, C. (1990). *Literacy for empowerment: The role of parents in children's education.* New York: Falmer Press.

Delgado-Gaitán, C. (1989). Classroom literacy activity for Spanish-speaking students. *Linguistics and Education, 1*, 285–297.

Droop, M., & Verhoeven, L. (1998). Background knowledge, linguistic complexity, and second-language reading comprehension. *Journal of Literacy Research, 30*(2), 253–271.

Durgunoğlu, A., Nagy, W., E., & Hancin-Bhatt, B. J. (1993). Cross-language transfer of phonological awareness. *Journal of Educational Psychology, 85*, 453–465.

Dworin, J. (in press). *Examining children's biliteracy in the classroom.* In A. I. Willis, G. E. García, V. J. Harris, & R. Barrera (Eds.), *Multicultural issues in literacy research and practice.* Mahwah, NJ: Lawrence Erlbaum Associates.

Elley, W. B. (1991). Acquiring literacy in a second language: The effect of book-based programs. *Language Learning, 41*(3), 375–411.

Escamilla, K., Andrade, A., Basurto, A., & Ruiz, O. (1990, 1991). Descubriendo la lectura: An early intervention Spanish language literacy project. *Annual Conference Journal, National Association for Bilingual Education,* pp. 31–43.

Fashola, O. S., Drum, P. A., Mayer, R. E., & Kang, S. (1996). A cognitive theory of orthographic transitioning: Predictable errors in how Spanish-speaking children spell English words. *American Educational Research Journal, 33*(4), 825–843.

Feldman, C., & Shen, M. (1971). Some language-related cognitive advantages of bilingual 5-year olds. *Journal of Genetic Psychology, 118*, 235–244.

Fernández, M. C., Pearson, B. Z., Umbel, V. M., & Oller, D. K. (1992). Bilingual receptive vocabulary in Hispanic preschool children. *Hispanic Journal of Behavioral Sciences, 14*, 268–276.

Fitzgerald, J. (1993). Views on bilingualism in the United States: A selective historical review. *Bilingual Research Journal, 17*, 35–56.

Fitzgerald, J. (1995a). English-as-second-language learners' cognitive reading processes: A review of research in the United States. *Review of Educational Research, 65*, 145–190.

Fitzgerald, J. (1995b). English-as-second-language reading instruction in the United States: A research review. *Journal of Reading Behavior, 27*, 115–152.

Galambos, S. J., & Goldin-Meadow, S. (1990). The effects of learning two languages on levels of metalinguistic awareness. *Cognition, 34*, 1–56.

García, G. E. (1991). Factors influencing the English reading test performance of Spanish-speaking Hispanic children. *Reading Research Quarterly, 26*(4), 371–392.

García, G. E. (1996, December). *Improving the English reading of Mexican-American bilingual students through the use of cognate recognition strategies.* Paper presented at the National Reading Conference, Charleston, SC.

García, G. E. (1998). Mexican-American bilingual students' metacognitive reading strategies: What's transferred, unique, problematic? *National Reading Conference Yearbook, 47*, 253–263.

García, G. E., & Godina, H. (1994). *Bilingual preschool children's classroom literacy experiences: 'Once upon a time' and its alternatives.* (ERIC Document Reproduction Service No. ED 381 770)

García, G. E., Jiménez, R. T., & Pearson, P. D. (1998). Metacognition, childhood bilingualism, and reading. In D. J. Hacker, J. Dunlosky, & A. C. Graesser (Eds.), *Metacognition in educational theory and practice* (pp. 193–219). Mahwah, NJ: Lawrence Erlbaum Associates.

García, G. E., Montes, J., Janisch, C., Bouchereau, E., & Consalvi, J. (1993). Literacy needs of limited-English proficient students: What information is available to mainstream teachers? In D. J. Leu & C. K. Kinzer (Eds.), *Examining central issues in literacy research, theory, and practice: Forty-second yearbook of the National Reading Conference* (pp. 171–177). Chicago: National Reading Conference.

García, G. E., & Nagy, W. (1993). Latino students' concept of cognates. In D. J. Leu & C. K. Kinzer (Eds.), *Examining central issues in literacy research, theory, and practice: Forty-second yearbook of the National Reading Conference* (pp. 367–373). Chicago: National Reading Conference.

García, G. E., & Pearson, P. D. (1994). Assessment and diversity. *Review of Research in Education, 20,* 337–391.

García, G. E., Pearson, P. D., & Jiménez, R. T. (1994). *The at-risk situation: A synthesis of reading research (Special report).* Champaign, IL: Center for the Study of Reading, University of Illinois.

García-Vázquez, E. (1995). Acculturation and academics: Effects of acculturation on reading achievement among Mexican-American students. *Bilingual Research Journal, 19,* 305–315.

Gersten, R. (1996). The language minority student in transition: Contemporary instructional research. *Elementary School Journal, 96*(3), 217–244.

Geva, E., Wade-Woolley, L., & Shany, M. (1993). The concurrent development of spelling and decoding in two different orthographies. *Journal of Reading Behavior, 25,* 383–406.

Godina, H. (1998). *Mexican-American high school students and the role of literacy across home–school–community settings.* Unpublished doctoral dissertation, University of Illinois at Urbana-Champaign.

Goldenberg, C. (1994). Promoting early literacy development among Spanish-speaking children: Lessons from two studies. In E. H. Hiebert and B. M. Taylor (Eds.), *Getting reading right from the start* (pp. 171–199). Boston: Allyn & Bacon.

Göncz, L., & Kodzopeljic, J. (1991) Exposure to two languages in the preschool period: Metalinguistic development and the acquisition of reading. *Journal of Multilingual and Multicultural Development, 12*(3), 137–163.

González, N., Moll, L., Tenery, M. F., Rivera, A., Rendon, P., Gonzales, R., & Amanti, C. (1995). Funds of knowledge for teaching in Latino households. *Urban Education, 29*(4), 443–470.

Hornberger, N. H. (1992). Biliteracy contexts, continua, and contrasts: Policy and curriculum for Cambodian and Puerto Rican students in Philadelphia. *Education and Urban Society, 24,* 196–211.

Hudelson, S. (1984). Kan yu ret an rayt en ingles: Children become literate in English as a second language. *TESOL Quarterly, 18,* 221–238.

Ianco-Worrall, A. D. (1972). Bilingualism and cognitive development. *Child Development, 43,* 1390–1400.

Jiménez, R. T. (1997). The strategic reading abilities and potential of five low-literacy Latina/o readers in middle school. *Reading Research Quarterly, 32,* 224–243.

Jiménez, R. T., García, G. E., & Pearson, P. D. (1995). Three children, two languages, and strategic reading: Case studies in bilingual/monolingual reading. *American Educational Research Journal, 32,* 31–61.

Jiménez, R. T., García, G. E., & Pearson, P. D. (1996). The reading strategies of bilingual Latina/o students who are successful English readers: Opportunities and obstacles. *Reading Research Quarterly, 31*(1), 90–112.

Krashen, S. (1985). *The input hypothesis: Issues and implications.* New York: Longman.

Langer, J. A., Bartolomé, L., Vásquez, O., & Lucas, T. (1990). Meaning construction in school literacy tasks: A study of bilingual students. *American Educational Research Journal, 27*(3), 427–471.

McLaughlin, B. (1984). *Second-language acquisition in childhood. Vol. 1: Preschool children.* Hillsdale, NJ: Lawrence Erlbaum Associates.

Miramontes, O. (1990). A comparative study of English oral reading skills in differently schooled groups of Hispanic students. *Journal of Reading Behavior, 22,* 373–394.

Moll, L. C. (1990, February). *Literacy research in community and classrooms: A sociocultural approach.* Paper presented at the conference on Multi-disciplinary Perspectives on Research Methodology in Language Arts, National Conference on Research in English, Chicago.

Moll, L. C., & González, N. (1994). Critical issues: Lessons from research with language-minority children. *Journal of Reading Behavior: A Journal of Literacy, 26*(4), 439–456.

Muñiz-Swicegood, M. (1994). The effects of metacognitive reading strategy training on the reading performance and fluent reading analysis strategies of third grade bilingual students. *Bilingual Research Journal, 18,* 83–97.

Nagy, W. E., García, G. E., Durgunoğlu, A., & Hancin-Bhatt, B. (1993). Spanish-English bilingual children's use and recognition of cognates in English reading. *Journal of Reading Behavior, 25*(3), 241–259.

Neuman, S. B., & Koskinen, P. (1992). Captioned television as comprehensible input: Effects of incidental word learning from context for language minority students. *Reading Research Quarterly, 27*(1), 95–109.

Nieto, S. (1993). We have stories to tell: A case study of Puerto Ricans in children's books. In V. J. Harris (Ed.), *Teaching multicultural literature in grades K–8* (pp. 171–201). Norwood, MA: Christopher-Gordon.

Padrón, Y. (1992). The effect of strategy instruction on bilingual students' cognitive strategy use in reading. *Bilingual Research Journal, 16,* 35–52.

Padrón, Y. (1994). Comparing reading instruction in Hispanic/limited English-proficient schools and other inner-city schools. *Bilingual Research Journal, 18,* 49–66.

Padrón, Y. N., Knight, S. L., & Waxman, H. C. (1986). Analyzing bilingual and monolingual students' perceptions of their reading strategies. *Reading Teacher, 39*(5), 430–433.

Peregoy, S. F., & Boyle, O. F. (1991). Second language oral proficiency characteristics of low, intermediate, and high second language readers. *Hispanic Journal of Behavioral Sciences, 13*, 35–47.

Pérez, B. (1994). Spanish literacy development: A descriptive study of four bilingual whole-language classrooms. *Journal of Reading Behavior: A Journal of Literacy, 26*, 75–94.

Pritchard, R. (1990, December). *Reading in Spanish and English: A comparative study of processing strategies.* Paper presented at the National Reading Conference, Miami, FL.

Pucci, S. L. (1994). Supporting Spanish language literacy: Latino children and free reading resources in California. *Bilingual Research Journal, 18*, 67–97.

Rámirez, J. D., Yuen, S. D., & Ramey, D. R. (1991). *Executive summary: Final report: Longitudinal study of structured English immersion strategy, early-exit and late-exit transitional bilingual education programs for language minority children.* San Mateo, CA: Aguirre International.

Reyes, M. de la Luz (1991). A process approach to literacy using dialogue journals and literature logs with second language learners. *Research on the Teaching of English, 25*, 291–313.

Rodriguez-Brown, F. V., & Mulhern, M. M. (1993). Fostering critical literacy through family literacy: A study of families in a Mexican-immigrant community. *Bilingual Research Journal, 17*, 1–16.

Rueda, R., & García, E. (1996). Teachers' perspectives on literacy assessment and instruction with language-minority students: A comparative study. *Elementary School Journal, 96*, 311–332.

Schmidt, P. R. (1993). Literacy development of two bilingual, ethnic-minority children in a kindergarten program. In D. J. Leu & C. K. Kinzer (Eds.), *Examining central issues in literacy research, theory, and practice: Forty-second yearbook of the National Reading Conference* (pp. 189–196). Chicago: National Reading Conference.

Schumm, J. S., Vaughn, S., Klingner, J. K., & Haager, D. (1992). A content analysis of basal readers: Teaching suggestions for ESL/LEP students learning to read in English. In C. K. Kinzer & D. J. Leu (Eds.), *Literacy research, theory, and practice: Views from many perspectives: Forty-first yearbook of the National Reading Conference* (pp. 425–434). Chicago: National Reading Conference.

Seda, I., & Abramson, S. (1990). English writing development of young, linguistically different learners. *Early Childhood Research Quarterly, 5*, 379–391.

Shanahan, T., Mulhern, M., & Rodriguez-Brown, F. (1995). Project FLAME: Lessons learned from a family literacy program for linguistic minority families. *Reading Teacher, 48*(7), 586–593.

Snow, C. E., Burns, M. S., & Griffin, P. (Eds.). (1998). *Preventing reading difficulties in young children.* Washington, DC: National Academy Press.

Teale, W. H. (1986). Home background and young children's emergent literacy development. In W. H. Teale & E. Sulzby (Eds.), *Emergent literacy: Writing and reading* (pp. 173–206). Norwood, NJ: Ablex.

Thornburg, D. (1993). Intergenerational literacy learning with bilingual families: A context for the analysis of social mediation of thought. *Journal of Reading Behavior, 25*(3), 321–352.

Titone, R. (1985). Early bilingual reading. *Prospects, 15*, 67–75.

Valdés, G. (1996). *Con respeto: Bridging the distances between culturally diverse families and schools: An ethnographic portrait.* New York: Teachers College Press.

Verhoeven, L. T. (1994). Transfer in bilingual development: The linguistic interdependence hypothesis revisited. *Language Learning, 44*, 381–415.

Weber, R. M. (1991). Linguistic diversity and reading in American society. In R. Barr, M. L. Kamil, P. Mosenthal, & P. D. Pearson (Eds.), *The handbook of reading research* (Vol. 2, pp. 97–119). New York: Longman.

CHAPTER 43

A Multicultural Perspective on Policies for Improving Literacy Achievement: Equity and Excellence

Kathryn H. Au
University of Hawaii

From the perspective of multicultural education, the key cultures are considered to be ethnicity or national origin, social class, primary language, gender/sex, religion, age, geographic region, urban–suburban–rural, and exceptionality (Gollnick & Chinn, 1990). Three of these cultural variables—ethnicity, social class, and primary language—are consistently related to schools' difficulties in serving students well and bringing them to high levels of literacy. In the United States, the students least well served by schools often are African American, Asian American, Latina/o, and Native American in ethnicity; come from poor and working-class families; and speak home languages other than standard American English. These students are referred to here as *students of diverse backgrounds*. Students of these ethnicities constitute a growing percentage of the U.S. school-age population, accounting for about 35% of the total enrollment in prekindergarten through Grade 12 (Nettles & Perna, 1997). Many of these children grow up in poverty. For example, in 1992, 44% of African American preschoolers lived in households with incomes under $10,000, a figure $5,000 below the poverty line for a family of four. At the same time, 2.3 million students in the United States spoke a first language other than standard American English and were considered to have "limited English proficiency" (U. S. Department of Education, 1992).

A gap between the literacy achievement of students of diverse background and students of mainstream backgrounds has long been recognized. The National Assessment of Educational Progress (NAEP) has monitored the literacy achievement of U.S. students at three grade levels for over 25 years. Results of the 1994 reading assessment for Grade 4 (9-year-olds) indicated the following percentages of students performing below a basic level of proficiency: Whites, 29%; African Americans, 69%; and Hispanics, 64% (Nettles & Perna, 1997). Comparable differences were observed at Grade 8 (13 year olds) and Grade 12 (17 year olds). Although the gap has narrowed somewhat over the years, differences between the literacy achievement of students of diverse backgrounds and mainstream students remain significant.

EXCELLENCE AND EQUITY

Literacy is high on the policy agenda in the United States (Elliott, 1996). A well-educated, literate workforce is seen as key to America's continued prosperity and competitiveness in the global marketplace. Goal 3, on student achievement and citizenship, of the National Educational Goals (1995) reads:

> By the year 2000, all students will leave grades 4, 8, and 12 having demonstrated competency over challenging subject matter including English, mathematics, science, foreign languages, civics and government, economics, arts, history, and geography, and every school in America will ensure that all students learn to use their minds well, so they may be prepared for responsible citizenship, further learning, and productive employment in our Nation's modern economy. (p. 11)

Goal 6 proclaims that every adult American will be literate. Given these goals, a priority from a policy perspective is to see that the benefits of high levels of achievement in a demanding curriculum are extended to students of diverse backgrounds, and not just to mainstream students. One of the objectives under Goal 3 refers directly to equity:

> The academic performance of all students at the elementary and secondary level will increase significantly in every quartile, and the distribution of minority students in each quartile will more closely reflect the student population as a whole. (National Education Goals Panel, 1995, p. 11)

The twin goals of excellence and equity, or quality and equality, in students' achievement are evident. *Excellence* is defined as students using their minds well when faced with challenging subject matter. In terms of literacy achievement, this definition points to an emphasis on higher level thinking with text. *Equity* is framed in terms of improving the achievement of students of diverse backgrounds to a level similar to that of mainstream students. Elliott (1996) believed that the question for U.S. policymakers is that of implementation, knowing what government can and should do to achieve these goals.

Considerable consensus among U.S. policymakers made the narrowing of the literacy achievement gap a priority. However, this consensus is by no means universal. Groups on the far right of the political spectrum attempted in the 1990s to dismantle affirmative action programs and to promote a meritocratic concept of equity, without regard to issues of cultural bias and community power. As Paquette (1998) noted, these groups argue from an economic perspective that educational resources should be concentrated on those most able to contribute to society in the future. In practice, of course, those judged most able are mainstream students who enter school with considerable cultural capital. In the view of the far right, equity and excellence are seen as competing goals, with excellence to be given priority and the low achievement of students of diverse backgrounds to be accepted as a given. Fortunately, this view has not yet prevailed. However, in Labaree's (1997) view, the trend is toward a social mobility, meritocratic view of education, and away from a democratic, egalitarian view.

Given the twin goals of equity and excellence, and the question of implementation, what are the key findings from research on the literacy achievement of students of diverse backgrounds? How are these findings related to issues of policy? The first section of this chapter presents an overview of research findings. The second section addresses equity policy and provides an understanding of existing efforts. In the final section, implications of research for policy, and implications of policy for research, are discussed.

RESEARCH ON THE LITERACY ACHIEVEMENT
OF STUDENTS OF DIVERSE BACKGROUNDS

Prior to the 1980s, reading researchers, often psychologists by training, gave scant attention to issues of equity, including the roles of ethnicity, social class, and primary language. As Willis and Harris (1997) pointed out, it is evident in hindsight that the omission of these issues in the large-scale First-Grade Studies (Bond & Dykstra, 1967) and other work resulted in missed opportunities to challenge the status quo in the reading instruction of students of diverse backgrounds. Beginning in the 1980s, considerable research began to appear on the language and culture of students of diverse backgrounds and the role of these factors in students' learning to read. Conducted primarily by linguists and anthropologists, these studies reflected the shift from a cultural deficit to a cultural differences paradigm. Reviews of this research are presented next.

Language Issues

In Volume II of the *Handbook of Reading Research*, Weber (1991) discussed research on learning to read in situations where more than one language is involved for the reader. Weber's review highlighted the predominance of English in the United States and the preference for bilingual programs that promoted the teaching of English over the maintenance of the mother tongue (see also Pease-Alvarez & Hakuta, 1992). A policy issue growing from Weber's review is the value attached to literacy in languages other than English in the United States. The irony is that the speaking of a first language other than English is considered a liability in young students who are from immigrant or low-income families. Yet the learning of second or foreign languages is a goal later in school, especially at elite high schools and colleges. As a consequence of the emphasis only on English, research tended to focus on young students' limited proficiency in English rather than on their knowledge of other languages. Considerable research had been conducted on the effectiveness of bilingual programs, but at this time, Weber judged much of this research to be flawed and inconclusive. Weber concluded that reading in a second language is much like reading in the first, with many processes being transferable from the first to the second language. Fitzgerald (1994) reached a similar conclusion in a review of U.S. research on the cognitive reading processes of English-as-a-second-language (ESL) learners. Taken together, the findings of these reviews suggested that, on the whole, the effective reading instruction of ESL learners follows the same general principles as for native speakers of English.

The nature of these general principles is summarized in Farr's (1991) review of studies of dialects, culture, and language arts instruction. Farr arrived at three principles of effective instruction for students of diverse backgrounds. The first and most important principle is that of "ethnosensitivity," that is, the need for teachers to understand and build upon students' home culture and language. The second principle involves emphasizing literacy activities that engage students in purposeful communication with a real audience, for example, exchanging thoughts with a teacher through dialogue journals. The third principle concerns the need for extensive involvement with written texts, such as novels, biographies, and poetry. Farr noted, "The more experience students have with such texts, the more easily they will acquire the particular linguistic devices and cultural orientation that they contain" (p. 369). This principle supports policy efforts to involve all students with challenging subject matter. Farr concluded by recommending instruction for all students consistent with these principles and coursework for current and future teachers to develop ethnosensitivity based on sociolinguistic research with students of diverse backgrounds. She also saw the need for further ethnographic research on community uses of language and literacy, so that classroom instruction can be modified to make connections to these practices.

Fitzgerald's (1995) review extended Farr's conclusions. Fitzgerald summarized studies of ESL reading instruction in the United States. The first topic addressed in her review was the usual nature of ESL classroom instruction. Research suggests that, at least in the primary grades, most instruction occurs in small groups and emphasizes lower level skills of word identification and oral reading, rather than higher level processes of comprehension and vocabulary meaning. In keeping with Farr's findings, Fitzgerald noted that the usual discourse patterns in reading lessons are incompatible with those of students' homes, although some teachers are able to adopt discourse patterns familiar to students. When working with ESL students in groups judged to be of lower ability, teachers place an even greater emphasis on low-level skills than when working with higher ability ESL groups. These patterns are of concern from a policy perspective, given the goal of moving all students toward higher level thinking about text.

Fitzgerald's second topic had to do with the role and timing of native-language and ESL reading instruction and their effects on reading achievement. The programs evaluated ranged from transitional bilingual, in which high use was made of the native language, to submersion, in which no special measures were taken for ESL learners. No program was shown to be clearly superior to the others in terms of effects on English reading achievement. However, a report of the National Research Council (1998) concluded that research supported beginning reading instruction in the native language (see also Cummins, 1996).

The third topic addressed in Fitzgerald's review concerns effective methods of ESL reading instruction. Systematic instruction directed at specific strategies or aspects of students' knowledge generally had positive effects. For example, such instruction helped students learn vocabulary and text structures and enabled them to acquire background knowledge related to text content. The final topic was professional materials for teachers, such as textbooks and journals. Fitzgerald's major finding was that these materials provide teachers with little information about theory and practice in the instruction of students in ESL reading.

Cultural Responsiveness

The importance to literacy achievement of teachers building on students' home language and culture, noted in Farr's and Fitzgerald's reviews, was further highlighted by Au and Kawakami (1994). These investigators summarized research on cultural congruence, or cultural responsiveness in instruction. The overall hypothesis in this research is that students of diverse backgrounds often do poorly in school because of a mismatch between their home culture and the culture of the school. Conversely, if lessons are conducted in a manner responsive to the home culture, students' learning opportunities will be improved. Culturally responsive instruction does not mean an exact match to home situations but a connecting to the patterns of participation and values expressed in such situations. Au and Kawakami found positive results when teachers accepted and built on students' home language; structured interaction with students in a manner consistent with their home values; kept expectations high and focused on meaning-making rather than lower level skills; recognized that storytelling and question answering may take different forms in different cultures; and capitalized on students' ability to learn from peers. Au and Kawakami noted that teachers who were outsiders to a culture could learn to teach in a culturally responsive manner, a finding reinforced in research by Ladson-Billings (1994). These findings point to the need for policies supporting teacher education programs designed to acquaint more teachers with the principles of culturally responsive instruction and to prepare them to use this type of instruction in their classrooms to improve students' literacy learning.

Although culturally responsive instruction may have a positive effect, other elements also appear important in closing the literacy achievement gap. Au (1998) reviewed research conducted from a social constructivist perspective on the school literacy learning of students of diverse backgrounds. From a social constructivist perspective, the literacy achievement gap is seen to be produced through the interactions of many systems and participants, including districts, schools, communities, teachers, students, and families. Au found this research to support seven recommendations for improving students' literacy learning. These recommendations are that educators:

1. Establish ownership of literacy as the overarching goal of the language arts curriculum.
2. Recognize the importance of students' home languages and promote biliteracy.
3. Increase the use of multicultural literature in classrooms.
4. Promote cultural responsiveness in classroom management and teachers' interactions with students.
5. Make stronger links to the community.
6. Provide students with authentic literacy activities and instruction in specific skills.
7. Use forms of assessment that reduce bias and more accurately reflect students' literacy achievement.

The problem of improving the literacy achievement of students of diverse backgrounds is complex, and the policy implication evident in Au's review is that multiple changes, rather than just one, will be required to make a difference.

Typical School Patterns

The need for deep, systemic changes to narrow the literacy achievement gap was demonstrated by Allington (1991). He summarized research that has looked at how schools typically respond to students of diverse backgrounds who find learning to read difficult. Instructional time is a major factor. Schools that serve large numbers of students of diverse backgrounds typically schedule less time for classroom literacy instruction than schools that serve middle-class, mainstream students. A disproportionate number of students of diverse backgrounds are placed in remedial and special education programs. Allington observes that these students, who struggle the most as readers, frequently miss the time allotted for classroom literacy instruction because they are removed from the classroom for these instructional support programs. Yet studies show that participation in these programs rarely leads to a net gain in time spent in literacy instruction. In the remedial or special education class, a higher proportion of time is devoted to nonacademic activities than in the regular classroom. Also, 50 or more hours per year are lost because time is needed for students to make the transition from one setting to the other.

Allington identified the mismatch between the curriculum of the regular classroom and the curriculum of remedial and special education programs as another factor hindering the literacy achievement of students of diverse backgrounds. The curricula students encounter in the two settings often reflect different philosophies about teaching, learning, and literacy, which lead to different instructional strategies and expectations for reading performance. Allington referred to the mismatch as "planned fragmentation" that only adds to the confusion and frustration students may already be experiencing in learning to read.

According to Allington, the lack of coherence and consistency in the literacy curriculum is evident even within the regular classroom itself. Typically, teachers use separate textbooks and instructional activities to teach reading, phonics, vocabulary, spelling, grammar, and other literacy skills. The more students are perceived to be struggling as readers, the greater the tendency to break the literacy curriculum into small bits. Students of diverse backgrounds, who tend to be categorized as poor readers, are likely to spend more time working on skills in isolation and less time actually reading and writing. They have less opportunity than their mainstream peers, who tend to be categorized as good readers, to understand and apply the full processes of reading and writing. Allington's finding that the instruction of students of diverse backgrounds is weighted in favor of low-level skills in isolation and against comprehension and higher level thinking about text reflects a broad pattern of bias that extends beyond the ESL learners in Fitzgerald's (1995) review.

One reason that students of diverse backgrounds seldom receive the high-quality, intensive literacy instruction they need is because schools are not organized to see that they receive these services. Often students are underserved because arrangements that will promote literacy achievement cannot be made within existing structures. Allington points out that the same student may qualify for several support programs (e.g., remedial reading and special education) but receive services from only one. To participate in any program, students generally need to leave the regular classroom and, as a consequence, they may be excluded from the literacy instruction that occurs there. Even if students were to receive the full range of literacy instruction available in both support programs and the regular classroom, the chances are that these services would be fragmented rather than well coordinated.

Allington argued that the key factor in creating and maintaining effective school literacy programs is the commitment of the school district to the education of all students. He emphasized the centrality of reforms at the district level, rather than at the school or classroom level, especially for students in remedial and special education programs. Allington's research suggested that principals and teachers are more likely to follow plans developed by the district than to create new plans themselves, and the attitudes of district administrators are passed on to principals, who, in turn, share these views with teachers. However, Allington noted, districts seldom allocate additional resources to schools with high numbers of students of diverse backgrounds, preferring to treat all schools as if they were the same.

The final review presented in this section provides a broader context for the problems identified by Allington and shows how the literacy achievement gap is just one manifestation of the negative effects of the existing educational system on students of diverse backgrounds. Darling-Hammond's (1995) review of research shows how schooling is structured to limit the learning opportunities of these students. Money makes a difference, and school districts and schools with large numbers of students of diverse backgrounds receive lower levels of funding than other districts and schools. More affluent schools and districts are able to hire and retain highly qualified teachers (those with experience and master's degrees), to keep classes smaller, and to invest in the materials and equipment needed for instruction. According to Darling-Hammond, much of the lower achievement of African American students is attributable to inferior opportunities to learn in school and severely limited access to high-quality teachers and teaching. Districts with the highest concentrations of students of diverse backgrounds generally have the largest numbers of poorly prepared teachers (Darling-Hammond, 1990; Pascal, 1987). These teachers are often unaware of current teaching methods, research on child development, and strategies for assisting struggling learners. Year after year, as they progress through the grades, students of diverse backgrounds in urban schools may face a succession of inexperienced and unqualified teachers. The cumulative effect is devastating, Darling-Hammond argued, because teacher expertise is the factor that contributes the most to the achievement of students of diverse backgrounds. For example, elementary students taught by less prepared teachers have lower achievement test scores in language arts than students taught by well-prepared teachers (Gomez & Grobe, 1990).

Darling-Hammond cited numerous studies indicating that, in comparison to mainstream students in suburban schools, students of diverse backgrounds in urban schools have limited access to advanced and college preparatory courses, up-to-date textbooks and materials, and equipment such as computers. Students of diverse backgrounds, in disproportionate numbers, find themselves placed in remedial and low-level courses, or in the bottom groups for reading and mathematics instruction. This system of tracking denies students of diverse backgrounds access to high-quality teaching, because the most qualified teachers are usually assigned to the top-track classes. Once assigned to the remedial and bottom groups, students of diverse backgrounds receive a rote-oriented curriculum with little opportunity to develop higher level thinking. Lessons are as likely to focus on behavior as on academic content. As a result, students who are tracked achieve at lower levels than students with similar entering aptitude who are placed in academic programs or untracked classes. Darling-Hammond highlighted the role played by standardized tests, which are used to justify the placement of students of diverse backgrounds in remedial and low track programs, thus limiting the learning opportunities available to them.

Darling-Hammond argued that a determined effort must be made to improve the quality of school learning opportunities for students of diverse backgrounds. Her recommendations for policy include equalizing the financial resources available to districts and schools with large numbers of students of diverse backgrounds, increasing the supply of highly qualified teachers, and changing curriculum and testing practices. According to her analysis, attention must be given to inequality at all levels of the educational system, because sources of inequality are apparent in the activities of states, districts, schools within districts, and classrooms and programs within schools. Darling-Hammond argued against current initiatives to categorize, or label, students and create special programs for students in the various categories. In her opinion, special programs, such as compensatory education, will never be effective in promoting the achievement of students of diverse backgrounds because these services are merely extensions of a larger system that is not designed to provide these students with a high-quality education.

Taken together, these reviews summarize much of what the existing research base shows about why the literacy achievement gap exists and how the gap might be narrowed. The next section presents research on equity policy and the concerns of policymakers. An understanding of the policy context forms the foundation for deriving implications of literacy research for policy, as well as implications of policy for literacy research.

EQUITY POLICY AT THREE LEVELS
OF GOVERNMENT

In the United States all three levels of government—federal, state, and local district—have developed policies to deal with problems of educational inequity. Wong (1994) reviewed research on equity policy efforts at each of these levels. In his analysis, the federal government is seen to have focused on social equity, or the needs of educationally disadvantaged students. These special populations are categorized according to factors such as poverty, ethnicity, language, and mental and physical challenges. State government has focused on interdistrict or territorial inequity, or the disparities in levels of funding among districts due to differences in taxable wealth. The local district has focused on distributive inequity, or the even distribution of resources among schools and classrooms within the district.

Federal Policy

The federal government has aimed at the social redistribution of educational opportunity for students of diverse backgrounds through programs such as compensatory education and bilingual education. Wong pointed out that these programs allocate resources to address inequities that result largely from differences in social class and ethnicity. Over the years the federal government has spent billions of dollars on programs with the aim of social equity. For example, in the 1990s, more than 5 million students in Grades K–12 were served by the Title I program of the Elementary and Secondary Education Act, a compensatory education effort targeting low-achieving students in schools in low-income communities.

When socially redistributive programs were introduced by the federal government, policymakers focused on issues of compliance in the implementation of these programs by states and districts. Policymakers have moved toward a focus on program effectiveness, a shift that Wong attributed to increased public concern about student achievement and America's ability to compete in the global marketplace. An example of this concern for program effectiveness is the 1988 Hawkins–Stafford amendments, designed to improve the quality of the Title I program. These amendments required coordination between the Title I program and the school's regular instructional program, supported the increased involvement of parents, allowed funds to be used for schoolwide projects in schools with high levels of students of poverty, and instructed districts to make improvements to ineffective programs. As Wong demonstrated, in the late 1980s and early 1990s, federal policy sought to promote equity through an emphasis on instructional effectiveness.

State Policy

Wong's analysis showed that by the mid 1980s, states had become the major funders of public education. States set educational policy in a number of different areas, including teacher certification and textbook adoption. Beginning in the mid 1980s, states began to pay increasing attention to issues of classroom instruction and curriculum. For example, states have increased requirements for instructional time in the classroom and sought to assist prospective teachers. However, in contrast to the federal government, state legislatures pay scant attention to issues of social equity. Instead, states concentrate on correcting the disparities in school funding among districts. Wong (1991) found that 78% of state funding was used to address interdistrict disparities in funding, whereas less than 8% was targeted for disadvantaged students. States tend to spread aid across almost all districts, although the poorest districts do receive a higher percentage of state monies than affluent districts. Because few state funds are directed at programs for students of diverse backgrounds, these students continue to be underserved, especially when they are concentrated in the poorest urban school districts. In Wong's view, the main reason that state legislatures follow such a roundabout strategy is that it enables them to address inequity without interfering in local decision making about curriculum and instruction.

Local District Policy

Local policies tend to concentrate on the equal distribution of resources among schools and, unlike federal policies, do not specifically address the needs of students of diverse backgrounds. Wong (1994) found that many local districts have policies allocating resources on the basis of the number of instructional staff in a school, not the number of students of diverse backgrounds. Districts tend to provide identical resources to teachers in schools with mainstream students and to teachers in schools with many students of diverse backgrounds. As a result, the latter do not receive the additional resources required—in the form of instructional materials, instructional support programs, or additional teacher education—to improve the learning opportunities of their students. Wong argued that distributive equity policies result in severe inequity for students of diverse backgrounds, because they are deprived of access to high-quality curriculum and instruction.

The school bureaucracy, especially in major urban districts, faces a complex task in coping with the demands of a large and disparate clientele. Wong examined the consequent dynamics within districts. On one hand, to make the task manageable, the school bureaucracy considers all students as equal in allocating resources, without attending to the greater educational needs of students of diverse backgrounds. On the other hand, the school bureaucracy has adopted policies to include rather than exclude participation by diverse ethnic groups. For example, since the 1980s, with the support of reform-minded community groups, businesses, and elected officials, schools with high enrollments of students of diverse backgrounds have sought to increase parental involvement (Jackson & Cibulka, 1992).

The increased participation of African Americans in the running of schools was studied by Meier, Stewart, and England (1989). They found that African American school-board members were able to endorse the hiring of African American administrators. These administrators promoted the hiring of African American teachers. In turn, these teachers improved distributive equity by reducing discrimination against African American students. African American teachers played a key role in decreasing the number of African American students assigned to special education classes and referred for disciplinary action, and in increasing the number assigned to classes for the gifted.

Efforts to develop policy to close the literacy achievement gap must take into account the complexities created by the differing strategies for promoting equity at the federal, state, and local levels. Taken together, these policies have not shown much success in giving less affluent districts and schools the resources needed to narrow the literacy achievement gap for students of diverse backgrounds. Yet although continuing difficulties are evident, Wong's review also points to some promising trends, to be discussed in the next section.

RELATIONSHIPS BETWEEN RESEARCH AND POLICY

This section presents a discussion of the relationships between equity policy and research on the literacy achievement of students of diverse backgrounds. What policy directions find support in the research? What implications does research hold for policy? What policy issues remain to be addressed by research?

Resource Allocation

A detailed discussion of the reform of governance structure and school finance is beyond the scope of this chapter. However, as Wong's (1994) review demonstrated, differences in funding must be corrected so that resources can be made available to support urgently needed reforms. As Allington (1991) and Darling-Hammond (1995) noted, districts and schools with large numbers of students of diverse backgrounds receive lower levels of funding than other districts and schools. This disparity in funding is the starting point for a complex and interrelated set of conditions that results in decreased learning opportunities for students of diverse backgrounds.

At the same time, it is unlikely that large infusions of additional funding will automatically result in improved achievement for students of diverse backgrounds. The problem is that districts and schools must know how to apply funding for the specific purpose of narrowing the achievement gap. For example, the problem of "planned fragmentation" identified by Allington (1991) results from the poor coordination of educational services, not a lack of funding for services. Elmore (1994) contended that public organizations, such as school districts, do not work according to principles of cost-benefit analysis, but think of budgeting in terms of past expenditures. This approach to budgeting prevents the district from knowing the cost components of a unit of service and how these components contribute to its performance. Without information on the relative contribution of these components, the district cannot know how additional funds should be spent to make a difference. For example, in the case of literacy achievement, it will be unclear whether monies are best spent on parent involvement programs, teachers' salaries, professional development workshops, books for classroom libraries, and so on. Elmore argued that educators will need to learn to think differently about the relationship between resources and student learning. He suggested that research in this area investigate the few situations in which schools and systems are starting to experiment with new models for using resources. This would appear to be a fruitful area for collaboration between literacy researchers and researchers with expertise in school finance.

Standards and Accountability

In the mid 1990s, federal efforts to narrow the literacy achievement gap through Title I were linked to the Goals 2000: Educate America Act. Goals 2000 was an effort to strengthen public education through a framework of goals and assessments. National goals for education included those quoted at the start of this chapter, with the nation's progress toward these goals measured annually. Goals 2000 supported states in developing their own challenging standards, along with assessments to measure students' progress toward meeting these standards. Federal policy required states to develop and implement student performance standards at least in reading/language arts and mathematics.

The research reviewed here (Allington, 1991; Au & Kawakami, 1994; Darling-Hammond, 1995; Farr, 1991; see also Oakes, 1992) indicates that the literacy achievement of students of diverse backgrounds suffers when they are held to lower expectations than other students and do not have the opportunity to read and discuss challenging material. Students of diverse backgrounds benefit when teachers hold high expectations and provide them with the high-quality instruction to meet these expectations (Mehan, Villanueva, Hubbard, & Lintz, 1996). There should not be a different set of standards for students of diverse backgrounds, but there should be a recognition that these students may require more powerful instruction and additional time to meet the standards. For example, ESL students may need extra teaching and time to develop the necessary English language skills. There is some evidence that the literacy achievement of students of diverse backgrounds can be improved through assessments based on standards, once high-quality instruction is in place (Au & Carroll, 1997). Much more research is needed to determine whether state standards and related assessments lead over time to a narrowing of the literacy achievement gap.

There is, however, ample research showing the negative effects of existing standardized (norm-referenced) testing on students of diverse backgrounds (Ascher, 1990; Darling-Hammond, 1995; Smith, 1991). For example, low scores on standardized tests may channel students into low-track classes, where they receive poor-quality instruction. Programs of standardized testing can reduce the time available for instruction and lead to a narrowing of the curriculum (Smith, 1991).

The danger is that challenging standards, like standardized tests, will not have a positive effect on the achievement of students of diverse backgrounds, but will simply serve as another means of identifying students of diverse backgrounds as losers in the educational game. Elmore (1994) warned that the implementation of high-stakes performance measures merely rewards or punishes educators for results, without supporting them in developing new ways of thinking about how to raise student achievement. Placing a premium on achievement results alone may discourage schools from making a commitment to serve struggling learners of diverse backgrounds or to keep these students from leaving school. An implication for policy is that standards and related assessments must be accompanied by sufficient resources to improve instruction, so that students of diverse backgrounds have the literacy learning opportunities needed to read and write at the demanding levels required.

Research conducted from a critical perspective calls into question the use of standards and the existence of a literacy achievement gap. The validity of the concept of a literacy achievement gap can be challenged for several reasons. First, an inherent problem is evident when the reference point for proficiency is determined by comparing one group to a second group. In this situation, students of diverse backgrounds will always be placed at a disadvantage, because of the assumption that the distribution of scores must follow the normal curve. Second, tests of reading proficiency, such as those used by NAEP, reflect an autonomous model of literacy. According to Street (1996), in an autonomous model, literacy is treated in technical and decontextualized terms as processes or practices to be valued in and of themselves. An autonomous model of literacy may be contrasted with an ideological model, in which literacy practices are believed to be embedded in and defined by particular social contexts shaped by cultural values and local ideologies. Heath (1983), for example, found differences in literacy contexts and practices among middle-class White, working-class White, and working-class Black communities. In an ideological model, literacy proficiency is examined in home and community as well as school contexts, and quite a different picture of students' performance emerges. Spanish-speaking students, for example, proved adept at translating English documents for their parents (Trueba, 1984), displaying literacy skills that went unrecognized in conventional reading tests. As this example suggests, multiple literacies in the lives of students of diverse backgrounds should be recognized (Gee, 1990).

Tests such as those used by NAEP cannot provide the fuller picture of the literacies of students of diverse backgrounds that can be obtained through research in community contexts. Such research is necessary to an understanding of the role that literacy plays in students' everyday lives (Taylor & Dorsey-Gaines, 1988). What the test results do show, however, is that schools generally have not been successful in helping students of diverse backgrounds to become as proficient as mainstream students in the literacy abilities valued by the larger society. These literacy abilities are essential if students are to have access to opportunities outside of their communities, including political influence and high-paying jobs. Furthermore, schools cannot restrict literacy instruction to skills measured by tests or tied to employment, but must involve students in critical literacy (Freire & Macedo, 1987), so that they will question inequities and work toward social justice.

Amount and Nature of Instruction

Substantial commitments of time must be made to literacy instruction, if students of diverse backgrounds are to progress well in developing higher level thinking about text. For example, the successful teachers in Grades K–6 studied by Au and Carroll (1997) spent a minimum of 60 minutes for reading plus 45 minutes for writing, four to five times per week. Districts typically have policies about the number of minutes to be allocated for instruction in language arts and other subjects. Policies stressing an adequate amount of time for language arts instruction appear particularly important in districts serving large numbers of students of diverse backgrounds.

Of course, not just time but the nature of instruction is important, and research reinforces the need for federal and state policies to address the quality and effectiveness of instruction. As indicated in numerous studies (Allington, 1991; Darling-Hammond, 1995; Fitzgerald, 1995), schools tend to provide students of diverse backgrounds with rote instruction in isolated skills and little opportunity to develop higher level thinking about text. Constructivist approaches to literacy instruction offer the possibility of reversing this pattern (Au, 1998). These approaches emphasize higher level thinking about text, encouraging students to arrive at well-reasoned interpretations and to make connections between texts and their own lives. In constructivist approaches, the learner takes an active role in constructing his or her own understandings. This is in contrast to traditional approaches, in which the learner adopts a more passive role in absorbing knowledge transmitted by the teacher (Au & Carroll, 1996). Constructivist approaches include literature-based instruction (Raphael & Au, 1998; Roser & Martinez, 1995), the process approach to writing (Calkins, 1994; Graves, 1994), and balanced literacy instruction (Au, Carroll, & Scheu, 1997; Freppon & Dahl, 1998; Strickland, 1994–1995).

A growing body of studies supports the effectiveness of constructivist approaches with students of diverse backgrounds (Au & Carroll, 1997; Dahl & Freppon, 1995; Guthrie et al., 1995; Morrow, 1992; Morrow, Pressley, Smith, & Smith, 1997). These studies reveal several features of constructivist approaches relevant to discussions of policy. First, constructivist approaches are effective not only in improving students' higher level thinking about text but also in fostering their motivation and interest in literacy. This motivation is likely to sustain students in pursuing further learning—for purposes of employment, citizenship, and personal fulfillment—that U.S. policy initiatives seek to promote (National Education Goals Panel, 1995). Research by Au (1997) indicates that motivation is a necessary but not sufficient condition for students to develop higher level thinking about text. Teacher-led instruction in higher level text processes, such as reading comprehension, vocabulary development, and the writing process, is also required. Research on constructivist approaches shows that the teaching of literacy can and should be motivating and responsive to children's backgrounds and interests, while at the same time providing them with systematic instruction in needed skills and strategies.

Second, these approaches are complex and involve a number of different components. They provide a variety of learning opportunities, including teacher-directed lessons and tasks requiring students' independent application of skills and strategies. Teachers do not limit students' reading to a single textbook but provide them with the chance to read an assortment of texts. Clearly, these approaches must be implemented by well-prepared teachers in well-supplied classrooms. To provide students with maximum benefits, constructivist approaches should be implemented in instructional support programs as well as in the regular classroom. To obtain this consistency, a schoolwide plan is needed.

Research supports changes in federal policies since 1994 directing Title I services away from pullout programs and toward schoolwide efforts (Allington, 1991; Allington & Johnston, 1989). Studies provide ample evidence showing that fragmentation in the literacy instruction of students of diverse backgrounds is all too common (Allington &McGill-Franzen, 1989; Johnston, Allington, & Afflerbach, 1985). However, research is needed on the programs developed by districts and schools that successfully restructure and coordinate literacy instruction for students of diverse backgrounds. Studies should document the gains in students' literacy achievement that result from exemplary programs, as well as the process by which these programs were developed and implemented.

Phonics

Phonics, or instruction in letter–sound correspondences, surfaces from time to time as the great debate in reading (Au, 1998; Chall, 1967; Taylor, 1998). An emphasis on phonics in beginning reading instruction was the focus of legislation in many states during the 1990s. If the overall goal is to improve the literacy achievement of students of diverse backgrounds, the issue of phonics must be approached with great caution. A repeated theme in the research is that students of diverse backgrounds benefit from instruction oriented toward higher level thinking and meaning making, rather than from instruction oriented toward lower level skills in isolation (Au & Kawakami, 1994; Farr, 1991; Guthrie et al., 1996). A greater emphasis on phonics might serve to subject these students to even greater amounts of instruction in low-level skills than they already receive.

Au (1998) provided a detailed discussion of the relationships among phonics, constructivist approaches, and the literacy learning of students of diverse backgrounds, organized around several understandings drawn from research. First, the literacy curriculum should be broadly defined to emphasize students' ownership of literacy, or valuing of reading and writing, reading comprehension, and the writing process. Maintaining a broad definition of literacy is essential to the successful education of students of diverse backgrounds, because these students typically receive a high degree of overly narrow skill instruction (Allington, 1991; Fitzgerald, 1995). Second, students of diverse backgrounds must be provided with instruction in comprehension and composition, processes requiring higher level thinking about text. Instruction in word identification or phonics is insufficient, because fluency in word identification does not lead automatically to improvements in comprehension (Anderson, Mason, & Shirey, 1984; Au, 1994). Third, systematic instruction in phonics should be properly timed, to occur when children have begun to attend to print and have gained a good understanding of the purposes for reading and writing. This timing is important, because an early over-emphasis on phonics and other low-level skills tends to give students of diverse backgrounds the impression that reading is nothing more than sounds, letters, and word identification, and their reading achievement is likely to suffer (Strickland, 1994; Tharp, 1982). If the literacy achievement gap is to be narrowed, instruction must lead students of diverse backgrounds to the understanding that reading involves higher level thinking about text, not just accurate word calling.

An implication to be drawn from the research is that states and districts should implement policies related to the quality of instruction, to ensure that the instruction provided to all students maintains a focus on higher level thinking about text. This emphasis is appropriate even in the primary grades, both for students of diverse backgrounds and others. Although systematic instruction in word identification should receive considerable attention at these grades, such instruction should not be isolated but should be directly connected to the development of students' higher level thinking about text. State and district policies related to the instruction of struggling readers of diverse backgrounds should have the aim of providing these students with high-quality instruction, rather than a steady diet of skills in isolation.

Other Policies

Two other topics noted in the research should be mentioned. The first is teacher education and recruitment. Research points to the importance of helping teachers gain knowledge of cultural and linguistic differences and how these differences relate to the literacy learning and academic performance of students of diverse backgrounds (Au & Kawakami, 1994; Farr, 1991; Heath, 1983). Research also suggests that teachers can improve students' literacy achievement through culturally responsive instruction (Au &

Mason, 1981; Lipka & McCarty, 1994), although other means of improving relationships with students and building trust may also be beneficial (Ogbu & Simon, 1998). Research supports the development of policies for making these topics central in preservice teacher education programs, as well as in professional development programs for inservice teachers (Au & Maaka, 1998; Grant, 1994; Ladson-Billings, 1995). Because new attitudes and practices are difficult to instill (Tatto, 1996), studies are needed to assess the effectiveness of these programs and to identify the components critical to their success.

Teacher recruitment issues are also important. Many studies indicate that increases in the proportion of students of diverse backgrounds have not been accompanied by increases in the proportion of teachers of diverse backgrounds (Gordon, 1994; King; 1993; Rong & Preissle, 1997). The positive contributions of teachers of diverse backgrounds to the education of students of diverse backgrounds have been noted in research (Ladson-Billings, 1994). For example, in addition to the study by Meier et al. (1989) discussed earlier, Foster (1994) summarized research indicating that African American teachers are likely to show solidarity and connectedness with students and the community, balance firmness and caring, engage in culturally responsive teaching, and demand high levels of achievement while also attending to students' social and emotional growth. Of course policies should not limit students' opportunities to benefit from the excellent literacy instruction and diverse perspectives that may be provided by well-prepared, committed teachers from mainstream or other cultural and linguistic backgrounds. However, the recruitment and preparation of teachers of diverse backgrounds is a key issue to be addressed in equity policies.

The second topic is parent and community involvement, and family literacy programs in particular. Policies promoting stronger connections among schools, parents, and the community find considerable support in the research (Au, 1998; Delgado-Gaitan, 1990; Goldenberg, 1987). The trend toward collaborative approaches is also reinforced by recent research (Keenan, Willett, & Solsken, 1993; Moll, Amanti, Neff, & Gonzalez, 1992). An overview of key issues in the development of family literacy programs was presented by Auerbach (1996). She highlighted the broad base of research showing that low-income and low-literate parents understand the importance of literacy, and that they can and do support their children's literacy learning in a variety of ways. She cautioned against intervention programs based on the assumption that literacy is absent in low-income homes or that parents do not care about their children's literacy. Auerbach advocates a multiple literacies perspective, based on the view that participants in family literacy programs already have literacy practices and ways of knowing rooted in their own cultures (cf. Gee, 1990). Educators should seek to understand these literacy practices and ways of knowing and collaborate with participants in the curriculum development process, as demonstrated in a project conducted by Neuman, Celano, and Fischer (1996). Auerbach suggested that family literacy programs will be effective to the extent that they include culturally relevant content, culturally familiar social contexts, and, in some cases, instruction in the first language.

REFERENCES

Allington, R. L. (1991). Children who find learning to read difficult: School responses to diversity. In E. H. Hiebert (Ed.), *Literacy for a diverse society: Perspectives, practices, and policies* (pp. 237–252). New York: Teachers College Press.

Allington, R. L., & Johnston, P. (1989). Coordination, collaboration, and consistency: The redesign of compensatory and special education interventions. In R. Slavin, N. Karweit, & N. Madden (Eds.), *Effective programs for students at risk* (pp. 320–354). Boston: Allyn & Bacon.

Allington, R. L., & McGill-Franzen, A. (1989). School response to reading failure: Chapter I and special education students in grades 2, 4, and 8. *Elementary School Journal, 89,* 529–542.

Anderson, R. C., Mason, J., & Shirey, L. (1984). The reading group: An experimental investigation of a labyrinth. *Reading Research Quarterly, 20,* 6–38.

Ascher, C. (1990). *Testing students in urban schools: Current problems and new directions.* Urban Diversity Series No. 100. New York: ERIC Clearinghouse on Urban Education, Institute for Urban and Minority Education, Teachers College, Columbia University.

Au, K. H. (1994). Portfolio assessment: Experiences at the Kamehameha Elementary Education Program. In S. W. Valencia, E. H. Hiebert, & P. P. Afflerbach (Eds.), *Authentic reading assessment: Practices and possibilities* (pp. 103–126). Newark, DE: International Reading Association.

Au, K. H. (1997). Ownership, literacy achievement, and students of diverse cultural backgrounds. In J. T. Guthrie & A. Wigfield (Eds.), *Reading engagement: Motivating readers through integrated instruction* (pp. 168–182), Newark, DE: International Reading Association.

Au, K. H. (1998). Social constructivism and the school literacy learning of students of diverse backgrounds. *Journal of Literacy Research, 20,* 297–319.

Au, K. H. (1998). Constructivist approaches, phonics, and the literacy learning of students of diverse backgrounds. In T. Shanahan & F. Rodriguez Brown (Eds.), *Forty-seventh yearbook of the National Reading Conference* (pp. 1–21). Chicago: National Reading Conference.

Au, K. H., & Carroll, J. H. (1996). Current research on classroom instruction: Goals, teachers' actions, and assessment. In D. Speece & B. Keogh (Eds.), *Research on classroom ecologies: Implications for inclusion of children with learning disabilities* (pp. 17–37). Mahwah, NJ: Lawrence Erlbaum Associates.

Au, K. H., & Carroll, J. H. (1997). Improving literacy achievement through a constructivist approach: The KEEP Demonstration Classroom Project. *Elementary School Journal, 97,* 203–221.

Au, K. H., Carroll, J. H., & Scheu, J. A. (1997). *Balanced literacy instruction: A teacher's resource book.* Norwood, MA: Christopher-Gordon.

Au, K. H., & Kawakami, A. J. (1994). Cultural congruence in instruction. In E. R. Hollins, J. E. King, & W. Hayman (Eds.), *Teaching diverse populations: Formulating a knowledge base* (pp. 5–23). Albany: State University of New York Press.

Au, K. H., & Maaka, M. J. (1998). Ka Lama O Ke Kaiaulu: Research on teacher education for a Hawaiian community. *Pacific Educational Research Journal, 9,* 65–85..

Au, K. H., & Mason, J. M. (1981). Social organizational factors in learning of read: The balance of rights hypothesis. *Reading Research Quarterly, 17,* 115152.

Auerbach, E. (1996). Critical issues: Deconstructing the discourse of strengths in family literacy. *JRB: A Journal of Literacy, 27,* 643–661.

Bond, G. L., & Dykstra, R. (1967). The cooperative research program in first-grade reading instruction. *Reading Research Quarterly, 2,* 5–142.

Calkins, L. M. (1994). *The art of teaching writing* (2nd ed.). Portsmouth, NH: Heinemann.

Chall, J. (1967). *Learning to read: The great debate.* New York: McGrawHill.

Cummins, J. (1996). *Negotiating identities: Education for empowerment in a diverse society.* Ontario, CA: California Association for Bilingual Education.

Dahl, K., & Freppon, P. (1995). A comparison of innercity children's interpretations of reading and writing instruction in the early grades in skills-based and whole language classrooms. *Reading Research Quarterly, 30,* 50–74.

Darling-Hammond, L. (1990). Teacher quality and equality. In J. Goodlad & P. Keating (Eds)., *Access to knowledge: An agenda for our nation's schools* (pp. 237–258). New York: College Entrance Examination Board.

Darling-Hammond, L. (1995). Inequality and access to knowledge. In J. A. Banks & C. A. M. Banks (Eds.), *Handbook of research on multicultural education* (pp. 465–483). New York: Macmillan.

Delgado-Gaitan, C. (1990). *Literacy for empowerment: The role of parents in children's education.* Bristol, PA: Falmer Press.

Elliott, E. J. (1996). Literacy: From policy to practice. *Journal of Literacy Research, 28,* 590–595.

Elmore, R. F. (1994). Thoughts on program equity: Productivity and incentives for performance in education. *Educational Policy, 8,* 453–459.

Farr, M. (1991). Dialects, culture, and teaching the English language arts. In J. Flood, J. M. Jensen, D. Lapp, & J. R. Squire (Eds.), *Handbook of research on teaching the English language arts* (pp. 365–371). New York: Macmillan.

Fitzgerald, J. (1994). English-as-a-second language learners' cognitive reading processes: A review of research in the United States. *Review of Educational Research, 65,* 145–190.

Fitzgerald, J. (1995). English-as-a-second-language reading instruction in the United States: A research review. *Journal of Reading Behavior, 27,* 115–152.

Foster, M. (1994). Effective Black teachers: A literature review. In E. R. Hollins, J. E. King, & W. C. Hayman (Eds.), *Teaching diverse populations: Formulating a knowledge base* (pp. 225–241). Albany: State University of New York Press.

Freire, P., & Macedo, D. (1987). *Literacy: Reading the word and the world.* New York: Bergin & Garvey.

Freppon, P. A., & Dahl, K. L. (1998). Balanced literacy instruction: Insights and considerations. *Reading Research Quarterly, 33,* 240–251.

Gee, J. P. (1990). *Social linguistics and literacies: Ideology in discourses.* London: Falmer Press.

Goldenberg, C. (1987). Low-income Hispanic parents' contributions to their first-grade children's word-recognition skills. *Anthropology & Education Quarterly, 18,* 149–179.

Gollnick, D. M., & Chinn, P. C. (1990). *Multicultural education in a pluralistic society* (3rd ed.). Columbus, OH: Merrill.

Gomez, D. L., & Grobe, R. P. (1990, April). *Three years of alternative certification in Dallas: Where are we?* Paper presented at the annual meeting of the American Educational Research Association, Boston.

Gordon, J. A. (1994). Why students of color are not entering the teaching profession: Reflections from minority teachers. *Journal of Teacher Education, 45,* 346–353.

Grant, C. A. (1994). Best practices in teacher education for urban schools: Lessons from the multicultural teacher education literature. *Action in Teacher Education, 16,* 1–18.

Graves, D. (1994). *A fresh look at writing.* Portsmouth, NH: Heinemann.

Guthrie, J. T., Van Meter, P., McCann, A. D., Wigfield, A., Bennett, L., Poundstone, C. C., Rice, M. E., Faibisch, F. M., Hunt, B., & Mitchell, A. M. (1995). Growth of literacy engagement: Changes in motivations and strategies during concept-oriented reading instruction. *Reading Research Quarterly, 31,* 306–332.

Heath, S.B. (1983). *Ways with words: Language, life, and work in communities and classrooms.* Cambridge: Cambridge University Press.

Jackson, B., & Cibulka, J. (1992). Leadership turnover and business mobilization: The changing political ecology of urban school systems. In J. Cibulka, R. Reed, & K. Wong (Eds.), *The politics of urban education in the United States* (pp. 71–86). London: Falmer Press.

Johnston, P. H., Allington, R. L., & Afflerbach, P. (1985). The congruence of classroom and remedial reading instruction. *Elementary School Journal, 85,* 465–478.

Keenan, J. W., Willett, J., & Solsken, J. (1993). Constructing an urban village: School/home collaboration in a multicultural classroom. *Language Arts, 70,* 204–214.

King, S. H. (1993). The limited presence of African-American teachers. *Review of Educational Research, 63,* 115–149.

Kirst, M. W. (1994). Equity for children: Linking education and children's services. *Educational Policy, 8,* 583–590.

Labaree, D. F. (1997). Public goods, private goods: The American struggle over educational goals. *American Educational Research Journal, 34,* 39–81.

Ladson-Billings, G. (1994). *The dreamkeepers: Successful teachers of African American children.* San Francisco: Jossey-Bass.

Ladson-Billings, G. (1995). Multicultural teacher education: Research, practice, and policy. In J. A. Banks & C. A. M. Banks (Eds.), *Handbook of research on multicultural education* (pp. 747–759). New York: Macmillan.

Lipka, J., & McCarty, T.L. (1994). Changing the culture of schooling: Navajo and Yup'ik cases. *Anthropology & Education Quarterly, 25,* 266–284.

Mehan, H., Villanueva, I., Hubbard, L., & Lintz, A. (1996). *Constructing school success: The consequences of untracking low-achieving students.* New York: Cambridge University Press.

Meier, K., Stewart, J., & England, R. (1989). *Race, class, and education.* Madison: University of Wisconsin Press.

Moll, L. C., Amanti, C., Neff, D., & Gonzalez, N. (1992). Funds of knowledge for teaching: Using a qualitative approach to connect homes and classrooms, *Theory Into Practice, 31,* 132–141.

Morrow, L. M. (1992). The impact of a literature-based program on literacy achievement, use of literature, and attitudes of children from minority backgrounds. *Reading Research Quarterly, 27,* 251–275.

Morrow, L. M., Pressley, M., Smith, J. K., & Smith, M. (1997). The effect of a literature-based program integrated into literacy and science instruction with children from diverse backgrounds. *Reading Research Quarterly, 32,* 54–76.

National Education Goals Panel. (1995). *The national education goals report: Building a nation of learners 1995.* Washington, DC: U. S. Government Printing Office.

National Research Council. (1998). *Preventing reading difficulties in young children.* Washington, DC: National Academy Press.

Nettles, M. T., & Perna, L. W. (1997). *The African American data book (Vol. II): Preschool thought high school education.* Fairfax, VA: Frederick D. Patterson Research Institute.

Neuman, S. B., Celano, D., & Fischer, R. (1996). The children's literature hour: A social-constructivist approach to family literacy. *Journal of Literacy Research, 28,* 499–523.

Oakes, J. (1992). Can tracking research inform practice? Technical, normative, and political considerations. *Educational Researcher, 21,* 12–21.

Ogbu, J. U., & Simon, H. D. (1998). Voluntary and involuntary minorities: A cultural-ecological theory of school performance with some implications for education. *Anthropology & Education Quarterly, 2,* 155–188.

Paquette, J. (1998). Equity in educational policy: A priority in transformation or in trouble? *Journal of Education Policy, 13,* 41–61.

Pascal, A. (1987). *The qualifications of teachers in American high schools.* Santa Monica, CA: RAND Corporation.

Pease-Alvarez, L., & Hakuta, K. (1992). Enriching our views of bilingualism and bilingual education. *Educational Researcher, 21*(2), 4–6, 19.

Raphael, T. E., & Au, K. H. (1998). *Literature-based instruction: Reshaping the curriculum.* Norwood, MA: Christopher-Gordon.

Rong, X. L., & Preissle, J. (1997). The continuing decline in Asian American teachers. *American Educational Research Journal, 34,* 267–293.

Roser, N. L., & Martinez, M. G. (Eds.). (1995). *Book talk and beyond: Children and teachers respond to literature.* Newark, DE: International Reading Association.

Smith, M. L. (1991). Put to the test: The effects of external testing on teachers. *Educational Researcher, 20*(5), 8–11.

Street, B. (1996). *Social literacies: Critical approaches to literacy development, ethnography and education.* New York: Longman.

Strickland, D. S. (1994). Educating African American learners at risk: Finding a better way. *Language Arts, 71*, 328–336.

Strickland, D. S. (1994–1995). Reinventing our literacy programs: Books, basics, and balance. *Reading Teacher, 48*, 294–306.

Tatto, M. T. (1996). Examining values and beliefs about teaching diverse students: Understanding the challenges for teacher education. *Educational Evaluation and Policy Analysis, 18*(2), 155–180.

Taylor, D. (1998). *Beginning to read and the spin doctors of science: The political campaign to change America's mind about how children learn to read.* Urbana, IL: National Council of Teachers of English.

Taylor, D., & Dorsey-Gaines, C. (1988). *Growing up literate: Learning from inner-city families.* Portsmouth, NH: Heinemann.

Tharp, R. G. (1982). The effective instruction of comprehension: Results and description of the Kamehameha Early Education Program. *Reading Research Quarterly, 17*, 503–527.

Trueba, H. T. (1984). The forms, functions, and values of literacy: Reading for survival in a barrio as a student. *NABE Journal, 9*, 21–40.

U. S. Department of Education (1992, June). *The condition of bilingual education in the nation: A report to the Congress and the President.* Washington, DC: United States Department of Education, Office of the Secretary.

Weber, R. (1991). Linguistic diversity and reading in American society. In R. Barr, M. L. Kamil, P. Mosenthal, & P. D. Pearson (Eds.), *Handbook of reading research* (Vol. II, pp. 97–119). New York: Longman.

Willis, A. I., & Harris, V. J. (1997). Expanding the boundaries: A reaction to the First-Grade Studies. *Reading Research Quarterly, 32*, 439–445.

Wong, K. K. (1991). State reform in education finance: Territorial and state strategies. *Publius: The Journal of Federalism, 21*, 125–142.

Wong, K. K. (1994). Governance structure, resource allocation, and equity policy. In L. Darling-Hammond (Ed.), *Review of research in education* (Vol. 20, pp. 257–289). Washington, DC: American Educational Research Association.

CHAPTER 44

Family Literacy

Victoria Purcell-Gates
Michigan State University

Family literacy, as an educational construct considered relevant as a focus of research, is relatively new. Although the practice of literacy within families is recognized to have existed over the centuries, it is only within the past few decades that it has emerged from the background of schooling and literacy development to appear highlighted and foregrounded for educational theorists, policymakers, teachers, and researchers. Suddenly, the ordinary has become extraordinary and special, and the subject of family literacy has become a topic of national attention and concern.

As we have begun to recognize and focus on the phenomenon of family literacy, its very definition has become elusive. At the moment, there is real lack of agreement as to what family literacy is, what it means for schooling, what it means for literacy development, and how, or if, we should go about researching it, instituting it, promoting it, or even "doing it," whatever "it" may be! Given this ambiguity, however, I attempt in this chapter to characterize the construct of family literacy as it now is viewed by researchers in the field of literacy and to synthesize the research that has been done with it as its focus, across the different perspectives. The reader must be aware, however, that this topic is a constantly evolving one and this synthesis is only a snapshot of that evolvement at this moment in time.

REVIEW PROCEDURES

Certain parameters constrained this review of family literacy research. I considered all research reports available to me that included the following: (a) a clearly stated research question or focus; (b) a description of the research design; (c) a description of the participants; (d) a description of the data collection procedures; (e) a description of the analysis procedures; and (f) results and interpretations based on the foregoing. Research from both quantitative and qualitative paradigms, including ethnographic, was included in the review if the reports met these criteria. Not included, thus, were the many anecdotal and descriptive accounts of programs and success stories that constitute so much of the literature around the topic of family literacy, unless these descriptions and anecdotes were embedded in data-based research studies. I also include in this review theoretical writings that help to clarify the nature of the paradigm debates as to the "true" nature of family literacy as a construct.

I begin with the research that provides the foundations on which family literacy research is based. This research spans the disciplines of psychology, emergent literacy, beginning reading, anthropology, and sociology. I then describe the differing perspectives on the construct of family literacy and the resulting debates revolving around family literacy programs and their different instantiations within the field. This is followed by a synthesis of the research conducted so far on existing family literacy programs, along with a brief discussion of the difficulty of carrying out such research. I conclude with a summary of where we are presently as regards family literacy research and some critical implications for further systematic study.

FAMILY LITERACY: THE FOUNDATIONAL RESEARCH

Family as Foundation for Learning

Research on child development began to highlight the importance of early environment for later development and academic success in the 1960s as behavioral theories of learning receded and social learning theories ascended (Bradley & Caldwell, 1987). This research documented the role of specific transactions between child and environment in the shaping of crucial cognitive and linguistic abilities (Bell, 1969; Bloom, 1964; Hunt, 1961). From such research, a variety of early intervention projects such as Head Start emerged (Caldwell & Freyer, 1983). Building on this foundation, a number of studies began documenting the positive relationships between home environment and IQ and language development (Bee et al., 1982; Bradley & Caldwell, 1980, 1984, 1987).

Embedded within most of these investigations were attempts to uncover causal links between socioeconomic status (SES) and academic underachievement by children from low-SES families. However, findings from study after study documented that SES, when examined as separate from specific home environment factors, was a weak or negative predictor (White, 1982). Rather, investigators identified specific home practices (mentioned earlier) that varied within SES and that were much more explanatory of academic achievement, IQ, and language development. From such beginnings, the focus of psychologists, linguists, and educators began to narrow onto literacy and literate practices, such as storybook reading, within the family and home as promising for a deeper understanding of language and literacy development as specific indices of academic achievement.

Family as Foundation for Language and Literacy Development

Correlational studies have repeatedly documented the significance of such factors as parents' educational level, the uses of print in the home, the number of books in the home, and the frequency of parent–child storybook reading events in children's reading achievement in school (Anglum, Bell, & Roubinek, 1990; Basic Skills Agency, 1993; Chaney, 1994; Downing, Ollila, & Oliver, 1975, 1977; Feitelson & Goldstein, 1986; Goldfield & Snow, 1984; Hiebert, 1980, 1981; Share, Jorm, Maclean, Mathews, & Waterman, 1983; Snow, Barnes, Chandler, Goodman, & Hemphill, 1991; Walberg & Tsai, 1985; Walker & Kuerbitz, 1979; Wells, 1979; Wells, Barnes, & Wells, 1984).

In two influential early studies on home literacy experiences for young children and their literacy learning, Hiebert (1980, 1981) studied sixty 3-, 4-, and 5-year-olds from middle-class homes. From data based on parent surveys and a series of tests for developing print knowledge, Hiebert concluded that home experiences with print, logical reasoning ability, and oral language comprehension accounted for .56 of the variance on the measures of print awareness. The dimension of the home experiences variable that proved to be a significant predictor was that of parents involving their young children with print, such as pointing out words on signs, reading to the child, or actual instruction in letter naming. Based on her findings, Hiebert concluded that all children know something about print when they start school.

Teale (1986) drew a similar conclusion based on his study of low-SES homes. Participant observers noted all literacy events experienced by focal children (ages 2.5–3.5) in 22 homes. This descriptive study documented literacy mediating social activity in the homes. Notable among the results were that by far the majority of the literacy events fell into the domain of daily living routines and the fewest were devoted to storybook time. Although noting his concern about the paucity of reading to children in these homes, Teale, as did Hiebert, concluded that "virtually all children in a literate society like ours have numerous experiences with written language before they ever get to school" (p. 192).

This assertion, however, which quickly became a tenet of the emergent literacy perspective, was challenged by Purcell-Gates (1995) with her ethnographic case study of a nonliterate family living and working within this same "literate" society. Based on observational, interview, instructional, and assessment data collected over a period of 2 years of teaching and associating with the mother and young son of this family, Purcell-Gates concluded that print in the world is "phenomena" and must be experienced in use in order to be recognized as semiotic and used for concept and skill development. This study strengthens the conclusion that the home is an essential locus of learning about print for young children.

Emergent Literacy Research

Looking at the emergent literacy research through a sociocultural frame (Purcell-Gates, 1986, 1995), researchers have documented that what young children learn about written language before schooling is constrained by the ways in which important others in their families and social communities use print (Clay in Goodman & Goodman, 1976; Heath, 1983; Purcell-Gates, 1995, 1996; Schieffelin & Cochran-Smith, 1984; Taylor, 1985; Taylor & Dorsey-Gaines, 1988; Teale, 1986). Within this, young children learn about the natures (e.g., different levels of decontextualization of language), the characteristics (e.g., the genre-related linguistic features of written text like syntax and wording), and the language forms (e.g., the form of personal letters, grocery lists, or written stories) that are used within their cultural environments (Butler & Clay, 1979; Ferreiro & Teberosky, 1982; Goodman, 1984; Harste, Woodward, & Burke, 1984; Holdaway, 1979; Purcell-Gates, 1988; Sulzby, 1985). Further, as young children participate in literacy events within their homes and communities, they learn that print is a language signifier, about the ways in which print represents meaning, the "code," and the conventions of encoding and decoding the print (Clay, 1975; Ferreiro & Teberosky, 1982; Goodman & Altwerger, 1981; Harste et al., 1984; Hiebert, 1980, 1981; Mason, 1980).

Although some of the emergent literacy research strove to explore the differences in the early literacy *experiences* between children of high-literate and those of low-literate homes, a study by Fitzgerald, Spiegel, and Cunningham (1991) explored the *perceptions* of low- and high-literate parents of early literacy learning, a topic of central importance to the establishment and success of family literacy interventions. One hundred and eight parents of kindergartners were interviewed and given a test of literacy level. Analysis using multiple analysis of variance (MANOVA) and multiple regression revealed that all parents were positive about the notion that literacy learning can begin during the preschool years. Lower literacy level parents put more importance on the presence of literacy artifacts in the home, and the desirable artifacts were seen as more skills oriented than for higher literate parents, who saw early literacy

more as cultural practice and who placed more importance on modeling of literate behaviors. The Fitzgerald et al. conclusion of a theoretical gulf between those who view
literacy learning as skills work, to be accomplished mainly in school, and those who
see it as cultural transmission, accomplished more indirectly and implicitly within
homes and communities as well as within school, is also suggested by Neuman's
(1995) work with teenage, minority mothers, Baker, Fernandez-Fein, Scher, and Williams's (1998) research of middle- and low-income urban parents, and Heath's (1983)
study of three different cultural and SES populations.

Research from a variety of disciplines has specified particular concepts, skills, and
attitudes relevant to learning to read and write that are learned within the family context as the result of specified literacy interactions. These are reviewed next.

Knowledge of Written Registers

The language one reads when reading books and written texts of different genres is not
the same language one speaks or hears. Written language differs in specific and identifiable ways from oral (Chafe & Danielewicz, 1986). Thus, developing readers and writers need to learn the different linguistic registers of the written texts they will read and
write. Written language differs from oral along a continuum reflecting degree of
decontextualization and formality as well as genre-related style. Its differences from
oral are marked primarily syntactically and lexically. Different syntax patterns and vocabulary are found in written texts as compared to the oral texts of speech. Some research has been done that documents what others have claimed: that young children
learn these registers from being read to (Bus, Ijzendoorn, & Pelligrini, 1995; Pappas,
1991; Pappas & Brown, 1988; Purcell-Gates, 1988; Purcell-Gates, McIntyre, & Freppon,
1995; Sulzby, 1985).

Storybook reading is the home literacy practice most widely perceived to be related
to young children's later success in learning to read and write in school (Burgess &
Lonigan, 1996; Scarborough & Dobrich, 1994). It is also the one most often recommended to parents in the course of family literacy programs. The research documenting the complex language learning that emanates from such home practices expands
the rationale for such practice beyond the affective domain and is reviewed in the following section. However, the magnitude of the effect of reading to young children has
been questioned by Scarborough and Dobrich (1994) in a meta-analysis of 30 years of
empirical research on the influence of shared reading on the development of language
and literacy skills. Scarborough and Dobrich found evidence for this association but an
overall effect size of only 8%.

Vocabulary/Language Knowledge

Several of the studies cited earlier (Pappas, 1991; Pappas & Brown, 1988; Purcell-Gates,
1988; Purcell-Gates et al., 1995) noted differential vocabulary knowledge as it was used
in the rendering of written registers (i.e., pretend reading or rereading familiar text).
Other studies, however, have looked at vocabulary from a general language development perspective, and vocabulary knowledge is generally measured in isolation on
such assessments as the Peabody Picture Vocabulary Test (PPVT), a receptive vocabulary measure. Most of these studies have noted positive relationships between vocabulary knowledge and home literacy practices, particularly shared reading
(Crain-Thoreson & Dale, 1992; Payne, Whitehurst, & Angell, 1994; Senechal, Thomas,
& Monker, 1995; Snow et al., 1991). Exposure to low-frequency words found in books
and participation in the oral language that surrounds book reading are suggested as
the operative factors in the positive relationship between being read to and vocabulary
knowledge (Snow et al., 1991). Strengthening the causal implications of this research,

Crain-Thoreson and Dale found that there was no relationship between linguistic pre-cocity and early reading. Rather, it was the frequency of story reading at 24 months that best predicted language ability, as measured by vocabulary and syntax knowl-edge, at 2½ years.

Several studies have examined qualitative aspects of the shared-reading event for differential effects on children's language development. Senechal et al. (1995) found significant effects for the level of involvement by the child during the reading. Children who only listened scored lower on comprehension and on production of new words than those children who participated actively by pointing and/or labeling.

Whitehurst et al. (1988) found that children of parents who asked more open-ended questions, function/attribute questions, and expansions; responded ap-propriately to children's attempts to answer these questions; and decreased their fre-quency of straight reading and questions that could be answered by pointing had significantly higher mean length of utterances (MLUs), higher frequency of phrases, and lower frequency of single words. Both the Senechal et al. and the Whitehurst et al. studies support the practice of teaching parents more effective ways of reading to their children.

Print Knowledge

The documentation of young children's developing print knowledge during the pre-school years (and thus assumed to have taken place in the context of the home) com-prises a large proportion of the body of emergent literacy research (Bissex, 1980; Clay, 1975; Ferreiro & Teberosky, 1982; Goodman & Altwerger, 1981; Harste et al., 1984; Hiebert, 1980, 1981; Lomax & McGee, 1987; Mason, 1980). Although it is assumed that this knowledge is gained through interactions with print, there has been relatively lit-tle research to directly explore this. What there is suggests that print knowledge results from explicit focusing on and/or teaching by parents within the context of home liter-acy activities (Baker et al., 1998; Hiebert, 1980).

Beyond correlational results based on survey studies, Purcell-Gates (1996) collected participant observation data within the homes of 20 low-SES families and assessed the focal children in these homes on an array of emergent literacy tasks, including Clay's Concepts of Print (1979) and a Concepts of Writing task. Findings revealed that the children's print knowledge was significantly related to the frequencies with which others in their home read and wrote texts at a more complex written discourse levels and to the frequencies with which parents focused their children onto print during such activities as writing out invitations or greeting cards, reading stories, or helping their children learn to write their names or individual letters.

Crain-Thoreson and Dale (1992), in their study of 25 linguistically precocious chil-dren, found significant relationships between exposure to home and school instruc-tion (they were unable to sort these out) in letter names and sounds and children's knowledge of print conventions and invented spellings. Similarly, Hess, Holloway, Price, and Dickson (1982) found that children who receive instruction from parents in letter naming score higher on tests of letter recognition than those who do not.

Phonological Awareness and Letter–Sound Knowledge

The evidence is less compelling regarding the acquisition of phonological awareness in the home environment. Burgess (1997), studying variation in home literacy environ-ments among 95 middle- to upper-middle-class children, found that the age at which children are first read to was moderately correlated with phonological awareness. However, other studies have failed to establish clear relationships between home ex-periences and phonological awareness (Baker et al., 1998).

Knowledge of letter–sound relationships, however, is more clearly related to home experiences, particularly those that involve children in writing (Bissex, 1980; Purcell-Gates, 1996; Read, 1971). This knowledge was also significantly related to parents' explicit teaching about words and letters in the context of home literacy activity (Purcell-Gates, 1996).

Motivation

The relationship between home literacy experiences and reading attitude or motivation has been empirically investigated by several studies. Durkin's study of early readers (1966) concluded that early readers had (a) rich home literacy environments with many opportunities for interaction with print, and (b) high interest in learning to read and write. In a study of preschoolers from working-class families in Britain, Lomax (1976) concluded that those children with higher interest in books and stories were read to at home more often. In the United States, Morrow (1983) found that kindergartners with a high interest in books had parents who reported reading to them daily and who had more books in the home as compared to low-interest children. Scher and Baker (reported in Baker, Scher, & Mackler, 1997) examining 65 first-grade students from low- and middle-class homes, however, found that children's home literacy experiences did not predict their scores on a Motivations for Reading Scale. They suggest that early experiences might better predict motivation in the later grades.

A few studies appear to confirm this prediction. Hansen (1969), exploring the relationships among IQ, achievement, and motivation among 48 fourth graders of mixed SES, found that only home literary environment was significantly related to motivation (defined as independent reading). Walberg and Tsai (1985), using National Assessment of Educational Progress (NAEP) 1979–1980 data, found significant relationships between home literary environment and reading attitude.

Conclusion: Home Literacy Practices Contribute
to Literacy Learning

In conclusion, the research documenting the many ways in which children experience and learn from home literacy practices suggests that these practices are facilitative of later literacy achievement in school. Further, the implication is there that at least some of the difference in literacy achievement among children can be explained by different experiences with print in their homes. Such thinking has led to a national focus on home literacy and to the establishment of family literacy programs around the country and abroad. It is at this point that real ideological differences emerge in the field, with some taking issue with the stance of family literacy programs that strive to change the behaviors of parents and family members and calling instead for (a) programs that place children's educational achievements in the context of restricted economic and political opportunities, and (b) collaborative approaches to working with parents, teachers, and schools to improve the academic performance of children, operating out of a posture of mutual respect of others' cultures and cultural practices (Auerbach, 1995; Cairney, 1997; Taylor, 1997).

THE DIFFERENT FACES OF FAMILY LITERACY

Should the term and construct of *family literacy* be interpreted as primarily descriptive or pedagogical? And if pedagogical, what should the nature of that pedagogy be? There is real difference and disagreement among researchers and educators as to the answers to these questions. There is general agreement that the term *family literacy* first emerged from descriptive ethnographies like Taylor's 1985 study of the same name. Her follow-up study, with Dorsey-Gaines (1988), of several inner-city, economically disadvantaged families balanced her first study of highly educated mainstream families and established the fact that literacy is woven into the lives of marginalised families as well. These works and others (e.g., Barton, 1994; Purcell-Gates, 1995, 1996; Teale, 1986) were meant to be viewed as descriptive of the ways in which literacy does and does not mediate the lives of families. However, during the span of time in which this research was conducted, the term *family literacy* was appropriated by those whose purpose was to teach parents to incorporate mainstream literacy practices into their lives as a way of improving the academic performance of their children. Thus, family literacy became known as a type of instructional program, one aimed at parents and their children. And from this, another type of research emerged, that of documenting the outcomes of those instructional programs. So we now have another version of family literacy research, one that is related to program effectiveness.

Within this, note should be taken of the ideological division between providers of family literacy instructional programs. On the one hand are those programs that appear to consider the goal of family literacy programs to teach, or train, parents to incorporate particular literacy and parenting practices into their homes and interactions with their children that are assumed to be related to the academic achievement of their children. Many of these assumptions rest, at least partially, on the body of literature synthesized and just described. Practices such as reading to their children, helping with their homework, and strategic communication with schools and teachers are among those commonly included in such family literacy programs. Underlying this stance is the belief that the targeted parents do not already practice these desirable behaviors, or that the literacy practices that are present in the home are not facilitative of academic success (Street, 1993), leading some to brand this stance as "deficit-driven." The commonly referred to exemplar of this type of program is the National Center for Family Literacy (NCFL), directed by Sharon Darling and privately funded.

Taylor (1997) and Auerbach (1995) have taken the lead in opposing these types of programs, asserting that research has documented that there are many ways of incorporating literacy into family life (Street, 1993), and that injecting academic, or school, literacy practices into homes in which they are viewed as "foreign" and from outside the culture is inadvisable, patronizing, and will not "work." As an alternative to the NCFL program standards which include indicators of effectiveness such as relevant content, balanced assessment design, and friendly intake procedures (cited in Taylor, 1997), Taylor and a group of family literacy researchers and providers have issued what they term "an international declaration of principles" (see Taylor, 1997). These principles, they believe, capture the need to view low-income, minority families as capable, cultural units, whose needs are the result of economic and political oppression and not the result of poor parenting or the failure to incorporate literacy into their lives. Family literacy programs must begin with a mutual respect and collaborative stance with families and view literacy as a vehicle for changing the oppressive forces in their lives, according to this perspective.

Although many of the family literacy programs that have documented results through outcome research assert that they do respect the cultures from which their participating families come (e.g., Paratore, 1993), and that their programs result in the empowerment of the families for tackling the policies that disadvantage them (e.g., Rodriguez-Brown & Meehan, 1998; Rodriguez-Brown & Mulhern, 1992), there has been no empirical research to date that addresses the issues raised in this debate.

FAMILY LITERACY PROGRAMS: DO THEY WORK?

Types of Family Literacy Programs

Nickse (1991) created a typology of family and intergenerational literacy programs to aid in description, research, and evaluation. She distinguished *family* and *intergenerational* programs by whether or not the relationships are between members of the same family or between unrelated adults and children (e.g., senior citizens reading to kindergarten children of the local school). Three of her four types of programs are family literacy-based and capture the array of programs currently in operation:

1. Instruction delivered directly to both adults and children, separately and together.
2. Instruction delivered directly to adults only with benefits expected to impact children.
3. Instruction delivered directly to children only, with expected indirect impact on parents.

I use these types to structure within sections the following discussion of impact of existing programs.

Evaluation Challenges and Issues

Evaluation of family literacy programs is extremely problematic and challenging (Hayes, 1996; Hibpshman, 1989). Although increasing numbers of large-scale, as well as small single-program, evaluations are being conducted, the central difficulty of eliminating competing explanations for results remains and weakens virtually all attempts at establishing program effectiveness. Thus, all reports that claim to "show" that programs "work" must be read and interpreted with extreme caution.

Evaluation Related to Goals of Family Literacy Programs

Family literacy programs have multiple goals and ways of addressing those goals (see Nickse, 1991, cited earlier) and evaluation and research need to be explicitly tied to these (Hayes, 1996). The findings of the research in the following section are organized according to the following broad goal areas: (a) impact on children's skills, achievement, and/or attitudes; (b) impact on parents' achievement, literate behaviors, and confidence/self-esteem; and (c) impact on parent/child literacy interactions.

Impact on Children's Skills, Achievement, and/or Attitudes.   By far the greatest amount of research has been done on the impact of family literacy programs on the academic achievement of children. The majority of the findings indicate that children of parents involved in some form of family literacy program did improve in areas relevant to school success. Most of these studies, however, lacked appropriate controls and must be taken as suggestive only.

Two large family literacy programs in the United States exemplify Nickse's Type 1 program— instruction delivered to both adults and children, separately and together. These are the National Center for Family Literacy (NCFL) and the Even Start program. Evaluations of these two programs have made attempts to incorporate control groups or norm controls (Darling & Hayes, 1996; St. Pierre, Swartz, Gamse, & Abt Associates, 1995). NCFL, based in Louisville, KY, is a privately funded program with locations across the United States. An outgrowth of the Parent and Child Education Program

(PACE), it provides direct service to adults and children in a structured program designed to address literacy and educational needs of parents and children, personal and social needs of parents, family-development needs, parent needs for working with their children, and preemployment needs of the parents (Darling & Hayes, 1966).

Studies have shown that NCFL children made significant gains in vocabulary, as measured by the norm-referenced PPVT, and gains three times what would be expected in the developmental domains on the normed Child Observation Record (COR). In an attempt to explore the children's school success, current teachers of children who had attended programs from 10 sites across the country were interviewed, usually by phone but some in person. Responses on 289 NCFL children and a randomly selected sample of 230 children from some of the same classes revealed the following areas in which the NCFL children were rated as average or above in their classes (areas where this criterion was not met were not reported): 78% on overall academic performance; 85% on motivation to learn; 86% on support from parents; 92% on relations with other students; 88% on attendance; 88% on classroom behavior; 81% on self-confidence; 86% on probable success in school. Follow-up studies are replicating these results, according to Darling and Hayes (1996).

The Even Start Family Literacy Program is federally funded and intended to "improve the educational opportunities of the Nation's children and adults by integrating early childhood education and adult education for parents into a unified program" (P.L. 100-297, Sec. 1051 in St. Pierre et al., 1995). According to St. Pierre et al., Even Start has three interrelated goals: (a) to help parents become full partners in the education of their children, (b) to assist children in reaching their full potential as learners, and (c) to provide literacy training for their parents. Evaluation of the program involved (a) the National Evaluation Information System (NEIS) for all Even Start projects to provide descriptive information on participating families, (b) an In-Depth Study of 10 purposively selected projects to document short-term outcomes, (c) other local evaluations by individual projects, and (d) data from local applications to enter the National Diffusion Network. The In-Depth Study included random assignment of participants to treatment and control groups.

Finding from this evaluation reveal that on the Preschool Inventory (PSI, a 32-item inventory of basic concepts important for preschool children to know before entering school), children from the NEIS made significant gains. Children from the In-Depth Study gained significantly on the PSI as compared to the control group at the first posttest (9 months after starting program), but at 18 months their scores did not differ from the controls. On the PPVT, there was no difference between the experimental children and the controls, with both groups making significant gains. Similarly, on an assessment of emergent literacy concepts, including orientation and directionality of text, recognition of letters and punctuation, and purposes for reading, there was no program effect, with both experimental and control children making significant gains.

Another Type 1 program whose evaluation used norm-referenced assessments as controls is the Basic Skills Agency's Family Literacy Program in Britain. Their evaluation has documented real gains for children. Funded by the government, the program holds as its overall aims to (a) raise standards of literacy among adults with difficulties and the children, and (b) to extend awareness of the importance of literacy and the role of family literacy (Brooks, Gorman, Harman, Hutchison, & Wilkin, 1996). Four demonstration programs were set up in low-income areas in England and Wales and provided the data for the evaluation. The delivery model was similar to both the NCAL and the Even Start ones: an adults-only component where the parents worked on their own literacy skills, learned about early literacy, and learned how they could help their children in this regard; a children-only component that blended nursery and infant (primary) school practices and approaches; and an adult–children component in which parents worked with their own children and applied what they had learned in the separate sessions about helping them. Evaluation of the program documented gains to the children in vocabulary, reading, and writing.

Neuman (1996) taught parents of preschoolers enrolled in Head Start classes to read and discuss children's books with their children. The parents went into the classes to read with their children following the adult-only sessions and then were given the books to take home. Neuman found significant increases on the PPVT and the Concepts of Print tests. However, there was no control group, nor were the PPVT norms used, only the raw scores.

Type 2 family literacy programs target only parents directly, with indirect benefits expected for their children (Nickse, 1991). Fossen and Sticht (1991) conducted an evaluation of educational programs aimed at mothers. Information on benefits to the children of the women participants was gathered via questionnaires, interviews, and family case studies. Mothers rated their children's performance across a number of categories (e.g., grades, test scores, attendance, attitude toward school) after having been in a women's program. Fossen and Sticht calculated that 65% of the children showed at least one indicator of improvement, as judged by their mothers. However, there was no attempt to obtain comparison data from control groups.

Another parent-only program, Project FLAME (Rodriguez-Brown & Meehan, 1998; Rodriguez-Brown & Shanahan, 1995), was designed for parents of children from 3 to 9 years old and serves primarily Hispanic parents in Chicago. The program encourages parents to use reading and writing around and with their children, to focus their children on uses of reading and writing, and to improve their own English proficiency and literacy skills. They are also shown how to more effectively read to their children and talk about the books. Further, they are given strategies for effectively interacting with schools and teachers.

Effects on the children of FLAME parents are measured each year with pre- and posttests of letter recognition, print awareness, and the Boehm Test of Basic Concepts. Analyses show statistically significant gains on each of these (Rodriguez-Brown & Meehan, 1998). Yet a comparative study of program effects, using a class of preschoolers from one of the FLAME schools, revealed no significant differences between the FLAME children and the comparison group.

Cairney and Munsie (1995) reported positive student outcomes of another parent-focused program. Talk to a Literacy Learner (TTALL) was developed in Australia to provide interactional strategies to parents to use with their children around literacy. Qualitative data (interviews, observations) indicated that children of TTALL parents were more positive about themselves as learners and more confident as readers and writers. Standardized achievement test results revealed that, as compared to a control group of randomly selected students, TTALL children had more positive attitudes toward reading more sophisticated vocabulary. Significant gains in comprehension were also reported for TTALL children, but no significant effects for spelling.

Several programs in the United Kingdom, designed to teach parents explicit response strategies to use with their children during reading and writing, have shown impressive results. Glynn (1996), in a review of 12 Pause, Prompt, Praise tutoring programs, reported reading age gains ranging from 1.5 and 2.0 months per month of trained tutoring to between 10 and 11 months per month of trained tutoring. Gains were particularly strong in programs introduced concurrently at home and at school. Topping (1996) reported results of evaluations of at least 215 Paired Learning Projects (Paired Reading, Cued Spelling, and Paired Writing). Reading achievement gains (across 60 published studies) included an average of 4.1 months of growth in accuracy for each month tutored, 5.4 months gain in comprehension for each month tutored. Of those studies with control groups, paired reading groups on the whole outperformed the controls. Spelling gains were reported on norm-referenced tests, along with increased confidence and generalization to other spelling tasks, compared to controls.

Descriptive and anecdotal data on the paired writing programs are also positive. Kemp (1996) reported on the Parents, Teachers, Children program, which teaches parents prompts to use when listening to kids read. Evaluating readings of the same text across three spaced occasions, Kemp found improvement in most areas of response at significant levels, with parents demonstrating widening repertoires of responses.

Another program in the United Kingdom, CAPER (Branston, 1996) was designed to encourage parents to read "real books" with their children and thus to support their children's reading development. Workshops were delivered within schools where parents participated in structured activities intended to add to their knowledge about ways of responding to and reading with their children, all the while emphasizing the goal of having fun. Two evaluations were carried out, using control groups. The first, a small pilot of 20 nursery school children, found significant gains for the experimental group on the British Picture Vocabulary Scale, the Verbal Comprehension and Naming Vocabulary Scales from the British Ability Scales, and Clay's Concepts of Print Test. A larger study, though, of 80 children in four nursery classes found no program effect on children's abilities.

Type 3 family literacy programs target children directly, with indirect impact on parent/home expected (Nickse, 1991). Morrow and Young (1997), in an example of this type of program, studied the effects on children's achievement and motivation of a school literacy program with a home component. Six first grades from two schools were randomly assigned to a treatment and control condition. Twelve children from each class were randomly selected for the data pool. Children in the experimental group received a home- and school-based program and those in the control group received only the school-based program. The home component included input from parents and contained materials and activities for storytelling, reading, and writing. Measurement outcomes revealed that children in the experimental group outscored the controls on all achievement measures and in teacher ratings of interest and motivation.

Phillips, Norris, and Mason (1996) conducted an intervention with 325 kindergartners in Nova Scotia by sending little books (see McCormick & Mason, 1986) into the homes for parents to read with their children. This study was carefully designed with three treatment and one control group. Measurements used were the Metropolitan Readiness Test, the Circus Listen to a Story Test, and an Emergent Literacy Concepts Test. At the end of kindergarten, there was only a small treatment effect on the emergent literacy test and none on the more general tests. Results from a 5-year follow-up study (Phillips et al., 1996) indicated that this increase in knowledge of early literacy concepts improved students' reading achievement for the next 4 years. Significantly, however, for family literacy concerns, the effects were strongest and longest lasting for the in-school-treatment-only group.

In conclusion, an increasing body of literature is documenting clear benefits to children of family literacy programs of all types. There continues to be, however, a real need for controlled studies using comparative groups to differentiate between development that will occur anyway as children experience reading and writing over time and through regular instruction and that which is a direct effect of family literacy intervention.

Impact on Parents' Academic Skills, Literate Behaviors, and Confidence/Self-Esteem.   Among parent/child instruction programs that have measured impact on parents, the NCFL, Even Start, and the Basic Skills Agency's Family Literacy Program evaluations all demonstrate modestly increased skills, as well as changed literate behaviors, and greater confidence by the parent participants. For the NCFL evaluation, Darling and Hayes (1996) reported that those adults who entered the program with the lowest levels of achievement on the Comprehensive Adult Student Assessment System (CASAS) gained an average of 4.4 scale-score points while in the program. According to Darling and Hayes, this gain is equivalent to slightly more than one grade level. One can infer that this gain was for people in the program for 1 year, but this is unclear, given the inclusion in the data pool of different evaluations from multiple sites. For adults who began the program reading at approximately a 6.7 grade level, the average gain was 1.2 months on the Test for Adult Basic Education (TABE). Darling and Hayes also reported that a higher percentage of adults in NCFL programs get the General Equivalency Degree (GED) as compared to those who attend adult-only programs. Self-report data documented increases in the amount of literacy-related activity in the home of parent participants and improvements in parents' self-confidence and confidence in parenting strategies.

The Even Start evaluation (St. Pierre et al., 1995) similarly documented significant gains on the CASAS for parents. However, when the In-Depth Study data were analyzed, with its control group factored in, there was no program effect for academic improvement. There was a program effect, though, for attainment of the GED. No change in home literacy activities was noted.

The Basic Skills Agency's Family Literacy Program evaluation (Brooks et al., 1996) documented an increase in the average reading test scores of 5% of the maximum score, and for writing, an increase of 10% of the starting level. Parents reported a growth in their confidence overall and especially as related to involving themselves in their children's schools.

Programs delivered directly to parents only have also reported gains by the participating adults. Paratore (1993), reporting on nine parents, found an average decrease in miscues of 13% after 40 instructional hours. Parents who participated in the English-as-a-second-language classes of the FLAME program for at least 10 months showed a significant gain in their English proficiency as measured by the BEST Test (Rodriguez-Brown & Shanahan, 1995). FLAME parents also reported increased confidence in their English-speaking abilities. Increased self-confidence was also reported by Branston (1996) as a result of the CAPER program, and by Cairney (1995) with regard to TTALL.

In summary, most programs that provided direct skill instruction to parents documented effects of that instruction, given sufficient instruction time. The relative paucity of data reported on this impact factor probably reflects the primary and ultimate focus of family literacy programs (as compared to adult-only literacy programs) on the academic achievements of the children. The indirect influence of parents literacy levels and education (see Hayes, 1996, discussed earlier) on children's academic success renders it difficult to factor it in as a direct intervention feature of family literacy programs.

Impact on Parent/Child Literacy Interactions. The influence of parent/child interactions around print, however, is well supported by the foundational research (discussed earlier) and is thus present in virtually every family literacy program as a primary focus. Either directly, or indirectly, family literacy programs all aim to increase the *frequency* of parent/child interactions around reading and writing in the home, and many programs targeted the *nature* of those interactions. As discussed previously, this often means increasing storybook reading but may also include other print-related activities such as letter/note writing, attention to environmental print, and help with homework. Workshops, modeling, and in-class practice are all activities that are used by different family literacy programs to teach and/or support strategies for these literacy-related interactions. However, measuring outcomes for these instructional practices is extremely problematic, especially for programs with large numbers of participants. Direct observation of parent/child interactions in the home is often considered inappropriate and/or too labor-intensive. Direct observation within classes is more possible but raises issues of ecological validity and is still very labor-intensive. Thus, most data on home-based interactions around print come from self-report measures from the parent, sometimes pre–post program participation, or sometimes at the end of the program as part of a participant evaluation procedure. The problems with self-report data, particularly if the respondents are well aware of what the questioners believe is important (as is the case with parents who have participated for a time in family literacy programs), are well known (Purcell-Gates, 1993).

Not surprisingly, given this effect, almost all programs with published evaluations report increases along this dimension, as documented by parental report. Significant increases in the frequency of the following home literacy interactions have been reported: (a) parent–child bookreading (Branston, 1996; Brooks et al., 1996; Cairney & Munsie, 1995; Darling & Hayes, 1996; Fossen & Sticht, 1991; Gambrell, Almasi, Xie, & Heland, 1995; Hannon, 1996; Paratore, 1993; Rodriguez-Brown & Shanahan, 1995; Somerfield, 1995); increased help with homework (Brooks et al., 1996; Darling & Hayes, 1996; Paratore, 1994; Rodriguez-Brown & Meehan, 1998); and increased and more effective use of the library (Brooks et al., 1996; Cairney & Munsie, 1995; Darling & Hayes, 1996; Paratore, 1993). A notable exception is the Even Start report (St. Pierre et al., 1995), which reported no significant increases in home literacy environment, with the exception of more reading materials in the home.

Regarding the *nature* of the print-related interactions occurring in the home, several studies report data that indicates a change toward "the better," but this is somewhat hazy and unspecified. For example, Darling and Hayes (1996) reported changes in "the patterns of language used in the home to be more consistent with patterns shown to be related to later school success of children" (p. 16). Brooks et al. (1996) reported that parents, in the course of interviews, indicated that they are more patient with their children now, pay more attention to their needs as regards school work, and have more fun with them. A few studies, however, have included interactional observations and thus have more interaction-specific data to document.

Cairney, Lowe, and Sproats (1995) incorporated observations of class, group, and home interactions in his evaluation of the TTALL program. Analysis of videotapes and direct observation data suggested the following: By the end of the programs, parents were (a) offering more positive feedback; (b) providing a different focus when listening to children reading (e.g., less emphasis on phonics); (c) asking qualitatively different questions; and (d) providing qualitatively better responses to their children's writing and reading.

Mulhern (1993) conducted in-home observational case studies of three FLAME parents in an attempt to triangulate the interview and testing data collected on the participants of the program. She found that the parents were incorporating the suggestions they had received from the program for reading with their children: They all read to their children; they read in ways that were appropriate to their reading levels; they involved their children in the reading through asking questions and relating the stories to experiences in the children's lives; and the children were active participants, asking questions and spontaneously commenting on the stories. Mulhern further noted that a problem seemed to exist around the fact that most of the storybooks were in English, which the parents would orally translate into Spanish as they read, rendering any print-specific learning that might come from the reading event problematic. She also noted that although FLAME parents were encouraged to involve their children in the home in writing events as well as reading events, none of the case-study families did so.

Neuman and Gallagher (1994) conducted an intervention to change the nature of the interactions between six low-income White teenage mothers and preschool-age children during literacy play. Using a multiple-baseline, different-behaviors, single-subject design, they documented clear increases in the mothers' uses of labeling, scaffolding, and contingent responsivity with their children. These increases declined with transfer and across time but continued at frequencies greater than at baseline for all but one of the mothers. The children's active turns increased and their unresponsive turns decreased, and their PPVT scores increased significantly from low average to high average.

Spreadbury (1994), as part of an analysis of the effects of a program designed to help parents learn to read to their children in interactive ways, videotaped 12 parents reading to their children before and after involvement in the program. She conducted an interactional analysis of the readings and found twice as much interaction during the second reading.

In summary, although parent/child interactions around print are at the heart of most family literacy programs, documentation of program impact on the frequency and nature of these interactions is difficult and thus insufficient at the present time. Further, except for the research of Neuman and Gallagher (1994), there is no documentation on the impact on children's literacy development of interventions that seek to change the nature of the interactions between parent and child around print. Given the critique of researchers like Taylor (1997) and Auerbach (1995), summarized earlier, it would behoove family literacy program researchers to explore directly the many issues arising from attempts to change the ways parents interact with their children.

SUMMARY

Research in the area of family literacy is lagging behind policy and practice. Public perception about its role in children's learning, public and private funding, and program implementations are all outpacing empirically based knowledge about the conditions for its occurrence, the different forms family literacy can take, the actual impact of the practice of these different forms on children's school achievement, and the differential impacts of the various types of intervention on children's long-term success with schooling and academic tasks, and/or parents' increased agency and self-efficacy regarding their children's schooling. The following can be concluded based on the research that has been done:

1. Children do learn many concepts, skills, attitudes, and behaviors relevant to the acquisition of literacy in their homes to the degree to which they participate in naturally occurring literacy events.
2. Many of these concepts, skills, attitudes, and behaviors appear to stand them in good stead when they begin school and proceed through the grades.
3. Intervention programs that target specific strategies for parents to use with their children around reading and writing are effective in improving children's achievement in school in areas directly related to those strategies.

Less well established are the following:

1. That family literacy interventions are effective in changing the ways in which print is viewed and operates within the culture of individual homes.
2. That the small gains documented so far for children of parents who have participated in family literacy programs will be sustained over time.
3. The optimal age of children for families to begin participation in family literacy programs.

Virtually unexplored by research is the issue of compatibility among the cultures of schools, homes, and family literacy programs. Studies that have documented significant differences in the attitudes and beliefs of families from nonmainstream cultures and those of the mainstream schools (e.g., Delgado-Gaitan, 1990; Fitzgerald et al., 1991;

Goldenberg, 1987; Neuman, 1995) regarding the ways children learn and the kinds of roles parents should be expected to play in this learning suggest a powerful cultural factor that needs to be directly addressed through inquiry. Studies need to be done on the comparative effectiveness, regarding children's academic achievement over time, of programs that operate out of a mainstream perspective and those that craft their programs to include and build on the cultural perspectives of the participants themselves (see Different Faces of Family Literacy section). These studies must be ethnographic and descriptive to capture the relevant nuances of individuals and context as well as experimental to speak to the issue of effectiveness. Relatedly, family literacy research needs to expand to look at the ways in which schools do and do not/can and cannot build on whatever abilities and beliefs children bring with them to achieve educational parity across class, race, and ethnicity.

REFERENCES

Anglum, B. S., Bell, M. L., & Roubinek, D. L. (1990). Prediction of elementary student reading achievement from specific home environment variables. *Reading Improvement, 27*, 173–184.

Auerbach, E. (1995). Deconstructing the discourse of strengths in family literacy. *Journal of Reading Behavior, 27*, 643–660.

Baker, L. Scher, D., & Mackler, K. (1997). Home and family influences on motivations for reading. *Educational Psychologist, 32*, 69–82.

Baker, L., Fernandez-Fein, S., Scher, S., & Williams, H. (1998). Home experiences related to the development of word recognition. In J. Metsala & L. Ehri (Eds.), *Word recognition in beginning literacy* (pp. 263–287). Mahwah, NJ: Lawrence Erlbaum Associates.

Barton, D. (1994). *Literacy: An introduction to the ecology of written language.* Oxford, UK: Blackwell.

Basic Skills Agency. (1993). *Parents and their children: The intergenerational effect of poor basic skills.* London: Adult Literacy and Basic Skills Unit.

Bee, H. L., Barnard, K. E., Eyres, S. J., Gray, C. A., Hammond, M. A., Spietz, A. L., Snyder, C., & Clark, B. (1982). Prediction of IQ and language skill from perinatal status, child performance, family characteristics, and mother-infant interaction. *Child Development, 53*, 1134–1156.

Bell, R. (1969). A reinterpretation of the direction of effects in studies of socialization. *Psychological Review, 75*, 81–95.

Bissex, G. (1980). *Gnys at wrk: A child learns to write and read.* Cambridge, MA: Harvard University Press.

Bloom, B. (1964). *Stability and change in human characteristics.* New York: Wiley.

Bradley, R. H., & Caldwell, B. M. (1980). Home environment, cognitive competence, and IQ among males and females. *Child Development, 51*, 1140–1148.

Bradley, R. H., & Caldwell, B. M. (1984). The relation of infants' home environment to achievement test performance in first grade: A follow-up study. *Child Development, 55*, 803–809.

Bradley, R. H., & Caldwell, B. M. (1987). Early environment and cognitive competence: The Little Rock study. *Early Child Development and Care, 27*, 307–341.

Branston, P. (1996). Children and parents enjoying reading (CAPER): Promoting parent support in reading. In S. Wolfendale & K. Topping, (Eds.), *Family involvement in literacy* (pp. 18–32). London: Cassell.

Brooks, G., Gorman, T., Harman, J., Hutchison, D., & Wilkin, A. (1996). *Family literacy works: The NFER evaluation of the Basic Skills Agency's demonstration programmes.* London: Basic Skills Agency.

Burgess, S. (1997). The role of shared reading in the development of phonological awareness: A longitudinal study of middle to upper class children. *Early Child Development and Care, 127–128*, 191–199.

Burgess, S. R., & Lonigan, C. J. (1996, April). *A meta-analysis examining the impact of the preschool home literacy environment on reading development: Paper lion or king of the reading jungle?* Paper presented at the Society for the Scientific Study of Reading. Chicago.

Bus, A. G., van Ijzendoorn, M. H., & Pelligrini, A. D. (1995). Joint book reading makes for success in learning to read: A meta-analysis on intergenerational transmission of literacy. *Review of Educational Research, 65*, 1–21.

Butler, D. & Clay, M. M. (1975). *Reading begins at home.* Exeter, NH: Heinemann.

Cairney, T. H. (1995). Developing parent partnerships in secondary literacy learning. *Journal of Reading, 38*, 520–526.

Cairney, T. H. (1997). Acknowledging diversity in home literacy practices: Moving towards partnership with parents. *Early Childhood Development and Care, 127–128*, 61–73.

Cairney, T. H., Lowe, K., & Sproats, E. (1995). *Developing partnerships: The home, school, and community interface* (Vols. 1–3). Canberra: DEET.

Cairney, T. H., & Munsie, L. (1995). Parent participation in literacy learning. *Reading Teacher, 48*, 392–403.

Caldwell, B., & Freyer, M. (1982). Day care and early education. In B. Spodek (Ed.), *Handbook of research in early childhood education* (pp. 110–117). New York: Free Press.

Chafe, W., & Danielewicz, J. (1986).Properties of spoken and written language. In R. Horowitz & S. J. Samuels (Eds.), *Comprehending oral and written language* (pp. 81–113). New York: Academic Press.

Chaney, C. (1994). Language development, metalinguistic awareness, and emergent literacy skills of three year old children in relation to social class. *Applied Psycholinguistics, 15*, 371–394.

Clay, M. M. (1975). *What did I write?* Auckland, NZ: Heinemann

Clay, M. M. (1979). *Early detection of reading difficulties.* Portsmouth, NH: Heinemann.

Crain-Thoreson, C., & Dale, P. S. (1992). Do early talkers become early reader? Linguistic precocity, preschool language, and emergent literacy. *Developmental Psychology, 28*, 421–429.

Darling, S., & Hayes, A. E. (1996). *The power of family literacy.* Louisville, KY: National Center for Family Literacy.

Delgado-Gaitan, C. (1990). *Literacy for empowerment: The role of parents in children's education.* London: Falmer Press.

Downing, J., Ollila, L., & Oliver, P. (1975). Cultural differences in children's concepts of reading and writing. *British Journal of Educational Psychology, 45*, 312–316.

Downing, J., Ollila, L., & Oliver, P. (1977). Concepts of language in children from differing socioeconomic backgrounds. *Journal of Educational Research, 70*, 277–281.

Durkin, D. (1966). *Children who read early.* New York: Teachers College Press.

Feitelson, D., & Goldstein, Z. (1986). Patterns of book ownership and reading to young children in Israeli school-oriented and nonschool-oriented families. *Reading Teacher, 39*, 924–930.

Ferreiro, E., & Teberosky, A. (1982). *Literacy before schooling.* Exeter, NH: Heinemann.

Fitzgerald, J., Spiegel, D. L., & Cunningham, J. W. (1991). The relationship between parental literacy level and perception of emergent literacy. *Journal of Reading Behavior, 23*, 191–213.

Fossen, S. V., & Sticht, T. G. (1991). *Teach the mother and reach the child: Results of the Intergenerational Literacy Action Research Project of Wider Opportunities for Women.* Washington, DC: Wider Opportunities for Women.

Gambrell, L. B., Almasi, J. F., Xie, Q., & Heland, V. J. (1995). Helping first graders get a running start in reading. In L. M. Morrow (Ed.), *Family literacy: Connections in schools and communities* (pp. 143–154). Newark, NJ: International Reading Association.

Glynn, T. (1996). Pause Prompt Praise: Reading tutoring procedures for home and school partnership. In S. Wolfendale & K. Topping (Eds.), *Family involvement in literacy* (pp. 33–44). London: Cassell.

Goldenberg, C. (1987). Low-income Hispanic parents' contributions to their first-grade children's word-recognition skills. *Anthropology & Education Quarterly, 18*, 149–179.

Goldfield, B. A., & Snow, C. E. (1984). Reading books with children: The mechanics of parental influence on children's reading achievement. In J. Flood (Eds.), *Promoting reading comprehension* (pp. 204–215). Newark, DE: International Reading Association.

Goodman, K., & Goodman, Y. (1976, April). *Learning to read is natural.* Paper presented at conference on Theory and Practice of Beginning Reading Instruction. Pittsburgh, PA.

Goodman, Y. (1984). The development of initial literacy. In H. Goelman, A. Oberg, & F. Smith (Eds.), *Awakening to literacy* (pp. 102–109). Exeter, NH: Heinemann.

Goodman, Y., & Altwerger, B. (1981). *Print awareness in preschool children: A working paper.* Tucson, AZ: University of Arizona, Program in Language and Literacy.

Hannon, P. (1996). School is too late: Preschool work with parents. In S. Wolfendale & K. Topping (Eds.), *Family involvement in literacy* (pp. 63–74). London: Cassell.

Hansen, H. S. (1969). The impact of the home literary environment on reading attitude. *Elementary English*, 17–24.

Harste, J., Woodward, V., & Burke, C. (1984). *Language stories and literacy lessons.* Exeter, NH: Heinemann.

Hayes, A. (1996). Longitudinal study of family literacy program outcomes. In L. A. Benjamin & J. Lord (Eds.), *Family literacy: Directions in research and implications for practice.* [Summary and papers of a national symposium sponsored by the U.S. Department of Education, Office of Educational Research and Improvement in collaboration with the Office of Vocational and Adult Education and the Office of Elementary and Secondary Education's Even Start Program] (pp. 45–54). Washington, DC: U.S. Government Printing Office.

Heath, S. B. (1983). *Ways with words.* New York: Cambridge University Press.

Hess, R. D., Holloway, S., Price, G. G., & Dickson, W. P. (1982). Family environments and acquisition of reading skills: Toward a more precise analysis. In L. M. Laosa & I. Siget (Eds.), *Families as learning environments for children* (pp. 87–113). New York: Plenum.

Hibpshman, T. (1989). *A review of the parent and child education (PACE) program* (Rep. No. PS019468). Lexington, KY: Kentucky Department of Education Office of Research and Planning. (ERIC Document Reproduction Service No. ED 329 366)

Hiebert, E. H. (1980). The relationship of logical reasoning ability, oral language comprehension, and home experiences to preschool children's print awareness. *Journal of Reading Behavior, 12*, 313–324.

Hiebert, E. H. (1981). Developmental patterns and interrelationships of preschool children's print awareness. *Reading Research Quarterly, 16*, 236–259.

Holdaway, D. (1979). *The foundations of literacy.* Auckland, NZ: Heinemann.

Hunt, J. (1961). *Intelligence and experience.* New York: Ronald.

Kemp, M. (1996). Parents, teachers, children: A whole literacy education system. In S. Wolfendale & K. Topping (Eds.), *Family involvement in literacy* (pp. 75–88). London: Cassell.

Lomax, C. M. (1976). Interest in books and stories at nursery school. *Educational Research, 19,* 100–112.

Lomax, R. G., & McGee, L. M (1987). Young children's concepts about print and reading: Toward a model of word reading acquisition. *Reading Research Quarterly, 22,* 237–256.

Mason, J. (1980). When do children learn to read: An exploration of four year old children's letter and word reading competencies. *Reading Research Quarterly, 15,* 203–221.

McCormick, C., & Mason, J. (1986). Intervention procedures for increasing preschool children's interest in and knowledge about reading. In W. Teale & E. Sulzby (Eds.), *Emergent literacy: Writing and reading* (pp. 90–115). Norwood, NJ: Ablex.

Morrow, L. M. (1983). Home and school correlates of early interest in literature. *Journal of Educational Research, 76,* 221–230.

Morrow, L., & Young, J. (1997). A collaborative family literacy program: The effects on children's motivation and literacy achievement. *Early Child Development and Care, 127–128,* 13–25.

Mulhern, M. (1993, April). *A further validation: An inside look at family literacy in the home.* Paper presented at the symposium Expanding and Using "Funds of Knowledge": Family Literacy in the Latino Community at the annual meeting of the American Educational Research Association, Atlanta, GA.

Neuman, S. (1995). Toward a collaborative approach to parent involvement in early education: A study of teenage mothers in an African-American community. *American Educational Research Journal, 32,* 801–827.

Neuman, S. (1996). Children engaging in storybook reading: The influence of access to print resources, opportunity, and parental interaction. *Early Childhood Research Quarterly, 11,* 495–513.

Neuman, S., & Gallagher, P. (1994). Joining together in literacy learning: Teenage mothers and children. *Reading Research Quarterly, 29,* 382–401.

Nickse, R. S. (1991, April). *A typology of family and intergenerational literacy programs: Implications for evaluation.* Paper presented at the Annual Meeting of the American Educational Research Association. Chicago.

Pappas, C. C. (1991). Young children's strategies in learning the "booklanguage" of information books. *Discourse Processes, 14,* 203–225.

Pappas, C. C. & Brown, E. (1988). The development of children's sense of the written story register: An analysis of the texture of kindergartners' "pretend reading" texts. *Linguistics and Education, 1,* 45–79.

Paratore, J. (1993). *An intergenerational approach to literacy: Effects on the literacy learning of adults and on the practice of family literacy.* ERIC Document. Washington, DC: U.S. Department of Education.

Paratore, J. (1994). Parents and children sharing literacy. In D. F. Lancy (Ed.), *Children's emergent literacy* (pp. 193–215). Westport, CT: Praeger.

Payne, A. C., Whitehurst, G. J., & Angell, A. L. (1994). The role of home literacy environment in the development of language ability in preschool children from low-income families. *Early Childhood Research Quarterly, 9,* 427–440.

Phillips, L. M., Norris, S. P., & Mason, J. M. (1996). Longitudinal effects of early literacy concepts on reading achievement: A kindergarten intervention and five-year-follow-up. *Journal of Literacy Research, 28,* 173–195.

Purcell-Gates, V. (1986). Three levels of understanding about written language acquired by young children prior to formal instruction. In J. Niles & R. Lalik (Eds.), *Solving problems in literacy: Learners, teachers, and researchers* (pp. 259–265). Rochester, NY: National Reading Conference.

Purcell-Gates, V. (1988). Lexical and syntactic knowledge of written narrative held by well-read-to kindergartners and second graders. *Research in the Teaching of English, 22,* 128–160.

Purcell-Gates, V. (1993).Issues for family literacy research: Voices from the trenches. *Language Arts, 70,* 670–677.

Purcell-Gates, V. (1995). *Other people's words: The cycle of low literacy.* Cambridge, MA: Harvard University Press.

Purcell-Gates, V. (1996). Stories, coupons, and the *TV Guide*: Relationships between home literacy experiences and emergent literacy knowledge. *Reading Research Quarterly, 31,* 406–428.

Purcell-Gates, V. McIntyre, E., & Freppon, P. A. (1995). Learning written storybook language in school: A comparison of low-SES children in skills-based and whole language classrooms. *American Educational Research Journal, 32,* 659–685.

Read, C. (1971). Preschool children's knowledge of English phonology. *Harvard Educational Review, 41,* 1–34.

Rodriguez-Brown, F. V., & Meehan, M. A. (1998). Family literacy and adult education: Project FLAME. In M. C. Smith (Ed.), *Literacy for the 21st century: Research, policy, practices and the National Adult Literacy Survey* (pp. 175–193). Westport, CT: Greenwood.

Rodriguez-Brown, F. V., & Mulhern, M. M. (1992, April). *Functional vs. critical literacy: A case study in a Hispanic community.* Paper presented at the American Education Research Association Annual Meeting, San Francisco, CA. (ERIC Document Reproduction Service No. ED 348 443)

Rodriguez-Brown, F. V., & Shanahan, T. (1995). *Exemplary program and practice: Request for nomination. Project Title: FLAME (Family Literacy: Aprendiendo, Mejorando, Educando).* Unpublished paper, University of Illinois at Chicago, Center for Literacy.

Scarborough, H. S., & Dobrich, H. S. (1994). On the efficacy of reading to preschoolers. *Developmental Review, 14,* 245–302.

Schieffelin, B., & Cochran-Smith, M. (1984). Learning to read culturally: Literacy before schooling. In H. Goelman, A. Oberg, & F. Smith (Eds.), *Awakening to literacy* (pp. 3–23). Exeter, NH: Heinemann.

Senechal, M., Thomas, E., & Monker, J. (1995). Individual differences in 4-year-old children's acquisition of vocabulary during storybook reading. *Journal of Educational Psychology, 87,* 218–229.

Share, D. L., Jorm, A. F., Maclean, R., Mathews, R., & Waterman, B. (1983). Early reading achievement, oral language ability, and a child's home background. *Australian Psychologist, 18,* 75–87.

Snow, C. E., Barnes, W. S., Chandler, J., Goodman, I. F., & Hemphill, L. (1991). *Unfulfilled expectations: Home and school influences on literacy.* Cambridge, MA: Harvard University Press.

Somerfield, B. (1995). Parents and children reading together; The Barbara Bush Foundation for Family Literacy. In L. Morrow (Ed.), *Family literacy: Connections in schools and communities* (pp. 184–195). Newark, DE: International Reading Association.

Spreadbury, J. (1994, July). *Families matter: Adults reading aloud to children at home and at school and its implications for language education.* Paper presented at the United Kingdom Reading Association, Coventry, England.

St. Pierre, R., Swartz, J., Gamse, B., & Abt Associates Inc. (1995). *National evaluation of the Even Start Family Literacy Program.* Washington, DC: U.S. Department of Education, Office of the Under Secretary.

Street, B. (1993). *Cross cultural approaches to literacy.* Cambridge: Cambridge University Press.

Sulzby, E. (1985). Children's emergent abilities to read favorite storybooks: A developmental study. *Reading Research Quarterly, 20,* 458–481.

Taylor, D. (1985). *Family literacy: Children learning to read and write.* Exeter, NH: Heinemann.

Taylor, D. (Ed.). (1997). *Many families, many literacies: An international declaration of principles.* Portsmouth, NH: Heinemann.

Taylor, D., & Dorsey-Gaines, C. (1988). *Growing up literate: Learning from inner city families.* Portsmouth, NH: Heinemann.

Teale, W. (1986). Home background and young children's literacy development. In W. H. Teale & E. Sulzby (Eds.), *Emergent literacy: Writing and reading* (pp. 173–206). Norwood, NJ: Ablex.

Topping, K. (1996). Tutoring systems for family literacy. In S. Wolfendale & K. Topping (Eds.), *Family involvement in literacy* (pp. 45–60). London: Cassell.

Walberg, H. J., & Tsai, S. L. (1985). Correlates of reading achievement and attitude: A national assessment study. *Journal of Educational Research, 78,* 159–167.

Walker, G. H., Jr., & Kuerbitz, I. E. (1979). Reading to preschoolers as an aid to successful beginning reading. *Reading Improvement, 16,* 149–154.

Wells, G. (1979). Language, literacy and educational success. *New Education, 1,* 23–34.

Wells, G., Barnes, S., & Wells, J. (1984). *Linguistic influences on educational attainment.* Final Report to DES Home and School Influences on Educational Attainment Project. Bristol, UK: University of Bristol.

White, K. R. (1982). The relation between socioeconomic status and academic achievement. *Psychological Bulletin, 91,* 461–481.

Whitehurst, G. J., Falco, F. L., Lonigan, C. J., Fischel, J. E., DeBaryshe, B. D., Valdez-Menchaca, M. C., & Caulfield, M. (1988). Accelerating language development through picture book reading. *Developmental Psychology, 24,* 552–559.

CHAPTER 45

Intergenerational Literacy Within Families

Vivian L. Gadsden
University of Pennsylvania

Whereas, "Knowledge is power," and an educated and intelligent people can neither be held in, nor reduced to slavery: Therefore [be it] Resolved, That we will insist upon the establishment of good schools for the thorough education of our children throughout the State; that, to this end, we will contribute freely and liberally of our means, and will earnestly and persistently urge forward every measure calculated to elevate us to the rank of a wise, enlightened and Christian people. Resolved, That we solemnly urge the parents and guardians of the young and rising generation, by the sad recollection of our forced ignorance and degradation in the past and by the bright and inspiring hopes of the future, to see that schools are at once established in every neighborhood, and when so established, to see to it that every child of proper age, is kept in regular attendance upon the same.

—Black Men's Convention (Proceedings 9–10, Charleston, SC, 1865)

The principle of schools, of education, is ... to elevate our families.

—James White, a black minister, Union Army veteran, and delegate
to the Arkansas Constitutional Convention in 1868 (see Gutman, 1987)

When I first came to the [literacy] program, I just wanted to get my reading together to get a job and help my children ..., but I see how knowing the things I'm learning about can make the difference for my children's whole life. It's not like I didn't know this before, but ... when you get a little time to think about your skills, then you spend more time thinking about how you can really help your children, and then you start planning for the future, you know; you know you should know about what they're learning in school and how I can help. I know that what I teach them, ... and what I show them, they'll do for their own children.

—Young participant mother in a family literacy program

Intergenerational literacy is associated often with deficit models and with the idea of "fixing" problems within families in order to create opportunity for future generations. Some analyses are as likely, if not more likely, to emphasize the lack of literate abilities that families pass on from one generation to another as to highlight the strengths that family members possess and share (Gadsden, 1994; Taylor, 1994; Taylor & Dorsey-Gaines, 1988). The perspectives that emerge from these analyses well might be labeled social-utilitarian or family-deficit. They deny the possibility and complexity of both intergenerationality and literacy as more than the simple production and transfer of knowledge within families and across different generations. However, as the Reverend White and the proclamation of the Black Men's Convention suggest, intergenerational literacy draws from beliefs about knowledge, its power, and its contributions to the future, but is not restricted by such beliefs and expectations. It houses vision and implicit meanings and purposes that are constructed and conveyed within families and communities, that are influenced by societal access and barriers, and that become a part of our own social and contextual historiography.

At the same time, intergenerational literacy embraces far more than beliefs or historiography. The mother's commentary in the quotation just given implies that intergenerational literacy is represented by high levels of activity in the present: that is, the processes of learning and teaching; the engagement of children by their parents, family members, and teachers in the acts of reading, writing, and problem solving; and the inculcation of values and practices that sustain such engagement. These processes, acts of reading and writing, and beliefs about and valuing of literacy may be used as predictors or consequences of generational practices. Depending on how they are conceptualized, framed, studied, or understood, they can enable us to move past the inherent constrictions of focusing on consequences and singular outcomes alone; rather, they can help us to investigate more deeply what constitutes important knowledge within social and cultural contexts and with what implications for learners over the short and long term.

This chapter focuses on conceptual and theoretical issues in intergenerational literacy within families by examining multiple stances within its primary domains of study. Drawing on work from a range of disciplines, the chapter explores fundamental issues related to future research in the field: that is, the degree to which reading research pushes the discourse of intergenerational literacy toward a deepening of knowledge and understanding of social, cultural, and gender factors that influence literacy within and across different generations; the extent to which it utilizes interdisciplinary knowledge about intergenerational learning within families; and the ways in which it can advance the construction of integrative frameworks that capture the nature and mode of literacy's transmission within diverse populations. Although the focus of this chapter is on families, the primary assumption that foregrounds the discussion is that intergenerational literacy is not exclusive to families. It may include a variety of individuals other than biological family members and contexts other than homes.

Intergenerational literacy has become an increasingly significant domain in educational research and practice over the past decade. The role of intergenerational literacy and its effects are studied in relationship to children's schooling and psychosocial well-being; parent–child, family, and adult learning; and family welfare and social support. The presumption of intergenerational connectedness in children's literacy and cognitive development is threaded throughout most empirical studies of children's achievement in school. Mothers' education, for example, has been used routinely as a predictor of children's school achievement, and studies regularly refer to parents as children's first socializers (Pellegrini, Brody, & Sigel, 1985).

The basic premises of intergenerational literacy, and the encompassing concept of intergenerational learning, revolve around families, parents in particular, and the transfer of behaviors, beliefs, practices, expectations, and potential to their progeny. The nature of these beliefs and practices—and the approaches and methods through which they are conveyed and sustained—are examined within an expanding complex of questions, ranging from what the relationship is between children's learning and parent and family involvement, to how schools build on literacy within the home, to whether an investment in the study of intergenerational literacy will result in positive change and effective practices. Despite increasing attention to these and other questions related to literacy learning and families, however, there is still relatively little work that connects intergenerational literacy to the larger scope of research on intergenerational learning or life-course family development, kinship and kin ties, or community relationships.

Most research on intergenerational literacy and on intergenerational learning is appropriately and uniquely situated within inquiry about the social and cultural processes that contribute to knowledge acquisition. It explores the approaches and mechanisms through which both knowledge and the processes used to transfer or transmit knowledge become embedded in family practices and folklore over time and the relationships between different approaches to learning. Although intergenerational research acknowledges children's neurological and biological predispositions to learning, it attempts to move outside circumscribed boundaries of cognitive science. The most cogent discussions of intergenerational literacy focus on the presence of specific behaviors in different generations and the accompanying concept of life-course development. They examine the continuum of acquired abilities and social constructs that influence reading, writing, and problem solving—not simply heritability of cognitive abilities within family lineage. Intergenerational research based on such discussions attends not only to the social and cultural contributions of families within the home but also to the influences of culture and social contexts that children experience outside of the home. Thus, it may center on a variety of relationships, such as, the impact of peers on learning; the reciprocal nature of transfer between different generations within and outside of families; the intersection of multiple settings that influence learning; and the ways in which these settings support, challenge, or thwart human development.

This chapter is divided into two broad parts intended to provide some of the historical and contemporary images associated with intergenerational literacy. The first part focuses on the development of an expansive discourse and integrative frameworks for intergenerational literacy. The second part explores contextual issues that contribute to integrative frameworks, specifically conceptualizations of intergenerational literacy within parent–child book reading and family literacy and models from intergenerational learning and family life course development. In the concluding section, I consider some of the implications of intergenerational literacy within and outside of current discussions about family literacy.

This chapter, like other writing on intergenerational literacy, draws heavily on issues examined within family literacy. The concepts *family literacy* and *intergenerational literacy* are often used interchangeably in reading research. In 1993, I suggested that rather than being synonymous with family literacy, intergenerational literacy should be considered a specific strand of inquiry, either parallel to or located within family literacy, because of its focus on the nature of the transmission of knowledge and behaviors (Gadsden, 1993). However, a broader and more global perspective on intergenerational literacy would consider a multiplicity of positions, including intergenerational literacy as a complement to family literacy, a strand of family literacy, or an overarching concept.

I have developed this chapter around two assumptions that guide my thinking and research on families; that allow me to cross some of the traditional boundaries of research, practice, and policy; and that take seriously issues of culture, race, class, and gender as defining features of the work with individual or collectives of learners. The first is that there is no appropriate, prototypical model of family structure. In fact, significant changes in family formation patterns have occurred, resulting in a vast range of family constellations. The second is that for all families, irrespective of ethnic background, their past and contemporary experiences have dictated or defined the family structures in which they function, with varying degrees of socially valued success. Each family brings a repertoire of beliefs, knowledge, skills, and experiences that are as likely to strengthen as to debilitate its members, depending on the family's access to resources and on the family's ability to rise above the constraints, social practices, and laws that circumscribe opportunities, whether our focus is literacy or other kinds of learning.

POSSIBILITIES FOR AN INTEGRATIVE FRAMEWORK

Intergenerational literacy as an area of study holds potential for creating an inclusive framework in which the variety of literacy studies focused on children, parents, and other family members and their relationships can be examined—from the role of parents in children's reading to the impact of family beliefs. This framework should lead to the development of a critical discourse that enhances the study of intergenerational effects, examines specific literate abilities, and augments "the sense of being literate." Heath (1991) describe this sense as deriving from "the ability to exhibit literate behaviors ... through which individuals can compare, sequence, argue with, interpret, and create extended chunks of spoken and written language in response to a written text in which communication, reflection, and interpretation are grounded" (p. 3). In order to construct this expansive framework, however, several issues about its construction, its components, and the intersection of influencing factors should be considered.

First, developing an integrative framework requires more than the combining of competing discourses and methodologies or the collapsing of related fields of knowledge and research. The simplistic approach to an integrative framework would be to seek out knowledge from intergenerational learning and literacy. Equally limited is focusing simply on how the two domains fit, demonstrating the oppositional philosophies that inform their development, or engaging in an intellectual power struggle over the value of cognitive domains over social, cultural, or contextual issues. An integrative framework for intergenerational literacy suggests a need to identify the different features of learning, literacy, families, human development, and intergenerationality. It is developed by examining the multiple layers of these domains in order to uncover the individual and social processes that define or dictate their salience in children and adults acquiring, using, and valuing literacy within families and from one generation to another.

Second, fundamental to the development of an integrative framework is a recognition and exploration of formerly unexamined, or seemingly peripheral or marginalized, issues within traditional discourses in the field. The most critical of these is a focus on diverse families, diverse not only in ethnicity, race, and culture, but also in family form, class, age, and stage within the life course. As is true of psychological and sociological research on families, research on intergenerational issues within literacy often appears to be developed around comparative models in which the knowledge and experiences of children with the least access and resources as a function of class or race are mapped against those of children who have had considerably more advantages. The resulting analysis informs us of how well or poorly one group—usually African American and Latino children, or low-income children and families—compares with another group—typically White children, or middle-income children and families. The greatest limitation of this analysis is that it minimizes the full range of factors that contribute to literacy learning and reduces the significance of the family's role in children's development past nominal investments. In short, the scope of issues related to families, the relationship of individual family members, and the factors that affect family life and families' interpretations of literacy's importance are left relatively unexplored.

Third, intergenerational literacy, like other forms of intergenerational learning, is steeped in history and the continuum of knowledge, abilities, behaviors, and beliefs that are accrued within and outside of families. As a historical tool and artifact, intergenerational literacy complements all literacy studies in the potential it offers to understand the sources and derivations of beliefs and practices, the ways in which they prepare children for learning, and the opportunities they lend for literacy access and reading success. Attention to intergenerational literacy is more than the history of context. It should invite rigorous analyses of context which locate the learner, family members, and tasks of literacy within a time frame that is affected by life transitions—that is, changes in class, sociopolitical factors, race, and gender. It should help in examining the responses to questions about whether children's literacy potential is a function of social statuses (Glass, Bengtson, & Dunham, 1986) in which children assume the social expectations of the previous generation, not only relative to familial access and ability but also relative to societal manipulations of opportunity. Are poor children, particularly poor children of color, confined to living out the imposed statuses of inequity and limited access? If the answer is no, then what do we need to know about the contributions of family members, and how do we reconcile the multiple streams of influence in children's reading and writing development?

Fourth, lacking in most analyses that link families, literacy, and intergenerationality is an examination of the variations in families—that is, in family forms and structures—and the role of non-parent family members. Studies of intergenerational literacy more often than not have focused primarily on two-generational (parent–child) relationships. Yet, there are considerable data that suggest that children access and have available to them a wider circle of caregivers who are likely to make equally significant, if not more significant, contributions to children's cognitive and social development (Taylor, Chatters, Tucker, & Lewis, 1990). These data raise several questions: Who are the members of families? What has the role of these family members been in relationship to children's literacy? How have these roles changed intergenerationally, and how have they been affected by social changes, such as women's entry into the workforce and changing social mores?

Fifth, even in two-generational (parent–child) studies, little research focuses on paternal roles and father–child reading patterns and relationships within intergenerational literacy and intergenerational learning. In my search for reading studies that include fathers, I was able to identify fewer than ten in the past 20 years. Through their presence or absence within the home, fathers play a role in children's preparation for learning literacy and valuing of literacy. They are both sources of knowledge about intergenerational literacy and vested recipients of information that can affect whether and how children access literacy, use literacy, and sustain interest in reading and writing. The current national attention to issues around fatherhood can serve as an impetus for intergenerational literacy research that joins other family research in focusing on both fathers and mothers. However, the emerging impetus around father involvement requires an analysis of the same issues that typify the study of mothers' expectations and family studies, particularly the diversity among fathers (e.g., fathers who are nonresidential, noncustodial; fathers who live in the home; poor and middle-class fathers; fathers limited by education; unemployed fathers; and fathers who differ by ethnicity, race, and culture; National Center on Fathers and Families, 1997; NICHD, 1998).

In addition, an expansive framework for intergenerational literacy would move outside of familiar domains and examine more intensively work that helps to thread

together relevant issues. The research since the 1980s on home–school–community relations is a reasonable prototype to initiate the revisions. Epstein (1995) and
Scott-Jones (1987; Scott-Jones & Clark, 1986), among others, offered a glimpse of the
varied family backgrounds and conditions that children bring and the ways that
schools accept, understand, and respond to them. Epstein (1990) provided a good
summary of the variations in families who are hard to reach, which is useful to consider in relationship to intergenerational literacy study with certain populations of
children and families.

The most useful approach for intergenerational literacy research is an examination of
the range of families and continuation of the focus on children and families who are at
the greatest risk of low literacy. What such an approach acknowledges is the presence of
strengths within all families, and it enables us to study the ways in which families with
apparent success acquire literate abilities and those families with less success negotiate
life demands across different generations. Rather than creating a template that can be
uniformly applied to all families, research would develop frameworks that focus on the
interactions among the multiple factors that contribute to literacy learning within and
across generations: that is, cognition, social processes, culture, and contexts.

Two basic questions persist in planning for intergenerational literacy research: (a)
who are the families, and (b) how do they describe literacy in their own words and
within their own family trajectories? Although we know more about
intergenerationality and families in reading research than we did a decade ago, we are
faced both with how much more there is to learn and with how to disentangle the complexities that arise from problems that interfere with learning, such as poverty and
poor schools. With seemingly begrudging frequency, studies are beginning to focus on
the entire family—mothers *and* fathers, grandmothers and grandfathers, other adults,
and children who are considered integral to the family structure (see Gadsden, 1998),
families with limited English fluency (e.g., Quintero & Velarde, 1990), families whose
children have special learning needs (e.g., Harry, 1995), and parents who while learning literacy have specific needs around parenting (e.g., Powell, 1991, 1990).

As public forums around family support increase and welfare devolution to the
states continues, the issue of literacy within and outside of families will be a critical
part of the public discourse. Welfare reform and family support initiatives are tied to
the ability of individuals to utilize existing literacies and to develop new ones. Social
policies that structure opportunities for people to use and value such learning and support their families are fundamental to any national or local agenda of family support,
as are policy investments in a developmental approach to strengthening families over
time. Having evolved from previous work in reading, the current and future focus encompasses a much wider set of goals and populations—from intergenerational learning to life-span development.

Intergenerational and family literacy has spurred a compelling movement in which
literacy educators and researchers work together to develop programs that promote
literacy activities between parents (and other adults in a family) and children. Research and programs that aim to link the concepts, intergenerational literacy and family literacy, might consider at least four broad questions:

1. How is intergenerational literacy conceptualized, and what characteristics of re-
    search and instruction in programs make them intergenerational?
2. What counts as knowledge and learning in intergenerational literacy, and how
    are changes charted and discussed?
3. What actually occurs in programs that promote reading, writing, and problem
    solving, and how are the activities around reading, writing, and problem solving
    integrated within the larger life issues of parenting, parent–child interactions,
    and family functioning?

4. How are issues around cultural difference, race, and poverty examined and addressed in research and practice?

The next section focuses on these questions and the issues that they suggest within several contributing research contexts.

CONTRIBUTING CONTEXTS TO AN INTEGRATIVE RESEARCH FRAMEWORK

Intergenerational literacy research draws on theoretical constructs within and across a range of disciplines that share a common concern about learning, fostering learning, and teaching within diverse settings. Intergenerationality within family literacy research and practice has not found its way to the mainstream of work in the field. In a review of studies that focused on intergenerational and family literacy, more than half of the citations were located outside of refereed journals or edited works in literacy. Fewer than one fourth of the citations in journals or edited books are in journals or works that are not literacy or reading-related. The research that has been reported is a blend primarily of ethnographic and qualitative analysis to case studies. These analyses typically describe the inherent complexities of developing a program, implementing the concept gaining acceptance within diverse low-income communities, and identifying useful approaches in response to the needs of practice and the demands of policy.

Research on intergenerational literacy may be linked to four domains of work: (a) parent–child book reading, (b) family literacy and parent (adult)–child literacy, (c) intergenerational learning, and (d) family life course. Each provides important theoretical frameworks about the nature and basis for the transfer of information within different settings; yet each differs in the history and rigor of the theories, frameworks, and models that are associated with it.

The study of intergenerational literacy as a formal area of inquiry is relatively recent, although reading research has focused for more than 30 years on two-generational issues, such as parents' influences on children's reading development and parent–child interactions around reading. However, there are few studies that provide in-depth analyses of direct relationships between children's acquisition of reading ability and parents' own development of literacy. That is, although many studies demonstrate the ways in which parents interact with children, there are few that provide a one-to-one analysis of the relationship between parent learning and child learning. Instead, studies that can be interpreted as intergenerational literacy have focused on the broad nature of practices—for example, verbal interactions, frequency of adult reading, and problem-solving tasks—that appear to contribute positively to children's desire to read and their success at reading (Snow, Barnes, Chandler, Goodman, & Hemphill, 1991).

Although a few longitudinal studies have been initiated (e.g., Gadsden, 1998; Purcell-Gates, 1995), and a proliferation of programs that are titled intergenerational exist, there is generally little research that makes any pronouncements about sustained effects of intergenerational literacy. Several studies in the 1960s set the stage for studying intergenerational literacy by examining the existence and applications of literacy practices in the home and suggesting that parents across cultural and ethnic groups, in fact, engage in a range of literate activities with their children. For example, by studying children and parents in low-income homes, Durkin's (1966, 1974–1975) research provided one of the most poignant analyses on the contributions of parents to children's early reading and role of family practices in black children's reading. Durkin's work was noteworthy not simply because of its contributions to the study of black children's reading development and the role of parents. It also engaged the field in a burgeoning discourse about how all children read and about how the field might rethink its approaches and the conduct of research on children's reading and parent support. Durkin and others whose work followed (e.g., Edwards, 1990, 1995; Strickland, 1981; Teale, 1981; Teale & Sulzby, 1986) contributed theoretical and pedagogical frameworks for the emerging family literacy. Their research and contributions to practice focused attention on familial derivations and sources of literacy practices and the influences of home and community as social contexts for two- and three-generational learners.

Parent–Child Book Reading

Intergenerational literacy also examines a common activity for young children—book reading. Doake (1981) observed that when parents and children participated in shared reading, children assumed more of the reading, reenacting what their parents had read to them. Either as emergent literacy (Teale & Sulzby, 1986), in which children interpret stories that are read to them in ways that reflect the text of the book, or as parents reading to their children, book reading continues to be seen as a convenient, realistic way to examine children's facility with print. Both emergent literacy and parent–child book reading focus, in some measure, on reading readiness in young children, that is, moving children from infancy to formal instruction in school. They are developed around the notion that specific practices and parent involvement generally improve children's literacy performance in school.

Home practices such as shared reading, availability of print materials, and reading aloud are but a few examples of activities or conditions that are thought to affect children's literacy development positively (Fitzgerald, Spiegel, & Cunningham, 1991; France & Meeks, 1987; Strickland & Morrow, 1989). The converse is an assumption that in homes where such behaviors and activities are not practiced, children's literacy development suffers a delay in the kind of active literacy engagement required to prepare for and perform well in school. There seems to be a kind of value assigned to routinized speech associated with storybook reading (Snow & Goldfield, 1983). Snow and her colleagues suggested that parents who were read to as children know how to read to their children; parents who have not been read to may experience difficulty in constructing or recreating the social routine.

The story routine includes parents engaging in a series of labeling questions while reading, such as "What's that?" and interacting with the young child as though the parent and child are participating in a two-way discussion. The parent and child are thought to be engaging together in the routine for which the parent can shift the responsibility of reading eventually to the child. Several research studies were developed to examine the process by which children assume this responsibility for print (i.e., scaffolding) and the nature of mutual engagement that occurs for parents and children during the literacy event (Dickerson, 1994; Pellegrini, Perlmutter, Galda, & Brody, 1990). Although the research appears conclusive for many middle-class, mainstream families, it has not provided equally informative data about how children from families that do not engage in these routines succeed or whether the strength of the process is intrinsic to the routine itself.

Family Literacy and Parent–Child Interactions Around Print

Like parent–child book reading, there was attention to families within literacy studies long before current discussions. Several studies in the 1960s and 1970s, for example, were generated in disciplines outside of reading and in response to national policies, they were centered on issues affecting children in poor Black families or poor families across ethnic groups (e.g., Billingsley, 1968; Coleman, Campbell, Hobson, McPartland,

Mood, Weinfeld, & York, 1966; Stack, 1974). Prior to the 1960s and 1970s, most studies of children's literacy and family influence were limited to upper-income families and focused on the genetic bases for reading ability (Demos, 1970; Harari & Vinovskis, 1989; Monaghan, 1991).The attention to lower income children and families reflected social changes around educational equality and equity, renewed national attention to reading and literacy research, and opened new directions and pathways to understand the variety of influences on children's learning. Research began to examine the intersections between and among parent knowledge, literacy processes in the home, and the connections that existed or could be established between home and school.

From the 1980s to the present, family literacy has become an active part of the lexicon within research, practice, and policy. The initial work was very much a part of the public discourse and acknowledged the presence of family relationships around literacy. Two, sometimes overlapping, lines of research emerged. One focused primarily on issues of context, culture, and social processes of literacy learning. Taylor's (1983) text offered both theoretical grounding and examples of literacy talk and activities within families. Heath (1982, 1983), whose work on parents' and children's uses of words highlighted intergenerationality in a variety of familial and community contexts and demonstrated the influences of culture, race, class, and dialect to enactments and meanings of literacy within home and community contexts. She described the ways in which literacy within these contexts cohered with or conflicted with school literacies.

One of the most provocative accounts that begs the question of intergenerational transfer is Taylor and Dorsey-Gaines's (1988) research, in which alternative perspectives to deficit models are examined within the lives of parents and children in low-income families. In this work about four families and the young learners in them, the authors approached the research process by seeking to understand the nature of the context in which the children were learning, to identify the places and times in which literate events occurred, and to explore what the relationships were between these events and the acts of knowing, caring, and investing in literacy. By acknowledging the class and race issues that limit access and opportunity from the outset, Taylor and Dorsey-Gaines placed the emphasis on what could be learned from the literate strengths of the families as a means to providing them with the resources that the children and families needed. The anthropological and literacy framework that the authors used enabled them to transcend preconceived notions about how the poor behave and the inherent limitations of poverty in relationship to literacy development and to offer a rich analysis in which we are asked to think about the relationships between parents and children, children and schools, and parents and schools.

In much the same way, Purcell-Gates (1995) challenged the prevailing race-centered analysis of low literacy by focusing on what Daisey (1991) would call the lack of intergenerational literacy transfer within low-income White families. Purcell-Gates's study of a poor, White, Appalachian boy and his mother and Auerbach's (1989) and Paratore's (1992) work with Latino families have contributed to critical discussions that have helped to transform family literacy from a policy-defined line of inquiry to an increasingly research- and practice-rich area of study.

A second line of research focuses on school-based literacy development and literacy within classrooms, particularly for children and parents from low-income homes, and contains two sublines, each representing different conceptualizations. One subline highlights skills approaches to help parents whose literate abilities are considered inadequate to ensure their children's success in school and to provide parents with strategies that support their children's literacy development (see Edwards (1990, 1993). The other subline refers implicitly to intergenerational learning but focuses primarily on classroom learning and practices and the bidirectionality of learning between home and school for low-income children (e.g., Morrow, 1994; Morrow & Young, 1997; Shanahan & Barr, 1995). Family literacy research has entertained divergent positions and has faced the same issues and controversies with which reading research has wrestled. The importance of these controversies within the context of intergenerational literacy is noteworthy, particularly in relationship to the frequent use of deficit models to explain the needs of children and families who are served by family literacy programs. A disproportionate number of these children and families are low income and of color. Thus, the likelihood of perpetuating racially coded explanations for reading difficulties, and for the inability to serve these children and their families, is substantially increased and foreboding.

Intergenerational Learning

A common feature of the studies described in the previous section is the absence of a discussion about intergenerational learning and its relationship to parent–child book reading, family literacy, or intergenerational literacy. Researchers in the social sciences use the term *intergenerational learning* as an all-encompassing concept for several kinds of human relationships across different generations. Intergenerational learning aims to respond to the question: What do children's lives reveal about their parents (Fishel, 1991)? In educational research, the study of intergenerational learning focuses on the ways in which parents and other family members contribute to or affect children's academic performance, school attendance, discipline, and valuing of schooling and education (see Gadsden, 1995). Developmental psychologists focus on cognitive transfers that influence children's linguistic patterns or psycho-socio-emotional well-being—from the inheritability of intelligence to parenting and environmental factors (Coles & Coles, 1988).

Although there is some agreement about the general uses of the concept, intergenerational learning researchers often have differing opinions about the definitions of *generation* itself. The term *generation* has been used to refer to a person's position in family lineage (Hagestad, 1981). Acock (1984) provides a useful framework and informative analysis on the commonly cited perspectives on generations: rank descent, cohort, developmental age, discrete time span, and zeitgeist. *Rank descent* is not a function of age; rather, an individual is placed in a generation based on his or her position in the family's hierarchy (Acock & Bengtson, 1975, 1978; Acock et al., 1982; Bengtson, 1975; Hill, Foote, Aldous, Carlson, & MacDonald, 1970; Troll, 1970). A self-sufficient, independent, adolescent parent is assigned the same status as a 60 year-old independent parent because of the ordering of their positions as parents in their respective families. Although rank descent makes it possible to study multiple generations, the age disparity does not address temporal or historical issues that affect family development or family members' perceptions.

Cohort as a generational indicator is based on age-homogeneous groupings (e.g., Elder's 1974 study of the children of the Great Depression). Children who are of the same age are assumed to have experienced certain social events in similar ways. These social events are thought to contribute to the life views of individuals as family members, suggesting consistency within age cohorts. Two primary limitations of cohorts are, first, that the differential ways that families mediate social events and circumstances are not acknowledged, and, second, that behaviors are attributed to generations as a function of social change when in fact more immediate and personal reasons unique to a family may be better explanations (see Rosow, 1978). Acock (1984) suggested that the cohort concept is relied on often, when "more proximate causes of generational cleavage" should be considered, such as when parent and child share an important or difficult series of life events.

In traditional perspectives on intergenerational learning, learning is discussed often as though all learning is unidirectional, that is, flowing from parent to child, and parents are the principal agents of socialization in childhood (Erikson, 1950; Freud,

1933; Heilbrun, & Gillard, 1966). The family is seen as the provider of stability and continuity to individual members and of the systematic socialization through which children come to understand the norms of the social order. Intergenerational similarity in attitudes is attributed to the socialization function and activities of the family (Glass et al., 1986). Children learn their parents' beliefs, values, and attitudes through both direct teaching and indirect observation; they actively seek out this information or passively accept it as a function of social conditioning. Implicit in traditional explanations is the assumption that childhood socialization is so powerful as to continue throughout adulthood (Campbell, 1969; Chodorow, 1978).

Some of the most compelling research from the 1980s to the present challenges the traditional approach along two primary lines. The first examines issues of race, class, gender, religious affiliation, and what Glass et al. (1986) described as other *social statuses* that affect an individual's life experiences. Acock (1984) referred to these social statuses when he suggested that parents and children share a common location in the social structure. Social structural forces may produce continuity or conflict. The similarity between children and parents is seen as a result of these social and cultural statuses as much as parental socialization. Social statuses provide a comfortable context for beliefs to persist unchallenged because they cohere with or explain the life circumstances of individuals. Thus, an upper-middle-class, 30-year-old, white, Protestant male might well express basic beliefs that appear remarkably similar to those of his parents. These similarities would be seen as the result of the social statuses of privilege, maleness, race, and religion that allow for the perpetuation of certain behaviors and practices from one generation to another.

The second line concerns the reverse direction or bidirectionality of intergenerational influence. Here, researchers examine children's influence on their parents and assume the occurrence of reciprocal learning from parent to child and from child to parent (Bronfenbrenner, 1986). Examples of this may be found in programs such as Head Start, which is designed for young children but results in significant changes in parents' behaviors and choices as well (Slaughter-Defoe & Richards, 1995). Proponents of this interactionist perspective argue that children increasingly influence their parents as both children and parents age and that the unidirectional flow from parent to child ignores the reciprocal relationships between children and parents (Bengtson & Troll, 1978; Featherman & Lerner, 1985; Glass et al., 1986; Hagestad, 1981, 1984; Lerner & Spanier, 1978).

A third line addresses changes in social structural location across each generation. Such changes can produce different values, adaptive to the contingencies of the generation, such as the generational distance created when a working-class or low-income family sends a child to college or when a middle-class student works with low-income children. As these students enter college and are exposed to different values and practices, they may become increasingly estranged from their parents over their life span or return home to their families and parents with new information and experiences to share. They may experience a generation break within lineages initially but may rebuild the relationship over time.

Family Life Course

Intergenerational learning is not limited to discrete points in a person's life but examines individual learning within the wider relationships of the family's life course. Family research has relied on life-course frameworks to connote the constantly changing role of family members and the family structures to which they belong (Germain, 1994; Kreppner & Lerner, 1989). Life span and life course, although similar in many ways, differ in their emphases. The work on life-span development describes human development as occurring in isolated, separable, fixed stages. Life-span approaches trace central phenomena such as sense of self or problem-solving abilities from infancy through old age to determine how they are transformed as a result of both psychological and social change (Baltes & Brim, 1979).

Life-course perspectives, in contrast, offer a wider array of situations and conditions; they consider life transitions, life events, and other life issues as ongoing processes that are constantly changing. Life-course approaches examine the relationship between individual change and the timing of major life events, such as the onset of schooling, the time at which someone leaves home, the beginning of childbearing, and retirement from the labor force (Elder, 1973).

Family life-course frameworks emphasize the continuity and reciprocity of life experiences and the ways in which new life experiences draw on others and are recycled over time—fluid rather than laconic role transitions (Germain, 1994). Families are seen as units of individuals, and the events, episodes, and activities that affect individual family members are thought to influence the unit and the course of family life. Each family member in each generation has a space that he or she shapes, and that shaping therefore becomes a part of the way families construct themselves and adapt to change. Germain (1983, 1994) noted that these transitions and events are both predictable and unpredictable and may be experienced as stressors or challenges, depending on the relationships among personal, cultural, and environmental factors. Some transitions and events are experienced by all families, and others differentiate families. Any one transition for an individual or within the family can precipitate a change or transformation for the entire family unit.

These and other issues in human development are embedded in a variety of disciplines that contribute to our understanding of human behavior—history (Hareven, 1977, 1982), sociology (Elder, 1985), and gerontology (Riley, 1985). In this interdisciplinary work, life changes and life events are seen as time specific rather than fixed. That is, the onset of these changes and events may occur within a specific period but may continue over time, is not always predictable, and may be affected by a variety of factors. Time may refer to historical and social changes that affect people born during a time period, such as gender role changes resulting from the women's movement; to individual time, reflecting how individuals shape and experience their lives; to social time, integrating individual human processes into collective activities within the family (Germain, 1990, 1994). Individual and family patterns of development vary as a function of gender, income, social class, culture, and the historical period of events and the way in which family members respond to events. However, life events and changes are experienced differently within different societies. Such contrasts are implied by comparisons of research such as that of Atchley (1975), who provided a picture of people in modern, industrialized societies, to that of Fry (1988), who found enormous cultural variability in socially accepted stages of adult development.

Difficult life circumstances result in families sometimes changing their perspectives and self-perceptions, in their constructing a collection of behaviors and practices that are associated internally and externally with the family. Several frameworks are used to represent these changes. My own work with multiple generations of African American and Puerto Rican families is developed around a theoretical framework to study literacy that I call *family cultures,* cumulative life texts of individual family members that contribute to the life course of the family as cultural artifacts. Intergenerational practices and learning within families are formed around an interplay of accepted ethnic traditions, cultural rituals, sociopolitical histories, religious practices and beliefs, and negotiated roles within families over time. Issues of race and culture are deeply embedded in family cultures, which are manipulated by societal events and affected by shifts in family mobility. They seem to revolve around a family-defined premise that family members hold as central to their purpose and to the life trajectory of children. Families vary in their level of desire to adapt these cultures, which may be fluid or static, depending on the degree to which family members adapt or accommodate change. In family cultures, family members construct traditions, practices, beliefs, and behaviors that they believe are critical to survival and achievement and that are embedded in their own family histories.

Reiss's (1981) *family paradigms*, for example, are defined by family members and include the shared, implicit beliefs that families have about themselves, their social worlds, and their relationship to social structures. He wrote that "the family, through the course of its own development, fashions fundamental and enduring assumptions about the world in which it lives. The assumptions are shared by all family members, despite the disagreements, conflicts, and differences that exist within the family" (p. 1). The assumptions about family and the world, Reiss suggested, are rarely conscious. Rather, paradigms are influenced by family history, culture, and the values and meanings assigned to experiences and perceptions. They are affected by the life views of family members, that is, views of the world as ordered or disorganized, predictable or unpredictable, and fair or inequitable. Family rituals and spatial and temporal conditions arise from and maintain family paradigms (Hartman & Laird, 1983; Kantor & Lehr, 1975). When families face stresses, they may move from implicit assumptions to stated alternatives to individual and family survival (Germain, 1994).

Stack and Burton (1993) expanded on their multigenerational research to focus on *kinscripts*. Kinscripts are developed on the premise that families have their own agenda, their own interpretation of cultural norms, and their own histories. Stack and Burton's model focuses on the temporal nature of the life course (e.g., lifetime, social time, family time, and historical time) and life-course independence (e.g., the ways that individual transitions and trajectories are affected by or contingent upon the life stages of others). The framework is developed around three critical issues: (a) temporal and interdependent factors in family role transitions, (b) creation and intergenerational transmission of family norms, and (c) negotiation, exchange, and conflict within families over the life course.

Antonucci and Akiyama's (1991) concept, *convoys of social support*, builds on Hagestad's (1981) work, which argued that researchers need to keep in mind that historical changes affect individual development in and out of relationships across the life course. Antonucci and Akiyama's convoy is "the group with whom one moves through life" (p. 106) and incorporates the concepts of both cohorts and generations. The construction, negotiation, and destruction of family norms, values, beliefs, and bonds cannot be assessed through analysis of aggregate data nor strictly through quantitative research. The concept was used in the authors' empirical study of social support among adults over 50. Subjects in this study identified people in their social networks, level of closeness, and type of functions provided. The authors found more similarities between the structure and support functions in parents' and adult children's networks and fewer for grandparents and grandchildren. Although Antonucci and Akiyama contended that their study provided some empirical support for the positive attributes of the convoy model, they suggested that convoys could have a negative impact.

Intergenerational learning issues may be described in terms of time, location, or social events. What is transmitted intergenerationally is as much a function of demographic features within a family line as direct socialization. How families respond to changes may be attributed in part to the family's solidarity (Roberts, Richards, and Bengtson, 1991). Associational solidarity is the amount of time a family spends together, either through face-to-face or distant interactions (e.g., letter writing and telephone conversations). It is related to parents' self-esteem (Small, Eastman, & Cornelius, 1988) and is predicated on the assumption that family members' participation in regularly shared activities results in the transmission of more elements of this family's cultural heritage than those of other families. Affective solidarity is based on theories, such as symbolic interaction, in which affect and support lead to concordance. In affective solidarity, the stronger the bonds between parents and children, the more likely it is that the parents will be seen as significant others. The most beneficial aspects of intergenerational solidarity pertain to the cultivation of high self-esteem among children and adolescents and act as a force mobilizing family members to provide emotional and material support for one another over the adult life course.

CONCLUSION

Beneath the surface of the relationships that exist in families and that in one way or another affect learning and ultimately literacy is a tension. In literacy research, this tension is a salient part of our conceptualization of the field and in learners' everyday responses to teaching. For families trying to convey meanings and specific knowledge to children, this tension at one and the same time is emancipated through individual acts of invention that remove the boundaries imposed by society and families and represented by the new ideas and ways of thinking and doing that contribute to generational identity. It is reconciled through acts of reinvention, revisiting, reconstructing, and reenacting old ideas and ways of thinking and doing that blur lines of generational difference. Through these acts of reinvention, child and adult learners of literacy, those who teach them, and those who study them are reminded of the fundamental reality that "little is new under the sun" and that the inherent possibilities imagined at the birth of a child will be transformed by history, innovation, and inattention to boundaries.

The historical context of research on intergenerational literacy is so intermingled with family literacy that it is difficult, and some might argue useless, to tease them apart. The facility of examining intergenerational literacy and family literacy as separate concepts is related to the fact that intergenerational literacy, although focused on families in this chapter, does and should examine relationships outside of families as well. The relationships that are created and fostered within schools, between teachers and students, are a special and differently studied area of intergenerational literacy, usually investigated within the context of research on teaching, teacher research, or teacher education.

We are still in the early stages of the field—of conducting research, understanding the broad scope of issues, achieving modest coherence among research studies, and providing responses that can improve assessment, learning, and teaching. We know a little about what kinds of studies may need to be pursued and some of the ways that intergenerational literacy as intervention is or is not effective. Longitudinal studies offer us the most important information to understand the nature of outcomes and enable us to focus on problems, not symptoms.

Within families, attention to intergenerational literacy should be expanded to capture the range of relationships, contributions, and contributors to literacy across ages. In addition, intergenerational literacy may be considered a tool or means to investigating and understanding individual learning, family influences to individual learning, or family learning and the effects of social change. Rather than connoting a specific domain in the way that we have come to think of family literacy, parent–child book reading, and emergent literacy, intergenerationality vacillates between being a subtext and an umbrella definition for all these and other studies in learning, literacy, and the processes involved in developing literacy. The issue facing the field is how to confront the complexity of conceptual issues that weaken the possibilities for the field, to project an agenda of rigorous research and practice that provides for intensive instruction and support to families, and to incorporate what has been learned about families to coordinate efforts for literacy learners across the life span and multiple generations.

REFERENCES

Acock, A. C. (1984). Parents and their children: The study of inter-generational influence. *Sociology & Social Research, 68*(2), 151–171.

Acock, A. C., & Bengtson, V. L. (1975). *Transmission of religious behavior and beliefs.* Victoria, Canada: Pacific Sociological Association Meetings.

Acock, A. C., & Bengtson, V. L. (1978). On the relative influence of mothers and fathers: A covariance analysis of political and religious socialization. *Journal of Marriage & the Family, 40*(3), 519–530.

Acock, A. C., Barker, D., & Bengtson, V. L. (1982). Mother's employment and parent–youth similarity. *Journal of Marriage & the Family, 44*(2), 441–455.

Antonucci, T. C., & Akiyama, H. (1991). Convoys of social support: Generational issues. *Marriage & Family Review, 16*(1–2), 103–123.

Atchley, R. C. (1975). Adjustment to loss of job at retirement. *International Journal of Aging & Human Development, 6*(1), 17–27.

Auerbach, E. R. (1989). Toward a socio-contextual approach to family literacy. *Harvard Educational Review, 59,* 165–187.

Baltes, P. B., & Brim, O. G., Jr. (1979). *Life-span development psychology: Personality and socialization* (Vol. 8). Hillsdale, NJ: Lawrence Erlbaum Associates.

Bengtson, V. L. (1975). Generation and family effects in value socialization. *American Sociological Review, 40*(3), 358–371.

Bengtson, V. L., & Troll, L. (1978). Youth and their parents: Feedback and intergenerational influence in socialization. In R. M. Lerner & G. B. Spanier (Eds.), *Child influences on marital and family interaction: A life-span perspective,* (pp. 215–240). New York: Academic Press.

Billingsley, A. (1968). *Black families in White America.* Englewood Cliffs, NJ: Prentice Hall.

Bronfenbrenner, U. (1986). Ecology of the family as a context for human development: Research perspectives. *Developmental Psychology, 22,* 723–742.

Campbell, E. Q. (1969). Adolescent socialization. In D. A. Goslin (Ed.), *Handbook of socialization theory and research* (pp. 821–859). Chicago: Rand McNally.

Chodorow, N. (1978). *The reproduction of mothering: Psychoanalysis and the sociology of gender.* Berkeley, CA: University of California Press.

Coleman, J. S., Campbell, E. Q., Hobson, C. J., McPartland, J. M., Mood, A. M., Weinfeld, F. D., & York, R. L. (1966). *Equality of educational opportunity.* Washington, DC: National Center for Educational Statistics.

Coles, M., & Coles, R. (1988). *The development of children.* New York: Freeman.

Daisey, P. (1991). Intergenerational literacy programs: Rationale, description, and effectiveness. *Journal of Clinical Child Psychology, 20,* 11–17.

Demos, J. (1970). *A little commonwealth: Family life in the Plymouth Colony.* New York: Oxford University Press.

Dickerson, D. K. (Ed.). (1994). *Bridges to literacy: Children, families and schools.* Cambridge, MA: Blackwell.

Doake, D. B. (1981). *Book experience and emergent reading behavior in preschool children.* Unpublished doctoral dissertation. University of Alberta, Canada.

Durkin, D. (1966). *Teaching young children to read.* Boston: Allyn & Bacon.

Durkin, D. (1974–1975). A six year study of children who learned to read in school at the age of four. *Reading Research Quarterly, 10,* 9–61.

Edwards, P. (1990). *Talking your way to literacy: A program to help non-reading parents prepare their children for reading.* Chicago: Children's Press.

Edwards, P. (1993). Connecting African-American parents and youth to the school's reading curriculum. In V. L. Gadsden & D. A. Wagner (Eds.), *Literacy and African American youth: Issues in learning, teaching, and schooling.* Norwood, NJ: Ablex.

Edwards, P. A. (1995). Empowering low-income mothers and fathers to share books with young children. *Reading Teacher, 48,* 558–564.

Elder, G. H. (Ed.). (1973). *Linking social structure to personality.* Beverly Hills, CA: Sage.

Elder, G. H. (1974). *Children of the Great Depression.* Chicago: University of Chicago Press.

Elder, G. H. (1985). Household, kinship, and the life course: Perspectives on Black families and children. In M. B. Spencer, G. K. Brookins, & W. R. Allen (Eds.), *Beginnings: The social and affective development of Black children* (pp. 29–43). Hillsdale, NJ: Lawrence Erlbaum Associates.

Epstein, J. L. (1990). What matters in the middle grades—Grade span or practices? *Phi Delta Kappan, 71,* 438–444.

Epstein, J. L. (1995, May). School/family/community partnerships: Caring for the children we share. *Phi Delta Kappan,* 701–712.

Erikson, E. (1950). *Childhood and society.* New York: Norton.

Featherman, D. L., & Lerner, R. M. (1985). Ontogenesis and sociogenesis: Problematics for theory and research about development and socialization across the lifespan. *American Sociological Review, 50*(5), 659–676.

Fishel, E. (1991). *Family mirrors: What our children's lives reveal about our selves.* Boston: Houghton Mifflin.

Fitzgerald, J., Spiegel, D. L., & Cunningham, J. W. (1991). The relationship between parental literacy level and perceptions of emergent literacy. *Journal of Reading Behavior, 23,* 191–213.

France, M., & Meeks, J. W. (1987). Parents who can't read: What schools can do. *Journal of Reading, 31*(3), 222–227.

Freud, S. (1933). *New introductory lectures on psycho-analysis.* New York: W. W. Norton.

Fry, C. L. (1988). Theories of age and culture. In J. Birren & V. Bengtson (Eds.), *Emergent theories of aging* (pp. 447–481). New York: Springer.

Gadsden, V. L. (1993). Literacy, education, and identity among African Americans: The communal nature of learning. *Urban Education, 27,* 352–369.

Gadsden, V. L. (1994). Understanding family literacy: Conceptual issues facing the field. *Teachers' College Record, 96,* 58–96.

Gadsden, V. L. (1995). Representations of literacy: Parents' images in two cultural communities. In L. M. Morrow (Ed.), *Family literacy: Connections in schools and communities* (pp. 287–303). New Brunswick, NJ: Rutgers.

Gadsden, V. L. (1998). Family cultures and literacy learning. In J. Osborn & F. Lehr (Eds.), *Literacy for all: Issues in teaching and learning* (pp. 32–50). New York: Guilford Press.

Gadsden, V. L. (1998). Black families within intergenerational and cultural perspective. In M. L. Lamb (Ed.), *Parenting and child development "nontraditional" families.* Mahwah, NJ: Lawrence Erlbaum Associates.

Germain, C. B. (1983). Time, social change, and social work. *Social Work in Health Care, 9*(2), 15–23.

Germain, C. B. (1990). Life forces and the anatomy of practice. *Smith College Studies in Social Work, 60*(2), 138–152.

Germain, C.B. (1994). Emerging conceptions of family development over the life course. *Families in Society, 75*(5), 259–268.

Glass, J., Bengtson, V. L., & Dunham, C. C. (1986). Attitude similarity in three-generational families: Socialization, status inheritance, or reciprocal influence? *American Sociological Review, 51*(5), 685–698.

Gutman, H. (1987). Historical consciousness in contemporary America. In I. Berlin (Ed.), *Power and culture: Essays on the American working class* (pp. 395–412). New York: Pantheon.

Hagestad, G. O. (1981). Problems and promises in the social psychology of intergenerational relations. In R. Fogel, E. Hatfield, S. Kiesler, & E. Shanas (Eds.), *Aging, stability, and change in the family* (pp. 11–46). New York: Academic Press.

Hagestad, G. O. (1984). The continuous bond: A dynamic multigenerational perspective on parent child relationships between adults. In M. Perlmutter (Ed.), *Parent–child interaction and parent–child relations in child development: Vol. 17. The Minnesota symposia on child psychology* (pp. 129–158). Hillsdale, NJ: Lawrence Erlbaum Associates.

Harari, S. E., & Vinovskis, M. A. (1989). Rediscovering the family in the past. In K. Kreppner & R. M. Lerner (Eds.), *Family systems and life-span development* (pp. 381–394). Hillsdale, NJ: Lawrence Erlbaum Associates.

Hareven, T. K. (1977). Family time and historical time. *Daedalus, 106,* 57–70.

Hareven, T. K. (1982). American families in transition: Historical perspectives on change. In F. Walsh (Ed.), *Normal family processes* (pp. 446–465). New York: Guilford Press.

Harry, B. (1995). Communication versus compliance: African-American parents' involvement in special education. *Exceptional Children, 61,* 364–377.

Hartman, A., & Laird, J. (1983). *Family-centered social work practice.* New York: Free Press.

Heath, S. B. (1982). What no bedtime story means: Narrative skills at home and school. *Language in Society, 11*(1), 49–76.

Heath, S. B. (1983). *Ways with words: Language, life, and work in communities and classrooms.* Cambridge: Cambridge University Press.

Heath, S. B. (1991). The sense of being literate: Historical and cross-cultural features. In R. Barr, M. L. Kamil, P. B. Mosenthal, & P. D. Pearson (Eds.), *Handbook of Reading Research* (Vol. II, pp.3–25). New York: Longman.

Heilbrun, A., & Gillard, B. (1966). Perceived maternal childrearing behavior and motivational effects of social reinforcement in females. *Perceptual and Motor Skills, 23*(2), 439–446.

Hill, R., Foote, N., Aldous, J., Carlson, R., & MacDonald, R. (1970). *Family development in three generations.* Cambridge, MA: Schenkman.

Kantor, D., & Lehr, W. (1975). *Inside the family.* San Francisco, CA: Jossey-Bass.

Kreppner, K., & Lerner, R. M. (Eds.). (1989). *Family systems and life-span development.* Hillsdale, NJ: Lawrence Erlbaum Associates.

Lerner, R. M., & Spanier, G. B. (1978). *Child influences on marital and family interaction: A life-span perspective.* New York: Academic Press.

Monaghan, E. J. (1991). Family literacy in early 18th-century Boston: Cotton Mather and his children. *Reading Research Quarterly, 26,* 342–70.

Morrow, L. M. (1994). *Family literacy: New perspectives, new opportunities.* Newark, DE: International Reading Association.

Morrow, L. M., & Young, J. A. (1997). Collaborative family literacy program: The effects on children's motivation and literacy achievement. *Early Child Development & Care, 127–128,* 13–25.

National Center on Fathers and Families. (1997). *Fathers and Families Roundtables: Discussions on the seven Core Learnings.* Philadelphia, PA: Author.

National Institute on Child Health Development. (1998, June). *Nurturing fatherhood: Improving data on research on male fertility, family formation, and fatherhood.* Washington, DC: Author.

Paratore, J. (1992) An intergenerational approach to literacy: Effects of literacy learning on adults and on the practice of family literacy. In *Examining central issues in literacy research, theory, and practice: Forty-second yearbook of the National Reading Conference* (pp. 83–92). Chicago: National Reading Conference.

Pellegrini, A., Brody, G., & Sigel, I. (1985). Parent's book-reading habits with their children. *Journal of Educational Psychology, 77,* 332–340.

Pellegrini, A., Perlmutter, J., Galda, L., & Brody, G. (1990). Joint reading between Black Head Start children and their mothers. *Child Development, 61*(2), 443–453.

Powell, D. (1991). *Strengthening parental contributions to school readiness and early school learning.* West Lafayette, IN: Purdue University, Department of Child Development and Family Studies.

Powell, D. (1990). The responsiveness of early childhood initiatives to families: Strategies and limitations. *Marriage and Family Review, 15*(1-2), 149–170.

Purcell-Gates, V. (1995). *Other people's words: The cycle of low literacy.* Cambridge, MA: Harvard University Press.

Quintero, E., & Velarde, C. (1990). Intergenerational literacy: A developmental, bilingual approach. *Young Children, 45,* 10–15.

Reiss, M. W. (1981). *The family's construction of reality.* Cambridge, MA: Harvard University Press.

Riley, M. W. (1985). Women, men, and the lengthening of the life course. In A. S. Rossi (Ed.), *Aging and the life course* (pp. 333–347). New York: Aldine.

Roberts, R. E., Richards, L. N., & Bengtson, V. L. (1991). Intergenerational solidarity in families: Untangling the ties that bind. *Marriage and Family Review, 16,* 11–46.

Rosow, I. (1978). What is a cohort and why? *Human Development, 21*(2), 65–75.

Scott-Jones, D. (1987). Mother-as-teacher in the families of high and low-achieving low-income Black first graders. *Journal of Negro Education, 56,* 21–34.

Scott-Jones, D., & Clark, M. L. (1986). The school experiences of black girls: The interaction of gender, race, and socioeconomic status. *Phi Delta Kappan, 67,* 520–527.

Shanahan, T., & Barr, R. (1995). Reading recovery: An independent evaluation of the effects of an early instructional intervention for at-risk learners. *Readers Research Quarterly, 30*(4), 958–996.

Slaughter-Defoe, D. T., & Richards, H. (1995). Literacy as empowerment: The case of African American males. In V. L. Gadsden & D. A. Wagner (Eds.), *Literacy among African American youth: Issues in learning, teaching, and schooling* (pp. 125–147). Cresskill, NJ: Hampton Press.

Small, S. A., Eastman, G., & Cornelius, S. (1988). Adolescent autonomy and parental stress. *Journal of Youth and Adolescence, 17*(5), 377–391.

Snow, C. E., Barnes, W. S., Chandler, J., Goodman, I. F., & Hemphill, L. (1991). *Unfulfilled expectations: Home and school influences on literacy.* Cambridge, MA: Harvard University Press.

Snow, C., & Goldfield, B. (1983). Turn the page please: Situation-specific language acquisition. *Journal of Child Language, 10,* 551–569.

Stack, C. B. (1974). *All our kin: Strategies for survival in the Black community.* New York: Harper and Row.

Stack, C. B., & Burton, L. M. (1993). Kinscripts. *Journal of Comparative Family Studies, 24*(Summer), 157–170.

Strickland, D., & Morrow, L. (1989). Family literacy and young children (emerging readers and writers). *Reading Teacher, 12,* 530–531.

Strickland, D. S. (1981) *The role of literature in reading instruction: Cross-cultural views.* Newark, DE: International Reading Association.

Taylor, D. (1983). *Family literacy: The social context of learning to read and write.* Portsmouth, NH: Heinemann.

Taylor, D. (1994). The trivial pursuit of reading psychology in the "real world": A response to West, Stanovich, and Mitchell. *Reading Research Quarterly, 29,* 276–288.

Taylor, D., & Dorsey-Gaines, C. (1988). *Growing up literate: Learning from inner city families.* Portsmouth, NH: Heinemann.

Taylor, R. J., Chatters, L. M., Tucker, M. B., & Lewis, E. (1990). Developments in research on Black families: A decade review. *Journal of Marriage and the Family, 52,* 993–1014.

Teale, W. H. (1981). Parents reading to their children: What we know and what we need to know. *Language Arts, 58,* 902–912.

Teale, W. H., & Sulzby, E. (Eds.). (1986). *Emergent literacy: Writing and reading.* Writing research: Multidisciplinary inquiries into the nature of writing series. Norwood, NJ: Ablex.

Troll, L. E. (1970). *Concepts of generation: Definitions and issues.* Detroit, MI: Wayne State University, Department of Psychology.

CHAPTER 46

Policy and Instruction: What Is the Relationship?

Anne McGill-Franzen
*National Research Center on English Learning
and Achievement and the University of Florida*

The present is a time of unprecedented public and governmental interest in reading instruction, "more interest … than at any time in the last 20 years" (Hart, 1996, p. 600). Not only are policymakers and researchers at a critical point in time, but Hart insisted, "a golden opportunity is presenting itself for all of us—researchers and policymakers alike—to join forces and influence one of the most important educational policy debates to present itself in quite some time" (p. 601). For better or for worse, federal and state policymakers are scrutinizing reading education as rarely before. Further, such policy is intruding on the "core technology" of teaching and learning (Cohen & Ball, 1997; Elmore, 1996). In this chapter, I describe the recent policy history of reading education, its place on the public policy agenda, and, relatedly, the research that relates reading policy to reading instruction. Although time periods and themes may overlap, the chapter is organized along a loose chronology of reading policy with an emphasis on contemporary issues.

BACKGROUND AND ORGANIZATION

Early federal education policy has its roots in the social reforms of the 1960s. The first generation of educational reform had as its purpose equal educational opportunity for children of the poor. The first of the sections that follow provides a brief recent history of federal education policy. In this section, I summarize what we know about the influence of federal policy on teaching and learning. Most often federal reading policy is associated with Elementary and Secondary Education Act (ESEA) Title 1 (or Chapter 1), but Individuals with Disabilities Education Act (IDEA) and earlier legislation establishing special education and the category of learning disabilities have profoundly affected the practice of reading education as well. The overidentification of learning disabled students with reading difficulties led to the National Institute of Child Health (NICHD) research agenda, one that now competes with that of the Office of Education Research and Improvement (OERI) and the national research centers for the attention of the U.S. Congress.

The second generation of educational reform was led by the states. Initially, states responded to the National Commission on Excellence in Education (1983) and the famous "tide of mediocrity" rhetoric by mandating higher standards for teachers and students in unprecedented state policymaking activity, the "first wave" of reform (McLaughlin, 1992). I revisit compensatory education, formerly Title 1, now Chapter 1, in the next section. I describe systemic reform, the theoretical underpinning of current state education policy, and review the effects of the so-called second wave of policy, that is, policy that deals with the harder issues of implementation and capacity building. Within this section I describe the effects of school organization on practice, with contrasting portraits of reading instruction in two restructured schools.

The third section emphasizes the research on implementation in Michigan, an early entrant into ambitious reading pedagogy and one whose implementation process has been carefully researched. I review the relation between school restructuring and reading instruction—in particular, whether changing school structures changes teaching and learning. Next, I describe the research on the nonmonolithic character of policy responses by teachers and administrators. Even among teachers using the same materials and curriculum guides within the same district, there is profound variability in the quality of the tasks and discourse of instruction.

In the fourth section I discuss the demise of constructivist reading policy in California. National attention to the crisis in California put literacy policy on the public agenda. I suggest an agenda-setting process that culminated with current federal reading policy initiatives. Finally, I close with a brief summary.

THE FIRST GENERATION OF POLICY FOR PRACTICE

A Federal Role to Ensure Equity

Until the mid 1960s, Lyndon Johnson's Great Society, and the passage of Title 1 and Head Start of the ESEA, there was little state or federal involvement in education policy. Title 1 marked the federal government's first attempt to influence local practice, what McLaughlin (1992) called the "first generation" of education policy. Title 1 distributed much money to local districts, based on the level of district poverty, to fund compensatory education programs—mostly in reading—that would supplement the regular classroom reading instruction of disadvantaged children. These first-generation policies were designed to redistribute educational opportunities, such as the opportunity to learn to read and preschool, more equitably, and to compensate for the lack of resources in impoverished school communities. Title 1 funds were earmarked for particular categories of services, such as supplemental reading instruction, and oversight initially focused on ensuring that federal dollars were actually spent on services within these categories. Implicit in these regulations was the assumption that lack of resources, not lack of professional knowledge on the part of teachers, was holding back low-income children (McLaughlin, 1992).

Early evaluations of Title 1 showed marginal gains, if any, for participating children, and demonstrated that policy alone, without local "will" and organizational capability, cannot bring about the intended change (Kennedy, Birman, & Demaline, 1986; McLaughlin, 1992; Timar, 1994), in this case, sustained reading achievement for disadvantaged children. Besides these marginal effects on children's achievement, Title 1 brought about other changes, most notably an infrastructure at the state and local levels for program disbursement, development, and oversight. Thus Title 1 created a separate administrative bureaucracy and a supplemental, and also separate, program of instructional services (mostly reading) for low-income children who were behind in school.

By 1981 the federal government had embarked on a campaign to decentralize federal functions, including education responsibilities. Under Ronald Reagan and the

New Federalism, federal education programs were consolidated under block grants and given to the states to administer and support. Title 1 aid was reduced, and barely maintained (and until 1994, was known as Chapter 1 of the Education Consolidation and Improvement Act, ECIA) even as poverty among children was increasing at an alarming rate. Title 1 funds were reduced under the assumption that state deregulation would lower the cost of oversight. Many provisions of Chapter 1 of ECIA remained the same, including the "supplement not supplant" requirement for reading services, and the emphasis on regulatory compliance rather than on the quality of the instructional services (Education Consolidation & Improvement Act, 20 U.S.C. 2701-2891 1965, as amended 1981; Timar, 1994). Title 1 was reauthorized in 1988, and again in 1994. I discuss these authorizations in a section that follows.

Special Education: An Underfunded Mandate

Responding to increasingly influential special education advocates, in 1976 Congress passed into law PL 94-142, thereby entitling disabled children to free and appropriate public education. Similar to the bureaucracy created by the passage of Title 1, PL 94-142 established the institution of special education and a concomitant bureaucracy to administer programs and certify service providers. This legislation was significant for the field of reading education because PL 94-142 set up a new category of children with reading problems (McGill-Franzen, 1987). As in compensatory education, the majority of children in special education were referred because they were experiencing reading difficulties. Unlike children in compensatory education who were provided reading services to presumably help them catch up, struggling readers referred to special education were assumed to have an organic disability that impaired their ability to learn to read—hence the label *learning disabled* (Spear-Swerling & Sternberg, 1996).

Between 1976 and 1993 the number of children placed in special education skyrocketed and overwhelmingly the growth was attributed to children who were labeled learning disabled. By 1995, approximately 10% of all school-aged children were classified as learning disabled (National Research Council, 1998), primarily because they could not read (Birman, 1981; Lyon, 1996). As funding for compensatory services in reading declined under ECIA and pressure for high standards and accountability for all students increased, as in the more recent waves of education policy, the demand for special education services continued to increase (McGill-Franzen & Allington, 1991). Public accountability raised the stakes for low-performing schools, motivating the placement of low-performing students in special education, outside the accountability stream (Allington & McGill-Franzen, 1992; McGill-Franzen & Allington, 1993). Because the federal initiative for handicapped students was an underfunded mandate (i.e., providing less than half of the cost of implementation), rising numbers of learning disabled students caused a substantive burden on the resources of local districts (Cohen & Spillane, 1992). The Center for Special Education Finance (Chambers, Parrish, Lieberman, & Wolman, 1998) estimated the 1995–1996 special education expenditures to be approximately $32.6 billion, or about 128% more than the cost of regular education. A recent survey of local district expenditures indicated that the extra resources allocated to education during the last decade or so were spent almost exclusively on services for handicapped students, with little resources allocated to improving the general education programs (Rothstein & Miles, 1995).

The high cost of special education and increasing demand for learning disability services for children with reading problems prompted a research agenda by the National Institute for Child Health (NICHD) funded by the federal government (Health Research Extension Act of 1985; Lyon, 1996). In order to identify research critical to the classification, causes and treatment of learning disabilities, NICHD in 1987 established the Learning Disability Research Network. The NICHD network promulgated the findings of major NICHD-funded studies, which consistently demonstrated that disabled readers had deficits in phonological processing. Several of the studies indicated that the difference between struggling readers and disabled readers lay on a continuum from proficiency to disability, and that learning disabled readers were not qualitatively different from other readers experiencing difficulty (Lyon, 1996). Further, intervention studies, such as that conducted by Scanlon and Vellutino (1996), demonstrated that phonological deficits can be remediated in all but 1% of young children. When 1990s reading policy faltered in California, Lyon (1995; 1997) was ready with the major findings of the NICHD-sponsored studies of the etiology and treatment of children with reading difficulties.

THE SECOND GENERATION OF POLICY FOR PRACTICE

Toward Excellence and Accountability

The period of time between 1980 and the present may be considered the "second generation of reform" (McLaughlin, 1992) marked by unprecedented education policy activity by the states. The federal presence in education policymaking waned somewhat during the 1980s, becoming more symbolic than substantive, as is suggested by the emergence of national commissions (National Commission on Excellence in Education, 1983; U.S. Department of Education, 1984; and so on). These commissions urged policymakers to establish accountability and excellence within the educational system. States responded with higher standards for curriculum and materials, more rigorous certification requirements for teachers, and new testing programs. All states but Nebraska, for example, now administer tests at different grade levels, about a third require a test for graduation, and Texas is moving toward a test to pass from grade to grade (Greene, 1998).

The National Governors' Association took the lead in coordinating these state efforts; their work led to the Education Summit in 1989, the establishment of the National Education Goals by George Bush, and the bipartisan support of the Goals 2000 legislation in 1994. Three of the National Goals relate to literacy[1]:

- All children will start school ready to learn.
- All students will leave Grades 4, 8, and 12 having demonstrated competency over challenging subject matter including English.
- Every adult American will be literate and will possess the knowledge and skills necessary to compete in a global economy and exercise the rights and responsibilities of citizenship.

The National Goals then provided a framework for evaluating federal and state reading programs as well as redefining expectations for learning and achievement.

Compensatory Education Revisited

During this time period, a number of empirical research studies described Title 1, now Chapter 1, as traditional, basic skills instruction that was neither congruent with the new intellectually rigorous standards nor related to children's achievement gains in the regular classroom (Allington & McGill-Franzen, 1989a & b; Jenkins, Pious, & Peterson, 1988). In 1988, Congress reauthorized Chapter 1, part of the Hawkins–Stafford El-

---

[1]Emerson Elliot (1996) noted that two National Goals related directly to literacy. I added the first goal to Elliot's two goals.

ementary and Secondary School Improvement Amendments, and changed the program in fundamental ways. No longer viewed as separate from the academic program of the regular classroom, Chapter 1 effectiveness was measured in terms of regular academic achievement. No longer targeting basic skills, Chapter 1 now emphasized mastery of advanced skills, and—rather than the "add on" program of the past—Chapter 1 resources could be used for school-wide classroom improvement (Hawkins–Stafford Elementary & Secondary School Improvement Amendments, PL 206-297, 1988; Timar, 1994).

However, the Prospects: The Congressional Mandated Study of Educational Growth and Opportunity (Puma et al., 1997) found 1990s Chapter 1 programs did not look that different from descriptions of earlier evaluations. At that time, Chapter 1 served 6 million children each year in most elementary schools in the country and half of the secondary schools. With funding of about $7 billion, Chapter 1 served 25% of all first through third graders, about 20% of children in the middle grades, and between 5% and 8% of secondary students. Most Chapter 1 students were primary grade children receiving reading instruction. But unlike earlier, highly regulated Title 1 programs, local school districts had many options for spending Chapter 1 funds so that services could look very different from school to school, depending on local context and need.

Nonetheless, Prospects researchers found that Chapter 1 was a marginal intervention. Like earlier Title 1 programs, Chapter 1 instruction in the 1990s added only 19 minutes of extra instructional time each day and typically consisted of pull-out instruction, often during reading and language arts instruction in the regular classroom. Half the staff hired with Chapter 1 funds were aides, not certified teachers, and these aides were most likely hired to work with students in push-in whole-class instruction in high poverty schools. Instructional assistance was weak, Prospects concluded, compared to the level of need.

Regardless of the form of the intervention or the staff hired, Chapter 1 did not seem to influence student achievement, just as earlier studies had found (Rowan & Guthrie, 1988). The average achievement of all students in high-poverty schools was approximately the same as the achievement of Chapter 1 students in low-poverty schools. Prospects found that the program had not closed the gap in academic achievement between advantaged and disadvantaged students. In fact, "the observed lockstep pattern of student growth clearly demonstrated that where students started out relative to their classmates is where they ended up in later grades" (Puma et al., 1997, p. vi). The longer students received Chapter 1 services, the further they lagged behind their peers.

Nonetheless, unlike earlier longitudinal evaluations of Title 1, the Prospects study found small school effects:

> Data from Prospects confirm the earlier findings by Coleman et al. (1966) that the characteristics of an individual student and his/her family account for the largest part of the overall variation in student achievement as measured by test scores. However, relatively smaller school factors do make an important contribution to student academic achievement and growth. (Puma et al., 1997, p. vi)

Other studies confirmed that schools have made a difference in the educational achievement of students from poor communities. Even though the scores of minorities on the National Assessment of Educational Progress (NAEP) are now stable or in decline, the achievement gap in reading between Whites and minorities was reduced by one third during the previous two decades, a time of increasing poverty for many families. This phenomenon has been attributed in part to federal educational interventions like Chapter 1 (Grissmer, Kirby, Berends, & Williamson, 1994).

The 1994 reauthorization of the Elementary and Secondary Education Act, the Improving America's Schools Act (IASA), again Title 1, substantively changed the program to make it more congruent with the national move toward excellence and accountability (Reinventing Chapter 1: The Current Chapter 1 Program and New Directions, U.S. Department of Education, 1993). According to the provisions of IASA, Title 1 students were expected to achieve the same rigorous standards and participate in the same challenging curriculum as all other students. Keeping with its historic mission to provide opportunity to disadvantaged students, Title 1 was to allocate more resources to the neediest schools and to initiate more school-wide programs to improve curriculum and instruction in high-poverty schools. Finally, in recognition of the emerging research on teacher development and the central role of teachers in the success of any reform, Title 1 provided resources to support professional development so that Title 1 service providers could themselves learn how to make challenging curriculum accessible to a range of learners.

Policymakers and the constituents of Title 1 are now preparing for upcoming reauthorization hearings. The National Center on Education in the Inner Cities, for example, recently held an invitational conference on Title 1. Conference participants identified a lack of information on effective and innovative strategies for implementing challenging curriculum in high-poverty schools. The most pressing need identified by service providers was opportunities for themselves to learn how to implement the Title 1 mandates for systemic reform (Wang, 1997; p. 16).

STATES TAKE THE POLICY INITIATIVE: AMBITIOUS TEACHING AND LEARNING

The early reforms requiring high standards for students and teachers have been called the "first wave" (of the second generation of reform) and, as such, represent the "easy" reforms to implement (Kirst, 1990; McLaughlin, 1992). It is easier to count course requirements for teacher certification or student requirements for graduation than to ensure that ambitious teaching and learning is in place, for example. Nonetheless, requirements for teacher education and certification, curriculum requirements, textbook adoption, and assessment of student achievement certainly constitute powerful and popular policy structures (Cohen & Spillane, 1992). Such policies may guide classroom instruction and mediate the influence of any other policy. However, "instructional guidance" (p. 11) may be consistent or not across domains, prescriptive or not, and mandated or not, leading to recognition by some policymakers that top-down, systemic reform needed to be in place for substantive educational change to take place.

Systemic Reform

Although some local sites across the country reported successful reforms, few states had developed coherent educational policy in reading. In 1988, policy analysts O'Day and Smith (Under Secretary of the U.S. Department of Education during Bill Clinton's presidency) promulgated the concept of *systemic reform*. Smith, who had written extensively on effective schools in the early 1980s, was a believer that schools can make a difference and that government can and should intervene with a combination of mandates and incentives to promote education policy (Purkey & Smith, 1983; Vinovskis, 1996). Early, wide-ranging, and ambitious initiatives by California and other states and the emerging research on teaching had convinced Smith and O'Day that top-down, state-wide curriculum frameworks aligned with assessments and teacher development were needed to effect substantive change:

We did not expect to suggest these policy directions when we started reviewing the research literature on teachers and teaching. The rationale for a state curriculum framework which structures the knowledge needed by the teacher, the content of the schools' curriculum, and student assessment instruments grows out of the research on the importance of content and pedagogical knowledge of teachers. (Smith & O'Day, 1988, in Vinovskis, 1996, p. 77)

Systemic reform holds that all children can achieve high academic standards, a new tenet of educational policy, and further, that schools must provide students with access to ambitious curriculum in the form of appropriate materials and effective teachers. That is, if students are to be held accountable for high standards of achievement, then they must have "opportunity to learn" (Vinovskis, 1996). Starting with the publication of the report "A Time for Results" (National Governors' Association, 1986), and with input from the educational community, states began to talk about building local capacity to implement more rigorous curriculum and just what that might take (McLaughlin, 1992). What has been called the "second wave" of instructional policy thus deals with improving practice by developing teacher knowledge and enhancing teacher control of curriculum and instruction (McLaughlin, 1992). Policymakers looked to site-based management and alternative governance and organizational structures so that teachers would have more authority along with more responsibility for student learning.

School Structures and Practice

In the late 1980s the Consortium for Policy Research in Education (CPRE) undertook a 3-year study to look at the processes and effects of school restructuring (Elmore, Peterson, & McCarthy, 1996). The basic premise of the school restructuring movement was that changing the organization of schools would improve the way teachers teach, providing support for more ambitious pedagogy and higher achievement on the part of students. CPRE researchers studied in depth the teachers in three restructured elementary schools, each with different structures to promote new ways of teaching, each at different stages of development, and each experiencing varying success. I consider here the reading instruction of two of those teachers from two different schools, one teacher (and school) involved for a few years with organizational and curricular change, and the other for over a decade; both schools were adequately supported in their efforts by the central administration.

Multigrade Classrooms, Teacher Teams, Cross-Age Single Classrooms, Professional Development: Do Organizational Structures Matter?

Mrs. Hancock was a member of a team of teachers who taught primary grades students in a school that was reorganized into multiage units. One of her responsibilities was to teach reading to first through second graders. For the past 2 years, Mrs. Hancock had been teaching reading by using literature instead of the basal reading program. She did not group students by ability. Instead, each week she introduced three books (from which each child could choose) and she used activity sheets developed at the district's teacher center:

> In September, Hancock introduced three books in the "Miss Nelson" series. Each group had a different worksheet to accompany each book: One had a "detective map" consisting of features to be filled in such as characters ... a second had an "activity sheet" of questions: "You are walking to school. Suddenly a dog runs up and pulls your lunchbox out of your hand. What would you do?"; and a third had a sheet to list characteristics of Miss Nelson. (p. 121)

Before introducing a writing activity, Mrs. Hancock had the children guess a long /I/ mystery item hidden in a bag. She randomly selected a student to wear the puppet High Hat (from the High Hat program) while she read a story with long /I/. Next, she found the long /I/ vowel on a vowel finder chart, and had children supply words with long /I/, which she wrote on the board and discussed with them. Hancock explained her instruction to the researchers as needing to do phonics:

> I have beginning readers and I also have second graders in there too, that I felt needed some extra work on phonics. We're really building hard on a phonics program for them, some word attack skills.... It gives them something to work with, when they come to unfamiliar words, besides context clues. (p. 123)

To a reading professional, it is clear that Mrs. Hancock probably did not know the subject matter of reading well enough to make a transition to teaching without the basal. As pointed out in the CPRE study, she tried to blend the old with the new and unsuccessfully adapted activities she had probably used in the past (p. 125). Rather than basing her practice on what children needed to learn, she seemed to depend on what she called a "teaching kit" for phonics unrelated to children's developmental levels, story starters for writing, and a selection of books that must have been too difficult for some and too easy for others.

By contrast, Mrs. Brezinski taught a self-contained classroom of fifth- and sixth-grade students in the most traditional of the restructured schools in the study. Each teacher there was responsible for a single cross-age class, an organization that the teachers ultimately selected because it was the most comfortable fit with their professional beliefs and pedagogy. Individual children were the focus of faculty meetings there, and Mrs. Brezinski kept a journal so that she could take notes and record her reflections on the learning of individual children, and in doing so, know them better. In the following example of part of a conversation between teacher and student, Mrs. Brezinski asks Chudney, a reluctant reader, what the quote (from Chudney's book), "She had to find herself, and she was still working on it," meant to her. Chudney responds, "She had to get away for awhile, and she had to fix herself.... I think she was in control of herself. She probably didn't yell at the kids, but she had to fix herself up. I think that is why she went away" (p. 174). Later, Mrs. Brezinski wrote in her journal:

> This is how Chudney translates or paraphrases "find herself"—reading into it her own understanding of the mother's behavior. She's also clear about the various relationships among characters and the sources of tension or dramatic conflict.... All this is very close to home as far as Chudney's own family relationships are concerned. (p. 174)

In this case, the researchers argue, Mrs. Brezinski interpreted "learning in her class primarily through the lens of individual students' developing knowledge" (p. 180). What concerned Mrs. Brezinski was how much she should control what her students read. Should she allow students like Chudney to always choose books close to their experiences, or should she insist that they read, for example, *Iliad*, because "myths like fairy tales are stories that have immense meaning and different meanings to different individuals. Reading them and knowing them is a way of putting that meaning inside your head so you can draw on it when you need to" (p. 183). Elmore et al. (1996) referred to this as the "constructivist dilemma"—how to bring expert knowledge to bear on children's learning without "displacing" the knowledge of children (p.182).

Additionally, Mrs. Brezinski's school was affiliated with a well-regarded alternative school in Vermont, where she and her colleagues met with the Vermont faculty each summer to discuss students, subject matter concerns, and issues of constructivist pedagogy.

In spite of the substantive differences between Mrs. Hancock and Mrs. Brezinski in their knowledge of reading and reading development, all teachers and administrators in each of the schools studied actually were doing what policy had asked them to do—to change teaching by changing school structures. They had initiated new grouping practices, more opportunities for professional development and team collaboration among teachers, more decentralized decision making at schools (p. 236). What was the problem? CPRE researchers concluded that there is only a "weak, problematic, and indirect" relationship between changing school structures and changing teaching practice (p. 237). A new kind of structure will unlikely lead to particular teaching practices. Teachers interpret new policy or new ideas about teaching in terms of their own variable experiences. It is unlikely that creating multiage structures, or cross-age classrooms, or any other organizational change will transform practice. Rather, the researchers argued, it is just as likely that practice should change structure (p. 238). In order to transform teaching, they argued, first enhance the knowledge and skill of individual teachers, then ask what kind of structure will support their work (p. 240).

Participative Decision Making and Practice: Does Governance Matter?

Besides changing the organization of classrooms, as in the CPRE study, policy can alter school governance, giving teachers more authority over the administration of school. Smylie, Lazarus, and Brownlee-Conyers (1996) studied the various ways teachers participated in school governance over a 4-year period in a mid-sized urban district and found a relationship between certain kinds of teacher participation and gains in reading achievement. Using survey, observations, and test score data, the researchers found that governance in schools reporting high and low teacher participation operated in fundamentally different ways. In governance councils with the highest participation, teachers studied curriculum and instruction issues, not just management issues. Within these high-participation councils, teachers' work was oriented toward instructional issues: Teachers selected literature-based textbooks, developed alternative assessments, integrated instructional units with language arts. Not only did teachers on these councils feel more pressure for accountability and report greater access to organizational learning opportunities, but students' reading achievement test scores improved significantly in these schools.

Teachers on councils with low-participative decision making, in contrast, were not focused on issues of academic content or instruction. The authors argue that participative governance structures may have negative influence on student outcomes if such governance is not well implemented, does not promote opportunities for professional development, and distracts teachers from their central mission of classroom instruction (p.194). Therefore, it is the type of decisions that involve teachers, not the process of participative decision making itself, that has potential to improve classroom instruction (p. 193).

Thus, even with higher standards, new school structures to accommodate new ways of teaching and learning, materials, assessments and other top-down reforms in place, without attention to teacher development and the local context within which policy is interpreted, many analysts thought the reforms would be for naught. Referred to as "the problem of the bottom over the top" (Elmore, 1983), this paradigm recognizes teachers (and administrators) are more than a "conduit" for instructional policy (Darling-Hammond, 1990): "Teachers teach from what they know," and thus new policy must attend closely to the support of teacher knowledge through professional development. Policies "land on top of other policies" (p. 240), and teachers understand new policy in terms of their experiences with other policy, and within the context of their own knowledge, beliefs and teaching circumstances (p. 235). In the following sections, I present research on the implementation of reading policy in two states, Michigan and California. The unexpected effects of state reading policy in California put reading on the national policy agenda, and that story is preceded by the section on policy implementation in Michigan. The research that follows suggests the ways local contexts, especially the knowledge, beliefs, and experiences of policy participants, shape state reading policy and its actualization in practice.

Michigan Redefines Reading But Local Contexts Transform State Policy

The state of Michigan was an early entrant into curriculum reform in reading. In 1985 the State Board of Education, under advisement from the Michigan Reading Association and a small group of university researchers, approved a new definition of reading:

> Reading is the process of constructing meaning through dynamic interaction among reader, the text, and the context of the reading situation. (Michigan State Board of Education, 1985)

Because the revised definition differed substantively from the previous definition, which emphasized word recognition, this step represented a shift in state reading policy. The State Department of Education (SDE) formed a Curriculum Review Committee (CRC) of innovative practitioners, sponsored conferences to help educators learn the concepts behind the new definition of reading and strategies for practice, and designed materials for staff developers to use locally. Next, the SDE revised the Michigan Educational Assessment Program (MEAP) to better align test items with the new definition of reading. The revised MEAP was administered in 1989 with the intention of "driving instruction," that is, as an inducement for teachers to change their practice in order to improve the test scores of their students.

Central Office Administrators Interpret Policy

Several policy analysts and researchers involved in the Educational Policy and Practice Study (EPPS), a longitudinal study of Michigan reading policy, followed its implementation at the local level. Spillane (1994, 1998) described how the state reading policy influenced the reading curriculum in two central Michigan school districts, one urban, one suburban, and conversely, how the central office and school level administrators' responses to the policy shaped the policy itself.

District office administrators in the suburban district revised curriculum guides, criteria for new textbooks, and report cards so that they were aligned with new state policy and allocated considerable resources for teacher development. In addition to promoting many of the main strategies of the reform, the district office included ideas, such as developmental education, that were not part of the state policy but important to central office staff, who were very involved with the Michigan Reading Association and National Association for Educators of Young Children. When later staff development was taken over by central office staff not originally involved, however, the focus of the training was much more narrow, reflecting the professional affiliations of this administrator with the Effective Schools Movement. Schools also responded differently, depending on the beliefs about reading instruction held by key staff. Where school administrators believed that decoding was as important as comprehension, the state reading policy was not supported to the same extent as in schools where administrators' beliefs were congruent with state policy. For example, it was clear that not all schools had banned basal readers and workbooks, as directed by central office. Instead, some combination of basal and literature was used in these schools because, in the words of one principal, "literature books don't have that same kind of controlled vocabulary" needed to increase sight vocabulary (Spillane, 1998, p. 46).

In the urban district, there was the same variable support for the state reading policy. Unlike the suburban district, however, administrative authority at the central office level here was segmented into the subunits of elementary, assessment, staff development, and Chapter 1, each with responsibilities that did not overlap. The only subunit that was cognizant of the new state reading policy was that of Chapter 1, the unit charged with oversight of reading teachers in the district. Chapter 1 administrators not only were aware of the state reading policy, but they felt it was consistent with their professional beliefs, affiliations, and experiences, as well as consistent with the 1988 reauthorization of Chapter 1, which was the source of funding for their program. Chapter 1 administrators fully supported the implementation of the state policy within the remedial reading program. The elementary division did not. They believed that the district-adopted basal reading program and the curriculum-referenced assessment that they used to monitor instruction were more suited to needs of an urban district than the instructional guidance offered by the state reading policy. The staff development subunit was primarily associated with the effective schools movement and geared the district's professional development toward that framework. The assessment division agreed with this view insofar as the two standardized tests administered by the District emphasized knowledge of discrete skills and comprehension of short passages over comprehension that was more interpretive. Even though the state MEAP test was aligned with the new definition of reading, the administrators overseeing the district assessment did not think that the MEAP provided them with valuable information.

Not all school-level administrators, however, thought that the MEAP was irrelevant. Although most of the urban communities served by the district were not concerned about MEAP scores, one of the schools, located in a suburban community, was very concerned because the parents kept close track of the school's performance. Within this school, the administrators went out of their way to understand and implement the new state reading policy so that the students were prepared for the state test. Thus, neither the suburban nor urban districts responded in a "monolithic" way (Spillane, 1998). Individual beliefs, knowledge, and professional affiliations of the administrators were the most important variables in how they implemented Michigan's reading policy.

Teachers Learn From Policy

Jennings (1996) examined implementation during the early years of Michigan reform from the teacher's perspective as a learner. Jennings held that policy implementation had two facets—opportunities provided for teachers to learn about the policy, and what teachers actually learned from the opportunities presented. Based on interviews and classroom observations, Jennings constructed case studies of teacher learning, looking at where these teachers started in terms of their knowledge, beliefs and experiences, and what changed. She argued that, ultimately, policy implementation was "an incident of teaching and learning rather than a process by which ideas are filtered though the educational system and enacted by practitioners" (p. 109). Policy implementation was *teaching* within this view, and policymakers should do what good teachers do, and that was "provide multiple paths to get to the ideas" (p. 108).

In another study, Spillane and Jennings (1997) argued that tasks and discourse of instruction must change—not just materials and activities—in order to implement ambitious reading pedagogy. They defined task as the "questions and exercises students engage with" and discourse as the interaction between teacher and students around task (p. 460). As evidence for their view, the researchers closely analyzed the reading and writing instruction of a number of Michigan teachers. The district itself had developed coherent policy that aligned materials, curriculum and assessment. All teachers used literature to teach reading (no basal textbook or practice workbook was allowed); all teachers had students read and discuss novels or nonfiction. There was little variation in the materials or activities across teachers, yet the researchers found great variation in the opportunities to learn that these teachers offered students. Consider, for example, the following description of interaction in a fifth-grade reading lesson:

> Mrs. Camps' students were reading a biography of Paul Revere as their reading text. The class had been studying the Revolutionary War and Camps chose this book to connect reading and social studies.... Camps asked students another question on the study sheet she had given them, whether Paul Revere wanted to be put on trial for cowardliness or not. One boy argued that he would have wanted to so that he could clear his name. This discussion went on for a long time and students vehemently argued their positions. No students, though , used the text to support their arguments. After quite a long time, a girl—Shirley—said that she thought the question asked if Revere wanted to be put on a trail and she said no because the British would have followed him too easily. Camps responded, "Now that's very interesting. That's one possible answer." When the girl asked if she was correct, Ms. Camps responded that she was because "that's how you interpreted the question." (pp. 465–466)

As this vignette illustrates, coherent policy environment was not enough to improve Mrs. Camp's instruction. Top-down reading policy usually does not help teachers to learn how to do it—how to get from policy to practice. External efforts to improve instruction, like aligned curriculum, materials, and assessment, rarely can make a difference because they rarely get to the core of teaching and learning (Cohen & Ball, 1997; Elmore, 1996). As Cohen and Ball argued, capacity to improve instruction resides in the "interactions among teachers and students around educational material" (p. 3), which comprise the tasks and discourse of the Spillane and Jennings work.

Thus, beyond developing consistent reading policy, policymakers must find ways for policy to educate, not simply put policies into practice. Teachers need opportunities to learn from policy. But what they take from these opportunities depends also on what they bring to policy—their own knowledge and beliefs. The research on policy implementation in Michigan may help inform our understanding of the failure of California reading policy to promote ambitious pedagogy and curriculum.

THE CALIFORNIA STORY:
READING POLICY GONE AWRY?

Throughout the 1980s, California was out in front of educational reforms, leading the way with content-driven, systemic state education policy (Carlos & Kirst, 1997). Over a decade or so, California enacted a series of policies designed to change teaching and learning in California. The Senate in 1983 required the State Department of Education (SDE) to develop model curriculum standards, established regional centers at universities to help teachers put the new standards into practice, established the California School Leadership Academy for administrators, and initiated changes in California's state assessment system from a focus on facts to a focus on application of knowledge (Chrispeels, 1997). In 1987 California adopted the English Language Arts Framework, which, consistent with the reform agenda of the time, emphasized the personal meaning-making function of literacy and literature-based instruction in reading. To help build teacher capacity, the California Literature Project and other subject-matter projects were founded and housed on university campuses for summer professional development for teachers with school-year follow-up. These professional development activities emphasized "whole-language" or constructivist approaches described in the English Language Arts Framework.

A long-time observer of professional development in California, Chrispeels (1997) longitudinally analyzed two dimensions of policymaking activity in California: 10 years of policy and policy implementation including mandates, inducements, capacity-building policy and hortatory policy developed by legislators, curriculum and instruction experts, and local and state leaders, and 3 years of local implementation by hundreds of participants in San Diego County. Within this analysis, policy inducements, such as textbook adoption, helped create a coherent, interrelated network of policies. Textbook adoption criteria were aligned with the frameworks, inducing schools to select from the state approved list in order to receive state funding for textbook purchase.

In 1989, the Senate passed the California Learning Assessment System (CLAS), an assessment and accountability system to be aligned with the curriculum frameworks. The involvement of teachers in the piloting and scoring of CLAS, the involvement with the Literature Project, and local school improvement programs helped build local capacity and high levels of teacher satisfaction with the frameworks. Teachers in San Diego Unified, for example, responded in the K–8 English Language Arts Evaluation Report that they routinely used "literature-based curriculum, variation in grouping, and open-ended questioning" and "endorsed the philosophy of integrating language arts through core literature and teaching vocabulary and writing in context" (Finley, Forest, Ferrer, & Dozier, 1994, in Chrispeels, 1997, p. 463). Even after CLAS had been eliminated, 87% of the district's K–8 teachers said that they had incorporated CLAS-like instruction and assessment into their classroom program (Finley et al., 1994, in Chrispeels, 1997), demonstrating, Chrispeels suggested, that local educators could sustain the direction of the state language arts policy even without state leadership. After state politicians shifted against CLAS, local educators continued to implement alternative assessments, Chrispeels argued, because they had developed the capacity to do so.

State policy adopted over the course of 10 years constituted a coherent policy system in literacy with a variety of policy instruments. As local educators interpreted and implemented the policies, they were themselves constructing their own policies and capacity to sustain them. As is known from the CPRE and EPPS studies of reading policy implementation in Michigan (Spillane & Jennings, 1997; Elmore et al., 1996), however, the policies teachers construct may bear little resemblance to those of intended by the state.

Cohen and Ball (1997) suggested that the new California state curriculum frameworks reform were enacted in an isolated and typically superficial way. Only a minority of teachers in California had the opportunity, like teachers in Chrispeels's San Diego study, to coordinate professional development with curriculum and assessment, and curriculum and assessment with teaching and learning. At least in math, teachers who did so had students with higher math achievement test scores. So, outside of teachers who participated in professional development (like that described by Chrispeels, 1997), few teachers had opportunities to deepen their knowledge of subject matter or work with the new materials or learn more about student response and capability (Cohen & Ball, 1997).

By 1995, new reading "policy texts" emerged in California, using the same variety of policy instruments to induce change in reading instruction, but in a different direction (Chrispeels, 1997; Carlos & Kirst, 1997). When NAEP results revealed that California children were last in the nation in reading achievement in 1992, and then again in 1994, the English Language Arts Framework, in particular, and "whole language" in general were blamed. According to NAEP, 87% of the teachers in California indicated that they had used the new approaches. California's newly developed state assessment, CLAS, supposedly aligned with the new curriculum frameworks, showed a similarly dismal performance in reading in 1994.

In the view of some observers of California's education policy, systemic curriculum reform had indeed changed reading instruction, but the reform itself was flawed (Carlos & Kirst, 1997). The chronic low test scores and accompanying media attention prompted an inquiry by state officials that led to the dismantling of California's state reading policy and the initiation of another.

Policy analysts Carlos and Kirst (1997) provided the following detailed story of California's shifting reading policy in the 1990s. After the media attention following the release of the 1994 NAEP scores, the California legislature, with the Governor's support, passed sweeping legislation "aimed at literacy and basic instruction, unprecedented in the history of the state" (p. 9), called ABC bills because of their intent to restore traditional instruction in reading and the last names of their sponsors (Assemblymen Apert, Burton, & Conroy). Assembly Bill 170 required that instructional materials be based on the "fundamental skills" including "systematic, explicit phonics, spelling" (p. 13), whereas Assembly Bill 1504 required that the materials be "reflective of current and confirmed research" (p. 14). During the following legislative session, after 8 hours of public hearings on reading pedagogy and practice, in which the professional literacy associations squared off with advocates of NICHD research on the importance of "phonics," the Assembly passed three bills (Assembly Bills 3482, 3075, and 1178) to authorize K–3 instructional materials and teacher training to implement the revised state reading policy. In the aftermath of the NAEP reading scores, the head of NICHD, who had been floating that research program for years, suddenly had an audience. In addition, research on the importance of the phonological component of learning to read had been steadily accumulating (Adams, 1990; Juel, 1994; Share & Stanovich, 1995), and these studies were getting finally getting the attention of policymakers and the media.

During that same session, the Senate passed legislation to support class size reduction in Grades K–3 from 30 students to 20 in service of reading improvement and authorized the use of Goals 2000 funds to educate teachers in the basic reading and phonics instruction proposed by the state. In contrast to previous lean times of state support for education, substantive resources were allocated to reduce class size, train teachers, and improve reading practice.

Also in 1995, the legislature established the Commission for the Establishment of Academic Content and Performance Standards, an advisory board appointed by the governor and legislature (and including the state superintendent), to oversee the development of new curriculum standards and an aligned assessment. In 1998 the state adopted the new Reading/ Language Arts Curriculum Frameworks, a document that explicitly lays out what students are expected to know and be able to do grade by grade. The Framework, unlike the broad approach taken in the 1987 Framework, which expected teachers to be able to fill in the details, is more similar to the California Department of Education (CDE) documents of the 1970s and 1980s in both form and content.

The California Reading Association (CRA) criticized the document for presenting reading as a "series of hierarchical tasks with an emphasis on one focused delivery system.... [I]t reflects strong bias toward direct instruction ... and decoding as the exclusive means by which students are taught... Little emphasis is placed on reading aloud, partner reading, independent silent reading ... shared and guided reading" (Schulz, 1998, p. 2). The International Reading Association sharply denounced the framework for "imposing a deficit or special education model on every student in California" (Board of Directors, IRA, 1998, p. 3).

In the aftermath of the state reading policy shift, Carlos and Krist noted that the CDE lost ground in the conflict over reading policy, having been criticized for putting into place policies that were "experimental" and without a basis in research. Of course, the research to which the analysts referred is that of the NICHD. Recently, policy analysts at the National Research Center on English Learning and Achievement (CELA) noted that much of the research conducted under the auspices of NICHD is not adequate to support the reading policy recommendations by the director (Allington & Woodside-Jiron, 1998).

Policy analysts hold that the 1990s intervention by the legislature into curriculum policy represented a break from the past. Top-down curriculum policy by elected officials, as in the reform of reading instruction, was unusual in the history of California's schools. Carlos and Krist attributed much of the responsibility for the policy shift in reading, and activity by the legislature, to the press, particularly the education reporter for the *Los Angeles Times*, who widely reported on declining test scores and the activities of parent coalitions that objected to what they called "outrageous" state policy.

Not only has the California legislature transformed state reading curriculum in California from a constructivist perspective to an emphasis on traditional teaching and basic curriculum, but by mid 1996, 18 so-called "phonics" bills had been introduced into 11 other state legislatures (Paterson, 1998). These bills mandated a type of "back to the basics" methodology that their sponsors claim is backed by research—the NICHD research program.

CURRENT ISSUES: EARLY LITERACY
ON THE POLICY AGENDA

How it happened is the subject of some discussion (see Allington & Woodside-Jiron, 1998; Elliot, 1996; Hart, 1996; Smith, Levin, & Cianci, 1997; Taylor, 1998). The literature on agenda setting (Kingdon, 1984; McGill-Franzen, 1993) suggests that for issues to reach the "decision" stage (i.e., when the government takes action on them), several things have to happen. The issue needs to be defined as a problem that government should address and labeled in a way that the public will support. Researchers often "soften up" the policy process by floating their ideas long before the issue is perceived as a problem, so that policymakers are more likely receptive to their solutions. Policy action depends on the convergence of a feasible solution to a pressing problem and the right political climate, creating an open window for an issue whose "time has come." Clearly, the perceived crisis in California, precipitated by the low NAEP test scores, created the sense of a pressing literacy problem that needed the attention of government. The NICHD research program had been around for years (Sweet, 1997), as had the research on phonemic awareness. Once the window opened for potential solutions to California's literacy crisis, the policy entrepreneurs—advocates, researchers, publishers, bureaucrats, so on—were ready.

Bitter debate continues over whether the state curriculum frameworks caused the decline in reading test scores as well as over whether the reading achievement of California youngsters did in fact decline (see, for example, The Literacy Crisis: False Claims, Real Solutions, McQuillan, 1998). The policy shift in California was transformed into a national policy debate on how to teach children to read, what proportion of the school population cannot read (and how is this defined), and what is research.

On the President's Agenda: NAEP Scores

President Clinton himself kept literacy an important policy issue in his 1996 campaign. As Clinton and other policymakers have pointed out, 40% of American fourth graders scored below the "basic" level on the 1994 NAEP. Clinton's goal—from the bully pulpit—is that all fourth-grade children be able to read at the basic level, and, to this end, he established the volunteer tutoring program America Reads. In 1997, with Republican control of Congress, Clinton made America Reads the centerpiece of his education program and one of the first examples of policymaking through a public campaign to develop awareness and mobilize support (Smith et al., 1997).

As most policymakers know, the National Assessment of Educational Progress (NAEP) developed a new framework for assessing reading, beginning in 1992. Instead of strictly multiple-choice items, NAEP changed its format to keep in step with the move toward more ambitious teaching and learning. The 1992 NAEP reading test included the dimension of reader's purpose (reading for literary response, information, to perform a task) as well as the dimension measuring depth of understanding, using authentic texts and extended responses (initial understanding, interpretation, personal reflection, and critical stance) (Elliot, 1996). To say that 40% of children read below a basic level on the NAEP is not to say that they can not read in absolute terms but, rather, that they may not be able to read well enough to participate fully in the technological society of tomorrow (National Research Council, 1998).

Research-Based Reading Pedagogy: What Counts as Research? What Counts as Reading?

Not only did the polemic surrounding beginning reading take over the education profession in California, but nationally as well (Taylor, 1998). The apparent lack of consensus on research-based reading curriculum and pedagogy prompted the U.S. Department of Education and the U.S. Department of Health and Human Services to ask the National Academy of Science to establish a committee to determine how reading difficulties can be prevented. The purpose of this committee was to synthesize the empirical research base on early literacy and present recommendations in an format accessible to parents, educators, publishers, and policymakers. The National Research Council (NRC) circulated a (prepublication) copy of the report (Preventing Reading Difficulties in Young Children) in 1998 that confirmed that reading ability is "determined by many factors":

> Many factors that correlate with reading fail to explain it; many experiences contribute to reading development without being prerequisite to it; and although there are many prerequisites, none by itself is considered sufficient. (p. 3)

The report identified reading for meaning and comprehension strategies as being essential to reading development, as well as understanding the nature of the alphabetic system, spelling–sound relationships, and the "structure" of spoken words. Further, the report claimed that all children experiencing difficulty—even children with learning disabilities—need the same high-quality instruction but more intensive support (p. 3). In addition, the report recognized preschool education as an untapped resource for the development of literacy. The Joint Policy Statement of the IRA and National Association for the Education of Young Children (NAEYC) issued in 1998, affirmed the commitment of these professional organizations to educate early childhood teachers about their responsibility to promote literacy development.

In order to build on the findings by the NRC, Congress requested that NICHD establish a National Reading Panel, in consultation with the Secretary of Education. The National Reading Panel is to review the research literature, including the effectiveness of different approaches to teaching children to read; to determine whether there can be classroom application of these findings; to develop a strategy for disseminating the findings; and to identify gaps in the research on reading instruction.

In early 1998, both the U.S. Senate and the House of Representatives considered a literacy bill that narrowly defined the research base for teacher development and provided for limited use of vouchers for reading tutors. The Reading Excellence Act (REA), sponsored by Rep. Goodling, Chair of the House Education and Workforce

Committee, passed the House but died a week before its self-imposed deadline as the Senate declined to act on it and recessed without approving a compromise bill (Sack, 1998). The $210 million (and perhaps an additional $260 million from Clinton's 1999 request for literacy) that was allocated to support reading initiatives under the literacy bill then reverted to special education state grants, a goal that some Republicans in Congress had all along—to find some money for this underfunded mandate. Some policy observers embraced the REA and others opposed it. For example, Carnine and Meeder (1997), of the National Center for Improving the Tools of Educators argued in the media that the REA was exactly what teachers needed to get back on track. On the other hand, the National Council of Teachers of English (NCTE) adamantly opposed the bill and worked to defeat its passage (Sack, 1998). What the NCTE opposed—control of reading pedagogy—the proponents of the bill applauded, believing that NICHD research program had "proven" that direct instruction was the appropriate methodology. As Cohen and Barnes (1993) pointed out, education policy is most often didactic itself but not often educative.

Ultimately, in the fall of 1998, Congress passed a revised Reading Excellence Act (REA), hailed by the Education Secretary as "the most significant law on child literacy passed by Congress in more than 30 years" (U.S. Department of Education, 1998, p. 1). By mid-1999, Congress had awarded more than $230 million to 17 states to support professional development for teachers, transition programs for kindergartners, family literacy and tutoring for struggling learners. The International Reading Association (IRA), representing more than 300,000 reading professionals, responded positively to aspects of the new version (1998). The IRA was pleased with the national emphasis on literacy instruction. Nonetheless, the IRA felt that the total allocation of funds was not enough to make a difference at the local level. Furthermore, the association expressed concern with the grant approval process, noting that it could diminish local control of education. IRA stated that the approval process was cumbersome, too dependent on government agencies, and vulnerable to voucher proposals.

SUMMARY AND CONCLUSIONS

Over the brief history of education policy that I have presented here, it is clear that problems were framed in different ways at different points in time. For example, Title 1 was originally framed as issue of insufficient resources, to an issue of regulation and compliance, and finally, it has been transformed into an issue of teaching and learning. The knowledge required of teachers today is complex, encompassing not only subject matter knowledge or curriculum expertise, but knowledge of children's development and the interactional competence to support children's learning and emerging control of their own literacy. But can policy facilitate this learning?

Instructional capacity, as Cohen and Ball (1997) reminded us, is the interaction of teachers with students around educational materials, and policy rarely targets all three components. What teachers do with curriculum, of course, influences what students learn, and teachers' knowledge of both content and development shapes the discourse of instruction. However, as implementation research in Michigan and California illustrated, educational policy does not tell teachers how to translate standards or assessments into instruction, often leading to superficial enactments of the intended policy (Cohen & Ball, 1997; Spillane & Jennings, 1997; see also Bridge, 1994, Miller, 1995, Miller, Hayes, & Atkinson, 1997, and Winograd, Petrosko, Compton-Hall, & Cantrell, 1997, for implementation research in other states).

It does not help that state reading policy shifts, as in California, created unstable contexts for teaching and learning and contributed to teacher cynicism about reform efforts (Cohen & Ball, 1997). Nonetheless, media attention to low performance on NAEP, the perception of rapidly increasing numbers of children with reading difficulties, increased costs associated with their education, and the NICHD research agenda have made literacy a national priority.

The recent National Research Council (NRC) report on preventing reading difficulties, as well as the small research on implementation and instruction, emphasized substantive teacher development in the core technology of teaching and learning. As a California educator told a CELA researcher, "Teachers are independent and you cannot tell them how to think and feel.... Because if you don't believe in a program whatever it happens to be, I can tell you whatever I want [but] it's not going to happen. Because when you go in that classroom and you close that door, you're going to teach what you feel and believe is right and what you feel and believe you can do" (McGill-Franzen, Machado, Jiron, & Veltema, 1998). To paraphrase policy analyst McLaughlin (1992), teaching may be too complicated, too embedded in context, and too tied to individual beliefs and knowledge for policy to have a predictable and consistent effect. That is not to say that policy has no effect, because it does, but it does so as one of myriad influences that make up the context of teaching and learning (p. 381).

REFERENCES

Adams. M. J. (1990). *Beginning to read: Thinking and learning abut print.* Cambridge, MA: MIT Press.

Allington, R. L., & McGill-Franzen, A. (1989a). Different programs, indifferent instruction. In A. Gartner & D. Lipsky (Eds.), *Beyond separate education: Quality education for all* (pp. 75–98). Baltimore, MD: Brookes.

Allington, R. L., & McGill-Franzen, A. (1989b). School response to reading failure: Chapter 1 and special education students in grades 2, 4, & 8. *Elementary School Journal, 89,* 529–542.

Allington, R. L., & McGill-Franzen, A. (1992). Unintended effects of educational reform in New York State. *Educational Policy, 6,* 396–413.

Allington, R., & Woodside-Jiron, H. (1998). 30 Years of research ...: When is a research summary not a research summary? In K. Goodman (Eds.), *In defense of good teaching: What teachers need to know about the reading wars.* (pp. 143–157). York, ME: Stenhouse.

Birman, B. F. (1981). Problems of overlap between Title I and P. L. 94-142: Implications for the federal role in education. *Educational Evaluation and Policy Development, 3,* 5–19.

Board of Directors, International Reading Association. (1998). International Reading Association's Response to CA Reading/Language Arts Curriculum Framework. [Online]. www.reading.org

Bridge, C. (1994). Implementing large-scale change in literacy instruction. In C. K. Kinzer and D. J. Leu (Eds.), *Multidimensional aspects of literacy research, theory, and practice: Forty-third yearbook of the National Reading Conference* (pp. 257–265). Chicago: National Reading Conference.

Carlos, L., & Kirst, M. (1997). *California curriculum policy in the 1990's: "We don't have to be in front to lead."* San Francisco: WestEd/PACE.

Carnine, D., & Meeder, H. (1997, September). Reading research into practice. *Education Week,* pp. 41, 43.

Chambers, J. G., Parrish, T. B., Lieberman, J. C., & Wolman, J. M. (1998). *What are we spending on special education in the U.S.?* (8) Palo Alto, CA: Center for Special Education Finance.

Chrispeels, J. H. (1997). Educational policy implementation in a shifting political climate: The California experience. *American Educational Research Journal, 34,* 453–481.

Cohen, D. K., & Ball, D. L. (1997). *Instruction, capacity and improvement.* University of Michigan, Ann Arbor.

Cohen, D. K., & Barnes, C. (1993). Pedagogy and policy. In D. K. Cohen, M. McLaughlin & J. Talbert (Eds.), *Teaching for understanding: Challenges for policy and practice* (pp. 207–240). San Francisco: Jossey-Bass.

Cohen, D. K. & Spillane, J. P. (1992). Policy and practice: The relations between governance and instruction. In G. Grant (Ed.), *Review of Research in Education* (pp. 3–49). Washington, DC: American Educational Research Association.

Darling-Hammond, L. (1990). Instructional policy into practice: "The power of the bottom over the top." *Educational Evaluation and Policy Analysis, 12,* 233–241.

Elliott, E. J. (1996). Literacy: From policy to practice. *Journal of Literacy Research, 28,* 590–595.

Elmore, R. (1983). Complexity and control: What legislators and administrators can do about implementing policy. In L. S. Shulman & G. Sykes (Eds.), *Handbook of Teaching and Policy.* New York: Longman.

Elmore, R. F. (1996). Getting to scale with good educational practice. *Harvard Educational Review, 66,* 1–26.

Elmore, R. F., Peterson, P. L., & McCarthy, S. J. (1996). *Restructuring in the classroom: Teaching, learning, and school organization.* San Francisco: Jossey-Bass.

Grissmer, D., Kirby, S. N., Berends, M., & Williamson, S. (1994). *Student achievement and the changing American family.* Santa Monica, CA: RAND Institute on Education and Training.

Greene, R. (1998, August 25). States use more standardized tests. *AOL News* [Online]. Available: www.aol.com.

Hart, G. K. (1996). A policymaker's response. *Journal of Literacy Research, 28,* 596–601.

International Reading Association. International Reading Association responds to the Reading Excellence Act at www.reading.org, October 1998.

Jenkins, J., Pious, C., & Peterson, D. (1988). Categorical programs for remedial and handicapped students: Issues of validity. *Exceptional Children, 55,* 147–158.

Jennings, N. E. (1996). *Interpreting policy in real classrooms: Case studies of state reform and teacher practice.* New York: Teachers College Press.

Juel, C. (1994). *Learning to read and write in one elementary school.* New York: Springer-Verlag.

Kennedy, M., Birman, B., & Demaline, R. (1986). *The effectiveness of chapter 1 services.* Washington, DC: U.S. Government Printing Office.

Kingdon, J. W. (1984). *Agendas, alternatives, and public policies.* Boston: Little, Brown.

Kirst, M. W. (1990). *Accountability: Implications for state and local policy makers.* Washington, DC: U.S. Government Printing Office.

Lyon, G. R. (1995). Research initiatives in learning disabilities: Contributions from scientists supported by the National Institute of Child Health and Development. *Journal of Child Neurology, 10,* 120–126.

Lyon, G. R. (1996). Learning disabilities. *Futures of Children, 6,* 54–76.

Lyon, G. R. (1997). *Statement of G. Reid Lyon, Ph.D before the Committee on Education and the Workforce, U.S. House of Representatives.* Bethesda, MD: National Institute of Child Health and Human Development, National Institutes of Health.

McGill-Franzen, A. (1987). Failure to learn to read: Formulating a policy problem. *Reading Research Quarterly, 22,* 475–490.

McGill-Franzen, A. (1993). *Shaping the preschool agenda: Early literacy, public policy and professional beliefs.* Albany: State University of New York Press.

McGill-Franzen, A., & Allington, R. L. (1991). The gridlock of low-achievement: Perspectives on policy and practice. *Remedial and Special Education, 12,* 20–30.

McGill-Franzen, A., & Allington, R. L. (1993). Flunk'em or get them classified: The contamination of primary grade accountability data. *Educational Researcher, 22,* 19–22.

McGill-Franzen, A., Woodside-Jiron, H., Machado, V., & Veltema, J. (1998, December). *A study of state education policymaking and implementation in English language arts curriculum and assessment in four states.* Paper presented at the National Reading Conference, Austin, TX.

McLaughlin, M. W. (1992). Educational policy, impact on practice. In M. Aiken (Ed.), American Educational Research Association encyclopedia of educational research (pp. 375–382). New York: Macmillan.

McLaughlin, M. W., & Talbert, J. E. (1993). *Contexts that matter for teaching and learning.* Center for Research on the Context of Secondary Teaching.

McQuillan, J. (1998). *The literacy crisis: False claims, real solutions.* Portsmouth, NH: Heinemann.

Michigan State Board of Education. (1985). *Michigan essential goals and objectives for reading education.* Lansing, MI: Author.

Miller, S. D. (1995). Teachers' responses to test-driven accountability: "If I change, will my scores drop?" *Reading Research and Instruction, 34,* 332–351.

Miller, S. D., Hayes, C. T., & Atkinson, T. S. (1997). State efforts to improve students' reading and language arts achievement: Does the left hand know what the right is doing? *Reading Instruction, 36,* 267–286.

National Commission on Excellence in Education. (1983). *A nation at risk.* Washington, DC: U.S. Government Printing Office.

National Governors' Association. (1986). *Time for results.* Washington, DC: National Governors' Association.

National Research Council. (1998). *Preventing reading difficulties in young children.* Washington, DC: National Academy.

Paterson, F. R. A. (1998). Mandating methodology: Promoting the use of phonics through state statute. In K. Goodman (Ed.), *In defense of good teaching: What teachers need to know about the "reading wars"* (pp. 107–125). York, ME: Stenhouse.

Puma, M. J., Karweit, N., Price, C., Ricciuti, A., Thompson, W., & Vaden-Kiernan, M. (1997). *Prospects: Final report on student outcomes.* Washington, DC: U.S. Department of Education, Planning and Evaluation Services.

Purkey, S. & Smith, M. (1983). Effective schools: A review. *Elementary School Journal, 83,* 427–454.

Rothstein, R., & Miles, K. H. (1995). *Where's the money gone? Changes in the level and composition of education spending.* Washington, DC: Economic Policy Institute.

Rowan, B. & Guthrie, L. F. (1989). The quality of chapter 1 instruction: Results from a study of twenty-four schools. In R. E. Slavin, N. Karweit, & N. Madden (Eds.), *Effective Programs for Students at Risk* (pp. 195–219). Boston: Allyn-Bacon.

Sack, J. L. (1998, August 21). Time runs out for literacy legislation. *AOL News* [Online]. Available: www.aol.com.

Scanlon, D. M., & Vellutino, F. R. (1996). Prerequisite skills, early instruction, and success in first-grade reading: Selected results from a longitudinal study. *Mental Retardation and Developmental Disabilities: Research and Review, 2,* 54–63.

Schulz, A. R. (1998). *California Reading Association response to CA Reading/Language Arts Curriculum Framework* [Online]. www.californiareads.org

Share, D., & Stanovich, K. (1995). Cognitive processes in early reading development: Accommodating individual differences into a model of acquisition. *Issues in Education: Contributions from Cognitive Psychology, 1,* 1–57.

Smith, M. S., Levin, J., & Cianci, J. E. (1997). Beyond a legislative agenda: Education policy approaches of the Clinton administration. *Educational Policy, 11,* 209–226.

Smylie, M. A., Lazarus, V., & Brownlee-Conyers, J. (1996). Instructional outcomes of school-based participative decision-making. *Educational Evaluation and Policy Analysis, 18,* 181–198.

Spear-Swerling, L., & Sternberg, R. J. (1996). *Off track: When poor readers become "learning disabled."* Boulder, CO: Westview Press.

Spillane, J. P. (1994). How districts mediate between state policy and teachers' practice. In R. Elmore & S. H. Fuhrman (Eds.), *The governance of curriculum* (pp. 167–185). Alexandria, VA: Association for Supervision and Curriculum Development.

Spillane, J. P. (1998). State policy and the non-monolithic nature of the local school district: Organizational and Professional considerations. *American Educational Research Journal, 35,* 33–64.

Spillane, J. P., & Jennings, N. E. (1997). Aligned instructional policy and ambitious pedagogy: Exploring instructional reform from the classroom perspective. *Teachers College Record, 98,* 449–481.

Sweet, R. W. (1997). Don't read, don't tell: Clinton's phony war on illiteracy. *Policy Review,* 38–42.

Taylor, D. (1998). *Beginning to read and the spin doctors of science: The political campaign to change America's mind about how children learn to read.* Urbana, IL: National Council of Teachers of English.

Timar, T. (1994). Federal education policy and practice: Building organizational capacity through Chapter 1. *Educational Evaluation and Policy Analysis, 16,* 51–66.

U.S. Department of Education. (1984, May). *The nation responds: Recent efforts to improve education.* Washington, DC: U.S. Government Printing Office.

U.S. Department of Education. (1993). *Reinventing Chapter 1: The current Chapter 1 program and new directions.* Washington, DC: Office of Policy and Planning.

U.S. Department of Education. Riley announces $231.8 million in grants to states to improve children's reading at www.ed.gov, October 1998.

Vinovskis, M. A. (1996). An analysis of the concept and uses of systemic educational reform. *American Educational Research Journal, 33,* 53–85.

Wang, M. C. (1997). *Improving our capacity for achieving student success: Recommendations from a national invitational conference on the Title 1 program.* Philadelphia PA: National Center on Education in the Inner Cities.

Winograd, P., Petrosko, J., Compton-Hall, M. & Cantrell, S.C. (1997). *The effects of KERA on Kentucky's elementary schools: Year one of a proposed five-year study.* University of Kentucky/University of Louisville Joint Center for the Study of Education Policy. Kentucky Institute for Education Research.

CHAPTER 47

Policy-Oriented Research on Literacy Standards and Assessment

Sheila W. Valencia
University of Washington

Karen K. Wixson
University of Michigan

This is the first edition of the *Handbook of Reading Research* to include policy chapters. During the 1980s and 1990s, instruments of policy reached into every facet of our educational lives. The "tools" of policy include everything from new content standards or instructional frameworks to teacher certification requirements, systems of assessment, Title I allocations and requirements, and textbook adoption guidelines. This chapter is focused on a discussion of policy-oriented research on literacy standards and assessment, as other literacy policy matters are addressed elsewhere in this *Handbook*. How policy instruments such as standards and assessments have risen to such high levels of prominence in subject matter learning is part of the story we must tell in this chapter.

Historically, state policymakers have delegated their authority over public education to local school districts, particularly in matters of curriculum and instruction. Districts, in turn, have entrusted the curriculum to teachers or indirectly to textbook publishers, and have done little to develop or provide instructional guidance (Massell, Kirst, & Hoppe, 1997). Since the publication of the now-famous report *A Nation at Risk* (National Commission on Excellence in Education, 1983), however, states and districts have made unprecedented forays into curriculum and instruction (Massell et al., 1997). This modern reform movement has been characterized by efforts to create new "policy instruments" to elicit, encourage, or demand changes in teaching and learning and reduce the tangles of regulation, bureaucracy, proliferating policy, and incoherent governance that would impede reform (Smith & O'Day, 1991). Included among the new policy instruments are the standards and assessments that are the subject of the research we examine in this review.

As we considered what literature to include in this review, we were conscious of how current reform efforts have resulted in an increased interest in policy research. For example, Office of Educational Research and Improvement (OERI) funded the Consortium for Policy Research in Education in 1985 and the Center for the Study of Teaching and Policy in 1998, and the American Educational Research Association established Division L on politics and policymaking in 1997. In addition to the growing number of policy researchers, researchers in the area of measurement and evaluation have also become interested in policy because many reform initiatives have focused on assessment as a primary vehicle for improving student achievement. Similarly, the many reform efforts aimed at improving the literacy levels of young Americans have led literacy researchers to become more interested in research on policy-related issues. The realization that policy-oriented research is being conducted from a variety of perspectives led us to approach this review on two levels. On one level, we characterize the nature of policy-oriented research on literacy standards and assessments. On another level, we review what research tells us about the impact of literacy standards and assessment on practice and student learning.

To characterize the nature of literacy policy research, we examine the literature on standards and assessment in relation to the policy, measurement, and literacy contexts from which it arises. As a result, we review three fairly distinct sets of literature. Policy researchers set out to address policy issues head-on, but are less concerned with subject matter specifics. Measurement researchers are also more concerned with general findings than with subject-matter specifics; however, they tend to focus on the qualities and influence of assessment policy tools rather than on policy questions per se. Similarly, literacy researchers rarely take the policy questions or issues as the driving force for their work; they are primarily interested in subject matter teaching and learning. Differences in perspective result in differences in research questions, conceptual frameworks, methodologies, perspectives on literacy, and audiences for publications, which, in turn, result in differences in what is learned about literacy standards and assessment.

To present these different perspectives and findings clearly, this chapter is organized into four sections. The first three sections present our review of the policy-oriented literature related to literacy standards and assessment in terms of the three research perspectives—policy, measurement, and literacy. Each of these sections has two parts—a brief background related to the context in which research from each perspective has arisen, and a review of the literacy policy research within each perspective. The fourth section focuses on what we have learned from these bodies of research with regard to the nature of the research and the results of policy-oriented research on literacy standards and assessment.

THE POLICY PERSPECTIVE

Following the publication of *A Nation at Risk* (National Commission on Excellence in Education, 1983), two "waves" of school reform emerged (Lusi, 1997). The first wave consisted of state efforts to accomplish three goals: (a) raise coursework standards for high school graduation, (b) implement and/or expand assessment programs, and (c) raise standards for prospective teachers (Goertz, Floden, & O'Day, 1995). The second wave of reform came in the form of school restructuring, and combined three complementary elements: (a) a call for higher and common expectations for all students, (b) an emphasis on new and more challenging teaching practices, and (c) dramatic changes in the organization and management of public schools (Elmore, 1990).

These initial waves of reform in the 1980s did little to change the content of instruction, especially with their focus on basic skills; nor did they result in the desired changes in teaching, learning, and student achievement (Cuban, 1990; Firestone, Fuhrman, & Kirst, 1989). Fragmented and contradictory policies diverted teachers' attention, provided little or no support for the type of professional learning necessary, and made it difficult to sustain the very promising reforms taking shape in individual schools or clusters of schools (Cohen & Spillane, 1992; Goertz et al., 1995).

Growing concerns about the educational preparation of the nation's youth prompted President Bush and the nation's governors to call an education summit in Charlottesville, VA, in September 1989. This summit resulted in six broad goals for education to be reached by the year 2000 (National Education Goals Panel, 1991). In pursuit of the National Education Goals, the bipartisan National Council on Education Standards and Testing (NCEST) issued a report in January 1992, recommending national content standards and a national system of assessments based on the new standards. Precedent for and guidance in developing national standards was to be found in the work of the National Council of Teachers of Mathematics (NCTM), published as Curriculum and Evaluation Standards for School Mathematics in 1989. The logic was that once broad agreement had been achieved on what is to be taught and learned, then everything else in the system including tests, professional development, textbooks, software, and so on could be redirected toward reaching those standards. This view has come to be known as *systemic reform*.

Systemic reform has, as its aim, changes in teaching as the most direct route to changes in students' learning (Cohen, 1995), and it is posited as a means of providing top-down support for bottom-up instructional improvement in classrooms, schools, and districts. The key question for reformers has been how to get there—how to foster (or mandate) changes in learning and teaching. Many systemic reformers have viewed government as their chief vehicle, although state and federal policies are not the only ways to pursue improved instruction, as demonstrated by efforts such as the Coalition for Essential Schools, the Accelerated Schools Network, and the New Standards Project, which operate largely outside the framework of governmental policy, although still with substantial resources. Systemic reformers have generally focused on creating new policy instruments such as content standards or curricular frameworks, assessments that are aligned with new content standards and changes in both preservice and inservice teacher education (Cohen, 1995).

According to McLaughlin (1987), policy research into the late 1980s generated a number of important lessons for policy, practice, and analysis by acknowledging the role of contextual factors such as local priorities, individual beliefs and motivation, and the balance between support and pressure to change. Furthermore, she saw these lessons as framing the conceptual and instrumental challenge for the next generation of policy analysts: one that described a model of implementation that highlighted individuals rather than institutions and viewed implementation issues in terms of individual actors' incentives, beliefs, and capacity. Darling-Hammond (1990) added that top-down policies could "constrain but not construct" change. She focused on policy enactment, arguing that local leadership and motivations for change are critical to policy success; that local agencies must adapt policies rather than adopting them, because local ideas and circumstances always vary; and "that teachers' and administrators' opportunities for continual learning, experimentation, and decision making during implementation determine whether policies will come alive in schools or fade away when the money or enforcement pressures end" (p. 235).

At a deeper level, though, Darling-Hammond (1990) argued that we knew little yet about the meaning of specific policies for educational life within classrooms. She indicated that advances in policy analysis during the 1980s made it possible to ask a number of new questions. For example, What differences do such advances actually make to teachers' and student's work together? How do teachers understand and interpret the intentions of new policies in the context of their knowledge, beliefs, and teaching circumstances? How and under what circumstances do policies intended to change teaching actually do so? These observations were presented in Darling-Hammond's introduction to a special issue of *Educational Evaluation and Policy Analysis* (EEPA) focused on case studies of California reform in K–12 mathematics education. These case studies were seen as leading the way toward a next generation of policy analysis that recognized "the importance of understanding the transformation of policy into teacher actions from the vantage point of the teachers, themselves, as well as from that of the policy system" (p. 175).

Our review of the policy research in the 1990s revealed relatively few studies that clearly addressed literacy standards and assessment. Of those that did, there were two types. First, there were large-scale investigations of state reform efforts that began to link macro and micro levels of analysis using classroom artifacts such as lesson assignments and interviews with teachers and administrators to get at the classroom perspective. Second, there were investigations, often case studies, that explored more deeply the impact of policy instruments on teachers, schools, and districts. In limiting our review to policy research related to literacy standards and assessments, we saw increased efforts to examine policy initiatives with what Darling-Hammond called a "pedagogical eye," but little attention to the role that different subject areas might play in implementation, although this too may be changing (see Ball & Cohen, 1995).

Research

A study by Goertz et al. (1995) provides an example of how large-scale policy research projects in the 1990s began to link macro and micro levels of analysis. The stated purposes for this study included expanding our knowledge of state approaches to education reform, examining district, school, and teacher responses to state reform policies in a small number of reforming schools and districts, and studying the capacity of the educational system to support education reform. The findings are based on case studies of 12 reforming schools located in six reforming school districts in three states that have taken somewhat different approaches to systemic reform—California, Michigan, and Vermont. The researchers interviewed educators, administrators and policymakers at the school, district, and state levels. They also surveyed and interviewed 60 teachers in each school. Because it was too early in the reform movement to assess the impact of any particular state, district, and/or school strategy, this study was intended more as a description of what was happening than "what works."

It is noteworthy that not until half-way through the seven-page Executive Summary did Goertz et al. mention that this research focused on reform in mathematics and language arts. Because we are concerned here with literacy-related policy research, we summarize only the section of the report that focuses specifically on language arts policy. From a policy researchers' perspective, however, we should remember that this report is not about mathematics or language arts reform. Rather, it is about systemic reform, and the attention given to mathematics and language arts merely provides some specificity to the findings.

The portion of the report dealing directly with language arts examines the degree to which teachers' reports on their instruction were consistent with explicit or implicit curriculum recommendations in policies, such as curriculum frameworks and state assessments. For example, some of the aims of California's "meaning-centered" English-language arts reform were reflected in survey data on reading instruction. Elementary teachers reported that during reading instruction, their students spent 3½ hours per week on comprehension strategies and responding to what they read. The least amount of time was spent on word recognition skills (30 minutes) and phonics (19 minutes). The California English Language Arts Framework (California Department of Education, 1987) also emphasized a literature-based curriculum that "engaged students with the vitality of ideas and values greater than those of the marketplace or video arcade" (p. 7). Elementary teachers indicated that 80% of instructional time was spent using literature trade books, with the remaining time distributed among reading or subject basals, workbooks or worksheets, or something else.

As in California, Michigan teachers emphasized content matching the "meaning-centered" view of Michigan's Essential Goals and Objectives in Reading (Michigan State Board of Education, 1986). For example, both elementary and secondary teachers reported spending over 3 hours per week on comprehension strategies and having students respond to what they read, and barely over one-half hour per week on basic skills, such as phonics and word recognition. Both California and Michigan teachers reported spending roughly the same amount of time per week on reading instruction. However, California teachers spent over 4½ hours per week with students engaged in small-group reading activities, such as working in pairs or teams and small-group discussion. In contrast, Michigan teachers spent less than 2½ hours per week engaging in these kinds of activities. These differences in instructional practices reported by Michigan and California teachers are consistent with the emphasis given to dissimilar aspects of the language arts reform policies in the two states.

Goertz et al. (1995) concluded that there is evidence of general patterns that incorporate new directions in both state and national reforms but also retain attention to more traditional topic areas. Teachers believed that they had been influenced by state policy instruments, such as assessments and curricular frameworks, but that these state influences were by no means the only influences on practice, or even the most important influences. Teachers reported that their own knowledge and beliefs about the subject matter and their students, for example, generally had a larger influence than state policies.

Other examples of policy research that reflect initial efforts to link macro and micro levels of analysis include the work of McDonnell (McDonnell, 1997; McDonnell & Choisser, 1997), Smith and colleagues (Smith et al., 1997), and the Kentucky Institute for Education Research (Lindle, Petrosko, & Pankratz, 1997), all of whom studied state reforms that included a literacy component. For example, McDonnell and Choisser examined the extent to which policymakers' expectations about the curricular effects of testing in Kentucky and North Carolina proved valid in local schools and classrooms. Their analysis was based on telephone and on-site interviews with teachers and administrators, and examinations of assignments and daily logs gathered from 23 teachers in each state. They concluded that transforming instruction through assessment was not a self-implementing reform because the tests alone lacked sufficient guidance for how teachers ought to change.

Smith et al. took a different methodological approach, conducting a 4-year, multimethod approach to study the effects of the now suspended Arizona Student Assessment Program (ASAP). They observed in classrooms and interviewed teachers and principals in four schools, and they used a survey approach to collect data from educators across the state. The results, reported as generalizations across subject areas, indicated that although educators knew about ASAP, their responses to it varied depending on how they understood it and how it fit with their underlying beliefs and the local conditions (material and knowledge resources, existing beliefs and ideologies about teaching, culture of accountability and authority). Smith et al. also concluded that having a dual focus on accountability and instructional improvement together with insufficient attention to capacity building resulted in marginal effects of the ASAP reform agenda.

In contrast to the large-scale investigations represented by the Goertz et al., McDonnell, and Smith et al. studies, some policy researchers have conducted more in-depth studies of the impact of policy instruments on teachers, schools, and districts. For example, Standerford (1997) studied two small districts in Michigan from 1988 until 1991. Both districts formed reading curriculum committees in an effort to interpret the state reading policy and design an official district response. To understand what happened in these districts, Standerford observed both the curriculum committees and the classroom practices of the teachers on these committees. Her results indicated that the district rules, objectives, players, audiences, and time frames made participation in the district effort quite separate from the state policy or from the classroom changes that individual teachers were making. Districts' responses to state reading reform were influenced by their need to reduce uncertainty, use standard operating procedures to effect change, advertise change by producing documents and plans, and respond selectively to policies based on the incentives attached. In contrast, the teachers made changes based on their individual professional development activities, but were often unsure just how those changes fit with the state policy.

Standerford concluded that state and district policies had influenced the teachers' efforts by making them aware that changes were expected in reading instruction, but had not made clear for the teachers what those instructional changes were, nor offered much support for their efforts to figure that out for themselves. As teachers learned more about the new ideas, they gradually changed the enacted curriculum in their classrooms. Yet those instructional changes were minimally represented in the written curriculum that they produced as members of the district committees because their roles and objectives were defined differently at the district and classroom levels.

In another series of studies, Spillane (1996, 1998), Spillane and Jennings (1997), and Jennings (1995) examined the impact of the reading policy in Michigan on both a racially and economically diverse urban district and a relatively affluent suburban district, as well as on a small group of teachers within the suburban district. Spillane's (1996) study revealed that state and local policies do not always support similar notions about instruction. The suburban district used the revision of the state reading test as a lever to move in another direction the central administrators, who preferred a basic skills curriculum. Within a short period of time, district administrators had developed a new curriculum guide for reading, adopted new curricular materials, revised their student assessment policies, and organized an extensive professional development program about reading that went beyond state policy. In contrast, the state's reading policy did not figure prominently in the reading program developed in the urban district. Curriculum guides supported traditional ideas about teaching reading such as encouraging teachers to teach isolated bits of vocabulary, decoding skills, and comprehension skills. A new basal reading program was mandated, accompanied by a traditional workbook that provided students with drill in reading skills, and central administrators made no effort to revise district policy on student assessment despite significant revisions of the state's reading test.

When Spillane and Jennings (1997) looked more closely at nine second- and fifth-grade teachers in the suburban district, they found that the extent to which teachers' practices reflected the district's literacy initiative depended on how well the reforms were elaborated by the district. Their initial data analysis suggested significant uniformity in language arts practice among the nine classrooms and offered striking evidence that the district's proposals for language arts reform were finding their way into practice. For example, they found that all nine teachers were using literature-based reading programs and trade books, engaging in activities such as Writer's Workshop, and focusing on comprehension over skills-based instruction. However, early discussions of the observation data revealed other differences that weren't being captured by the analytical framework. This led to a revised analytical frame focused on classroom tasks and discourse patterns that helped track these "below-the-surface" differences in pedagogy.

Comparing results using the two analytical frameworks, Spillane and Jennings showed that it is relatively easy to arrive at very different conclusions about the extent to which reforms that call for more ambitious pedagogy have permeated practice. They argued that if reforms are meant to help all students encounter language arts in a more demanding and authentic manner, then policy analysts cannot rely solely on indicators such as the materials and the activities teachers use. Rather, they must sit in classrooms and figure out what type of knowledge is supported by classroom tasks and discourse patterns. We would add that to be able to explore these issues effectively, one needs to understand a great deal about the subject matter instruction that is the focus of the reform. Spillane and Jennings amassed a great deal of knowledge about language arts and language arts instruction over their years of studying reform in this area, and we would argue that without this knowledge, they might never have even seen the differences that led them to revise their analytical framework and uncover these important differences in classroom practice.

Collectively, these studies provide insight regarding both policy research related to literacy standards and assessments, and the impact of literacy standards and assessments on district and teacher practices. On the one hand, very few policy studies provide sufficient subject matter information to warrant inclusion in this review. On the other hand, several studies probe deeply into the details of the classroom discourse and tasks related to language arts instruction, revealing important differences in teachers' implementation of reform efforts. In terms of the impact of literacy standards and assessments, it is clear that policy tools such as conceptual frameworks, curriculum guides, and assessments can and do influence district and classroom practice. It is also evident that the relations between language arts policy and practice are complex and at least partly dependent on the knowledge, beliefs, goals, and experience of the administrators and teachers working with these types of policy tools. These findings speak clearly to the need to understand thoroughly the context of policy implementation from both the system perspective and the day-to-day lives of teachers and students. They also suggest that without some form of professional development the effects of such policies are highly variable.

THE MEASUREMENT PERSPECTIVE

Assessment has been part of educational reform efforts for the past 40 years (Linn, 1998), initially serving as an indicator of reform or progress and more recently serving as a lever for reform. In the 1960s, testing increased substantially to meet the demands of evaluation and accountability for Title I. Then in the 1970s and 1980s, measurement researchers became intimately involved in policy-related issues during the minimal competency testing (MCT) movement when high stakes were attached to test performance. In Florida, for example, where MCT graduation requirements gained a great deal of attention, test results revealed gains for low-achieving students but differential passing rates for African American, Hispanic, and White students. In addition, the Federal District Court decision in the landmark *Debra P. vs. Turlington* (1981) case directed that students must be provided with ample opportunity to learn the material tested when high stakes, such as high school graduation, are in place. Events such as these quickly propelled assessment and assessment researchers into the policy arena. Following this trend, a new movement, measurement-driven reform (Popham, Cruse, Rankin, Sandifer, & Williams, 1985), gained in popularity, emphasizing large-scale assessment as a "catalyst to improve instruction" (p. 628). Measurement-driven reform expanded the role of assessment into the policy arena in two important ways: (a) It focused attention on what students should learn (outcomes) and (b) it made teaching toward the test a valued instructional strategy.

Many measurement researchers explored the effects of early high-stakes assessments on student performance, curriculum, and teachers' instructional practices. In general, studies indicated that high-stakes standardized basic skills tests led to narrowing of the curriculum; overemphasis on basic skills and test-like instructional methods; reduction in effective instructional time and an increase in time for test preparation; inflated test scores; and pressure on teachers to improve test scores (Herman &

Golan, 1993; Nolen, Haladyna, & Haas, 1992; Resnick & Resnick, 1992; Shepard, 1991; Shepard & Dougherty, 1991; Smith, 1991; Smith, Edelsky, Draper, Rottenberg, & Cherland, 1990). These studies led educators and the public alike to question the effectiveness of educational reform efforts and the assessments themselves (Linn, Grau, & Sanders, 1990). As a result of this line of research and renewed interest in the intended and unintended consequences of assessment (Messick, 1989), the "alternative" or "authentic" assessment movement was launched.

From past research it was clear that assessment could be a lever for reform—that what gets tested, gets taught, and what doesn't get tested, doesn't get taught. Therefore, it was reasoned that if better, more authentic assessments could be created to measure the "thinking curriculum" (Resnick & Resnick, 1992), then better teaching and learning would follow. Publicly acknowledged content standards in specific subject areas would guide the content of the new assessments, and high performance standards, rather than norms, would guide goals for student achievement learn (NCEST, 1992). Furthermore, it was argued that if teachers were more involved in the development, administration, and scoring of the assessments, there would be a greater chance that teaching would be enhanced. Performance assessment, portfolios, and projects (Resnick & Resnick, 1992) were advanced by both educators and measurement experts as assessment models that might foster effective teaching, learning and measurement of worthwhile outcomes (Shepard, 1989; Simmons & Resnick, 1993; Wiggins, 1993). In many respects, the authentic assessment movement is an extension of the measurement-driven reform of the 1980s, only now the form of the assessment, criteria for content selection and student performance, focus on opportunity to learn, and people involved in assessment development have changed.

The measurement community cautioned that the field would require new models and methods of determining the technical merit of new assessments (Linn, Baker, & Dunbar, 1991; Moss, 1994), many of which were not yet in place. Furthermore, many argued that it was impossible to test the logical assertion that these new measures would yield more positive results until the assessments were in place for some time. Nevertheless, pressure for new, better assessments and for public accountability placed new assessments on a fast track. By 1997, 46 out of 50 states had some form of statewide assessment, and 36 of those included extended responses typical of performance assessments (Roeber, Bond, & Braskamp, 1997). Linn (1998) suggested that policymakers have placed enormous emphasis on assessment reform because it is relatively inexpensive and easy to mandate, can be implemented rapidly, and is easily reported by the press, when compared to the type of professional development and restructuring/reculturing of schools that is needed for deep, second-order educational change (Fullan & Miles, 1992). So in the 1990s, we witnessed an enormous growth in new assessments as the levers for reform.

The research we review in this section falls into two general categories: on-demand forms of performance assessments, and classroom-based assessments such as portfolios. We use the term *on-demand performance assessments* to define uniform assessments administered under controlled conditions; they are usually given on a particular day or days under standard conditions across classrooms, schools, and districts. Most statewide assessments in reading and writing are on-demand assessments. Recent efforts have focused on improving the quality of the assessment tasks and expanding response modes while, at the same time, trying to maintain high levels of reliability and validity. In this section of the review, we include research on the on-demand performance assessments that require students to demonstrate higher order cognitive processes and to provide some extended responses to comprehension questions or to write in response to a prompt. We do not include research on more traditional assessments, which are comprised only of multiple-choice items. For the second category, classroom-based assessments, we include assessment evidence that is systematically collected as an ongoing part of the instructional program. In some cases, the evidence is scored and then reported for accountability purposes either at the state or school district level. Because we are focusing on policy-related research, we do not include research on individual classroom assessment projects.

Research

On-Demand Performance Assessment.   First attempts at performance assessment in literacy can be traced back to the 1960s and the use of direct writing assessment instead of indirect measures such as multiple choice tests (cf. Freedman, 1993). Direct writing assessment requires students to write in response to an assigned topic under timed conditions; papers are scored using a standard rubric. Many statewide assessments (Roeber et al., 1997) and the National Assessment of Educational Progress (NAEP) still use this approach with considerable success. Measurement researchers have focused on issues of interrater reliability and generalizability with respect to scoring writing samples. Interrater reliability is generally high, although studies indicate it can vary from .3 to .91 (Dunbar, Koretz, & Hoover, 1992; Hieronymus, Hoover, Cantor, & Oberley, 1987; Welch, 1991). Measurement researchers seem to have a good understanding about how to raise reliability to an acceptable level by implementing more extensive training of carefully selected scorers, more specific scoring guidelines, and the like (Mehrens, 1992; Miller & Legg, 1993). Issues of generalizability across modes of writing or even topics within modes are not as clear, however, and continue to present challenges for measurement experts (Dunbar et al., 1992; Herman, 1991; Hieronymus et al., 1987). Language arts educators, however, are now raising questions regarding the authenticity of direct writing assessment and the validity of the results when students are required to write under these unnatural, on-demand conditions (e.g., constrained by time, topic, audience, and process) (Freedman, 1993; Lucas, 1988a, 1988b). Although these criticisms are appealing on the surface, Messick (1994), a noted measurement researcher, pointed out that concerns about both authenticity and directness need to be supported empirically rather than simply claimed. This is a good example of how differences in perspective shape the questions and the nature of the evidence sought.

Although direct writing assessment is still a mainstay of many assessment programs, more recent efforts at performance assessment in reading and writing go further; many include longer and more complex reading selections from a variety of genres, higher level comprehension questions, extended written responses, and cross-text analyses. The few studies from a measurement perspective that are available on new statewide assessments (e.g., Maryland, Kentucky, Arizona) do not distinguish among reading, language arts, and mathematics in design or analyses, making it difficult for literacy educators to interpret the implications for curriculum, instruction, or research. For example, in two parallel studies, researchers at RAND (Koretz, Barron, Mitchell, & Stecher, 1996; Koretz, Mitchell, Barron, & Keith, 1996) used telephone and written surveys to examine the influence of the Maryland School Performance Assessment Program (MSPAP) and the Kentucky Instructional Information System (KIRIS)—both of which had assessments in several subject areas. By focusing only on responses of elementary teachers included in these reports, we can get some idea of language arts-related results. Across both studies, teachers supported the new assessments, even in terms of encouraging reluctant teachers to change; however, they did not support the use of test results for accountability. On the positive side, teachers aligned curriculum with the assessments, especially spending more time on writing (a dominant response mode for both assessments), although they felt that more specific curriculum frameworks would be helpful. On the negative side, teachers reported spending considerable time in test preparation activities and a tendency to deemphasize untested material. Data from both studies indicated that teachers' expectations rose for high-achieving students rather than low-achieving students and that teachers credited student gains to specific test practice and test familiarity rather than to true improvements in capabilities. These findings led the researchers to call for further research on issues related to the specificity of the frameworks, effects on equity, inflated test scores, and the validity of the measures.

One of the few studies of on-demand assessment to report specifically by subject area is based on data from the New Standards Project, a multistate effort designed to involve educators in the creation of state and district performance-based assessments in reading, writing, and mathematics (Resnick, Resnick, & DeStefano, 1993). This shared emphasis on new assessments and professional development involved teachers in the development, piloting, and scoring of the assessments. Researchers found "moderate" interrater reliability for both the reading and writing sections of the test—too low to use for judging students or educational programs. More interesting, reliability varied depending on the task being scored, the approach to calculating reliability (correlation or agreement), and the scoring method used (holistic or a combination of analytic and holistic); moreover, individual students' scores varied depending on the scoring method used. The researchers suggested that more intensive training, a more selective scoring team, clearer rubrics, and better exemplars might improve interrater agreement. These findings mirror the findings discussed earlier related to direct writing assessment.

Classroom-Based Assessment. The classroom-based measurement research has largely been conducted on portfolios. Interest in portfolios and policy stemmed from an attempt to join the advantages of classroom-embedded assessment with the need for large-scale public accountability. From the beginning, many were leery of trying to accomplish both purposes with one instrument, but the advantages in terms of teacher development, instructional practice, and student engagement motivated educators to try (Aschbacher, 1994; Haney, 1991; Mehrens, 1998; Valencia, 1991).

The most widely studied of the large-scale portfolio projects is the Vermont Portfolio Assessment Program, although more measurement researchers have studied the mathematics portfolio than the writing portfolio (Koretz, McCaffrey, Klein, Bell, Stecher, 1993; Koretz, Stecher, Deibert, 1992; Koretz, Stecher, Klein, & McCaffrey, 1994; Koretz, Stecher, Klein, McCaffrey, & Deibert, 1993). Because statewide assessment was new in Vermont, this project was conceptualized as a system that would take hold gradually—it would be decentralized and would require "a very long effort" (Mills & Brewer, 1988, in Koretz et al., 1994). According to state officials, it was designed to support sound educational practice, encourage professional development of education, encourage local autonomy, and provide comparable information across schools. The writing assessment was designed to be administered in Grades 4 and 8 (in 1994–1995, the writing assessment was moved to Grades 5 and 8) and is comprised of two main components in writing: (a) a portfolio of student work, which includes a set number and specified types of pieces of writing collected over the course of a year, and (b) a "uniform test" of writing (i.e., a standard prompt to which all students respond using standard procedures). The portfolio contents and the Uniform Test are scored by a wide range of Vermont teachers other than the students' own, using an analytic scoring rubric.

Studies of reliability indicated interrater correlations ranging from .46 to .63 (45% agreement based on exact match) depending on how the scores were aggregated (e.g., within or across scoring dimensions; by individual piece or across sections of the portfolio), a finding that led researchers to conclude that the state could not report on the percentage of students scoring at each point on each of the writing traits, nor could it provide comparative data across districts and schools (Koretz, Stecher, Klein, McCaffrey, & Deibert, 1993). Researchers suggested that inadequate rubrics, insufficient training of scorers, and lack of standardization of portfolio tasks most likely contributed to the lack of reliability.

In terms of validity, the Vermont results were "not persuasive" (Koretz, Stecher, Klein, & McCaffrey, 1994). The correlation between the portfolio scores and the Uniform Writing assessment was moderate, as one might expect from other research; however, these same levels of correlations were found between writing portfolios and a multiple-choice math test. In addition, researchers found little difference between scores on papers students selected as "best pieces" and scores for the rest of the writing portfolio, a finding that is inconsistent with other evidence suggesting lack of generalizability across different writing tasks (Dunbar et al., 1991). Validity was also brought into question in terms of portfolio implementation. In keeping with local autonomy, researchers found great variability in teachers' implementation of portfolios, resulting in a wide range of types of work included in the portfolios, as well as a wide range of teacher support for the work, all of which would raise validity questions. Principals reported that although the assessment system placed sizable demands on schools for resources—especially in the area of time and support—they thought it was a worthwhile burden (Koretz, Stecher, Klein, McCaffrey, & Deibert, 1993). Because they felt the burden fell primarily on the teachers, the majority of principals provided release time to help ease the stress.

In contrast to statewide initiatives on portfolios, several school districts tried to implement literacy portfolios with the dual focus of accountability and improvement of instruction. Measurement researchers have studied both the ARTS PROPEL middle/high school writing portfolios in Pittsburgh and early literacy portfolios in Rochester, NY. Portfolios from Pittsburgh Public Schools (LeMahieu, Eresh, & Wallace, 1992) grew out of the ARTS PROPEL project, a privately funded project to design instruction-based assessment in visual arts, music, and imaginative writing. The writing portfolios were compiled by students in Grades 6–12 from a folder of their classroom writing. Using a set of guidelines, students selected four pieces (including drafts as well as final copies) and provided several written reflections on their writing processes, rationale for their selections, and the criteria they used for judging their work. As a result, there was less required commonality across portfolios than in the Vermont Portfolio Assessment. Portfolios were scored by a small group of highly trained district teachers and administrators using a rubric that reflected a decade-long district-wide history of professional development in writing. Judges assigned identical scores for 45% to 56% of the portfolios. Interrater correlations ranged from .80 to .84 across three scoring dimensions (accomplishment, processes/strategies, growth). In addition, researchers found that portfolio scores were highly related to the classroom opportunities students had in writing. Students in classrooms judged to have teachers with an "intense" writing practice scored significantly better than those in classrooms judged to be moderately intense or not intense at all. Interestingly, portfolio scores were most strongly correlated with a standardized reading test rather than with a standardized direct writing measure.

The Rochester portfolios grew out of curriculum reform initiated 3 years before portfolios were sequentially implemented in the primary grades. The portfolios were designed by teachers to be scored by classroom teachers rather than by external scorers. They include both required (e.g., writing samples, letter–sound assessments, observations, and anecdotal records) and optional pieces for reading and writing collected on a regular schedule. Teachers scored the portfolios and then assigned each child to a developmental stage specified in a "rubric." Supovitz, MacGowan, and Slattery (1997) compared the ratings given by Rochester classroom teachers and outside evaluators. They found interrater correlations between .58 and .77 with more consistency in reliability for writing than for reading. They found that external reviewers had difficulty scoring "thin" evidence found for reading both because few reading pieces were required in the portfolios and because teachers rarely included the required (or any additional) reading evidence. When reading evidence was included, they found that outside raters had difficulty judging the work and applying judgments to developmental levels. Findings also suggest that classroom teachers scored students significantly higher than outside raters did in the area of reading, where the lack of portfolio evidence was most likely supplemented by teachers' knowledge. There were no significant differences across scorers in writing. In a second study, Supovitz and Brennan (1997) found that gender, socioeconomic, and racial inequities existed when portfolio performance was compared to standardized test performance, although the Rochester portfolios closed the gaps between Blacks and Whites and widened the gaps between boys and girls.

Questions about the variability in portfolio contents across students have been raised with respect to the influence on reliability, but the issue is pertinent with respect to validity as well. If students receive different levels of support or if evidence is simply not available, then judgments about students' abilities will be open to question. Two studies shed light on this point. In one, Herman, Gearhart, and Baker (1993) were able to get satisfactory levels of interrater agreement for portfolios containing only narrative and summary writing, but they discovered that students' scores were substantially different across different contexts (standard writing prompt vs. portfolio work; analytic vs. holistic rubrics; scoring of individual pieces vs. the total portfolio; narrative vs. summaries). In fact, two-thirds of the students classified as competent using portfolio scores were not judged competent on the standard writing assessment. This led the researchers to question the validity of portfolio scores and to look further behind the actual work. So, in another study, Gearhart, Herman, Baker, and Whittaker (1993) asked, "Who's work is it?" that is contained in students' writing portfolio. Teachers were asked to rate the level of instructional support for writing assignments in students' portfolios (Grades 1–6). They found variability in the amount of support that teachers provided to students, time students spent on assignments, and extent to which work was copied. Furthermore, students received different levels of support depending on whether they were low or high achieving, and teachers with more portfolio experience provided more teacher support. Not only was student work influenced by the level of teacher support, but this support was provided differentially across students and classrooms.

In an effort to look more closely at classroom-embedded performance assessment, Shepard and her colleagues (Shepard et al., 1996) examined the effects of a professional development project to help teachers use performance assessments as part of regular instruction in reading and mathematics. They reasoned that embedded performance assessments would improve learning by introducing challenging tasks that were consistent with curricular goals and by helping teachers clarify their understanding of their students, thereby informing their instruction. This study represents a shift from the other studies in this section in two important ways: (a) It integrates expertise in subject matter, teacher change, and assessment in the design, implementation, and analysis; and (b) it integrates professional development with a study of new assessments and student learning. Although the authors reported no gains in student learning in reading on the outcome measure (Maryland School Performance Assessment Program), they offered explanations that are consistent with other studies in both the policy and literacy sections. Specifically, they found that although teachers were familiar with the district curricular framework before the project began, their motivation and instructional practices were not congruent with the framework. So what the researchers thought was a professional project to introduce classroom performance assessment, evolved into more of a project on literacy instruction and assessment. They concluded that performance assessments themselves are not enough to improve teaching—long-term professional development is also needed.

Measurement researchers tend to focus on the feasibility of new assessments from a technical perspective (reliability and validity) and on their desirability (consequential validity), often relying on statistical procedures and self-reports. Like policy researchers, measurement researchers generally have not distinguished among different subject areas either in their targets for study or in their conclusions and recommendations, even though Linn (1998), a prominent measurement researcher, has found differences in student performance across subject areas as well within subscales of the same subject area. Overall, the measurement research on literacy assessment reform suggests that there is still uncertainly about the ability of performance assessments to provide reliable and valid data for accountability. As we might expect, contextual factors such as the nature of the classroom instruction and support provided to students are difficult to control across classrooms. Another source of difficulty is the degree of teacher involvement and teacher choice in the assessment. Several studies suggest that if there were more standardization in the assessment artifacts, more expertise in the scorers, or more specificity in the outcomes, problems of reliability and validity could be addressed. However, these suggestions fly in the face of an important rationale for new standards and assessment—the professional development of teachers that is fostered through their involvement in the development and scoring of new assessments. In terms of consequential validity, data indicate that new assessments and standards have some influence on teachers' practices but that the accountability factor introduces stress for teachers and raises questions about how well they implement new assessments. Whether we look at issues of feasibility or desirability of new assessments, the studies in this section highlight the tension between assessment for accountability and assessment for instructional improvement, and they raise questions about the quality and the influence of assessment as a policy tool (see Linn, 1998, and Mehrens, 1998, for more in-depth measurement perspectives across subject areas).

THE LITERACY PERSPECTIVE

Literacy has been a centerpiece in efforts to push ambitious reforms in teaching and learning. National reports such as *A Nation at Risk* noted the failure of schools to provide the nation with a more literate populace as evidenced by allegedly declining verbal SAT scores and less than encouraging results of National Assessment of Educational Progress (NAEP) reading assessments. At the same time, the research community expressed concern about the skills-based conceptualizations that were guiding assessment and instruction in reading (see Curtis & Glaser, 1983; Guthrie & Kirsch, 1984; Linn, 1986); they were less concerned with writing because, as we noted previously, writing process and direct assessment of writing had gained popularity in the 1970s. These concerns led the National Academy of Education's Commission on Reading to issue the report entitled *Becoming a Nation of Readers* (BNR) (Anderson, Hiebert, Scott, & Wilkinson, 1985). The essence of BNR was that reading is a holistic, constructive process rather than the aggregate of a series of isolated subskills and that curriculum, instruction, and assessment should reflect this view of reading. In many respects, BNR represented a subject-matter-specific version of the national reports calling for more attention to higher order thinking, and it became a conceptual framework for literacy researchers who were becoming involved in local, state, and national policy initiatives.

A constructivist view of reading was also evident in a number of state efforts to develop curriculum frameworks, objectives, and assessments in reading and language arts. For example, in 1984, Michigan put forward a "new" definition of reading as "the process of constructing meaning through the dynamic interaction among the reader, the text, and the context of the reading situation" (Wixson & Peters, 1984). This definition then served as the basis for new state Essential Goals and Objectives in Reading

(Michigan State Board of Education, 1986). Given that BNR was written in Illinois, and Michigan was promoting a similar conceptualization of reading through its new definition, it is not surprising that these two states led the way in developing statewide reading assessments that better reflected constructivist reading theory and knowledge (Valencia, Pearson, Peters, & Wixson, 1989; Wixson, Peters, Weber, & Roeber, 1987).

Literacy researchers and state curriculum specialists worked together with measurement specialists in Michigan and Illinois to develop a new generation of reading assessments consistent with new views of reading and new student outcomes (Peters, Wixson, Valencia, & Pearson, 1993). Although there was precedent for this type of collaboration in the development of the NAEP tests, NAEP had little impact on the development of curriculum, instruction, and assessment at state, district, and school levels because it had been designed to provide information only at the national level. Rather, it was the large-scale reform efforts of the 1980s described previously in this chapter that brought together literacy researchers and curriculum and measurement specialists to effect the types of changes being called for by the research community, policymakers, and the public at large.

The constructivist perspective on reading being promoted in various national and state policy documents also influenced the development in of a new Reading Framework for NAEP reading tests. The 1992 Reading Framework, which was also used in 1994 and 1998, indicated that, "Reading for meaning involves a dynamic, complex interaction among three elements: the reader, the text, and the context" (National Assessment Governing Board, p. 10). Although NAEP continued to use direct writing assessment as it had done in the past, it now included some open-ended reading items to address the new definition of reading and recommendations for new forms of reading assessment. The first year this Reading Framework was in effect was also the first year of the voluntary, trial program to administer NAEP in a way that allowed for state-by-state comparisons, and the year in which the NAEP special study on oral reading fluency was conducted (Pinnell et al., 1995). Both of these innovations came in response to demands by many that NAEP respond to higher levels of accountability in general and specifically in the area of reading.

With the publication of the California English-Language Arts Framework in 1987, the treatment of reading and writing as separate subject areas began to give way to the idea of integrated language arts consisting of listening, speaking, reading, and writing. "Language arts became a discipline concerned with major universal themes, the human condition, exploring life experiences, and social agendas introduced through quality literature" (Gonzales & Grubb, 1997, p. 696). The California Framework pushed the definition of reading and language arts beyond a purely constructivist perspective to a more social-constructivist perspective with its emphasis on "transactions" as opposed to interactions with text and considerations of the sociocultural experiences students bring to text.

Prominent among the policy initiatives adopted by the California State Department of Education to support its framework was the California Learning Assessment System (CLAS). The CLAS reading assessment was designed to evaluate the success of the language arts curriculum, and to help districts and schools understand how well students were internalizing the strategies that encourage them to construct understandings beyond the school setting. CLAS took seriously the call for integration of the language arts by including open-ended written responses to reading selections, having students work collaboratively on some sections of the assessment, and tying some of the direct writing prompts to reading selections (Weiss, 1994).

In 1992, when the new CLAS assessments were being implemented, the contract to develop national English language arts standards was let by the U.S. Department of Education (DOE) to the Center for the Study of Reading at the University of Illinois in collaboration with the International Reading Association (IRA) and the National

Council of Teachers of English (NCTE). Before these standards were completed, however, the contract was terminated by the U.S. DOE for lack of satisfactory progress reflecting differences in perceptions about what constitute appropriate standards in English language arts. The project continued under the auspices of IRA and NCTE and concluded with the publication of the Standards for English Language Arts in 1996.

Consistent with the California Framework, the NCTE/IRA standards defined English language arts as listening, speaking, reading, writing, viewing, and representing. By the time the NCTE/IRA standards were published in 1996, there was widespread concern about the direction in which constructivist and sociocultural views of teaching and learning were taking curriculum, instruction, and assessment in all subject areas including reading. Legislation to continue funding for CLAS was vetoed by Governor Wilson in 1994 after yielding to pressure from conservative groups (Gonzales & Grubb, 1997), and the results of the 1992 and 1994 NAEP state-by-state comparisons placed California close to the bottom of the rankings in reading (Campbell, Donahue, Reese, & Phillips, 1996; Mullis, Campbell, & Farstrup, 1993). The "whole-language" California framework was blamed for the failure of many California children to learn to read, fueling a nationwide resurgence of the "reading wars" that have surfaced every 10 or 20 years since the turn of the century (e.g., Chall, 1967; Flesch, 1955).

Most recently, there has been a shift away from attention on comprehension, writing, and integrated language arts to early reading, especially phonemic awareness and phonics. In 1998, some policymakers and educators promoted a return to skills-based definitions of reading that emphasized decoding as the only or primary concern of reading instruction. At the state level, there was a virtual firestorm of legislation focused on early reading that included new curriculum frameworks and standards, assessment mandates, textbook adoption guidelines, and mandates for teacher credentialing and professional development. For the first time since its inception in the mid 1970s, the U.S. DOE funded the National Center for Improvement of Early Reading Achievement (CIERA) in 1997. At the same time, the National Research Council of the National Academy of Science commissioned a blue-ribbon panel report on preventing reading difficulties (National Research Council, 1998) and the National Institute for Child Health Development (NICHD) impaneled a group of experts to point educators and policymakers to the best research in reading instruction. With these most recent events, national involvement in standards, assessment, and instructional strategies gained momentum.

The policy-oriented research we review in this section focuses on three areas related to literacy standards and assessments—on-demand reading and writing assessments, classroom-based assessments such as portfolios, and statewide language arts standards. What distinguishes policy-oriented research conducted by literacy researchers—in comparison with policy and measurement researchers—is a primary emphasis on the subject-matter content of standards and assessment as well as their validity and consistency with current literacy theory and research. Literacy researchers also focus on ways that policies shape classroom literacy practices, frequently gathering direct evidence of teaching and of student learning as well as self-reported responses to policy. Literacy researchers tend to be less interested in the overall, or more systemic, effects of policy and reform.

Research

On-Demand Performance Assessments.   Several literacy researchers have explored the influence of on-demand literacy assessments. In a series of studies, literacy researchers at NRRC (Afflerbach, Almasi, Guthrie, & Schafer, 1996; Almasi,

Afflerbach, Guthrie, & Schafer, 1995; Guthrie, Schafer, Afflerbach, & Almasi, 1994) investigated the effects of the Maryland State Performance Assessment Program (MSPAP), a multipronged reform that includes learning outcomes, a performance assessment, guidelines for school decision making, and suggestions for staff development. Using semistructured interviews, similar to those used by measurement researchers, they found that, 1 year after implementation, there was some limited understanding of the Maryland learning outcomes among country/district language arts administrators but no widespread consensus on the reading/language arts outcomes included in the MSPAP. Nevertheless, the administrators believed that the performance assessment was moderately aligned with their local curricula.

Although there was little-to-no reported change in school governance or teacher decision-making, administrators did report some change in instructional practices, including integrating reading and writing within content areas and the use of more trade books. In schools nominated as implementing positive innovations in response to MSPAP, teachers and administrators reported changes in instructional tasks, methods, materials, and learning environments that reflected the nature of the MSPAP and learner outcomes in literacy. They also reported administrative support for change, including professional development, and a positive influence on students' motivation for reading and writing. The researchers also identified several barriers to the implementation even in these schools that were identified as successful implementors: lack of alignment between classroom instruction and assessment and the MSPAP assessment; insufficient resources such as time and money for professional development; testing logistics; and communication between the state and schools about the rationale and nature of the assessment program. They suggested that better communication and support is needed between state and local school districts if implementation is to be effective; change, they argued, requires more than development of assessment materials and procedures.

Other researchers examined more directly the relationship between new statewide writing assessments and classroom instruction. Two studies highlighted the difficulties in achieving effective reciprocity between instructional practice and assessment. Goldberg, Roswell and Michaels (1995/1996) examined whether the Maryland School Performance Assessment (MSPAP) in writing, which required students to engage in the writing process (including drafting, peer response, revision, and writing a final draft), produced improved performance. Specifically, researchers were interested in the extent to which students engaged in effective peer response, revision, and final drafts during testing. Using results from the MSPAP and observations from test taking in Grades 3, 5, and 8, they found that students did not use revision or peer response to improve their final writing; their changes were minimal and focused on surface-level features, and their peer responses were unengaged. Goldberg et al. suggested that the constraints of large-scale assessment (i.e., assigned topics, limited and prescribed time blocks, use of revision and response worksheet, collaboration with assigned partners rather than classmates) may inhibit students' motivation and ability to engage in revision and peer response. They concluded that testing situations may not be able to mirror some aspects of good instructional practice.

Similarly, Loofbourrow (1994) conducted a case study of how two eighth-grade teachers interpreted and enacted the California Assessment Program (CAP) in writing into their classroom instruction. This study was conducted at a time when CAP was a high-stakes assessment and when it was not aligned with California curriculum guidelines for teaching writing. She found that when there was misalignment between a high-stakes test and statewide recommendations for curriculum and instruction, teachers attended more to the form and content of the assessment. In this case, although middle school teachers had students write across a wider variety of genres (an emphasis of both CAP and instructional recommendations), most of their writing assignments mirrored the test-like setting of CAP (e.g. limited time, one- to two-page writing assignments, teacher-assigned topic, focus on one of the eight CAP modes, emphasis on form over function). Many sound curricular and instructional recommendations were put aside as teachers attended to the specific form and content of the assessment.

Allington and his colleagues took a different approach to on-demand assessments, exploring the effects of on-demand assessment policies on special needs students and on the system as a whole. In several studies, Allington and McGill-Franzen (1992a, 1992b; McGill-Franzen & Allington, 1993) highlighted the changes in the incidence of retention, remediation, and identification of students as handicapped across a 10-year period when New York State increased high-stakes assessment and accountability. An increasing proportion of elementary children were retained or identified as handicapped in Grades K–2, the grades that preceded the Grade 3 high-stakes reading assessment. There was no corresponding trend for remediation. The researchers suggested that although it was unlikely that the reform was intended to increase numbers of children retained or placed in special education, the net effect was that these low-achieving students were removed or delayed from the accountability stream. As a result, scores at the targeted grades were likely to rise without improved learning—the sample of students tested was simply limited. In fact, these researchers found that across all grades, schools that had been historically low-performing, but since the implementation of high-stakes assessment seemed to be improving, had three times the number of students identified for special education or retained as compared with historically high-performing schools. Retention and identification, they argued, are expensive and ineffective ways to produce real gains.

Classroom-Based Assessment.   Most studies of classroom-based assessment literacy have investigated the effects of portfolio assessment; some have focused on statewide policies, and others on district-wide efforts. Two interesting lines of research have come from literacy researchers who have examined effects of statewide writing portfolio assessments in Vermont and Kentucky. Studies of the Vermont writing portfolio (Lipson, 1997; Lipson & Mosenthal, 1997; Mosenthal, Lipson, Mekkelsen, Daniels, & Jiron, 1996, Mosenthal, Mekkelsen, & Jiron, 1997) examined teachers' perspectives on the influence of the portfolio mandate and how they used the portfolios in classroom instruction and assessment. Unlike the research on Vermont portfolios cited in the previous assessment section, this work focused specifically on the writing portfolio and used a combination of surveys, interviews, and in-depth case studies and observations of 12 teachers. In addition, these researchers analyzed their findings in terms of teachers' different theoretical perspectives and beliefs about writing instruction.

Surveys were administered to fifth-grade teachers before and after the first year of implementation. The majority of teachers reported that their writing instruction had improved; they incorporated more writing into their classrooms and, once more writing was in place, they used the portfolio scoring criteria as part of their instructional talk with students. Although teachers embraced portfolios for instructional purposes, they did not seem to use portfolios or the criteria for assessing writing in the classroom, which suggested that they may not have a "shared standard" for student performance. What's more, teachers were strongly opposed to the scoring and public reporting of results.

Most interesting, surveys and observations revealed that teachers with different beliefs about teaching writing changed in different ways. Those who already emphasized writing processes in their instruction felt most positively about the state assessment but changed very little because they had little need to change. In contrast, those teachers who were more dependent on curriculum and less child centered used portfolios for organizing writing, but didn't integrate them into their teaching. Finally, those teachers who paid little attention to writing processes or portfolios were most negative and changed their practices very little.

The Kentucky writing portfolios also have been studied by literacy researchers. Bridge, Compton-Hall, and Cantrell (1997) replicated a 1982 study to determine changes in the amount and type of writing elementary students were engaged in and the nature of writing instruction provided by teachers. They studied changes in one school district using written surveys of more than 200 teachers and classroom observations of teachers' instruction and writing activities of targeted students in 12 classrooms. Across both observations and surveys, they found a twofold increase in amount of time students spent engaged in writing as compared to 1982; the biggest increase occurred at Grade 1. This finding confirms results of other studies of reform in Kentucky (Bridge, 1994; Raths & Fanning, 1993).

Bridge et al. also looked closely at quality of the writing. They found a sizable increase in the amount of time spent on higher level writing tasks such as crafting and revising and a decrease in the time students spent filling in words on worksheets or copying, which were dominant in 1982. In addition, teachers reported major changes in the way they responded to students' writing, shifting to greater use of teacher and group conferences and a decrease of assigning grades to students writing. Teachers reported that, in large part, changes in their writing instruction could be attributed to the Kentucky assessments, although the authors acknowledged that most teachers were more knowledgeable about the writing process in 1995 than in 1982. Although more than 50% of teachers reported substantive changes in their writing instruction since the Kentucky Education Reform Act (KERA), about one third of them reported little change because their instruction was already in line with the new assessments. Like the Vermont studies, this study highlights the increase in amount of writing and the differential impact of policy on teachers whose instruction is more or less aligned with new assessments.

A slightly different perspective on the Kentucky reform comes from a case study of nine high school English teachers faced with implementing the state portfolios in the second year of the mandate (Callahan, 1997). This study found that teachers had not yet received much professional development regarding the assessment and that they viewed the portfolio as a "test of their competence." Consequently, although the assessment did change the amount and kind of writing students did to fit with portfolio requirements and prompted teachers to internalize and use scoring criteria during instruction, teachers put their energy into "the visible, procedural elements of the assessment," rather than integrating it into their instruction. It remained a separate and intimidating burden to them. This lack of attention to professional development is also reported in studies by Gooden (1996) and by Miller, Hayes, and Atkinson (1997). Their work suggests that in some states, having a high-stakes assessment in place was assumed to be sufficient to promote teacher change or to encourage local districts to provide support for change. Unfortunately, this didn't happen.

Several literacy researchers have focused on classroom-based assessment at the district level (Hoffman et al., 1996; Salinger & Chittenden, 1994; Valencia & Au, 1997). In all three of these studies, the researchers were interested in whether assessments could serve the dual purpose of improving instruction and providing accountability information. And in all cases, the researchers worked directly with teachers and school districts in ongoing professional development activities focused on literacy curriculum and instruction as well as assessment implementation. Two studies focused early literacy assessment at the district level—the South Brunswick Early Literacy Portfolio (Salinger & Chittenden, 1994) and the Primary Assessment of Language Arts and Mathematics (PALM) (Hoffman et al., 1996). The South Brunswick portfolio included specific contents aimed at early literacy (K–2), and specific procedures and timelines for data collection. Using a developmental scale, teachers rated students on one component, strategies for making sense of and with print. The PALM model was somewhat different in that it combined three assessment elements: classroom-embedded assessments, a week-long on-demand assessment, and "taking a closer look" assessments, which teachers used to gather additional information on particular students. The on-demand assessment and a developmental profile based on classroom-embedded and "take a closer look" information were scored. Using a combination of artifacts, interviews, and documents as data sources, Hoffman et al. and Salinger and Chittenden combined qualitative and quantitative analyses. In both studies, teachers reported that they were able to use assessment information for instructional purposes and that using these assessments was consistent with and enhanced their practice. Although teachers at both sites struggled with management and time issues, they all felt that the results justified the effort Teachers viewed participation in professional development as critical to their success. Student data from both sites were able to be reliably scored, making the assessments useful for accountability purposes at a district level. In addition, statistical analysis of the PALM data revealed that all three components of PALM (classroom-embedded, on-demand, taking a closer look) contributed significantly to the prediction of students' scores on a norm-referenced reading test.

The third example in this group of district-level efforts involved a cross-district study (Au & Valencia, 1997; Valencia & Au, 1997). This approach is different from others in that it addressed the question of whether common but not identical curriculum standards and portfolio structures could produce effective cross-site analysis and cross-site teacher learning. In addition, it examined the contextual factors that influenced portfolio implementation and used a portfolio model in which students chose a substantial number of pieces. Valencia and Au found that classroom portfolios contained artifacts consistent with the constructivist literacy curriculum frameworks at both sites. Although teachers were expected to include several required or "on-demand" pieces, some portfolios were missing needed evidence. This was a result of different emphases in different classrooms and teachers' difficulty documenting particular aspects of reading, yet once teachers were aware of what was missing, they were confident they could include it. Teachers reached a high level of agreement when rating portfolios from both sites, and they enhanced their knowledge of teaching, learning, and assessment through the scoring process. Valencia and Au suggested that results were a function of a supportive system for implementation that included district support, low-stakes, long-term professional development focused on assessment and instruction, and gradual implementation with an emphasis first on curriculum and instruction. They also suggested that the combination of required and optional pieces and the scoring process encouraged the flexibility of implementation and specificity of performance standards needed for portfolios to address both accountability and improved instruction.

Stephens et al. (1995) also addressed contextual influences in their study of the relationship between assessment and instruction. Using in-depth case studies of elementary schools in four school districts, they examined how decisions were made and how that process influenced the relationship between assessment and instruction. Qualitative analysis revealed that the relationship was not straightforward; the unique decision-making model in each district influenced the relationship. When the teachers had little authority or power over instructional decision making, or when administrators were controlled by district staff, "assessment-as-test" drove instruction. In other words, when responsibility and accountability were to external forces, tests did drive instruction, and not necessarily in positive ways. When the culture of the district was one of responsibility to individual learners and decisions were based on individual or collective perspectives of teachers, "assessment as test" did not appear to drive instruction. Stephens et al. raised the question of whether reform aimed at teacher empowerment can coexist with external accountability when school culture exerts such a strong force on teachers' practice.

Language Arts Standards.   Few literacy researchers have conducted research aimed directly at either state or national English language arts and, as we noted previously, policy researchers interested in standards often analyze them in terms of larger reforms efforts, without specific regard for subject area. Three types of studies characterize the nature of standards research from a literacy perspective: document analysis, study of teachers' practices, and the alignment of standards with assessment.

Wixson and Dutro (1999) conducted a document analysis of 42 state standards in early reading/language arts as a way to gauge how the variability in standards might influence their translation into local curriculum, instruction, and assessment. They found that the majority of state documents did not provide specific benchmarks or outcomes at Grades K–3, that they varied in the way they conceptualized and organized the area of reading, and that many included inappropriate content and/or ignored important content. When documents did provide benchmarks, many did not provide a logical developmental progression across grades, and many of the benchmarks themselves were overly specific or overly broad. In the former case, Wixson and Dutro concluded, districts are provided insufficient guidance; in the later, the curriculum becomes prescriptive without much flexibility for local interpretation. They recommended balance between specificity and generality if standards are to help local educators engage in conversation needed to advance teaching and learning.

In a different approach to examining standards, McGill-Franzen and Ward (1997) first reviewed documents to determine the fit between New York State Language Arts and Social Studies frameworks with national standards; then they conducted case study interviews with K–4 teachers in four districts to determine how state standards were incorporated into teachers' practices. All the participants in their case studies had been involved in some sort of school-wide language arts curriculum development projects aimed at helping teachers reconceptualize teaching. Consistent with Wixson and Dutro's (in press) recommendations, they found New York State standards reflected the national standards in orientation to reading process and learning, and actually went beyond national standards to provide a level of specificity that helps teachers know what students should know and be able to do at different developmental levels. However, they also found that teachers interpreted the state standards differentially. If teachers were under pressure to improve scores on tests (which were not aligned with the standards), and worked under conditions that restricted their authority and responsibility for instructional decision making, they were less likely to reconceptualize curriculum and evaluation in their schools. Since this study, New York State has restructured its assessments to align with its curriculum. We do not yet have data to know if the results of McGill-Franzen and Ward (1997) will be replicated with the new assessments.

The last approach to research on standards is found in a study by Bruce, Osborn, and Commeyras (1993) in which they examined the alignment between NAEP Reading assessment items and the NAEP reading framework (standards). Using data from interviews, expert panels, and surveys of hundreds of literacy educators, Bruce et al. concluded that although most literacy experts agreed that the NAEP framework reflected current research and practice, the experts judged the alignment between framework and test items to be "murky." Items could not be mapped clearly onto the framework and, in practice, the items often failed to capture the intent behind the framework. Even with a sound framework, the translation into large-scale assessment items was problematic.

Literacy researchers bring a deliberate subject-matter focus to bear on questions of standards and assessment. For the most part, they look more deeply at literacy than either policy or measurement researchers by examining specific aspects of literacy instruction (e.g., writing process, qualities of writing, alignment of assessment with constructivist curriculum frameworks in literacy, specificity of state standards) and by situating much of their work in classrooms or in direct interactions with teachers. The studies in this section suggest that instructional change in language arts does occur with reform but that it is mediated by teachers' beliefs, knowledge, and their sense of accountability pressure. In studies that integrate professional development with assessment reform, results are most positive both in terms of teachers' learning and attitudes toward change, and in terms of useable assessment information; reform without this support seems to produce more surface-level change and questionable assessment practices. At the same time, the work on standards and implementation of new assessments suggests that the translation from literacy research to standards and from standards to assessment is not straightforward. Overall, an emerging theme is one of tension between the need for accountability and specificity on the one hand, and teacher decision making and flexibility in interpretation on the other.

CONCLUSIONS AND FUTURE DIRECTIONS

Throughout this review we have attended to both the nature of policy-oriented research on literacy standards and assessments and the impact of standards and assessment on literacy practice and student learning. Our conclusions address both of these issues.

With regard to the nature of policy-oriented research, it is clear that the research differs with regard to questions, methods, and audience as a function of the perspective from which it arises. In general, we see policy researchers concerned with broad reforms involving standards, assessments, reorganization, governance, and the like; literacy is simply one of the subjects, and standards and assessment are two of "tools" or levers of reform they study. Policy researchers' questions focus on the system, and their data are gathered through teachers' reported and actual practices. For the most part, we found few policy researchers distinguishing among subject areas within policy or spending extended time in literacy classrooms. Measurement researchers, as we might expect, are most interested in the assessment components of reform and are particularly concerned with validity issues and with the psychometric qualities of new assessments that are needed for accountability and policy purposes. For the most part, they rely on statistical analysis and, to some extent, self-reports, interviews, and artifacts to address their questions. And literacy researchers generally ask questions about instruction and learning in relation to research and theory. Do new standards and assessments result in better reading and writing instruction? Do they advance teacher understanding? Are the reforms consistent with sound research and theory on literacy learning? Just as literacy is the vehicle for many policy studies, policy is the vehicle for many literacy studies. Literacy researchers typically look closely at actual classroom practices, teachers' understanding, and artifacts of students literacy learning, and they work more directly with teachers than either policy or measurement researchers. For the most part, their new assessments are not subjected to the rigor of measurement researchers' criteria, and the policy contexts for their work are not considered in a systemic way.

The picture that emerges is a trade-off between general and in-depth understandings. Studies that address general questions provide information that is useful for understanding the larger issues of systemic reform such as restructuring, governance, standards, and assessment, and the contexts in which these reforms are implemented. In contrast, research that addresses questions about classroom practice in relation to specific subject matter provides insight into what happens at the individual teacher and student levels. It attends to teacher understanding and practice, and student learning, often without specific attention to the policy environment in which change is enacted. As policy-oriented research grows and matures, we see a greater need to attend to both the macro and micro view of reform, practice, and learning, and we suspect there will be more crossover among the studies representing policy, measurement, and literacy perspectives.

With respect to the influence of policy, it is clear that literacy standards and assessment do have an influence on teachers' beliefs and practice, but the influence is not always in the expected or the desired direction. The effect is mediated by a large number of factors such as teachers' knowledge, beliefs, and existing practices; the economic, social, philosophical, and political conditions of the school or district; the stakes attached to the policy; and the quality of the support and lines of communication provided to teachers and administrators. It is equally clear that policy by itself is not sufficient to promote desired change; simply implementing new assessments or creating new standards does not insure improved teaching or learning. What is less clear, however, is just what it would take to promote change in the desired direction or to insure improved teaching and learning. To be sure, discipline-specific professional development is implicated in many studies, but we need to know more about both professional development processes and the quality of those processes. How, for example, do teachers and districts learn about new literacy standards and assessments? How are districts and teachers supported to understand the theory and research that underlie new assessments or new content standards? How do these experiences shape teachers' understanding and practices? What are effective models for professional development? Not only are these important questions for educators but they are critical to policymakers who are being asked to support professional development as part of reform (Elliott, 1996; Hart, 1996).

Among the factors mediating the effects on literacy teaching and learning, the research suggests that more specificity in standards and assessment promotes changes in the desired direction. A caution we would offer in this regard, however, is that many of the deeper levels of change in teacher beliefs and practices associated with literacy learning do not lend themselves to simple directives. There is a very fine line between offering sufficient guidance for teachers and districts to undertake substantive change and being prescriptive in ways that work against teacher learning, decision making, and flexibility. Similarly, the influence of standards and assessments is likely mediated by teachers' and administrators' stance toward policy—do they see policy as a means for monitoring, controlling, or helping educators do their work? Why, for example, would teachers bring impoverished understandings of assessments and standards to policy work in their districts yet demonstrate deep understanding in their classrooms? How do the messages teachers receive about standards and assessments fit or conflict with other policies in their environments such as mandated curriculum and materials, alternative teacher certification programs, site-based decision making, and the like?

And finally, there is still uncertainty about the quality of the new literacy assessments and standards that must stand the test of scrutiny of policymakers outside education as well as educators themselves. It seems that if the tools themselves are problematic, political credibility and deeper order change are highly improbable. That said, we also suggest that although there is a move in 1998 away from the more elaborate forms of performance assessments (i.e., California, Arizona, Kentucky), these decisions are rarely based on psychometric qualities alone; policy, resources, and politics weigh heavily in decisions about the feasibility and desirability of new assessments and new standards.

We conclude from our synthesis that there is a pressing need to conduct research on policy issues, such as standards and assessments, with specific attention to subject matter. There has been an almost tacit assumption among policy and measurement researchers that whatever holds true for one subject matter will likely be the case for others. When there are possibilities to look across subject areas such as mathematics and literacy, the analyses are rarely done. More important, however, is attention to depth of understanding of literacy processes, learning, and instruction. At the heart of this issue are questions about what it means to read and write with understanding; what teaching for understanding looks like in different classrooms; and what constitutes the domain of English language arts curriculum. Future research must look both across and within the subject matter of literacy; this requires subject-matter expertise and it requires more than self-report data.

Issues of student achievement will need to be confronted as well. Few studies we reviewed included direct measures of student learning. In one sense, this is understandable because most reform is fairly new and change is a long-term process. Nevertheless, pressure is mounting on educators to show results in terms of achievement. Future researchers will need to address the challenge, finding meaningful ways to document student achievement while at the same time documenting formative measures of progress such as parents' understanding of instructional goals, teachers' priorities and their practice, teacher understanding, and even more surface level changes in materials and activities.

As we write this chapter in the late 1990s, there continues to be a groundswell of new policies related to literacy standards and assessment, and there is new interest in policies related to instructional strategies. Whether we like it or not, literacy researchers have been drawn into policy. At worst we will be recipients of policy; at best we will be informers of policy. In our opinion, the best way to influence policy and teacher development is for policy, measurement, and literacy researchers to work together and to communicate the findings of their collaborative work in a wide range of journals and reports, and through participation in state and national councils. Literacy researchers need to become knowledgeable about policy research and about the policy contexts in which their research is conducted. At the same time, we must reach out to policy researchers and measurement researchers, bringing to their work a deep understanding of the subject matter of literacy and the pedagogical content knowledge needed to teach well. Without this collaborative commitment, policy will not reflect or inform meaningful changes in literacy teaching and learning; measurement will not encourage substantive instructional change or provide useful assessment information to literacy educators; and literacy educators will not have a voice in policy and measurement arenas. With a collaborative research agenda and a wider audience, we can improve the lives of children and the lives of teachers.

REFERENCES

Afflerbach, P. P., Almasi, J., Guthrie, J. T., & Schafer, W. (1996). *Barriers to implementation of a statewide performance program: School personnel perspectives* (Reading Research Rep. No. 51). Athens, GA: National Reading Research Center.

Allington, R. L., & McGill-Franzen, A. (1992a). Unintended effects of educational reform in New York. *Educational Policy, 6*, 397–414.

Allington, R. L., & McGill-Franzen, A. (1992b). Does high stakes testing improve school effectiveness? *Spectrum, 10*, 3–12.

Almasi, J. F., Afflerbach, P. P., Guthrie, J. T., & Schafer, W. D. (1995). *Effects of a statewide performance assessment program on classroom instructional practice in literacy* (Reading Research Rep. No. 32). Athens, GA: National Reading Research Center.

Anderson, R. C., Hiebert, E., Scott, J. A., & Wilkinson, A. G. (1985). *Becoming a nation of readers: The report of the commission on reading.* Washington, DC: National Institute of Education.

Aschbacher, P. R. (1994). Helping educators to develop and use alternative assessments: Barriers and facilitators. *Educational Policy, 8*, 202–223.

Au, K. H. & Valencia, S. W. (1997). The complexities of portfolio assessment. In D. Hansen & N. Burbules (Eds.), *Teaching and its predicaments* (pp. 123–144). Boulder, CO: Westview.

Ball, D. L., & Cohen, D. K. (1995, April). *What does the educational system bring to learning a new pedagogy of reading or mathematics?* Paper presented at the annual meeting of American Educational Research Association, San Francisco, CA.

Bridge, C. A. (1994). Implementing large scale change in literacy instruction. In C. Kinzer & D. Leu (Eds.), *Multidimensional aspects of literacy research, theory, and practice: Forty-third yearbook of the National Reading Conference* (pp. 257–265). Chicago: National Reading Conference.

Bridge, C. A., Compton-Hall, M., & Cantrell, S. C. (1997). Classroom writing practices revisited: The effects of statewide reform on writing instruction. *Elementary School Journal, 98*, 151–170.

Bruce, B., Osborn, J., & Commeyras, M. (1993). Contention and consensus: The development of the 1992 National Assessment of Educational Progress in reading. *Educational Assessment, 1*, 225–254.

California Department of Education. (1987). *English-language arts framework for California public schools.* Sacramento, CA: Author.

Callahan, S. (1997). Tests worth taking?: Using portfolios for accountability in Kentucky. *Research in the Teaching of English, 31*, 295–336.

Campbell, J. R., Donahue, P. L., Reese, C. M., & Phillips, G. W. (1996). *NAEP 1994 reading reports card for the nation and the states.* Washington, DC: Government Printing Office.

Chall, J. (1967). *Learning to read: The great debate.* New York: McGraw-Hill.

Cohen, D. K. (1995). What is the system in systemic reform? *Educational Researcher, 24*(9), 11–17.

Cohen, D. K., & Spillane, J. (1992). Policy and practice: The relations between governance and instruction. In G. Grant (Ed.), *The review of research in education* (pp. 3–49). Washington, DC: American Educational Research Association.

Cuban, L. (1990). Reforming again, again, and again. *Educational Researcher, 19*(1), 3–13.

Curtis, M. E., & Glaser, R. (1983). Reading theory and the assessment of reading achievement. *Journal of Educational Measurement, 20*, 133–148.

Darling-Hammond, L. (1990). Instructional policy into practice: "The power of the bottom over the top." *Educational Evaluation and Policy Analysis, 12*, 233–241.

Dunbar, S. B., Koretz, D. M., & Hoover, H. D. (1992). Quality control in the development and use of performance assessments. *Applied Measurement in Education, 4*, 289–303.

Elliott, E. J. (1996). Literacy: From policy to practice. *Journal of Literacy Research, 28*, 590–595.

Elmore, R. F. (1990). Introduction: On changing the structure of public schools. In R. F. Elmore (Ed.), *Restructuring schools: The next generation of educational reform* (pp. 1–28). San Francisco: Jossey-Bass.

Firestone, W. A., Fuhrman, S. H., & Kirst, M. W. (1989). *The progress of reform: An appraisal of state education initiatives.* New Brunswick, NJ: Consortium for Policy Research in Education, Rutgers University.

Flesch, R. (1955). *Why Johnny can't read.* New York: Harper & Brothers.

Freedman, S. W. (1993). Linking large-scale testing and classroom portfolio assessments of student writing. *Educational Assessment, 1*, 27–52.

Fullan, M. G., & Miles, M. B. (1992). Getting reform right: What works and what doesn't. *Phi Delta Kappan, 73*, 744–752.

Gearhart, M., Herman, J. L., Baker, E. L., & Whittaker, A. K. (1993). *Whose work is it? A question for the validity of large-scale portfolio assessment* (CSE Tech. Rep. No. 363). Los Angeles: National Center for the Research on Evaluation, Standards, and Student Testing, University of California.

Goertz, M. E., Floden, R. E., & O'Day, J. (1995). *Studies of education reform: systemic reform (Vol. 1): Findings and conclusions.* New Brunswick, NJ: Consortium for Policy Research in Education, Rutgers University.

Goldberg, G. L., Roswell, B. S., & Michaels, H. (1995/1996). Can assessment mirror instruction? A look at peer response and revision in a large-scale writing test. *Educational Assessment, 3*(4), 287–314.

Gonzales, P. C., & Grubb, M. (1997). California's literature-based curriculum and the California literature project. In J. Flood, S. B. Heath, & D. Lapp (Eds.), *Handbook for literacy educators: Research on teaching and communicative and visual arts* (pp. 695–703). Newark, DE: International Reading Association.

Gooden, S. (1996). A comparison of writing assessment portfolios in two states: Implications for large-scale writing assessment. In D. J. Leu, C. K. Kinzer, & K. A. Hinchman (Eds.), *Literacies for the 21st century: Research and practice: Forty-fifth yearbook of the National Reading Conference* (pp. 88–99). Chicago: National Reading Conference.

Guthrie, J. T., & Kirsch, I. (1984). The emergent perspective on literacy. *Phi Delta Kappan, 65*, 351–355.

Guthrie, J. T., Schafer, W. D., Afflerbach, P. P., & Almasi, J. F. (1994). *Systemic reform of literacy education: State and district-level policy changes in Maryland* (Reading Research Rep. No. 27). Athens, GA: National Reading Research Center.

Haney, W. (1991). We must take care: Fitting assessments to functions. In V. Perrone (Ed.), *Expanding student assessment* (pp. 142–163). Alexandria, VA: Association for Supervision and Curriculum Development.

Hart, G. K. (1996). A policymaker's response. *Journal of Literacy Research, 28*, 596–601.

Herman, J. L. (1991). Research in cognition and learning: Implications for achievement testing practice. In M. C. Wittrock & E. L. Baker (Eds.), *Testing and cognition* (pp. 154–165). Englewood Cliffs, NJ: Prentice Hall.

Herman, J. L., & Golan, S. (1993). The effects of standardized testing on teaching and schools. *Educational Measurement: Issues and Practice, 12*(4), 20–25, 41–42.

Herman, J. L., Gearhart, M., & Baker, E. L. (1993). Assessing writing portfolios: Issues in the validity and meaning of scores. *Educational Assessment, 1*, 201–224.

Hieronymus, A. N., Hoover, H. D., Cantor, N. K., & Oberley, K. R. (1987). *Writing supplement teacher's guide: Iowa Tests of Basic Skills.* Chicago: Riverside.

Hoffman, J. V., Worthy, J., Roser, N. L., McKool, S. S., Rutherford, W. L., & Strecker, S. (1996). Performance assessment in first grade classrooms: The PALM model. In D. J. Leu, C. K. Kinzer, & K. A. Hinchman (Eds.), *Literacies for the 21st century: Research and practice: Forty-fifth yearbook of the National Reading Conference* (pp. 100–112). Chicago: National Reading Conference.

Jennings, N. E. (1995). *Interpreting policy in real classrooms: Case studies of state reform and teacher practice.* New York: Teachers College Press.

Koretz, D. M., Barron, S., Mitchell, K. J., & Stecher, B. M. (1996). *Perceived effects of the Kentucky Instructional Results Information System (KIRIS).* Santa Monica, CA: RAND.

Koretz, D., McCaffrey, D., Klein, S., Bell, R., & Stecher, B. (1993). *The reliability of scores from the 1992 Vermont Portfolio Assessment Program* (CSE Tech. Rep. No. 355). Los Angeles: RAND Institute on Education and Training, National Center for Research on Evaluation, Standards, and Student Testing.

Koretz, D., Mitchell, K., Barron, S., & Keith, S. (1996). Final *report: Perceived effects of the Maryland School Performance Assessment Program* (CSE Tech. Rep. No. 409). Los Angeles: National Center for Research on Evaluation, Standards, and Student Testing, University of California.

Koretz, D., Stecher, B., & Deibert, E. (1992). *The Vermont Portfolio Assessment Program: Interim report on implementation and impact, 1991–92 school year* (CSE Tech. Rep. No. 350). Los Angeles: National Center for Research on Evaluation, Standards, and Student Testing, University of California.

Koretz, D., Stecher, B., Klein, S., & McCaffrey, D. (1994). The Vermont Portfolio Assessment Program: Findings and implications. *Educational Measurement: Issues and Practice, 13*(3), 5–16.

Koretz, D., Stecher, B., Klein, S., McCaffrey, D., & Deibert, E. (1993). *Can portfolios assess student performance and influence instruction? The 1991–1992 Vermont experience* (CSE Tech. Rep. No. 371). Los Angeles: National Center for the Research on Evaluation, Standards, and Student Testing, University of California.

LeMahieu, P. G., Eresh, J. T., & Wallace, R. C. (1992). Using student portfolios for a public accounting. *School Administrator, 49*(11), 8–15.

Lindle, J. C., Petrosko, J., & Pankratz, R. (1997, May). *1996 Review of research on the Kentucky education reform act.* Frankfort, KY: Kentucky Institute for Education Research.

Linn, R. L. (1986). Educational testing and assessment: Research needs and policy issues. *American Psychologist, 41*, 1153–1160.

Linn, R. L. (1998, April). *Assessments and accountability.* Paper presented at the annual meeting of the American Educational Research Association, San Diego, CA.

Linn, R. L., Baker, E. L., & Dunbar, S. B. (1991). Complex, performance-based assessment: Expectations and validation criteria. *Educational Researcher, 20*(8), 15–21.

Linn, R. L., Grau, E., & Sanders, N. M. (1990). Comparing state and district test results to national norms: The validity of claims that "Everyone is above average." *Educational Measurement: Issues and Practice, 9*(3), 5–14.

Lipson, M. Y. (1997, April). *Teacher diversity as an influence on change: Capturing the multiple dimensions of teacher beliefs.* Paper presented at the annual meeting of the American Educational Research Association, Chicago.

Lipson, M. Y., & Mosenthal, J. (1997, April). *The differential impact of Vermont's writing portfolio assessment on classroom instruction.* Paper presented at the annual meeting of the American Educational Research Association, Chicago.

Loofbourrow, P. T. (1994). Composition in the context of the CAP: A case study of the interplay between composition assessment and classrooms. *Educational Assessment, 2*, 7–49.

Lucas, C. K. (1988a). Toward ecological evaluation. *Quarterly of the National Writing Project and the Center for the Study of Writing, 10*(1), 13, 12–17.

Lucas, C. K. (1988b). Recontextualizing literacy assessment. *Quarterly of the National Writing Project and the Center for the Study of Writing, 10*(2), 4–10.

Lusi, S. F. (1997). The *role of state departments of education in complex school reform.* New York: Teachers College Press.

Massell, D., Kirst, M., & Hoppe, M. (1997). *Persistence and change: Standards-based reform in nine states.* Philadelphia: Consortium for Policy Research in Education, University of Pennsylvania.

McDonnell, L. (1997, February). *The politics of state testing: Implementing new student assessments.* Los Angeles: National Center for Research on Evaluation, Standards, and Student Testing, University of California.

McDonnell, L., & Choisser, C. (1997, September). *Testing and teaching: Local implementation of new state assessments.* Los Angeles: National Center for Research on Evaluation, Standards, and Student Testing, University of California.

McGill-Franzen, A., & Allington, R. L. (1993). Flunk'em or get them classified: The contamination of primary grade accountability data. *Educational Researcher, 22*(1), 19–22.

McGill-Franzen, A., & Ward, N. (1997, April). *Teachers' use of new standards, frameworks, and assessments for English language arts and social studies: Local cases of New York State primary grade teachers.* Paper presented at the annual meeting of the American Educational Research Association, Chicago.

McLaughlin, M. W. (1987). Learning from experience: Lessons from policy implementation. *Educational Evaluation and Policy Analysis, 9*, 171–178.

Mehrens, W. A. (1998). Consequences of assessment: What is the evidence? *Education Policy Analysis Archives* [Online serial], *6*(13). Available http://olam.ed.asu.edu/epaa/

Mehrens, W. A. (1992). Using performance assessment for accountability purposes. *Educational Measurement: Issues and Practice, 11*(1), 3–9, 20.

Messick, S. (1989). Validity. In R. L. Linn (Ed.), *Educational measurement* (3rd ed., pp. 13–103). New York: Macmillan.

Messick, S. (1994). The interplay of evidence and consequences in the validation of performance assessments. *Educational Researcher, 23*(2), 13–23.

Michigan State Board of Education. (1986). *Essential Goals and Objectives for Reading Education.* Lansing, MI: Author.

Miller, M. D., & Legg, S. M. (1993). Alternative assessment in a high-stakes environment. *Educational Measurement: Issues and Practice, 12*(2), 9–15.

Miller, S. D., Hayes, C. T., & Atkinson, T. S. (1997). State officials' efforts to improve students' reading and language arts achievement with their newly designed end-of-grade assessments. In C. K. Kinzer, K. A. Hinchman, & D. J. Leu (Eds.), *Inquiries in literacy theory and practice: Forty-sixth yearbook of the National Reading Conference* (pp. 91–100). Chicago: National Reading Conference.

Mosenthal, J., Lipson, M. Y., Mekkelsen, J., Daniels, P., & Jiron, H. W. (1996). The meaning and use of portfolios in different literacy contexts: Making sense of the Vermont Assessment Program. In D. J. Leu, C. K. Kinzer, & K. A. Hinchman (Eds.), *Literacies for the 21st century: Forty-fifth yearbook of the National Reading Conference* (pp. 113–123). Chicago: National Reading Conference.

Mosenthal, J. H., Mekkelsen, J. E., & Jiron, H. W. (1997). Agents of their own instruction: The teacher's perspective on the influence of the Vermont Assessment Program. In D. J. Leu, C. K. Kinzer, & K. A. Hinchman (Eds.), *Literacies for the 21st century: Forty-fifty yearbook of the National Reading Conference* (pp. 113–123). Chicago: National Reading Conference.

Moss, P. (1994). Can there be validity without reliability. *Educational Researcher, 23*(2), 5–12.

Mullis, I. V. S., Campbell, J. R., & Farstrup, A. E. (1993). *NAEP 1992 reading report card for the nation and the states.* Washington, DC: Government Printing Office.

National Assessment Governing Board (NAGB). *Reading framework for the 1992 and 1994 National Assessment of Educational Progress.* Washington, DC: Author.

National Commission on Excellence in Education. (1983). *A nation at risk: The imperative for educational reform.* Washington, DC: U.S. Government Printing Office.

National Council on Education Standards and Testing. (1992). *Raising standards for American Education.* Washington, DC: U.S. Government Printing Office.

National Educational Goals Panel. (1991). *National educational goals report: Building a nation of learners.* Washington, DC: U.S. Government Printing Office.

National Research Council. (1998). *Preventing reading difficulties in young children.* Washington, DC: National Academy Press.

Nolen, S. B., Haladyna, T. M., & Haas, N. S. (1992). Uses and abuses of achievement test scores. *Educational Measurement: Issues and Practice, 11*(2), 9–15.

Peters, C. W., Wixson, K. K., Valencia, S. W., & Pearson, P. D. (1993). Changing statewide reading assessment: A case study of Michigan and Illinois. In B. R. Gifford (Ed.), *Policy perspectives on educational testing* (pp. 295–391). Boston: Kluwer.

Pinnell, G. S., Pikulski, J. J., Wixson, K. K., Campbell, J. R., Gough, P. B., & Beatty, A. S. (1995). *Listening to children read aloud.* Washington, DC: Government Printing Office.

Popham, J. W., Cruse, K. L., Rankin, S. C., Sandifer, P. D., & Williams, P. L. (1985). Measurement-driven instruction: It's on the road. *Phi Delta Kappan, 66*, 628–634.

Raths, J., & Fanning, J. (1993). *Primary school reform in Kentucky revisited.* Lexington, KY: Prichard Committee for Academic Excellence.

Resnick, L. B., & Resnick, D. L. (1992). Assessing the thinking curriculum: New tools for educational reform. In B. R. Gifford & M. C. O'Connor (Eds.), *Future assessments: Changing views of aptitude, achievement, and instruction* (pp. 37–75). Boston: Kluwer.

Resnick, L., Resnick, D., & DeStefano, L. (1993). *Cross-scorer and cross-method comparability and distribution of judgments of student math, reading and writing performance: Results from the New Standards Project Big Sky Scoring Conference.* Los Angles: Center for Research on Evaluation, Standards and Student Testing.

Roeber, E., Bond, L. A., & Braskamp, D. (1997). *Trends in statewide student assessment programs, 1997.* North Central Regional Educational Laboratory and Council of Chief State School Officers, Washington, DC.

Salinger, T., & Chittenden, E. (1994). Analysis of an early literacy portfolio: Consequences for instruction. *Language Arts, 71*(6), 446–452.

Shepard, L. A. (1989). Why we need better assessments. *Educational Leadership, 46*(7), 4–9.

Shepard, L. A. (1991). Will national tests improve student learning? *Phi Delta Kappan, 72*, 232–238.

Shepard, L. A., & Dougherty, K. C. (1991, April). *Effects of high-stakes testing on instruction.* Paper presented at the annual meeting of the American Educational Research Association, Chicago.

Shepard, L. A., Flexer, R. J., Hiebert, E. H., Marion, S. F., Mayfield, V., & Weston, J. T. (1996). Effects of introducing classroom performance assessments on student learning. *Educational Measurement: Issues and Practice, 15*(3), 7–18.

Simmons, W., & Resnick, L. (1993). Assessment as the catalyst of school reform. *Educational Leadership, 50*(5), 11–16.

Smith, M. L. (1991). Put to the test: The effects of external testing on teachers. *Educational Researcher, 20*(5), 8–11.

Smith, M. L., Edelsky, C., Draper, K., Rottenberg, C., & Cherland, M. (1990). *The role of testing in elementary schools* (CSE Tech. Rep. No. 321). Los Angeles: Center for Research on Evaluation, Standards, and Student Testing, University of California.

Smith, M. L., Noble, A. J., Heinecke, W., Seck, M., Parish, C., Cabay, M., Junker, S. C., Haag, S., Taylor, K., Safran, Y., Penley, Y., & Bradshaw, A. (1997). *Reforming Schools by Reforming Assessment: Consequences of the*

Arizona Student Assessment Program (ASAP): Equity and Teacher Capacity Building (CSE Tech. Rep. No. 425). Los Angeles: Center for Research on Evaluation, Standards, and Student Testing, University of California.

Smith, M. S., & O'Day, J. (1991). Systemic school reform. In S. Furhman (Ed.), *The politics of curriculum and testing: The 1990 yearbook of the Politics of Education Associations* (pp. 233–267). Philadelphia: Falmer.

Spillane, J. P. (1996). School districts matter: Local educational authorities and state instructional policy. *Educational Policy, 10*, 63–87.

Spillane, J. P. (1998). State policy and the non-monolithic nature of the local school district: Organizational and professional considerations. *American Educational Research Journal, 35*, 33–63.

Spillane, J. P., & Jennings, N. E. (1997). Aligned instructional policy and ambitious pedagogy: Exploring instructional reform from the classroom perspective. *Teachers College Record, 98*, 449–481.

Standerford, N. S. (1997). Reforming reading instruction on multiple levels: Interrelations and disconnections across the state, district, and classroom levels. *Educational Policy, 11*, 58–91.

Stephens, D., Pearson, P. D., Gilrane, C., Roe, M., Stallman, A. C., Shelton, J., Weinzierl, J., Rodriguez, A., & Commeyras, M. (1995). Assessment and decision making in schools: A cross-site analysis. *Reading Research Quarterly, 30*, 478–499.

Supovitz, J. A., & Brennan, R. T. (1997). Mirror, mirror on the wall, which is the fairest test of all? An examination of the equitability of portfolio assessment relative to standardized tests. *Harvard Educational Review, 67*, 472–506.

Supovitz, J. A., MacGowan, A., III, & Slattery, J. (1997). Assessing agreement: An examination of the interrater reliability of portfolio assessment in Rochester, New York. *Educational Assessment, 4*, 237–259.

Valencia, S. W. (1991). Portfolios: Panacea or Pandora's box? In F. Finch (Ed.), *Educational performance testing* (pp. 33–46). Chicago: Riverside.

Valencia, S. W., & Au, K., H. (1997). Portfolios across educational contexts: Issues of evaluation, professional development, and system validity. *Educational Assessment, 4*, 1–35.

Valencia, S. W., Pearson, P. D., Peters, C. W., & Wixson, K. K. (1989). Theory and practice in statewide reading assessment: Closing the gap. *Educational Leadership, 47*(7), 57–63.

Weiss, B. (1994). California's new English-Language Arts assessment. In S. W. Valencia, E. H. Hiebert, & P. P. Afflerbach (Eds.), *Authentic reading assessment: Practices and possibilities*. Newark, DE: International Reading Association.

Welch, C. (1991, April). *Estimating the reliability of a direct measure of writing through generalizability theory*. Paper presented at the annual meeting of the American Educational Research Association, Chicago.

Wiggins, G. P. (1993). *Assessing student performance*. New York: Jossey-Bass.

Wixson, K. K., & Peters, C. W. (1984). Reading redefined: A Michigan Reading Association position paper. *Michigan Reading Journal, 17*, 4–7.

Wixson, K. K., & Dutro, E. (1999). Standards for primary-grade reading: An analysis of state frameworks. *Elementary School Journal, 100*, 89–110.

Wixson, K. K., Peters, C. W., Weber, E. M., & Roeber, E. (1987). New directions in statewide reading assessment. *Reading Teacher, 40*, 749–754.

Author Index

Subject Index

A

Ability, 50, 184, 191, 854, 864. *See also* Cognitive abilities; Decoding; Literacy; Reading; Spelling
  metacognitive, 650–651
  phonological processing, 493–494
  student, 299–300
Abstracts, 218, 365, 503, 646
Academic achievement, 352. *See also* Student achievement
  communicative competence and, 339–340
  emergent literacy research and, 437–439
  family literacy and, 860–864
  family literacy research and, 854–867
  parent, 863–864
Academic community, 135–136
Academic domain, 292–293, 301, 649
Academic research, xii, 30, 35–36
Academics, 48, 125, 135, 293
Academic tasks, 649–650, 658–660
Academic writing, 124, 127
Accelerated Schools Network, 911
Acción Popular Cultural Hondurena, 45
Accountability, 352. *See also* Standards
  and excellence, 892, 894
  policy research and, 913, 918, 921
Achievement, 18, 20, 184, 300, 756, 890. *See also* Academic achievement; Literacy achievement
  focus, 24–26
  gains, 11, 23, 892, 897
  patterns, 456t–466t, 459t, 465t–466t, 471, 472t
  variation, 9, 11, 682
Acoustics, 441, 445, 484
Acquisition. *See* Knowledge; Language; Reading acquisition; English
Active learning, 32, 344, 352, 617
  college studying and, 645, 647, 654
  vocabulary instruction and, 504–506
Adaptation, 504, 882
  teacher, 732–734
  vocabulary learning and, 510–517
Administrators, 33, 413, 843, 898, 899, 924

Adolescents, 366, 392, 577, 622, 623, 637, 856
Adult, 434, 570, 877
  education, 44, 46, 861, 864, 963
  literacy, 3, 4, 9, 54
  readers, contextual effects and, 20–21
  styles, storybook reading, 429–430
  young, literature, 638, 640
Aesthetics, 131–133
Affect, 66, 163, 165, 167, 797, 798. *See also* Reading processes
Affective solidarity and, 883–884
African-Americans, 142, 148, 340, 618, 621
  children's literature and, 363, 364
  intergenerational literacy and, 874, 877–879, 882
  literature response research and, 390, 394, 397
  multicultural education and, 835, 840, 843, 845
Age, 339, 366, 404, 673, 680, 830, 835
  reading motivation and, 408–409
  reading preference and, 367, 368
Alan Duff Charitable Foundation, 10
Albania, 37
Alfabetización, 45–46, 48–50
Alliteration, 18, 262, 263
Alphabet, 229, 255, 326, 347, 484, 531. *See also* Alfabetización; Letter
  code, 490, 495
  knowledge, 5, 11
  principle, 352, 464, 467, 488
  recognition, 673
  and speech, 483–484
Alternative education, Latin America, 44–46, 48–50
American Association of Colleges of Teacher Education, 727
American Heritage Dictionary, 127
American Psychological Association (APA), 119
Americans with Disabilities Act (1990), 352
America Reads, 903–904
Analysis, 49, 328, 505. *See also* Content analysis; Critical analysis: Data analysis; Meta-analytic procedures; Protocol analysis; Single-subject experiments; Textual analysis
  computer aided, 55, 58, 71